AQA GCSE Mathematics

HIGHER TIER

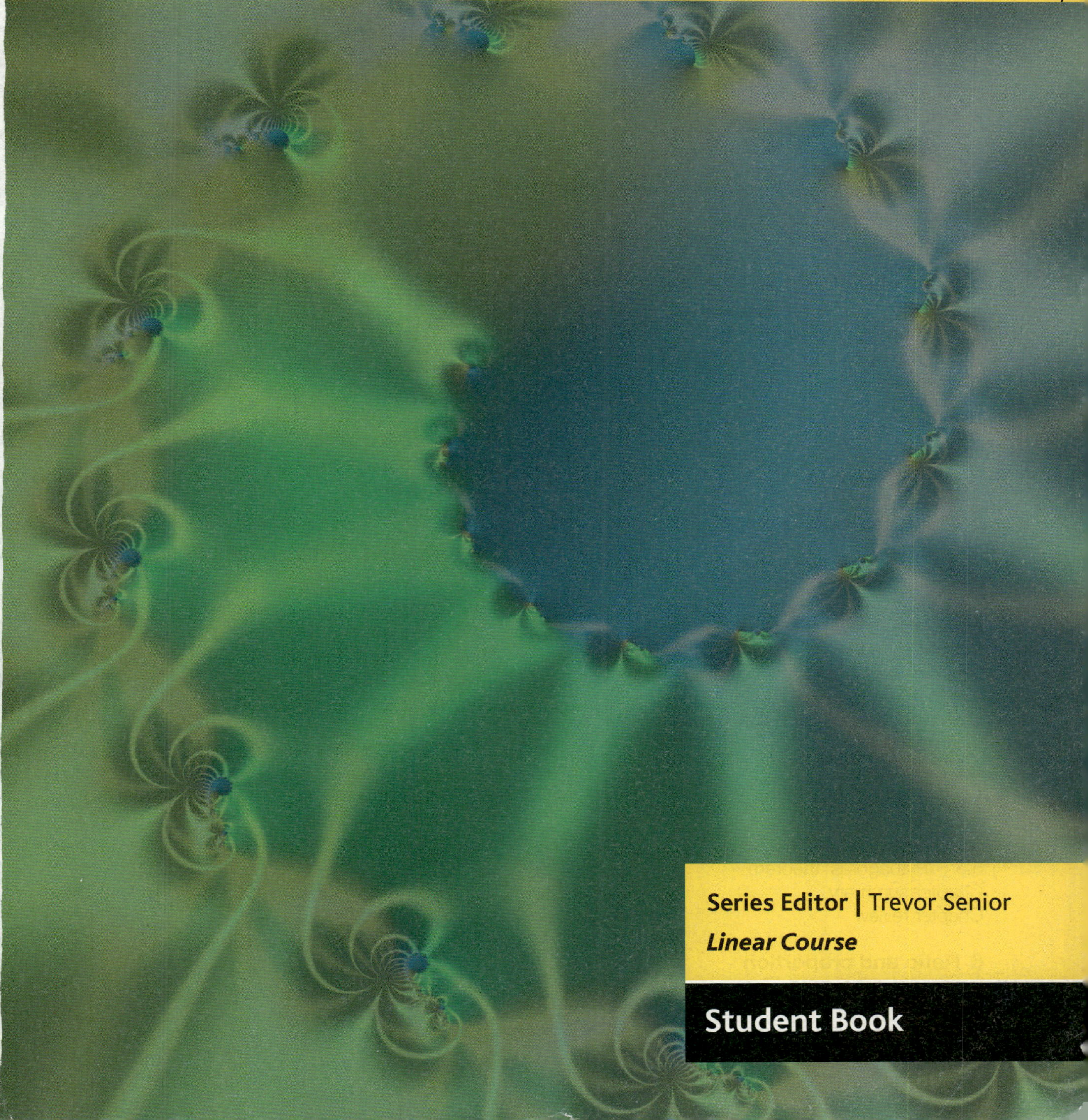

Series Editor | Trevor Senior

Linear Course

Student Book

Contents

Introduction

Welcome to *Longman AQA GCSE Mathematics Linear Higher Student Book and ActiveBook*. It has been written to cover all the skills and knowledge required for AQA's GCSE Mathematics Higher Tier Specification.

The Student Book

Each chapter has a number of units to work through, with full explanations of each topic, numerous worked examples and plenty of exercises, followed by a Chapter Summary and chapter review questions.

Each unit is introduced by a 'Can you remember' box, which tells you what you need to know before you can tackle the unit. There is then a box highlighting the learning objectives for each unit.

The text and worked examples that follow have been written to support you through the subsequent exercises. In Exercise A you will practice the skills and knowledge required for that topic.

The further explanatory text and worked examples lead into Exercise B. Exercise B questions have been written to stretch you a bit further than Exercise A and will require you to use and apply the knowledge you have learnt from the unit. The questions in all exercises have been written to progress from easy to more difficult.

At the end of each chapter, there is a Chapter Summary which will help you remember all the key points and concepts you need to know from the chapter and tell you what you should be able to do for the exam.

Following the Chapter Summary is a Chapter Review which comprises further questions, all of which are exam-style questions and have been written by examiners for the new specifications. Like the questions in the exercise sections, these progress from easy to hard.

In the exercise sections and Chapter Reviews

by a question shows that it and those that follow are non-calculator questions.

by a question shows that it and those that follow are calculator questions.

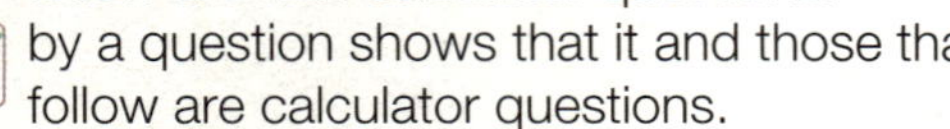

The ActiveBook

The ActiveBook CD-ROM is found in the back of this book. It is a digital version of this Student Book, with links to additional resources and extra support. Using the ActiveBook you can:

- See what vocabulary you will need to know for the unit
- Click on glossary words to see and hear their definitions
- Easily access and display answers to the questions in the exercise sections (these do not appear in the printed Student Book)
- Access a complete glossary for the whole book
- Practice exam questions and improve your exam technique with *Exam Tutor* model questions and answers. Each question that has an *Exam Tutor* icon beside it links to a worked solution with audio and visual annotation to guide you through it

Recommended specification
Pentium 3 500 Mhz processor
128MB RAM
8× speed CD-ROM
1GB free hard disc space
800 × 600 (or 1024 × 768) resolution screen at 16 bit colour
sound card, speakers or headphones

Windows 2000 or XP. This product has been designed for Windows 98, but will be unsupported in line with Microsoft's Product Life-Cycle policy.

Installation
Insert the CD. If you have autorun enabled the program should start within a few seconds. Follow on-screen instructions. Should you experience difficulty, please locate and review the readme file on the CD.

Technical support
If after reviewing the readme you are unable to resolve your problem, contact customer support:

- telephone 0870 6073777 (between 8.00 and 4.00)
- email schools.cd-romhelpdesk@pearson.com
- web http://centraal.uk.knowledgebox.com/kbase/

CHAPTER 1

Mental and written methods

1.1 Squares, square roots, cubes and cube roots

CAN YOU REMEMBER

- The meanings of 'square' and 'square root'?
- That square root is the inverse of square (and vice versa)?
- How to work out cubes of numbers?

IN THIS SECTION YOU WILL

- Learn and use the square numbers up to 225
- Learn that any positive number has both a positive and a negative square root.
- Use the cube numbers 1, 8, 27, 64, 125 and 1000

The inverse of squaring a number is finding its *square root*.

For example, $\sqrt{144} = 12$ because $12 \times 12 = 144$

Also, $-12 \times -12 = 144$. So the square root of 144 is also -12

This is written as $\sqrt{144} = 12$ or -12 or $\sqrt{144} = \pm 12$

Any positive number has both a positive and a negative square root.

To *cube* a number, multiply it by itself 3 times.

$1^3 = 1 \times 1 \times 1 = 1$ $\quad 2^3 = 2 \times 2 \times 2 = 8$

$3^3 = 3 \times 3 \times 3 = 27$ $\quad 4^3 = 4 \times 4 \times 4 = 64$

$5^3 = 5 \times 5 \times 5 = 125$ $\quad 10^3 = 10 \times 10 \times 10 = 1000$

The inverse of cubing a number is finding its *cube root*, written $\sqrt[3]{\ }$.

For example, $\sqrt[3]{125} = 5$ because $5 \times 5 \times 5 = 125$

Learn:

- the square numbers up to 225 and their corresponding square roots
- the cubes of 1, 2, 3, 4, 5 and 10 and the corresponding cube roots.

They are often used in calculations.

Example 1

Work out the value of $13^2 + 2^3$

Solution 1

$13^2 = 169$ and $2^3 = 8$
$13^2 + 2^3 = 169 + 8 = 177$

Square and cube numbers can be used to work out other squares and cubes.

Example 2

Use the square numbers up to 225 to work out:

a 20^2 **b** 400^2

Use $4^3 = 64$ to work out:

c 40^3 **d** 0.4^3

Solution 2

a $20^2 = (2 \times 10)^2 = 2^2 \times 10^2 = 4 \times 100 = 400$

b $400^2 = (4 \times 100)^2 = 4^2 \times 100^2 = 16 \times 10\,000 = 160\,000$

c $40^3 = (4 \times 10)^3 = 4^3 \times 10^3 = 64 \times 1000 = 64\,000$

d $0.4^3 = \left(\frac{4}{10}\right)^3 = \frac{4^3}{10^3} = \frac{64}{1000} = 0.064$

Square roots can be found using the square root button on a calculator. Make sure you know how to work out square roots using your own calculator.

Exercise A

1 Write down the values of each of the following:

a 1^2 **b** 9^2 **c** 12^2 **d** 15^2
e 7^2 **f** 13^2 **g** 11^2 **h** 14^2

2 Work out the values of each of the following:

a $4^2 + 12^2$ **b** $5^2 + 14^2$ **c** $12^2 + 7^2$ **d** $13^2 + 2^2$
e $15^2 - 12^2$ **f** $11^2 - 10^2$ **g** $14^2 - 11^2$ **h** $15^2 - 13^2$

3 Work out the values of each of the following:

a 30^2 **b** 50^2 **c** 110^2 **d** 200^2
e 800^2 **f** 1200^2 **g** 7000^2 **h** $14\,000^2$

4 Work out the values of each of the following:

a 20^3 **b** 50^3 **c** 300^3 **d** 4000^3

5 Use the square numbers up to 225 to work out:

a 0.1^2 **b** 0.5^2 **c** 0.8^2 **d** 0.9^2
e 1.5^2 **f** 1.3^2 **g** 1.1^2 **h** 1.4^2

6 Use the cube numbers up to 125 to work out:

a 0.2^3 **b** 0.3^3 **c** 0.5^3

7 Write down the positive and negative values of each of the following:

a $\sqrt{36}$ **b** $\sqrt{81}$ **c** $\sqrt{121}$ **d** $\sqrt{225}$
e $\sqrt{100}$ **f** $\sqrt{144}$ **g** $\sqrt{196}$ **h** $\sqrt{169}$

8 Write down the values of each of the following:

a $\sqrt[3]{8}$ **b** $\sqrt[3]{27}$ **c** $\sqrt[3]{125}$

9 Copy and complete the following sentences using consecutive integers:

a The positive square root of 20 is between .... and ....
b The positive square root of 75 is between .... and ....
c The positive square root of 125 is between .... and ....
d The positive square root of 150 is between .... and ....
e The negative square root of 20 is between .... and ....
f The negative square root of 75 is between .... and ....
g The negative square root of 125 is between .... and ....
h The negative square root of 150 is between .... and ....

10 Work out the values of each of the following using **positive** square roots:

a $12^2 + \sqrt{225}$ **b** $\sqrt{144} - 3^3$ **c** $\sqrt{121} + \sqrt{144}$ **d** $5^3 + \sqrt{196}$
e $\sqrt{225} - \sqrt{81}$ **f** $10^3 - \sqrt{169}$ **g** $\sqrt{169} + 4^3$ **h** $\sqrt{225} + \sqrt{225}$

11 Use a calculator to show that $\sqrt{56}$ is greater than 7.4 and less than 7.5

12 $196 = 4 \times 49$
Use a calculator to show that $\sqrt{196} = \sqrt{4} \times \sqrt{49}$

A square number has an integer (whole number) square root.

Example 3

Explain how you know that
a 10 and **b** 40 are not square numbers.

Solution 3

a 10 is between the square numbers 9 and 16
So the positive square root of 10 is between $\sqrt{9} = 3$ and $\sqrt{16} = 4$
$\sqrt{10}$ is not a whole number, so 10 is not a square number.

b The positive square root of 40 is between 6 and 7 so 40 is not a square number.

Exercise B

1 Write down the square numbers from the list:
16 30 49 81 90 121 140 196

2 Explain how you know that 200 is **not** a square number.

3 Harriet says that the units digit of a square number is always one of the following:
0 1 4 5 9
Give an example to show that she is **not** correct.

4 $\sqrt{2916} = 54$
Write down the values of:
a $\sqrt{291\,600}$ **b** $\sqrt{29.16}$ **c** 0.54^2

5 Andrew says that all even square numbers are also multiples of 4. Give an example to show that this is true.

6 Here is a pattern using squares and cubes:

$1^2 = 1^3$

$(1 + 2)^2 = 1^3 + 2^3$

$(1 + 2 + 3)^2 = 1^3 + 2^3 + 3^3$

a Write down the sixth line of the pattern.

b Use a calculator to check that the pattern works for the sixth line.

7 **a** Copy and complete the table for square numbers up to 225

Number	1		2		3		4		5		...	
Square number	1		4		9		16		25		...	
Difference		3		5		7		9				

b What do you notice about the differences?

8 Use a calculator to find

a two integers between which $\sqrt{850}$ lies

b the greatest square number that is less than 1000

c the smallest square number that is greater than 1000

d two integers between which $\sqrt[3]{200}$ lies.

1.2 Significant figures

CAN YOU REMEMBER

- How to round numbers to the nearest 10, 100, 1000?
- How to round numbers to the nearest whole number (integer)?
- How to round numbers to an accuracy of up to three decimal places?
- How to round numbers to one significant figure?

IN THIS SECTION YOU WILL

- Learn how to round to a given number of significant figures.
- Understand the limitations on the accuracy of rounded data and measurements.

Quantities are *rounded* to make data or measurements more manageable.
A rounded number is an approximation of the accurate value of the number.

It is often sensible to round the answer to a calculation.
For example, using a calculator the answer to an area calculation is 4.121 134 1 m^2
It is sensible to round this answer to 4 m^2

The most *significant* digit in a number is the digit with the largest place value.
For example, in the number 7008 the most significant digit is 7, the thousands digit.
This is called the first significant figure.

Number	First significant figure	Second significant figure	Third significant figure	Fourth significant figure
7008	7 thousands	0 hundreds	0 tens	8 units
0.004 95	4 thousandths	9 ten thousandths	5 hundred thousandths	

Notice that all the digits after the first non-zero digit are significant, even the zeros.

Example 1

Round each number to one significant figure:

a 923.456 **b** 0.004 95

Solution 1

a The most significant figure is the 9. It has value 900
So for this number, rounding to one significant figure means rounding to the nearest hundred.
The number is between 900 and 1000. The digit 2 in the tens column shows that it is closer to 900
Answer = 900

b The most significant figure is the 4. It has value 0.004
So for this number, rounding to one significant figure means rounding to the nearest thousandth (0.001).
The number is between 0.004 and 0.005. The digit 9 in the ten thousandths column shows that it is closer to 0.005
Answer = 0.005

To round to one significant figure, round to the place value of the most significant digit in the number.
A number rounded to one significant figure has only one non-zero digit.

To round to two significant figures, round to the place value of the second significant digit in the number.
A number rounded to two significant figures has only two non-zero digits.

Example 2

Round each number to two significant figures:

a 923.456 **b** 7008

Solution 2

a The two most significant figures are the 9 and the 2
The second significant figure is 2 tens.
So for this number, rounding to two significant figures means rounding to the nearest ten.
Answer = 920

b The two most significant figures are the 7 and the following 0
The second significant figure is 0 hundreds.
So for this number, rounding to two significant figures means rounding to the nearest hundred.
Answer = 7000

Exercise A

1 Round the following numbers to one significant figure:

a	21	**b**	18	**c**	47	**d**	34
e	97	**f**	129	**g**	432	**h**	899
i	201	**j**	1200	**k**	3070	**l**	2008

2 Round the following decimals to one significant figure:

a	0.14	**b**	0.25	**c**	0.73	**d**	0.87
e	0.042	**f**	0.058	**g**	0.039	**h**	0.077
i	0.0708	**j**	0.0045	**k**	0.003 05	**l**	0.004 745

3 Round the following decimals to one significant figure:

a	8.7	**b**	1.55	**c**	21.8	**d**	1.71
e	8.34	**f**	3.76	**g**	9.14	**h**	12.6
i	142.1	**j**	203.5	**k**	591.4	**l**	301.2

4 Round the following numbers to two significant figures:

a	324	**b**	475	**c**	671	**d**	898
e	1247	**f**	1254	**g**	3946	**h**	4788
i	8303	**j**	9027	**k**	4093	**l**	10 356

5 Round the following decimals to two significant figures:

a	0.164	**b**	0.552	**c**	0.293	**d**	0.475
e	0.648	**f**	0.389	**g**	0.0256	**h**	0.048 52
i	0.0995	**j**	0.007 962	**k**	0.004 060 4	**l**	0.001 949 2

6 Round the following decimals to two significant figures:

a	1.56	**b**	3.24	**c**	7.81	**d**	10.25
e	2.68	**f**	12.71	**g**	26.02	**h**	18.95
i	32.16	**j**	102.4	**k**	281.7	**l**	202.8
m	213.7	**n**	595.2	**o**	1050.8	**p**	2121.21

7 Round the following numbers to three significant figures:

a	1026	**b**	3685	**c**	20 060	**d**	15 675
e	60 291	**f**	544 546	**g**	100 500	**h**	109 090

8 Round the following decimals to three significant figures:

a	0.2045	**b**	0.3092	**c**	0.4865	**d**	0.3764
e	0.399 54	**f**	0.189 97	**g**	0.523 68	**h**	0.051 35
i	0.067 78	**j**	0.072 77	**k**	0.090 460 2	**l**	0.070 809
m	0.004 651	**n**	0.007 892	**o**	0.004 080 4	**p**	0.001 958 1

9 Round the following decimals to three significant figures:

a	8.762	**b**	3.498	**c**	1.385	**d**	3.141 59
e	2.1828	**f**	8.2376	**g**	11.4192	**h**	101.65

In a 100 metre sprint, two runners both have a time of 10.3 seconds.

These times are rounded to three significant figures.

The exact times are between 10.25 seconds and 10.35 seconds.

10.25 seconds and 10.35 seconds are called the *bounds* or *limits*.

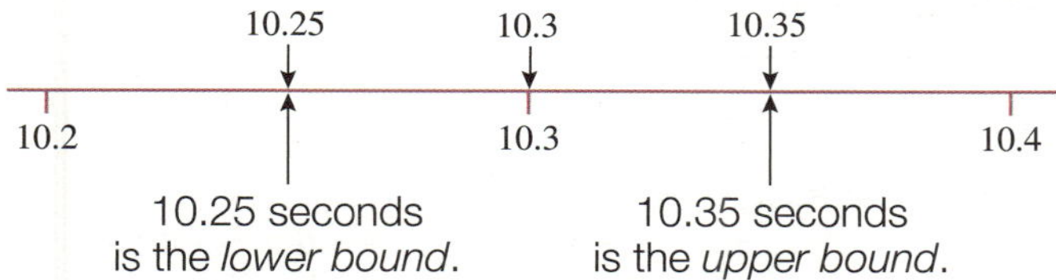

10.25 seconds is the *lower bound*.

10.35 seconds is the *upper bound*.

Example 3

Darren spends £5, correct to the nearest pound.
What are the minimum and maximum amounts that Darren could have spent?

Solution 3

4.5 is the smallest number that rounds to 5
£4.50 is the lower bound. The minimum amount is £4.50
5.5 is the smallest number that rounds to 6, which means that £5.50 rounds up to £6
So £5.49 is the largest amount that rounds down to £5
£5.49 is the upper bound. The maximum amount is £5.49

Example 4

A bag contains 120 sweets, correct to two significant figures.
What are the least and greatest possible numbers of sweets in the bag?

Solution 4

The least number of sweets is 115, because 115 is the smallest number that rounds to 120
The greatest number of sweets is 124, because 124 is the largest number that rounds to 120

Example 5

A bag of sand weighs 20 kg to the nearest kilogram.
What are the lower and upper bounds of the amount of sand in the bag?

Solution 5

The lower bound is 19.5 kg.
The upper bound is 20.5 kg.

Exercise B

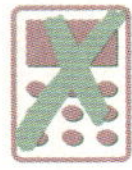

1 The following amounts of money are given to the nearest pound.
Write down the maximum and minimum possible amounts of money for each amount.

a £3 **b** £10 **c** £15 **d** £30 **e** £100 **f** £2000

2 Three students guess the amount of money they each have in their pockets.
These are their answers:

£5 £2 £3.20

They are all correct to the nearest 10 pence.
What is the least amount that they could have altogether?

3 The distance from Manchester to Birmingham is 90 miles to the nearest 5 miles.
Tom drives from Manchester to Birmingham and back again.
What is the shortest distance his journey could be?

4 The following quantities are given to the nearest whole number.
Write down the lower and upper bounds for each quantity.

a 5 grams **b** 10 metres **c** 25 kg **d** 50 litres
e 124 miles **f** 4 pints **g** 100° **h** 32 cm

5 The following measures are each given to one significant figure.
Write down the lower and upper bounds for each number.

a 20 grams **b** 40 km **c** 100 metres **d** 6 pints
e 200 feet **f** 0.2 litres **g** 0.05 mm

6 The diagram shows a rectangle.
The length is 16 cm and the width is 12 cm.
Both measurements are correct to two significant figures.

a Write down the minimum possible length of the rectangle.
b Write down the minimum possible width of the rectangle.
c Use your answers to **a** and **b** to work out the minimum possible perimeter of the rectangle.

7 The diagram shows an equilateral triangle.
The length of one side is 300 mm correct to one significant figure.

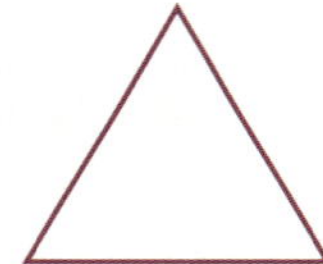

a Write down the upper bound for the length of one side.
b Work out the maximum perimeter of the equilateral triangle.

8 The height of the Eiffel Tower in Paris is 300 metres correct to one significant figure.
The height of the Stratosphere Tower in Las Vegas is 350 metres correct to two significant figures.
Richard says that this means that the two towers could be the same height.
Explain why Richard is correct.

9 A giant Armadillo is 1.5 m high and weighs 50 kg.
A fairy Armadillo is 15 cm high and weighs 90 g.
The heights are correct to two significant figures.
The weights are correct to one significant figure.

a What is the minimum possible total of their heights?
Give your answer in metres.
b What is the maximum possible total of their weights?
Give your answer in kilograms.

10 The area of Jordan is 92 000 km^2 correct to two significant figures.
Jabal Ramm is Jordan's highest point. It is 1750 m high correct to the nearest 50 m.
Mutasem says that the exact area of Jordan is 91 880 km^2 and the exact height of Jabal Ramm is 1754 m.
Could he be correct?
Explain your answer.

1.3 Estimation

CAN YOU REMEMBER

- How to round numbers to one significant figure?
- How to divide by a decimal?

IN THIS SECTION YOU WILL

- Round to one significant figure in order to estimate answers to calculations.
- Understand that answers can be checked using estimation.
- Check answers by approximating values to one significant figure.

The answer to a calculation can be estimated using approximations.
Round each value in the calculation to one significant figure.

In the calculation $\frac{19.8 \times 50.2}{99}$

19.8 rounds to 20   50.2 rounds to 50   99 rounds to 100

So an estimate of the answer to the calculation is $\frac{20 \times 50}{100} = \frac{1000}{100} = 10$

Using a calculator, the exact answer to $\frac{19.8 \times 50.2}{99} = 10.04$

So the estimate is close to the exact answer.

Example 1

Use approximations to estimate the value of:

a 4.9×30.4 **b** $59.7 \div 10.3$

Solution 1

a 4.9×30.4
Rounding each value to one significant figure gives:
$5 \times 30 = 150$
4.9×30.4 is approximately equal to 150

b $59.7 \div 10.3$
Rounding each value to one significant figure gives:
$60 \div 10 = 6$
$59.7 \div 10.3$ is approximately equal to 6

Example 2

Estimate the cost of 9.8 metres of pipe at 39 pence per metre.

Solution 2

The calculation for the cost is 9.8×39 pence.
Rounding each value to one significant figure gives: $10 \times 40 = 400$ pence = £4
9.8 m of pipe costs approximately £4

Exercise A

1 Use approximations to estimate the value of each of the following:

a $8.9 + 6.2$ **b** $1.2 + 8.4$ **c** $9.3 + 3.6$ **d** $2.7 + 8.1$
e $4.6 + 9.1$ **f** $8.2 + 10.4$ **g** $20.1 + 29.7$ **h** $6.1 - 4.2$
i $7.9 - 1.1$ **j** $9.8 - 3.1$ **k** $6.7 - 2.3$ **l** $19.9 - 5.01$
m $10.2 - 9.99$ **n** $39.6 - 20.3$

2 Use approximations to estimate the value of each of the following:

a 6.1×8.7 **b** 1.03×7.98 **c** 9.99×2.17 **d** 14.9×1.98
e 7.1×3.2 **f** 5.8×8.8 **g** 3.89×6.04 **h** 10.2×7.14
i 3.14×21.98 **j** 4.68×5.21

3 Use approximations to estimate the value of each of the following:

a $3.85 \div 2.01$ **b** $9.9 \div 1.89$ **c** $18.2 \div 3.7$ **d** $11.2 \div 1.78$
e $29.3 \div 3.05$ **f** $39.8 \div 5.2$ **g** $59.6 \div 5.59$ **h** $83.4 \div 19.7$
i $49.5 \div 10.1$ **j** $99 \div 20.2$

4 Use approximations to estimate the value of each of the following:

a $\frac{2.8 \times 8.7}{3.1}$ **b** $\frac{4.2 \times 4.9}{9.9}$ **c** $\frac{6.03 \times 5.98}{6.2}$ **d** $\frac{3.9 \times 5.9}{1.9}$
e $\frac{7.2 \times 4.1}{2.02}$ **f** $\frac{10.16 \times 8.02}{19.7}$ **g** $\frac{8.3 \times 3.9}{7.9}$ **h** $\frac{29.2 \times 2.11}{5.79}$

5 Use approximations to estimate the value of each of the following:

a $\frac{203.1 \times 1.9}{3.8 + 6.1}$ **b** $\frac{104.3 \times 5.9}{1.8 + 4.3}$ **c** $\frac{975 \times 3.1}{0.9 + 1.9}$ **d** $\frac{52.2 \times 4.1}{8.6 + 0.9}$
e $\frac{501 \times 7.8}{10.02 - 5.91}$ **f** $\frac{48.7 \times 2.95}{20.3 - 9.99}$ **g** $\frac{38.3 + 62.5}{5.9 - 1.07}$ **h** $\frac{28.9 - 5.43}{7.12 - 1.95}$

6 Estimate the cost of:

a 5 ice-creams at 99p each **b** 20 biros at 49p each
c 4.2 m of cloth at 99p per metre **d** 19 pens at £1.99 each
e 8.7 kg of fruit at 31p per kg **f** 31 litres of diesel at 97p per litre
g 18 drinks at £1.07 each **h** 11 books at £18.99 each.

7 Use the formula

$$\text{Distance} = \text{speed} \times \text{time}$$

to estimate the distance for each of the following journeys:

a 20.3 mph for 9.7 hours **b** 42.1 km/h for 1.2 hours
c 68 mph for 3 hours 10 minutes **d** 96 km/h for 4 hours 50 minutes.

8 Use the formula

$$\text{Average speed} = \frac{\text{distance}}{\text{time}}$$

to estimate the average speed for each of the following journeys:

a 98 miles in 1 hour 56 minutes **b** 103 km in 2 hours 5 minutes
c 3200 miles in 10.5 hours
d 10 000 metres in 30 minutes 22 seconds. Give your answer in metres per hour.

9 Use a calculator to work out the exact answers to question **4**.
If they are very different to your estimates, check your working.

Example 3

Sian calculates the answer to 3.5×0.61 to be 0.2135

a Estimate an answer to her calculation using approximations.

b Is her answer correct? Explain how you know.

Solution 3

a Rounding each value to one significant figure gives:
$4 \times 0.6 = 2.4$
The correct answer is approximately 2.4

b Sian is not correct. The decimal point is not in the correct place.
The correct answer is 2.135

Example 4

Use approximations to estimate the value of $\dfrac{310 \times 29}{0.49}$

Solution 4

$\dfrac{310 \times 29}{0.49}$ Rounding each value to one significant figure gives $\dfrac{300 \times 30}{0.5}$

Multiplying the numerator and denominator by 10 gives:

$$\frac{300 \times 30}{0.5} = \frac{300 \times 30 \times 10}{0.5 \times 10} = \frac{90\,000}{5} = 18\,000$$

$\dfrac{310 \times 29}{0.49}$ is approximately equal to 18 000

Exercise B

1 Use approximations to estimate the value of each of the following:

a $\dfrac{1.1}{0.51}$ **b** $\dfrac{6.03}{0.302}$ **c** $\dfrac{7.96}{0.17}$ **d** $\dfrac{4.89}{0.09}$

e $\dfrac{10.2}{0.49}$ **f** $\dfrac{9.05}{0.28}$ **g** $\dfrac{5.78}{0.59}$ **h** $\dfrac{7.11}{0.51}$

2 Use approximations to estimate the value of each of the following:

a $\dfrac{29}{0.51}$ **b** $\dfrac{41}{0.215}$ **c** $\dfrac{99}{0.19}$ **d** $\dfrac{39}{0.099}$

e $\dfrac{10.2}{0.51}$ **f** $\dfrac{29.7}{0.279}$ **g** $\dfrac{60.1}{0.58}$ **h** $\dfrac{49.6}{0.52}$

3 Use approximations to estimate the value of each of the following:

a $\dfrac{605 \times 4.99}{0.212}$ **b** $\dfrac{18.9 \times 22.3}{0.401}$ **c** $\dfrac{3.14 \times 7.9}{0.578}$

d $\dfrac{87.9 - 30.2}{0.62}$ **e** $\dfrac{6.9 \times 201}{0.71}$ **f** $\dfrac{5.04 \times 198.3}{0.507}$

4 Use approximations to estimate the value of each of the following:

a $\sqrt{5.1 \times 19.6}$ **b** $\sqrt{39.7 \times 41.2}$ **c** $\sqrt{\frac{1001}{9.7}}$ **d** $\sqrt{\frac{200.3}{49.5}}$

e $\sqrt{\frac{91\,200}{(10.1)^2}}$ **f** $\sqrt{\frac{413}{9.9^2}}$ **g** $\sqrt{\frac{3980}{5.01 \times 1.98}}$ **h** $\sqrt{\frac{1997}{2.05 \times 10.2}}$

5 Use approximations to estimate the value of each of the following:

a $3.9^2 + 6.2^2$ **b** $9.9^3 - 5.02^3$ **c** $6.01^2 + 7.95^2 - 2.88^2$

d $10.2^3 - 8.1^2$ **e** $\sqrt{3.99^2 + 3.01^2}$ **f** $\sqrt{4.96^2 + 12.02^2}$

g $\sqrt{10.21^2 - 6.04^2}$ **h** $\sqrt{4.1^3}$

6 Which is greater:

$7 \div 0.69$, $4 \div 0.79$ or $5 \div 0.11$?

Use estimation to work out your answer.

7 Which is smaller:

$8 \div 0.81$, $8 \div 0.41$ or $8 \div 0.21$?

a Use estimation to work out your answer.

b What do you notice about the divisor and the answer?

8

Trevor is correct.
Explain how he worked it out.

9 Akuji says that $84 \times 9.1 = 7644$
Use estimation to show that he is **not** correct.

10 Jill says that $19.1 \times 0.043 = 0.8213$
Use estimation to decide whether she could be correct.

11 a Round each number to one significant figure to estimate the value of $\frac{3.98}{0.13}$

b Work out the difference between the estimated value of $\frac{3.98}{0.13}$ and the exact value.

12 Use a calculator to work out the exact answers to questions **4** and **5**.
If they are very different to the estimated answers, check your working.

1.4 Reciprocals

CAN YOU REMEMBER

- How to multiply and divide by whole numbers, decimals and fractions?
- How to write an improper fraction as a mixed number?
- That to find the product of two numbers is to multiply them?
- How to input fractions on a calculator?

IN THIS SECTION YOU WILL

- Learn the meaning of the term 'reciprocal'.
- Work out the reciprocal of numbers in different forms: integers, fractions and decimals.
- Use reciprocals to carry out divisions.

The *reciprocal* of any number is 1 divided by the number. For example:

The reciprocal of 5 is $1 \div 5 = \frac{1}{5} = 0.2$

The reciprocal of $\frac{2}{3}$ is $1 \div \frac{2}{3} = 1 \times \frac{3}{2} = \frac{3}{2} = 1.5$

The reciprocal of a fraction is the fraction inverted.

Example 1

a Work out the reciprocals of: **i** 7 **ii** -5
Give your answers as fractions.

b Work out the reciprocal of $\frac{1}{9}$

c Work out the reciprocals of: **i** 0.3 **ii** $\frac{3}{4}$
Give your answers as mixed numbers.

Solution 1

a **i** Reciprocal of $7 = 1 \div 7 = \frac{1}{7}$ **ii** Reciprocal of $-5 = 1 \div -5 = \frac{1}{-5} = -\frac{1}{5}$

b Reciprocal of $\frac{1}{9} = 1 \div \frac{1}{9} = 1 \times \frac{9}{1} = 9$

c **i** Reciprocal of $0.3 = 1 \div 0.3 = \frac{1}{0.3} = \frac{1 \times 10}{0.3 \times 10} = \frac{10}{3} = 3\frac{1}{3}$

ii Reciprocal of $\frac{3}{4} = \frac{4}{3} = 1\frac{1}{3}$

The product of any number and its reciprocal is equal to 1, e.g.

$5 \times \frac{1}{5} = 1$ or $\frac{2}{3} \times \frac{3}{2} = \frac{2 \times 3}{3 \times 2} = \frac{6}{6} = 1$

The reciprocal of a number can be worked out using a calculator.

Example 2

For each part, work out whether the numbers are reciprocals of each other.

a 8 and $\frac{1}{8}$ **b** -4 and $\frac{1}{4}$ **c** 0.25 and 4 **d** 0.6 and $1\frac{2}{3}$

Solution 2

If two numbers are reciprocals of each other their product is equal to 1

a $8 \times \frac{1}{8} = 1$
8 and $\frac{1}{8}$ are reciprocals of each other.

b $-4 \times \frac{1}{4} = -1$
-4 and $\frac{1}{4}$ are **not** reciprocals of each other.

c $0.25 \times 4 = 1$
0.25 and 4 are reciprocals of each other.

d $0.6 \times 1\frac{2}{3} = \frac{6}{10} \times \frac{5}{3} = \frac{30}{30} = 1$
0.6 and $1\frac{2}{3}$ are reciprocals of each other.

Exercise A

1 Write down the reciprocal of the following numbers.
Leave your answer as a fraction.

a 8 **b** 12 **c** 6 **d** 50
e 100 **f** 11 **g** −10 **h** −3
i −8 **j** −5 **k** −25 **l** −7

2 Write down the reciprocal of the following fractions.
Leave your answer as a whole number.

a $\frac{1}{8}$ **b** $\frac{1}{5}$ **c** $\frac{1}{7}$ **d** $\frac{1}{10}$ **e** $\frac{1}{11}$ **f** $\frac{1}{3}$

3 Write down the reciprocal of the following fractions.
Leave your answer as an improper fraction.

a $\frac{3}{8}$ **b** $\frac{2}{5}$ **c** $\frac{5}{7}$ **d** $\frac{3}{10}$ **e** $\frac{8}{11}$ **f** $\frac{2}{7}$

4 Work out the reciprocal of the following fractions.
Give your answer as a mixed number.

a $\frac{4}{7}$ **b** $\frac{2}{9}$ **c** $\frac{4}{11}$ **d** $\frac{7}{10}$ **e** $\frac{2}{15}$ **f** $\frac{3}{20}$

5 Work out the reciprocal of the following integers.
Leave your answer as a decimal.

a 4 **b** 10 **c** 2 **d** 5 **e** 100 **f** 20

6 Work out the reciprocal of the following integers.
Give your answer as a decimal to two decimal places.

a 3 **b** 9 **c** 11 **d** 13 **e** 7 **f** 19

7 Use a calculator to work out the reciprocal of the following mixed numbers.
Leave your answer as a fraction or as a decimal to two decimal places.

a $1\frac{1}{2}$: $1 \div 1\frac{1}{2} = 1 \div \frac{3}{2} = ?$ **b** $3\frac{1}{4}$
c $5\frac{1}{2}$ **d** $2\frac{1}{3}$ **e** $1\frac{1}{5}$ **f** $4\frac{1}{2}$

8 Use a calculator to work out the reciprocal of the following decimals.
Where necessary, give your answer as a decimal to two decimal places.

a 0.2 **b** 0.5 **c** 0.8 **d** 0.75
e 0.6 **f** 0.4 **g** 1.2 **h** 1.5
i 2.5 **j** 3.2 **k** 4.5 **l** 2.7

9 For each part, work out whether the numbers are reciprocals of each other.

a 7 and $\frac{1}{7}$ **b** 0.75 and 1.3 **c** 0.4 and 2.5
d $2\frac{1}{3}$ and $\frac{3}{7}$ **e** 0.6 and $1\frac{2}{3}$ **f** $\frac{3}{4}$ and $1\frac{1}{3}$

10 Match the pairs of reciprocals.

One way of dividing by a number is to multiply by its reciprocal.

For example, $3 \div 5 = 3 \times \frac{1}{5} = \frac{3}{5}$ $\frac{2}{3} \div \frac{3}{4} = \frac{2}{3} \times \frac{4}{3} = \frac{8}{9}$

Exercise B

1 Use reciprocals to work out these divisions.

a $7 \div 10$ **b** $6 \div \frac{1}{2}$ **c** $7 \div \frac{2}{3}$ **d** $\frac{1}{2} \div \frac{3}{5}$ **e** $\frac{3}{5} \div 7$ **f** $\frac{1}{4} \div \frac{3}{10}$

2 Here is a number machine.

a What is the output when the input is 2?
b What is the output when the input is −4?
c What is the input when the output is 3?

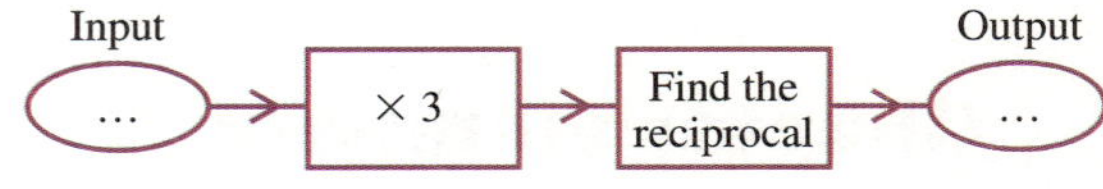

3 Here is a number machine.

a What is the output when the input is 5?
b What is the output when the input is 6?
c What is the input when the output is $\frac{1}{2}$?

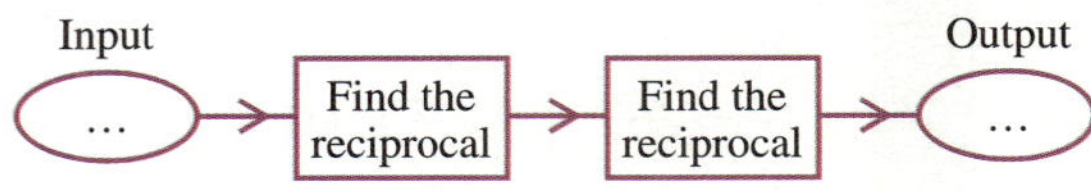

4 Which is the greater, the reciprocal of 5 or the reciprocal of 3?
Explain your answer.

5 x and y are both positive.
x is less than y.
Which is the greater, the reciprocal of x or the reciprocal of y?
Explain your answer.

6 I think of a number.
The reciprocal of the number is equal to the number.
What number am I thinking of?

7 Pietro says, 'Zero has no reciprocal.'
He is correct.
Explain why he is correct.

8 Here is a number machine.

Input ... → Find the reciprocal → ÷ 0.5 → Output ...

a What is the output when the input is $1\frac{1}{4}$?
b What is the output when the input is −7.5?
c What is the input when the output is 10?

9 Here is a number machine.

Input ... → Find the reciprocal → Add 5 → Find the reciprocal → Output ...

a What is the output when the input is $\frac{1}{4}$?
b What is the output when the input is 6?
c What is the input when the output is 1?

10 Add together the reciprocal of 8 and the reciprocal of 10. Give your answer as a decimal.

11 I choose any number.
I square my number and then find the reciprocal of the answer.
If I find the reciprocal of my number first and then square it, the answer is the same.
Give an example to show that this works.

12 I choose any number.
I cube my number and then find the reciprocal of the answer.
If I find the reciprocal of my number first and then cube it, the answer is the same.
Give an example to show that this works.

Chapter summary

- The square numbers from 1 (1^2) to 225 (15^2) are

$1^2 = 1$	$2^2 = 4$	$3^2 = 9$	$4^2 = 16$	$5^2 = 25$
$6^2 = 36$	$7^2 = 49$	$8^2 = 64$	$9^2 = 81$	$10^2 = 100$
$11^2 = 121$	$12^2 = 144$	$13^2 = 169$	$14^2 = 196$	$15^2 = 225$

- Any positive number has both a positive and a negative square root, e.g. $\sqrt{225} = \pm 15$
- The square numbers up to $15^2 = 225$ can be used to work out other squares.
- A square number has an integer (whole number) square root.
- Some cube numbers are
  $1^3 = 1$ $2^3 = 8$ $3^3 = 27$ $4^3 = 64$ $5^3 = 125$ $10^3 = 1000$
- The most significant digit in a number is the digit with the largest place value.
- To round to one significant figure, round to the place value of the most significant digit in the number.
- To round to two significant figures, round to the place value of the second significant digit in the number, and so on.
- The lower bound for a rounded value is the lowest possible value it could have.
- The upper bound for a rounded value is the highest possible value it could have.
  For example, 7 g to the nearest gram: lower bound = 6.5 g, upper bound = 7.5 g.
- The answer to a calculation can be estimated using approximations.
  Round each value in the calculation to one significant figure.
- The *reciprocal* of any number is 1 divided by the number, e.g. the reciprocal of 5 is $1 \div 5 = \frac{1}{5}$
- The reciprocal of a fraction is the fraction inverted, e.g. the reciprocal of $\frac{2}{3}$ is $\frac{3}{2}$
- The product of any number and its reciprocal is equal to 1
- One way of dividing by a number is to multiply by its reciprocal,
  e.g. $7 \div 5 = 7 \times \frac{1}{5}$ $\frac{1}{2} \div \frac{3}{4} = \frac{1}{2} \times \frac{4}{3}$

Chapter review

1 Pat wants to calculate 53.76 ÷ 6.17, but she doesn't have a calculator.
 a Write each of the numbers in the calculation to the nearest whole number.
 b Use these numbers to find an estimate of the answer to the calculation.

2 Estimate the value of $\dfrac{(3.8 \times 41.2)}{(6.15 + 1.87)}$

3 A tea-bag weighs 3 grams, correct to the nearest gram.
a What is the maximum possible weight of a tea-bag?
b What is the minimum possible weight of a tea-bag?

4 **a** Write down the reciprocal of 3
b Write the reciprocal of $\frac{3}{8}$ as a mixed number.
c Which is greater, the reciprocal of 4 or the reciprocal of 5?
Explain your answer.

5 Dina spends £12 on a DVD.
The amount is correct to the nearest pound.
Write down:
a the minimum price that Dina could have paid
b the maximum price that Dina could have paid.

6 **a** The number of students in a school is 1278
What is the number of students to two significant figures?
b Another school has 1100 students, correct to the nearest hundred.
i What is the least possible number of students in the school?
ii What is the greatest possible number of students in the school?

7 **a** Work out $\frac{1}{2} \div \frac{1}{8}$
b Find the value of:
i 196
ii $\sqrt{(2^2 \times 5^2)}$

8 Jason makes a true statement.
a Write down the minimum age that Jason could be.
b Write down the maximum age that Jason could be.

9 Use your calculator to find the value of $\dfrac{(3.76 \times 0.82)}{(6.23 - 5.04)}$
Give your answer correct to three significant figures.

10 Calculate $\dfrac{(35.1 \times 27.9)}{24.8^2}$
a Write down your full calculator display.
b Write your answer to three significant figures.

11 Find the value of $\sqrt{(27.97^2 - 14.1^2)}$
a Write down your full calculator display.
b Write your answer to three significant figures.

CHAPTER 2

Charts and diagrams

2.1 Pie charts

CAN YOU REMEMBER

- How many degrees are in a full circle?
- How to multiply by a fraction?
- How to use a protractor?

IN THIS SECTION YOU WILL

- Understand how a pie chart represents data.
- Learn how to calculate the angles for the sectors of a pie chart.
- Learn how to draw a pie chart.
- Learn how to interpret information from a pie chart.

A pie chart is a circular diagram split into sectors.
The angle of each sector of the pie chart is in proportion to the amount of information it represents.
There are 360° in a full circle.
The angles of the sectors in a pie chart add up to 360°.
The pie chart below shows how sales in a large store are divided between departments.

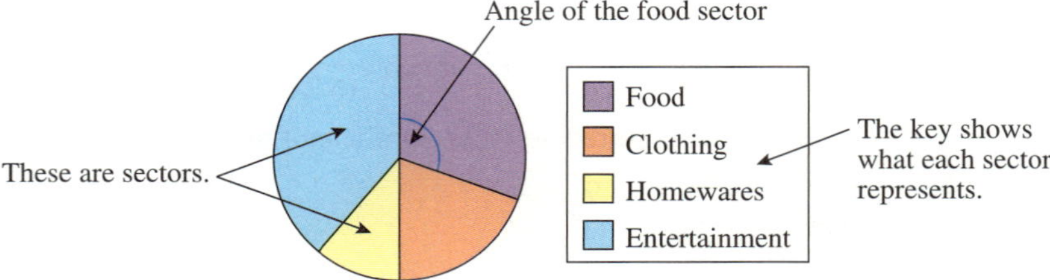

Entertainment is the largest sector. More money is spent on entertainment than the other items in the store.

Example 1

Draw a pie chart to represent this data.

Fish	Perch	Roach	Eel	Pike	**Total**
Number caught	12	16	5	3	**36**

Solution 1

Step 1: Calculate the angle for one fish.

360° in a circle represent 36 fish.

So 360° ÷ 36 represent one fish.

10° represent one fish.

Step 2: Calculate the angle for each sector.

There are 12 perch. Angle for perch = 12 × 10° = 120°

There are 16 roach. Angle for roach = 16 × 10° = 160°

Angle for eel = 5 × 10° = 50°

Angle for pike = 3 × 10° = 30°

Step 3: Check that the sum of all of the angles equals 360°

120° + 160° + 50° + 30° = 360°

Step 4: Draw a circle. Draw a straight line (a radius) from the centre of the circle to the circumference. Use a protractor to measure accurately and then draw the angle for each sector. Complete the pie chart by labelling each sector or using a key (but not both).

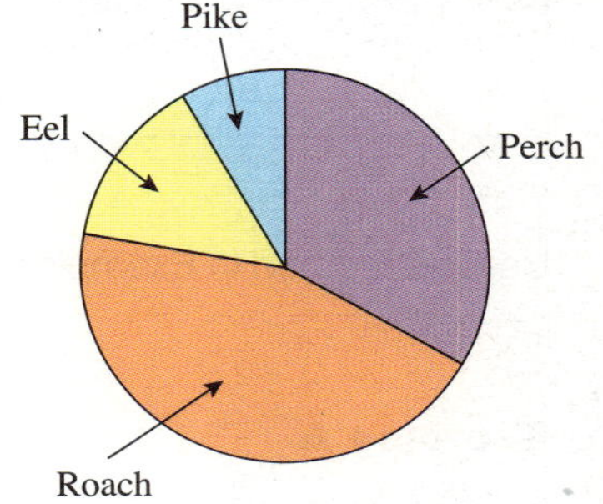

Use the method in Example 1 when the total number is a multiple or factor of 360.

Example 2

The table shows a family's gas bills.
They receive one bill every three months.
Draw a pie chart to represent the data.

	Cost of gas (£)
Jan–Mar	95
Apr–Jun	55
Jul–Sep	45
Oct–Dec	105

Solution 2

Step 1: Calculate the fraction of the whole that each sector represents.

Add up the values in the table to find the total amount.

95 + 55 + 45 + 105 = 300

The value for Jan–Mar is £95

So the Jan–Mar sector is $\frac{95}{300}$ of the whole circle (360°).

In the same way, Apr–Jun is $\frac{55}{300}$, Jul–Sep is $\frac{45}{300}$, Oct–Dec is $\frac{105}{300}$

Step 2: Calculate the angles for each sector.

The angle of the sector for Jan–Mar is $\frac{95}{300} \times 360° = 114°$ (using a calculator)

In the same way:

Apr–Jun	Jul–Sep	Oct–Dec
$\frac{55}{300} \times 360 = 66°$	$\frac{45}{300} \times 360 = 54°$	$\frac{105}{300} \times 360 = 126°$

Step 3: Check that the sum of all of the angles equals 360°

$114° + 66° + 54° + 126° = 360°$

Step 4:

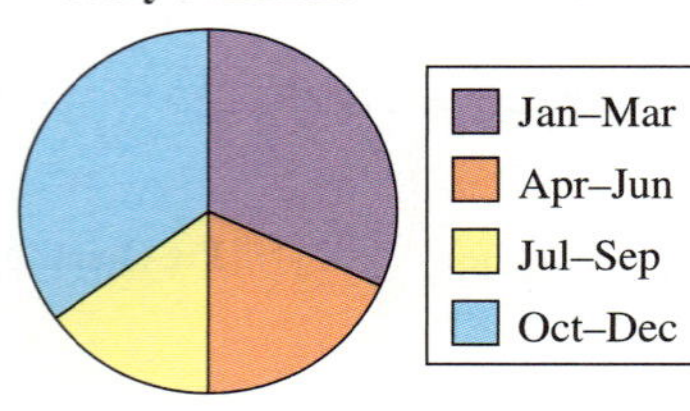

Use the method in Example 2 when the total number is not a multiple or factor of 360

Exercise A

1 **a** Copy the table below.

Transport	Frequency	Angle
Car	45	
Bus	35	
Train	10	40°
Total	**90**	**360°**

There are 90 'items'. Work out the angle for one item.

Work out the angle for each type of transport. Write the angles in the table.

b Draw a pie chart to represent the data.

2 For each part:

i copy and complete the table **ii** draw a pie chart to represent the data.

a

Drink	Frequency	Angle
Cola	25	
Orange	20	
Lemon	10	
Other	5	
Total	**60**	**360°**

b

House	Frequency	Angle
Detached	60	
Semi-detached	80	
Terraced	40	
Total	**180**	

3 The following goods were sold by a clothes shop in one week.

a Copy and complete the table opposite.

b Draw a pie chart to represent the data.

Goods	Value (£)	Angle
T-shirts	100	
Shorts	64	
Jackets	306	
Suits	250	
Total	**720**	

4 **a** Copy the table opposite.
Work out the fraction of the whole that each type of transport represents.
Work out the angle for each type of transport.
Write the angles in the table.

b Draw a pie chart to represent this data.

Transport	Frequency	Angle
Bus	200	
Car	370	
Bicycle	85	
Taxi	25	
Total	**680**	

5 A travel company arranges visits to the town, seaside or countryside.
The number of these visits, over a year, is shown in the table.
Draw a pie chart to show this information.

Visit	Number
Town	25
Seaside	45
Countryside	30

6 The costs of a family holiday are shown in the table.
Draw a pie chart to represent this information.

Item	Costs (£)
Flights	600
Accommodation	350
Food	490
Spending money	720

On a pie chart, the largest sector represents the modal group.

Example 3

30 students were asked to choose their favourite leisure activity.
The pie chart shows the results.

a What is the modal leisure activity?

b Calculate the number of students who chose cinema.

c **i** Measure and write down the angle of the gym sector.

ii How many students chose gym?

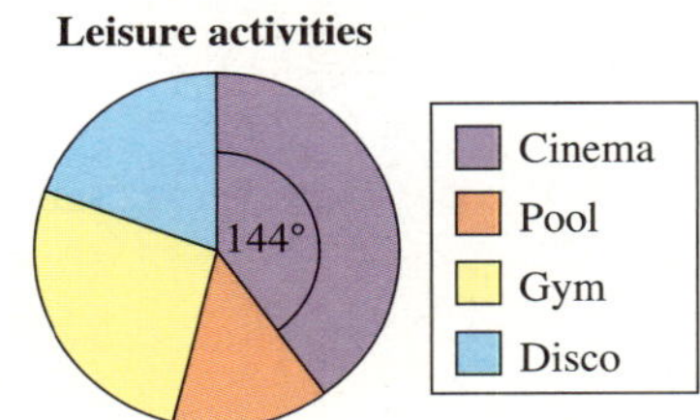

Solution 3

a Cinema is the modal activity, as it has the largest sector in the pie chart.

b **Step 1:** Find the angle.

Cinema sector angle = 144°

Step 2: Work out what fraction of the whole the sector represents.

Cinema is $\frac{144}{360} = \frac{2}{5}$ of the whole.

Step 3: Calculate the fraction of the total amount.

$\frac{2}{5}$ of 30 students $= \frac{2}{5} \times 30 = 12$ students

12 students chose cinema.

c **i** **Step 1:** Gym sector angle = 96°

ii **Step 2:** Gym is $\frac{96}{360}$ of the whole.

Step 3: $\frac{96}{360} \times 30 = 8$

Eight students chose gym.

Exercise B

1 The table opposite shows how 90 students travel to school one day. Copy and complete the pie chart.

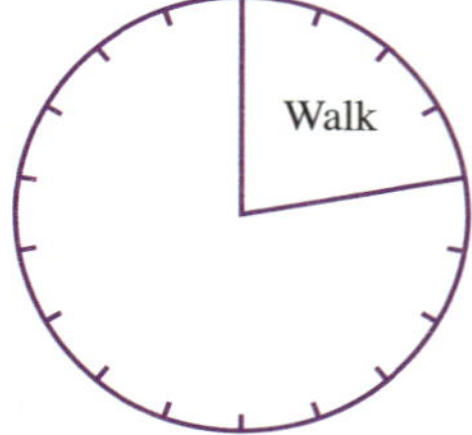

Transport	Frequency
Walk	20
Cycle	5
Bus	25
Car	40

2 There are 60 admissions to a hospital one day. The table shows the number of each type of admission.

Draw a pie chart to represent the data in the table.

Type of admission	Frequency
Medical (M)	18
Surgical (S)	12
Children (C)	6
Geriatric (G)	24

3 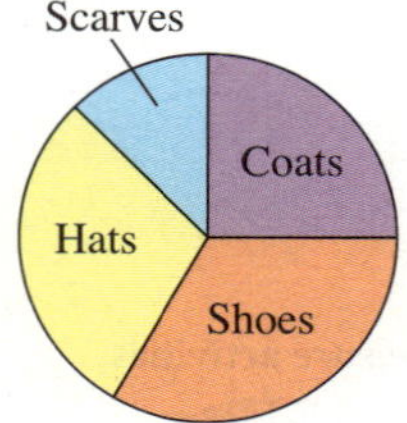

The pie chart shows the value of the sales of goods by a shop in September.

a Measure the size of the angle for coats.

b What fraction of the total sales were coats?

The goods in the table were sold by the shop in the month of October.

The total value of all the sales was £180.

c Draw a pie chart to represent these sales.

Goods	Value (£)
Hats	70
Scarves	50
Gloves	40
Umbrellas	20

4 The table shows the number of each type of house on an estate.
a What fraction of the houses were terraced houses?
b Draw a pie chart to represent this data.

Type of house	Number
Terraced (T)	180
Semi-detached (S)	141
Detached (D)	123
Bungalow (B)	96

5 The pie chart shows the annual costs of running a small family car.
a What fraction of the annual cost is petrol?
b The annual cost of maintenance is £350
Work out the total annual cost of running this car.

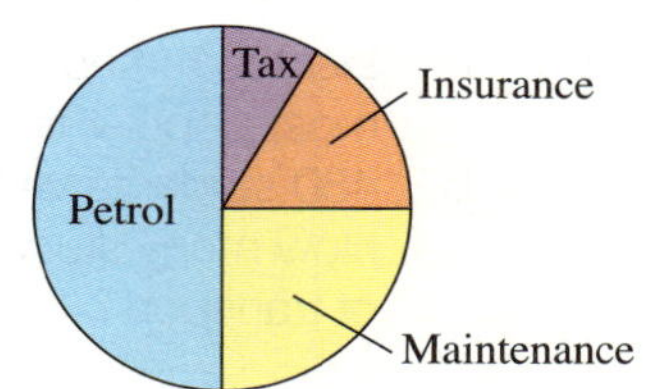

6 The IT staff at a college recorded how the computers were being used at lunchtime.
The table shows the results.
Draw a pie chart to represent this data.

Used for	Number of computers
E-mail	30
Games	22
Work	25
Internet	23

7 The table shows the average weekly water use for a family of four.
Draw a pie chart to represent these figures.

Use of water	Amount of water (litres)
Washing machine	240
Bathing	500
Flushing toilet	820
Other	350

8 There are three types of day-visits which people take in the UK.
The table shows the percentages for each type of day-visit last summer.
A pie chart is to be drawn to represent the data.
a Calculate the angle for countryside.
b Draw a pie chart to represent this information.

Destination	Percentage
Countryside	40
Seaside	25
Town	35

9 The road distances travelled by different types of vehicle in Great Britain in 2005 are shown in the table.
Draw a pie chart to represent this data.

The government expects the road distances to increase by 10% each year.
Shaun says, 'This means that in 2007 the distance travelled will be more than 800 billion kilometres.' Is he correct?
Explain your answer.

Type of vehicle	Distance (billion km)
Car	420
Lorry	100
Bus	130
Motorcycle	50

10 The 900 customers who shopped in a department store one day paid for their purchases using either cash, cheque or credit card.
One quarter used cash and 120 used cheques.
- **a** How many people used credit cards?
- **b** Draw a pie chart to show this information.

11 The pie chart shows the usual method of travel to school for students at a particular school.
- **a** List the methods of transport in order of popularity, most popular first.
- **b** 480 students walk to this school.
How many students use each of the other methods of transport?

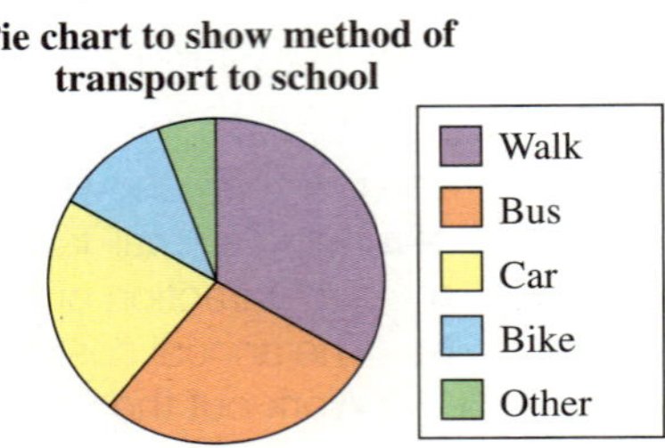

2.2 Stem and leaf diagrams

CAN YOU REMEMBER

- The meaning of the word 'frequency'?
- How to find the median, the mode and the range?

IN THIS SECTION YOU WILL

- Learn how to draw an ordered stem and leaf diagram to represent data.
- Learn how to interpret data in a stem and leaf diagram.
- Find the median, the mode and the range from a stem and leaf diagram.
- Understand the advantages of using a stem and leaf diagram.

The *ordered stem and leaf* diagram below shows the number of passengers on each of 17 bus journeys.

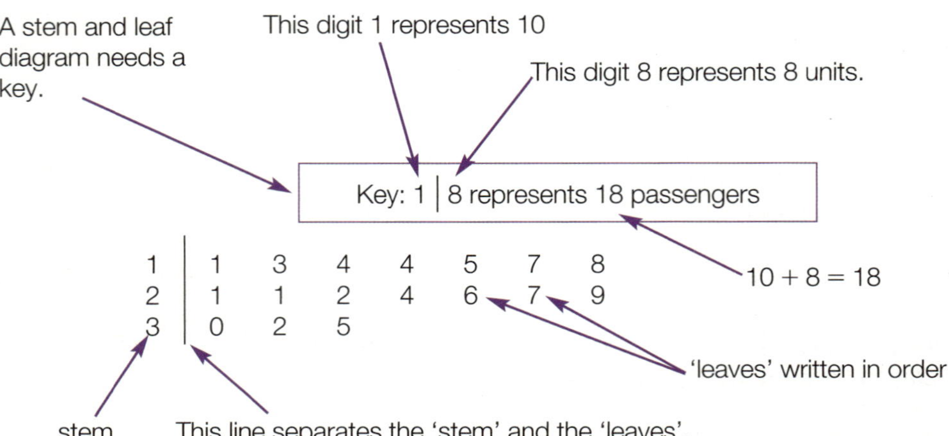

The mode, median and range can be found directly from a stem and leaf diagram.

Example 1

a Draw an ordered stem and leaf diagram to represent the following data.

12 14 32 9 15 23 31 19 14 6 25 20 16 28 7

b Work out the:

i mode **ii** median **iii** range.

Solution 1

a Rewrite the data in order of size:

6	7	9	12	14
14	15	16	19	20
23	25	28	31	32

Key: 2 | 3 represents 23

Values less than 10 have 'stem' 0

Stem	Leaves
0	6 7 9
1	2 4 4 5 6 9
2	0 3 5 8
3	1 2

b **i** The **mode** is the value that occurs most times.

Mode = **14**

ii The **median** is the middle value in an ordered list.
In the stem and leaf diagram the values are in order.
There are 15 values.

$$\text{Median} = \frac{(15 + 1)}{2}\text{th value} = \textbf{eighth value} = \textbf{16}$$

iii Range = **largest value** − **smallest value** = **32** − **6** = 26

Exercise A

1 Copy and complete the stem and leaf diagram for the following data.
Remember to complete the key.

12 15 16 11 18 20 22 25 29 14 22 23 28 31 33 35

Key: ...... | ...... represents ....

1 | ....
2 | ....
3 | ....

2 The number of students in each of 20 classes is listed below.

14 17 22 23 24 22 15 16 10 31 15 21 25 20 13 18 25 12 18 21

Draw a stem and leaf diagram with a key to represent this data.

3 The number of customers queuing at a town's main post office each day at 12 noon is recorded for twenty days. The results are:

21 13 15 23 31 14 10 6 12 14 18 18 31 30 24 20 18 11 8 3

a Draw a stem and leaf diagram to represent this data. Include a key.
b Write down the mode.
c Work out the range of the number of customers queuing.

4 Pupils in a class were asked to count how many CDs they owned.
The results are:

25	35	44	15	24	34	18	20	31	12	32	45	50
64	19	13	23	52	55	16	42	44	46	53	24	

a Draw an ordered stem and leaf diagram with a key to represent this data.
b Work out the range of the number of CDs owned.
c Find the median.

5 The stem and leaf diagram represents the number of cars parked in a car park each day at 10 am for 15 days.
a Work out the range.
b Write down the mode.
c Calculate the median.

Key: 4 | 5 represents 45 cars

4	2	3	5	7	8	9	
5	0	1	2	6	6	8	9
6	2	3					

6 The number of customers using a barber is recorded each week and is listed below:

123 131 129 111 102 105 117 119 120 128 135

a Copy and complete the ordered stem and leaf diagram.
b Work out the range.
c Find the median.

Key: 10 | 5 represents 105 customers

10	2	5
11		
12		
13		

A stem and leaf diagram shows the shape of a distribution, similar to a bar chart.

1	**2**	**3**	**5**			
2	**4**	**5**	**8**	**9**		
3	**1**	**2**	**4**	**6**	**6**	**9**

The raw data can be read from a stem and leaf diagram.
In a bar chart, the raw data is 'lost'.

Example 2

The stem and leaf diagram shows the number of driving lessons people had before they passed their driving test.

a How many people were asked?
b Write down the range of the number of driving lessons.
c Calculate the median number of driving lessons.
d Saleem passes his test. When his number of driving lessons is added to the stem and leaf diagram the median increases by 1 and the range increases by 1
Work out the number of driving lessons Saleem had.

Key: 2 | 3 represents 23 lessons

1	0	3	5	5	8
2	0	3	5	9	
3	1	6			
4	4				
5	0	1			

Solution 2

a Count the number of leaves: 14 people were asked.

b Range = largest value − smallest value = 51 − 10 = 41 lessons

c Median $= \frac{(14 + 1)}{2}$ th value = 7.5th value

The 7.5th value is the average of the seventh value and the eighth value.

So median $= \frac{23 + 25}{2} = \frac{48}{2} = 24$ lessons

d The range increases by 1 so the value is either 1 less than the smallest value (10 − 1 = 9) or 1 more than the largest value (51 + 1 = 52).
The median increases by 1 so the new number of driving lessons must be above the old median.
Saleem had 52 driving lessons.

Exercise B

1 A company records the number of days that employees are off sick.
The stem and leaf diagram shows the results.

Key: 0 | 3 represents 3 days absent

0	0	0	2	3	5	7	8
1	0	1	2	3	5		
2	1	3					
3	1						

a How many employees had no days off sick?
b What was the greatest number of days off sick?
c How many employees were off sick for more than 10 days?
d Work out the median number of days off sick.
e Explain an advantage of a stem and leaf diagram over a bar chart.

2 Dayton Rugby Club recorded the number of matches its supporters attended last season.
The stem and leaf diagram shows the number of matches from last season.

Key: 1 | 2 represents 12 games

0	8	9						
1	0	0	2	3	3	5	6	9
2	0	1	1	2	2	2	3	

a Work out the range. **b** Write down the mode. **c** Find the median.

Annie's data was missed off the diagram. When it is added to the stem and leaf diagram the range did not change but the median was reduced.

d How many matches could Annie have attended? Explain your reasons.

3 The ordered stem and leaf diagram represents the number of e-mails that each of 12 students received last week.
It contains three errors.
Describe each error.

1	0	5	3	5	8
2	0	3	9		
3	1	6			
4	4				

4 A manager of a grocery shop recorded how much, to the nearest pound, each of 15 customers had spent.
The range was £19
The median was £11
Three customers spent over £20
The smallest amount spent was £2
Draw a stem and leaf diagram to represent this information. Invent the entries to complete the diagram.

5 The stem and leaf diagram shows the number of patients a doctor saw each day for 20 days.

Key: 1 | 0 represents 10 patients

0	6	7	8	9	9	9		
1	0	1	3	3	5	7	8	8
2	0	1	2	2	3	5		

- **a** Work out the range of the number of patients seen.
- **b** Write down the mode of the number of patients seen.
- **c** Calculate the median number of patients seen.
- **d** On the 21st day the doctor saw 28 patients. Write down the new range and the new median when this number of patients is added to the diagram.

6 A group of students measured their pulse rate after exercising. The results were:

65	72	69	82	85	94	76	104
67	120	118	95	128	122	86	63

- **a** Draw a stem and leaf diagram to represent this data. Include a key.
- **b** Work out the range.
- **c** Calculate the median.
- **d** Any student with a pulse rate above 90 was not allowed to do further exercise. What are the range and the median of the pulse rates of the students who could carry on exercising?

2.3 Scatter graphs

CAN YOU REMEMBER

- How to plot points on a graph?
- How to read values from a graph?

IN THIS SECTION YOU WILL

- Understand the meaning of 'positive correlation', 'negative correlation' and 'no correlation'.
- Learn how to use and interpret a scatter diagram.
- Learn how to draw and use a line of best fit on a scatter graph.
- Learn when **not** to use a line of best fit.

Scatter graphs are used to investigate relationships between two sets of data.
A scatter graph may show a link or *correlation* between two variables.

For example, this scatter graph shows the hours of sunshine each day and the amount of rainfall (in mm) each day for 12 days.

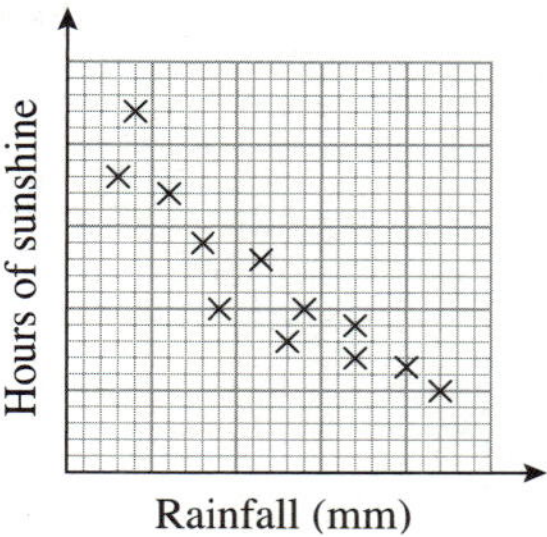

The graph shows that as the amount of rainfall increases, the hours of sunshine decrease. This suggests that the two variables 'hours of sunshine' and 'rainfall' are linked.

Correlation can be shown by a *line of best fit*. This is a straight line which is as close to the points as possible, drawn by eye. The line should have roughly the same number of points above it as below it.

If the line of best fit on a scatter graph has a positive gradient then the correlation is positive. If it has a negative gradient then the correlation is negative.

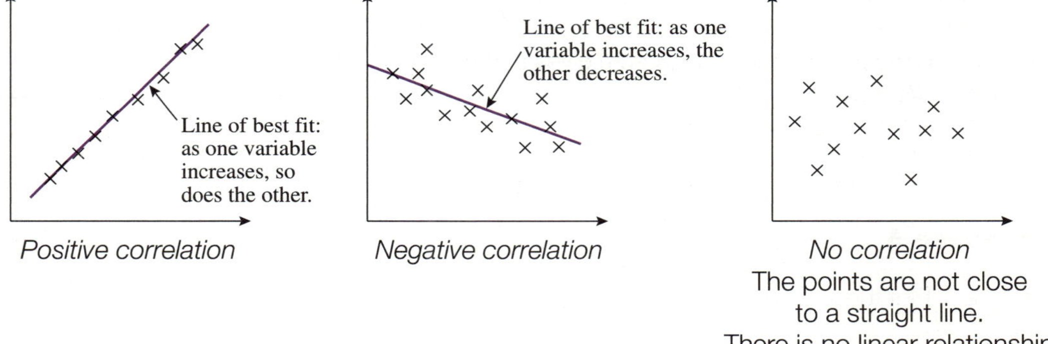

Positive correlation

Negative correlation

No correlation
The points are not close to a straight line.
There is no linear relationship between the two variables.

A line of best fit can be used to predict the value for one variable given a value of the other variable.

Example 1

The table shows the heights and weights of ten men.

Height (cm)	155	157	164	169	172	177	181	185	190	195
Weight (kg)	71	70	76	80	79	85	82	94	96	94

a Plot the points on a scatter graph.
b Draw a line of best fit on the scatter graph.
c Describe the relationship between height and weight.
d Use the line of best fit to estimate the weight of a man who is 182 cm tall.

Solution 1

a, b

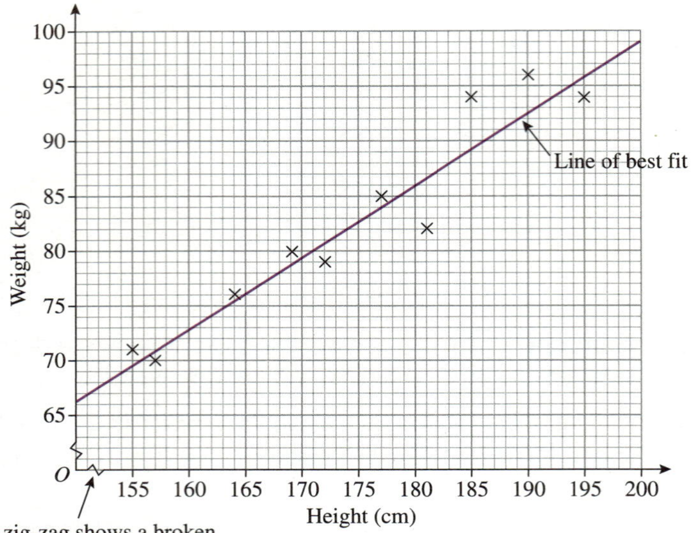

c As the heights increase, so do the weights.
There is positive correlation between height and weight.

d Reading from a height of 182 cm gives a weight of 87.5 kg.

Exercise A

1 a Plot these points as a scatter graph.

Length and weight of pike

Length, inches	10	12	13	14	15	16	18	21	32
Weight, lb	3	10	18	14	22	25	28	32	36

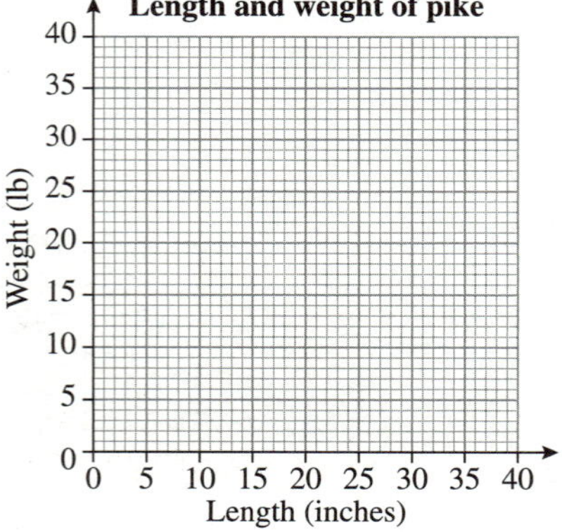

b Draw a line of best fit.

c Comment on the relationship between length and weight of pike.

2 The shoe sizes and waist sizes of eight teenagers are recorded in the table.

Shoe size	3	3.5	4	5	6	6.5	8	9
Waist size (inches)	22	23	25	26	28	30	32	34

a Plot the data as a scatter graph.

b Comment on the relationship shown by your graph.

c Draw a line of best fit.

d Use your line of best fit to estimate the waist size of a teenager with shoe size 5.5

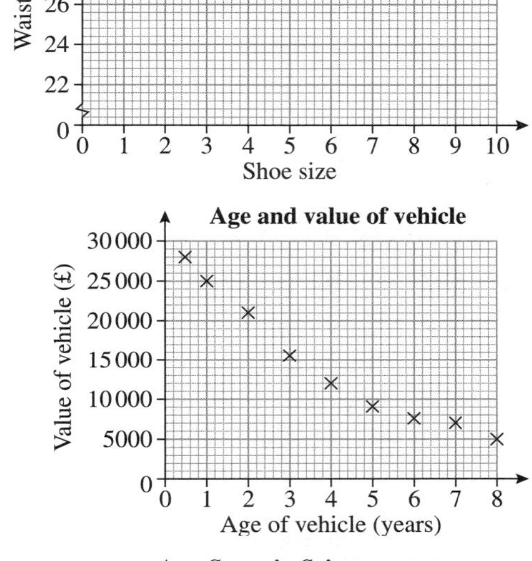

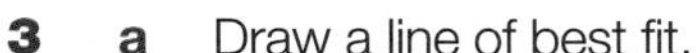

3 **a** Draw a line of best fit.

b Describe the type of correlation in the scatter graph.

c Use your line of best fit to estimate the value of the vehicle when it was $2\frac{1}{2}$ years old.

4 **a** Draw a line of best fit.

b Describe the type of correlation shown.

c Use your line of best fit to estimate the score in Science test paper 1 for a student who scored 23 in Science test paper 2

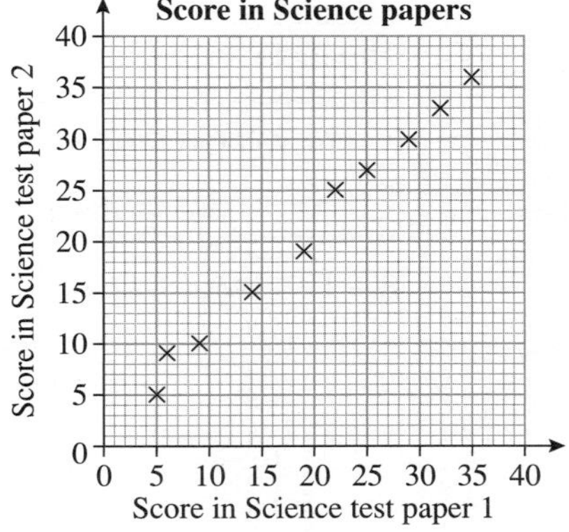

5

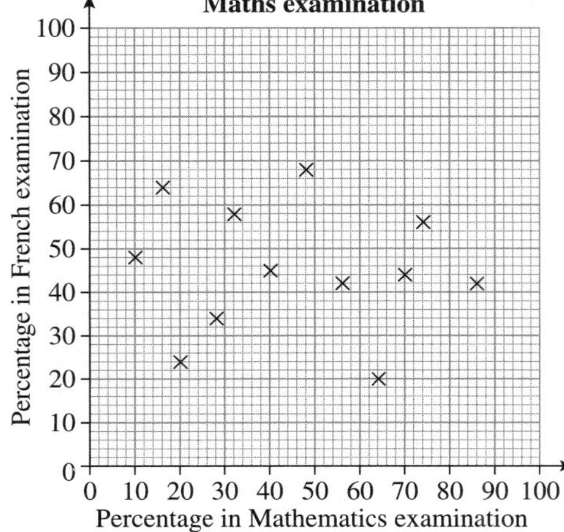

a What type of correlation is shown in the scatter graph on the left?

b Is there a relationship between the percentage marks in the French and the percentage marks in the Mathematics examinations?
Explain your answer.

6 Eight pupils were asked how much time each of them spent on their computer and each of them spent watching TV on one day.
Their results are shown in the table.

Time spent on the computer (min)	10	20	30	35	40	45	50	60
Time spent watching TV (min)	120	100	80	60	50	30	40	20

a Plot the data as a scatter diagram.
b Draw a line of best fit.
c Describe the relationship between the time spent on the computer and the time spent watching TV.
d Another pupil spent 25 minutes on his computer that day.
Estimate the time he spent watching TV.

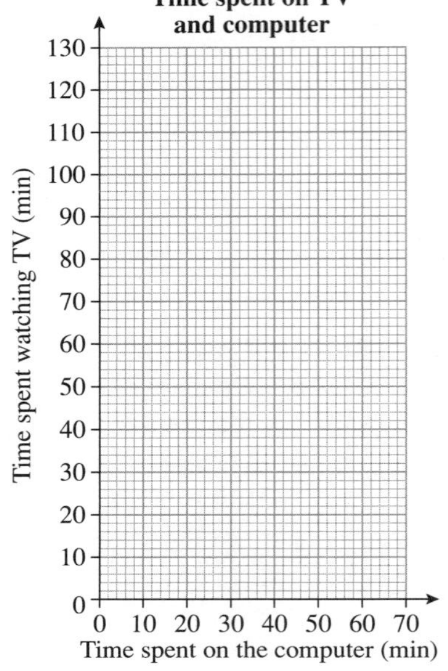

7 In a science experiment eight students were asked to time how fast they could catch a moving object.
The table shows their times before and after practising the experiment.

Time without practice (s)	2.5	3	3.5	4	4	5	5	6
Time with practice (s)	2	3	3	3.5	4	4	5.5	7

a Plot this data as a scatter graph.

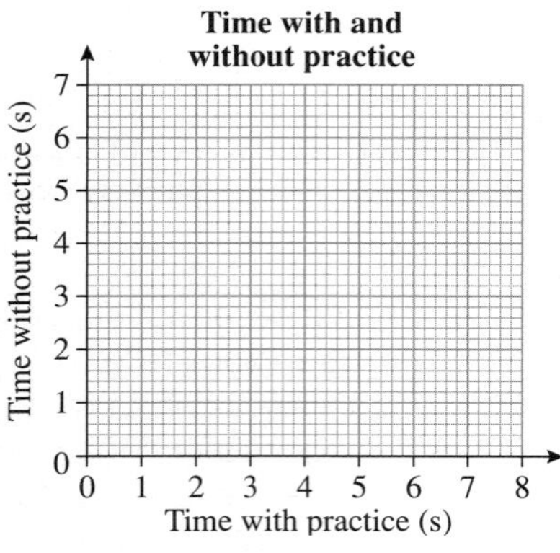

b Draw a line of best fit.
c Describe the relationship between the times without practice and times with practice.
d Use your line of best fit to estimate the time with practice of a pupil who took 5.5 seconds to catch the object without practice.

The closer the points are to a straight line, the stronger the correlation.

Strong correlation
(points close to being in a straight line)

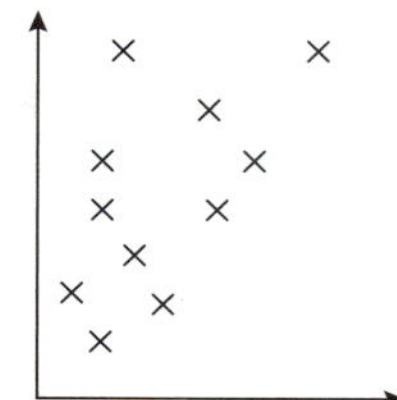

Weak correlation
(points follow a general pattern)

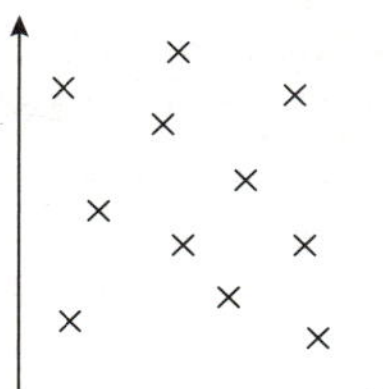

No correlation
(points well scattered)

A line of best fit should only be used to estimate values within the range of a set of data. This is called *interpolation.* The line of best fit must not be extended beyond the actual data to make predictions, because there is no evidence that any pattern in the data will continue. Extending the line outside the data values is called *extrapolation.*

Example 2

The scatter diagram shows the amount of time spent on revision and the score obtained in a Mathematics examination for eight students.

a Draw a line of best fit on the scatter graph.

b What type of correlation is shown in the scatter graph?

c Use your line of best fit to estimate the exam score of a student who revised for 8 hours.

d Comment on the reliability of your estimate in part **c**.

e Explain why it is not sensible to use the line of best fit to estimate the exam score of a student who revised for 10 hours.

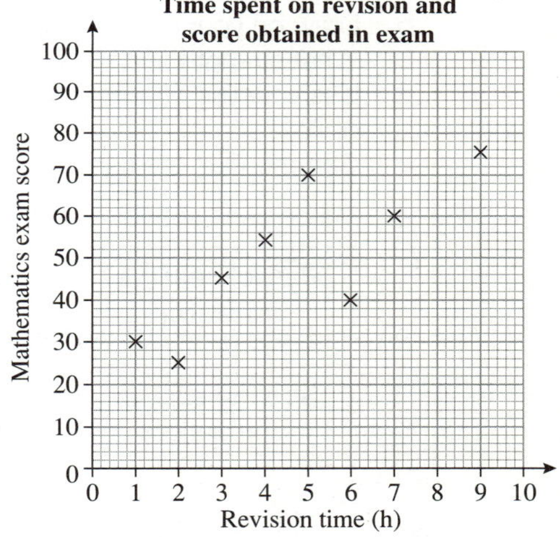

Solution 2

a

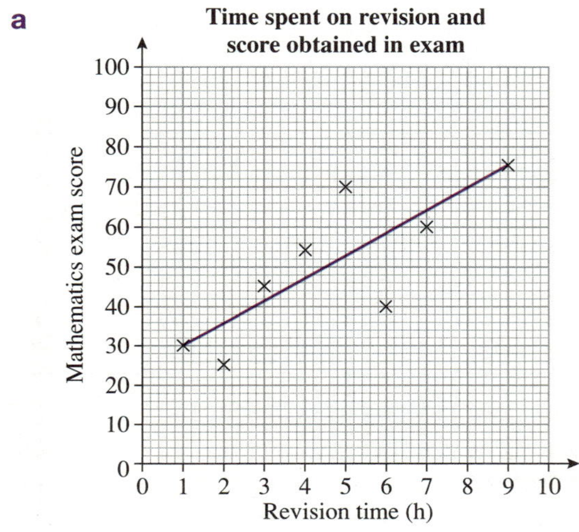

b Weak positive correlation, as the points are not very close to the line.

c Reading from 8 hours on the horizontal axis, the estimated exam score is 70

d The estimate is within the range of the data but the correlation is quite weak. So it may not be a very reliable estimate.

e This value is outside the given range of data. The pattern in the relationship may not continue.

Exercise B

1 Twelve people followed a special diet.
The scatter diagram shows the number of weeks on the diet and the amount of weight in kilograms lost by each person.

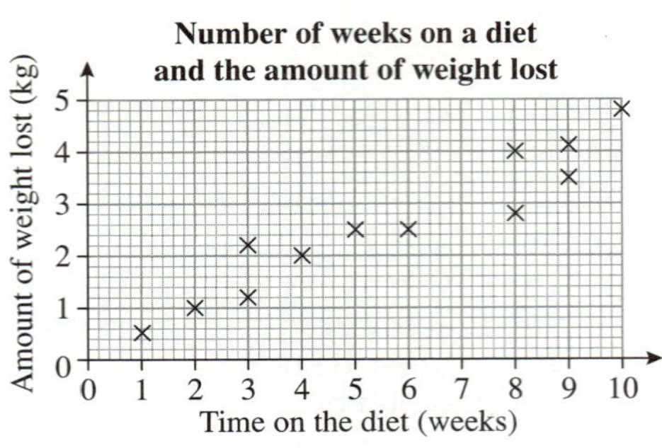

a Draw a line of best fit on a copy of the diagram.
b What type of correlation is shown?
c Use your line of best fit to estimate how much weight a person would be expected to lose after seven weeks on the diet.
d Is your estimate in part **c** interpolation or extrapolation? Explain your answer.

2 At a job interview six candidates were tested for their numeracy and IT skills.
The table shows their scores.

Numeracy score	3	5	6	8	9	10
IT score	1	4	6	9	6	9

a Plot a scatter graph of this data.
b Draw on your scatter graph a line of best fit.
c What strength and type of correlation is shown in the scatter graph?
d Use your line of best fit to estimate the numeracy score of a candidate who had an IT score of 7
e Comment on the reliability of your estimate.

3 **a** Match each scatter graph below with one of the following labels.

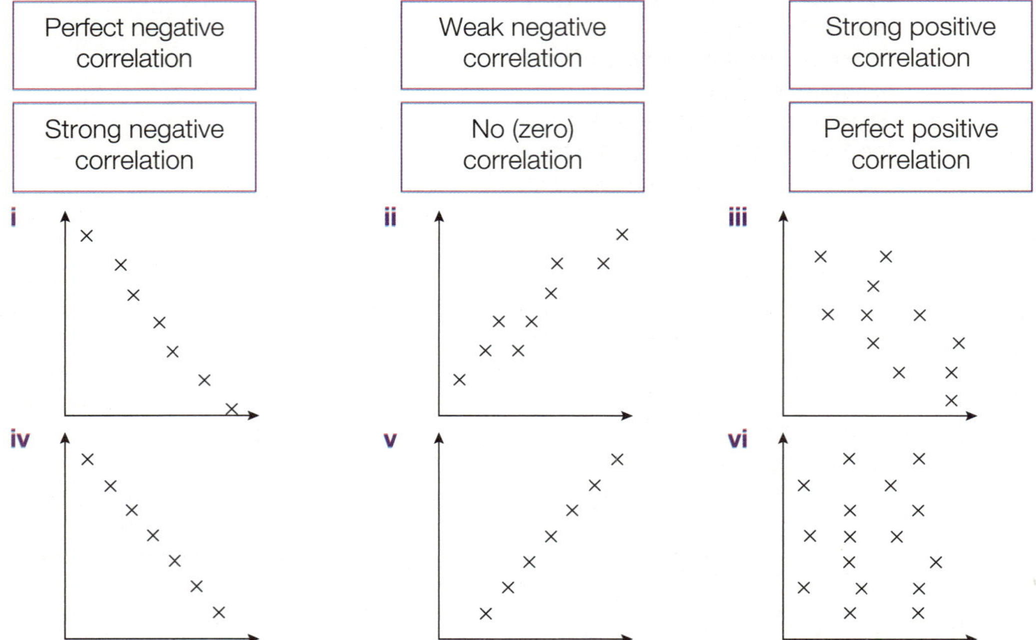

b What type of correlation would you expect with these pairs of variables?
i The heights and weights of a group of 11-year-old girls.
ii The heights of fathers and their eldest son.
iii The amount of time practising and the number of errors in a spelling test.
c Write down a pair of variables which would show strong negative correlation.

4 Eight new cars with different engine sizes were tested for their fuel consumption during motorway driving.
The table shows the results.

Engine size (cm^3)	950	1000	1200	1400	1500	1800	2000	2200
Fuel consumption (mpg)	62	57	55	48	45	42	40	36

a Draw a scatter graph for this data.
(Hint: Use 'broken' scales. Start the horizontal axis at 900 cm^3 and let 1 cm = 100 cm^3. Start the vertical axis at 30 and let 2 cm = 10 mpg.)
b Draw a line of best fit on the scatter graph.
c Describe the strength and type of correlation shown.
d Use the line of best fit to estimate:
  i the consumption for a car with engine size 1300 cm^3
  ii the engine size of a car that has a consumption rate of 50 mpg.
e Explain why the line of best fit should not be used to estimate the fuel consumption for cars with an engine size greater than 2200 cm^3

5 In a survey on weekly spending habits six families recorded the amount they spent in one week on groceries.
The results are shown in the table.

Family size	2	3	4	4	6	6
Amount spent (£)	50	65	80	94	120	135

a Plot the data as a scatter graph.
b Describe the relationship shown by the scatter graph.
c Draw a line of best fit on the scatter graph.
d Use your line of best fit to estimate the weekly spend on groceries by:
  i a family of size 5
  ii a single person (a family of size 1).
e Which of your estimates in part **d** is the less reliable?
Give a reason for your answer.
f Explain why you should not use your line of best fit to estimate the weekly spend by a family of nine people.

Chapter summary

- The angle of each sector of a pie chart is in proportion to the amount of information it represents.
- There are 360° in a full circle.
- The angles of the sectors in a pie chart add up to 360°.
- To draw a pie chart:
  Step 1: When the total number is a multiple or factor of 360, calculate the angle for one item.
  OR
  When the total number is not a multiple or factor of 360, calculate the fraction of the whole that each sector represents.
  Step 2: Calculate the angle for each sector.

Step 3: Check that the sum of all of the angles equals 360°.
Step 4: Draw a circle.
Draw a straight line (a radius) from the centre of the circle to the circumference.
Use a protractor to measure accurately and then draw the angle for each sector.
Complete the pie chart by labelling each sector or using a key (not both).

- To interpret a pie chart:
  Step 1: Measure the angle for a sector.
  Step 2: Work out what fraction of the whole the sector represents.
  Step 3: Calculate the fraction of the total amount.
- On a pie chart, the largest sector represents the modal group.
- In a stem and leaf diagram:
  - the data is written in order
  - a key is needed; for example 1 | 7 represents 17
- The mode, median and range can be found from a stem and leaf diagram.
- A stem and leaf diagram shows the shape of a distribution.
- The raw data can be read from a stem and leaf diagram.
- Scatter graphs are used to investigate relationships between two sets of data.
- A scatter graph may show a link or *correlation* between two variables.
- Correlation can be shown by a line of best fit. This is a straight line which is as close to the points as possible, drawn by eye. The line should have roughly the same number of points above it as below it.

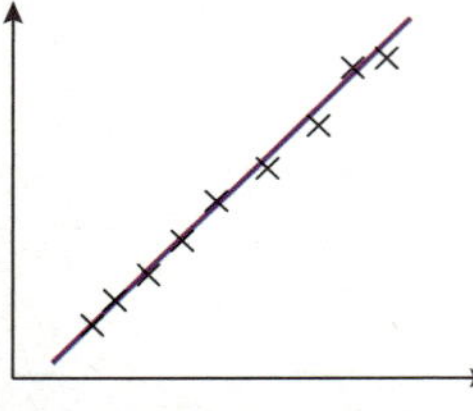

Positive correlation

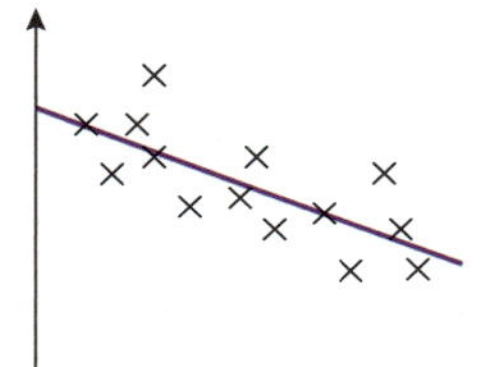

Negative correlation

No correlation
The points are not close to a straight line.
There is no linear relationship between the two variables.

- The closer the points are to a straight line, the stronger the correlation.

Strong correlation
(points close to a straight line)

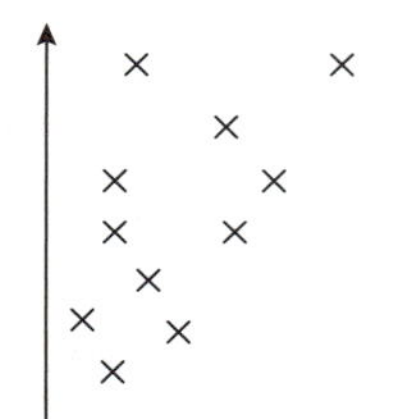

Weak correlation
(points follow a general pattern)

- A line of best fit should only be used to estimate values within the range of a set of data. This is called *interpolation*.
- The line of best fit must not be extended beyond the actual data to make predictions, because there is no evidence that any pattern in the data will continue. Extending the line outside the data values is called *extrapolation*.

Chapter review

1 The graph shows the number of passengers going through airports in the UK between 1953 and 2004

a Use the graph to estimate the number of passengers going through UK airports in 1980

b Use the graph to estimate in which year the number of passengers was 120 million.

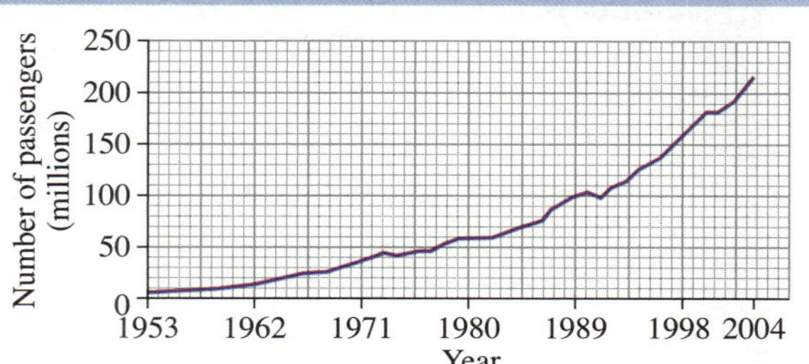

2 **a** Write down the type of correlation shown in each of the scatter graphs below.

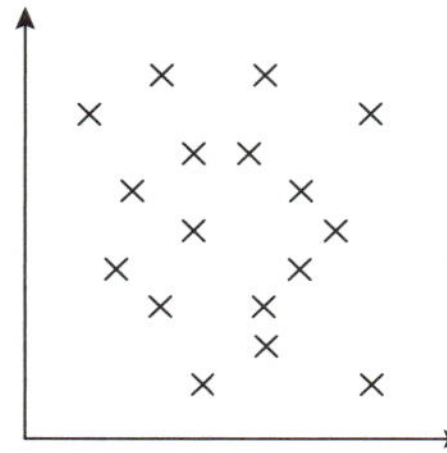

Scatter graph i

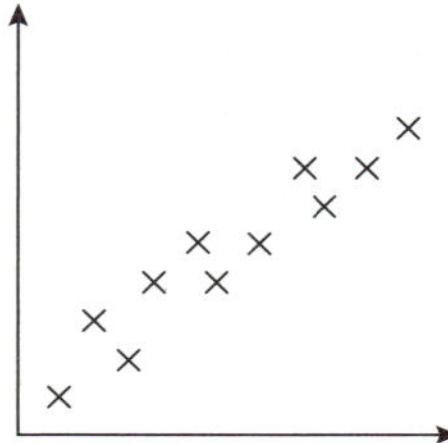

Scatter graph ii

b The marks for a group of pupils who sat two tests are shown in the scatter graph opposite.

i Draw a line of best fit on a copy of the graph.

ii Use your line of best fit to estimate the French test mark for a pupil who scored 50 marks in the Physics test.

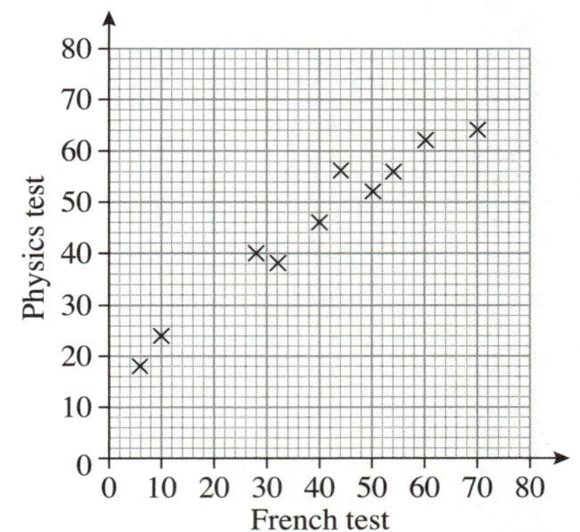

3 Abigail listed the favourite summer sports of the pupils in her class.

Sport	Tennis	Cricket	Swimming	Athletics	Golf
Number of pupils	7	6	11	4	2

Abigail wants to illustrate this information with a pie chart.

a How many degrees on the pie chart will represent one student?

b How many degrees on the pie chart will represent the students whose favourite summer sport is swimming?

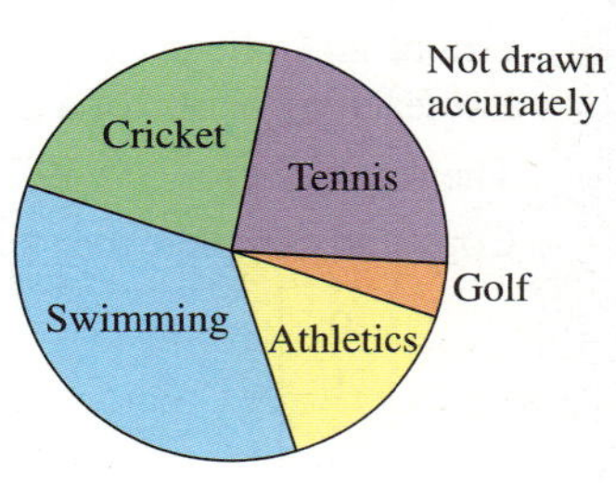

4 The stem and leaf diagram shows the number of miles travelled by a doctor on call each day for 21 days.

Stem	Leaf						
1	1	6	8	8			
2	0	0	2	2	3	5	9
3	2	4	5	6			
4	4	5	6				
5	0	7					
6	6						

Key: 1 | 6 represents 16 miles travelled

a Find the range of this data.
b What is the median value?
c On how many days did the doctor travel between 30 and 60 miles?

5 The table shows the type of weather James recorded in his diary over 30 days.
a Display the data in a fully labelled pie chart.
b What was the modal type of weather?

Type of weather	Number of days
sunny	10
rain	9
cloudy but dry	8
snow	1
fog	2

6 The pie chart shows the proportions of destination countries for people going on holiday.
a What proportion of people went on holiday in the UK?
b 200 people went on holiday in Europe. How many people went on holiday altogether?
c Work out the number of people who went on holiday in the USA.

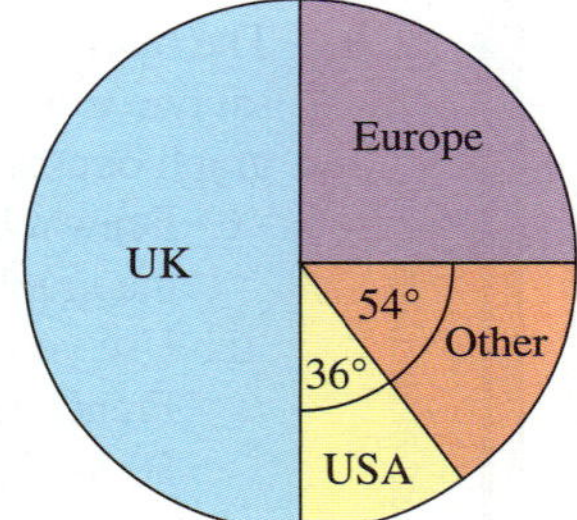

7 The time that eight teenagers spent on their mobile phones and spent watching TV one day is recorded in the table.

Time on mobile phone (minutes)	20	30	30	50	60	60	70	70
Time spent watching TV (minutes)	60	50	40	45	35	25	15	20

a Plot this data as a scatter graph.
b Draw a line of best fit on your scatter graph.
c Describe the relationship shown in the scatter graph.

8 Cambford College carried out a survey of the number of students in each year 13 class during the last teaching period of a day.

The results were: 9 12 15 19 10 6 12 18 20 12 19 8 14 9 22 21

Copy and complete the stem and leaf diagram to show these results.

Stem	Leaf
0	
1	
2	

Key: .... | ...... represents .... students

9 The table shows the type of transport used by 80 commuters. Draw and label a pie chart to represent this information.

Type of transport	Number of commuters
Car	35
Bus	25
Bike	18
Walk	2

10 A number of people were asked how many car journeys they had taken in a week.
The results are shown in the stem and leaf diagram.

Stem	Leaf
0	7
1	1 5 5 6 9
2	0 1 2 4 4 5 9
3	2 5 8
4	2

Key: 1 | 5 represents 15 car journeys

a How many people were asked?
b What was the median number of car journeys?
c Work out the range of the number of car journeys.

CHAPTER

3 Percentages

3.1 Expressing one quantity as a percentage of another

CAN YOU REMEMBER

- How to express one quantity as a fraction of another?
- How to change from one unit to another?
- How to simplify a fraction (by cancelling common factors)?
- Simple conversions from fractions to percentages, e.g. $\frac{1}{2} = 50\%$, $\frac{1}{3} = 33.3\%$?

IN THIS SECTION YOU WILL

- Learn how to write one number as a percentage of another number.
- Use percentages to compare quantities using the same or different units.
- Learn how to write one quantity as a percentage of another quantity.

In this test, the score was 7 out of 10

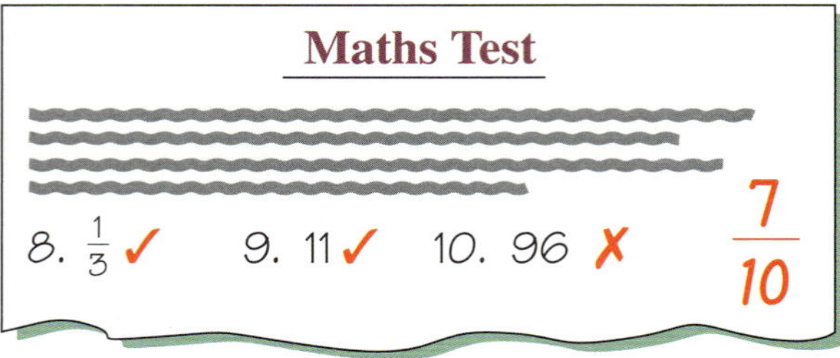

7 written as a fraction of 10 is $\frac{7}{10}$

$\frac{7}{10} = \frac{70}{100} = 70\%$

7 written as a percentage of 10 = 70%.

To write a quantity as a percentage of another quantity:

Method 1

Step 1: Make sure that both quantities have the same units.

Step 2: Write the fraction $\frac{\text{first quantity}}{\text{second quantity}}$ as a fraction with a denominator of 100

Step 3: Write the fraction as a percentage.
For example, $\frac{70}{100} = 70\%$

Method 2

Step 1: Make sure that both quantities have the same units.

Step 2: Use the formula $\frac{\text{first quantity}}{\text{second quantity}} \times 100\%$

For example,
$\frac{7}{10} \times 100\% = 70\%$

Example 1

a Write 60 as a percentage of 150

b Write 3 kg as a percentage of 10 kg.

c Write 70 cm as a percentage of 1 metre.

Solution 1

a **Method 1**

Write $\frac{60}{150}$ as a fraction and cancel:

$\frac{60}{150} = \frac{6}{15} = \frac{2}{5}$

Write $\frac{2}{5}$ as a fraction with a denominator of 100

$\frac{2}{5} = \frac{2 \times 20}{5 \times 20} = \frac{40}{100} = 40\%$

Method 2

Use the formula

$\frac{\text{first quantity}}{\text{second quantity}} \times 100\%$

$\frac{60}{150} \times 100\% = 40\%$

b **Step 1:** Both quantities have the same units.

Method 1

Step 2: $\frac{3\,\text{kg}}{10\,\text{kg}}$ simplifies by cancelling the common units to $\frac{3}{10}$

$\frac{3}{10} \times 100\% = 30\%$

Method 2

$\frac{3}{10} = \frac{3 \times 10}{10 \times 10} = \frac{30}{100} = 30\%$

c **Step 1:** 1 metre = 100 cm

Step 2: $\frac{70\,\text{cm}}{1\,\text{metre}} = \frac{70\,\text{cm}}{100\,\text{cm}} = \frac{70}{100} = 70\%$

Exercise A

1 Copy and complete:

a $\frac{9}{10} = \frac{}{100} = \ldots\%$ **b** $\frac{21}{50} = \frac{}{100} = \ldots\%$ **c** $\frac{4}{25} = \frac{}{100} = \ldots\%$

d $\frac{7}{20} = \frac{}{100} = \ldots\%$ **e** $\frac{3}{4} = \frac{}{100} = \ldots\%$ **f** $\frac{4}{5} = \frac{}{100} = \ldots\%$

2 **a** Write 1 as a percentage of 10
b Write 3 as a percentage of 5
c Write 4 as a percentage of 16
d Write 8 as a percentage of 20
e Write 1 as a percentage of 4
f Write 18 as a percentage of 20
g Write 80 as a percentage of 160
h Write 50 as a percentage of 200

3 In each part, remember to simplify by cancelling the common units.

a Write 2 cm as a percentage of 8 cm.
b Write 4 litres as a percentage of 20 litres.
c Write 6 grams as a percentage of 25 grams.
d Write 9 cm^3 as a percentage of 90 cm^3
e Write 4 kg as a percentage of 8 kg.
f Write 3 metres as a percentage of 10 metres.

4 In each part, change to common units. Then cancel the common units before converting to a percentage.

- **a** Write 40 cm as a percentage of 1 metre (hint: 100 cm = 1 metre).
- **b** Write 6 inches as a percentage of 1 foot (hint: 12 inches = 1 foot).
- **c** Write 9 inches as a percentage of 3 feet.
- **d** Write 20 cl as a percentage of 1 litre (hint: 100 cl = 1 litre).
- **e** Write 300 grams as a percentage of 1 kg (hint: 1000 grams = 1 kg).
- **f** Write 250 kg as a percentage of 1 tonne (hint: 1000 kg = 1 tonne).
- **g** Write 75p as a percentage of £1
- **h** Write 500 metres as a percentage of 1 kilometre (hint: 1000 metres = 1 km).

5 In each part, give your answer to one decimal place.

- **a** Write 1 as a percentage of 3
- **b** Write 6 as a percentage of 9
- **c** Write 5 as a percentage of 7
- **d** Write 9 as a percentage of 11
- **e** Write 18 as a percentage of 27
- **f** Write 8 as a percentage of 13
- **g** Write 7 as a percentage of 21
- **h** Write 25 as a percentage of 42

6 In each part, give your answer to one decimal place.

- **a** Write 6 cm as a percentage of 9 cm.
- **b** Write 5 tonnes as a percentage of 15 tonnes.
- **c** Write 12 miles as a percentage of 72 miles.
- **d** Write £14 as a percentage of £98
- **e** Write 8 km as a percentage of 12 km.
- **f** Write 25 kg as a percentage of 30 kg.
- **g** Write 21 cl as a percentage of 26 cl.
- **h** Write 12 cm^2 as a percentage of 34 cm^2

7 Use the fact that 1 mile = 1760 yards to write 440 yards as a percentage of 1 mile.

8 2460 fish are caught in a net. 820 are too small and are thrown back in the sea.
What percentage of the fish is thrown back in the sea?
Write your answer to one decimal place.

9 936 people visit a theatre in London. 104 are from Yorkshire.
What percentage of the total is from Yorkshire?
Write your answer to one decimal place.

10 21 600 people attend a football match. 8640 support the away team.
What percentage of the total attendance supports the away team?

11 Belinda spends £97.62 at the supermarket.
£32.54 of this is on wine.
What percentage of her total bill is spent on wine?
Write your answer to one decimal place.

Exercise B

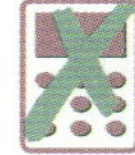

1 60 children visit a show. 36 are boys.
What percentage of the children are girls?

2 A shape has ten sides. Three of the sides are curved.
The rest are straight. What percentage of the sides is straight?

3 A bag contains 13 red marbles, seven blue marbles and five yellow marbles.
What percentage of the marbles is **not** yellow?

4 In test 1 a student scores 13 out of 20
In test 2 the same student scores 24 out of 30
In which test did the student do better?

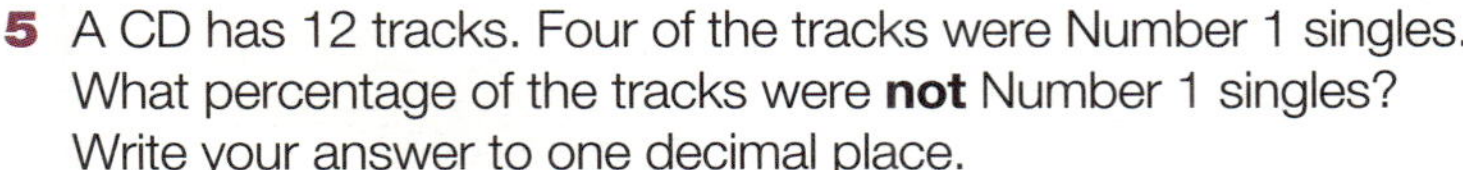

5 A CD has 12 tracks. Four of the tracks were Number 1 singles.
What percentage of the tracks were **not** Number 1 singles?
Write your answer to one decimal place.

6 A shop has two offers.
Which is the better value?
Use percentages to explain your answer.

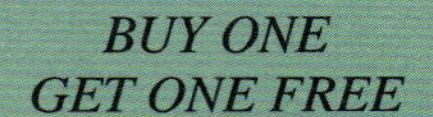

BUY TWO GET THE THIRD FREE

7 In test 1 a student scores 13 out of 15
In test 2 the same student scores 38 out of 45
In which test did the student do better?
Explain your answer by giving the percentage mark for each test.

8 An 800 ml bottle contains 500 ml of water.
Darren says that the bottle is more than 50% but less than 60% full.
Is he correct? Explain your answer.

9 A book contains 750 pages.
300 of the pages have pictures and no writing.
100 pages have pictures and writing.
The rest have just writing.
What percentage of the pages have pictures on them?
Give your answer to one decimal place.

10 In a survey 13 out of 20 girls have fair hair and 11 out of 25 boys have fair hair.
What percentage of the whole survey has fair hair?
Write your answer to one decimal place.

11 A shop has two offers:

Spend £5
Get £1 back

Buy any three items
of the same value
Get the fourth free

Which is the better value? Explain your answer.

3.2 Increasing and decreasing by a percentage

CAN YOU REMEMBER

- How to find a percentage of a quantity?
- How to use mental methods to work out 10%, 5%, 20%, 25%?

IN THIS SECTION YOU WILL

- Learn how to increase or decrease an amount by a percentage.
- Use the multiplier method to increase or decrease an amount by a percentage.

There are two methods for working out the sale price.

Method 1

Work out the decrease, 10% of £17
Subtract the decrease
from the original price.
10% of £17 = 0.1 × £17
= £1.70
Sale price = £17 − £1.70
= £15.30

Method 2

Original price = 100%, decrease = 10%
100% − 10% = 90%
90% written as a decimal = 0.9
Sale price = 90% of original price
= £17 × 0.9 = £15.30
0.9 is called the *multiplier*.
New value = original value × multiplier

Example 1

a Increase 40 kg by 25%.

b Decrease £6.50 by 18%.

Solution 1

a **Method 1**

Work out the increase: 25% of 40 kg = 0.25 × 40 kg = 10 kg
Add on the increase to the original amount.
Increased amount = 40 kg + 10 kg = 50 kg

Method 2

Original = 100%, increase = 25%
100% + 25% = 125%
125% written as a decimal = 1.25, so the multiplier = 1.25
Increased amount = original amount × multiplier
= 40 kg × 1.25 = 50 kg

b Original = 100%, decrease = 18%
100% − 18% = 82%
82% written as a decimal = 0.82, so the multiplier = 0.82
Decreased amount = original amount × multiplier
= £6.50 × 0.82 = £5.33

Exercise A

1 Increase each of the following quantities by 10%.

a	£200	**b**	1000 tonnes	**c**	900 people	**d**	300 buttons
e	80 cm	**f**	70 litres	**g**	40 pence	**h**	20 kg
i	£10	**j**	30 km	**k**	120 minutes	**l**	180°

2 Decrease each of the following quantities by 25%.

a	£400	**b**	800 tonnes	**c**	2000 fish	**d**	100 buttons
e	80 cm	**f**	60 g	**g**	8 litres	**h**	120 m
i	£16	**j**	32 miles	**k**	600 km	**l**	180°

3 Increase each of the following quantities by 5%.

a	£100	**b**	20 tonnes	**c**	500 fish	**d**	12 g
e	70 litres	**f**	£2.20	**g**	18 m	**h**	24 kg
i	£26	**j**	32 miles	**k**	36 km	**l**	90 minutes

4 Decrease each of the following quantities by 20%.

a	£100	**b**	40 people	**c**	50 fish	**d**	80 buttons
e	30 cm	**f**	12 g	**g**	18 m	**h**	24 kg
i	£26	**j**	32 miles	**k**	36 km	**l**	90 minutes

5 **a** Increase 75p by 20%.
b Increase £36 by 15%.
c Increase 80 grams by 25%.
d Increase £2.40 by 50%.
e Decrease £20 by 2%.
f Decrease 40 litres by 15%.

6 Write down the multiplier for each of the following percentage increases.
a 18% **b** 22% **c** 30% **d** 70% **e** 100% **f** 8% **g** 6% **h** 9%

7 Write down the multiplier for each of the following percentage decreases.
a 19% **b** 24% **c** 40% **d** 60% **e** 5% **f** 7% **g** 9% **h** 2%

8 Match the multipliers to the percentage changes.

9 Use the multiplier method to work out the following.
a Increase £4.50 by 12%.
b Increase 82 cl by 18%.
c Increase 90 g by 23%.
d Increase £2.50 by 38%.
e Increase $94 by 19%.
f Increase 45 tonnes by 6%.

10 Use the multiplier method to work out the following.
a Decrease £54 by 22%.
b Decrease 90 minutes by 17%.
c Decrease 34 kg by 8%.
d Decrease 220 g by 53%.
e Decrease £57 by 14%.
f Decrease 75 litres by 7%.

Example 2

Calculate the price of the van including VAT.

Solution 2

Original amount = 100%, VAT = 17.5%
100% + 17.5% = 117.5%
117.5% written as a decimal = 1.175, so the multiplier = 1.175
Price of van including VAT = original amount × multiplier
= £3500 × 1.175 = £4112.50

Exercise B

1 A new car costs £15 000
After one year the value of the car has decreased by 35%.
Work out the value of the car after one year.

2 A meal in a restaurant costs £36
A service charge of 15% is added.
Work out the cost of the meal including the service charge.

3 A statue is sold at an auction for £800
Commission is charged to the buyer at 5% of the selling price.
What is the total cost of the statue including the commission?

4 Amina invests £950 for one year at 6% interest.
What is the total value of the investment after one year?

5 Pablo has €750
He spends 5% on clothes.
How much does he have left?

6 Harriet receives a gas bill for £70
VAT is added at 5%.
How much is the total bill?

7 A computer costs £450 plus VAT at 17.5%.
What is the total cost of the computer?

8 A man who weighed 14 stone lost 6% of this weight.
Work out his new weight.

9 The area of a football pitch is 7000 m^2
This is increased by 0.5%.
What is the new area of the football pitch?

10 A fashion shop sells 250 dresses in a week. The following week, sales decrease by 12%.
How many dresses are sold in the following week?

11 The population of Somalia is 9.9 million.
It is estimated to be increasing at the rate of 3.3% per year.
Calculate an estimate for the population next year.

3.3 Finding a percentage change

CAN YOU REMEMBER

- How to express one quantity as a percentage of another?
- How to increase or decrease by a percentage?
- How to simplify a fraction?

IN THIS SECTION YOU WILL

- Learn how to work out an increase as a percentage.
- Learn how to work out a decrease as a percentage.

When a value increases or decreases, the change is often given as a percentage of the original amount. To calculate percentage change, use the formula

$$\text{Percentage change} = \frac{\text{Change (increase or decrease)}}{\text{Original amount}} \times 100\%$$

Example 1

The number of tickets on sale for a concert increases from 5000 to 6000
Calculate the percentage increase.

Solution 1

The increase in the number of tickets is 1000. The original number was 5000

$$\text{Percentage increase} = \frac{\text{Increase}}{\text{Original amount}} \times 100\% = \frac{1000}{5000} \times 100\% = 20\%$$

Example 2

The weight of bags of potatoes is reduced from 15 kg to 10 kg.
Find the percentage reduction in the weight of the bags.

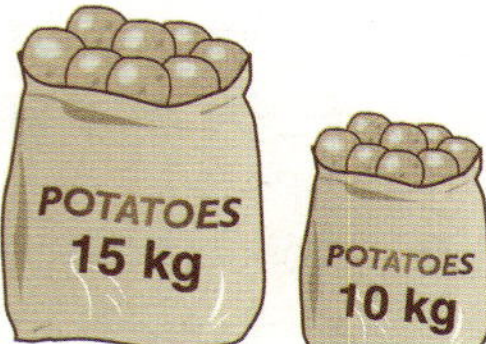

Solution 2

The reduction in the weight is 5 kg. The original weight was 15 kg.

$$\text{Percentage reduction} = \frac{\text{Reduction}}{\text{Original amount}} \times 100\% = \frac{5\text{ kg}}{15\text{ kg}} \times 100\% = 33\tfrac{1}{3}\%$$

Exercise A

1 Work out the percentage change for each of the following.

a	Increasing 50 by 5	**b**	Increasing 30 by 6
c	Increasing 100 by 20	**d**	Increasing 36 by 9
e	Decreasing 60 by 12	**f**	Decreasing 25 by 20
g	Decreasing 50 by 30	**h**	Decreasing 44 by 11

2 Work out the percentage change for each of the following.

- **a** Increasing from 40 to 50
- **b** Increasing from 100 to 130
- **c** Increasing from 160 to 200
- **d** Increasing from 48 to 60
- **e** Decreasing from 60 to 48
- **f** Decreasing from 80 to 40
- **g** Decreasing from 300 to 200
- **h** Decreasing from 72 to 18

3 Copy and complete the table.

	Initial quantity	Change	Final quantity	Percentage change
a	£20	£2 increase		
b	40 g	8 g increase		
c	36 litres		54 litres	
d	100 minutes	20 minute decrease		
e	18 kg	6 kg decrease		
f	70 km		35 km	

4 Match each statement to the correct percentage change.

In questions **5** to **8** give any decimal answers to one decimal place.

5 Work out the percentage change for each of the following.

- **a** Increasing £90 by £5
- **b** Increasing 76 g by 4 g
- **c** Increasing 84 litres by 24 litres
- **d** Decreasing 92 cm by 8 cm
- **e** Decreasing 124 kg by 24 kg
- **f** Decreasing 750 km by 100 km

6 Work out the percentage change for each of the following.

- **a** Increasing from 600 mm to 840 mm
- **b** Increasing from €1200 to €1250
- **c** Increasing from £185 to £200
- **d** Decreasing from $844 to $800
- **e** Decreasing from 580 km to 500 km
- **f** Decreasing from 72 hours to 50 hours

7 Which of the following statements represent a 30% change?

- **a** 40 changes to 52
- **b** 40 changes to 10
- **c** 40 changes to 28

8 A candle is 40 cm tall. As it burns, it shrinks by 5 cm each hour.

- **a** Work out the percentage change after one hour.
- **b** Work out the percentage change after three hours.
- **c** After how many hours is the percentage change 50%?

Percentage profit or percentage loss can be calculated in the same way as percentage increase or decrease.

$$\text{Percentage profit} = \frac{\text{Profit}}{\text{Original amount}} \times 100\% \qquad \text{Percentage loss} = \frac{\text{Loss}}{\text{Original amount}} \times 100\%$$

Example 3

Jon buys a car for £1200. He then sells it for £1500. Work out the percentage profit.

Solution 3

Profit = £1500 − £1200 = £300. Original amount = £1200

$$\text{Percentage profit} = \frac{\text{Profit}}{\text{Original amount}} \times 100\% = \frac{£300}{£1200} \times 100\% = 25\%$$

Exercise B

1 A television is bought for £1000 and then sold for £750
Find the percentage loss.

2 A chef makes a meal for £20
The price on the menu is £23
Calculate the percentage profit.

3 Mick buys a toy for £4 and sells it for £5
Work out the percentage profit.

4 There are 250 fish in a lake.
50 of the fish are caught by anglers.
Calculate the percentage caught by anglers.

5 The price of fish and chips is increased from £4.00 to £4.40
Work out the percentage increase.

6 Pavel's salary is reduced from £30 000 a year to £21 000 a year.
What is the percentage reduction in Pavel's salary?

7 A computer is bought for £450
It is then sold for £400
Calculate the percentage loss.
Give your answer to one decimal place.

8 Matt buys a watch for £80
He sells it for £50
Calculate his percentage loss.

9 Peter and his son Jack each take two tests.
The results are shown in the table.
Whose test mark has improved by the greatest percentage?
Show your working.

	Test A	Test B
Peter	60	34
Jack	75	43

10 Terry invests £875 in shares. The value of the shares falls by £150
He says that this is a loss of between 15% and 20%.
Is he correct? Show your working.

11 **a** Work out the percentage increase when 240 kg is increased to 300 kg.
b Work out the percentage decrease when 300 kg is decreased to 240 kg.
c Explain why your answers to parts **a** and **b** are different.

12 The average attendance for a football team last season was 11 500
This season the average has fallen by 800
What is the percentage fall in the average attendance this season?
Give your answer to the nearest whole number.

13 The value of a luxury coach depreciates (decreases) from £240 000 when new to £160 000 one year later.
Calculate the percentage depreciation.

3.4 Percentages in real life

CAN YOU REMEMBER

- How to work out a percentage of a quantity?
- How to increase or decrease by a percentage?
- How to write one quantity as a percentage of another?

IN THIS SECTION YOU WILL

- Understand the meaning of 'interest', 'inflation' and 'income tax'.
- Learn how to calculate simple interest.
- Learn how to calculate income tax.
- Solve real-life problems using percentages.

Interest is the cost of borrowing or lending money.
Interest is earned when money is invested.
Interest is charged when a loan is taken out.

INVEST £1000
Interest paid annually at a fixed rate of 5% of the initial investment

For this account the interest for one year is 5% of £1000 = £50
In three years the interest = £50 × 3 = £150
This account pays *simple interest*. The amount paid is the same each year.
After three years the value of the investment is
£1000 + £150 = £1150

Simple interest can also be calculated using the formula $I = \frac{PRT}{100}$

where I is the interest, P is the amount invested, R is the rate of interest and T is the time invested.

Example 1

Chico borrows £800 for two years. Simple interest is charged at 10% per year.
How much does Chico have to pay back altogether?

Solution 1

Method 1
Interest per year = 10% of £800
= 0.1 × 800 = £80
Interest charged for two years
= £80 × 2 = £160
Total to pay back = £800 + £160 = £960

Method 2
Using the formula $I = \frac{PRT}{100}$

$P = £800$, $R = 10\%$, $T = 2$ years

$$I = \frac{800 \times 10 \times 2}{100} = £160$$

Total to pay back = £800 + £160 = £960

Example 2

Tim invests £1000 for 1 year. He earns interest of £75
What is the interest rate?

Solution 2

Method 1
£75 as a percentage of £1000

$= \frac{75}{1000} \times 100\%$

$= 7.5\%$

Interest rate = 7.5%

Method 2
Using the formula $I = \frac{PRT}{100}$

$P = £1000$, $T = 1$ year, $I = £75$

$75 = \frac{^{10}\cancel{1000} \times R \times 1}{\cancel{100}_1}$ Cancel

$75 = 10R$ Divide both sides by 10

$R = 7.5$

Interest rate = 7.5%

Exercise A

1 Work out the simple interest on each of the following for:
i 1 year **ii** 3 years **iii** 5 years.

a £500 at 10% per year **b** £400 at 5% per year **c** £2000 at 3% per year
d £1000 at 8% per year **e** £200 at 2.5% per year **f** £1500 at 4% per year

2 Work out the value of the following investments after:
i 1 year **ii** 2 years.

a £300 at 10% per year **b** £500 at 2% per year **c** £1000 at 5% per year
d £1200 at 4% per year **e** £100 at 2.5% per year **f** £2500 at 7% per year

3 For each of the following loans, use the formula $I = \frac{PRT}{100}$ to work out:
i the simple interest **ii** the total amount repaid.

a £250 at 10% per year for 2 years **b** £400 at 2% per year for 2 years
c £1000 at 6% per year for 3 years **d** £500 at 4% per year for 3 years
e £1500 at 3% per year for 3 years **f** £800 at 5% per year for 6 years
g £1000 at 2.5% per year for 5 years **h** £2000 at 8% per year for 4 years

4 Jo invested £500 at 6% simple interest. She received £90 interest in total.
For how many years did she invest?

5 Copy and complete this simple interest table.

	Initial amount	Interest rate per year	Simple interest per year	Simple interest for 5 years	Total amount after 5 years
a	£675	8%			
b	£450	5.5%			
c	£280	3.5%			
d	£520	4.5%			
e	£650	3.2%			

6 Norris invests £2500 in a bond paying 3.8% simple interest.
He says that in three years his bond will be worth over £3000
Is he correct? Explain your answer.

7 For each of the following loans work out:

i the simple interest using the formula $I = \frac{PRT}{100}$ **ii** the total amount repaid.

a £32 000 at 4% per year for 2 years
b £1800 at 2.5% per year for 2 years
c £4500 at 6.2% per year for 3 years
d £7200 at 4.8% per year for 3 years
e £1600 at 3.4% per year for 3 years
f £900 at 5.6% per year for 4 years
g £5000 at 7.5% per year for 5 years
h £4000 at 2.1% per year for 10 years

8 Greg takes out a loan of £3500 for 3 years.
He pays £525 simple interest.
Work out the interest rate.

9 Terry lends £2200 to his daughter.
She agrees to pay back 5% of the initial loan each year.
How long will it take her to pay off the loan?

Inflation is the increase in prices or costs.
The *annual rate of inflation* is the percentage increase over one year.

Example 3

The annual rate of inflation is 6% per year.
A house is valued at £125 000 this year.
Use the annual rate of inflation to work out the value of the house next year.

Solution 3

6% of £125 000 = 0.06 × £125 000 = £7500
New value = £125 000 + £7500 = £132 500

The Government takes a percentage of people's earnings as *income tax*. The rate of income tax paid depends on the total income.

Example 4

A man earns £8000 per year.
The first £5000 is tax free. The remainder is taxed at 20%.
How much tax does he pay?

Solution 4

He pays tax on £8000 − £5000 = £3000
20% of £3000 = 0.2 × £3000 = £600
He pays £600 tax.

Exercise B

1 The annual rate of inflation is 5%.
Use the annual rate of inflation to work out the prices after one year of:

a a car costing £8000 this year
b a trolley of food costing £50 this year
c a tank of petrol costing £40 this year
d a three-piece suite costing £800 this year.

2 Mrs Farthing earns $20 000 per year.
The first $5000 is tax free.
She pays income tax at the rate of 25%.
How much tax does she pay?

3 Mr Shilling earns £10 000 per year.
The first £4800 is tax free.
He pays income tax at the rate of 20%.
How much tax does he pay?

4 Miss Halfpenny earns £5000 per year.
The first £4000 is tax free.
She pays income tax at the rate of 10%.
How much does she have left after tax?

5 The annual rate of inflation is 7.5%.
Use the annual rate of inflation to work out the prices after one year of:

a a house costing £95 000 this year
b a dress costing £80 this year
c a shirt costing £17.50 this year
d a tyre costing £63 this year.

6 Mrs Florin earns £25 000 per year.
The first £4600 is tax free.
She pays income tax at the rate of 25%.
How much tax does she pay?

7 Mr Crown earns £12 500 per year.
The first £5200 is tax free.
He pays income tax at the rate of 22%.
How much tax does he pay?

8 The first £4300 of income is tax free.
Income tax is paid at the rate of 10% on £5000
Income tax is paid at the rate of 22% on the remainder.

a Miss Guinea earns £17 000 per year. How much tax does she pay?
b Mr Penny earns £15 700 per year. How much tax does he pay?

Chapter summary

- To write a quantity as a percentage of another quantity:
  - **Method 1**
    Step 1: Make sure that both quantities have the same units.
    Step 2: Use the formula $\dfrac{\text{first quantity}}{\text{second quantity}} \times 100\%$
  - **Method 2**
    Step 1: Make sure that both quantities have the same units.
    Step 2: Write the fraction $\dfrac{\text{first quantity}}{\text{second quantity}}$ as a fraction with a denominator of 100
    Step 3: Write the fraction as a percentage.

- There are two methods for working out a percentage increase or decrease.
  - **Method 1**
    Work out the decrease.
    Subtract the decrease from the original value.

    Work out the increase.
    Add the increase to the original value.
  - **Method 2** – Use a multiplier.
    New value = original value × multiplier

    Original value = 100%,
    decrease = 20%
    100% − 20% = 80%
    80% written as a decimal = 0.8
    so the multiplier = 0.8

    Original value = 100%,
    increase = 10%
    100% + 10% = 110%
    110% written as a decimal = 1.1
    so the multiplier = 1.1
- $\text{Percentage change} = \dfrac{\text{Change (increase or decrease)}}{\text{Original amount}} \times 100\%$
- $\text{Percentage profit} = \dfrac{\text{Profit}}{\text{Original amount}} \times 100\%$
- $\text{Percentage loss} = \dfrac{\text{Loss}}{\text{Original amount}} \times 100\%$
- Interest is the cost of borrowing or lending money.
- With simple interest, the amount of interest is the same each year.
- Simple interest can be calculated using the formula $I = \dfrac{PRT}{100}$, where I is the interest, P is the amount invested, R is the rate of interest and T is the time invested.
- Inflation is the increase in prices or costs.
- The annual rate of inflation is the percentage increase over one year.
- Income tax is the percentage of people's earnings taken by the Government.

Chapter review

1 There are 50 members of a rowing club.
a There are 32 male members.
What percentage is male?
b The number of members increases by 20% of the original number of members each year.
Calculate the number of members in the rowing club after two years.

2 Tara has a weekend job. She earns £4.50 per hour on Saturdays.
On Sundays her pay per hour is 50% more than it is on Saturdays.
a What is her pay on Sundays?
b Last weekend Tara worked for 6 hours on Saturday and for 5 hours on Sunday.
How much did she earn in the two days?

3 The recommended price of a guitar is £240
Sanjay discovers that he can order the guitar on the Internet and get a discount of 30% off the recommended price.
Calculate the amount Sanjay would pay if he ordered the guitar on the Internet.

4 Owen receives his gas bill. The bill is for £120 plus VAT at 5%.
a Calculate the amount of VAT.
b Find the total amount which Owen has to pay.

5 This year Mr Day attended 50 meetings. Mr Day wants to decrease the number of meetings he attends by 10%. Which calculation should he use to work out the number of meetings he wants to attend?

50×0.1 50×0.9 50×1.1 50×10

Explain your answer.

6 Rosemary and her sister are getting ready for the new term.
They go to Suzie's Stationery to buy paper, pens and pencils.
Paper costs 87 pence per pad.
Pens cost £1.05 each.
Pencils cost 35 pence each.
a Copy and complete their bill.
b Because they are students, they are given a reduction of 10% of the total cost.
By how much is their bill reduced?

Suzie's Stationery	
8 pads of paper	£ ....
...... pens	£ 12.60
6 pencils	£ ....
Total	£ ....

7 Roy invests £5000 for two years.
Simple interest is paid annually at the rate of 4.5%.
How much is the investment worth after two years?

8 The cost of a camera is £250, plus VAT at 17.5%.
Calculate the amount of VAT charged on the camera.

9 A fish increases in weight from 28 kg to 30 kg.
Calculate the percentage increase in the weight of the fish.

10 An antiques dealer buys a table for £450. He sells the table for 60% more than the price he paid for it.
It costs the dealer £70 to restore the table before he sells it.
a For how much does the dealer sell the table?
b Calculate the amount of profit the dealer made.
c Calculate this profit as a percentage of the price the dealer paid for the table.

CHAPTER 4

Basic algebraic skills

4.1 Indices

CAN YOU REMEMBER

- The square numbers from 1 to 225 and the cube numbers from 1 to 125?
- That x^2 means $x \times x$ and x^3 means $x \times x \times x$?
- How to substitute values into an algebraic expression?
- That $p \times q$ simplifies to pq?

IN THIS SECTION YOU WILL

- Learn the rules for multiplying and dividing index numbers.

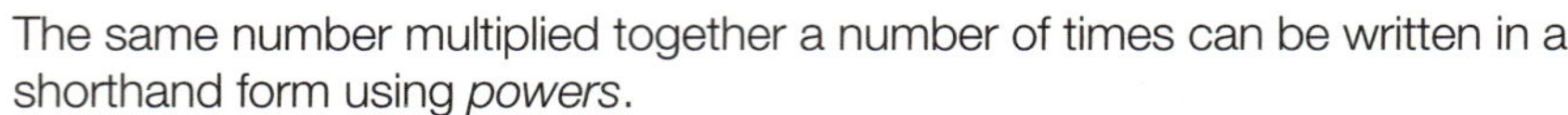

The same number multiplied together a number of times can be written in a shorthand form using *powers*.

For example

$3 \times 3 = 3^2$	'3 squared' or '3 to the power 2'
$4 \times 4 \times 4 = 4^3$	'4 cubed' or '4 to the power 3'
$5 \times 5 \times 5 \times 5 \times 5 \times 5 \times 5 = 5^7$	'5 to the power 7'

In the expression 5^7, 5 is the *base number* and 7 is the power or *index*.
The power is the number of times that the base number is multiplied together.

Example 1

a Write each of the following in index form.

- **i** $3 \times 3 \times 3 \times 3$
- **ii** $2 \times 2 \times 2 \times 5 \times 5 \times 5 \times 5 \times 5 \times 5$
- **iii** $p \times p \times p \times p$
- **iv** $q \times q \times q \times r \times r \times r \times r \times r \times r$

b Write each of the following using multiplication symbols.

- **i** $5^3 \times 7^4$
- **ii** y^5z^2

Solution 1

a

- **i** $3 \times 3 \times 3 \times 3 = 3^4$
- **ii** $2 \times 2 \times 2 \times 5 \times 5 \times 5 \times 5 \times 5 \times 5 = 2^3 \times 5^6$
- **iii** $p \times p \times p \times p = p^4$
- **iv** $q \times q \times q \times r \times r \times r \times r \times r \times r = q^3 \times r^6 = q^3r^6$

b

- **i** $5^3 \times 7^4 = 5 \times 5 \times 5 \times 7 \times 7 \times 7 \times 7$
- **ii** $y^5z^2 = y \times y \times y \times y \times y \times z \times z$

Make sure you know how to work out powers using your calculator.

Example 2

Calculate the value of each of the following expressions when $x = 3$ and $y = 4$

a x^3 **b** y^2 **c** $x^5 + y^6$ **d** x^5y^6

Solution 2

a $x^3 = x \times x \times x$
When $x = 3$
$x^3 = 3 \times 3 \times 3 = 27$

b When $y = 4$
$y^2 = 4 \times 4 = 16$

c $x^5 + y^6 = 3^5 + 4^6$
$= 4339$

d $x^5y^6 = 3^5 \times 4^6$
$= 995\,328$

Exercise A

1 Write each of the following in index form.

- **a** $3 \times 3 \times 3 \times 3 \times 3 \times 3 \times 3$
- **b** $5 \times 5 \times 5 \times 5 \times 5 \times 5$
- **c** 4×4
- **d** $2 \times 2 \times 2 \times 3 \times 3$
- **e** $2 \times 2 \times 5 \times 5 \times 5 \times 5 \times 5 \times 5$
- **f** $2 \times 2 \times 3 \times 3 \times 3 \times 4 \times 4 \times 4 \times 4$
- **g** $3 \times 3 \times 4 \times 4 \times 4 \times 5 \times 5 \times 5 \times 5$
- **h** $7 \times 7 \times 7 \times 9 \times 9 \times 9 \times 11 \times 11 \times 11$
- **i** $4 \times 4 \times 4 \times 4 \times 4 \times 4 \times 4 \times 4 \times 4 \times 4 \times 4 \times 4 \times 4 \times 4 \times 4$
- **j** $2 \times 2 \times 2 \times 2 \times 2 \times 2 \times 2 \times 2 \times 2 \times 2 \times 2 \times 2 \times 2 \times 2 \times 2$

2 Write each of the following in index form.

- **a** $x \times x \times x \times x \times x \times x \times x$
- **b** $y \times y \times y \times y \times y$
- **c** $z \times z$
- **d** $a \times a \times b \times b \times b$
- **e** $p \times p \times p \times q \times q \times q \times q \times q$
- **f** $r \times r \times s \times s \times s \times t$
- **g** $v \times v \times v \times v \times w \times w \times w \times w \times w$
- **h** $a \times a \times a \times b \times b \times b \times c \times c \times c$
- **i** $x \times y \times y \times z \times z \times z \times z \times z \times z \times z$
- **j** $a \times a \times b \times b \times b \times c \times c \times c \times c \times c \times c \times c \times d \times d \times d \times d$

3 Write each of the following using multiplication symbols.

a 4^2 **b** 6^3 **c** 7^1 **d** 2^{10}
e $2^2 \times 3^3$ **f** $4^5 \times 6^3$ **g** $4^5 \times 5^4$ **h** $2^2 \times 3^3 \times 4$
i $3 \times 4^3 \times 5^4$ **j** $2^4 \times 3^3 \times 4^2 \times 5$

4 Write each of the following using multiplication symbols.

a a^3 **b** a^5 **c** b^7 **d** b^9 **e** a^2b^3
f x^3y^2 **g** x^5y^4 **h** p^3q^7r **i** pq^2r^5 **j** $a^5b^4c^2$

5 Copy and complete this table. The first one has been done for you.

	x	y	x^2	y^3	$x^2 + y^3$	x^2y^3
a	3	2	9	8	$9 + 8 = 17$	$9 \times 8 = 72$
b	2	3				
c	10	5				
d	5	10				
e	1	4				
f	4	1				

6 Use your knowledge of squares and cubes to work out the value of each letter symbol in the following.

a $2^a = 4$ **b** $3^b = 27$ **c** $4^c = 64$
d $10^d = 1000$ **e** $5^e = 125$

7 You are given that $A = x^4 + y^5$ and $B = x^4y^5$
Find the values of A and B when

a $x = 4$ and $y = 5$ **b** $x = 5$ and $y = 4$

8 The letter symbols in the following expressions represent positive integers.
Use the power button on a scientific calculator to find their values.

a $5^a = 625$ **b** $7^b = 343$ **c** $8^c = 32\,768$
d $9^d = 729$ **e** $2^e = 256$

Multiplying index numbers with the same base

$$2^5 \times 2^4 = (2 \times 2 \times 2 \times 2 \times 2) \times (2 \times 2 \times 2 \times 2)$$
$$= 2 \times 2 \times 2 \times 2 \times 2 \times 2 \times 2 \times 2 \times 2 = 2^9$$

So $2^5 \times 2^4 = 2^{5+4} = 2^9$

In general, $x^a \times x^b = x^{a+b}$

To **multiply** index numbers with the same base **add** the powers.

Dividing index numbers with the same base

$$7^{10} \div 7^4 = \frac{7 \times 7 \times 7 \times 7 \times 7 \times 7 \times \cancel{7} \times \cancel{7} \times \cancel{7} \times \cancel{7}}{\cancel{7} \times \cancel{7} \times \cancel{7} \times \cancel{7}} = 7^6$$

So $7^{10} \div 7^4 = 7^{10-4} = 7^6$

In general, $x^a \div x^b = x^{a-b}$

To **divide** index numbers with the same base **subtract** the powers.

Example 3

a **i** Simplify $x^5 \times x^3 \times x$ **ii** Simplify $z^3 \times z^2 \div z^2$

Solution 3

a **i** $x^5 \times x^3 \times x = x^{5+3+1} = x^9$ x can be written as x^1
ii $z^3 \times z^2 \div z^2 = z^{3+2-2} = z^3$

When terms include numbers and letters, deal with the numbers and letters separately.

Example 4

Simplify: **a** $2x^3 \times 3x^2$ **b** $8y^6 \div 2y^4$

Solution 4

a $2x^3 \times 3x^2 = 2 \times 3 \times x^3 \times x^2 = 6 \times x^{3+2} = 6x^5$

Multiply the numbers (2×3) and **add** the powers ($3 + 2$).

b $8y^6 \div 2y^4 = \dfrac{8 \times y^6}{2 \times y^4} = \dfrac{8}{2} \times \dfrac{y^6}{y^4}$

$\dfrac{8}{2} = 4$ and $\dfrac{y^6}{y^4} = y^{6-4} = y^2$

Divide the numbers ($8 \div 2$) and **subtract** the powers ($6 - 4$).

So $8y^6 \div 2y^4 = 4 \times y^2 = 4y^2$

Exercise B

1 **a** Sadik says that the value of 2^3 is 6
By working out the correct answer show that Sadik is wrong.
b Tom says that the expressions $5x$ and x^5 are the same. Explain why Tom is wrong.

2 Match pairs of equivalent expressions in each set. In set **a** one has been done for you.

a

$3 + 3 + 3 + 3$	3^4
$3 \times 3 \times 3 \times 3$	4^3
$4 + 4 + 4$	3×4
$4 \times 4 \times 4$	4×3

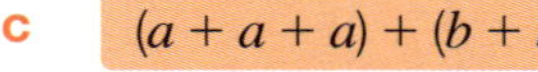

b

$x + x + x + x$	x^5
$x \times x \times x \times x \times x$	$4x$
$x \times x \times x \times x$	$5x$
$x + x + x + x + x$	x^4

c

$(a + a + a) + (b + b)$	a^3b^2
$(a \times a \times a) \times (b \times b)$	$3a + 2b$
$(a + a + a) \times (b + b)$	$a^3 + b^2$
$(a \times a \times a) + (b \times b)$	$3a + b^2$
$(a + a + a) + (b \times b)$	$a^3 + 2b$
$(a \times a \times a) + (b + b)$	$6ab$

3 Find the value of the letter symbol in each of the following.

a $2^a = 2^5 \times 2^4$ **b** $3^b = 3^5 \times 3^3$ **c** $5^c = 5^2 \times 5^3 \times 5^4$ **d** $7^d = 7 \times 7^2 \times 7^5$
e $2^e = 2^7 \div 2^4$ **f** $3^f = 3^5 \div 3^3$ **g** $5^g = 5^4 \div 5^3$ **h** $7^h = 7^5 \div 7^4$
i $2^i = 2^4 \times 2^5 \div 2^3$ **j** $3^j = \dfrac{3^4 \times 3^5}{3^7 \div 3^4}$

4 Simplify each of the following.

a $t^2 \times t^3$ **b** $p^5 \times p^4$ **c** $x \times x^5$ **d** $a^4 \times a^7$ **e** $a^2 \times a^4$
f $q^4 \div q$ **g** $y^5 \div y^2$ **h** $d^7 \div d^2$ **i** $z^{12} \div z^9$ **j** $g^9 \div g^2$

5 Simplify each of the following.

a $a^3 \times a^2 \times a$ **b** $b^4 \times b^3 \times b^2$ **c** $c^5 \times c^2 \times c^2$ **d** $d^5 \times d^3 \div d^2$
e $e \times e^3 \div e^2$ **f** $\dfrac{f^5}{f^2 \times f^2}$ **g** $\dfrac{g^7 \div g^2}{g \times g^2}$ **h** $\dfrac{h^4 \times h^2}{h^3 \times h}$
i $\dfrac{i^3 \times i^2}{i^6 \div i^2}$ **j** $\dfrac{j^3 \times j^2 \div j}{j^5 \times j^3 \div j^4}$

6 Emma is asked to simplify $4x^3 \times 7x^5$. She writes down $11x^8$

a What has Emma done wrong? **b** Simplify $4x^3 \times 7x^5$ correctly.

7 Simplify each of the following.

a $2x^2 \times 5x^3$ **b** $3x \times 4x^5$ **c** $5x^4 \times 4x^5$ **d** $3x^2 \times 2x^3 \times 2x$

e $7x \times 2x^3 \times 5x^4$ **f** $12x^5 \div 3x^2$ **g** $15x^3 \div 5x$ **h** $16x^9 \div 8x^3$

i $24x \div 3x^2$ **j** $5x^3 \times 4x \div 2x^6$

8 The table shows a list of the powers of 2 up to 2^{12}

2^1	2^2	2^3	2^4	2^5	2^6	2^7	2^8	2^9	2^{10}	2^{11}	2^{12}
2	4	8	16	32	64	128	256	512	1024	2048	4096

a **i** Write 64 and 32 as powers of 2 **ii** Use the table to work out the value of 64×32

b **i** Write 2048 and 16 as powers of 2 **ii** Use the table to work out $2048 \div 16$

9 Copy and complete this table of the powers of 3

3^1	3^2	3^3	3^4	3^5	3^6	3^7	3^8	3^9	3^{10}	3^{11}	3^{12}

a Use the table to find the value of

i 81×2187 **ii** 243^2 **iii** $531\,441 \div 19\,683$

You **must** show your working.

b Use the table to show that

i $243 \times 2187 = 729^2$

ii $243 \times 177\,147 = 6561^2$

iii $(531\,441 \div 2187)^2 = 59\,049$

You **must** show your working.

10 Use the powers of 5 to show that $9\,765\,625 = 5 \times 25 \times 125 \times 625$

4.2 Expanding brackets and simplifying expressions 1

CAN YOU REMEMBER

- How to simplify expressions by collecting like terms?
- The rules for multiplying and dividing index numbers with the same base?
- The order of operations (BIDMAS or BODMAS)?
- The grid method for multiplying numbers?

IN THIS SECTION YOU WILL

- Reinforce and extend skills in simplifying expressions.
- Learn how to multiply an expression in brackets by a single term.
- Learn how to simplify expressions that include brackets.

Each bag contains $x + 2$ marbles.

The total number of marbles in the three bags can be written as:

$3 \times (x + 2)$ or $3(x + 2)$ or $x + 2 + x + 2 + x + 2$ or $3 \times x + 3 \times 2$ or $3x + 6$

This shows that $3(x + 2) = 3 \times x + 3 \times 2$

This can also be shown using the *grid method*.

$3(x + 2)$

So $3 \times (x + 2) = 3 \times x + 3 \times 2$
$= 3x + 6$

$\times$	x	2	
3	$3 \times x$	3×2	$3 \times x + 3 \times 2 = 3x + 6$

$a(b + c)$

In general, $a(b + c) = ab + ac$

$\times$	b	c	
a	$a \times b = ab$	$a \times c = ac$	$ab + ac$

Multiplying $3(x + 2)$ to get $3x + 6$ is called *expanding* or multiplying out the brackets.

Example 1

a Use the grid method to expand $-4(y - 5)$.

b Expand $3(x + y)$.

Solution 1

a $-4(y - 5)$

$\times$	y	-5	
-4	$-4 \times y = -4y$	$-4 \times -5 = 20$	$-4y + 20$

So $-4(y - 5) = -4 \times y + -4 \times -5 = -4y + 20$

b $3(x + y) = 3 \times x + 3 \times y = 3x + 3y$

When an expression contains brackets and other terms, expand the brackets and then collect like terms.

Example 2

a Expand and simplify $3(4x + 2y) + 5y$.

b Expand $3(2a + 3b - 4c)$.

c Expand and simplify $-4(3p - 2) - 5$

Solution 2

a Expand the brackets.

$3(4x + 2y) + 5y = 3 \times 4x + 3 \times 2y + 5y = 12x + 6y + 5y$

Collect like terms:

$12x + 6y + 5y = 12x + 11y$

b $3(2a + 3b - 4c) = 3(2a + 3b + -4c)$
$= 3 \times 2a + 3 \times 3b + 3 \times -4c = 6a + 9b - 12c$

c $-4(3p - 2) - 5 = -4(3p + -2) - 5$
$= -4 \times 3p + -4 \times -2 - 5 = -12p + 8 - 5 = -12p + 3$

Exercise A

1 Copy and complete this table.

a	$2(a + 6)$	$(a + 6) + (a + 6)$	$2a + 12$
b	$3(b + 4)$	$(b + 4) + (b + 4) + (b + 4)$	
c	$2(4c - 5)$		$8c - 10$
d	$4(d + 2)$		
e		$(e + 1) + (e + 1) + (e + 1)$	
f			$5f + 10$
g	$6(g - 3)$		
h	$4(2h + 7)$		
i		$(3i - 2) + (3i - 2) + (3i - 2) + (3i - 2)$	
j		$(2j + 3) + (2j + 3) + (2j + 3) + (2j + 3) + (2j + 3)$	
k			$6k - 12$
l	$7(3l - 1)$		

2 Copy and complete the grids to expand the expressions given.
The first one has been done for you.

a $5(x + 4)$

$\times$	x	4	
5	$5 \times x = 5x$	$5 \times 4 = 20$	$5x + 20$

b $3(x + 6)$

$\times$	x	6	
3			

c $2(4x + 3)$

$\times$	$4x$	3	
2			

d $3(2x - 7)$

$\times$	$2x$	-7	
3			

e $-3(-2x + 3y - 4)$

$\times$			

3 Match the pairs of equivalent expressions in these boxes.

4 Match the pairs of equivalent expressions in these boxes.

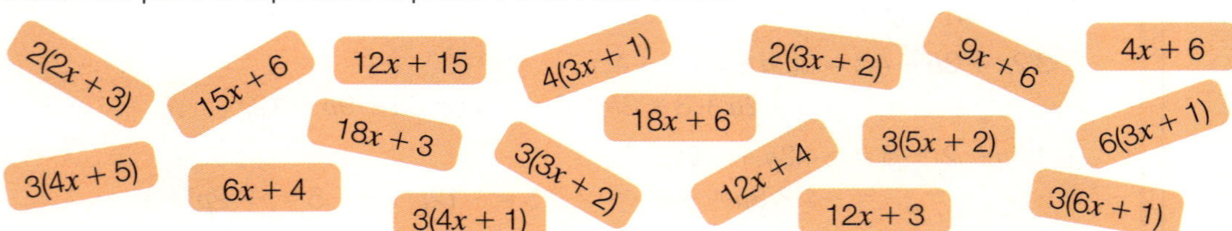

5 Expand each of these expressions.

a	$2(a + 4)$	**b**	$3(b + 7)$	**c**	$4(c + 3)$	**d**	$5(d + 1)$
e	$4(e - 1)$	**f**	$7(f - 2)$	**g**	$3(g + 9)$	**h**	$4(h - 3)$
i	$3(2 - i)$	**j**	$4(5 - j)$	**k**	$-4(2 - k)$	**l**	$-2(l + 9)$
m	$-5(m - 6)$	**n**	$5(x + y - 1)$	**o**	$3(x - y + 1)$	**p**	$-2(x - y - 1)$

6 Expand each of these expressions.

a	$2(3a + 5)$	**b**	$3(2b + 1)$	**c**	$4(3c + 2)$	**d**	$5(3d + 7)$
e	$3(4e - 1)$	**f**	$5(4f - 3)$	**g**	$3(5g + 3)$	**h**	$4(4h - 3)$
i	$2(6 - 5i)$	**j**	$3(4 - 3j)$	**k**	$-3(1 - 5k)$	**l**	$-6(2l + 7)$
m	$-3(5m - 2)$	**n**	$3(2x + 3y - 1)$	**o**	$3(3x - 2y + 4)$	**p**	$-5(2x - 4y - 3)$

7 Multiply out the brackets and simplify each of the following expressions.

a	$3(a + 5) + 7$	**b**	$2(b + 1) + 3$	**c**	$4(c + 3) - 3$
d	$5(d + 3) + 2d$	**e**	$3(e + 1) + 4e$	**f**	$6(2f + 1) + 5$
g	$4(2g - 3) + 5g$	**h**	$5(2h - 3) + 4$	**i**	$3(6 - 5i) + 15i$
j	$3(2 - 5j) - 6$	**k**	$-4(1 - 2k) + 4$	**l**	$-5(2l + 1) + 11l$
m	$-2(4m - 2) + 6$	**n**	$3(4x + 2y - 1) + 3x + 3$		
o	$2(5x - 3y + 1) + 6y - 2$	**p**	$-5(x - 2y + 3) + 5x - 10y$		

8 Sakshi expands $3(2a + 4)$. Her answer is $6a + 4$. Explain what Sakshi has done wrong.

9 Sue and Bill use different methods to show that $8x + 14 = 4(2x + 3) + 2$

Sue's method

$$8x + 14 = (2x + 3) + (2x + 3) + (2x + 3) + (2x + 3) + 2 = 4(2x + 3) + 2$$

Bill's method

$$4(2x + 3) + 2 = 4 \times 2x + 4 \times 3 + 2 = 8x + 12 + 2 = 8x + 14$$

a Use both Sue's and Bill's methods to show that
  i $6(x + 2) + 3 = 6x + 15$ **ii** $3(x + 5) + 3x = 6x + 15$

b **i** Use Sue's method to show that $6a - 10b = 6(a - 2b) + 2b$
  ii Use Bill's method to show that $5(a - 2b) + a = 6a - 10b$

10 a **i** Work out $8 \times 70 + 8 \times 9$
  ii Work out $8 \times (70 + 9)$. **iii** What do you notice?

b **i** Work out $9 \times 200 + 9 \times 70 + 9 \times 6$
  ii Work out $9 \times (200 + 70 + 6)$. **iii** What do you notice?

c **i** Work out $6 \times 400 + 6 \times 80 + 6 \times 9 + 7 \times 90 + 7 \times 8$
  ii Work out $6 \times (400 + 80 + 9) + 7 \times (90 + 8)$. **iii** What do you notice?

Example 3

Use the grid method to expand **a** $x(x + 4)$ **b** $2x(3x + 2)$.

Solution 3

a $x(x + 4)$

$\times$	x	4	
x	$x \times x = x^2$	$x \times 4 = 4x$	$x^2 + 4x$

So $x(x + 4) = x \times x + x \times 4 = x^{1+1} + 4x = x^2 + 4x$

b $2x(3x + 2)$

$\times$	$3x$	2	
$2x$	$2x \times 3x = 6x^2$	$2x \times 2 = 4x$	$6x^2 + 4x$

So $2x(3x + 2) = 2x \times 3x + 2x \times 2$
$= 2 \times 3 \times x \times x + 2 \times 2 \times x = 6x^2 + 4x$

Example 4

Expand and simplify: **a** $2(x + 5) + 3(x - 2)$ **b** $3(4x - 5) - 3(2x - 1)$

Solution 4

a
$2(x + 5) = 2 \times x + 2 \times 5$
$= 2x + 10$
$3(x - 2) = 3 \times x + 3 \times -2$
$= 3x + -6 = 3x - 6$
$2(x + 5) + 3(x - 2)$
$= 2x + 10 + 3x - 6 = 5x + 4$

b
$3(4x - 5) - 3(2x - 1)$
$= 3(4x + -5) + -3(2x + -1)$
$= 3 \times 4x + 3 \times -5 + -3 \times 2x + -3 \times -1$
$= 12x + -15 + -6x + 3$
$= 6x - 12$

Two expressions in brackets can be multiplied together.

- Multiply **all** terms in the first bracket by **all** terms in the second bracket.
- Simplify by collecting like terms.

Example 5

a Expand and simplify $(x + 5)(x + 2)$.
b Multiply out the brackets and simplify $(x - 4)(x + 1)$.

Solution 5

a $(x + 5)(x + 2)$

Method 1
$= x \times (x + 2) + 5 \times (x + 2)$
$= x \times x + x \times 2 + 5 \times x + 5 \times 2$
$= x^2 + 2x + 5x + 10$
$= x^2 + 7x + 10$

Method 2

$\times$	x	5
x	x^2	$5x$
2	$2x$	10

$= x^2 + 2x + 5x + 10$
$= x^2 + 7x + 10$

b $(x - 4)(x + 1)$

Method 1
$= x \times (x + 1) - 4 \times (x + 1)$
$= x \times x + x \times 1 - 4 \times x - 4 \times 1$
$= x^2 + x - 4x - 4$
$= x^2 - 3x - 4$

Method 2

$\times$	x	-4
x	x^2	$-4x$
1	x	-4

$= x^2 + x - 4x - 4$
$= x^2 - 3x - 4$

Exercise B

1 Expand each of these expressions.

a $a(a + 5)$ **b** $b(b + 1)$ **c** $c(c - 2)$ **d** $d(2d + 3)$
e $e(3e - 1)$ **f** $f(2f - 5)$ **g** $g(3g + 7)$ **h** $h(5h - 2)$
i $i(3 - 2i)$ **j** $j(1 - j)$ **k** $-k(3 - 2k)$ **l** $x(x + y)$
m $x(5x - 2y)$ **n** $x(2x + 3y - 1)$ **o** $-x(2x - 3y)$ **p** $-x(2x - 4y - 3)$

2 Expand each of these expressions.

a $2a(4a + 3)$ **b** $5b(2b + 3)$ **c** $3c(4c + 1)$ **d** $7d(2d + 3)$
e $3e^2(2e - 5)$ **f** $4f^2(2f - 1)$ **g** $3g^2(5g^2 + 2)$ **h** $4h^3(4h^2 - 3)$
i $2i(6 - 5i + i^2)$ **j** $3j^2(4j^2 - 3j + 1)$ **k** $-3k^4(1 - 3k^2)$ **l** $x^4(2x + 3y)$
m $3x^3(x - 2y)$ **n** $3x(2x^2 + 3xy - y^2)$ **o** $xy(x - y + 1)$ **p** $5xy(3x^2 - 2xy - 4y^2)$

3 Multiply out the brackets and simplify each of the following expressions.

a $4(a + 3) + 7(a + 4)$
b $3(b + 1) + 3(b + 5)$
c $4(2c + 3) + 3(3c - 1)$
d $7(3d + 3) - 2(4d - 3)$
e $e(5e + 4) - 4e(e + 1)$
f $f(4f + 3) - 3f(f + 1)$
g $2g(2g - 5) + 5g(g + 2)$
h $5h(3h - 2) + 2h(3h + 5)$
i $2i(4 - 5i) + 5i(3i + 4) + i(i + 1)$
j $3j(1 - 5j) - 2j(1 - 4j) + 7j^2$
k $-4k(1 - 2k) + 4k(2 - 3k)$
l $x(x + y) + x(x - y)$
m $x(x + y) - x(x - y)$
n $xy(x + y) + xy(x - y)$
o $2x^3(3x^2 + 4x - 1) + x^2(3x^3 - 8x^2 + 2x + 1)$
p $3x^2(2x^2 + x - 3) - 2x(3x^3 - x^2 + 2x + 1)$

4 Look at Ben's homework.

1 $2(5x + 3) = 2 \times 5x + 2 \times 3$ ✓ **1 mark**
$= 10x + 6$ ✓ **1 mark**

2 $x(x + 3)$

×	x	3	
x	$x \times x = x^2$	$x \times 3 = 3x$	$x^2 + 3x$

$x(x + 3) = x \times x + x \times 3$
$= 2x + x^3$

3 $3(a - b) + 4(a + 2b) = 3 \times a + 3 \times -b + 4 \times a + 4 \times 2b$
$= 3a - 3b + 4a + 8b$
$= 7a - 11b$

4 $4(p + q) + 4(p - q) = 4 \times p + 4 \times q + 4 \times p + 4 \times -q$
$= 4p + 4q + 4p - 4q$
$= 8p$

5 $4x(3x^2 + 2x) = 4x \times 3x^2 + 4x \times 2x$
$= 7x^3 + 6x^2$

a Ben scores one mark for using the right method to expand the brackets.
He scores another mark if he gets the correct answer.
The first question has been marked.
Check the rest of Ben's homework and show that he scores 7 out of 10

b Correct Ben's mistakes.
Write some notes to help Ben work out what he has done wrong.

5 In each row of the table one expression is not equivalent to the other three.
Which expression is the odd one out in each row?
Give a reason for each of your answers.

a	$3(2a + 4)$	$2(3a + 6)$	$6a + 12$	$2(3a + 5)$
b	$5(4b - 3)$	$2(10b - 8) + 1$	$4(5b - 4) - 1$	$10(2b - 1) - 5$
c	$6(1 - 3b)$	$9(1 - 2b) + 3$	$3(2 - 5b) - 3b$	$18(1 - b) - 12$
d	$6d^2 + 8d$	$6d(d + 1) + 2d$	$2d(3d + 4)$	$3d(3d + 4) - 3d^2 - 4$
e	$2(3e + 5) + 3(e - 2)$	$3(3e + 1)$	$9(e + 2) - 15$	$3(3e + 5) - 12$

6 Show that $3(2x + 7) + 5(2x - 1) = 16(x + 1)$.

7 Show that $3x(4x + 3y) - 6x(2x - y) = 15xy$.

8 Jim, Kay and Emma try to expand $3x^2(4x^5 + 2y^3)$.
Jim gets $7x^{10} + 5xy^6$
Kay gets $12x^7 + 6x^2y^3$
Emma gets $12x^7 + 3x^2$
a Who is correct?
b Describe the mistakes that the other two have made.

9 Multiply out the brackets and simplify.
a $(x + 4)(x + 3)$
b $(x + 2)(x + 7)$
c $(x + 1)(x + 5)$
d $(x - 3)(x + 5)$
e $(x + 1)(x - 4)$
f $(x + 7)(x + 8)$
g $(x + 7)(x - 8)$
h $(x - 7)(x - 8)$

10 Expand and simplify.
a $(a + 2)(a - 5)$
b $(b - 2)(b - 4)$
c $(c + 8)(c - 3)$
d $(d - 1)(d - 2)$
e $(e + 9)(e - 5)$
f $(f + 1)(f - 1)$
g $(g - 2)(g - 5)$
h $(h + 2)(h - 5)$

4.3 Factorising simple expressions

CAN YOU REMEMBER

- How to find the factors of a number?
- How to find the common factors of two numbers?
- How to expand or multiply out brackets?

IN THIS SECTION YOU WILL

- Learn how to factorise simple algebraic expressions with common factors.
- Extend skills in simplifying expressions.

The factors of a number can be found using multiplication facts.
For example, the factors of 6 are found from $6 = 1 \times 6$ and $6 = 2 \times 3$
The factors of an algebraic expression can be found in the same way.
For example, $10x = 1 \times 10x$, $10x = 2 \times 5x$, $10x = 5 \times 2x$, $10x = 10 \times x$

So

Factors of 6	**1**, **2**, 3 and 6
Factors of $10x$	**1**, **2**, 5, 10, x, $2x$, $5x$ and $10x$

1 and **2** are the common factors of 6 and $10x$.

The common factors of $10x$ and 6 can be used to *factorise* $10x + 6$
Factorise means 'write an expression as the *product* of its factors'.

Using the common factor 2:

$10x + 6 = \mathbf{2} \times 5x + \mathbf{2} \times 3 = \mathbf{2} \times (5x + 3) = \mathbf{2}(5x + 3)$

So $10x + 6$ factorises to $2(5x + 3)$.

Check by *expanding* the brackets.
$2(5x + 3) = 2 \times 5x + 2 \times 3 = 10x + 6$

Factorising is the inverse of *expanding* brackets.
To factorise an expression completely:

Step 1: Find the common factors of the terms of the expression.

Step 2: Choose the highest of the common factors.

Step 3: Write the expression as a product of its factors.

Example 1

Factorise completely $12a - 16b$.

Solution 1

Step 1: The common factors of $12a$ and $16b$ are 2 and 4

Step 2: The highest of the common factors is **4**

Step 3: $12a + 16b = \mathbf{4} \times 3a + \mathbf{4} \times 4b = \mathbf{4} \times (3a + 4b) = \mathbf{4}(3a + 4b)$

Check: Expand $4(3a + 4b) = 4 \times 3a + 4 \times 4b = 12a + 16b$.

Exercise A

1 **a** Copy and complete the following to find the factors of 20 and $12x$.

1×20	$2 \times \ldots$	$4 \times \ldots$			
$1 \times 12x$	$2 \times 6x$	$3 \times \ldots$	$4 \times \ldots$	$6 \times \ldots$	$12 \times \ldots$

Factors of 20	1, 2, 4, …, … and …
Factors of $12x$	1, 2, 3, 4, 6, 12, …, …, …, …, … and $12x$

b What is the highest of the common factors of $12x$ and 20?

c Factorise $12x + 20$

2 **a** **i** Copy and complete the following to find the factors of $18p$.

$1 \times \ldots$	$2 \times \ldots$	$\ldots \times 6p$	$\ldots \times 3p$	$\ldots \times \ldots$	$18 \times \ldots$

ii Write a similar list of the factors of $12q$.

b Copy and complete this table.

Factors of $18p$	1, 2, …, …, …, 18, …, …, $3p$, $6p$, … and …
Factors of $12q$	

c Factorise **i** $18p + 12q$ **ii** $12p + 18q$.

3 **a** Write a list of the factors of **i** $8a$ **ii** $20b$.

b Factorise **i** $8a + 20b$ **ii** $20a + 8b$.

4 | $6x$ | 1 | $3x$ | x | 9 | $2x$ | 3 | $9x$ | 6 | $4x$ | 2 |

a Which of the cards above show the factors of
 i 3 **ii** 6 **iii** 9?

b Which of the cards above show the factors of
 i $3x$ **ii** $6x$ **iii** $9x$?

c Factorise
 i $6x + 3$ **ii** $3x + 9$ **iii** $9x + 6$ **iv** $6x + 9$

5 The diagram on the left shows the relation 'is a factor of'.

a Copy and complete the diagram on the right.

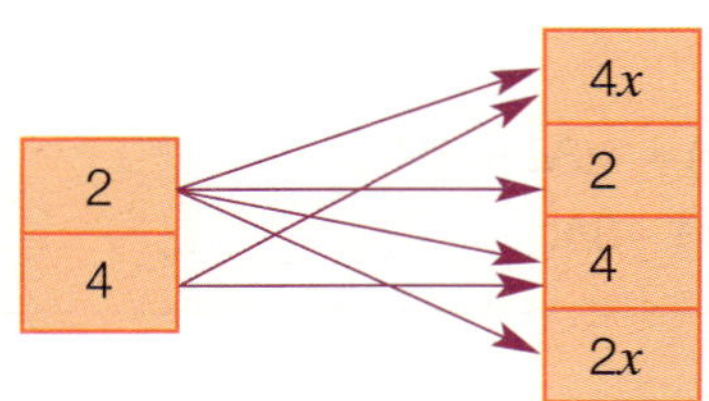

The arrow says, '8 is a factor of $16x$'

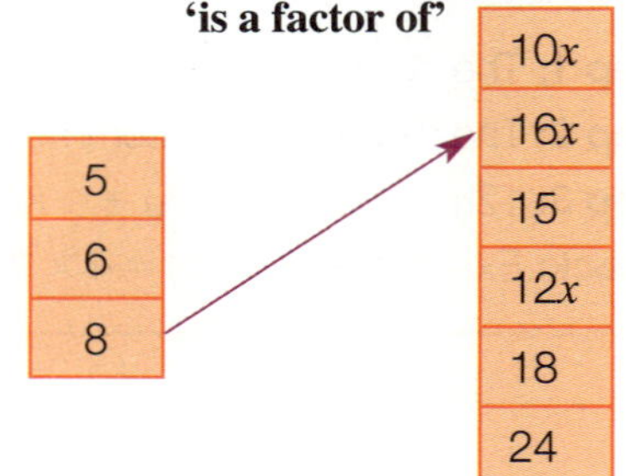

b Use the diagram to help you factorise completely
 i $10x + 15$ **ii** $16x + 24$ **iii** $12x + 18$

6 Copy and complete this table.

a	$2a + 4$	$2(a + 2)$	**b**	$2b - 6$	$2(b - \ldots)$
c	$4c + 6$	$2(2c + \ldots)$	**d**	$4d - 10$	$2(\ldots - 5)$
e	$6e + 18$	$6(\ldots + \ldots)$	**f**	$12f - 18$	$6(\ldots - \ldots)$
g	$18g + 12$	$6(\ldots + \ldots)$	**h**	$21h - 14$	$\ldots(3h - 2)$
i	$26i + 8$	$\ldots(13i + 4)$	**j**	$16j - 24$	$\ldots(2j - 3)$
k	$4x + 6y$	$2(\ldots + \ldots)$	**l**	$8x - 2y$	$2(\ldots - \ldots)$
m	$12x + 30y$	$6(\ldots + \ldots)$	**n**	$12x - 9y$	$\ldots(\ldots - \ldots)$
o	$14x + 8y$	$\ldots(\ldots + \ldots)$			

7 Factorise completely

a $18a + 24$ **b** $18b - 27$ **c** $25c + 15$
d $21d - 35$ **e** $32e + 16$ **f** $32f - 24$
g $32g + 20$ **h** $18h - 45$ **i** $33i + 22$
j $40x - 60y$ **k** $26x + 39y$ **l** $24x - 60y$
m $4x + 6y$ **n** $6x - 8y$ **o** $12x + 40y$
p $60x - 90y$ **q** $56x + 48y$ **r** $48x - 72y$
s $50x + 75y$ **t** $80x - 32y$.

Example 2

a Factorise $a^2 + a$.

b Factorise completely $b^3 - 2b^2$

Solution 2

a **Step 1:** Find the common factors of a^2 and a:

$a^2 = 1 \times a^2,\ a^2 = a \times a$
$a = 1 \times a$

Step 2: a is the highest common factor of a and a^2

Factors of a^2	**1**, a and a^2
Factors of a	**1** and a

Step 3:

$a^2 + a = a \times a + a \times 1 = a \times (a + 1) = a(a + 1)$

So $a^2 + a = a(a + 1)$.

Check: Expand $a(a + 1) = a \times a + a \times 1 = a^2 + a$.

b **Step 1:**

$b^3 = 1 \times b^3 = b \times b^2$
$2b^2 = 1 \times 2b^2 = 2 \times b^2 = b \times 2b$

Step 2: b^2 is the highest common factor of b^3 and $2b^2$

Factors of b^3	**1**, b, b^2 and b^3
Factors of $2b^2$	**1**, 2, b, $2b$, b^2 and $2b^2$

Step 3:

$b^3 - 2b^2 = b^2 \times b - b^2 \times 2 = b^2 \times (b - 2) = b^2(b - 2)$

So $b^3 - 2b^2 = b^2(b - 2)$.

Check: Expand $b^2(b - 2) = b^2 \times b + b^2 \times -2 = b^3 - 2b^2$

Exercise B

1 **a** Dave is asked to **completely** factorise $20x + 40$
He gives the answer $10(2x + 4)$. Explain why he is wrong.

b Melanie is asked to factorise $3x^2 + 2x$.
She gives the answer $x(3x + 1)$. Explain why she is wrong.

2 Two of the expressions in the boxes are factors of the given expression.
In each case find the two factors.

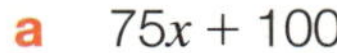

a $75x + 100$	15	$3x + 4$	50	$5x + 2$	25
b $36x + 54$	18	$9x + 2$	27	$2x + 3$	4
c $80x + 60$	40	$4x + 3$	20	$2x + 5$	12
d $75x + 30$	25	$5x + 2$	30	$3x + 1$	15

3 **a** Copy and complete the diagram to show the factors of $20x + 30$

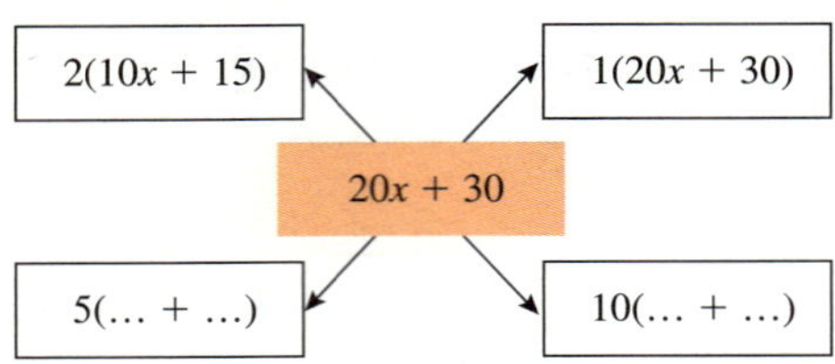

b Copy and complete the diagram to show the factors of $40x - 60y$.

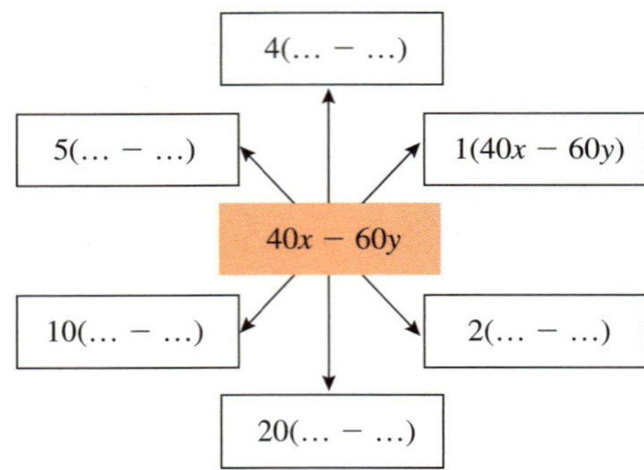

c Copy and complete the diagram to show the factors of $x^3 - 2x^2$

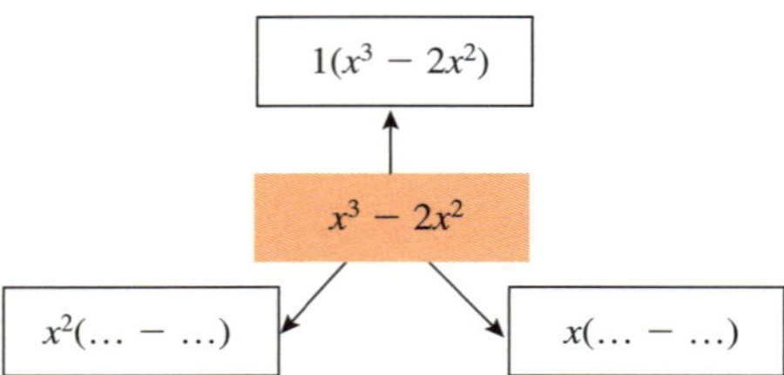

4 Find the value of a in each of the following.

a $16x + 8 = a(2x + 1)$

b $25x - 15 = 5(ax - 3)$

c $12x + 20y = a(3x + 5y)$

d $18p - 27q = 9(2p - aq)$

e $35p + 63q = a(5p + 9q)$

5 Find the values of b and c in each of the following.

a $35x + 45 = b(cx + 9)$

b $42x + 70 = b(3x + c)$

c $30p - 48q = b(5p - cq)$

d $20x + 55y = b(4x + cy)$

e $84p - 60q = b(cp - 5q)$

6 **a** **i** Write down all the factors of x^2

ii Write down all the factors of $5x$.

iii Factorise $x^2 + 5x$.

b **i** Write down all the factors of xy.

ii Write down all the factors of $2x^2$

iii Factorise $2x^2 - xy$.

7 Copy and complete this table.

a	$a^2 + 2a$	$a(a + 2)$	**b**	$b^2 - 4b$	$b(\ldots - \ldots)$
c	$e^2 + 6e$	$\ldots(e + \ldots)$	**d**	$5f^2 - 2f$	$\ldots(5f - \ldots)$
e	$7g^2 + 6g$	$g(\ldots + \ldots)$	**f**	$4h^3 - h$	$h(\ldots - \ldots)$
g	$i^3 + 6i^2$	$i^2(\ldots + \ldots)$	**h**	$5j^4 - j^2$	$\ldots(\ldots - 1)$
i	$x^2 + xy$	$\ldots(\ldots + y)$	**j**	$4x^4 - 3xy$	$x(\ldots - \ldots)$

8 Factorise completely

a	$a^2 + 4a$	**b**	$5b^2 - b$	**c**	$c^2 + 8c$	**d**	$8d^2 + d$
e	$4e - 3e^2$	**f**	$ax + bx$	**g**	$x - 6xy$	**h**	$2x + 3xy$
i	$4x - xy$	**j**	$12x^2 + 8y^2$	**k**	$75x^2 - 50y^2$	**l**	$56x^2 + 63y^2$
m	$x^3 - x$	**n**	$x^3 + x^2$	**o**	$x^3 - 3x^2$	**p**	$x^5 + 5x^2$
q	$ax^6 - bx^3$	**r**	$x^5 + 5xy$	**s**	$3x^5 - 7x^3$	**t**	$x^5 + xy^3$

9 **a** You are given that $6(3x - 5) + 3(4x - 5) = 15(ax + b)$.
Find the values of a and b.

b You are given that $5(4x - 5y) - 2(3x - 2y) = c(2x + dy)$.
Find the values of c and d.

Expand $6(3x - 5) + 3(4x - 5)$ first and then factorise.

10 Factorise completely

a	**i** $6x + 12y - 30z$	**ii** $14x - 21y + 70z$	**iii** $25p + 35q + 50r$
b	**i** $24x - 60y - 72z$	**ii** $16x - 48y - 144$	**iii** $36p + 54q - 144$
c	**i** $x^4 + x^3 + x^2$	**ii** $2x^4 + 4x^3 + 6x^2$	**iii** $24x^4 - 60x^3 - 72x^2$

Chapter summary

- In the expression b^a, b is called the *base* and a the *power*.
- b^a is shorthand for multiplying b by itself a times.
- x^a is 'x to the power a'.
- To multiply and divide powers with **the same base** follow these rules:
  - to multiply **add** the powers: $x^a \times x^b = x^{a+b}$
  - to divide **subtract** the powers: $x^a \div x^b = x^{a-b}$
- When multiplying terms that include both numbers and letters, deal with the numbers and letters separately.
- Expanding or multiplying out brackets:
  $a(b + c) = a \times b + a \times c = ab + ac$
- When an expression contains brackets and extra terms, or more than one set of brackets, first expand the brackets and then collect like terms.
- To multiply two expressions in brackets together, multiply **all** terms in the first bracket by **all** terms in the second bracket.
- Factorising is the inverse of expanding brackets.
  To factorise an expression completely:
  - Find the common factors of the terms in the expression.
  - Choose the highest common factor.
  - Write the expression as a product of its factors.
  - **Check** by expanding the factorised expression.

Chapter review

1 Work out the value of $2^7 \div 2^4$

2 Simplify

a $x^5 \times x^2$ **b** $y^5 \div y^2$ **c** $w^6 \times w^2$ **d** $x^5 \div x^3$

3 Simplify

a $c \times c \times c \times c$ **b** $d^5 \times d^3 \times d$ **c** $\frac{e^8}{e}$

4 Simplify

a $5y^3 \times 3y^5$ **b** $2a^5 \times 3a^2$ **c** $8y^6 \div 4y^2$ **d** $\dfrac{36a^6}{9a^2}$

5 Expand

a $4(m - 1)$ **b** $3(4y + 1)$ **c** $p(p + 3)$ **d** $s(s^2 + 6)$ **e** $4(p + 3q - r)$.

6 Expand and simplify

a $4(x + 1) + 3(2x - 5)$ **b** $5(2a - c) + 3(4a + 2c)$

c $5(2a - 1) - 3(a - 4)$ **d** $3(5x - 4) - 5(2 - x)$.

7 **a** Simplify **i** $x + x + 2x$ **ii** $x \times 2x$.

b Multiply out the brackets and simplify $12 - 3(x + 2)$.

8 Factorise

a $9x + 18$ **b** $4c + 12$ **c** $10a + 5$ **d** $x^2 + 5x$ **e** $4a^2 + a$.

9 Factorise completely

a $12y - 54$ **b** $2a^2 - 4a$ **c** $3xy - 6y^2$

10 **a** Expand $4x(x^2 + 5)$. **b** Expand and simplify $4(x - 2) + 3(x + 2)$.

c Factorise $c^2 - 5c$. **d** Factorise completely $3x^2 - 9x$.

11 **a** Calculate the value of $6^4 - 2^{10}$

b x is a positive integer.

$4^x = 1\,048\,576$

Find the value of x.

Properties of two-dimensional shapes

CHAPTER 5

5.1 Parallel lines

CAN YOU REMEMBER

- That parallel lines are lines which are always the same distance apart?
- That angles at a point add up to 360°?
- That angles on a straight line add up to 180°?
- That vertically opposite angles are equal?

IN THIS SECTION YOU WILL

- Understand and use the terms 'alternate', 'corresponding' and 'allied angles'.
- Calculate the sizes of angles between parallel lines.

The diagram shows two *parallel* lines cut by a third line. The arrowheads indicate that the lines are parallel. The third line is called a *transversal*.

Several equal pairs of angles are formed.

Alternate angles form a Z-shape using the parallel lines.

The angles are on opposite sides of the transversal.

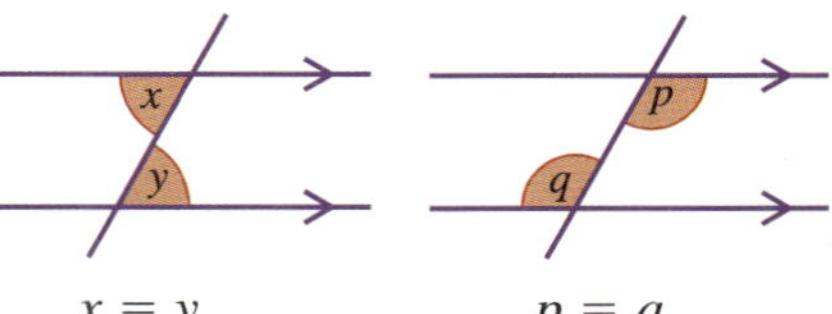

$x = y$ $p = q$

Alternate angles are always equal.

Corresponding angles are formed within an F-shape. These angles are in similar positions on the same side of the transversal.

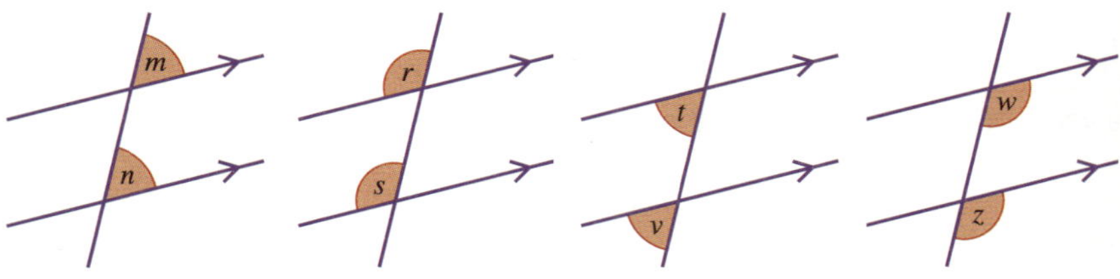

$m = n$ $r = s$ $t = v$ $w = z$

Corresponding angles are always equal.

Allied angles are inside a pair of parallel lines.

$a + b = 180°$

Allied angles always add up to 180°.

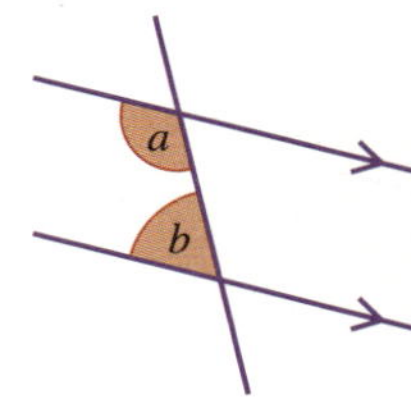

Example 1

Work out the value of the angles marked by letters. Give reasons for your answers.

a

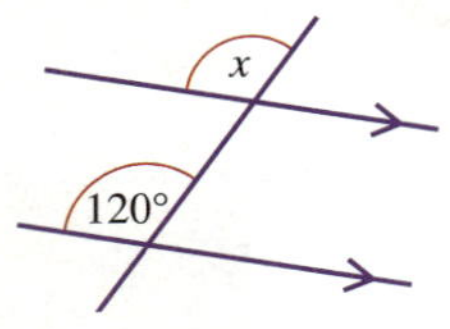

b

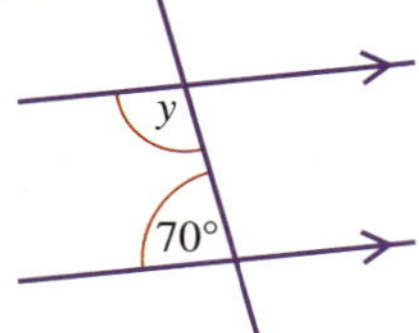

c

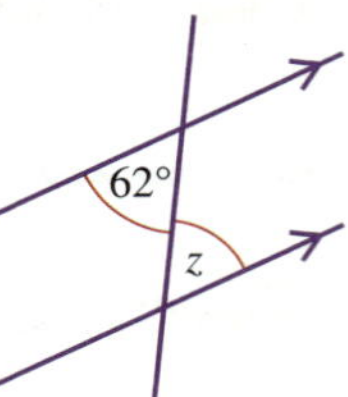

Solution 1

a $x = 120°$ (corresponding angles)
b $y = 180° - 70° = 110°$ (allied angles)
c $z = 62°$ (alternate angles)

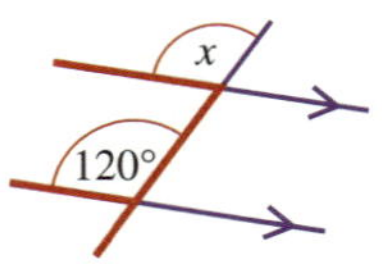

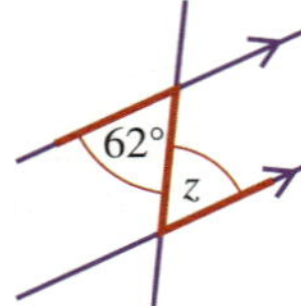

Exercise A

In the following exercise the diagrams are not drawn accurately.

1 Write down the value of angle x in each of these diagrams.

a

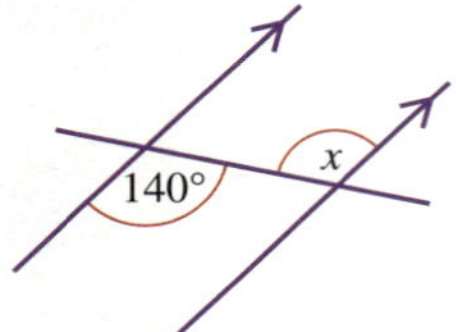

b

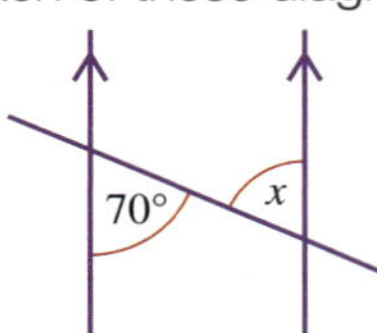

c

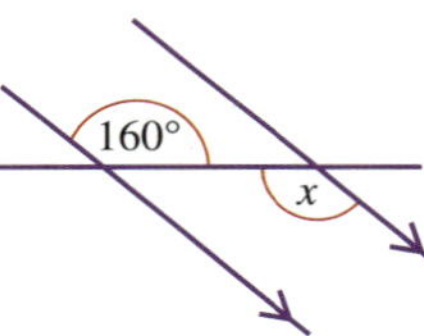

d

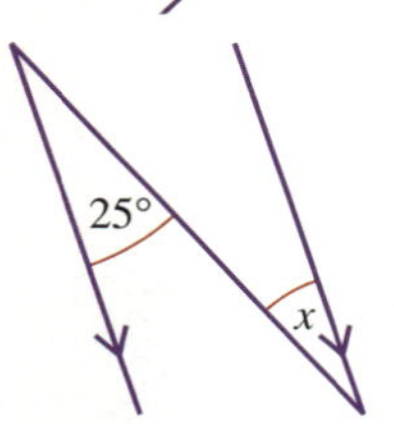

e

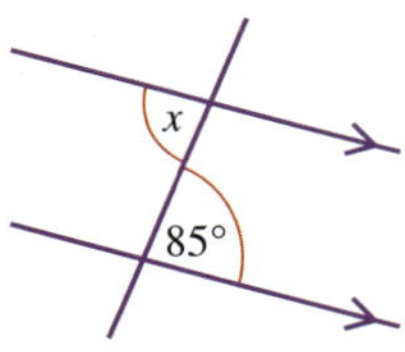

f

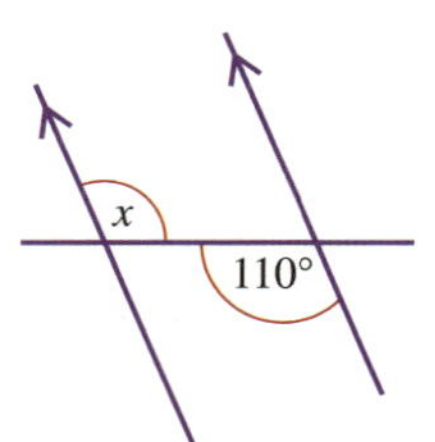

2 Write down the value of angle y in each of these diagrams.

a

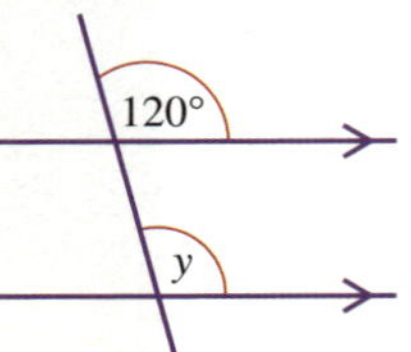

b

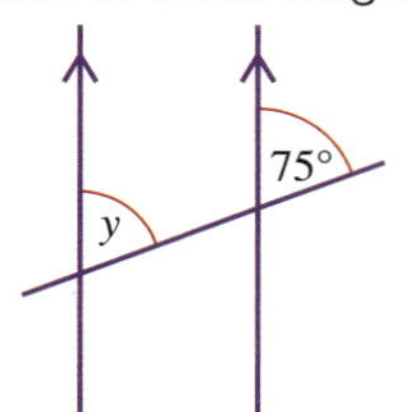

c

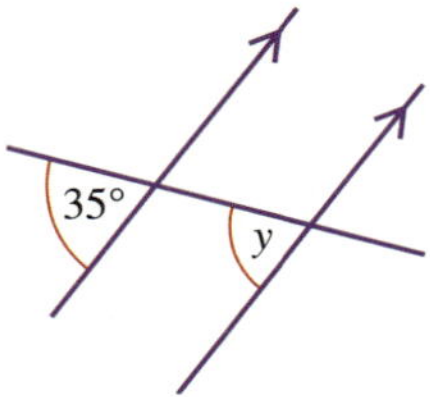

d

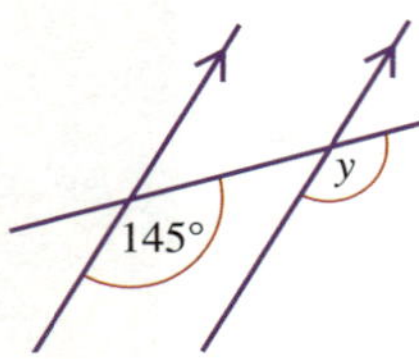

e

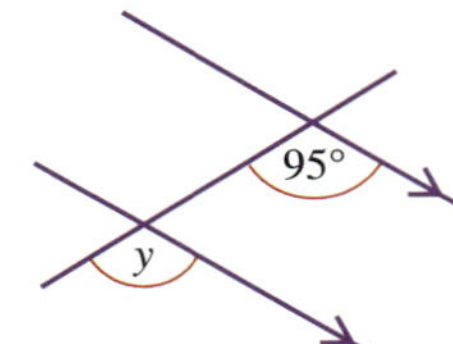

f

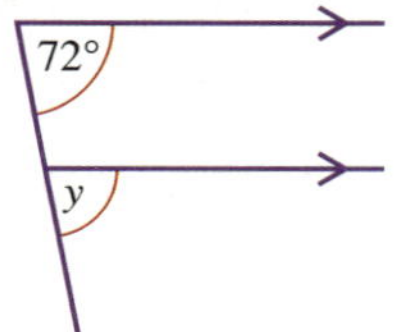

3 Work out the value of the angles marked by letters.

a

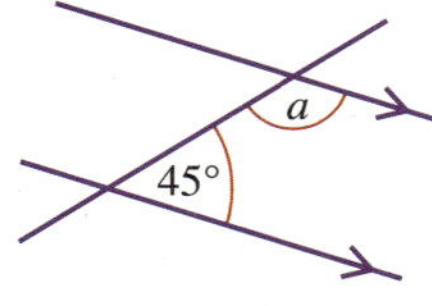

b

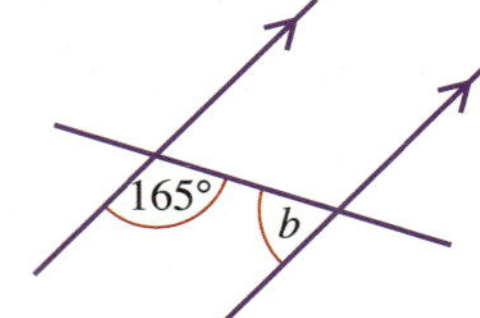

c

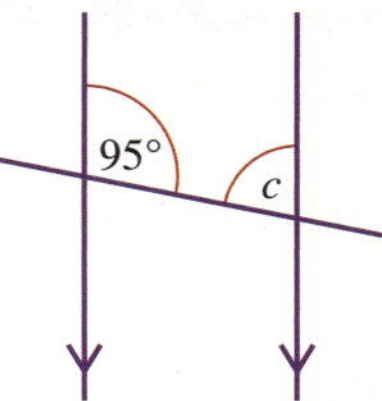

d

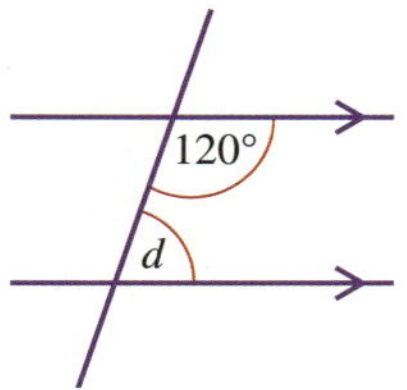

e

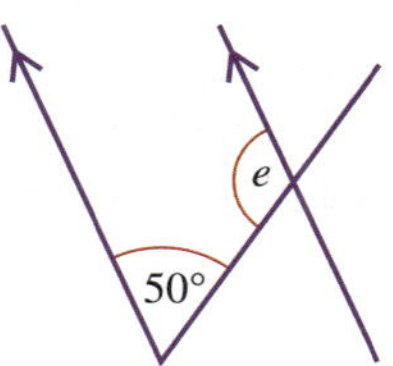

f

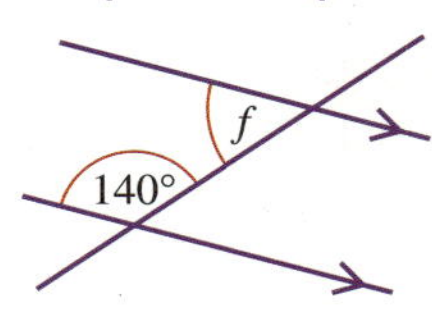

4 Calculate the value of each of the angles marked by letters. Give reasons for your answers.

a

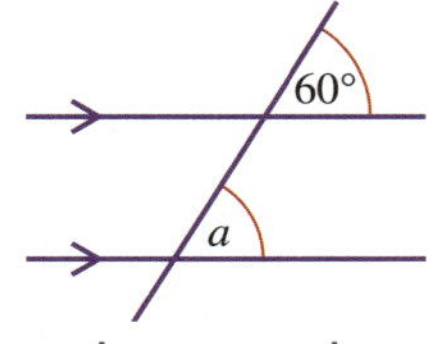

b

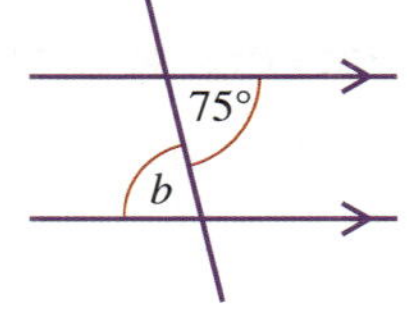

c

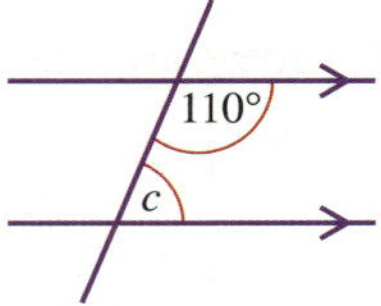

d

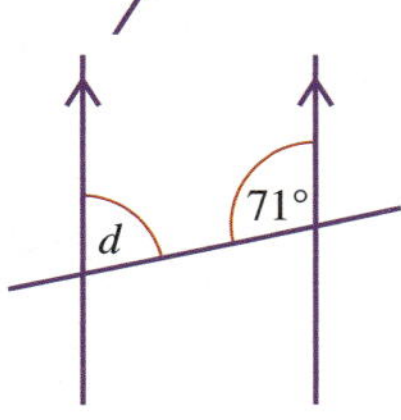

e

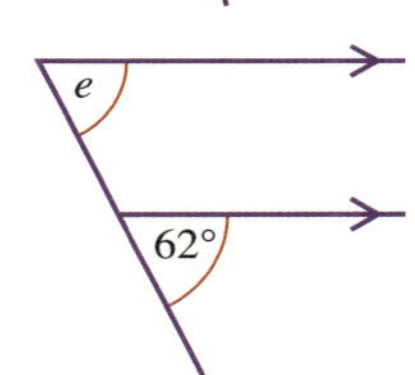

f

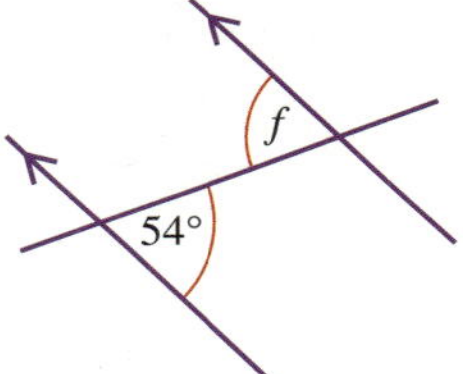

5 Calculate the value of each of the angles marked by letters. Give reasons for your answers.

a

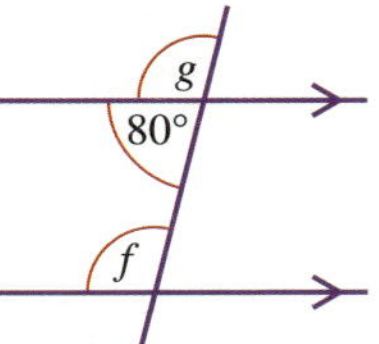

b

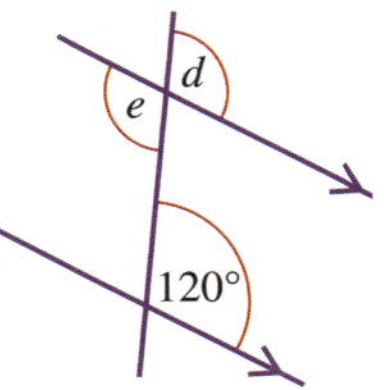

c

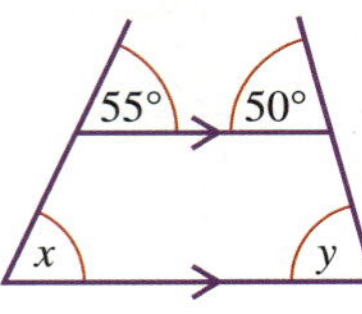

d

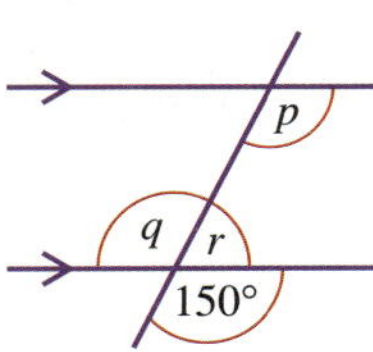

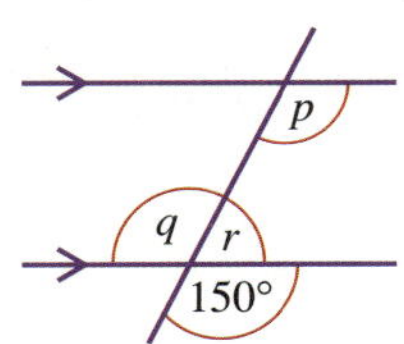

e

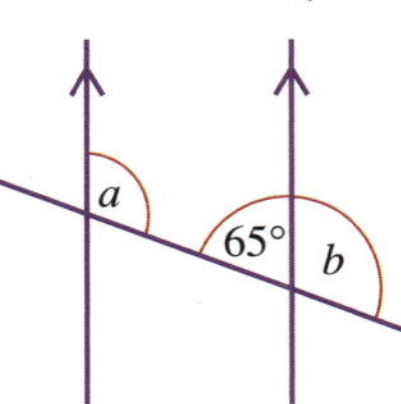

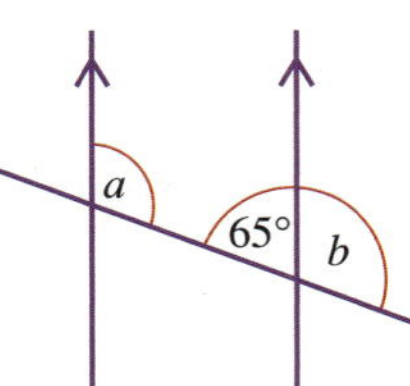

6 Work out the size of each angle marked by a letter in the following diagrams.
Give reasons for your answers.

a

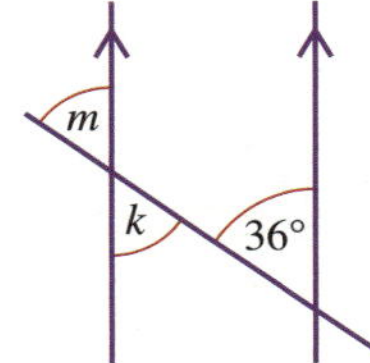

b

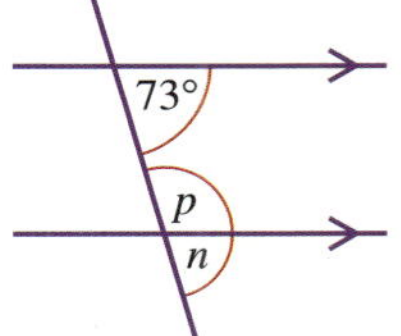

c

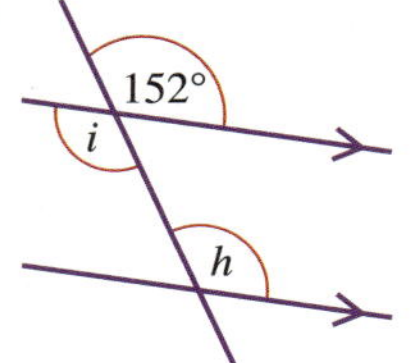

d

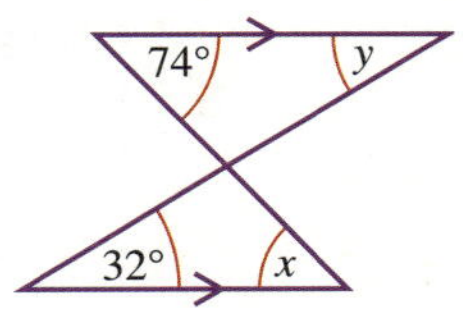

Example 2

Calculate the values of the marked angles in this diagram.
Give reasons for your answers.

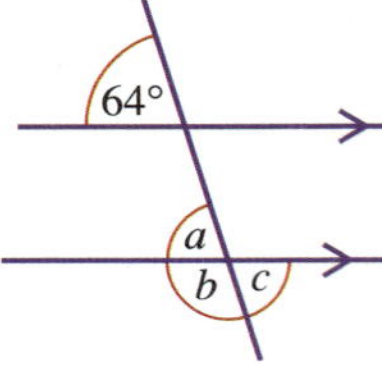

Solution 2

$a = 64°$ (corresponding angles)
$b = 180° - 64° = 116°$ (angles on a straight line total 180°)
$c = 64°$ (vertically opposite to a)

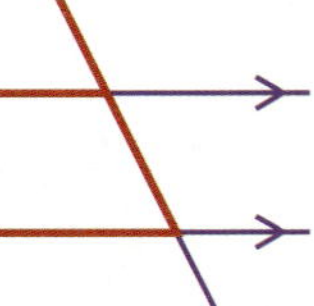

Exercise B

In the following exercise the diagrams are not drawn accurately.

1 In each part, work out the values of the angles marked by letters.

a

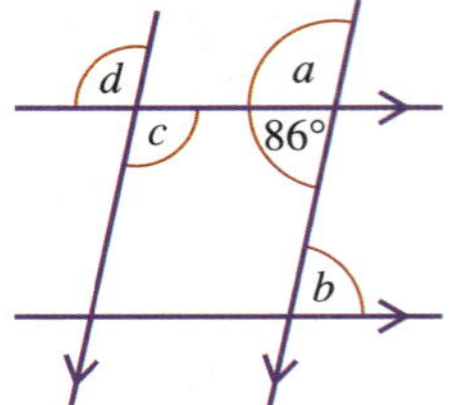

b

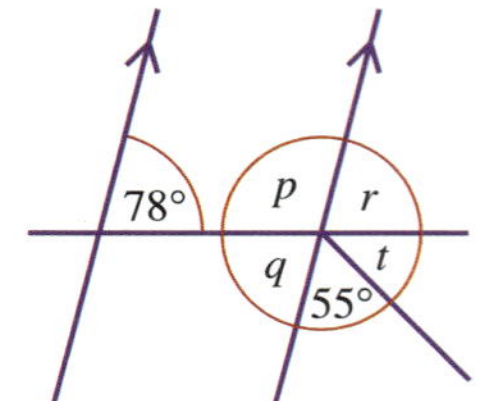

c

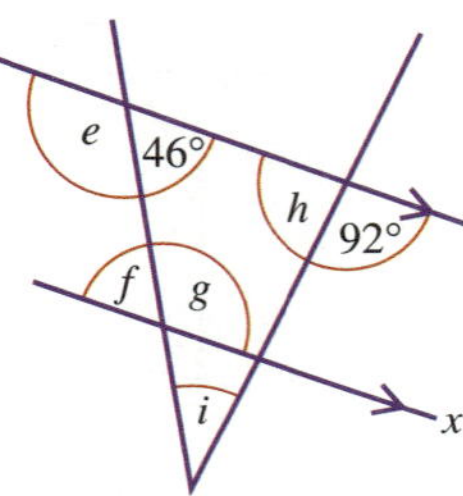

d

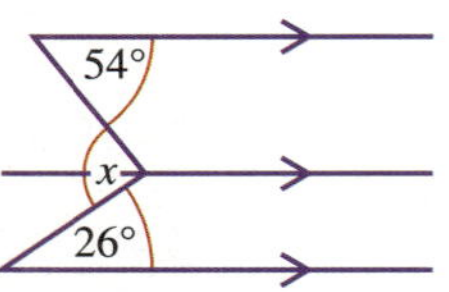

e

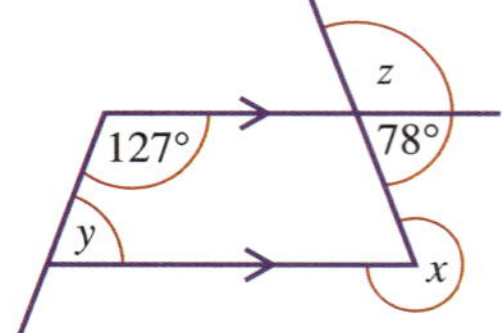

f

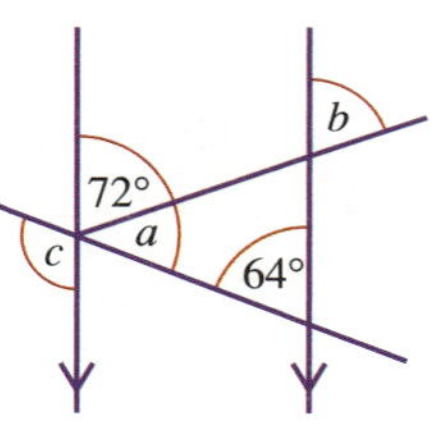

g

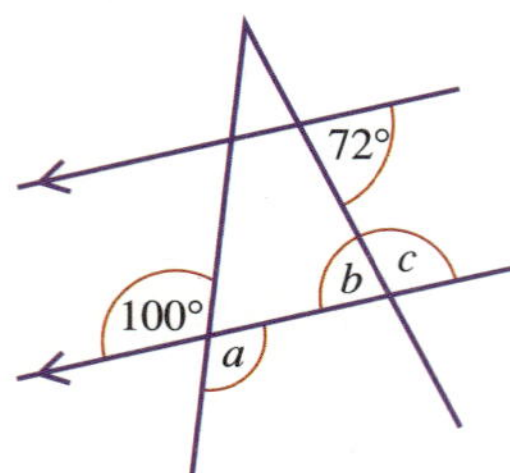

h

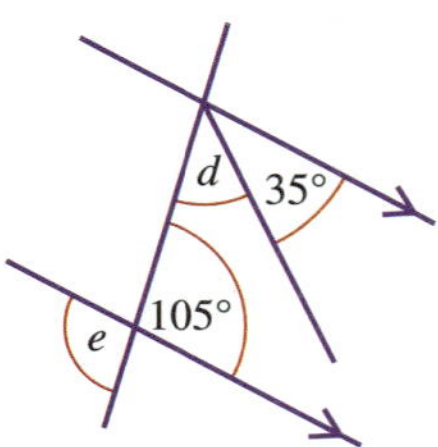

i

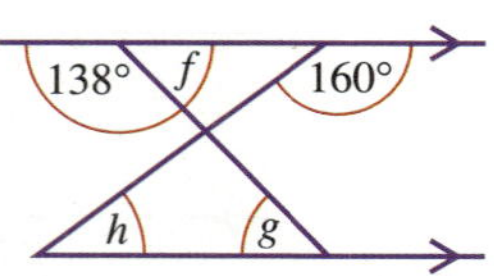

2 In the diagram AB is parallel to CD.

a Write down the value of x.
Give a reason for your answer.

b Find the value of y.

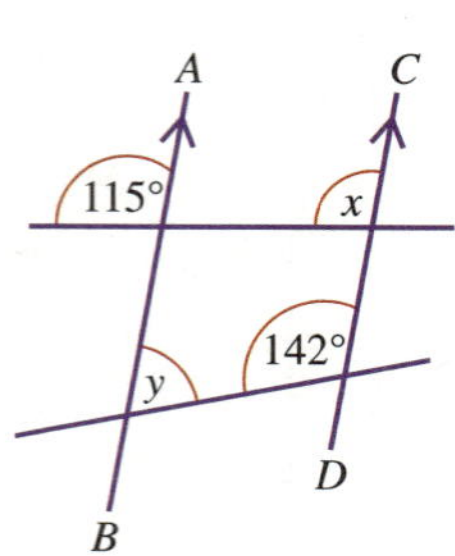

3 Work out the values of angles x, y and z.

a

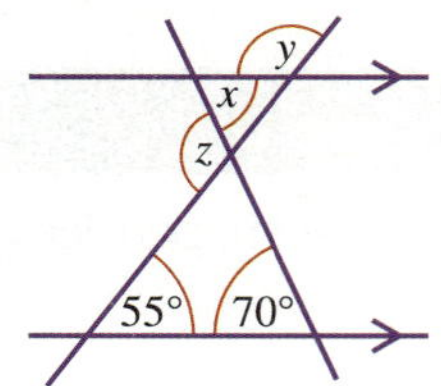

b

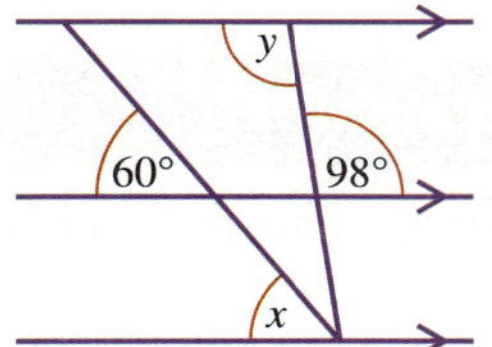

4 Find the size of p and q.
Give reasons for your answer.

a

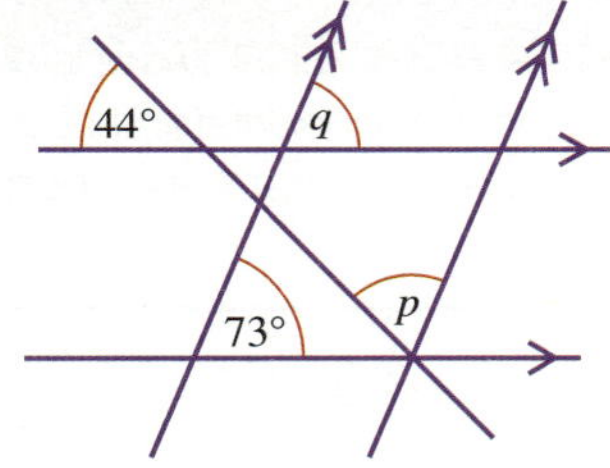

b

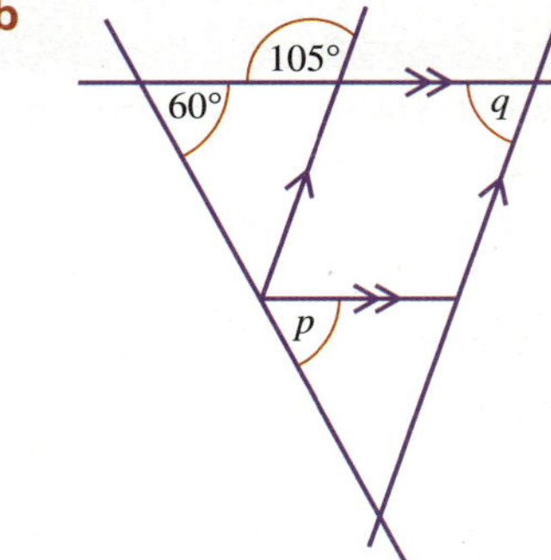

5 **a** Write down the size of angle a.
b Work out the size of angle b.

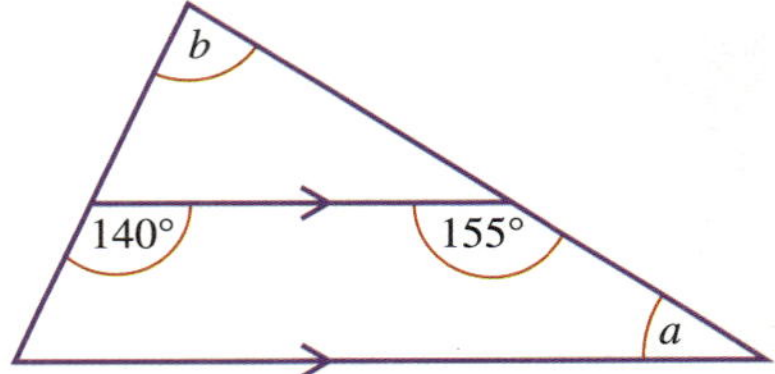

6 Work out the sizes of angles p, q, r and s.

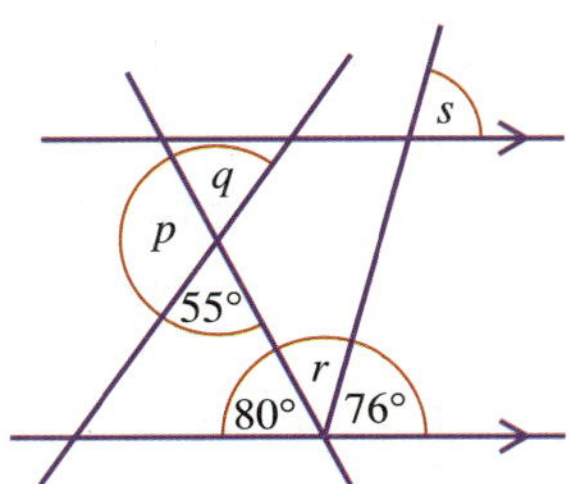

7 Look at these diagrams. Give reasons for your answers.

a Are lines AB and CD parallel?

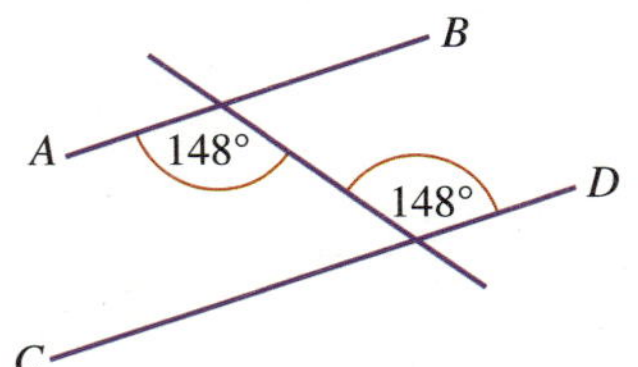

b Are lines PQ and RS parallel?

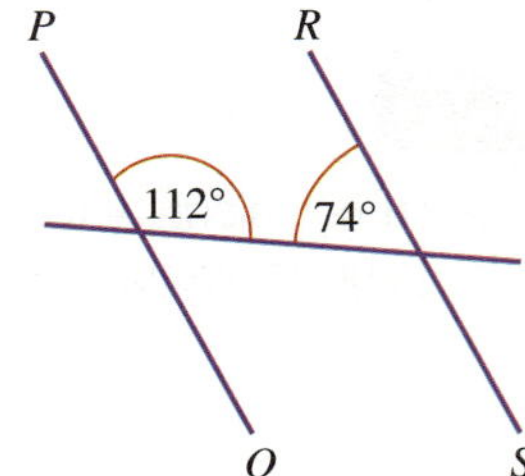

5.2 Angles in quadrilaterals

CAN YOU REMEMBER

- The properties of special quadrilaterals – square, rectangle, trapezium, parallelogram, rhombus and kite?
- That angles in a triangle add up to 180°?
- That allied angles between parallel lines add up to 180°?
- That equal lengths are shown with matching dashes?

IN THIS SECTION YOU WILL

- Use your knowledge of triangles to show that the angles in any quadrilateral add up to 360°.
- Understand and use the angle properties of a trapezium, parallelogram and rhombus.
- Calculate the interior angles of any quadrilateral.

Any quadrilateral can be divided into two triangles by drawing a diagonal.

The angles in each triangle add up to 180°.

$a + b + c = 180°$ $\qquad d + e + f = 180°$

So $a + b + c + d + e + f = 180° + 180° = 360°$.

The angles in any quadrilateral add up to 360°.

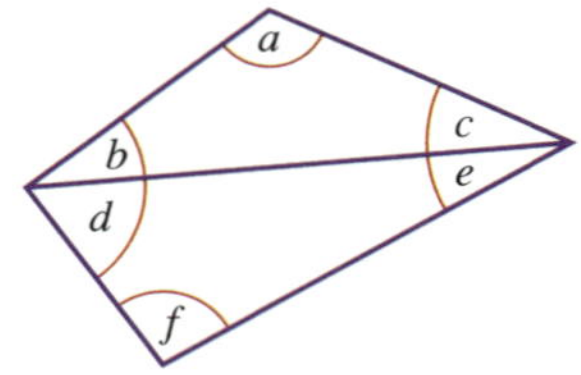

Example 1

Calculate the size of angle x.

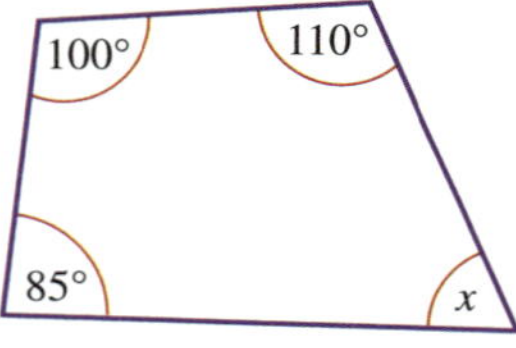

Solution 1

$110° + 100° + 85° = 295°$

The angles in any quadrilateral add up to 360°.

$x = 360° - 295° = 65°$

These quadrilaterals have one or two pairs of parallel sides.

rectangle

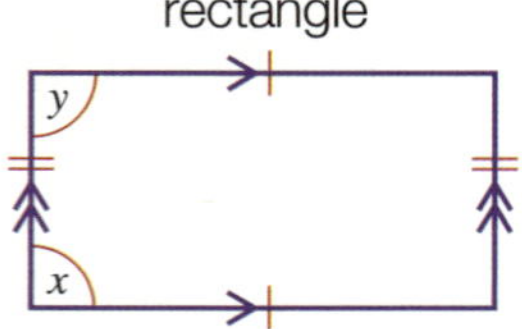

parallelogram

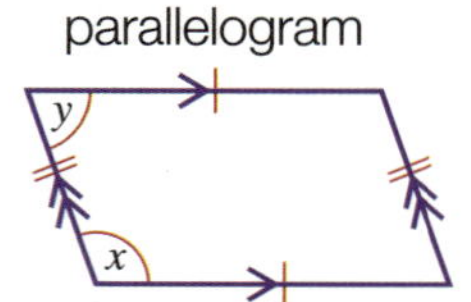

rhombus

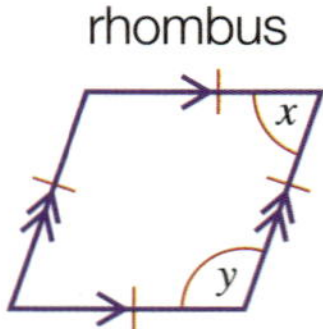

trapezium

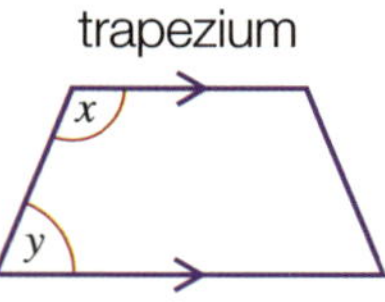

In each diagram x and y are allied angles between parallel lines. So $x + y = 180°$.

Example 2

ABCD is a trapezium. Calculate the size of angles a and b. Give reasons for your answers.

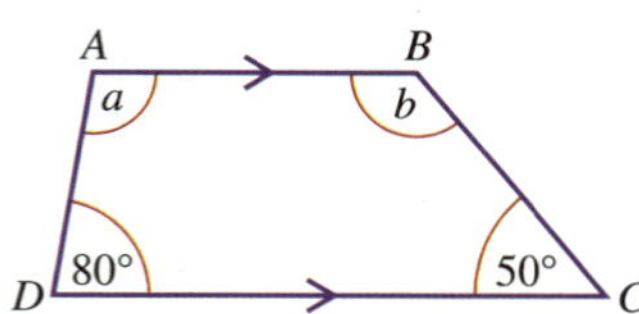

Solution 2

AB and CD are parallel.
So $a + 80° = 180°$ (allied angles), $a = 100°$
$b + 50° = 180°$ (allied angles), $b = 130°$

Exercise A

1 Calculate the size of angle x in each of these quadrilaterals.

a
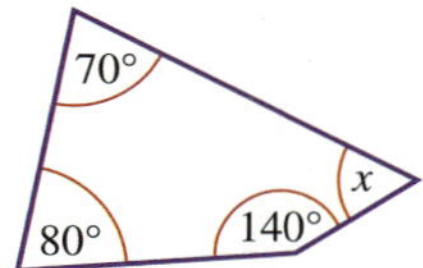

b
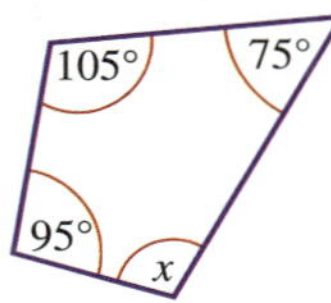

c
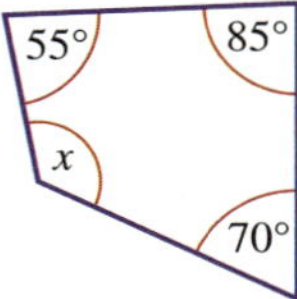

2 Each diagram shows a trapezium.
Calculate the sizes of the angles marked by letters.

a
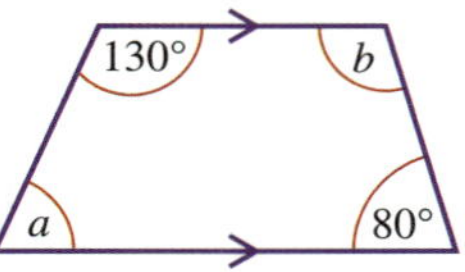

b
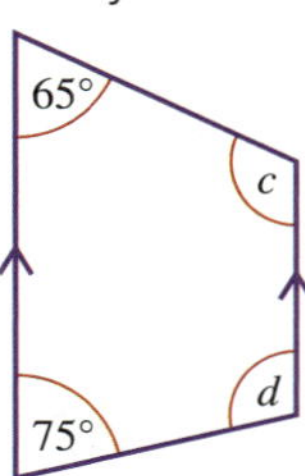

c
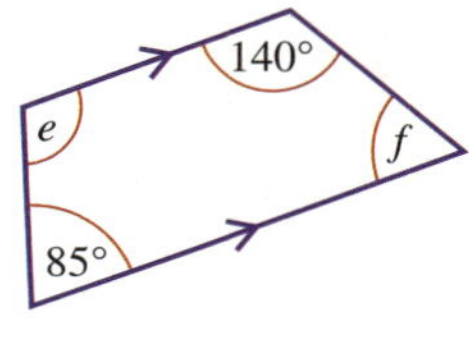

3 Each diagram shows a rhombus.
Calculate the sizes of the angles marked by letters.

a
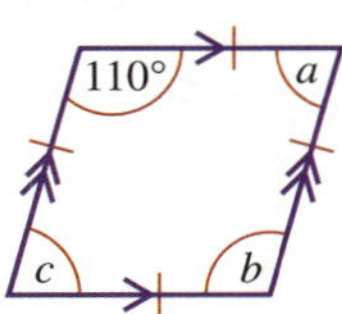

b
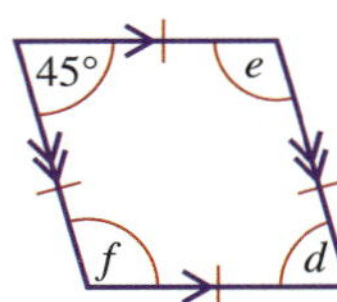

4 Each diagram shows a kite. Calculate the sizes of the angles marked by letters.

a
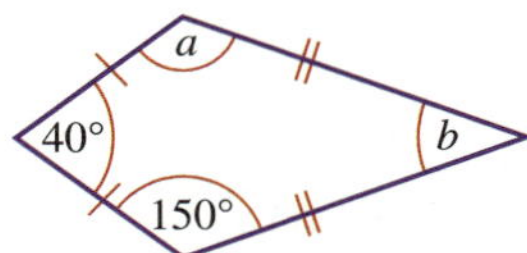

b
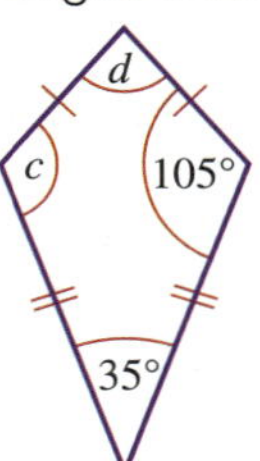

5 Each diagram shows a parallelogram.
Calculate the sizes of the angles marked by letters.

a
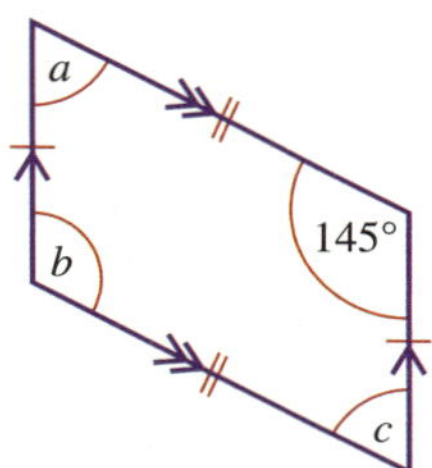

b
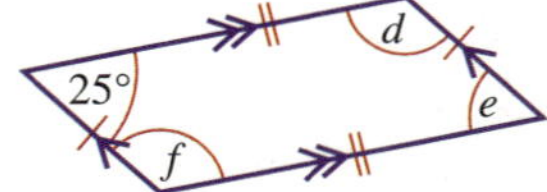

In each of the questions below calculate the size of the angles marked by letters.

6 a

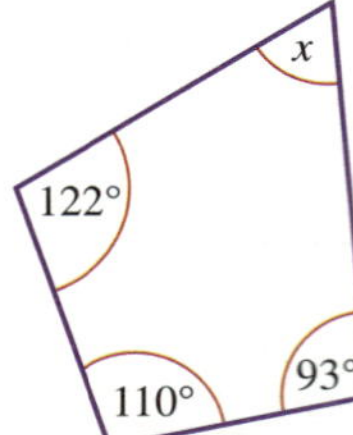

b

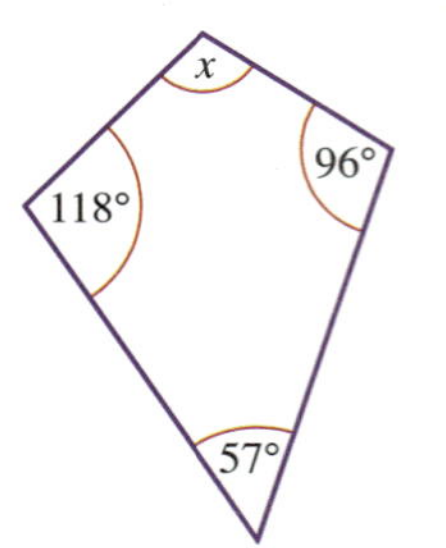

c

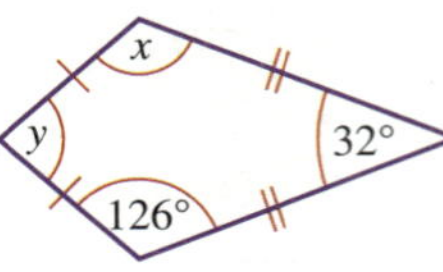

7 a

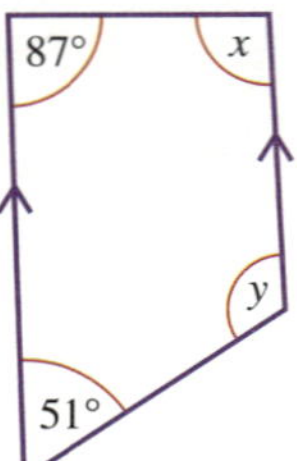

b

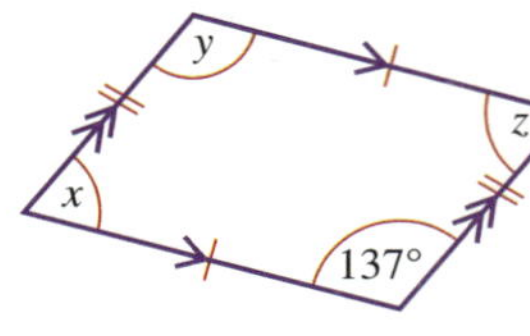

c

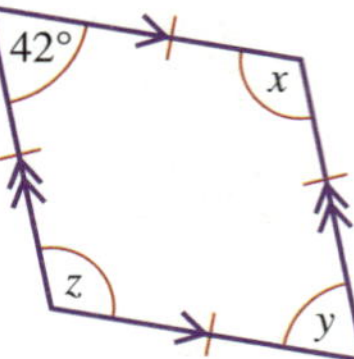

8 a

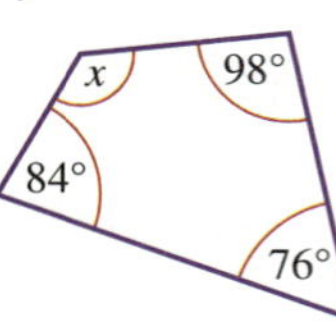

b

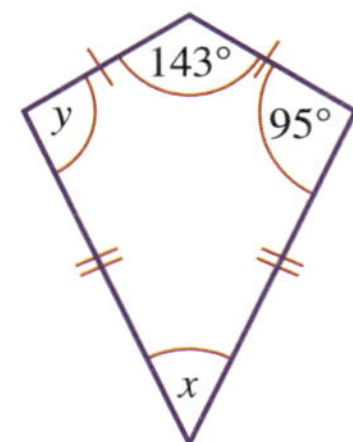

c

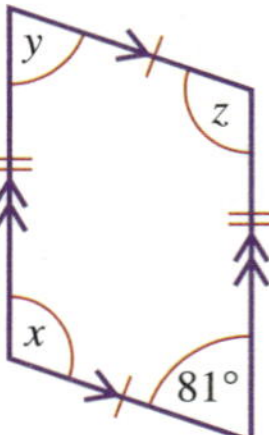

Example 3

Calculate the size of the angles marked by letters in the diagram. Give a reason for each answer.

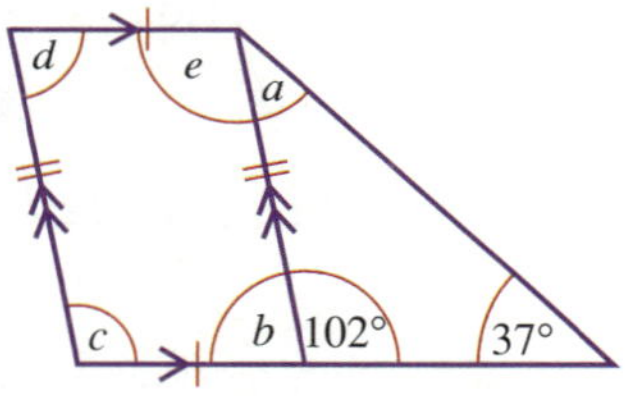

Solution 3

$a + 102° + 37° = 180°$ (angles in a triangle add up to 180°)
$a = 180° - 139° = 41°$
$b = 180° - 102°$ (angles on a straight line add up to 180°)
$b = 78°$
$b + c = 180°$ (allied angles)
$c = 180° - 78° = 102°$
$e = c = 102°$ (opposite angles of a parallelogram are equal)
$d = b = 78°$ (opposite angles of a parallelogram are equal)

Exercise B

1 Calculate the values of the angles marked by letters. Give a reason for each answer.

a

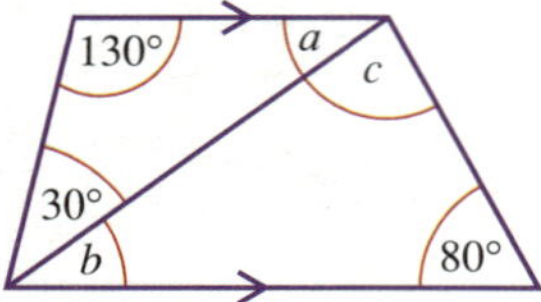

b

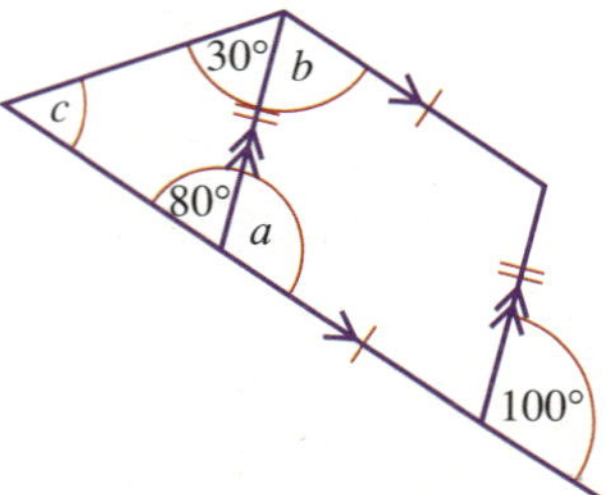

2 The diagram shows a kite.
Calculate the size of the angle marked x.
(Hint: other angles may need to be worked out first.)

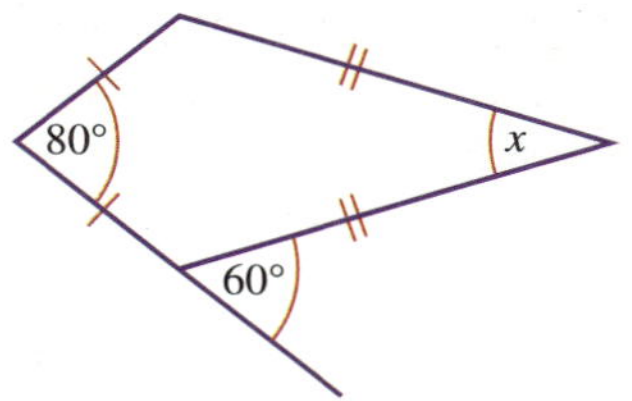

3 The diagram shows a rhombus with one diagonal drawn in.
Calculate the size of angle x.

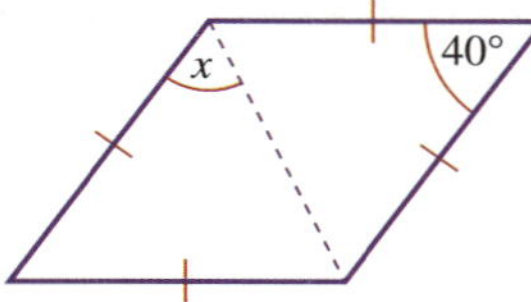

4 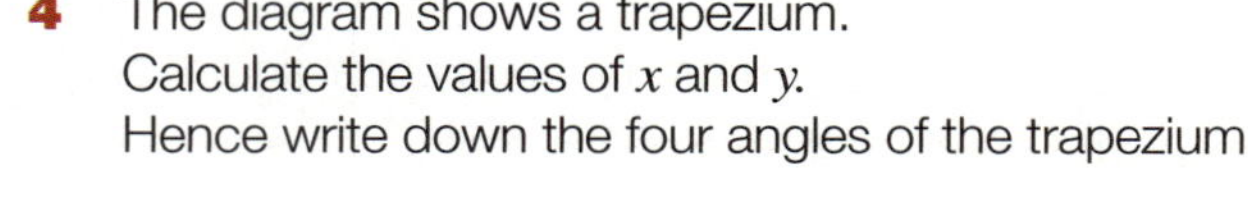
The diagram shows a trapezium.
Calculate the values of x and y.
Hence write down the four angles of the trapezium.

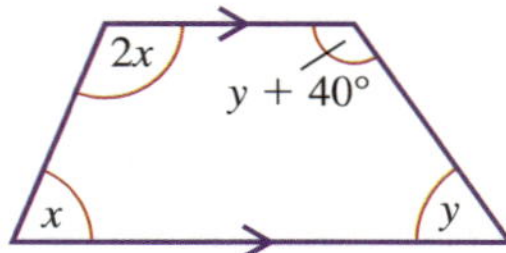

5 Calculate the **a** size of angle x

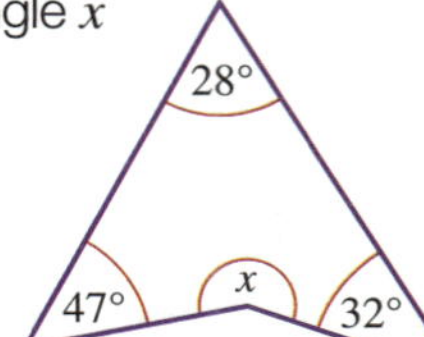

b value of y.

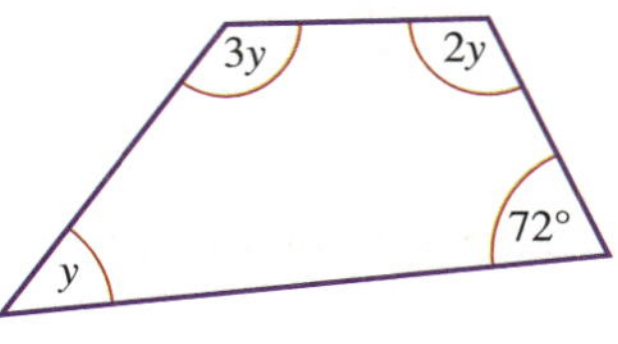

6 Find the values of angles x and y.

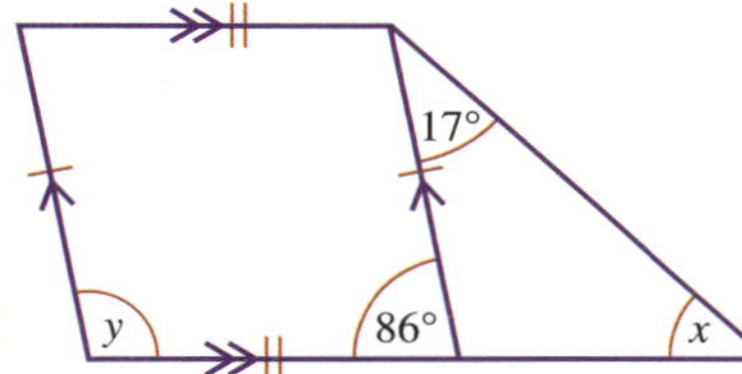

7 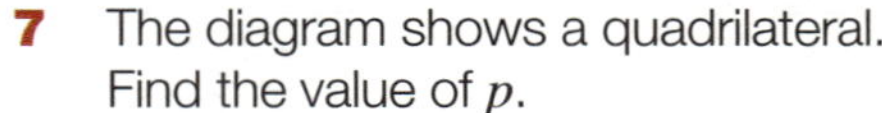
The diagram shows a quadrilateral.
Find the value of p.

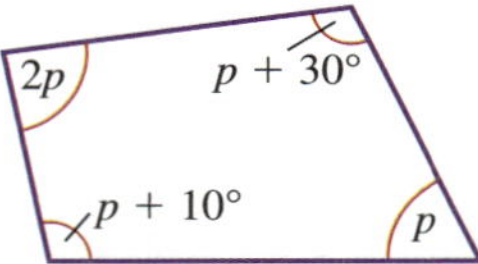

8 $ABCD$ is a quadrilateral.
Find the value of q and hence write down the size of each angle.

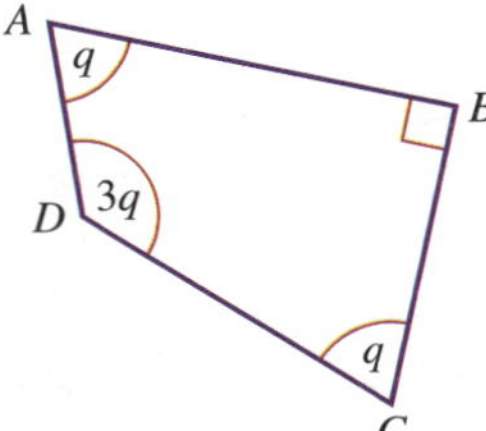

5.3 Properties of polygons

CAN YOU REMEMBER

- That angles on a straight line total 180°?
- That there are 360° in a full turn?
- How to draw lines of symmetry?
- How to find the order of rotational symmetry of a 2-D shape?

IN THIS SECTION YOU WILL

- Recognise and name polygons.
- Understand the symmetry of regular polygons.
- Learn how to calculate interior and exterior angles of polygons.

A *polygon* is a two-dimensional shape made by straight lines.
A triangle is a polygon with three sides.
A quadrilateral is a polygon with four sides.

Other polygons include:

pentagon – five sides
hexagon – six sides
heptagon – seven sides
octagon – eight sides
nonagon – nine sides
decagon – ten sides

regular hexagon

regular octagon

A *regular polygon* has all sides equal and all angles equal.

The number of lines of symmetry of a regular polygon is equal to the number of sides.

regular pentagon
five lines of symmetry

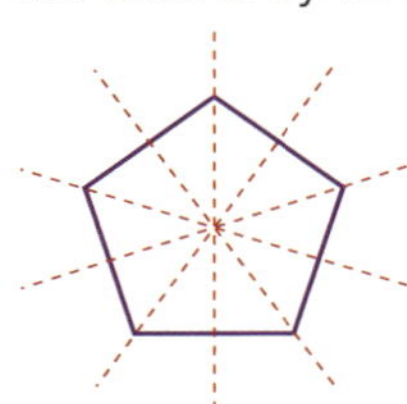

regular hexagon
six lines of symmetry

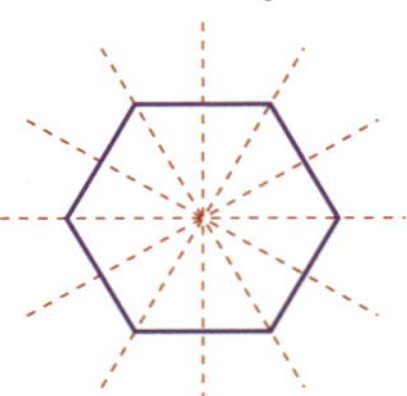

The order of rotational symmetry of a regular polygon is equal to the number of sides.

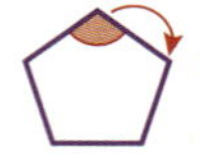
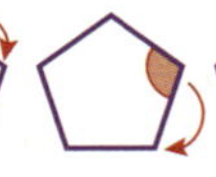
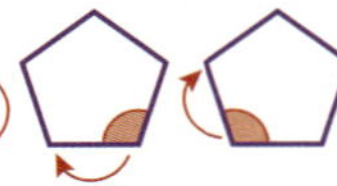
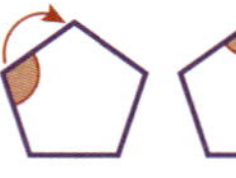
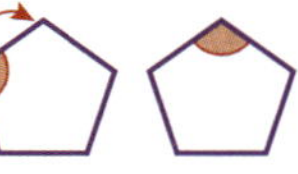

order 5

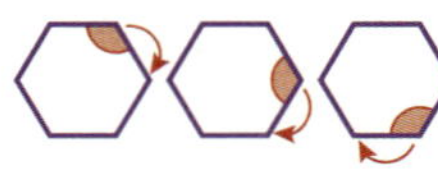

order 6

A regular polygon can be drawn using a circle.

Example 1

Use the circle method to draw a regular hexagon.

Solution 1

Step 1: Use compasses to draw a circle.
Step 2: Divide 360° by the number of sides of a hexagon.
$360° \div 6 = 60°$
Step 3: Use a protractor to divide the circle into six equal *sectors*, each with angle 60° at the centre.
Step 4: Join the points where the sector lines meet the circle, to form the hexagon.

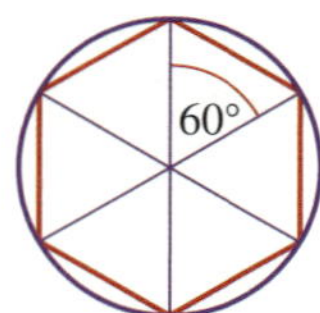

Exercise A

1 Write down the name of each of these polygons.

a

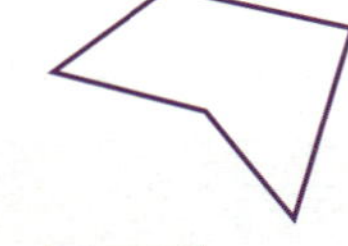

b

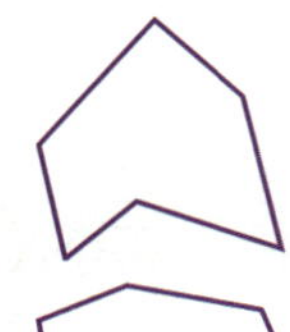

c

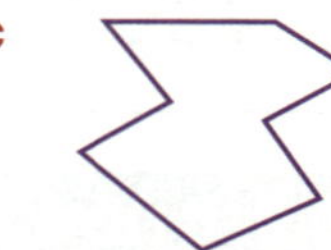

d

e

f

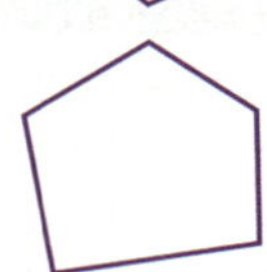

2 Copy and complete this table.

Name of regular polygon	Number of sides	Number of lines of symmetry	Order of rotational symmetry
pentagon	5	5	5
hexagon			
heptagon			7
octagon			
nonagon		9	
decagon			

3 Trace each of these regular polygons and draw in all the lines of symmetry.

a 

b 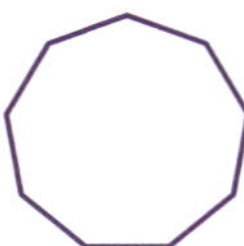

c 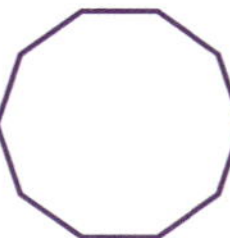

4 Use the circle method to draw:

a a regular pentagon

b a regular octagon.

5 A regular icosagon has 20 sides.
How many lines of symmetry does the icosagon have?

6 Use the circle method to draw a regular decagon.

7 A regular dodecagon has 12 sides.
Write down the order of rotational symmetry of a regular dodecagon.

8 Write down the number of lines of symmetry of

a a regular polygon with 15 sides

b a regular polygon with 18 sides.

9 Use the circle method to draw a regular nonagon.

Angles inside a polygon at the vertices are called *interior angles*.
If a side of the polygon is extended, the angle formed outside the polygon is called an *exterior angle*.
Interior and exterior angles form a straight line.

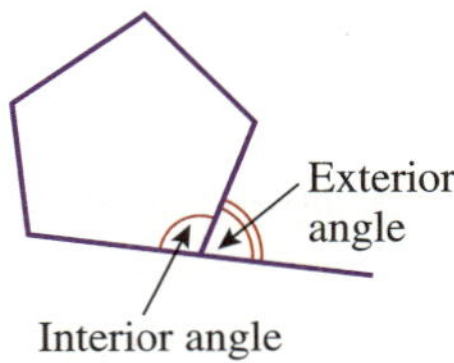

So at each vertex

interior angle + exterior angle = 180°

In any regular polygon:

- interior angles are all equal
- exterior angles are all equal.

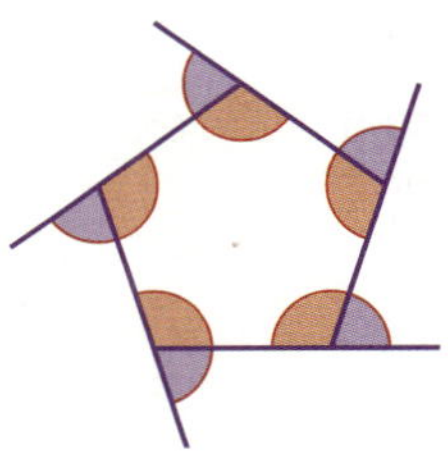

Example 2

A regular polygon has exterior angles of 36°.
Find the size of an interior angle of this polygon.

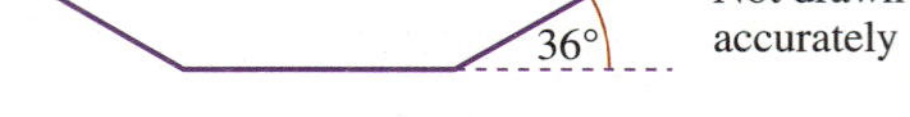

Solution 2

Interior angle + exterior angle = 180°
Interior angle + 36° = 180°
So interior angle = 144°

Exercise B

1 The exterior angle of a regular polygon is 60°.
Find the size of the interior angle of this polygon.

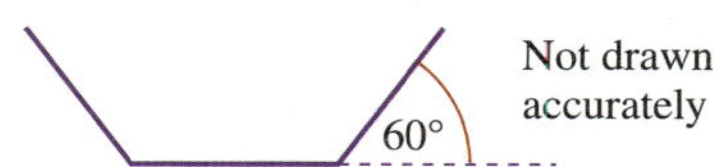

2 Here are the exterior angles of some polygons.
Work out the interior angles.
a 50° **b** 30° **c** 45° **d** 80° **e** 75° **f** 110°

3 The interior angle of a regular polygon is 160°.
Work out the size of the exterior angle.

4 Here are the interior angles of some polygons.
Work out the exterior angles.
a 65° **b** 120° **c** 55° **d** 95° **e** 140° **f** 25°

5 One vertex of a pentagon has interior angle 100°.
What is the exterior angle at this vertex?

6 Here are the exterior angles of some polygons.
Work out the interior angles.
a 40° **b** 72° **c** 36° **d** 120°

7 Here are the interior angles of some polygons.
Work out the exterior angles.
a 108° **b** 135° **c** 168° **d** 150°

8 Each interior angle of a regular pentagon is 108°.
Calculate the total sum of all the interior angles of a regular pentagon.

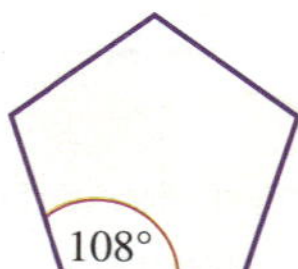

9 Each exterior angle of a regular hexagon is 60°.
a How many exterior angles does a hexagon have?
b Calculate the total sum of the exterior angles of a hexagon.

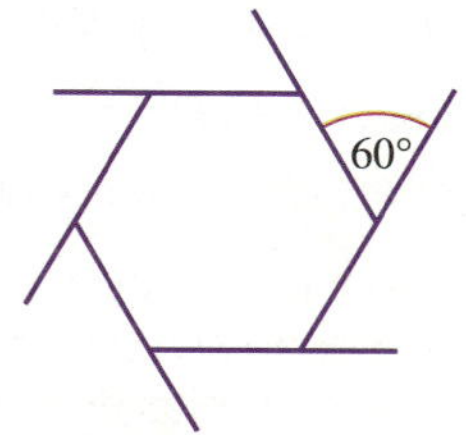

10 Each exterior angle of an octagon is 45°.
Calculate the sum of the exterior angles of an octagon.

5.4 Angles in polygons

CAN YOU REMEMBER

- That angles in a triangle total 180° and angles in a quadrilateral total 360°?
- That in any polygon the interior angle + the exterior angle = 180°?
- That a regular polygon has all sides equal and all angles equal?

IN THIS SECTION YOU WILL

- Learn how to calculate the sum of the interior angles of any polygon.
- Use a formula to calculate the exterior angle of a regular polygon.
- Use angle properties to work out the number of sides of a given polygon.

The sum of the angles of a quadrilateral is 360° because the quadrilateral can be divided into two triangles.

$2 \times 180° = 360°$

All polygons can be divided into triangles by drawing the diagonals from one vertex.

A pentagon divides into three triangles.

So the sum of the interior angles in a pentagon is $3 \times 180° = 540°$

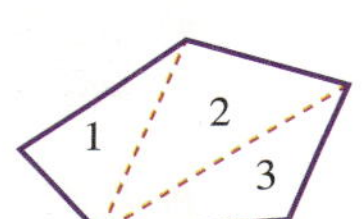

The five exterior angles on this pentagon fit together round a point.

$a + b + c + d + e = 360°$

The same is true for any polygon.

For any polygon:

- the sum of the exterior angles of the polygon is equal to 360°
- the number of exterior angles = the number of sides.

In a regular polygon all exterior angles are equal.
Each exterior angle can be found using the formula:

$$\text{Exterior angle} = \frac{360°}{\text{Number of sides}}$$

The number of sides of a regular polygon can be found using the formula:

$$\text{Number of sides} = \frac{360°}{\text{Exterior angle}}$$

Example 1

By drawing the diagonals from one vertex, work out the sum of the interior angles in a hexagon.

Solution 1

A hexagon divides into four triangles.
So the sum of the interior angles in a hexagon is $4 \times 180° = 720°$

Example 2

A regular polygon has an exterior angle of 36°.
How many sides has the polygon?

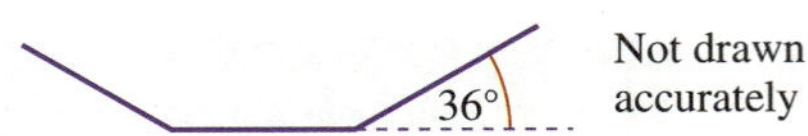

Solution 2

$$\text{Number of sides} = \frac{360°}{\text{Exterior angle}} = \frac{360°}{36°} = 10$$

The polygon has ten sides.

Exercise A

1 Draw an octagon. By drawing the diagonals from one vertex, work out the sum of the interior angles of an octagon.

2 Copy these diagrams. By drawing the diagonals from one vertex, work out the sum of the angles of each polygon.

a

b

3 A regular polygon has 12 sides.
Calculate the size of each exterior angle of the polygon.

4 A regular polygon has nine sides. Find the size of:
a each exterior angle **b** each interior angle.

5 Each exterior angle of a regular polygon is 60°.
How many sides has this polygon?

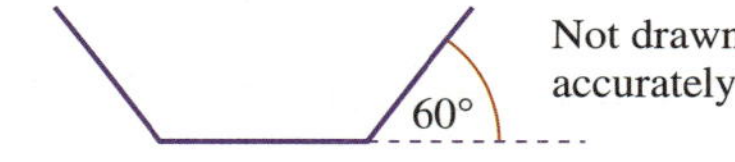

6 A regular polygon has 18 sides.
Calculate the size of the exterior angle.

7 Each interior angle of a regular polygon is 162°.
How many sides has this polygon?

8 A regular polygon has an interior angle of 135°.
a Calculate the size of each exterior angle.
b How many sides has this polygon?
c Write down the name of this polygon.

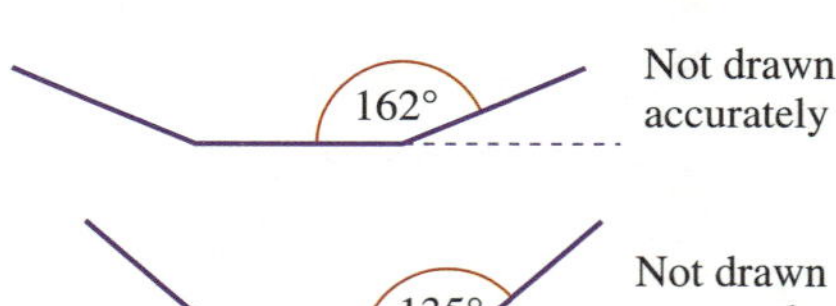

9 A regular polygon has 15 sides.
What is the size of each exterior angle?

10 Calculate the value of each missing exterior angle in these polygons.

a

95°
x
35°
65°
85°
50°

b

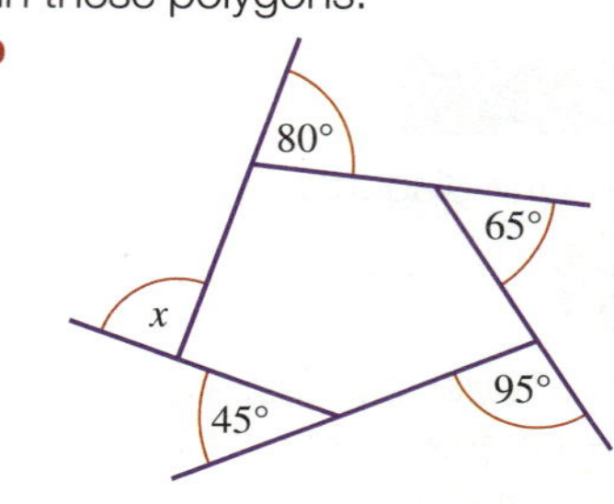

The table shows the sum of the interior angles of some polygons.

Each time the number of sides increases by 1 the sum of the angles increases by 180°.

With **3** sides the sum is **1** × 180°

With **4** sides the sum is **2** × 180°

With ***n*** sides the sum is **(*n* − 2)** × 180°

Sum of the interior angles of a polygon $= (n - 2) \times 180°$, where n is the number of sides.

Polygon	Number of sides	Sum of interior angles
Triangle	3	180°
Quadrilateral	4	360°
Pentagon	5	540°
Hexagon	6	720°

Example 3

The diagram shows a hexagon. Calculate the size of angle x.

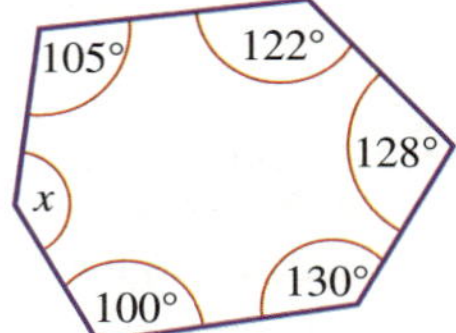

Solution 3

Sum of the interior angles of a hexagon

$= (n - 2) \times 180° = (6 - 2) \times 180° = 4 \times 180° = 720°$

So $105° + 122° + 128° + 130° + 100° + x = 720°$

$585° + x = 720°$

$x = 135°$

Exercise B

1 Calculate the sum of the interior angles of a decagon.

2 A polygon has 22 sides.
Calculate the sum of the interior angles.

3 Work out the size of the missing angle in each of these polygons.

a

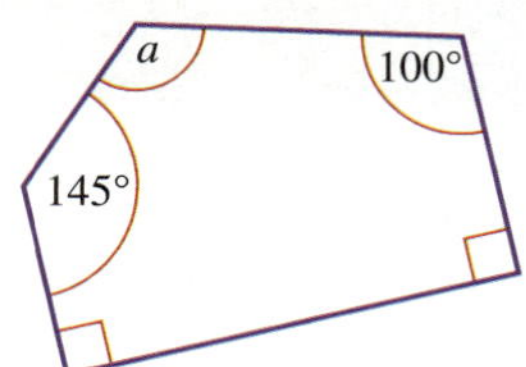

b

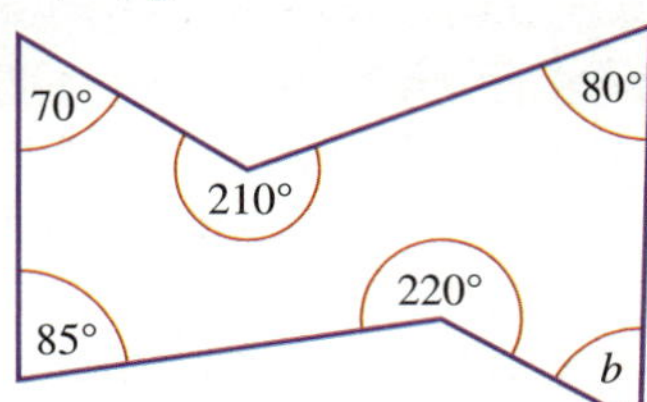

4 The sum of the interior angles of a polygon is 1800°.
How many sides has the polygon?

5 The diagram shows an octagon.
Calculate the size of the angle marked c.

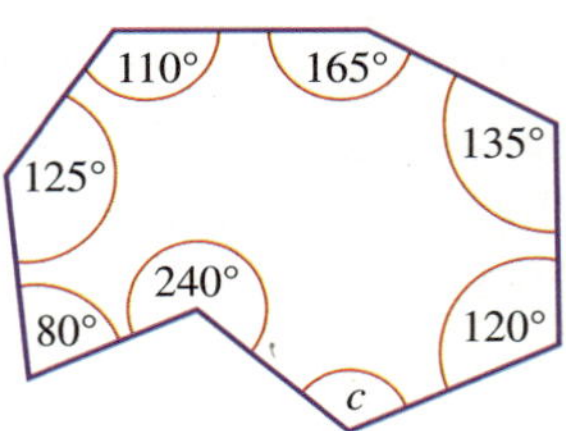

6 Calculate the size of the angle marked with a letter in each of these polygons.

a

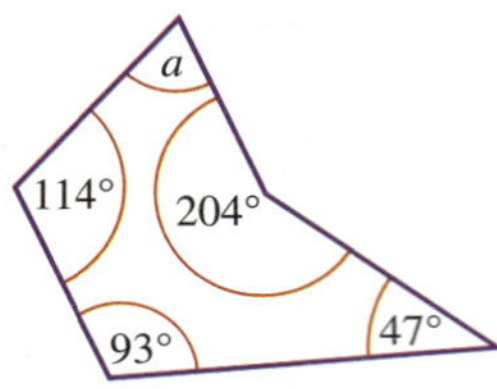

b

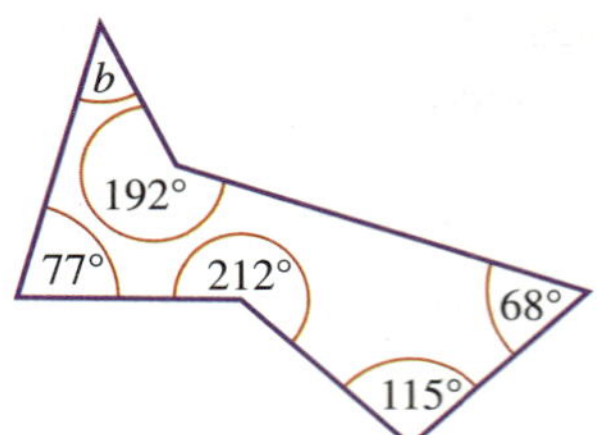

c

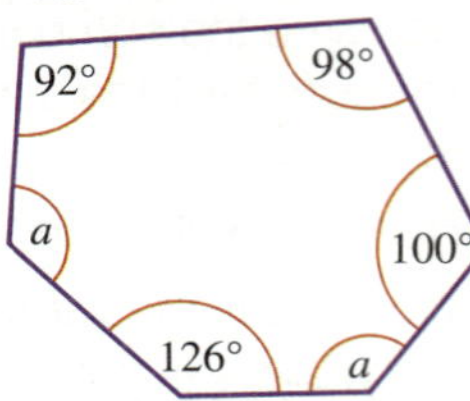

d

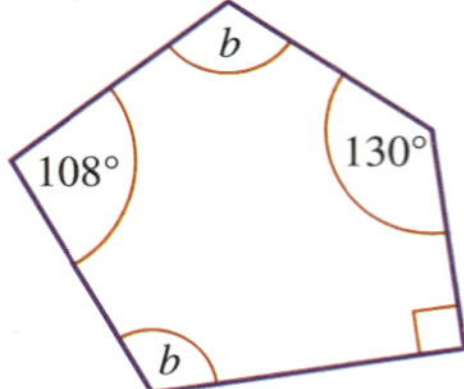

e

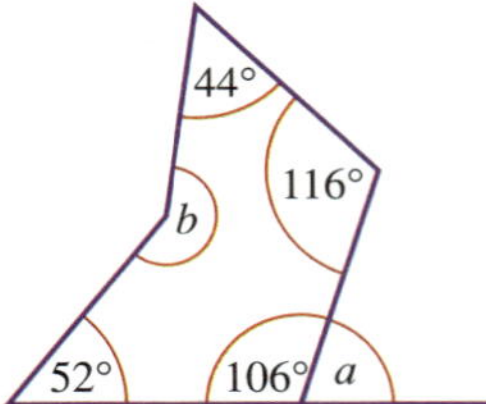

f

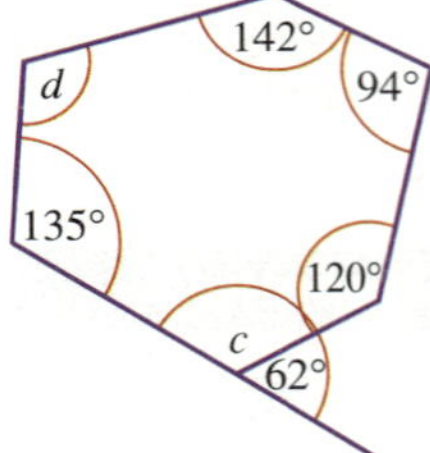

7 A regular hexagon and a regular pentagon are joined together as shown.
Calculate the size of angle x.

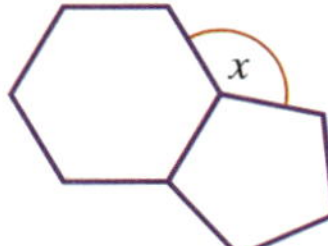

8 This diagram shows three regular polygons.
Calculate the size of angle x.

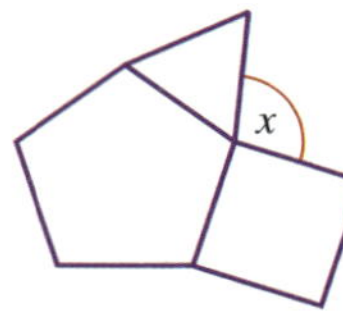

5.5 Pythagoras' theorem

CAN YOU REMEMBER

- That a right-angled triangle has one angle of 90°?
- The square numbers up to $15^2 = 225$?
- How to find squares and square roots using a calculator?

IN THIS SECTION YOU WILL

- Use Pythagoras' theorem to calculate the lengths of sides of right-angled triangles.
- Use Pythagoras' theorem to work out whether a triangle is right-angled.

In a right-angled triangle the longest side of the triangle is opposite to the right angle. This side is called the *hypotenuse*.

The diagram shows a right-angled triangle with sides of length 3 cm, 4 cm and 5 cm. Squares have been constructed on each side of the triangle.

The areas of these squares are 9, 16 and 25 cm^2.

The area of the large square is equal to the sum of the areas of the other two squares.
$9 + 16 = 25$ so $3^2 + 4^2 = 5^2$

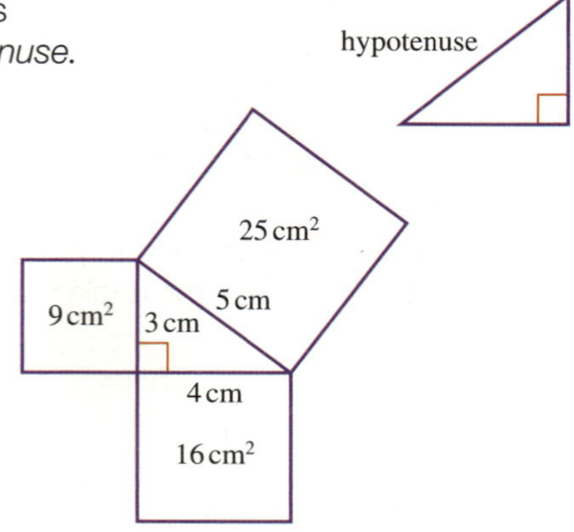

Pythagoras, an ancient Greek mathematician, found that this was true for all right-angled triangles.
Pythagoras' theorem: In any right-angled triangle the square of the hypotenuse is always equal to the sum of the squares of the two shorter sides.

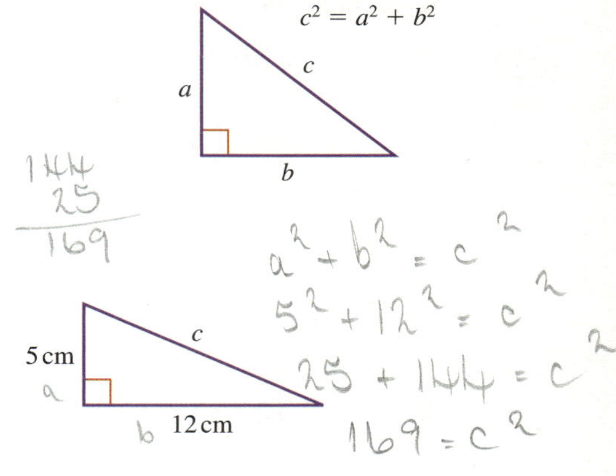

Example 1

Calculate the missing length on this triangle.

Solution 1

The triangle is right-angled so use Pythagoras' theorem:

$c^2 = a^2 + b^2 = 5^2 + 12^2 = 25 + 144$

$c^2 = 169$ Take the square root of each side.

$c = \sqrt{169} = 13$ cm

Example 2

Calculate the length of side c.
Give your answer

a as a square root
b to one decimal place.

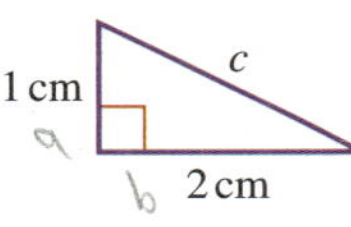

Solution 2

The triangle is right-angled so use Pythagoras' theorem:

$c^2 = a^2 + b^2 = 1^2 + 2^2 = 1 + 4$

$c^2 = 5$ Take the square root of each side.

a $c = \sqrt{5}$ **b** $c = 2.23606... = 2.2$ (to 1 d.p.)

Example 3

Calculate the length of side b.
Give your answer to one decimal place.

14 cm, 8 cm, b

Solution 3

As the triangle is right-angled use Pythagoras' theorem.
The longest side is 14cm.
So using $c^2 = a^2 + b^2$

$14^2 = 8^2 + b^2$

$196 = 64 + b^2$ Subtract 64 from both sides.

$196 - 64 = b^2$

$132 = b^2$ Take the square root of each side.

$\sqrt{132} = b$

$b = 11.5$ cm (to 1 d.p.)

Exercise A

1 Find the length of the hypotenuse in each of these triangles.

a

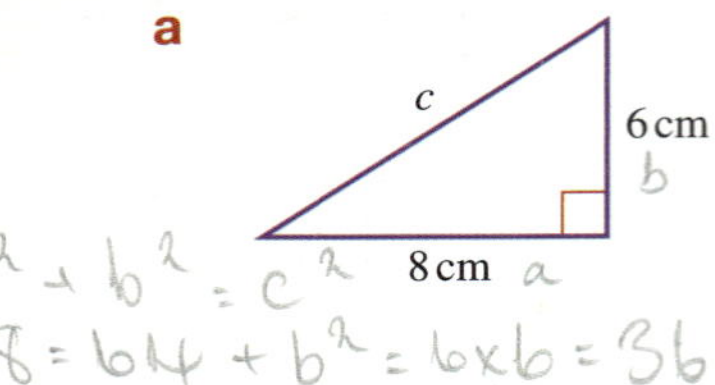

b

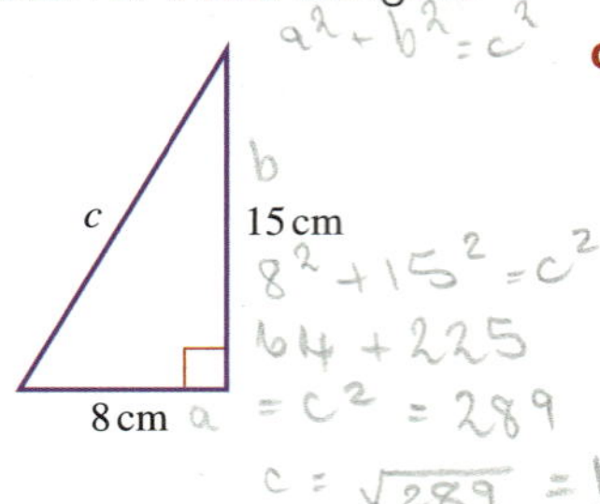

c

2 Find the length of the hypotenuse, marked c, in each of these triangles.
Leave each answer as a square root.

a

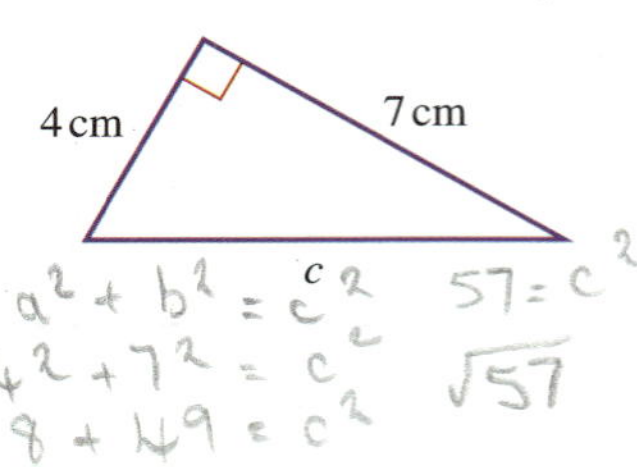

b

c

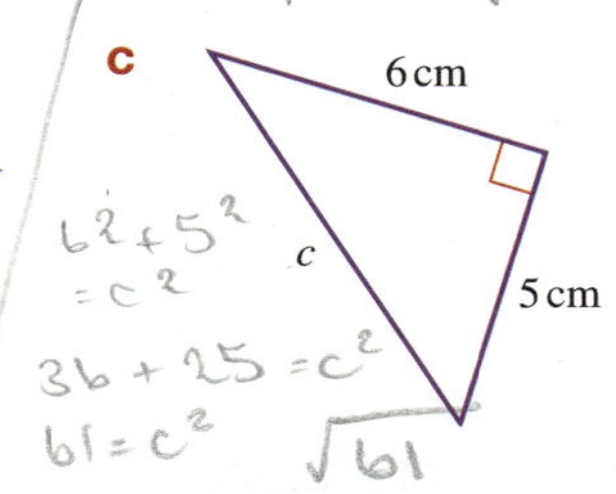

3 Calculate the length of the missing side, marked x, in each of these triangles.

a

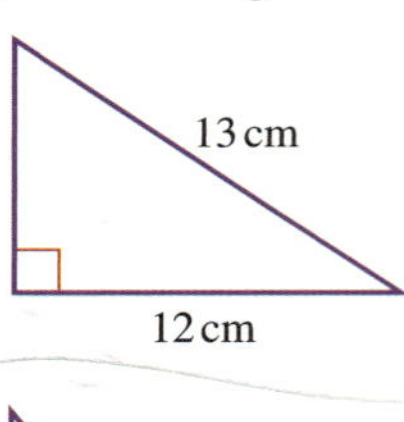

b

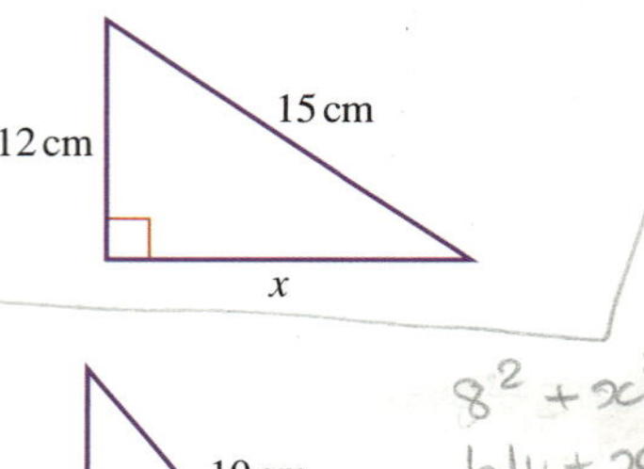

c

d

4 Calculate the length of the missing side, marked x, in each of these triangles.
Leave each answer as a square root.

a

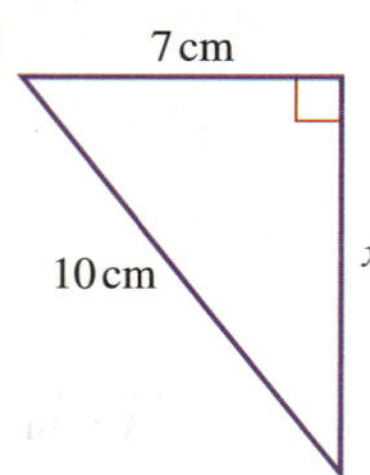

b

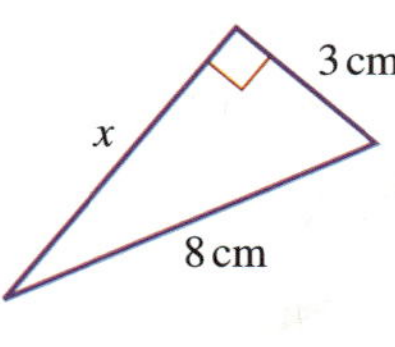

c

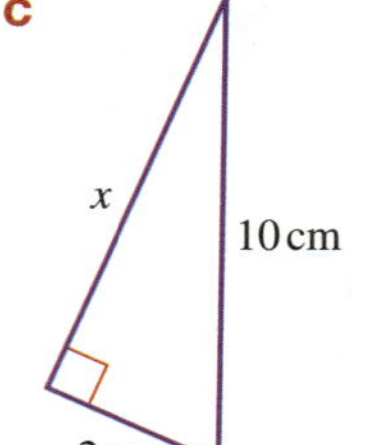

d

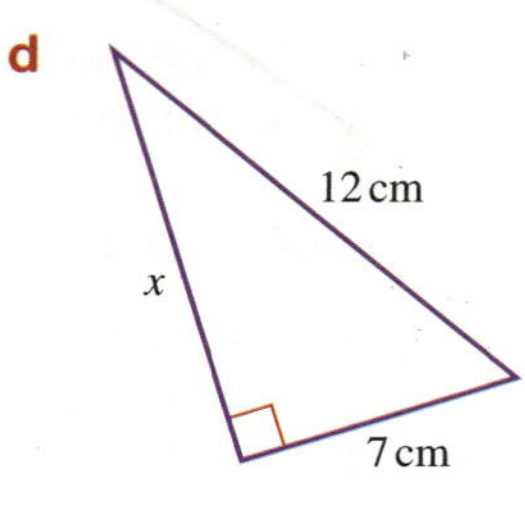

5 A rectangle has a length of 9 cm and a width of 5 cm.
Calculate the length of the diagonal.
Leave your answer as a square root.

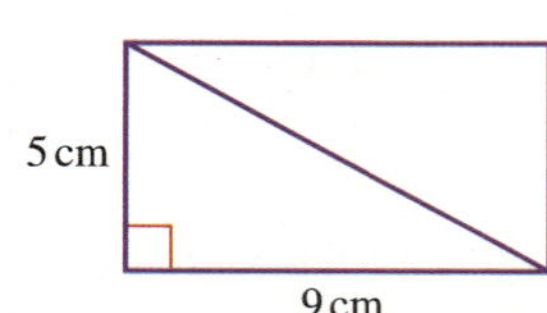

6 Calculate the length of the diagonal of each of these rectangles.
Give your answers to one decimal place.

a
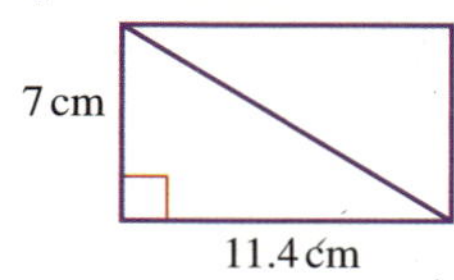

b
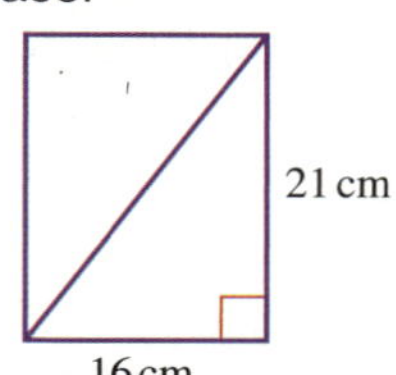

c
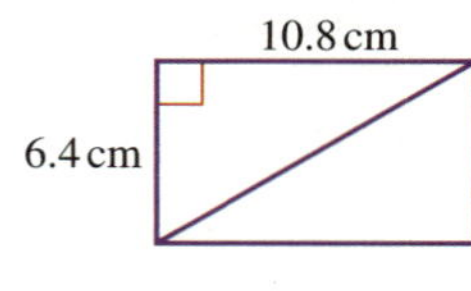

7 Calculate the length of the hypotenuse in each of these right-angled triangles.
Give your answers to one decimal place.

a
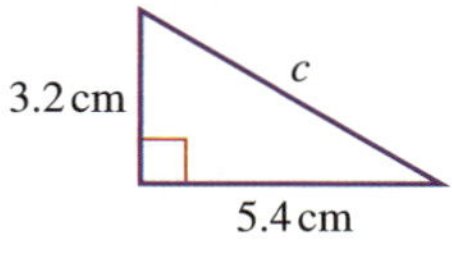

b
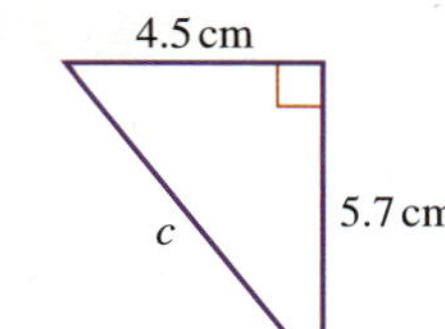

c
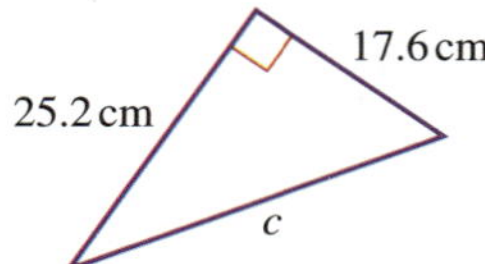

d
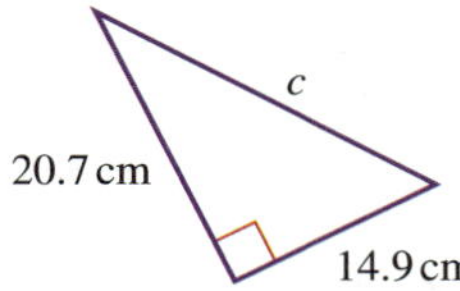

8 Calculate the length of side b in each of these triangles.
Give your answers to two decimal places.

a
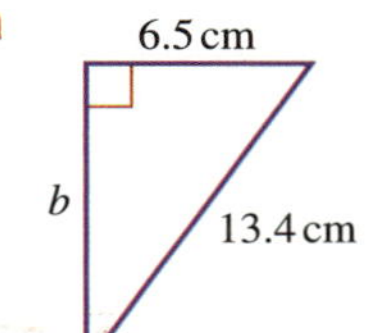

b
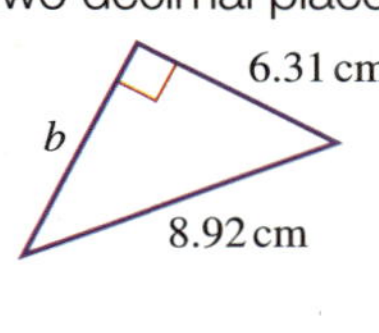

c
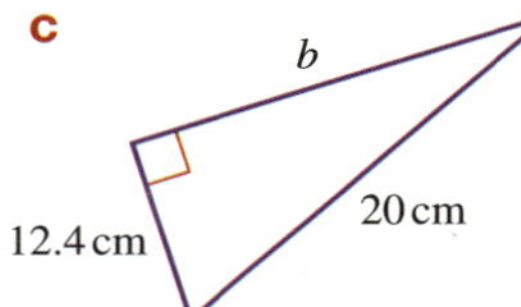

d
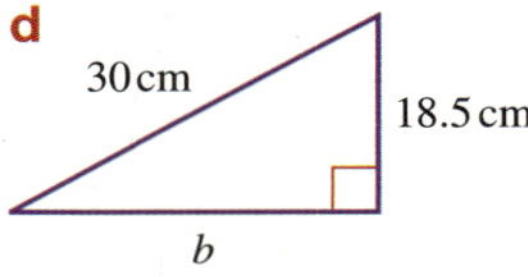

9 Calculate the width of each of these rectangles.
Give your answers to two decimal places.

a
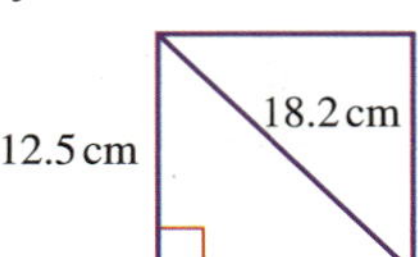

b
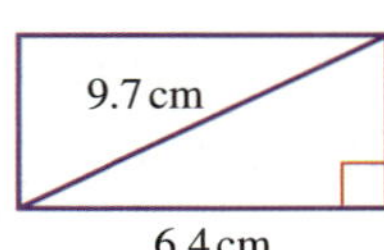

c
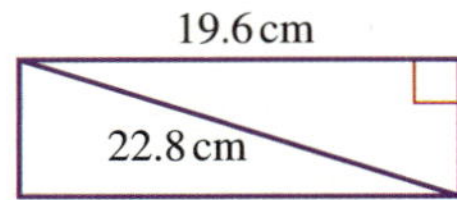

10 Calculate the length of the missing side in each of these triangles.

a
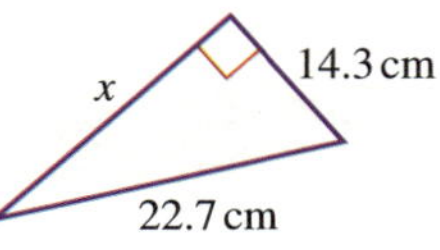

b
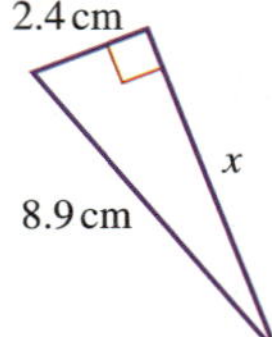

c
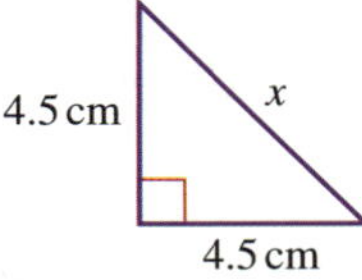

d
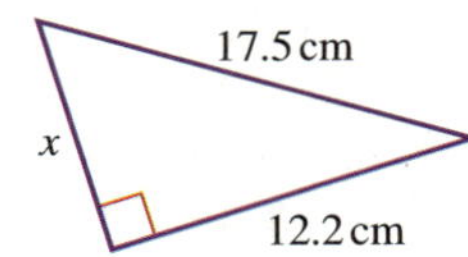

e
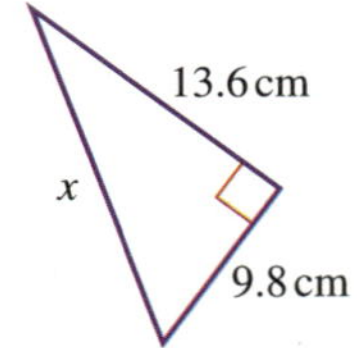

Example 4

An equilateral triangle has sides 8 cm long. What is its vertical height?

Solution 4

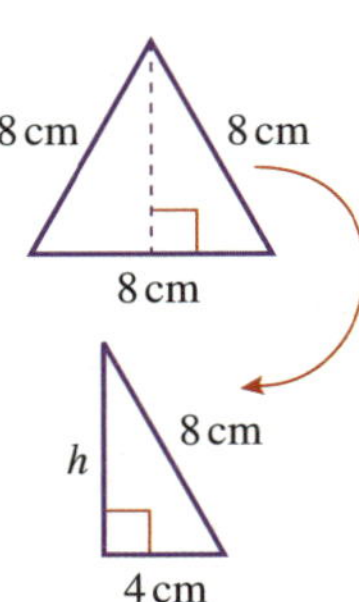

The vertical height divides the equilateral triangle into two right-angled triangles of equal size. Pythagoras' theorem can be used with one of these right-angled triangles to find the vertical height (h).

$h^2 + 4^2 = 8^2$

$h^2 + 16 = 64$ — Subtract 16 from both sides.

$h^2 = 64 - 16 = 48$

$h = \sqrt{48} = 6.9$ cm (1 d.p.)

Exercise B

1 Calculate the vertical height, h, of this equilateral triangle.

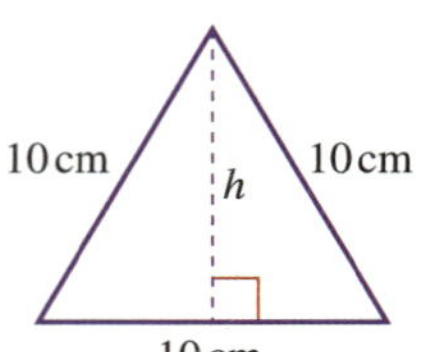

2 Copy the tables.
Use the patterns in the tables to complete them.
Check your answers using Pythagoras' theorem.

a

Side a	Side b	Hypotenuse c
3	4	5
6	8	10
9	12	15
12		

b

Side a	Side b	Hypotenuse c
5	12	13
0.5	1.2	
50		130
	1200	1300

3 A man walks 6.7 km due south and then turns to walk 3.8 km due west.
How much shorter would the distance be if he walked straight from his starting point to his finishing point?

4 Check whether each of these triangles is right-angled. Show your working.

a Side lengths 2 cm, 3 cm and 4 cm.
b Side lengths 12 cm, 16 cm and 20 cm.
c Side lengths 6 cm, 9 cm and 12 cm.
d Side lengths 9 cm, 40 cm and 41 cm.
e Side lengths 7 cm, 24 cm and 25 cm.

Hint: check that they satisfy $a^2 + b^2 = c^2$

5 An isosceles triangle has two sides 9.2 cm long and a third side which is 7.4 cm long.
Calculate the height of the triangle.

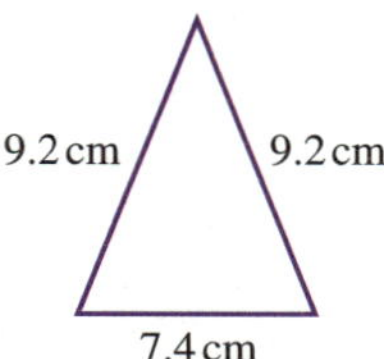

6 A ladder 8.4 m long rests against a wall. The foot of the ladder is 1.7 m away from the wall.
How high up the wall does the ladder reach?

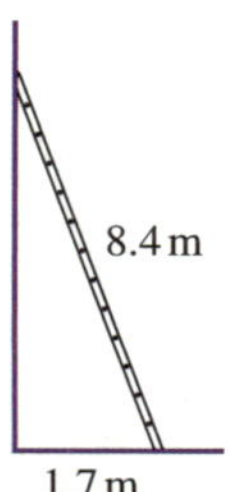

7 A flagpole 9.8 m high is held firm by a wire fixed to its top and to a point on the ground 6.4 m from the foot of the pole.
How long is the wire?

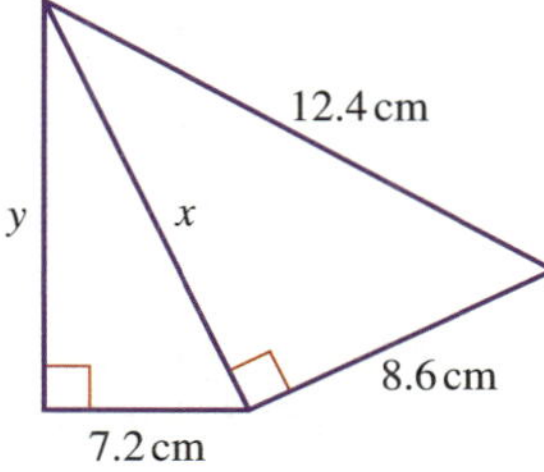

8 Find the length of AB.

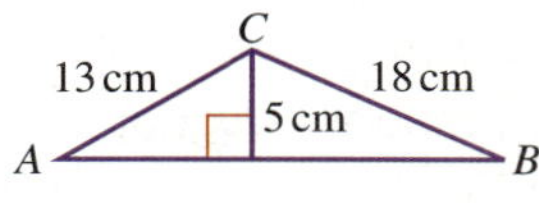

9 Calculate the lengths of x and y in these diagrams.

a

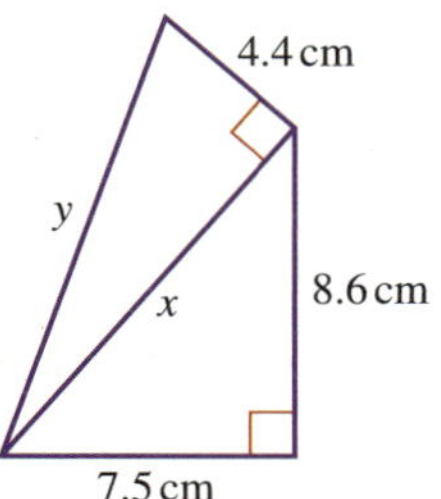

b

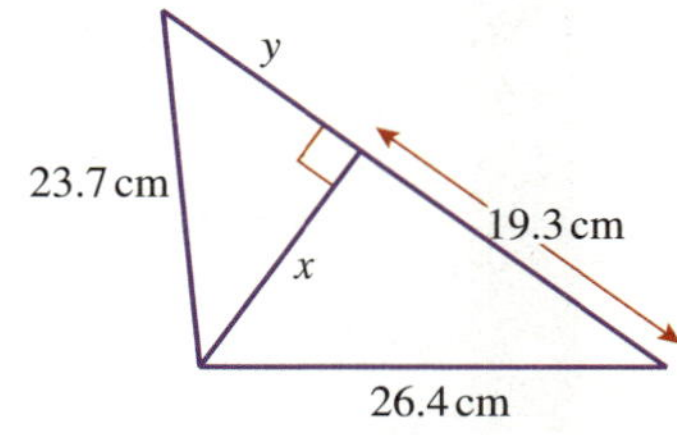

c

Chapter summary

- When two parallel lines are cut by a third line:

Alternate angles are equal.

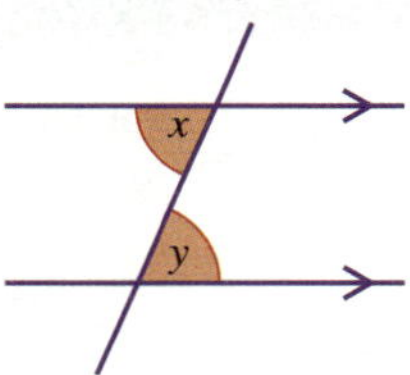

$x = y$

Corresponding angles are equal.

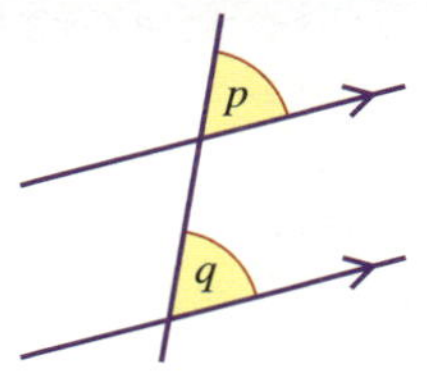

$p = q$

Allied angles add up to 180°.

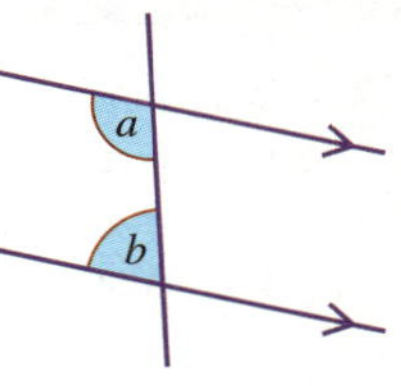

$a + b = 180°$

- The angles in any quadrilateral add up to 360°.
120° + 50° + 130° + 60° = 360°

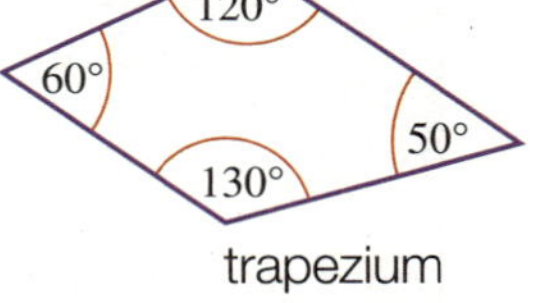

- Quadrilaterals with parallel sides have pairs of allied angles.

rectangle

parallelogram

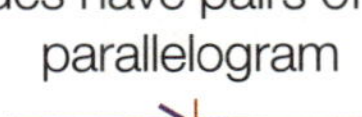
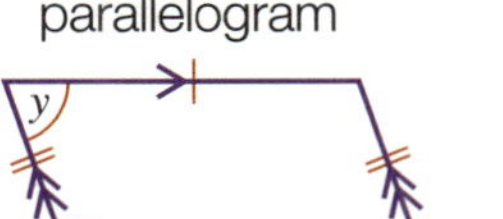

rhombus

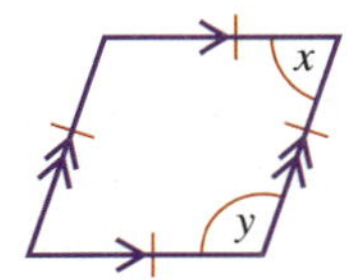

trapezium

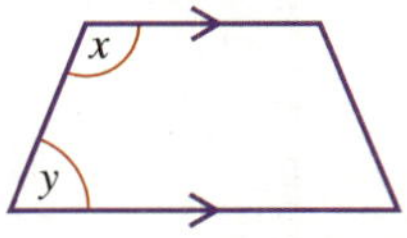

In each diagram $x + y = 180°$.

- A polygon is a two-dimensional shape made by straight lines.

pentagon – five sides | hexagon – six sides | heptagon – seven sides
octagon – eight sides | nonagon – nine sides | decagon – ten sides

- A regular polygon has all sides equal and all angles equal.
- Number of lines of symmetry of a regular polygon = number of sides
- Order of rotational symmetry of a regular polygon = number of sides

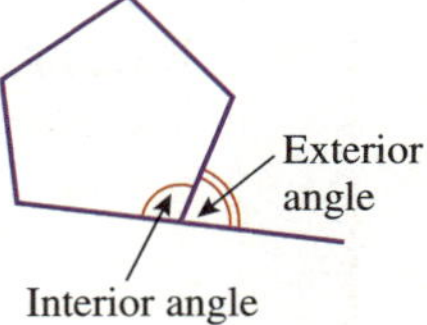

- At each vertex of any polygon the sum of the exterior and interior angles is 180°.
- In any regular polygon:
  - interior angles are all equal
  - exterior angles are all equal.

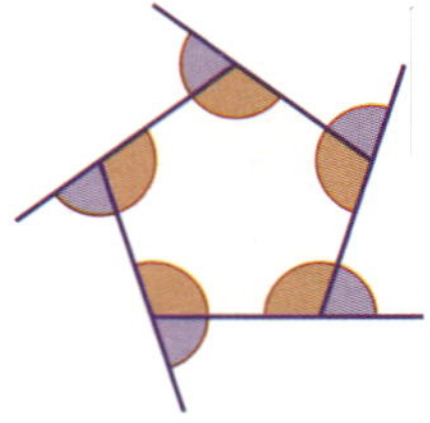

- The sum of the exterior angles of any polygon is equal to 360°.
- An exterior angle of a regular polygon can be found using the formula:

$$\text{Exterior angle} = \frac{360°}{\text{Number of sides}} \qquad \text{Number of sides} = \frac{360°}{\text{Exterior angle}}$$

- Sum of the interior angles of a polygon $= (n - 2) \times 180°$, where n is the number of sides.
- Pythagoras' theorem: In any right-angled triangle the square of the hypotenuse is always equal to the sum of the squares of the two shorter sides.

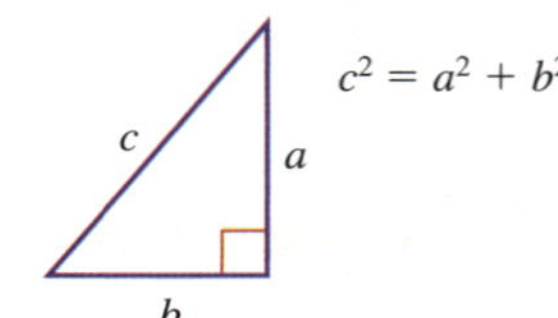

Chapter review

1 The diagram shows a kite.

a Write down the value of p.
Give a reason for your answer.

b Work out the value of q.

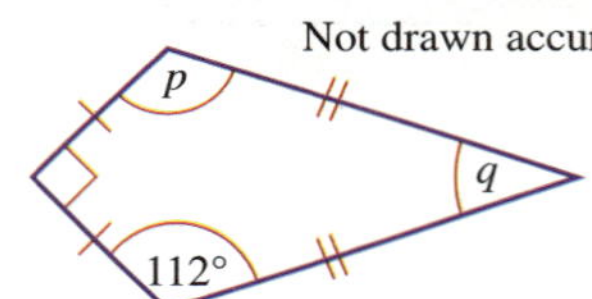

2 Two sides of a regular pentagon have been drawn in the circle.
Trace the circle and lines.
Complete the regular pentagon.

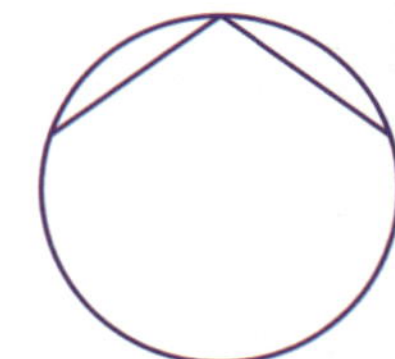

3 **a** ABC is a right-angled triangle.
Angle $B = 63°$.
Work out the size of angle A.

b The diagram shows a regular decagon.
Calculate the size of the exterior angle, marked x on the diagram.

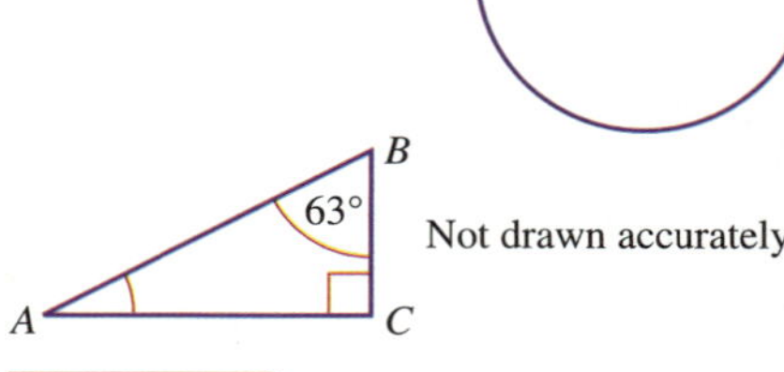

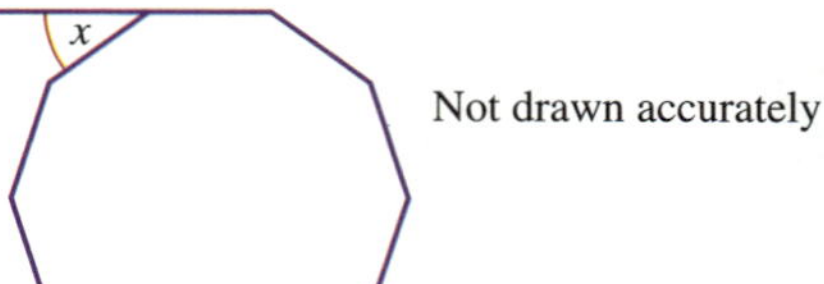

4 The diagram shows a trapezium.
Calculate the values of x and y.

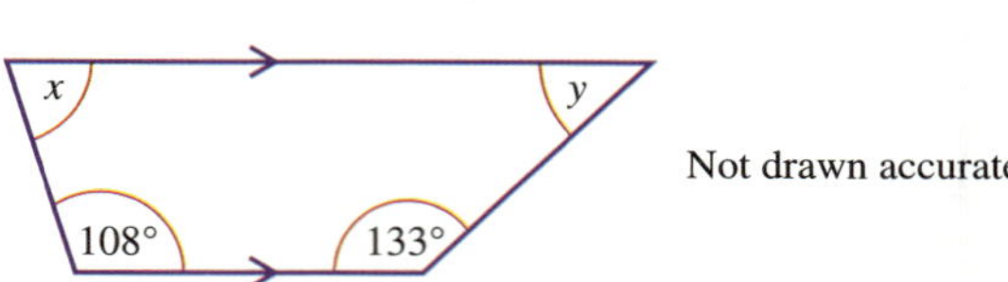

5 **a** The diagram shows a regular hexagon.

i How many axes of symmetry does a regular hexagon have?

ii Calculate the size of the exterior angle x.

b Work out the value of y in the triangle below.

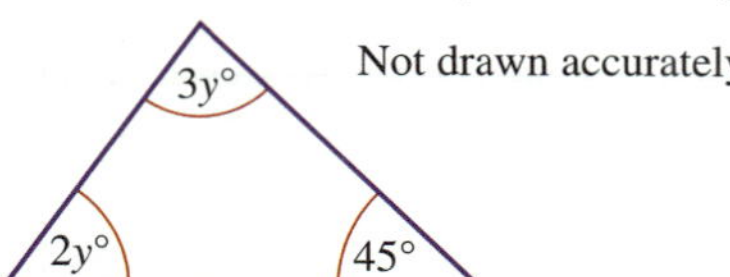

6 The diagram shows a field.
The length of the field, $AB = 130$ m.
The width of the field, $AD = 85$ m.
Calculate the length of the diagonal BD.
Give your answer to one decimal place.

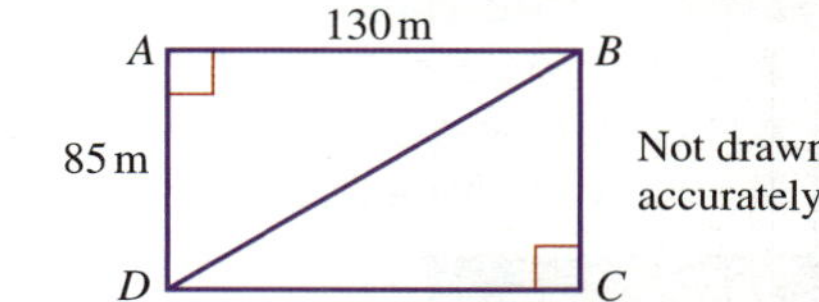

7 The triangle ABC has angles $3x°$, $4x°$ and $5x°$.
Form an equation and solve it to find the value of x.

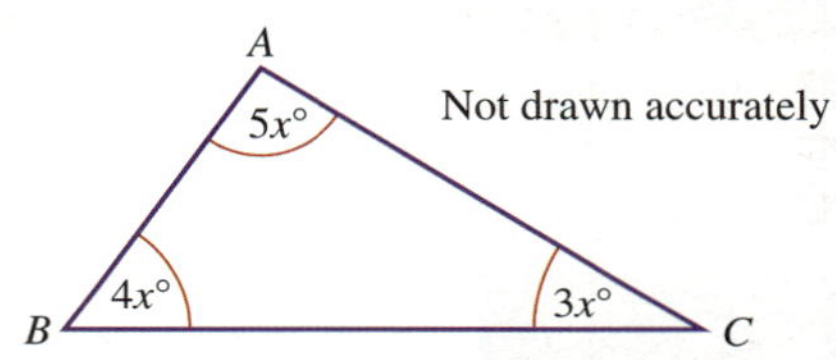

8 Each exterior angle of a regular polygon is 18°.

a How many sides does the polygon have?

b Calculate the sum of the interior angles of the polygon.

9 ABC is a right-angled triangle.
$AC = 29$ cm and $AB = 19$ cm.
Calculate the length of BC.

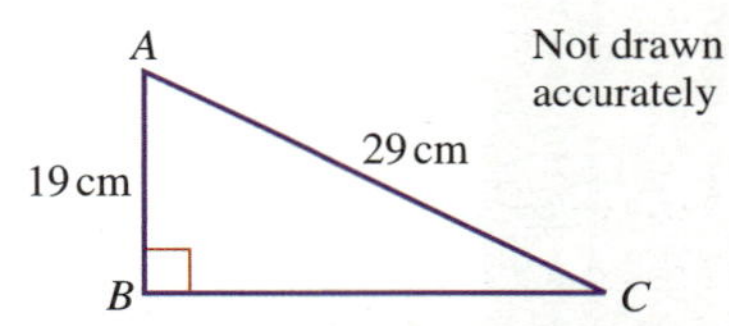

CHAPTER

6

Ratio and proportion

6.1 Ratio

CAN YOU REMEMBER

- How to cancel a fraction to its simplest form?
- How to find common factors of two numbers?
- How to divide by an integer?

IN THIS SECTION YOU WILL

- Use ratio notation.
- Write ratios in their simplest form.
- Divide quantities in a given ratio.

A *ratio* compares two or more quantities.

The ratio of red beads to blue beads on this necklace is 3 : 1

For every 3 red beads on the necklace there is 1 blue bead.

The numbers in a ratio can be multiplied or divided by the same number to get an *equivalent ratio.*

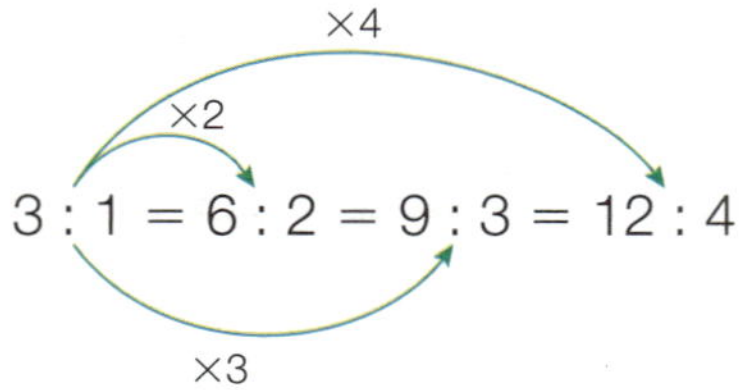

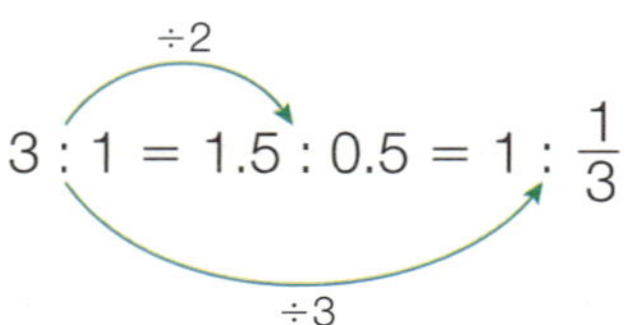

The *simplest form* of a ratio has whole numbers with no common factors apart from 1 – for example 3 : 1 and 5 : 2
The ratio 6 : 4 is not in simplest form because 6 and 4 have a common factor of 2

$1 : \frac{1}{3}$ is not in simplest form because $\frac{1}{3}$ is not a whole number.

To write a ratio in its simplest form:

- if the ratio includes fractions or decimals, multiply to make both parts whole numbers
- divide both parts by their common factors.

Example 1

Write each ratio in its simplest form.

a 9 : 6 **b** 12 : 15 : 18 **c** 1.6 : 2.4 **d** $\frac{1}{2} : 7$

Solution 1

a 9 : 6 = 3 : 2 (dividing both parts by 3)
b 12 : 15 : 18 = 12 ÷ 3 : 15 ÷ 3 : 18 ÷ 3 = 4 : 5 : 6
c Write the ratio 1.6 : 2.4 using whole numbers, by multiplying each value by 10
1.6 : 2.4 = 1.6 × 10 : 2.4 × 10 = 16 : 24
Divide by the common factor 8
16 : 24 = 16 ÷ 8 : 24 ÷ 8 = 2 : 3
d Write the ratio $\frac{1}{2}$: 7 using whole numbers, by multiplying each value by 2
$\frac{1}{2}$: 7 = $\frac{1}{2}$ × 2 : 7 × 2 = 1 : 14

Example 2

The ratio of green counters to yellow counters in a bag is 3 : 5
There are 45 green counters.
How many yellow counters are there?

Solution 2

For every three green counters there are five yellow counters.
45 ÷ 3 = 15
45 green counters = 15 lots of three green counters
15 lots of five yellow counters = 15 × 5 = 75 yellow counters

Exercise A

1 Copy and complete the following equivalent ratios.

a 1 : 4 = 2 : ... **b** 3 : 1 = ... : 2
c 1 : 5 = 3 : ... **d** 4 : 1 = 16 : ...
e 2 : 3 = ... : 9 **f** 6 : 1 = 18 : ...
g 3 : 2 = ... : 8 **h** 5 : 3 = ... : 9

2 Each set of cards shows four equivalent ratios and a different ratio.
Which is the odd one out?

a

b

c

d

3 **a** Which of these ratios are equivalent to 3 : 2?

b Which of these ratios are equivalent to 5 : 3?

4 Here are some necklaces with blue and white beads.

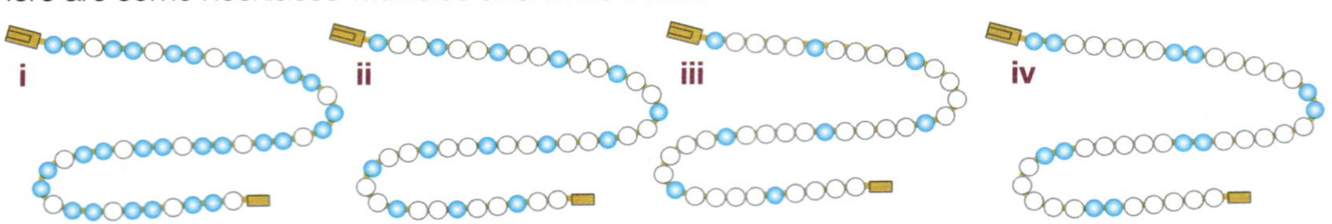

a Match the necklaces to the ratios of blue to white beads.

b One necklace is missing. Draw the necklace.

2:5 3:2 2:1 1:4 1:2

5 Write each ratio in its simplest form.

a	3 : 6	**b**	8 : 4	**c**	9 : 3	**d**	2 : 6
e	15 : 10	**f**	21 : 7	**g**	4 : 24	**h**	20 : 25
i	24 : 32	**j**	25 : 40	**k**	36 : 48	**l**	60 : 45

6 Write each ratio in its simplest form.

a	1.2 : 2.4	**b**	0.5 : 1.5	**c**	3.2 : 1.6	**d**	1.5 : 4.5
e	1.6 : 0.8	**f**	2.1 : 1.4	**g**	2.5 : 5	**h**	7.5 : 2.5
i	0.4 : 1.6	**j**	3.5 : 0.5	**k**	4.8 : 3.6	**l**	1.2 : 6
m	2.7 : 1.8	**n**	3.2 : 3.6	**o**	3.6 : 7.2	**p**	4.2 : 2.8

7 Write each ratio in its simplest form.

a	$1\frac{1}{2} : 3$	**b**	$\frac{1}{2} : 4$	**c**	$5 : \frac{1}{3}$	**d**	$2\frac{1}{2} : 5$
e	$1\frac{1}{4} : 2\frac{1}{2}$	**f**	$5 : 1\frac{1}{4}$	**g**	$\frac{1}{5} : 1$	**h**	$2 : \frac{1}{3}$
i	$\frac{2}{3} : 1$	**j**	$4 : \frac{3}{4}$	**k**	$1\frac{1}{4} : 2\frac{3}{4}$	**l**	$1\frac{1}{3} : 2\frac{1}{4}$

8 A waiter pours out two glasses of juice in the ratio 2 : 3
The larger glass contains 180 ml of juice.
How much does the smaller glass contain?

9 The numbers of apples and pears on a fruit stall are in the ratio 3 : 2
There are 360 apples. How many pears are there?

10 Write each ratio in its simplest form.

a	15 : 12 : 9	**b**	24 : 36 : 48	**c**	20 : 40 : 30	**d**	9 : 3 : 12
e	12 : 8 : 16	**f**	20 : 36 : 24	**g**	18 : 32 : 40	**h**	10 : 90 : 28
i	14 : 21 : 35	**j**	36 : 48 : 24	**k**	72 : 36 : 18	**l**	100 : 20 : 25
m	84 : 72 : 60	**n**	40 : 50 : 70	**o**	27 : 81 : 9	**p**	48 : 36 : 72

11 The area of a garden is made up of lawns and plants in the ratio 2 : 3
The area of plants is 85 hectares. What is the area of the lawns?

12 The ratio of soft sweets to hard sweets in a bag is 3 : 1
There are 16 hard sweets. How many soft sweets?

13 Mr and Mrs Khan share the driving in the ratio 4 : 5
Mr Khan drives 60 miles. How many miles does Mrs Khan drive?

Example 3

Divide £24 in the ratio 1 : 3

Solution 3

The money is divided into lots of £1 and £3
£1 + £3 = £4
£24 ÷ £4 = 6. There are six lots of £4 in £24
6 lots of £1 = £6; 6 lots of £3 = £18
£24 divided in the ratio 1 : 3 = £6 : £18

Check: £6 + £18 = £24

Example 4

Matt and Viki share £72 in the ratio 2 : 7 with Viki having the larger share.
How much more is Viki's share than Matt's share?

Solution 4

For every £2 that Matt gets, Viki gets £7. £2 + £7 = £9
£72 ÷ £9 = 8. There are eight lots of £9 in £72

Method 1
8 lots of £2 = £16
8 lots of £7 = £56
£72 divided in the ratio 2 : 7 = £16 : £56
Matt gets £16 and Viki gets £56
So Viki's share = £40 more than Matt's share.

Method 2
For each £2 that Matt gets, Viki gets £5 more.
8 lots of £5 = £40
So Viki's share = £40 more than Matt's share.

Exercise B

1 **a** Divide £21 in the ratio 6 : 1
b Divide 25 metres in the ratio 1 : 4
c Divide $40 in the ratio 7 : 1
d Divide €18 in the ratio 1 : 5
e Divide £36 in the ratio 5 : 4
f Divide 20 litres in the ratio 3 : 5
g Divide 48 sweets in the ratio 5 : 3
h Divide £28 in the ratio 4 : 3
i Divide £28 in the ratio 3 : 2 : 2
j Divide 75 litres in the ratio 2 : 3 : 5
k Divide $100 in the ratio 5 : 2 : 3
l Divide €48 in the ratio 2 : 3 : 3

2 In each part find the smaller share when:
a £80 is divided in the ratio 3 : 2
b 70 cm is divided in the ratio 2 : 5
c $30 is divided in the ratio 2 : 3
d €27 is divided in the ratio 4 : 5

3 In each part find the larger share when:
a 36 g is divided in the ratio 4 : 5
b 42 sweets are divided in the ratio 3 : 4
c £110 is divided in the ratio 7 : 4
d 130 cm is divided in the ratio 5 : 8

4 **a** Divide $100 in the ratio 5 : 2 : 3
b Divide 70 sweets in the ratio 2 : 2 : 3
c Divide £120 in the ratio 4 : 3 : 5
d Divide 40 cm in the ratio 2 : 3 : 3

5 Jack and Jill share 24 litres of water in the ratio 5 : 3
How much more water does Jack have than Jill?

6 **a** Divide £96 in the ratio 1 : 7
b Divide 144 metres in the ratio 1 : 15
c Divide $108 in the ratio 8 : 1
d Divide €180 in the ratio 1 : 8
e Divide £550 in the ratio 4 : 1
f Divide 2424 cm in the ratio 1 : 11

7 In each part find the smaller share when:

- **a** £120 is divided in the ratio 4 : 1
- **b** 480 m is divided in the ratio 1 : 15
- **c** $750 is divided in the ratio 9 : 1
- **d** €1200 is divided in the ratio 1 : 7
- **e** 3600 g is divided in the ratio 5 : 3 : 1
- **f** £840 is divided in the ratio 3 : 3 : 1

8 In each part find the larger share when:

- **a** 300 m is divided in the ratio 1 : 14
- **b** $500 is divided in the ratio 9 : 1
- **c** €1024 is divided in the ratio 1 : 7
- **d** 189 g is divided in the ratio 3 : 5 : 1
- **e** £560 is divided in the ratio 5 : 1 : 1
- **f** 400 cm is divided in the ratio 1 : 1 : 2

9 Juice is made by mixing orange and water in the ratio 2 : 5

- **a** If 280 litres of juice are mixed, how much orange is required?
- **b** Bill says that to mix 105 litres of juice he uses 30 litres of water. Is he correct? Explain your answer.
- **c** Ben mixes 20 litres of orange with 55 litres of water. Is this correct? Explain your answer.

10 Tom travels 290 miles. His journey is made up of walking, taxi and train in the ratio 3 : 10 : 45
Work out the distances for each part of his journey.

11 A garage has three models of car for sale.
The manager says "We have sold 45 of the cars in the ratio 7 : 6 : 5"
Is this possible? Explain your answer.

12 David and Dawn share £75 in the ratio 11 : 4
David says that he received £35 more than Dawn.
Is he correct? Show your working.

6.2 Proportion and best value

CAN YOU REMEMBER

- How to work out a fraction of a quantity?
- How to work out a percentage of a quantity?
- How to compare two or more quantities using ratios?

IN THIS SECTION YOU WILL

- Use direct proportion in simple contexts.
- Solve simple problems involving direct proportion.
- Identify when proportional reasoning is needed to solve a problem.

Proportion compares parts of a quantity to the whole quantity.
Proportions can be written in words, fractions, percentages or decimals.

For example, 1 out of 4, 1 in 4, $\frac{1}{4}$, 25% or 0.25 are different ways of writing the same proportion.

Example 1

There are 120 visitors to a park. 90 are female and 30 are male.
What proportion of the visitors is female?

Solution 1

There are 90 female visitors out of a total of 120 visitors.
The proportion of female visitors is 90 out of 120, or 9 out of 12, or 3 out of 4, or $\frac{3}{4}$, or 75%, or 0.75

A bar of chocolate costs 50 pence.
So two bars of chocolate cost £1, three bars cost £1.50 and so on.
The total cost is *proportional* to the number of bars bought.
For each extra bar, the cost increases by 50 pence.
When two values are in proportion, as one changes, the other changes at a steady rate.
To solve problems using proportional reasoning, start by working out the cost or amount for one item.

Example 2

Four ice-creams cost £1.20
What is the cost of:

a one ice-cream **b** five ice-creams?

Solution 2

Four ice-creams cost £1.20

a One ice-cream costs 30 pence (Divide by 4)
b Five ice-creams cost 5×30 pence = £1.50

Example 3

Here is a recipe for white sauce for two people.
How many grams of plain flour does a recipe for three people need?

Solution 3

30 g flour for two people.

15 g flour for one person. (Divide by 2)

$15 \times 3 = 45$ g for three people. (Multiply by 3)

Exercise A

1 A bag contains 20 coloured counters – five red, ten green, one blue and four yellow. Find the proportion of:

a red counters **b** green counters **c** blue counters
d counters that are **not** yellow.

2 A toolbox contains five spanners, two wrenches, one hammer and four screwdrivers.
Write down the proportion of tools that are:

a screwdrivers **b** wrenches **c** spanners
d **not** wrenches or a hammer.

3 1 litre of juice contains 250 ml of grapefruit juice.
How much grapefruit juice is there in 5 litres of juice?

4 5 miles is approximately equal to 8 kilometres.
Find the number of kilometres in:
a 1 mile **b** 30 miles **c** 300 miles.

5 Three tins of paint cost £10.50. Find the cost of:
a one tin **b** five tins **c** 15 tins.

6 Here is a recipe for Yorkshire pudding to serve four people.
Find the number of grams of flour for a recipe for:
a eight people **b** six people.

7 Shaheen has £45. She spends two thirds and saves the rest.
a What proportion does she save?
b How much does she save?

8 Making 10 litres of orange paint uses 7 litres of yellow paint and 3 litres of red paint.
How many litres of yellow paint and red paint are needed to make:
a 15 litres of orange paint **b** 25 litres of orange paint?

9 There are seven soft sweets out of every nine sweets in a tin.
Altogether there are 72 sweets in the tin.
a What proportion are soft sweets? **b** How many are soft sweets?
c How many are **not** soft sweets?

10 At a party there are 57 children.
There are twice as many girls as boys.
a What proportion are girls? **b** How many girls are there?
c How many boys are there?

11 At an athletics meeting the number of competitors and the number of spectators are recorded.
Show that the proportion of male to female is the same for both competitors and spectators.

	Competitors	Spectators
Male	35	245
Female	15	105

Two small boxes contain 160 tea bags, the same as one large box.

Two small boxes cost $2 \times$ £1.41 = £2.82
One large box costs £2.95
The small box is better value.
To decide which pack is the better value, work out the cost of each for the same quantity.

Example 4

Which packet is the better value?

Solution 4

Method 1 – Cost per gram

Cost of 1 g of small packet = £1.78 ÷ 750
= 178 ÷ 750 pence = 0.237… pence

Cost of 1 g of large packet = £2.28 ÷ 1000
= 228 ÷ 1000 pence = 0.228 pence

The large packet is better value.

Method 2 – Number of grams per penny

Number of grams for one penny in small packet = 750 ÷ 178 = 4.21… g

Number of grams for one penny in large packet = 1000 ÷ 228 = 4.38… g

The large packet is better value.

Method 3 – Scaling

Work out the cost of 250 g for each packet.

Small packet: 750 g cost £1.78

250 g cost £1.78 ÷ 3 = 59.3 pence

Large packet: 1000 g cost £2.28

250 g cost £2.28 ÷ 4 = 57 pence

The large packet is better value.

Exercise B

1 Show that both offers are the same value.

2 Are four fish for £10 better value than ten fish for £25?
Explain your answer.

3 Which is the better value?
Show your working.

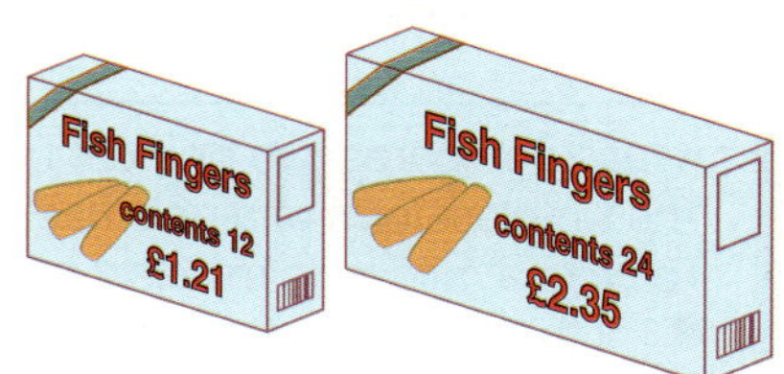

4 40 tea bags cost 71 pence.
80 tea bags cost £1.43
Which is the better value?

5 Two cogs, A and B, are connected as shown.
The number of turns made by the small cog is proportional to the number of turns made by the large cog.
When cog A makes nine turns, cog B makes two turns.
When cog A makes 360 turns, how many turns does cog B make?

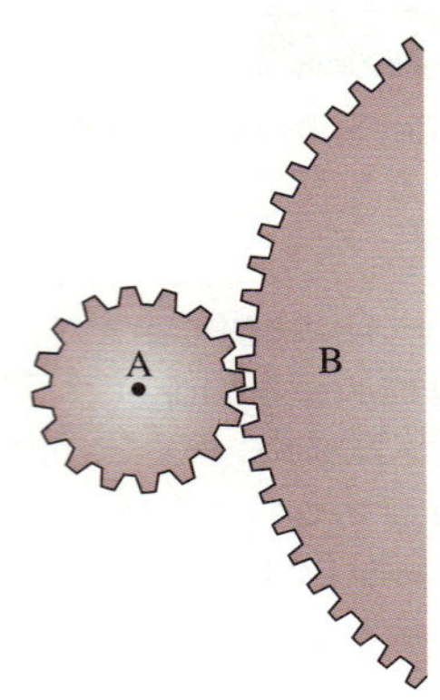

6 The table shows the number of male and female relatives for Pavel and Andy.
Who has the greater proportion of male relatives?
Show your working.

	Male	Female
Pavel	17	20
Andy	22	25

7 In a large hotel, the manager estimates that the proportion of light bulbs not working is 1 out of 30
If 29 870 lights are working, estimate the number of lights there are altogether.

8 Zanib and Tracey went fishing.
The table shows the number of days that each of them went fishing and the number of fish caught.
Who caught the highest proportion of fish per day?

	Number of days fishing	Number of fish caught
Zanib	140	253
Tracey	85	151

9 Which bottle is the better value?
Show your working.

10 5 miles = 8 km
Which is further, 60 miles or 88 km?
Show your working.

Chapter summary

- A *ratio* compares two or more quantities.
- The simplest form of a ratio has whole numbers with no common factors apart from 1
- To write a ratio in its simplest form:
  - if the ratio includes fractions or decimals, multiply to make both parts whole numbers
  - divide both parts by their common factors.
- *Proportion* compares parts of a quantity to the whole quantity.
- Proportions can be written in words, fractions, percentages or decimals, e.g. 1 out of 4, 1 in 4, $\frac{1}{4}$, 25% or 0.25
- When two values are in proportion, as one changes, the other changes at a steady rate.
- To solve problems using proportional reasoning, start by working out the cost or amount for one item.
- To decide which pack is the better value, work out the cost of each for the same quantity.

Chapter review

1 Four apples cost £1.40. How much will five apples cost?

2 In Class 3B, the ratio of City supporters to United supporters is 4 : 1
There are 30 students in Class 3B. How many are City supporters?

3 Rosie and Sophie share some chocolates in the ratio 3 : 2
Sophie gets 12 chocolates. How many does Rosie get?

4 Danny and Richard share £49 in the ratio 4 : 3
How much is the smaller share?

5 Pietro walks 9 miles in 3 hours. Adriana walks 8 miles in 2 hours.
Who is the slower walker? You **must** show your working.

6 A shop sells milk in different sizes.
Which size is the best value for money?
You **must** show your working.

7 Packets of sausages are sold in two sizes.
Which packet is the better value?
You **must** show your working.

8 A business spends £387 000 in one year.
£9 out of every £10 is spent on salaries.
How much is spent on salaries?

9 1250 people watch a school concert.
The numbers of teachers, pupils and visitors are in the ratio 1 : 6 : 3
a How many pupils watched the concert?
b How many visitors watched the concert?

10 At an auction the number of cars and vans for sale is recorded on two days.
Is the proportion of cars for sale greater on Wednesday or Friday?
You **must** show your working.

	Cars	Vans
Wednesday	180	32
Friday	85	17

11 Making 5 litres of tree green paint uses 3.5 litres of yellow paint and 1.5 litres of blue paint.
How many litres of yellow paint and blue paint are needed to make:
a 10 litres of tree green paint **b** 3 litres of tree green paint?

CHAPTER 7

Using formulae

7.1 Substituting into expressions and formulae

CAN YOU REMEMBER

- The difference between an 'algebraic expression' and a 'formula'?
- The order of operations (BODMAS or BIDMAS)?
- How to calculate with negative numbers, fractions and decimals, using written methods and a calculator?
- How to solve equations using the balance method?

IN THIS SECTION YOU WILL

- Substitute values into algebraic expressions and formulae.
- Evaluate formulae.

To substitute numbers into an algebraic expression (or formula):

- replace the letter symbols with numbers and insert all the operation symbols
- work out the value of the expression, using the correct order of operations.

Example 1

a If $a = 3$ and $b = -4$, work out the value of: **i** $2ab + 5$ **ii** $2a(b + 5)$.

b Find the value of $5x - \frac{8}{y}$ when $x = 3$ and $y = -2$

Solution 1

a **i** When $a = 3$ and $b = -4$

$2ab + 5 = 2 \times 3 \times -4 + 5 = -24 + 5 = -19$

ii When $a = 3$ and $b = -4$

$2a(b + 5) = 2 \times 3 \times (-4 + 5) = 2 \times 3 \times 1 = 6$

b When $x = 3$ and $y = -2$

$5x - \frac{8}{y} = 5 \times 3 - 8 \div -2$

$= 15 - -4$

Dividing a positive by a negative gives a negative.

$= 15 + 4 = 19$

Subtracting a negative is the same as adding a positive.

Example 2

You are given the formula $S = 3p^2 + \frac{q}{5}$ and the formula $T = \frac{c + 4d}{e^3}$

a Work out S when $p = -5$ and $q = 15$
b Work out T when $c = -12$, $d = 7$ and $e = -2$

Solution 2

a When $p = -5$ and $q = 15$

$S = 3 \times (-5)^2 + 15 \div 5$

$= 3 \times 25 + 15 \div 5$

$S = 75 + 3 = 78$

A negative number squared is always positive.

b When $c = -12$, $d = 7$ and $e = -2$

$T = \frac{-12 + 4 \times 7}{(-2)^3}$

$= \frac{-12 + 28}{-8}$

A negative number cubed is always negative.

$= \frac{16}{-8}$

$T = -2$

Example 3

$P = \frac{2x^2}{y^3}$

Find the value of P when $x = 8$ and $y = \frac{2}{5}$

Solution 3

When $x = 8$ and $y = \frac{2}{5}$, $P = \frac{2 \times 8^2}{\left(\frac{2}{5}\right)^3} = 2 \times 8^2 \div \left(\frac{2}{5}\right)^3$

Using a calculator, $P = 2000$

Make sure you know how to work out fractions using your calculator.

Exercise A

1 **a** If $p = -4$ and $q = 2$ work out:

i $6pq$ **ii** $\frac{p}{q} + 6$ **iii** $pq + 6$ **iv** $p(q - 5)$ **v** $\frac{p}{q - 5}$

vi $5p + 4q$ **vii** $2p - 3q$ **viii** $3pq - \frac{2p}{q}$ **ix** $\frac{8}{p} + q$ **x** $\frac{30}{p - q}$

b Repeat **a** for the values $p = 10$ and $q = -5$

2 **a** If $a = 10$, $b = -4$ and $c = 2$ work out:

i abc **ii** $ab - c$ **iii** $\frac{ab}{c}$ **iv** $a(b - c)$ **v** $a - bc$

vi $\frac{a}{b} - c$ **vii** $\frac{a}{b - c}$ **viii** $a - \frac{b}{c}$ **ix** $\frac{a - b}{c}$ **x** $a \div \frac{b}{c}$

b Repeat **a** for the values $a = 20$, $b = -5$ and $c = -10$

3 **a** If $w = 12$, $x = 4$, $y = 8$ and $z = -2$ work out:

i $wx + yz$ **ii** $w(x + y + z)$ **iii** $\frac{w}{x} + \frac{y}{z}$ **iv** $\frac{w(x + y)}{z}$ **v** $\frac{wx}{yz}$

vi $\frac{wxy}{z}$ **vii** $\frac{w}{y - x} + z$ **viii** $\frac{w}{x + y - z}$ **ix** $(w + x)(y + z)$ **x** $\frac{w + x}{y + z}$

b Repeat **a** for the values $w = 12$, $x = -3$, $y = -6$ and $z = 3$

4 $P = x^2 + y^2$ $Q = x^3 + y^3$ $R = \sqrt{(x^2 + y^2)}$ $S = 2x^2 + 3y^2$ $T = (2x)^2 + (3y)^2$

Work out the values of P, Q, R, S and T when:

a $x = 3$ and $y = 4$ **b** $x = -3$ and $y = -4$

c $x = 3$ and $y = -4$ **d** $x = -3$ and $y = 4$

5 **a** $A = \frac{5x^3}{4}$ $B = \frac{4x^2(x - 5)}{8x}$ $C = 2x^3(x - 1)^2$ $D = \frac{2x + 15}{(x - 15)^2}$

Find the values of A, B, C and D when: **i** $x = 10$ **ii** $x = -10$

b Work out the value of $\frac{2ab^2}{(a - b)^3}$ when $a = 5$ and $b = -5$

6 If $r = 0.7$, $s = 2.75$ and $t = \frac{3}{4}$ work out:

a rs^2 **b** $(r + s)^3$ **c** $2r(s - t)(r + t)$ **d** $rs(1 + 2t)^3$

e $\frac{15(5s + 1)}{rt}$ **f** $\frac{1}{r} + \frac{1}{s} + \frac{1}{t}$ **g** $\left(\frac{1}{r}\right)^2 + \left(\frac{2}{s}\right)^2 + \left(\frac{3}{t}\right)^2$ **h** $\frac{1}{r^2} + \frac{1}{s^2} + \frac{1}{t^2}$

i $r^3 + s^4 + t^5$ **j** $2r^3 + (3s)^3$

Sometimes substituting into a formula leads to an equation to solve.

Example 4

The formula $l = 30 + 0.2W$ gives the length, l cm, of a spring when a weight, W grams, is added to it.

a Find l when $W = 100$ g. **b** Find W when $l = 36$ cm.

Solution 4

a When $W = 100$

$l = 30 + 0.2 \times 100 = 30 + 20 = 50$ cm

b When $l = 36$

$36 = 30 + 0.2 \times W$ — Solve this equation using the balance method.

$36 - 30 = 30 - 30 + 0.2 \times W$ — Subtract 30 from both sides.

$6 = 0.2 \times W$

$6 \div 0.2 = 0.2 \div 0.2 \times W$ — Divide both sides by 0.2

$\frac{6}{0.2} = W$

$W = \frac{6 \times 10}{0.2 \times 10}$ — Multiply numerator and denominator by 10

$= \frac{60}{2} = 30$ g

Exercise B

1 This formula is used to convert temperatures from °C to °F.

$F = \frac{9C}{5} + 32$

Work out F when C is:

a 30 **b** 0 **c** −5 **d** 8

2 This formula is used to convert temperatures from °F to °C.

$C = \frac{5(F - 32)}{9}$

Work out C when F is:

a 41 **b** 212 **c** 68 **d** −4

3 The formula $f = \frac{uv}{u + v}$ is used in the study of light.

Calculate f when:

a $u = 2$ and $v = 8$ **b** $u = 5$ and $v = -3$

c $u = 80$ and $v = 20$ **d** $u = 0.3$ and $v = 0.7$

4 The area of a trapezium is given by the formula $A = \frac{1}{2}(a + b)h$

a Find A when:

i $a = 5$, $b = 7$ and $h = 6$

ii $a = 3$, $b = 12$ and $h = 10$

iii $a = 4.8$, $b = 15.2$ and $h = 6.375$

iv $a = 0.55$, $b = 1.45$ and $h = 17.5$

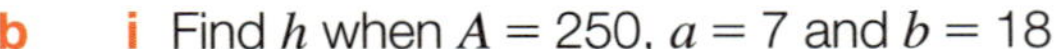

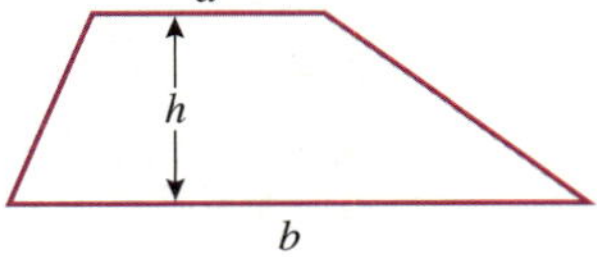

b **i** Find h when $A = 250$, $a = 7$ and $b = 18$

ii Find h when $A = 250$, $a = 21$ and $b = 29$

iii Find values of a, b and h for another trapezium with $A = 250$

5 The formula $v = u + at$ is used in the study of motion.

a Work out v when:

i $u = 12$, $a = 4$ and $t = 5$ **ii** $u = 1.2$, $a = 0.4$ and $t = 20$

b Work out u when:

i $v = 16$, $a = 0.4$ and $t = 5$ **ii** $v = 34.2$, $a = 2.38$ and $t = 10$

c Work out t when:

i $v = 18$, $u = 3$ and $a = 3$ **ii** $v = 22$, $u = 4$ and $a = 10$

d Work out a when:

i $v = 26.5$, $u = 2.5$ and $t = 60$ **ii** $v = 102$, $u = 27$ and $t = 7.5$

6 Another formula used in the study of motion is $s = ut + \frac{1}{2}at^2$

a Work out s when:

i $u = 11$, $a = 4$ and $t = 5$ **ii** $u = 4.5$, $a = 2$ and $t = 20$

b Work out u when:

i $s = 200$, $a = 4$ and $t = 8$ **ii** $s = 27.2$, $a = 0.36$ and $t = 10$

c Work out a when:

i $s = 32$, $u = 5$ and $t = 4$ **ii** $s = 180$, $u = 6.5$ and $t = 20$

7 **a** Copy and complete this table of values for $a^2 + a$ and $a(a + 1)$ for the values of a given.

a	$a^2 + a$	$a(a + 1)$
2	$4 + 2 = 6$	$2 \times 3 = 6$
5		
−2		
−5		
$\frac{1}{2}$		

b What do you notice? Give a reason for your answer.

8 The volume of this solid is given by the formula $V = \frac{4}{3}a^3$

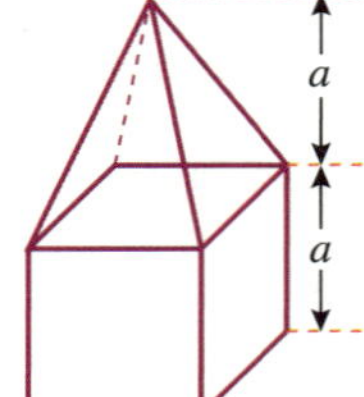

a Work out V when a is:

i 9

ii 15

b Work out a when V is 36

9 R is given by the formula $R = \dfrac{xyz}{xy + xz + yz}$

Work out R when:

a $x = 5$, $y = 2$ and $z = 10$

b $x = 8.6$, $y = 3.7$ and $z = 9.8$

c $x = 12.5$, $y = 32.7$ and $z = 19.8$

d $x = 0.465$, $y = 0.326$ and $z = 1.072$

In each case, give your answer to an appropriate degree of accuracy.

10 x is a positive integer.

Terry says that $(x + 1)^3 - x^3$ is *always* a prime number.

He gives this example:

> When $x = 2$
> $(2 + 1)^3 - 2^3 = 3^3 - 2^3 = 27 - 8 = 19$
> 19 is a prime number

Find a counter-example to show that Terry is wrong.

11 $P = \dfrac{x^2 + y^2}{x - y}$ $\qquad$ $Q = \dfrac{x^2 - y^2}{x + y}$

$R = P^2Q + Q^2P$ $\qquad$ $S = PQ(P + Q)$

a Work out R and S when:

i $x = 8$ and $y = 6$ $\qquad$ **ii** $x = 14$ and $y = 4$

b What do you notice about your answers for **a**?
Give a reason for this.

7.2 Writing expressions, formulae and equations

CAN YOU REMEMBER

- The difference between an algebraic expression and a formula?
- How to expand brackets in expressions like $3(2x + 1)$?
- How to simplify expressions by collecting like terms?
- How to find the perimeter and area of a rectangle?

IN THIS SECTION YOU WILL

- Understand the difference between an equation and a formula.
- Write expressions, formulae and equations using letter symbols.

The *formula* for the area, A, of a trapezium is $A = \frac{1}{2}(a + b)h$.
The letter symbols a, b and h represent lengths and can take **any** value.
Given the values of a, b and h, the value of A can be calculated.

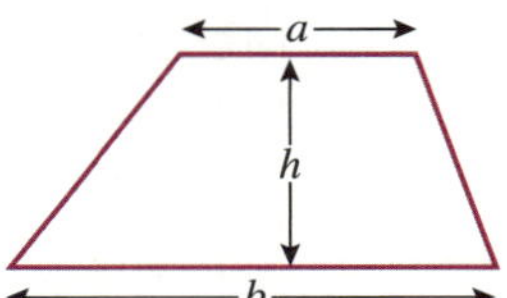

A formula always includes an '=' symbol.
In a formula the letter symbols can take **any** value.
An *equation* also includes an '=' symbol.
In an equation, the letter symbols have fixed values.
For example, $3x + 2 = 11$ is an equation with one letter symbol, x.
There is only **one** fixed value of x that fits this equation, $x = 3$

Example 1

Bags labelled X each contain x counters.

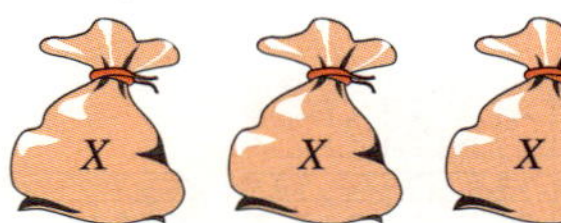

Bags labelled Y each contain y counters.

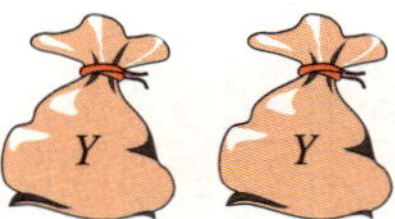

a Write an expression for the number of counters in:
  i A bag labelled X with three counters taken out.
  ii A bag labelled Y with half the counters taken out.
  iii Three bags labelled X.
  iv Three bags labelled X and two bags labelled Y.

b Write a *formula* for T, the total number of counters in a bags labelled X and b bags labelled Y.

c There are two bags labelled X.
Five counters are removed.
The total number of counters left is 15
Use this information to write an *equation* in terms of x.

Solution 1

a **i** $x - 3$ **ii** $\frac{y}{2}$ or $\frac{1}{2}y$ **iii** $3x$

  iv Three bags labelled X contain $3x$ counters.
  Two bags labelled Y contain $2y$ counters.
  So an expression for the total number of counters is $3x + 2y$.

b a bags labelled X contain ax counters.
b bags labelled Y contain by counters.
So the formula for T, the total number of counters in the bags, is $T = ax + by$.

c Two bags labelled X contain $2x$ counters.
When five counters are removed there are $2x - 5$ counters left.
So the equation is $2x - 5 = 15$

Exercise A

1 Boxes of matches each contain b matches.
- **a** Write an expression for the number of matches in three boxes when one match has been removed.
- **b** James uses half the matches in one box and five matches from another box.
  Write a formula for T, the total number of matches that James uses.

2 Michael is m years old.
Naomi is n years old.
Andrew is five years older than Michael.
Ben is three years younger than Naomi.
Peter's age, p, is the sum of Andrew's age and Ben's age.
Write a formula giving p in terms of m and n.

3 Afzal saves £5 each week.
After saving for w weeks Afzal spends £8
Write an expression for the amount that Afzal has left.

4 Billy is using building blocks to build towers and walls.
Each tower contains five blocks.
Each wall contains eight blocks.

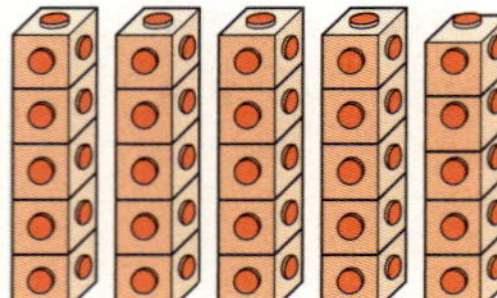
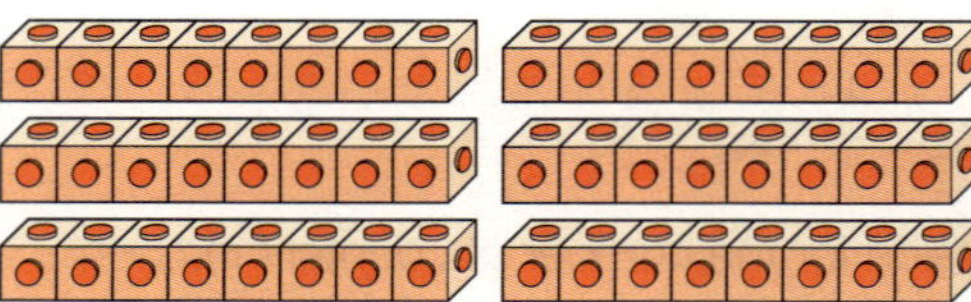
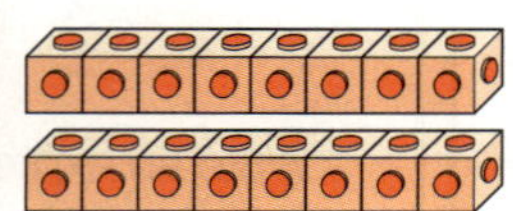

Write a formula for B, the number of blocks that Billy uses to build t towers and w walls.

5 Tickets for the school play cost £5 for adults and £3 for children.
Write a formula for £T, the total cost of x adult tickets and y children's tickets.

6 A window cleaner charges £5 for visiting a house and £3 for each window he cleans.
Write a formula for £A, the total amount of money that the window cleaner charges for visiting h houses and cleaning w windows.

7 Amy has p packets each containing x sweets.
Jade has b bags each containing y sweets.
Amy has more sweets than Jade.
How many more?
Give your answer as an algebraic expression in terms of p, x, b and y.

8 Sally buys five chocolate bars costing c pence each.
She pays with a £10 note and gets £6 change.
Use this information to write an equation in terms of c.

9 Zack buys three boxes of sweets each containing x sweets.
He also has seven sweets left in an opened box.

a How many sweets does Zack have in total?
Give your answer as an expression in terms of x.

b Altogether Zack has 55 sweets.
Use this information to write an equation in terms of x.

Example 2

The diagram shows a white square inside a shaded rectangle.

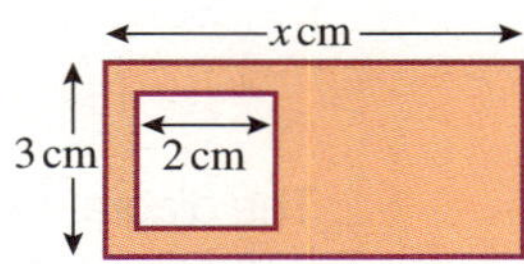

a Write an expression for the shaded area in terms of x.

b The shaded area is 20 cm^2
Use this information to write an equation in terms of x.

c Solve the equation to find the value of x.

Solution 2

a Area of rectangle $= x \times 3 = 3x$ cm^2

Area of square $= 2 \times 2 = 4$ cm^2

So shaded area $= 3x - 4$ cm^2

b $3x - 4 = 20$

c

$$3x - 4 = 20$$

$$3x - 4 + 4 = 20 + 4$$ Add 4 to both sides.

$$3x = 24$$

$$3x \div 3 = 24 \div 3$$ Divide both sides by 3

$$x = 8$$

Exercise B

1 The diagram shows a rectangle with length $(x + 3)$ cm and width $(3x - 5)$ cm.

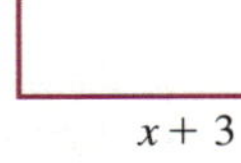

a Write an expression for the perimeter of the rectangle in terms of x.

b The perimeter of the rectangle is 20 cm.

i Write an equation in terms of x.

ii Solve the equation to find the value of x.

2 A list of consecutive integers starts x, $x + 1$, $x + 2$

a **i** Copy the list and continue it up to six consecutive integers starting with x.

ii Write down the list when $x = 8$

b The sum of four consecutive integers starting with x is 14

i Use this information to write an equation in terms of x.

ii Solve the equation to find the value of x.

c The sum of six consecutive integers starting with y is 39

i Use this information to write an equation in terms of y.

ii Solve the equation to find the value of y.

d Prove that the sum of any three consecutive integers is a multiple of 3

e Prove that the sum of any five consecutive integers is a multiple of 5

3 Sally buys x chocolate bars costing y pence each.
She pays with a £10 note.
- **a** Write an expression for the change that Sally gets in pence.
- **b** Write a formula for C, the change that Sally gets in pounds.
- **c** Write an equation for working out y when $x = 5$ and $C = £8$

4 The diagram shows a shape made up of two rectangles.
- **a** Show that the area of this shape, A cm², is given by the formula $A = 13x - 2$
- **b** Write an equation to find x when $A = 37$
- **c** Solve the equation to find x.

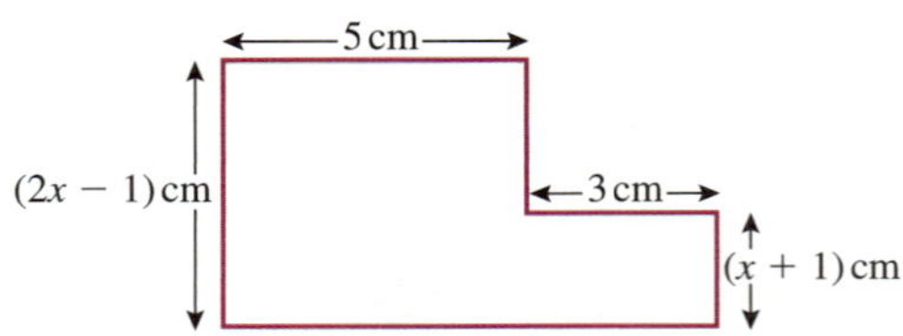

5 The diagram shows a path of width x metres surrounding a rectangular lawn.
The lawn has length L metres and width W metres.
- **a** Use each of the following methods to write down a possible formula for P, the area of the path.
  - **i** Subtract the area of the lawn from the area of the lawn and path.
  - **ii** Split the path up into the sections shown in the diagram and add the area of each section.

- **b** By splitting the path up into different sections find another possible formula for P.
- **c** Use $L = 5$, $W = 3$ and $x = 2$ to show that all of the formulae you have found give the same value of P.
  You **must** show your working.

6 Look at the number machines A and B below.

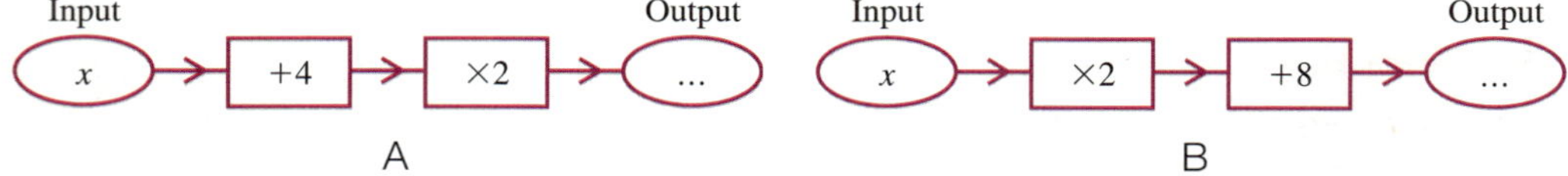

- **a** Write an expression in terms of x for the output of each machine.
- **b** Show that the output for machine A equals the output for machine B when the input value, x, is:
  i 2 **ii** −2 **iii** 0 **iv** 0.5 **v** −0.5
- **c** Repeat **b** for some other values of x.
- **d** Explain your answers to **b** and **c**.
- **e** Find some other pairs of number machines that have equal output for the same input.

7 In the year 2000 Tim was x years old. Mary was 3 years older than Tim. John was twice Tim's age.
- **a** Write an expression in terms of x for the sum of Tim's, Mary's and John's ages in 2000. Write the expression as simply as possible.
- **b** Write an expression in terms of x for:
  i Tim's age in 2005 **ii** Mary's age in 2005 **iii** John's age in 2005
- **c** In 2005 the sum of Tim's, Mary's and John's ages is twice the sum of their ages in 2000
  i Show that $4x + 18 = 8x + 6$ **ii** Is this a formula or an equation? Explain your answer.

8 The table shows the number of marbles in six bags labelled A, B, C, D, E and F.

Bag	Number of marbles
A	x
B	y
C	Three more than in bag A
D	Four times the number in bag B
E	Twice as many as bag C
F	Five less than in bag D

Find a formula for the total number of marbles, M, in all of bags A to F.

9 Shape A and shape B are made up of rectangles with dimensions as shown.
In parts **a** and **b** write your answers as simply as possible.

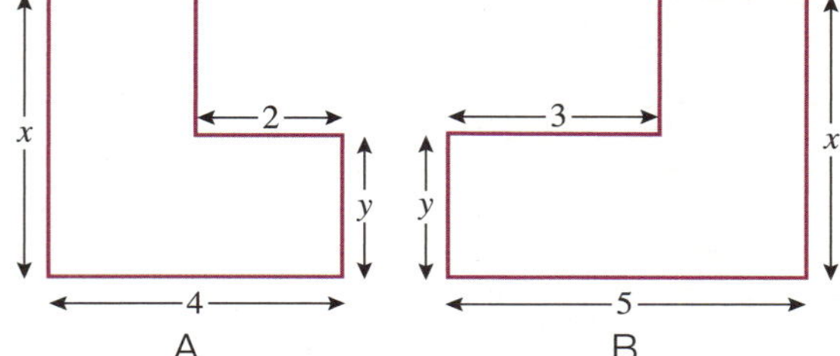

a i Write a formula for a, the total area of shape A.
ii Write a formula for b, the total area of shape B.
iii Write a formula for t, the total area of both shapes.

b i Write an equation to find x when $a = 30$ and $y = 3$
ii Write an equation to find x when $b = 30$ and $y = 3$

c Tom is told that $t = 70$ and $x = 6$
Explain clearly how Tom can work out a and b.

7.3 Changing the subject of a formula

CAN YOU REMEMBER

- That a formula is a rule for working out the value of one quantity from the value of other quantities?
- How to construct number machines and inverse number machines?
- How to solve equations using the balance method?

IN THIS SECTION YOU WILL

- Learn how to change the subject of a formula.

The formula $F = 1.8C + 32$ can be used to change temperatures in degrees Celsius (°C) to degrees Fahrenheit (°F).

The *subject* of this formula is F.

The subject of a formula is the single letter symbol on one side of the equals sign.

The formula can be *rearranged* to make C the subject. Then it can be used to change temperatures in degrees Fahrenheit (°F) to degrees Celsius (°C).

One method of changing the subject of a formula uses inverse number machines.

The formula $F = 1.8C + 32$ can be written using number machines:

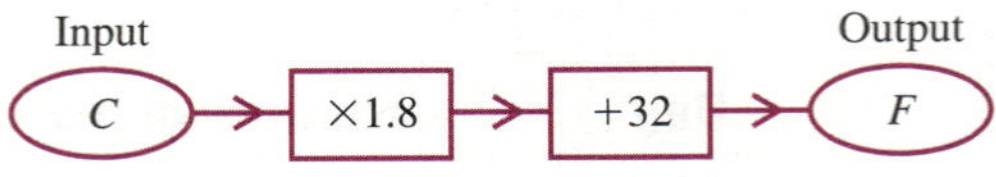

The inverse number machine is:

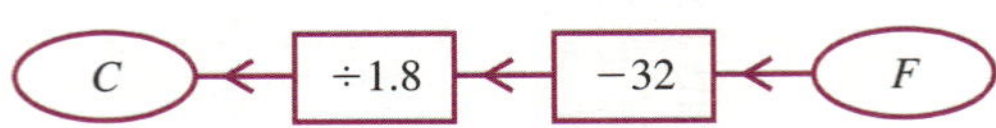

The output of the inverse number machine is

$C = (F - 32) \div 1.8$

This is the rearranged formula with C as the subject.

Example 1

Use inverse number machines to make x the subject of each of these formulae.

a $y = \dfrac{x}{4} + 3$ **b** $y = 2x - 5$

Solution 1

a $y = \dfrac{x}{4} + 3$

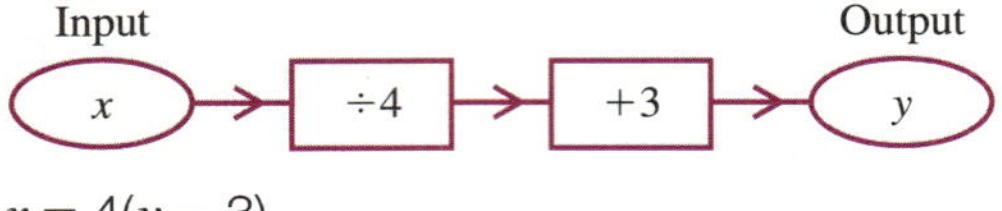

$x = 4(y - 3)$

x ← $\times 4$ ← -3 ← y

b $y = 2x - 5$

Input x → $\times 2$ → -5 → y Output

$x = (y + 5) \div 2$

x ← $\div 2$ ← $+5$ ← y

Example 2

Use number machines to make:

a b the subject of the formula $a = \dfrac{b}{c} - d$

b r the subject of the formula $p = q(r - 3)$

Solution 2

a Input b → $\div c$ → $-d$ → a Output

b ← $\times c$ ← $+d$ ← a

$b = c(a + d)$

b Input r → -3 → $\times q$ → p Output

r ← $+3$ ← $\div q$ ← p

$r = \dfrac{p}{q} + 3$

Example 3

a In the formula $A = bx^2$, A, b and x are positive numbers.
Rearrange the formula to make x the subject.

b Rearrange the formula $B = \sqrt{y} + p$ to make y the subject.

Solution 3

a $A = bx^2$

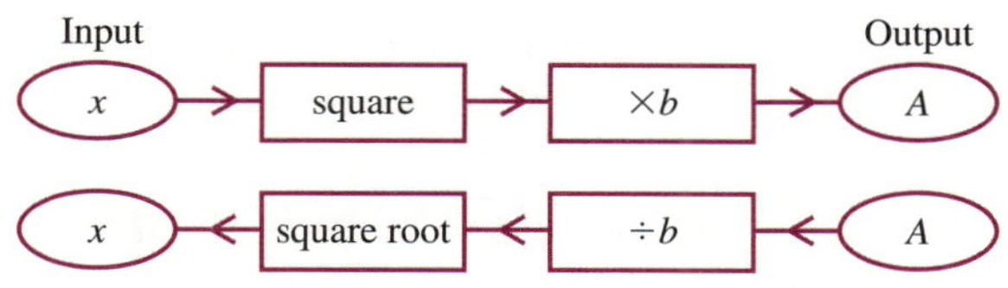

So $x = \sqrt{\left(\frac{A}{b}\right)}$

b $B = \sqrt{y} + p$

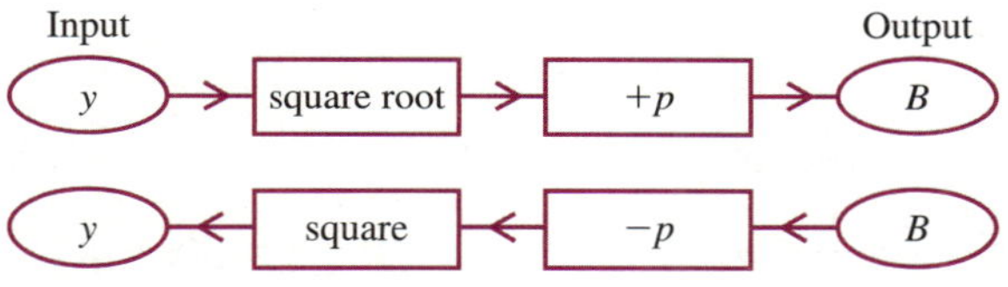

So $y = (B - p)^2$

Exercise A

1 Make w the subject of:

a $a = w + 4$ **b** $b = w + 9$ **c** $c = w + t$ **d** $d = w - 4$
e $e = w - 1$ **f** $f = w - t$ **g** $g = 5 - w$ **h** $h = t - w$

2 Make x the subject of:

a $a = 5x$ **b** $b = 6x$ **c** $c = px$ **d** $d = -2x$
e $e = -px$ **f** $f = \frac{x}{2}$ **g** $g = \frac{x}{5}$ **h** $h = \frac{x}{q}$

3 Make y the subject of:

a $a = 2y + 8$ **b** $b = 3y + 2$ **c** $c = 5y + t$ **d** $d = my + 2$
e $e = ny + p$ **f** $f = 5y - 3$ **g** $g = py - 5$ **h** $h = qy - s$

4 Make z the subject of:

a $a = \frac{z}{2} + 4$ **b** $b = \frac{z}{8} - 5$ **c** $c = \frac{z}{8} - r$
d $d = \frac{z}{m} + 2$ **e** $e = \frac{z}{a} + b$ **f** $f = \frac{z}{p} - q$

5 Make p the subject of:

a $a = 2(p + 3)$ **b** $b = x(p + y)$ **c** $c = r(p - q)$
d $d = p(a + 1)$ **e** $e = p(a - 5)$ **f** $f = p(a - b)$

6 Make q the subject of:

a $a = \frac{q+3}{2}$ **b** $b = \frac{q-3}{5}$ **c** $c = \frac{q+x}{10}$

d $\frac{d = q - x}{y}$ **e** $e = \frac{q+a}{b}$ **f** $f = \frac{2q-c}{d}$

7 In this question all letter symbols represent positive numbers.
Make t the subject of:

a $a = t^2$ **b** $b = 9t^2$ **c** $c = xt^2$ **d** $d = \frac{t^2}{4}$

e $e = \frac{t^2}{a}$ **f** $f = t^2 + 5$ **g** $g = (t-5)^2$ **h** $h = (t+a)^2$

8 Make m the subject of:

a $a = \sqrt{m}$ **b** $b = \sqrt{m} + 2$ **c** $c = \sqrt{m-2}$ **d** $d = \frac{\sqrt{m}}{5}$

e $e = \sqrt{\frac{m}{5}}$ **f** $f = a\sqrt{m}$ **g** $g = \sqrt{m+x}$ **h** $h = \sqrt{m} - y$

The subject of a formula can be changed using the *balance method.*

Example 4

Use the balance method to make x the subject of:

a $y = px + q$ **b** $y = \frac{x}{a} - b$ **c** $y = p(x+q)$

d $y = \frac{x-b}{a}$ **e** $y = x^2 + p$ **f** $y = \sqrt{x+p}$

Solution 4

a $y = px + q$ — Subtract q from both sides.

$y - q = px$ — Divide both sides by p.

$\frac{y-q}{p} = x$

So $x = \frac{y-q}{p}$

b $y = \frac{x}{a} - b$ — Add b to both sides.

$y + b = \frac{x}{a}$ — Multiply both sides by a.

$a(y+b) = x$

So $x = a(y+b)$

c $y = p(x+q)$ — Divide both sides by p.

$\frac{y}{p} = x + q$ — Subtract q from both sides.

$\frac{y}{p} - q = x$

So $x = \frac{y}{p} - q$

d $y = \dfrac{x - b}{a}$ — Multiply both sides by a.

$ay = x - b$ — Add b to both sides.

$ay + b = x$

So $x = ay + b$

e $y = x^2 + p$ — Subtract p from both sides.

$y - p = x^2$ — Take the square root of both sides.

$\sqrt{y - p} = x$

So $x = \sqrt{y - p}$

f $y = \sqrt{x + p}$ — Square both sides.

$y^2 = x + p$ — Subtract p from both sides.

$y^2 - p = x$

So $x = y^2 - p$

Example 5

The volume, V, of the square-based cuboid shown in the diagram is given by the formula $V = x^2h$.
A square-based cuboid has volume 900 cm^3 and height 4 cm.
Calculate the length of the base of the cuboid.

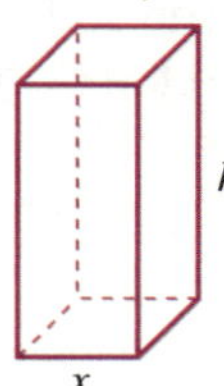

Solution 5

Method 1: Substitute values into the formula and solve the equation.

$900 = x^2 \times 4$ — Divide both sides by 4

$900 \div 4 = x^2 \times 4 \div 4$

$225 = x^2$ — Take the square root of both sides.

$\sqrt{225} = x$

So $x = 15$ cm

Method 2: Rearrange the formula to make x the subject and then substitute.

$V = x^2h$ — Divide both sides by h.

$\dfrac{V}{h} = x^2$ — Take the square root of both sides.

$\sqrt{\left(\dfrac{V}{h}\right)} = x$

So $x = \sqrt{\left(\dfrac{V}{h}\right)}$

When $V = 900$ cm^3 and $h = 4$ cm, $x = \sqrt{900 \div 4} = \sqrt{225} = 15$ cm.
Method 2 is useful when x has to be calculated a number of times for different values of V and h.

Exercise B

1 Repeat **Exercise A** using the balance method to rearrange each formula.
You **must** show your working.

2 A rectangle has length l and width w.
The perimeter, P, of the rectangle is given by the formula
$P = 2l + 2w$
The area, A, of the rectangle is given by the formula $A = lw$

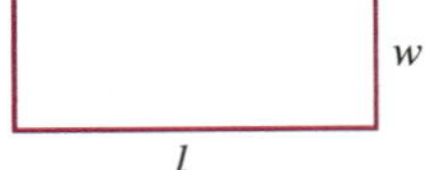

- **a** Rearrange $P = 2l + 2w$ to make l the subject.
- **b** A rectangle has width 7.5 cm and perimeter 31 cm.
  - **i** Work out l.
  - **ii** Work out A.
- **c** Find A when $w = 4$ cm and $P = 25$ cm.

3 The area of a trapezium is given by the formula $A = \frac{1}{2}(a + b)h$

This formula can also be written in the form $A = \dfrac{(a + b)h}{2}$

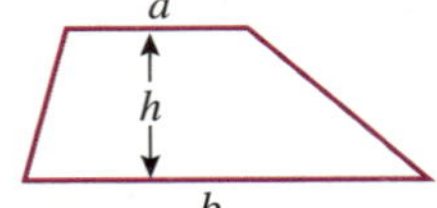

- **a** Calculate A when $a = 12$ cm, $b = 18$ cm and $h = 20$ cm.
- **b** Rearrange the formula to make a the subject.
- **c**
  - **i** Calculate a when $A = 500\text{ cm}^2$, $b = 6.5$ cm and $h = 40$ cm.
  - **ii** Calculate a when $A = 165\text{ cm}^2$, $b = 20.2$ cm and $h = 7.5$ cm.
- **d** Calculate h when $A = 12\text{ cm}^2$, $a = 6.3$ cm and $b = 3.7$ cm.

4 The surface area, A, of the square-based cuboid shown in the diagram is given by the formula $A = 2x^2 + 4hx$

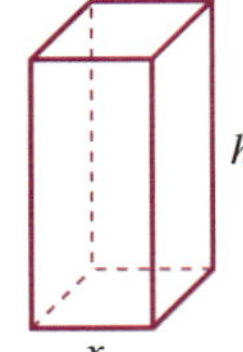

- **a** Rearrange this formula to make h the subject.
- **b** Work out h when $A = 250\text{ cm}^2$ and $x = 5$ cm.

5
- **a** Rearrange the formula $v = u + at$ to make:
  - **i** u the subject
  - **ii** a the subject
  - **iii** t the subject.
- **b** Rearrange the formula $v^2 = u^2 + 2as$ to make:
  - **i** a the subject
  - **ii** s the subject
  - **iii** u the subject.

6 $X = ab + c \qquad Y = b + ac$
- **a** By rearranging each of these formulae to make b the subject show that

  $$\frac{X - c}{a} = Y - ac$$
- **b** Hence show that $X = a(Y - ac) + c$

7 The letter symbols a, b and c are connected by the formula $a = \sqrt{b^2 + c^2}$
- **a** Show that $b = \sqrt{a^2 - c^2}$
- **b**
  - **i** Calculate a when $b = 14$ and $c = 48$
  - **ii** Calculate b when $a = 17$ and $c = 15$
  - **iii** Calculate c when $a = 1.23$ and $b = 0.27$

8 A triangle has sides of length a, b and c.
The area, A, of the triangle is given by the formula

$A = \sqrt{s(s - a)(s - b)(s - c)}$ where $s = \dfrac{a + b + c}{2}$

- **a** Rearrange the formula $s = \dfrac{a + b + c}{2}$ to make c the subject.
- **b** Work out the area of a triangle when $a = 6$ cm, $b = 8$ cm and $s = 12$ cm.

7.4 Harder formulae

CAN YOU REMEMBER

- How to use the balance method to change the subject of a formula?
- How to expand brackets and factorise algebraic expressions?

IN THIS SECTION YOU WILL

- Extend skills in changing the subject of a formula to formulae where the subject occurs twice and formulae with powers, roots and fractions.

The balance method can be used to rearrange formulae where the variable(s) occur more than once.

Example 1

a Rearrange the formula $am + b = cm + d$ to make m the subject.
b Make p the subject of the formula $a(p - b) = b(p + a)$

Solution 1

a $am + b = cm + d$ — Collect terms in m on the left-hand side (LHS) of the formula by subtracting cm from both sides.

$am - cm + b = d$ — Collect the other terms on the RHS by subtracting b from both sides.

$am - cm = d - b$ — Factorise the terms involving m.

$m(a - c) = d - b$ — Divide both sides by $a - c$.

$$m = \frac{d - b}{a - c}$$

b $a(p - b) = b(p + a)$ — Expand the brackets on both sides.

$ap - ab = bp + ab$ — Collect terms in p on the LHS by subtracting bp from both sides.

$ap - bp - ab = ab$ — Collect other terms on the RHS by adding ab to both sides.

$ap - bp = 2ab$ — Factorise terms involving p.

$p(a - b) = 2ab$ — Divide both sides by $(a - b)$.

$$p = \frac{2ab}{a - b}$$

Exercise A

1 Make a the subject of:

a $5a - b = a + b$ **b** $4a + b = 2a + c$ **c** $4a + 3b = a + 3c$
d $a - b = ab$ **e** $5a - b = ab + 1$ **f** $a - 3 = ab + b$

2 Make x the subject of:

a $x - y = xw + w$ **b** $xy + w = xw + 3z$ **c** $xy - w = xw$
d $2x - wy = xy + w$ **e** $3x + 3y = w + xy$ **f** $w - xy = wy - xw$

3 Make m the subject of:

a $2(m - n) = m + n$ **b** $5m = 3(m + n)$ **c** $3(m - n) = mn$
d $4(m - n) = n(m - 1)$ **e** $5(m - 2) = 2(n - m)$ **f** $8(m - 2n) = 2n(m + 5)$

4 Make b the subject of:

a $a(b-1)=a+b$ **b** $ab=3(b+1)$ **c** $a(b-c)=bc$

d $a(c-b)=c(2a-b)$ **e** $a(b-2)=2(3-b)$ **f** $c(b-a)=a(b+c)$

5 Make p the subject of:

a $4(p-3)=q(p+4)+2(p+1)$

b $4(p-q)=q(2p-1)-2(3p+q)$

c $q(p-2)=2(p+3)-p(q-1)$

d $4(p-1)+q(p-2)=3(p+q)-2(3p+q)$

e $q(p-r)=r(p+q)+2(p-q)$

f $q(2p-q)=r(2p+r)-2(p+q+r)$

g $p(q+2)+q(2p-q)=q(p+2q)+p$

h $q(p-r)+r(p-q)=qr(p+1)+2pqr$

More complex formulae may involve fractions together with powers and roots.

Example 2

Make x the subject of:

a $w=\dfrac{x+y}{x-y}$ **b** $z=\sqrt{\dfrac{x}{x+y}}$

Solution 2

a

$w=\dfrac{x+y}{x-y}$ Remove the fraction by multiplying both sides by $x-y$.

$w(x-y)=x+y$ Expand the brackets on the LHS.

$wx-wy=x+y$ Collect terms in x on LHS and other terms on RHS.

$wx-x=y+wy$ Factorise terms involving x and terms involving y.

$x(w-1)=y(1+w)$ Divide both sides by $w-1$

$x=\dfrac{y(1+w)}{w-1}$

b

$z=\sqrt{\dfrac{x}{x+y}}$ Remove the square root by squaring both sides.

$z^2=\dfrac{x}{x+y}$ Remove the fraction by multiplying both sides by $x+y$.

$z^2(x+y)=x$ Expand the brackets.

$xz^2+yz^2=x$ Collect terms in x on LHS and other terms on RHS.

$xz^2-x=-yz^2$ Factorise terms involving x.

$x(z^2-1)=-yz^2$ Divide both sides by z^2-1

$x=\dfrac{-yz^2}{z^2-1}$ Remove the minus sign in the denominator by multiplying numerator and denominator by -1

$x=\dfrac{yz^2}{1-z^2}$

Example 3

Rectangles A and B are equal in area.

Show that $y = \dfrac{1 - x}{x + 2}$

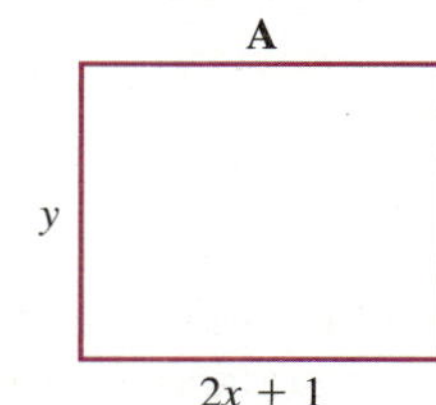

B
$x - 1$
$y - 1$

Solution 3

Area of rectangle A $= y(2x + 1) \equiv 2xy + y$
Area of rectangle B $= (y - 1)(x - 1) \equiv xy - y - x + 1$
Area of rectangle A = area of rectangle B

$2xy + y = xy - y - x + 1$ — Collect terms in y on LHS and other terms on RHS.

$xy + 2y = 1 - x$ — Factorise LHS.

$y(x + 2) = 1 - x$ — Divide both sides by $x + 2$

$y = \dfrac{1 - x}{x + 2}$

Exercise B

1 Make x the subject of:

a $y = \dfrac{(x + 3)}{(x - 3)}$ **b** $y = \dfrac{x + 2}{x - 2}$ **c** $y = \dfrac{2(1 - 5x)}{x - 5}$

d $y = \dfrac{5(2 - 3x)}{2x - 3}$ **e** $y = \dfrac{1 - x^2}{1 + x^2}$

2 Rearrange each of the following formulae to make a the subject.

a $b = \dfrac{a + 1}{a}$ **b** $b = \dfrac{a}{a - 1}$ **c** $b = \dfrac{ac}{a - c}$

d $b = \dfrac{a + c}{a - c}$ **e** $b = \dfrac{a^2 + c^2}{a^2c^2}$

3 **a** Make x the subject of the formula $A = \sqrt{\dfrac{s(s - x)}{ax}}$

b Make A the subject of the formula $P = \dfrac{A}{\sqrt{(A^2 + B^2)}}$

c Make cos A the subject of the formula $a^2 = b^2 + c^2 - 2bc \cos A$

4 **a** Rearrange the formula $f = \dfrac{2mg}{(M + 2m)}$ to make m the subject.

b Make x the subject of the formula $P = \dfrac{h(x + 3y)}{2(x + 2y)}$

5 A cylinder has radius x cm and height y cm.
A different cylinder has radius r cm and height $9y$ cm.
The two cylinders have equal volume.
Find a formula for r in terms of x.

6 Rectangle A has length x and width y.
Rectangle B has length $(x - 3)$ and width $(y + 6)$.
The area of rectangle B is twice the area of rectangle A.
Find a formula that gives y in terms of x.

7 x, y and z are variables connected by $\dfrac{x}{a - x} = \dfrac{b - x}{x}$

Show that $x = \dfrac{ab}{a + b}$

8 A cylinder has radius y and height $2x$.
The total surface area of the cylinder is given by the formula $A = 2\pi y^2 + 4\pi xy$
The cylinder has the same surface area as a sphere of radius x.
The formula for the surface area of the sphere is $4\pi x^2$.
Show that $y = \sqrt{(2x(x - y))}$

Chapter summary

- To substitute numbers into an algebraic expression (or formula):
  - replace the letter symbols with numbers and insert all the operation symbols
  - work out the value of the expression, using the correct order of operations.
- A *formula* always includes an '=' symbol. For example, $A = l \times w$
  In a formula the letter symbols can take **any** value.
- An *equation* also includes an '=' symbol.
  In an equation the letter symbols have fixed values. For example, $x = 7$ in $x + 5 = 12$
- The subject of a formula is the single letter symbol on one side of the equals sign.
  The subject of a formula can be changed using inverse number machines or the balance method.
- The balance method can also be used in formulae in which variables occur more than once.

Chapter review

1 **a** Find the value of $x^2 + 5xy$ when $x = -6$ and $y = 2$

b You are given that $m = \frac{3}{4}$, $p = \frac{1}{2}$ and $t = 2$
Find the value of: **i** $mp + t$ **ii** $t(m + p)$

2 **a** Tara buys x rulers at 25 pence each and y pens at 60 pence each.
Write down an expression for the total cost of the rulers and the pens.

b Tom buys x biros.
Each biro costs 18 pence.
Tom pays with a £2 coin.
Write down an expression for the change, in pence, Tom should receive.

3 The diagram shows an isosceles triangle.
Write down an expression, in terms of x,
for the size of angle B.

Not drawn accurately

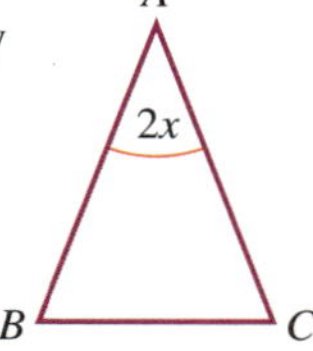

4 Make x the subject of the formula $5x + 2y = 12y - 5$
Simplify your answer as much as possible.

5 Make q the subject of the formula $p = \dfrac{q}{5} + 3$

6 **a** Make b the subject of the formula $a = b^2 + c$

b Rearrange the formula $E = mc^2$ to make c the subject.

c Make t the subject of the formula $x = \sqrt{t} + y$

7 **a** **i** Make x the subject of the formula $y = 12 + 3x$

ii Hence find the value of x when $y = 0$

b **i** Make p the subject of the formula $r = \dfrac{4(p + 3)}{q}$

ii Hence find the value of p when $r = -5$ and $q = 8$

8 You are given the formula $t = \sqrt{\dfrac{r}{s}}$

Calculate t when $r = 720$ and $s = 20$

9 A small paving slab weighs x kilograms.
A large paving slab weighs $(2x + 3)$ kilograms.

a Show that the total weight of 16 small slabs and four large slabs is $12(2x + 1)$.

b The total weight of the slabs is 132 kilograms. Write down an equation in x.

10 Make x the subject of the formula

$$a = \frac{b + 2x}{2b - x}$$

11 Rearrange the formula $P = \dfrac{2m}{\sqrt{m^2 - 3}}$ to make m the subject.

12 A cuboid has a square base of side x cm.
The volume of the cuboid is V cm^3 and the height is h cm.

a Write down an expression for x in terms of V and h.

b Find the value of x when $V = 150$ and $h = 24$

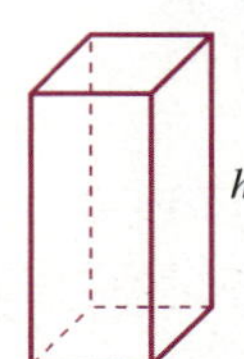

13 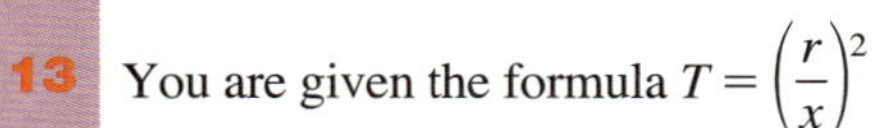
You are given the formula $T = \left(\dfrac{r}{x}\right)^2$

Calculate the value of T when $r = -0.9$ and $x = \frac{3}{8}$

14 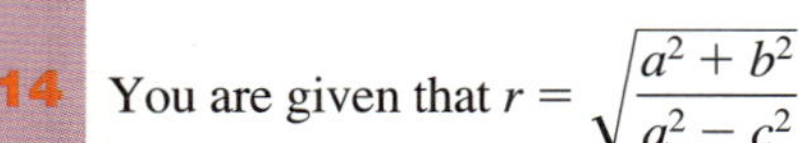
You are given that $r = \sqrt{\dfrac{a^2 + b^2}{a^2 - c^2}}$

a Calculate r when $a = 3$, $b = \frac{2}{5}$ and $c = -0.8$
Give your answer to 3 significant figures.

b Rearrange the formula to give a in terms of b, c and r.

CHAPTER

8 Probability 1

8.1 Two-way tables

CAN YOU REMEMBER

- How to work out simple fractions and percentages of quantities?
- How to read data from a dual bar chart?

IN THIS SECTION YOU WILL

- Read information from a two-way table.
- Work out missing information in a two-way table.
- Design two-way tables.
- Complete a two-way table using data from a graph.

A *two-way table* shows two linked sets of information.

	Age 14	Age 15
Male	8	9
Female	4	7

For example, the table above shows the gender and age of a class of Year 10 pupils.

- There are eight boys aged 14
- There are nine boys aged 15
- There are four girls aged 14
- There are seven girls aged 15
- There are 17 boys (8 + 9).
- There are 11 girls (4 + 7).
- There are 12 students aged 14 (8 + 4).
- There are 16 students aged 15 (9 + 7).
- There are 28 students altogether (8 + 9 + 4 + 7).

Example 1

200 people are asked which petrol station they usually use.
An equal number of males and females are asked.
Altogether 90 people use station A, but only half that number use station C.

Use this information to complete the two-way table.

	A	B	C
Males	52	32	
Females			

Solution 1

Total number of males = 100
Number of males who use station C = 100 − 52 − 32 = 16
90 people use station A.
Number of females who use station A = 90 − 52 = 38
Total number who use station C = total number who use station A ÷ 2
= 90 ÷ 2 = 45
Number of females who use station C = 45 − 16 = 29
Number of females who use station B = 100 − 38 − 29 = 33

	A	B	C
Males	52	32	16
Females	38	33	29

Exercise A

1 The two-way table shows the year group and gender of the students on a trip to France.
How many:
a Year 7 students went to France
b female students went to France
c students in total went to France?

	Year 7	Year 8	Year 9
Male	12	15	13
Female	20	18	12

2 The two-way table shows items sold in the restaurant and take-away sections of a fish-and-chip shop during a 20-minute period.

	Fish	Sausage	Fishcake	Pie
Restaurant	12	8	5	7
Take-away	23	15	10	11

a Find the total number of pies sold.
b Find the number of fish sold in the take-away.
c Find the total number of sausages and pies sold in the restaurant.

3 The two-way table shows the destination and gender of 100 travellers.
One of the entries is missing.
a Copy and complete the table.
b How many travellers are female?
c How many travellers are going to the USA?
d Copy and complete this sentence.

	Europe	USA	Other
Female	26	13	4
Male	35	20	

'Seven more .... travellers than .... travellers are going to ....'

4 The two-way table shows the numbers of child, adult, home and away supporters at a football match.
a How many home supporters are at the match?
b How many children are at the match?
c Charlie said, 'There were over 40 000 people at the match.' Is Charlie correct?
Explain your answer.

	Home	Away
Adult	25 152	3087
Child	8559	231

5 The incomplete two-way table shows information about the visitors to a theme park.

	Young child	Teenager	Adult
Male	2304		565
Female	3121	1143	

a Copy the table. Use the following information to complete it.
- There are 2010 teenage visitors.
- The total number of adults is half the total number of teenagers.

b Calculate the total number of visitors.

6 The incomplete two-way table shows the numbers of different vehicles recorded on a local road and a motorway in a 30-minute period.

	Car	Lorry	Bus	Motorbike	Bicycle
Local road		4	6	3	19
Motorway	141		2	4	

a Copy the table. Use the following information to complete it.
- Bicycles are not allowed on the motorway.
- 61 lorries are recorded in total.
- There are six times more cars than buses on the local road.

b Calculate the total number of vehicles on:
i the local road **ii** the motorway.

c Copy and complete this sentence.
'There were .... times more vehicles in total on the motorway than on the local road.'

Example 2

520 people play in a charity golf tournament.

$\frac{3}{4}$ of the players are male.

90% of the male players are professionals.

60% of the female players are professionals.

Design and complete a two-way table to show this information.

Solution 2

Step 1: Identify the headings for the table.
The information given is on male/female and professional players.
The headings are as opposite.

Step 2: Work out the entries for the table.

	Professional	Non-professional
Male	351	39
Female	78	52

$\frac{3}{4}$ of the 520 players are male. $\frac{3}{4}$ of $520 = \frac{3}{4} \times 520 = 390$

There are 390 male players. So there are $520 - 390 = 130$ female players.
90% of the males are professional. 90% of $390 = 0.9 \times 390 = 351$
So $390 - 351 = 39$ males are non-professional.
60% of the female players are professional. 60% of $130 = 0.6 \times 130 = 78$
So $130 - 78 = 52$ females are non-professional.

Example 3

The dual bar chart shows the data for the number of people joining a book club over three years.

a Construct a two-way table for the data shown in the bar chart.
b Describe two patterns in the data.
c Work out the total number of people joining the book club in the three years.

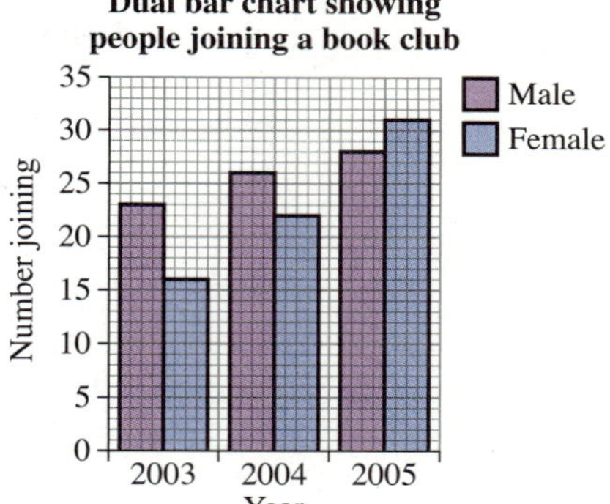

Solution 3

a **Step 1:** Identify the headings for the table.
The information is given by year and by gender.
Step 2: Read the entries for each section from the bar chart.

	2003	2004	2005
Male	23	26	28
Female	16	22	31

b The numbers of both males and females joining increase each year.
The number of females is increasing at a faster rate than the number of males.

c Total number joining = 23 + 16 + 26 + 22 + 28 + 31 = 146

Exercise B

1 Josie travels around different countries. In total she makes 60 journeys, $\frac{1}{4}$ of them at night.
During the day she travels by aeroplane five times, train 29 times and by boat.
During the night she travels by train for all journeys, except one.
Design and complete a two-way table to show Josie's travel by day and night.

2 The dual bar chart shows the animals Javed sees in his garden over three months.

a Construct a two-way table for the data shown in the bar chart.
b How many animals does Javed see in total?
c Javed says, 'I saw more cats than hedgehogs and foxes put together.'
Explain why Javed is correct.

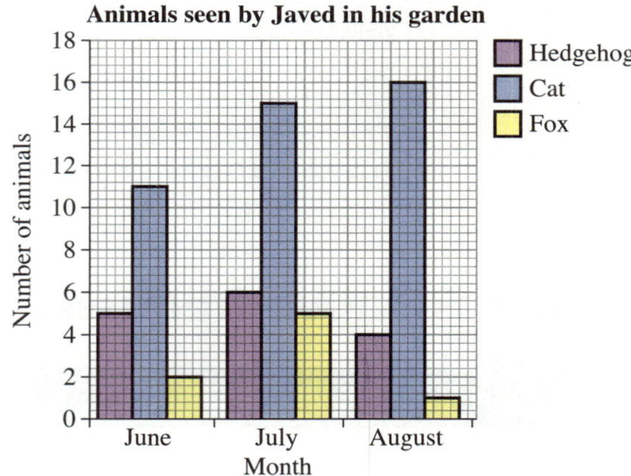

3 In a crowd of 5000 at a rugby match, 10% of the home supporters and 5% of the away supporters are female. Four fifths of the crowd are home supporters.
Design and complete a two-way table for the data.

4 Jade records the musical tastes of 400 people and whether they are right- or left-handed.
The choices of music are classical, rock or pop.
52 right-handed people choose classical music.
Twice as many right-handed people choose rock music as classical music.
Of the 120 left-handed people, 12 choose classical and the rest choose rock or pop in equal numbers.
Design and complete the two-way table for the data.

5 The two-way table shows some of the numbers of people from a town and the country who own no car, one car or more than one car.
200 people from the town are asked which they own.
50 people from the country are asked which they own.

	Do not own a car	Own one car	Own more than one car
Town	24	86	
Country	1		19

a Copy and complete this two-way table.
b Construct a two-way table showing the **percentage** of people from the town in each category and the **percentage** of people from the country in each category.
c Comment on one similarity and one difference in car ownership between people from the town and people from the country.
d Which of the two two-way tables was more useful when trying to answer part **c**?

6 200 people from Wales, 200 people from England and 200 people from Scotland are asked if they have visited London, Cardiff or Edinburgh. The results are shown in the chart.

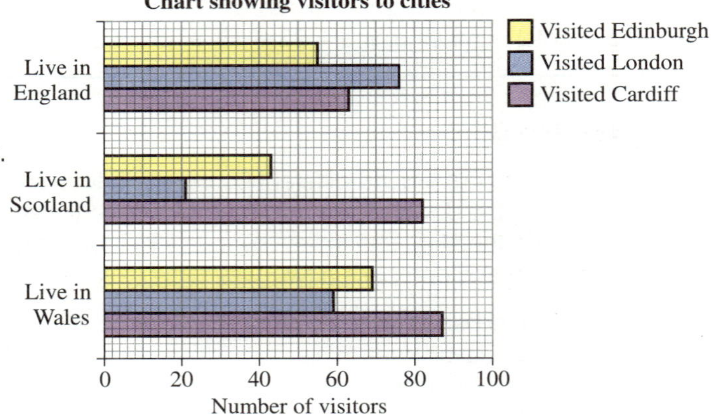

a Design and complete a two-way table for the results.
b Calculate the total number of people from the sample of 600 who have:
  i visited Cardiff
  ii visited London
  iii visited Edinburgh.
c How many of the people who live in Scotland have visited either Cardiff or London?

8.2 Relative frequency

CAN YOU REMEMBER

- How to calculate the probability of an event using equally likely outcomes?
- How to convert a fraction to a decimal?
- How to multiply whole numbers by fractions and decimals?

IN THIS SECTION YOU WILL

- Learn the meaning of 'trial' and 'relative frequency'.
- Learn how to use relative frequency to estimate probabilities from the results of experiments or surveys.
- Learn that the reliability of relative frequency as a measure of probability increases with the number of trials or observations.

For some events, the probability cannot be calculated using equally likely outcomes.

For example, for the probability of a train from Newcastle to Manchester being late, 'being late' and 'being on time' may not be equally likely.

In cases like this, the probability can be estimated using the results of an experiment or a survey and the *relative frequency.*

$$\text{The relative frequency of an event} = \frac{\text{number of times the event occurs in an experiment (or survey)}}{\text{total number of } \textit{trials} \text{ in the experiment (or observations in the survey)}}$$

Relative frequency is usually written as a fraction or a decimal. It can also be written as a percentage.

Probability based on relative frequency is called *experimental probability.*

Probability calculated from equally likely outcomes is called *theoretical probability.*

Example 1

2000 children take a cycling proficiency test.
1860 of these children pass the test.
Estimate the probability that a child passes the test.

Solution 1

Relative frequency $= \frac{1860}{2000} = 0.93$

An estimate for the probability that a child passes the test = 0.93

Example 2

Eric throws a dart at a dartboard 100 times. The table shows his results.

Result	Hits treble	Hits double	Hits single	Misses board
Frequency	12	5	80	3
Relative frequency				

a Complete the table.

b Use the answer to part **a** to estimate the probability that Eric throws a double.

Solution 2

a Total number of trials = 100

Result	Hits treble	Hits double	Hits single	Misses board
Frequency	12	5	80	3
Relative frequency	$\frac{12}{100}$	$\frac{5}{100}$	$\frac{80}{100}$	$\frac{3}{100}$

b The estimated probability that Eric hits a double $= \frac{5}{100}$ or 5% or 0.05

Exercise A

1 100 vehicles are observed passing the school gate.
14 of the vehicles are vans.
What is the relative frequency of a van passing the school gate?

2 Chandra drops a drawing pin and records whether it lands point up or point down.
She repeats this trial 100 times.
The number of times the drawing pin lands point up is 28

a What is the relative frequency of the drawing pin landing point up?
b Estimate the probability that the drawing pin lands point down.

3 A gardener plants 50 bulbs.
45 of the bulbs grow into healthy plants.

a What is the relative frequency of a bulb growing into a healthy plant?
b Estimate the probability of a bulb not producing a healthy plant.

4 Some students do this experiment with a bag of coloured counters.

- *Take a counter from the bag.*
- *Record its colour.*
- *Put the counter back in the bag.*
- *Repeat this trial a number of times.*

Their results are shown in this table.

a What is the relative frequency of David taking a red counter from the bag?
b What is the relative frequency of Suki taking a white counter from the bag?
c Estimate the probability of Leon taking a blue counter from the bag.

Name of student	Number of trials	Colour of counter		
		Red	White	Blue
David	50	22	15	13
Suki	100	48	32	20
Leon	200	102	60	38

5 In an experiment a marble is picked from a bag at random.
Its colour is recorded and it is replaced in the bag.
This trial is repeated ten times.
The results of the experiment are    
Copy and complete this table for the results.

Colour	Blue	Yellow	Red	Green
Frequency				
Relative frequency				

6 A four-sided spinner is spun 20 times.
The results are shown in the table.

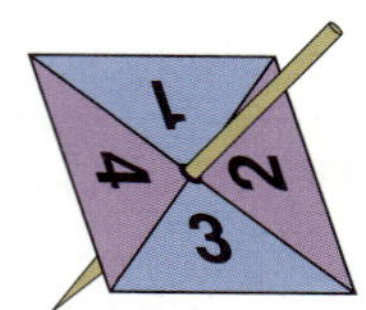

Number on spinner	1	2	3	4
Frequency	4	7	3	6

Use the results to calculate the relative frequency of each number.

7 A supermarket records the amount of money spent by 50 shoppers.
The results are shown in the table.

Amount spent	Less than £10	£10–£19.99	£20–£29.99	£30 or more
Frequency	2	10	25	13

a Work out the relative frequency of a shopper spending:
  i less than £10 **ii** between £10 and £30
b Estimate the probability that a shopper chosen at random will spend £30 or more.

8 In a survey, James records the colours of 25 cars on a motorway as either red (R), silver (S) or other (O). Here are his results.

S S R S O R S S O R O O R S S S S R R O S R S S O

Copy and complete the table.

Colour	R	S	O
Frequency			
Relative frequency			

9 Pavel is a footballer. His scoring record for attempts at goal with his left foot, his right foot and his head are shown below.

Left foot:	✓	✗	✗	✓	✓	✓	✓	✗	✓	✗
Right foot:	✓	✓	✗	✓	✗	✓	✓	✓	✓	✓
Head:	✗	✗	✗	✓	✗	✓	✓	✓	✗	✓

a Work out the relative frequency of Pavel scoring:
  i with his right foot **ii** with his left foot.
b Estimate the probability of Pavel scoring with his head.
c If you were Pavel's coach, what advice would you give him?

Relative frequency gives a more reliable estimate of probability when its value is based on a large number of trials or observations.

Example 3

A bead is taken from a bag of coloured beads and then replaced.
This trial is repeated 200 times.
The number of red beads taken from the bag every 20 trials is recorded.
This table shows the relative frequency of the number of red beads after each 20 trials.

Total number of beads	20	40	60	80	100	120	140	160	180	200
Number of red beads	2	7	14	18	21	26	28	33	37	40
Relative frequency	$\frac{2}{20}$ 0.1	$\frac{7}{40}$ 0.175	$\frac{14}{60}$ 0.233	$\frac{18}{80}$ 0.225	$\frac{21}{100}$ 0.21	$\frac{26}{120}$ 0.217	$\frac{28}{140}$ 0.2	$\frac{33}{160}$ 0.206	$\frac{37}{180}$ 0.206	$\frac{40}{200}$ 0.2

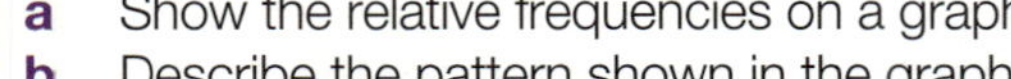

a Show the relative frequencies on a graph.
b Describe the pattern shown in the graph.
c Estimate the probability of picking a red bead from the bag.

Solution 3

a

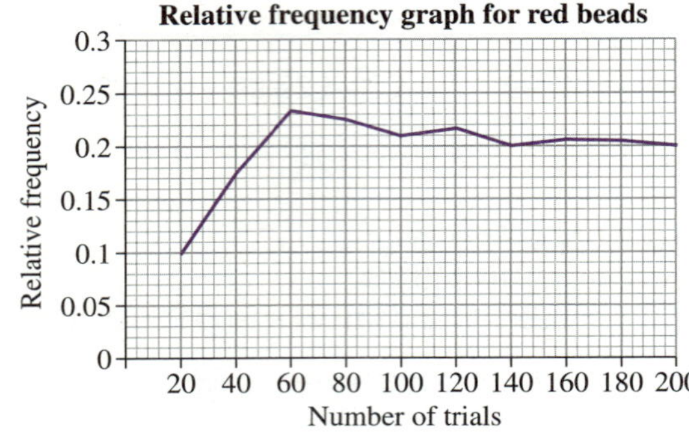

b At first, when the number of trials is small, the relative frequency changes a lot. As the number of trials increases the relative frequency changes less.

c The best estimate of the probability is 0.2, the relative frequency for the largest number of trials in the experiment.

For a large number of trials the relative frequency gives a reliable estimate of the theoretical probability.

Example 4

Adrian carries out an experiment with this spinner.
He spins the spinner 100 times and calculates the relative frequency of the spinner landing on red after every 20 spins.
Some of the results are shown on the graph.

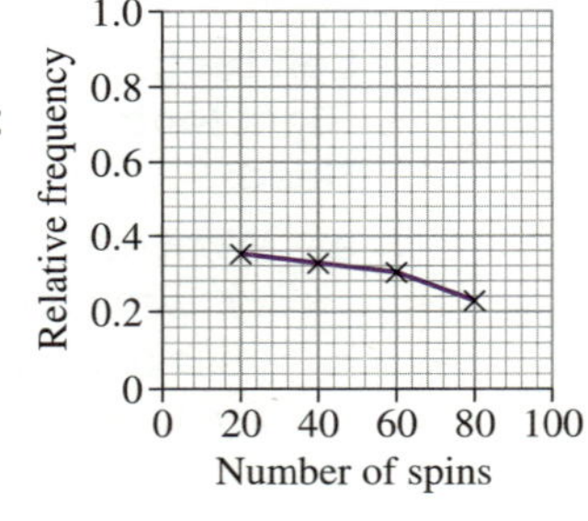

a Use the graph to find the number of times the spinner lands on red:
  i after 20 spins
  ii after 40 spins.

b After 100 spins red had appeared 24 times.
Calculate the relative frequency.

c What is the most reliable estimate of the spinner landing on red? Explain your answer.

d Assuming the spinner is fair, work out the theoretical probability of the spinner landing on red. Compare this with your answer to part **c**.

Solution 4

a Relative frequency $= \dfrac{\text{number of times spinner lands on red}}{\text{total number of spins}}$

  i When the total number of spins is 20, the relative frequency is 0.35

  $0.35 = \dfrac{\text{number of times spinner lands on red}}{20}$

  Number of times spinner landed on red $= 0.35 \times 20 = 7$
  The spinner lands on red seven times.

  ii When the total number of spins is 40, the relative frequency is 0.325
  Number of times spinner lands on red $= 0.325 \times 40 = 13$

b Relative frequency $= \frac{24}{100} = 0.24$

c The most reliable estimate of the probability that the spinner lands on red is 0.24
This is the relative frequency of the spinner landing on red for the largest number of trials in the experiment.

d The theoretical probability = number of successful outcomes ÷ total number of outcomes
$= \frac{1}{4} = 0.25$
The experimental probability, 0.24, is very close to the theoretical probability.

Exercise B

1 Tom takes a counter from a bag, records its colour and then replaces it.
He does this for 50 trials.

a Copy and complete this table.

Number of trials	10	20	30	40	50
Number of red counters	3	10	15	18	20
Relative frequency of a red counter	$\frac{3}{10}$ 0.3		$\frac{15}{30}$	$\frac{18}{40}$ 0.45	

b Copy and complete the graph to show how the relative frequency changes as the number of trials increases.

c Describe the pattern shown in the graph.

d What is the best estimate of the probability of taking a red counter from the bag?

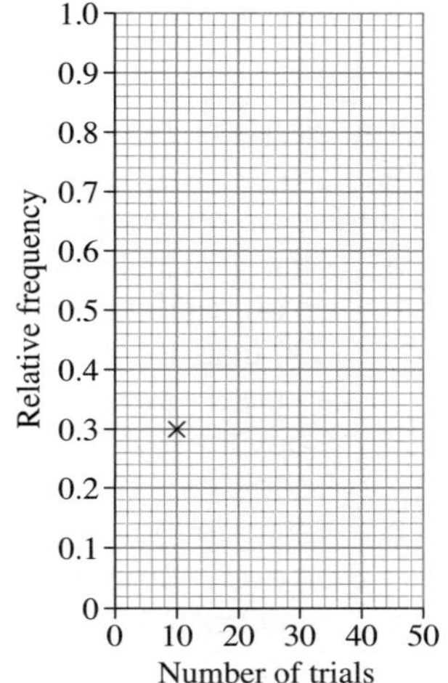

2 The diagram shows the number of trials and the relative frequency of a head when a coin is thrown 100 times.

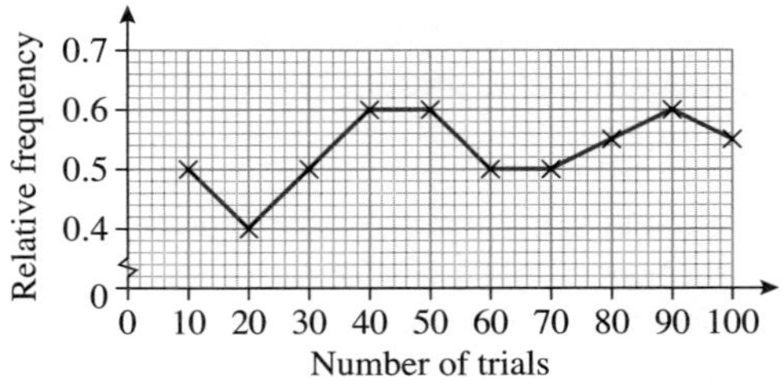

a Copy and complete the table.

Number of trials	10	20	30	40	50	60	70	80	90	100
Relative frequency	0.5	0.4								
Number of heads	5									

b Write down the best estimate of the probability of throwing a head.
Explain your answer.

c Assuming the coin is fair, work out the theoretical probability of throwing a head.
Compare this with the estimated probability.

3 The diagram shows the number of trials and the relative frequency of a spinner landing on green when it is spun 100 times.

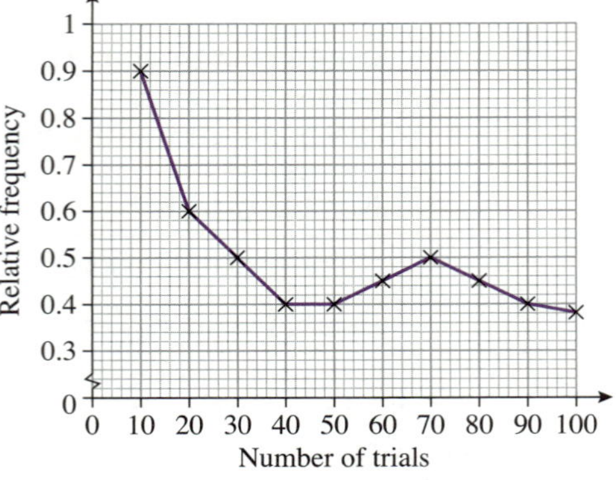

a Copy and complete the table.

Number of trials	10	20	30	40
Relative frequency	0.9	0.6	0.5	
Frequency of green				

b What is the best estimate of the probability of the spinner landing on green? Explain your answer.

4 The diagram shows the number of trials and the relative frequency of a dice landing on an even number.

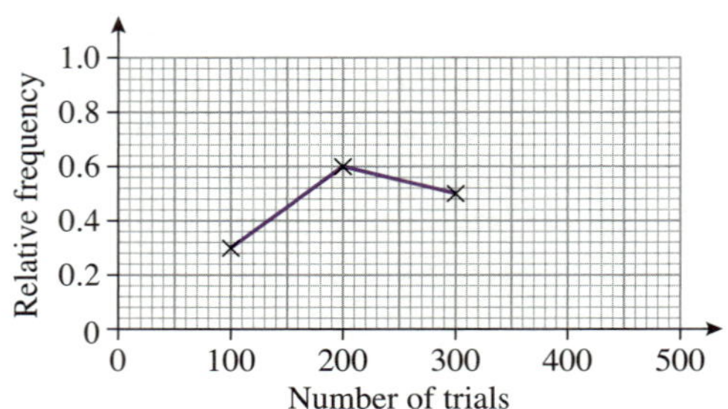

a After 400 trials the dice has landed on an even number 200 times. After 500 trials the dice has landed on an even number 250 times.
Copy the graph and plot the relative frequencies at 400 and 500 trials.

b Estimate the probability that the dice lands on an even number.

c How does the answer to **b** compare with the theoretical probability?

5 Paul records the number of left-handed students he meets at regular intervals. The table shows his results.

Number of students	20	50	80	100	120
Number of left-handed students	3	9	15	18	21

a Draw a graph to show the relative frequency of a student being left-handed.

b Estimate the probability of a student being left-handed.

6

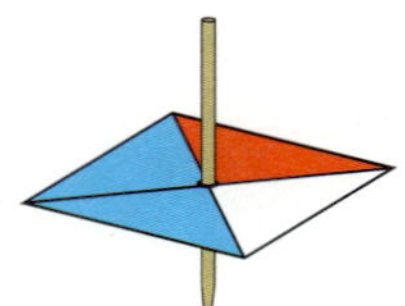

Shania spins the spinner 50 times and calculates the relative frequency of blue after every ten spins.
The results are shown on the graph.

a Use the graph to calculate the number of times that the spinner lands on blue:

i after the first ten spins

ii after the first 50 spins.

b What is the best estimate of the theoretical probability that the spinner lands on blue?

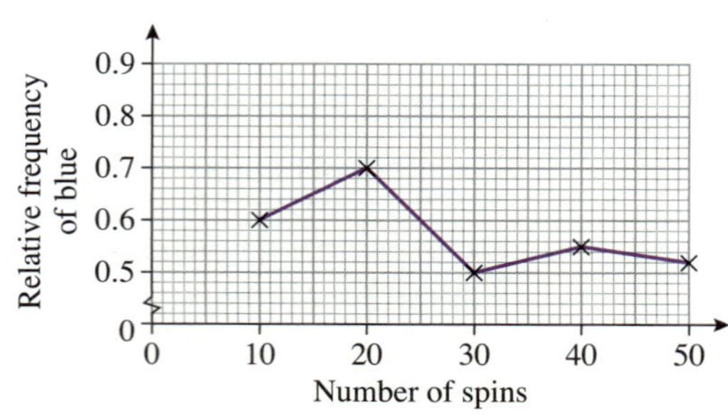

7 The table shows the results of a survey of the number of red cars passing a school.
The results are running totals after every 25 cars.

Number of cars	25	50	75	100	125	150
Number of red cars	4	12	20	25	32	38
Relative frequency of red						

a Copy and complete the table of relative frequencies.
b Show the information on a relative frequency graph.

8 Jo and Owen are trying to estimate the probability of their team winning a football match.
Jo says that so far this season the team have won nine of their 20 games.
Owen says that the team have won 84 of their 420 games in the previous ten seasons before this season.

a **i** Using Jo's figures, what is the team's relative frequency of winning?
ii Using Owen's figures, what is the team's relative frequency of winning?

b Give a reason why Jo's figures may provide a better estimate of the probability of the team winning.

c Give a reason why Owen's figures may provide a better estimate of the probability of the team winning.

8.3 Using relative frequency

CAN YOU REMEMBER

- How to calculate the probability of an event using equally likely outcomes?
- How to use relative frequency to estimate probability for an experiment or survey?
- How to multiply whole numbers by fractions and decimals?
- How to round to the nearest integer?

IN THIS SECTION YOU WILL

- Use theoretical probability and relative frequency to estimate the result of an experiment or survey.
- Use theoretical probability and relative frequency to judge whether a situation is fair or biased.

In an experiment a coin is thrown 1000 times.

The theoretical probability of throwing a head is: $\frac{\text{number of successful outcomes}}{\text{total number of outcomes}} = \frac{1}{2}$

1000 is a large number of trials. For a large number of trials, the relative frequency is close to the theoretical probability.

So for 1000 trials: $\frac{\text{number of heads}}{1000} = \frac{1}{2}$

Number of heads $= \frac{1}{2} \times 1000 = 500$

500 is a good estimate for the number of heads when the coin is thrown 1000 times.
Estimated number of successful outcomes = probability × total number of trials

Relative frequency and theoretical probability can be used to estimate the result of an experiment.

The larger the number of trials in the experiment, the more accurate the estimate.

Example 1

The probability of scoring 1 on a four-sided dice is $\frac{1}{4}$
The dice is rolled 20 times.

a Estimate the number of times a 1 is likely to occur.
b How reliable is this estimate? Give a reason for your answer.

Solution 1

a Estimated number of results = probability × total number of trials
Estimated number of 1s = $\frac{1}{4} \times 20 = 5$
b The estimate is not reliable because the number of trials is small.

If a situation is fair, the relative frequency for a large number of trials is close to the theoretical probability.
If the relative frequency for a large number of trials is not close to the theoretical probability, the situation could be unfair or biased.

Example 2

A coin is spun 500 times and shows heads 160 times.
Is the coin fair? Explain your answer.

Solution 2

The relative frequency of a head = $\frac{160}{500} = 0.32$. This is lower than the theoretical probability of 0.5
The number of trials is large, so the relative frequency is a reliable estimate of probability.
So it is likely that the coin is biased.

Example 3

Dan spins a coin 10 times and gets three heads.
Is the coin biased?

Solution 3

The relative frequency of a head = $\frac{3}{10} = 0.3$

The relative frequency is lower than the theoretical probability of 0.5. But 0.3 is not a reliable estimate of probability, because the number of trials is small.

So it is not possible to say whether the coin is biased.

Exercise A

1 An ordinary fair dice is thrown 60 times.
Estimate the number of times that a 6 is likely to be thrown.

2 An ordinary dice is thrown 600 times.
The dice lands on a square number 120 times.
Is the dice fair?
Give a reason for your answer.

3 The probability of winning a game is 0.4
Steve plays the game 20 times.
- **a** Estimate the number of times Steve is likely to win.
- **b** How reliable is this estimate?
  Explain your answer.

4
- **a** Jenny throws a coin 200 times.
  She gets 107 heads and 93 tails.
  Is the coin fair? Give a reason for your answer.
- **b** Tim throws two coins 400 times.
  He gets two heads 112 times and two tails 88 times.
  He says that the coins are biased towards heads.
  Give a reason why he might be wrong.

5 A survey of 100 men is carried out in a town. 30 of the men are married.
- **a** Estimate the probability that a man selected at random in the town is married.
- **b** The population of men in the town is 5000
  Estimate the number of married men in the town.

6 An ordinary fair dice is thrown. A score is given according to these rules:

If the dice lands on an odd number, **score = 2 × number on the dice**

If the dice lands on an even number, **score = number on the dice**

- **a** Complete the table to show the possible scores.

Number on dice	1	2	3	4	5	6
Score	2	2				

- **b** Write down the probability of a score of:
  i 1 **ii** 2 **iii** less than 6
- **c** The dice is thrown 120 times.
  Estimate the number of scores of 2 that is likely to be obtained.
- **d** A different dice is thrown 120 times.
  Scores are given in the same way.
  57 scores of 2 are obtained.
  Is this dice fair? Give a reason for your answer.

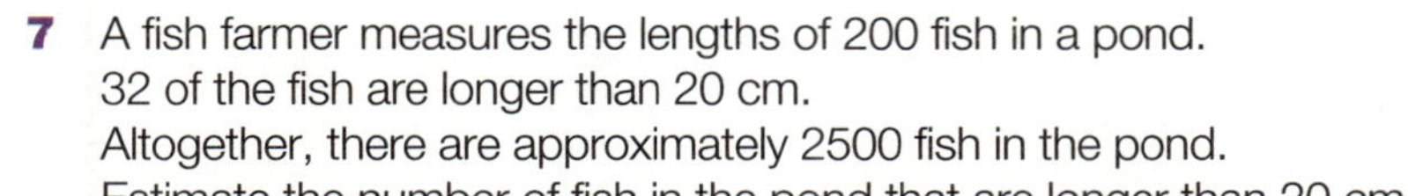

7 A fish farmer measures the lengths of 200 fish in a pond.
32 of the fish are longer than 20 cm.
Altogether, there are approximately 2500 fish in the pond.
Estimate the number of fish in the pond that are longer than 20 cm.

8 Two fair five-sided spinners are spun.
A score is obtained by adding the numbers on each spinner.

- **a** Copy and complete the table of scores.

+	1	2	3	4	5
1	2	3	4		
2	3	4			
3					
4					
5					

b Write down the probability of a score of:
  i 3 **ii** 8 or more.

c The spinners are spun 500 times.
Estimate the number of times that a score of 8 or more is likely to occur.

9 In a game, a fair coin is thrown and an ordinary fair dice is rolled.
A score is given according to these rules:

If the coin lands on heads, score $= 2 \times$ number on the dice

If the coin lands on tails, score $=$ number on the dice $+1$

a Copy and complete the table of scores.

	1	2	3	4	5	6
Head			6			
Tail		3				

b Write down the probability of a score of: **i** 3 **ii** more than 4

c The game is played 120 times.
Estimate the number of times that a score more than 4 is likely to be obtained.

d The same game is played 500 times using a different coin and dice.
A score of more than 4 was obtained 320 times.
Is this game fair? Explain your answer.

10 A group of 2500 people were asked which party they would vote for in an election.
The group were typical of the people who vote in the election.
1360 of the people said they would vote for the Democrats.

a What is the probability that a person chosen at random will vote Democrat?

b 55 000 000 people are expected to vote in the election.
Estimate the number of people who are likely to vote for the Democrats.

Example 4

The probability that a clover has four leaves is 0.02
Sally picks 1000 clovers.
Estimate the number she is likely to find that do **not** have four leaves.

Solution 4

Method 1
The probability of **not** getting a four-leaf clover $= 1 - 0.02 = 0.98$

$0.98 \times 1000 = 980$

Method 2
$0.02 \times 1000 = 20$

The estimated number of clovers with four leaves $= 20$

$1000 - 20 = 980$

The estimated number of clovers that do not have four leaves is 980

Example 5

Here are some instructions for an experiment.

Bill and Sally both complete this experiment.
Their results are shown in the table.

Take a bead at random from a bag containing 500 beads.

Record the colour of the bead and then put it back in the bag.

Repeat this trial a number of times.

Student	Number of trials	Number of red beads obtained
Bill	35	8
Sally	300	78

a **i** What is the relative frequency of Bill taking a red bead from the bag?
ii What is the relative frequency of Sally taking a red bead from the bag?

b **i** Use Bill's results to estimate the number of red beads in the bag.
ii Use Sally's results to estimate the number of red beads in the bag.

c Whose experiment should give the more accurate estimate of the number of red beads in the bag?
Explain your answer.

Solution 5

a **i** $\frac{8}{35}$ or 0.229 **ii** $\frac{78}{300}$ or 0.26

b Theoretical probability $= \frac{\text{number of red beads in bag}}{500}$

i Estimated probability $= \frac{8}{35}$

$$\frac{\text{Number of red beads}}{500} = \frac{8}{35}$$

Number of red beads $= \frac{8}{35} \times 500 = 114.28\ldots$

From Bill's experiment, the estimated number of red beads = 114

ii $$\frac{\text{Number of red beads}}{500} = \frac{78}{300}$$

Estimated number of red beads $= \frac{78}{300} \times 500 = 130$

From Sally's experiment, the estimated number of red beads = 130

c Sally's experiment should give a more accurate estimate of the number of red beads in the bag. The relative frequency from Sally's experiment is a more reliable estimate of the probability of taking a red bead from the bag.

Exercise B

1 A fair dice is thrown thousands of times. Estimate the relative frequency of throwing a six.
Explain your answer.

2 **a** The probability that Daisy wins a game is 0.2 She plays the game 20 times.
How many times would you expect Daisy **not** to win?

b The probability that a number 289 bus is late is 0.1
Over one week the number 289 bus makes 80 journeys.
How many times would you expect the bus **not** to be late?

3 The diagram shows a fair spinner.
The results of the first 20 spins are shown below.

A B C D B C A A D E
E E B C D C D E A A

a What is the relative frequency of the letter A for these results?

b The results of the next ten spins are:

B C D C A B C D B E

What is the relative frequency of the letter A after 30 spins?

c The spinner is spun some more times.
Estimate the number of times the letter A will occur after 1000 spins.

4 The table shows the probabilities of four players playing for a team.
The team plays 60 games.
Andy and Danny never play in the same team.
Estimate the number of times that neither Andy nor Danny play.

Paul	Andy	Danny	Nathan
$\frac{1}{2}$	$\frac{3}{4}$	$\frac{1}{10}$	$\frac{2}{3}$

5 A sack contains a number of gold and silver discs.
A disc is taken from the sack at random and its colour is recorded.
The disc is then replaced.
This trial is repeated a number of times. The table shows the results.

Number of trials	10	50	100	150	200
Number of gold discs	3	8	23	30	38

a On a copy of this grid draw a graph to show how the relative frequency of a gold disc changes as the number of trials increases.

b Write down an estimate of the probability of taking a gold disc from the sack.
Give a reason for your answer.

c The sack contains 1000 discs.
Estimate the number of gold discs in the sack.

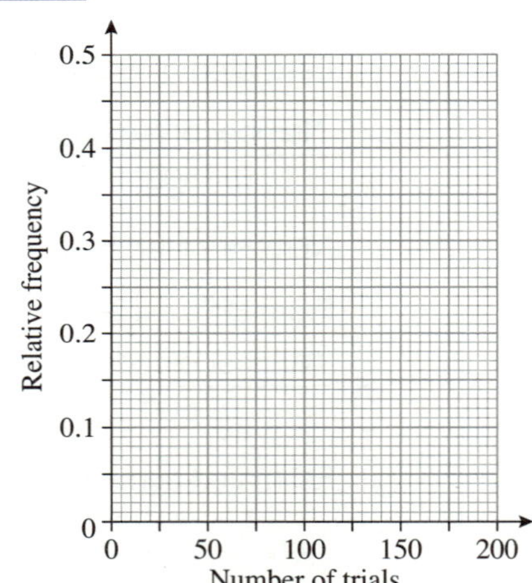

6 Bags A, B and C each contain coloured counters.
Counters are taken at random from each bag and then replaced.
This trial is repeated a different number of times for each bag.

a The relative frequency of taking a blue counter from bag A is shown in the graph.
Explain why this graph is unlikely to give a reliable estimate of the probability of taking a blue counter from bag A.

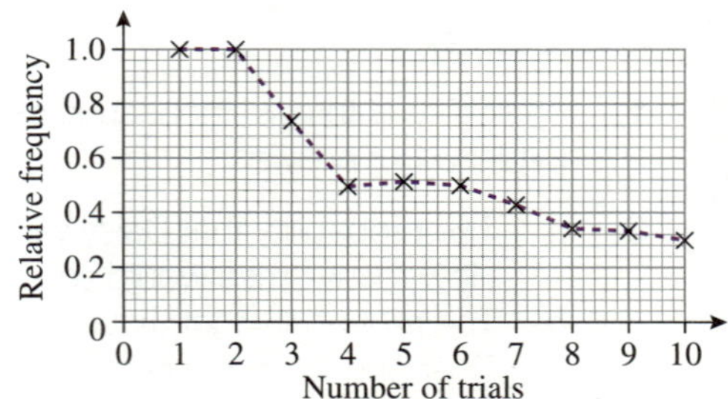

b Bag B contains 80 counters.
The relative frequency of taking a blue counter from bag B is shown on this graph.
Estimate the number of blue counters in bag B.

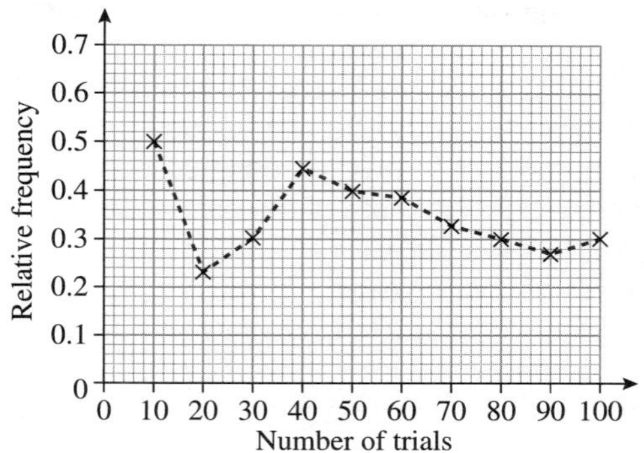

c Bag C contains 120 counters. 72 of the counters are blue.
Copy and complete this graph to show possible relative frequencies of taking a blue counter from bag C.

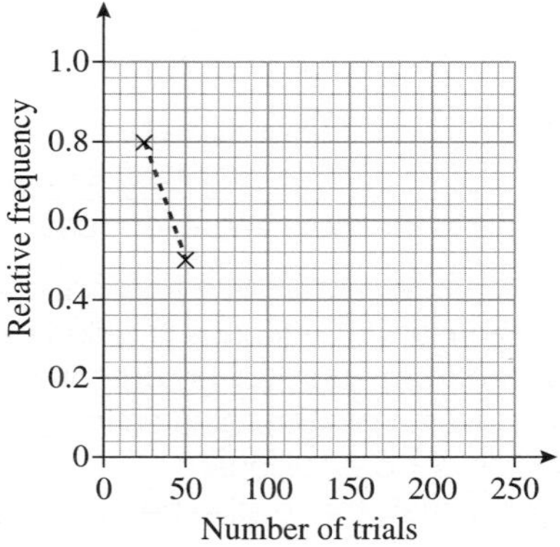

7 A survey of the age groups of 170 rail passengers is shown.

Age	16 or under	17–59	60 or over
Number of passengers	38	72	60

Estimate the number of passengers aged 17 or over on a train carrying 1000 passengers.

8 An internet shop has the following delivery charges:

Delivery	Super saver (5 days)	Saver (3 days)	Express (next day)
Charge	Free	£3.50	£5

Customer records show the following probabilities.
Probability that a customer chooses Super saver = 0.8
Probability that a customer chooses Saver = 0.15
On average, the company makes 2320 deliveries per month.

a Estimate the average number of Express deliveries each month.

b Estimate the average amount the company receives in delivery charges each month.

9 Matthew throws darts at a target.
His results are shown in this table.

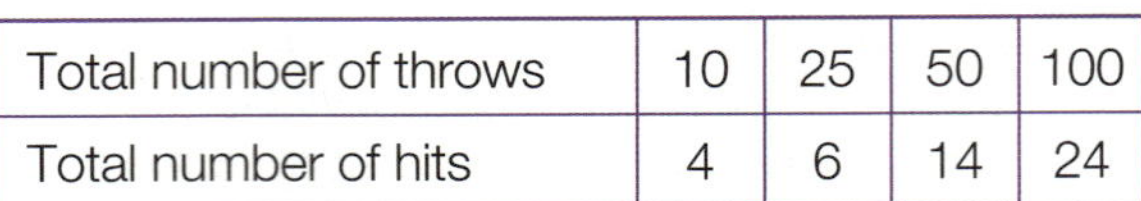

Total number of throws	10	25	50	100
Total number of hits	4	6	14	24

a Work out the relative frequency that Matthew hits the target after:
i 10 throws **ii** 25 throws

iii 50 throws **iv** 100 throws.

b On a copy of this grid draw a graph to show how the relative frequency of a hit changes as the total number of throws increases.

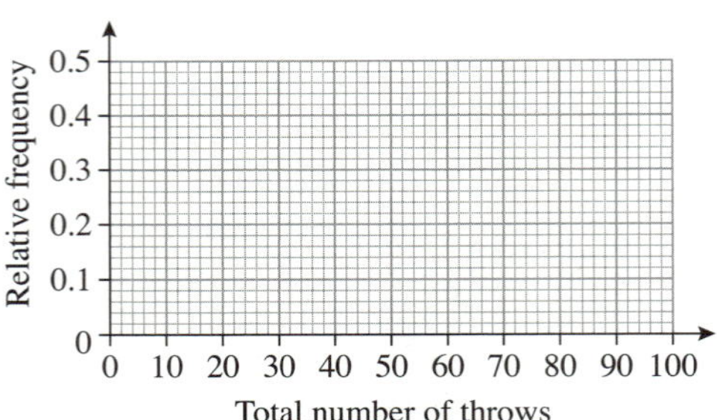

c Write down the best estimate of the probability that Matthew hits the target.
Give a reason for your answer.

d During one week Matthew throws darts at the target 1000 times.
Estimate the number of hits he gets.

Chapter summary

- A two-way table shows two linked sets of information.
- Probabilities can be estimated from the results of an experiment or a survey using relative frequency.
- The relative frequency of an event is:

$$\frac{\text{number of times the event occurs in an experiment (or survey)}}{\text{total number of trials in the experiment (or observations in the survey)}}$$

- Relative frequency can be written as a fraction, decimal or a percentage.
- Probability based on relative frequency is called experimental probability.
  Probability calculated from equally likely outcomes is called theoretical probability.
- Relative frequency gives a more reliable estimate of probability when its value is based on a large number of trials or observations.
- For a large number of trials the relative frequency gives a reliable estimate of the theoretical probability.
- Estimated number of successful outcomes = probability × total number of trials
- Relative frequency and theoretical probability can be used to estimate the result of an experiment.
- The larger the number of trials in the experiment, the more accurate the prediction.
- If a situation is fair, the relative frequency for a large number of trials is close to the theoretical probability.
- If the relative frequency for a large number of trials is not close to the theoretical probability, the situation could be unfair or biased.

Chapter review

1 40 families are asked how many adults there are in the family and how many cars the family owns. The two-way table shows the results.

a How many families own two cars?
b How many families have four adults?
c How many households have the same number of cars as adults?

	1 adult	2 adults	3 adults	4 adults
1 car	6	4	2	0
2 cars	1	4	8	1
3 cars	0	1	3	3
4 cars	0	1	1	5

2 The diagram shows a fair spinner.
The results of the first ten spins are:

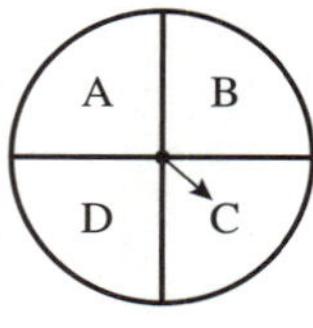

A B C A B D C C D B

a What is the relative frequency of the letter C?
b Describe what will happen to the relative frequency of the letter C as the number of spins increases.

3 25 students each shuffle a pack of cards labelled A, B, C and D and choose a card at random.
A list of the cards chosen is shown.

A B B C D C D B A A B D A
A B A A C D B C A B A D

a Work out the relative frequency of each letter.
b Estimate the number of times that a letter A is likely to be chosen if 100 students choose a letter at random.

4 James takes a bead at random from a box of coloured beads.
He records its colour and then puts the bead back in the box.
He repeats this trial 300 times. The table shows his results.

Colour	Red	Blue	Green	White
Frequency	81	90	114	15

a What is the relative frequency of James taking a red bead from the box?
b There are 500 beads in the box.
Estimate the number of red beads in the box.

5 Kali has a spinner with coloured sections of equal size.
She does an experiment to find the probability that her spinner lands on blue.
In her experiment Kali spins the spinner 100 times.
She works out the relative frequency of a blue after every ten spins.
Her results are shown on the graph.

a Use the graph to work out the number of times that the spinner lands on blue:
i after the first ten spins
ii after the first 50 spins.

b Estimate the probability of the spinner landing on blue.

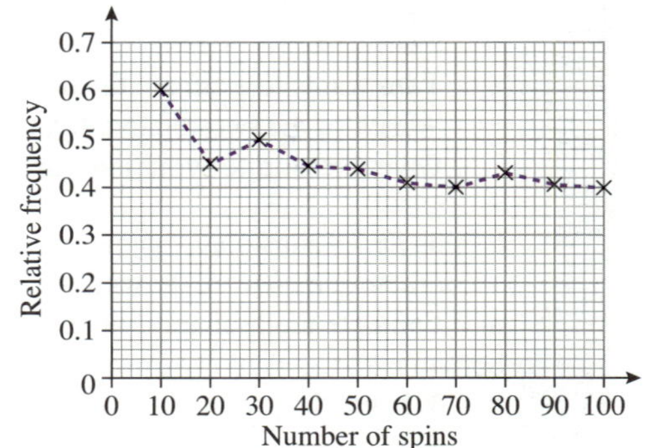

6 A circular spinner has a red sector (R) and a blue sector (B).
The arrow is spun 1000 times.

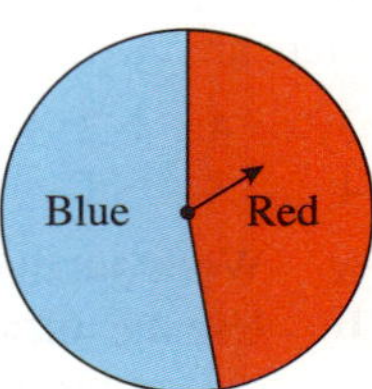

a The results for the first ten spins are:

R R B B B R B B B R

Work out the relative frequency of the spinner landing on red after ten spins.

b The table shows the relative frequency of the spinner landing on red after different numbers of spins.

Number of spins	Relative frequency of a red
50	0.42
100	0.35
200	0.36
500	0.3
1000	0.31

i How many times did the spinner land on red after 500 spins?
ii Give an estimate of the probability of a red.
Explain your answer.

7 A circular spinner has sections coloured red (R), white (W) and blue (B).
The spinner is spun 20 times. The results are shown below.

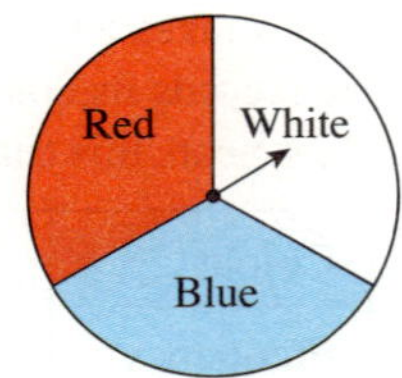

R	R	B	W	W	R	B
W	W	R	W	B	W	B
W	R	W	B	W	B	

a Copy and complete the relative frequency table.

Colour	Red (R)	White (W)	Blue (B)
Relative frequency			

b The table shows the relative frequencies after the spinner has been spun 200 times.

Colour	Red (R)	White (W)	Blue (B)
Relative frequency	$\frac{42}{200}$	$\frac{102}{200}$	$\frac{56}{200}$

Tom wants to estimate the probability of the spinner landing on red.
Which of the two relative frequencies for red should he use?
Give a reason for your answer.

8 Serena and Venus play a game of cards. They have played 150 times before.
15 of their games were drawn.
a Estimate the probability that their next game will be drawn.
Serena is twice as likely to win as Venus.
b What is the probability that Venus wins?

9 It is suspected that a dice is unfair.
Here are the results of 20 throws.

3	4	2	3	1	5	6	2	4	3
4	3	1	1	6	2	5	6	5	3

a Work out the relative frequency of each score.
b Use the relative frequency of a 3 to estimate the number of scores of 3 you are likely to obtain with 60 throws of the dice.
c Compare the answer to **b** with the most likely number of scores of 3 you obtain with 60 throws of a fair dice.

10 Matthew has a dice with three red faces, two blue faces and one green face.
He throws the dice 300 times and gets:

153 reds   98 blues   49 greens

a What is the relative frequency of throwing red?

b Is the dice fair?
Explain your answer.

c Emmie has a dice with four red faces and two blue faces.
She throws the dice ten times and gets two reds.
Emmie says the dice is biased.
Explain why Emmie could be wrong.

11 Tim, Sam and Joe carry out this experiment with the same bag of ten counters.

> *Take a counter from the bag at random.*
> *Record its colour.*
> *Replace the counter in the bag.*
> *Repeat this trial a number of times.*

Their results are shown in this table.
Estimate the number of each different coloured counter in the box.
State the set of results that you use to make the estimate.
Give a reason for your choice.

Name of pupil	Number of trials	Colour of counters		
		Black	White	Green
Tim	10	0	7	3
Sam	40	4	17	19
Joe	200	23	78	99

CHAPTER

9 Perimeter and area

9.1 Area of parallelograms and triangles

CAN YOU REMEMBER

- The formula for the area of a rectangle: area = length $\times$ width?
- That area is measured in square units, e.g. cm^2, mm^2, m^2, km^2?

IN THIS SECTION YOU WILL

- Understand how the formulae for the area of a parallelogram and area of a triangle can be worked out from the formula for the area of a rectangle.
- Learn the meaning of 'base' and 'perpendicular height'.
- Calculate the area of triangles and parallelograms.
- Use area formulae to work out lengths in triangles and parallelograms.

The diagram shows a rectangle drawn on centimetre-squared paper.
There are ten squares in the rectangle.
Area of rectangle = length $\times$ width = $10\,cm^2$

This parallelogram is drawn on centimetre-squared paper.

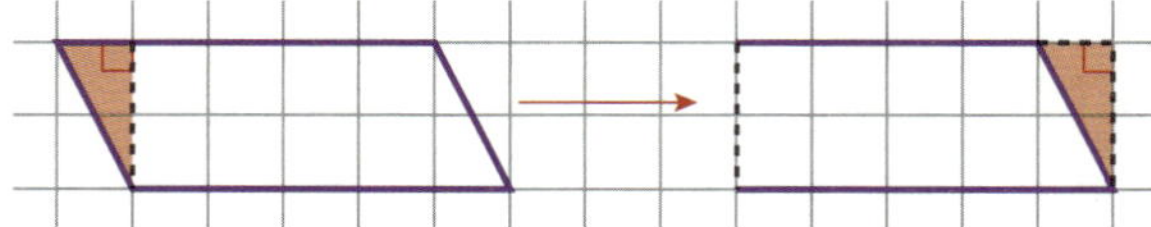

The shaded triangle is cut from one end of the parallelogram.
It fits onto the other end to form a rectangle.

Area of parallelogram = area of rectangle = $10\,cm^2$

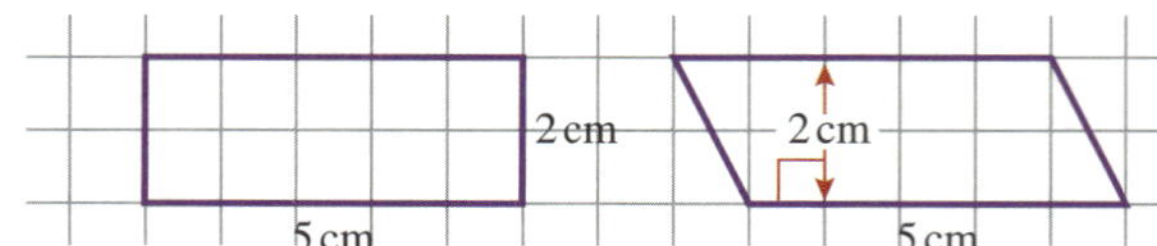

The *base* of the parallelogram is 5 cm.
The *perpendicular height* is at right angles to the base.
The perpendicular height of this parallelogram is 2 cm.
The area of the parallelogram can be calculated using the formula

area = base $\times$ perpendicular height

Example 1

Find the area of each of these parallelograms.

a

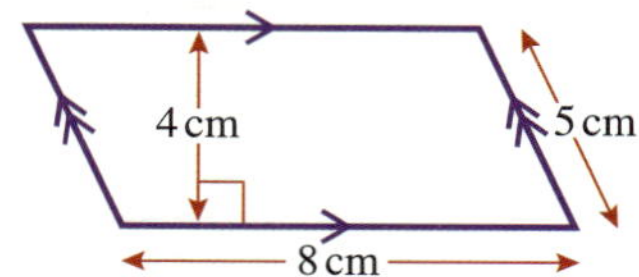

b

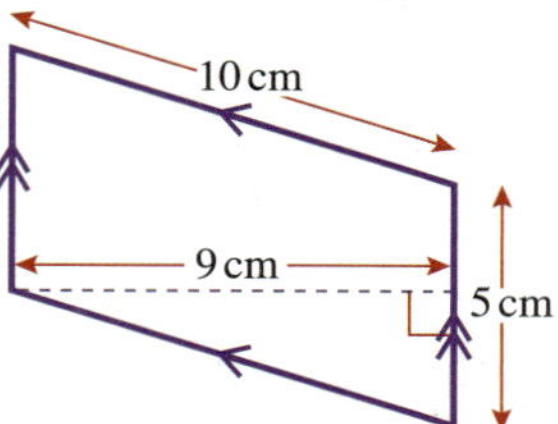

Solution 1

a base = 8 cm,
perpendicular height = 4 cm
(The 5 cm measurement is not used.)
area = base × perpendicular height
= 8 × 4 = 32 cm²

4 cm perpendicular height 5 cm
8 cm base

b The base must be at right angles to the height.
So base = 5 cm, perpendicular height = 9 cm.
(The 10 cm measurement is not used.)
area = base × perpendicular height
= 5 × 9 = 45 cm²

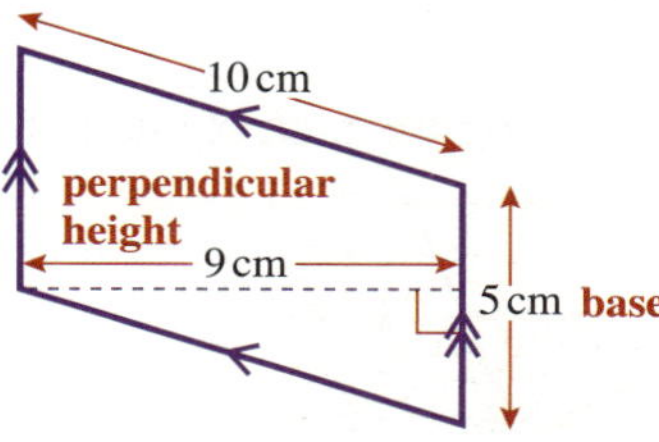

In the diagram, a diagonal has been drawn on the rectangle and the parallelogram.

The diagonal divides each shape into two triangles of the same size and area.
The area of each triangle is half the area of the rectangle or parallelogram.
This gives the formula for the area of a triangle:

area of triangle = $\frac{1}{2}$ × base × perpendicular height

$$A = \frac{1}{2}bh$$

Example 2

Calculate the area of this triangle.

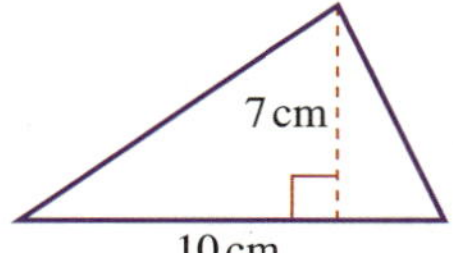

Solution 2

base = 10 cm, perpendicular height = 7 cm
area = $\frac{1}{2}$ × base × perpendicular height
= $\frac{1}{2}$ × 10 × 7 = 35 cm²

Exercise A

1 Work out the area of each of these parallelograms.

a
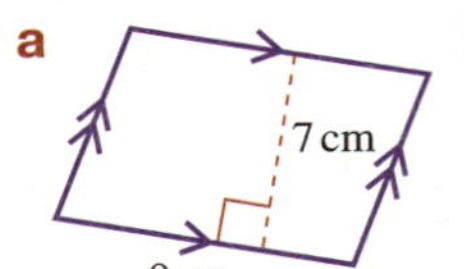

b
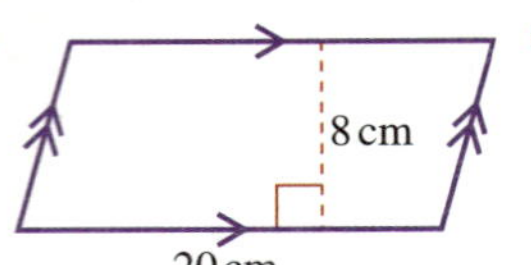

c
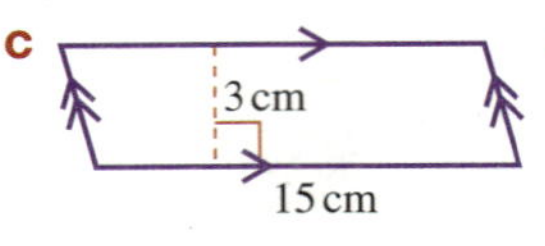

d
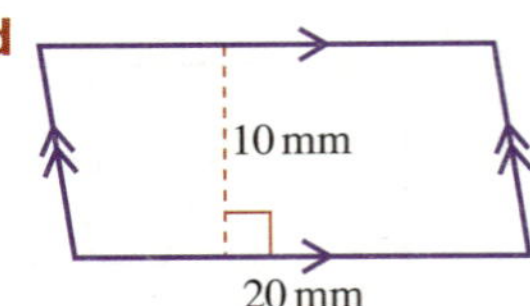

2 Find the area of each of these parallelograms.

a
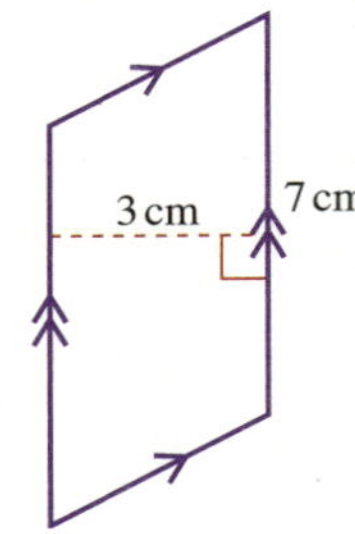

b
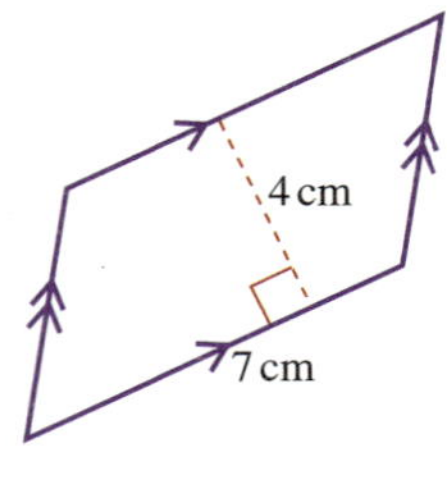

c
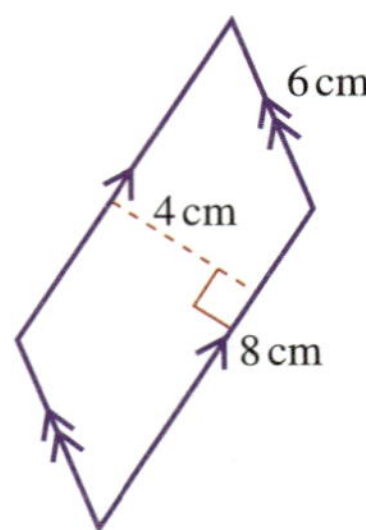

d
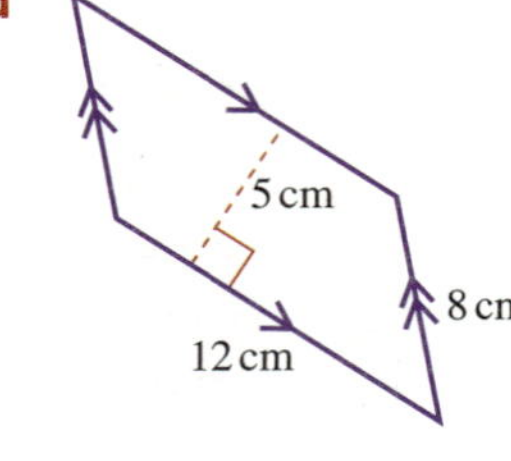

3 Find the area of each of these triangles.

a
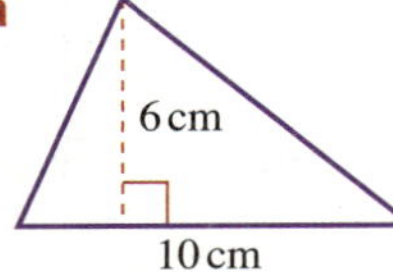

b
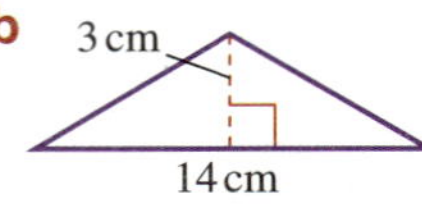

c
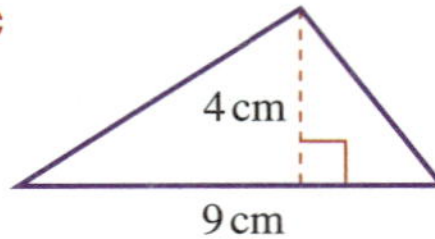

d
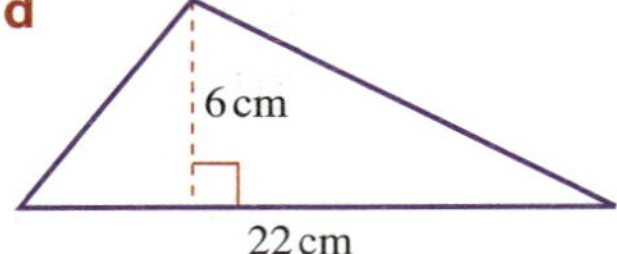

4 Find the area of each of these triangles.

a
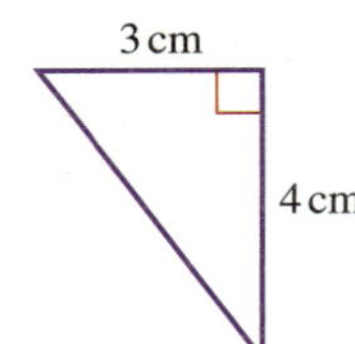

b
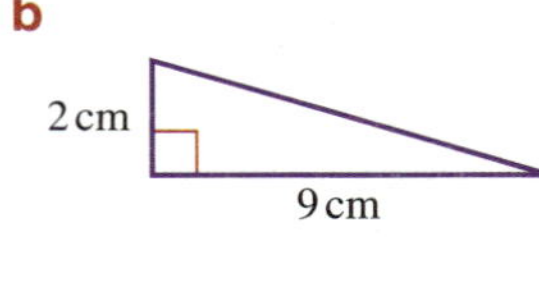

c
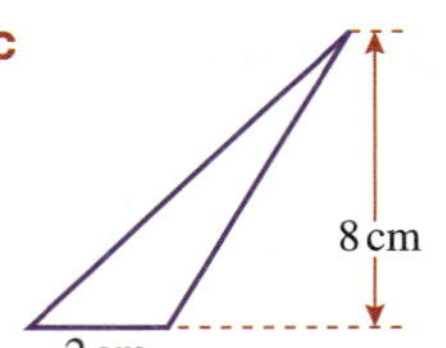

d
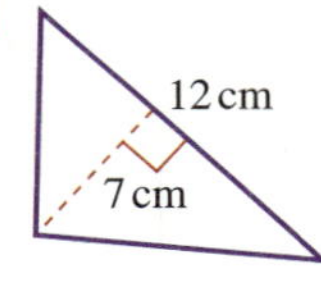

5 Find the area of each of these shapes.

a
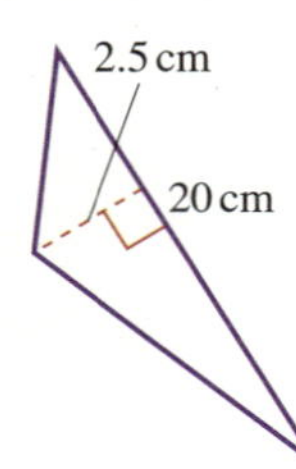

b
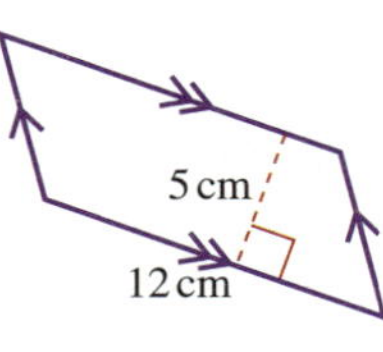

c
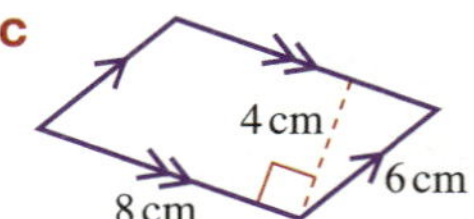

d
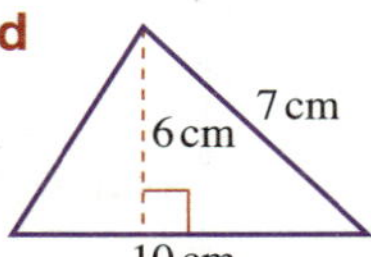

6 Calculate the area of each of these parallelograms.

a
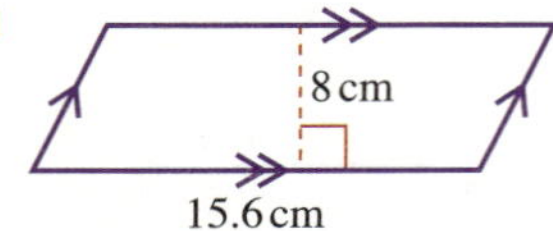

b
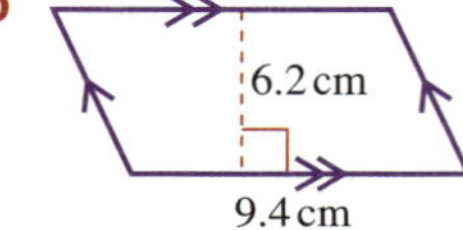

c
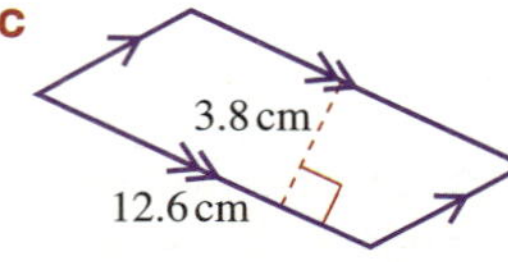

d
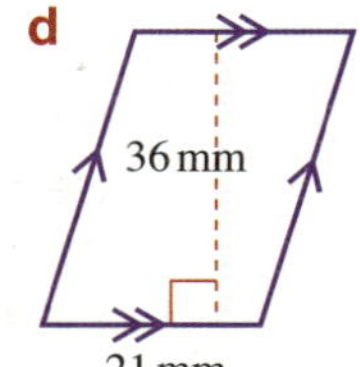

7 Calculate the area of each of these parallelograms.

a
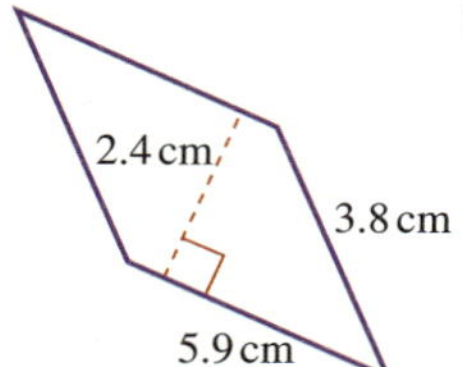

b
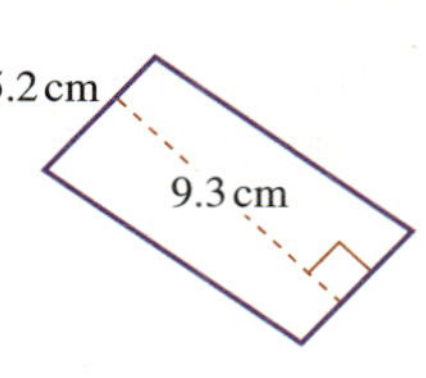

c
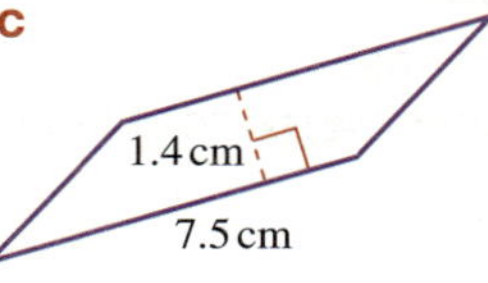

d
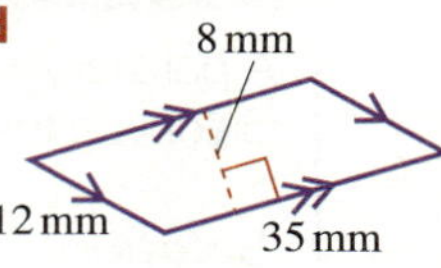

8 Calculate the area of each of these triangles.

a
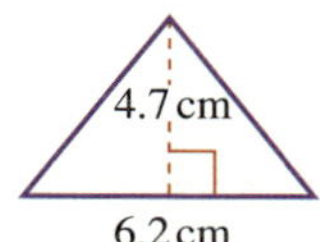

b
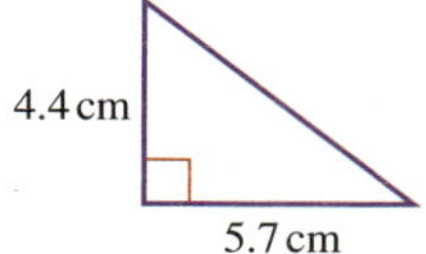

c
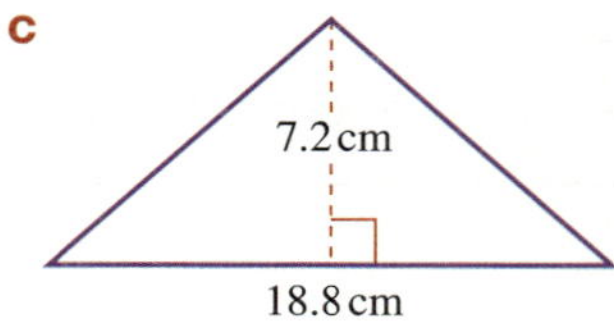

d
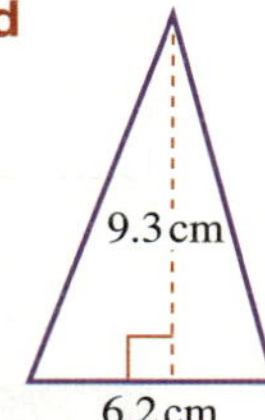

9 Calculate the area of each of these triangles.

a
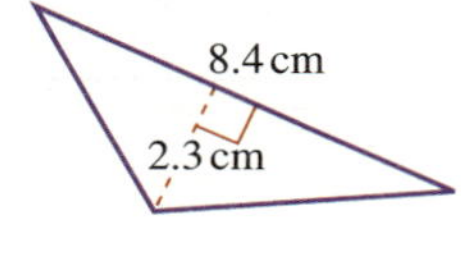

b
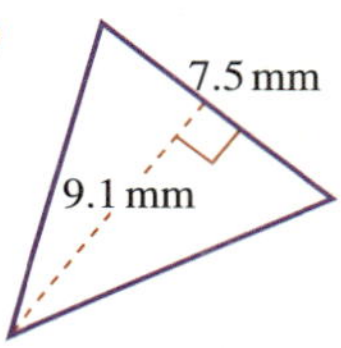

c
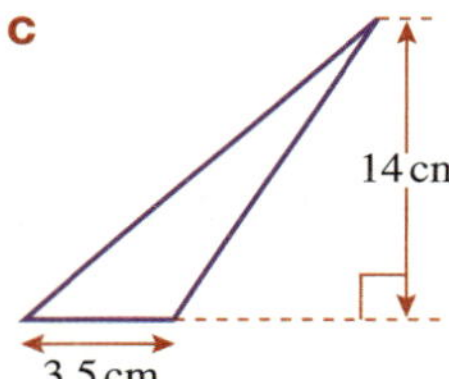

d
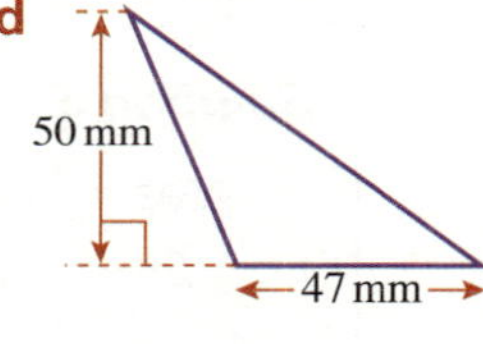

10 Calculate the area of these shapes.

a
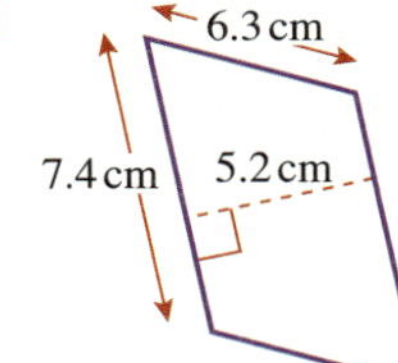

b
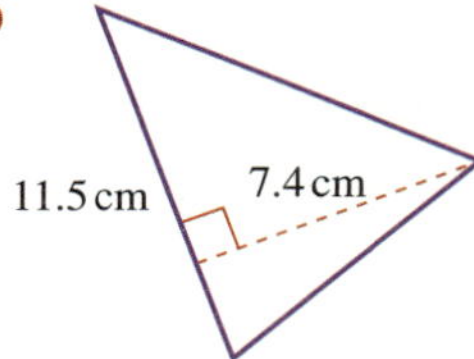

c
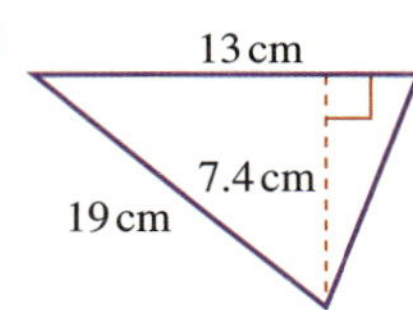

d
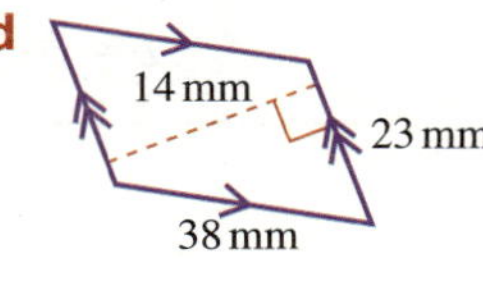

Example 3

Calculate the area of the parallelogram.
Give your answer in square centimetres.

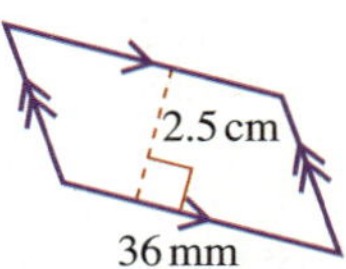

Solution 3

The base is 36 mm.
The perpendicular height is 2.5 cm.
The two measurements are given in different units.
Convert 36 mm to centimetres: 10 mm = 1 cm

36 mm = 36 ÷ 10 = 3.6 cm

Area = base × perpendicular height = $3.6 \times 2.5 = 9\ \text{cm}^2$

Example 4

A parallelogram of base 20 cm has an area of 280 cm^2
Calculate the perpendicular height of the parallelogram.

Solution 4

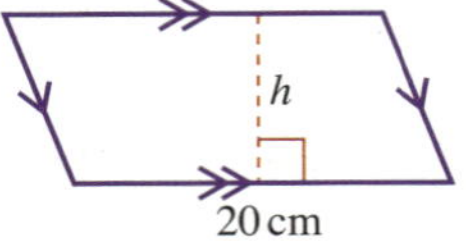

Area = base × perpendicular height
$280 = 20 \times h$
$280 \div 20 = h$ — Dividing both sides by 20
$14 = h$

The perpendicular height is 14 cm.

Example 5

The area of this triangle is 24 cm^2
Calculate the length of the base, b, of the triangle.

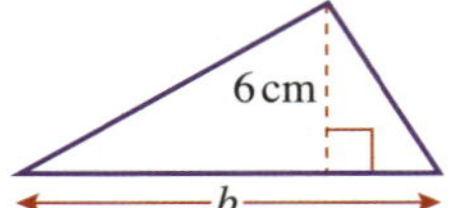

Solution 5

Area = $\frac{1}{2}$ base × perpendicular height
$24 = \frac{1}{2} \times b \times 6$
$24 \div 6 = \frac{1}{2} \times b$ — Dividing both sides by 6
$4 = \frac{1}{2} \times b$
$4 \times 2 = b$ — Multiplying both sides by 2
$b = 8$ cm

Exercise B

1 Calculate the area of each of these shapes.
Give your answers in square centimetres.

a
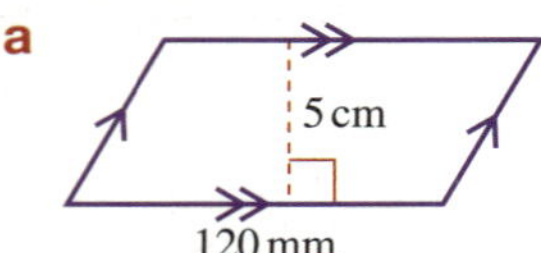

b

c
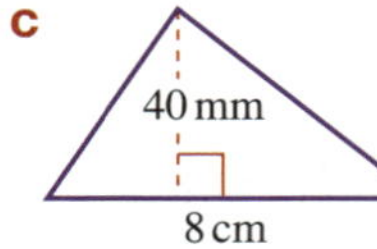

d
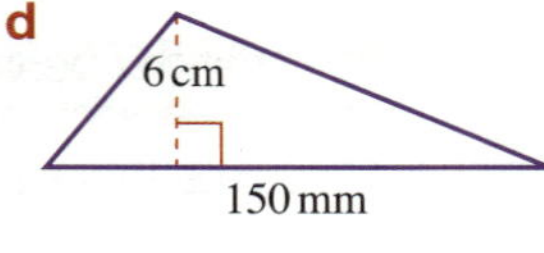

2 Which of the following shapes has the largest area?
Show your working.

a
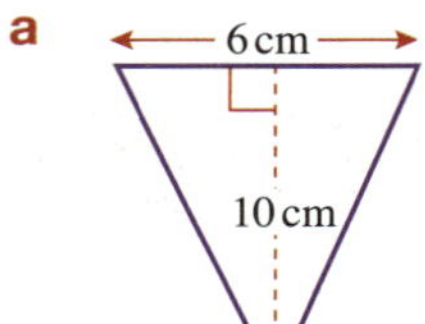

b

c
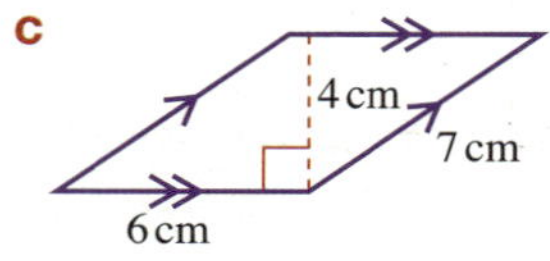

3 Three of these shapes have the same area. Which is the odd one out? Show your working.

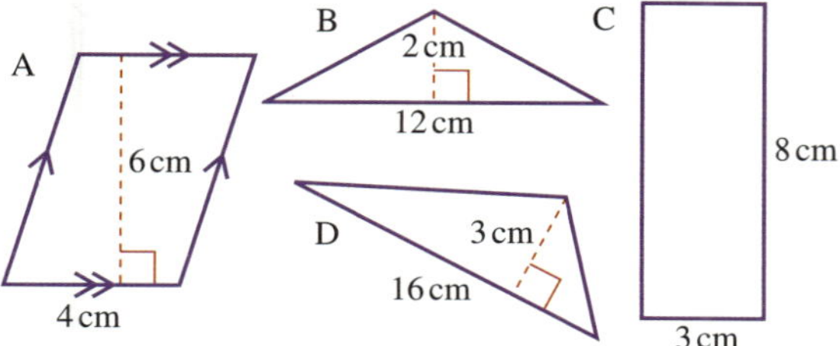

4 A parallelogram has an area of 75 cm^2 If the base of the parallelogram is 25 cm, what is the perpendicular height?

5 A triangle has a base of 14 cm. The area of the triangle is 70 cm^2 Calculate the perpendicular height of the triangle.

6 A parallelogram of base 14.6 cm has an area of 124.1 cm^2 Calculate the perpendicular height of the parallelogram.

7 A triangle of base 10 cm and perpendicular height 8.5 cm is cut from a rectangle of length 14 cm and width 12 cm. What area of the rectangle is left?

8 A triangle has a perpendicular height of 26 cm. If the area of the triangle is 447 cm^2, what is the length of the base of the triangle? Give your answer to one decimal place.

9 An arrowhead is made from two parallelograms of the same size. Calculate the area of the arrowhead.

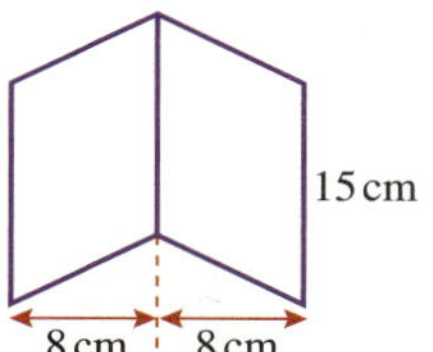

10 Mr Green's lawn is in the shape of a parallelogram. Mr Green sows each square metre with 40 grams of grass seed. The seed costs £1.05 for 140 grams. Calculate the cost of the grass seed.

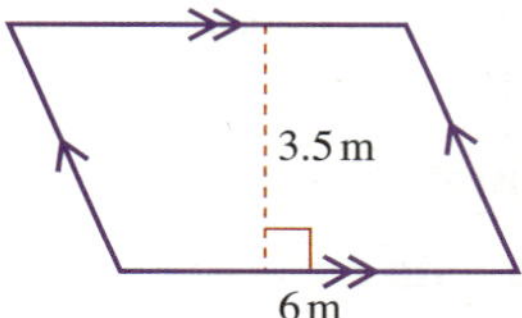

9.2 Circle definitions and circumference

CAN YOU REMEMBER

- That the perimeter is the distance around a shape?
- That the circumference of a circle is the distance around the edge or the perimeter of the circle?
- That the centre of the circle is an equal distance from every point on the circumference?
- That the diameter is a line across the circle passing through the centre?

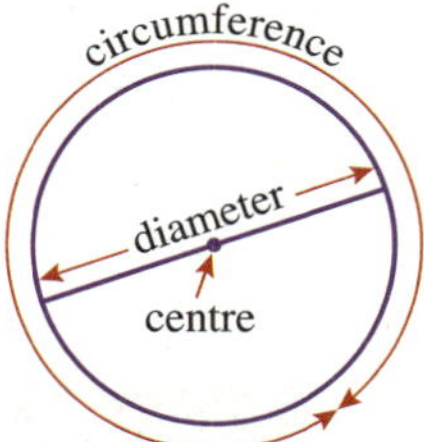

IN THIS SECTION YOU WILL

- Recognise and name parts of a circle.
- Calculate the circumference of a circle or part of a circle.

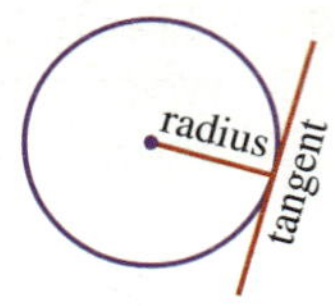

The *radius* is a straight line from the centre to any point on the circumference. So the length of the radius is half the length of the diameter. The plural of radius is *radii.*

A *tangent* is a straight line outside the circle that touches the circle at only one point.

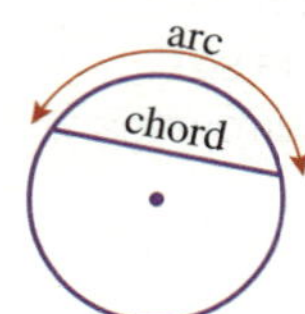

A *chord* is a straight line that joins any two points on the circumference.
An *arc* is a section of the circumference.

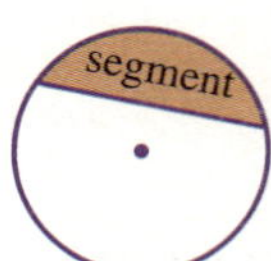

A *segment* is an area between a chord and an arc.
A *sector* is an area between two radii and an arc.

Circumference of a circle

The circumference of a circle can be calculated accurately using the formulae:

$C = \pi d$ or $C = 2\pi r$

where d is the diameter, r is the radius and π (pi) is the Greek letter which represents a value of 3.1415 ...

To **estimate** the area use $\pi = 3$

To **calculate** the area use $\pi = 3.14$ or the π button on a calculator.

Example 1

Estimate the circumference of a circle with diameter 5 cm.
Take the value of π to be 3

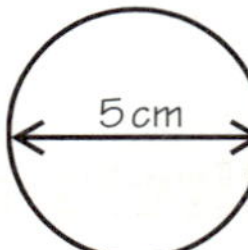

Solution 1

Using $C = \pi d$
$C = 3 \times 5 = 15$ cm

Using $C = 2\pi r$
$d = 5$ cm, so $r = 2.5$ cm
$C = 2 \times 3 \times 2.5 = 15$ cm

An estimate for the circumference is 15 cm.

Example 2

Find the circumference of a circle of radius 8 cm.
Leave your answer in terms of π.

Solution 2

$C = 2\pi r = 2 \times \pi \times 8 = 16\pi$ cm

Example 3

Calculate the circumference of a circle of radius 5 cm.
Take the value of π to be 3.14

Solution 3

Using $C = 2\pi r$

$r = 5$ cm

$C = 2 \times 3.14 \times 5 = 31.4$ cm

Using $C = \pi d$

$r = 5$ cm so $d = 10$ cm

$C = 3.14 \times 10 = 31.4$

The circumference is 31.4 cm.

Exercise A

1 Copy each diagram and write the names of the parts of the circle in the boxes.

a

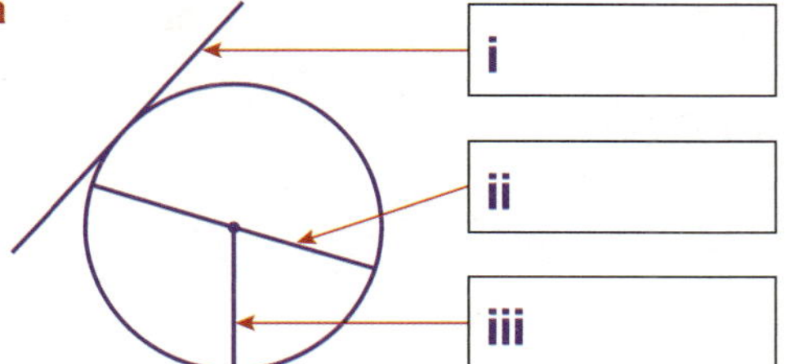

b

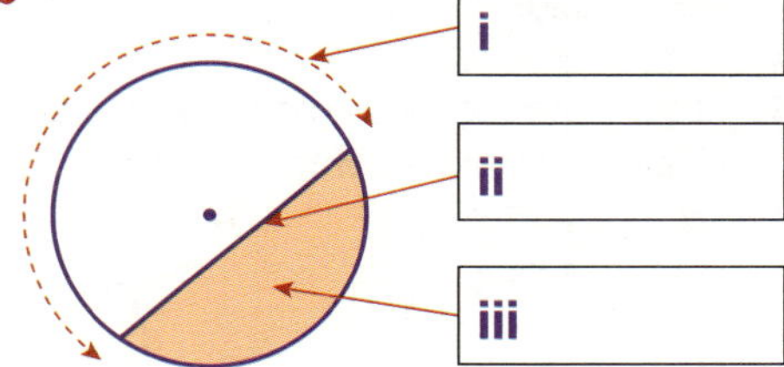

2 Copy and complete these statements with the correct word.

a The .... is a special name for the perimeter of a circle.

b The shaded area between a chord and an arc is called a ....

c A straight line from the centre of a circle to a point on the edge of the circle is called a ....

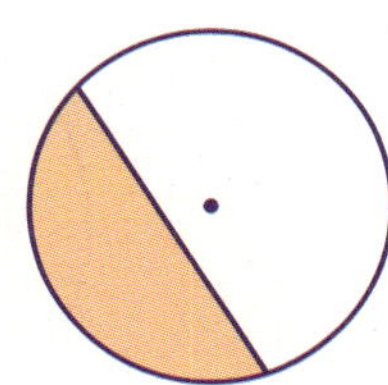

3 Estimate the circumference of these circles.

Take the value of π to be 3

a

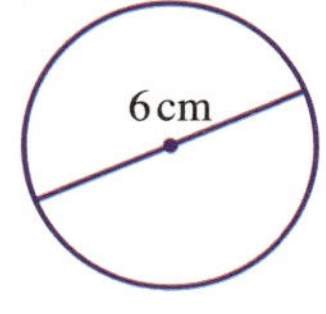

b

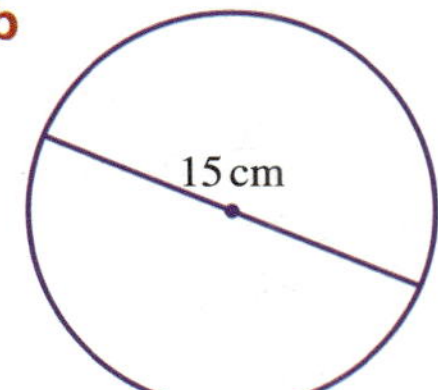

c

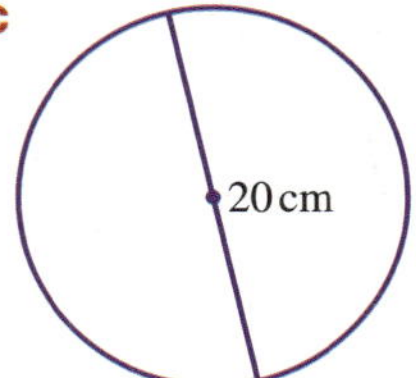

d

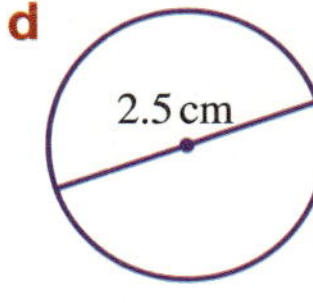

e

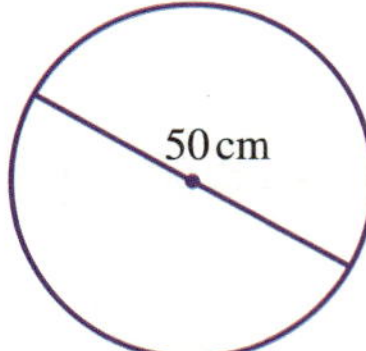

f

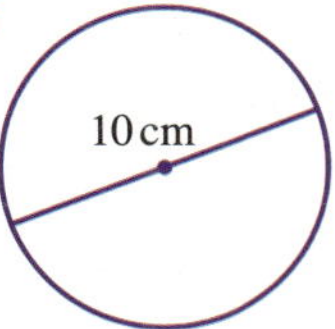

g

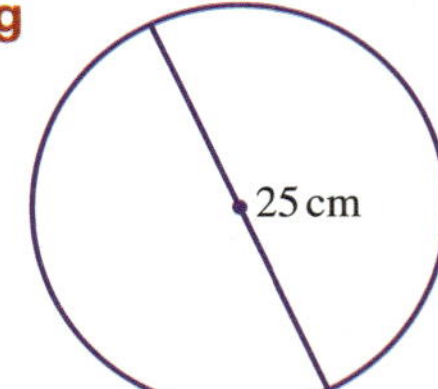

h

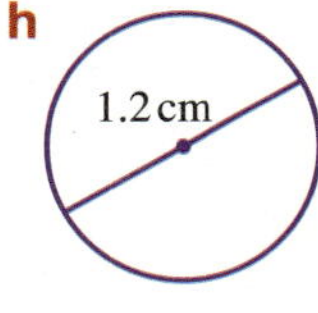

4 Estimate the circumference of these circles. Take the value of π to be 3

a 4 cm
b 1.5 cm
c 25 cm
d 10 cm
e 16 mm
f 7 cm
g 50 mm
h 11 cm

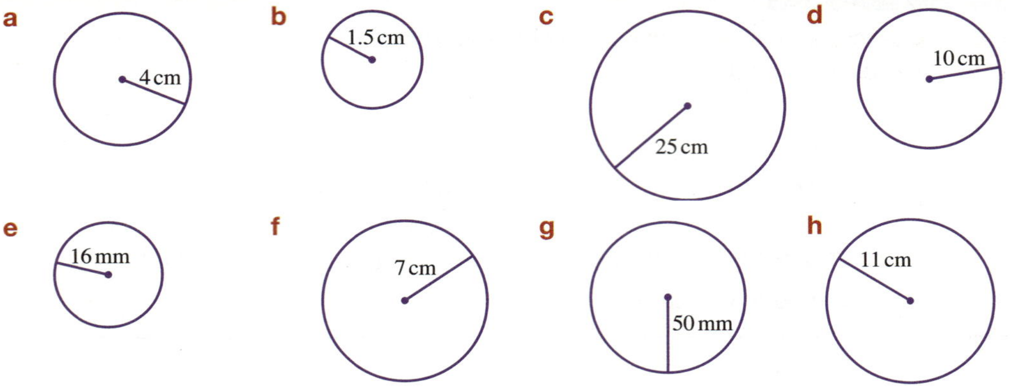

5 Calculate the circumference of each of the following circles.
Leave your answers in terms of π.

a	diameter =	**i** 12 cm	**ii** 17 cm	**iii** 35 cm
b	radius =	**i** 4.5 cm	**ii** 22 cm	**iii** 7.1 cm

6 Calculate the circumference of each of these circles.
Take the value of π to be 3.14

a 4.9 cm
b 15.7 cm
c 11.5 cm
d 124 mm
e 36.5 cm
f 0.45 cm
g 22 cm
h 13.6 cm

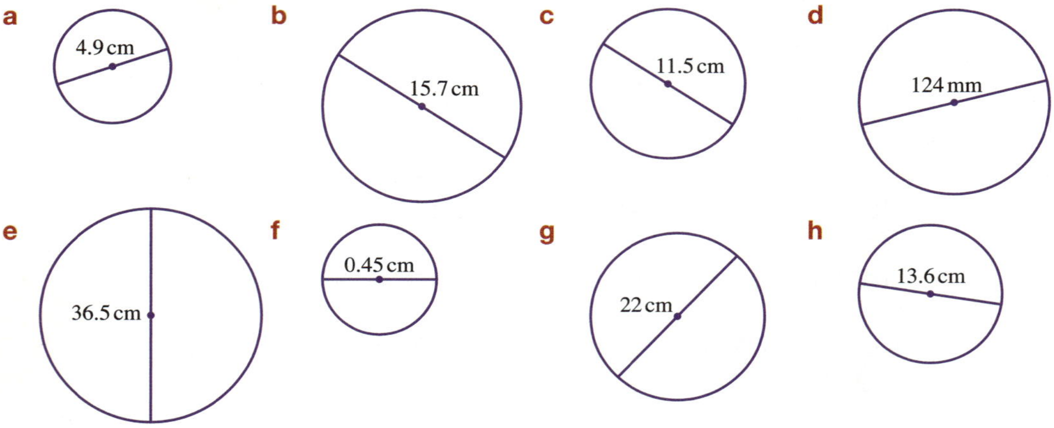

7 Calculate the circumference of each of these circles.
Take the value of π to be 3.14

a 3.4 cm
b 9.6 cm
c 0.8 cm
d 10.5 cm
e 12.5 mm
f 105 mm
g 14.1 cm
h 0.3 cm

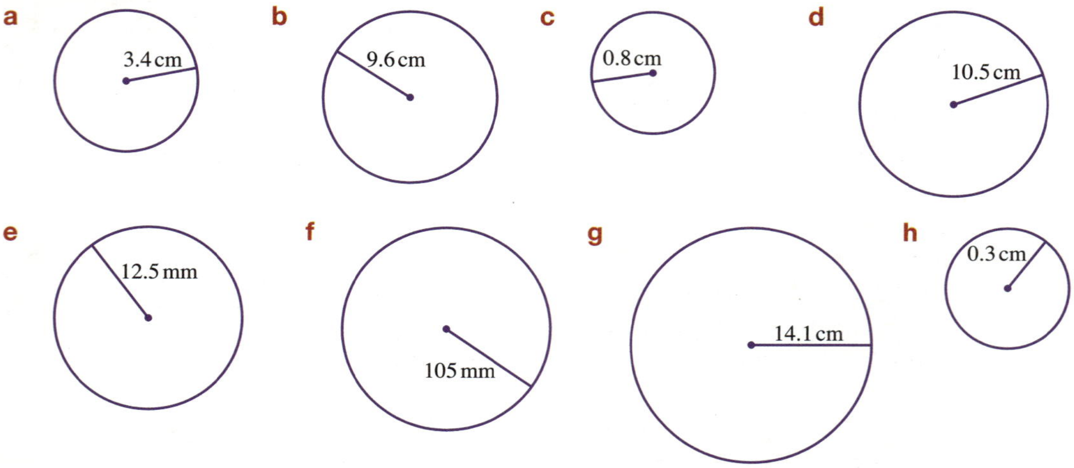

In questions **8–10** use the π button on a calculator.

8 Calculate the circumference of each of these circles.
Give your answers to one decimal place.

a

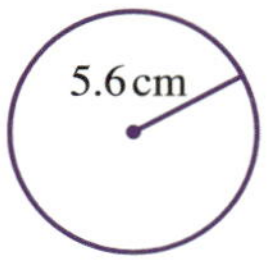

b

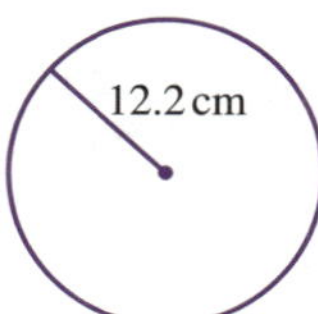

c

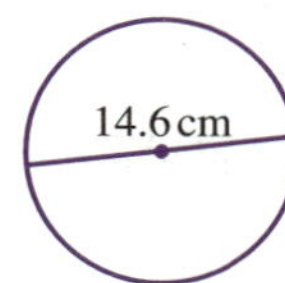

d

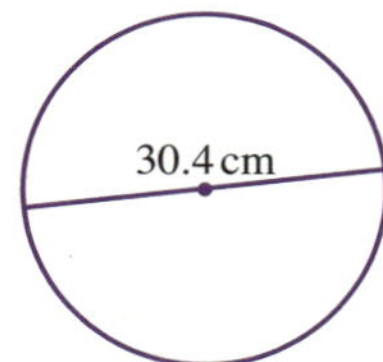

e

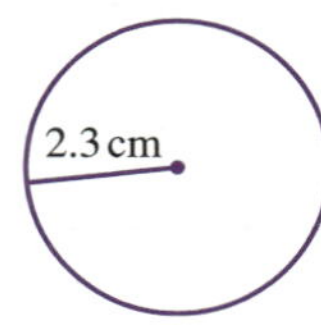

f

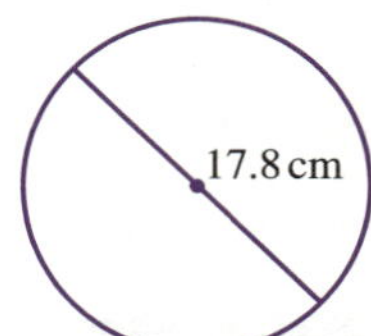

9 The radius of a bicycle wheel is 56 cm.
What is the circumference of the wheel?
Give your answer to the nearest whole number.

10

A ten-pence piece has a diameter of 2.8 cm.
Work out the circumference of the ten-pence piece.
Give your answer to one decimal place.

Example 4

A doormat is in the shape of a semicircle of diameter 75 cm.

Calculate the perimeter of the mat.

Give your answer to the nearest centimetre.

Solution 4

Perimeter of the mat = circumference of half a circle + straight side of 75 cm

So $P = \dfrac{\text{circumference}}{2} + 75$

Circumference of circle diameter 75 cm = $\pi \times 75 = 235.619\,449$ cm

Perimeter of the mat $= \dfrac{235.619\,449}{2} + 75 = 192.809\,724\,5$

$= 193$ cm (to the nearest cm)

Example 5

Calculate the perimeter of this shape.

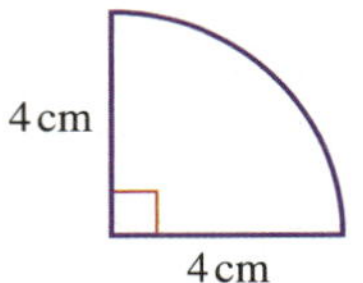

Solution 5

The shape is one quarter of a circle of radius 4 cm.
Perimeter = circumference of quarter circle + the lengths of the two straight sides

So perimeter $= \dfrac{\text{circumference}}{4} + 4 + 4$

Circumference of a circle of radius 4 cm $= 2 \times \pi \times 4 = 25.132\,741$ cm

Perimeter of the shape $= \dfrac{25.132\,741}{4} + 8 = 14.283\,185 = 14.3$ cm (to 1 d.p.)

Example 6

The circumference of a circle is 36 cm. Calculate the diameter of this circle.

Solution 6

$C = \pi d$, so $36 = \pi \times d$

$\dfrac{36}{\pi} = d$ — Dividing both sides by π.

$11.459\,155 = d$

The diameter is 11.46 cm (to 2 d.p.).

Example 7

The circumference of a circle is 40.84 cm. Calculate the radius of this circle.

Solution 7

$C = 2\pi r$, so $40.84 = 2 \times \pi \times r$

$\dfrac{40.84}{\pi} = 2 \times r$ — Dividing both sides by π.

$12.999\,775 = 2 \times r$

$6.499\,888 = r$ — Dividing both sides by 2

The radius is 6.5 cm (to 1 d.p.).

Exercise B

1 Estimate the diameter of each of the circles with the following circumferences.
Take π to be 3

a 21 cm **b** 333 cm **c** 96 mm **d** 0.6 m

2 Estimate the radius of each of the circles with the following circumferences.
Take π to be 3

a 66 cm **b** 12.6 cm **c** 186 mm **d** 0.9 m

3 A wheel of diameter 70 cm makes five complete revolutions.
How far does the wheel travel? Leave your answer in terms of π.

4 Ann has four circular pillowcases and a roll of ribbon. Each pillowcase has a radius of 11 cm.
Ann sews ribbon around the circumference of each pillowcase.
How many centimetres of ribbon does she need? Leave your answer in terms of π.

In questions **5–10** use the π button on your calculator.

5 Find the perimeter of these shapes. Give your answers to two decimal places.

a

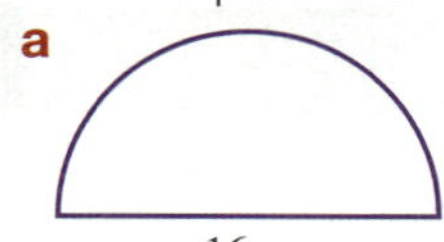

semicircle

b

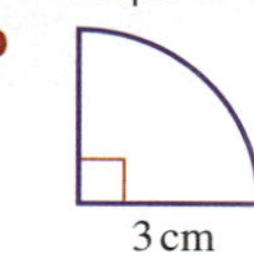

quarter circle

c

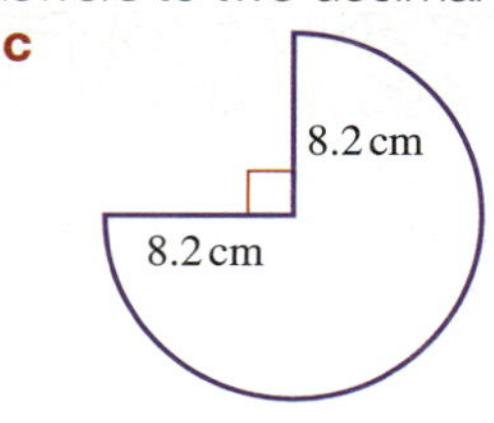

three-quarter circle

d

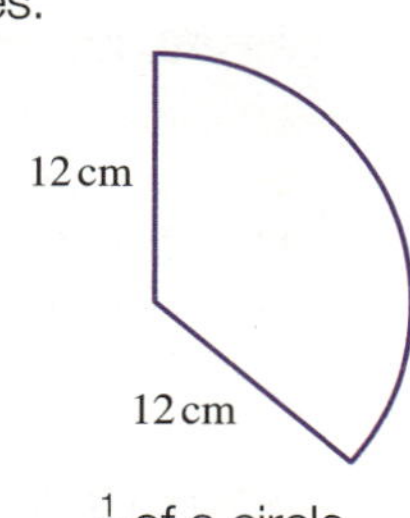

$\frac{1}{3}$ of a circle

6 Calculate the diameter of each of the circles with the following circumferences.
Give your answers to one decimal place.

a 13.7 cm **b** 46.8 cm **c** 804 mm **d** 2.85 m

7 Calculate the radius of each of the circles with the following circumferences.
Give your answers to two decimal places.

a 4.72 cm **b** 112 mm **c** 0.475 m **d** 76.45 cm

8 A circular sweet tin has a diameter of 14.2 cm.
The lid is sealed with tape. The ends of the tape overlap by 2 cm.
Calculate the length of tape needed to seal the tin.

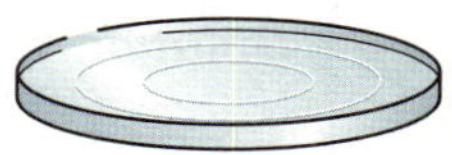

9 A cycling track has two straight sections of length 150 m and two semicircular ends of diameter 65 m.

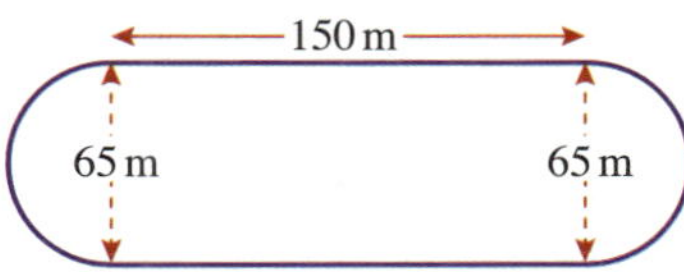

Jacob says that three times round the track is greater than 1500 metres.
Is he correct? Show your working.

10 A bicycle wheel has a diameter of 30 cm.
Calculate the number of complete revolutions made by the wheel when the bicycle travels 50 metres.

9.3 Area of a circle

CAN YOU REMEMBER

- That π represents the number 3.1415 ... and can be approximated depending on the accuracy required?
- That area is measured in square units, e.g. mm^2, cm^2, m^2, km^2?
- That the radius of a circle is half the length of the diameter?
- That the area of a rectangle = length × width?

IN THIS SECTION YOU WILL

- Use a formula to calculate the area of circles, semicircles and quarter circles.
- Calculate the area of shapes made from parts of circles and rectangles.

The area of a circle can be found using the formula

area = $\pi \times (\text{radius})^2$ or $A = \pi r^2$

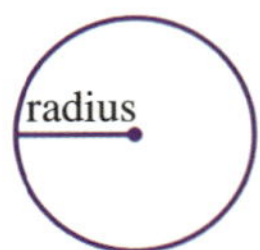

Example 1

Work out the area of a circle of radius 4 cm.
Leave your answer in terms of π.
Remember to state the units in your answer.

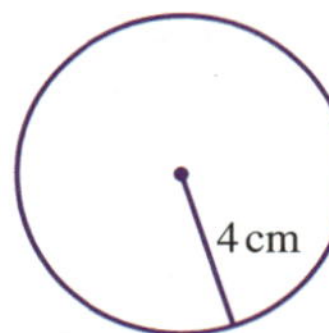

Solution 1

$A = \pi r^2 = \pi \times 4^2 = \pi \times 4 \times 4 = 16\pi$

Area of circle = 16π cm^2

Example 2

Calculate the area of a circle of diameter 5.6 mm.

Solution 2

Diameter = 5.6 mm, so radius = 5.6 mm ÷ 2 = 2.8 mm

$A = \pi r^2 = \pi \times 2.8^2 = \pi \times 2.8 \times 2.8$

$= 24.630\,086$

Using the π button on a calculator.

Area of circle = 24.63 mm^2 (to 2 d.p.)

Exercise A

For questions **1** and **2**, take π to be 3

1 Estimate the area of each of the following circles.

a

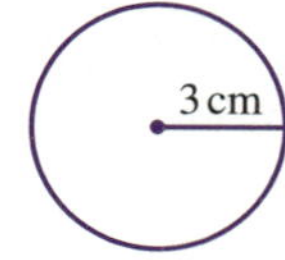

b

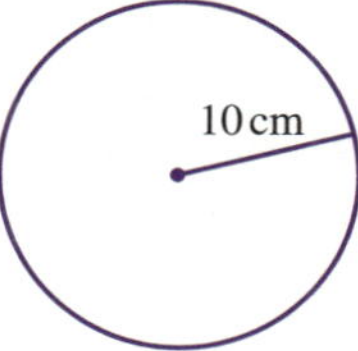

c

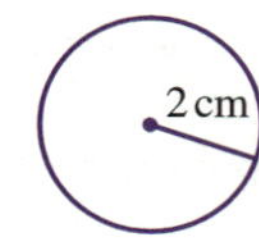

2 Estimate the area of each of the following circles.

a

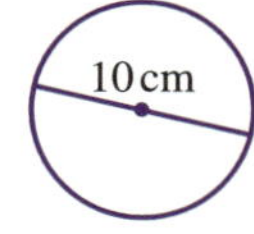

b

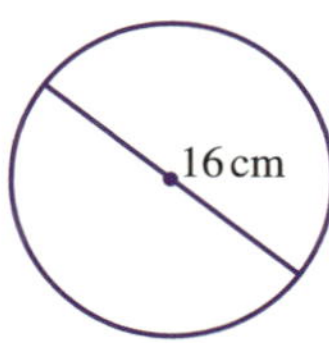

c

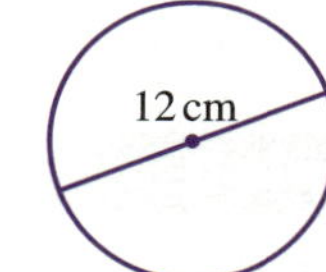

For questions **3** and **4**, leave your answers in terms of π.
State the units of your answers.

3 Work out the area of each of the circles with the following radii.
a 7 cm **b** 11 mm **c** 8 km **d** 15 cm **e** 9 m **f** 6 mm

4 Work out the area of each of the circles with the following diameters.
a 2 km **b** 8 cm **c** 24 mm **d** 6 m **e** 20 cm **f** 26 mm

For questions **5**–**7**, use $\pi = 3.14$ or the π button on a calculator.

5 Calculate the area of each of the following circles.
Give your answers to the nearest whole number.
a radius = 4.5 mm **b** radius = 17.4 cm **c** radius = 7.36 cm

6 Calculate the area of each of the following circles.
Give your answers to one decimal place.
a diameter = 26.2 cm **b** diameter = 4.06 cm **c** diameter = 104 mm

7 Calculate the area of each of the following circles.
Give your answer to two decimal places.

a

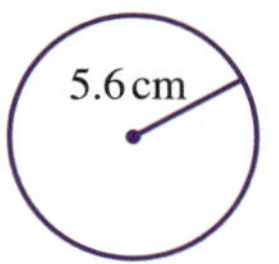

b

c

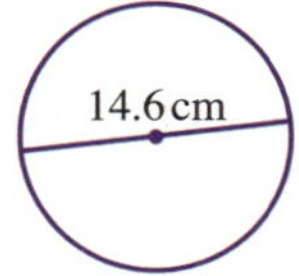

d

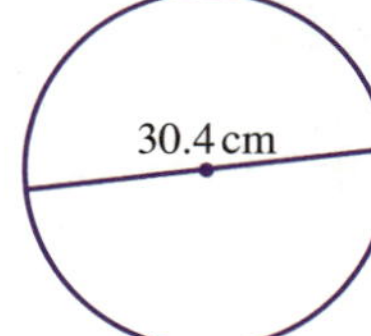

e

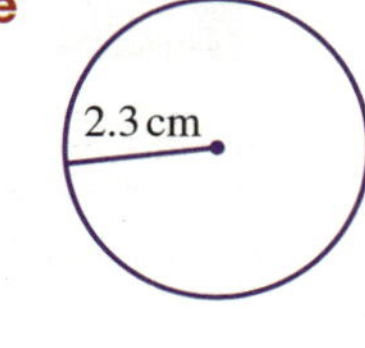

f

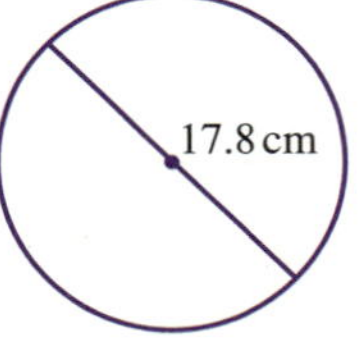

g

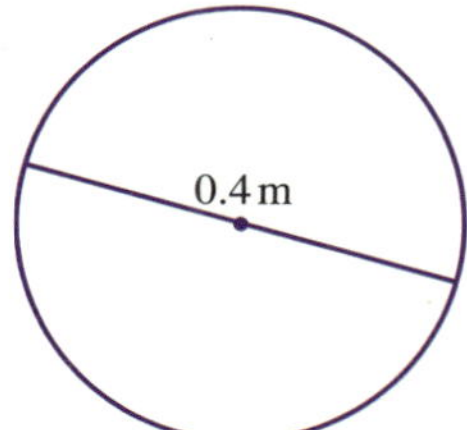

h

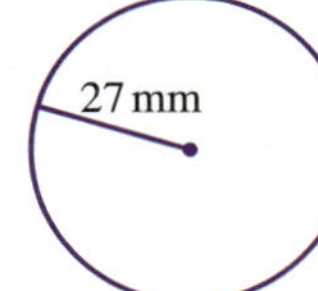

i

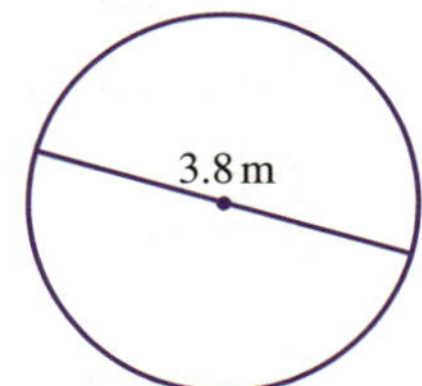

8 A circular rug has a diameter of 1.6 m.
Calculate the area covered by the rug.
Give your answer to the nearest square metre.

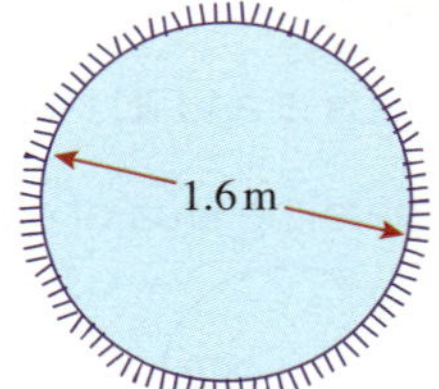

9 A circular window has a diameter of 34 cm.
Calculate the area of glass needed for the window.
Give your answer to the nearest square centimetre.

10 A two-pence piece has a diameter of 2.5 cm.
Find the total area of both faces of the coin.
Give your answer to one decimal place.

Example 3

A plate has a radius of 6 cm.

a Calculate the area of the plate. Leave your answer in terms of π.

b How many plates will fit side by side on a tray of length 50 cm and width 25 cm?

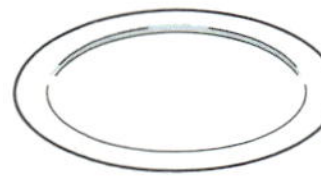

Solution 3

a $A = \pi r^2 = \pi \times 6 \times 6 = 36\pi$

Area of the plate = 36π cm^2

b Each plate has radius 6 cm, so diameter $2 \times 6 = 12$ cm.

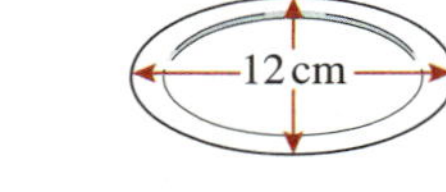

Length of tray = 50 cm

4×12 cm = 48 cm

so four plates will fit along the length of the tray.

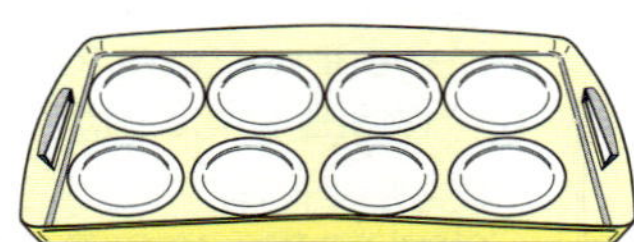

Width of tray = 25 cm

2×12 cm = 24 cm

so two plates will fit along the width of the tray.

$2 \times 4 = 8$ plates will fit on the tray.

Example 4

A shape is made up of a semicircle of diameter 8 cm and a square of side 8 cm.
Calculate the total area of this shape.

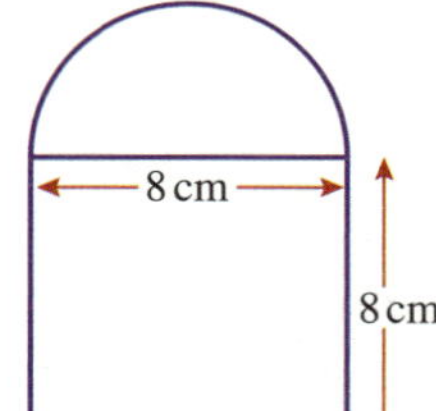

Solution 4

Diameter of semicircle = 8 cm so radius = 4 cm

Area of circle of radius 4 cm = $\pi \times 4^2 = 50.265$ cm^2

Area of semicircle = 50.265 cm$^2 \div 2 = 25.133$ cm^2

Area of square = $8 \times 8 = 64$ cm^2

So total area of shape = $25.133 + 64 = 89.1$ cm^2 (to 1 d.p.)

Exercise B

1 A semicircular rug has a radius of 20 cm.
Calculate the area covered by the rug.
Leave your answer in terms of π.

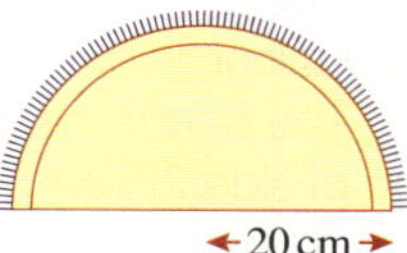

2 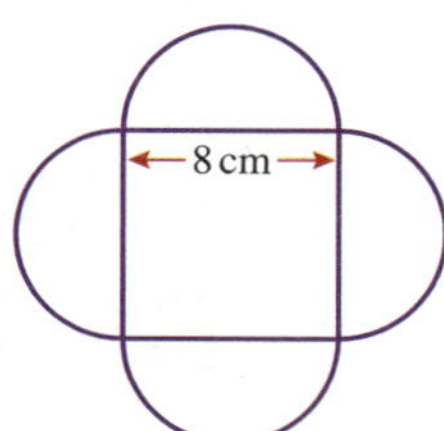

A shape is made from a square of side 8 cm surrounded by four semicircles of diameter 8 cm as shown.
Estimate the area of the shape.
Take the value of π to be 3

3 Calculate the area of each of the following shapes.
Give your answers in terms of π.

a 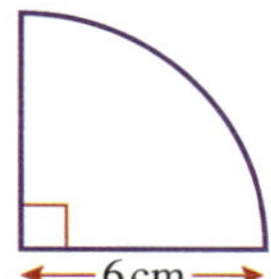

b 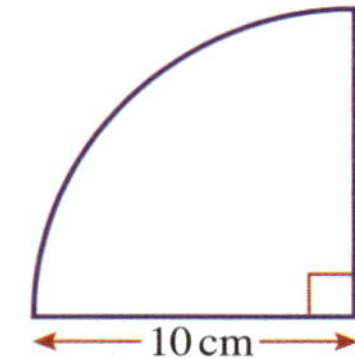

4 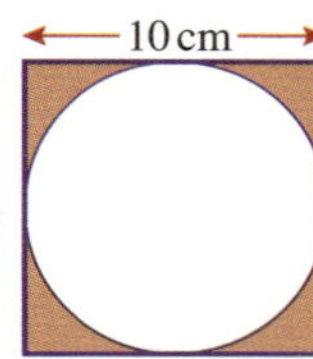

The diagram shows a circle of diameter 10 cm inside a square of side 10 cm.
Estimate the area of the square not covered by the circle.
Take the value of π to be 3

5 A mug has a radius of 4 cm.

a Calculate the area of the base of the mug.
Give your answer in terms of π.

b How many of these mugs will fit on a tray of length 40 cm and width 24 cm?

6 A circular flower bed has a radius of 1.5 metres.

a Calculate the area of the flower bed.
Give your answer to the nearest square metre.

Six plants can be grown in each square metre.

b Calculate the number of plants that can be grown in this flower bed.

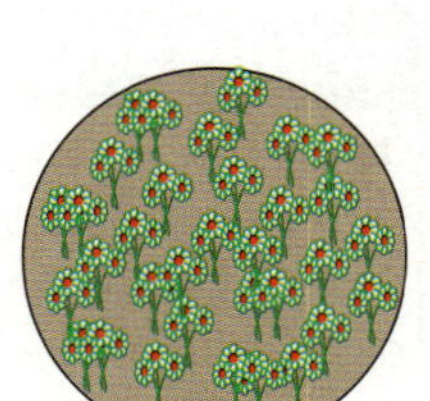

7 The diagram shows a solid wooden gate which is made up of a rectangle and a semicircle.

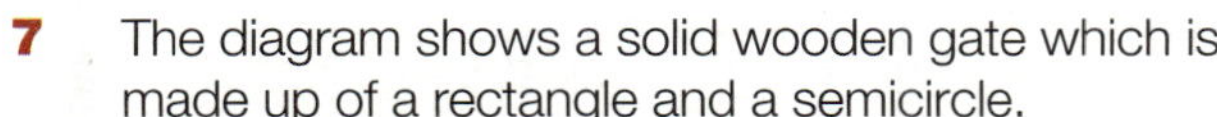

a Write down the height of the gate.

b Calculate the area of wood needed to make the gate.

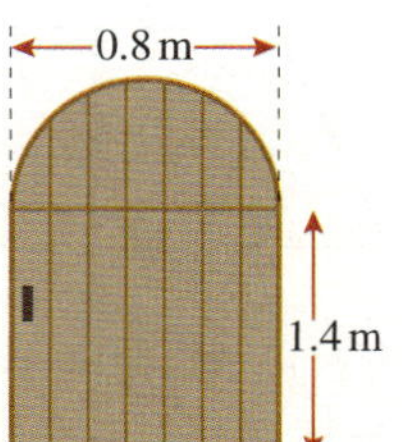

8 A badge is made out of two semicircles as shown.
The diameter of each semicircle is 2.5 cm.
- **a** Calculate the area of the badge.
- **b** The badge is cut from a square piece of metal of side 2.5 cm.
  Calculate the amount of metal wasted.

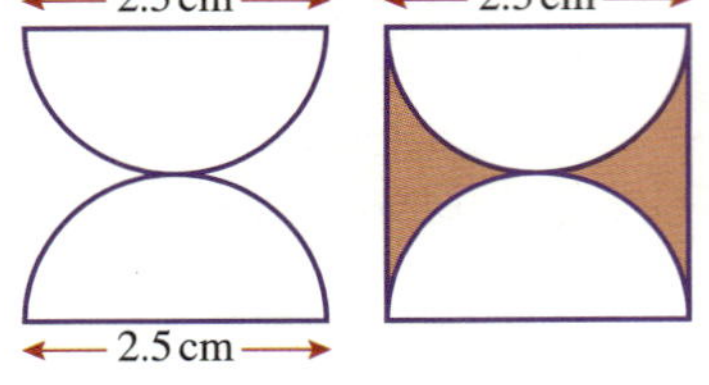

9 A quadrant (quarter circle) is cut from each side of a square piece of card as shown in the diagram.
The square has side length 16 cm.
Each quadrant has a radius of 5 cm.
Calculate the area of card remaining (shown shaded).
Give your answer to one decimal place.

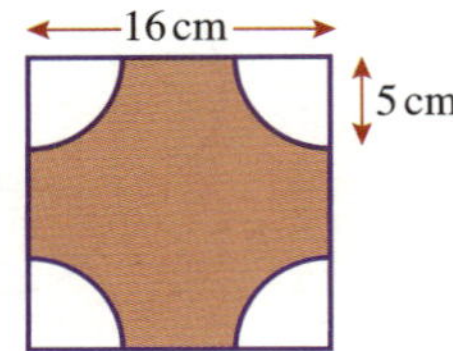

10 

A circular flower bed of radius 1.2 m is surrounded by a path 55 cm wide.
Calculate the area of the path in square metres.
Give your answer to one decimal place.

9.4 Composite shapes

CAN YOU REMEMBER

- That the perimeter is the distance all the way round a shape?
- The properties of a parallelogram and a trapezium?
- That for a rectangle $A = lw$, for a parallelogram $A = bh$, and for a triangle $A = \frac{1}{2}bh$?

IN THIS SECTION YOU WILL

- Work out the perimeter of shapes made from rectangles and triangles.
- Use a formula to calculate the area of a trapezium.
- Calculate the area of shapes made from rectangles and triangles.

This shape is formed from a rectangle and a triangle.

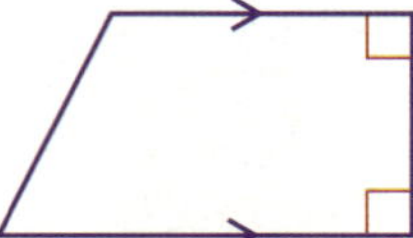 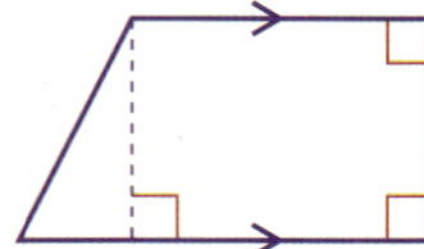  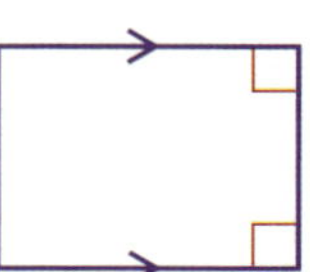

The perimeter of a shape is the total length of the sides of the shape.

Area of the shape = area of rectangle + area of triangle

Example 1

Calculate

a the perimeter

b the area of this shape.

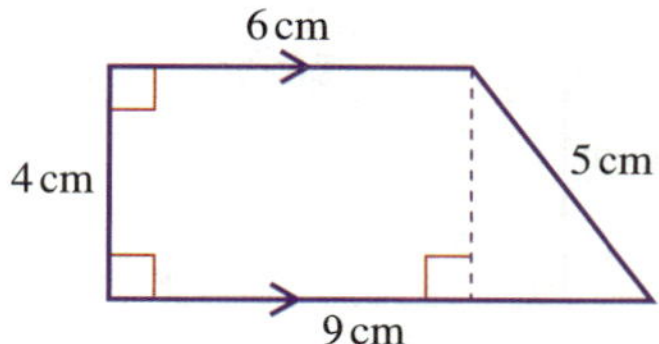

Solution 1

a Perimeter = 6 + 4 + 9 + 5 = 24 cm

b The shape is made from a rectangle A and a triangle B.

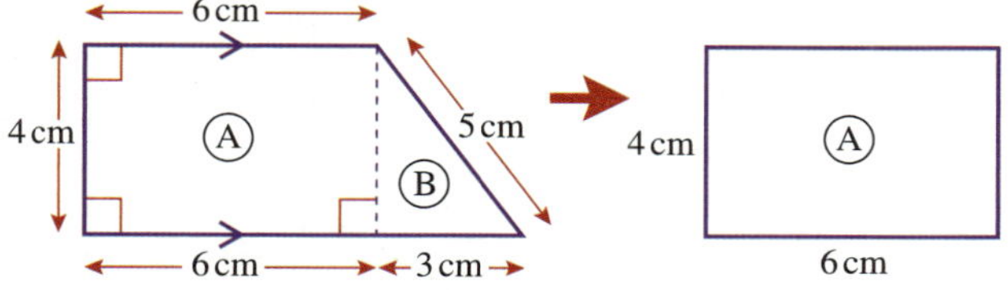

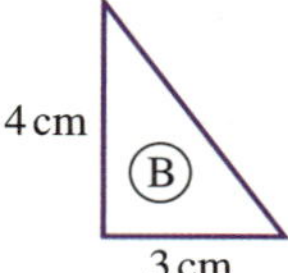

Area of rectangle A = 6 × 4 = 24 cm^2

Area of triangle B = $\frac{1}{2}$ × 3 × 4 = 6 cm^2

Total area of shape = 24 + 6 = 30 cm^2

The shape in Example 1 is a trapezium.

The area of a trapezium can also be found by using the formula

area = $\frac{1}{2}(a + b)h$

where a and b are the lengths of the parallel sides and h is the perpendicular height.

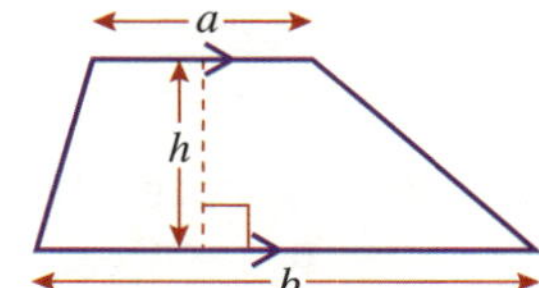

Example 2

Find the area of this trapezium.

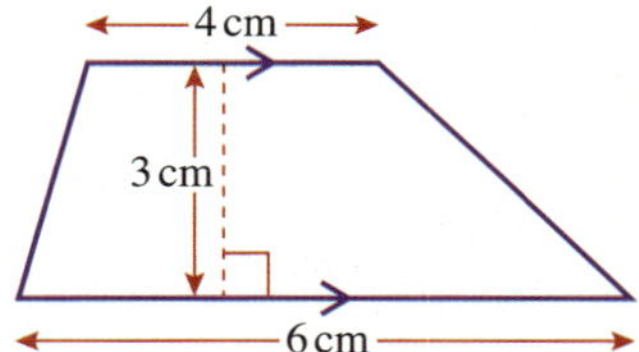

Solution 2

Area of trapezium = $\frac{1}{2}(a+b)h$

a = 4 cm, b = 6 cm, h = 3 cm

Area of trapezium = $\frac{1}{2}$ × (4 + 6) × 3 = $\frac{1}{2}$ × 10 × 3 = 15 cm^2

Exercise A

1 Work out the perimeter of these shapes.

a

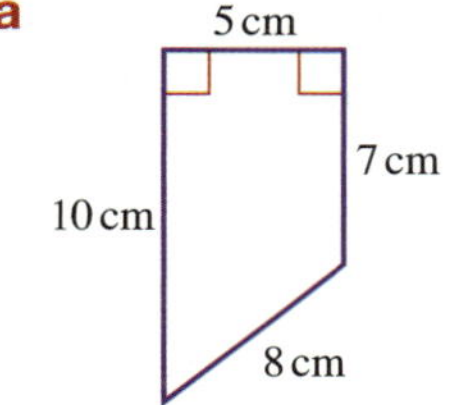

b

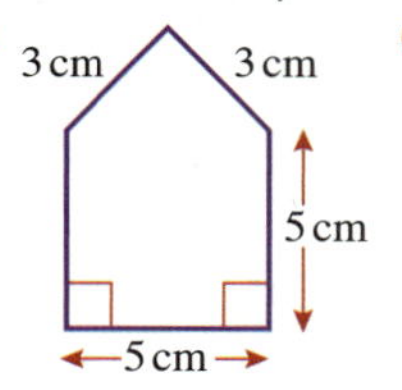

c

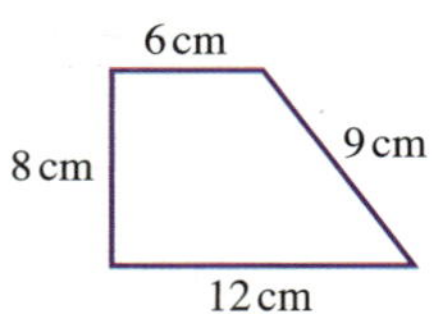

d

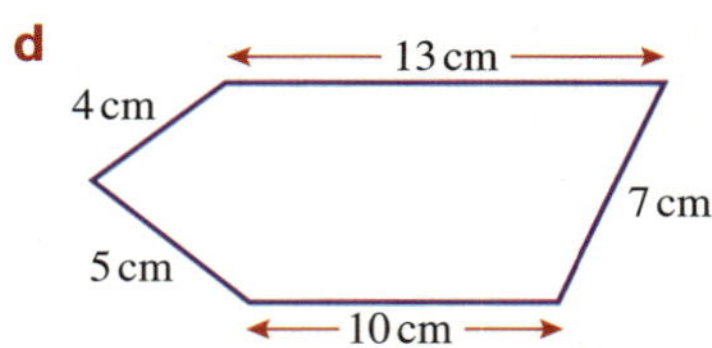

2 Work out the area of these shapes.

Divide them into rectangles.

a

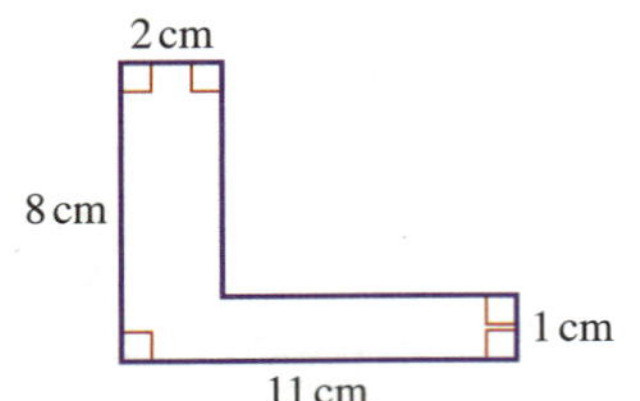

b

6 cm 6 cm 9 cm 15 cm 20 cm

c

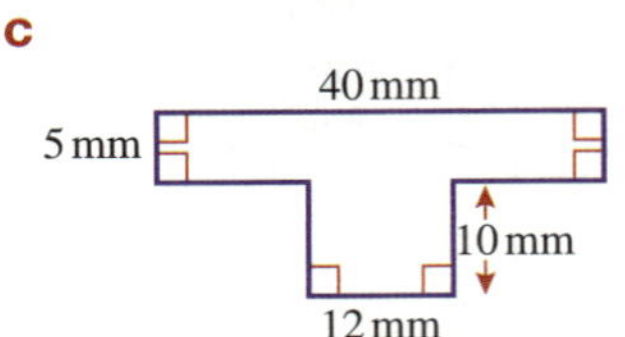

3 Calculate the area of each of these shapes.

a

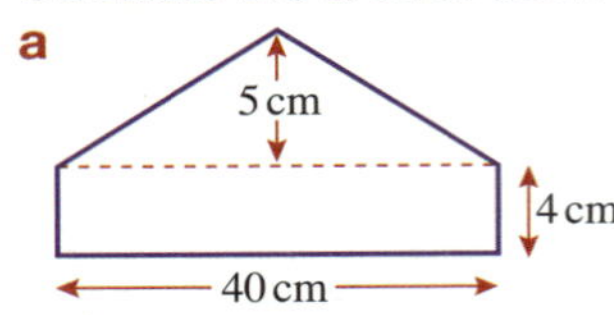

b

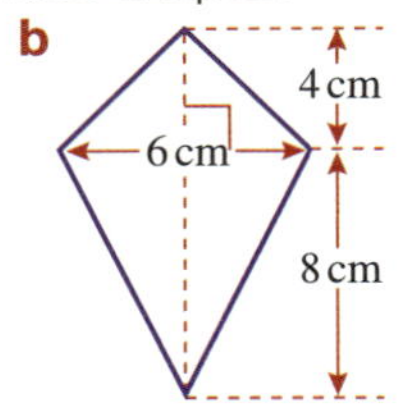

c

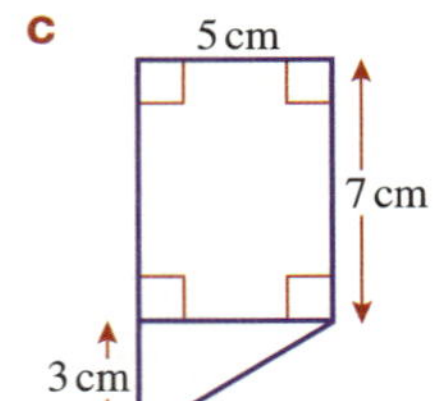

d

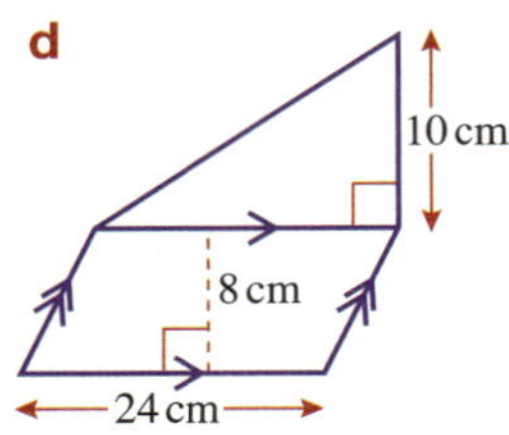

4 Calculate the area of each of these shapes.

a

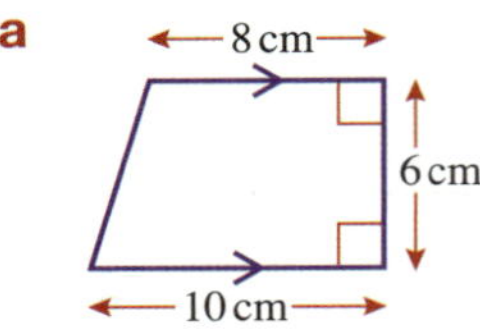

b

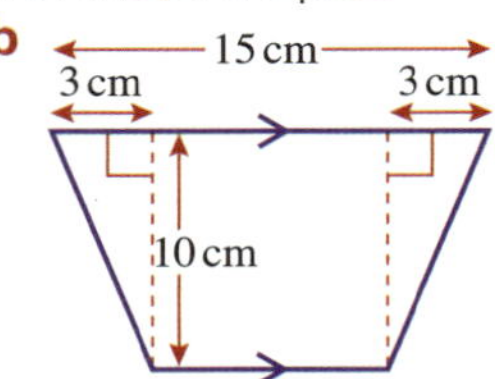

c

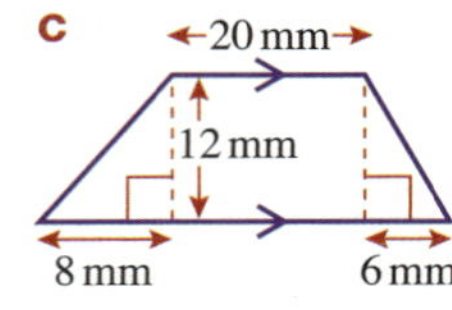

d

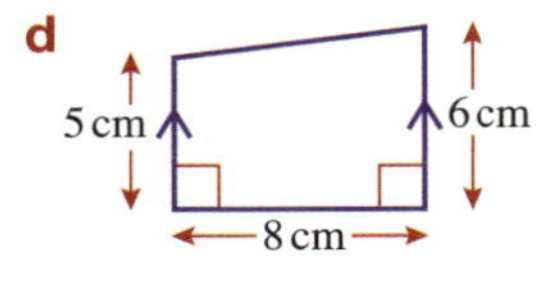

5 Calculate the area of each trapezium.

a

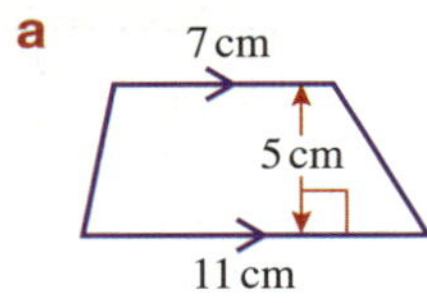

b

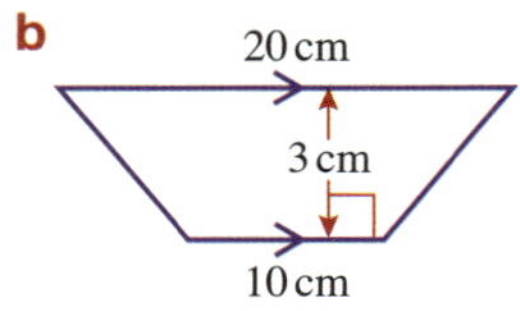

c

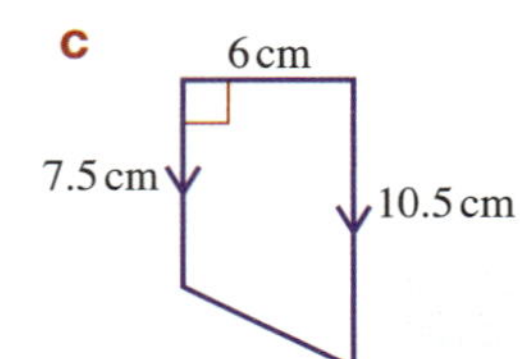

d

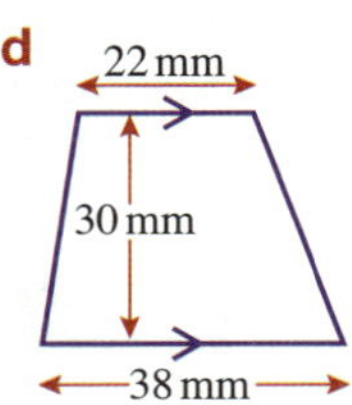

6 Calculate the perimeter of these shapes.

a

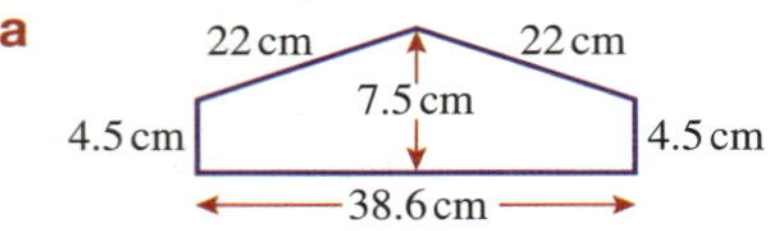

b

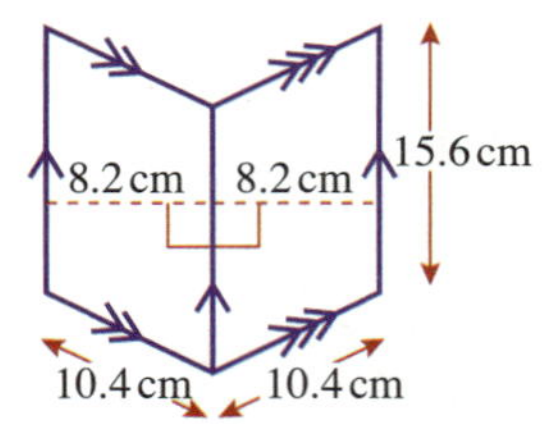

c

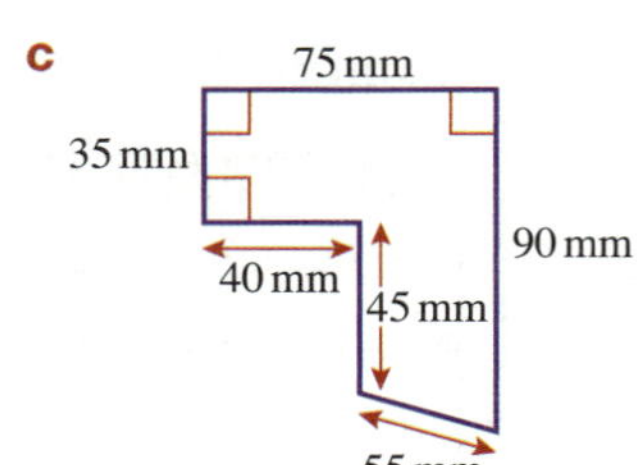

7 Each of the following shapes is a trapezium. Calculate the area of each shape.

a

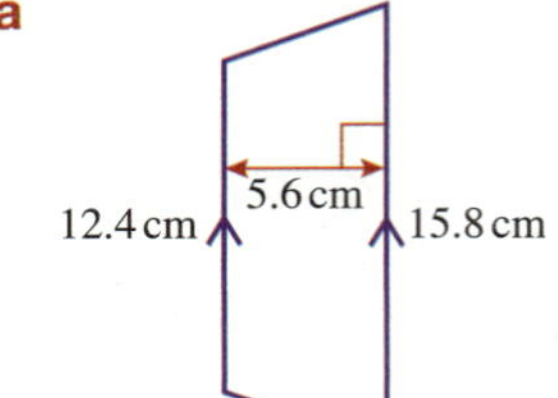

b

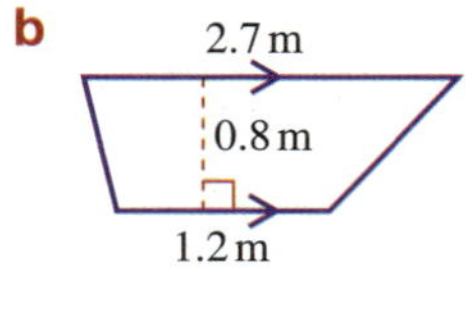

c

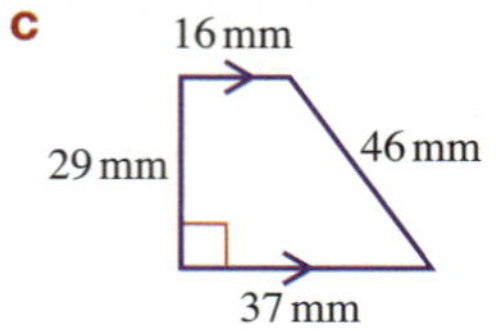

d

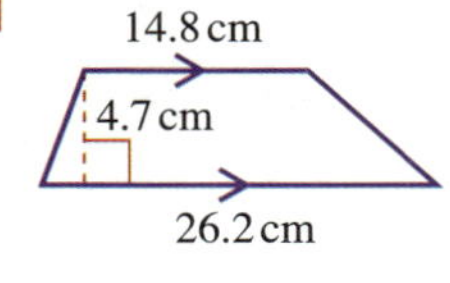

8 Calculate the area of the shapes given in question **6**.

9 This shape is made from a square of side 2.5 cm and four isosceles triangles of base 2.5 cm and perpendicular height 1.8 cm.
Calculate the area of the shape.

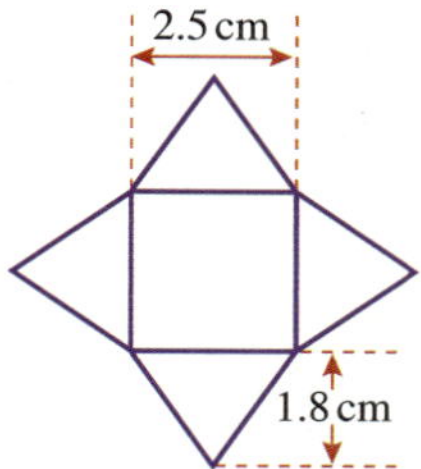

10 Calculate the area of these shapes.

a

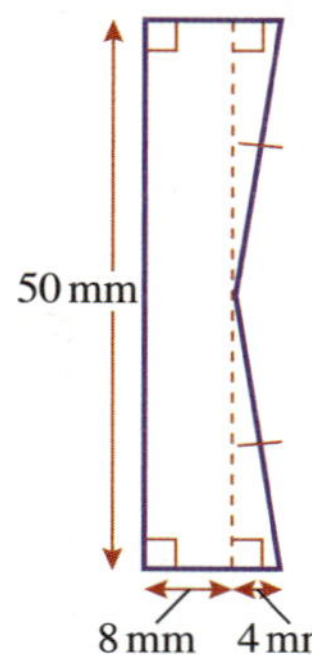

b

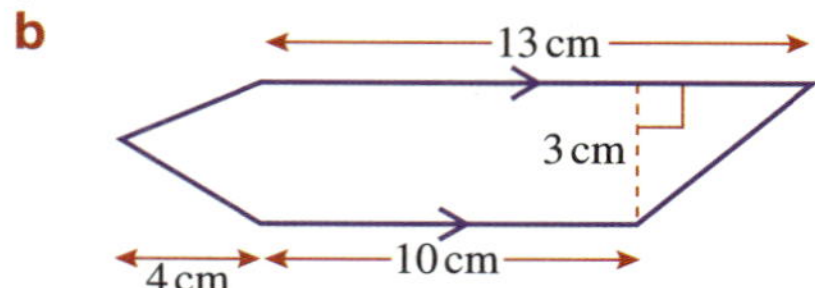

Example 3

Find the area of the shaded part of this diagram.

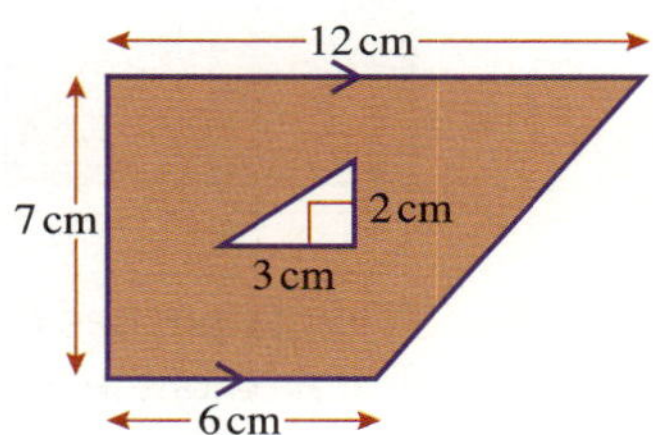

Solution 3

Shaded area shown
= area of trapezium – area of unshaded triangle

Area of trapezium $= \frac{1}{2}(a+b)h$

$= \frac{1}{2}(12 + 6) \times 7 = \frac{1}{2} \times 18 \times 7 = 63\ \text{cm}^2$

Area of triangle $= \frac{1}{2}bh = \frac{1}{2} \times 3 \times 2 = 3\ \text{cm}^2$

Shaded area $= 63\ \text{cm}^2 - 3\ \text{cm}^2 = 60\ \text{cm}^2$

Example 4

This trapezium has area 90 cm^2
The parallel sides of the trapezium measure 11 cm and 19 cm.
Calculate the perpendicular height of the trapezium.

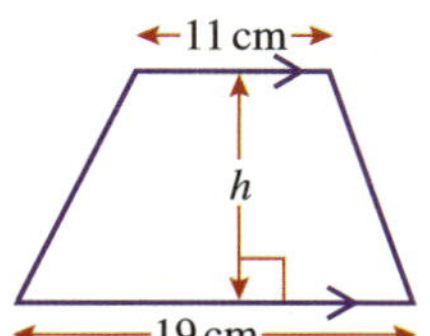

Solution 4

Area of a trapezium $= \frac{1}{2}(a+b)h$

$90 = \frac{1}{2} \times (11 + 19) \times h$

$90 = \frac{1}{2} \times 30 \times h$

$90 = 15 \times h$

$\frac{90}{15} = h = 6$ Dividing both sides by 15

The perpendicular height of the trapezium is 6 cm.

Exercise B

1 Find
a the perimeter
b the area of this shape.

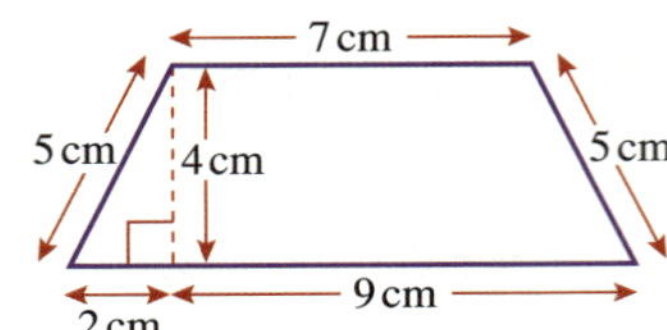

2 Calculate the area of each of these shapes.

a

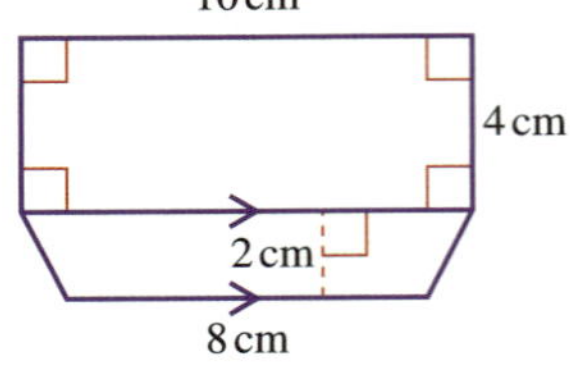

b

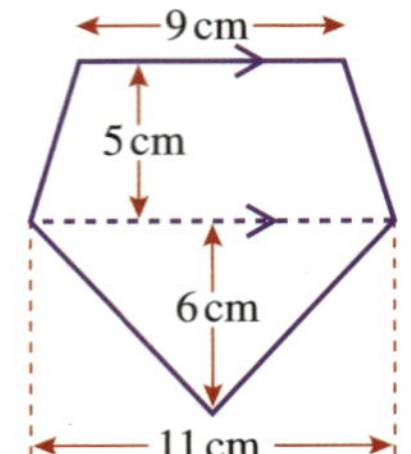

3 A small square of side 6 cm is cut from a large square of side 8 cm as shown. Calculate the shaded area.

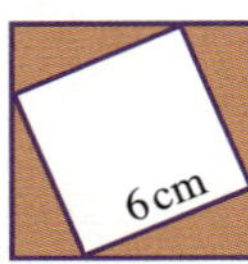

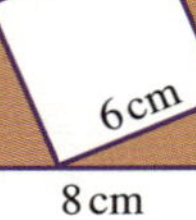

4 A trapezium is cut from a rectangular piece of card as shown. Calculate the shaded area.

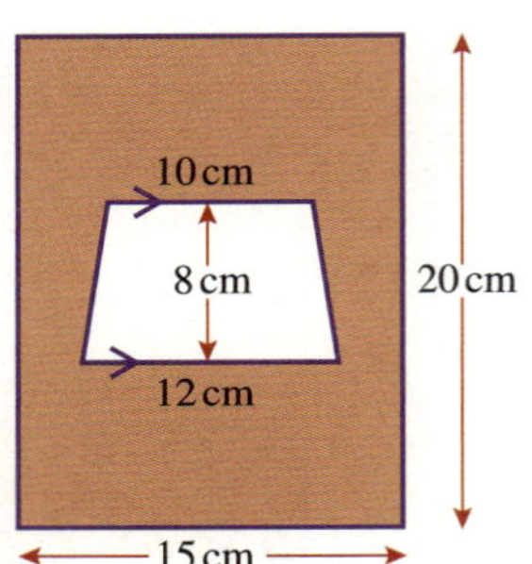

5 A trapezium has parallel sides of 14 cm and 26 cm. The area of the trapezium is 160 cm^2 Calculate the perpendicular height of the trapezium.

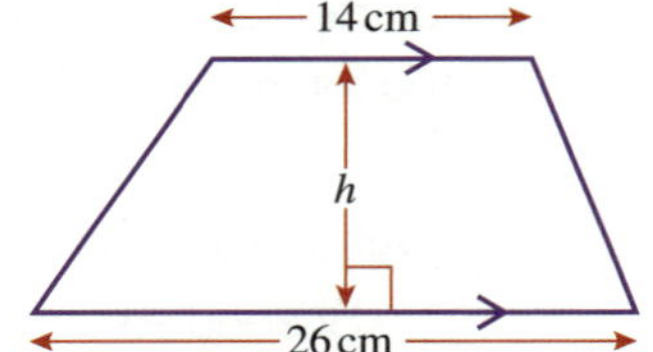

6 Calculate the shaded area of the following shapes.

a

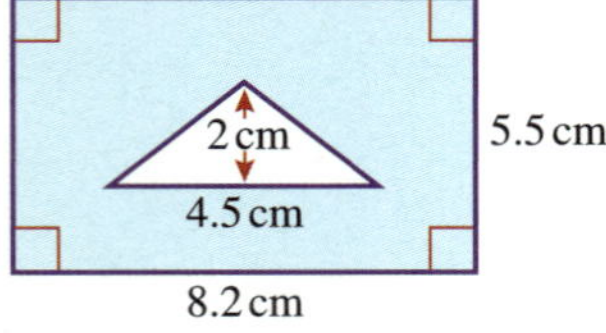

b

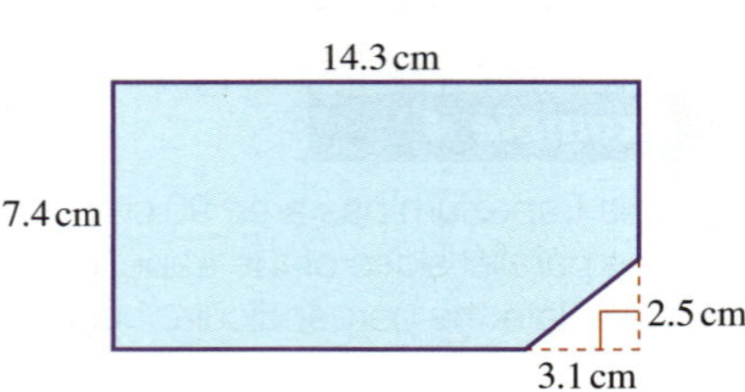

c

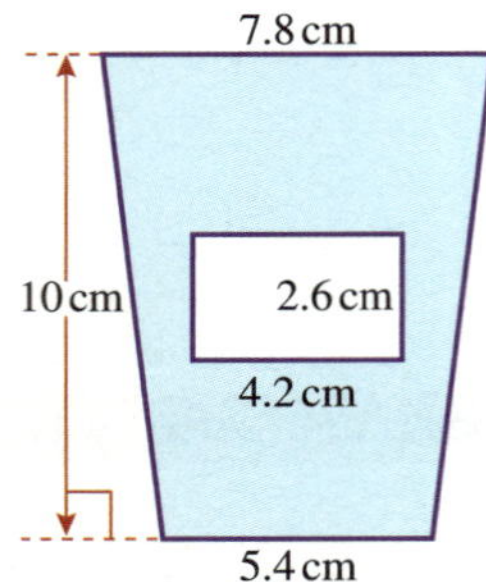

d

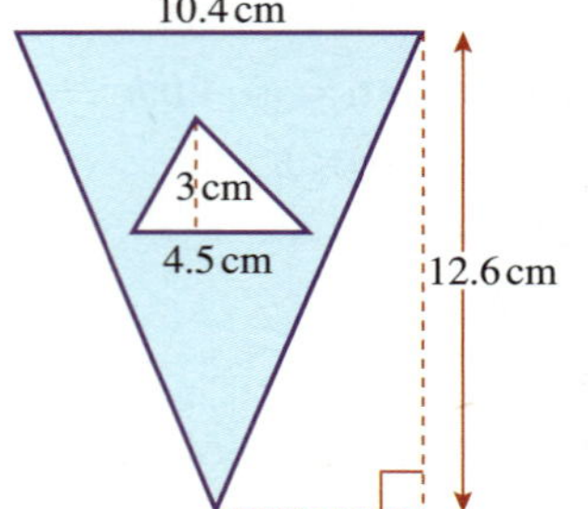

7 Which of the following shapes has the smallest area?
Show your working.

a

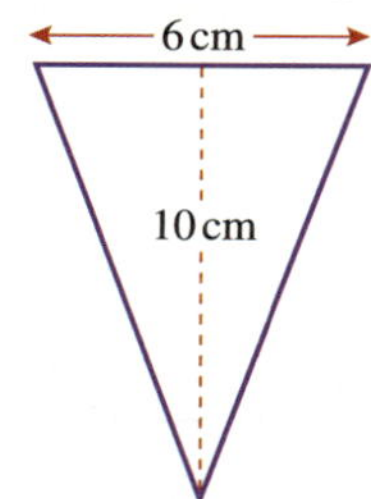

b

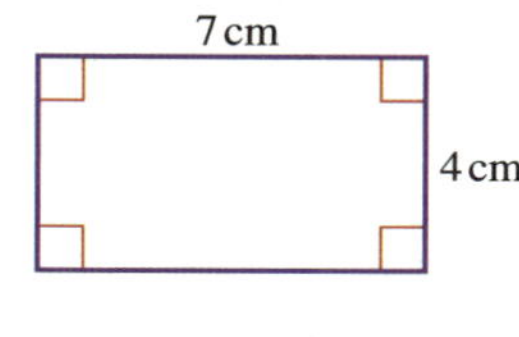

c

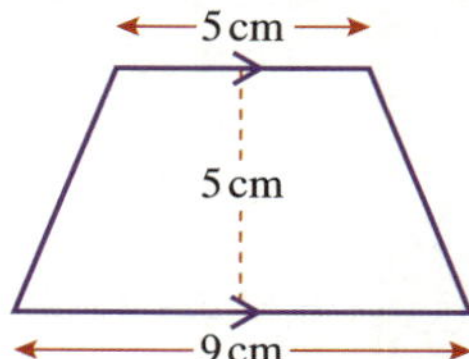

8 Here is a sketch of an L-shaped lawn.
Turf is bought in rolls. Each roll covers 1 square metre and costs £2.50
Calculate the cost of turfing the lawn.

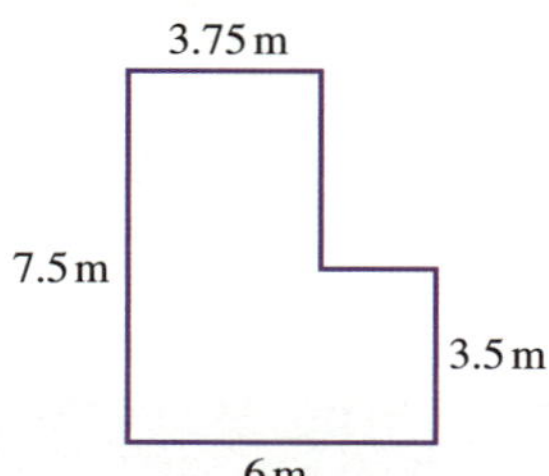

9 The diagram shows a trapezium $ABCD$ of area 245.68 mm^2
$AB = 22.4$ mm and $CD = 36.8$ mm.
Calculate the perpendicular height, h, of the trapezium.

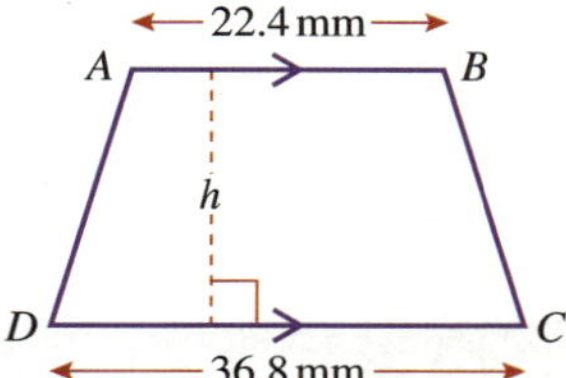

10 A field is in the shape of a trapezium.
There is a gate, 3 m wide, in the longest side of the field.

a Calculate the area of the field.

b The farmer wants to build a new fence to enclose the field, leaving the gate in the same place.
He has £2000 to spend. The cost of the fencing is £8.50 per metre.
Does the farmer have enough money to complete the fence?
Show your working.

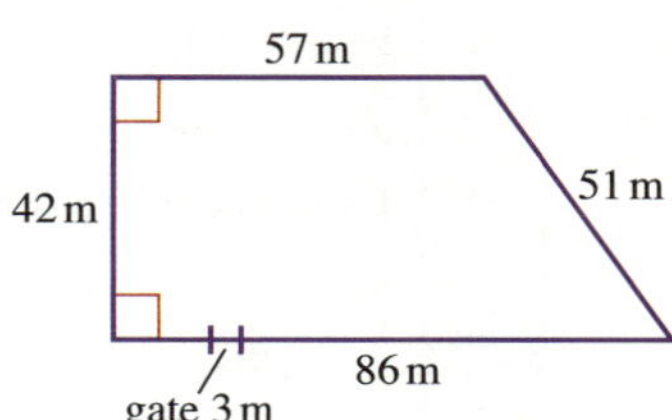

Chapter summary

- Area of a parallelogram = base × perpendicular height
$A = bh$

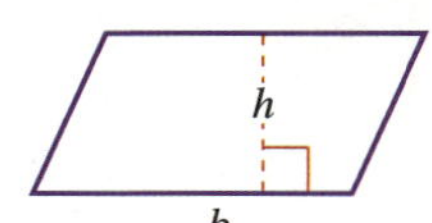

- Area of a triangle = $\frac{1}{2}$ × base × perpendicular height
$A = \frac{1}{2}bh$

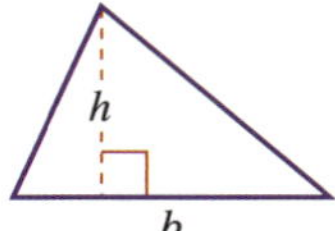

- The names given to parts of a circle are shown below.

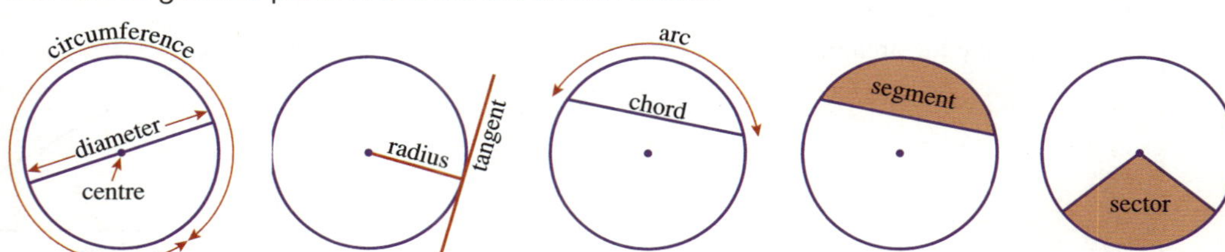

- The diameter (d) of a circle is twice the length of the radius (r).
- The circumference of a circle $C = \pi d$ or $C = 2\pi r$
- The area of a circle $A = \pi r^2$
- The perimeter of a shape is the total length of the sides of the shape.
- The area of a trapezium can sometimes be found by dividing the trapezium into a rectangle and triangles.

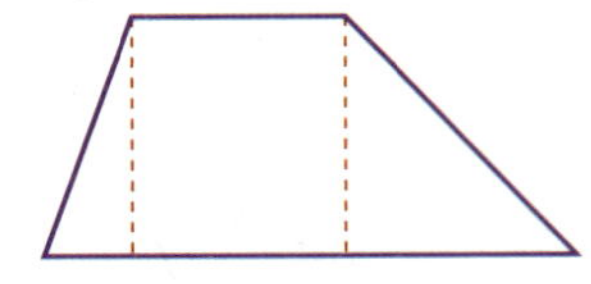

- The area of a trapezium can also be found using the formula: area $= \frac{1}{2}(a+b)h$ where a and b are the lengths of the parallel sides and h is the perpendicular height.

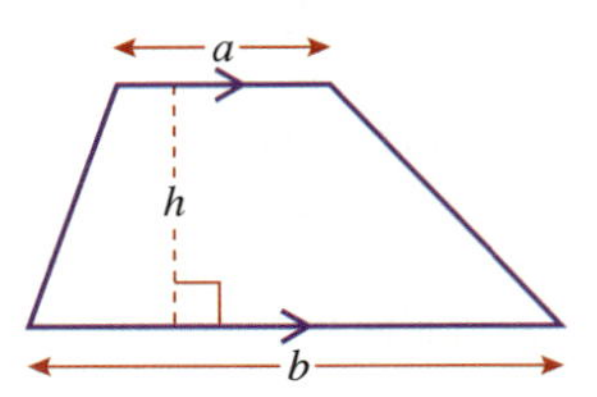

Chapter review

1 Here is a list of words that are connected with circles.

arc chord diameter radius sector segment tangent

Label the lettered parts on the diagram, by choosing the correct words from the list.

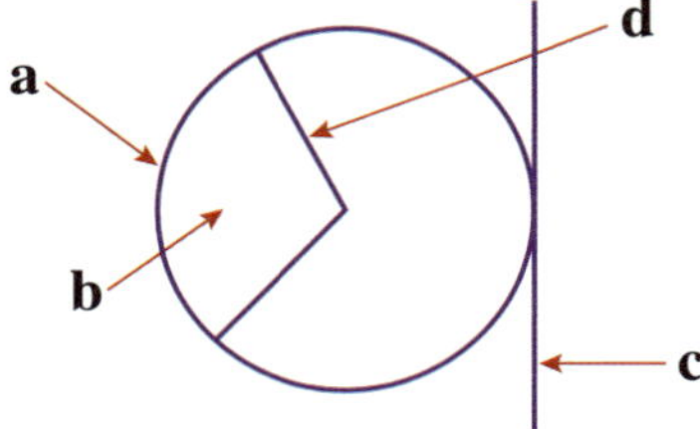

2 A parallelogram is drawn on a centimetre-square grid.
Calculate the area of the parallelogram.

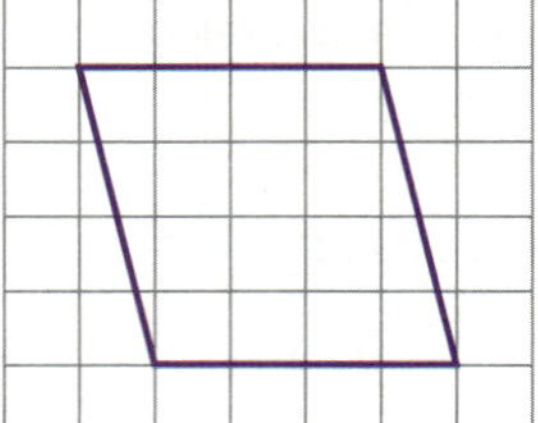

3 PQR is a right-angled triangle.
Calculate the area of triangle PQR.

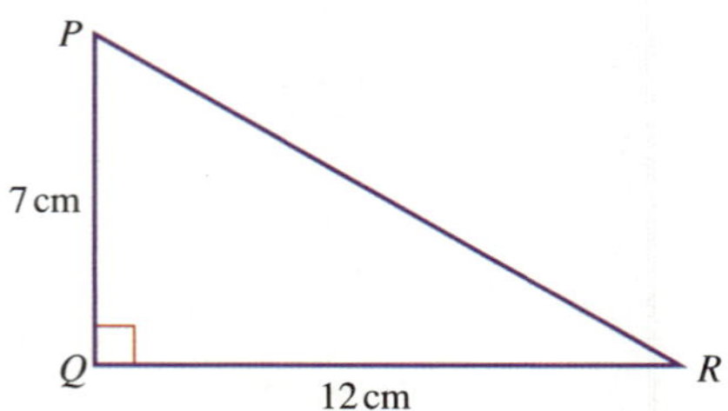

4 **a** The diagram shows a circle of radius 4 cm.
Work out the area of the circle.
Give your answer in terms of π.

b A badge is made out of a semicircle and an isosceles triangle as shown.
The radius of the semicircle is 5 cm.
The height of the isosceles triangle is 6 cm.

i Work out the area of the badge.
Give your answer in terms of π.

ii Write down the height of the badge, marked h on the diagram.

iii The badge is cut from a strip of metal.
The metal strip is 10 cm wide and 1 metre long.
How many badges can be cut from the strip?
Show your working.

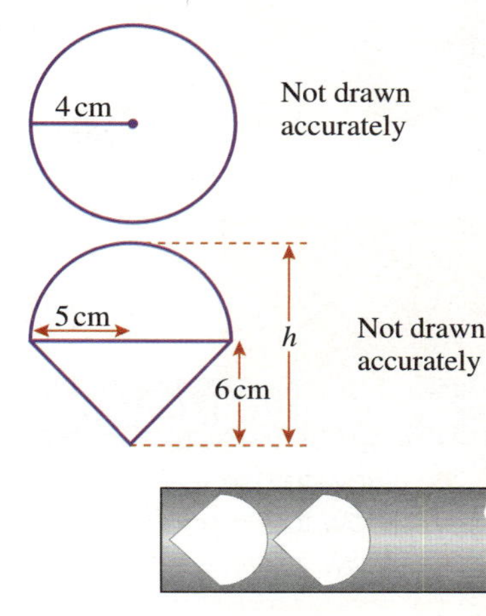

5 The diagram shows a trapezium.
Calculate the area of the trapezium.

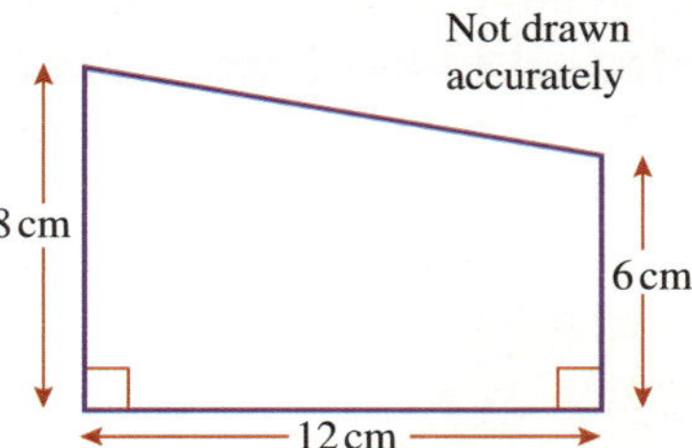

6 The diagram shows one rectangle drawn inside another rectangle.
Calculate the area of the shaded region.

9 cm
20 cm
12 cm
30 cm
Not drawn accurately

7 Calculate the value of πr^2 when $r = 5.4$
Give your answer correct to two decimal places.

8 **a** A circle has a diameter of 6 cm. Write down the length of the radius.

b Draw a circle. On the circle:

i draw a radius **ii** draw a chord

iii mark with a cross a point on the circumference.

9 **a** Calculate the area of a circle with diameter 3 metres.

b A semicircular table has a radius of 0.8 metres.
Calculate the perimeter of the table.

0.8 m

10 Hazel's back garden is in the shape of a trapezium. In the middle of the garden there is a circular pond of diameter 2 m. The rest of the garden is covered with grass.
Calculate the area of grass in the garden to the nearest square metre.

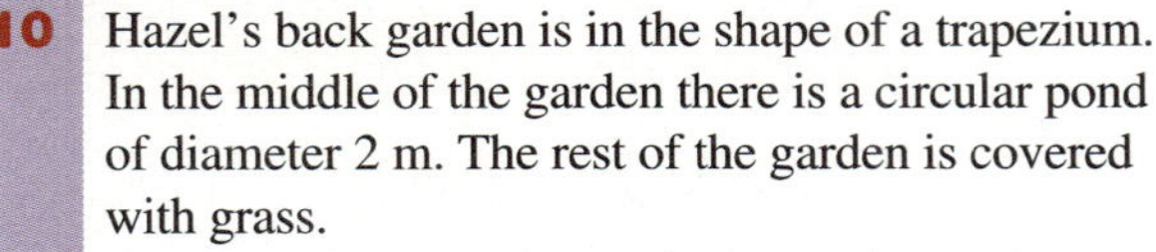

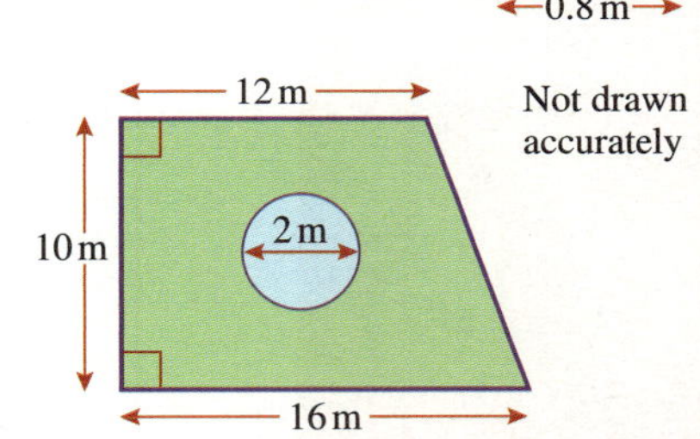

CHAPTER 10

Equalities and inequalities

10.1 Linear equations

CAN YOU REMEMBER

- How to use the balance method to solve simple equations?
- How to expand brackets and simplify algebraic expressions by collecting like terms?
- How to write statements in words as algebraic expressions?

IN THIS SECTION YOU WILL

- Solve equations with the unknown on both sides of the equation, including those with brackets and fractions.
- Set up and solve equations from given situations.

The balance method can be extended to solve equations with the unknown on both sides.

Example 1

Solve each of the following equations.

a $\frac{2}{3}a + 8 = 5$ **b** $8b - 3 = 6b + 7$ **c** $\frac{3 - 2c}{4} = 5$

Solution 1

a $\frac{2}{3}a + 8 = 5$

$\frac{2}{3}a = -3$ To remove the number term from the LHS subtract 8 from both sides.

$\frac{2}{3}a \times \frac{3}{2} = -3 \times \frac{3}{2}$ To remove the fraction ($\frac{2}{3}$) term on the LHS multiply both sides by its reciprocal $\frac{3}{2}$

$a = -4.5$

Check: When $a = -4.5$, $\frac{2}{3}a + 8 = \frac{2}{3} \times -4.5 + 8 = -3 + 8 = 5$ ✓

b $8b - 3 = 6b + 7$

$2b - 3 = 7$ To remove the b term from the RHS subtract $6b$ from both sides.

$2b = 10$ To remove the number term from the LHS add 3 to both sides.

$\frac{2b}{2} = \frac{10}{2}$ Divide both sides by 2

$b = 5$

Check: When $b = 5$, $8b - 3 = 8 \times 5 - 3 = 40 - 3 = 37$

$6b + 7 = 6 \times 5 + 7 = 30 + 7 = 37$ ✓

c $\dfrac{3-2c}{4}=5$ — To remove the fraction from the LHS multiply both sides by 4

$3-2c=20$ — To remove the number term from the LHS subtract 3 from both sides.

$-2c=17$ — Divide both sides by -2

$$\frac{-2c}{-2}=\frac{17}{-2}=17\div-2$$

$$c=-8.5$$

Check: When $c=-8.5$, $\dfrac{3-2c}{4}=\dfrac{3-2\times-8.5}{4}=\dfrac{3--17}{4}$

$=20\div4=5$ ✓

To solve an equation with brackets, first *expand* the brackets and then, if necessary, *simplify*. Then solve the resulting equation using the balance method.

Example 2

Solve the following equations.

a $3(2x+1)=9$ **b** $3(5y-2)+5=7y+3$

Solution 2

a $3(2x+1)=9$

Method 1

$3(2x+1)=6x+3$

$6x+3=9$ — Expand brackets.

$6x=6$ — Subtract 3 from both sides.

$\dfrac{6x}{6}=\dfrac{6}{6}$ — Divide both sides by 6

$x=1$

Method 2

$3(2x+1)=9$

$\dfrac{3(2x+1)}{3}=\dfrac{9}{3}$ — Divide both sides by 3

$2x+1=3$

$2x=2$ — Subtract 1 from both sides.

$\dfrac{2x}{2}=\dfrac{2}{2}$ — Divide both sides by 2

$x=1$

Check: When $x=1$, $3(2x+1)=3\times(2\times1+1)=3\times3=9$ ✓

b $3(5y - 2) + 5 = 7y + 3$

$3(5y - 2) + 5 = 15y - 6 + 5 = 15y - 1$ — Expand brackets and simplify.

$15y - 1 = 7y + 3$ — Subtract $7y$ from both sides.

$8y - 1 = 3$ — Add 1 to both sides.

$8y = 4$ — Divide both sides by 8

$y = \frac{4}{8} = \frac{1}{2}$

Check: When $y = \frac{1}{2}$, $3(5y - 2) + 5 = 3 \times (5 \times \frac{1}{2} - 2) + 5 = 3 \times \frac{1}{2} + 5 = 6\frac{1}{2}$

$7y + 3 = 7 \times \frac{1}{2} + 3 = 3\frac{1}{2} + 3 = 6\frac{1}{2}$ ✓

Equations are often used to solve problems.
Step 1: Use the information given to set up an equation.
Step 2: Solve the equation using the balance method.

Example 3

The two rectangles shown are equal in area.

a Write down an equation in x.

b Solve the equation to find the value of x.

Rectangle A

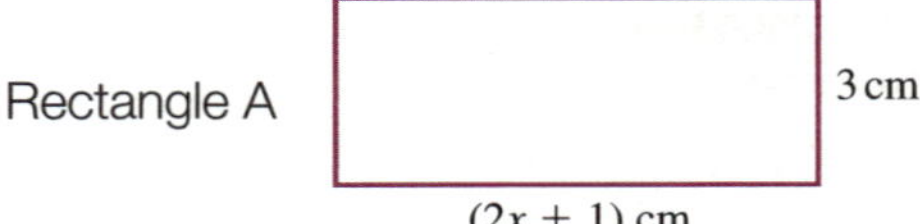

Rectangle B

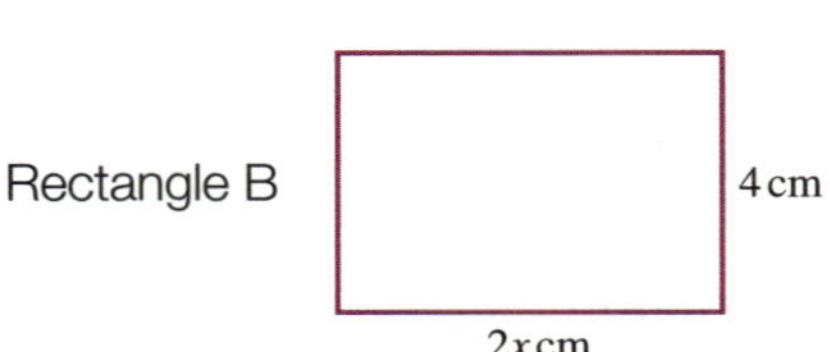

Solution 3

a Area of rectangle A $= 3(2x + 1)$

Area of rectangle B $= 4 \times 2x = 8x$

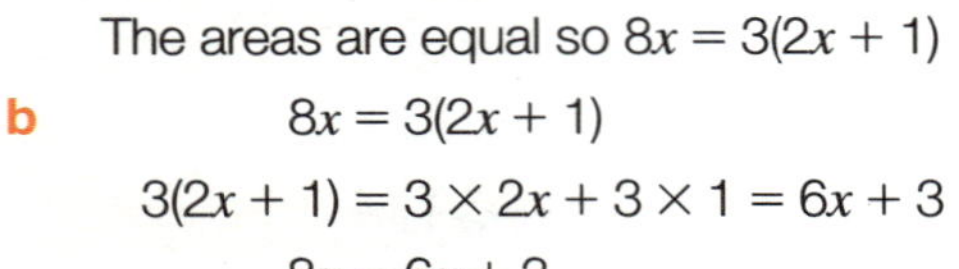

The areas are equal so $8x = 3(2x + 1)$

b $8x = 3(2x + 1)$

$3(2x + 1) = 3 \times 2x + 3 \times 1 = 6x + 3$ — Expand the brackets.

$8x = 6x + 3$ — Subtract $6x$ from both sides.

$2x = 3$ — Divide both sides by 2

$\frac{2x}{2} = \frac{3}{2}$

$x = 1.5$

Check: Rectangle A: area $= 3 \times (2 \times 1.5 + 1) = 3 \times (3 + 1) = 3 \times 4 = 12$ cm^2

Rectangle B: area $= 4 \times 2 \times 1.5 = 12$ cm^2

Exercise A

1 Solve each of the following equations.

a $5a - 2 = 8$ **b** $3b + 1 = 10$ **c** $2c + 6 = 0$ **d** $4d - 3 = -7$

e $4e + 1 = -5$ **f** $-5f - 2 = -12$ **g** $4g - 1 = -7$ **h** $-3h + 5 = -7$

2 Solve each of the following equations.

a $\frac{a}{3} + 1 = 2$ **b** $\frac{b}{2} - 12 = 0$ **c** $\frac{c}{2} + 14 = 2$ **d** $\frac{d}{2} - 2 = -2$

e $\frac{2}{5}e = 4$ **f** $\frac{5}{7}f = 10$ **g** $\frac{3}{10}g = 9$ **h** $\frac{6}{11}h = 3$

i $\frac{3}{4}i + 5 = 8$ **j** $\frac{2}{7}j - 4 = 3$ **k** $\frac{4}{5}k + 10 = 2$ **l** $\frac{2}{9}l - 4 = 7$

m $\frac{2 - m}{5} = 4$ **n** $\frac{8 - 5n}{2} = 6$ **o** $\frac{6(2 - q)}{5} = 3$ **p** $\frac{10 - 7p}{4} = 6$

3 Solve each of the following equations.

a $4a + 7 = 2a + 3$ **b** $5b - 3 = 3b + 5$ **c** $9c + 1 = 4c + 11$
d $6d - 4 = 3d + 11$ **e** $8e - 12 = 3e - 2$ **f** $5f - 8 = 2f + 1$
g $5g - 2 = 10 - g$ **h** $9h - 5 = 5h + 7$ **i** $7i - 15 = 5 - 3i$
j $-3j + 2 = 10 - 5j$

4 Solve each of the following equations.

a $5a + 12 = 3a + 5$ **b** $6b - 5 = 4b - 13$ **c** $5c - 2 = 3c - 5$
d $8d + 14 = 3d - 1$ **e** $11e - 9 = 3e - 2$ **f** $6f + 1 = 2f + 8$
g $-8g + 6 = -3g + 2$ **h** $2h - 1 = 4 - 4h$ **i** $-i + 7 = 5 - 3i$
j $3j + 7 = 6 - 2j$

5 Solve each of the following equations.

a $4(a + 1) = 8$ **b** $5(4b - 1) = 25$ **c** $3(5c - 7) = 9$
d $2(6d - 1) = 4$ **e** $7(2e - 3) = 14$

6 Solve each of the following equations.

a $4(a + 2) = 2a - 6$ **b** $2(3b - 4) = 4b - 7$ **c** $5(3c + 2) = 5c + 1$
d $4(3d - 7) = 2 - 3d$ **e** $2(5e - 2) = e + 2$ **f** $3(4f - 5) = 8f + 9$
g $2(5g - 2) = 5g + 7$ **h** $7(3h - 1) = 5 - 4h$ **h** $4(3i + 1) = 7(i + 2)$
i $3(2j + 11) = 2(5 - 2j)$

7 Solve each of the following equations.

a $14a + 249 = -73$ **b** $23b - 325 = -26$ **c** $46c + 171 = 12c - 373$
d $23d - 12 = 180 - 9d$ **e** $12(13e - 2) = 15$ **f** $8(14f + 5) = 432$
g $-5(12g - 7) = -13$ **h** $7(4h - 5) + 12h = -7$ **i** $6(5 - 3i) - 6i = 81$
j $7(11j - 9) = 3(9j + 7)$

8 The two rectangles shown are equal in area.

Rectangle A

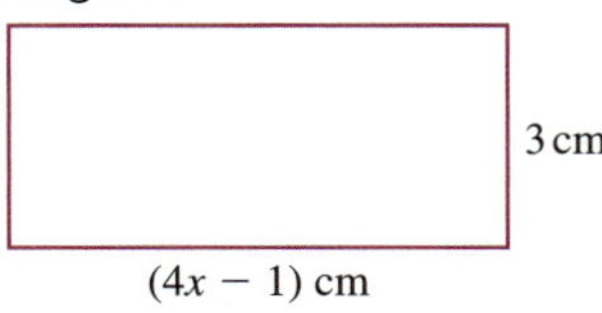

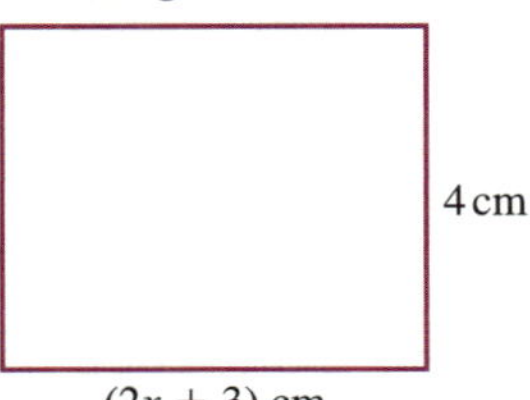

a Write down an equation in x.
b Solve the equation to find the value of x.

9 **a** A triangle has angles $x°$, $2x°$ and $(x + 20)°$.
 i Write down an equation in x.
 ii Solve the equation to find x.

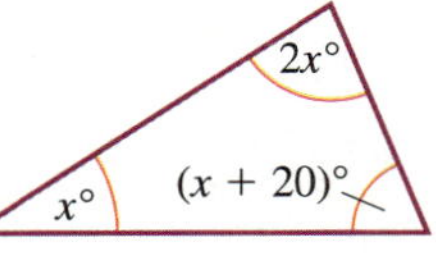

b Repeat **a** for these triangles.

i

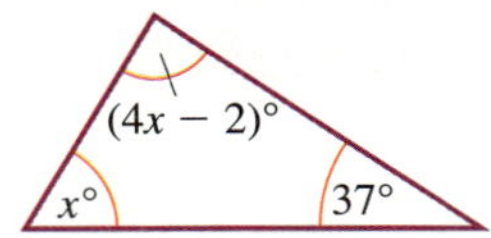

ii

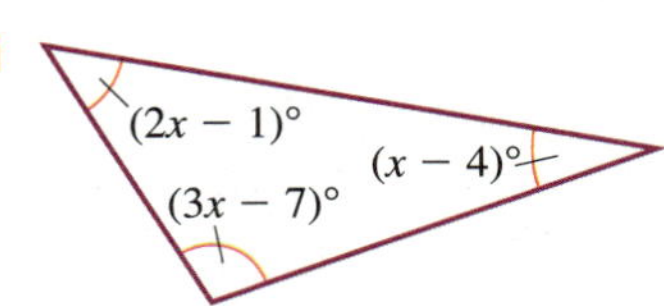

10 For each of the following diagrams

a Write down an equation in y.

b Solve the equation to find the value of y.

i

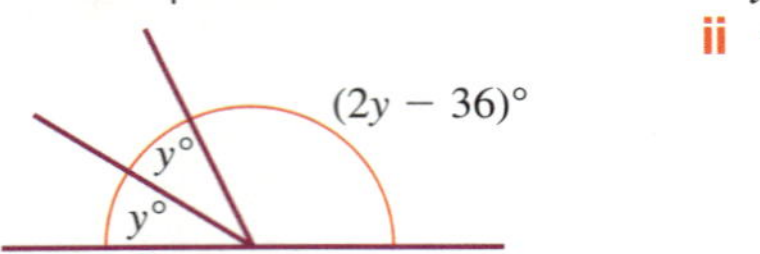

ii

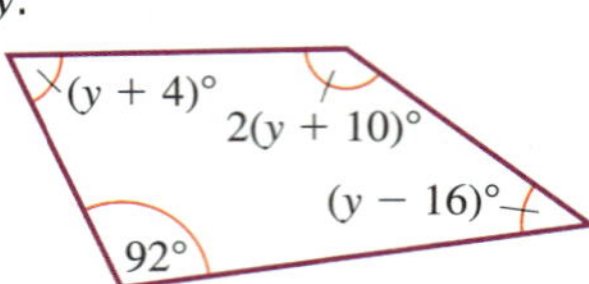

In some equations, terms include fractions with different denominators.

Example 4

Solve each of the following equations.

a $\frac{2}{3}x - 8 = \frac{1}{4}x + 2$

b $\dfrac{2x + 1}{3} = \dfrac{3(x + 3)}{2}$

c $\dfrac{2(5y - 1)}{5} + 3 = \dfrac{7y + 3}{3}$

Solution 4

a $\frac{2}{3}x - 8 = \frac{1}{4}x + 2$

Method 1

$\frac{2}{3}x - 8 = \frac{1}{4}x + 2$ — Subtract $\frac{1}{4}x$ from both sides.

$\frac{2}{3}x - 8 - \frac{1}{4}x = 2$ — Add 8 to both sides.

$\frac{2}{3}x - \frac{1}{4}x = 10$ — Simplify the LHS
$\frac{2}{3}x - \frac{1}{4}x = \frac{8}{12}x - \frac{3}{12}x$
$= \frac{5}{12}x$

$\frac{5}{12}x = 10$ — Multiply both sides by the reciprocal of $\frac{5}{12}$

$x = 10 \times \frac{12}{5}$

$x = 10 \times 12 \div 5 = 24$

Method 2

The denominators of the fractions in the equation are 3 and 4

The least common multiple (LCM) of 3 and 4 is 12

$12(\frac{2}{3}x - 8) = 12(\frac{1}{4}x + 2)$ — Multiply both sides by 12

$\frac{2}{3}x \times 12 - 8 \times 12 = \frac{1}{4}x \times 12 + 2 \times 12$

$8x - 96 = 3x + 24$ — Subtract $3x$ from both sides.

$5x - 96 = 24$ — Add 96 to both sides.

$5x = 120$ — Divide both sides by 5

$x = 120 \div 5 = 24$

Check: When $x = 24$, $\frac{2}{3}x - 8 = \frac{2}{3} \times 24 - 8 = 16 - 8 = 8$
$\frac{1}{4}x + 2 = \frac{1}{4} \times 24 + 2 = 6 + 2 = 8$ ✓

b $\dfrac{2x+1}{3} = \dfrac{3(x+3)}{2}$

The denominators of the fractions in the equation are 3 and 2. The LCM of 3 and 2 is 6

$\dfrac{2x+1}{\cancel{3}^{1}} \times \cancel{6}^{2} = \dfrac{3(x+3)}{\cancel{2}^{1}} \times \cancel{6}^{3}$ — Multiply both sides by 6

$2(2x+1) = 9(x+3)$

$4x + 2 = 9x + 27$ — Expand the brackets and simplify $2(2x+1) = 4x + 2$ $9(x+3) = 9x + 27$

$-5x + 2 = 27$ — Subtract $9x$ from both sides.

$-5x = 25$ — Subtract 2 from both sides.

$x = 25 \div -5$ — Divide both sides by -5

So $x = -5$

Check: When $x = -5$, $\dfrac{2x+1}{3} = \dfrac{-10+1}{3} = \dfrac{-9}{3} = -3$

$\dfrac{3(x+3)}{2} = \dfrac{3(-5+3)}{2} = \dfrac{3 \times -2}{2} = -3$ ✓

c $\dfrac{2(5y-1)}{5} + 3 = \dfrac{7y+3}{3}$

The denominators of the fractions in the equation are 3 and 5. Their LCM is 15

$\dfrac{2(5y-1)}{\cancel{5}^{1}} \times \cancel{15}^{3} + 3 \times 15 = \dfrac{7y+3}{\cancel{3}^{1}} \times \cancel{15}^{5}$ — Multiply each term by 15

$6(5y-1) + 45 = 5(7y+3)$ — Expand the brackets and simplify. $6(5y-1) + 45 = 30y - 6 + 45 = 30y + 39$ $5(7y+3) = 35y + 15$

$30y + 39 = 35y + 15$

$39 = 5y + 15$ — Subtract $30y$ from both sides.

$24 = 5y$ — Subtract 15 from both sides.

$y = \frac{24}{5}$ — Divide both sides by 5

So $y = 4\frac{4}{5}$ or 4.8

Check: When $y = 4.8$, $\dfrac{2(5y-1)}{5} + 3 = \dfrac{2(5 \times 4.8 - 1)}{5} + 3 = \dfrac{2(24-1)}{5} + 3 = 12.2$

$\dfrac{7y+3}{3} = \dfrac{7 \times 4.8 + 3}{3} = 12.2$ ✓

Example 5

The diagram shows a triangle with angles $x°$, $(x + 30)°$ and $(2x - 10)°$
Show that the triangle is an isosceles triangle.

$(x + 30)°$

$x°$

$(2x - 10)°$

Solution 5

The sum of the angles in the triangle $= x + (x + 30) + (2x - 10) = 4x + 20$
The sum of the angles of a triangle is 180°

So $\quad 4x + 20 = 180$

$4x = 160$ — Subtract 20 from both sides.

$x = 40$ — Divide both sides by 4

So the angles of the triangle are

$x = 40°$, $x + 30 = 70°$, $2x - 10 = 70°$

The triangle has two equal angles and, therefore, is isosceles.

Exercise B

1 Solve each of the following equations.

a $\frac{3}{4}a + 5 = \frac{1}{2}a - 3$ **b** $\frac{2}{5}b - 7 = \frac{1}{10}b - 4$ **c** $\frac{3}{8}c + 2 = \frac{1}{4}c - 9$

d $\frac{5}{6}d - 8 = \frac{1}{3}d + 11$ **e** $\frac{7}{8}e + 1 = \frac{3}{4}e + 2$ **f** $\frac{7}{10}f + 3 = \frac{2}{5}f + 9$

g $\frac{5}{6}g - 2 = \frac{2}{3}g$ **h** $\frac{2}{3}h + 4 = \frac{1}{2}h - 3$ **i** $\frac{3}{7}i - 2 = \frac{1}{3}i + 1$

j $\frac{3}{5}j + 3 = \frac{3}{4}j - 9$

2 Solve each of the following equations.

a $\frac{3x + 1}{2} = \frac{4x - 1}{3}$ **b** $\frac{2x - 5}{3} = \frac{4x + 2}{4}$ **c** $\frac{x - 7}{3} = \frac{4(x - 3)}{5}$

d $\frac{2x - 3}{3} = \frac{3(2x - 5)}{2}$ **e** $\frac{2(x - 1)}{3} = \frac{3(x + 1)}{2}$ **f** $\frac{3(2y - 1)}{4} - 1 = \frac{3y - 2}{3}$

g $\frac{2(4y - 3)}{5} = \frac{5(2y + 7)}{2} - 5$ **h** $\frac{4(3y + 10)}{5} - 6 = \frac{5(2y - 8)}{7} + 15$

3 Sally has a piece of ribbon 1 metre long.
She cuts the ribbon into eight pieces each of length x cm.
She has exactly 8 cm of ribbon left over.
Write down and solve an equation to find x.

4 **a** **i** Explain why the three consecutive integers starting with x are x, $x + 1$ and $x + 2$

ii The sum of three consecutive integers starting with x is 24
Write down and solve an equation to find the three integers.

b The sum of five consecutive integers is 60
Find the median of the five integers.

5 Tom and Sally investigate the numbers they can make using different rules.

a **Tom**
Use x to stand for the number that Tom thinks of.
Write down and solve an equation to find x when Tom's answer is 12

b **Sally**
Use y to stand for the number that Sally thinks of.
Write down and solve an equation to find y when Sally's answer is 28

c Both Tom and Sally think of the same number, z.
They both get the same answer.
Write down and solve an equation to find z.

6 **a** Here are two number machines.
There is a value of x that gives the **same** value of y for **both** machines.
Write the output for each machine in the form $y = \ldots$
Hence write down and solve an equation to find this value of x.

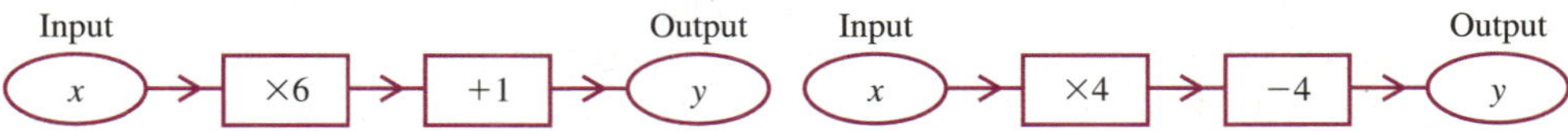

b Repeat **a** for each of the following pairs of number machines.

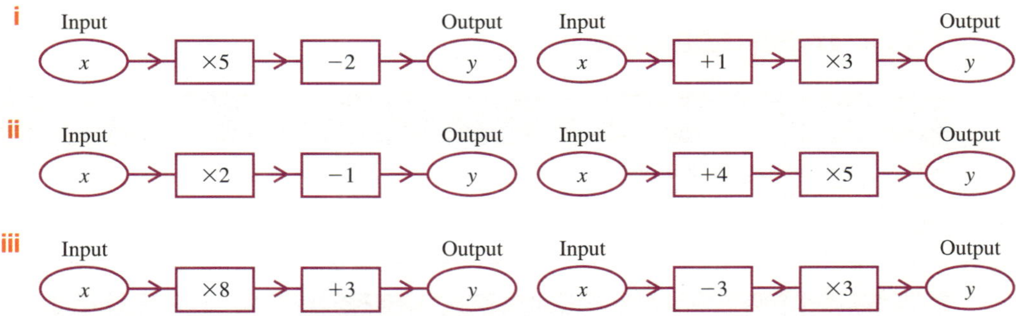

7 **a** Rectangle A has sides of length 4 cm and $(3x - 2)$ cm.
Work out x if the perimeter of rectangle A is 16 cm.

b Rectangle B has sides of length 5 cm and $(2y + 1)$ cm.
Work out y if the area of rectangle B is 50 cm^2

c Rectangle C has sides of length 3 cm and $(4z - 1)$ cm.
Rectangle D has sides of length 5 cm and $(3z - 2)$ cm.
Work out z if the area of rectangle C equals the area of rectangle D.

8 **a** Show that this triangle is equilateral.

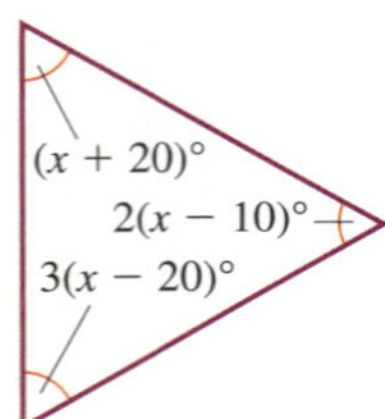

b This triangle is also equilateral.

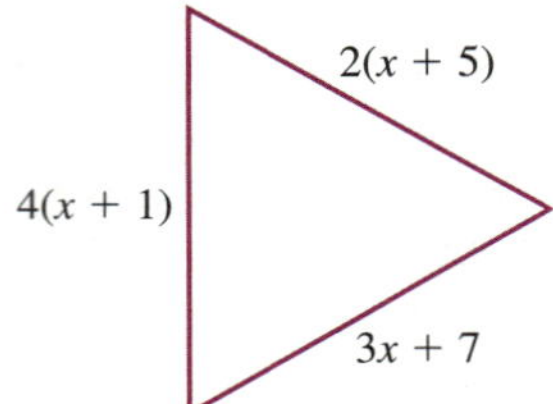

Work out the value of x.

9 **a** A rectangle has the measurements shown on the diagram.

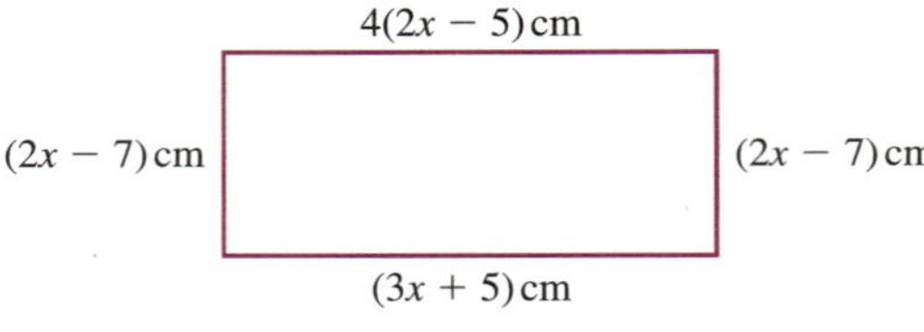

i Explain why $4(2x - 5) = 3x + 5$

ii Solve the equation $4(2x - 5) = 3x + 5$

iii Show that the area of the rectangle is 60 cm^2

b Show that this rectangle has a perimeter of 54 cm.

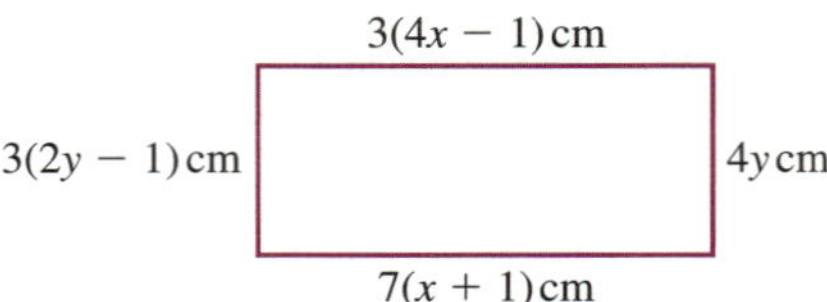

10 In bag A there are x counters.
In bag B there are 4 fewer counters than in bag A.
In bag C there are twice as many counters as there are in bag B.
In bag D there are five times as many counters as there are in bag A.
Afzal says that the number of counters in bag C equals the number of counters in bag D.
Explain why this is impossible.

10.2 Inequalities

CAN YOU REMEMBER

- The meaning of 'integer'?
- How to use a number line?
- How to solve an equation using the balance method?

IN THIS SECTION YOU WILL

- Learn how to represent an inequality on a number line.
- Learn how to use the balance method to solve a simple inequality.

An *inequality* is written using one of these symbols $< \leqslant > \geqslant$

$x < 2$ means that the value of the letter symbol x is *less than* 2
$x > -3$ means that the value of the letter symbol x is *greater than* −3
$x \leqslant -1$ means that the value of the letter symbol x is *less than or equal to* −1
$x \geqslant 3$ means that the value of the letter symbol x is *greater than or equal to* 3

Inequalities can be shown on a number line.

$x < 2$

The values covered by the solid line are the values of x that fit the inequality.
The hollow circle at 2 means that 2 is **not** included in the inequality.

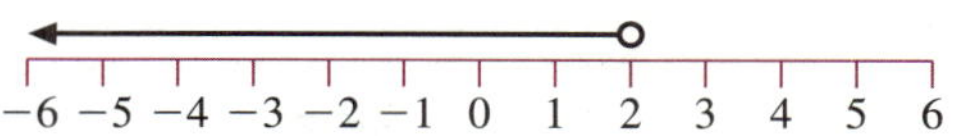

$x \geqslant -3$

The values covered by the solid line are the values of x that fit the inequality.
The full circle at −3 means that −3 **is** included in the inequality.

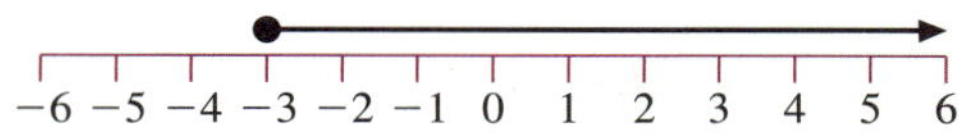

x is greater than 2 means the same as 2 is less than x.
So $x > 2$ and $2 < x$ are equivalent.

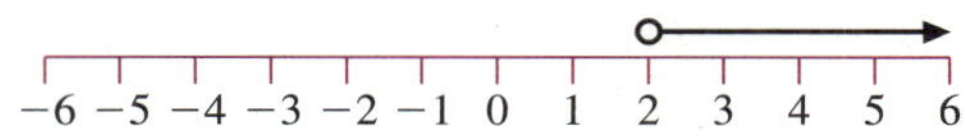

Example 1

Write down the inequality shown on each of these number lines.

a −6 −5 −4 −3 −2 −1 0 1 2 3 4 5 6

b

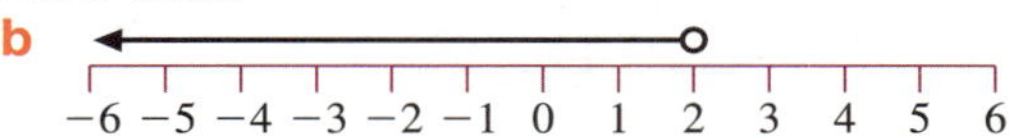

Solution 1

a $x \geqslant -5$ or $-5 \leqslant x$

b $x < 2$ or $2 > x$

The balance method can be used to solve simple linear inequalities.
The solution can be written as an inequality or shown on a number line.

For example

$$3x + 4 \geqslant -2$$

Subtract 4 from both sides.

$$3x \geqslant -6$$

Divide both sides by 3

$$x \geqslant -2$$

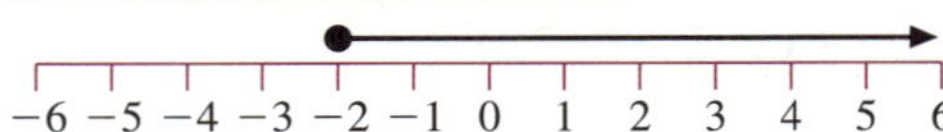

Example 2

Solve the inequalities:

a **i** $\frac{1}{2}x - 4 < -1$ **ii** $2x - 5 > 4x$

b Show the solution to each of the following inequalities on a number line.

i $7x - 7 \leqslant 2x - 2$ **ii** $\frac{x-2}{3} \geqslant \frac{2x-3}{4}$

Solution 2

a **i** $\frac{1}{2}x - 4 < -1$

Add 4 to both sides.

$$\frac{1}{2}x < 3$$

Multiply both sides by 2

$$x < 6$$

ii **Method 1** Make sure the x terms remain positive

$2x \geqslant 4x - 5$	Subtract $2x$ from both sides.
$0 \geqslant 2x - 5$	Add 5 to both sides.
$5 \geqslant 2x$	Divide both sides by 2
$2.5 \geqslant x$	

Method 2

$2x \geqslant 4x - 5$	Subtract $4x$ from both sides.
$-2x \geqslant -5$	Divide both sides by -2

When dividing (or multiplying) both sides by a negative value **reverse** the inequality

$x \leqslant 2.5$

$2.5 \geqslant x$ and $x \leqslant 2.5$ are equivalent

b **i**

$7x - 7 \leqslant 2x - 2$	Subtract $2x$ from both sides.
$5x - 7 \leqslant -2$	Add 7 to both sides.
$5x \leqslant 5$	Divide both sides by 5
$x \leqslant 1$	

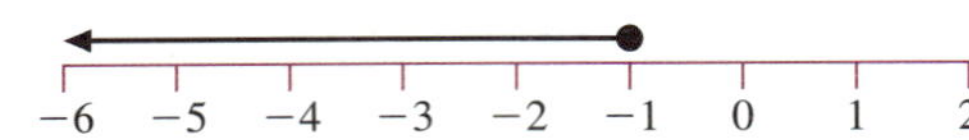

ii $\dfrac{x-2}{3} \geqslant \dfrac{2x-3}{4}$

The denominators of the fractions in the equation are 3 and 4. The LCM of 3 and 4 is 12

$\overset{4}{\cancel{12}} \times \dfrac{x-2}{\cancel{3}_1} > \overset{3}{\cancel{12}} \times \dfrac{2x-3}{\cancel{4}_1}$	Multiply both sides by 12
$4(x-2) > 3(2x-3)$	Expand the brackets.
$4x - 8 > 6x - 9$	Subtract $4x$ from both sides.
$-8 > 2x - 9$	Add 9 to both sides.
$1 > 2x$	Divide both sides by 2

$0.5 > x$

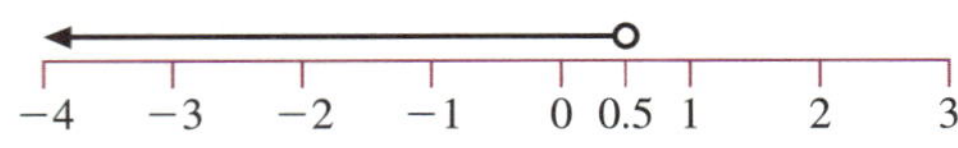

Exercise A

1 Show the following inequalities on a copy of this number line.
Use a different number line for each inequality.

−6 −5 −4 −3 −2 −1 0 1 2 3 4 5 6

a $x < 4$ **b** $x \geqslant 1$ **c** $x > -3$ **d** $x \leqslant -1$

e $-5 > x$ **f** $-5 \leqslant x$ **g** $3 \geqslant x$ **h** $3 < x$

2 The number lines show values of x.
Write down each of the inequalities.

a
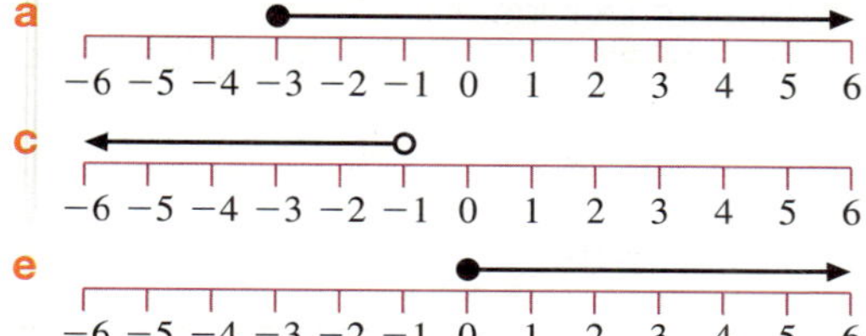

b
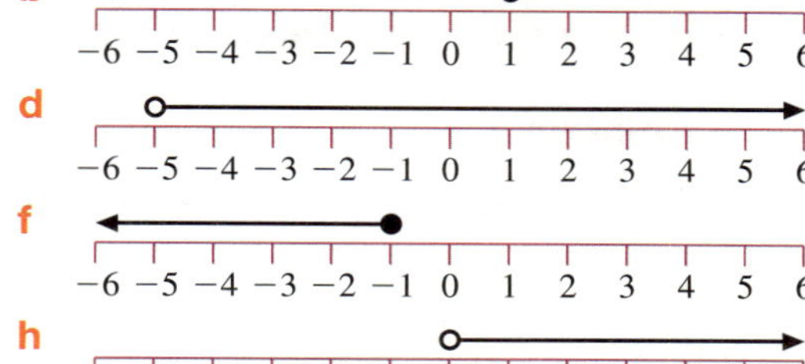

c

d

e

f

g

h

3 The smallest integer that satisfies the inequality $x \geqslant 2$ is $x = 2$
Write down the smallest integer that satisfies each of these inequalities.

a $a > 3$ **b** $b > 7$ **c** $c \geqslant -1$ **d** $d \geqslant -6$
e $e > -1$ **f** $f > -4$ **g** $g \geqslant -4$ **h** $h \geqslant -2$
i $i > 1\frac{1}{4}$ **j** $j > 2\frac{5}{8}$ **k** $k \geqslant 1\frac{1}{4}$ **l** $l \geqslant 2\frac{5}{8}$
m $m \geqslant -3\frac{4}{5}$ **n** $n \geqslant -1\frac{1}{3}$ **o** $o \geqslant -7.964$ **p** $p \geqslant -1.007$

4 The largest integer that satisfies the inequality $x < 2$ is $x = 1$
Write down the largest integer that satisfies each of these inequalities.

a $a < 3$ **b** $b < 7$ **c** $c \leqslant -1$ **d** $d \leqslant -6$
e $e < -1$ **f** $f < -4$ **g** $g \leqslant -4$ **h** $h \leqslant -2$
i $i < 1\frac{1}{4}$ **j** $j < 2\frac{5}{8}$ **k** $k \leqslant 1\frac{1}{4}$ **l** $l \leqslant 2\frac{5}{8}$
m $m \leqslant -3\frac{4}{5}$ **n** $n \leqslant -1\frac{1}{3}$ **o** $o \leqslant -7.964$ **p** $p \leqslant -1.007$

5 Solve each of the following inequalities.

a $a + 2 \leqslant 1$ **b** $b - 5 > -1$ **c** $4c \geqslant 12$ **d** $\frac{1}{4}d < -3$
e $2e + 3 \leqslant -1$ **f** $4f < 2f + 12$ **g** $5g - 3 \geqslant -8$ **h** $3(h - 6) \geqslant h$
i $3i - 3 \leqslant i - 5$ **j** $10j - 15 \geqslant 4j - 24$

6 Solve each of the following inequalities. Show your answers on a number line.

a $a - 3 > -7$ **b** $b - 5 \leqslant -2$ **c** $3c < -12$ **d** $\frac{1}{3}d \geqslant -1$
e $3e - 2 \leqslant -5$ **f** $6f > 2f - 8$ **g** $\frac{1}{5}g - 3 \geqslant -2$ **h** $\frac{1}{2}(h - 4) < -4$

7 Solve each of the following inequalties. Show your answer on a number line.

a $5i - 6 \leqslant 2i - 3$ **b** $3(2j + 1) \geqslant 2j - 5$ **c** $5y - 3 > 2y + 6$
d $3(d + 2) \leqslant 5d + 9$ **e** $5e - 6 \geqslant 6e + 5$ **f** $2f - 7 < 5(f + 1)$
g $\frac{x + 1}{2} < \frac{x - 5}{4}$ **h** $\frac{h - 9}{3} \geqslant \frac{2h + 1}{4}$ **i** $\frac{3h - 7}{2} \leqslant \frac{4h + 3}{3}$
j $\frac{5j - 9}{3} \leqslant \frac{2(6j - 7)}{5}$

Two single inequalities can be combined into a double inequality.
For example, the values of x that fit both of the inequalities $-4 < x$ and $x \leqslant 2$ can be described by the double inequality $-4 < x \leqslant 2$
The integers that satisfy this double inequality are $-3, -2, -1, 0, 1$ and 2

Example 3

Show each of the following double inequalities on a number line.

a $-4 \leqslant x < 3$ **b** $-4 < x \leqslant 3$ **c** $-3 \geqslant x$ and $x > 4$

Solution 3

a The values of x that fit the inequality $-4 \leqslant x < 3$ fit **both** $-4 \leqslant x$ and $x < 3$

$-4 \leqslant x$ (or $x \geqslant -4$)

$x < 3$

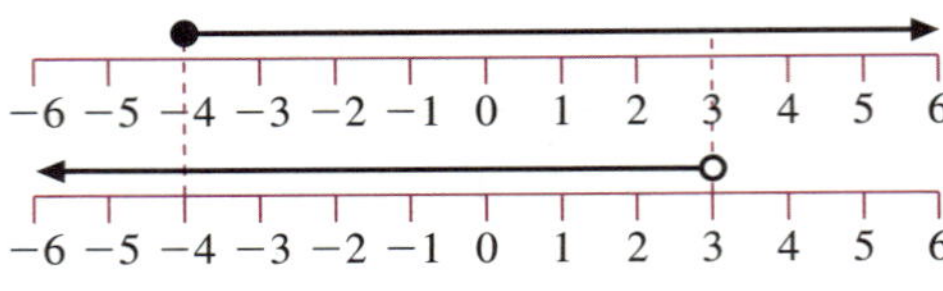

So the values of x that fit $-4 \leqslant x < 3$ are

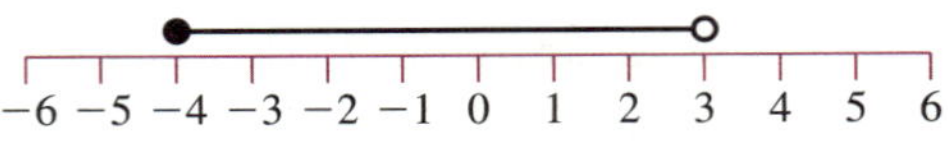

b $-4 < x \leqslant 3$

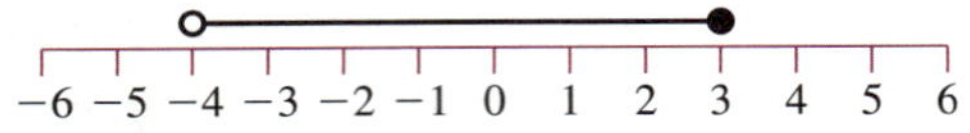

c $-3 \geqslant x$ and $x > 4$

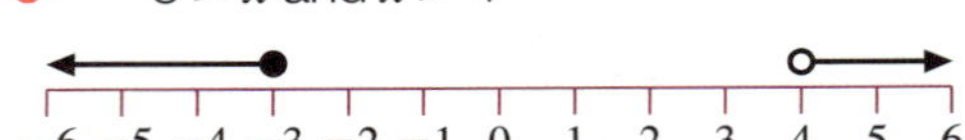

To solve double inequalities

Step 1: Write the double inequality as two separate inequalities.

Step 2: Use the balance method to solve each of the separate inequalities.

Step 3: Combine the two solutions into one double inequality.

Example 4

a Solve the inequality $1 \leqslant x + 4 < 5$

b Show the solution of the inequality $-5 \leqslant 2x + 3 < 9$ on a number line.

c Find the integer values that satisfy $-3 < 3(2x - 3) \leqslant 9$

Solution 4

a Separating $-1 \leqslant x + 4 < 5$ into two inequalities gives

$-1 \leqslant x + 4$ $\quad x + 4 < 5$ Subtract 4 from both sides.

$-5 \leqslant x$ $\quad x < 1$

Combining the single inequalities gives the double inequality $-5 \leqslant x < 1$

b Separating $-5 \leqslant 2x + 3 < 9$ into two inequalities gives

$-5 \leqslant 2x + 3$ $\quad 2x + 3 < 9$ Subtract 3 from both sides.

$-8 \leqslant 2x$ $\quad 2x < 6$ Divide both sides by 2

$-4 \leqslant x$ $\quad x < 3$

So the solution is the double inequality $-4 \leqslant x < 3$

On a number line the solution is

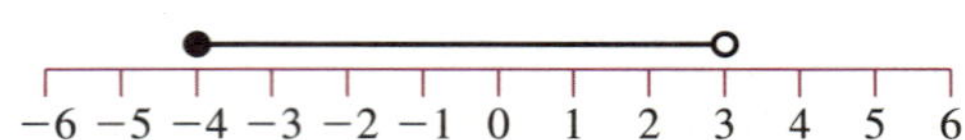

c Separating $-3 < 3(2x - 3) \leqslant 9$ into two inequalities gives

$-3 < 3(2x - 3)$	$3(2x - 3) \leqslant 9$	Expand the brackets.
$-3 < 6x - 9$	$6x - 9 \leqslant 9$	Add 9 to both sides.
$6 < 6x$	$6x \leqslant 18$	Divide both sides by 6
$1 < x$	$x \leqslant 3$	

So the solution is the double inequality $1 < x \leqslant 3$

So x can have values between 1 and 3, not including 1 but including 3

So the integer values satisfying $-3 < 3(2x - 3) \leqslant 9$ are 2 and 3

Exercise B

1 Tim says that the integers $-2, -1, 0, 1$ and 2 fit the double inequality $-3 \leqslant x < 2$
Explain why Tim is wrong.

2 Sally says that the integers $-1, 0$ and 1 fit the inequalities $-1 \geqslant x$ and $x \geqslant 1$
Explain why Sally is wrong.

3 Find the values of each of the integers p, q, r, s, t and u where
a the integers $-3, -2, -1, 0, 1, 2$ and 3 fit the inequality $p < x \leqslant q$
b the integers $-2, -1, 0, 1, 2, 3$ and 4 fit the inequality $r \leqslant x \leqslant s$
c the integers $-5, -4, -3, -2$ and -1 fit the inequality $t < x < u$.

4 You are given the following inequalities:
A $-4 \leqslant x < 1$ B $-1 < x \leqslant 3$
C $2 > x$ and $x \geqslant 4$ D $1 > x$ and $x > 3$
a Show each of inequalities A, B, C and D on a number line.
b Write down the integers that fit both A and B.
c Write down the integers that fit both A and C.
d Write down the integers that fit all of A, B, C and D.

5 Write down the inequalities shown on each of these number lines.

a
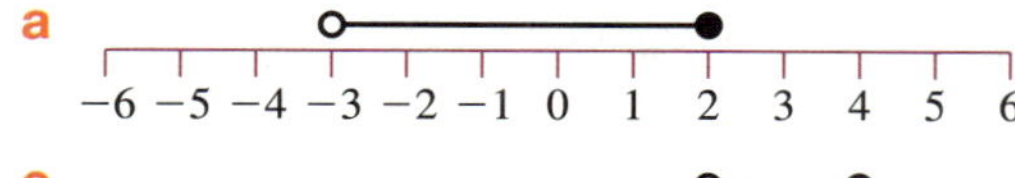

b
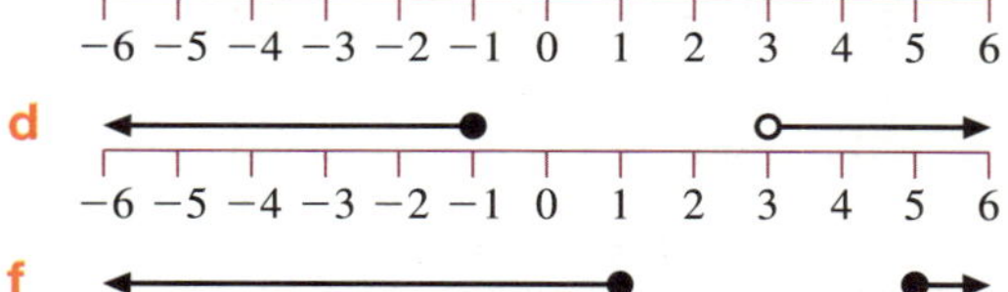

c
d
e
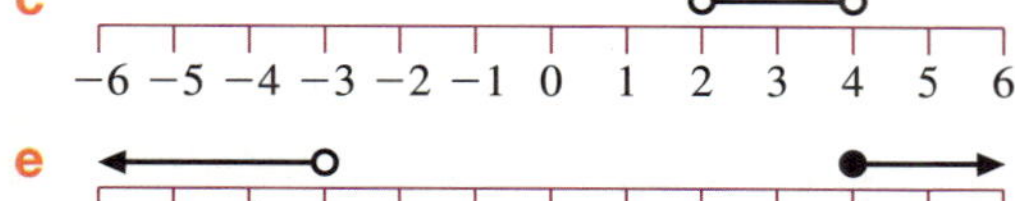

f
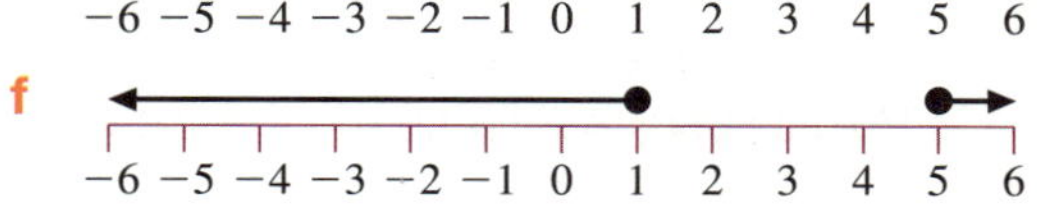

6 **a** Write the following pairs of inequalities as a single inequality.
i $-2 \leqslant x$ and $x < 5$ **ii** $-3 \leqslant x$ and $x \leqslant 2$ **iii** $0 < x$ and $x \leqslant 3$
iv $-1 \leqslant x$ and $x \leqslant 2$ **v** $-6 < x$ and $x < 3$
b Write down two separate inequalities that are equivalent to each of these double inequalities.
i $-1 \leqslant x < 2$ **ii** $-4 \leqslant x \leqslant 6$ **iii** $-4 < x \leqslant 0$
iv $1 \leqslant x \leqslant 2$ **v** $-1 < x < 1$
c List the integers that fit each of the inequalities in **a** and **b**.

7 Solve each of these inequalities.

a $-1 < x + 3 < 1$ **b** $-3 \leqslant x - 1 < 2$ **c** $-2 < x + 4 \leqslant 3$

d $-5 \leqslant x - 2 \leqslant -1$ **e** $-4 < 2x \leqslant 8$ **f** $-8 < 4x < 4$

g $-1 \leqslant \frac{1}{2}x \leqslant 3$ **h** $-2 \leqslant \frac{1}{4}x < 1$

8 Write down the integer values that satisfy each of these inequalities.

a $2 < x + 5 < 8$ **b** $-5 \leqslant x - 2 < -1$ **c** $-1 < x + 4 \leqslant 4$

d $-8 \leqslant x - 6 \leqslant -4$ **e** $-20 < 5x \leqslant 5$ **f** $-9 < 3x < 3$

g $-1 \leqslant \frac{1}{3}x \leqslant 1$ **h** $-2 \leqslant \frac{1}{2}x < 0$

9 Show the solution of each inequality on a number line.

a $-2 \leqslant x + 5 \leqslant 4$ **b** $0 \leqslant 2x + 4 \leqslant 10$ **c** $7 < 3x - 2 < 13$

d $-11 < 5x - 1 \leqslant 24$ **e** $-14 \leqslant 8x + 2 \leqslant 42$ **f** $-4 \leqslant 10x - 4 < 96$

g $-30 \leqslant 2(x - 5) \leqslant 10$ **h** $-7.5 < \dfrac{x - 3}{2} < 1.5$

10 Find the integer values that satisfy:

a $-2 \leqslant 3x + 1 < 7$ **b** $7 \leqslant 2x + 3 \leqslant 21$ **c** $-8 < 2(x - 4) < 0$

d $-3 < 3(3x - 1) < 9$ **e** $-7 < \dfrac{5x - 4}{2} < 1$ **f** $-5 < 2(5x + 1) \leqslant 9$

g $-100 < 10(3x + 2) < 200$ **h** $-9 < \dfrac{20x - 3}{5} + 2 < 14$

10.3 Inequalities in two variables

CAN YOU REMEMBER

- The meaning of the symbols $< \leqslant > \geqslant$?
- How to draw a straight line graph?
- How to find the equation of a straight line graph?

IN THIS SECTION YOU WILL

- Learn how to represent an inequality involving one or two variables on a grid.
- Learn how to represent several linear inequalities as a region on a grid.

The graph of $x + y = 4$ divides the grid into three sets of points.

At P, $x = 1$, $y = 3$ and $x + y = 4$
Points such as P that lie on the line satisfy the equality $x + y = 4$

At Q, $x = 3$, $y = 4$ and $x + y > 4$
Q is in the *region* **above** the line.
Points above the line satisfy the inequality $x + y > 4$

At R, $x = 2$, $y = 1$ and $x + y < 4$
R is in the region **below** the line.
Points below the line satisfy the inequality $x + y < 4$
When an inequality involves two variables, it can be shown as a region on a graph.

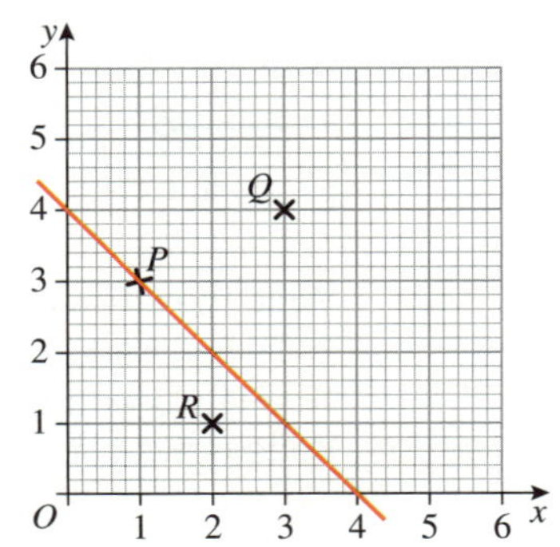

For example

$x < 4$

All points in the shaded region satisfy the inequality $x < 4$

The line $x = 4$ is **broken** because points on the line are **not** included in the inequality.

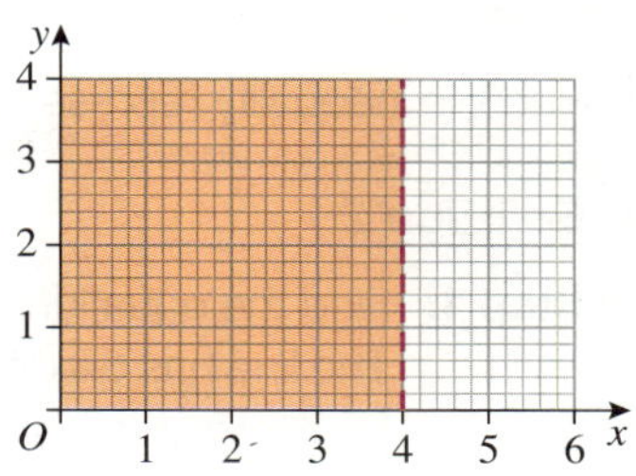

$y \geqslant -2$

All points in the shaded region satisfy the inequality $y \geqslant -2$

The line $y = -2$ is **solid** because points on the line are included in the inequality.

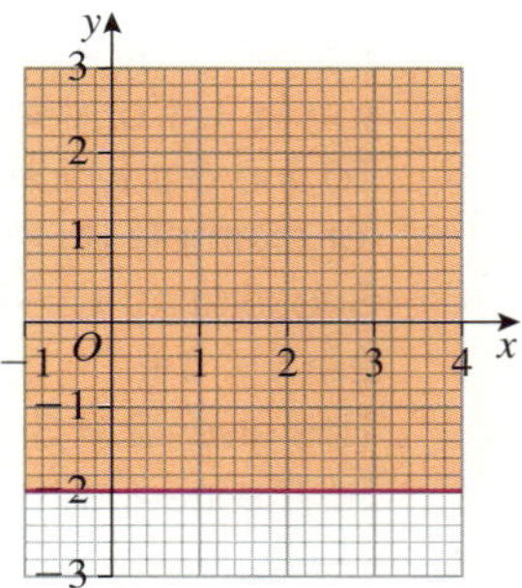

$y > 2x$

All points in the shaded region satisfy the inequality $y > 2x$.

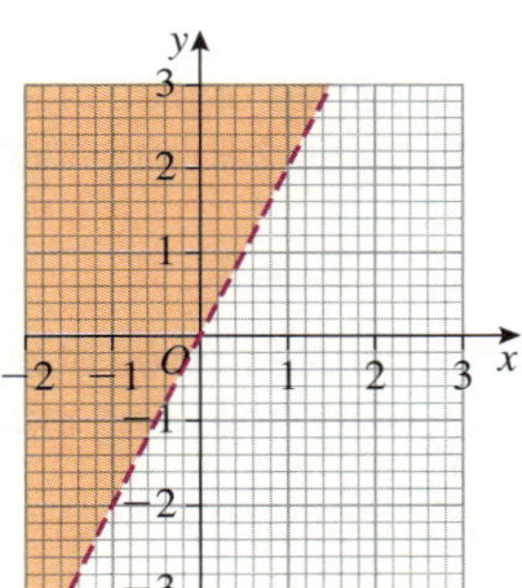

Example 1

Shade the region that satisfies the inequality $y \leqslant 3x - 2$

Solution 1

Step 1: Draw the line $y = 3x - 2$

Method 1

The line $y = 3x - 2$ passes through $(0, -2)$ and has gradient 3

Method 2

The line passes through $(0, -2)$, $(1, 1)$ and $(2, 4)$

Points on the line $y = 3x - 2$ are included in $y \leqslant 3x - 2$ so draw a solid line.

Step 2: Test any point not on the line to see whether it satisfies the inequality.

For example, test the point $(1, 3)$

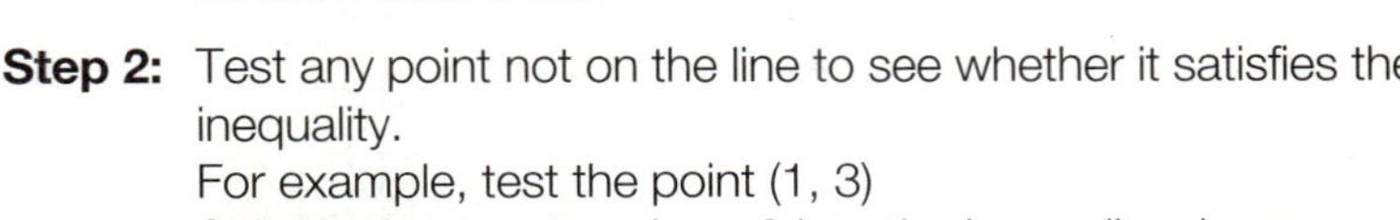

Substituting $x = 1$ and $y = 3$ into the inequality gives

$3 \leqslant 3 \times 1 - 2$

This gives $3 \leqslant 1$ which is **false**.

So $(1, 3)$ is **not** in the region satisfying the inequality.

So the other side of $y = 3x - 2$ should be shaded.

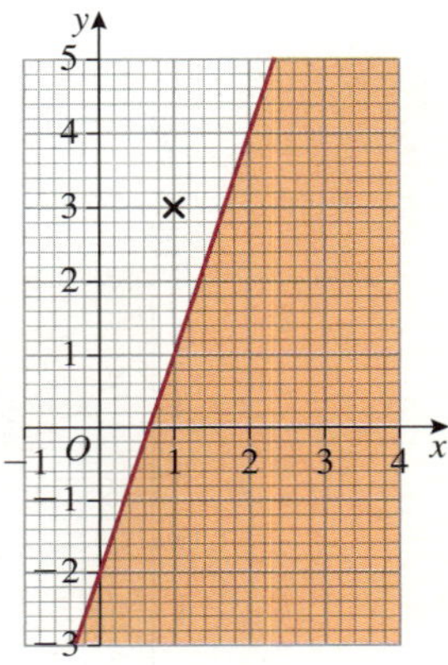

Example 2

Find the inequality represented by the shaded region on this grid.

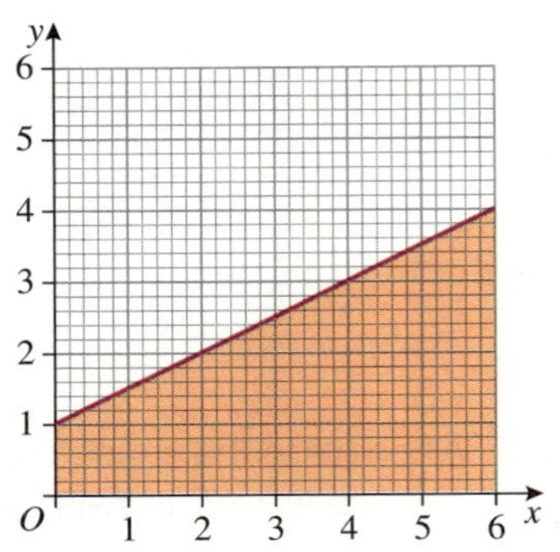

Solution 2

Step 1: Find the equation of the line.
The line has gradient $(m)\ \frac{1}{2}$ and y-intercept (c) 1
So its equation is $y = \frac{1}{2}x + 1$

Step 2: Find the inequality.
$y = \frac{1}{2}x + 1$ is a solid line so the inequality is
$y \geqslant \frac{1}{2}x + 1$ or $y \leqslant \frac{1}{2}x + 1$
To find out which, test a point in the shaded region, for example (4, 2)
Substituting $x = 4$ and $y = 2$ in $y \geqslant \frac{1}{2}x + 1$ gives
$2 \geqslant \frac{1}{2} \times 4 + 1$
This gives $2 \geqslant 3$ which is **false**.
So the inequality is $y \leqslant \frac{1}{2}x + 1$

Exercise A

1 On separate copies of a grid with x and y from 0 to 6, shade and label the regions that satisfy each of the following inequalities.

a $x > 2$ **b** $y \leqslant 1$ **c** $x + y < 5$
d $x + 2y \geqslant 4$ **e** $y \leqslant 2x$ **f** $y > -\frac{1}{2}x + 1$

2 On separate copies of a grid with x and y from -6 to 6, shade and label the regions that satisfy each of the following inequalities.

a $y \geqslant x + 2$ **b** $y \leqslant 3x - 4$ **c** $4x + y > 8$
d $x + 2y \leqslant -4$ **e** $y > 3 - 2x$ **f** $x + y < -3$

3 Find the inequality represented by each of the following regions.

a

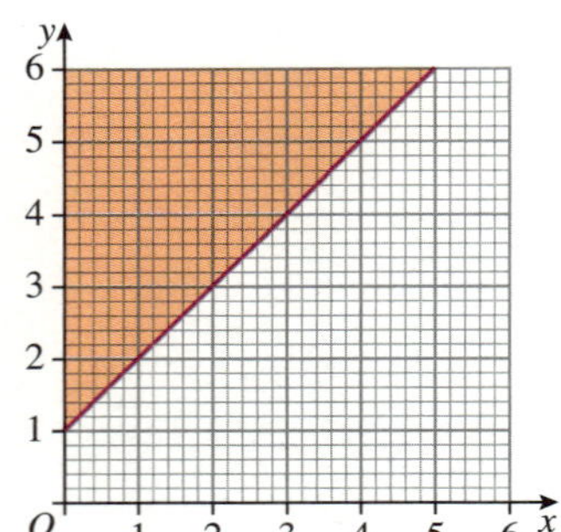

b

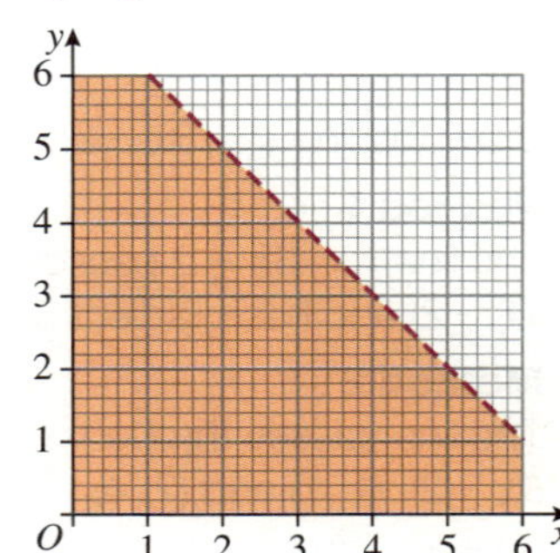

c

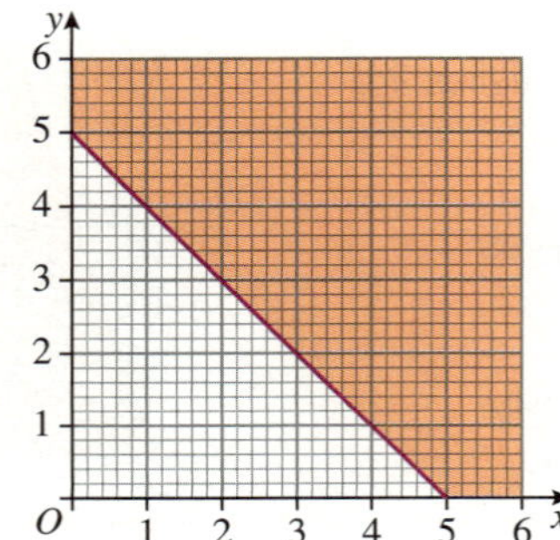

d

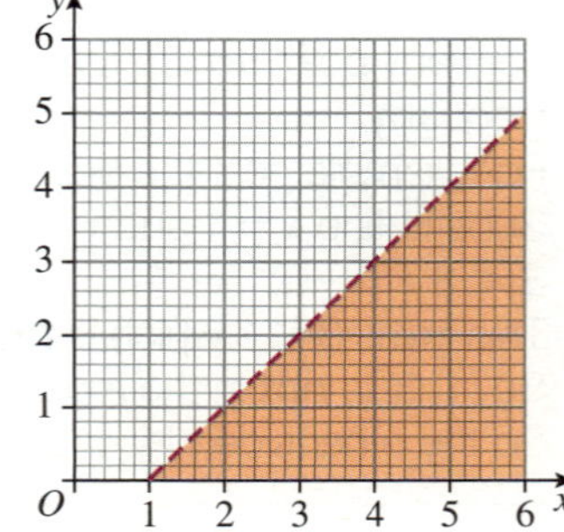

4 Find the inequality represented by each of the following **shaded** regions.

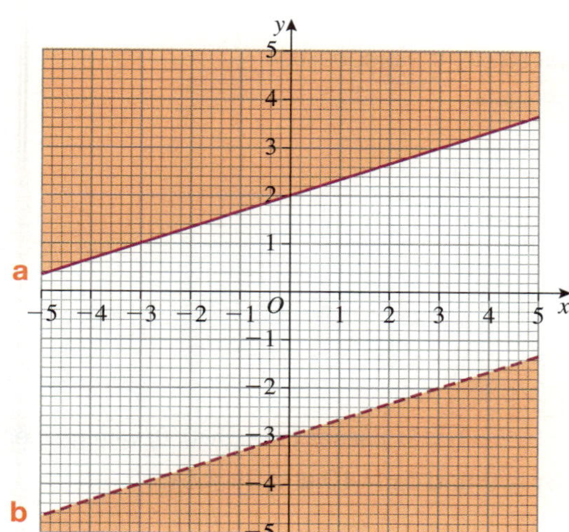

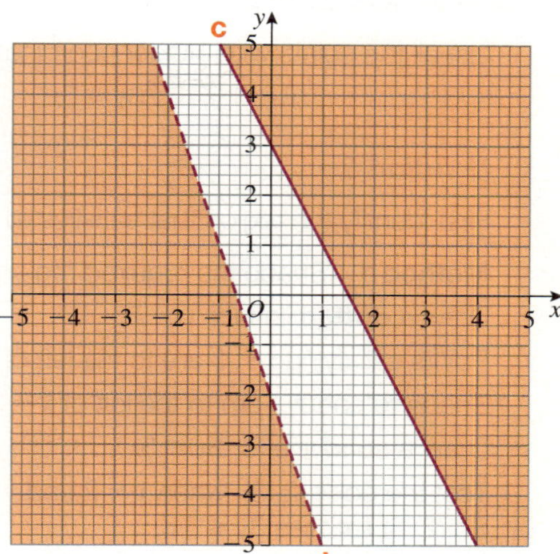

5 On the same grid, shade the regions that satisfy the inequalities.

a $x - 2y < 4$ and $x - 2y \geqslant 6$ **b** $y - 2x > 0$ and $y + 2x \leqslant 0$

6 Match each of these inequalities to one of the **unshaded** regions below.

a $2x + y < 4$ **b** $3x - 2y > 6$ **c** $y > 4 - 2x$ **d** $x + 2y < 4$

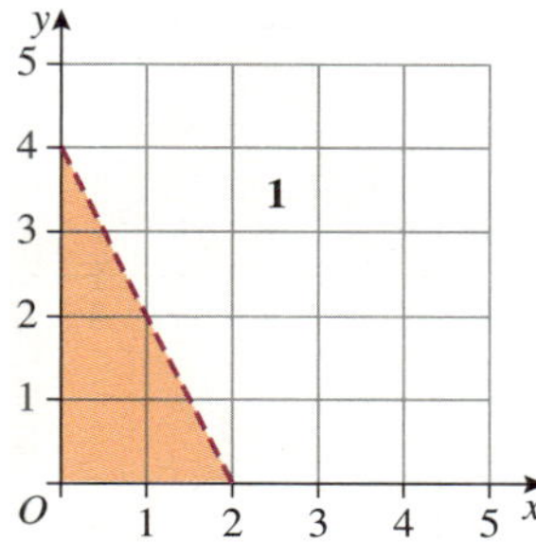

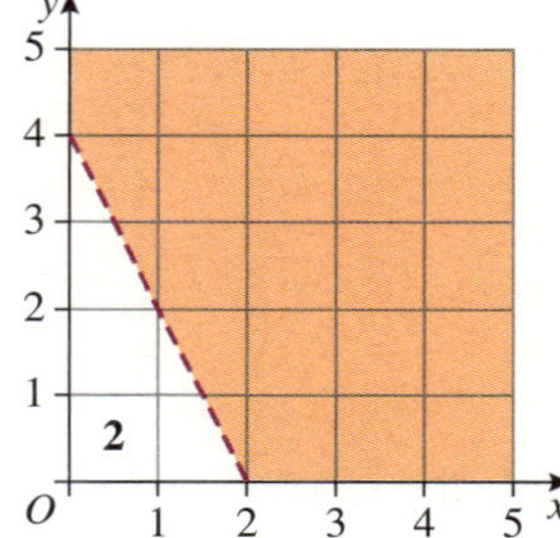

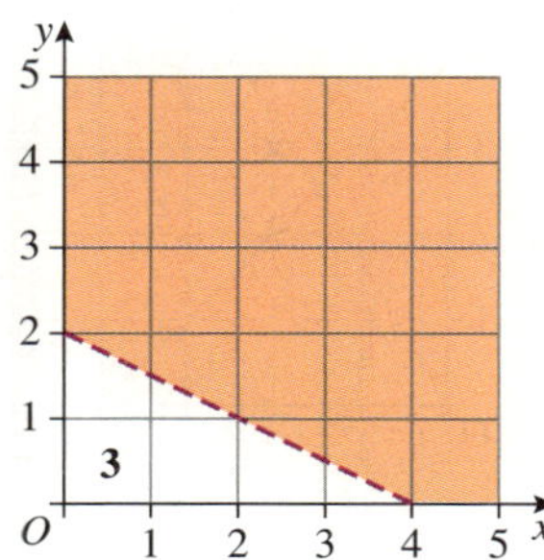

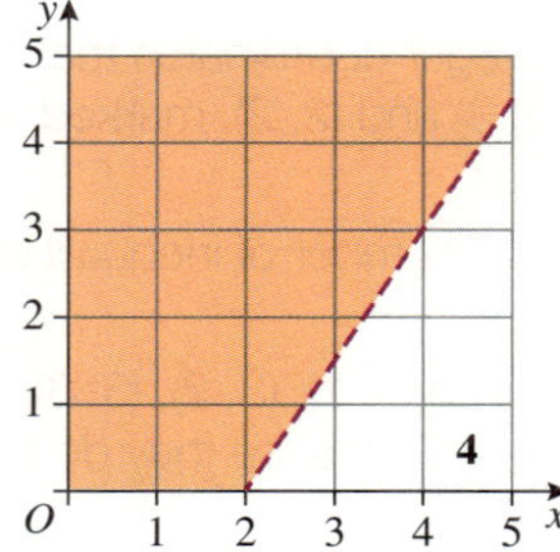

Regions can be described by more than one inequality.

Example 3

List all the points with integer coordinates that satisfy the inequalities

$$x < 3 \qquad 3y \leqslant 5x \qquad x + y \geqslant 4$$

Solution 3

First identify the region that satisfies all the inequalities.

Method 1 Shade the required region.

Draw a **dotted** line for $x = 3$

Points satisfying $x < 3$ are to the left of this line.

Shade to about 1 cm to the left of $x = 3$

Draw a **solid** line for $3y \leqslant 5x$.

$3y = 5x$ passes through (0, 0) with gradient $\frac{5}{3}$

Test the point (2, 3): when $x = 2$ and $y = 3$, $3y = 9$ and $5x = 10$ and $3y \leqslant 5x$.
So (2, 3) satisfies $3y \leqslant 5x$.
Shade to about 1 cm below $3y = 5x$.

Draw a **solid** line for $x + y \geqslant 4$

$x + y = 5$ passes through (0, 4) and (4, 0)

Test the point (0, 0): when $x = 0$ and $y = 0$, $x + y = 0$ and $x + y \leqslant 4$
So (0, 0) does **not** satisfy $x + y \geqslant 4$
Shade to about 1 cm above $x + y = 4$
The region satisfying the three inequalities is the triangle that has been shaded 3 times.
Points on the solid boundary lines are included in the region but points on the dotted line are not.

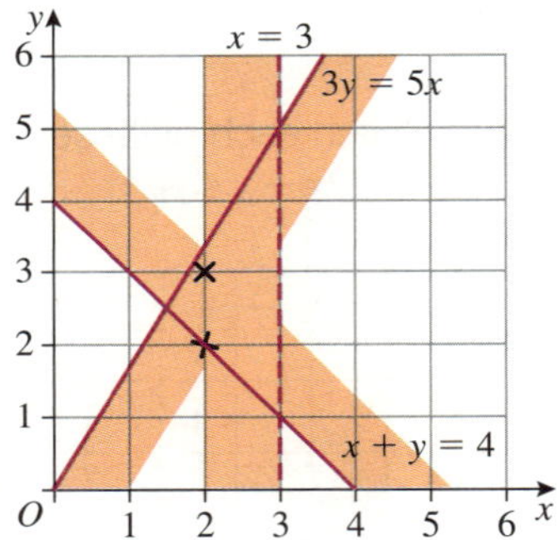

Method 2 Shade the regions **not** required.

Again there is no need to shade each entire region.

In this case the required region is **not** shaded.

The points with integer coordinates that satisfy the three inequalities are (2, 3) and (2, 2), marked with a cross on the grids.

Points that satisfy a number of inequalities are called the *solution set*.

Notice that the points (3, 1), (3, 2), (3, 3), (3, 4) and (3, 5) are not in the solution set because they do **not** satisfy the inequality $x < 3$

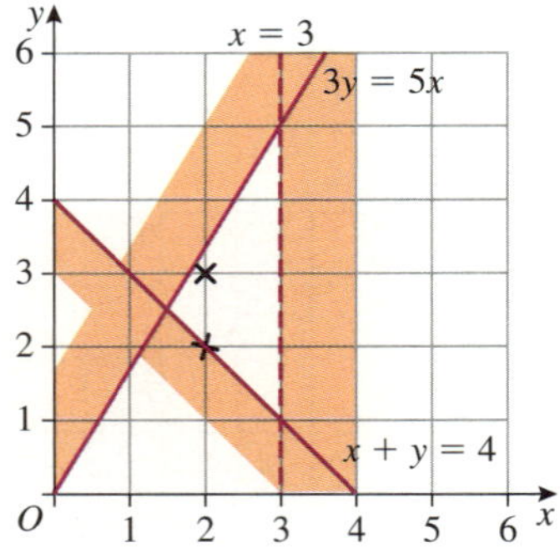

Exercise B

1 Show on a labelled grid the region satisfied by each of the following sets of three inequalities.

a $x \leqslant 3$, $y \geqslant x + 2$ and $y \leqslant 3x$

b $y \geqslant -1$, $x \leqslant 5$ and $y \leqslant x$

c $x + y \leqslant 4$, $y \geqslant \frac{1}{2}x$ and $x \geqslant 2$

d $y > 1$, $2y + 3x < 6$ and $y < 2x + 1$

e $y \leqslant x + 3$, $y \geqslant -\frac{1}{2}x + 3$ and $x \leqslant 6$

f $y \geqslant -2x + 4$, $y < \frac{1}{2}x + 4$ and $y \geqslant 2x - 4$

2 Each of these diagrams shows a region that satisfies a set of inequalities.
For each diagram find the inequalities.

a

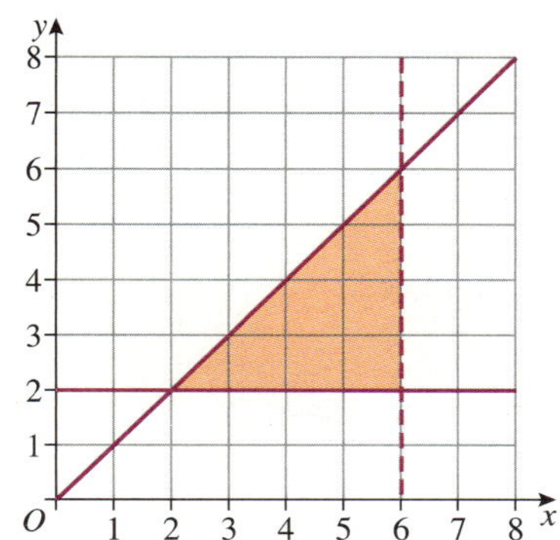

b

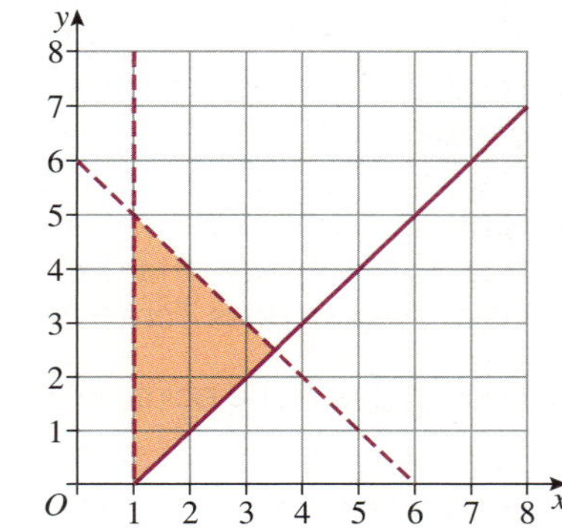

c

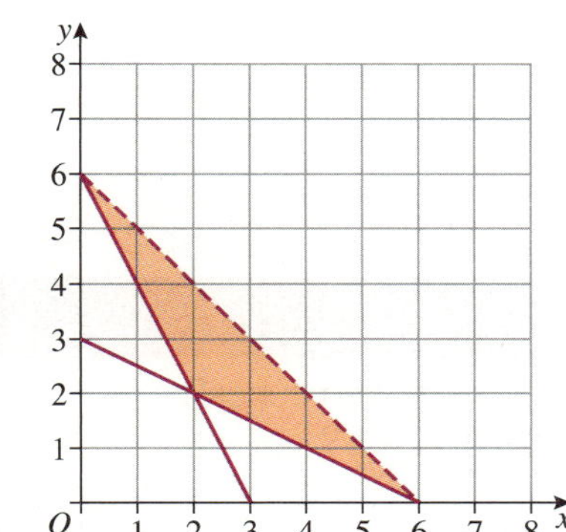

d

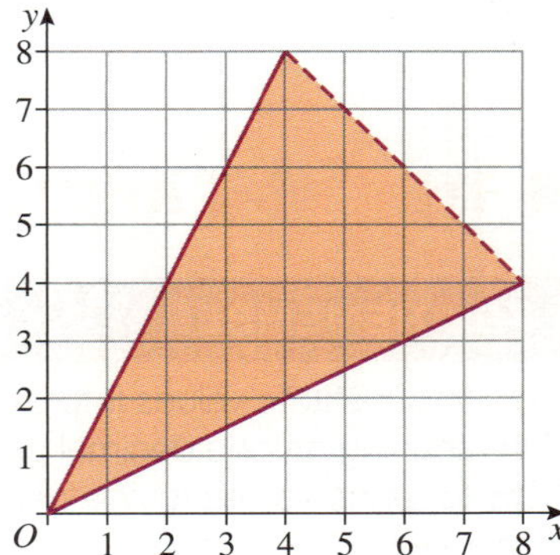

e

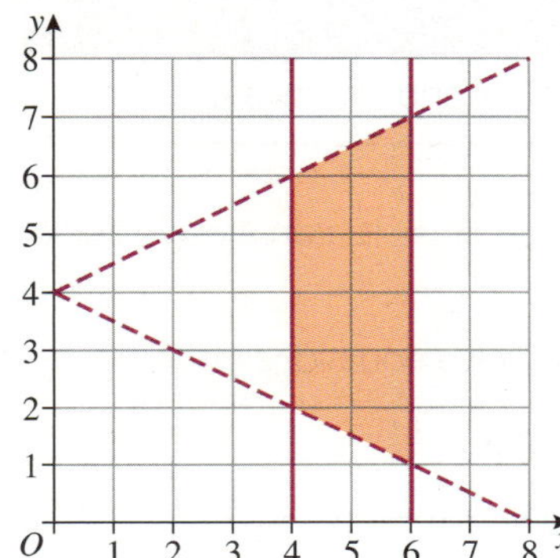

f

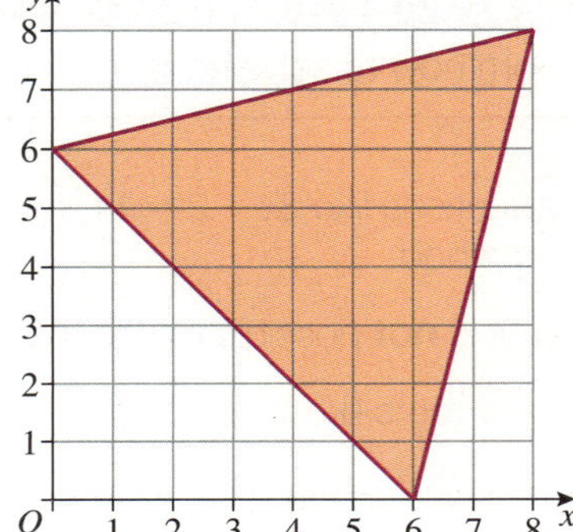

3 **a** Draw and label a grid with x and y going from 0 to 8
b Shade the region that satisfies the inequalities $y \leqslant x + 4$, $y \leqslant 8 - x$ and $y > 4$
c Explain why the point with coordinates (2, 4) does **not** lie in the region shaded in part **b**.
d Explain why the point with coordinates (1, 5) does lie in the region shaded in part **b**.

4 **a** Draw and label a grid with x and y going from 0 to 9
b Label R the region where the inequalities $y \geqslant x + 2$ and $3x + 4y \leqslant 24$ are satisfied.
c The values of x and y are positive integers.
Use your answer to part **b** to write down one possible pair of values that satisfies the inequalities $y \geqslant x + 2$ and $3x + 4y \leqslant 24$

5 Tom is thinking of two positive integers, x and y.
He gives these clues about the numbers.
The sum of the numbers is less than 12
The larger integer, y, is more than twice the smaller integer.
The smaller integer is greater than 2
a Draw and label a grid with x and y from 0 to 12
b Represent Tom's clues as a region on the grid.
c Both of the integers that Tom thinks of are prime numbers.
What integers does Tom think of?

6 The coordinates of the points in the region R satisfy the inequalities

$$x \leqslant 4, \qquad y \leqslant 2x + 1, \qquad y > x + 1$$

a Draw a grid with x and y from 0 to 9
b Show the region R on the grid.
c Circle all the points with integer coordinates that are in region R.

10.4 Trial and improvement

CAN YOU REMEMBER

- How to substitute values into expressions involving squares and cubes?
- The meaning of 'one decimal place', 'two decimal places', etc.?
- How to round values to one decimal place?

IN THIS SECTION YOU WILL

- Learn how to solve equations using the method of trial and improvement.

Simple equations like $3x + 2 = 11$, $5y - 2 = 4 + y$ and $5(z + 7) = 12$ can always be solved using the balance method.

However, it is **not** possible to use the balance method to solve equations involving powers and roots like $x^3 + 2x = 12$, $y^2 - \frac{1}{y} = 17$ and $\sqrt{y} + y = 11$

One way of solving these equations is the method of *trial and improvement*.

Estimate a solution, try it in the equation, and use the result to improve the estimate.

Trial and improvement should only be used to solve equations that cannot easily be solved by other methods.

Example 1

The equation $x^3 + 2x = 33$ has a solution that is a whole number.
Use the method of trial and improvement to find this solution.

Solution 1

Trial value of x	$x^3 + 2x$	Comment	Conclusion
2	$2^3 + 4 = 8 + 4 = 12$	Too small	$x > 2$, x is bigger than 2
4	$4^3 + 8 = 64 + 8 = 72$	Too big	$x < 4$, x is smaller than 4
3	$3^3 + 6 = 27 + 6 = 33$	Correct	$x = 3$

The solution of $x^3 + 2x = 33$ is $x = 3$

Example 2

Use the method of trial and improvement to solve the equation $x^3 - x = 30$
Give your answer to two decimal places.

Solution 2

Step 1: Try whole numbers.

x	$x^3 - x$	Comment	Conclusion
2	$2^3 - 2 = 6$	Too small	$x > 2$, x is bigger than 2
3	$3^3 - 3 = 24$	Too small	$x > 3$, x is bigger than 3
4	$4^3 - 4 = 60$	Too big	$3 < x < 4$, x is between 3 and 4

The solution lies between $x = 3$ and $x = 4$

Step 2: Try numbers between 3 and 4, with one decimal place.

x	$x^3 - x$	Comment	Conclusion
3.5	$3.5^3 - 3.5 = 39.375$	Too big	$3 < x < 3.5$, x is between 3 and 3.5
3.2	$3.2^3 - 3.2 = 29.568$	Too small	$3.2 < x < 3.5$, x is between 3.2 and 3.5
3.3	$3.3^3 - 3.3 = 32.637$	Too big	$3.2 < x < 3.3$, x is between 3.2 and 3.3

The solution lies between $x = 3.2$ and $x = 3.3$

Step 3: Try numbers between 3.2 and 3.3, with two decimal places.

x	$x^3 - x$	Comment	Conclusion
3.25	$3.25^3 - 3.25 = 31.078$	Too big	$3.2 < x < 3.25$, x is between 3.2 and 3.25
3.22	$3.22^3 - 3.22 = 30.166$	Too big	$3.2 < x < 3.22$, x is between 3.2 and 3.22
3.21	$3.21^3 - 3.21 = 29.866$	Too small	$3.21 < x < 3.22$, x is between 3.21 and 3.22

The solution lies between $x = 3.21$ and $x = 3.22$

Step 4: Try 3.215

x	$x^3 - x$	Comment	Conclusion
3.215	$3.215^3 - 3.215 = 30.016$	Too big	$3.21 < x < 3.215$

The solution lies between 3.21 and 3.215
All numbers between 3.21 and 3.215 round to 3.21 to two decimal places.
The solution of $x^3 - x = 30$ is $x = 3.21$ to two decimal places.

Exercise A

1 Each of the following equations has a solution that is a whole number.
Use the method of trial and improvement to find the exact solution.
You **must** show your trials.

a $a^2 + a = 56$ **b** $b^2 + b = 210$ **c** $c^2 - c = 210$ **d** $d^2 - d = 156$
e $e^2 + 2e = 99$ **f** $f^3 + f = 130$ **g** $g^3 + 3g = 36$ **h** $h^2 + \sqrt{h} = 84$
i $i^2 + \frac{1}{i} = 16.25$ **j** $j^3 - j^2 = 100$ **k** $k + \sqrt{k} = 20$

2 Lara, Bill and Sunita are solving an equation in x using trial and improvement.

a Lara finds that the solution lies between $x = 3.5$ and $x = 4$
What is the solution to the nearest whole number?

b Bill finds that the solution lies between $x = 3.6$ and $x = 3.65$
What is the solution to one decimal place?

c Sunita finds that the solution lies between $x = 3.63$ and $x = 3.64$

i Write this information as an inequality.

ii What value of x should Sunita try so that she can give the solution to two decimal places?

3 **a** The solution of the equation $x^3 - x = 20$ lies between $x = p$ and $x = q$ where p and q are consecutive whole numbers.

i Find the values of p and q. **ii** Write this information as an inequality.

b Repeat **a** for

i $x^3 + x^2 = 60$ **ii** $x^3 + x^2 - x = 100$ **iii** $x^3 - x^2 + x - \frac{1}{x} = 52$

4 **a** Use trial and improvement to solve the equation $x^3 = 16$
Give your answer to an accuracy of two decimal places.
Use a starting trial value of $x = 2$. You **must** show your trials.

b James wants to find the cube root of 1100

i What equation should James solve?

ii Find the cube root of 1100 to two decimal places using trial and improvement.
You **must** show your trials.

c Use trial and improvement to find the cube root of 425 to an accuracy of two decimal places. You **must** show your trials.

5 Copy and complete the following to solve the equation $x^3 + x = 20$ using the method of trial and improvement.
Give your answer to an accuracy of one decimal place.

Trial value of x	$x^3 + x$	Comment	Conclusion
2	$2^3 + 2 = \ldots$	Too …	$x > 2$
3	…	…	$\ldots < x < \ldots$

The solution lies between $x = \ldots$ and $x = \ldots$

Trial value of x	$x^3 + x$	Comment	Conclusion
2.5	$2.5^3 + 2.5 = \ldots$	…	$\ldots < x < \ldots$
…	…	…	$\ldots < x < \ldots$

The solution lies between $x = \ldots$ and $x = \ldots$

Trial value of x	$x^3 + x$	Comment	Conclusion
…	…	…	$\ldots < x < \ldots$

So to one decimal place the solution of $x^3 + x = 20$ is $x = \ldots$

6 Copy and complete the following to solve the equation $x^3 - x^2 = 95$ using the method of trial and improvement.
Give your answer to two decimal places.

Trial value of x	$x^3 + x^2$	Comment	Conclusion
4	$4^3 - 4^2 = \ldots$	Too …	$\ldots x > 4$
5	…	…	$\ldots < x < \ldots$

The solution lies between $x = \ldots$ and $x = \ldots$

Trial value of x	$x^3 - x^2$	Comment	Conclusion
4.5	$4.5^3 - 4.5^2 = \ldots$	…	$\ldots < x < \ldots$
4.9	…	…	$\ldots < x < 5$

The solution lies between $x = \ldots$ and $x = \ldots$

Trial value of x	$x^3 - x^2$	Comment	Conclusion
4.95	…	…	$\ldots < x < \ldots$
4.92	…	…	$\ldots < x < \ldots$
…	…	…	$\ldots < x < \ldots$

The solution lies between $x = \ldots$ and $x = \ldots$

Trial value of x	$x^3 - x^2$	Comment	Conclusion
…	…	…	$\ldots < x < \ldots$

So to two decimal places the solution of $x^3 - x^2 = 95$ is $x = \ldots$

7 Use trial and improvement to solve each of the following equations.
Use the starting values given. Give each of your answers to one decimal place.
You **must** show your trials.

a $a^2 + a = 60$ (start with $a = 7$) **b** $b^2 - b = 250$ (start with $b = 16$)

c $c^3 + 3c = 42$ (start with $c = 3$)

Example 3

Use trial and improvement to complete the table to find a solution to the equation
$x^2 + \sqrt{x} = 90$
Give your answer to one decimal place.

x	$x^2 + \sqrt{x}$	**Comment**
9	$9^2 + \sqrt{9} = 84$	Too small, $x > 9$, x is bigger than 9
10	$10^2 + \sqrt{10} = 103.162\ldots$	Too big, $9 < x < 10$, x is between 9 and 10

Solution 3

x	$x^2 + \sqrt{x}$	**Comment**	
Try one decimal place numbers between $x = 9$ and $x = 10$			
9.5	$9.5^2 + \sqrt{9.5} = 93.332\ldots$	Too big, $9 < x < 9.5$	x is between 9 and 9.5
9.4	$9.4^2 + \sqrt{9.4} = 91.425\ldots$	Too big, $9 < x < 9.4$	x is between 9 and 9.4
9.3	$9.3^2 + \sqrt{9.3} = 89.539\ldots$	Too small, $9.3 < x < 9.4$	x is between 9.3 and 9.4
Try $x = 9.35$			
9.35	$9.35^2 + \sqrt{9.35} = 90.480\ldots$	Too big, $9.3 < x < 9.35$	x is between 9.3 and 9.35

The solution lies between 9.3 and 9.35
All numbers between 9.3 and 9.35 round to 9.3 to one decimal place.
So the solution of $x^2 + \sqrt{x} = 90$ is $x = 9.3$ (to 1 d.p.).

Exercise B

1 Use trial and improvement to solve each of the following equations.
Use the starting values given. Give each of your answers to one decimal place.
You **must** show your trials.

a $d^2 + \sqrt{d} = 95$ (start with $d = 9$) **b** $e^2 + \frac{1}{e} = 43$ (start with $e = 6$)

c $f^3 - f^2 = 286$ (start with $f = 7$) **d** $g + \sqrt{g} = 4$ (start with $g = 2$)

e $h^3 - h^2 + h - \frac{1}{h} = 200$ (start with $h = 6$)

2 **a** Derek uses trial and improvement to solve an equation.
He finds that the solution lies between 3.731 and 3.734
Derek makes three statements.
Which statements are true?

Write a correct statement to replace any false statement.

b Derek finds that the solution of another equation is between 4.73 and 4.78
Derek gives the solution as 4.8. Explain why he could be wrong.

3 John is trying to solve the equation $x^3 + 2x = 45$ using trial and improvement.
He has been asked for the solution to an accuracy of one decimal place.
John's work is shown on the right.

Write down three (or more) pieces of advice for John.
Point out where he has gone wrong and how he could improve his method.

x	$x^3 + 2x$	Comment
3.5	$3.5^3 + 7 = 50$	Too big
3	$3^3 + 6 = 33$	Too small
3.25	$3.25^3 + 6.5 = 40$	Too small
3.24	$3.24^3 + 6.48 = 40$	Too small
3.28	$3.28^3 + 6.56 = 42$	Too small
3.32	$3.32^3 + 6.64 = 43$	Too small
3.325	$3.325^3 + 6.65 = 43$	Too small
3.4	$3.4^3 + 6.8 = 46$	Too big
3.35	$3.35^3 + 6.7 = 44.29$	Too small
3.36	$3.36^3 + 6.72 = 44.65$	Too small
3.37	$3.37^3 + 6.74 = 45.01$	Too big
3.369	$3.369^3 + 6.738 = 44.98$	Too small
3.3695	$3.3695^3 + 6.739 = 44.994 \ldots$	Too small

Answer 44.994 …

4 Megan is using trial and improvement to solve this problem.
Number × 2.7 = 6.2

Megan shows her working in this table.
Copy the table and continue Megan's work until you know the number correct to two decimal places.

Try	Result	Comment
2	$2 \times 2.7 = 5.4$	Too small
2.5	$2.5 \times 2.7 = 6.75$	Too big

5 Copy the table. Use trial and improvement to complete it to find a solution to the equation $x^3 + 5x = 167$

Give your answer to one decimal place.

x	$x^3 + 5x$	Comment
5		

6 Copy the table. Use trial and improvement to complete it to find a solution to the equation $x^3 - 2x = 50$

Give your answer to one decimal place.

x	$x^3 - 2x$	Comment
3		

7 You are asked to solve the equation $x(x + 1)(x + 2) = 3$

a Find two consecutive whole numbers between which x must lie.

b Solve the equation using the method of trial and improvement.
Give your answer to one decimal place. You **must** show your trials.

8 The following equations each have two solutions, some of which are negative. Use the method of trial and improvement to find both the solutions for each equation to an accuracy of one decimal place.

a $x^2 + x = 55$ **b** $x^2 - 5x = 7$ **c** $x^2 + 6x = 24$

9 Use the method of trial and improvement to solve each of these equations. Give your answer to one decimal place. You **must** show your trials.

a $a^3 + 3a = 82$ **b** $b^3 - 2b = 147$ **c** $c^3 + 3c = 75$

d $d^3 + 4d = 94$ **e** $e^3 + 2e^2 = 1055$ **f** $f^3 - 3f^2 = 170$

g $3g^3 - 4g = 60$ **h** $h^3 - 2h^2 + 3h = 54$

Chapter summary

- The balance method can be extended to solve equations with the unknown on one or both sides.
- Equations are often used to solve problems.
  Step 1: Use the information given to set up an equation.
  Step 2: Solve the equation using the balance method.
- An inequality is written using one of these symbols $< \leqslant > \geqslant$
- Inequalities can be shown on a number line.
  $x < 4$ or $4 > x$

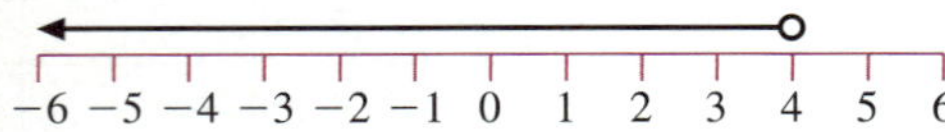

  The hollow circle indicates that 4 is **not** included in the inequality.
  $x \leqslant 4$ or $4 \geqslant x$

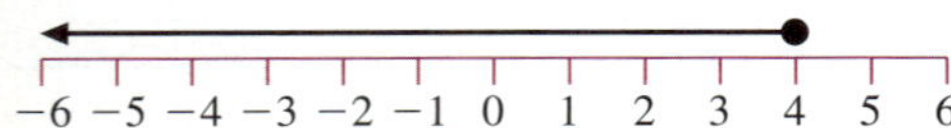

  The full circle indicates that 4 **is** included in the inequality.
- The balance method can be used to solve simple inequalities.
- Two single inequalities can be combined into a double inequality.
- The balance method can be used to solve double inequalities.
  Separate the double inequality into two inequalities and solve each using the balance method. Then combine the two solution inequalities.
- Inequalities involving one or two variables can be shown as regions on a graph.
- One way of solving equations involving powers and roots is the method of trial and improvement.

Chapter review

1 Solve these equations.

a $8s + 2 = 6s + 3$

b $\frac{20 - y}{3} = 5.5$

c $2(y + 3) = 24$

d $8z + 2 = 9 - 2z$

2 Solve these equations.

a $9x - 4 = 8 + x$

b $\frac{9 - y}{3} = 4$

c $2(z - 3) = 5 - 3z$

3 Solve these equations.

a $\frac{10 - x}{4} = x - 2$

b $\frac{2}{3}(5x - 2) = 12$

c $\frac{3}{4}x - 1 = \frac{2}{5}x + 6$

d $\frac{3x - 1}{2} - \frac{2x - 1}{6} = 6$

4 The diagram shows a triangle with the lengths of its sides given in centimetres.

a Write down an expression for the perimeter of the triangle. Give your answer in its simplest form.

b The perimeter of the triangle is 22 cm. By forming an equation, find the value of y.

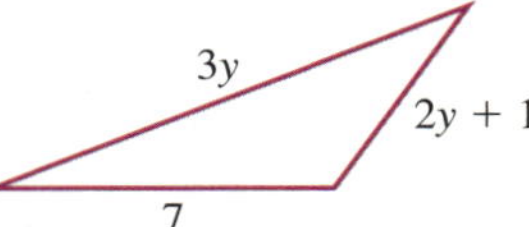

5 A test has 25 questions. The test score is calculated like this:

Start with 50 marks.
Add 2 marks for every correct answer.
Deduct 1 mark for every wrong answer.

a What is the range of possible marks in the test?

b A candidate gets x questions correct.
Write an expression in terms of x for the candidate's total mark.
Write the expression as simply as possible.

c Sally scores 85 in the test.
Write and solve an equation in x to calculate the number of questions that Sally gets correct.

6 Solve the inequalities.

a $4w + 9 < 1$

b $9x < 5x + 6$

c $y + 20 < 12 - 3y$

7 List the values of x, where x is an integer, such that

a $-1 \leqslant x - 2 < 1$

b $3 < 2x \leqslant 11$

c $-1 \leqslant 3x + 2 < 8$

8 a Solve the inequality $3x + 4 \geqslant 1$

b Write down the inequality shown by the following diagram.

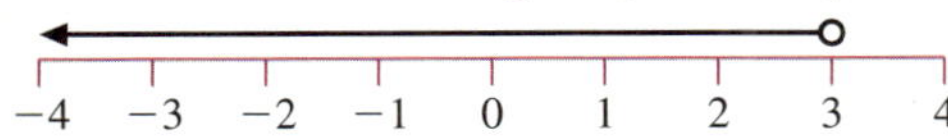

c Write down all the integers that satisfy both inequalities shown in parts **a** and **b**.

9 Find all pairs of integer values of x and y that satisfy all the inequalities
$2 < x < 6, \quad 0 < y < 3, \quad 2 < x + y < 7$

10 **a** On a copy of a grid with x and y from -6 to 6 indicate clearly the region defined by the three inequalities $y \leqslant 4$, $\quad x \geqslant -3$, $\quad y \geqslant x + 1$

b Write down the three inequalities that describe the shaded region.

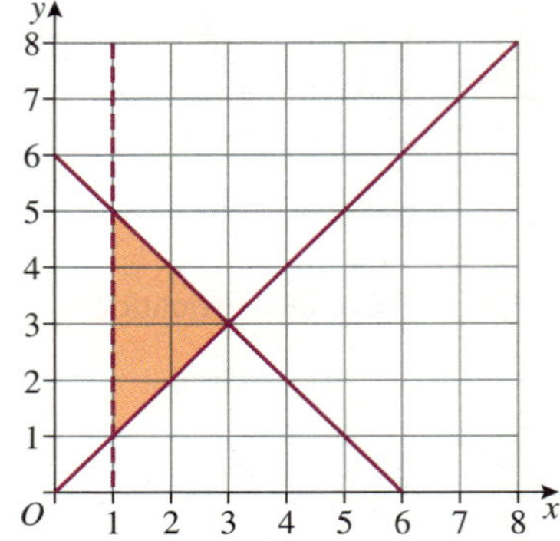

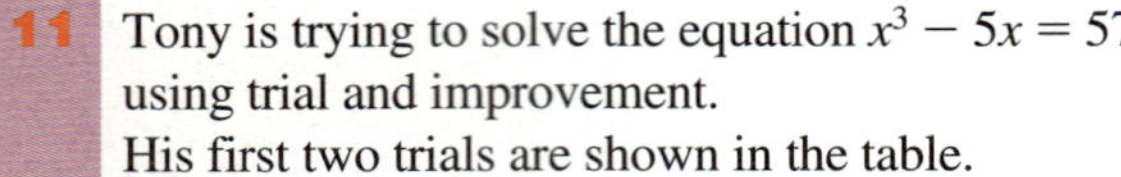

11 Tony is trying to solve the equation $x^3 - 5x = 57$ using trial and improvement.
His first two trials are shown in the table.

x	$x^3 - 5x$	**Comment**
4	44	Too small
5	100	Too big

Find the solution of the equation.
Give your answer to one decimal place.

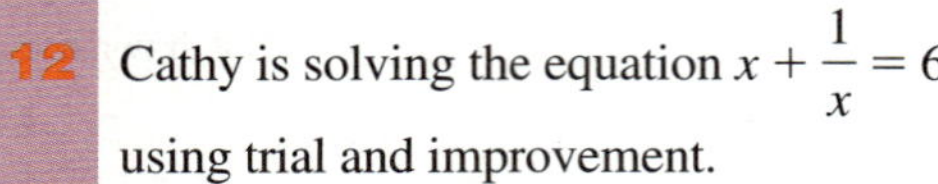

12 Cathy is solving the equation $x + \dfrac{1}{x} = 6$ using trial and improvement.

The table shows her first two trials.
Find the solution of the equation.
Give your answer to one decimal place.

x	$x + \dfrac{1}{x}$	**Comment**
5	5.2	Too small
6	6.17	Too big

CHAPTER 11

Accuracy and speed

11.1 Accuracy and measures

CAN YOU REMEMBER

- How to show inequalities on a number line?
- The rules for rounding numbers?
- The difference between discrete and continuous data?

IN THIS SECTION YOU WILL

- Learn the meaning of 'approximation', 'lower bound' and 'upper bound'.
- Estimate solutions to problems using approximate data.
- Write numbers to an appropriate level or degree of accuracy.

An *approximation* is a rounded value.
For example, an approximation for the number of people at a party is 120 people to the nearest ten.
There could be as few as 115 people, because 115 rounds up to 120 to the nearest ten.
There could be as many as 124 people, because 124 rounds down to 120 to the nearest ten.

This can be shown on a number line, as on the right.

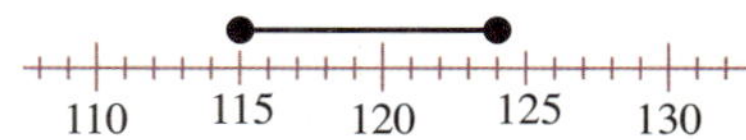

The approximation, 120, lies between the *lower bound* 115 and the *upper bound* 124.
The smallest possible value is called the lower bound or *lower limit*.
The largest possible value is called the upper bound or *upper limit*.

For example, the cost of a car journey is £9 to the nearest pound.

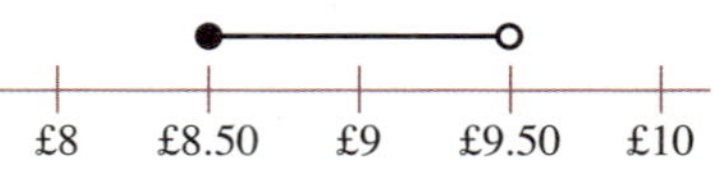

£8.50 ⩽ cost < £9.50

The lower bound is £8.50

The upper bound is £9.49

£9.50 is not included as it rounds to £10

Here are some statements using continuous data.

A car is travelling at 30 miles per hour to the nearest whole number.

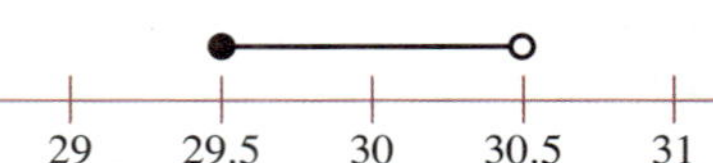

The approximate speed, 30 mph, lies between the lower bound 29.5 mph and the upper bound 30.5 mph.

The greatest possible speed is actually 30.499 99… mph, as this is the greatest value that rounds down to 30 mph. 30.499 99… mph is very close to 30.5 mph.

It is more convenient to give the maximum possible speed as 30.5 mph.

Example 1

The River Don is 70 miles long to the nearest 10 miles.
Write down the smallest and largest possible lengths of the river.

Solution 1

Smallest possible length = 65 miles

Largest possible length = 74.999 999 9 = 75 miles

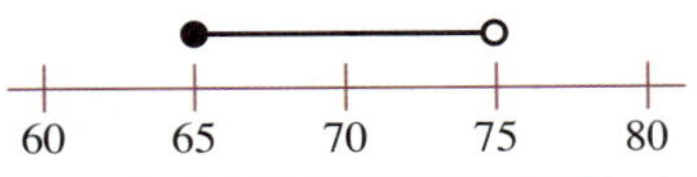

Example 2

On a shopping trip Mrs Senior spent £50 to the nearest £5
What is the most that she could have spent?

Solution 2

£47.50 ⩽ spent < £52.50

Most she could have spent = £50 + £2.49 = £52.49

The answer is not £52.50 as this would round up to £55

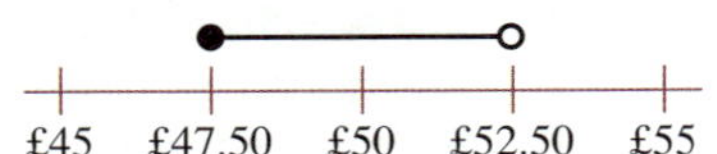

Exercise A

1 Each of the following values is given to the nearest whole number. Write down the largest and smallest possible values.

a	£5	**b**	£12	**c**	£20	**d**	£100
e	30 kg	**f**	25 miles	**g**	17 km	**h**	30 seconds

2 Write down the minimum and maximum values of each of the following.

- **a** £10 given to the nearest pound
- **b** 60 pence given to the nearest 10 p
- **c** £1.40 given to the nearest 10 p
- **d** 85 pence given to the nearest 5 p
- **e** £5.55 given to the nearest 5 p
- **f** 80 pence given to the nearest 20 p
- **g** £4.60 given to the nearest 20 p
- **h** £25 given to the nearest £5
- **i** £70 given to the nearest £5
- **j** £90 given to the nearest £10
- **k** £130 given to the nearest £10

3 Write down the minimum and maximum values of each of the following.

- **a** 30 miles to the nearest mile
- **b** 14 miles to the nearest mile
- **c** 16 kg to the nearest kilogramme
- **d** 25 kg to the nearest kilogramme
- **e** 27 seconds to the nearest second
- **f** 60 seconds to the nearest second

4 Write down the minimum and maximum values of each of the following.

- **a** 50 miles to the nearest 10 miles
- **b** 180 kg to the nearest 10 kg
- **c** 30 tonnes to the nearest 10 tonnes
- **d** 80 km to the nearest 10 km
- **e** 25 metres to the nearest 5 metres
- **f** 70 grams to the nearest 5 grams
- **g** 120 cm to the nearest 5 cm
- **h** 175 cl to the nearest 5 cl

5 The signpost is accurate to the nearest mile.
What is the shortest possible distance to Todwick?

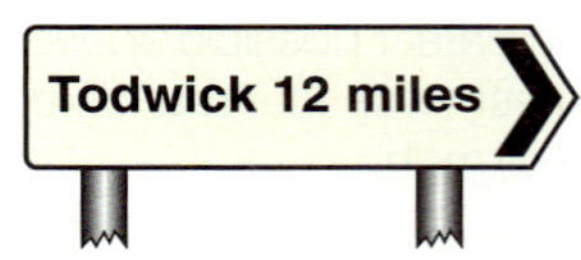

6 Lawrence is working out his salary on his calculator.
He says that his salary is £83 000 to the nearest thousand pounds.
a What is the least possible value of his salary?
b What is the highest possible value of his salary?

7 A car is for sale. The advertisement says that the car has travelled 65 000 miles, to the nearest thousand miles.
What is the smallest possible mileage the car could have travelled?

8 A television commentator said that the attendance at Old Trafford was 53 000 to the nearest thousand. What was the largest possible attendance?

Here are three statements.

The height of the Empire State Building is 1453 feet, $8\frac{9}{16}$ inches – very accurate.
The height of the Empire State Building is 1450 feet – accurate but rounded sensibly.
The height of the Empire State Building is 1500 feet – not very accurate, rounded to the nearest 100 feet.

To write answers to an appropriate or suitable degree of accuracy, round the number to a value that would be used in conversation.

Example 3

Write each of the following values to a suitable degree of accuracy.
a The average salary of a consultant is £82 147.34
b The number of units of electricity that the average household uses in winter is 1678
c The average speed on a motorway is 63.2143 mph.

Solution 3

a Write to the nearest thousand → £82 000
b Write to the nearest 50 → 1700
c Write to the nearest whole number → 63 mph or to the nearest 10 mph → 60 mph.

For a calculation, a suitable degree of accuracy often means giving the answer to the same number of decimal places as the values in the question.

Example 4

A rectangle has length = 3.1 cm and width = 4.7 cm.
Calculate the area, giving your answer to a suitable degree of accuracy.

Solution 4

Area $= l \times w = 3.1 \times 4.7 = 14.57$ cm^2
The values in the question are to one decimal place.
So the answer should be given to the same degree of accuracy, one decimal place:
area $= 14.6$ cm^2

Exercise B

1 Write each of the following values to a suitable degree of accuracy, giving a reason for your answer.
   a An average wage of £187.50 per week
   b An average attendance at a football ground of 34 127
   c The height of a mountain 1203.1 metres
   d The distance between two towns is 32.157 miles
   e The average number of patients per dentist is 971.2

2 Match the most appropriate degree of accuracy to each measurement.

Distance between planets and the sun	to the nearest km	Distance between British towns
Diameter of planets	to the nearest 1 000 000 km	to the nearest 1000 km

3 The length of a rectangle is 11.3 cm. The width of the rectangle is 7.1 cm.
Each length is approximate.
Work out the perimeter of the rectangle.
Give your answer to a suitable degree of accuracy.

4 Daniel says he lives 472 metres from school. Give this distance to a suitable degree of accuracy and state the degree of accuracy used.

5 The radius of a circle is 4.2 cm.
Find the area of the circle. Give your answer to a suitable degree of accuracy.

6 Megan is 5 feet 3 inches tall. Use 1 foot = 12 inches = 30 centimetres to calculate Megan's height in centimetres. Give your answer to an appropriate degree of accuracy.

7 The radius of a circle is 10.42 cm.
Calculate the circumference.
Give your answer to a suitable degree of accuracy.

8 A 70 cl bottle of wine costs £2.99
Work out the cost of 1 litre.

9 A man is paid at the rate of £7.125 per hour.
He works 15 hours.
How much is he paid?

10 Paul travels 6.7 km in 4.15 minutes.
He works out his speed using $6.7 \div 4.15$
He says his speed is 1.614 457 831 km/min.
Explain why this is not an appropriate degree of accuracy.

11 $f = \dfrac{u + v}{uv}$

Work out the value of f given that $u = 3.4$ and $v = 7.2$, where u and v are given to one decimal place.
   a Write down the full calculator display.
   b Write your answer to a suitable degree of accuracy.

11.2 Speed

CAN YOU REMEMBER

- How to convert fractions of an hour into minutes, e.g. 20 minutes = $\frac{1}{3}$ of an hour?
- Units for distance, e.g. metres (m), kilometres (km), miles?
- That there are 60 seconds in a minute and 60 minutes in an hour?
- How to divide by fractions?

IN THIS SECTION YOU WILL

- Learn the units for speed.
- Use fractions of an hour to work out speed.
- Use a formula to work out average speed.

Speed measures how fast or slow something is travelling. *Constant speed* means the speed does not increase or decrease.

A constant speed of 15 metres per second (m/s) means that a distance of 15 metres is travelled in every second.

In a journey, speed is not usually constant. A car may slow down for traffic, or speed up on a clear stretch of road. If a car travels 30 miles in 1 hour, its *average speed* is 30 miles per hour or 30 mph.
Average speed = total distance ÷ time taken

Example 1

A car travels 80 miles in 2 hours.
What is the average speed of the car? Give the answer in miles per hour.

Solution 1

$$\text{Average speed} = \frac{\text{total distance}}{\text{time taken}} = \frac{80}{2} = 40 \text{ miles per hour or } 40 \text{ mph}$$

Example 2

A boy travels 10 miles in 15 minutes.
What is his speed? Give the answer in miles per hour.

Solution 2

To calculate speed in miles per hour, the time needs to be in hours.

$$15 \text{ minutes} = \frac{15}{60} \text{ hours} = 0.25 \text{ hours}$$

$$\text{Average speed} = \frac{10}{0.25} = \frac{1000}{25} = 40$$

His speed is 40 miles per hour.

Example 3

A girl runs 12 kilometres in 1 hour 30 minutes.
Work out her average speed. Give your answer in kilometres per hour.

Solution 3

1 hour 30 minutes = 1.5 hours

Average speed $= \frac{12}{1.5} = \frac{120}{15} = 8$

Her average speed is 8 km/h.

Exercise A

1 Write the following times as fractions of an hour.
The first one has been done for you.

a 30 minutes $= \frac{30}{60}$ hours $= \frac{1}{2}$ hour

b 15 minutes **c** 45 minutes **d** 20 minutes
e 40 minutes **f** 10 minutes **g** 6 minutes
h 12 minutes **i** 1 hour 30 minutes **j** 2 hours 15 minutes

2 Work out the average speed for these journeys in miles per hour.
a 60 miles in 2 hours **b** 30 miles in 3 hours **c** 45 miles in 5 hours

3 Work out the average speed for these journeys in kilometres per hour.
a 24 km in 2 hours **b** 36 km in 4 hours **c** 28 km in 7 hours

4 Work out the average speed for these journeys in metres per second.
a 40 metres in 20 seconds **b** 60 metres in 15 seconds

5 Work out the average speed for these journeys.
a 60 miles in $\frac{1}{2}$ hour **b** 30 miles in 15 minutes
c 20 miles in $\frac{1}{4}$ hour **d** 36 miles in 45 minutes
e 44 km in $\frac{1}{2}$ hour **f** 25 km in 30 minutes
g 40 km in 20 minutes **h** 60 km in 15 minutes

6 A cheetah runs 90 metres in 3 seconds.
What is its average speed in metres per second?

7 Work out the average speed for these journeys.
a 30 miles in $1\frac{1}{2}$ hours **b** 50 miles in 2 hours 30 minutes
c 30 miles in $\frac{3}{4}$ hour **d** 24 miles in 15 minutes
e 45 km in $1\frac{1}{2}$ hours **f** 90 km in 1 hour 30 minutes
g 40 km in 1 hour 20 minutes **h** 105 km in 3 hours 30 minutes

8 Sushma walks to Silkstone.
It takes her 20 minutes.
At what speed does she walk?

The formula $\text{Average speed} = \dfrac{\text{total distance}}{\text{time taken}}$ can be rearranged to give

$$\text{Total distance} = \text{average speed} \times \text{time taken}$$

$$\text{Time} = \frac{\text{total distance}}{\text{average speed}}$$

This can be remembered by using the diagram.

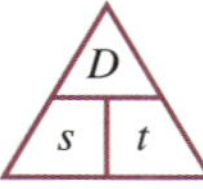

$D = s \times t$

Example 4

A person travels 45 miles in 2 hours and then a further 30 miles in 1 hour.
Calculate the average speed for the whole journey.

Solution 4

Total distance = 45 miles + 30 miles = 75 miles
Time taken = 2 hours + 1 hour = 3 hours

$$\text{Average speed} = \frac{\text{total distance}}{\text{time taken}} = \frac{75}{3} = 25\text{ mph}$$

Example 5

The average speed of a train on a journey is 120 km/h.
The time taken is 2.5 hours. How far is the journey?

Solution 5

Average speed = 120 km/h   Time taken = 2.5 hours
Distance = average speed × time = 120 × 2.5 = 300 km

Example 6

A woman drives at an average speed of 60 km/h.
How long will it take her to travel 75 km? Give your answer in hours and minutes.

Solution 6

$D = s \times t$

To make t the subject, divide both sides by s.

$\dfrac{D}{s} = t$

Time taken $= \frac{75}{60} = \frac{15}{12} = \frac{5}{4}$

Cancelling by 5 and then by 3

$= 1\frac{1}{4}$ hours = 1 hour 15 minutes

Exercise B

1 Work out the distance travelled at an average speed of:

a	30 mph for 2 hours	**b**	25 mph for 3 hours	**c**	32 km/h for 2 hours
d	56 km/h for 3 hours	**e**	40 m/s for 6 seconds	**f**	60 m/s for 8 seconds.

2 Work out the distance travelled at an average speed of:

a	40 mph for 30 minutes	**b**	60 mph for 15 minutes	**c**	30 mph for 10 minutes
d	33 mph for 20 minutes	**e**	48 km/h for 30 minutes	**f**	48 km/h for 45 minutes
g	90 km/h for 20 minutes	**h**	60 km/h for 12 minutes.		

3 Work out the time taken, in minutes, to travel:

a	5 miles at 10 mph	**b**	30 miles at 30 mph	**c**	20 miles at 60 mph
d	10 miles at 40 mph	**e**	20 km at 40 km/h	**f**	30 km at 40 km/h
g	25 km at 100 km/h	**h**	20 km at 30 km/h.		

4 Use a formula to work out the time taken, in minutes, to travel:

a	70 miles at 35 mph	**b**	35 miles at 70 mph	**c**	10 miles at 60 mph
d	25 miles at 75 mph	**e**	16 km at 64 km/h	**f**	20 km at 80 km/h
g	45 km at 15 km/h	**h**	30 km at 6 km/h.		

5 A sprinter runs 100 metres in 10 seconds.
- **a** Work out his average speed.
- **b** Explain why his top speed is greater than his average speed.

6 Fred drives his taxi on two journeys. The first journey is 8 miles and takes 35 minutes. The second journey is 17.5 miles and takes 55 minutes. Calculate the average speed for the two journeys combined. Give your answer in miles per hour.

7 A bus drives 2500 km in a week. Its average speed is estimated at 30 km/h. Estimate how long the bus spends driving in the week. Give your answer to the nearest hour.

8 You are given that 5 miles = 8 kilometres. A car travels 45 miles in 1 hour 30 minutes. A lorry travels 50 kilometres in 1 hour. Which vehicle has the greater average speed? Show your working.

9 The distance between two towns is 30 miles on the motorway or 25 miles on other roads. At rush hour, the average speed on the motorway is 36 mph and the average speed on other roads is 37.5 mph. Which is the quicker journey? You **must** show your working.

Chapter summary

- An *approximation* is a rounded value that lies between two values.
- The smallest possible value is called the *lower bound* or *lower limit*.
- The largest possible value is called the *upper bound* or *upper limit*.
- *Speed* measures how fast or slow something is travelling. *Constant speed* means the speed does not increase or decrease.
- The formula Average speed $= \dfrac{\text{total distance}}{\text{time taken}}$ can be rearranged to give

  Total distance = average speed × time taken
- Time $= \dfrac{\text{total distance}}{\text{average speed}}$

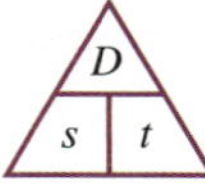

Chapter review

1 Two towns X and Y are connected by a country lane of length 30 miles and motorway of length 40 miles as shown.
A tractor travels down the country lane at an average speed of 20 mph.
A car travels on the motorway at an average speed of 60 mph.
Which vehicle gets from X to Y in the shortest time?
What is the difference in their journey times?
Give your answers in minutes.

Country lane
X Y
Motorway

2 A packet of biscuits weighs 250 grams to the nearest 10 grams.
What is the minimum possible weight of this packet of biscuits?

3 A hockey pitch is 91 metres long to the nearest metre.
Write down the least and greatest possible length of the pitch.

4 A book costs £8 to the nearest pound. Write down:
- **a** the maximum possible price of the book
- **b** the minimum possible price of the book.

5 Wales High School has 1500 students to the nearest hundred.
- **a** What is the least possible number of students?
- **b** What is the greatest possible number of students?

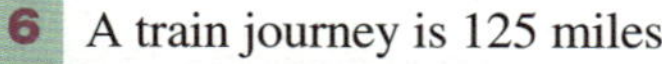

6 A train journey is 125 miles.
- **a** The journey takes 2 hours 30 minutes.
  What is the average speed of the train in miles per hour?
- **b** The average speed of another train on the same journey is 100 mph.
  How long does the journey take?

7 A 15 mile journey takes 20 minutes.
What is the average speed for the journey in miles per hour?

8 Mr Day travels 60 miles in 2 hours. Mrs Thompson travels 98 miles in 3.5 hours.
Who has the fastest average speed? You **must** show your working.

9 Mike runs 3 km in 15 minutes.
Calculate his average speed in kilometres per hour.

10 A cycle route is 20 miles long. Paul completes the route in 1 hour 15 minutes.
Norris completes the route at an average speed of 15 mph. Who is quicker?
You **must** show your working.

11 Nicola drives 183 miles at an average speed of 42 mph. Work out how long it takes her.
Give your answer in hours and minutes to a suitable degree of accuracy.

CHAPTER 12

Collecting data

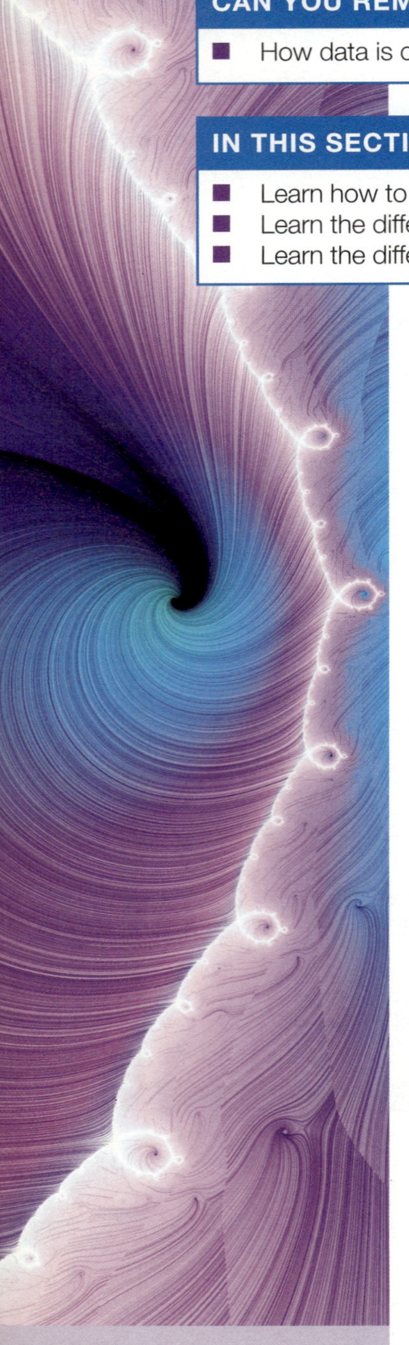

12.1 Questionnaires and surveys

CAN YOU REMEMBER

- How data is often arranged in groups?

IN THIS SECTION YOU WILL

- Learn how to design and improve questions for a questionnaire.
- Learn the different methods of carrying out a survey.
- Learn the difference between a sample and a census.

A *questionnaire* is a set of questions. Questionnaires are often used in a *survey* to collect data on people's opinions on a particular topic.

A questionnaire needs to be carefully planned to make sure that the information obtained is appropriate and relevant.

The following checklist should be considered when producing a questionnaire:

- Use simple language that is easily understood.
- Keep the questionnaire short and to the point.
- Avoid *open questions*, where there is no restriction on possible answers.
- Use *closed questions*, which give a choice of answer. Use a *response section* containing tick boxes. Restricting the choice of answer makes analysing the results much easier.
- If giving options or tick boxes for answers, make sure they are exclusive. This means that every possible answer can only go in **one** box.
- Avoid *leading questions* like 'Don't you agree …?' or 'Do you agree …?' which encourage a particular answer. *Biased questions* like these make the questionnaire invalid.
- Unless it is essential, avoid personal questions such as 'How old are you?'
- Test the questions on a small number of people before carrying out the full survey. This is called carrying out a *pilot survey.*

A pilot survey may show up problems with the questionnaire.

Example 1

Here are two possible questions for a questionnaire.

1 How old are you?

2 Tick the box which indicates your age.

Under 10 ☐ 11–20 ☐ 20 or over ☐

a Criticise these questions.

b Write a better question to find out age.

Solution 1

a Question 1 is an open question. The answers will be lots of different numbers and it will be difficult to process the data.
Question 2 is better as it is a closed question with a response section but:
- there is overlap – someone aged 20 would not know which box to tick
- there is a gap in the ages – someone aged 10 has no option to tick
- more age groups above 20 are needed.

b How old are you? Tick one box.

under 10 ☐ 10–19 ☐ 20–29 ☐ 30–39 ☐
40–49 ☐ 50–59 ☐ 60 and over ☐

Example 2

In her questionnaire about school Dana asked:
'Don't you think it's about time they got rid of school uniform?'

Yes, definitely ☐ Yes, probably ☐ No ☐

a Criticise this question. **b** Rewrite the question.

Solution 2

a The question is biased – it gives away Dana's own opinion.
There are two response boxes for Yes and only one for No. It is better to have balance in the boxes. It is not possible to answer 'Don't know'.

b What is your opinion on school uniform? Tick the box for your answer.

Keep it ☐ Get rid of it ☐ Unsure/Don't know ☐

Exercise A

1 The school caterers decide to ask students these questions.
- **a** What is your age?
- **b** We think it would be great to offer Chinese food on the school dinner menu. Do you agree?
  - **i** Criticise each question.
  - **ii** Write a better version of each question.

2 For each of the following questions, say whether it is suitable, leading or biased.
For each question that is not suitable, write a new question.
- **a** Smoking kills people and should be totally banned. What do you think?
- **b** How far do you travel to school?

  Less than 3 miles ☐ More than 3 miles ☐
- **c** Name the country of your birth.
- **d** What is your favourite type of music?

3 Write a question which would effectively find out the following.
Remember to give a response section where appropriate.
- **a** The total number of brothers and sisters a person has.
- **b** The time it takes for a student to get home from school.
- **c** Whether people think that footballers are paid too much.
- **d** Where a person went on holiday last year.

4 **a** Design a short questionnaire on a topic of your choice.
b Use your questionnaire in a pilot survey of about five people.
c If necessary, improve your questionnaire based on the results of your pilot.
d Give your questionnaire to about 30 people. Collect the results and write two sentences to explain what they show.

5 **a** Explain what a pilot survey is in the context of a questionnaire.
b Why might it be useful to use a pilot survey?

A survey finds out information about a topic or situation. Most surveys use a questionnaire. They can be carried out by face-to-face or telephone interviews, or the questionnaire can be sent out by post.

Surveys may also be carried out by observation, for example recording the gender of people using a shop.

Surveys need to be carried out in a fair way to avoid *bias*.

For example, if a school wants to find out about students' eating habits, it is not a fair survey if only the students who use the school canteen are included. All the students who have other lunch arrangements will be omitted from the survey and the results will be biased.

The group of people a survey is interested in is called the *population*.
For example, the population for a survey on school lunches is the students at the school.
If a survey asks the views of the whole population, this is called a *census*. A census will find out more accurate information but can be expensive and time-consuming. For example, the UK National Census takes place every ten years. Every household in the UK is sent a questionnaire.
A survey about a large population uses a sample of the population. A *sample* is a small group selected from the larger population.
A sample needs to be *representative* – this means that it should reflect the population fairly. For example, for a survey on uniform, a representative sample will include students from each year.

Example 3

Mushtaq is finding out about the cost of new computers. He goes to a supermarket near his home and records the cost of every computer on sale there.

a Is this a survey or a census? Explain your answer.
b Is this a fair way of finding out the cost of new computers? Explain your answer.

Solution 3

a Mushtaq is interested in the cost of new computers and so the population is all new computers. He has only recorded costs from one shop, a sample. This is a survey not a census.
b No, he should go to a range of different shops that sell computers and obtain a sample of prices from each.

Exercise B

1 Two schools are considering merging their sports teams to try to win the National Finals. School A asks 10% of its staff and students whether they think this is a good idea. School B asks all of its staff and students the same question.
a Which school is carrying out a survey? Explain your answer.
b Give one advantage and one disadvantage of school A's approach.
c Give one advantage and one disadvantage of school B's approach.

2 Pauline is interested in finding out who uses the launderette she owns.
She decides to ask everyone who comes into the launderette about their age, family and job one Monday from 9 am to 11 am.

a Explain why this is not a good method.

b Suggest how Pauline might find her information in a better way.

3 A company wants to test the lifetime of the new light bulbs it has developed.
It produces 1000 light bulbs each hour.

a Explain why the company must test a sample and not the population.

b The company suggests three possible methods of choosing the light bulbs to be tested.
Method 1: Take the first light bulb produced every day for one month.
Method 2: Take 30 light bulbs produced on 1 March.
Method 3: Take every 50th light bulb produced each day for three months.
Comment on each suggested method.

4 Search on the Internet to answer the following questions about the UK National Census.

a How often is there a National Census in the UK?

b When is the next National Census?

c Who has to respond to the National Census?

d Find out five pieces of information which the National Census asks about.

5 Imagine you are going to find out information about the amount of homework the average Year 10 student does each evening.

a Write down some questions you would ask.

b Describe how you could choose a sample of people for your survey.

12.2 Observation sheets and data logging

CAN YOU REMEMBER

- How to construct a two-way table?
- How to construct a tally chart?

IN THIS SECTION YOU WILL

- Learn the meaning of the phrase 'observation sheet'.
- Learn how to construct an observation sheet.
- Learn the meaning of data logging.
- Interpret data from an observation sheet.

An *observation sheet* or *data collection sheet* is a chart or table for recording data from a survey or experiment or from observation.

Tally charts and two-way tables are types of observation sheet.
An observation sheet should be drawn before the data is collected.
It is a good idea to test the sheet using a pilot survey and then improve it as necessary.

Example 1

Billy says that primary school pupils eat chips more often than secondary school pupils. Design an observation sheet to investigate Billy's claim.
Invent the first 20 possible responses.

Solution 1

A time period needs to be stated even though this was not mentioned in the question: for example, 'number of times chips are eaten per week'.
The first category is age of pupil – primary or secondary.
The second category is the number of times chips are eaten per week.

Number of times chips are eaten per week / School	0	1	2	3	4 or more
Primary	||	||||	|||	|	
Secondary	|	~~||||~~	|	||	|

Data logging is when data is collected automatically by a machine. For example, the numbers of cars entering and leaving a car park are logged by a machine, so that no cars can enter when the car park is full.

Exercise A

1 Javed wants to know whether his friends prefer pizza, burgers or fish and chips. He wants to know if this is different for boys and girls.
Design an observation sheet to collect this information.

2 The observation sheet below is designed to collect data about the number of visits abroad made by children of different ages.

Visits / Age	0	1 or 2	4 or 5	7 or 8	More than 10
Under 10					
11–14					
Older teenagers					

a Criticise the observation sheet.
b Design a better observation sheet.

3 Julian thought that his teacher gave tests much more often in the afternoon than in the morning and did practical work much more often in the morning than the afternoon.
a Design an observation sheet to collect data to test Julian's ideas.
b Invent the first 20 entries.

4 **a** Describe how data logging might be used to collect data about the number of people entering a shop at different times.
b How might this data be useful to the owners of the shop?

5 **a** Design an observation sheet which would collect data for the following question.
'Does it rain more often at weekends than during the week?'

b **i** Invent data for four weeks. Try to make the data realistic.

ii Use the invented data to answer the question 'Does it rain more often at weekends than during the week?'
What extra factor should be considered to make the question fair?

6 **a** Criticise and improve on the observation sheet below for a survey on pocket money of boys and girls in Year 10.

Pocket money Gender	£1	£2–£5	£5–£10	£10–£20
Boys				
Girls				

b Ask a sample of students for their responses and fill in the improved observation sheet.

Example 2

This observation sheet is designed to collect data about the preferred method of transport of adults and children.

	Car	Bus	Train	Plane
Adults				
Children				

a What problems may arise in the use of this observation sheet?
b Suggest an improved version of the observation sheet.

Solution 2

a There is no definition of adults and children, e.g. which box does a 17 year-old go into?
There are other transport methods apart from those listed.
It may also be fair to say that there is not enough space to collect much data.

b An improved observation sheet is:

	Car	Bus	Train	Plane	Boat	Other
Age 16 or over						
Age under 16						

Example 3

Look at this completed version of the observation sheet from Example 2 and determine whether the statements about it are true or false. Explain your answers.

	Car	Bus	Train	Plane	Boat	Other
Age 16 or over	𝍸	|||	𝍸 𝍸 |	||	|	||
Age under 16	||	||||	𝍸 ||	𝍸 ||||	|||	|

a More under-16s prefer planes than 16s or over.
b The same number of people in each age category were asked.
c 10% of under-16s preferred cars.

Solution 3

a True, nine under-16s prefer planes whereas only two 16s or over do.
b False, 24 people aged 16 or over were asked whereas 26 under-16s were asked.
c False, as there were 26 under-16s, 10% of 26 is not 2.

Exercise B

1 This observation sheet was designed to collect data about the favourite fruit of people of different ages.

	Apple	Banana	Strawberry	Peach
Under 10				
Under 20				
Under 40				
Over 40				

a Explain two distinct problems with this observation sheet.
b Design an improved version of this observation sheet.

2 This observation sheet shows data collected on favourite colour.

	Red	Blue	Purple	Green	Yellow	Other
Boys	~~||||~~ |||	~~||||~~ ~~||||~~ ~~||||~~ |||	||||	||	|	~~||||~~ ||
Girls	~~||||~~ ||||	|||	~~||||~~ ~~||||~~ ||	|||	~~||||~~ ||	|

State whether each of these statements about the observation sheet is true or false. Give a reason each time.
a More girls than boys preferred purple.
b Green was the least favourite colour overall.
c 20% of boys chose red as their favourite colour.

3 A data logging machine recorded this table of information about the numbers of vehicles in a car park at different times.
a How many extra vehicles entered the car park between 9 am and 10 am?
b 17 vehicles left the car park between 10 am and 11 am. How many vehicles entered the car park between 10 am and 11 am?
c How many spaces are there for vehicles in the car park? Give a reason for your answer.

Time	Number of vehicles
9 am	36
10 am	125
11 am	170
12 pm	170
1 pm	156
2 pm	168
3 pm	170
4 pm	152
5 pm	87

4 Jodie asked a sample of 60 people, two thirds of whom were men, to name a city in the USA.

Half of the women and ten of the men named New York.

20% of the women and 40% of the men named Washington.

Three women and six men named San Francisco.

The rest of the sample named various other US cities.

Jodie collected all of this information on an observation sheet.

Given that she had predicted the responses well, draw a suitable observation sheet and complete it with her data.

5 This observation sheet was used to record the number of goals scored by home teams and goals scored by away teams in 100 football fixtures. The tallies have been converted into figures.

Number of goals scored	0	1	2	3	4	5	6	7
Goals scored by home team	18	37	20	14	8	2	0	1
Goals scored by away team	32	38	16	8	4	1	1	0

a Compare the goals scored by the home teams and away teams by looking at the figures on the observation sheet.

b **i** Calculate the mean and range of both sets of data.

ii Do these measures confirm your observations in part **a**?

c Illustrate the data using a suitable graph.

6 The data logging equipment on the doors at a nightclub keeps a record of the number of people inside the nightclub.
The data for each night is recorded every hour. The table shows one night's data.

Time	Number of people inside nightclub
9 pm	120
10 pm	246
11 pm	287
12 am	378
1 am	400
2 am	367
3 am	112

a The club opened at 8 pm. On average how many people per minute entered the club in the first hour?

b 87 people left the nightclub between 11 pm and 12 am. How many people entered the nightclub between 11 pm and 12 am?

c According to safety inspectors the nightclub is full when 400 people are inside.
At 1 am the nightclub was full.

Only five people entered the nightclub between 1 am and 2 am.

How many people left the nightclub between 1 am and 2 am?

12.3 Social statistics

CAN YOU REMEMBER

- How to draw and interpret time series graphs?
- How to calculate with percentages?

IN THIS SECTION YOU WILL

- Learn the meaning of 'index number'.
- Use and interpret data collected by the Government.

The Government's Office for National Statistics (ONS) collects and publishes a vast amount of information about the population of the UK and patterns of spending.

For example, the Retail Prices Index (RPI) measures the changing cost of selected items. The information is given as an *index number*. An index number represents a value by giving it as a percentage of an original value or *base value.*

For example, using January 2003 as the base value (100%), the RPI for September 2005 was 114.

Month	January 2003	September 2005
RPI	100	114

This means that, on average, prices were 14% higher in September 2005 than in January 2003.

Example 1

The cost of a banana in January 2004 was 40 pence.
Using January 2004 as a base, the index number for the cost in January 2006 was 105.
Find the cost of a banana in January 2006

Solution 1

The index number of 105 indicates that the January 2006 cost is 5% higher than the January 2004 cost.

January 2006 cost = 105% of January 2004 cost

105% written as a decimal = 1.05, so the multiplier is 1.05

January 2006 cost = January 2004 cost × multiplier = 40 pence × 1.05 = 42 pence

The cost in January 2006 was 42 pence.

Example 2

A car was bought for £8000 in January 2005 and sold for £6000 in September 2006.
Find the index number for September 2006 using January 2005 as the base.

Solution 2

The price has decreased from the original, so the index number will be less than 100

The calculation is equivalent to finding the new value as a percentage of the old value.

$$\text{Index number} = \frac{\text{new value}}{\text{old value}} \times 100 = \frac{6000}{8000} \times 100 = 0.75 \times 100 = 75$$

Government data is also presented as time series, such as unemployment rates, and in graphs and charts, such as data from the National Census about the number of people living in each house.

Example 3

The time series below shows the car and commercial vehicle production figures for the United Kingdom for 1999–2004 with 2000 as base.

Year	1999	2000	2001	2002	2003	2004
Index	108.8	100.0	90.9	99.3	101.0	100.3

(Source: www.statistics.gov.uk)

a Explain why this data is a time series.

b In which year from this period was the car and commercial vehicle production:
i lowest **ii** highest?

c In which years were the production figures lower than the previous year?

Solution 3

a This data is a time series as the values are recorded over a period of time.

b **i** 2001 **ii** 1999

c 2000, 2001, 2004

Exercise A

1 The cost of a loaf of bread in 1990 was 30 pence.
The index value for 2006 using 1990 as base year is 150
Find the cost of a loaf of bread in 2006

2 The cost of a litre of petrol in 2000 was 60 pence.
The cost of a litre of petrol in 2012 is predicted to be £1.50
Find the predicted index number for 2012 using 2000 as the base year.

3 The price of an item doubles.
Write down the index value of the new price compared to the old price.

4 The time series data shows the numbers (in thousands) of self-employed people for the period 1995–2005

Year	1995	1996	1997	1998	1999	2000	2001	2002	2003	2004	2005
Number of people	3820	3777	3724	3588	3614	3517	3526	3585	3801	3860	3840

(Source: www.statistics.gov.uk)

a Draw a time series graph for the data.

b Describe any patterns in the data.

c In which year was the greatest increase in the number of self-employed?

5 The average cost of a CD in 2000 was £12.40
The index number for 2006 using 2000 as the base year was 81
Find, to the nearest penny, the average cost of a CD in 2006

6 In 1980 a field was valued at £12 500
In 2005 the same field was valued at £230 000
Find the index number for this field in 2005 using 1980 as the base year.

7 The graph shows the percentages of households with Internet access according to Government surveys for 2000 to 2005

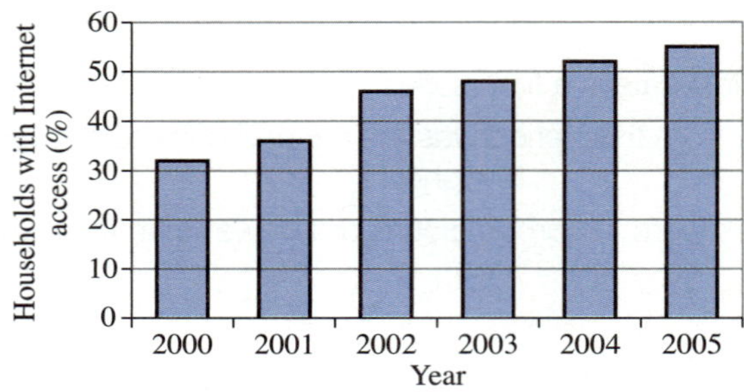

(Source: www.statistics.gov.uk)

a In which year did the value first rise above 50%?

b Use the graph to estimate the index number for 2005 with 2000 as base year.

c If 2005 were taken as the base year, approximately what would the index number for 2000 be?

8 The time series graph shows the percentage change in the Retail Prices Index (RPI) and the Consumer Prices Index (CPI) compared with the same month one year before, for September 2003–September 2005

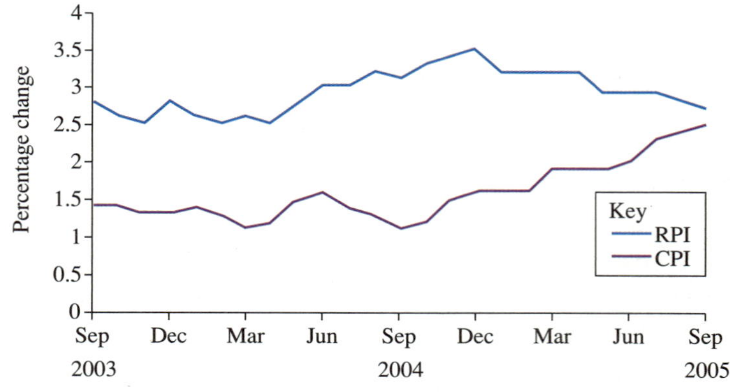

(Source: www.statistics.gov.uk)

a In which month and year was the change in the:
  i RPI at its highest for this period
  ii CPI at its lowest for this period?

b Estimate the difference between the changes in the two indices for June 2004

Exercise B

The table shows the percentage change for the average cost of items from September 2004 to September 2005

Use the data in the table to answer questions **1–7**

Sections	Percentage change September 2004–September 2005
All items	6.9
Food and non-alcoholic beverages	23.1
Alcoholic beverages and tobacco	2.7
Clothing and footwear	–1.3
Housing, water, electricity, gas and other fuels	1.8
Home ownership	1.6
Rent	6.1
Water, electricity, gas and other fuels	0.5
Furnishings, household equipment and routine maintenance of the house	1.4
Health	4.6
Transport	2.1
Communication	–9.1
Recreation and culture	11.1
Education	4.0
Hotels, cafés and restaurants	7.0
Miscellaneous goods and services	2.3

1 **a** Which items showed the greatest percentage increase in price?
b Use the answers to part **a** to work out the index number for September 2005, using September 2004 as a base.

2 **a** Which items decreased in price during the period?
b Give the September 2005 index numbers for these items using September 2004 as a base.

3 Which item had the smallest percentage change in price during the period?

4 Display the data in the table using a suitable graph.

5 In September 2004, a room in Green's hotel cost £71 per night. If Green's hotel's prices moved in line with the average for that sector, how much did the room cost in September 2005?

6 **a** Calculate the mean of all the values in the table excluding the 'All items' value.
b Explain why the 'All items' value of 6.9 is different from your answer to part **a**.

7 Which would cost more in September 2005?
- A pair of shoes that cost £40 in September 2004 or
- A small piece of household equipment that cost £39 in September 2004

You may assume that each item's price moved in line with the average for its sector.

Chapter summary

- A *questionnaire* is a set of questions. Questionnaires are often used in a *survey* to collect data on people's opinions on a particular topic.
- An observation sheet or data collection sheet is a chart or table for recording data from a survey or experiment or from observation.
- Tally charts and two-way tables are types of observation sheet.
- *Data logging* is when data is collected automatically by a machine.
- The Retail Prices Index (RPI) measures the changing cost of selected items. The information is given as an *index number.* An index number represents a value by giving it as a percentage of an original value or *base value.*
- Government data is also presented as time series, such as unemployment rates, and in graphs and charts, for example data from the National Census.

Chapter review

1 Justin is asking for opinions on the quality of the local bus service.
He wants to find out the age of each person he asks.
a Give two reasons why he should not ask 'What is your age?'
b One of his questions asks, 'Are you fed up with being let down by the local bus service?'
Explain what is wrong with this question.

2 April wants to collect data about the numbers of cats and dogs owned by her friends.
Design an observation sheet for this purpose. Use a two-way table with headings 'cats' and 'dogs'.

3 Nitin is investigating where people go on holiday.
He thinks of three possible ways of finding out information for his survey.
Method 1: Stand outside a travel agent and ask the people who enter.
Method 2: Ask all his family and friends where they went on holiday.
Method 3: Put questionnaires through some letter boxes in a range of houses around his town.
a Give one disadvantage of each method.
b Which of the three methods is likely to produce the best data?

4 The table shows the index values for service industries' costs for some months of 2005, using January 2002 as the base.

Month in 2005	March	April	May	June	July	August
Index value	108.0	108.3	108.4	109.0	108.9	109.2

a By what percentage are the March 2005 service industry costs higher than in January 2002?
b Which of the given months in 2005 had the highest costs?
c Find the cost in May 2005 of an item that cost £50 in January 2002

5 A consumer magazine is investigating the cost of washing machines.
A reporter for the magazine visits an electrical shop in the town centre and records the cost of all the washing machines in the shop.
a Explain whether this is a census or a sample.
b Give reasons why the reporter's choice of survey method may not be ideal.

6 **a** What is a pilot survey? **b** Why might a pilot survey be useful?

7 Zarina is writing a questionnaire about people's choice of supermarket.
One of the questions is about the distance people travel to their favourite supermarket.
The question states,
'How far do you travel to your favourite supermarket?
1 mile 2 miles 3 miles more'

a Comment on Zarina's response section. **b** Write an improved response section.

8 The table shows the number of registrations (in thousands) for new vehicles from 1991 to 2002

Year	1991	1992	1993	1994	1995	1996	1997	1998	1999	2000	2001	2002
Registrations	1921.5	1901.5	2073.9	2249.0	2306.5	2410.1	2597.7	2740.3	2765.8	2870.9	3136.6	3229.5

a What is the name given to this type of data which changes over time?
b Show the data on an appropriate graph.
c Comment on the trend in the data.

9 A company which manufactures fireworks wishes to test the performance of their new rocket.
a Explain why the company must test a sample and not the population.
b They propose to test the first five rockets produced the following day.
Give two reasons why this is not an ideal way to take the sample.

10 The graph shows the voting intentions of the people who responded to surveys in the run-up to the 2005 General Election.

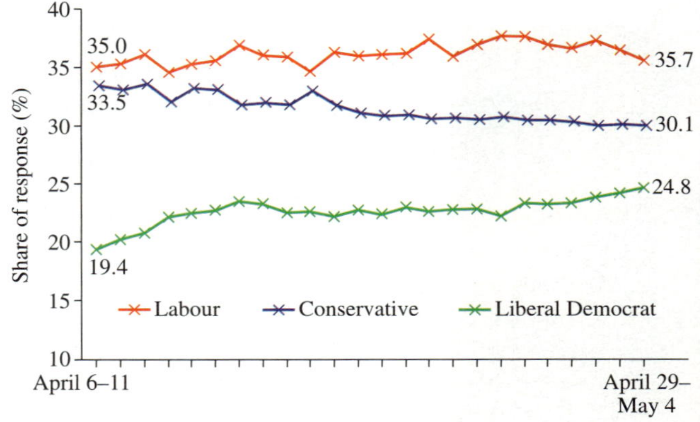

a Which party always had the greatest share of the vote?
b Which party's support increased the most over the period?
c **i** For each party, calculate the index number of the final value, using the first value as base.
ii Which party showed the greatest percentage increase in popularity?
d Explain why the percentages at the end of the time series do not add to 100%.

CHAPTER 13

Three-dimensional shapes

13.1 Plans and elevations

CAN YOU REMEMBER

- The area of a rectangle can be found by counting squares or by using the formula area = length × width?
- The volume of a cuboid can be found by counting cubes or by using the formulae volume = length × width × height or volume = area of base × height?

IN THIS SECTION YOU WILL

- Draw 2-D views of 3-D objects.
- Draw 3-D objects from 2-D projections.
- Calculate the surface area of 2-D views.
- Calculate volumes of 3-D objects made from cubes.

This picture shows the roof, front and side of a garage.

The roof, front and side can be drawn as three separate two-dimensional views.

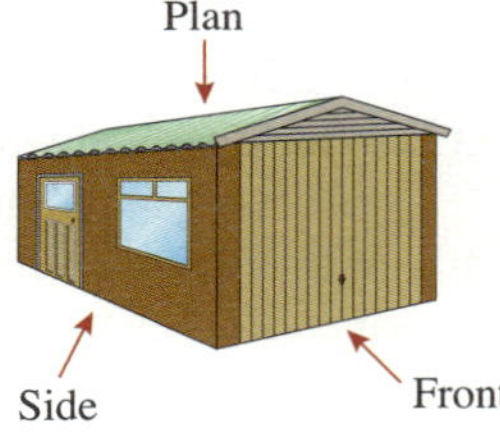

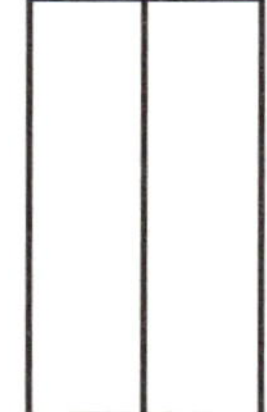

The view from above is called the *plan view*.

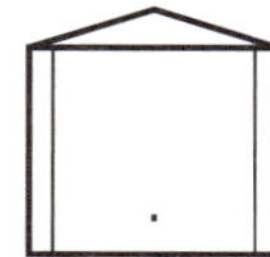

The view from the front is called the *front elevation*.

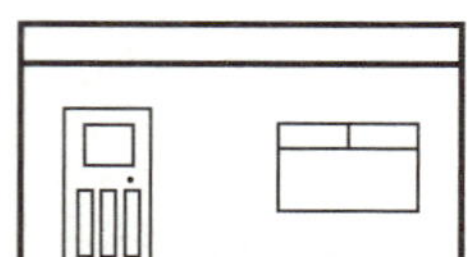

The view from the side is called the *side elevation*.

The side elevation is from one side of the garage. The side elevation from the other side may be different.
For example, there may be no door or window on the other side.

Example 1

A solid is made from a cube of side 2 cm and two cubes of side 1 cm. Draw on square grids:

a the front elevation
b the side elevation from the direction shown
c the plan view of this solid.

Solution 1

Colour the faces for each view.

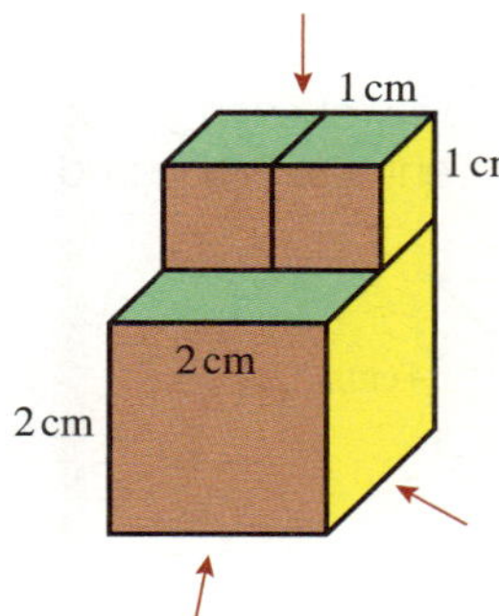

a

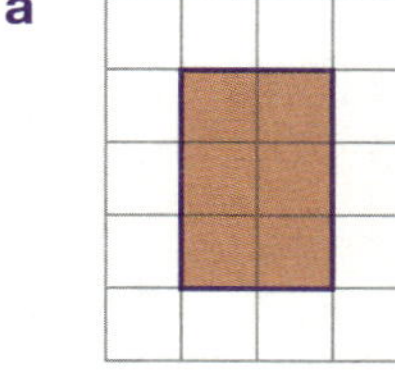
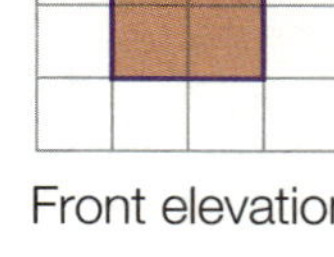

Front elevation

b

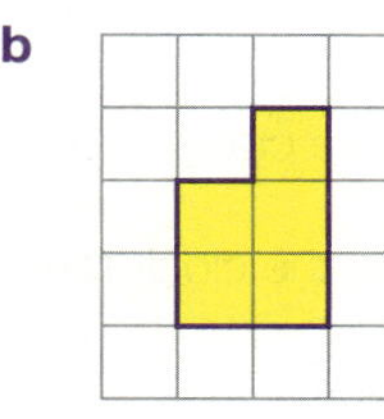

Side elevation

c

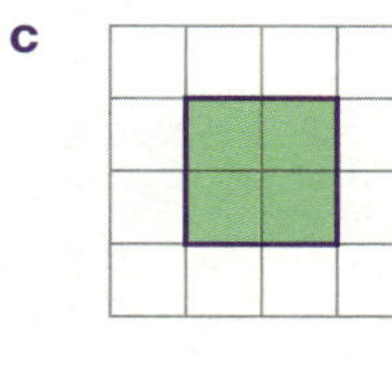

Plan view

Example 2

The plan view, front elevation and side elevation of a 3-D solid made up of cubes are shown below.

plan view

front elevation

side elevation

Draw the solid on isometric paper.

Solution 2

The plan view shows how the cubes are arranged on the base.
The front and side elevations show that the tallest parts of the solid are two cubes high.
The side elevation shows a gap in the centre.

plan view

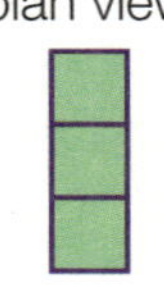

front elevation

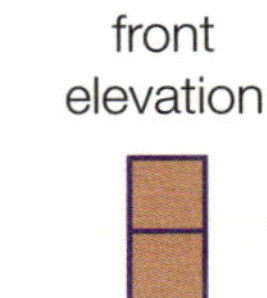

side elevation

If only one side elevation is shown then the views from both sides are the same.
This is the solid.

Exercise A

1 Here are some pictures of solid objects together with the plan view of each.
Match the object with its plan view.

a 
b 
c 
d 
e 

i 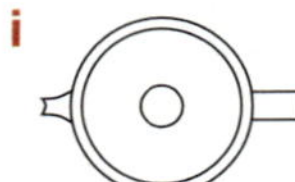
ii 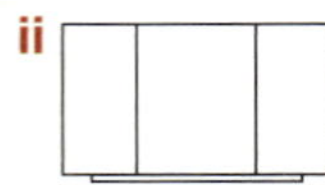
iii 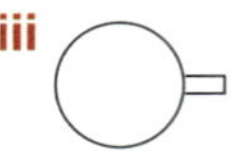
iv 
v 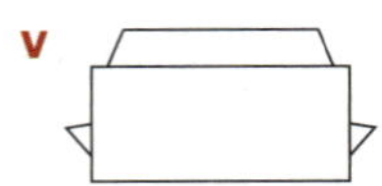

2 The diagram shows a clock tower.
Draw a sketch of:

a the plan view of the clock tower
b the front elevation
c the side elevation.

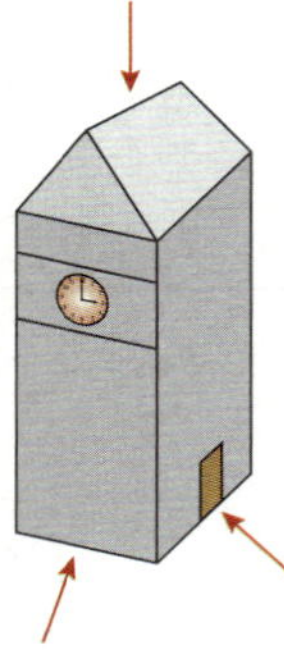

3 Draw the plan view of each shape accurately on centimetre-squared paper.

a

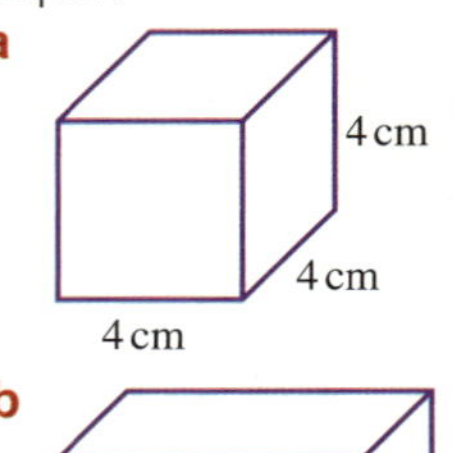

b

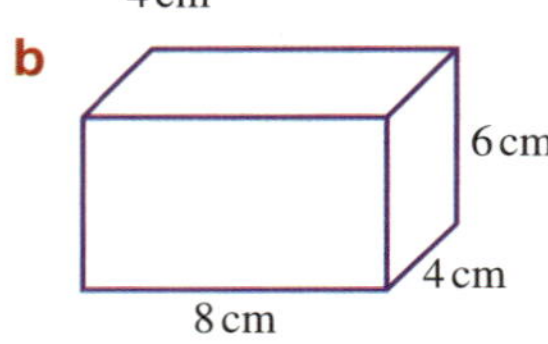

4 Draw the plan view of each solid on squared paper.

a 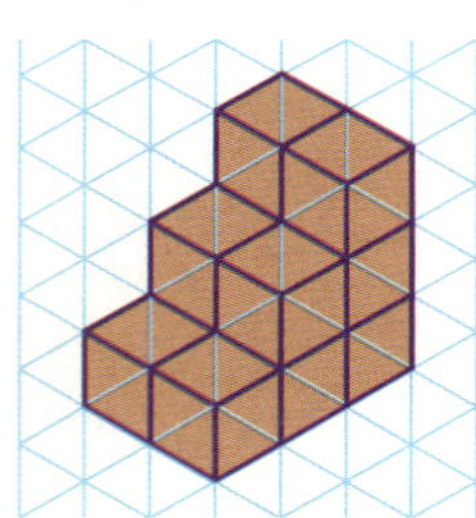
b 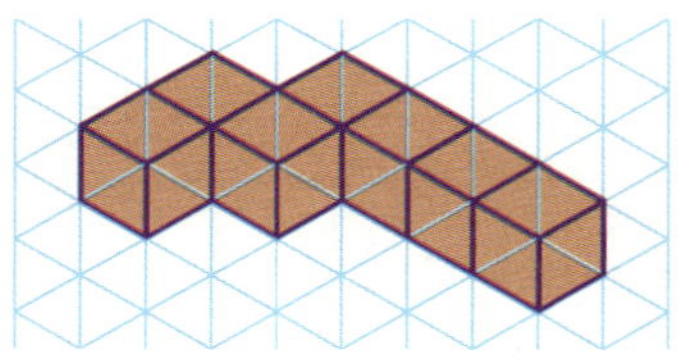
c 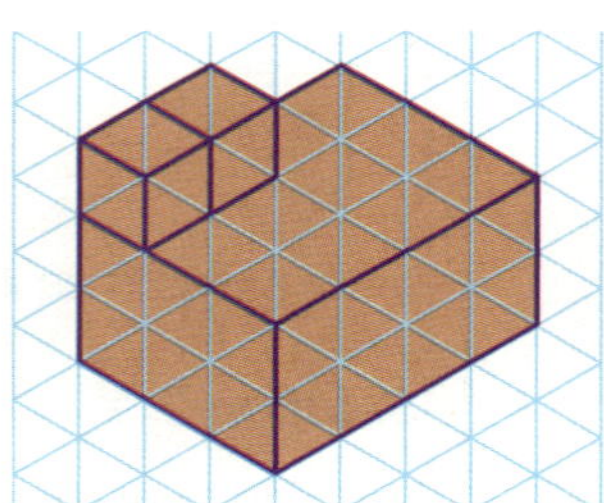

5 The plan view, front elevation and side elevation of a 3-D solid made from cubes are shown.
Draw the solid on isometric paper.

plan view | front elevation | side elevation

6 Each solid is made from centimetre cubes.
For each solid, draw on centimetre-squared paper:
i the plan view **ii** the front elevation **iii** the side elevation.

a

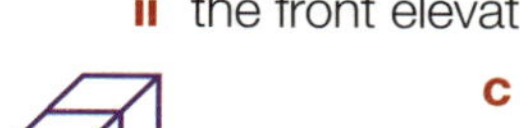

b

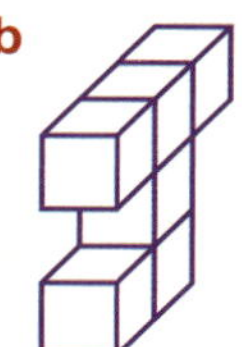

c

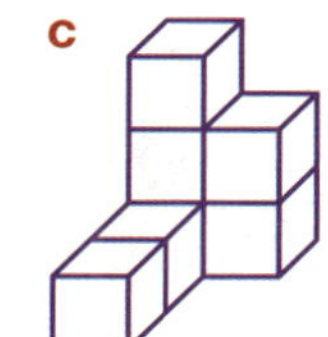

d

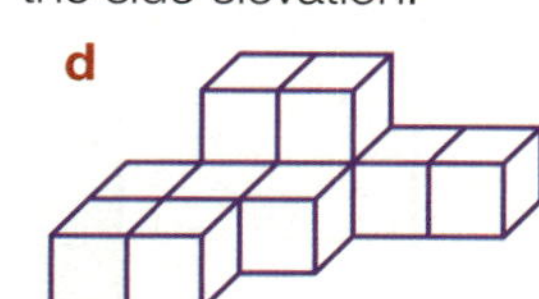

7 The plan view, front elevation and side elevation of a 3-D solid made from cubes are shown. Draw the solid on isometric paper.

plan view front elevation side elevation

8 The diagram represents a solid made from seven small cubes.
On squared paper, draw the view of the solid:
a from direction A
b from direction B.

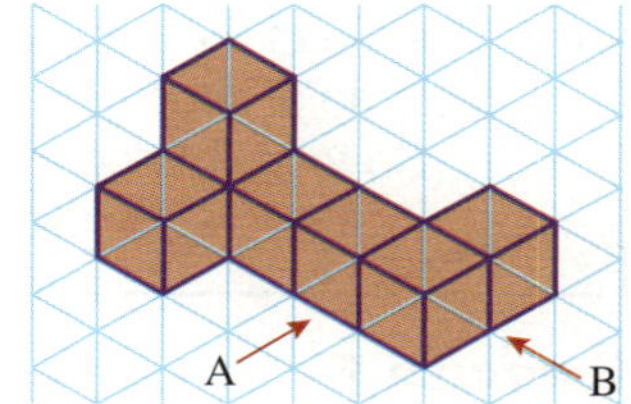

9 plan view front elevation side elevation

The plan view, front elevation and side elevation of a 3-D solid made from cubes are shown on the left. Draw the solid on isometric paper.

The surface area of a solid is the total area of all the faces in the solid.
The plan view, side and front elevations of the solid can be used to work out the surface area and the volume of a solid.

Example 3

A solid is made from a cube of side 2 cm and three cubes of side 1 cm as shown.

a Draw the plan view, front elevation and side elevation of the solid, on centimetre-squared paper.
b Work out the surface area of the solid.
c Calculate the volume of the solid.

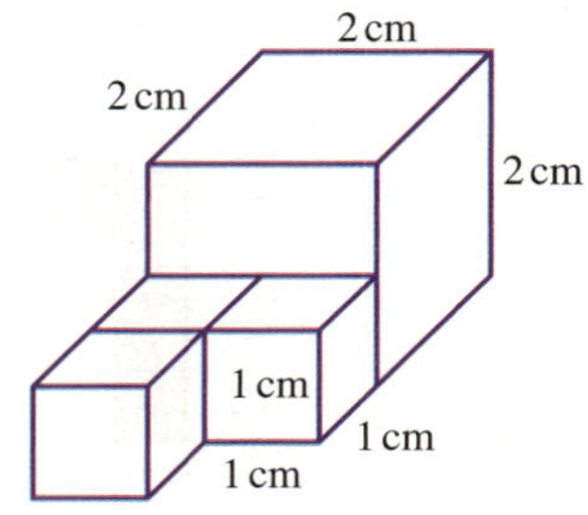

Solution 3

a

plan view

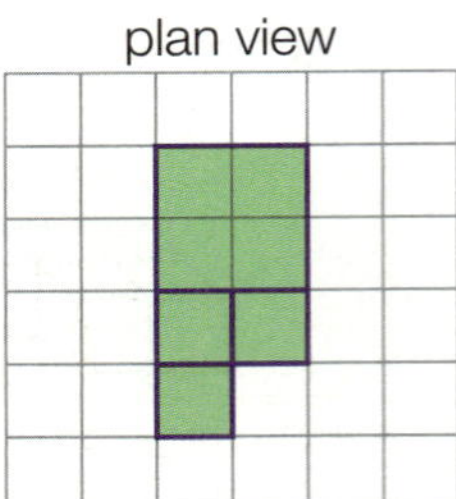

front elevation

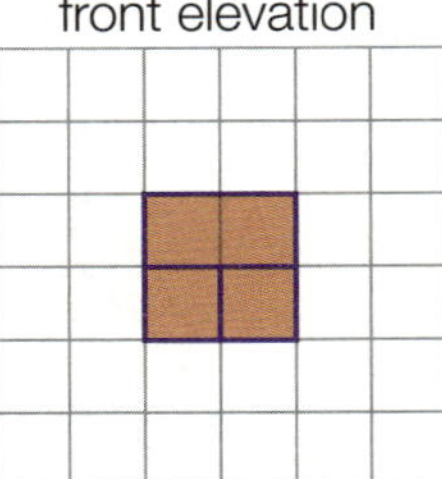

side elevation

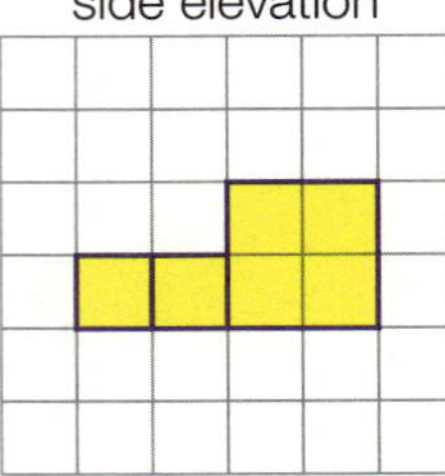

b The plan view shows the surface area of the top and the base of the solid.
The front elevation shows the surface area of the front and the back of the solid.
The side elevation shows the surface area of each side of the solid.
By counting squares,

Area of plan view $= 7\,\text{cm}^2$

Area of front elevation $= 4\,\text{cm}^2$

Area of side elevation $= 6\,\text{cm}^2$

Total surface area $= (2 \times 7) + (2 \times 4) + (2 \times 6) = 14 + 8 + 12 = 34\,\text{cm}^2$

c Volume of the cube with side 2 cm $= 2 \times 2 \times 2 = 8\,\text{cm}^3$

Volume of each cube with side 1 cm $= 1 \times 1 \times 1 = 1\,\text{cm}^3$

So total volume = volume of 2 cm cube + volume of three 1 cm cubes
$= 8 + 1 + 1 + 1 = 11\,\text{cm}^3$

Exercise B

1 This solid is made from cubes of side 1 cm.

a Draw the plan view, front elevation and side elevation of the solid on centimetre-squared paper.

b Calculate the surface area of the solid.

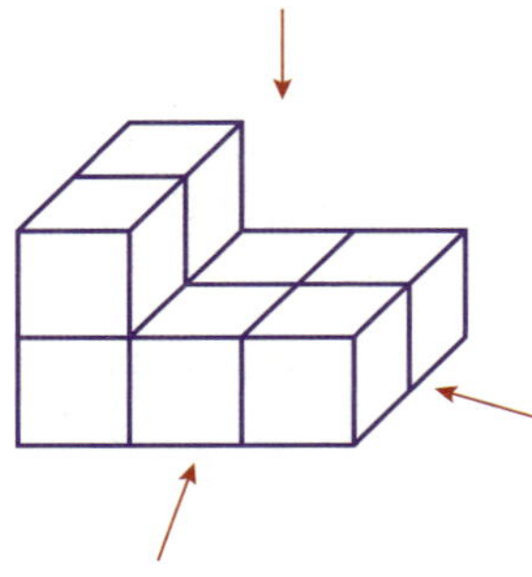

2 Here are three solids and three plan views.
Match each solid with the correct plan view.

A

B

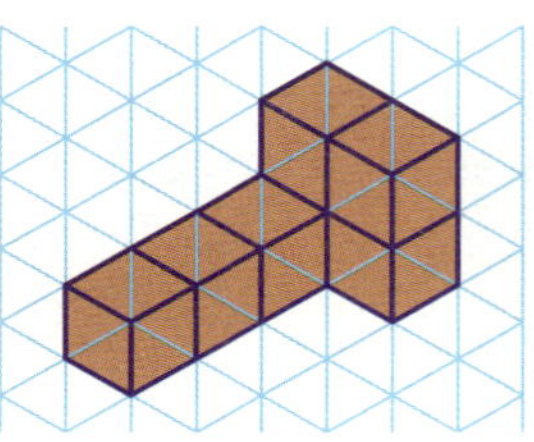

C

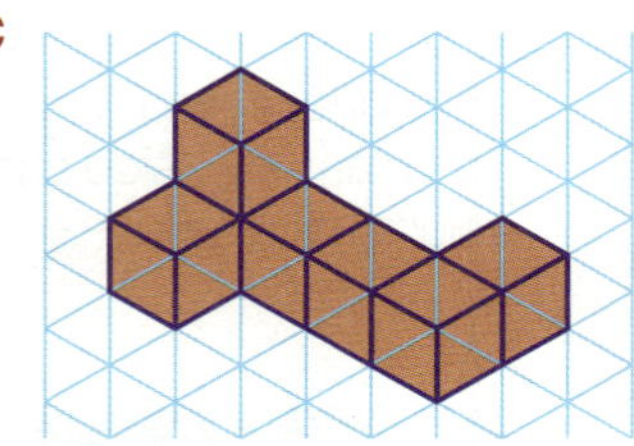

①

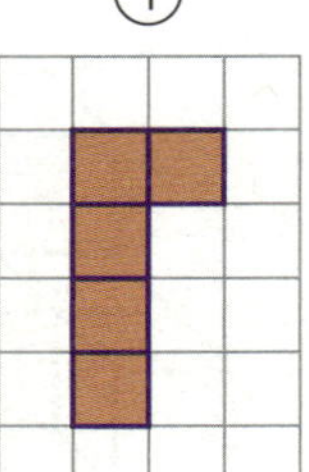

②

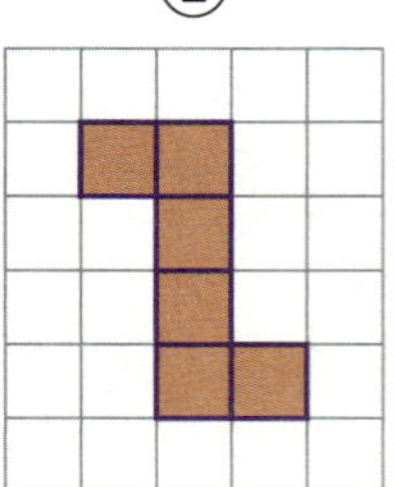

③

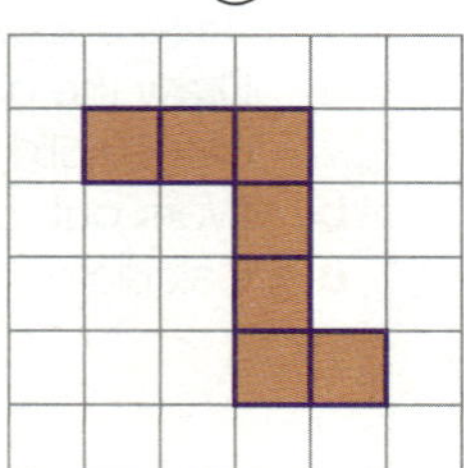

3 Here are three views of a solid made from centimetre cubes.

a Draw the solid on isometric paper.

b Calculate the volume of the solid.

plan view   front elevation   side elevation

4 These solids are built from cubes of side 1 cm.
Work out the volume of each solid.

a

b

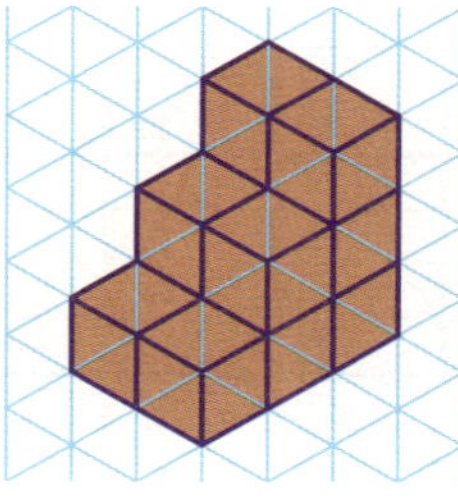

c

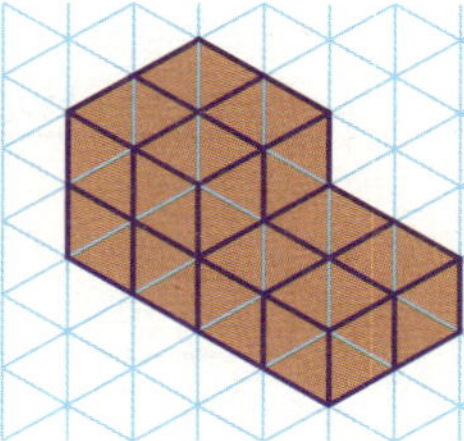

Some of the cubes are not visible in the drawing.

5 These solids are made from cubes of side 1 cm.
Calculate the surface area of each solid.

a

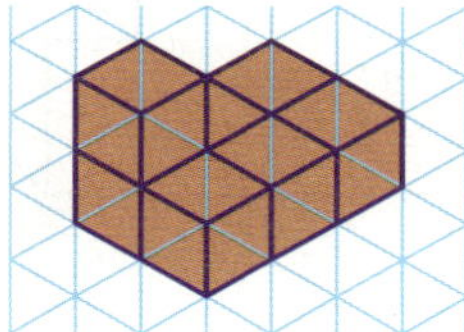

b

6 The solid shown is made up of a cuboid and two cubes of side 1 cm.

a Draw the plan view, front elevation and side elevation of this solid.

b Calculate the volume of this solid.

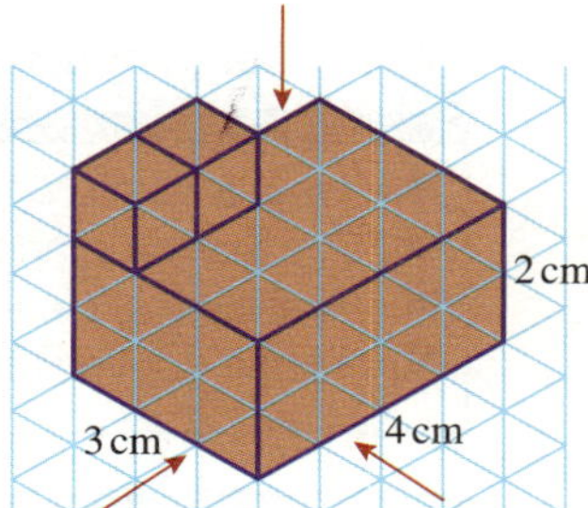

7 A stage is made from one cube of side 3 metres and two cubes of side 2 metres as shown.

a Draw the plan view of the stage.

b Calculate the area of the plan view of the stage.

c Calculate the volume of the stage.

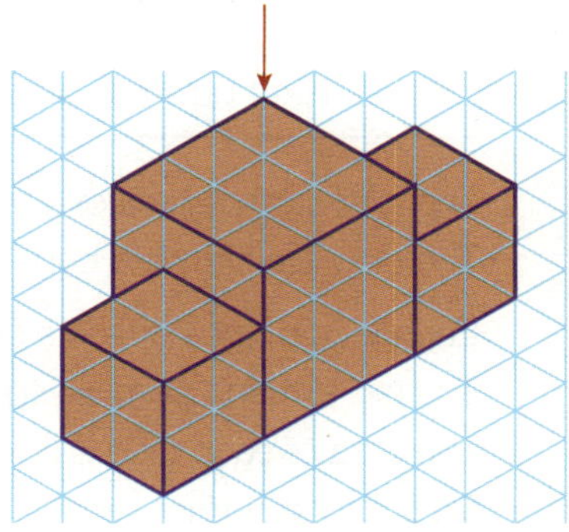

8 The diagrams show the plan view, front elevation and side elevation of a cuboid drawn on centimetre-squared paper. Calculate the volume of the cuboid.

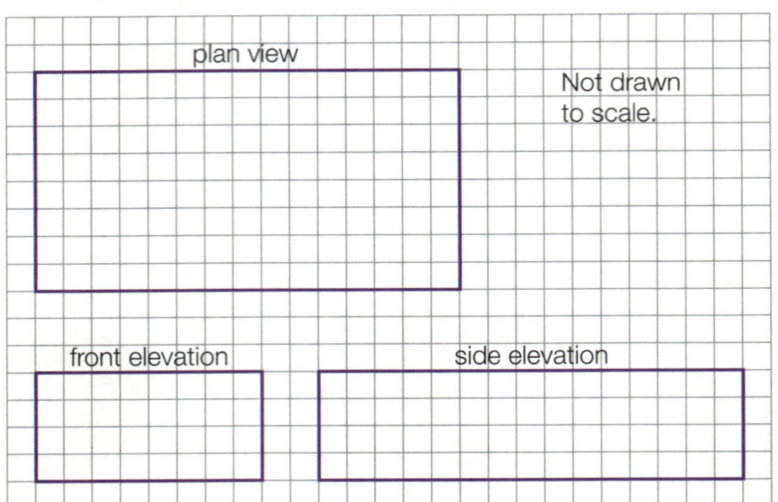

9 Each diagram shows a solid. For each diagram: draw the front elevation and calculate its area.

a

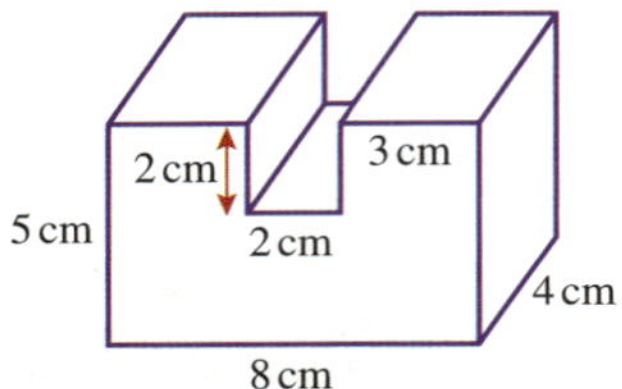

b

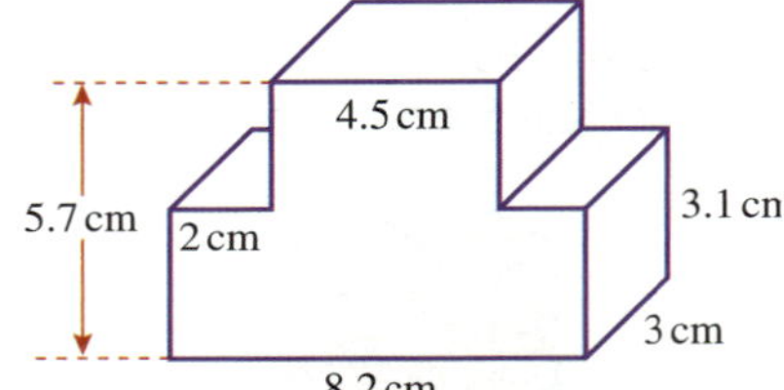

13.2 Surface area of prisms

CAN YOU REMEMBER

- How to sketch nets of cubes, cuboids and triangular prisms?
- Area of a rectangle = length × width, area of a triangle = $\frac{1}{2}$ × base × perpendicular height?
- Area of a circle = πr^2, circumference of a circle = $2\pi r$?
- Metric conversions for lengths: 1 m = 100 cm, 1 cm = 10 mm?

IN THIS SECTION YOU WILL

- Calculate the surface area of cubes, cuboids, triangular prisms and cylinders.
- Convert between area measures, e.g. cm^2 to m^2

The total surface area of a three-dimensional shape is the sum of the areas of all the faces of the shape.

The diagram shows a cube of side 5 cm and its net.

Each face of the cube is a square of side 5 cm.

The net is made from six squares.

The area of each face is 5 × 5 = 25 cm^2

So the total surface area = 6 × 25 = 150 cm^2

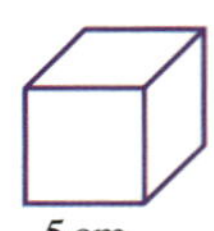

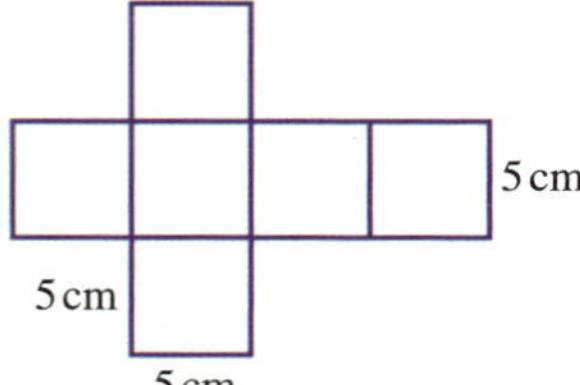

Example 1

Work out the total surface area of this cuboid.

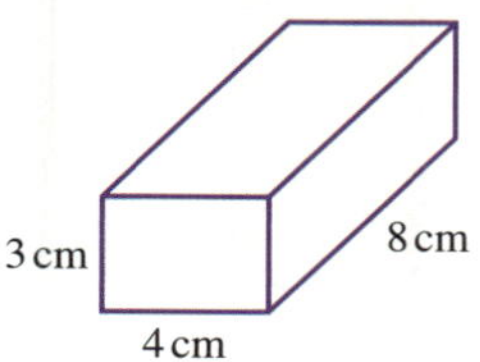

Solution 1

Draw the net.

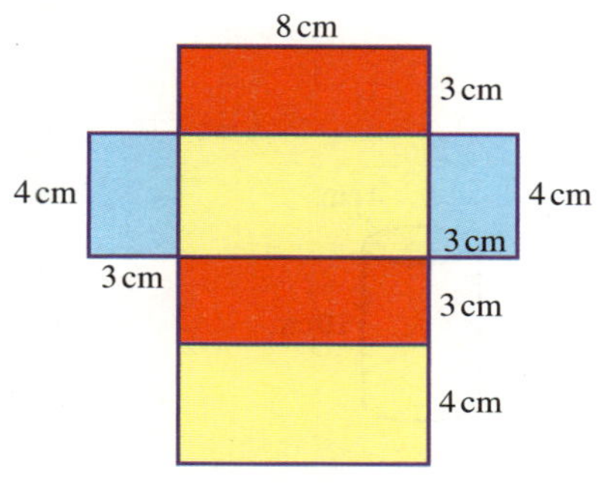

Two blue faces (front and back) are rectangles of length 4 cm and width 3 cm.

The total area of these rectangles is $2 \times (4 \times 3) = 24\text{ cm}^2$

Two yellow faces (top and base) are rectangles of length 4 cm and width 8 cm.

The total area of these rectangles is $2 \times (4 \times 8) = 64\text{ cm}^2$

Two red faces (sides) are rectangles of length 8 cm and width 3 cm.

The total area of these rectangles is $2 \times (8 \times 3) = 48\text{ cm}^2$

Total surface area $= 24 + 64 + 48 = 136\text{ cm}^2$

Example 2

Calculate the total surface area of this triangular prism.

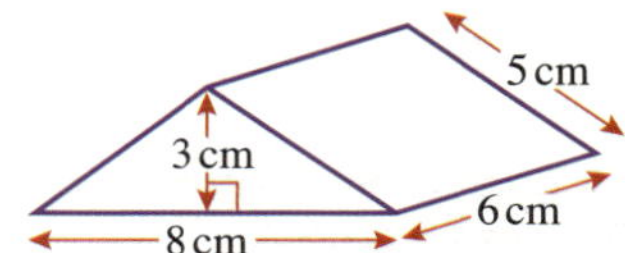

Solution 2

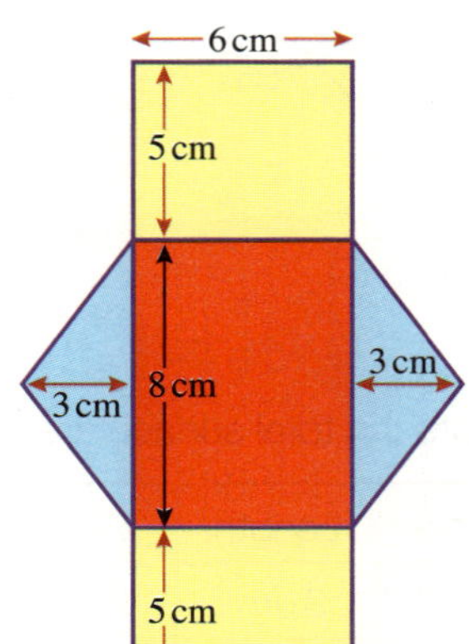

Draw the net.

Two blue faces are triangles.

Area of each triangle

$= \frac{1}{2} \times \text{base} \times \text{perpendicular height}$

$= \frac{1}{2} \times 8 \times 3 = 12\text{ cm}^2$

Two yellow faces (sides) are rectangles.

Area of each rectangle $= 6 \times 5 = 30\text{ cm}^2$

One red face (base) is a rectangle.

Area $= 6 \times 8 = 48\text{ cm}^2$

Total surface area $= (2 \times 12) + (2 \times 30) + 48 = 24 + 60 + 48 = 132\text{ cm}^2$

Surface area of a cylinder

The diagram shows a hollow cylinder. It has no base or top.

This is called an *open cylinder*.

The area of the surface is called the *curved surface area.*
The net of the curved surface is a rectangle.

The length of the rectangle is equal to the circumference of the circular end.

So length $= 2\pi r$

The area of the curved surface $= 2\pi r \times h = 2\pi rh$

Example 3

Calculate the curved surface area of a cylinder of radius 4 cm and height 10 cm.
Leave your answer in terms of π.

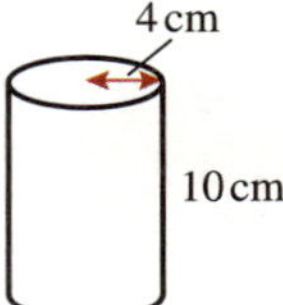

Solution 3

$r = 4$ cm, $h = 10$ cm
Curved surface area $= 2\pi rh = 2 \times \pi \times 4 \times 10 = 80\pi\ \text{cm}^2$

Exercise A

1 Calculate the total surface area of the cubes with the following sides.
a 3 cm **b** 7 cm **c** 10 cm **d** 2 cm

2 For each of these cuboids:
i sketch a net **ii** calculate the total surface area of the cuboid.

a

4 cm
7 cm
8 cm

b

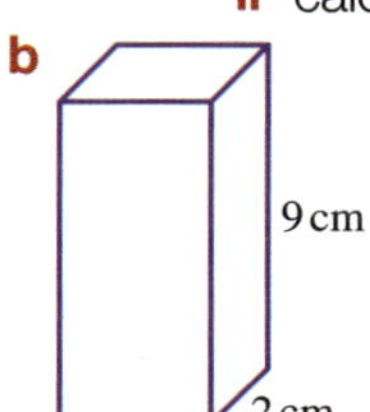

c

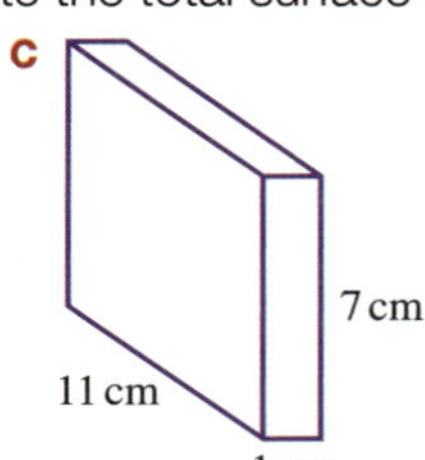

d

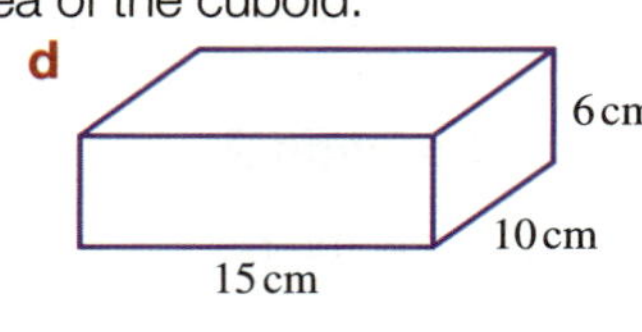

3 Calculate the total surface area of the following cuboids.

Cuboid	Length	Width	Height
a	3 cm	9 cm	5 cm
b	7 cm	2 cm	4 cm
c	4 m	4 m	10 m
d	5 cm	8 cm	12 cm

4 Here is a triangular prism.

a Sketch a net of the prism.

b Calculate the total surface area of the prism.

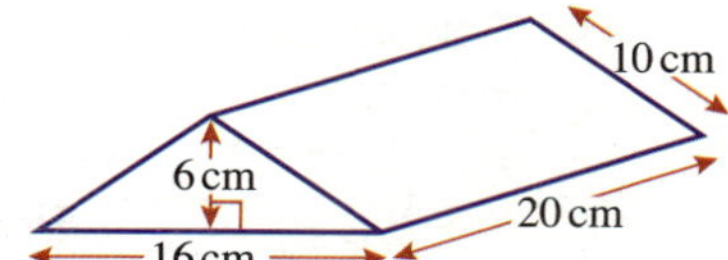

5 Calculate the curved surface area of these open cylinders.
Leave your answers in terms of π.

a

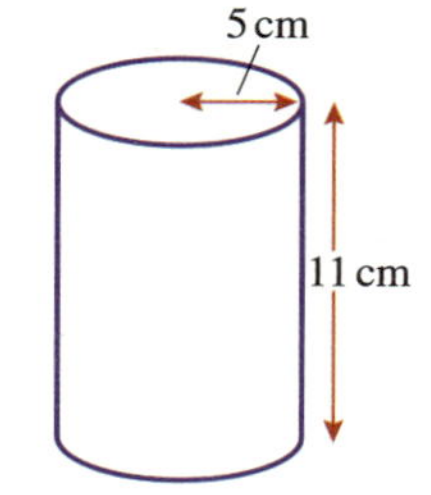

b

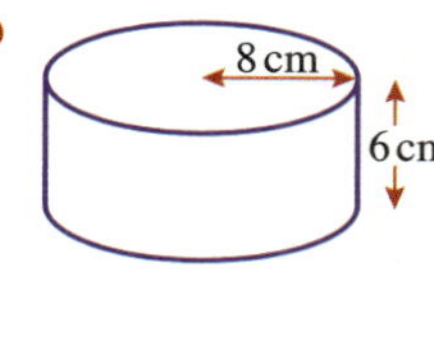

c

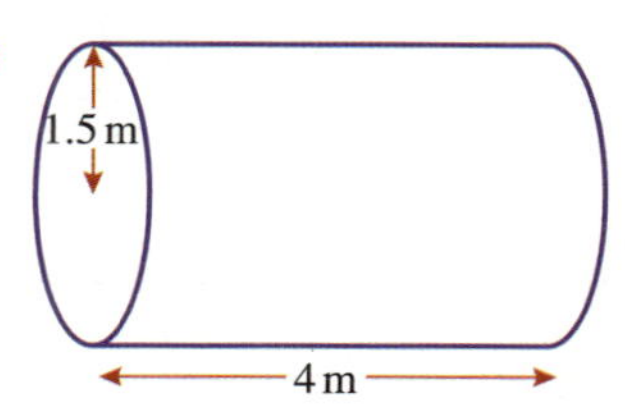

d

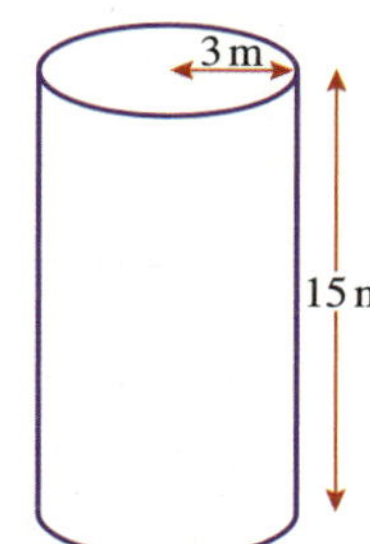

6 Calculate the total surface area of the cubes with the following sides.

a 2.4 cm **b** 3.1 cm **c** 27 cm **d** 8.7 m

7 Calculate the total surface area of each cuboid.

a

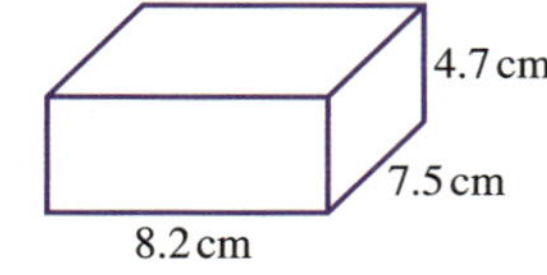

b

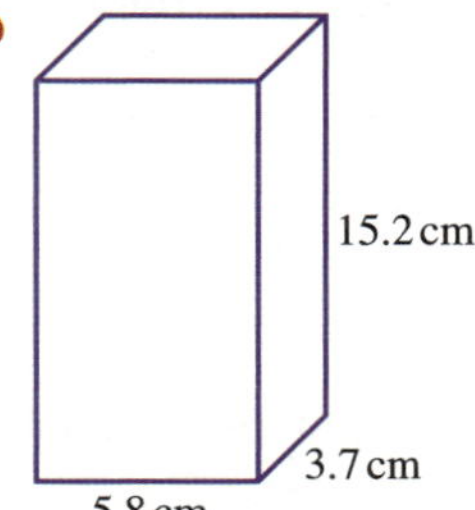

c

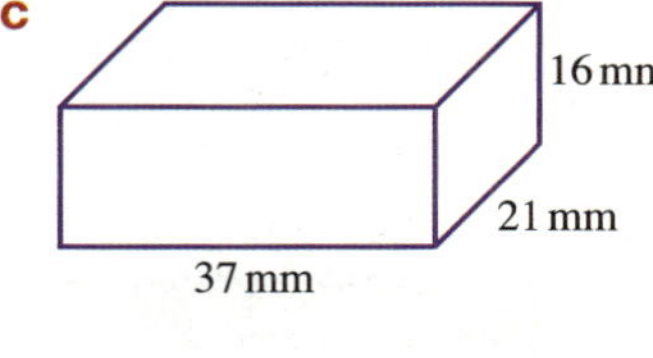

8 Calculate the total surface area of the following cuboids.

Cuboid	Length	Width	Height
a	1.7 cm	0.9 cm	2.1 cm
b	14 cm	46 cm	52 cm
c	3.2 m	2.5 m	4.1 m
d	12.5 cm	8 cm	12.5 cm

9 Here is a triangular prism.

a Sketch a net of this prism.

b Calculate the total surface area of the prism.

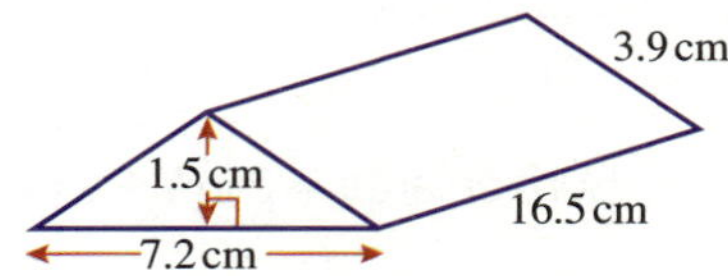

10 Calculate the curved surface area of each cylinder. Take the value of π to be 3.14 or use the π button on a calculator. Give each answer to one decimal place.

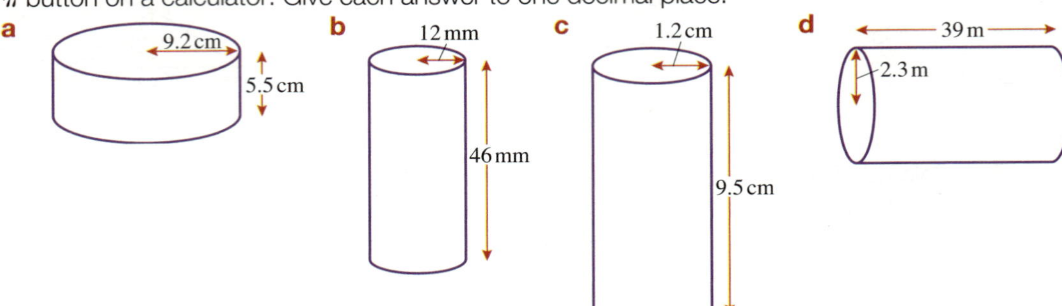

This square has side 1 metre.
The area of the square is 1 m^2

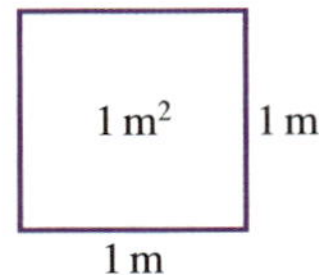

Here is the same square with the units given in centimetres.
Each side is 100 cm.
The area of the square is 100 cm × 100 cm = 10 000 cm^2
So 1 m^2 = 10 000 cm^2

Other units of area can be converted using this method.
For example, 1 cm = 10 mm
1 cm^2 = 10 mm × 10 mm = 100 mm^2

Example 4

a Work out the number of square centimetres there are in: **i** 3 m^2 **ii** 4.2 m^2
b Convert 15 500 cm^2 to square metres.

Solution 4

a 1 m^2 = 10 000 cm^2
To convert m^2 to cm^2 multiply by 10 000
i 3 m^2 = 3 × 10 000 cm^2 = 30 000 cm^2
ii 4.2 m^2 = 4.2 × 10 000 cm^2 = 42 000 cm^2
b To convert cm^2 to m^2 divide by 10 000
15 500 cm^2 = 15 500 ÷ 10 000 cm^2 = 1.55 m^2

A closed cylinder has a circular top and a circular base.
The net of a closed cylinder is shown on the right.

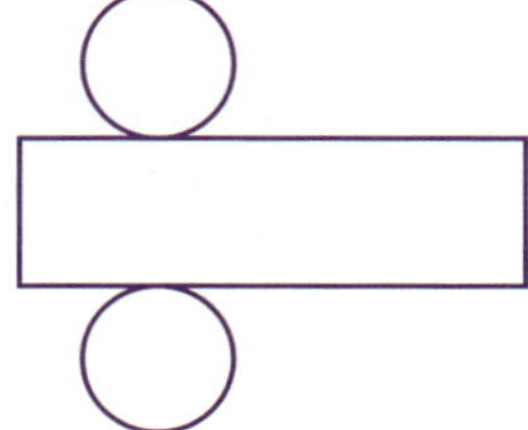

The total surface area
= curved surface area + area of top + area of base
$= 2\pi rh + \pi r^2 + \pi r^2$
Surface area $= 2\pi rh + 2\pi r^2$

Example 5

The diagram shows a closed cylinder.
Calculate the total surface area of the cylinder.
Give your answer:

a to the nearest cm^2

b in square metres to one decimal place.

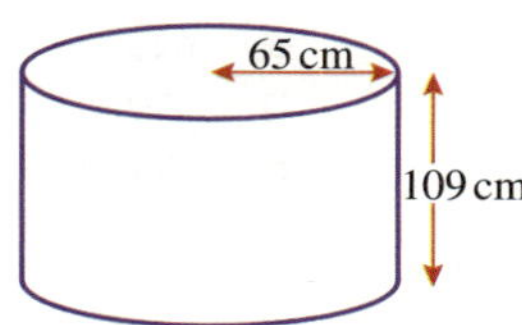

Solution 5

Curved surface area $= 2\pi rh = 2 \times \pi \times 65 \times 109 = 44\,516.3679\ cm^2$

Area of top **and** base $= 2 \times \pi r^2 = 2 \times \pi \times 65 \times 65 = 26\,546.457\,92\ cm^2$

a Total surface area $= 44\,516.3679 + 26\,546.457\,92 = 71\,062.825 = 71\,063\ cm^2$

b Dividing by 10 000

Total surface area $= 71\,062.825 \div 10\,000\ cm^2 = 7.1\ m^2$ (to 1 d.p.)

Exercise B

1 Convert the following areas to square metres.

a $34\,500\ cm^2$ **b** $200\,000\ cm^2$ **c** $4563\ cm^2$ **d** $97\,480\ cm^2$

2 Convert the following areas to square centimetres.

a $7\ m^2$ **b** $3.4\ m^2$ **c** $0.75\ m^2$ **d** $13.8\ m^2$

3 A cuboid measures 12 mm by 9 mm by 11 mm.
Calculate the total surface area of the cuboid.

a Give your answer in mm^2

b Convert your answer to part **a** into cm^2

4 A circular cake tin has a base radius of 11 cm and a depth of 6 cm.
The sides and the base of the tin are to be lined with paper.
Work out the area of paper needed to line the tin.
Leave your answer in terms of π.

5 Sam makes wooden toy boxes.
The boxes are cuboids measuring 50 cm by 30 cm by 25 cm and have no lid.
Sam paints the outside of each box.
A tin of paint covers an area of $5.5\ m^2$
How many toy boxes can Sam complete with one tin of paint?

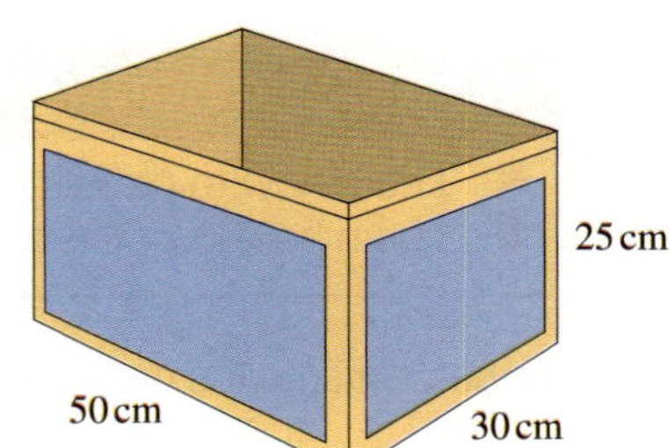

6 Which of the following has the largest surface area?

a A cube of side 25 cm.

b A cuboid measuring 30 cm by 26 cm by 18 cm.

Show your working.

7 A tent is in the form of a triangular prism as shown.
The ends of the prism are equilateral triangles of side 80 cm.
Calculate the total surface area of the tent not including the groundsheet.
Give your answer in square metres.

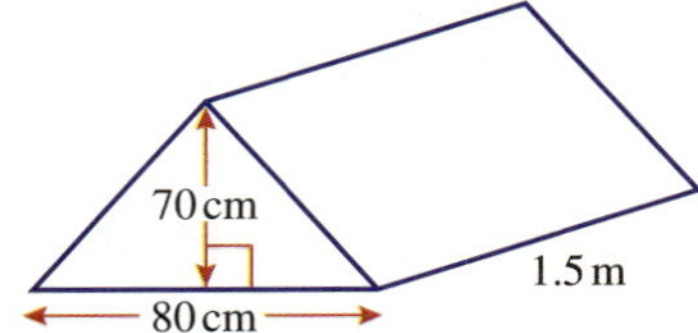

8 Calculate the total surface area of the following closed cylinders.
Give each answer to two decimal places.
a radius 7.2 cm, height 12.8 cm
b radius 0.7 m, height 3.6 m
c diameter 12.4 cm, height 20 cm

9 The diagram shows a wooden wedge.
Calculate the total surface area of the wedge.

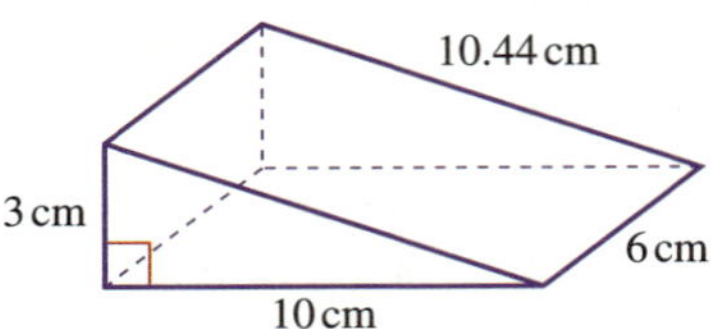

10 Two cylindrical pipes are shown below.

a

radius 0.5 m, length 37 m

b

radius 1.2 m, length 15 m

Which pipe has the smallest curved surface area? Show your working.

13.3 Volumes of prisms

CAN YOU REMEMBER

- A prism is a three-dimensional shape which has the same cross-section all the way through the shape?
- Volume is measured in cube units: mm^3, cm^3, m^3?
- 1 litre = 1000 cm^3?

IN THIS SECTION YOU WILL

- Learn how to calculate the volume of prisms.
- Learn how to convert between volume measures, e.g. cm^3 to m^3

In these prisms the cross-sections are shaded.

  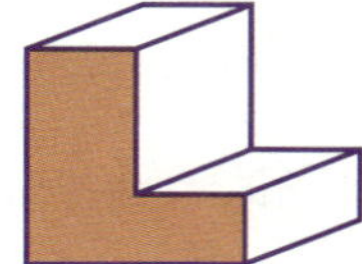 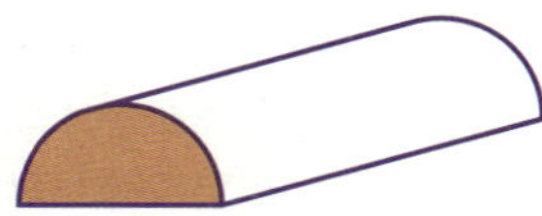

The formula for calculating the volume of a prism is:
volume of a prism = area of cross-section × length
Remember that you should always state the units of your answer.

Density is mass per unit volume. Total mass can be calculated using the formula

Total mass = volume × density.

Example 1

Work out the volume of this triangular prism.

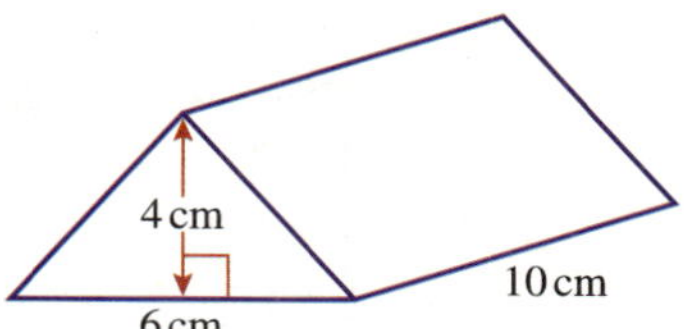

Solution 1

The cross-section is a triangle.

Area of cross-section $= \frac{1}{2} \times \text{base} \times \text{height}$

$= \frac{1}{2} \times 6 \times 4 = 12\ \text{cm}^2$

Volume = area of cross-section × length = 12 × 10 = 120

Volume of the prism = 120 cm^3

Example 2

A cylinder has a base radius of 3 cm and a height of 8 cm.
Calculate the volume of the cylinder. Leave your answer in terms of π.

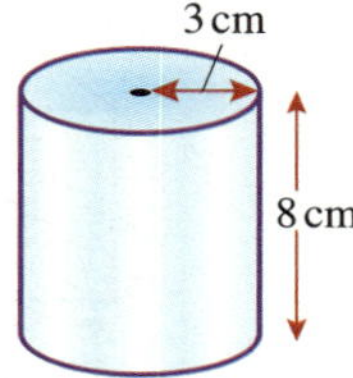

Solution 2

The cross-section is a circle.

Area of cross-section $= \pi r^2 = \pi \times 3^2 = \pi \times 3 \times 3 = 9\pi\ \text{cm}^2$

Volume of the cylinder = area of cross-section × length $= 9\pi \times 8 = 72\pi\ \text{cm}^3$

Example 3

Here is a prism.

a Calculate the area of the cross-section.
b Calculate the volume of the prism.
c Calculate the mass of the prism.

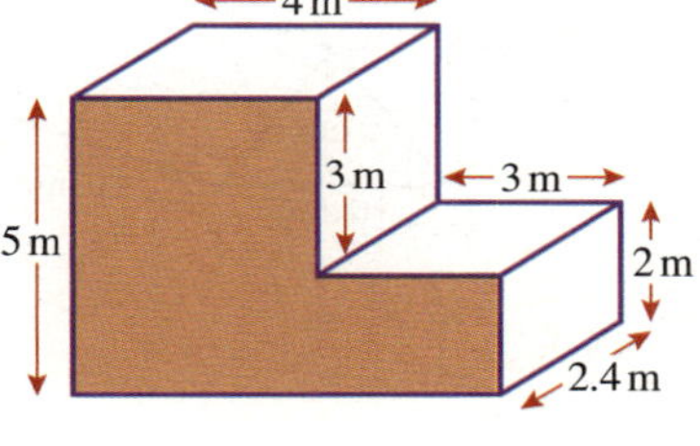

Solution 3

a Divide the cross-section into rectangles

Area of cross-section = (5 × 4) + (3 × 2)

= 20 + 6 = 26 m^2

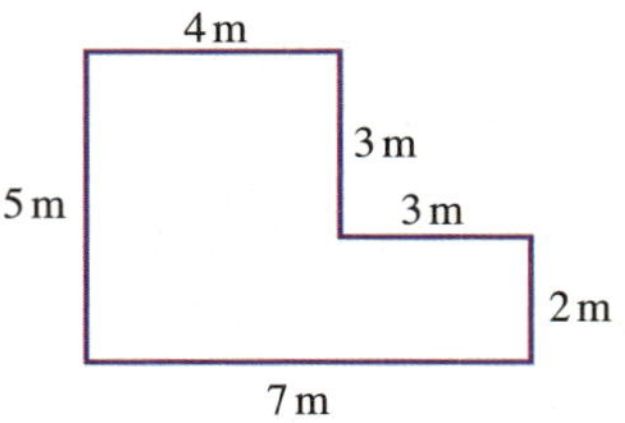

b Volume of prism = area of cross-section × length

= 26 × 2.4 = 62.4 m^3

c The density of the prism is 250 kg/m^3

Total mass = 62.4 × 250 = 15 600 kg

Exercise A

1 For each triangular prism:

i sketch the cross-section **ii** work out the area of the cross-section
iii work out the volume of the prism.

State the units of your answer.

a

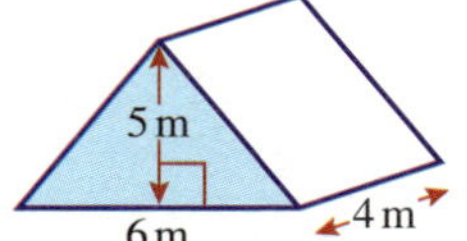

b

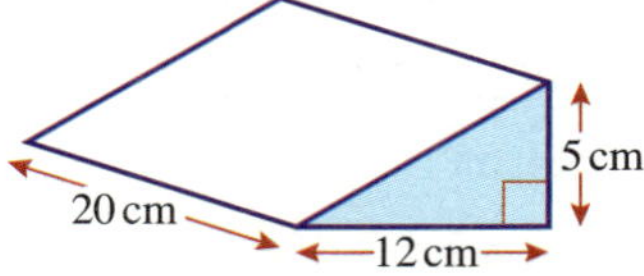

c

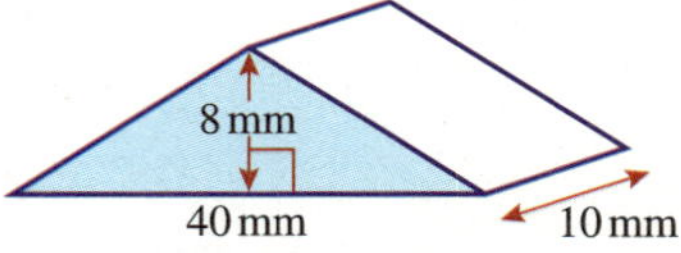

2 Calculate an estimate of the volume of each cylinder. Take the value of π to be 3

a **b** 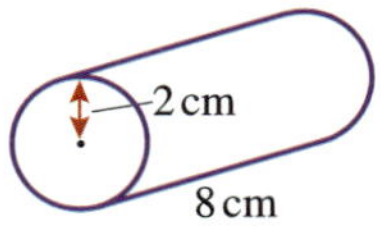 **c** 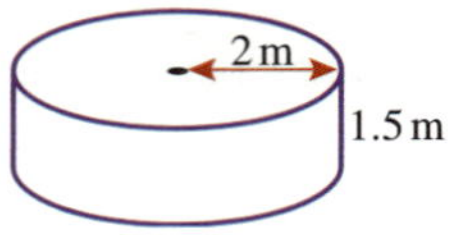 **d**

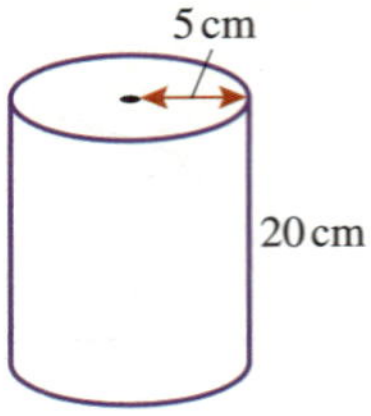

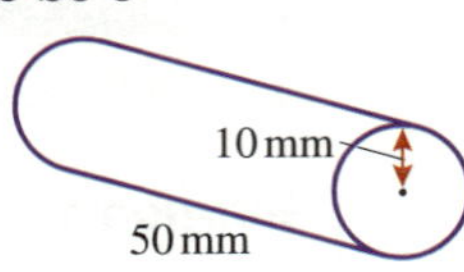

3 For each prism shown:

i sketch the cross-section **ii** work out the area of the cross-section

iii work out the volume of the prism.

a **b** 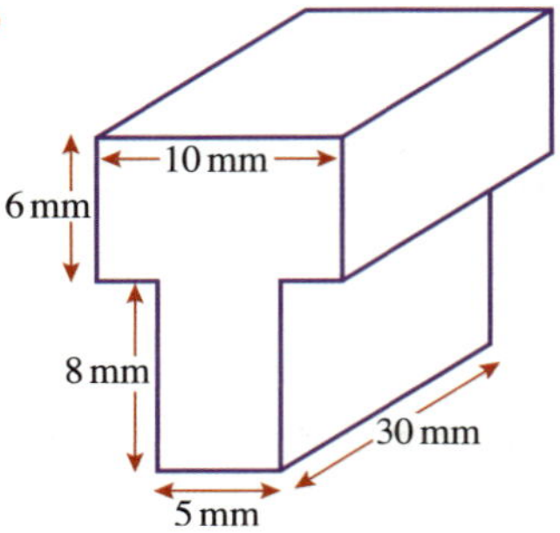 **c**

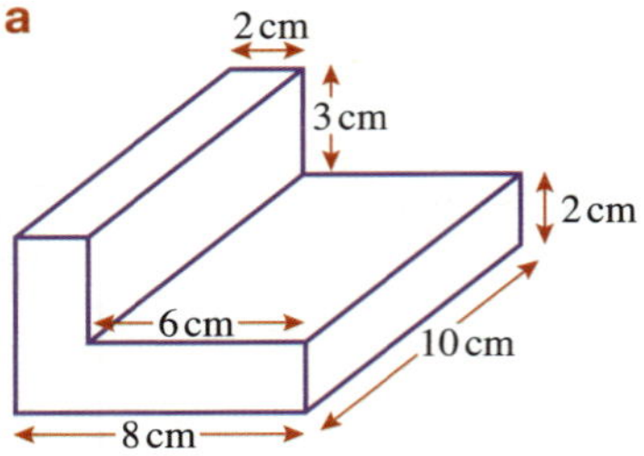

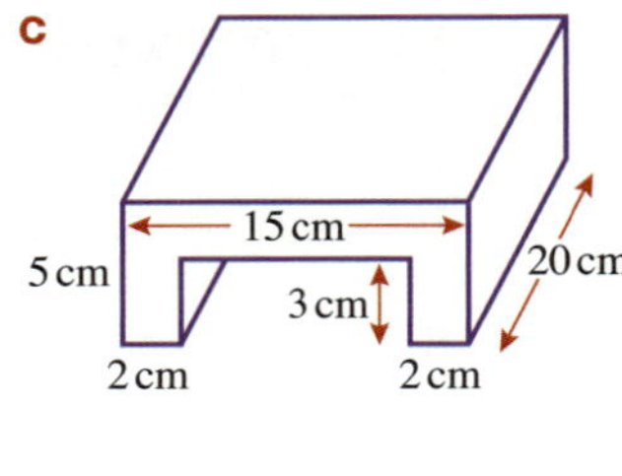

4 Work out the volume of each of these triangular prisms.

a **b** **c** 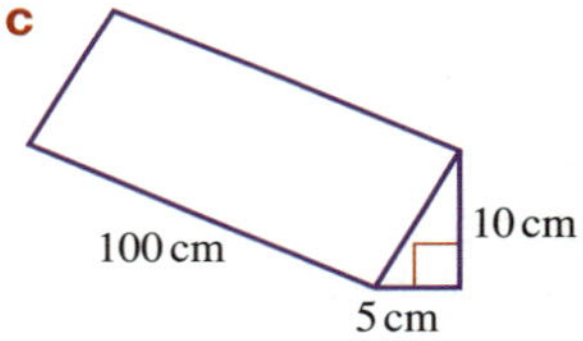 **d**

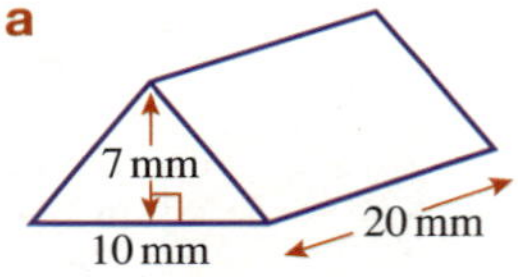

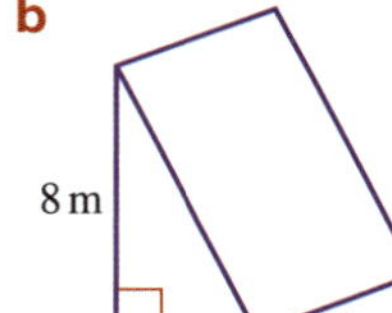

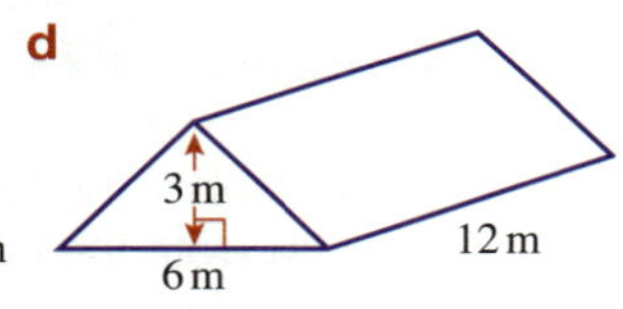

5 Work out the volume of each cylinder. Leave your answer in terms of π.

a **b** **c**

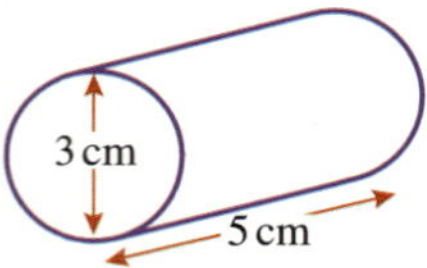

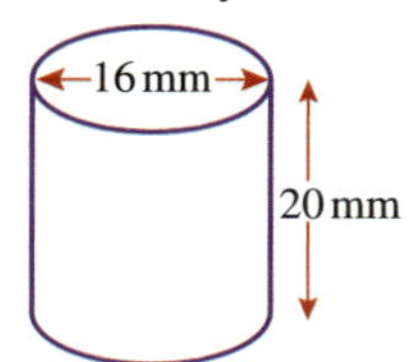

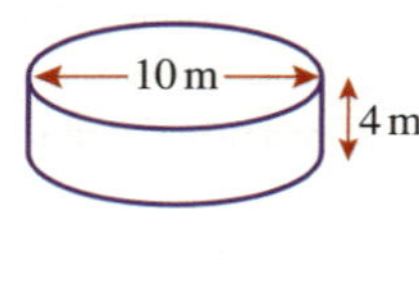

6 **a** Calculate the area of the cross-section of this prism.

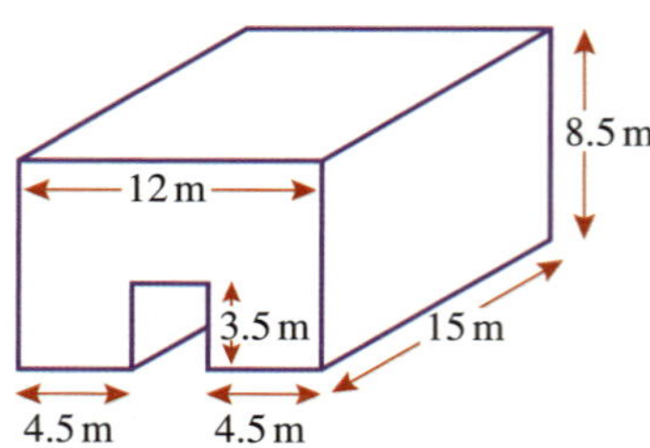

b Calculate the volume of the prism.

7 **a** Calculate the volume of the prism below.

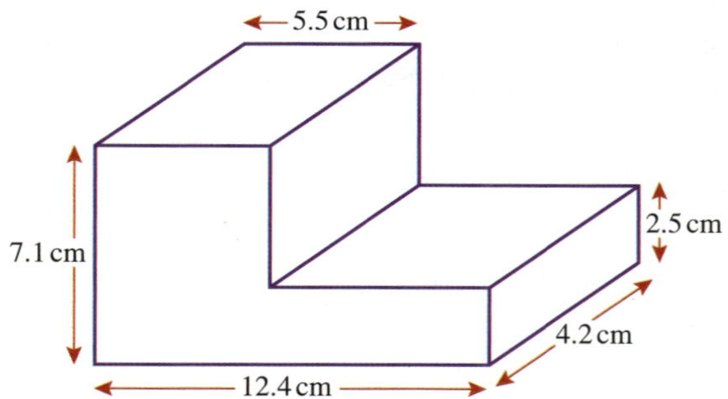

b 1 cm^3 has a mass of 30 grams.
What is the mass of the prism?

8 The prism below has a cross-section in the shape of a right-angled triangle.

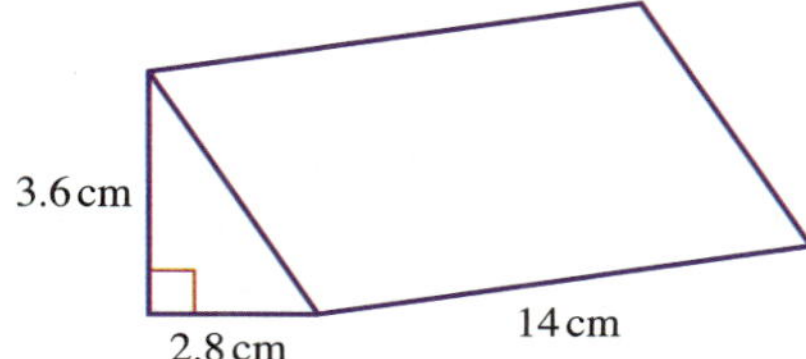

a Calculate the volume of the prism.
b The density of the prism is 30 g/cm^3. What is the total mass of the prism?

9 A drinks can is in the shape of a cylinder of radius 3.5 cm and height 12 cm.
Calculate the volume of the can.
Give your answer to the nearest cm^3

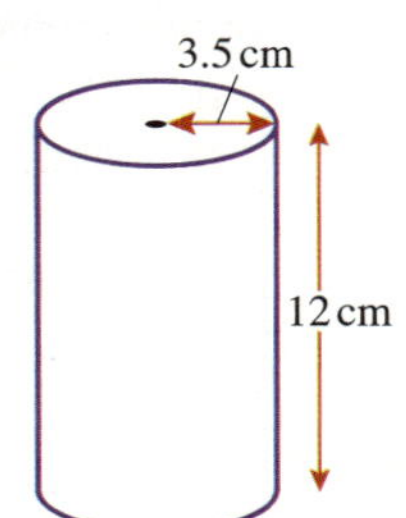

10 Calculate the volume of each of these semicircular prisms.
Give each answer to one decimal place.

a

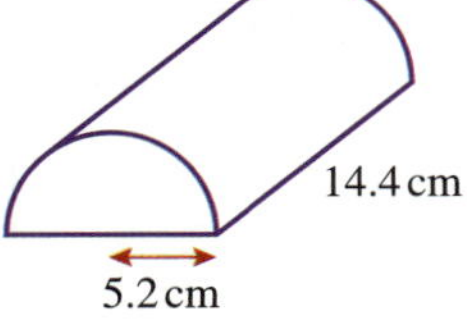

b

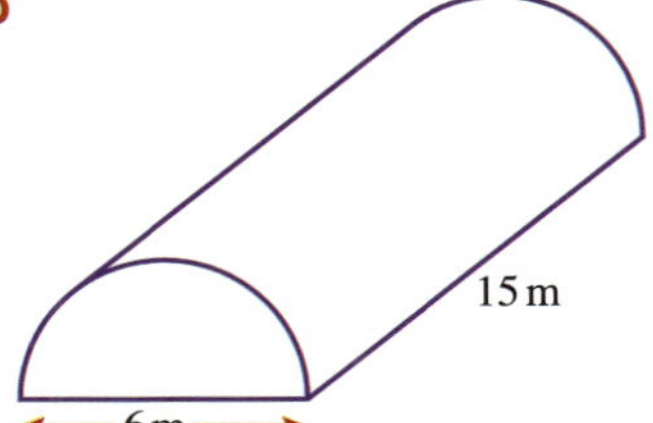

c

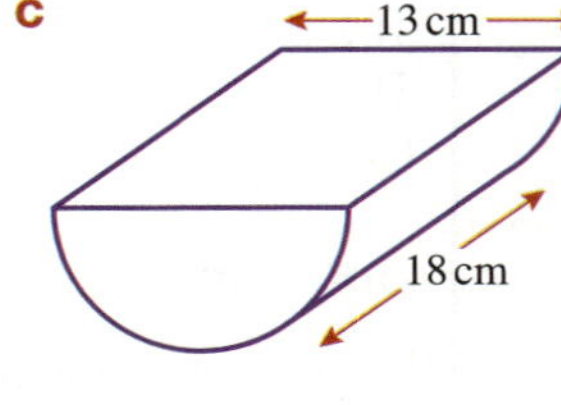

This cube has side 1 metre.
The volume of the cube is 1 m^3

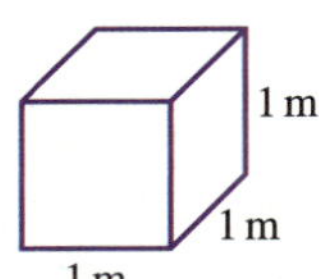

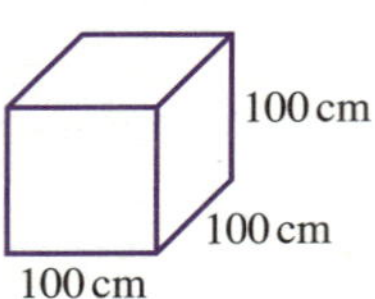

Here is the same cube with the units given in centimetres.
Each side is 100 cm.
The volume of the cube is
100 cm × 100 cm × 100 cm = 1 000 000 cm^3
So 1 m^3 = 1 000 000 cm^3

Other units of volume can be converted using this method.

For example, 1 cm = 10 mm
1 cm^3 = 10 mm × 10 mm × 10 mm = 1000 mm^3

Remember also that 1000 cm^3 = 1 litre

Example 4

a Work out the number of cubic centimetres (cm^3) there are in:
i 4 m^3 **ii** 2.7 m^3
b Convert 2 350 000 cm^3 to cubic metres (m^3).

Solution 4

a 1 m^3 = 1 000 000 cm^3
To convert m^3 to cm^3 multiply by 1 000 000
i 4 m^3 = 4 × 1 000 000 cm^3
= 4 000 000 cm^3
ii 2.7 m^3 = 2.7 × 1 000 000 cm^3
= 2 700 000 cm^3
b To convert cm^3 to m^3 divide by 1 000 000
2 350 000 cm^3 = 2 350 000 ÷ 1 000 000 cm^3 = 2.35 m^3

Example 5

a Shaun says that length × width is the formula for the volume of a cuboid. Is he correct?
b Which is the correct unit for volume: cm^2, cm^3 or cm?

Solution 5

a No he is not correct as length × width is the formula for **area** of a rectangle.
(Volume of a cuboid = length × width × height)
b Volume is measured in cubic units so cm^3 is correct. (cm^2 = area, cm = length)

Example 6

The diagram shows a cylinder of volume 80π cm^3
The radius of the base of the cylinder is 4 cm.
Calculate the height of the cylinder.

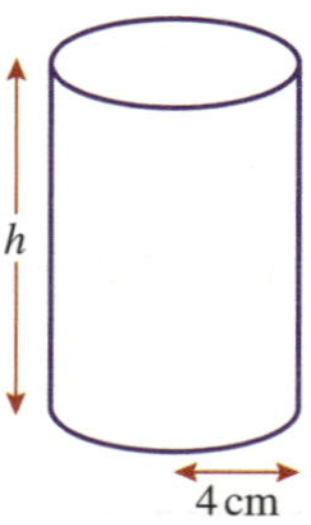

Solution 6

Volume of a cylinder = $\pi r^2 h$
Substitute volume = 80π and $r = 4$ into the formula:

$80\pi = \pi \times 4 \times 4 \times h$

$80 = 4 \times 4 \times h$ Divide both sides by π

$80 = 16 \times h$ Divide both sides by 16

$5 = h$

The height of the cylinder is 5 cm.

Exercise B

1 Convert the following to cubic metres (m^3).

a 1 940 000 cm^3 **b** 31 000 000 cm^3 **c** 826 700 cm^3

2 Convert the following to cubic centimetres (cm^3).

a 8 m^3 **b** 7.9 m^3 **c** 0.25 m^3 **d** 37.4 m^3

3 Match the words to the units.

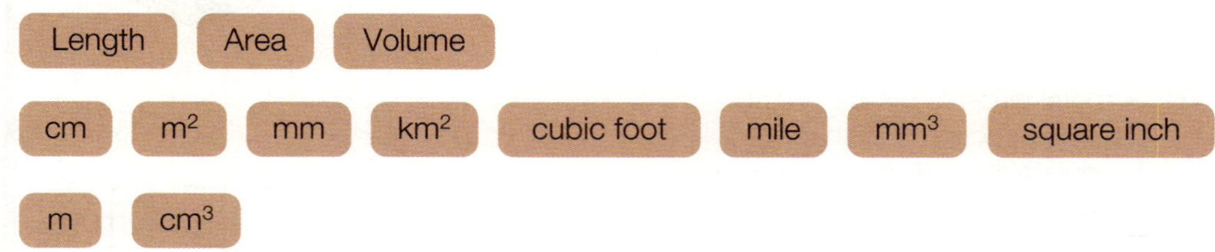

4 A vase is a cuboid with a square base of side 8 cm and a height of 30 cm.
The vase is half full of water.
One litre of water is added. Will the water overflow?
Show your working.

5 The diagram shows a cylinder.
The volume of the cylinder is 100π cm^3
The radius of the cylinder is 5 cm.
Calculate the height of the cylinder.

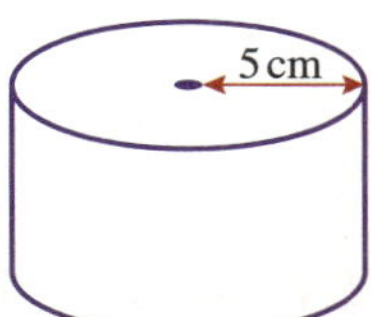

6 Here is a list of formulae:
Copy these headings and write each formula in the correct column.

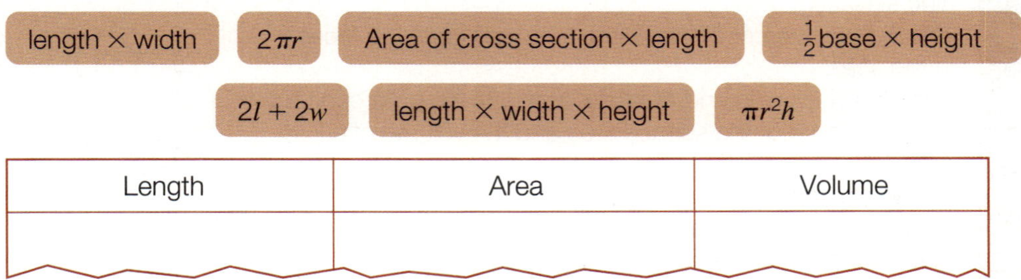

Length	Area	Volume

7 Pete says that πr^2 is the formula for circumference of a circle. Is he correct?
Give a reason for your answer.

8

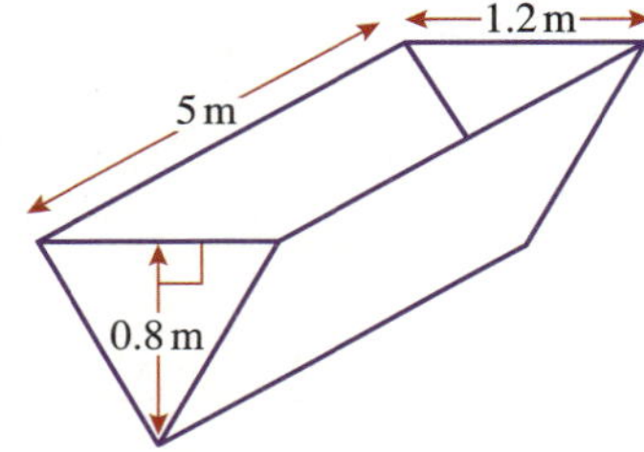

A farmer has a water trough in the shape of a triangular prism.

a Calculate the volume of the trough.

b How many litres of water will the trough hold when full?

1 m^3 = 1000 litres

9 A carton holds 2 litres of apple juice. Cylindrical glasses of height 8 cm and radius 3.5 cm are to be filled from the carton. How many glasses can be filled? Show your working.

10 A metal girder is 4 metres long. Its cross-section is L-shaped. Calculate the volume of the girder. State the units of your answer.

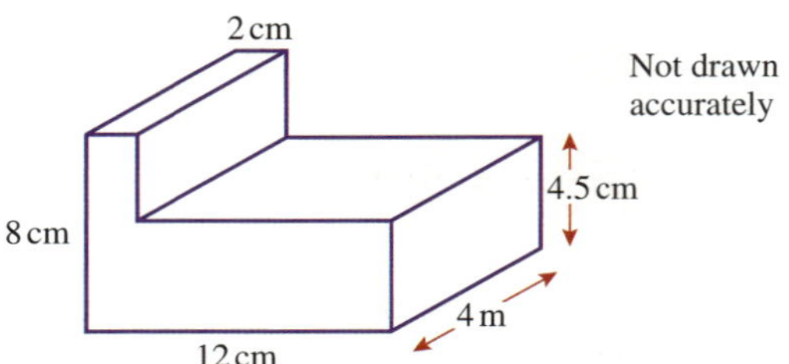

Chapter summary

- Solids can be represented by two-dimensional views.
- The views are plan view, front elevation and side elevation.
- The surface area of a solid is the total area of all the faces in the solid.
- The plan view, side and front elevations of the solid can be used to work out the surface area and the volume of a solid.

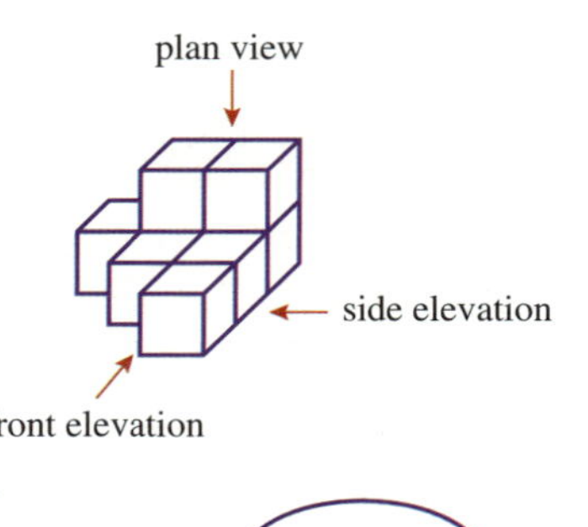

- The total surface area of a three-dimensional shape is the sum of the areas of all the faces of the shape.
- The curved surface area of a cylinder $= 2\pi rh$
- A closed cylinder has a circular top and a circular base. The total surface area
  $=$ curved surface area $+$ area of top $+$ area of base
  $= 2\pi rh + \pi r^2 + \pi r^2 = 2\pi rh + 2\pi r^2$

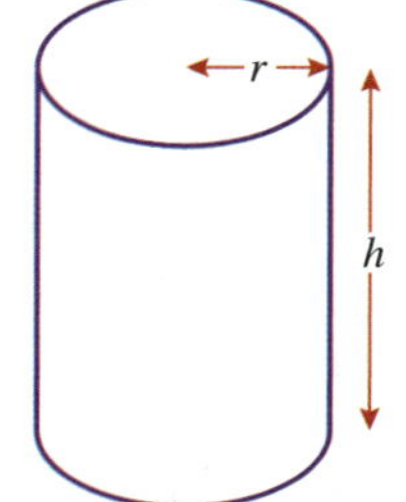

- To convert units of area, e.g.
  $1\text{ m}^2 = 100\text{ cm} \times 100\text{ cm} = 10\,000\text{ cm}^2$
- $1\text{ cm}^2 = 10\text{ mm} \times 10\text{ mm} = 100\text{ mm}^2$
- Volume of a prism $=$ area of cross-section $\times$ length
- To convert units of volume, e.g.
  $1\text{ m}^3 = 100\text{ cm} \times 100\text{ cm} \times 100\text{ cm} = 1\,000\,000\text{ cm}^3$
  $1\text{ cm}^3 = 10\text{ mm} \times 10\text{ mm} \times 10\text{ mm} = 1000\text{ mm}^3$
- $1\text{ litre} = 1000\text{ cm}^3$

Chapter review

1 The diagram opposite shows a solid.
On a grid, draw the elevation of this solid as seen from the direction of the arrow.

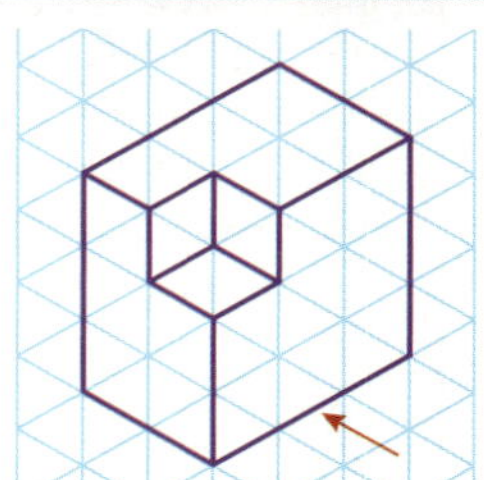

2 The diagram shows an isometric representation of a house.
On a grid, draw the plan of the house.
The plan is the view from above the house.

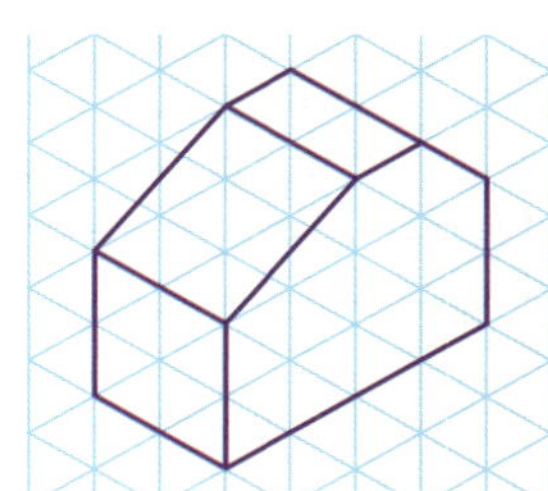

3 The diagram shows a triangular prism.
The cross-section of the prism is a right-angled triangle.
Calculate the volume of the prism.

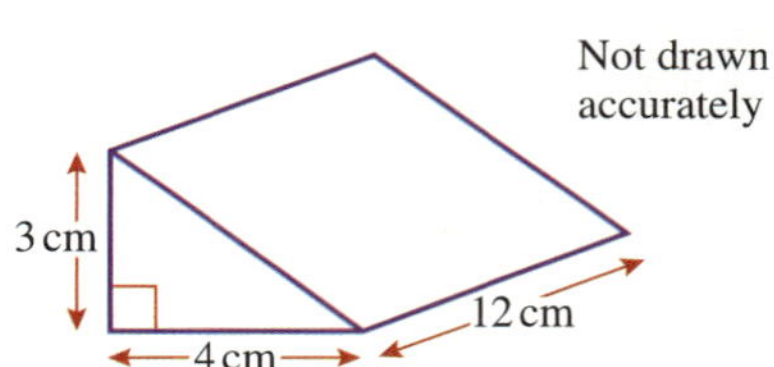

4 The diagram shows a cylinder.
The volume of the cylinder is $540\pi\ \text{cm}^3$
The radius of the cylinder is 10 cm.
Calculate the height of the cylinder.

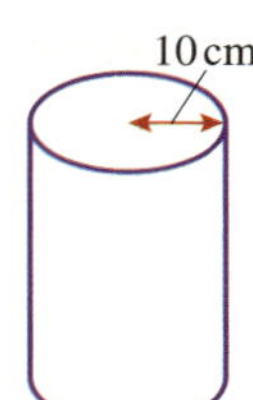

5 A child's swimming pool is in the shape of a cuboid.
The area of the floor of the swimming pool is $50\ \text{m}^2$
Calculate the number of litres of water needed to fill the pool to a height of 1.2 m.

6 The diagram shows a gold bar.
The cross-section of the gold bar is a trapezium.

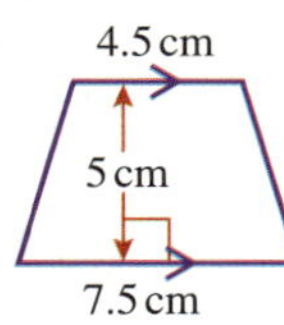

a Calculate the area of the cross-section.
b Calculate the volume of the gold bar.
The density of the gold bar is $19.3\ \text{g/cm}^3$
c What is its total mass?

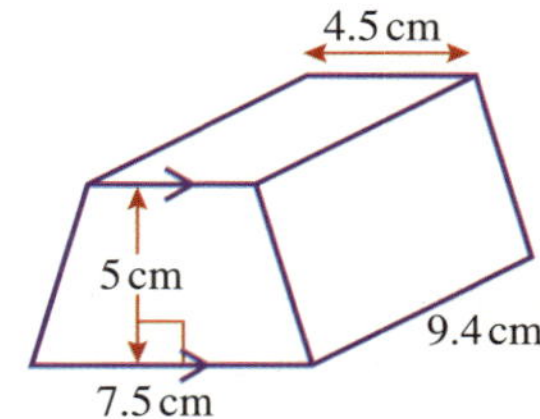

7 A cylinder has a radius of 6 cm.
a Calculate the circumference of a circular end of the cylinder.
b The cylinder has a volume of $950\ \text{cm}^3$
Calculate the height of the cylinder.

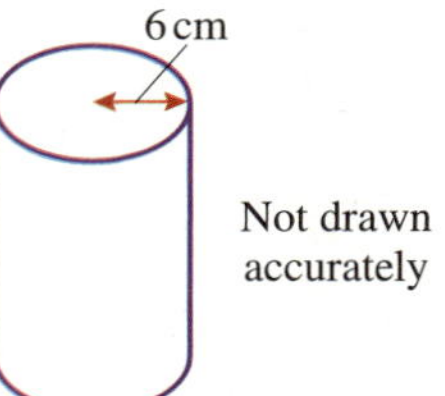

8 A metal girder is 5.6 m long and has an L-shaped cross-section as shown.
Calculate the volume of the girder:

a in cm^3

b in m^3

Give each answer correct to two significant figures.

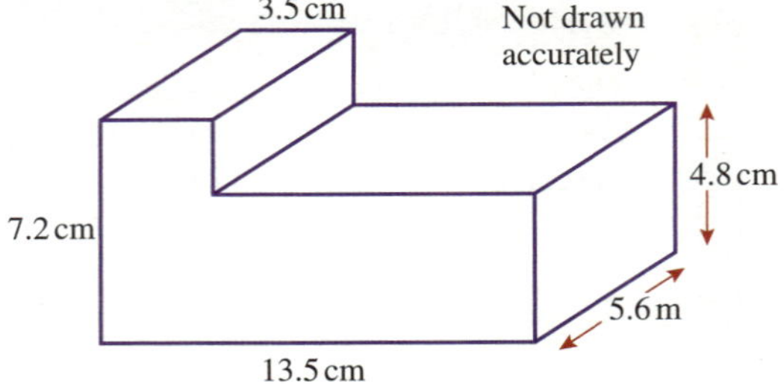

9 The diagram shows a cylindrical tin of fruit.
The height of the tin is 5.1 cm.
The radius of the base is 4.2 cm.
Calculate the **total** surface area of the tin.
Give your answer correct to one decimal place.

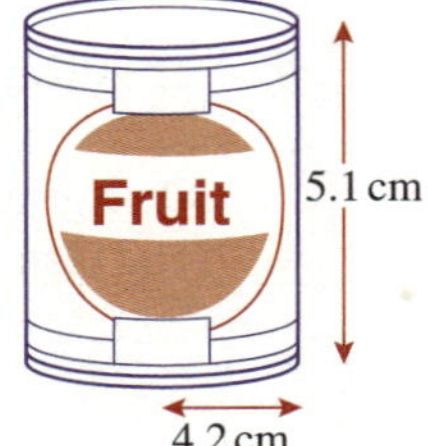

10 The diagram shows a ridge tent which is 3.6 m long.
Calculate the volume of the ridge tent.

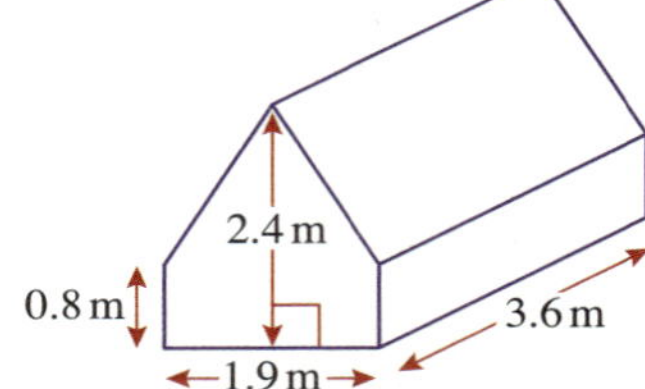

CHAPTER

14

Sequences

14.1 Generating sequences using *n*th term rules

CAN YOU REMEMBER

- That a sequence is a list of numbers or terms that follow a pattern?
- How to continue a sequence using the term-to-term rule?
- How to substitute numbers for letter symbols in algebraic expressions and formulae?

IN THIS SECTION YOU WILL

- Learn how to use position-to-term rules to generate sequences.

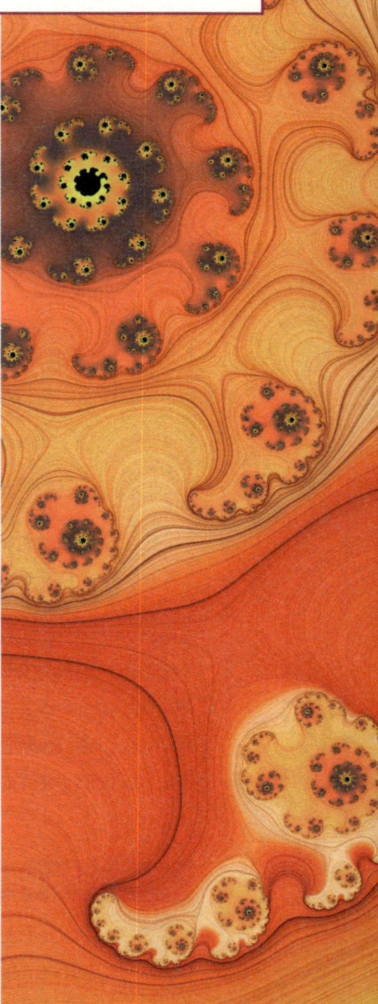

Sequences can be generated using a *term-to-term rule* provided that one term in the sequence is known.

For example: The first term in a sequence is 5

The term-to-term rule is add 4

first term = 5

second term = 5 + 4 = 9

third term = 9 + 4 = 13

fourth term = 13 + 4 = 17

So the first four terms of the sequence are 5, 9, 13, 17

Sequences can also be generated using *position-to-term* rules.

The nth term of a sequence is a position-to-term rule where n represents the position of a term in the sequence.

Example 1

Find the first three terms of the sequences with the following nth terms.

Describe each sequence in words.

a $3n$ **b** $3n - 1$

Solution 1

a nth term = $3n$, where n stands for the term number or the position of the term in the sequence.

Term number	**1**st term	**2**nd term	**3**rd term
n	**1**	**2**	**3**
$3n$	$3 \times \mathbf{1} = 3$	$3 \times \mathbf{2} = 6$	$3 \times \mathbf{3} = 9$
Sequence	3	6	9

The first three terms are 3, 6, 9

The sequence with nth term $3n$ consists of the multiples of 3

b nth term = $3n - 1$

Term number	**1**st term	**2**nd term	**3**rd term
n	**1**	**2**	**3**
$3n - 1$	$3 \times \mathbf{1} - 1 = 2$	$3 \times \mathbf{2} - 1 = 5$	$3 \times \mathbf{3} - 1 = 8$
Sequence	2	5	8

The first three terms are 2, 5, 8
The terms in the sequence are one less than the multiples of 3

Example 2

Find the first three terms and term-to-term rule of the sequences with these nth terms.
Describe each sequence in words.

a $5n$ **b** $5n + 2$

Solution 2

a nth term = $5n$

Term number	**1**st term	**2**nd term	**3**rd term
n	**1**	**2**	**3**
$5n$	$5 \times \mathbf{1} = 5$	$5 \times \mathbf{2} = 10$	$5 \times \mathbf{3} = 15$
Sequence	5	10	15

The first three terms are 5, 10, 15. Term-to-term rule add 5
The sequence with nth term $5n$ consists of the multiples of 5

b nth term = $5n + 2$

Term number	**1**st term	**2**nd term	**3**rd term
n	**1**	**2**	**3**
$5n + 2$	$5 \times \mathbf{1} + 2 = 7$	$5 \times \mathbf{2} + 2 = 12$	$5 \times \mathbf{3} + 2 = 17$
Sequence	7	12	17

The first three terms are 7, 12, 17. Term-to-term rule add 5
The terms in the sequence are two more than the multiples of 5

The nth term can be used:

- to work out the terms in a sequence
- to check whether a given term is in a sequence
- to find the position of a given term in a sequence.

Example 3

A sequence has nth term $3n + 5$

a Is 145 a term in the sequence?

b What is the position of the term 80 in the sequence?

Solution 3

a $3n + 5 = 145$ — Subtract 5 from both sides.

$3n = 140$ — Divide both sides by 3

$n = 140 \div 3 = 46\frac{2}{3}$

There is no $46\frac{2}{3}$ term (n must be a positive integer), so 145 is not a term in the sequence.

b $3n + 5 = 80$ — Subtract 5 from both sides.

$3n = 75$ — Divide both sides by 3

$n = 75 \div 3 = 25$

So 80 is the 25th term in the sequence.

Exercise A

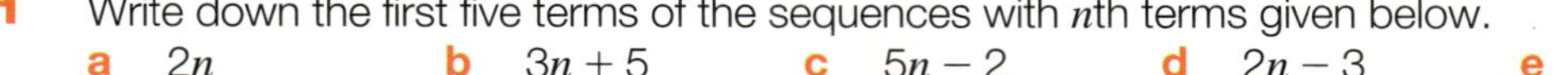

1 Write down the first five terms of the sequences with nth terms given below.

a $2n$ **b** $3n + 5$ **c** $5n - 2$ **d** $2n - 3$ **e** $5n + 3$

f $3n - 3$ **g** $5n - 3$ **h** $2n + 5$ **i** $3n - 2$ **j** $5n + 2$

2 Write down the first five terms of the sequences with nth terms given below.
Describe each sequence in words.

a **i** $4n$ **ii** $4n - 1$ **iii** $4n + 3$ **iv** $4n - 5$ **v** $4n + 9$

b **i** $10n$ **ii** $10n - 3$ **iii** $10n + 7$ **iv** $10n - 11$ **v** $10n + 6$

3 **a** A sequence has nth term $2n - 5$
- **i** Find the fifth term of this sequence.
- **ii** Find the tenth term of this sequence.
- **iii** Find the 15th term of this sequence.

b Find the second, fourth and sixth terms of the sequence with nth term $3n$.

c Find the third, fifth and seventh terms of the sequence with nth term $6n - 1$

d Find the 10th, 20th and 30th terms of the sequence with nth term $5n + 1$

e Find the 100th, 200th and 300th terms of the sequence with nth term $4n + 1$

4 **a** A sequence has nth term $7 - 2n$.
- **i** Find the first three terms of this sequence.
- **ii** How many terms of the sequence are positive integers? Work out as many terms as you need to find out.

b A sequence has nth term $10 - 4n$.
- **i** Find the fourth term of this sequence.
- **ii** How many terms of this sequence are positive integers?

5 The cards below give the nth terms of some sequences.

$3n + 7$	$5n + 1$	$3n + 4$
$8n - 5$	$5n + 7$	$8n - 3$

a Which two sequences have a term equal to 11?

b Which three sequences have a first term equal to a prime number?

c Which two sequences have a third term equal to a square number?

d Which three sequences have a term equal to 13?

e Which three sequences have the term 16 in common?

f Which two sequences have the term-to-term rule add 8 ?

6 **a** A sequence has nth term $2n - 5$
Find the first term and term-to-term rule of this sequence.

b Repeat part **a** for the sequence with nth term:
i $4n + 3$ **ii** $3n - 7$ **iii** $8 - 3n$ **iv** $20 - 5n$

7 **a** Match the nth term rules with the sequences.

Sequences	nth term rules
Sequence 1 1, 8, 15, 22, 29, …	**nth term rule A** $4n - 3$
Sequence 2 1, 7, 13,19, 25, …	**nth term rule B** $7n - 6$
Sequence 3 1, 4, 7, 10, 13, …	**nth term rule C** $6n - 5$
Sequence 4 1, 5, 9, 13, 17, …	**nth term rule D** $3n - 2$
Sequence 5 1, 6, 11, 16, 21, …	**nth term rule E** $5n - 4$

b Write the nth term rule for the sequence 1, 9, 17, 25, 33, …

8 **a** This number machine gives the nth term of a sequence.

Term number, n → $\times 2$ → $+7$ → nth term

i Use the number machine to complete this table.

Term number, n	1	2	3	4	5
Term					

ii Write down the term-to-term rule for the sequence.
iii Find the nth term rule for the sequence.

b Repeat part **a** for the sequences given by these number machines.

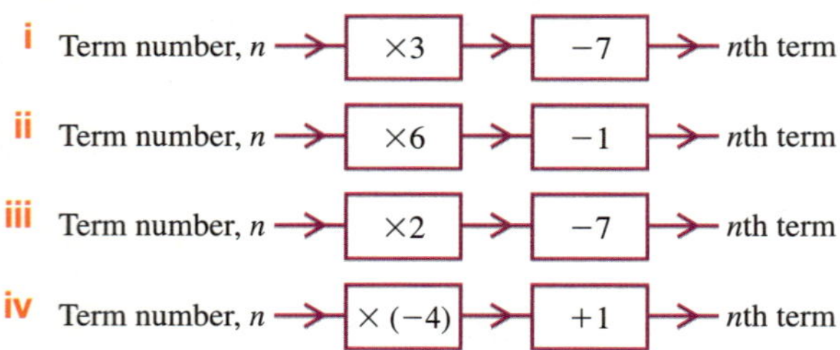

9 Match each of these nth terms with the term-to-term rule for its sequence.

nth terms
$4n - 1$
$7n + 1$
$3n - 1$
$6n + 1$
$5n - 1$

Term-to-term rules
Add 7
Add 4
Add 6
Add 5
Add 3

What do you notice?

10 Which of the following statements are true and which are false?
- **a** 396 is the 44th term of the sequence with nth term $9n$.
- **b** 95 is the 17th term in the sequence with nth term $6n - 7$
- **c** 89 is a term in the sequence with nth term $14n - 3$
- **d** 323 is a term in the sequence with nth term $40n + 3$
- **e** 137 is a term in the sequence with nth term $27n + 3$
- **f** 26 is a term in the sequence with nth term $100 - 13n$.
- **g** -12 is a term in the sequence with nth term $78 - 15n$.
- **h** -126 is a term in the sequence with nth term $130 - 16n$.

Sequences with a *constant difference* between consecutive terms:
- have a term-to-term rule of the form **+ constant difference**
- have a position-to-term rule or nth term of the form **nth term $= an + b$** where a is the constant difference and b is a positive or negative integer.

For example, the sequence 5, 11, 17, 23, 29, … has a constant difference of **6**

	5		11		17		23		29
Differences		**+6**		**+6**		**+6**		**+6**	

The constant difference is **6**, so the term-to-term rule is **add 6**

The nth term rule is $\mathbf{6}n - 1$

Some sequences do **not** have a constant difference between consecutive terms.

For example, the first five terms of the sequence with nth term n^2 are 1, 4, 9, 16, 25, …

Term	1		4		9		16		25
Differences		**+3**		**+5**		**+7**		**+9**	
			+2		+2		+2		

All sequences that contain an n^2 term have a similar sort of difference pattern.

Example 4

A sequence has nth term $2(n - 3)^2$
- **a** Find the first five terms of this sequence.
- **b** Find the pattern of differences between consecutive terms of the sequence. What do you notice?

Solution 4

a nth term $2(n - 3)^2$

Term number	**1**st term	**2**nd term	**3**rd term	**4**th term	**5**th term
n	**1**	**2**	**3**	**4**	**5**
$n - 3$	$\mathbf{1} - 3 = -2$	$\mathbf{2} - 3 = -1$	$\mathbf{3} - 3 = 0$	$\mathbf{4} - 3 = 1$	$\mathbf{5} - 3 = 2$
$(n - 3)^2$	$(-2)^2 = 4$	$(-1)^2 = 1$	$0^2 = 0$	$1^2 = 1$	$2^2 = 4$
$2(n - 3)^2$	$2 \times 4 = 8$	$2 \times 1 = 2$	$2 \times 0 = 0$	$2 \times 1 = 2$	$2 \times 4 = 8$
Sequence	8	2	0	2	8

The first five terms are 8, 2, 0, 2, 8

b

Sequence	8		2		0		2		8
Differences		**−6**		**−2**		**+2**		**+6**	
			+ 4		+ 4		+ 4		

The differences between the terms in the sequence follow a pattern with constant difference 4

Exercise B

1 The cards show the first five terms of some sequences with first term 2

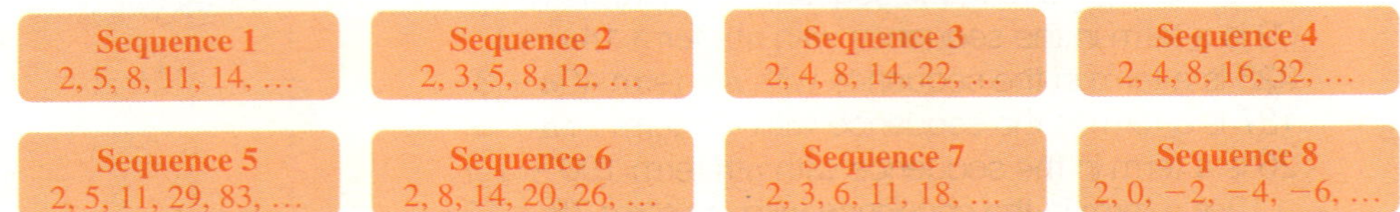

Which of the sequences have a constant difference between consecutive terms?

2 **a** A sequence has nth term $4n + 7$
What is the constant difference between consecutive terms of this sequence?
b The constant difference between the terms of a linear sequence is 5
Write down three possible nth terms for this sequence.

3 **a** A sequence has nth term $n^2 + 1$
i Write down the first five terms of this sequence.
ii Describe the pattern of differences between consecutive terms.
b Repeat part **a** for the sequences with nth terms:
i $n^2 + n$ **ii** $n(n + 1)$ **iii** $(n + 1)^2$
iv $(n - 1)^2$ **v** $2n^2 + 1$ **vi** $(n + 2)(n - 3)$

4 A sequence has nth term $2n$.
Explain why it is not possible for 1001 to be a term in this sequence.

5 Tom says that 503 is a term in the sequence with nth term $5n$.
Explain why he is wrong.

6 **a** Explain why 122 is **not** a term in the sequence with nth term $4n$.
b Explain why 151 is a term in the sequence with nth term $10n + 11$

7 **a** A linear sequence contains the term 101
One possible nth term for such a sequence is $5n + 1$ because 101 is 1 more than a multiple of 5
Write down five other possible nth terms for a linear sequence containing 101.
Give a reason for each of the nth terms you choose.
b Show that $n^2 + 1$ and $2n^2 + 3$ are both possible nth terms for a sequence that contains the term 101

8 The nth terms of some linear sequences are shown below.
$2n + 1$ $3n + 2$ $4n - 3$ $5n + 2$ $6n - 3$ $10n + 15$
a **i** In which of the sequences do multiples of 3 occur?
ii Which of the sequences contain **only** multiples of 3?
b **i** In which of the sequences do odd numbers occur?
ii Which of the sequences contain **only** odd numbers?
c **i** In which of the sequences do multiples of 5 occur?
ii Which of the sequences contain **only** multiples of 5?
Explain your answer.

9 **a** The number machine gives the nth term of a sequence.

Term number, n → square → ×2 → nth term

Describe the pattern of differences between consecutive terms of this sequence.

b Repeat for the sequences given by these number machines.

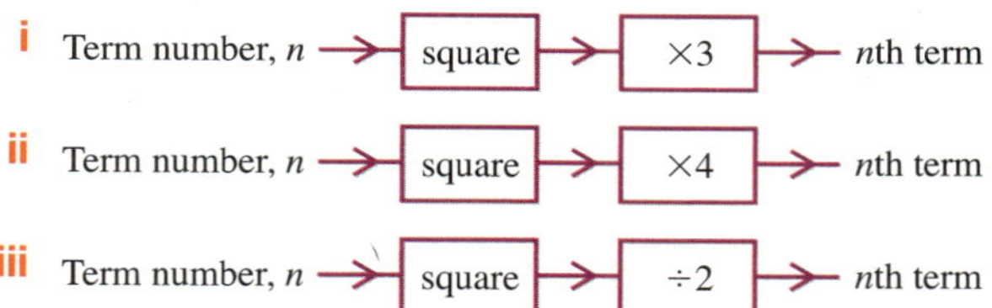

10 A sequence has nth term $2n^2 + 4n + 5$
Use trial and improvement to show that 75 is a term in this sequence.

14.2 Finding the nth term of a sequence

CAN YOU REMEMBER

- How to use the nth term of a sequence to generate terms in the sequence?

IN THIS SECTION YOU WILL

- Learn how to find the nth term of a sequence with a constant difference between consecutive terms.
- Work out the nth terms of sequences based on patterns of shapes and numbers.
- Connect nth term rules to the patterns of shapes upon which they are based.

Some sequences of multiples are shown below.

Multiples of **2**	2		4		6		8
Differences		**+2**		**+2**		**+2**	

Term-to-term rule **add 2**
nth term $2n$

Multiples of **3**	3		6		9		12
Differences		**+3**		**+3**		**+3**	

Term-to-term rule **add 3**
nth term $3n$

Multiples of **10**	10		20		30		40
		+10		**+10**		**+10**	

Term-to-term rule **add 10**
nth term $10n$

This sequence is based on the multiples of 2

The multiples of 2	**2**		**4**		**6**		**8**
1 more than the multiples of 2	3		5		7		9
Differences		**+2**		**+2**		**+2**	

Term-to-term rule **add 2**
nth term $2n + 1$

This sequence is based on the multiples of 3

The multiples of 3	**3**		**6**		**9**		**12**
4 more than the multiples of 3	7		10		13		16
Differences		**+3**		**+3**		**+3**	

Term-to-term rule **add 3**
nth term $3n + 4$

This sequence is based on the multiples of 10

The multiples of 10	**10**		**20**		**30**		**40**
2 less than the multiples of 10	8		18		28		38
Differences		**+10**		**+10**		**+10**	

Term-to-term rule **add 10**
nth term $10n - 2$

Example 1

a Find the nth term of each of the following linear sequences.

i 1, 6, 11, 16, … **ii** 5, 9, 13, 17, …

b Use the nth term to find the 250th term of each of the sequences.

Solution 1

a **i** 1 6 11 16

+5 +5 +5

Term-to-term rule **add 5**
The sequence is based on the multiples of 5

Term number (n)	1	2	3	4	n
Multiple of **5** (**5** × n)	**5** × 1 = 5	**5** × 2 = 10	**5** × 3 = 15	**5** × 4 = 20	**5**n
Term	1	6	11	16	
Term − **5**n	1 − 5 = −4	6 − 10 = −4	11 − 15 = −4	16 − 20 = −4	−4

Term − **5**n = −4
The nth term is **5**n − 4

So each term is 4 less than a multiple of 5

ii 5 9 13 17

+4 +4 +4

Term-to-term rule **add 4**
The sequence is based on the multiples of 4

Term number (n)	1	2	3	4	n
Multiple of **4** (**4** × n)	**4** × 1 = 4	**4** × 2 = 8	**4** × 3 = 12	**4** × 4 = 16	**4**n
Term	5	9	13	17	
Term − **4**n	5 − 4 = 1	9 − 8 = 1	13 − 12 = 1	17 − 16 = 1	1

Term − **4**n = 1
The nth term is **4**n + 1

So each term is 1 more than a multiple of 4

b **i** nth term $5n - 4$
When $n = 250$,
$5n - 4 = 5 \times 250 - 4 = 1246$
So the 250th term is 1246

ii nth term $4n + 1$
When $n = 250$,
$4n + 1 = 4 \times 250 + 1 = 1001$
So the 250th term is 1001

Example 2

Matchsticks are used to make this pattern of shapes.

pattern 1

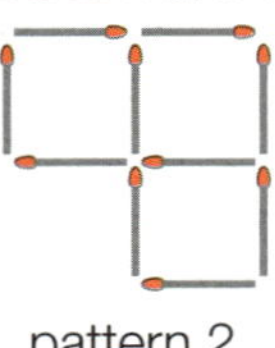

pattern 2

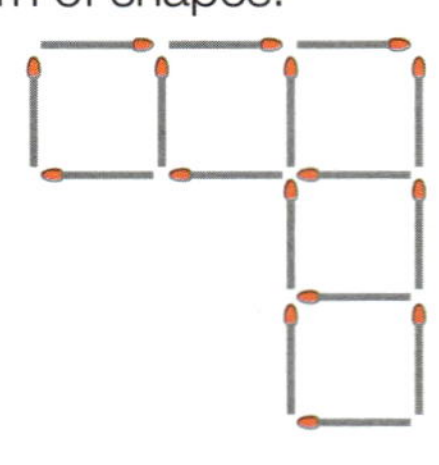

pattern 3

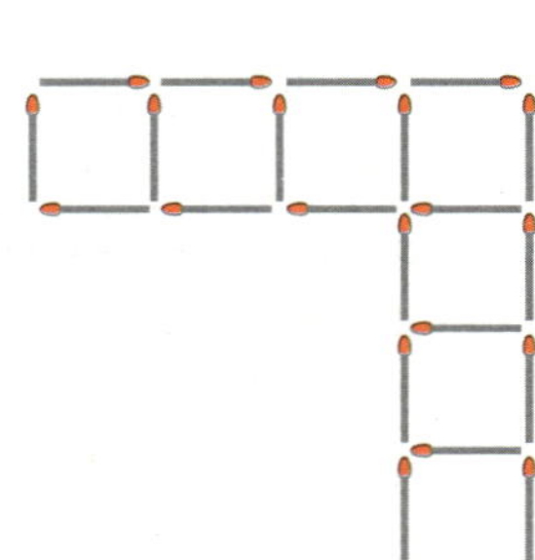

pattern 4

a Find an expression for the number of matchsticks needed to make pattern n.
b Find the number of the pattern that uses 304 matchsticks.

Solution 2

a The number of matchsticks in each pattern is shown in the table.

Pattern number	1	2	3	4
Number of matchsticks	4	10	16	22

The number of matchsticks forms the sequence 4, 10, 16, 22, …

Difference = **6**

Term-to-term rule **add 6**

This can be seen from the diagram, where six blue matchsticks are added each time to make the next pattern.
So the sequence is based on the multiples of **6**

Term number (n)	1	2	3	4	n
Multiple of **6** (**6** $\times n$)	**6** $\times 1 = 6$	**6** $\times 2 = 12$	**6** $\times 3 = 18$	**6** $\times 4 = 24$	**6n**
Term	4	10	16	22	
Term − **6n**	$4 - 6 = -2$	$10 - 12 = -2$	$16 - 18 = -2$	$22 - 24 = -2$	-2

So the number of matchsticks in pattern n is $6n - 2$

b When there are 304 matchsticks

$6n - 2 = 304$ (Add 2 to both sides)

$6n = 306$ (Divide both sides by 6)

$n = 51$

So pattern 51 uses 304 matchsticks.

Exercise A

1 The nth term of the sequence 5, 10, 15, 20, 25, … is $5n$.
Write down the nth term of the following sequences.

a 6, 12, 18, 24, 30, …
b 12, 24, 36, 48, 60, …
c 8, 16, 24, 32, 40, …
d $\frac{1}{2}$, 1, $1\frac{1}{2}$, 2, $2\frac{1}{2}$, …
e $\frac{1}{4}$, $\frac{1}{2}$, $\frac{3}{4}$, 1, $1\frac{1}{4}$, …
f −2, −4, −6, −8, −10, …
g −5, −10, −15, −20, −25, …
h $-\frac{1}{2}$, −1, $-1\frac{1}{2}$, −2, $-2\frac{1}{2}$, …

2 The sequence 5, 10, 15, 20, 25, … has nth term $5n$.
Write down the nth term of these sequences.

a 6, 11, 16, 21, 26, ….
b 4, 9, 14, 19, 24, …
c 8, 13, 18, 23, 28, …
d 1, 6, 11, 16, 21, …
e −4, 1, 6, 11, 16, …

3 **a** Write down the nth term of the sequence 3, 6, 9, 12, 15, …
b Write down the nth term of these sequences.
i 4, 7, 10, 13, 16, …
ii 2, 5, 8, 11, 14, …
iii 8, 11, 14, 17, 20, …
iv −2, 1, 4, 7, 10, …
v 13, 16, 19, 22, 25, …

4 For each of these sequences write down the term-to-term rule and find the nth term.

a 5, 11, 17, 23, 29, …
b 7, 11, 15, 19, 23, …
c 8, 14, 20, 26, 32, …
d 20, 17, 14, 11, 8, …
e −2, 5, 12, 19, 26, …
f 5, $5\frac{1}{2}$, 6, $6\frac{1}{2}$, 7, …
g 102, 105, 108, 111, 114, …
h 21, 29, 37, 45, 53, …
i 4, $6\frac{1}{2}$, 9, $11\frac{1}{2}$, 14, …
j 100, 91, 82, 73, 64, …

5 These patterns are made from dots.

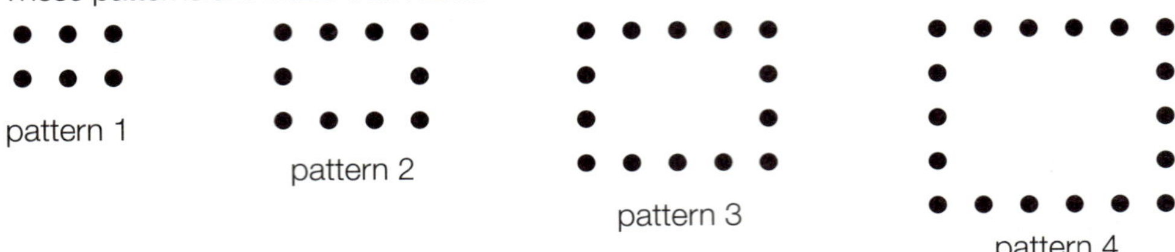

a Find an expression for the number of dots in pattern n.
b How many dots form pattern 100?
c Which pattern in the sequence has 502 dots?

6 The diagrams show patterns made from matchsticks.

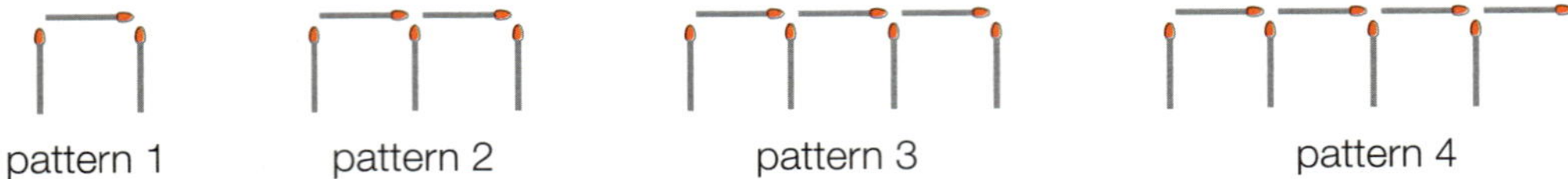

a Find an expression for the number of matchsticks in pattern n.
b How many matchsticks will be needed to make pattern 50?
c James has 300 matchsticks. Can he make pattern 150?

7 The diagrams show hexagon patterns made from matchsticks.

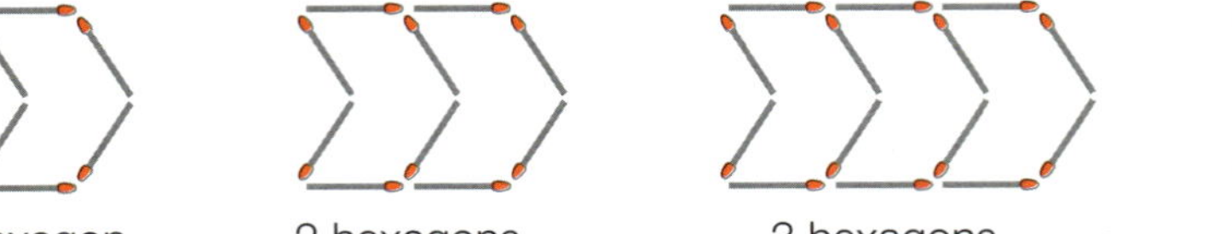

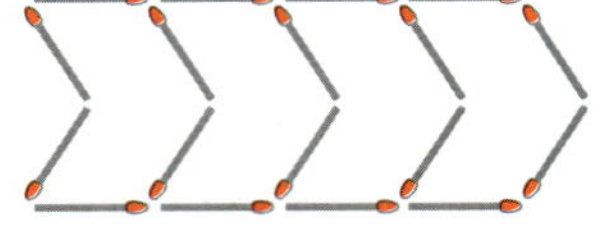

a Find an expression for the number of matchsticks needed to make n hexagons.
b How many hexagons can be made with 82 matchsticks?

8 These pentagon patterns are made from matchsticks.

Copy and complete this table.

Number of pentagons	1	2	3	4	n		200
Number of matchsticks	5	9	13			101	

9 These diagrams show patterns made from orange and white squares.

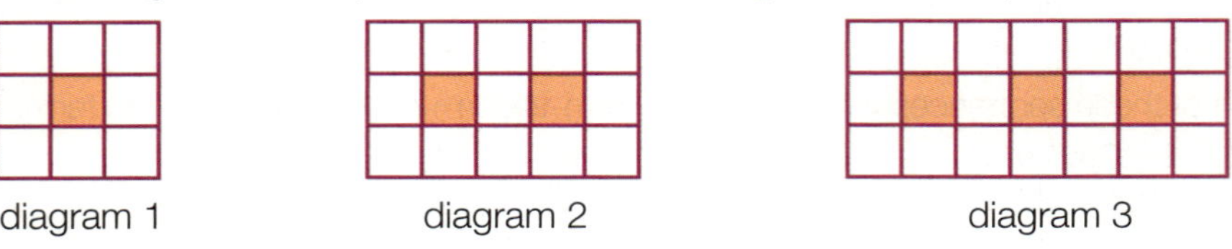

a Find an expression for the number of white squares in diagram n.
b In which diagram are there 328 white squares?

10 These diagrams are made from black square tiles.

diagram 1

diagram 2

diagram 3

a Find an expression for the number of tiles in diagram n.
b Helen has 100 black tiles. What is the biggest diagram she can make?

Some sequences involve the products of pairs of numbers.
To find the nth term of sequences like this:

- find the nth term of each sequence of numbers separately
- multiply these nth terms together to find the nth term for the sequence of products.

Do the same for a sequence involving one number divided by another.

Example 3

Find the nth term of each of these sequences.

a $1 \times 3, 3 \times 7, 5 \times 11, 7 \times 15, \ldots$ **b** $\frac{1}{5}, \frac{4}{8}, \frac{9}{11}, \frac{16}{14}, \frac{25}{17}, \ldots$

Solution 3

a Look at each of the numbers in the products separately.
The first numbers form the sequence 1, 3, 5, 7, …
This sequence has constant difference 2, so it is based on the multiples of **2**

Term number (n)	1	2	3	4	n
Multiple of **2** (**2** $\times n$)	**2** $\times 1 = 2$	**2** $\times 2 = 4$	**2** $\times 3 = 6$	**2** $\times 4 = 8$	**2**n
Term − **2**n	$1 - 2 = -1$	$3 - 4 = -1$	$5 - 6 = -1$	$7 - 8 = -1$	-1

So the first number in the product has nth term $2n - 1$
The second numbers form the sequence 3, 7, 11, 15, …
This sequence has constant difference 4, so it is based on the multiples of **4**

Term number (n)	1	2	3	4	n
Multiple of **4** (**4** $\times n$)	**4** $\times 1 = 4$	**4** $\times 2 = 8$	**4** $\times 3 = 12$	**4** $\times 4 = 16$	**4**n
Term − **4**n	$3 - 4 = -1$	$7 - 8 = -1$	$11 - 12 = -1$	$15 - 16 = -1$	-1

So the second number in the product has nth term $4n - 1$
So the nth term of the sequence $1 \times 3, 3 \times 7, 5 \times 11, 7 \times 15, \ldots$ is $(2n - 1)(4n - 1)$.

b Look at each of the numbers in the fractions separately.
The numerators are the square numbers 1, 4, 9, 16, 25, … and have nth term n^2
The denominators 5, 8, 11, 14, 17, … have constant difference 3
This sequence is 2 more than the multiples of 3 and has nth term $3n + 2$

So the nth term of the sequence $\frac{1}{5}, \frac{4}{8}, \frac{9}{11}, \frac{16}{14}, \frac{25}{17}, \ldots$ is $\dfrac{n^2}{3n + 2}$

Sometimes the nth term can be found from looking at the way the patterns in a sequence grow.

Example 4

These patterns are made from square counters.

pattern 1

pattern 2

pattern 3

pattern 4

Explain why the number of counters in pattern n is $n^2 + n$.

Solution 4

Pattern 1 has one black square + one red square
Pattern 2 has a 2×2 square of black squares + two red squares
Pattern 3 has a 3×3 square of black squares + three red squares
…
Pattern n has an $n \times n$ square of black squares + n red squares.
So the number of counters in pattern n is $n \times n + n = n^2 + n$.

This expression can be obtained directly from the pattern.
The black squares form a square and the red squares form a line.
The side of the square and the line are both the same size as the pattern number.

Exercise B

1 Each of the sequences in the table has an nth term of the form an^2

Term number, n	1	2	3	4	5	nth term
Sequence 1	1	4	9	16	25	n^2
Sequence 2	2	8	18	32	50	$2n^2$
Sequence 3	10	40	90	160	250	
Sequence 4	0.5	2	4.5	8	12.5	
Sequence 5	5	20	45	80	125	

Find the nth terms of sequences 3, 4 and 5

2 Each of the sequences in the table has an nth term of the form $n^2 + b$.

Term number, n	1	2	3	4	5	nth term
Sequence 1	1	4	9	16	25	n^2
Sequence 2	3	6	11	18	27	$n^2 + 2$
Sequence 3	0	3	8	15	24	
Sequence 4	6	9	14	21	30	
Sequence 5	−4	−1	4	11	20	

Find the nth terms of sequences 3, 4 and 5

3 Write down the nth term of each of these sequences.

a $2 \times 3, 3 \times 4, 4 \times 5, 5 \times 6, \ldots$ **b** $2 \times 3, 5 \times 5, 8 \times 7, 11 \times 9, \ldots$

c $2 \times 3, 6 \times 7, 10 \times 11, 14 \times 15, \ldots$ **d** $2 \times 2, 4 \times 8, 6 \times 14, 8 \times 20, \ldots$

4 Write down the nth term of each of these sequences.

a $\frac{2}{3}, \frac{3}{5}, \frac{4}{7}, \frac{5}{9}, \frac{6}{11}, \ldots$ **b** $\frac{1}{5}, \frac{4}{6}, \frac{9}{7}, \frac{16}{8}, \frac{25}{9}, \ldots$ **c** $\frac{4}{3}, \frac{7}{12}, \frac{10}{21}, \frac{13}{30}, \frac{16}{39}, \ldots$

d $\frac{7}{7}, \frac{4}{17}, \frac{1}{27}, -\frac{2}{37}, -\frac{5}{47}, \ldots$ **e** $\frac{9}{7}, \frac{14}{12}, \frac{19}{17}, \frac{24}{22}, \frac{29}{27}, \ldots$

5 **a** The first five terms of a sequence are 2, 5, 8, 11, 14, …

i What are the differences between terms?

ii Explain why the sequence has nth term $3n - 1$

b The first five terms of a sequence are 7, 9, 11, 13, 15, …

Tom says that the nth term of this sequence is $5n + 2$

Explain why Tom is wrong.

c A sequence has nth term $(n - 5)^2 + 4$

Explain why all the terms in this sequence are positive.

6 Sarah is trying to find the nth term of the sequence 5, 12, 21, 32, 45, …

She starts by subtracting the square numbers 1, 4, 9, 16, 25, … from each term in the sequence.

$5 - 1 = 4$
$12 - 4 =$
$21 -$

a **i** Copy and complete Sarah's list.

ii Write down the nth term of the linear sequence she obtains.

b Explain why the nth term of the sequence 5, 12, 21, 32, 45, … is $n^2 + 4n$.

7 **a** **i** Show that the equation $5n - 6 = 3n + 2$ has the solution $n = 4$

ii Explain why this shows that the fourth terms of the sequences with nth terms $5n - 6$ and $3n + 2$ are equal.

iii Show that the equal fourth term has the value 14

b Two sequences have nth terms $6n - 10$ and $3n + 14$

i What term of these sequences is equal?

ii What is its value?

c Two sequences have nth terms $7n - 13$ and $5n + 16$

Do these sequences have an equal term? Explain your answer.

8 This pattern is made from small square tiles.

pattern 1

pattern 2

pattern 3

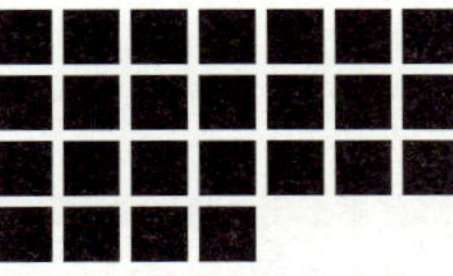

pattern 4

a Billy says

Use the patterns to explain why Billy is right.

b Sasha looks at pattern 3 like this.

$2 \times 5 + 3 = 13$

i Explain why Sasha writes $3 \times 7 + 4 = 25$ for pattern 4

ii Sasha says

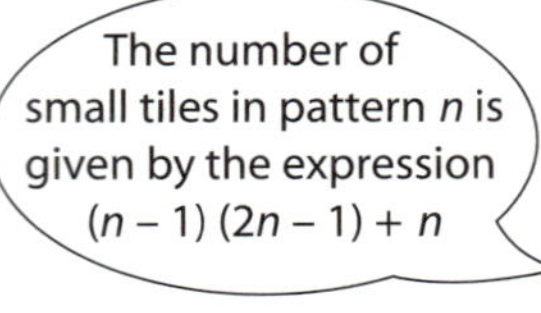

Use Sasha's work to explain why she is also right.

Chapter summary

- The nth term of a sequence is a *position-to-term* rule where n represents the position of a term in the sequence.
- The nth term can be used:
  - to work out the terms in a sequence
  - to check whether a given term is in a sequence
  - to find the position of a given term in a sequence.
- Sequences with *a constant difference* between consecutive terms:
  - have a term-to-term rule of the form **+ constant difference**
  - have a position-to-term rule or nth term of the form **nth term $= an + b$**

    where a is the constant difference and b is a positive or negative integer.
- Some sequences involve the products of pairs of numbers.

  To find the nth term of sequences like this:
  - find the nth term of each sequence of numbers separately
  - multiply these nth terms together to find the nth term for the sequence of products.

  Do the same for a sequence involving one number divided by another.
- Sequences can be shown as patterns made, for example, from dots, squares or matchsticks. Sometimes the nth term can be found from looking at the way the patterns in a sequence grow.

Chapter review

1 **a** The nth term of a sequence is $4n + 3$

i Write down the first three terms of the sequence.

ii Is 82 a term in the sequence? Explain your answer.

b Tim builds fence patterns from matchsticks as shown below.

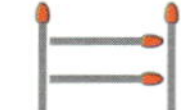

pattern 1
4 matchsticks

pattern 2
7 matchsticks

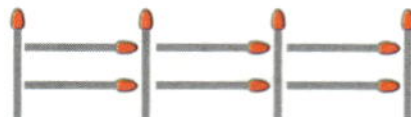

pattern 3
10 matchsticks

How many matchsticks are in Pattern n?

2 Matchsticks are used to make this pattern of pentagons.

pattern 1
5 matchsticks

pattern 2
9 matchsticks

pattern 3
13 matchsticks

a How many matchsticks are needed for pattern 5?
b Write down an expression for the number of matchsticks in pattern n.
c Which pattern uses 101 matchsticks?

3 The nth term of a sequence is $5n - 1$
a Write down the first and second terms of the sequence.
b Which term of the sequence is equal to 54?
c Explain why 100 is not a term in the sequence.

4 Patterns are made from green and white squares.

1st pattern 2nd pattern 3rd pattern 4th pattern

a How many green squares are there in the nth pattern?
b How many white squares are there in the nth pattern?

5 A sequence of numbers is shown: 5 8 11 14 17
a Find an expression for the nth term of the sequence.
b Explain why 99 will not be a term in this sequence.

6 **a** Stars are arranged to form a sequence of patterns as shown.

☆ ☆☆☆ ☆☆☆☆☆ ☆☆☆☆☆☆☆

pattern 1 pattern 2 pattern 3 pattern 4

Write an expression for the number of stars in pattern n.

b Counters are arranged to form a sequence of patterns as shown.

pattern 1 pattern 2 pattern 3 pattern 4

Write an expression for the number of counters in pattern n.

7 **a** A sequence begins $-2,\quad -1,\quad 0,\quad 1,\quad 2,\quad \ldots$
Write an expression for the nth term of the sequence.
b The nth term of a different sequence is $7n + 1$
What is the difference between the first and second terms of this sequence?

8 Sticks are arranged to form a sequence of patterns as shown.

pattern 1

pattern 2

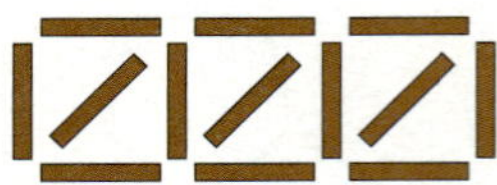
pattern 3

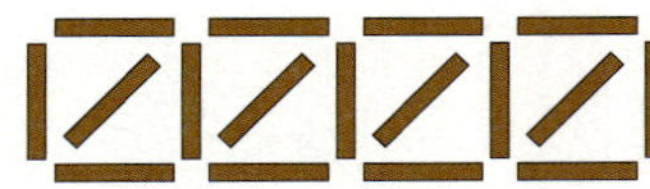
pattern 4

Write an expression for the number of sticks in pattern n.

9 John and Sarah are each asked to continue a sequence that begins 2, 5, …

a John writes 2, 5, 8, 11, 14, … Write down the nth term of John's sequence.

b Sarah writes 2, 5, 10, 17, 26, … Write down the nth term of Sarah's sequence.

Common factors and common multiples

CHAPTER 15

15.1 Products of prime factors

CAN YOU REMEMBER

- That a prime number has only two factors, 1 and the number itself?
- How to work out all the factors of a number?
- The meaning of 'index form' or 'power form'?

IN THIS SECTION YOU WILL

- Learn the meaning of 'prime factor'.
- Learn how to write a number as a product of prime factors.
- Learn how to write a number as a product of prime factors using index form.

Here is a list of prime numbers starting with the smallest:

2, 3, 5, 7, 11, 13, 17, 19, ...

The factors of 20 are 1, 2, 4, 5, 10 and 20
2 and 5 are the *prime factors* of 20
The prime factors of a number are all its factors that are also prime numbers.

Every number can be written as a product of prime factors.
20 written as the product of its prime factors is $2 \times 2 \times 5$

There are two methods of writing a number as a product of prime factors – the *repeated division* method and the *factor tree* method.

Example 1

Write 18 as a product of prime factors.

Solution 1

Repeated division method
Start by dividing 18 by its smallest prime factor, 2
Dividing by 2 $18 \div \mathbf{2} = 9$
9 is not divisible by 2, so divide by the next smallest prime factor.
Dividing by 3 $9 \div \mathbf{3} = 3$
Dividing by 3 again $3 \div \mathbf{3} = 1$
Stop when you get to 1
18 written as a product of prime factors is $\mathbf{2 \times 3 \times 3}$

This can be set out as:

$$\begin{array}{r|l} 2 & 18 \\ 3 & 9 \\ 3 & 3 \\ & 1 \end{array}$$

Example 2

Write 45 as a product of prime factors.

Solution 2

Factor tree method

Start with any multiplication that gives 45

$45 = 5 \times 9$

5 is prime so shade that branch to show it is complete.

9 is not a prime number, so find the factors of 9

$9 = 3 \times 3$

3 is a prime number so all the branches now end in primes.

45 written as a product of prime factors is $3 \times 3 \times 5$

The same method can be used without showing the products on a factor tree

$45 = 5 \times 9$

$45 = 5 \times 3 \times 3$

Exercise A

1 Work out these products of primes.

a 5×7 **b** $2 \times 2 \times 3 \times 3$ **c** $3 \times 5 \times 5$

d $3 \times 5 \times 7$ **e** $2 \times 2 \times 2 \times 3$ **f** $3 \times 3 \times 11$

g $2 \times 2 \times 2 \times 5 \times 5$

2 For each of the following numbers, write them as a product of two factors, not including 1

a 8 **b** 20 **c** 25 **d** 30

e 32 **f** 35 **g** 36 **h** 42

i 48 **j** 60 **k** 81 **l** 90

3 Write down the prime factors of each of the following numbers.

a 8 **b** 14 **c** 15 **d** 25

e 27 **f** 35 **g** 49 **h** 50

i 81 **j** 100 **k** 121

4 Copy and complete to find the prime factors:

a 2)16
2) 8
)
)
)

b 2)54
3)
)
)
)

c 3)39
)
)

5 Copy and complete the factor trees.

a

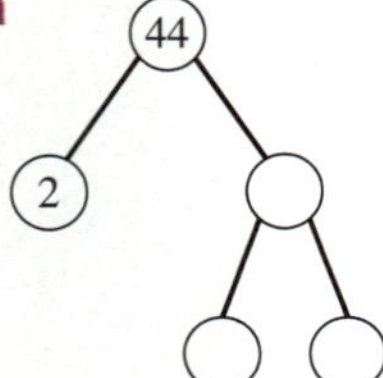

b

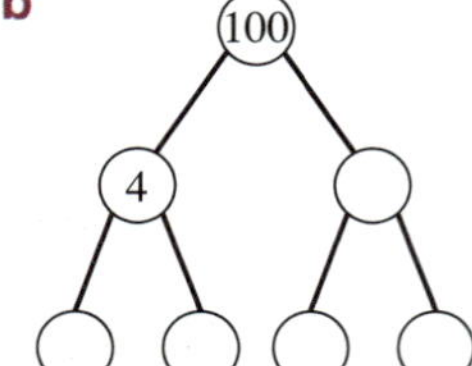

c

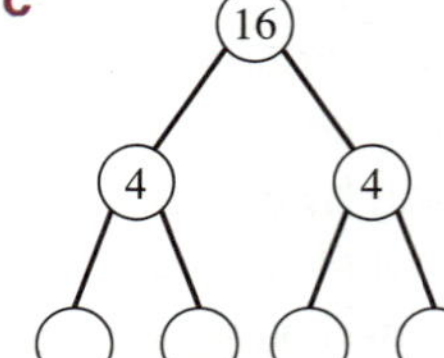

6 Write each of these numbers as a product of its prime factors.

a 10	**b** 15	**c** 24	**d** 28
e 30	**f** 36	**g** 42	**h** 45
i 50	**j** 60	**k** 81	**l** 90

7 Work out these products.

a $5 \times 7 \times 7$ **b** $2 \times 3 \times 3 \times 11$

c $5 \times 5 \times 7 \times 11$ **d** $5 \times 7 \times 11 \times 11$

e $2 \times 2 \times 3 \times 13 \times 23$ **f** $3 \times 17 \times 19$

g $2 \times 2 \times 5 \times 5 \times 17 \times 23$ **h** 23×29

8 Use a calculator to find a prime factor greater than 10 for each of the following numbers.

a 184	**b** 153	**c** 116	**d** 275
e 369	**f** 124	**g** 620	**h** 5800

9 Write each of these numbers as a product of its prime factors.

a 112	**b** 125	**c** 144	**d** 150
e 180	**f** 184	**g** 200	**h** 500

A number can be written as a product of its prime factors using *index form* (or *power form*).

Example 3

Write 54 as a product of prime factors. Give your answer in index form.

Solution 3

Repeated division method

2)54
3)27
3)9
3)3
1

$54 = 2 \times 3 \times 3 \times 3 = 2 \times 3^3$

Factor tree method

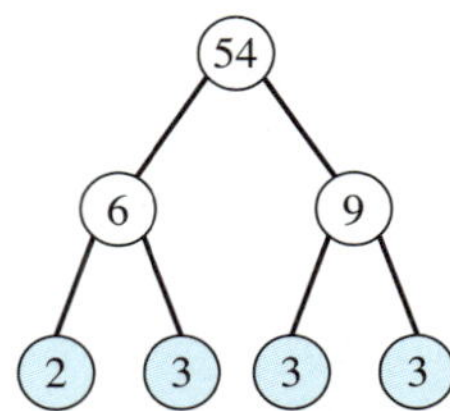

$54 = 2 \times 3 \times 3 \times 3 = 2 \times 3^3$

Exercise B

1 Write each product in index form.

a $2 \times 2 \times 2 \times 3 \times 3$ **b** $2 \times 5 \times 5 \times 5 \times 5$

c $3 \times 3 \times 5 \times 5 \times 7$ **d** $2 \times 3 \times 5 \times 7 \times 7 \times 7$

e $3 \times 3 \times 5 \times 5 \times 5 \times 7 \times 11 \times 11$ **f** $2 \times 2 \times 2 \times 5 \times 11 \times 11 \times 13 \times 13 \times 13$

2 Write each product in index form by sorting the numbers into order first.

a $3 \times 5 \times 2 \times 2 \times 3$ **b** $7 \times 2 \times 3 \times 2 \times 7$

c $11 \times 11 \times 2 \times 11 \times 11$ **d** $5 \times 3 \times 5 \times 3 \times 5 \times 3$

e $7 \times 5 \times 5 \times 5 \times 7 \times 7 \times 3 \times 2$ **f** $17 \times 13 \times 3 \times 5 \times 13 \times 7 \times 17 \times 13 \times 5$

3 Write each of these numbers as a product of its prime factors.
Give your answer in index form.

a 20	**b** 28	**c** 48	**d** 56
e 72	**f** 162	**g** 90	**h** 100

4 **a** Write the numbers 48, 144 and 432 as a product of their prime factors.
Give your answers in index form.
b Comment on a pattern.
c Write down the next number in the pattern, in index form.

5 **a** Here are two possible different factor trees for 40
Find two more different factor trees for 40
What do you notice?
b Draw all possible factor trees for 18

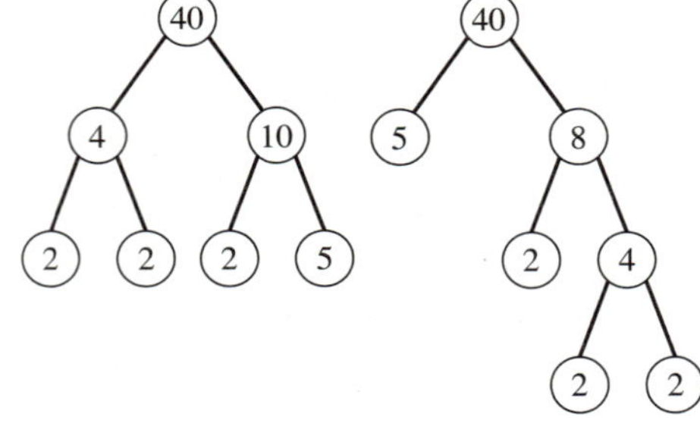

6 Write each of these numbers as a product of its prime factors.
Give your answers in index form.
a 132 **b** 156 **c** 250 **d** 400 **e** 480 **f** 620 **g** 720 **h** 900

7 Mark says that 2×6^3 is the same as 12^3
Show that he is not correct.

8 Bev says that $(2 \times 3 \times 5)^2$ is the same as $2^2 \times 3^2 \times 5^2$
Is she correct?
Show your working.

9 Here are two numbers written as products of their prime factors.
$2 \times 3 \times 5$ and $2 \times 3 \times 7$
Is 6 a factor of both numbers? Explain your answer.

15.2 Highest common factor (HCF)

CAN YOU REMEMBER

- The meaning of 'factor', 'multiple', 'common factor', 'prime factor'?
- How to work out all the factors of a number?
- That every number has at least two factors, 1 and the number itself?
- How to write a number as a product of prime factors?

IN THIS SECTION YOU WILL

- Learn how to identify common factors of two numbers.
- Learn how to work out the highest common factor of two or more numbers.

Two numbers may have factors in common. The *highest common factor* (HCF) of two or more numbers is the *common factor* with the highest value.

To find the HCF of two or more numbers:

Method 1

- List all the factors of both numbers.
- Highlight the common factors.
- Find the common factor with the highest value.

Example 1

Work out the highest common factor (HCF) of 24 and 54

Solution 1

Work systematically to find the factors of both numbers.
Start with 1 and the number itself.

The factors of 24	The factors of 54
$1 \times 24 = 24$	$1 \times 54 = 54$
$2 \times 12 = 24$	$2 \times 27 = 54$
$3 \times 8 = 24$	$3 \times 18 = 54$
$4 \times 6 = 24$	$6 \times 9 = 54$

The factors of 24 are **1**, **2**, **3**, 4, (**6**), 8, 12, 24

The factors of 54 are **1**, **2**, **3**, (**6**), 9, 18, 27, 54

The highest common factor of 24 and 54 is 6

Exercise A

1 i Write down the factors of each number.
ii Underline the common factors.
iii Draw a circle around the highest common factor.

a 8 and 12 **b** 15 and 25 **c** 12 and 24
d 25 and 40 **e** 14 and 20 **f** 12 and 18

2 Find the highest common factor (HCF) of each of the following pairs of numbers.

a 12 and 16 **b** 20 and 25 **c** 24 and 36
d 18 and 32 **e** 16 and 28 **f** 14 and 42
g 25 and 35 **h** 36 and 48

3 Find the highest common factor (HCF) of each of the following sets of numbers.

a 10, 15 and 40 **b** 8, 12 and 20 **c** 9, 15 and 18
d 8, 16 and 32 **e** 12, 18 and 22 **f** 18, 24 and 42
g 25, 35 and 55 **h** 24, 36 and 48

4 Find the highest common factor (HCF) of each of the following pairs of numbers.

a 48 and 54 **b** 36 and 72 **c** 24 and 84
d 28 and 42 **e** 30 and 65 **f** 36 and 108
g 40 and 88 **h** 56 and 108

5 Find the highest common factor (HCF) of each of the following sets of numbers.

a 36, 42 and 54 **b** 16, 24 and 60 **c** 15, 24 and 39

d 24, 60 and 72 **e** 15, 36 and 48 **f** 32, 42 and 56

g 36, 48 and 90 **h** 25, 75 and 100

For very large numbers, it can take a long time to work out all the factor pairs.
Another method for finding the highest common factor of two or more numbers is:

Method 2

- Write each number as a product of its prime factors.
- Highlight any prime factors that are common to both numbers.
- Work out the product of the common prime factors – this is the HCF.

To simplify a fraction fully, divide both numbers by their highest common factor.
To factorise an expression completely, write the HCF of the terms outside the bracket.

Example 2

a Work out the highest common factor (HCF) of 16 and 24

b Use the highest common factor of 16 and 24 to:

i simplify $\frac{16}{24}$ **ii** factorise $16x + 24$

Solution 2

a Write each number as a product of its prime factors.

$16 = \mathbf{2} \times \mathbf{2} \times \mathbf{2} \times 2$

$24 = \mathbf{2} \times \mathbf{2} \times \mathbf{2} \times 3$

Work out the product of the common factors:

$2 \times 2 \times 2 = 8$

The highest common factor (HCF) of 16 and 24 is 8

Show the factors on a diagram.

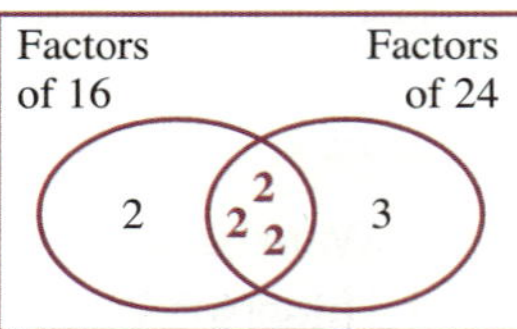

b **i** $\frac{16}{24} = \frac{16 \div 8}{24 \div 8} = \frac{2}{3}$

ii $16x = 8 \times 2x \quad 24 = 8 \times 3$

$16x + 24 = 8(2x + 3)$

Exercise B

1 **a** Work out the highest common factor of 32 and 48

b Use the highest common factor of 32 and 48 to simplify $\frac{32}{48}$

2 Work out the highest common factor (HCF) of 30 and 25. Use the answer to factorise $30x + 25$

3 John says that the highest common factor of two numbers cannot be 1
Give an example to show that he is **not** correct.

4 Mary says that the highest common factor of two numbers cannot be one of the two numbers.
Give an example to show that she is **not** correct.

5 **a** Here are the first five multiples of 12

12 24 36 48 60

i What is the highest common factor (HCF) of all these multiples of 12?
ii What is the highest common factor (HCF) of all multiples of 12?

b Here are the first five multiples of 8

8 16 24 32 40

What is the highest common factor (HCF) of all multiples of 8?

c Here are the first five multiples of x.

x $2x$ $3x$ $4x$ $5x$

What is the highest common factor (HCF) of all multiples of x?

6 **a** The HCF of 32 and another number is 16
The other number is between 40 and 50
What is it?

b The HCF of 72 and another number is 24
The other number is between 90 and 100
What is it?

7 The highest common factor of two expressions is $2x$.
One of the two expressions is $6x$.
The other expression is larger than $6x$.
Write down one possibility for the other expression.

8 The highest common factor of two expressions is $5y$.
One of the two expressions is $20y$.
The other expression is smaller than $20y$.
Write down all the possibilities for the other expression.

15.3 Least common multiple (LCM)

CAN YOU REMEMBER

- The meaning of 'multiple'?
- The difference between a multiple and a factor?

IN THIS SECTION YOU WILL

- Find common multiples of two or more numbers.
- Learn how to work out the least common multiple of two or more numbers.
- Solve problems using least common multiples.

The *least common multiple* (LCM) of two or more numbers is the *common multiple* with the least (lowest) value.

For example,

3 has multiples 3, 6, 9, (12), 15, 18, 21, **24**, 27, 30, 33, **36**, …

4 has multiples 4, 8, (12), 16, 20, **24**, 28, 32, **36**, …

12, 24, 36, … are common multiples of 3 and 4
The least common multiple of 3 and 4 is 12

To find the LCM of two or more numbers:

Method 1

- List the first few multiples of both numbers.
- Highlight the common multiples.
- Find the common multiple with the least value.

Example 1

Work out the least common multiple (LCM) of 8 and 12

Solution 1

The multiples of 8 are: 8, 16, **24**, 32, 40, **48**, 56, 64, **72**, 80, …

The multiples of 12 are: 12, **24**, 36, **48**, 60, **72**, 84, …

The common multiples of 8 and 12 are: 24, 48, 72, … The LCM of 8 and 12 is 24

Exercise A

1 Write down the first ten multiples of each number.
Find the least common multiple of each pair of numbers.

a 3 and 4 **b** 5 and 6 **c** 3 and 9 **d** 6 and 8
e 8 and 10 **f** 6 and 9 **g** 10 and 15 **h** 6 and 7

2 Find the least common multiple of each of the following sets of numbers.

a 3, 5 and 6 **b** 4, 5 and 10 **c** 3, 6 and 8
d 2, 4 and 7 **e** 5, 6 and 10 **f** 4, 5 and 6
g 2, 7 and 9 **h** 5, 8 and 10

3 Sausages are sold in packets of 10. Bread rolls are sold in packets of 12
Mrs Pate wants exactly the same number of each. She can only buy whole packets.

a Write down the first six multiples of 10 and 12
b What is the smallest number of sausages and bread rolls she can buy?
c Use the answer to **b** to work out the least number of packets of each she should buy.

4 Arnold bangs his drum once every 4 seconds.
Fretwell bangs his drum once every 5 seconds.
Boswell bangs his drum once every 6 seconds.
They all start together.
How long is it before they again bang the drums at the same time?

5 Find the least common multiple of each of the following pairs of numbers.

a 12 and 16 **b** 10 and 12 **c** 15 and 18 **d** 9 and 11
e 11 and 14 **f** 15 and 20 **g** 8 and 18 **h** 7 and 16

6 Find the least common multiple of each of the following sets of numbers.

a 10, 12 and 15 **b** 8, 12 and 18 **c** 9, 12 and 15 **d** 8, 11 and 16
e 7, 8 and 12 **f** 7, 9 and 15 **g** 6, 15 and 20 **h** 8, 12 and 20

7 Rosie runs around a track in 54 seconds. Charlie runs around the same track in 72 seconds. They start together. How long is it before Rosie overtakes Charlie?

8 Trevor buys beans costing 28p per tin.
Belinda buys spaghetti costing 32p per tin.
They both spend the same amount.
What is the least amount that each could have spent?

The least common multiple (LCM) can be found without writing out lists of multiples.
Another method for finding the LCM of two or more numbers is:

Method 2

- Write each number as a product of its prime factors.
- Show all the factors of both numbers in a diagram.
- Work out the product of **all** these factors – this is the LCM.

Example 2

Work out the least common multiple (LCM) of 18 and 24

Solution 2

Write each number as a product of prime factors:

$18 = 2 \times 3 \times 3$

$24 = 2 \times 2 \times 2 \times 3$

The least common multiple is the product of **all** the factors of 18 and 24

So the LCM of 18 and 24 is $2 \times 2 \times 2 \times 3 \times 3 = 72$

Show the factors on a diagram.

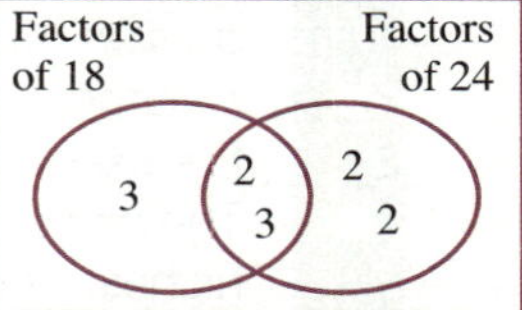

Exercise B

1 Write each number as a product of its prime factors and use a diagram to work out the least common multiple of

a 15 and 40 **b** 14 and 35

2 Dietrich says that the least common multiple of two numbers cannot be one of the two numbers.
Give an example to show that he is **not** correct.

3 Polly says that the least common multiple of two numbers cannot be the product of the two numbers.
Give an example to show that she is **not** correct.

4 **a** Here are the factors of 12: 1 2 3 4 6 12
What is the least common multiple of all the factors of 12?

b Here are the factors of 15: 1 3 5 15
What is the least common multiple of all the factors of 15?

c What is the least common multiple of all the factors of 80?

5 **a** Find the least common multiple of the denominators of these two fractions: $\frac{1}{6}$ and $\frac{3}{10}$

b Write each fraction as an equivalent fraction with the LCM of 6 and 10 as the denominator.

c Add the two fractions. Write the answer in its simplest form.

d Use the method from parts **a–c** to work out $\frac{2}{5} + \frac{3}{8}$

6 **a** The least common multiple of 16 and one other number is 48
The other number is between 20 and 30
What is it?

b The least common multiple of two numbers is 180
One of the numbers is between 40 and 50
The other number is between 30 and 40
What are the numbers?

7 x and y are both prime numbers.
Write down the least common multiple of x and y.

8 x is even and y is odd.
Which statement is true?
A: The least common multiple of x and y is even.
B: The least common multiple of x and y is odd.
C: The least common multiple of x and y could be odd or even.

Chapter summary

- The prime factors of a number are all its factors that are also prime numbers.
- Every number can be written as a product of prime factors.
- There are two methods of writing a number as a product of prime factors – the *repeated division* method and the *factor tree* method.
- A number can be written as a product of its prime factors using *index form*.
  For example, $36 = 2 \times 2 \times 3 \times 3 = 2^2 \times 3^2$
- The *highest common factor* (HCF) of two or more numbers is the common factor with the highest value.
- To find the HCF of two or more numbers:
  Method 1
  - List all the factors of both numbers.
  - Highlight the common factors.
  - Find the common factor with the highest value.

  Method 2
  - Write each number as a product of its prime factors.
  - Highlight any prime factors that are common to both numbers.
  - Work out the product of these common factors – this is the HCF.
- To simplify a fraction fully, divide the numerator and denominator by their highest common factor.
- To factorise an expression completely, write the HCF of the terms outside the bracket.
- The *least common multiple* (LCM) of two or more numbers is the common multiple with the least value.
- To find the LCM of two or more numbers:
  Method 1
  - List the first few multiples of both numbers.
  - Highlight the common multiples.
  - Find the common multiple with the least value.

  Method 2
  - Write each number as a product of its prime factors.
  - Show all the factors of both numbers in a diagram.
  - Work out the product of **all** these factors – this is the LCM.

Chapter review

1 **a** Express 24 as a product of its prime factors.
b Find the least common multiple (LCM) of 24 and 30

2 **a** Write 28 as a product of its prime factors.
b Find the least common multiple (LCM) of 28 and 35

3 **a** Write 18 as a product of its prime factors.
b What is the least common multiple (LCM) of 18 and 30?

4 **a** Express 48 as a product of its prime factors.
Give your answer in index form.
b Find the highest common factor (HCF) of 18 and 48

5 **a** x and y are prime numbers.
$xy^2 = 50$
Find the values of x and y.
b Find the highest common factor (HCF) of 50 and 75

6 **a** Express 54 as a product of its prime factors.
Give your answer in index form.
b Find the highest common factor (HCF) of 54 and 36

7 45 expressed as a product of prime factors in index form is $3^2 \times 5$
a Express 36 as a product of its prime factors.
Give your answer in index form.
b What is the highest common factor (HCF) of 45 and 36?

8 Drinks are in packs of 24
Sandwiches are in packs of 18
A café wants the same number of drinks and sandwiches.
What is the lowest number of packs of drinks and sandwiches they could have?

9 What is the lowest number that is a multiple of both 14 and 15?

10 Cereal is sold in 500 gram boxes and costs £1.60 per box.
Coffee is sold in 300 gram jars and costs £4.20 per jar.
Harriet buys the same number of grams of cereal and coffee.
What is the least that she could have spent?

CHAPTER 16

Averages for large data sets

16.1 Mean for grouped data

CAN YOU REMEMBER

- How to calculate the mean of a discrete frequency distribution?
- The meaning of Σfx and Σf?
- The meaning of the symbols $\leqslant$ and $<$?

IN THIS SECTION YOU WILL

- Learn how to write data in groups.
- Learn how to find the midpoint of a group.
- Learn how to find an estimate of the mean for a grouped frequency distribution.
- Understand why the value found is only an estimate.

A large set of data can be put into groups.

For example, data on the heights, in metres, of 40 sunflower plants has been grouped in this table.

Height, h (metres)	Frequency, f
$0.8 \leqslant h < 1.0$	1
$1.0 \leqslant h < 1.2$	5
$1.2 \leqslant h < 1.4$	12
$1.4 \leqslant h < 1.6$	16
$1.6 \leqslant h < 1.8$	4
$1.8 \leqslant h < 2.0$	2

A frequency distribution where the data is in groups is called a *grouped frequency distribution.*

The group $0.8 \leqslant h < 1.0$ includes all the plants with heights from 0.8 m up to but not including 1.0 m. A plant with height 1.0 m would be recorded in the next group.

In grouped data, the groups are sometimes called *class intervals.*

A grouped frequency distribution does not show the exact values of the original data, so an exact mean cannot be calculated.
Instead, the *midpoints* or *mid-values* of the groups are used to calculate an estimate of the mean, using the formula $\frac{\Sigma fx}{\Sigma f}$, where f is the frequency for each group and x is the midpoint for each group.

Always check that the mean calculated is sensible. For most data sets it will be close to the 'middle' of the data values.

Example 1

a Calculate an estimate of the mean height of the sunflower plants from the previous table.
b Explain why the value in part **a** is only an estimate.

Solution 1

a Add two extra columns to the table, one for the midpoints h and one for the calculation of fh.
Add an extra row to the table for the totals of f and fh.
Calculate the midpoint for each group. For the group $0.8 \leqslant h \leqslant 1.0$, the midpoint is
$\frac{0.8 + 1.0}{2} = 0.9$ and so on.

Height, h (metres)	Frequency, f	Midpoint, h	fh
$0.8 \leqslant h < 1.0$	1	0.9	0.9
$1.0 \leqslant h < 1.2$	5	1.1	5.5
$1.2 \leqslant h < 1.4$	12	1.3	15.6
$1.4 \leqslant h < 1.6$	16	1.5	24.0
$1.6 \leqslant h < 1.8$	4	1.7	6.8
$1.8 \leqslant h < 2.0$	2	1.9	3.8
	$\Sigma f = 40$		$\Sigma fh = 56.6$

An estimate for the mean is $\frac{\Sigma fh}{\Sigma f} = \frac{56.6}{40} = 1.415$ metres

Check: the range of data values is from 0.8 to 2.0, so the middle of this range is 1.4
The value calculated is close to this middle value.

b This value is only an estimate because the exact values of each of the 40 heights are not known. The midpoints are estimates for the mean value for each group.

Exercise A

1 The grouped frequency distribution represents the lengths of 20 phone calls Natasha made.

Length of call, l (minutes)	Frequency, f	Midpoint, l	fl
$0 \leqslant l < 6$	4	4x 3	12
$6 \leqslant l < 12$	7	7x 9	63
$12 \leqslant l < 18$	9	9x 15	135
	$\Sigma f =$ 20		$\Sigma fl =$ 210

a Explain why the midpoint of the first group is 3
b Copy the table and complete the midpoint column.
c Complete the fl column.
d Calculate Σfl and Σf.
e Find an estimate of the mean length of Natasha's phone calls.

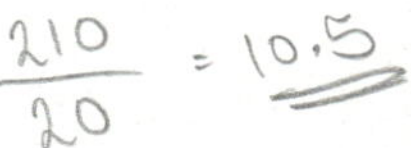

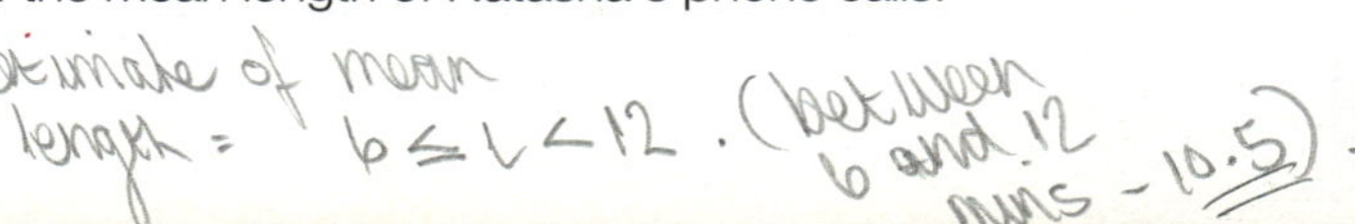

2 The grouped frequency distribution shows the length of ten worms (in cm) that Zoë dug up in her garden.

Length of worm, l (cm)	Frequency, f	Midpoint, l	fl
$2 \leqslant l < 6$	4		
$6 \leqslant l < 10$	5		
$10 \leqslant l < 14$	1		
	$\Sigma f =$		$\Sigma fl =$

a Copy and complete the table.
b Find an estimate of the mean length of worm dug up.

3 Jarnail collects information from a police officer about the speeds of the first 30 cars going past his school. The data is in the form of the grouped frequency distribution here.

Speed, s (mph)	Frequency, f
$20 \leqslant s < 30$	21
$30 \leqslant s < 40$	6
$40 \leqslant s < 50$	3

a Copy the table.
Add extra columns for the midpoint of each group and the value of fs.
Complete these columns.
b Hence find an estimate of the average speed of these 30 cars.

4 For each part, calculate an estimate of the mean of the grouped frequency distributions.

a The table shows the heights of 50 men (in cm).

Height, h (cm)	Frequency, f
$120 \leqslant h < 140$	4
$140 \leqslant h < 160$	17
$160 \leqslant h < 180$	21
$180 \leqslant h < 200$	8

b The table shows the length (in seconds) of 117 hit records.

Length of time, t (s)	Frequency, f
$120 \leqslant t < 150$	1
$150 \leqslant t < 180$	7
$180 \leqslant t < 210$	34
$210 \leqslant t < 240$	54
$240 \leqslant t < 270$	19
$270 \leqslant t < 300$	2

c The table shows the weight (in grams) of 59 apples.

Weight of apple, w (g)	Frequency, f
$20 \leqslant w < 40$	5
$40 \leqslant w < 50$	16
$50 \leqslant w < 55$	13
$55 \leqslant w < 60$	22
$60 \leqslant w < 100$	3

When grouping data:

- use equal-sized groups or class intervals where possible
- use the lowest value in the data to decide where to start the first group
- use the highest value in the data to decide where to end the last group
- choose class intervals that give between four and ten class intervals in total.

Example 2

The data shows the time taken (in seconds) for 30 teachers to complete an obstacle course. The data has been rounded to one decimal place.

57.6	45.2	87.3	64.0	55.6
59.1	40.6	60.0	49.8	63.7
78.5	46.2	72.7	96.0	78.9
67.3	66.1	64.5	50.3	47.2
66.8	44.4	99.3	50.2	64.7
71.5	84.3	88.8	67.1	53.4

a Calculate the mean of this data.

b Construct a grouped frequency distribution using groups of width 10

c Calculate an estimate of the mean of the grouped frequency distribution.

d **i** Use your answers to parts **a** and **c** to calculate the percentage error generated by grouping the data and calculating an estimate of the mean.

ii Comment on your answer.

e 30 sixth-form students also completed the obstacle course. The students' fastest time was 37.5 seconds, their slowest time was 116.7 seconds, and their mean was 62.8 seconds. Compare the students' and teachers' times.

Solution 2

a $$\text{The mean} = \frac{\text{total of all the values}}{\text{total number of values}}$$

$$= \frac{1941.1}{30} = 64.703\ldots = 64.7 \text{ seconds (1 d.p.)}$$

b Lowest = 40.6 so the first group should start at 40
Highest = 99.3 so the final group should end at 100
The groups have width 10, so are $40 \leqslant t < 50$ and so on.

Time taken, t (seconds)	Tally	Frequency
$40 \leqslant t < 50$	𝍸 I	6
$50 \leqslant t < 60$	𝍸 I	6
$60 \leqslant t < 70$	𝍸 IIII	9
$70 \leqslant t < 80$	IIII	4
$80 \leqslant t < 90$	III	3
$90 \leqslant t < 100$	II	2

c Add two extra columns for the midpoints, t, and for ft, and an extra row for totalling.

Time taken, t (seconds)	Frequency, f	Midpoint, t	ft
$40 \leqslant t < 50$	6	45	270
$50 \leqslant t < 60$	6	55	330
$60 \leqslant t < 70$	9	65	585
$70 \leqslant t < 80$	4	75	300
$80 \leqslant t < 90$	3	85	255
$90 \leqslant t < 100$	2	95	190
	$\Sigma f = 30$		$\Sigma ft = 1930$

An estimate for the mean $= \frac{\Sigma ft}{\Sigma f} = \frac{1930}{30} = 64.333\ldots = 64.3$ seconds (1 d.p.)

d **i** Error = 64.333 – 64.703 = –0.37

$$\text{Percentage error} = \frac{\text{actual error}}{\text{correct value}} \times 100$$

$$= \frac{-0.37}{64.703} \times 100 = -0.57184\ldots = -0.57\% \text{ (2 d.p.)}$$

ii The error value is negative, which means that the estimate for the mean is lower than the true value. The percentage error is very small, because the estimate is close to the true value.

e The range for the teachers' times is 99.3 – 40. 6 = 58.7 seconds.
The students had a larger range of times (79.2 seconds).
The mean time for the teachers (64.7 seconds) is greater than the mean time for the students (62.8 seconds). So on average, the teachers took longer than the students.

Exercise B

1 The lengths of 40 bananas are measured. The smallest banana is 14.6 cm.
The largest banana is 29.4 cm. The data is grouped into class intervals of length 5 cm.
The first group is labelled $10 \leqslant l < 15$
Write down the labels for the rest of the groups.

2 Lawrence looks up the lengths of some motorways in a road atlas.
The shortest motorway is 3.2 miles. The longest motorway is 204.6 miles.
Lawrence groups the data into groups of 50 miles.
List the group labels Lawrence should have in his table.

3 Louise says that it is not possible for the estimated mean of a grouped frequency distribution to be exactly the same as the true mean for the original data.
Is Louise correct? Explain your answer.

4 The times taken for 40 Year 11 pupils to complete a set of maths questions are recorded below (to the nearest 0.1 minutes).

15.2	21.0	14.9	8.6	7.2	16.3	20.5	16.6	19.2	18.1
9.1	26.3	24.1	15.8	17.3	6.4	12.5	20.8	14.6	22.2
15.5	15.0	7.8	16.2	14.6	21.6	29.4	10.4	21.6	15.5
10.0	21.5	14.7	17.4	13.5	23.4	16.6	11.1	28.0	16.7

a Find the range of the times taken.

b Copy and complete the grouped frequency distribution table.

Time taken, t (minutes)	Tally	Frequency, f
$5 \leqslant t < 10$		
$10 \leqslant t < 10$		

c Add extra columns to the table for the midpoints and ft.

d Add an extra row for the totals Σf and Σft. Hence find an estimate for the mean time taken by the Year 11 pupils to complete the set of questions.

e The same questions were attempted by 40 Year 9 pupils. The mean time was 21.7 seconds and the range was 32.5 seconds.
Compare the performances of the Year 9 and Year 11 pupils on these maths questions.

5 Terry has spilt water on his book.
The first label in his grouped frequency table is now missing but he suspects it is $10 \leqslant l < 20$
The estimated mean based on this table is 37
Show that Terry is correct.

Length, l (metres)	Frequency
	5
$20 \leqslant l < 30$	12
$30 \leqslant l < 40$	24
$40 \leqslant l < 50$	22
$50 \leqslant l < 60$	7

6 20 snails were raced over a course of 25 centimetres. The times for each snail to complete the course are given below, in seconds, to one decimal place.

39.6	45.1	76.4	54.7	30.2	70.0	54.7	33.3	63.6	54.1
58.4	62.7	44.7	75.8	51.9	64.3	40.7	52.3	60.8	37.8

a Calculate the mean time for the snails to complete the course.

b Hence calculate the mean time for a snail to travel 1 metre.

c Put the data in groups of length 10. Make the first group $30 \leqslant t < 40$ and the final group $70 \leqslant t < 80$
Draw up a grouped frequency distribution table and fill in the frequencies.

d Hence calculate an estimate of the mean for this grouped frequency distribution.

e Explain why the value calculated in part **d** is an estimate.

f What is the percentage error caused by grouping the data and finding the estimate? Comment on your answer.

16.2 Finding the median for frequency distributions

CAN YOU REMEMBER

- How to find the median for a list of numbers?

IN THIS SECTION YOU WILL

- Find the median for a discrete frequency distribution.
- Find the group containing the median for a grouped frequency distribution.

When discrete data has been collected in a frequency table, the data is already ordered.

To find the median:

Step 1 Work out the total frequency $n = \Sigma f$.

Step 2 Work out $\frac{n+1}{2}$ to find the position of the median in the data.

Step 3 Count along the frequencies until the class containing the median is reached.

If n is 50 or more, $\frac{n}{2}$ can be used to calculate the position of the median.

Example 1

A fair four-sided dice is rolled several times.
The discrete frequency distribution shows the number of times each score occurs.

Find the median score on the dice.

Dice score	Number of times
1	8
2	7
3	10
4	5

Solution 1

Step 1 $n = 8 + 7 + 10 + 5 = 30$

Step 2 The position of the median is the $\frac{30+1}{2}$th = 15.5th value.

Add a third column showing the running total of the frequencies. This makes it easier to find the position of the median.
So the median is the mean of the 15th and 16th values

Dice score	Number of times	Running total
1	**8**	8
2	**7**	8 + **7** = 15
3	**10**	15 + **10** = 25
4	**5**	25 + **5** = 30

Step 3 The 15th value is a 2 and the 16th value is a 3

So the median is $\frac{2+3}{2} = 2.5$

Exercise A

1 The number of fish caught by some anglers one morning is shown in the table.

Number of fish caught	Frequency
0	3
1	12
2	21
3	10
4	4

Find the median number of fish caught.

2 The number of times the children in a class of 25 are going on holiday in the next year is recorded in the table.

Find the median number of holidays.

Number of holidays, x	Frequency, f
0	6
1	14
2	4
3	1

3 The table shows the number of days of rain each week for 10 weeks.

Find the median number of days of rain per week.

Days of rain, x	Number of times, f
0	1
1	0
2	2
3	3
4	1
5	1
6	2
7	0

4 The table shows the number of weddings held per week at a large hotel over a long period of time.

Find the median number of weddings held per week.

Number of weddings, x	Frequency, f
3	21
4	63
5	57
6	14
7	7

5 The number of red sweets in 50 mixed bags of the sweets is counted. The table shows the results.

Find the median number of red sweets per bag.

Number of red sweets	Frequency
3	21
4	15
5	10
6	2
7	1
8	1

6 The frequency distribution shows the number of times Oliver goes fishing per week over one year.

Find the median number of times Oliver goes fishing during the year.

Number of times Oliver went fishing	Frequency
1	7
2	19
3	13
4	10
5	3

A grouped frequency distribution does not give the original data values.

For a grouped frequency distribution:
- the median value cannot be found (instead, find the group that contains the median)
- the range cannot be found, as the exact highest and lowest values are not known
- the modal class (the class with the highest frequency) can be identified.

Example 2

The frequency distribution on page 272 shows the heights, h, of 40 sunflower plants in metres.

a Find the group that contains the median.
b Find the modal class.

Solution 2

a **Step 1** $n = 40$

Step 2 The position of the median is the $\frac{40+1}{2}$th $= 20.5$th value.

This is the average of the 20th and 21st values.

Step 3 Add a running total column to the table.

Height, h (metres)	Frequency	Running total
$0.8 \leqslant h < 1.0$	1	1
$1.0 \leqslant h < 1.2$	5	6
$1.2 \leqslant h < 1.4$	12	18
$1.4 \leqslant h < 1.6$	16	34
$1.6 \leqslant h < 1.8$	4	38
$1.8 \leqslant h < 2.0$	2	40

The 20th and 21st values both lie in the group $1.4 \leqslant h < 1.6$

Step 4 The median is in the group $1.4 \leqslant h < 1.6$

b The modal class is also $1.4 \leqslant h < 1.6$

Exercise B

1 The grouped frequency distribution represents the lengths of 20 internet sessions

Find the group which contains the median.

Length of session, t (minutes)	Frequency, f
$1 \leqslant t < 7$	4
$7 \leqslant t < 13$	7
$13 \leqslant t < 19$	9

2 The grouped frequency distribution shows the widths of 10 toy cars (w cm).

Find the group which contains the median width of toy car.

Width of toy car, w (cm)	Frequency, f
$2 \leqslant w < 8$	4
$8 \leqslant w < 14$	5
$14 \leqslant w < 20$	1

3 A speed trap records the following information about the speeds of 30 cars.
The data is in the form of the grouped frequency distribution.

a Find the group which contains the median speed.

b Which is the modal group?

Speed, s (mph)	Frequency, f
$20 \leqslant s < 30$	14
$30 \leqslant s < 40$	13
$40 \leqslant s < 50$	3

4 The table shows the heights of 50 athletes (h, in cm)

a Find the group that contains the median height.

b Which is the modal group?

Height, h (cm)	Frequency, f
$120 \leqslant h < 140$	4
$140 \leqslant h < 160$	22
$160 \leqslant h < 180$	16
$180 \leqslant h < 200$	8

5 The table shows the lengths (in seconds) of 100 speeches in the House of Commons.

Find the group that contains the median length of speech.

Length of speech, t (seconds)	Frequency, f
$120 \leqslant t < 150$	2
$150 \leqslant t < 180$	7
$180 \leqslant t < 210$	31
$210 \leqslant t < 240$	50
$240 \leqslant t < 270$	8
$270 \leqslant t < 300$	2

6 The table shows the weight, w (in grams) of 59 oranges.

Find the group within which the median weight of orange lies.

Weight of orange, w (g)	Frequency, f
$10 \leqslant w < 40$	5
$40 \leqslant w < 70$	16
$70 \leqslant w < 95$	13
$95 \leqslant w < 130$	22
$130 \leqslant w < 160$	3

7 20 snails were raced over a course of 25 centimetres. The times for each snail to complete the course are given below in seconds to one decimal place.

39.6	45.1	76.4	54.7	30.2
70.0	54.7	33.3	63.6	54.1
58.4	62.7	44.7	75.8	51.9
64.3	40.7	52.3	60.8	37.8

a Write the data in order. Find the median length of snail.

b Write the data in a frequency distribution table, with groups $30 \leqslant t < 40$, $40 \leqslant t < 50$, etc.

c Find the group within which the median length lies.

d Comment on your answers to parts **a** and **c**.

8 The grouped frequency table shows the time taken, t, for a group of Year 11 students to complete some maths problems.

a Show that the median lies in the group $15 \leqslant t < 20$

b Three absent pupils who completed the test at a later date, all took under 15 minutes to complete the test. Does this change which group contains the median?

Time taken, t (minutes)	Frequency
$5 \leqslant t < 10$	6
$10 \leqslant t < 15$	13
$15 \leqslant t < 20$	10
$20 \leqslant t < 25$	9
$25 \leqslant t < 30$	2

9 The incomplete frequency distribution table shows the weights of 37 cookies (in g).

The median lies in the group $30 \leqslant w < 35$
Copy and complete the table to show one possible set of frequencies.

Weight, w (g)	Frequency
$15 \leqslant w < 20$	3
$20 \leqslant w < 25$	
$25 \leqslant w < 30$	
$30 \leqslant w < 35$	
$35 \leqslant w < 40$	17

16.3 Frequency polygons

CAN YOU REMEMBER

- How to collect data into a grouped frequency distribution?
- How to find the midpoint of a group?

IN THIS SECTION YOU WILL

- Learn how to draw a frequency polygon for a grouped frequency distribution.

A *frequency polygon* is a line graph that shows the shape of a grouped frequency distribution. It is constructed by plotting the frequency against the midpoint for each class interval.

Example 1

The frequency distribution shows the heights of 40 sunflower plants in metres measured to the nearest centimetre.

Draw a frequency polygon for this frequency distribution.

Height, h	Frequency, f
$0.8 \leqslant h < 1.0$	1
$1.0 \leqslant h < 1.2$	5
$1.2 \leqslant h < 1.4$	12
$1.4 \leqslant h < 1.6$	16
$1.6 \leqslant h < 1.8$	4
$1.8 \leqslant h < 2.0$	2

Solution 1

Work out the midpoint for each group, then plot it against the frequency for that group.

Height, h	Midpoint	Frequency, f	Coordinates
$0.8 \leqslant h < 1.0$	0.9	1	(0.9, 1)
$1.0 \leqslant h < 1.2$	1.1	5	(1.1, 5)
$1.2 \leqslant h < 1.4$	1.3	12	(1.3, 12)
$1.4 \leqslant h < 1.6$	1.5	16	(1.5, 16)
$1.6 \leqslant h < 1.8$	1.7	4	(1.7, 4)
$1.8 \leqslant h < 2.0$	1.9	2	(1.9, 2)

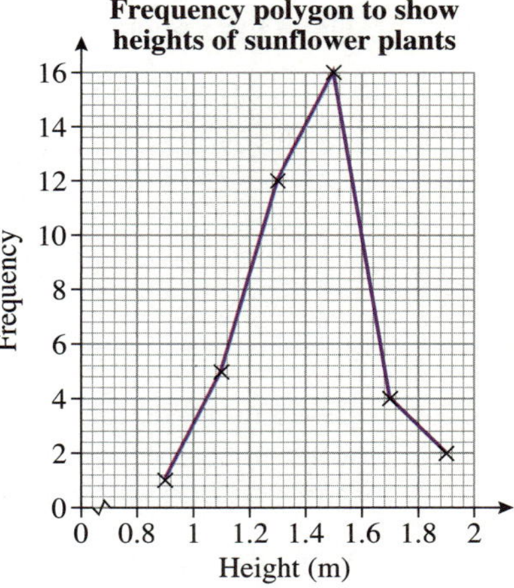

Join the points with straight lines.

Exercise A

1 The frequency distribution shows the heights of 50 horses (in cm).

Height, h (cm)	Midpoint	Frequency, f	Coordinates
$120 \leqslant h < 140$		4	
$140 \leqslant h < 160$		17	
$160 \leqslant h < 180$		21	
$180 \leqslant h < 200$		8	

a Copy the table and complete the midpoints column.
b Complete the coordinates column.
c Draw the frequency polygon.
Use a horizontal scale of 1 cm to 10 cm, starting at 100 cm.

2 The table shows the lengths of time of 117 theatre shows (in minutes).

Length of time, l (min)	Frequency, f
$120 \leqslant l < 150$	1
$150 \leqslant l < 180$	7
$180 \leqslant l < 210$	34
$210 \leqslant l < 240$	54
$240 \leqslant l < 270$	19
$270 \leqslant l < 300$	2

Draw the frequency polygon.

3 The frequency table shows the time taken (in minutes) for 30 people to complete a fun run.

Draw the frequency polygon.

Time taken, t (min)	Frequency, f
$45 \leqslant t < 55$	6
$55 \leqslant t < 65$	6
$65 \leqslant t < 75$	9
$75 \leqslant t < 85$	4
$85 \leqslant t < 95$	3
$95 \leqslant t < 105$	2

4 The time taken for 40 Year 7 pupils to complete a set of science questions is recorded in the grouped frequency distribution.

Draw the frequency polygon.

Time taken, t (min)	Frequency, f
$5 \leqslant t < 10$	5
$10 \leqslant t < 15$	9
$15 \leqslant t < 20$	14
$20 \leqslant t < 25$	9
$25 \leqslant t < 30$	3

5 The table shows the weight (in grams) of 53 pears.

Draw the frequency polygon.

Weight of pear, w (g)	Frequency, f
$20 \leqslant w < 40$	5
$40 \leqslant w < 50$	16
$50 \leqslant w < 55$	13
$55 \leqslant w < 60$	16
$60 \leqslant w < 100$	3

6 The data represents the weights of 30 babies (in kg) born during the same week at a maternity hospital.

3.4 2.1 4.7 3.5 4.4 2.5 2.6 3.0 4.5 5.2
3.4 3.6 2.0 4.9 1.8 3.3 3.6 3.7 3.4 4.5
4.8 1.5 3.8 2.7 2.2 3.6 4.2 4.0 4.9 3.4

Collect the data into a copy of the table below.
Draw a frequency polygon to illustrate the data.

Weight of baby, w (kg)	Tally	Frequency, f
$1 \leqslant w < 2$		
$2 \leqslant w < 3$		
$3 \leqslant w < 4$		
$4 \leqslant w < 5$		
$5 \leqslant w < 6$		

Example 2

Scarlett drew the following frequency polygon for the lengths of 50 films.
Construct the grouped frequency table from which the frequency polygon was drawn.

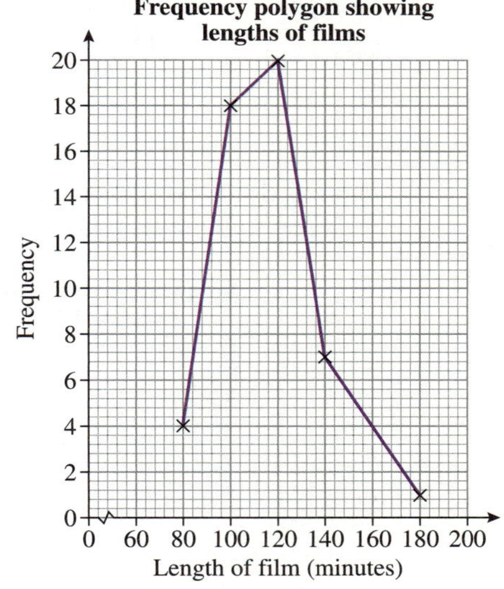

Solution 2

The points are plotted at the midpoints of the groups.
So the midpoints are 80, 100, 120, 140, 180
These are mostly 20 minutes apart, so the width of most groups is 20 minutes.
The 20 minute group with midpoint 80 is $70 \leqslant x < 90$
The next group is $90 \leqslant x < 110$ and so on.

The last group is $150 \leqslant x < 210$

The frequency for each group can be read off the graph.
The grouped frequency table is:

Length of film, x (min)	Frequency
$70 \leqslant x < 90$	4
$90 \leqslant x < 110$	18
$110 \leqslant x < 130$	20
$130 \leqslant x < 150$	7
$150 \leqslant x < 210$	1

Exercise B

1 The frequency polygon below represents the time before the Terriers football team concede their first goal in each game. (Assume that they always concede at least one goal.)

Construct the grouped frequency table that corresponds to this frequency polygon.

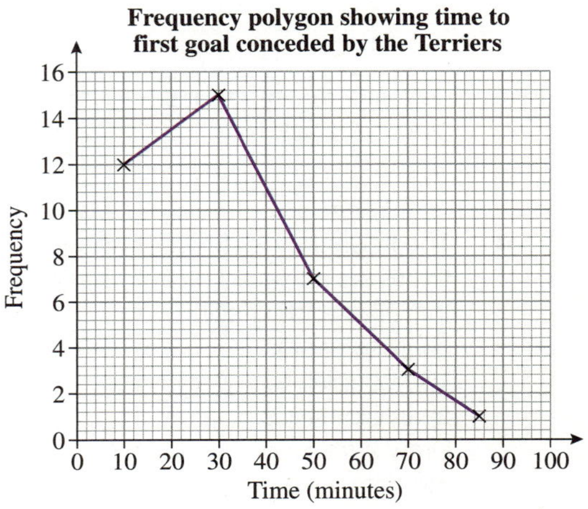

2 The grouped frequency distribution on the right shows the weights of 40 steaks served in a restaurant.

Weight of steak, w (ounces)	Frequency
$6 \leqslant w < 8$	4
$8 \leqslant w < 10$	11
$10 \leqslant w < 12$	13
$12 \leqslant w < 16$	9
$16 \leqslant w < 24$	3

Ishmail drew the following frequency polygon to illustrate this data.

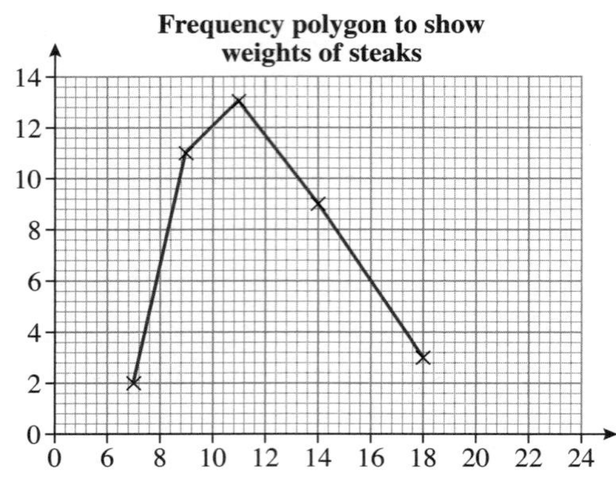

There are four errors in Ishmail's graph. Make a list of his errors.

3 The frequency polygon below shows the heights of some primary school students in cm.

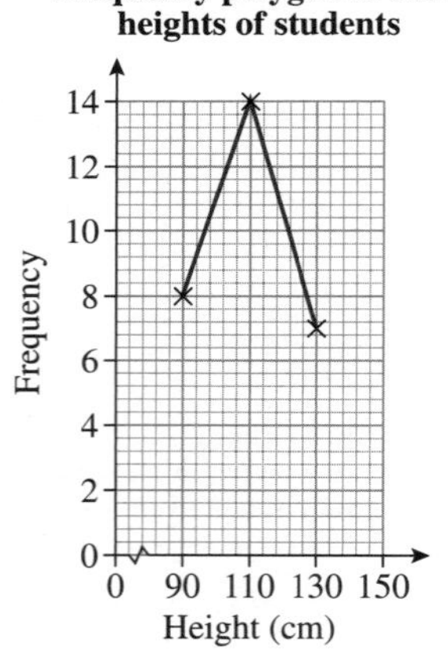

Use the frequency polygon to calculate an estimate of the mean height of the students.

> You may want to construct the grouped frequency distribution and add an fx column.

4 The frequency distribution shows the times achieved by couples in the UK standing-still championships.
100 couples took part in the championships.
Draw a frequency polygon for the data. Use graph paper.

Time standing still, t (minutes)	Frequency
$0 \leqslant t < 100$	$4x$
$100 \leqslant t < 200$	$3x$
$200 \leqslant t < 300$	$2x$
$300 \leqslant t < 400$	x

16.4 Histograms for continuous data with equal class widths

CAN YOU REMEMBER

- How to draw bar charts for discrete data?

IN THIS SECTION YOU WILL

- Learn how to draw a histogram for grouped continuous data with equal class widths.
- Understand the differences between a histogram and a bar chart.

A *histogram* is a frequency diagram drawn to show grouped continuous data.

A histogram looks similar to a bar chart but with some very important differences.

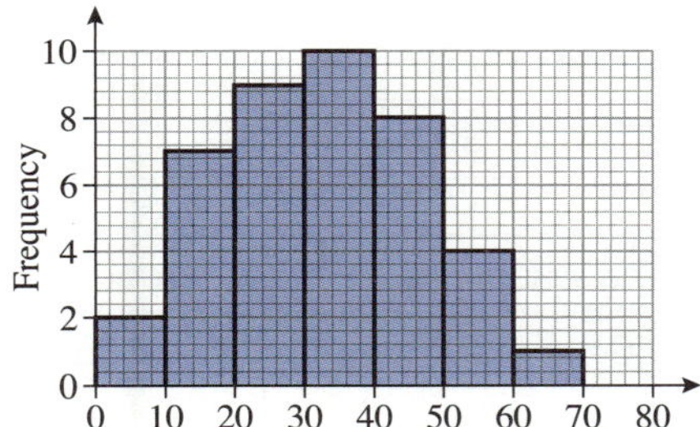

On a histogram:

- there are no gaps between the bars
- the x-axis is labelled as a continuous scale, in the same way as a graph axis
- The **area** of each bar represents the frequency. In this section, all the groups are of equal width, so the height also represents the frequency.

Example 1

The frequency distribution shows the lengths of 20 roads in one town in kilometres.

Draw a histogram for this grouped frequency distribution.

Length, l (kilometres)	Frequency, f
$0.8 \leqslant l < 1.0$	0
$1.0 \leqslant l < 1.2$	3
$1.2 \leqslant l < 1.4$	6
$1.4 \leqslant l < 1.6$	8
$1.6 \leqslant l < 1.8$	2
$1.8 \leqslant l < 2.0$	1

Solution 1

The widths of the bars are given by the class intervals. The bars are all the same width, so the heights of the bars are given by the frequency.

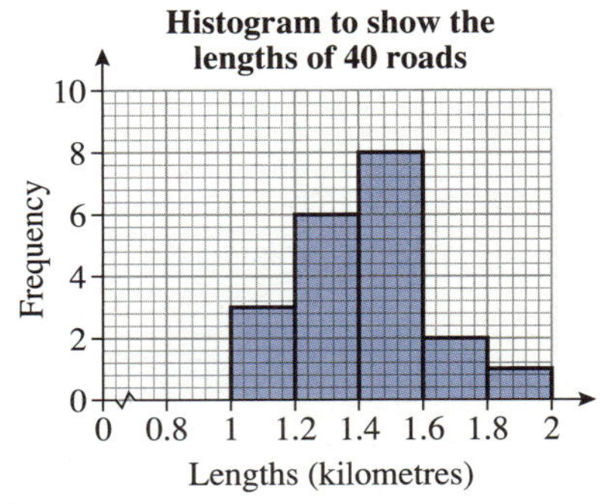

Exercise A

1 The table shows the weights of 50 cows (in kg).

Draw a histogram for this data.
Begin the horizontal axis at 200 kg.
Use a scale of 1 cm to 20 kg.
Use a scale of 1 cm to 2 cows for the vertical axis.

Weight, w (kg)	Frequency, f
$220 \leqslant w < 240$	4
$240 \leqslant w < 260$	17
$260 \leqslant w < 280$	21
$280 \leqslant w < 300$	8

2 The table shows the length, in seconds, of 100 songs by a famous group.

Draw a histogram to show this data.

Length of time, t (s)	Frequency, f
$120 \leqslant t < 150$	1
$150 \leqslant t < 180$	7
$180 \leqslant t < 210$	26
$210 \leqslant t < 240$	45
$240 \leqslant t < 270$	19
$270 \leqslant t < 300$	2

3 The frequency table shows the time taken (in seconds) for 30 teachers to complete an obstacle course.

Use this information to draw a histogram.

Time taken, t (s)	Frequency, f
$40 \leqslant t < 50$	6
$50 \leqslant t < 60$	6
$60 \leqslant t < 70$	9
$70 \leqslant t < 80$	4
$80 \leqslant t < 90$	3
$90 \leqslant t < 100$	2

4 The time taken for 50 pupils to complete a questionnaire on homework is recorded in the grouped frequency distribution.

Draw a histogram.

Time taken, t (minutes)	Frequency, f
$15 \leqslant t < 20$	5
$20 \leqslant t < 25$	9
$25 \leqslant t < 30$	24
$30 \leqslant t < 35$	9
$35 \leqslant t < 40$	3

5 The table shows the weight (in grams) of 60 apples.

Draw a histogram to show this data.

Weight of apple, w (g)	Frequency, f
$20 \leqslant w < 30$	5
$30 \leqslant w < 40$	16
$40 \leqslant w < 50$	13
$50 \leqslant w < 60$	22
$60 \leqslant w < 70$	4

Example 2

The histogram shows the weights of 30 baskets of strawberries.

a What is the modal group?

b Use the histogram to find an estimate of the mean weight of a basket of strawberries.

c Ayeisha says, 'The range of the weights of the baskets is 4 kg.'
Is Ayeisha correct? Explain your answer.

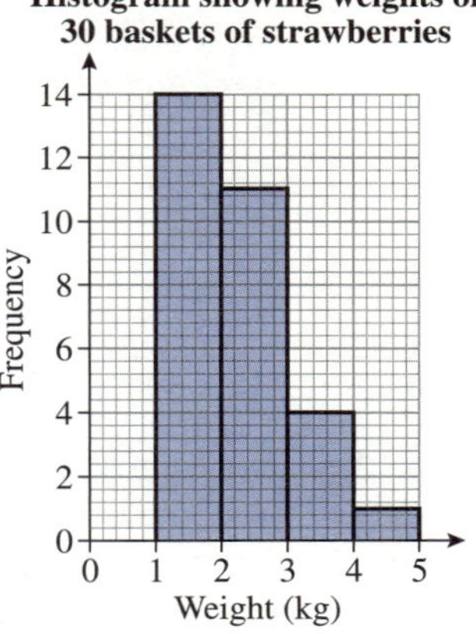

Solution 2

a Modal group is $1 \leqslant w < 2$

b

Weight, w (kg)	Frequency, f	Midpoint, w	fw
$1 \leqslant w < 2$	14	1.5	21
$2 \leqslant w < 3$	11	2.5	27.5
$3 \leqslant w < 4$	4	3.5	14
$4 \leqslant w < 5$	1	4.5	4.5
	$\Sigma f = 30$		$\Sigma fx = 67$

$$\text{Mean} = \frac{\Sigma fw}{\Sigma f} = \frac{67}{30} = 2.233\ldots \text{ kg}$$

c Since the data is grouped, the actual weights are not known, so it is not possible to calculate the range.

Exercise B

1 The histogram shows the ages of 40 tourists on a visit to London.

a What is the modal age group?

b Calculate an estimate of the mean age of the tourists.

c In which group does the median age lie?

d Jack says, 'There are more tourists in their 20s than in their 40s.' Jill says that you cannot tell. Who is correct? Explain your answer.

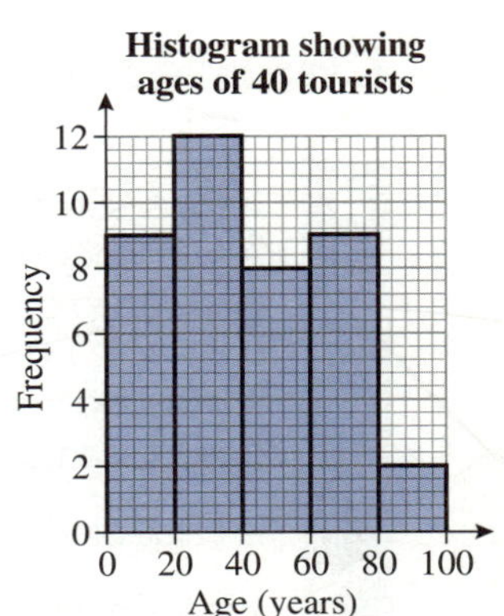

2 The frequency polygon shows the lengths of 49 films.

Construct the histogram for this data.

> You may wish to construct the grouped frequency distribution first.

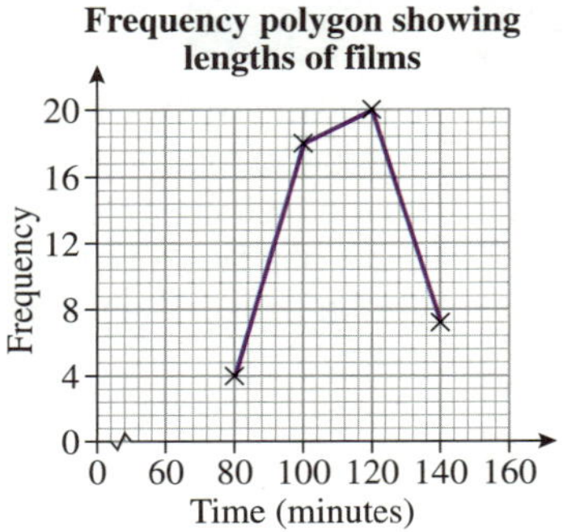

3 Data is collected for the length of time, t, that 40 people can hold their breath.
The data is put into 20-second groups. The first group is $20 \leqslant t < 40$
The longest any of the people could hold their breath was 1 minute 52 seconds.

a How many groups of data are there?

b The frequency for the first group is 14. The frequencies for the remaining groups decrease in equal 'steps' finishing at 2 for the last group.
Draw a histogram to show the data.

4 The times taken, t minutes, for customers' meals to arrive in a restaurant are recorded.
The results are:

8	12	16	9	18	19	24	7	16	24	11	29
14	10	18	9	12	24	22	16	23	20	10	7
16	17	25	13	6	18	15	16	24	20	16	17

Draw a histogram for this data. Use equal-sized groups starting with $5 \leqslant t < 10$

5 The histogram shows the lengths of a number of fossils dug up on an archaeological site.

a Explain why the median fossil length could not be 31 mm.

b If the fossils were measured in centimetres, in what way would the histogram change?

c More fossils are found. It **is** possible now that the median is 31 mm.
Draw a histogram which could represent **all** the fossils.

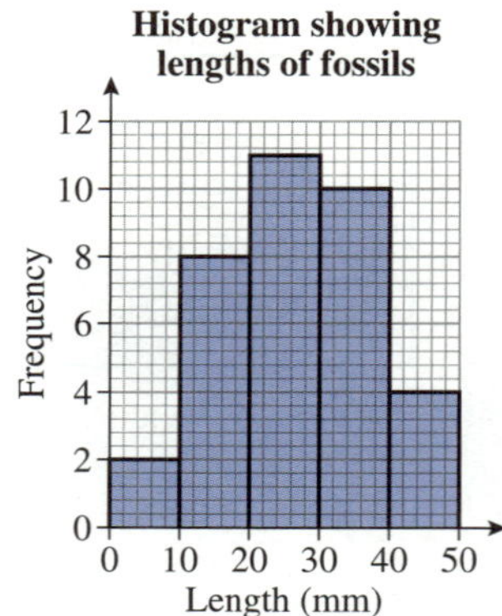

Chapter summary

- A large set of data should be put into groups.
- A frequency distribution where the data is in groups is called a *grouped frequency distribution*.
- In grouped data, the groups are sometimes called *class intervals*. The group $0.8 \leqslant x < 1.0$ includes all the values from 0.8 up to but not including 1.0
- A grouped frequency distribution does not show the exact values of the original data, so an exact mean cannot be calculated. Instead, an estimate of the mean is calculated, using the formula $\frac{\Sigma fx}{\Sigma f}$, where f is the frequency for each group and x is the midpoint for each group.

- Always check that the mean calculated is sensible. For most data sets it will be close to the 'middle' of the data values.
- When grouping data:
  - use equal-sized groups or class intervals
  - use the lowest value in the data to decide where to start the first group
  - use the highest value in the data to decide where to end the last group
  - choose class intervals that give between four and ten class intervals in total.
- To find the median for a set of discrete data in a frequency table:

  Step 1 Work out the total frequency $n = \Sigma f$.

  Step 2 Work out $\frac{n+1}{2}$ to find the position of the median in the data.

  Step 3 Count along the frequencies until the class containing the median is reached.
- If n is 50 or more, $\frac{n}{2}$ can be used to calculate the position of the median.
- For a grouped frequency distribution:
  - The median value cannot be found (instead find the group that contains the median).
  - The range cannot be found, as the exact highest and lowest values are not known.
  - The modal class (the class with the highest frequency) can be identified.
- A *frequency polygon* is a line graph that shows the shape of a grouped frequency distribution. It is constructed by plotting the frequency against the midpoint for each class interval.
- A *histogram* is a frequency diagram drawn to show grouped continuous data.
- On a histogram:
  - there are no gaps between the bars
  - the x-axis is labelled as a continuous scale, in the same way as a graph axis
  - the **area** of each bar represents the frequency. When the groups are of equal width, the height also represents the frequency.

Chapter review

1 The frequency polygon shows the height of 45 male pole-vaulters.

a From the frequency polygon, what is the modal height for a male pole-vaulter?

b Construct the grouped frequency distribution of pole-vaulter heights.

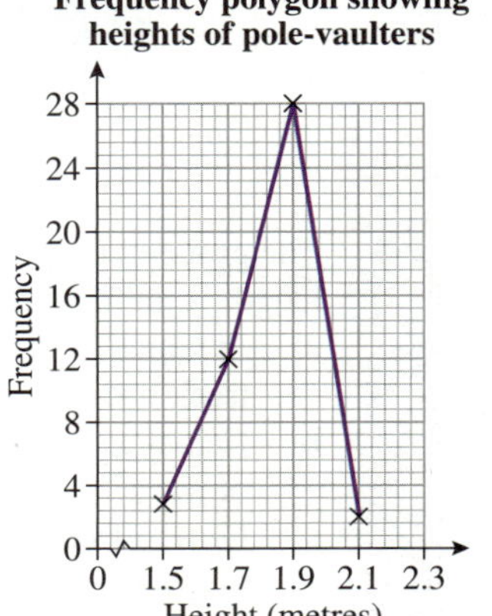

2 Five more pole-vaulters were added to the data for question 2
Their heights were 1.57 m, 2.00 m, 1.88 m, 2.24 m and 2.13 m.
Construct a histogram to represent all 50 pole-vaulters' heights.

3 Victoria keeps a record of the time it takes the school bus to take her from her home to school. Her record for last month is shown in the table.

Time, t (min)	Frequency	Midpoint
$10 < t \leqslant 12$	5	
$12 < t \leqslant 14$	10	
$14 < t \leqslant 16$	4	
$16 < t \leqslant 18$	1	

a Complete the midpoint column and use it to calculate an estimate of the mean time.
b There are 200 school days in the year. Use the information in the table to estimate the number of days in a year on which Victoria's bus journey takes more than 14 minutes. (Victoria never misses a day of school!)
c What is the probability that, on a randomly chosen day, the journey takes less than or equal to 12 minutes?

4 For this frequency distribution the estimated mean was calculated to be 10
The total frequency is 40
a Find the missing frequency *.
b Hence show the estimated mean was calculated correctly.

Length, x (cm)	Frequency
$0 \leqslant x < 4$	4
$4 \leqslant x < 8$	8
$8 \leqslant x < 12$	16
$12 \leqslant x < 16$	8
$16 \leqslant x < 20$	*

5

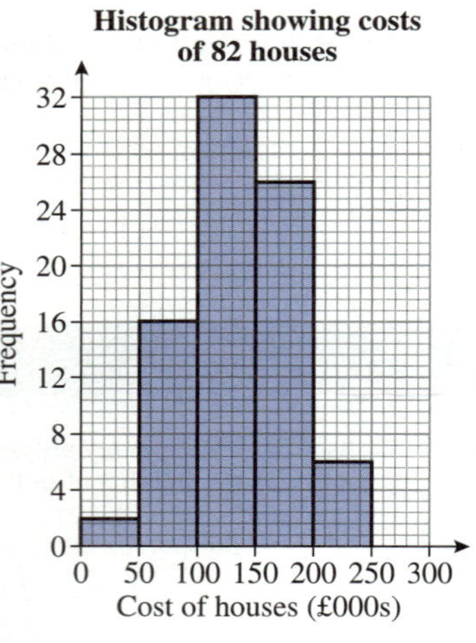

The histogram shows the cost of 82 different houses sold in one city.
a What is the modal group?
b In which group does the median lie?
c Calculate an estimate of the mean house price.

6 The grouped frequency distribution shows the length, x, in minutes of 100 tracks on rock CDs.
a In which group does the median length of track lie?
b Calculate an estimate of the mean length of track.
c Draw a frequency polygon to display this data.

Length (min)	Frequency
$0 \leqslant x < 2$	3
$2 \leqslant x < 4$	24
$4 \leqslant x < 6$	60
$6 \leqslant x < 8$	8
$8 \leqslant x < 10$	3
$10 \leqslant x < 12$	1
$12 \leqslant x < 14$	1

7 The table shows the heights of 40 plants.

Height, h (cm)	Number of plants
$5 \leqslant h < 7$	8
$7 \leqslant h < 9$	15
$9 \leqslant h < 11$	12
$11 \leqslant h < 13$	5

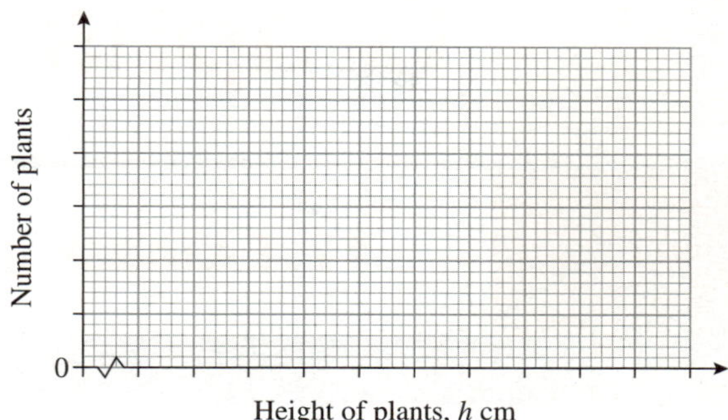

a Draw a frequency diagram.

b Calculate an estimate of the mean height of these 40 plants.

8 The grouped frequency table shows the speeds of cars measured by a police speed trap.

Speed, s (miles per hour)	Frequency
$25 \leqslant s < 30$	65
$30 \leqslant s < 35$	17
$35 \leqslant s < 40$	12
$40 \leqslant s < 45$	5

a Calculate an estimate of the mean of this frequency table.

It was later found that the trap was recording a speed 3 miles per hour lower than it should have been.

b Estimate the mean actual speed of the cars represented by the frequency table.

9 The amount of rain (measured in millimetres) was recorded for 60 days.

The grouped frequency table shows the results.

Rain (mm)	Frequency
$0 \leqslant x < 4$	41
$4 \leqslant x < 8$	6
$8 \leqslant x < 12$	7
$12 \leqslant x < 16$	3
$16 \leqslant x < 20$	2
$20 \leqslant x < 24$	0
$24 \leqslant x < 28$	0
$28 \leqslant x < 32$	0
$32 \leqslant x < 36$	1

a Calculate an estimate of the mean rainfall per day.

b Give a reason why the estimate might be higher than the actual mean.

c Suggest another method for obtaining a more reliable average.

CHAPTER 17

Graphs

17.1 Linear graphs

CAN YOU REMEMBER

- How to substitute values into an expression or a formula?
- How to use a table of values to draw a linear graph?
- How to draw and identify straight lines with equations like $x = 2$, $y = -3$, $y = x$ and $y = -x$?

IN THIS SECTION YOU WILL

- Learn the meaning of 'linear function'.
- Increase skills in drawing the graphs of linear functions.
- Use graphs to solve linear equations.
- Learn the meaning of 'gradient' and work out the gradients of simple linear graphs.

In algebra a function is a special formula that connects values of **one** letter symbol with values of **one** other letter symbol.

For example $y = x + 2$, $y = 2x$, $x + 2y = 3$ and $y = x^2 + 2x$ are all functions.

Functions can be shown on a graph. Functions that give a straight-line graph are called *linear functions.* Linear functions involve only an x term and a y term and possibly a number term. They do not include squares, cubes or other powers.

The *gradient* measures the slope of a line.

It can be worked out from the formula $\text{Gradient} = \dfrac{\text{distance up}}{\text{distance across}}$

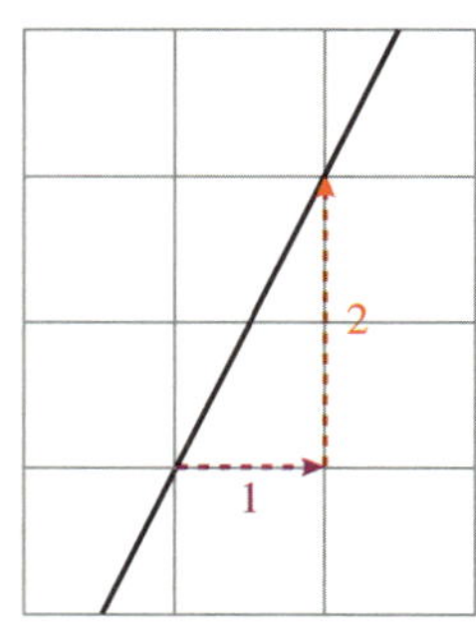

$\text{Gradient} = \dfrac{2}{1} = 2$

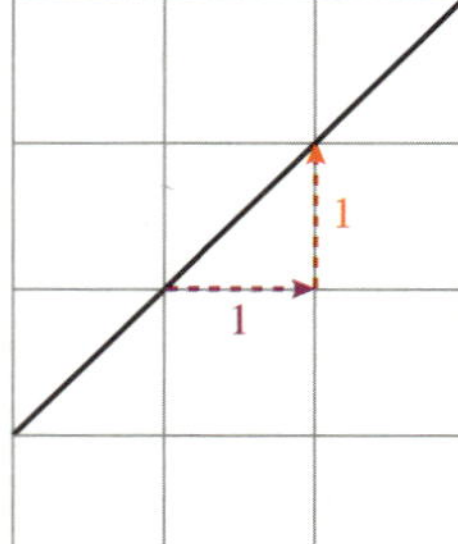

$\text{Gradient} = \dfrac{1}{1} = 1$

Example 1

a Draw the graph of $y = 3x - 1$ for values of x from -1 to 3
b Find the gradient of the graph.

Solution 1

a **Step 1:** Choose three values of x from -1 to 3 (include $x = 0$ if possible).
$x = 0$, $x = 1$ and $x = 2$

Step 2: Substitute these values of x into $y = 3x - 1$ and obtain the corresponding values of y.

x	0	1	2
y	−1	2	5

When $x = \mathbf{0}$, $y = 3 \times \mathbf{0} - 1 = 0 - 1 = \mathbf{-1}$

When $x = \mathbf{1}$, $y = 3 \times \mathbf{1} - 1 = 3 - 1 = \mathbf{2}$

When $x = \mathbf{2}$, $y = 3 \times \mathbf{2} - 1 = 6 - 1 = \mathbf{5}$

Write the pairs of values of x and y as coordinates.

So the points with coordinates (**0**, **−1**), (**1**, **2**) and (**2**, **5**) lie on the graph of $y = 3x - 1$

Step 3: Plot the coordinates on the grid and draw a straight line through them.

Check Only two points are needed to draw a straight line. The third point acts as a check.

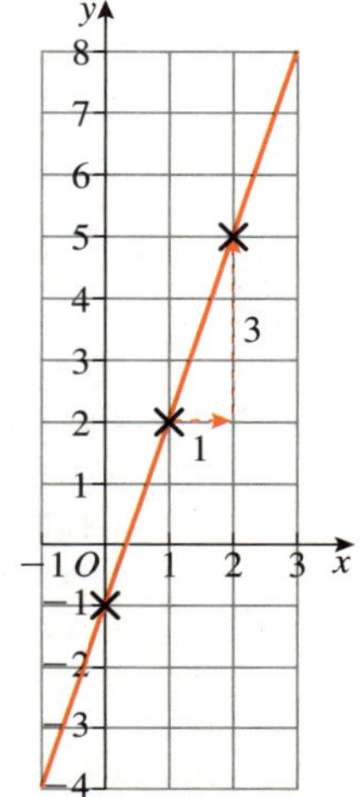

b From the graph, gradient $= \dfrac{\text{distance up}}{\text{distance across}} = \dfrac{3}{1} = 3$

To draw the graph of a linear function written in the form $2x + y = 8$, find coordinates on the x-axis and the y-axis by substituting the values $y = 0$ and $x = 0$ into the function.

Example 2

Draw the graph of $2x + y = 8$ from $x = 0$ to $x = 5$

Solution 2

Find coordinates of points on $2x + y = 8$ at $x = 0$ and at $y = 0$

When $x = \mathbf{0}$ $2 \times \mathbf{0} + y = 8$ $y = \mathbf{8}$

When $y = \mathbf{0}$ $2x + \mathbf{0} = 8$ $x = \mathbf{4}$

x	0	4
y	8	0

So the points with coordinates (**0**, **8**) and (**4**, **0**) lie on the graph of $2x + y = 8$

Check Choose a point on the line, say (3, 2).
Substitute the x-coordinate and y-coordinate into $2x + y$ and check that it gives the value 8
$2 \times \mathbf{3} + \mathbf{2} = 6 + 2 = 8$ ✓

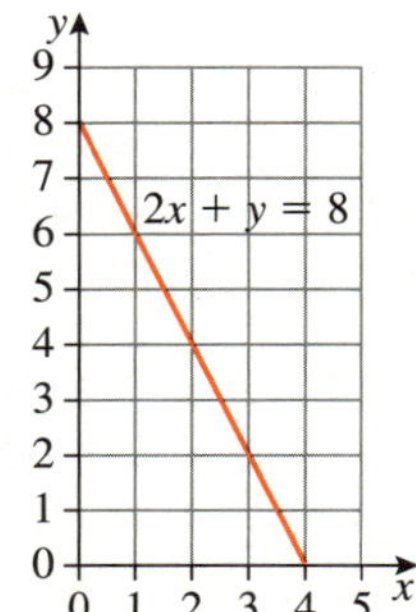

Exercise A

1 **a** Draw and label a grid with the x-axis from -4 to 4 and the y-axis from -10 to 10
b Find the coordinates of points that lie on the graph of $y = x + 5$ at $x = -2$, $x = 0$ and $x = 2$
c On the grid draw and label the graph of $y = x + 5$
d Repeat parts **b** and **c** for the graphs of:
i $y = x + 3$ **ii** $y = x + 1$ **iii** $y = x - 1$
iv $y = x - 3$ **v** $y = x - 5$
e Work out the gradient of each graph drawn in this question. What do you notice?

2 **a** Draw and label a grid with the x-axis from -3 to 3 and the y-axis from -9 to 9
b Find the coordinates of points that lie on the graph of $y = 3x$ at $x = -2$, $x = 0$ and $x = 2$
c On the grid draw and label the graph of $y = 3x$
d Repeat parts **b** and **c** for the graph $y = 4x$
e Work out the gradients of the graphs of $y = 3x$ and $y = 4x$
f On a new copy of the grid, draw the graphs of:
i $y = -3x$ **ii** $y = -4x$ What do you notice?

3 **a** Draw and label a grid with the x-axis from -3 to 3 and the y-axis from -8 to 10
b Find the coordinates of points that lie on the graph of $y = 2x + 5$ at $x = -2$, $x = 0$ and $x = 2$
c On the grid draw and label the graph of $y = 2x + 5$
d Repeat parts **b** and **c** for the graphs of:
i $y = 2x + 3$ **ii** $y = 2x + 1$ **iii** $y = 2x - 1$ **iv** $y = 2x - 3$
e Work out the gradient of each graph drawn in this question. What do you notice?

4 **a** Draw and label a grid with the x-axis from -3 to 3 and the y-axis from -10 to 10
b On the grid draw and label the graphs of:
i $y = 3x + 2$ **ii** $y = 4x + 1$ **iii** $y = 5x - 2$
c Work out the gradient of each graph in part **b**
d On a new grid draw the graphs of:
i $y = 3 - 5x$ **ii** $y = 5 - 3x$ What do you notice?

5 **a** Draw and label a grid with both the x-axis and y-axis from -8 to 8
b On the grid draw and label the graphs of:
i $x + y = 8$ **ii** $x + y = 4$ **iii** $x + y = 0$
iv $x + y = -4$ **v** $x + y = -8$

6 In this question use a new grid for each pair of graphs.
Draw both the x-axis and the y-axis from 0 to 16
a **i** Find the value of y when $x = 0$ in $x + 3y = 15$ and complete the coordinate (0, ...).
ii Find the value of x when $y = 0$ in $x + 3y = 15$ and complete the coordinate (..., 0).
iii On the grid draw and label the graph of $x + 3y = 15$
iv Repeat parts **i**, **ii** and **iii** for $3x + y = 15$
b Repeat part **a** for each of these pairs of graphs.
i $4x + y = 16$ and $x + 4y = 16$ **ii** $3x + 5y = 30$ and $5x + 3y = 30$
iii $3x + 4y = 24$ and $4x + 3y = 24$ **iv** $2x + 5y = 20$ and $5x + 2y = 20$

7 **a** Draw and label a grid with the x-axis from -2 to 5 and the y-axis from -11 to 9
b On the grid draw and label the graph of $y = 3x - 4$ from $x = -2$ to $x = 4$
c Write down the coordinates of the point where the graph of $y = 3x - 4$ crosses each of these lines.
i $y = -7$ **ii** $y = x$ **iii** $y = -x$ **iv** $x + y = 2$

8 **a** Draw and label a grid with both the x-axis and the y-axis from 0 to 8
b On the grid draw and label the graph of $x + 2y = 6$
c Write down the coordinates of the point where the graph of $x + 2y = 6$ crosses the line $y = x$.
Check that the coordinates of this point satisfy $x + 2y = 6$

9 Graphs **A** to **E** are shown on the grid.
Match each equation to its graph.
a $y = 6x - 5$
b $y = x$
c $y = 1$
d $y = 5 - 4x$
e $x + y = 1$

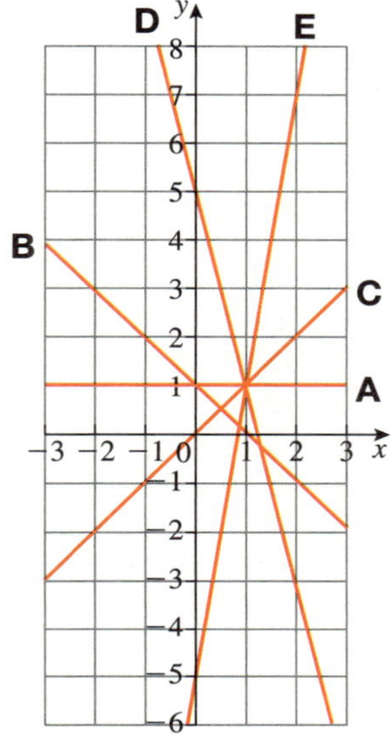

10 **a** Each of the coordinates **A** to **D** lies on the graph of one of functions **1** to **4**
Match the functions and coordinates.

Function 1 $y = 2x - 5$	**Function 2** $y = 5 - 2x$	**Function 3** $y = 3x - 7$	**Function 4** $y = 7 - 3x$
Coordinate A (3, −1)	**Coordinate B** (1, 4)	**Coordinate C** (1, −3)	**Coordinate D** (−1, −10)

b Draw graphs of functions **1** and **3** on the same grid.
Find the coordinates of the point where they cross.
c Draw graphs of functions **2** and **4** on the same grid.
Find the coordinates of the point where they cross.

Linear graphs can be used to solve equations.

For example the solution of the equation $3x + 4 = 2$ is the x-coordinate of the point where the line $y = 3x + 4$ crosses the line $y = 2$

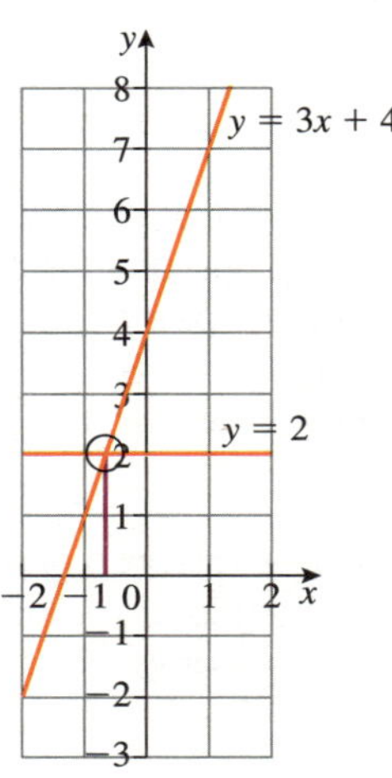

Exercise B

1 **a** Match each graph with its gradient. The first one has been done for you.

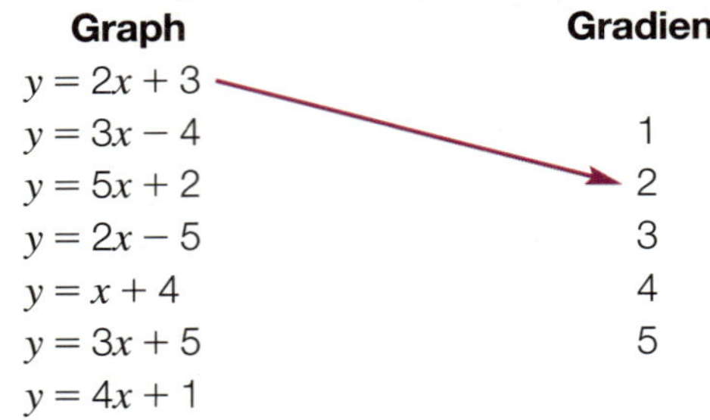

b Which of the graphs in **a** are parallel?

2 **a** Draw and label a grid with the x-axis from -3 to 3 and the y-axis from -2 to 12

b On the grid draw and label the graphs:

i $y = 2x + 6$

ii $y = 2x + 2$

iii $y + 2x = 8$

iv $y + 2x = 4$

c Write down the coordinates of the points where:

i the graph of $y = 2x + 6$ crosses the graph of $y + 2x = 8$

ii the graph of $y = 2x + 4$ crosses the graph of $y + 2x = 2$

3 The diagram shows the graph of $y = 4x + 1$
Copy the diagram.
Use the diagram to solve the equations below.

a $4x + 1 = 5$

b $4x + 1 = -2$

Show your method.

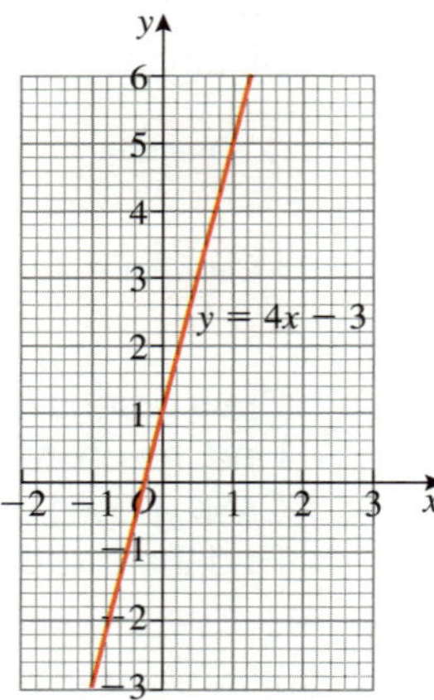

4 **a** Draw and label a grid with the x-axis from -2 to 3 and the y-axis from -9 to 8

b On the grid draw and label the graph of $y = 5x - 3$

c Use your graph to solve the following equations.

i $5x - 3 = -8$ **ii** $5x - 3 = 7$

Show your method.

5 **a** Draw and label a grid with the x-axis from -4 to 3 and the y-axis from -3 to 13

b On the grid draw and label the graph of $y = 2x + 6$

c Use your graph to solve the following equations.

i $2x + 6 = 9$ **ii** $2x + 6 = -1$

6 The points $A(2, 1)$, $B(2, 5)$, $C(4, 3)$, $D(4, 5)$ and $E(4, 7)$ are shown on the grid.
Find which of the points lie on the following lines:

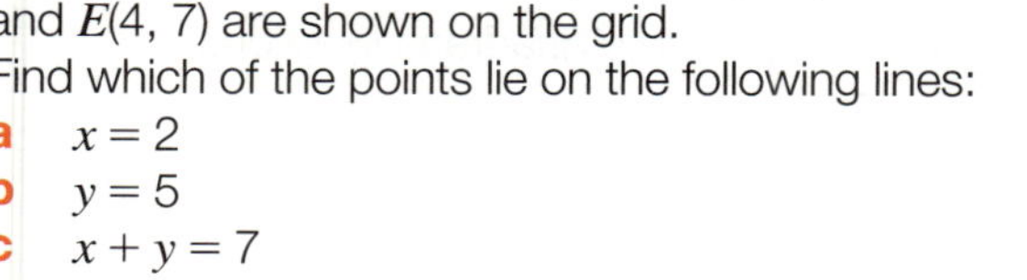

a $x = 2$
b $y = 5$
c $x + y = 7$
d $y = x - 1$
e $y = 2x - 5$
f $y = 3x - 5$

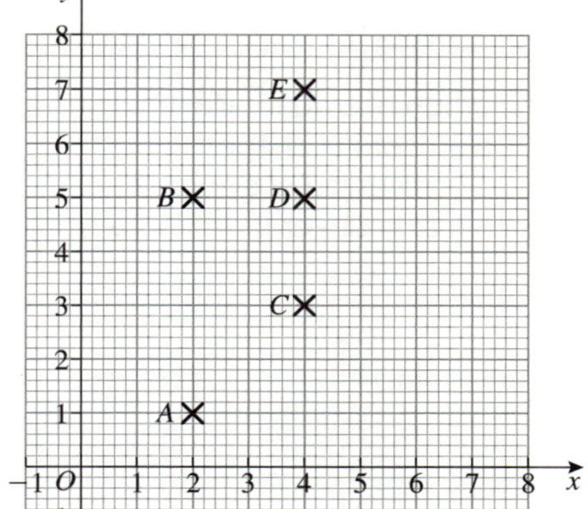

7 The points on the grid show John's attempt at drawing the line $y = 5 - 3x$
a How does John know he has made a mistake?
b Which point is wrong? Explain your answer.
c Draw the correct graph and use it to solve the equation $5 - 3x = 8$

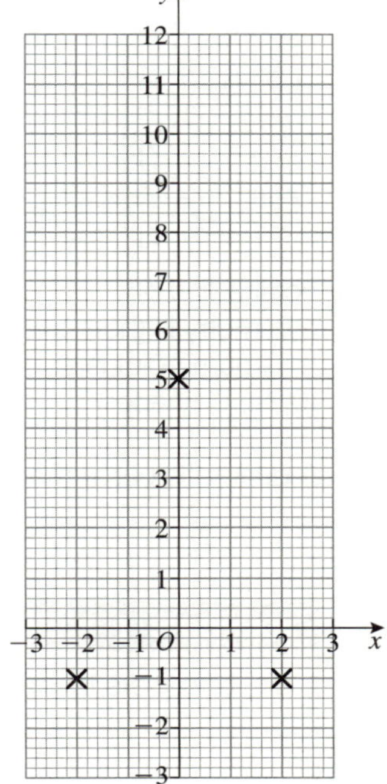

8 Use a graphical method to solve each of these equations.
a $5x - 2 = 4$
b $2x + 3 = -2$

17.2 Quadratic graphs

CAN YOU REMEMBER

- How to substitute positive and negative integers into an expression that contains a square term such as x^2 or $2x^2$?
- How to draw a graph from a table of values?
- How to use graphs to solve linear equations?

IN THIS SECTION YOU WILL

- Learn the meaning of 'quadratic function'.
- Complete tables of values for quadratic functions and draw their graphs.
- Start to use quadratic graphs to solve quadratic equations.

Quadratic functions have an x^2 term. They can also have an x term and/or a number term.

For example $y = x^2 - 1$, $y = x^2 + 5x$ and $y = x^2 + 3x - 5$ are quadratic functions.

The graph of a quadratic function has:

- a smooth U-shaped curve
- a vertical line of symmetry
- a maximum or a minimum point.

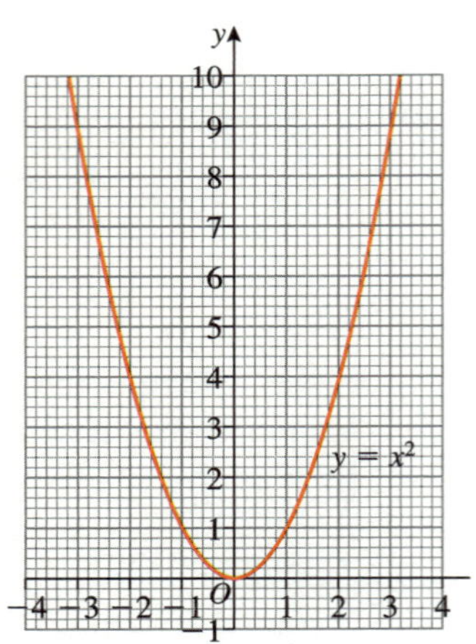

vertical line of symmetry is the y-axis; minimum point is at (0, 0); U-shape

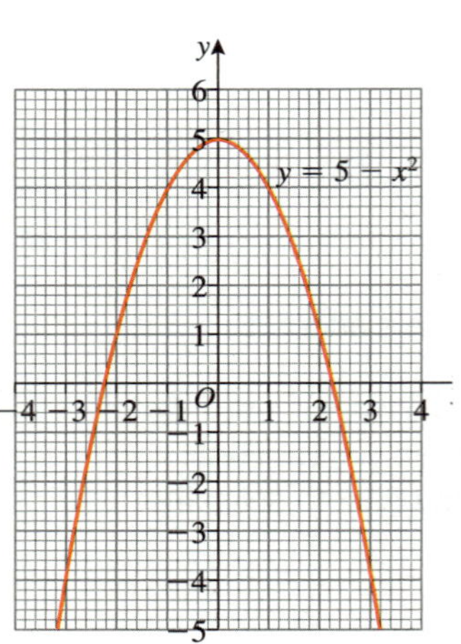

vertical line of symmetry is the y-axis; maximum point is at (0, 5); $-x^2$ gives an inverted U-shape

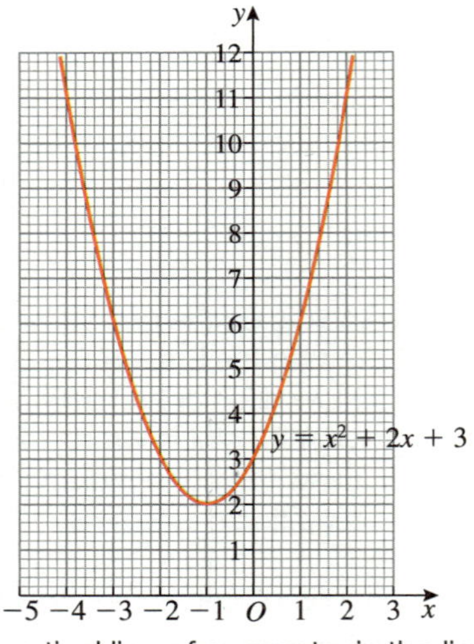

vertical line of symmetry is the line $x = -1$; minimum point is at $(-1, 2)$; U-shape

A quadratic curve may touch the x-axis, cross it twice or lie completely above or below it.

Example 1

a Complete the table and draw the graph of $y = 3 - x^2$

x	−3	−2	−1	0	1	2	3
y			2	3	2	−1	−6

b Write down the coordinates of the maximum point on the graph.

Solution 1

a **Step 1:** Complete the table of values.

When $x = -3$ $\quad y = 3 - (-3)^2 = 3 - 9 = -6$

When $x = -2$ $\quad y = 3 - (-2)^2 = 3 - 4 = -1$

x	−3	−2	−1	0	1	2	3
y	−6	−1	2	3	2	−1	−6

Step 2: Write a list of coordinates from the table.

(−3, −6), (−2, −1), (−1, 2), (0, 3), (1, 2), (2, −1), (3, −6)

Step 3: Plot the points on a grid and join them with a smooth curve.

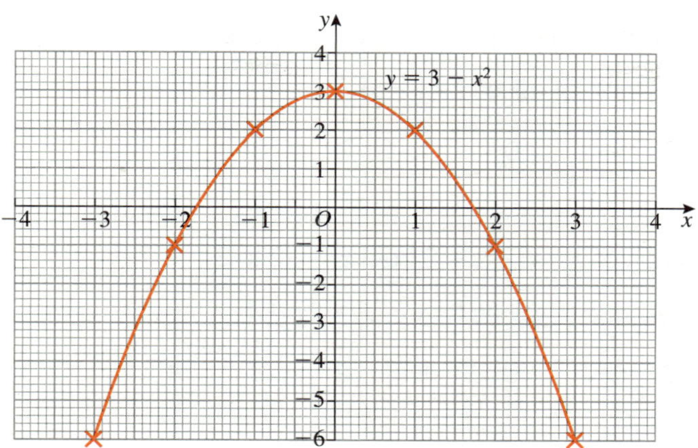

Check Maximum point ✓
Vertical line of symmetry ✓
Inverted smooth U-shaped curve ✓

b The maximum point has coordinates (0, 3)

Exercise A

1 Draw all the graphs in this question on a grid with the x-axis from −4 to 4 and the y-axis from −10 to 14

a Complete the table of values for $y = x^2 - 3$

x	−3	−2	−1	0	1	2	3
y							

b On the grid draw and label the graph of $y = x^2 - 3$ from $x = -3$ to 3

c Repeat parts **a** and **b** for:

i $y = x^2 + 4$ **ii** $y = x^2 - 9$ **iii** $y = x^2 + 2$ **iv** $y = x^2 - 6$

d At what point does the graph of $y = x^2 + 50$ cross the y-axis?

2 Draw all the graphs in this question on a grid with the x-axis from −4 to 4 and the y-axis from −30 to 30
Use a scale on the x-axis of 2 cm to 1 unit and a scale on the y-axis of 1 cm to 5 units.

a Complete the table of values for $y = 2x^2$

x	−3	−2	−1	0	1	2	3
y							

b On the grid draw and label the graph of $y = 2x^2$ from $x = -3$ to 3

c Repeat parts **a** and **b** for:

i $y = x^2$ **ii** $y = -x^2$ **iii** $y = -2x^2$ **iv** $y = 3x^2$ **v** $y = -3x^2$

3 Draw all the graphs in this question on a grid with the x-axis from −4 to 4 and the y-axis from −15 to 10

a Complete the table of values for $y = 5 - x^2$

x	−3	−2	−1	0	1	2	3
y							

b On the grid draw and label the graph of $y = 5 - x^2$ from $x = -3$ to 3

c Repeat parts **a** and **b** for:

i $y = 8 - x^2$ **ii** $y = -2 - x^2$ **iii** $y = 1 - x^2$ **iv** $y = -5 - x^2$

d At what point does the graph of $y = 50 - x^2$ cross the y-axis?

4 **a** Complete the table of values for $y = x^2 - x + 3$

x	−2	−1	0	1	2	3
y						

b Draw the graph of $y = x^2 - x + 3$ from $x = -2$ to 3

5 **a** Complete the table of values for $y = x^2 - 2x - 4$

x	−2	−1	0	1	2	3	4
y							

b Draw the graph of $y = x^2 - 2x - 4$ from $x = -2$ to 4

c Write down the coordinates of the points where the graph of $y = x^2 - 2x - 4$ crosses the x-axis.

6 **a** Complete the table and draw the graph of $y = x^2 + 3x - 3$

x	−5	−4	−3	−2	−1	0	1	2
y								

b On the same grid draw the line $y = 2x + 3$

c Write down the coordinates of the points where the line $y = 2x + 3$ crosses the curve $y = x^2 + 3x - 3$

7 Make a table of values and draw a graph using a suitable grid for each of the following quadratic functions:

a $y = 2x^2 - 5$ from $x = -3$ to 3

b $y = x^2 + x - 3$ from $x = -4$ to 3

c $y = x^2 - 4x + 2$ from $x = -1$ to 5

d $y = x^2 + 4x - 1$ from $x = -5$ to 1

8 Match each graph to a function.

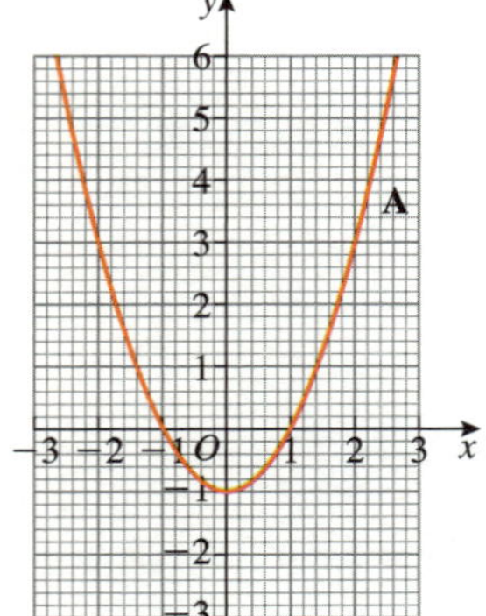

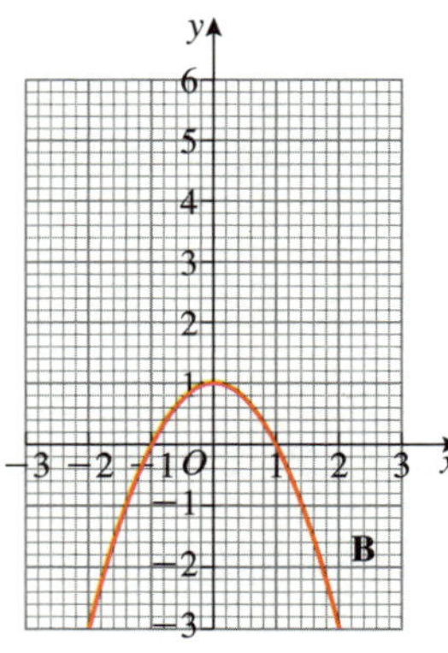

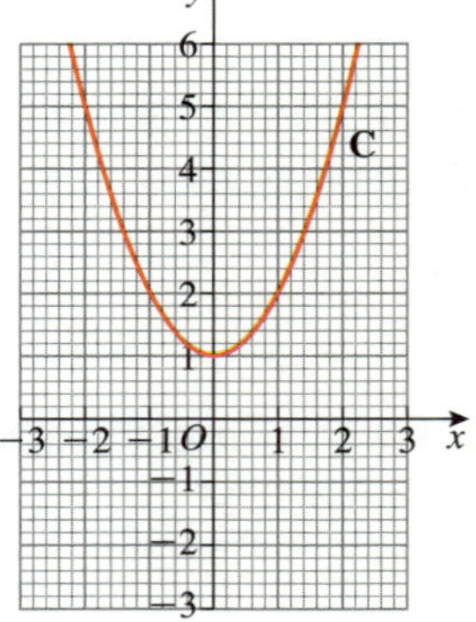

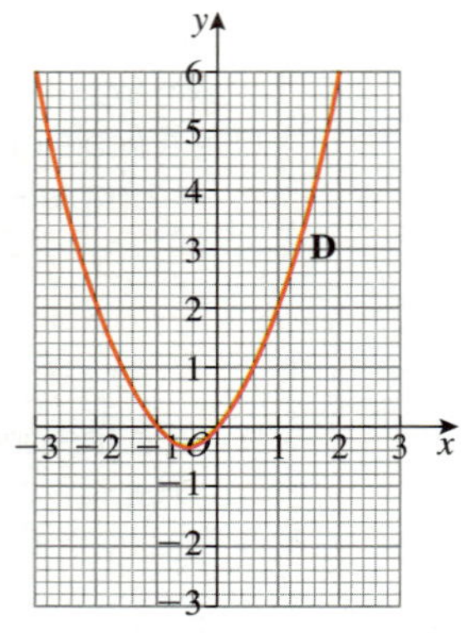

a $y = x^2 + 1$ **b** $y = x^2 + x$ **c** $y = 1 - x^2$ **d** $y = x^2 - 1$

9 **a** Complete the table for $y = x^2 - 4x - 3$

x	−2	−1	0	1	2	3	4	5	6
y									

b Complete the table for $y = 9 - x^2$

x	−4	−3	−2	−1	0	1	2	3	4
y									

c Draw a grid with the x-axis from −5 to 7 and the y-axis from −8 to 10. Draw the graphs of $y = x^2 - 4x - 3$ and $y = 9 - x^2$ on the grid.

d Write down the coordinates of the points where the graph of $y = 9 - x^2$ crosses the graph of $y = x^2 - 4x - 3$

10 a Make a table of values for the following quadratic functions.

i $y = x^2 + x - 7$ for $x = -4$ to 3 **ii** $y = 8 - x^2$ for $x = -4$ to 4

b On a grid with the x-axis going from −4 to 5 and the y-axis going from −9 to 14, draw the graphs of $y = x^2 + x - 7$ and $y = 8 - x^2$

c Write down the coordinates of the points where the graph of $y = x^2 + x - 7$ crosses the graph of $y = 8 - x^2$

Using graphs to solve quadratic equations

A quadratic equation is normally written x^2 term ± x term ± number = 0

For example $x^2 - 5x - 4 = 0$

$(x + 2)(x + 5) = 0$ is also a quadratic equation.

×	x	5
x	x^2	$5x$
2	$2x$	10

Expanding $(x + 2)(x + 5) = x^2 + 2x + 5x + 10$

$= x^2 + 7x + 10$

So the equation $(x + 2)(x + 5) = 0$ can be written $x^2 + 7x + 10 = 0$

Quadratic graphs can be used to solve quadratic equations.

Example 2

The graph of $y = x^2 + 3x - 3$ for values of x from −5 to 2 is shown on the grid.

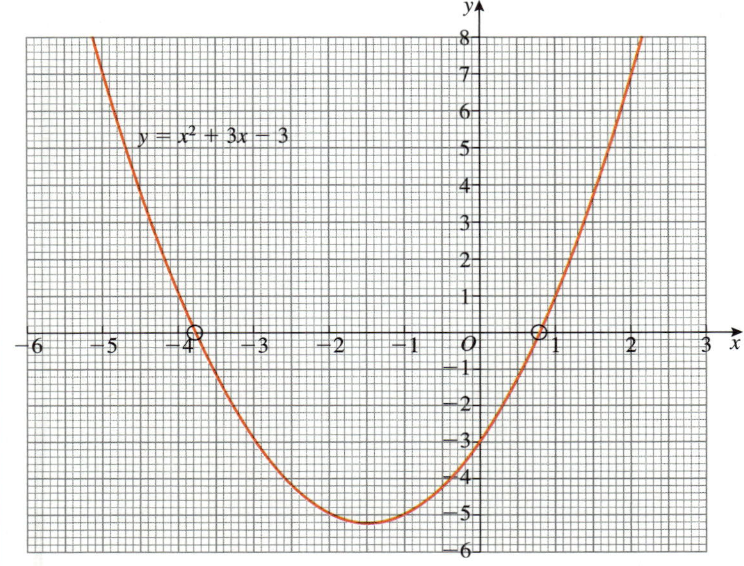

Use the graph to find the solutions of the equation $x^2 + 3x - 3 = 0$

Solution 2

To solve the equation $x^2 + 3x - 3 = 0$, find the x-coordinates of the points where the graph of $y = x^2 + 3x + 3$ crosses the line $y = 0$ (the x-axis).

The graph of $y = x^2 + 3x - 3$ crosses the line $y = 0$ (the x-axis) at the points (**−3.8**, 0) and (**0.8**, 0).

The solutions of the quadratic equation $x^2 + 3x - 3 = 0$ are $x =$ **−3.8** and $x =$ **0.8**

Example 3

a Complete the table and draw the graph of $y = (x - 2)(x + 1)$.

b Use your graph to solve the equation $(x - 2)(x + 1) = 0$

x	−3	−2	−1	0	1	2	3	4
y	10	4		−2		0	4	10

Solution 3

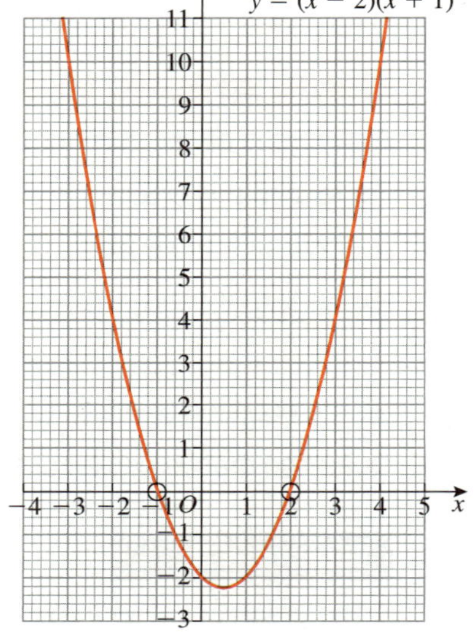

a When $x = -1$
$y = (-1 - 2)(-1 + 1) = -3 \times 0 = 0$
When $x = 1$
$y = (1 - 2)(1 + 1) = -1 \times 2 = -2$

x	−3	−2	−1	0	1	2	3	4
y	10	4	0	−2	−2	0	4	10

b The graph of $y = (x - 2)(x + 1)$ crosses the line $y = 0$ (the x-axis) at the points (**−1**, 0) and (**2**, 0).
The solutions of the quadratic equation $(x - 2)(x + 1) = 0$ are $x =$ **−1** and $x =$ **2**

Check When $x = -1$ $\quad (-1 - 2)(-1 + 1) = -3 \times 0 = 0$ ✓

When $x = 2$ $\quad (2 - 2)(2 + 1) = 0 \times 3 = 0$ ✓

Exercise B

1 The graph of $y = x^2 + x - 2$ for values of x from −4 to 3 is shown on the grid.
Explain how the graph shows that the solutions of the equation $x^2 + x - 2 = 0$ are $x = -2$ and $x = 1$

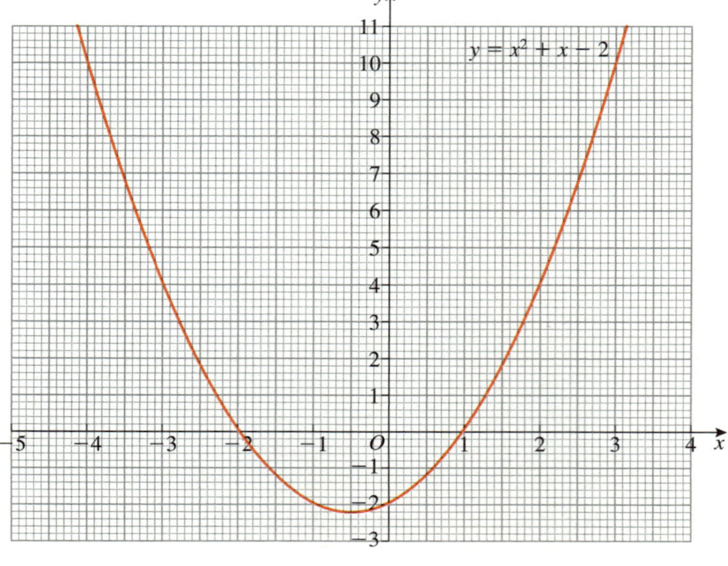

2 The diagrams show the graphs of $y = x^2 + 3$, $y = x^2 + 2x + 1$ and $y = x^2 - 3$

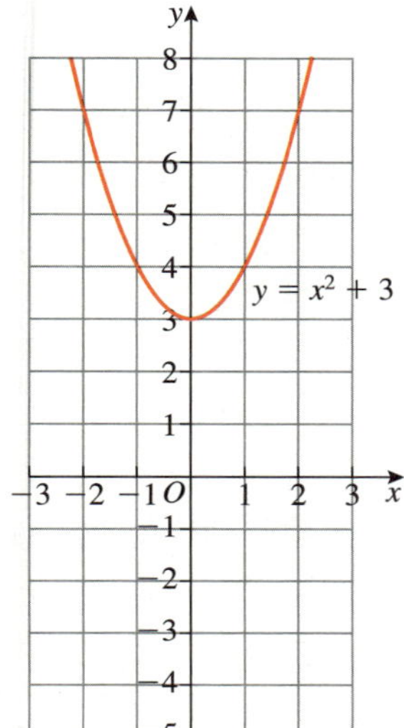

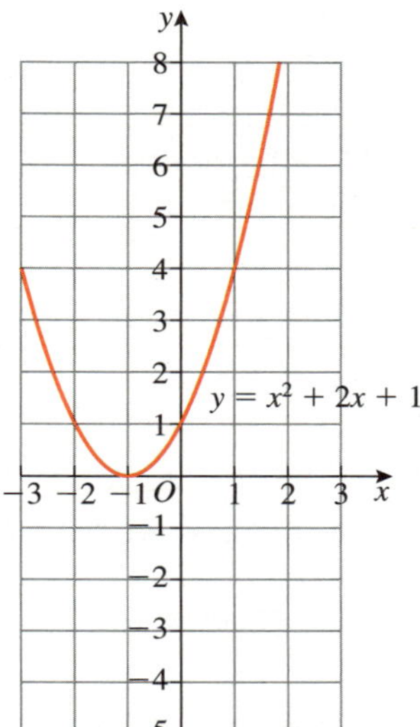

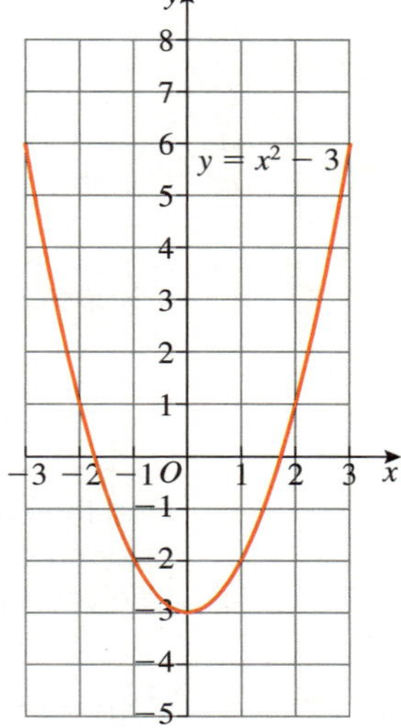

Are the following statements true or false? Use the graphs to explain each answer.

a The equation $x^2 + 3 = 0$ has two solutions.

b The equation $x^2 + 2x + 1 = 0$ has only one solution.

c The equation $x^2 - 3 = 0$ has two solutions.

d The minimum point of the graph of $y = x^2 + 2x + 1$ lies on the y-axis.

e The graph of $y = x^2 + 3$ has a maximum point at (0, 3).

3 **a** Complete the table for values of $y = x^2 + 3x + 1$

x	−5	−4	−3	−2	−1	0	1	2
y								

b Draw the graph of $y = x^2 + 3x + 1$ for values of x from −5 to 2

c Use your graph to solve the equation $x^2 + 3x + 1 = 0$

4 Here is the graph of $y = x^2 - 6x + 3$

a Write down the coordinates of the minimum point on the graph.

b Use the graph to solve the equation $x^2 - 6x + 3 = 0$
Explain how you obtained your answer.

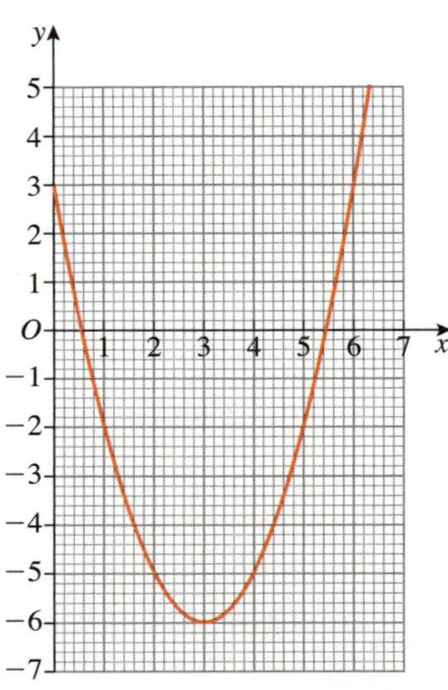

5 **a** Complete the table for $y = 15 - 2x^2$

x	−3	−2	−1	0	1	2	3
y							

b Draw the graph of $y = 15 - 2x^2$ for values of x from −3 to 3

c Use the graph to solve the equation $15 - 2x^2 = 0$

6 **a** Complete the table and draw the graph of $y = (x - 4)(x - 1)$.

x	−1	0	1	2	3	4	5	6
y								

b Find the coordinates of the point where the graph of $y = (x - 4)(x - 1)$ crosses its line of symmetry.

c Use your graph to solve the equation $(x - 4)(x - 1) = 0$

7 **a** Complete the table and draw the graph for $y = (x - 3)(x + 2)$.

x	−4	−3	−2	−1	0	1	2	3	4	5
y										

b Use your graph to solve the equation $(x - 3)(x + 2) = 0$

8 Amy is trying to draw the graph of $y = x^2 - 3x - 2$
Here is her work.

x	−2	−1	0	1	2	3	4	5
y	−4	2	−2	−4	−4	−2	2	8

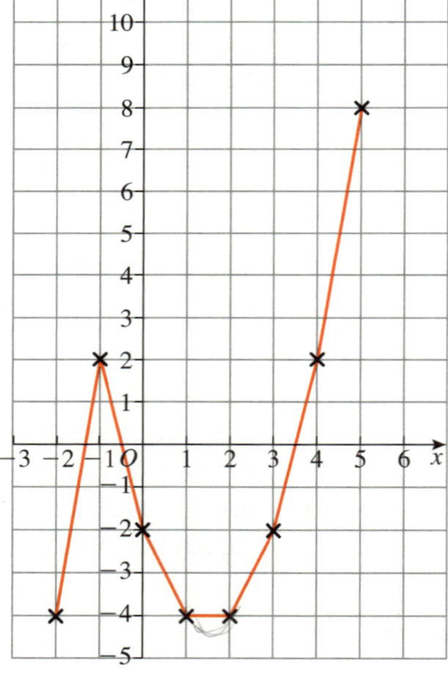

Amy's teacher says she has made two mistakes.

a What mistakes has Amy made?

b Correct Amy's mistakes and draw the correct graph of $y = x^2 - 3x - 2$

c Use your graph to solve the equation $x^2 - 3x - 2 = 0$

9 **a** Complete the table for $y = 4x - x^2$

x	−1	0	1	2	3	4	5
y							

b On a suitable grid draw the graph of $y = 4x - x^2$ from $x = -1$ to 5

c Use your graph to solve the equation $4x - x^2 = 0$

10 a Complete the table for $y = (x + 1)(3 - x)$.

x	−2	−1	0	1	2	3	4
y							

b On a suitable grid draw the graph of $y = (x + 1)(3 - x)$ from $x = -2$ to 4

c Use your graph to solve the equation $(x + 1)(3 - x) = 0$

17.3 Real-life graphs

CAN YOU REMEMBER

- How to interpret points on graphs?

IN THIS SECTION YOU WILL

- Draw graphs that model real-life situations.
- Develop skills in interpreting real-life graphs.

Graphs are used in science and other real-life situations to show how one quantity changes with another.

The *gradient* of a graph shows the *rate* of the change. The steeper the slope of the graph the faster the change.

Example 1

The distance, d kilometres, that Ben walks in t minutes is given by $d = \frac{t}{10}$

a Draw the graph of $d = \frac{t}{10}$

b Use the graph to find the time it takes Ben to walk 4 km.

Solution 1

a When $t = 0$ minutes, $d = 0 \div 10 = 0$ km

When $t = 30$ minutes, $d = 30 \div 10 = 3$ km

When $t = 60$ minutes, $d = 60 \div 10 = 6$ km

So the points with coordinates (0, 0), (30, 3) and (60, 6) lie on the graph of $d = \frac{t}{10}$

Check All three points lie on a straight line. ✓

b The line passes through the point (**40**, 4).
Ben takes **40** minutes to walk 4 km.

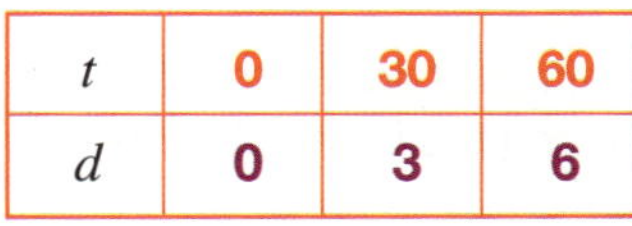

t	0	30	60
d	0	3	6

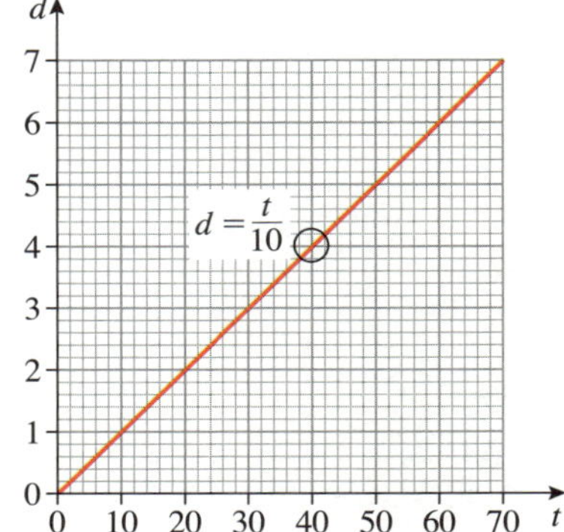

Distance–time graphs are used to represent journeys.
On a distance–time graph:

- the gradient equals the speed, so a steeper line means higher speed
- a straight line means constant speed
- a horizontal straight line means zero speed.

Example 2

The distance–time graph shows a short journey.

a Work out the speed on the first 10 seconds of the journey.
b Between what times from the start is the speed zero?
c Work out the average speed over the whole journey.

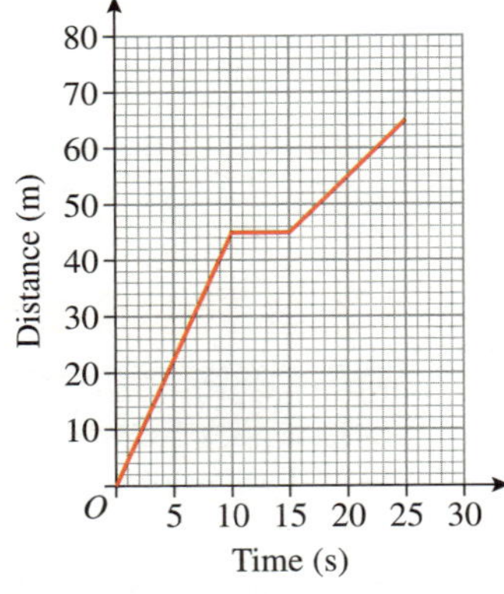

Solution 2

a Time across = 10 seconds
Distance up = 45 m
Gradient = speed = $\frac{45}{10}$ = 4.5 m/s

b The speed is zero when the gradient of the distance–time graph is zero.
This occurs between 10 and 15 seconds.

c Total time across = 25 seconds
Total distance up = 65 m
Average speed = $\frac{\text{Total distance}}{\text{Total time}} = \frac{65}{25}$ = 2.6 m/s

Exercise A

1 To convert the mark in a test, m, to a percentage, p, a teacher uses the graph of $p = 5m$.

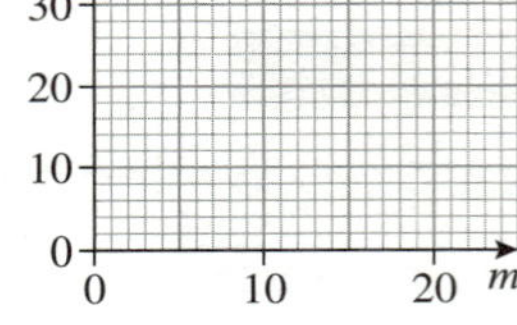

a Copy these axes and extend the vertical axis to 100.
Draw the graph of $p = 5m$ from $m = 0$ to 20
b Bill scored 12 marks. Use the graph to find his percentage.
c Betty's percentage is 85%.
What mark did Betty score in the test?

2 The time it takes to cook a joint of meat is given by $T = 30W + 20$
T is the time in minutes. W is the weight in pounds.

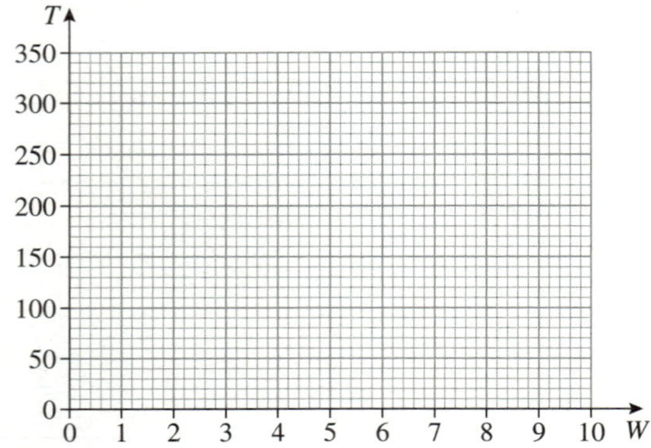

a On a copy of the grid, draw the graph of $T = 30W + 20$
b A joint of meat weighs 4 pounds.
Use the graph to find how long it takes to cook this joint.
c To cook a joint of meat it takes 1 hour 20 minutes.
Use the graph to find the weight of this joint.

3 The distance–time graphs show the journeys of three different people walking from home to a local shop.

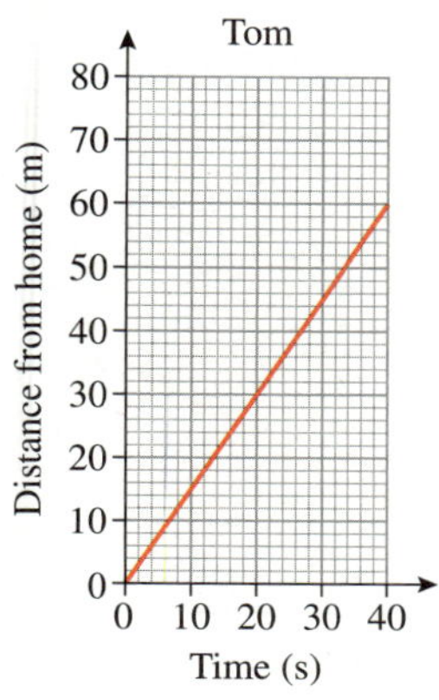

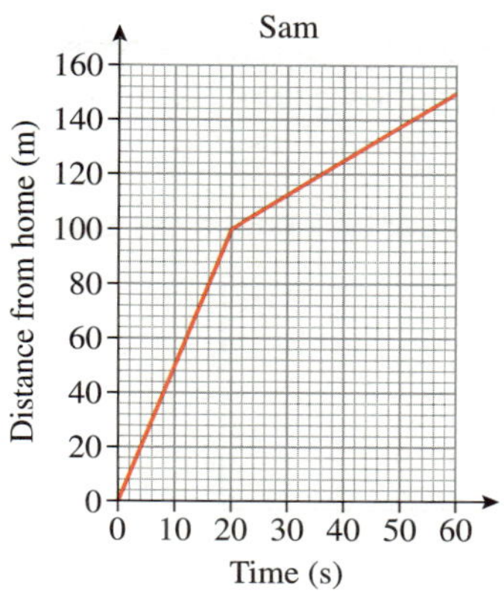

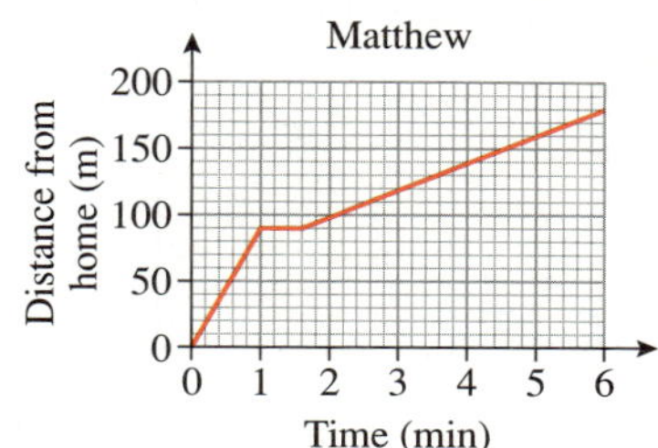

- **a** Who lives furthest from the shop?
- **b** Who stops and for how many seconds?
- **c** Work out Tom's speed on his walk in m/s.
- **d** Work out Sam's speed for the first 20 seconds of his walk.
- **e** Work out Sam's average speed in m/s for his complete journey.
- **f** Work out Matthew's average speed in m/s for his complete journey.

4 The height of a candle as it burns is given by $h = 20 - 4t$
t is the time in minutes and h is the height in centimetres.

- **a** On a grid with t from 0 to 5 and h from 0 to 25, draw the graph of $h = 20 - 4t$
- **b** What feature of the graph shows that the height of the candle is decreasing?
- **c** **i** What is the initial height of the candle?
  ii How long does it take the candle to burn from a height of 3 cm to a height of 1 cm?
- **d** The candle burns for 3 minutes 30 seconds. What is its decrease in height?

5 A hardware shop sells large screws in packs of 10
The graph shows the cost of buying up to 100 large screws.

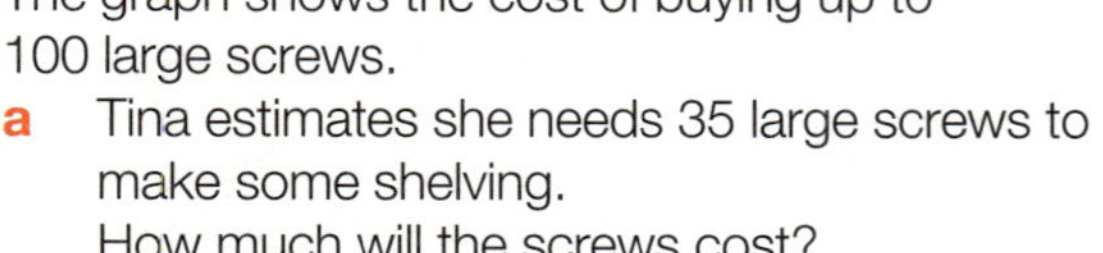

- **a** Tina estimates she needs 35 large screws to make some shelving.
  How much will the screws cost?
- **b** Explain why there is no line through the points on this graph.

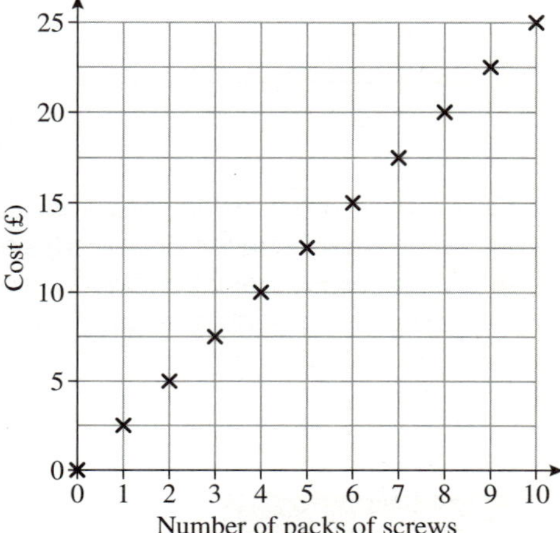

6 Bill spends £20 on bottles of pop and chocolate bars for the school tuck shop.
The cost of a large bottle of pop is £1
The cost of a pack of chocolate bars is £2
Bill draws the graph of $x + 2y = 20$ to help him decide how many bottles of pop and packs of chocolate bars he can buy for **exactly** £20

- **a** On a grid with values of x from 0 to 20 and values of y from 0 to 10, draw the graph of $x + 2y = 20$

b What do x and y represent on this graph?
c Use the graph to write down all the possible ways that Bill can spend exactly £20 on pop and chocolate bars.
d **i** Explain why a line should **not** be drawn through the points on this graph.
ii Explain why the graph slopes down.

7 Water flows into each of these containers at a constant rate.

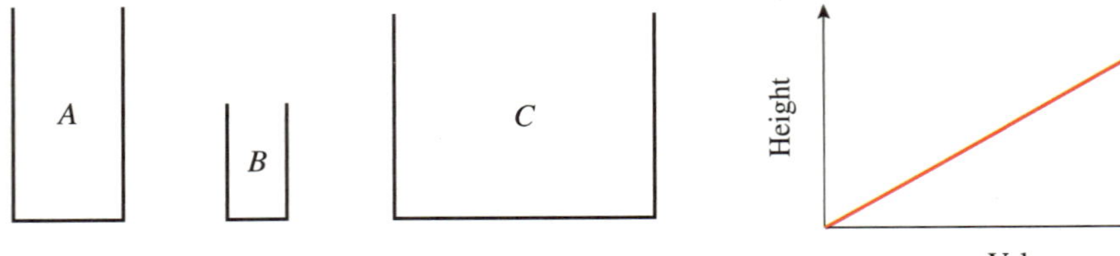

The graph shows how the height of the water in container A changes as the volume of water in the container increases.
On a copy of the same graph sketch the lines for containers B and C.

8 The weight of salt, W grams, that can be dissolved in a beaker of water at different temperatures is given by $W = 0.4t + 50$ where t is the temperature of the water in degrees Celsius.
a On a copy of the grid, draw the graph of $W = 0.4t + 50$
b Use the graph to find:
i W when $t = 45°C$
ii t when $W = 62.8$ grams.

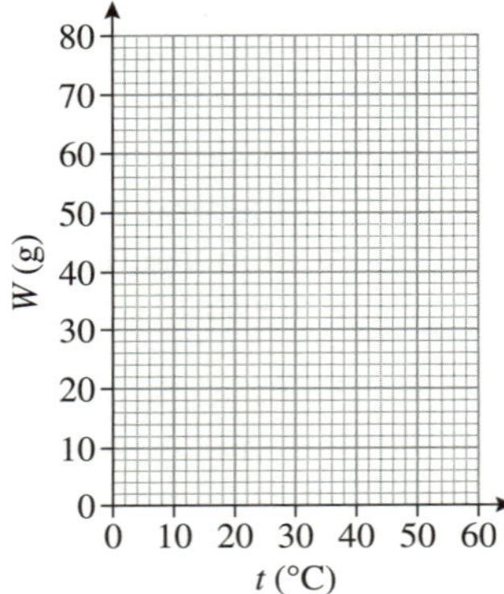

Graphs that show real-life situations can be curved.

- When lines (straight or curved) slope **upwards** they show an **increasing** quantity.
- When lines (straight or curved) slope **downwards** they show a **decreasing** quantity.

The steeper the slope, the faster the increase or decrease.

Example 2

Water flows into this container at a constant rate.
Sketch a graph to show how the depth of water in the container changes with time.
Give reasons for the shape of the graph.

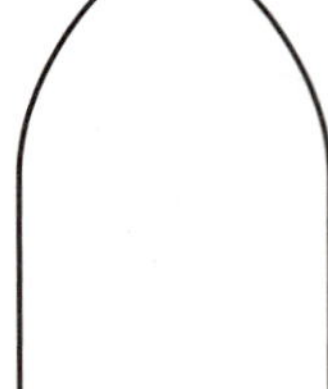

Solution 3

Straight-sided section of container:
The depth of water increases at a constant rate, so the graph is a straight line.

Curved section of the container:
As the container narrows, the depth of water increases at a faster and faster rate.
This means that the graph gets steeper and steeper, and starts to curve up.

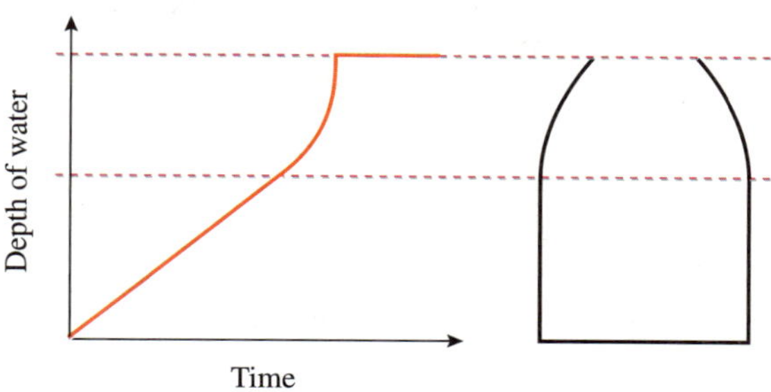

The container is full:
The depth of water does not increase, so the graph is horizontal.

Exercise B

1 Match the graphs with the statements.
Statement **1**: The birth rate fell for a number of years but more recently it has been steady.
Statement **2**: Unemployment decreased rapidly but then started to rise slowly.
Statement **3**: The price of oil fell steadily.
Statement **4**: Profits increased rapidly but then started to fall gradually.

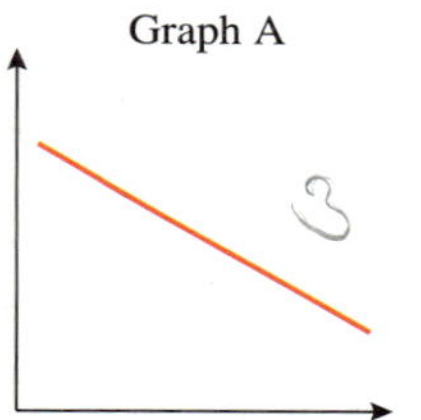

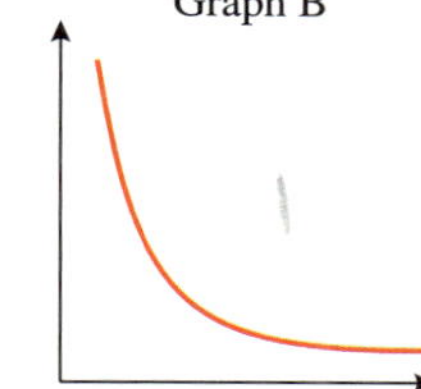

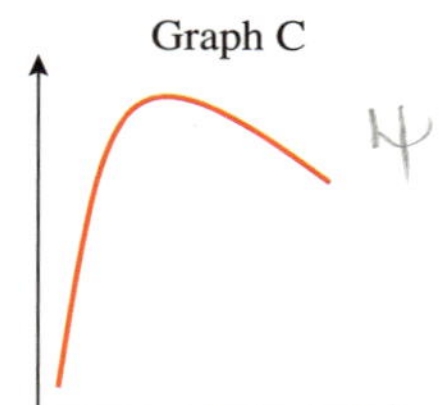

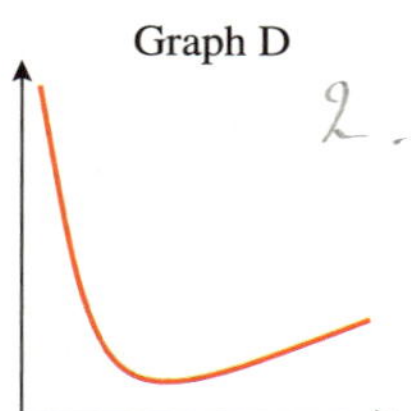

2 This graph shows how the percentage of male and female smokers varies with age.

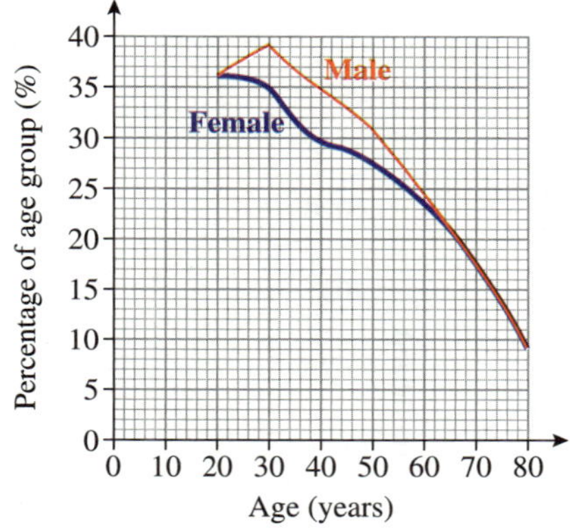

a At what ages is the percentage of male and female smokers equal?

b At what age is there the greatest **decrease** in the percentage of smokers:
 i for men
 ii for women?
 Explain your answers.

c At what age is there the biggest difference between the percentage of male and female smokers?

d **i** In what age range do more than 30% of males smoke?
 ii In what age range do more than 30% of females smoke?

3 The graph shows how numbers of deaths from lung disease changed between 1920 and 1960.

a In which year did the number of deaths from lung cancer first exceed the number of deaths from tuberculosis?

b In which five-year period did the number of deaths from lung cancer increase the most?

c Which year had the greatest total number of deaths from both lung cancer and tuberculosis?

d What percentage of the total number of deaths was from lung cancer:
i in 1920 **ii** in 1960?

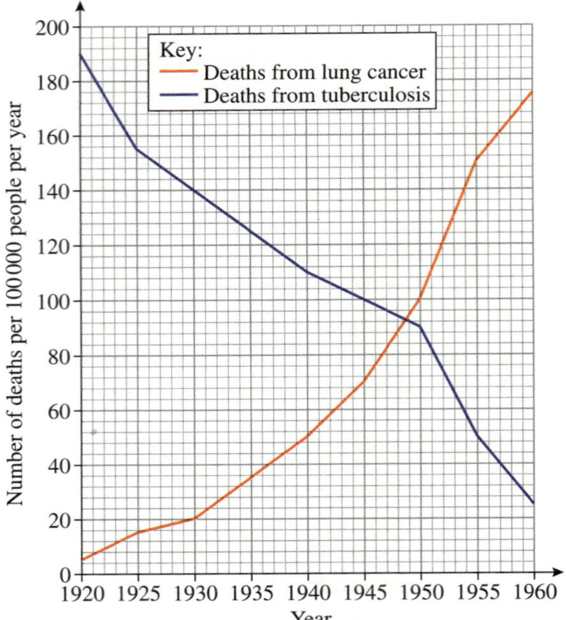

4 The graph shows the temperature of water in a pan when cooking boil-in-the-bag fish.
The instructions say cook for 20 minutes.

a For how long is the water at 100°C?

b How long is the temperature of the water below 80°C?

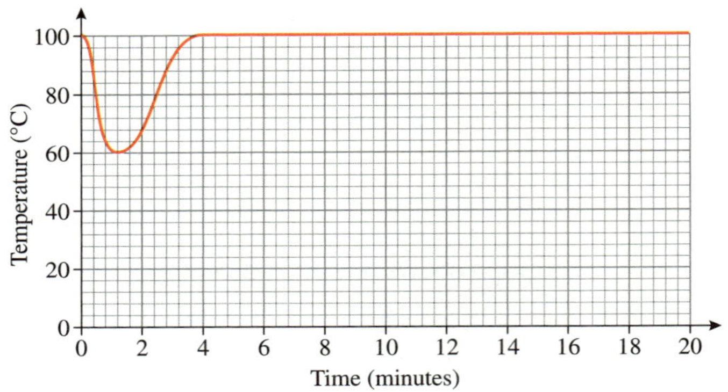

5 Atmospheric pressure can be used to forecast the weather.
This graph shows how atmospheric pressure changes over a period of about 40 hours on a Monday and Tuesday.

a How many times during the 40-hour period is the atmospheric pressure 1005 millibars?

b When is the atmospheric pressure lowest?

c For how long is the atmospheric pressure below 1005 millibars?

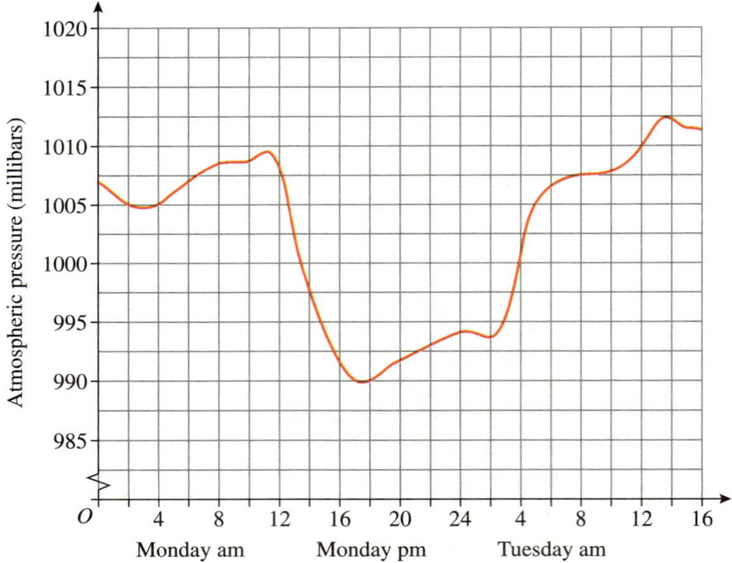

Bad weather is likely to occur if there is a quick **decrease** in atmospheric pressure.
For example: if atmospheric pressure drops by 5 or more millibars over a three-hour period, then **bad** weather can be forecast.

Better weather is likely to follow bad weather if there is a quick **increase** in atmospheric pressure.
For example: if atmospheric pressure has risen by 5 or more millibars over a three-hour period of bad weather, then **improved** weather can be forecast.

d Use the graph to forecast when bad or better weather occurs.
Explain your answer.

6 The graph shows the depth of water in a harbour on one day.

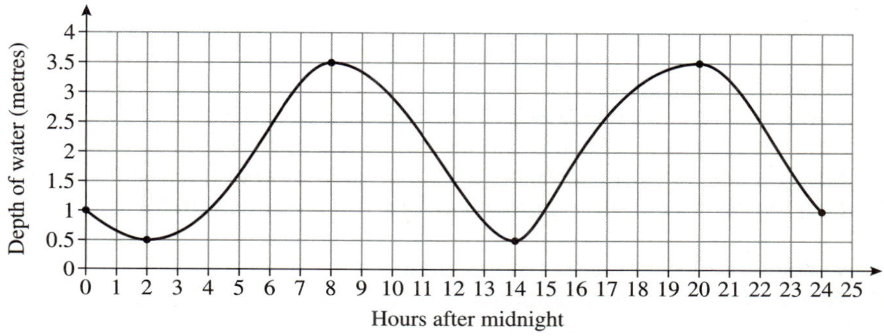

a What times are low tide?

b A loaded trawler can only enter the harbour when the depth of water is greater than 2 metres.
An empty trawler can only leave when the depth is greater than 1.5 metres.
It takes the trawler 30 minutes to enter the harbour. It takes seven hours to unload the trawler.
What is the earliest time that a trawler arriving at midnight can:
i enter the harbour **ii** leave the harbour?

7 The graph shows the average fuel consumption in miles per gallon for cars at different speeds.

a Use the graph to work out:
i the speeds where fuel consumption is maximum.
ii the speeds that the average fuel consumption is below 30 mpg.

b Comment on the idea of raising the motorway speed limit.
Use the information on the graph to help you.

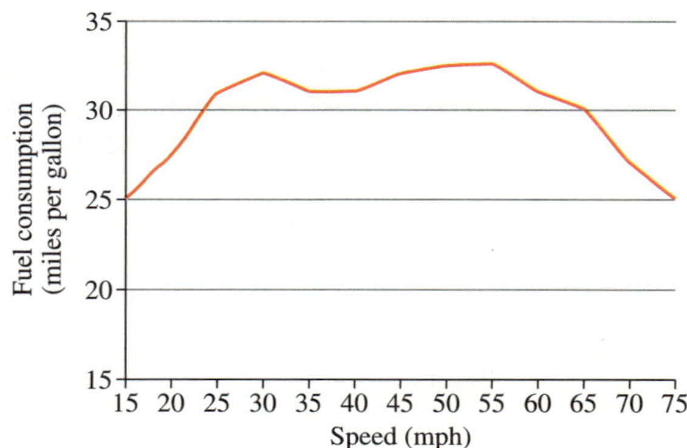

8 A farmer has 40 metres of fencing.
He uses it to make this rectangular enclosure.

a What is the area of this enclosure?

b Find the areas of some more rectangular enclosures that can be made with 40 metres of fencing.

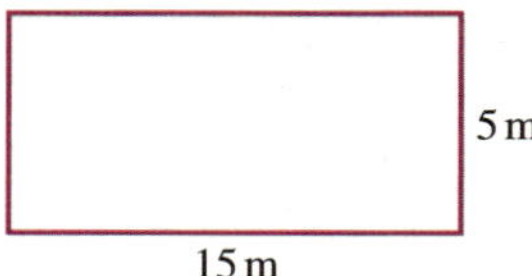

c Copy and complete this graph to show the areas of **all** the different rectangular enclosures that can be made with 40 metres of fencing.

d Give a reason for the shape of the graph.

e Repeat with 100 metres of fencing.

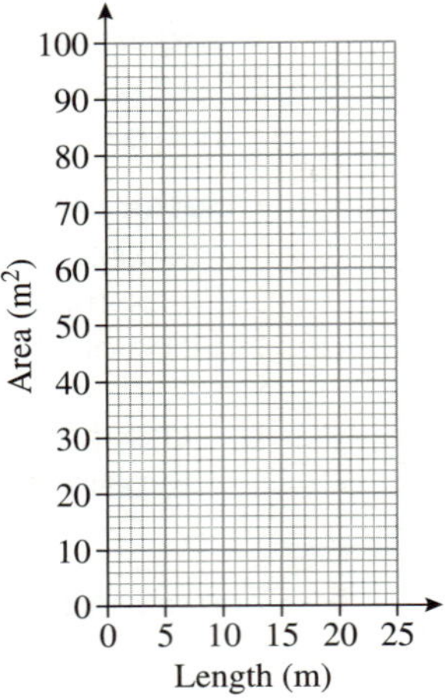

9 Sketch graphs to show:

a how the area of a circle changes as its radius increases

b how the volume of a sphere changes as its radius increases

c how the time taken to complete a 200-km journey changes with the average speed

d how the number of items purchased for £100 changes with the cost of the item.

10 Draw sketch graphs for each of these situations.

a As x increases by equal amounts, y increases by equal amounts.

b As x increases by equal amounts, y increases by amounts that get larger.

c As x increases by equal amounts, y increases by amounts that get smaller.

d As x increases by equal amounts, y decreases by equal amounts.

e As x increases by equal amounts, y decreases by amounts that get larger.

f As x increases by equal amounts, y decreases by amounts that get smaller.

11 **a** Water flows into each of these containers at a constant rate.

Sketch a graph of the depth of water against time for each container.

b The graph shows depth changes with time as water flows into a container at a constant rate. Sketch the container.

12 The graph shows postal charges for first-class letters. Explain why the graph is drawn in steps.

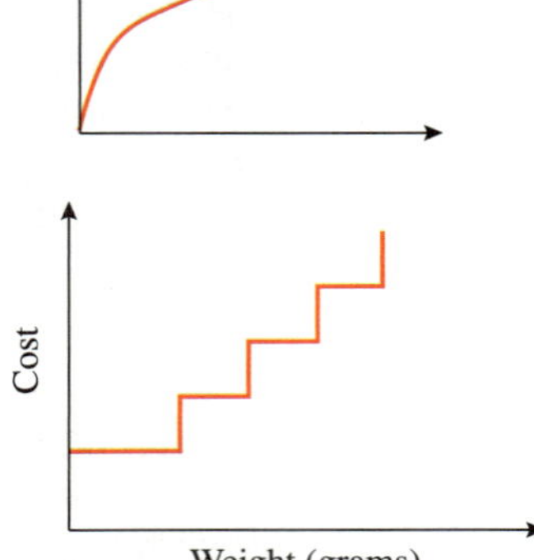

Chapter summary

- In algebra a function is a special formula that connects values of **one** letter symbol with values of **one** other letter symbol.
- Functions that give a straight-line graph are called *linear functions*. Linear functions involve only an x term and a y term and possibly a number term.
  They do not include squares, cubes or other powers.
- To draw the graph of a linear function:
  Step 1 Choose three values of x that span the grid for the graph.
  Step 2 Substitute these values of x into the function and work out the values of y.
  This can be done using a table of values.
  Write the values of x and y as coordinates (x, y).
  Step 3 Plot the coordinates on the grid and draw a straight line through them.
  Check that the three points lie on a straight line.
- To draw the graph of a linear function written in the form $2x + y = 8$, find coordinates on the x-axis and the y-axis by substituting the values $y = 0$ and $x = 0$ into the function.
- Linear graphs can be used to solve equations.
  For example, the solution of the equation $3x + 4 = 2$ is the x-coordinate of the point where the line $y = 3x + 4$ crosses the line $y = 2$
- The gradient measures the slope of a line. It can be worked out from the formula
  $\text{gradient} = \dfrac{\text{distance up}}{\text{distance across}}$
- Quadratic functions have an x^2 term. They can also have an x term and/or a number term.
  For example $y = x^2 - 1$ and $y = x^2 + 3x - 5$ are quadratic functions.
- To draw the graph of a quadratic function:
  Step 1 Complete a table of values of x and y.
  Step 2 Write a list of coordinates from the table.
  Step 3 Plot the points on a grid and join them with a smooth curve.
  Check that the graph:
  - has a maximum or minimum point
  - has a vertical line of symmetry
  - is a smooth U-shaped curve (inverted if the function includes $-x^2$).
- Quadratic graphs can be used to solve quadratic equations.
  For example, the solutions of the equation $x^2 + 2x - 1 = 0$ are the x-coordinates of the points where the line $y = x^2 + 2x - 1$ crosses the line $y = 0$ (the x-axis).
- Graphs are used in science and other real-life situations to show how one quantity changes with another.
- The gradient of a graph shows the rate of the change. The steeper the slope of the graph the faster the change.
  On a distance–time graph:
  - the gradient equals the speed, so a steeper line means faster speed
  - a straight line means constant speed
  - a horizontal straight line means zero speed.
- Graphs that show real-life situations can be curved.
  - When lines (straight or curved) slope **upwards** they show an **increasing** quantity.
  - When lines (straight or curved) slope **downwards** they show a **decreasing** quantity.

  The steeper the slope the faster the increase or decrease.

Chapter review

1 **a** On a copy of the grid, draw the graph of $y = x - 1$
b Write down the gradient of the graph.
c The line $y = -4$ crosses the line $y = x - 1$ at the point P.
What are the coordinates of P?

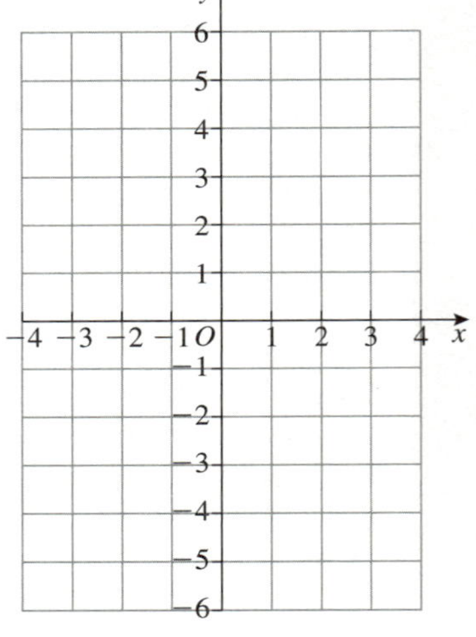

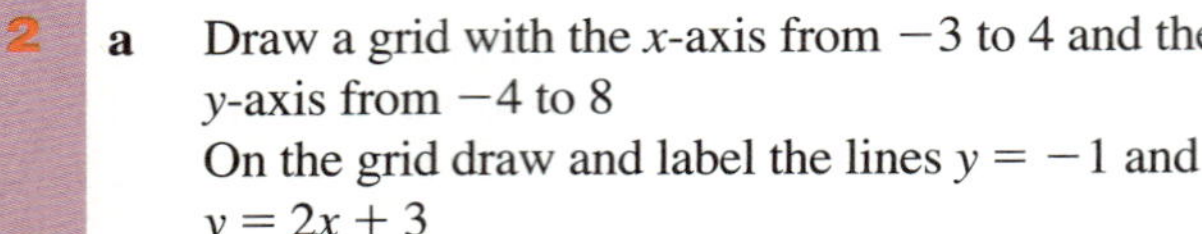

2 **a** Draw a grid with the x-axis from -3 to 4 and the y-axis from -4 to 8
On the grid draw and label the lines $y = -1$ and $y = 2x + 3$
b Write down the gradient of the graph.
c Write down the coordinates of the point where the lines $y = -1$ and $y = 2x + 3$ cross.

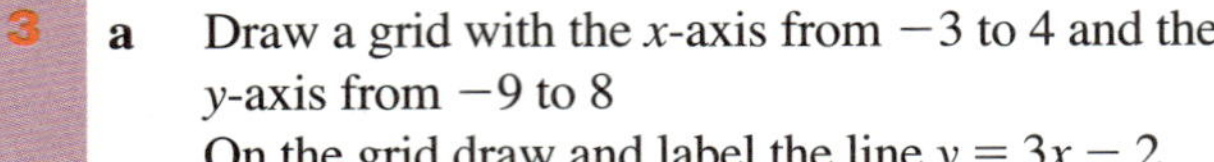

3 **a** Draw a grid with the x-axis from -3 to 4 and the y-axis from -9 to 8
On the grid draw and label the line $y = 3x - 2$
b Write down the gradient of the graph.
c The line $y = -5$ crosses $y = 3x - 2$ at Q.
Write down the coordinates of Q.
d Use the graph to solve the equation $3x - 2 = -8$

4 **a** Copy this grid and draw the graph of $x + y = 6$
b A is a point on the line $x + y = 6$
Peter says, 'The x-coordinate of A is one less than the y-coordinate of A.'
Write down the coordinates of A.

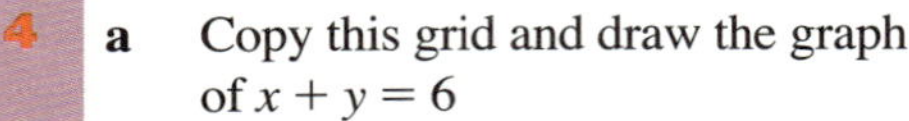

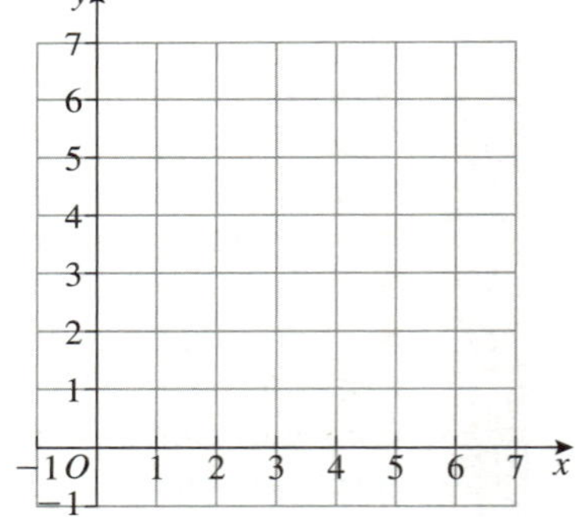

5 The line $y = 3x - 1$ goes through the point $P(-5, a)$.
What is the value of a?

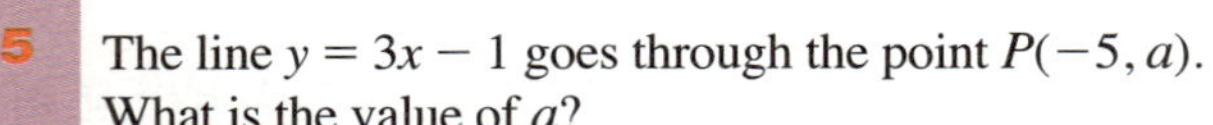

6 **a** On a copy of the grid from question **4**, draw the graph of $2x + 5y = 10$
b Show that the point $(-5, 4)$ lies on this line.

7 **a** Show that the graphs of $y = x + 2$ and $y = 6 - x$ cross at the point $(2, 4)$.
b Find the coordinates of the point where the graphs of $y = 3x - 4$ and $y = -x$ cross.

8 **a** Complete the table of values for $y = x^2 - 4$

x	-3	-2	-1	0	1	2	3
y	5	0			-3	0	

b On a copy of the grid from question **1**, draw the graph of $y = x^2 - 4$ for values of x from -3 to 3
c Write down the values of x at the point where the line $y = 2$ crosses the graph.

9 An electrician charges £C for a repair depending on t, the time taken in minutes, according to the relationship $C = 0.6t + 40$

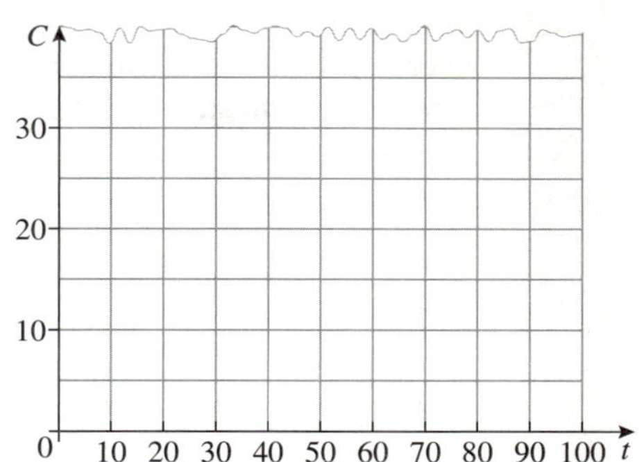

a Copy the grid with the vertical axis extended to $C = 100$

Draw the graph of $C = 0.6t + 40$

b Use the graph to find:

i how much the electrician charges for a repair lasting 20 minutes

ii the length of a repair costing £66

c Explain why a repair cannot cost less than £40

10 **a** Complete the table of values for $y = x^2 - 2x - 1$

x	-2	-1	0	1	2	3	4
y		2	-1		-1	2	7

b Draw a grid with the x-axis from -3 to 5 and the y-axis from -3 to 8

On the grid draw and label the graph of $y = x^2 - 2x - 1$ for values of x from -2 to 4

c Use the graph to solve the equation $x^2 - 2x - 1 = 0$

11 **a** Complete the table of values for $y = (2 + x)(3 - x)$.

x	-2	-1	0	1	2	3	4
y		4	6	6	4	0	

b Copy the grid from question **1**.

Draw the graph of $y = (2 + x)(3 - x)$ for values of x from -2 to 4

12 The graph shows the number of species of endangered mammals and birds in the USA between 1980 and 2000

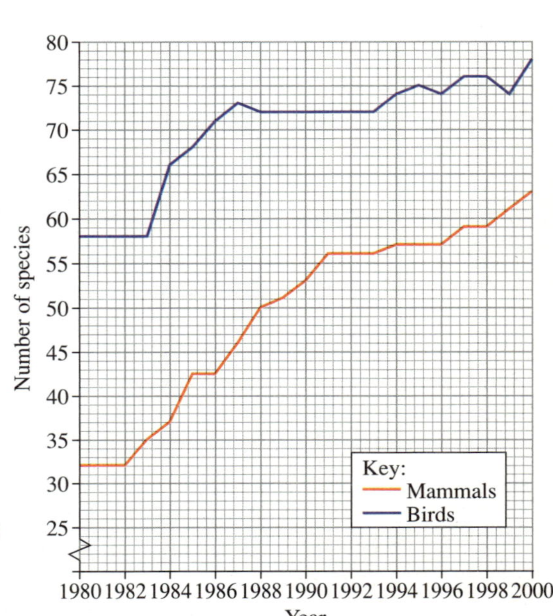

a Use the graph to work out the difference between the number of endangered mammal species and endangered bird species in 1995

b What was the longest length of time that the number of endangered bird species stayed the same.

Explain how the graph tells you this.

c When did the number of endangered bird species increase the fastest?

Explain how the graph tells you this.

d Use the graph to compare the percentage increase from 1980 to 2000 in the number of:

i endangered mammal species

ii endangered bird species.

13 The diagram shows the cross-section of a container.
Water is poured at a constant rate into the container.
Sketch a graph to show the height of water in the container as it is being filled.

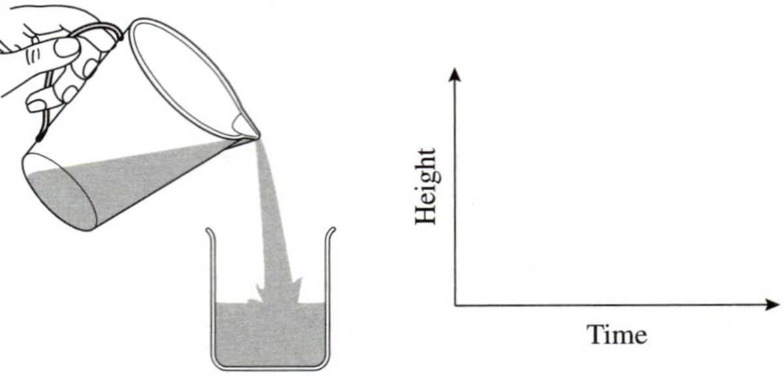

Constructions

CHAPTER 18

18.1 Two-dimensional and three-dimensional coordinates

CAN YOU REMEMBER

- How to plot (x, y) coordinates in all four quadrants on a grid?
- The properties of 2-D shapes such as rectangles and parallelograms?
- How to find the length of a line using Pythagoras' theorem?

IN THIS SECTION YOU WILL

- Use 2-D coordinates to draw and complete shapes.
- Find the coordinates of the midpoint of a line.
- Find the length of a line joining two points.
- Describe points in space using 3-D coordinates.

Two-dimensional shapes can be drawn on a grid by plotting the coordinates of the vertices. A missing *vertex* can be found by using the properties of the shape, for example knowing that the sides are of equal length.

Example 1

a On a square grid plot the points A (3, 2), B (5, 2) and C (5, 6).

b Plot the point D such that $ABCD$ is a rectangle.

c Write down the coordinates of point D.

Solution 1

a, b

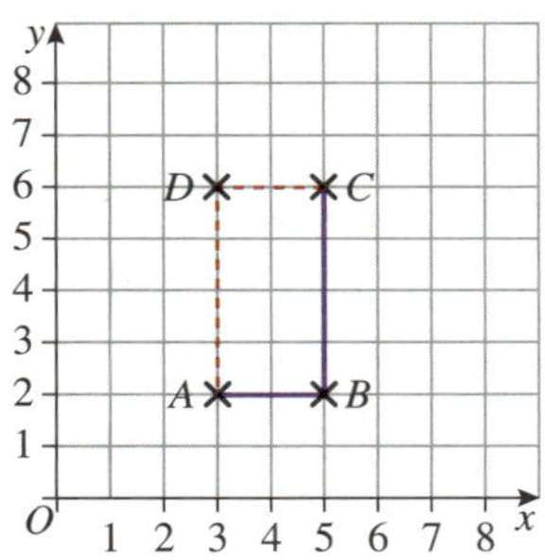

c The coordinates of D are (3, 6).

Example 2

a Find the coordinates of the midpoint of AB.
b Calculate the length of the line AB.

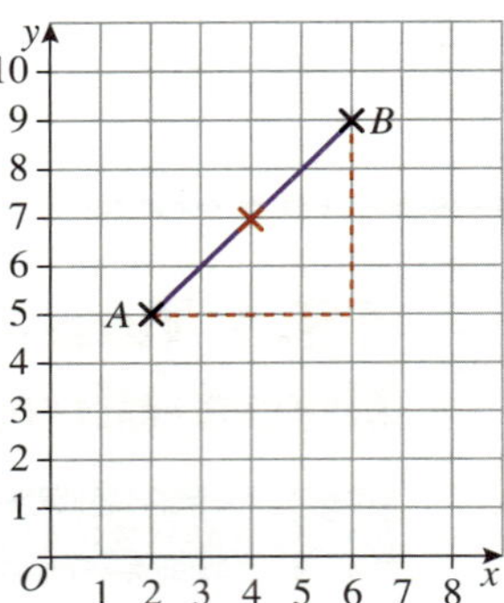

Solution 2

a By measuring the line AB or counting the squares, mark the midpoint.
The coordinates of the midpoint are (4, 7).

b Draw a right-angled triangle ABC on the graph with AB as the hypotenuse.
Find the lengths of the shorter sides of the triangle by counting squares or by finding the difference between the coordinates A (2, 5) and B (6, 9).
Difference in x-coordinates (length AC) is $6 - 2 = 4$
Difference in y-coordinates (length BC) is $9 - 5 = 4$
Then use Pythagoras' theorem to calculate the length of AB.
Using $c^2 = a^2 + b^2$
$AB^2 = 4^2 + 4^2 = 16 + 16 = 32$
$AB = \sqrt{32} = 5.7$ units.

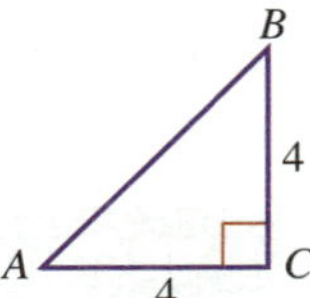

The midpoint of a line joining two points is given by:
(mean of the two x-coordinates, mean of the two y-coordinates)

Example 3

Find the midpoint of the line AB joining the points A (2, 5) and B (6, 9) without drawing a graph.

Solution 3

Midpoint of x-coordinates $= \dfrac{2+6}{2} = 4$ Midpoint of y-coordinates $= \dfrac{5+9}{2} = 7$

Midpoint of AB is (4, 7).

This is the same answer as found by the drawing method in Example 2

Exercise A

For questions **1–3** draw a grid with x- and y-values from −4 to 8

1 $EFGH$ is a square.
The coordinates of E, F and G are (4, 5), (7, 5) and (7, 2) respectively.

a Plot E, F and G on a grid.
b Plot the point H on the grid to complete the square.
c Write down the coordinates of H.

2 $ABCD$ is a rectangle.
$A = (2, -3)$, $B = (-3, -3)$, $C = (-3, 5)$

a Plot A, B and C on a grid. **b** Work out the coordinates of D.

3 $PQRS$ is a parallelogram.
$P = (-2, 3)$, $Q = (3, 3)$, $R = (5, -1)$
a Plot P, Q and R on a grid. **b** Work out the two possible coordinates of S.

4 The diagram shows four lines.
Write down the coordinates of the midpoint of:
a AB
b CD
c EF
d GH.

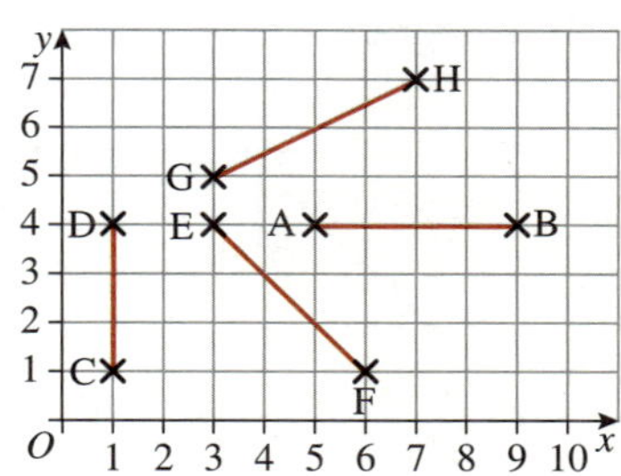

5 $ABCD$ is a parallelogram.

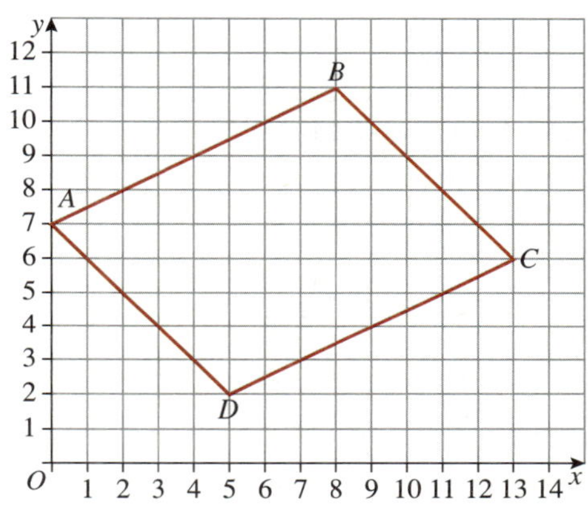

a Write down the coordinates of the midpoint of:
i AB **ii** BC **iii** CD **iv** AD.
b Calculate the lengths of the sides of the parallelogram.
Leave your answers as square roots.

6 Work out:
i the midpoint of each of the following pairs of points
ii the length of the line joining the two points.
a A (3, 4) and B (5, 8)
b C (−3, 2) and D (1, 6)
c E (0, −1) and F (5, 3)
d G (−2, −6) and H (−4, −4)

7 Triangle ABC has vertices A (−2, 1), B (3, 4) and C (1, −1).
Work out the coordinates of the midpoint of each side of the triangle.

8 The midpoint of a line PQ is (9.5, 3).
P is the point (7, −2).
Work out the coordinates of Q.

9 $EFGH$ is a rectangle.
$E = (-2, 2)$, $F = (1, 2)$, $G = (1, -2)$
a Work out the coordinates of H.
b Work out the coordinates of the midpoint of:
i FG **ii** GH.

10 S is the point (−5, 1).
The midpoint of the line ST is (−1, −2).
Work out the coordinates of T.

Three-dimensional coordinates can be used to represent points in space.

Example 4

The diagram shows a cuboid drawn on a three-dimensional grid.

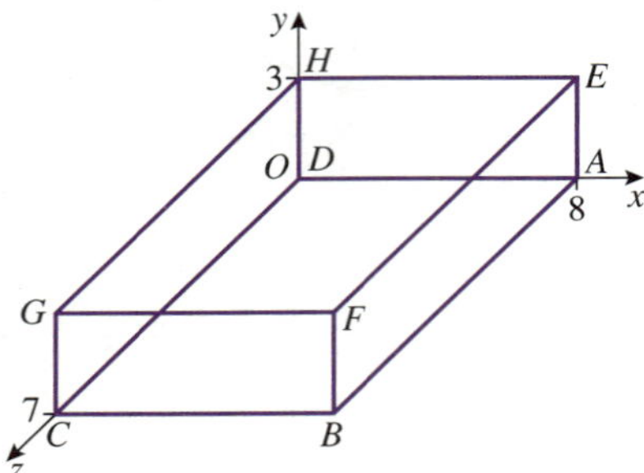

Each vertex has three coordinates (x, y, z) representing the distances along the x, y and z axes.

Point A has coordinates (8, 0, 0).
Point H has coordinates (0, 3, 0).
Point C has coordinates (0, 0, 7).

Write down the 3-D coordinates of points B and F.

Solution 4

Point B is 8 units in the x-direction, 0 units in the y-direction and 7 units in the z-direction.

B has coordinates (8, 0, 7).

Point F is 8 units in the x-direction, 3 units in the y-direction and 7 units in the z-direction.

F has coordinates (8, 3, 7).

Exercise B

1 The diagram shows a cuboid drawn on a 3-D grid.
A is the point (0, 0, 0).
B is the point (5, 0, 0).
D is the point (0, 0, 10).
E is the point (0, 3, 0).
Write down the 3-D coordinates of
a C **b** F **c** G **d** H.

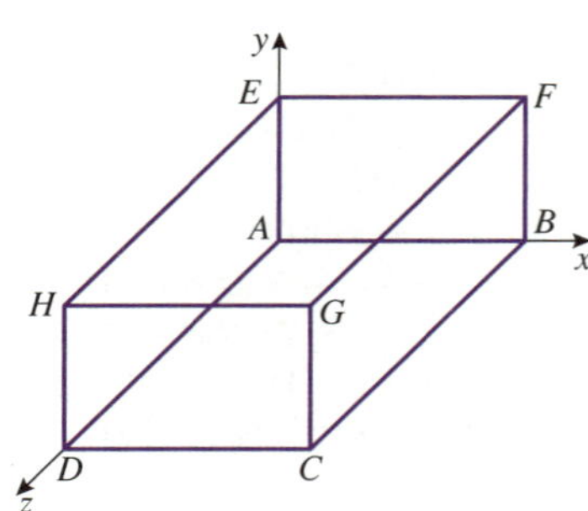

2 The diagram shows a cuboid drawn on a 3-D grid.
B is the point (9, 0, 0).
G is the point (9, 3, 8).
Write down the 3-D coordinates of
a E **b** F **c** H.

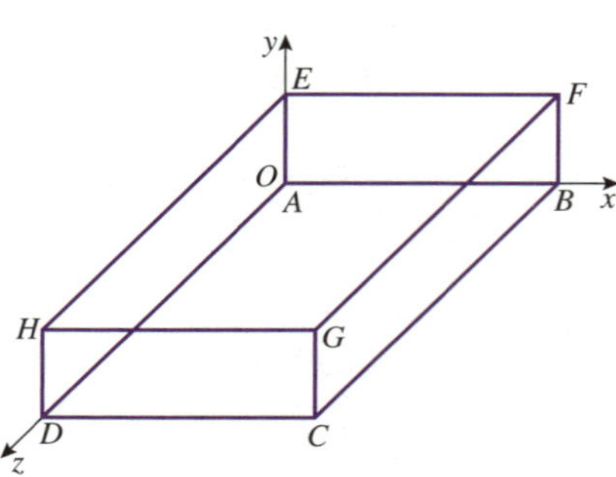

3 Which of the following 3-D coordinates are for vertex G in the diagram?

a (9, 2, 7)
b (7, 2, 9)
c (7, 9, 2)
d (2, 7, 9)

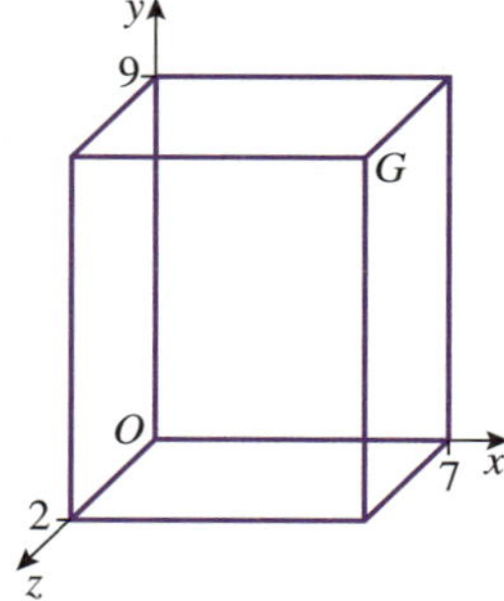

4

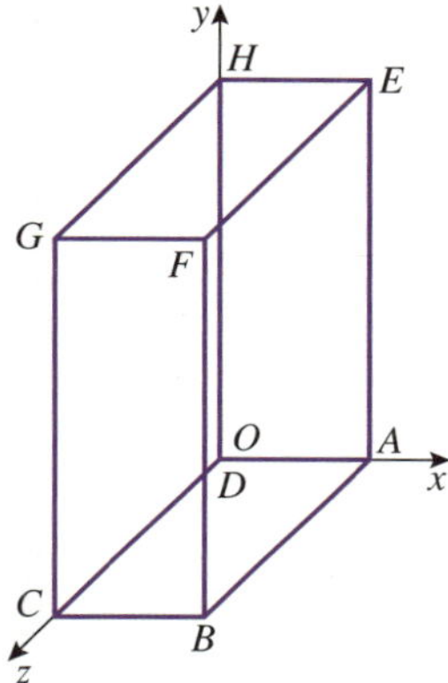

This 3-D diagram shows a cuboid.
F has 3-D coordinates (4, 11, 6).

Write down the coordinates of the other vertices of the cuboid.

5 The 3-D diagram shows a cuboid.

a Write down the coordinates of
i A **ii** F **iii** H.

b Work out the volume of the cuboid.

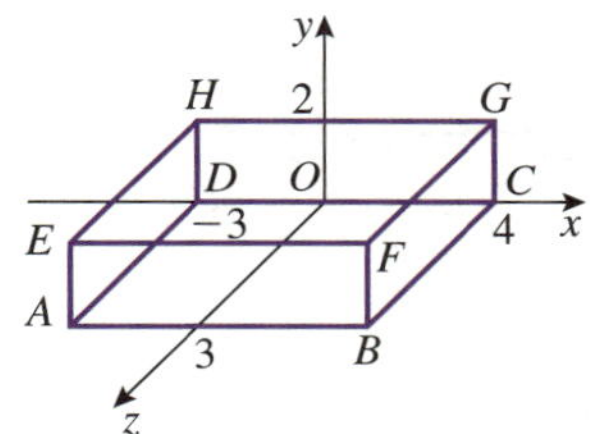

18.2 Constructions and loci

CAN YOU REMEMBER

- That 'bisect' means to divide into two equal parts?
- How to use a pair of compasses to draw a circle accurately?
- How to construct a triangle using a ruler and compasses?
- How to use and draw scale diagrams?

IN THIS SECTION YOU WILL

- Learn how to construct the perpendicular bisector of a straight line.
- Learn how to construct the bisector of an angle.
- Understand the meaning of the words 'locus' and 'loci'.
- Learn how to draw the locus of points with given rules.

The *perpendicular bisector* of a line bisects the line (divides it into two equal sections) at an angle of 90°.

The perpendicular bisector of the line AB is shown.

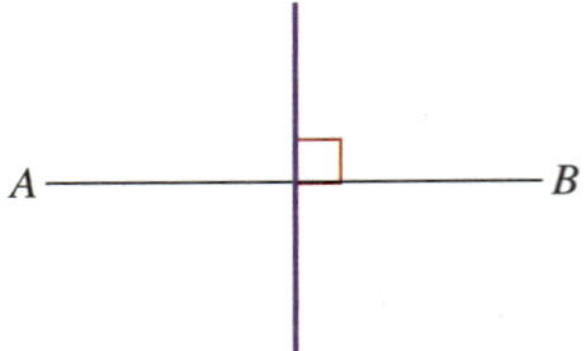

All the points on the perpendicular bisector of AB are *equidistant* from A and B (an equal distance from A and from B).

The perpendicular bisector of a line can be constructed accurately using a ruler and compasses.

Example 1

Draw a line AB of length 7 cm.
Using ruler and compasses only, construct the perpendicular bisector of AB.

Solution 1

Step 1: Draw line AB accurately.

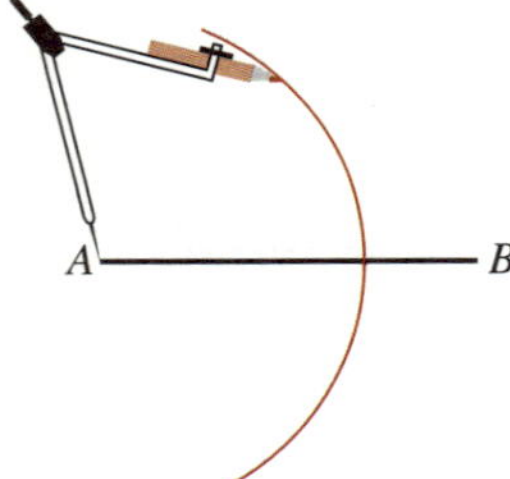

Step 2: Open the compasses to a radius greater than half the length of AB.
Keep the compasses at this setting throughout the construction.
Put the compass point at A and draw an arc through the line AB.

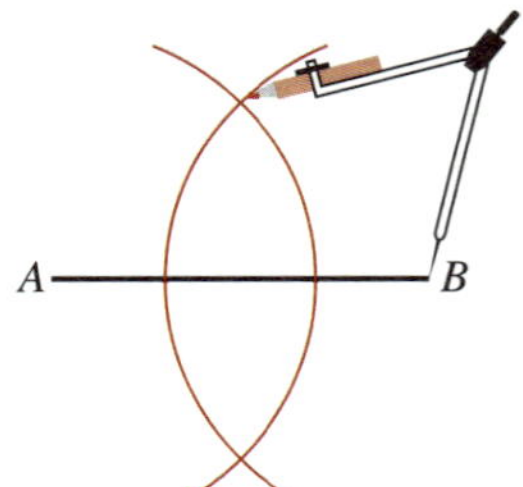

Step 3: Repeat Step 2 with the compass point at B.

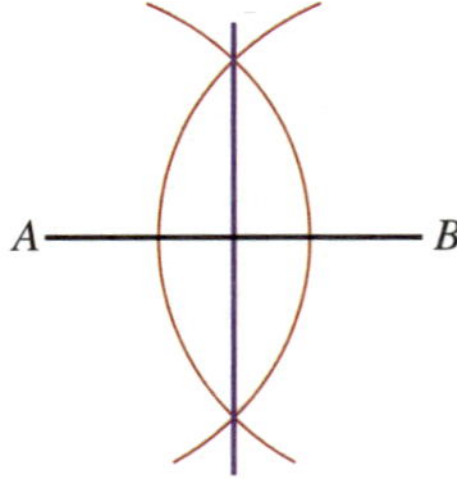

Step 4: Join the points of intersection of the two arcs with a straight line.
This line is the perpendicular bisector of AB.
Leave in all the arcs to show how the construction was drawn.

Other lines can be constructed perpendicular to a given line.

Example 2

Use ruler and compasses to construct a perpendicular line from point P to the line shown.

×P

Solution 2

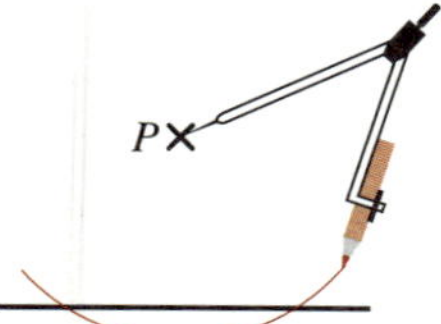

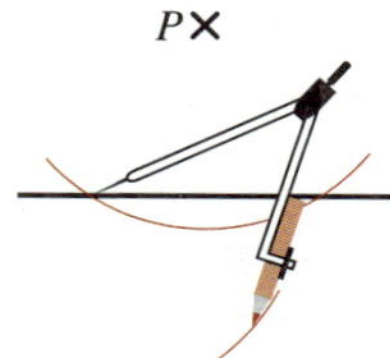

Step 1: Open the compasses to a radius greater than the distance between point P and the line. Put the compass point on P and draw an arc cutting the line in two places.

Step 2: Put the compass point at the first point of intersection and draw another arc below the line.

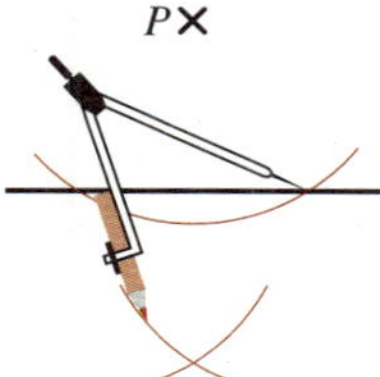

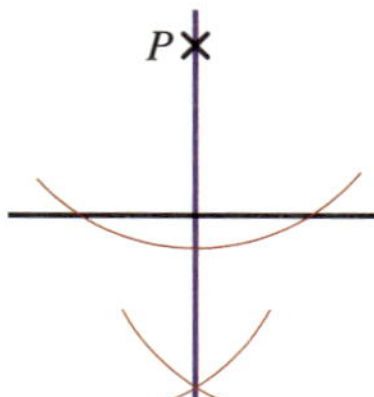

Step 3: Keeping the compasses at the same radius, repeat Step 2 from the other point of intersection. Make sure the arcs cross as shown.

Step 4: Join the intersection of these two arcs to point P with a straight line. This line is perpendicular to the original line.

Example 3

Draw a line perpendicular to AB such that angle A is 90°.

Solution 3

The perpendicular line must cut AB at A.

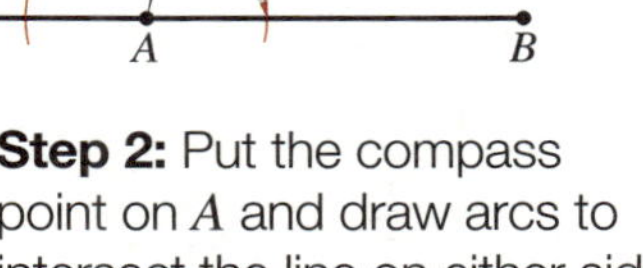

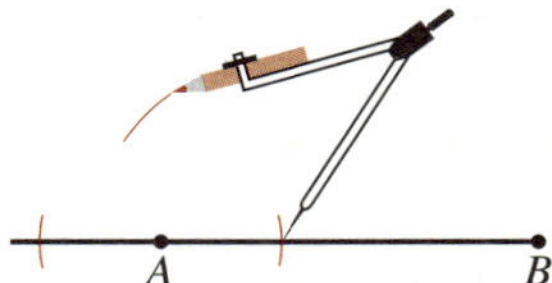

Step 1: Extend the line past point A.

Step 2: Put the compass point on A and draw arcs to intersect the line on either side of A.

Step 3: Open your compasses wider. Put the compass point on the first point of intersection of the line and draw an arc above (or below) the line.

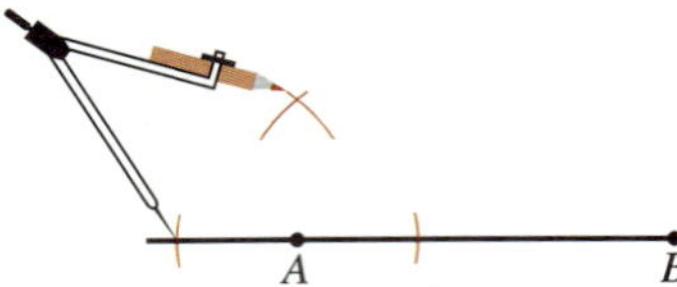

Step 4: Keeping the compasses at the same radius, repeat Step 3 from the other point of intersection. The two arcs should intersect.

Step 5: Join point A to the point where the arcs intersect. This line is perpendicular to AB and forms a 90° angle at A.

This construction can also be used to draw a right-angled triangle.

An *angle bisector* is a line that bisects an angle.
Any point on the angle bisector is equidistant from the lines that form the angle.
The angle bisector can be constructed accurately using a ruler and compasses.

Example 4

Using ruler and compasses only, construct the bisector of angle A.

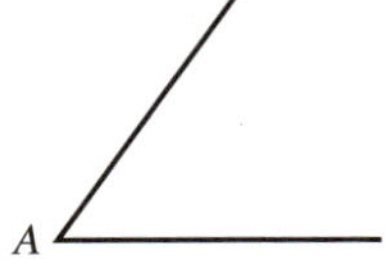

Solution 4

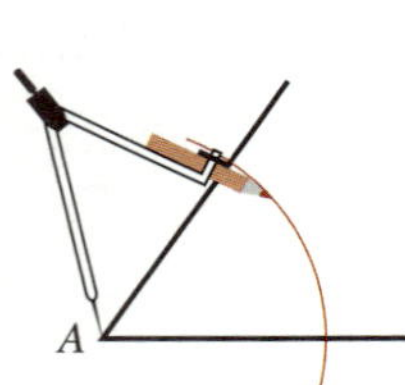

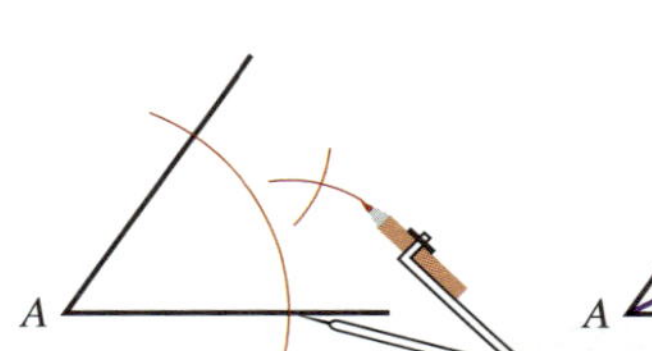

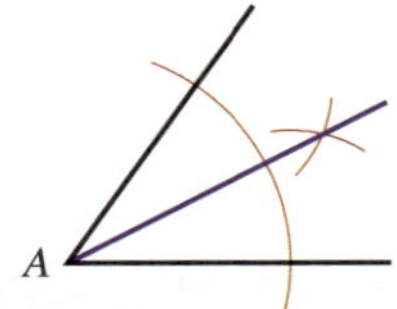

Step 1: Put the point of the compasses on A. Draw an arc to cut both lines.

Step 2: Put the compass point on the intersection of the arc and one line. Draw an arc inside the angle.

Step 3: Repeat Step 2 with compasses on the intersection of the arc and the other line. The two new arcs should intersect.

Step 4: Join the point of intersection of these two arcs to point A. This line is the angle bisector of angle A. Leave in all the arcs.

Exercise A

1 Draw each line to the size stated, leaving space for the construction.
Using ruler and compasses only, construct the perpendicular bisector of each line.

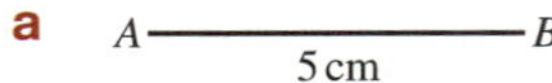

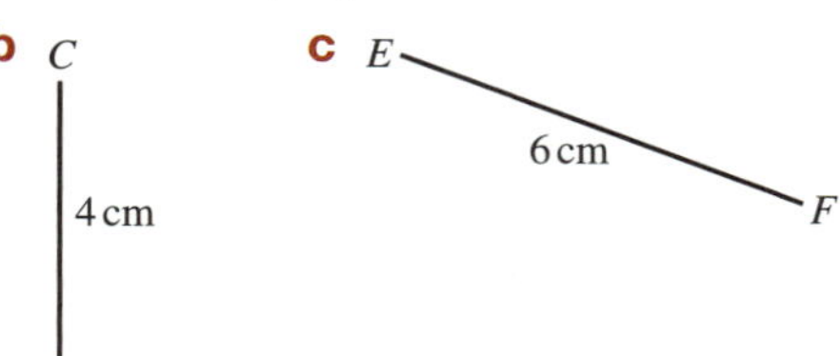

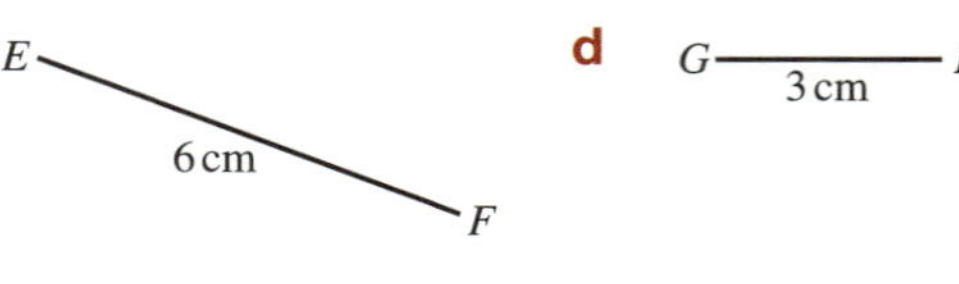

2 Copy the following diagrams.
Using ruler and compasses only, construct the angle bisector.

a Angle $ABC = 60°$

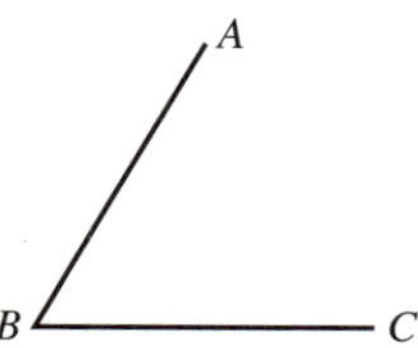

Check that each new angle measures 30°.

b Angle $DEF = 40°$

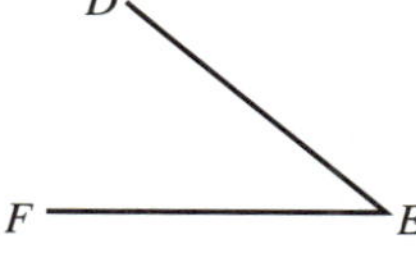

Check that each new angle measures 20°.

c Angle $LMN = 130°$

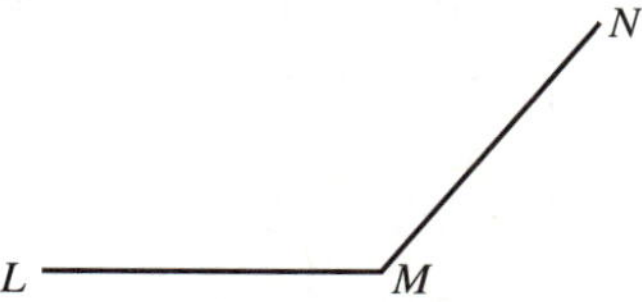

Check that each new angle measures 65°.

d Angle $PQR = 150°$

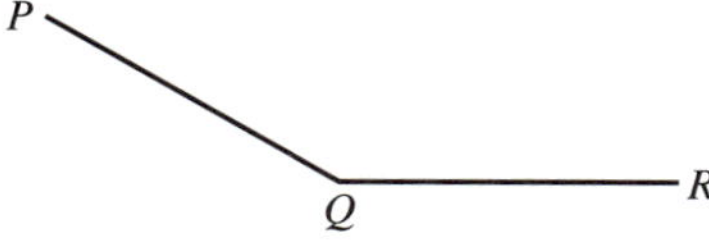

Check that each new angle measures 75°.

3 Copy the following diagrams.
Using ruler and compasses only, construct a perpendicular line from the point to the line.

a

b

4 Draw a line AB 8 cm long.
Using ruler and compasses only, construct the perpendicular bisector of AB.
Use compasses to mark a point 10 cm from A on the perpendicular bisector.

5 Use a protractor to draw an angle of 70°.
Using ruler and compasses only, construct the bisector of the angle.
Mark the point on the bisector which is 3 cm from the angle.

6 Use ruler and compasses only to:

a construct an equilateral triangle ABC of side 7 cm

b construct the bisector of angle A. Draw it long enough to intersect BC

c measure and write down the distance from angle A to the intersection with BC.

7 Use ruler and compasses only to:

a construct triangle PQR with $PQ = 8$ cm, $QR = 7$ cm and $PR = 4.5$ cm

b construct the perpendicular bisector of QR

c mark the point, S, where the perpendicular bisector cuts PQ

d measure and write down the distance from the midpoint of QR to S.

8 The diagram shows a sketch of a right-angled triangle.
Using ruler and compasses only, construct an accurate drawing of the triangle.

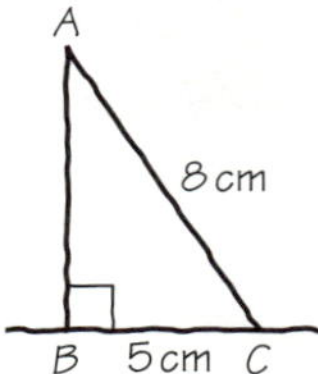

9 **a** Draw a large triangle.
b Using ruler and compasses only, construct the perpendicular bisectors of each side of your triangle.
c These bisectors should meet at a point. Mark the point Y.

A *locus* (plural *loci*) is the path of a point which moves according to a rule.

The locus of a point which moves so that it is always 2 cm away from a fixed point C is a circle of radius 2 cm with centre C.

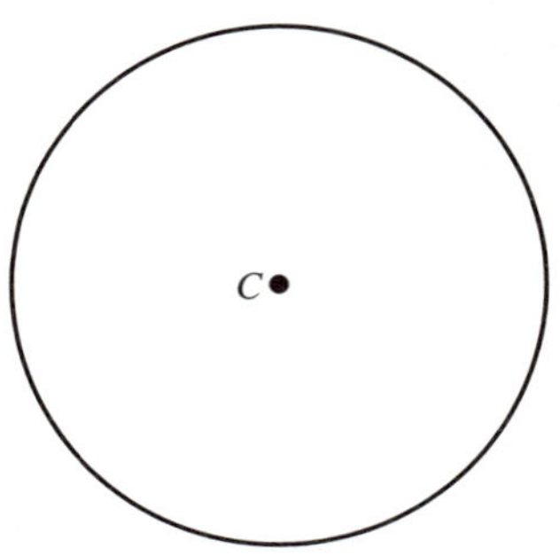

Every point on the circumference of the circle is 2 cm from C.

The locus of all the points that are equidistant from two fixed points is the perpendicular bisector of the line joining the points.

locus
A B

The locus of all the points that are equidistant from two straight lines that form an angle is the angle bisector.

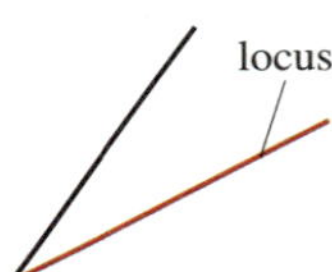

Example 5

The diagram shows a triangle ABC.

a Make an accurate drawing of the triangle.
Draw the locus of points that are 3 cm from B.
b Shade the region inside the triangle which is less than 3 cm from B.

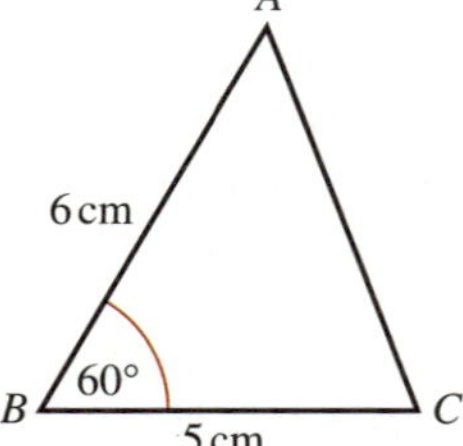

Solution 5

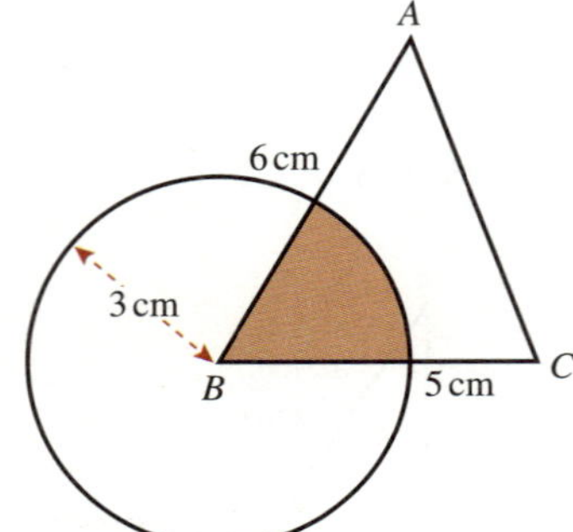

a The locus of points that are 3 cm from B is a circle, centre B and radius 3 cm.
b The shaded region shows the area within the triangle which is less than 3 cm from B.

Example 6

A line ST is 8 cm long.
Draw the locus of points that are exactly 2 cm from the line.

Solution 6

The locus has two straight edges and two semicircular ends.
All points on the locus are 2 cm from the line ST.

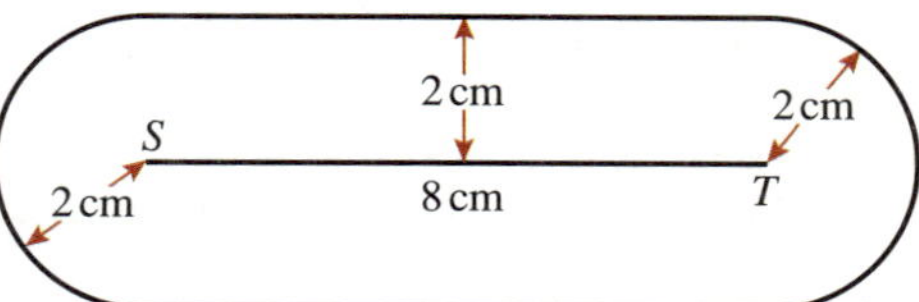

Example 7

The diagram shows a triangular cornfield.

A scarecrow stands in the field.
It is equidistant from BC and AC and 6 m from A.

Using ruler and compasses, find the position of the scarecrow.

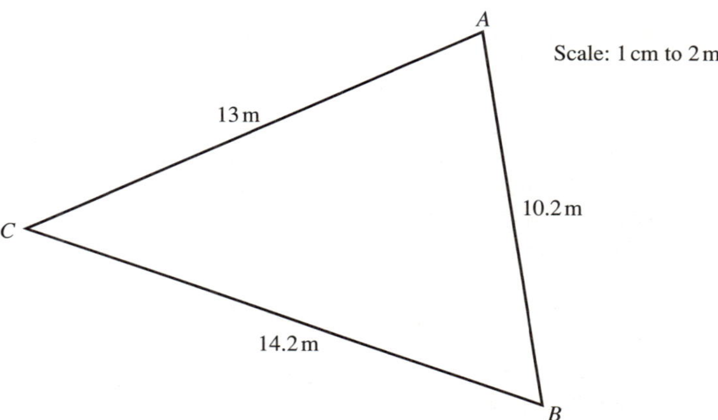

Solution 7

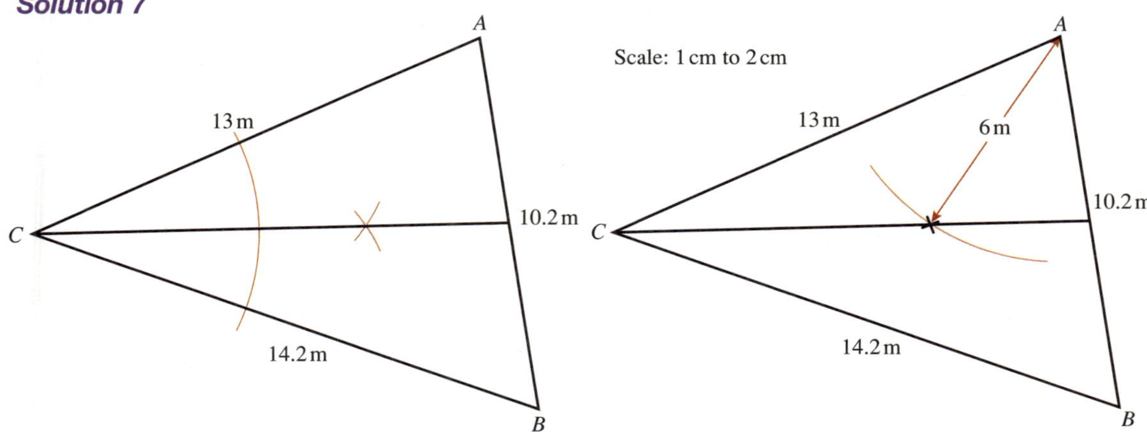

All points equidistant from BC and AC lie on the angle bisector of C.

The points 6 m from A lie on a circle with centre A and radius 6 m.

6 m is represented by 3 cm on the diagram.

Draw the arc of the circle of radius 3 cm and centre A which is inside the triangle.

The scarecrow stands where the arc and the angle bisector intersect (marked with a cross).

Exercise B

1 A, B and C are three points on a straight line.

Draw the line accurately.
Draw the locus of points that are:

a 3 cm from A **b** 4.5 cm from B **c** 2 cm from C.

2 Draw a line AB 6 cm long.
Construct the locus of points that are exactly 3 cm from AB.

3 Draw a rectangle with length 4 cm and width 3 cm.
Draw the locus of points outside the rectangle that are 1 cm from the rectangle.

4 The diagram shows an equilateral triangle of side 9 cm.

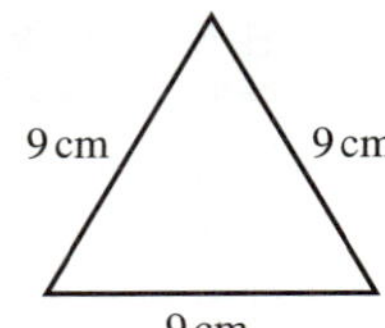

a **i** Sketch the triangle.
ii Sketch the locus of points outside the triangle that are 1 cm from the triangle.

b Draw the equilateral triangle using a ruler and protractor.
Remember: the angles of an equilateral triangle are 60°.

c Using ruler and compasses only, show all the points inside the triangle that are at least 4 cm from each vertex.

5 The diagram shows a rectangle $PQRS$.
Copy the diagram.
Using ruler and compasses only, construct the locus of points inside the rectangle that are equidistant from RQ and RS.

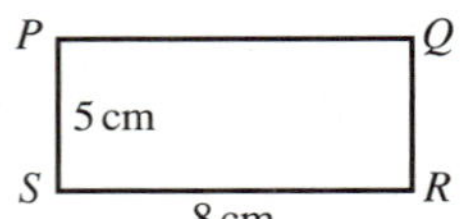

6 A dog is tied to the corner of a shed by a rope of length 4 m.
Copy the diagram and construct the locus of points that show the boundary of where the dog can go.

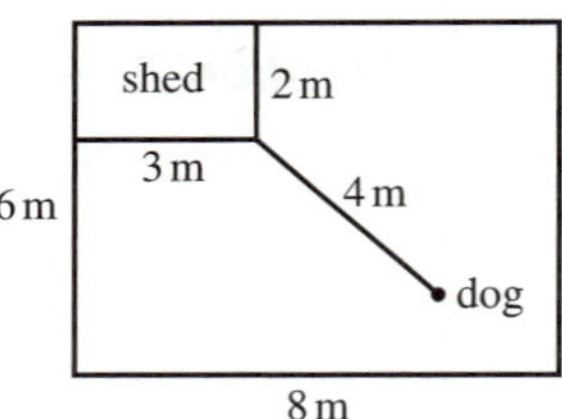

7 A radio transmitter is designed to give good reception in an area between 50 km and 150 km from the transmitter.
Using a scale of 1 cm to 25 km, draw a scale diagram to show the area within which there is good reception.

8 The diagram shows a sketch of a rectangular field.

a Make a scale drawing of the field using a scale of 1 cm to 50 m.

b A well is 200 m from corner A and 325 m from corner B.
Mark the position of the well on the scale drawing.

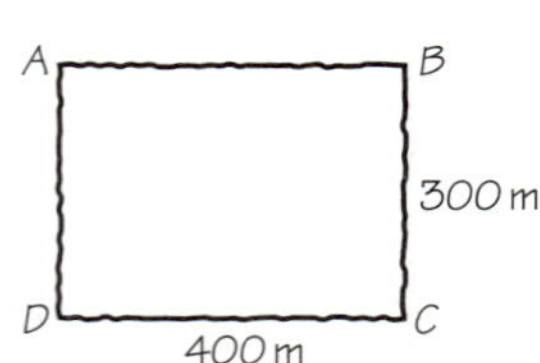

9 Two boats X and Y are 30 km apart. Boat X is due west of boat Y.

a Use a scale of 1 cm to 5 km to make a scale drawing showing the position of the two boats.

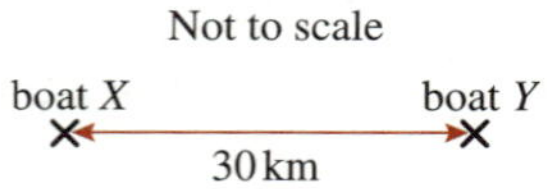

b Shade the region which is less than 15 km from boat X and less than 25 km from boat Y.

10 A rectangular plot of land $PQRS$ measures 10 m by 7 m.
A gold coin is buried on the plot of land. The coin is equidistant from PQ and QR and equidistant from R and S.

a Using a scale of 1 cm to 1 m, draw the plot of land.

b Using ruler and compasses only, find and mark the position of the gold coin.

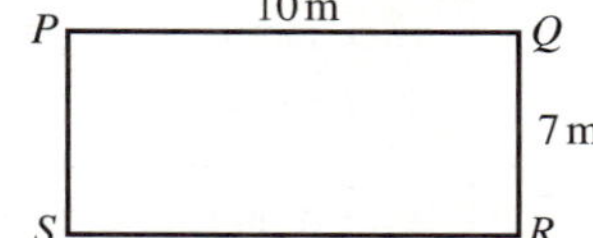

Chapter summary

- The midpoint of a line joining two points is given by (mean of the two x-coordinates, mean of the two y-coordinates).
- Three-dimensional coordinates can be used to represent points in space, e.g. F is the point (6, 5, 8).
- The *perpendicular bisector* of a line bisects the line at an angle of 90°.
- An *angle bisector* is a line that bisects an angle.
- A *locus* (plural *loci*) is the path of a point which moves according to a rule.
- The locus of all the points at a distance d from point A is a circle centre A, radius d.

- The locus of all the points that are equidistant from two fixed points is the perpendicular bisector of the line joining the two points.
- The locus of all the points that are equidistant from two straight lines that form an angle is the angle bisector.

Chapter review

1 A rectangle $ABCD$ has vertices at A (−2, 6), B (−2, 1) and C (4, 1).

a Plot these points on a grid.

b Work out the coordinates of D.

2 The diagram shows the line PQ which joins points P (−1, −3) and Q (5, 2).

a Find the coordinates of the midpoint of PQ.

b Calculate the length of PQ.
Leave your answer as a square root.

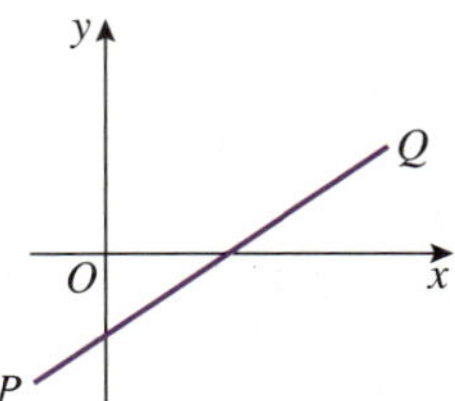

3 Draw a line ST 10 cm long.

a Use ruler and compasses to construct the perpendicular bisector of ST.
You **must** show clearly all your construction arcs.

b Mark a point on the perpendicular bisector which is 6 cm from T.

4 The diagram shows a triangle ABC.

a On a copy of the diagram draw accurately the locus of points that are 3 cm from C.

b Shade the region inside the triangle which is more than 3 cm from C.

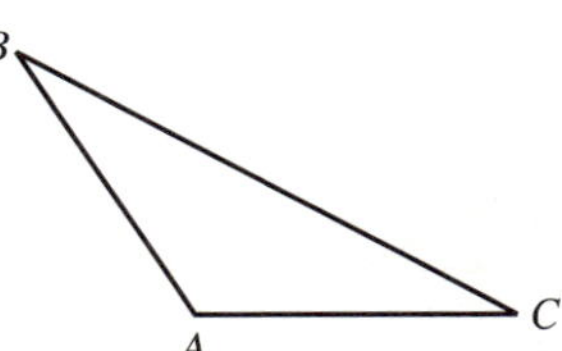

5 Draw an angle of 110°.
Label it angle *A*.
Use ruler and compasses to construct the bisector of the angle *A*.
You **must** show clearly all your construction arcs.

6 The diagram shows a cuboid drawn on a 3-D grid.
A is the point (0, 0, 0).
B is the point (7, 0, 0).
D is the point (0, 0, 9).
E is the point (0, 5, 0).
Write down the 3-D coordinates of

a *C* **b** *F*
c *G* **d** *H*.

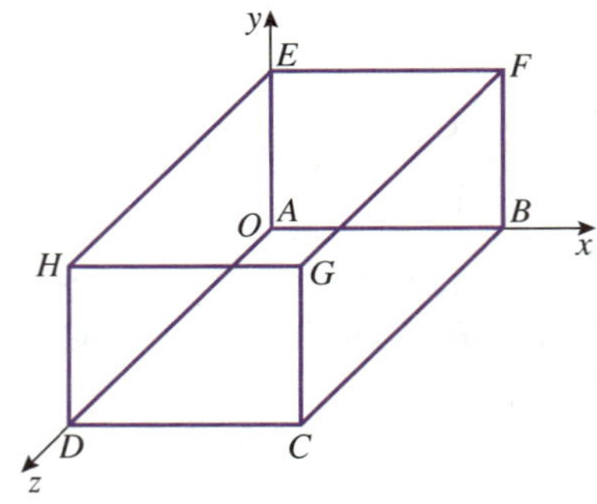

7 *A* is the point (2, 9).
The midpoint of the line *AC* is the point *B* with coordinates (7, 13).
Work out the coordinates of *C*.

8 Draw a line *AB* 6 cm long.
Using ruler and compasses only, construct a line perpendicular to *AB* which goes through point *B*.

9 **a** Draw a square of side 4 cm.
b Draw the locus of points outside the square that are 2 cm from the square.

10 *ABC* is an equilateral triangle of side 6 cm.
a Using ruler and compasses only, construct the triangle.
b A point *T* is inside the triangle.
T is nearer to *AB* than to *AC*.
T is more than 5 cm from *C*.
T is more than 3 cm from *B*.
Shade the region in which *T* could lie.

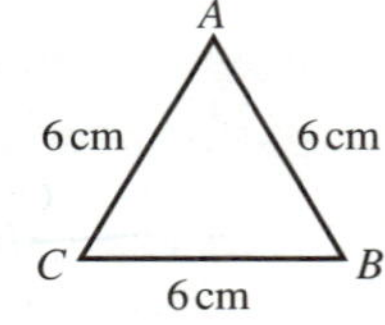

11 Peter wants to plant a tree in his garden.
The garden is shown drawn to scale.
The line *AD* represents the outside wall of Peter's house.
The tree must be closer to the wall *AB* than to the house.
It must also be closer to *C* than *D*.
Copy the diagram and shade the area in which the tree may be planted.
All your construction lines **must** be shown clearly.

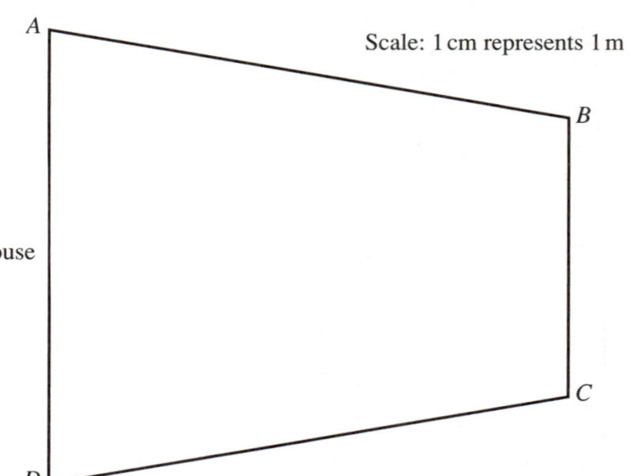

Cumulative frequency

CHAPTER 19

19.1 Cumulative frequency and cumulative frequency graphs

CAN YOU REMEMBER

- How to interpret frequency tables?
- How to plot coordinates?
- The position of the median in a set of data?

IN THIS SECTION YOU WILL

- Learn how to calculate cumulative frequencies.
- Learn how to draw cumulative frequency graphs.
- Interpret data from cumulative frequency graphs.

Cumulative frequency is a running total of all the data up to a certain point. When the data is continuous, a *cumulative frequency diagram* or graph can be drawn.

Example 1

The frequency distribution shows the heights (in metres) of 40 buildings.

Height (h)	Frequency
$8 \leqslant h < 10$	1
$10 \leqslant h < 12$	5
$12 \leqslant h < 14$	12
$14 \leqslant h < 16$	16
$16 \leqslant h < 18$	4
$18 \leqslant h < 20$	2

a Calculate the cumulative frequencies for the data.
b Construct a cumulative frequency graph for this data.

Solution 1

a Add extra columns to the table.

This is the *upper bound* for the class interval $8 \leqslant h < 10$

Height (h)	Frequency	Height (h)	Cumulative frequency
$8 \leqslant h < 10$	1	< 10	1
$10 \leqslant h < 12$	5	< 12	$1 + 5 = 6$
$12 \leqslant h < 14$	12	< 14	$6 + 12 = 18$
$14 \leqslant h < 16$	16	< 16	$18 + 16 = 34$
$16 \leqslant h < 18$	4	< 18	$34 + 4 = 38$
$18 \leqslant h < 20$	2	< 20	$38 + 2 = 40$

1 building is less than 10 metres high.

6 buildings are less than 12 metres high.

b To draw the cumulative frequency diagram plot the cumulative frequency value at the upper bound of each class interval.

It is useful to redraw the table using the upper class bound as the label in the left-hand column.

Height (x)	Cumulative frequency	Coordinate to plot
$x < 10$	1	(10, 1)
$x < 12$	6	(12, 6)
$x < 14$	18	(14, 18)
$x < 16$	34	(16, 34)
$x < 18$	38	(18, 38)
$x < 20$	40	(20, 40)

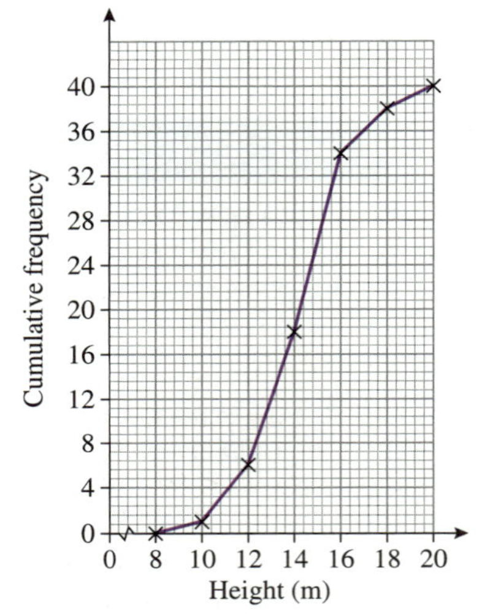

The point (8, 0) can also be plotted as it is known that there are no values below 8

The points are then joined with a curve or straight lines.

Example 1 shows the typical shape of a cumulative frequency graph.

Exercise A

1 The numbers of brothers and sisters of 30 students are given in the table.

Number of brothers and sisters	Frequency	Number of brothers and sisters	Cumulative frequency
0	3	$\leqslant 0$	3
1	12	$\leqslant 1$	15
2	9	$\leqslant 2$	24
3	5	$\leqslant 3$	29
4	1	$\leqslant 4$	30

Work out the remaining values for the cumulative frequency column.

2 A dice is rolled 50 times. The scores are shown in the table.

Score	Frequency	Score	Cumulative frequency
1	8	$\leqslant 1$	8
2	9	$\leqslant 2$	17
3	7	$\leqslant 3$	24
4	10	$\leqslant 4$	34
5	5	$\leqslant 5$	39
6	11	$\leqslant 6$	50

Copy and complete the table.

3 The table shows the lengths (in cm) of 100 sausages.

Length of sausage, l (cm)	Frequency	Length (cm)	Cumulative frequency
$5 \leqslant l < 6$	23	$l < 6$	23
$6 \leqslant l < 7$	38	$l < 7$	61
$7 \leqslant l < 8$	30	$l < 8$	91
$8 \leqslant l < 9$	9	$l < 9$	100

a Copy and complete the table.
b Draw a cumulative frequency diagram on a copy of these axes.

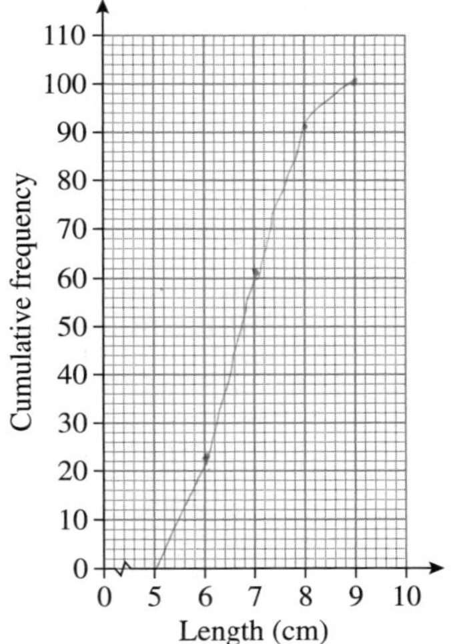

4 A weather forecaster measured the amount of rain each month for four years.
The data is shown in the table.

Amount of rain (cm)	Frequency	Amount of rain (cm)	Cumulative frequency
$0 \leqslant x < 5$	2	$x < 5$	2
$5 \leqslant x < 10$	11	$x < 10$	13
$10 \leqslant x < 15$	20	$x < 15$	33
$15 \leqslant x < 20$	12	$x < 20$	45
$20 \leqslant x < 30$	3	$x < 30$	48

a Copy and complete the table.
b Draw a cumulative frequency diagram for the data.

5 The lengths of 1000 calls to a telephone hotline were measured and recorded, as shown in the table.

Length of call (s)	Frequency	Length of call (s)	Cumulative frequency
$0 \leqslant t < 30$	24	$t < 30$	24
$30 \leqslant t < 60$	108	$t < 60$	132
$60 \leqslant t < 90$	128	$t < 90$	260
$90 \leqslant t < 120$	297	$t < 120$	557
$120 \leqslant t < 150$	261	$t < 150$	818
$150 \leqslant t < 180$	111	$t < 180$	929
$180 \leqslant t < 210$	71	$t < 210$	1000

✓**a** Copy the table and complete the third column.
✓**b** Calculate the cumulative frequencies.
c Construct the cumulative frequency diagram for this data.

6 **a** A bank records the amount of money in its customers' accounts at the end of each month. The table shows the data for the customers who were not overdrawn.

Amount in account (£)	Frequency	A in acc (£)	cum freq
$0 \leqslant x < 1000$	357	$x < 1000$	357
$1000 \leqslant x < 2000$	1276	$x < 2000$	1633
$2000 \leqslant x < 3000$	3087	$x < 3000$	4720
$3000 \leqslant x < 4000$	2221	$x < 4000$	6941
$4000 \leqslant x < 5000$	745	$x < 5000$	7686
$5000 \leqslant x < 6000$	198	$x < 6000$	7884

Construct the cumulative frequency diagram for this data.

b The table shows the amounts by which the remaining customers were overdrawn.

Amount overdrawn (£)	Frequency	A. overdrawn (£)	cum freq
$0 \leqslant x < 1000$	3042	$x < 1000$	3042
$1000 \leqslant x < 2000$	1209	$x < 2000$	4251
$2000 \leqslant x < 3000$	308	$x < 3000$	4559
$3000 \leqslant x < 4000$	21	$x < 4000$	4580
$4000 \leqslant x < 5000$	5	$x < 5000$	4585
$5000 \leqslant x < 6000$	1	$x < 6000$	4586

Construct the cumulative frequency diagram for this data.

7 The table shows the cumulative frequencies for the lengths of 60 theatre performances. Copy the table and complete the frequency column.

Length of performance (min)	Frequency	Cumulative frequency
$60 \leqslant t < 90$		3
$90 \leqslant t < 120$		19
$120 \leqslant t < 150$		42
$150 \leqslant t < 180$		55
$180 \leqslant t < 210$		60

The median can be estimated from a cumulative frequency diagram.
Step 1: Draw a horizontal line from the value of half the total cumulative frequency.
Step 2: Read off the value of the median on the horizontal scale.
The *lower quartile*, the median and the *upper quartile* divide the data into four equal parts.
To find the lower and upper quartiles, read off the values on the horizontal scale from $\frac{1}{4}$ and $\frac{3}{4}$ of the total cumulative frequency.
Interquartile range (IQR) = upper quartile − lower quartile.
The IQR is a measure of spread for the central 50% of the data. This means that it is not affected by any extreme values in the data (unlike the range). It is sometimes used to compare the spread of two different distributions.

Example 2

The cumulative frequency graph shows the ages of the people living in a village.
Estimate the:

a median **b** lower quartile **c** upper quartile
d interquartile range.

Solution 2

a **Step 1:** Half of 2000 = 1000. Draw a line from 1000
Step 2: Read off the value from the x-axis, which is (just under) 44
So an estimate of the median age is 44 years old.

b $\frac{1}{4}$ of 2000 is 500
Drawing a line from 500 and reading off from the x-axis gives 27, so an estimate of the lower quartile is 27 years old.

c $\frac{3}{4}$ of 2000 is 1500
Drawing a line from 1500 and reading off from the x-axis gives 61, so an estimate of the upper quartile is 61 years old.

d Interquartile range = upper quartile − lower quartile
= 61 − 27 = 34 years.

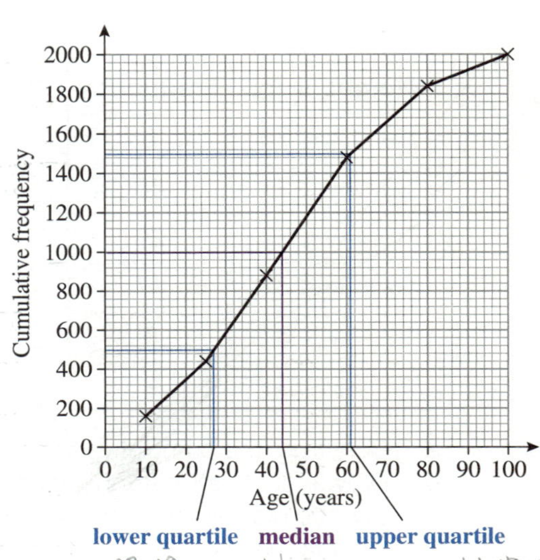

Exercise B

1 The cumulative frequency diagram shows the heights of 120 children.
Use it to estimate the:
- **a** median
- **b** lower quartile
- **c** upper quartile
- **d** interquartile range.

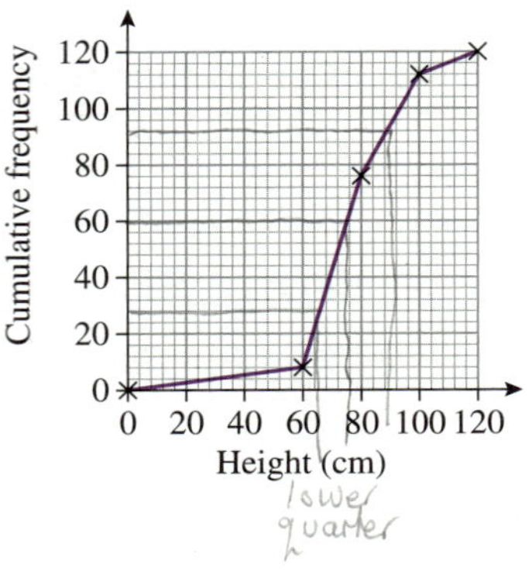

2 The cumulative frequency diagram shows the time taken by Year 9 to finish the school sponsored walk in minutes.
- **a** Use the graph to estimate the:
  - **i** median
  - **ii** lower quartile
  - **iii** upper quartile
  - **iv** interquartile range.
- **b** What is the range of the finishing times?

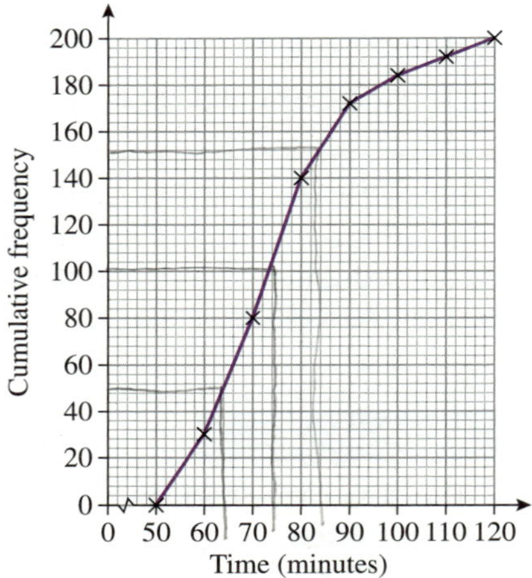

3 The table shows the weights of 100 packets of crisps.

Weight, w (g)	Frequency
$29 \leqslant w < 30$	6
$30 \leqslant w < 31$	46
$31 \leqslant w < 32$	20
$32 \leqslant w < 33$	17
$33 \leqslant w < 34$	9
$34 \leqslant w < 35$	2

- **a** Construct the cumulative frequency distribution for the data.
- **b** Draw a cumulative frequency diagram.
- **c** Use the diagram to estimate:
  - **i** the median
  - **ii** the lower quartile
  - **iii** the upper quartile
  - **iv** the interquartile range.
- **d** The crisp packets are supposed to have a weight of at least 30 g. Comment on this, referring to the above data and your answers to part **c**.

4 The tables show the distances achieved in the long jump for boys (Table A) and girls (Table B) in the Year 10 sports day at Glanford High School.

Table A

Distance jumped, l (m)	Frequency
$2 \leqslant l < 2.5$	4
$2.5 \leqslant l < 3$	7
$3 \leqslant l < 3.5$	23
$3.5 \leqslant l < 4$	11
$4 \leqslant l < 4.5$	5

Table B

Distance jumped, l (m)	Frequency
$2 \leqslant l < 2.5$	2
$2.5 \leqslant l < 3$	5
$3 \leqslant l < 3.5$	18
$3.5 \leqslant l < 4$	16
$4 \leqslant l < 4.5$	9

a Draw two cumulative frequency diagrams on the same axes to show the data. Label the graphs clearly.

b Use the graphs to estimate, for both the boys and the girls:

i the median **ii** the lower quartile
iii the upper quartile **iv** the interquartile range.

c Use your answers to part **b** to compare the performances of the boys and girls. (Hint: In this type of question it is necessary to make a statement about the average and a statement about the spread of the two sets of data.)

d One student jumped 4.45 metres. This was a new sports-day record. Explain whether this student is more likely to be a boy or a girl.

5 500 students took part in a general knowledge competition for charity. They each received a percentage score at the end of the competition. The table shows the distribution of the scores.

Percentage score, x	Frequency
$0 \leqslant x < 20$	24
$20 \leqslant x < 40$	107
$40 \leqslant x < 60$	265
$60 \leqslant x < 80$	88
$80 \leqslant x < 100$	16

a Construct the cumulative frequency distribution for this data.

b Draw a cumulative frequency diagram for this data.

c Use the diagram to estimate the:

i median **ii** lower quartile
iii upper quartile **iv** interquartile range.

d The top 10% of students won a prize. Use the diagram to estimate the minimum score achieved by the top 10%.

e Every student scoring 50 or above entered another competition against another school. Use the graph to estimate the number of students scoring 50 or above.

6 The table shows the relative performances of 136 students in both a Maths test and a Biology test.

Score, x	Frequency (Maths)	Frequency (Biology)
$0 \leqslant x < 10$	18	9
$10 \leqslant x < 20$	23	44
$20 \leqslant x < 30$	37	52
$30 \leqslant x < 40$	35	27
$40 \leqslant x < 50$	23	4

a On the same axes draw cumulative frequency diagrams for the data.
b Use the graphs to estimate appropriate measures for the data so that the performances in the two subjects can be compared.
c The pass mark in Maths was 15 out of 50
Estimate the percentage of students who passed the Maths test.

7 **a** Find the values given by the letters a, b, c and d in the table below.

Score, x	Frequency	Cumulative frequency
$0 \leqslant x < 15$	a	7
$15 \leqslant x < 30$	12	c
$30 \leqslant x < 45$	25	44
$45 \leqslant x < 60$	b	55
$60 \leqslant x < 75$	2b	d

b Hence estimate the interquartile range of the distribution.

8 Draw a cumulative frequency graph for the heights of 100 camels given the following information.
- The shortest camel was 2.1 metres tall.
- The median height was 2.9 metres tall.
- The tallest camel was 3.6 metres tall.
- The interquartile range was exactly half of the actual range.

19.2 Box plots

CAN YOU REMEMBER
- The meaning of 'median', 'lower quartile', 'upper quartile' and 'interquartile range'?
- How to compare two distributions?

IN THIS SECTION YOU WILL
- Learn what the different parts of a box plot represent.
- Learn how to draw a box plot.
- Learn how to use box plots to compare distributions.

A box plot is a diagram that shows the minimum value, lower quartile, median, upper quartile and the maximum value for a distribution.
A box plot should be drawn on a marked scale on graph paper.
A box plot is also sometimes called a *box and whisker plot.*

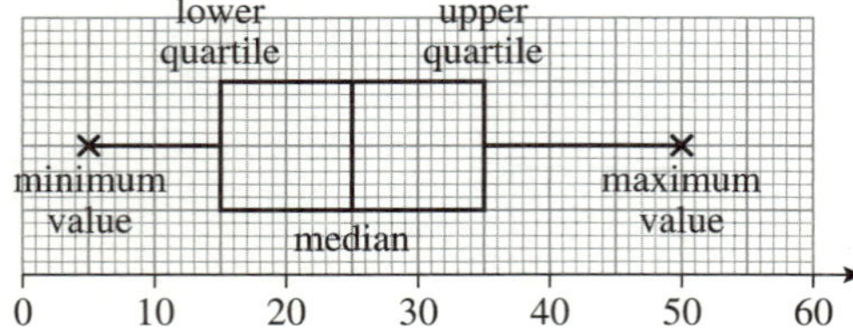

Example 1

A group of shoppers was timed for how long they spent in a supermarket.
The shortest time was 8 minutes, the longest time was 1 hour 12 minutes.
The lower quartile was 26 minutes, the upper quartile was 48 minutes.
The median time was 38 minutes.
Illustrate this data on a box plot.

Solution 1

Remember box plots should be drawn on graph paper with a numbered scale.

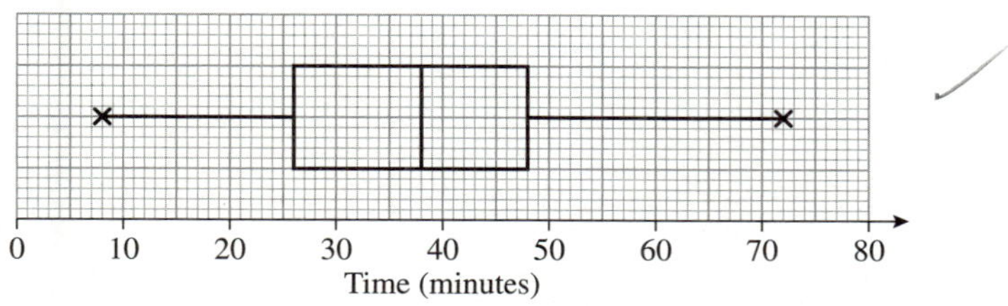

Example 2

The cumulative frequency diagram shows the distribution of the lengths of time 50 light bulbs lasted before breaking.

a Use the diagram to estimate the:
- **i** median
- **ii** lower quartile
- **iii** upper quartile.

b Given that the lowest value was 61 hours and the highest was 120 hours, draw a box plot to illustrate the data.

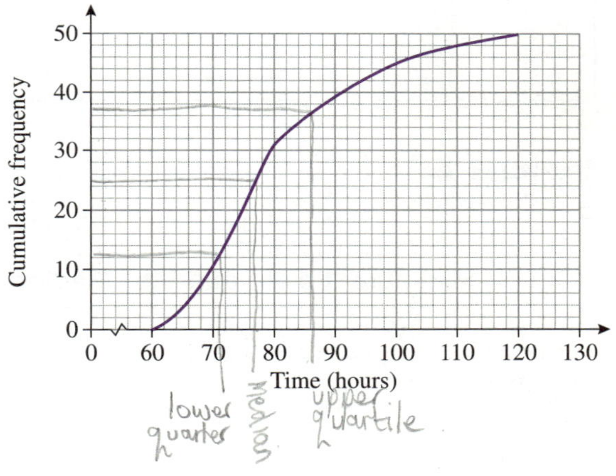

Solution 2

Method 1

Work out the median and quartiles from the cumulative frequency graph.

a **i** median = 77 hours **ii** lower quartile = 71 hours
iii upper quartile = 88 hours

b minimum value = 61, maximum value = 120

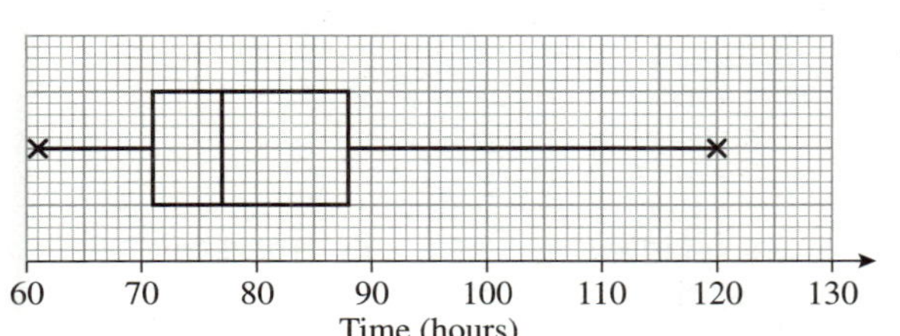

Method 2

The box plot can be drawn underneath the cumulative frequency graph by drawing lines vertically downwards as shown below.

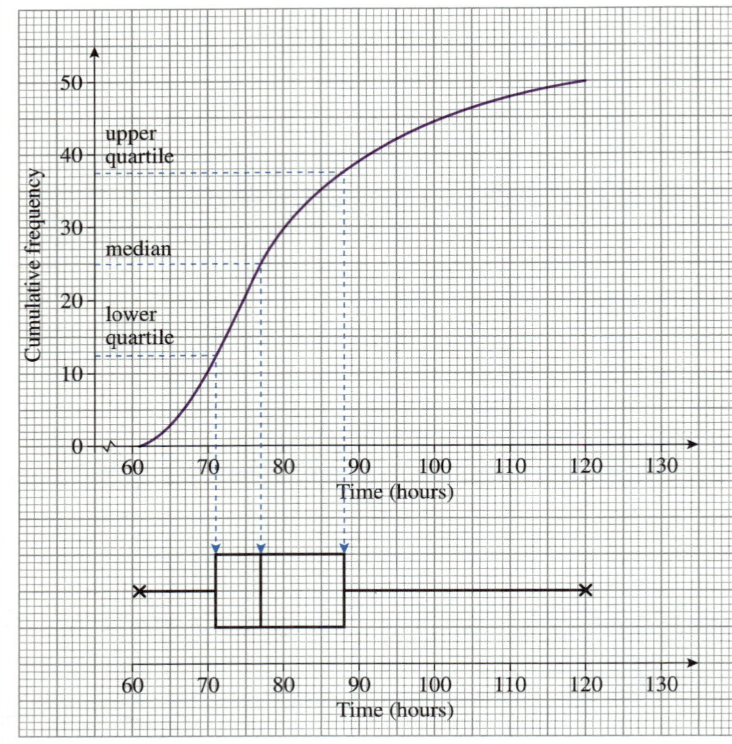

Exercise A

1 Draw a box plot for each of these sets of data.

	Minimum	Lower quartile	Median	Upper quartile	Maximum
a	10	20	25	30	40
b	6	14	21	27	35
c	80	120	150	200	300

2 The box plot below shows information about the lengths of time 100 people took to fill in their National Census form.

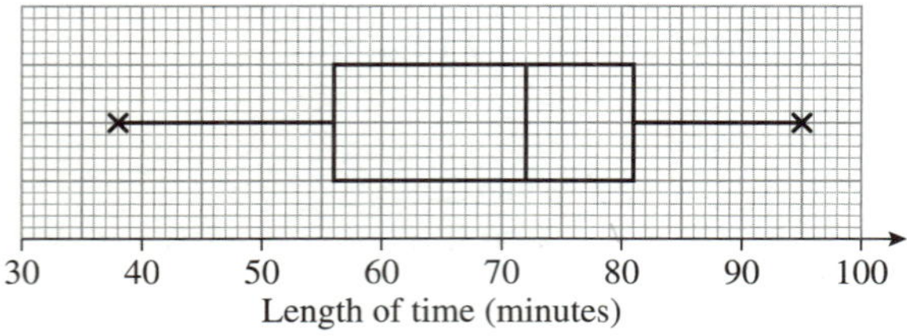

a From the box plot write down the
i shortest time **ii** lower quartile **iii** median
iv upper quartile **v** longest time.

b Use your answers from part **a** to work out the interquartile range.

3 The cumulative frequency graph shows the weights of 40 rugby players.

a Use the cumulative frequency graph to estimate the

 i median

 ii lower quartile

 iii upper quartile.

b Find an estimate of the interquartile range.

c Use your answers to part **a** and the fact that the lightest player weighed 72 kg and the heaviest player weighed 145 kg to construct a box plot for the data.

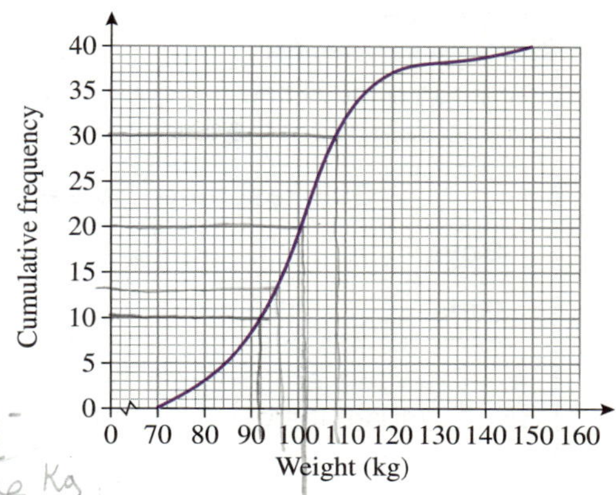

4 The cumulative frequency graph shows the heights of 2000 students in a large school.

a Find estimates of the median, lower quartile and upper quartile.

b Hence draw a box plot.
Assume the minimum value is 1.1 and the maximum value is 1.99

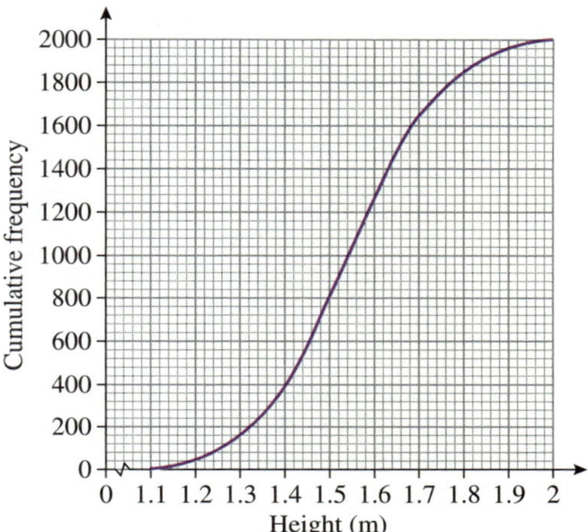

5 The grouped frequency distribution shows the speeds of a sample of 500 cars passing a police radar on a motorway.

Speed, s (miles per hour)	Frequency
$45 \leqslant s < 50$	1
$50 \leqslant s < 55$	28
$55 \leqslant s < 60$	54
$60 \leqslant s < 65$	120
$65 \leqslant s < 70$	249
$70 \leqslant s < 75$	48

a Draw a cumulative frequency diagram to show the data.

b Use the diagram to estimate the measures required to draw a box plot.

c Draw a box plot based on your answers to **b**. Assume the minimum value is 45 and the maximum is 74.9

Box plots are used to compare the spread (range or interquartile range) and the average (median) of two distributions.
When comparing two distributions using box plots it is important to use the same scale.

Example 3

A group of boys and a group of girls took part in a treasure hunt in the grounds of a school.
Some data about the times taken, in minutes, to finish by the boys and girls is given in the table.

	Quickest time	Lower quartile	Median	Upper quartile	Slowest time
Boys	23	34	41	49	62
Girls	19	29	42	52	71

a Draw two box plots on the same axes for the boys' and girls' data.
b Compare the boys' and girls' performance in the treasure hunt.

Solution 3

a

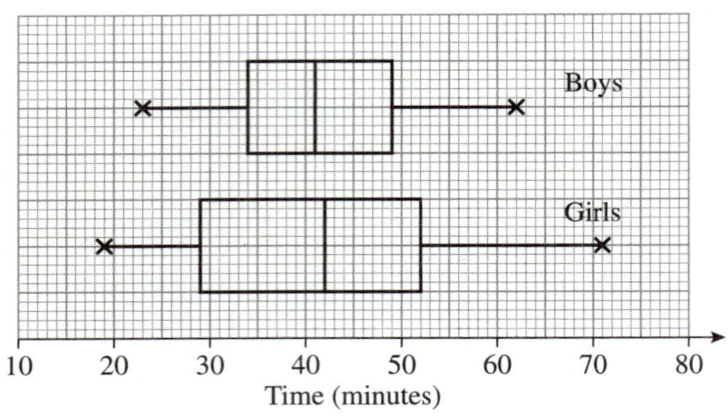

b Median: boys = 41 minutes, girls = 42 minutes.
The boys and girls had a very similar average (median) time with the boys finishing slightly quicker.
Interquartile range: boys = 15 minutes, girls = 23 minutes.
The girls' times were more spread out than the boys' times, and the girls had both the slowest and quickest times.

Exercise B

1 A group of students and a group of teachers all entered a charity walk.
Some information about the times taken, in minutes, to complete the walk is given in the table.

	Quickest	Lower quartile	Median	Upper quartile	Slowest
Students	55	68	80	99	125
Teachers	50	62	74	91	108

a Draw two box plots on the same axes for the students' and teachers' data.
b Compare the times taken in the walk for teachers and students.

2 Two groups of pupils took a test in Science.
The first group had special revision classes.
The second group revised on their own.
The table shows some information (in %) about their results in the test.

	Lowest	Lower quartile	Median	Upper quartile	Highest
Group 1	42	50	57	66	92
Group 2	42	49	55	61	73

a Draw two box plots on the same axes for groups 1 and 2
b Compare the performance of the two groups.

3 80 cows were fed on a special diet to try to help them put on weight.
The table shows some information about their weights (in kg) before the special diet and six months later.

	Lowest	Lower quartile	Median	Upper quartile	Highest
Before diet	123	137	152	159	170
Six months later	135	142	154	160	170

a Draw two box plots on the same axes for the data before and after the diet.
b Does it appear that the diet has had any effect?
Explain your answer.

4 The cumulative frequency diagram shows the times taken for 100 of Kevin's journeys to work using route A.

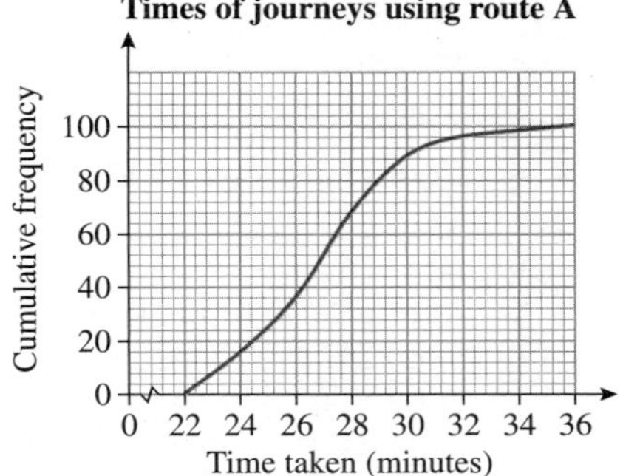

a **i** Use the diagram to find estimates for the median and quartiles.
ii Hence find the interquartile range.

b This is the data for 100 of Kevin's journeys to work using route B.

Minimum time	15 minutes
Lower quartile	25 minutes
Median	31 minutes
Upper quartile	35 minutes
Maximum time	44 minutes

For route A, Kevin's minimum time was 22 minutes and his maximum time was 36 minutes.
i Draw box plots for the times using routes A and B.
ii Use the box plots to compare the time taken by the different routes.

c Kevin left home at 9:23 am one day. He had an important meeting at work starting at 10 am.
Which route should Kevin take?
Give a reason for your answer.

5 The grouped frequency table shows the lengths of two different species of vole.

Length, l (cm)	Number of voles of species A	Number of voles of species B
$4 \leqslant l < 6$	23	45
$6 \leqslant l < 8$	86	107
$8 \leqslant l < 10$	182	132
$10 \leqslant l < 12$	54	67
$12 \leqslant l < 14$	20	9

a Draw cumulative frequency diagrams for the two species on the same axes.
b Draw box plots for the two species on the same axes.
Assume the minimum length for each species is 4 cm and the maximum length for each species is 14 cm.
c Compare the two distributions.

6 The box plot shows some information about the lengths of 100 feature films.

a Work out the interquartile range.

b Draw a possible cumulative frequency diagram for this data.

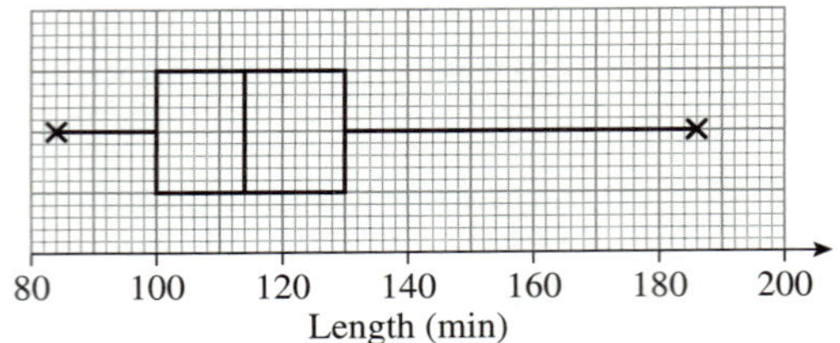

Chapter summary

- Cumulative frequency is a running total of all the data up to a certain point. The cumulative frequency is found by adding successive frequencies.
- When the data is continuous, a cumulative frequency diagram or graph can be drawn. To draw the cumulative frequency diagram plot the cumulative frequency value at the upper bound (top value) of each class interval. Join the points with straight lines or a smooth curve.
- The median can be estimated from a cumulative frequency diagram.
  - **Step 1:** Draw a horizontal line from the value of half the total cumulative frequency.
  - **Step 2:** Read off the value of the median on the horizontal scale.
- The lower quartile, the median and the upper quartile divide the data into four equal parts.
- To find the lower and upper quartiles read off the values on the horizontal scale from $\frac{1}{4}$ and $\frac{3}{4}$ of the total cumulative frequency.
- Interquartile range (IQR) = upper quartile − lower quartile. The IQR is a measure of spread for the central 50% of the data.
- A box plot is a diagram that shows the minimum value, lower quartile, median, upper quartile and the maximum value for a distribution.
- A box plot should be drawn on a marked scale on graph paper.
- A box plot is also sometimes called a *box and whisker plot.*
- Box plots are used to compare the spread (range or interquartile range) and the average (median) of two distributions. When comparing two distributions using box plots it is important to use the same scale.

Chapter review

1 The table shows the scores when an octahedral dice is rolled 50 times.

Score	Frequency	Score	Cumulative frequency
1	5	$\leqslant 1$	
2	8	$\leqslant 2$	
3	3	$\leqslant 3$	
4	5	$\leqslant 4$	
5	9	$\leqslant 5$	
6	10	$\leqslant 6$	
7	4	$\leqslant 7$	
8	6	$\leqslant 8$	

Copy and complete the table.

2 The cumulative frequency graph shows the results (in %) for a Maths test taken by 160 students.

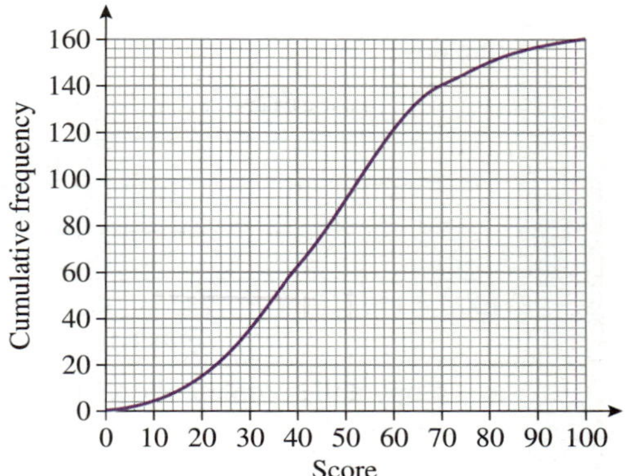

a Use the diagram to find the:
   i median
   ii lower quartile
   iii upper quartile.

b Calculate the interquartile range.

c The pass mark was set at 45%. Estimate the number of students who passed the test.

3 Copy the table and tick the appropriate box for each line.

Statement	Always true	Might be true	Always false
a The median is 50% of the way along the data.			
b The lower quartile will be higher than the upper quartile.			
c The interquartile range is exactly half of the range.			
d The interquartile range covers the central 50% of the data.			
e The median and upper quartile are equal.			

4 This grouped frequency distribution shows the queuing times for 100 customers in a bank.

Queuing time, t (minutes)	Frequency
$0 \leqslant t < 2$	23
$2 \leqslant t < 4$	35
$4 \leqslant t < 6$	30
$6 \leqslant t < 8$	9
$8 \leqslant t < 10$	3

a Construct a cumulative frequency diagram for this data.

b The bank manager claimed that customers, on average, waited less than 4 minutes. By finding an estimate of the median from the graph, comment on the bank manager's claim.

5 The box plot shows some information about the weights of 80 parcels delivered by Royal Mail one day.

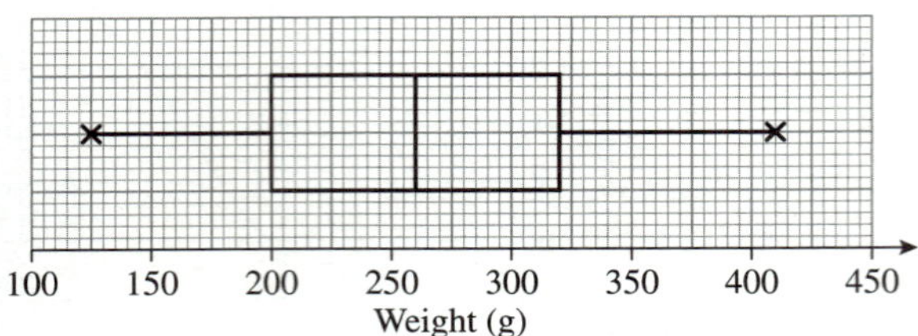

a Copy and complete the table.

Measure	Weight (g)
Minimum	
Lower quartile	
Median	
Upper quartile	
Maximum	
Interquartile range	

b Construct a possible cumulative frequency diagram for this data.

6 120 students took an examination paper. The table gives a summary of their results.

a Draw a box plot to show this information.
b Write down the interquartile range for this data.
c Draw a cumulative frequency diagram to show the information.
d Grade 1 is awarded to students who score 65 marks or more. Use the cumulative frequency diagram to estimate the number of pupils awarded grade 1

	Marks
Minimum	17
Lower quartile	46
Median	58
Upper quartile	72
Maximum	92

7 The table gives information about the waiting times (in minutes) at Doctor Gloucester and Doctor Foster's surgeries.

Measure	Doctor Gloucester	Doctor Foster
Minimum wait	3	6
Lower quartile	8	11
Median	14	15
Upper quartile	22	21
Maximum wait	31	25

a On the same axes draw a pair of labelled box plots to illustrate this data.
b Compare the waiting times for the two doctors.

8 The lifetime of two types of batteries, Supercell and Staywell, were tested by using a sample of 200 of each in a particular type of torch. The length of time the torch shone was recorded for each battery.
The box plots show some information about the recorded data.

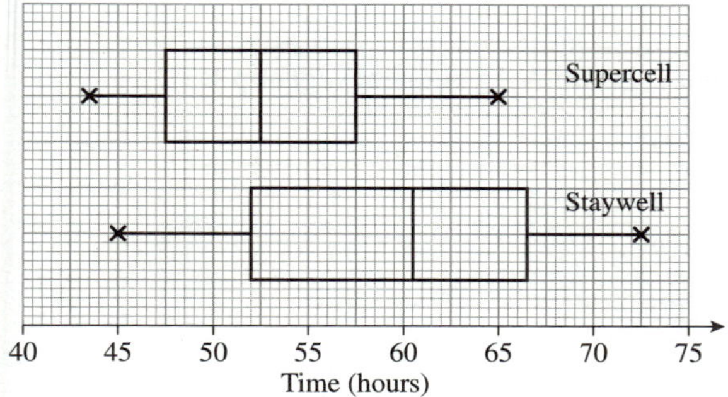

a Compare the medians for the two types of battery.
b Compare the interquartile ranges for the two types of battery.
c The Staywell batteries cost 20% more than the Supercell batteries.
Explain your answer.

9 The grouped frequency table gives the times 200 customers were kept on hold after calling a customer services centre for a particular company.

Time on hold, t (min)	Frequency	Time on hold (min)	Cumulative frequency
$0 \leqslant t < 4$	78	$t < 4$	
$4 \leqslant t < 8$	55	$t < 8$	
$8 \leqslant t < 12$	41		
$12 \leqslant t < 16$	22		
$16 \leqslant t < 20$	4		

a Copy and complete the table.
b Draw a cumulative frequency diagram to illustrate the data.
c Use the diagram to estimate the:
i median
ii lower quartile
iii upper quartile
iv interquartile range.
d The company promises customers that anyone kept on hold for more than 15 minutes will receive a £20 gift voucher.
Use your diagram to estimate the percentage of these 200 customers who should receive the voucher.

10 The contents of a bag of sweets is advertised as weighing 100 grams.
Clive buys 100 bags of these sweets and weighs the contents.
The results are given in the table.
a Draw a cumulative frequency diagram.
b Use your diagram to estimate the:
i interquartile range
ii the percentage of these bags of sweets within 3% of the advertised weight.

Weight, w (g)	Frequency
$94 \leqslant w < 96$	4
$96 \leqslant w < 98$	7
$98 \leqslant w < 100$	19
$100 \leqslant w < 102$	62
$102 \leqslant w < 104$	7
$104 \leqslant w < 106$	1

11 Two groups of people are trying to diet.
Group A are given a training routine to follow.
Group B are given a special diet to follow.
The table below shows the actual weight loss for each of the groups three months after the trial began.

Weight loss, w (kg)	**Frequency, group A**	**Frequency, group B**
$-2 \leqslant w < 0$	4	6
$0 \leqslant w < 2$	9	8
$2 \leqslant w < 4$	17	11
$4 \leqslant w < 6$	22	15
$6 \leqslant w < 8$	6	17
$8 \leqslant w < 10$	2	10

a What does a weight loss of -1 kg mean?
b Draw two cumulative frequency diagrams on the same axes.
c Draw box plots and compare the weight losses of the two groups. Assume the minimum value is -2 and the maximum value is 9.9
d Mabel lost 6 kg in weight. Which group was she more likely to be from? Explain your answer.

Index numbers

CHAPTER 20

20.1 Powers and indices

CAN YOU REMEMBER

- How to simplify simple powers, for example $x^2 \times x^3 = x^5$, $x^9 \div x^4 = x^5$?
- Square and cube numbers?

IN THIS SECTION YOU WILL

- Learn how to work out powers of numbers when the powers are positive or negative integers.
- Learn how to work out powers of numbers when the powers are fractions.
- Simplify expressions involving powers.

Here is a table of powers of 7

7^4	7^3	7^2	7^1
$7 \times 7 \times 7 \times 7 = 2401$	$7 \times 7 \times 7 = 343$	$7 \times 7 = 49$	7

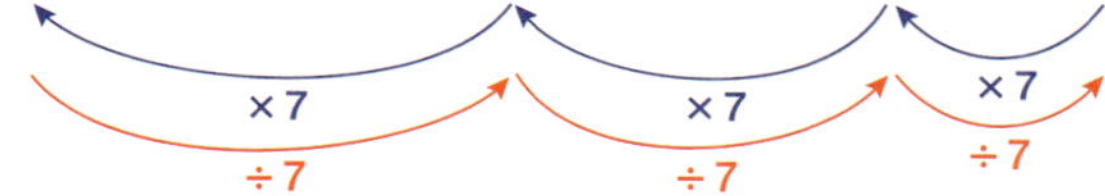

In the table, moving to the **left** multiplies by 7 and increases the power by 1 each time.
Moving to the **right** divides by 7 and decreases the power by 1 each time.
This table continues the pattern into negative powers:

7^4	7^3	7^2	7^1	7^0	7^{-1}	7^{-2}	7^{-3}	7^{-4}
2401	343	49	7	$7 \div 7 = 1$	$1 \div 7 = \frac{1}{7}$	$\frac{1}{7} \div 7 = \frac{1}{49}$	$\frac{1}{49} \div 7 = \frac{1}{343}$	$\frac{1}{343} \div 7 = \frac{1}{2401}$

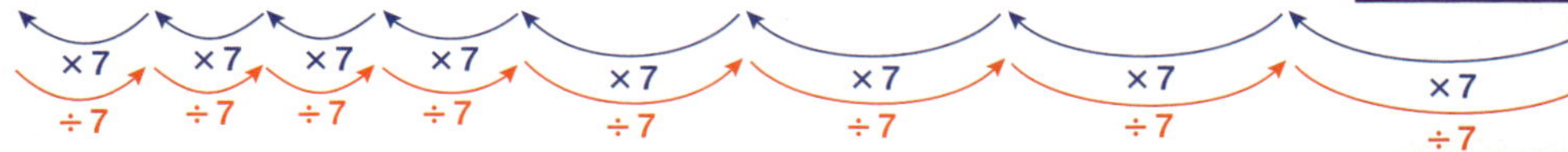

Writing these powers in pairs gives:

$7^4 = 2401,\ 7^{-4} = \frac{1}{2401}$ $\qquad$ $7^3 = 343,\ 7^{-3} = \frac{1}{343}$

$7^2 = 49,\ 7^{-2} = \frac{1}{49}$ $\qquad$ $7^1 = 7,\ 7^{-1} = \frac{1}{7}$

leaving $7^0 = 1$

In general $x^{-n} = \frac{1}{x^n}$ and $x^0 = 1$

Any number to the power zero equals 1, for example $12^0 = 1$

Example 1

a Work out the values of:
 i 2^4 **ii** 3^2 **iii** 1^5

b Use the answers to part **a** to write down the values of:
 i 2^{-4} **ii** 3^{-2} **iii** 1^{-5}

Solution 1

a **i** $2^4 = 2 \times 2 \times 2 \times 2 = 16$ **ii** $3^2 = 3 \times 3 = 9$ **iii** $1^5 = 1 \times 1 \times 1 \times 1 \times 1 = 1$

b **i** $2^{-4} = \frac{1}{2^4} = \frac{1}{16}$ **ii** $3^{-2} = \frac{1}{3^2} = \frac{1}{9}$ **iii** $1^{-5} = \frac{1}{1^5} = \frac{1}{1} = 1$

The index rule for multiplication is $x^a \times x^b = x^{a+b}$
$\sqrt{x} \times \sqrt{x} = x$ and using the index rule $x^{\frac{1}{2}} \times x^{\frac{1}{2}} = x^1 = x$
so $\sqrt{x} = x^{\frac{1}{2}}$
Similarly $\sqrt[3]{x} = x^{\frac{1}{3}}$, $\sqrt[4]{x} = x^{\frac{1}{4}}$ and so on.

Raising a number to the power $\frac{1}{2}$ gives the **positive** square root.

Raising a number to the power $\frac{1}{3}$ gives the cube root.

For example $25^{\frac{1}{2}} = \sqrt{25} = 5$ and $64^{\frac{1}{3}} = \sqrt[3]{64} = 4$

Exercise A

1 Copy the table. Use patterns to complete the table of values for the following.

a

3^4	3^3	3^2	3^1	3^0	3^{-1}	3^{-2}	3^{-3}	3^{-4}
		9				$\frac{1}{9}$		

b

2^4	2^3	2^2	2^1	2^0	2^{-1}	2^{-2}	2^{-3}	2^{-4}
16				1				

2 **a** Work out the values of:
 i 5^3 **ii** 2^6 **iii** 4^2 **iv** 9^0

b Use the answers to part **a** to write down the values of:
 i 5^{-3} **ii** 2^{-6} **iii** 4^{-2}

3 Work out:
a $\sqrt{36}$ **b** $49^{\frac{1}{2}}$ **c** $\sqrt[3]{27}$ **d** $1000^{\frac{1}{3}}$
e 6^0 **f** $81^{\frac{1}{2}} + 25^{\frac{1}{2}}$ **g** $8^{\frac{1}{3}} - 1^{\frac{1}{3}}$ **h** $64^{\frac{1}{3}} - 64^{\frac{1}{2}}$

4 Work out:
a $\sqrt{16} \times \sqrt{9}$ **b** $\sqrt{16 \times 9}$
c What do you notice about your answers to parts **a** and **b**?
d $16^{\frac{1}{2}} + 9^{\frac{1}{2}}$ **e** $25^{\frac{1}{2}}$
f What do you notice about your answers to parts **d** and **e**?

5 Work out:
a 2^{-5} **b** 3^{-1} **c** 5^0 **d** 10^{-2} **e** 1^{-4}

6 a Use a calculator to work out:

i $1 - 5^{-3}$ **ii** $(1 - 5^{-1})(1 + 5^{-1} + 5^{-2})$

b What do you notice about your answers to parts **i** and **ii**?

7 a Use a calculator to work out:

i $1 - 4^{-3}$ **ii** $(1 - 4^{-1})(1 + 4^{-1} + 4^{-2})$

b What do you notice about your answers to parts **i** and **ii**?

Using the index law for multiplication:

$(2^4)^3 = 2^4 \times 2^4 \times 2^4 = 2^{3 \times 4} = 2^{12}$ $(3^{-2})^3 = 3^{-2} \times 3^{-2} \times 3^{-2} = 3^{-6}$

In general $(x^a)^b = x^{ab}$

So $x^{\frac{a}{b}} = x^{\left(\frac{1}{b}\right)^a} = (\sqrt[b]{x})^a$

For example, $25^{\frac{3}{2}} = (25^{\frac{1}{2}})^3 = (\sqrt{25})^3 = 5^3 = 125$

and $64^{\frac{2}{3}} = (64^{\frac{1}{3}})^2 = (\sqrt[3]{64})^2 = 4^2 = 16$

Also, for negative powers

$x^{-\frac{a}{b}} = \dfrac{1}{x^{\frac{a}{b}}}$ $8^{-\frac{2}{3}} = \dfrac{1}{8^{\frac{2}{3}}} = \dfrac{1}{(\sqrt[3]{8})^2} = \dfrac{1}{2^2} = \dfrac{1}{4}$

It is sensible to work out the root before the power, to give smaller values to work with.

Example 2

Write 27 in the form 9^x.

Solution 2

$27 = 3^3$ and $3 = \sqrt{9} = 9^{\frac{1}{2}}$

So $27 = (9^{\frac{1}{2}})^3 = 9^{\frac{3}{2}}$

Exercise B

1 a Work out the values of:

i $16^{\frac{3}{2}}$ **ii** $4^{\frac{3}{2}}$ **iii** $25^{\frac{3}{2}}$ **iv** $9^{\frac{3}{2}}$

v $100^{\frac{3}{2}}$ **vi** $1^{\frac{3}{2}}$

b Use your answers to part **a** to write down the values of:

i $16^{-\frac{3}{2}}$ **ii** $4^{-\frac{3}{2}}$ **iii** $25^{-\frac{3}{2}}$ **iv** $9^{-\frac{3}{2}}$

v $100^{-\frac{3}{2}}$ **vi** $1^{-\frac{3}{2}}$

2 Work out the values of:

a $4^{\frac{5}{2}}$ **b** $100^{\frac{7}{2}}$ **c** $0^{\frac{3}{2}}$ **d** $8^{\frac{2}{3}}$

e $125^{\frac{2}{3}}$ **f** $64^{-\frac{1}{3}}$ **g** $1^{\frac{3}{4}}$ **h** $27^{-\frac{2}{3}}$

3 a Write 16 in the form 2^x **b** Write 32 in the form 4^x

c Write 9 in the form 27^x **d** Write 4 in the form 8^x

4 Evaluate: **a** $25^{0.5} \times 3^{-2}$ **b** $64^{\frac{1}{2}} \div 2^{-2}$

5 Write $4^{-\frac{3}{2}}$ in the form $\dfrac{1}{n}$, where n is an integer.

6 a $2^x = 32$. Write down the value of x.

b $9^y = 27$. Write down the value of y.

7 Use a calculator to work out the value of:
a $729^{\frac{5}{2}}$ **b** $256^{-0.5}$ **c** $81^{\frac{3}{2}}$ **d** $125^{\frac{4}{3}}$ **e** $1024^{-\frac{9}{10}}$

8 Show that $50^{\frac{1}{4}}$ lies between 2 and 3
Hint: work out 2^4

9 Louis says that $100^{\frac{1}{3}}$ is greater than 5
Is he correct?
Explain your answer.

20.2 Standard index form

CAN YOU REMEMBER

- Powers of 10?
- The rules of indices: $x^a \times x^b = x^{a+b}$ and $x^a \div x^b = x^{a-b}$?

IN THIS SECTION YOU WILL

- Convert numbers between ordinary and standard index form.
- Calculate with standard index form.
- Use a calculator for standard form calculations.

Very large and very small powers of 10 can be written using index form.

For example, 1 000 000 can be written as 10^6 and 0.0001 can be written as 10^{-4}.

All numbers can be written in standard index form, also called standard form.

Numbers in standard form are written as $a \times 10^n$, where $1 \leqslant a < 10$ and n is an integer (whole number).

For example, $5718 = 5.718 \times 1000 = 5.718 \times 10^3$

Standard form numbers can be converted back to ordinary numbers.

For example, $4.2 \times 10^4 = 4.2 \times 10\,000 = 42\,000$

Example 1

a Write each number in standard form:
i 346 **ii** 80 **iii** 0.024

b Write each number as an ordinary number:
i 7.6×10^2 **ii** 6.01×10^{-3} **iii** 7×10^6

Solution 1

a **i** $346 = 3.46 \times 100 = 3.46 \times 10^2$ **ii** $80 = 8 \times 10^1$

iii $0.024 = 2.4 \times \frac{1}{100} = 2.4 \times 10^{-2}$

b **i** $7.6 \times 10^2 = 7.6 \times 100 = 760$

ii $6.01 \times 10^{-3} = 6.01 \times \frac{1}{1000} = 0.006\,01$

iii $7 \times 10^6 = 7 \times 1\,000\,000 = 7\,000\,000$

Example 2

Write each number in standard form correct to one significant figure:

a 106 234 **b** 0.007 872 5

Solution 2

a $106\,234 = 1.062\,34 \times 100\,000 = 1.062\,34 \times 10^5$
$1.062\,34$ correct to 1 s.f. $= 1$
So $106\,234 = 1 \times 10^5$ correct to 1 s.f.

b $0.007\,872\,5 = 7.8725 \times \frac{1}{1000} = 7.8725 \times 10^{-3}$
7.8725 correct to 1 s.f. $= 8$
So $0.007\,872\,5 = 8 \times 10^{-3}$ correct to 1 s.f.

Exercise A

1 Write each number as a power of 10

a 1000 **b** 100 **c** 10 **d** 1

e $\frac{1}{10}$ **f** $\frac{1}{100}$ **g** $\frac{1}{1000}$

2 Write each of these numbers in standard form.

a 186 **b** 23.1 **c** 57.2 **d** 4206

e 900 **f** 17 million **g** 8 thousand **h** 0.26

i 0.147 **j** 0.081 **k** 0.0045 **l** 0.000 933

3 Write each of these numbers as an ordinary number.

a 7.6×10^2 **b** 2.19×10^4 **c** 8.02×10^3

d 9.4×10^1 **e** 5.51×10^0 **f** 3.5×10^6

g 9×10^3 **h** 1.2×10^{-2} **i** 9.35×10^{-1}

j 2.47×10^{-4} **k** 6.24×10^{-2} **l** 4×10^{-6}

4 Write each number in standard form to one significant figure.

a 412 **b** 7853 **c** 18.69 **d** 315.6

e 0.475 **f** 0.002 91 **g** 0.000 732

5 Put these numbers in ascending order.

7×10^4 0.098 3 million 5237 1.2×10^6 4.6×10^{-4}

6 Make these cards into three calculations.
The first one has been done for you.

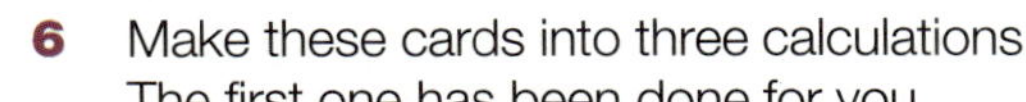

7.2×10^3 1.3×10^4 6×10^2 3600 604 = 39 000

× + ÷ = 2 3 4

7.2×10^3 ÷ 2 = 3600

For calculations with numbers in index form, remember:

- the rules of indices for multiplication and division
- numbers can only be added or subtracted in index form if they are the *same power* of the *same base*. If not, convert them to ordinary numbers first.

Example 3

Calculate, giving each answer in standard form.

a $(2 \times 10^5) \times (4.1 \times 10^3)$ **b** $\dfrac{(4.2 \times 10^5)}{(7 \times 10^{-6})}$ **c** $(7.1 \times 10^4) + (3.2 \times 10^4)$

d $(1.4 \times 10^3) + (2.5 \times 10^2)$ **e** $(3.7 \times 10^2) - (2.8 \times 10^{-1})$

Solution 3

a $(2 \times 10^5) \times (4.1 \times 10^3) = 2 \times 4.1 \times 10^5 \times 10^3$ — Numbers, then powers of 10
$= 8.2 \times 10^{5+3} = 8.2 \times 10^8$

b $\dfrac{(4.2 \times 10^5)}{(7 \times 10^{-6})} = \dfrac{4.2}{7} \times \dfrac{10^5}{10^{-6}}$
$= 0.6 \times 10^{5--6}$ — Numbers, then powers of 10
$= 0.6 \times 10^{11}$ — Not standard form, because 0.6 is less than 1
$= 6 \times \dfrac{1}{10} \times 10^{11} = 6 \times 10^{-1} \times 10^{11} = 6 \times 10^{10}$

c $(7.1 \times 10^4) + (3.2 \times 10^4)$ — Same powers of same base, so add the number parts.
$= 10.3 \times 10^4$ — Not standard form, because 10.3 is greater than 1
$= 1.03 \times 10 \times 10^4 = 1.03 \times 10^5$

d $(1.4 \times 10^3) + (2.5 \times 10^2) = (1.4 \times 1000) + (2.5 \times 100)$
$= 1400 + 250$ — Converting to ordinary numbers.
$= 1650 = 1.65 \times 1000$
$= 1.65 \times 10^3$ — Converting back to standard form.

e $(3.7 \times 10^2) - (2.8 \times 10^{-1}) = (3.7 \times 100) - (2.8 \times \dfrac{1}{10})$
$= 370 - 0.28$ — Converting to ordinary numbers.
$= 369.72$
$= 3.6972 \times 100$ — Converting back to standard form.
$= 3.6972 \times 10^2$

Calculations in standard form can be entered on a calculator. Some calculators have an EXP or $\times 10^n$ button for this. Make sure you know how to enter numbers in standard form, and read the display, on your own calculator.

Exercise B

1 Write the answer to each of the following in index form.

a 10×10^2 **b** $10^4 \times 10^3$ **c** $10^2 \times 10^7$ **d** $10^9 \times 10$
e $10^{-5} \times 10^8$ **f** $10^{-6} \times 10^{-1}$ **g** $10^4 \div 10^3$ **h** $10^6 \div 10^2$
i $10^5 \div 10^{-5}$ **j** $10^{-7} \div 10^{-1}$ **k** $10^{-2} \div 10^2$ **l** $10^{-6} \div 10^4$

2 Calculate, giving each answer in standard form.

a $(4 \times 10^3) \times (2 \times 10^4)$ **b** $(3.2 \times 10^2) \times (3 \times 10^5)$
c $(2.12 \times 10^4) \times (4 \times 10^2)$ **d** $(1.7 \times 10^6) \times (2 \times 10^{-3})$
e $(3 \times 10^{-2}) \times (1.1 \times 10^{-4})$ **f** $(4 \times 10^{-1}) \times (2.03 \times 10^{-5})$

3 Calculate, giving each answer in standard form.

a $(7 \times 10^3) \times (3 \times 10^4)$ **b** $(5.2 \times 10^2) \times (4 \times 10^5)$

c $(6.1 \times 10^4) \times (8 \times 10^2)$ **d** $(3.9 \times 10^6) \times (6 \times 10^{-3})$

e $(5 \times 10^{-2}) \times (8.2 \times 10^{-4})$ **f** $(9 \times 10^{-1}) \times (2.4 \times 10^{-1})$

4 Calculate, giving each answer in standard form.

a $(8 \times 10^6) \div (2 \times 10^4)$ **b** $(9.3 \times 10^2) \div (3 \times 10^5)$

c $(8.04 \times 10^5) \div (4 \times 10^2)$ **d** $(6.2 \times 10^6) \div (2 \times 10^{-5})$

e $\dfrac{9.63 \times 10^5}{3 \times 10^6}$ **f** $\dfrac{7.5 \times 10^{-1}}{5 \times 10^{-3}}$

5 Calculate, giving each answer in standard form.

a $(3.2 \times 10^3) \div (4 \times 10^4)$ **b** $(4.8 \times 10^2) \div (8 \times 10^5)$

c $(3.1 \times 10^4) \div (6.2 \times 10^2)$ **d** $(3.9 \times 10^6) \div (6 \times 10^{-3})$

e $\dfrac{1.5 \times 10^{-3}}{3 \times 10^{-4}}$ **f** $\dfrac{1.6 \times 10^{-7}}{4 \times 10^2}$

6 Calculate, giving each answer in standard form.

a $(7.2 \times 10^3) + (2.4 \times 10^4)$ **b** $(5.6 \times 10^2) + (7.8 \times 10^4)$

c $(1.8 \times 10^5) + (9.8 \times 10^5)$ **d** $(9.3 \times 10^7) - (4.2 \times 10^7)$

e $(3.4 \times 10^3) - (1.9 \times 10^2)$ **f** $(6.7 \times 10^5) - (6.5 \times 10^5)$

7 Calculate:

a $(4 \times 10^3) + (2 \times 10^4)$ **b** $(7 \times 10^3) + (2 \times 10^3)$

c $(2.6 \times 10^5) + (1.2 \times 10^2)$ **d** $(2.4 \times 10^4) - (1.7 \times 10^4)$

e $(6 \times 10^4) - (3.5 \times 10^3)$ **f** $(1.8 \times 10^2) - (1.4 \times 10^{-1})$

8 The table shows the masses of five planets and their average speed of orbit around the Sun.

Planet	Mass of planet (kg)	Average speed of orbit (km/h)
Jupiter	1.9×10^{27}	4.7×10^4
Saturn	5.7×10^{26}	3.5×10^4
Uranus	8.7×10^{25}	2.5×10^5
Neptune	1.0×10^{26}	1.2×10^4
Pluto	1.5×10^{22}	1.7×10^4

a Which planet travels the slowest?

b Which planet has approximately six times the mass of Neptune?

c Which planet travels at approximately half the speed of Saturn?

d What is the difference in speed between Neptune and Pluto? Give your answer in standard form.

e What is the combined mass of Jupiter and Saturn? Give your answer in standard form.

9 Callisto is a moon of Jupiter. It completes one orbit in 400 hours.
The distance travelled in one orbit is approximately 7.5 million miles.
Work out the average speed of Callisto. Give your answer in standard form.

10 Check your answers to questions **2** to **7** using a calculator.

Chapter summary

- $x^{-n} = \frac{1}{x^n}$, for example $2^{-3} = \frac{1}{2^3}$
- $x^0 = 1$, for example $12^0 = 1$
- $\sqrt{x} = x^{\frac{1}{2}}$, for example $25^{\frac{1}{2}} = \sqrt{25} = 5$
- $\sqrt[3]{x} = x^{\frac{1}{3}}$, for example $27^{\frac{1}{3}} = \sqrt[3]{27} = 3$
- $x^{\frac{a}{b}} = x^{\left(\frac{1}{b}\right)^a} = (\sqrt[b]{x})^a$, for example $64^{\frac{2}{3}} = (64^{\frac{1}{3}})^2 = (\sqrt[3]{64})^2 = 4^2 = 16$
- $x^{-\frac{a}{b}} = \frac{1}{x^{\frac{a}{b}}}$ for example $8^{-\frac{2}{3}} = \frac{1}{(\sqrt[3]{8})^2} = \frac{1}{2^2} = \frac{1}{4}$
- Numbers in standard form are written as $a \times 10^n$, where $1 \leqslant a < 10$ and n is an integer. For example, $5718 = 5.718 \times 1000 = 5.718 \times 10^3$
- Standard form numbers can be converted back to ordinary numbers. For example, $4.2 \times 10^4 = 4.2 \times 10\,000 = 42\,000$
- Numbers can only be added or subtracted in index form if they are the *same power* of the *same base*. If not, convert them to ordinary numbers first.

Chapter review

1 **a** Evaluate $81^{\frac{1}{2}} + 4^{-2}$ **b** Work out $1000^{\frac{2}{3}}$

2 **a** Add 2.4×10^4 and 8.1×10^4
Give your answer in standard form.
b Multiply 4×10^7 and 1.3×10^{-3}

3 **a** Find the value of 14^0
b Work out $\frac{2 \times 10^7}{5 \times 10^{-4}}$

4 Write $64^{-\frac{2}{3}} \times 27^{\frac{1}{3}}$ in the form $\frac{a}{b}$ where a and b are integers.

5 The speed of light is approximately 3×10^8 metres per second.
It takes light approximately 1.3 seconds to travel from the Earth to the Moon.
Use these facts to work out the approximate distance, in standard form, between the Earth and the Moon.
Give your answer in kilometres.

6 **a** Calculate $5.4 \times 10^4 \times 7.2$
Give your answer in standard form.
b Calculate $5.4 \times 10^4 \div 7.2$
Give your answer in standard form.

7 In January 2006 the world population was approximately 6 530 000 000
a Write this number in standard form.
The world population is increasing by approximately 6 million each month in 2006
b Estimate the population in January 2007
Give your answer in standard form.

8 The population of the UK in 2005 was 60.5 million.

a Write 60.5 million in standard form.

b The area of land in the UK is 2.4×10^5 km^2

Use the following formula to work out the average area per person in the UK:

$$\text{average area per person} = \frac{\text{area}}{\text{population}}$$

Give your answer, in standard form, to a suitable degree of accuracy.

9 Use a calculator to work out the value of:

a $4096^{\frac{1}{2}}$

b $1024^{-\frac{1}{2}}$

10 Use a calculator to work out the value of:

a $\sqrt{729^{\frac{1}{3}} \times 256^{\frac{1}{2}} \times 8^0}$

b $64^{-\frac{1}{6}} \div (0.5)^{-3}$

11 The planet Mars is approximately a sphere of radius 3400 km.
Calculate the approximate surface area of the planet Mars in km^2
Give your answer in standard form to a suitable degree of accuracy.
Surface area of a sphere $= 4\pi r^2$

CHAPTER

21 Algebraic identities 1

21.1 Identities involving indices

CAN YOU REMEMBER

- The meaning of 'power', 'index' and 'base number'?
- The rules for multiplying and dividing index numbers?
- The meaning of 'reciprocal', 'square root' and 'cube root'?

IN THIS SECTION YOU WILL

- Learn the meaning of 'identity'.
- Learn how to raise a power to a power.
- Learn the result of raising any number to the power zero.
- Use fractional and negative powers in algebra.

In the expression $x(x + 1)$, the letter symbol, x, is a *variable*.
This means that x can have **any value**.
$x(x + 1) \equiv x^2 + x$ is an *identity* because it is true for **all** possible values of the variable, x.
An *identity* is formed when two algebraic expressions are equal for any values of the letter symbols.
The symbol $\equiv$ means 'is identically equal to'.
It shows that two expressions form an identity.

The rules of *indices*

To multiply index numbers with the same base, add the powers $\quad x^a \times x^b \equiv x^{a+b}$

To divide index numbers with the same base, subtract the powers $\quad x^a \div x^b \equiv x^{a-b}$

To raise a power to a power, multiply the powers $\quad (x^a)^b \equiv x^{ab}$

For example, $(x^5)^3 \equiv x^5 \times x^5 \times x^5 \equiv x^{5 \times 3} \equiv x^{15}$

Example 1

Simplify: **a** $2x^3 \times 3x^4$ **b** $6x^7 \div 2x^3$ **c** $(x^2y^3)^2$

Solution 1

a $2x^3 \times 3x^4 \equiv 2 \times x^3 \times 3 \times x^4$
$\equiv 2 \times 3 \times x^3 \times x^4$
$\equiv 6 \times x^{3+4}$
$\equiv 6x^7$

Multiply the numbers, add the powers.

b $6x^7 \div 2x^3 \equiv \dfrac{6x^7}{2x^3}$

$\equiv \dfrac{6}{2} \times \dfrac{x^7}{x^3}$ Divide the numbers, subtract the powers.

$\equiv 3x^4$

c $(x^2y^3)^2 \equiv (x^2)^2 \times (y^3)^2 \equiv x^{2 \times 2} \times y^{3 \times 2} \equiv x^4 \times y^6 \equiv x^4y^6$

Exercise A

1 Simplify:

a $a^3 \times a^5$ **b** $b \times b^5$ **c** $c^2 \times c \times c^3$

d $d^3 \times d^5 \times d^2$ **e** $e^4 \div e$ **f** $f^5 \div f^2$

g $g^4 \times g^2 \div g$ **h** $h^4 \div h^2 \times h$ **i** $\dfrac{(i^3 \times i^5)}{i^2}$

j $\dfrac{(j^7 \times j^2)}{j}$ **k** $\dfrac{(k^5 \times k^3)}{(k^2 \times k)}$ **l** $\dfrac{(l^4 \times l^5)}{(l^2 \times l^3)}$

2 **a** $2a^3 \times 4a^4$ **b** $3b^5 \times 5b^3$ **c** $4c^3 \times 2c^2$

d $7d^5 \times 3d$ **e** $4e^4 \times 5e^2 \times e^3$ **f** $2d^4 \times 3d^3 \times 4d^2$

g $8g^7 \div 2g^3$ **h** $12h^4 \div 4h$ **i** $30i^8 \div 10i^3$

j $12j^3 \div 4j \times 2j^4$ **k** $\dfrac{(9k^3 \times 4k^2)}{12k^4}$ **l** $\dfrac{12l^8}{(3l \times 2l^2)}$

3 Simplify:

a $\dfrac{(2a^7 \times 8a^2)}{(4a \times a^3)}$ **b** $\dfrac{(9b^3 \times 4b^2)}{(3b^2 \times 2b)}$ **c** $\dfrac{(6c^4 \times 8c^4)}{(4c \times 2c^3)}$ **d** $\dfrac{(12d^3 \times 4d^7)}{(8d^4 \times 2d)}$

4 Simplify:

a $x^3y^2 \times xy$ **b** $xy^4 \times x^3y^2$ **c** $x^2y^5 \times x^2y^2$

d $x^5y^2 \div x^2y$ **e** $x^7y^3 \div xy^2$ **f** $x^8y^4 \div x^5y^2$

g $\dfrac{(x^2y \times xy^2)}{(x^2y^2)}$ **h** $\dfrac{(x^3y^2 \times x^2y^3)}{(x^5y^4)}$ **i** $\dfrac{(xy^2 \times y)}{(xy^2)}$

5 Simplify:

a $(x^3)^4$ **b** $(x^4)^3$ **c** $(x^6)^2$ **d** $(x^2)^6$

e $(x^2)^5$ **f** $(x^5)^2$ **g** $(x^7)^2 \times x^7$ **h** $(x^3)^2 \times (x^2)^5$

i $(x^4)^3 \times (x^3)^2$ **j** $(x^2)^4 \div x^4$ **k** $(x^5)^3 \div (x^3)^2$ **l** $(x^3)^{10} \div (x^4)^5$

6 Simplify:

a $(xy^3)^4$ **b** $(x^4y^4)^3$ **c** $(x^2y^3)^2$

d $(x^3y^2)^3$ **e** $(x^5y)^3$ **f** $(x^2y^5)^4$

g $(x^3y^5)^2 \times xy^2$ **h** $(x^3y)^4 \times (x^2y^2)^2$ **i** $(x^5y^3)^2 \times (xy^4)^3$

j $(x^3y^5)^3 \div xy^3$ **k** $(x^2y^3)^5 \div (x^3y^5)^3$ **l** $\dfrac{(x^5y^4)^5}{(x^4y^5)^3}$

Example 2

Simplify: **a** $(2x^3)^4$ **b** $(4x^3y^4z)^3$

Solution 2

a $(2x^3)^4 \equiv 2^4 \times (x^3)^4 \equiv 16 \times x^{3 \times 4} \equiv 16x^{12}$

b $(4x^3y^4z)^3 \equiv 4^3 \times (x^3)^3 \times (y^4)^3 \times (z)^3 \equiv 64 \times x^{3 \times 3} \times y^{4 \times 3} \times z^3 \equiv 64x^9y^{12}z^3$

$x^n \div x^n \equiv x^{n-n} \equiv x^0$

$x^n \div x^n$ is a number divided by itself which must be 1

Any number raised to the power zero equals 1 $\quad x^0 = 1$

For example, $5^0 = 1$

$1 \div x^n \equiv x^0 \div x^n \equiv x^{0-n} \equiv x^{-n}$

The *reciprocal* of x^n is x^{-n} $\quad x^n \equiv \dfrac{1}{x^{-n}}$

Similarly, the reciprocal of x^{-n} is x^n $\quad x^{-n} \equiv \dfrac{1}{x^n}$

For example, $x^{-2} \equiv \dfrac{1}{x^2}$

Finding the square root of a positive number is the *inverse* of raising the number to the power 2
Finding the cube root of a number is the *inverse* of raising the number to the power 3

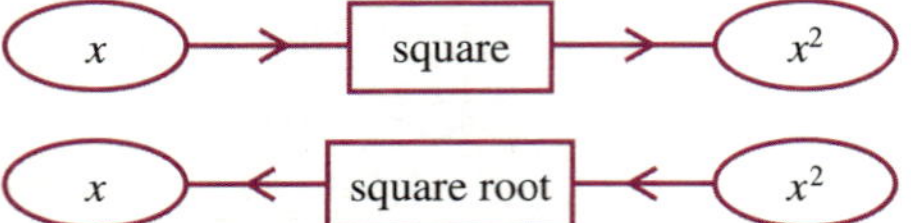

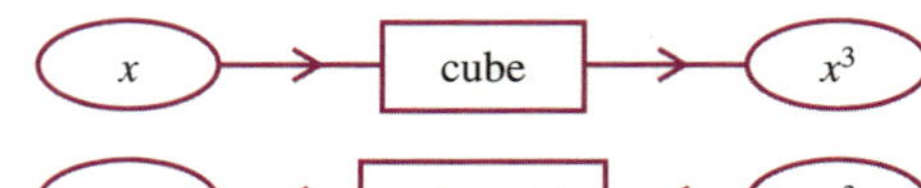

However,

$(x^2)^{\frac{1}{2}} \equiv x^{2 \times \frac{1}{2}} \equiv x \qquad (x^3)^{\frac{1}{3}} \equiv x^{3 \times \frac{1}{3}} \equiv x$

Raising a number to the power $\frac{1}{2}$ is the same as finding the positive square root of the number. $\quad x^{\frac{1}{2}} \equiv \sqrt{x}$

Raising a number to the power $\frac{1}{3}$ is the same as finding the cube root of the number. $\quad x^{\frac{1}{3}} \equiv \sqrt[3]{x}$

For example: $\quad 64^{\frac{1}{2}} = \sqrt{64} = 8 \qquad 64^{\frac{1}{3}} = \sqrt[3]{64} = 4$

Example 3

Simplify:

a $\dfrac{10x^{-3}}{5x}$ **b** $(x^2)^{-3}$ **c** $\sqrt[3]{x^6}$ **d** $\sqrt{(16x^{-4}y^6)}$

Solution 3

a $\dfrac{10x^{-3}}{5x} \equiv \dfrac{10}{5} \times \dfrac{x^{-3}}{x} \equiv 2 \times x^{-3-1} \equiv 2x^{-4} \equiv \dfrac{2}{x^4}$

b $(x^2)^{-3} \equiv x^{2 \times -3} \equiv x^{-6} \equiv \dfrac{1}{x^6}$

c $\sqrt[3]{x^6} \equiv (x^6)^{\frac{1}{3}} \equiv x^{6 \times \frac{1}{3}} \equiv x^2$

d $\sqrt{(16x^{-4}y^6)} \equiv (16x^{-4}y^6)^{\frac{1}{2}} \equiv 16^{\frac{1}{2}} \times (x^{-4})^{\frac{1}{2}} \times (y^6)^{\frac{1}{2}} \equiv 4 \times x^{-4 \times \frac{1}{2}} \times y^{6 \times \frac{1}{2}} \equiv 4 \times x^{-2} \times y^3 \equiv \dfrac{4y^3}{x^2}$

Exercise B

1 Find the value of:

a a^0 **b** $2b^0$ **c** $(2c)^0$ **d** $5d^0$ **e** $(5e)^0$
f $(f+1)^0$ **g** $(2g-3)^0$ **h** $4(h-5)^0$ **i** $6(2i-7)^0$

2 Simplify:

a $(2a^3)^2$ **b** $(2b^2)^3$ **c** $(4c^5)^2$ **d** $(2d^5)^4$
e $(4e^5)^3$ **f** $(2d^3)^5$ **g** $(5g^3)^2 \times 2g^3$ **h** $(10h^4)^2 \div 4h$
i $(5i^5)^2 \times (2i^3)^2$

3 Simplify:

a $(2x^2y^3)^3$ **b** $(3xy^3)^2$ **c** $(4x^2y^5)^2$ **d** $(5x^3y^2)^3$
e $(2x^3y^5)^4$ **f** $(6x^5y^3)^2$ **g** $(3x^4y^4)^3$ **h** $(7x^6y)^2$
i $(10x^5y^2)^3$

4 Simplify:

a $5x^4y^3 \times 2xy^2$ **b** $6xy^3 \times 4x^2y$ **c** $12x^3y^5 \times 3x^4y^3$
d $20x^7y^2 \div 4x^2y$ **e** $12x^3y^5 \div 2x^2y^2$ **f** $18x^3y^2 \div 9x^2y^2$
g $4xy \times 5xy \div x^2y^2$ **h** $8xy^4 \times 4x^5y^3 \div 2x^3y^2$ **i** $12xy^2 \div 6y \times 3xy^2$

5 Simplify:

a $(5x^2y^3z^4)^2$ **b** $(2x^3yz^2)^3$ **c** $(5xy^2z^3)^2 \times (2x^3y^2z)^3$
d $(3x^2y^4z^5)^2 \times (2x^5y^4z^3)^3$ **e** $(8x^4y^4z^2)^2 \div (2x^2yz)^3$ **f** $(10x^2y^3z^4)^3 \div (5x^2y^3z^4)^2$

6 Write each of the following expressions as simply as possible with **no** negative powers.

a x^{-1} **b** x^{-2} **c** $\frac{x^2}{x^3}$ **d** $x^3 \times x^{-5}$
e $(x^3)^{-1}$ **f** $(x^{-3})^2$ **g** $1 \div x^5$ **h** $\frac{1}{x^7} \times x^3$
i $\frac{(x^3)^2}{(x^4)^3}$ **j** $x^3 \times x^{-5}$ **k** $x^{-3} \times x^{-5}$ **l** $x^{-3} \div x^5$
m $2x^{-5}$ **n** $2x^{-6} \times 4x^2$ **o** $8x^3 \div 2x^8$

7 Copy and complete.

a The inverse of squaring is finding the ....
b The inverse of squaring is raising to the power ....
c The inverse of cubing is finding the ....
d The inverse of cubing is raising to the power ....

8 Simplify the following expressions.

a $(x^2)^{\frac{1}{2}}$ **b** $(4x^2)^{\frac{1}{2}}$ **c** $\sqrt{(4x^2)}$
d $(x^6)^{\frac{1}{3}}$ **e** $(27x^6)^{\frac{1}{3}}$ **f** $\sqrt[3]{(27x^6)}$
g $(x^3y^9)^{\frac{1}{3}}$ **h** $(64x^3y^9)^{\frac{1}{3}}$ **i** $\sqrt[3]{(64x^3y^9)}$
j $\sqrt{(64x^6y^2)}$ **k** $\sqrt[3]{(8x^6y^3)}$ **l** $\sqrt{(100x^2y^8z^4)}$

9 Simplify the following expressions.
Write your answers using **positive** powers only.

a $(x^4)^{-\frac{1}{2}}$ **b** $(x^{-2})^4$ **c** $(x^3)^{-\frac{1}{3}}$ **d** $\sqrt[3]{(x^{-6})}$
e $(x^2y^4)^{-\frac{1}{2}}$ **f** $\sqrt{(16x^{-4})}$ **g** $(x^3y^{-3})^{-\frac{1}{3}}$ **h** $(8x^3y^{-3})^{-\frac{1}{3}}$
i $\sqrt[3]{(27x^{-3}y^{-6})}$

10 Show that:

a $5x^{-2} \times 2x^{-3} \equiv \dfrac{10}{x^5}$ **b** $\dfrac{24x^3}{6x^6} \equiv \dfrac{4}{x^3}$

c $2(x^{-2})^3 \equiv \dfrac{2}{x^6}$ **d** $\sqrt{(25x^{-2})} \equiv \dfrac{5}{x}$

11 a Find the value of w in $2^w = 1$ **b** Find the value of x in $2^x = \dfrac{1}{4}$

c Find the value of y in $8^y = 2$ **d** Find the value of z in $16^{z+3} = 2^z$

12 You are given that $x^2 = a^3$
Write each of the following expressions in terms of a.
Write your answers using **positive** powers only.
a x^{-2} **b** x^4 **c** x **d** x^{-1} **e** x^3 **f** $\sqrt[3]{x^{-2}}$

21.2 Expanding brackets and simplifying expressions 2

CAN YOU REMEMBER

- How to multiply an expression in brackets by a single term?
- How to simplify expressions that include brackets?
- The meaning of 'identity' and the symbol '$\equiv$'?

IN THIS SECTION YOU WILL

- Reinforce and extend skills in expanding brackets and simplifying.

The process of removing brackets from an algebraic expression is called *expanding*.
Multiply **each** term in the bracket by the term outside the bracket.

Example 1

Expand $2x^2(3x + 5)$

Solution 1

Method 1

$2x^2(3x + 5) \equiv 2x^2 \times 3x + 2x^2 \times 5$

$2x^2(3x + 5) \equiv 6x^3 + 10x^2$

Method 2

$\times$	$3x$	5
$2x^2$	$6x^3$	$10x^2$

Multiply **each** term in the first bracket by **each** term in the second bracket.

Example 2

Expand and simplify $(x + 5)(3x - 2)$

Solution 2

Method 1

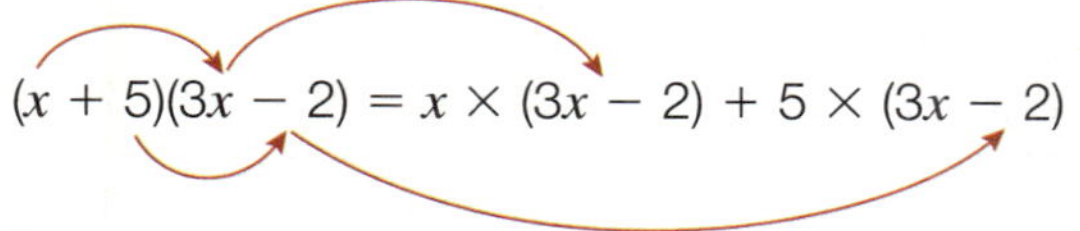

$(x + 5)(3x - 2) = x \times (3x - 2) + 5 \times (3x - 2)$

Method 2

$\times$	x	5
$3x$	$3x^2$	$15x$
-2	$-2x$	-10

$(x + 5)(3x - 2) \equiv 3x^2 - 2x + 15x - 10 \equiv 3x^2 + 13x - 10$
$(x + 5)(3x - 2) \equiv 3x^2 + 13x - 10$ is an identity.

Example 3

Expand and simplify $(2x - 5)(3x - 1)$

Solution 3

Method 1

$(2x - 5)(3x - 1) \equiv 2x(3x - 1) - 5(3x - 1)$
$\equiv 2x \times 3x + 2x \times -1 - 5 \times 3x - 5 \times -1$

Method 2

$\times$	$2x$	-5
$3x$	$6x^2$	$-15x$
-1	$-2x$	5

$(2x - 5)(3x - 1) \equiv 6x^2 + -2x - 15x + 5$
$(2x - 5)(3x - 1) \equiv 6x^2 - 17x + 5$

Exercise A

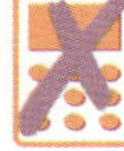

1 Expand each of the following expressions.

a $5x(x + 3)$ **b** $3x(x - 6)$ **c** $2x^2(4x + 3)$
d $3x^2(2x - 7y)$ **e** $7xy(5x + 2y)$ **f** $-3xy^2(-2x^2 + 3y)$

2 Match the pairs of equivalent expressions in these boxes.
Write each answer as an identity.

$2x(x + 9)$	$12x^3 + 3x$	$12x^3 + 4x$	$2x^2(3x + 4)$	$4x^2(3x + 1)$
$3x^3 + 6x$	$6x^3 + 8x^2$	$2x(3x + 1)$	$6x^2(x + 2)$	$12x^3 + 4x^2$
$3x^3 + 18x$	$3x(x^2 + 2)$	$2x^2 + 18x$	$6x^2 + 2x$	$3x(x^2 + 6)$
$6x^3 + 12x^2$		$3x(4x^2 + 1)$		$4x(3x^2 + 1)$

3 Expand each of these expressions.

a $3a(a + 2)$ **b** $3b(2b + 1)$ **c** $2c(3c + 2)$ **d** $5d(d^2 + 1)$
e $4e^2(e - 2)$ **f** $7f(2f - 3)$ **g** $g^3(2g - 7)$ **h** $4h^2(2h - 5)$
i $3i^2(2 - 5i)$ **j** $4j(3 - 2j^2)$ **k** $-4k^2(1 - 3k)$ **l** $-2l(6l^3 + 1)$

4 Complete each of these identities.

a $2x(3x - 1) \equiv 6x^2 - \ldots\ldots$ **b** $3x^2(2x + 1) \equiv \ldots\ldots + 3x^2$
c $xy(x + y) \equiv$ **d** $5xy(3x + 7y) \equiv$ **e** $3xy^2(4x - y) \equiv$
f $2x^2y^2(3xy - 1) \equiv$ **g** $2x^2y(5x + 3y) \equiv$ **h** $4xy(4x^2 - 3y^2) \equiv$
i $xyz(x + y + z) \equiv$ **j** $xyz(x - 2y - z^2) \equiv$

5 Expand and simplify each of the following expressions.

a $(x + 7)(x + 2)$ **b** $(x + 2)(x - 7)$ **c** $(x - 5)(x - 6)$
d $(x - 2)(x + 3)$ **e** $(x - 1)(x - 7)$ **f** $(2x + 5)(x + 3)$
g $(3x + 2)(x - 4)$ **h** $(4x + 1)(3x - 2)$ **i** $(2x - 1)(5x - 3)$

6 Complete each of these identities.

a $(x + 2)(x + 1) \equiv$ **b** $(2x - 3)(x + 2) \equiv$ **c** $(5x + 3)(x - 1) \equiv$
d $(4x - 3)(x - 5) \equiv$ **e** $(x + 3)(2x - 1) \equiv$ **f** $(x - 2)(2x - 5) \equiv$
g $(4x - 1)(2x - 5) \equiv$ **h** $(3x - 1)(5x + 2) \equiv$ **i** $(x + 3)(2x - 7) \equiv$
j $(3x + 4)(1 - 2x) \equiv$ **k** $(4x - 3)(3x - 5) \equiv$ **l** $(5x - 1)(3x - 5) \equiv$
m $(2x + 1)(1 - x) \equiv$ **n** $(3x - 1)(2x - 3) \equiv$ **o** $(3x - 2)(6x - 1) \equiv$
p $(2x + 7)(5 - 2x) \equiv$

7 Match the pairs of equivalent expressions in these boxes.
Write each answer as an identity.

$(2x + 1)(x + 9)$	$2x^2 - 19x + 9$	$2x^2 + 17x - 9$	$(2x + 1)(x - 9)$
$2x^2 - 17x - 9$	$2x^2 - 11x + 9$	$(2x + 9)(x + 1)$	$(2x - 9)(x + 1)$
$2x^2 + 11x + 9$	$2x^2 + 7x - 9$	$(2x + 9)(x - 1)$	$2x^2 + 19x + 9$
$(2x - 1)(x + 9)$	$(2x - 9)(x - 1)$	$(2x - 1)(x - 9)$	$2x^2 - 7x - 9$

8 Expand and simplify:

a $(x + 9)(x + 2)$ **b** $(x + 9)(x - 2)$ **c** $(x - 9)(x + 2)$
d $(x - 9)(x - 2)$ **e** $(4x + 1)(x + 4)$ **f** $(4x + 1)(x - 4)$
g $(4x - 1)(x + 4)$ **h** $(4x - 1)(x - 4)$ **i** $(5x + 7)(4x + 3)$
j $(5x + 7)(4x - 3)$ **k** $(5x - 7)(4x + 3)$ **l** $(5x - 7)(4x - 3)$
m $(3x + 5)(2x + 7)$ **n** $(3x + 5)(2x - 7)$ **o** $(3x - 5)(2x + 7)$
p $(3x - 5)(2x - 7))$ **q** $(7x + 2)(2x + 7)$ **r** $(7x - 2)(2x + 7)$
s $(7x + 2)(2x - 7)$ **t** $(7x - 2)(2x - 7)$ **u** $(4x + 3)(3x + 5)$
v $(4x + 3)(3x - 5)$ **w** $(4x - 3)(3x + 5)$ **x** $(4x - 3)(3x - 5)$

Example 4

Expand and simplify $3x^2(5x - 2y) - 2y(x^2 - 4y)$
Write the answer as an identity.

Solution 4

$$3x^2(5x - 2y) - 2y(x^2 - 4y) \equiv (3x^2 \times 5x) + (3x^2 \times -2y) - (2y \times x^2) - (2y \times -4y)$$
$$\equiv 15x^3 + (-6x^2y) - 2x^2y - (-8y^2)$$
$$\equiv 15x^3 - 6x^2y - 2x^2y + 8y^2$$

$3x^2(5x - 2y) - 2y(x^2 - 4y) \equiv 15x^3 - 8x^2y + 8y^2$

Exercise B

1 Jim, Kay and Emma try to expand $3x^2(4x^5 + 2y^3)$
Jim writes $3x^2(4x^5 + 2y^3) \equiv 7x^{10} + 5xy^6$
Kay writes $3x^2(4x^5 + 2y^3) \equiv 12x^7 + 6x^2y^3$
Emma writes $3x^2(4x^5 + 2y^3) = 12x^7 + 3x^2$

a Who is correct?
b Describe the mistakes that the other two have made.

2 Tim expands $(2y + 4)(y - 3)$
His answer is $2y^2 - 12$
Explain what Tim has done wrong.

3 Expand and simplify.
Write each answer as an identity.

a $a(5a + 4) - 4a(a + 1)$
b $b(4b+ 3) - 3b(b+ 1)$
c $2c(2c - 5) + 5c(c + 2)$
d $5d(3d - 2) + 2d(3d + 5)$
e $2e(4 - 5e) + 5e(3e + 4) + e(e + 1)$
f $3f(1 - 5f) - 2f(1 - 4f) + 7f^2$
g $-4g(1 - 2g) + 4g(2 - 3g)$

4 Expand and simplify:

a $x(x + y) + x(x - y)$
b $x(x + y) - x(x - y)$
c $xy(x + y) + xy(x - y)$
d $2x^3(3x^2 + 4x - 1) + x^2(3x^3 - 8x^2 + 2x + 1)$
e $3x^2(2x^2 + x - 3) - 2x(3x^3 - x^2 + 2x + 1)$

5 Show that:

a $(2x + 1)(x + 3) - (2x + 3)(x + 1) \equiv 2x$
b $(3x + 1)(x + 1) - (2x + 1)(x + 1) \equiv x^2 + x$
c $(3 + 5x)(x + 2) + (3 - 5x)(x + 2) \equiv 6(x + 2)$
d $(5x + 4)(3x - 1) - (3x - 4)(5x + 1) \equiv 24x$
e $(2x + y)(2x - y) - (x + y)(x - y) \equiv 3x^2$
f $(3x + 2y)(3x - 2y) - (2x + 3y)(2x - 3y) \equiv 5(x^2 + y^2)$

6 The diagram shows four rectangles, A, B, C and D.
Rectangle A has length $(3x + 1)$ cm and width $(x + 2)$ cm.
Rectangle B has length $(3x - 2)$ cm and width $(x + 3)$ cm.
Rectangle C has length $(3y + 2)$ cm and width $(y + 1)$ cm.
Rectangle D has length $(2y + 1)$ cm and width $(y + 2)$ cm.

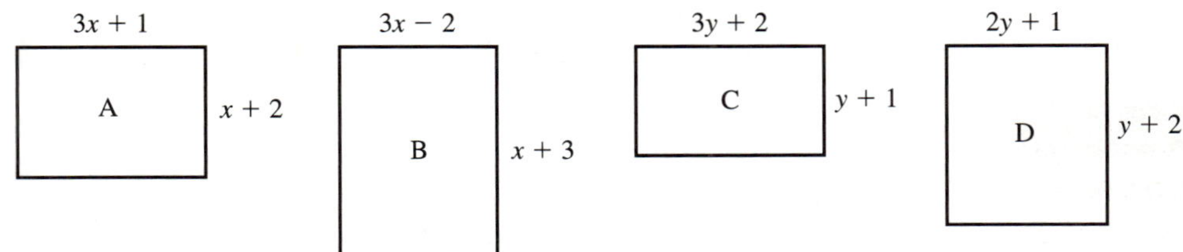

a Write out an expression for the area of rectangle A.
b Write out an expression for the area of rectangle B.
c Use your answers to **a** and **b** to show that the difference between the areas of rectangles A and B is 8 cm^2.
d Show that the area of rectangle C is never less than the area of rectangle D, for any value of y.
e Find the sum of the areas of all four rectangles.

7 The diagram shows a rectangular flower bed with a path on three sides.
The flower bed is 1 metre wide and 5 metres long.
The path is x metres wide.
Show that the total area of the flower bed and path is $2x^2 + 11x + 5$

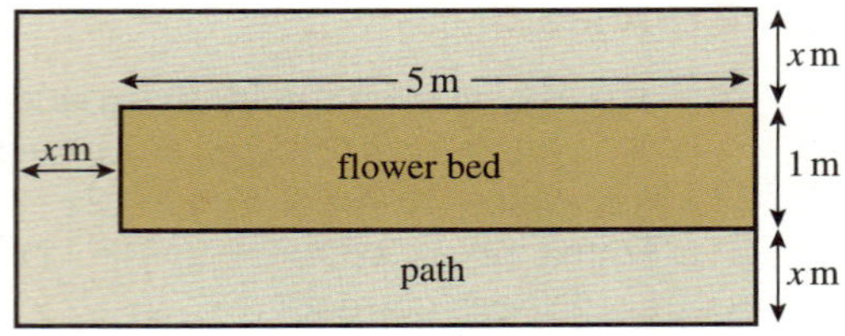

8 The diagram shows a rectangular lawn with a path on three sides.
The lawn is x metres wide and $2x$ metres long.
The path is 1 metre wide.
Show that the total area of the lawn and path is $2x^2 + 5x + 2$ m^2

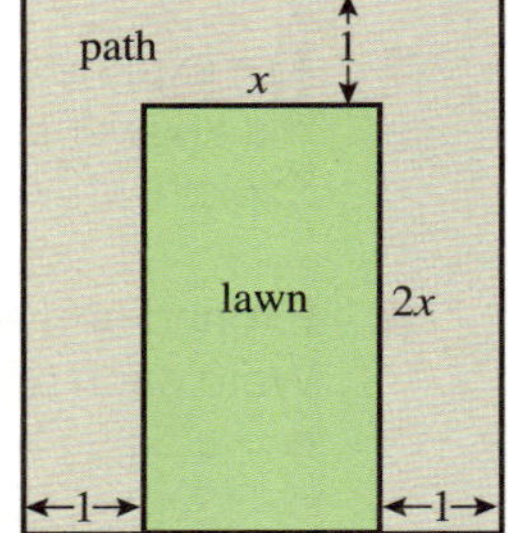

21.3 More factorisation

CAN YOU REMEMBER

- That the inverse of expanding brackets is called factorising?
- How to factorise simple algebraic expressions?
- How to find the highest common factor (HCF) of two numbers or terms?

IN THIS SECTION YOU WILL

- Extend skills in factorising.
- Learn about quadratic expressions.
- Learn how to factorise quadratic expressions.

Factorising is the inverse of expanding brackets.
To factorise an algebraic expression first find the *highest common factor* (HCF) of all the terms in the expression. In a complex expression, do this systematically by looking at numbers and each of the variables separately.

Example 1

Factorise: **a** $4x^2y^3z^4 + 6xy^3z^2$ **b** $7xy^2 + 21x^2y^3 - 35x^3y^4$

Solution 1

a The HCF of 4 and 6 is **2**
The HCF of x^2 and x is $\mathbf{x}$
The HCF of y^3 and y^3 is $\mathbf{y^3}$
The HCF of z^4 and z^2 is $\mathbf{z^2}$
So the HCF of $4x^2y^3z^4$ and $6xy^3z^2$ is $\mathbf{2xy^3z^2}$
So $4x^2y^3z^4 + 6xy^3z^2 \equiv \mathbf{2xy^3z^2} \times 2xz^2 + \mathbf{2xy^3z^2} \times 3 \equiv \mathbf{2xy^3z^2}(2xz^2 + 3)$
$2xy^3z^2(2xz^2 + 3)$ is the **fully** factorised form of $4x^2y^3z^4 + 6xy^3z^2$

Check by expanding:

$\times$	$2xz^2$	3
$2xy^3z^2$	$4x^2y^3z^4$ ✓	$6xy^3z^2$ ✓

b The HCF of $7xy^2$, $21x^2y^3$ and $35x^3y^4$ is $7xy^2$

$7xy^2 + 21x^2y^3 - 35x^3y^4 \equiv 7xy^2 \times 1 + 7xy^2 \times 3xy - 7xy^2 \times 5x^2y^2$

$\equiv 7xy^2(1 + 3xy - 5x^2y^2)$

Check by expanding:

$\times$	1	$3xy$	$-5x^2y^2$
$7xy^2$	$7xy^2 \times 1 = 7xy^2$ ✓	$7xy^2 \times 3xy = 21x^2y^3$ ✓	$7xy^2 \times -5x^2y^2 = -35x^3y^4$ ✓

Example 2

Factorise: **a** $ac + bc$ **b** $ad + bd$ **c** $ac + bc + ad + bd$

Solution 2

a $ac + bc \equiv c(a + b)$

b $ad + bd \equiv d(a + b)$

c $ac + bc + ad + bd \equiv (ac + bc) + (ad + bd)$

$\equiv c(a + b) + d(a + b)$

$\equiv (a + b)(c + d)$

$(a + b)$ is the highest common factor (HCF).

Exercise A

1 Find the highest common factor (HCF) of:

a $4x$ and $6x^2$ **b** $12x^2$ and $18x^5$ **c** $6x^7$ and $9x^3$

d $16xy^2$ and $24x^2y$ **e** $20x^3y^2$ and $30x^2y^4$ **f** $15xy^3$ and $25x^2y^3$

g $24xyz$ and $36x^2y$ **h** $45x^3y^2z$ and $36x^2yz^2$ **i** $12xyz$ and $15x^2y^2z^2$

2 Use your answers to question **1** to factorise each of the following expressions.

a $4x + 6x^2$ **b** $12x^2 - 18x^5$ **c** $9x^3 + 6x^7$

d $16xy^2 - 24x^2y$ **e** $30x^2y^4 - 20x^3y^2$ **f** $15xy^3 + 25x^2y^3$

g $24xyz + 36x^2y$ **h** $45x^3y^2z - 36x^2yz^2$ **i** $15x^2y^2z^2 - 12xyz$

3

$8x$	$4x^2$	$3xy$	$8x^2y$	$6x^2yz$	$3xy^2z$	$9x^2yz^3$

Which of the cards above show the highest common factor (HCF) of:

a $12x^2y$ and $8x^3$ **b** $18x^3y^2z$ and $6x^2yz^3$ **c** $18x^2y^3z^4$ and $27x^2yz^3$

d $8x^2y^3$ and $16x^3y$ **e** $16x^2z$ and $24xy$ **f** $16x^4y$ and $12x^2$

g $24x^2y^3$ and $40x^3y$ **h** $9xy^3z$ and $6x^2y^2z^5$ **i** $15xy^2$ and $9x^2y$

4 Copy and complete this table.

a	$2x^2 + 4x$	$2x(x + \ldots)$
b	$2x^3 - 6x^2$	$2x^2(\ldots - \ldots)$
c	$4xy + 6x^2y^2$	$\ldots (2 + \ldots)$
d	$6xy^2 - 10x^2y$	$2xy(\ldots - \ldots)$
e	$6x^3y^4 + 18xy$	$\ldots (\ldots + 3)$
f	$12x^2yz^3 - 18xy^2z^2$	$\ldots (\ldots - 3y)$
g	$18x^4y^3z^5 + 12x^5y^2z^4$	$\ldots (3yz + \ldots)$
h	$21x^2y^3z^4 - 14x^4y^3z^2$	$7x^2y^3z^2 (\ldots - \ldots)$
i	$26x^2y^2z^2 + 39x^3y^3z^3$	$\ldots(2 + \ldots)$
j	$16x^3y^3z^3 - 24x^2y^2z^2$	$\ldots(2xyz - \ldots)$

5 Factorise **fully**:

a $18x + 24$ **b** $18x^2 - 27x$ **c** $ax - ax^2$
d $15xy - 5y^2$ **e** $24xy + 56x^2$ **f** $25xy + 15x^2$
g $25xy + 15x^2y$ **h** $16xy + 8yz + 8xyz$ **i** $21xy - 35x^2y^2$
j $6a^3x + 10ax^3$ **k** $39xyz^2 - 52x^2yz$ **l** $4ab - 10ab^2 + 6a^2b$
m $6x^3y^2z^3 - 15x^2y^3z^2$ **n** $6xy^2z^3 - 8x^3yz^2$ **o** $12a^2b^2 + 6ab^2 - 9a^2b$

6 Factorise the following expressions.

a **i** $xy + zy$ **ii** $xw + zw$ **iii** $xy + zy + xw + zw$
b **i** $cy + dy$ **ii** $cz + dz$ **iii** $cy + dy + cz + dz$
c **i** $pr + qr$ **ii** $ps + qs$ **iii** $pr + qr - ps - qs$
d **i** $xy - x^2y$ **ii** $a - ax$ **iii** $xy - x^2y + a - ax$
e $xy - 4ay + 3xb - 12ab$ **f** $ax^2 + x - abx - b$
g $x^2 + xy + xz + yz$ **h** $2x + 4x^2 - y - 2xy$

7 Copy and complete the following.
The first one has been done for you.

a $x^2 + 5x + 6 \equiv (x^2 + 2x) + (3x + 6) \equiv x(x + 2) + 3(x + 2) \equiv (x + 2)(x + 3)$
b $x^2 + 6x + 8 \equiv (x^2 + 2x) + (4x + 8) \equiv \ldots$
c $x^2 + 7x + 12 \equiv (x^2 + 4x) + (\ldots\ldots + \ldots\ldots) \equiv \ldots$
d $x^2 + 13x + 12 \equiv (x^2 + x) + (\ldots + \ldots) \equiv \ldots$
e $x^2 + 8x + 15 \equiv (x^2 + \ldots) + (\ldots + \ldots) \equiv \ldots$
f $x^2 + 9x + 14 \equiv (x^2 + \ldots) + (\ldots + \ldots) \equiv \ldots$

Quadratic expressions

The general form of a quadratic expression is $ax^2 + bx + c$.
Quadratic expressions must have an x^2 term, so $a \neq 0$
They can also have an x term and/or a number term.
This means that b and/or c can be zero.
The table shows examples of quadratic expressions and the values of a, b and c.

Expression	a	b	c
$x^2 - 5x + 6$	1	−5	6
$2x^2 + 3x - 7$	2	3	−7
$x^2 - 2x$	1	−2	0
$8 - 5x^2$	−5	0	8

The expression $(x + 2)(x + 3)$ expands and simplifies to a quadratic expression
$(x + 2)(x + 3) \equiv x^2 + 5x + 6$
Factorising $x^2 + 5x + 6$ means rewriting it in the form $(x + 2)(x + 3)$.
A quadratic expression of the form $x^2 + bx + c$ can be factorised to the form $(x + p)(x + q)$.

Example 3

Factorise: **a** $a^2 + 9a + 20$ **b** $b^2 - 2b - 15$

Solution 3

a **Step 1:** $a^2 + 9a + 20 \equiv (a + p)(a + q)$

×	a	p
a	a^2	pa
q	qa	pq

$= a^2 + pa + qa + pq$

Comparing with $a^2 + 9a + 20$ gives $p + q = 9$ and $pq = 20$

Step 2: $p + q$ is positive and pq is positive, so both p and q are positive.

List possible pairs of positive values of p and q that multiply to give 20 and work out $p + q$

p	q	pq (= 20)	$p + q$
1	20	1 × 20	1 + 20 = 21✗
2	10	2 × 10	2 + 10 = 12✗
4	5	4 × 5	4 + 5 = 9✓

So $p = 4$ and $q = 5$

So $a^2 + 9a + 20 \equiv (a + 4)(a + 5)$

Check by expanding the brackets:

×	a	4
a	a^2	$4a$
5	$5a$	20

$a^2 + 9a + 20 \equiv (a + 4)(a + 5)$✓

b **Step 1:** $b^2 - 2b - 15 \equiv (b + p)(b + q)$

$p + q = -2$ and $pq = -15$

Step 2: $p + q$ is negative and pq is negative.

So one of p and q is positive and the other is negative.

p	q	pq (= −15)	$p + q$
−1	15	−1 × 15 = −15	−1 + 15 = 14✗
1	−15	1 × −15 = −15	1 + −15 = −14✗
−3	5	−3 × 5 = −15	−3 + 5 = 2✗
3	−5	3 × −5 = −15	3 + −5 = −2✓

So $p = 3$ and $q = -5$
So $b^2 - 2b - 15 \equiv (b + 3)(b - 5)$
Check by expanding the brackets:

$\times$	b	3
b	b^2	$3b$
-5	$-5b$	-15

$b^2 - 2b - 15 \equiv (b + 3)(b - 5)$✓

Example 4

Factorise: **a** $2x^2 - 13x + 15$ **b** $6y^2 - 13y + 2$

Solution 4

a **Step 1:** $2x \times x = 2x^2$
This is the **only** way that the product of the x terms can give $2x^2$
So $2x^2 - 13x + 15 \equiv (2x + p)(x + q)$

$\times$	$2x$	p
x	$2x^2$	px
q	$2qx$	pq

$p + 2q = -13$ and $pq = 15$
Step 2: $p + 2q$ is negative and pq is positive.
So both p and q are negative.
List possible pairs of values of p and q and work out $p + 2q$.

p	q	pq (=15)	$p + 2q$
−1	−15	$-1 \times -15 = 15$	$-1 + 2 \times -15 = -31$✗
−15	−1	$-15 \times -1 = 15$	$-15 + 2 \times -1 = -17$✗
−3	−5	$-3 \times -5 = 15$	$-3 + 2 \times -5 = -13$✓
−5	−3	$-5 \times -3 = 15$	$-5 + 2 \times -3 = -11$✗

So $p = -3$ and $q = -5$
So $2x^2 - 13x + 15 \equiv (2x - 3)(x - 5)$
Check by expanding the brackets:

$\times$	$2x$	-3
x	$2x^2$	$-3x$
-5	$-10x$	15

$2x^2 - 13x + 15 \equiv (2x - 3)(x - 5)$✓

b **Step 1:** $6y \times y = 6y^2$ or $3y \times 2y = 6y^2$
There are **two** ways that the product of the y terms can give $6y^2$.
$6y^2 - 13y + 2 \equiv (6y + p)(y + q)$ $6y^2 - 13y + 2 \equiv (3y + p)(2y + q)$.

$\times$	$6y$	p
y	$6y^2$	py
q	$6qy$	pq

$\times$	$3y$	p
$2y$	$6y^2$	$2py$
q	$3qy$	pq

$p + 6q = -13$ and $pq = 2$ or $2p + 3q = -13$ and $pq = 2$

Step 2: $p + 6q$ and $2p + 3q$ are both negative and pq is positive.
So both p and q are negative.
List possible pairs of values of p and q and work out $p + 6q$ and $2p + 3q$.

p	q	pq (=2)	$p + 6q$	$2p + 3q$
−1	−2	$-1 \times -2 = 2$	$-1 + 6 \times -2 = -13$ ✓	$2 \times -1 + 3 \times -2 = -8$ ✗
−2	−1	$-2 \times -1 = 2$	$-2 + 6 \times -1 = -8$ ✗	$2 \times -2 + 3 \times -1 = -7$ ✗

So $p = -1$ and $q = -2$
So $6y^2 - 13y + 2 \equiv (6y - 1)(y - 2)$
Check by expanding the brackets:

×	$6y$	-1
y	$6y^2$	$-y$
-2	$-12y$	2

$6y^2 - 13y + 2 \equiv (6y - 1)(y - 2)$ ✓

A quadratic expression of the form $ax^2 + bx + c$ can be factorised to the form $(px + q)(rx + s)$.
A quadratic expression written in the form $(px + q)(rx + s)$ can be expanded and simplified to the form $ax^2 + bx + c$.

Exercise B

1 Factorise each of the following expressions.

a $x^2 + 8x + 15$ **b** $x^2 + 9x + 14$ **c** $x^2 + 7x + 12$
d $x^2 + 7x + 10$ **e** $x^2 + 16x + 15$ **f** $x^2 + 5x + 4$
g $x^2 + 3x + 2$ **h** $x^2 + 12x + 32$ **i** $x^2 + 6x + 5$
j $x^2 + 9x + 18$ **k** $x^2 + 20x + 19$ **l** $x^2 + 40x + 144$
m $x^2 + 14x + 33$ **n** $x^2 + 14x + 24$ **o** $x^2 + 8x + 12$

2 Factorise each of the following expressions.

a $x^2 - x - 20$ **b** $x^2 - 4x - 21$ **c** $x^2 - 4x - 5$
d $x^2 + 3x - 28$ **e** $x^2 - 8x - 9$ **f** $x^2 - x - 30$
g $x^2 - 3x + 2$ **h** $x^2 - 18x + 45$ **i** $x^2 + x - 2$
j $x^2 - 11x + 30$ **k** $x^2 - 14x + 45$ **l** $x^2 - 10x - 39$
m $x^2 + 12x - 45$ **n** $x^2 - 8x + 12$ **o** $x^2 - x - 72$
p $x^2 - x - 42$ **q** $x^2 + 3x - 10$ **r** $x^2 - 7x + 10$
s $x^2 - 40x + 144$ **t** $x^2 - 13x + 36$ **u** $x^2 + 5x - 14$

3 Copy and complete each of the following factorisations.

a $2x^2 + 3x + 1 \equiv (2x + 1)(x + \ldots)$ **b** $2x^2 + 7x + 3 \equiv (2x + \ldots)(\ldots + 3)$
c $3x^2 + 4x + 1 \equiv (\ldots + 1)(x + \ldots)$ **d** $2x^2 - 9x - 5 \equiv (2x - 1)(x + \ldots)$
e $5x^2 - 6x + 1 \equiv (\ldots - 1)(\ldots - 1)$ **f** $5x^2 + 3x - 2 \equiv (\ldots - \ldots)(x + 1)$
g $6x^2 + 5x + 1 \equiv (\ldots + \ldots)(2x + \ldots)$ **h** $8x^2 - 6x + 1 \equiv (4x - \ldots)(\ldots - \ldots)$
i $6x^2 - 17x + 5 \equiv (\ldots - \ldots)(2x - \ldots)$ **j** $4x^2 + x - 3 \equiv (\ldots - \ldots)(x + \ldots)$
k $12x^2 - 11x + 2 \equiv (\ldots - \ldots)(3x - \ldots)$ **l** $6x^2 - x - 2 \equiv (\ldots + \ldots)(3x - \ldots)$

4 Factorise each of the following expressions.

a $3x^2 + 5x + 2$ **b** $2x^2 + 9x + 7$ **c** $5x^2 + 16x + 3$
d $2x^2 + 5x + 3$ **e** $5x^2 + 26x + 5$ **f** $3x^2 + 10x + 7$
g $3x^2 + 11x + 6$ **h** $2x^2 + 11x + 12$ **i** $5x^2 + 17x + 6$
j $7x^2 + 37x + 10$ **k** $3x^2 + 16x + 21$ **l** $2x^2 + 19x + 35$
m $6x^2 + 13x + 5$ **n** $8x^2 + 10x + 3$ **o** $15x^2 + 22x + 8$

5 **a** $3x^2 - 4x + 1$ **b** $2x^2 - 7x + 5$ **c** $3x^2 - 10x + 3$
d $5x^2 - 8x + 3$ **e** $3x^2 - 16x + 5$ **f** $2x^2 - 9x + 7$
g $3x^2 - 14x + 8$ **h** $3x^2 - 13x + 12$ **i** $5x^2 - 13x + 6$
j $5x^2 - 27x + 10$ **k** $2x^2 - 11x + 14$ **l** $5x^2 - 28x + 15$
m $6x^2 - 13x + 6$ **n** $15x^2 - 22x + 8$ **o** $9x^2 - 27x + 20$

6 **a** $3x^2 + 8x - 3$ **b** $2x^2 - 3x - 5$ **c** $3x^2 + 14x - 5$
d $2x^2 - x - 6$ **e** $7x^2 + 9x - 10$ **f** $2x^2 + 5x - 12$
g $6x^2 + 19x - 7$ **h** $8x^2 - 2x - 3$ **i** $10x^2 + x - 2$
j $6x^2 - x - 15$ **k** $5x^2 + 9x - 18$ **l** $12x^2 - 5x - 2$
m $14x^2 + 17x - 6$ **n** $6x^2 - 7x - 10$ **o** $15x^2 + 19x - 10$

7 A quadratic expression of the form $ax^2 + bx + c$ has factors $7x - 2$ and $2x + 5$
Write down the values of a, b and c.

8 Adil factorises $3x^2 + 11x - 4$ and writes $3x^2 + 11x - 4 \equiv (3x - 1)(x + 4)$.
Explain why Adil has used the identity symbol, $\equiv$.

21.4 Special cases

CAN YOU REMEMBER

- How to expand two brackets to form a quadratic expression?
- How to factorise a quadratic expression?
- The meaning of 'square'?

IN THIS SECTION YOU WILL

- Learn about expressions that are the difference of two squares.
- Learn about expressions that are perfect squares.
- Learn how to write a quadratic expression in the form $(ax + b)^2 + c$.

Expanding $(a - b)(a + b)$ gives

$\times$	a	$-b$
a	a^2	$-ab$
b	ab	$-b^2$

$(a - b)(a + b) \equiv a^2 - b^2$
$a^2 - b^2$ is the *difference of two squares*.

Example 1

a Expand: **i** $(x - 3)(x + 3)$ **ii** $(2y + 5)(2y - 5)$
b Factorise: **i** $x^2 - 49$ **ii** $2x^2 - 18y^2$
c Calculate: $43^2 - 33^2$

Solution 1

a **i** $(x - 3)(x + 3) \equiv x^2 - 3^2 \equiv x^2 - 9$
ii $(2y + 5)(2y - 5) \equiv (2y)^2 - 5^2 \equiv 4y^2 - 25$
b **i** $x^2 - 49 \equiv x^2 - 7^2 \equiv (x - 7)(x + 7)$
ii $2x^2 - 18y^2 \equiv 2(x^2 - 9y^2) \equiv 2(x^2 - (3y)^2) \equiv 2(x - 3y)(x + 3y)$
c $43^2 - 33^2 = (43 - 33)(43 + 33) = 10 \times 76 = 760$

Expanding $(ax + b)^2$ gives

$\times$	ax	b
ax	a^2x^2	abx
b	abx	b^2

$(ax + b)^2 \equiv a^2x^2 + 2abx + b^2$
$a^2x^2 + 2abx + b^2$ is a *perfect square*.
Similarly, $(ax - b)^2$ is also a perfect square.
$(ax - b)^2 \equiv a^2x^2 - 2abx + b^2$

Example 2

a Expand: **i** $(x - 3)^2$ **ii** $(4y + 3)^2$
b Factorise: **i** $x^2 - 12x + 36$ **ii** $4x^2 + 12xy + 9y^2$

Solution 2

a **i** $(x - 3)^2 \equiv (x - 3)(x - 3)$

$\times$	x	-3
x	x^2	$-3x$
-3	$-3x$	3^2

$\equiv x^2 + 2 \times -3x + 3^2 \equiv x^2 - 6x + 9$

ii $(4y + 3)^2 \equiv (4y)^2 + 2 \times 4y \times 3 + 3^2 \equiv 16y^2 + 24y + 9$

b **i** **Method 1**
$x^2 - 12x + 36 \equiv x^2 - 2 \times 6x + 6^2$
$x^2 - 12x + 36 \equiv (x - 6)^2$
Method 2
$x^2 - 12x + 36 \equiv (x + p)(x + q)$
$p + q = -12$ and $pq = 36$
$p + q$ is negative and pq is positive.
So both p and q are negative.
$p = q = -6$
$x^2 - 12x + 36 \equiv (x - 6)^2$
Check by expanding the brackets:
$(x - 6)^2 \equiv (x - 6)(x - 6) \equiv x(x - 6) - 6(x - 6)$
$\equiv x^2 - 6x - 6x + 36$
$x^2 - 12x + 36 \equiv (x - 6)^2$✓

ii $4x^2 + 12xy + 9y^2 \equiv (2x)^2 + 2 \times (2x) \times (3y) + (3y)^2$
$4x^2 + 12xy + 9y^2 \equiv (2x + 3y)^2$
Check by expanding the brackets:

$\times$	$2x$	$3y$
$2x$	$4x^2$	$6xy$
$3y$	$6xy$	$9y^2$

$4x^2 + 12xy + 9y^2 \equiv (2x + 3y)^2$✓

Exercise A

1 Expand and simplify each of the following expressions.

a $(x-1)(x+1)$ **b** $(p-5)(p+5)$ **c** $(x+6)(x-6)$
d $(z+9)(z-9)$ **e** $(x+10)(x-10)$ **f** $(w+15)(w-15)$
g $(2a-1)(2a+1)$ **h** $(3y-2)(3y+2)$ **i** $(5y-4)(5y+4)$
j $(1-b)(1+b)$ **k** $(2-7t)(2+7t)$ **l** $(8-5a)(8+5a)$

2 Expand and simplify each of the following expressions.

a $(x-y)(x+y)$ **b** $(2x-y)(2x+y)$ **c** $(2x-3y)(2x+3y)$
d $(2a+5b)(2a-5b)$ **e** $(3a+4b)(3a-4b)$ **f** $(a+10b)(a-10b)$

3 Expand and simplify each of the following expressions.

a $(x+1)^2$ **b** $(x+2)^2$ **c** $(x+3)^2$ **d** $(x+4)^2$
e $(x-1)^2$ **f** $(x-2)^2$ **g** $(x-3)^2$ **h** $(x-4)^2$
i $(x+10)^2$ **j** $(x-10)^2$ **k** $(x+15)^2$ **l** $(x-15)^2$

4 Expand and simplify each of the following expressions.

a $(2x+1)^2$ **b** $(2x-1)^2$ **c** $(2x+3)^2$ **d** $(2x-3)^2$
e $(3x-4)^2$ **f** $(3x+4)^2$ **g** $(5x-2)^2$ **h** $(5x+2)^2$

5 Expand and simplify each of the following expressions.

a $(3x+y)^2$ **b** $(3x-2y)^2$ **c** $(3x+4y)^2$ **d** $(2x-3y)^2$
e $(4x+5y)^2$ **f** $(3x-5y)^2$ **g** $(5x+3y)^2$ **h** $(3x-7y)^2$

6 Use the identity $a^2-b^2 \equiv (a-b)(a+b)$ to work out the following:

a 34^2-33^2 **b** 134^2-133^2 **c** 44^2-34^2
d 55^2-45^2 **e** 36^2-26^2 **f** 85^2-15^2
g 145^2-55^2 **h** 855^2-145^2 **i** 9524^2-476^2

7 Factorise:

a x^2-64 **b** x^2-36 **c** x^2-49
d $4x^2-9$ **e** $4x^2-25$ **f** $4x^2-1$
g $9x^2-1$ **h** $9x^2-16$ **i** $16x^2-49$
j $9x^2-y^2$ **k** $9x^2-4y^2$ **l** $4x^2-9y^2$
m $3x^2-3$ **n** $8x^2-50$ **o** $27x^2-12$
p $12x^2-27y^2$ **q** $72x^2-50y^2$ **r** $16x^2-900y^2$

8 Factorise:

a $x^2-8x+16$ **b** $x^2+22x+121$ **c** $x^2-20x+100$
d $x^2+16x+64$ **e** $16x^2+8x+1$ **f** $25x^2-10x+1$
g $9x^2+6x+1$ **h** $49x^2-14x+1$ **i** $36x^2-12x+1$
j $4x^2-4xy+y^2$ **k** $4x^2-12x+9$ **l** $9x^2+12xy+4y^2$
m $16x^2-40x+25$ **n** $9x^2+60x+100$ **o** $4x^2-36xy+81y^2$
p $2x^2-32xy+128y^2$ **q** $72x^2+96x+32$ **r** $12x^2-36xy+27y^2$

9 Use the identity $a^2-b^2 \equiv (a-b)(a+b)$ to work out the following:

a $2.34^2-1.34^2$ **b** $23.46^2-6.54^2$ **c** $12.64^2-2.36^2$

10 Use the identity $(a+b)^2 \equiv a^2+2ab+b^2$ to show that $1.6^2 = 2.56$

Example 3

Prove the identity $(4x + 3)^2 - (3x + 4)^2 \equiv 7(x^2 - 1)$

Solution 3

Method 1: Use the difference of two squares.
$(4x + 3)^2 - (3x + 4)^2 \equiv [(4x + 3) + (3x + 4)] \times [(4x + 3) - (3x + 4)]$
$\equiv (7x + 7)(x - 1) \equiv 7(x + 1)(x - 1) \equiv 7(x^2 - 1)$

Method 2: Expand and simplify.
$(4x + 3)^2 - (3x + 4)^2 \equiv (16x^2 + 24x + 9) - (9x^2 + 24x + 16)$
$\equiv 7x^2 - 7 \equiv 7(x^2 - 1)$

Quadratics of the form $x^2 + bx + c$ can be written in the form $(x + p)^2 + q$.

Example 4

a Write $x^2 + 6x + 4$ in the form $(x + p)^2 + q$.
b You are given that $4x^2 + 12x - 7 \equiv (px + q)^2 - 16$
Find the values of p and q.

Solution 4

a **Method 1**
$(x + p)^2 + q \equiv x^2 + 2px + p^2 + q$
So $x^2 + 6x + 4 \equiv x^2 + 2px + p^2 + q$
$2p = 6$, so $p = 3$ — Comparing the x terms.
$p^2 + q = 4$ — Comparing the number terms.
So $3^2 + q = 9 + q = 4$
$q = -5$
$x^2 + 6x + 4 \equiv (x + 3)^2 - 5$

Method 2
Step 1: Look at $x^2 + 6x$
$\frac{1}{2}$ of $6 = 3$
$(x + 3)^2 = x^2 + 6x + 9$
Step 2: $x^2 + 6x + 4 \equiv x^2 + 6x + 9 - 5$
$x^2 + 6x + 4 \equiv (x + 3)^2 - 5$

b **Method 1**
Using $(px + q)^2 + r \equiv p^2x^2 + 2pqx + q^2 + r$
$4x^2 + 12x - 7 \equiv p^2x^2 + 2pqx + q^2 + r$
$p^2 = 4$ — Comparing the x^2 terms.
$2pq = 12$ — Comparing the x terms.
$q^2 + r = -7$ — Comparing the number terms.
This gives $p = \sqrt{4} = 2$ or -2

$2pq = 2 \times 2 \times q = 12$	or	$2pq = 2 \times -2 \times q = 12$
$q = 3$		$q = -3$
$q^2 + r = 3^2 + r = 9 + r = -7$	or	$q^2 + r = (-3)^2 + r = 9 + r = -7$
$r = -16$		$r = -16$
$4x^2 + 12x - 7 \equiv (2x + 3)^2 - 16$	or	$4x^2 + 12x - 7 \equiv (-2x - 3)^2 - 16$

But $(2x + 3)^2 \equiv (-2x - 3)^2$, so
$4x^2 + 12x - 7 \equiv (2x + 3)^2 - 16$

Method 2

Step 1: Look at $4x^2 + 12x$

$\sqrt{4} = 2$ or -2

-2 can be ignored, as it gives the same identity as $+2$ (see Method 1)

$\frac{1}{2}$ of $12 = 6$

$6 \div 2 = 3$

$(2x + 3)^2 = 4x^2 + 12x + 9$

Step 2: $4x^2 + 12x - 7 \equiv 4x^2 + 12x + 9 - 16$

$4x^2 + 12x - 7 \equiv (2x + 3)^2 - 16$

Exercise B

1 **a** $(3x + 2)^2 - (2x + 3)^2 \equiv (ax + b)(x - 1)$
Use the difference of two squares to find the values of a and b.
b Hence or otherwise show that $(3x + 2)^2 - (2x + 3)^2 \equiv 5(x^2 - 1)$

2 Show that:
a $(x + 1)^2 - (x - 1)^2 \equiv 4x$
b $(x + 2)^2 - (x - 2)^2 \equiv 8x$
c $(x + 3)^2 - (x - 3)^2 \equiv 12x$
d $(x + n)^2 - (x - n)^2 \equiv 4nx$

3 Prove each of the following identities:
a $(x + 5)^2 - (x + 1)^2 \equiv 8(x + 3)$
b $(2x + 5)^2 - (2x + 1)^2 \equiv 8(2x + 3)$
c $(8x + 5)^2 - (8x + 1)^2 \equiv 8(8x + 3)$
d $(nx + 5)^2 - (nx + 1)^2 \equiv 8(nx + 3)$

4 Show that:
a $(2x + 1)^2 - (x + 2)^2 \equiv 3(x^2 - 1)$
b $(3x + 1)^2 - (x + 3)^2 \equiv 8(x^2 - 1)$
c $(4x + 1)^2 - (x + 4)^2 \equiv 15(x^2 - 1)$
d $(nx + 1)^2 - (x + n)^2 \equiv (n^2 - 1)(x^2 - 1)$

5 Prove each of the following identities:
a $(x + 2)^2 + (2x - 1)^2 \equiv 5(x^2 + 1)$
b $(x + 3)^2 + (3x - 1)^2 \equiv 10(x^2 + 1)$
c $(x + 4)^2 + (4x - 1)^2 \equiv 17(x^2 + 1)$
d $(x + n)^2 + (nx - 1)^2 \equiv (n^2 + 1)(x^2 + 1)$

6 **a** **i** $x^2 + 10x + c$ is a perfect square.
What is the value of c?
Explain your answer.
ii Repeat part **ai** for $x^2 + 5x + c$.
b $x^2 + bx + 81$ is a perfect square.
What is the value of b?
Explain your answer.

7 Find the values of p and q in each of the following.
a $x^2 + 6x + p \equiv (x + q)^2$
b $x^2 + px + q \equiv (x - 5)^2$
c $x^2 + px + q \equiv (x - 4)^2 + 1$
d $x^2 + 8x + p \equiv (x + q)^2 - 3$
e $4x^2 + px + 5 \equiv (2x + 3)^2 - q$

8 Write each of the following in the form $(x + p)^2 + q$
a $x^2 + 16x + 50$
b $x^2 - 16x + 50$
c $x^2 + 10x - 15$
d $x^2 + 10x + 30$
e $x^2 - 3x + 2$
f $x^2 - 7x - 11$

9 **a** Show that $4x^2 + 12x + 5 \equiv (2x + 3)^2 - 4$
b You are given that $9x^2 - 24x + 5 \equiv (px + q)^2 - 11$
Find the values of p and q.
c You are given that $16x^2 - 8x + 7 \equiv (px + q)^2 + r$
Find the values of p, q and r.

Chapter summary

- An *identity* is formed when two algebraic expressions are equal for any values of the letter symbols.
- The symbol ≡ means 'is identically equal to'. It shows that two expressions form an identity.
- The rules of indices are as follows.
  - To multiply index numbers with the same base add the powers $x^a \times x^b \equiv x^{a+b}$
  - To divide index numbers with the same base subtract the powers $x^a \div x^b \equiv x^{a-b}$
  - To raise a power to a power multiply the powers $(x^a)^b \equiv x^{a \times b}$
  - Any number raised to the power zero equals 1 $x^0 = 1$
  - The reciprocal of x^{-n} is x^n $x^{-n} \equiv \frac{1}{x^n}$
  - Raising a number to the power $\frac{1}{2}$ is the same as finding the square root of the number $x^{\frac{1}{2}} \equiv \sqrt{x}$
  - Raising a number to the power $\frac{1}{3}$ is the same as finding the cube root of the number $x^{\frac{1}{3}} \equiv \sqrt[3]{x}$
- To *expand* an expression of the form $a(b + c)$, multiply each term inside the bracket by the single term outside the bracket.
  $a(b + c) \equiv ab + ac$
- To expand an expression of the form $(a + b)(c + d)$, multiply each term in the first bracket by each term in the second bracket.
  $(a + b)(c + d) \equiv ac + ad + bc + bd$
- Factorising is the inverse of expanding brackets.
- To factorise an algebraic expression first find the *highest common factor* (HCF) of all the terms in the expression. In a complex expression find the HCF of numbers and each letter symbol separately.
- A quadratic expression written in the form $ax^2 + bx + c$ can be factorised to the form $(px + q)(rx + s)$.
- A quadratic expression written in the form $(px + q)(rx + s)$ can be expanded and simplified to the form $ax^2 + bx + c$.
- There are special forms of quadratic expressions.
  The difference of two squares $x^2 - n^2 \equiv (x - n)(x + n)$
  The perfect square $(ax + b)^2 \equiv a^2x^2 + 2abx + b^2$
  $(ax - b)^2 \equiv a^2x^2 - 2abx + b^2$
- Quadratics of the form $x^2 + bx + c$ can be written in the form $(x + p)^2 + q$.

Chapter review

1 Simplify:

a $3a^5 \times 4a^2$ **b** $42a^7 \div 7a^9$ **c** $(a^4)^3$
d $(3xy^2)^4$ **e** $(2a^2b^{-3})^3$ **f** $2a^2b^3 \times (3ab)^2$

2 Simplify fully:

a $12x^6 \div 3x^3$ **b** $(3xy)^2$ **c** $2x^3y^2 \times \frac{(6x^4y^2)}{4xy^3}$ **d** $\frac{(\sqrt{x})^{-3}}{x^{-2}}$

Leave your answer to part **d** as a power of x.

3 **a** Expand and simplify.
i $x(2x - 5) + 4(x^2 + 3)$ **ii** $(x - 5)(x + 2)$ **iii** $(3x + 2)(x + 4)$
iv $(3x + 1)^2$ **v** $(2x - 3)(3x - 5)$ **vi** $(x - 3y)(x + 3y)$
b **i** Expand and simplify $(a + b)(a - b)$
ii Use your answer to calculate $760^2 - 240^2$

4 **a** Multiply out and simplify $(a - 5)^2$
b Simplify $4y^3 \times 3y^4$

5 Factorise $x^2 - 9$

6 Factorise fully:
a $10x - 15x^2$ **b** $8x^2 + 6xy$ **c** $x^2 - 25y^2$
d $x^2 - 3x - 4$ **e** $5x^2 - 14x - 3$ **f** $3x^2 + 2x - 8$

7 **a** Work out the value of $2^{-1} + 4^{\frac{1}{2}} + 6^0$
b You are given that $2^{-2} \times 4 \equiv 2^m$
Find the value of m.
c You are given that $2^3 \div \sqrt[3]{\left(\frac{1}{8}\right)} \equiv 2^n$
Find the value of n.

8 Factorise fully
a $2x^2 + 4x + 2$ **b** $4x^2 - 20xy + 25y^2$ **c** $4x^2 - 36$
d $3x - 12x^2$ **e** $3x^2 - 12y^2$ **f** $2x^2 - 50y^2$

9 **a** Write the expression $x^2 - 10x + 8$ in the form $(x - a)^2 + b$
b You are given that $x^2 - 10x + 14 + a \equiv (x - b)^2$ where a and b are integers.
Find the values of a and b.

10 You are given that $4x^2 - 12x - 2 \equiv (ax + b)^2 - 11$
Find the values of a and b.

11 You are given that $ax^2 - 72x + b \equiv (2x + c)^2$
Find the values of a, b and c.

12 Show that:
a $(3x + 4)^2 - (3x + 2)^2 \equiv 12(x + 1)$
b $(2y + 3)^2 - (y + 1)^2 \equiv (3y + 4)(y + 2) \equiv (3y + 1)(y + 3) + 5$

13 Two squares have side length $(4n + 3)$ cm and $(3n + 4)$ cm.

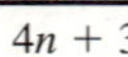

$4n + 3$

$3n + 4$

a Show that the sum of the areas of the two squares is $25(n + 1)^2 - 2n$
b Show that the difference between the areas of the two squares is $7(n^2 - 1)$.

CHAPTER 22

Transformations

22.1 Reflections

CAN YOU REMEMBER

- That a line of symmetry is also called a mirror line?
- How to draw lines such as $x = 3$ and $y = -1$?
- How to draw the lines $y = x$ and $y = -x$?
- That congruent shapes are exactly the same shape and size?

IN THIS SECTION YOU WILL

- Transform shapes by reflection in a mirror line.
- Transform shapes by reflection in the x-axis, y-axis and lines parallel to the axes.
- Transform shapes by reflection in the lines $y = x$ and $y = -x$.
- Describe reflections.

A *transformation* is the movement of a shape from one position to another.

A *reflection* is the *mirror image* of a shape or *object* in a given line.

This diagram shows a reflection of a shape in a mirror line.
The white triangle is the original shape or object.
The coloured triangle is the reflection or *image*.

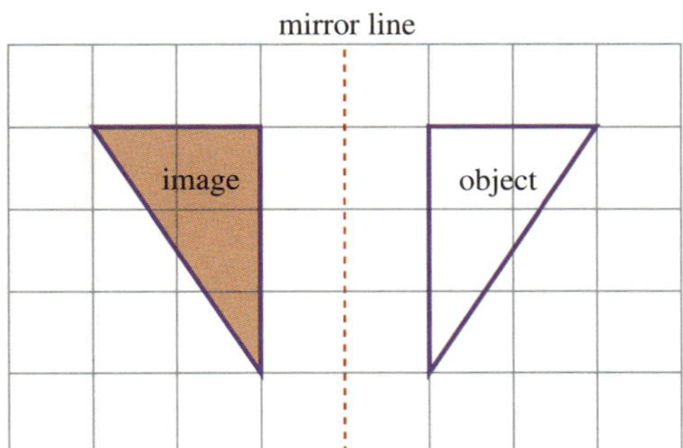

- The image is the same distance from the mirror line as the object.
- The image is the same shape and size as the object.
- The object and the image are *congruent*.

These are true for all reflections.

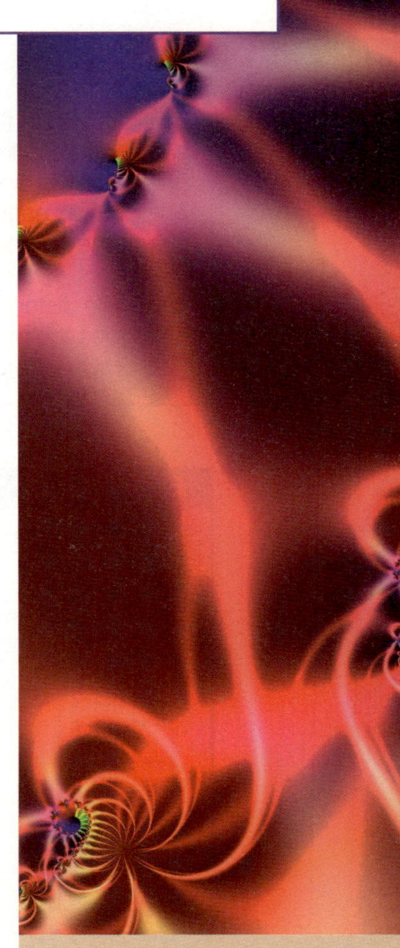

Example 1

Draw the reflection of each shape in the line AB.

Solution 1

a

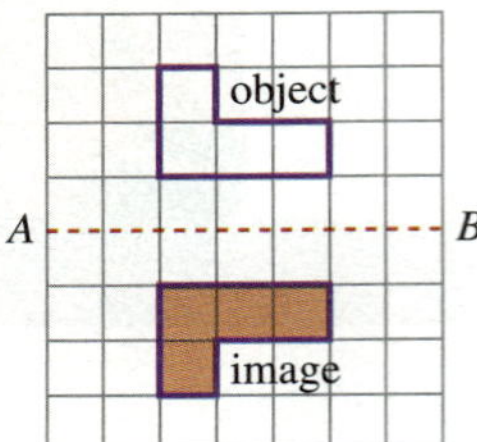

b

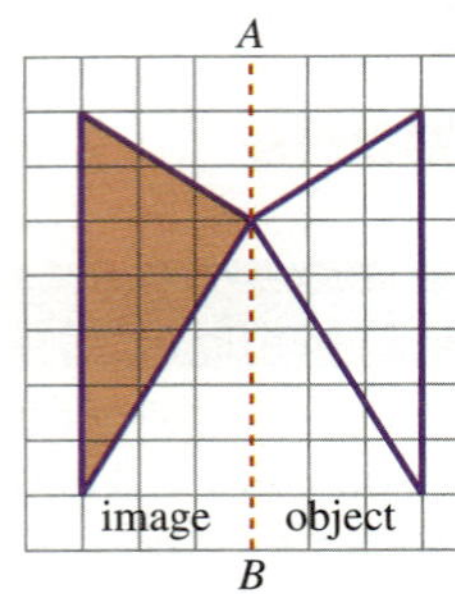

A point on the mirror line is reflected onto itself.

Example 2

This diagram shows an object and its image after reflection in a mirror line.
Draw in the mirror line.

Solution 2

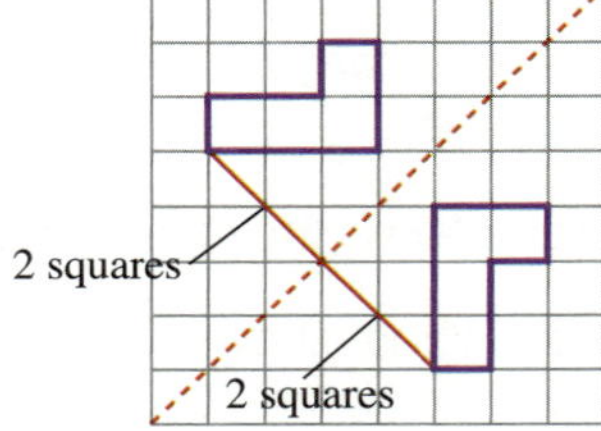

The object and the image must both be the same distance from the mirror line. Choose two matching points, one on the object and one on the image.
Count the number of squares between the points.
Halve the distance between them.
This gives the position of the mirror line.
Check with another pair of matching points.

Example 3

Draw the image of this shape after reflection in the x-axis.

Solution 3

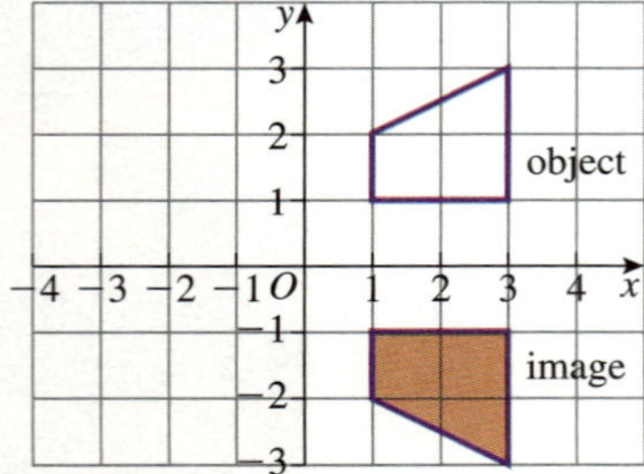

Exercise A

1 For each shape:
 i copy the shape and the mirror line onto squared paper
 ii draw the image of the shape after reflection in the mirror line.

a

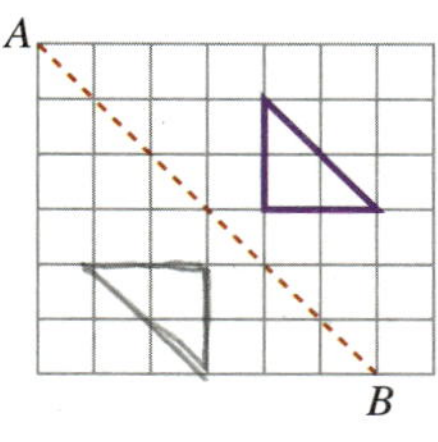

b

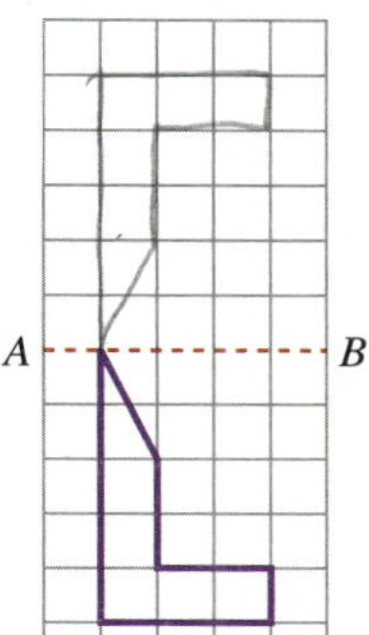

c

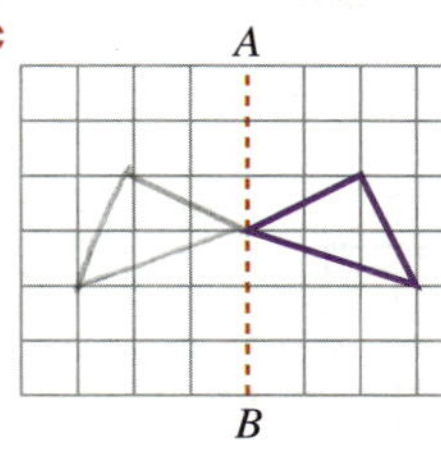

d

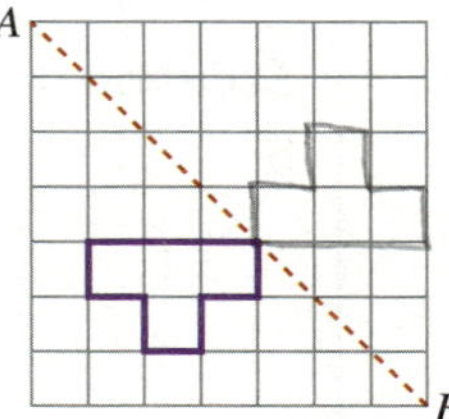

2 Each diagram shows an object and its image after reflection in a mirror line.
Copy each diagram onto squared paper. Draw in the mirror line.

a

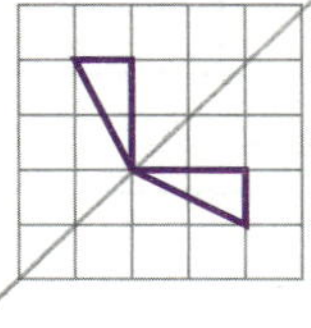

b

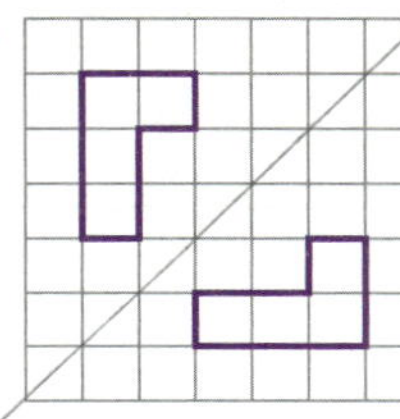

c

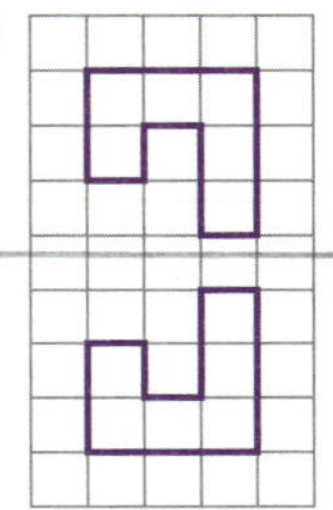

d

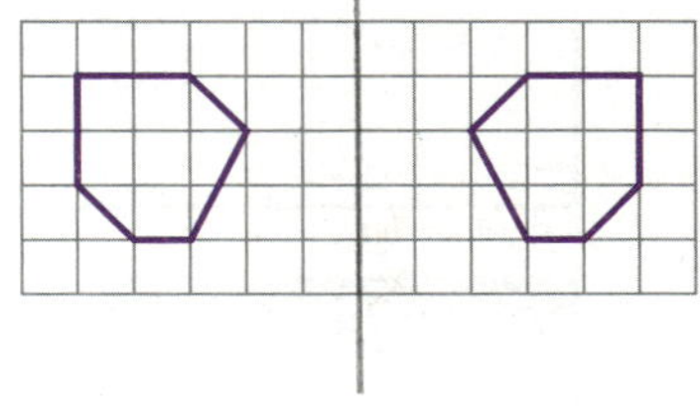

3 For each diagram:
 i copy the axes and the shape onto squared paper
 ii draw the image of the shape after reflection in the x-axis.

a

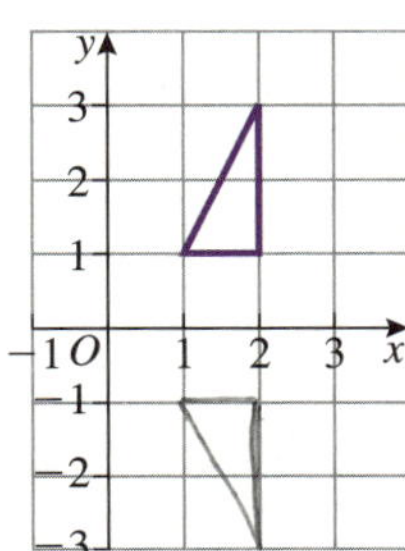

b

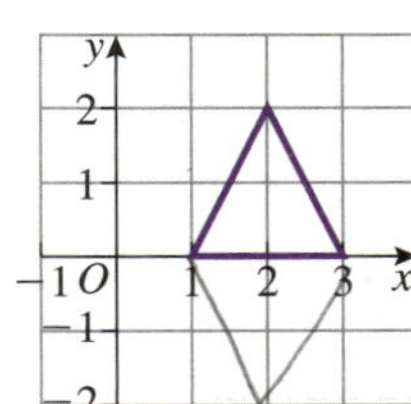

c

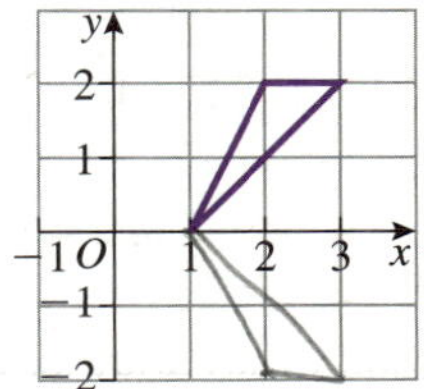

4 Copy the diagrams in question **3**.
Draw the image of each shape after reflection in the y-axis.

Any line on a graph may be used as a mirror line.
These lines are often used:

- horizontal lines, e.g. $y = 4$
- vertical lines, e.g. $x = -2$
- the diagonal lines $y = x$ and $y = -x$

A description of a reflection must include:

- the word 'reflection'
- the name of the mirror line, e.g. $y = 2$, the x-axis.

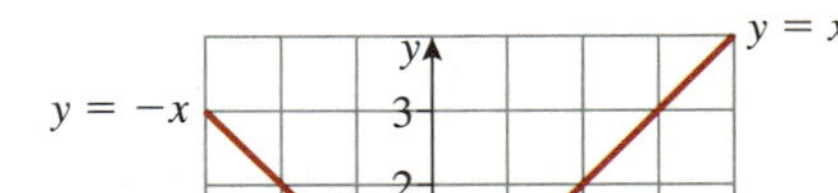

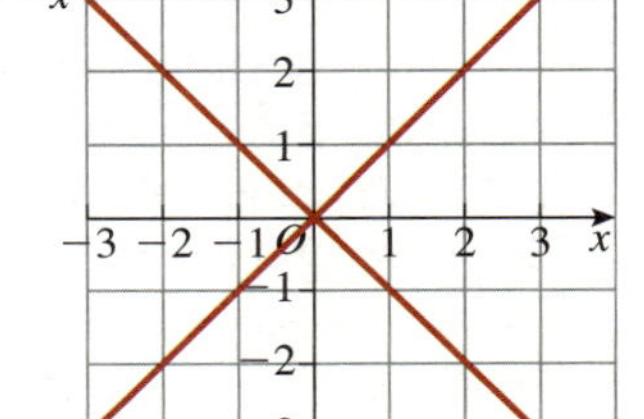

Example 4

Draw the image of shape A after reflection in the line

a $x = 2$ **b** $y = 1$

Solution 4

a

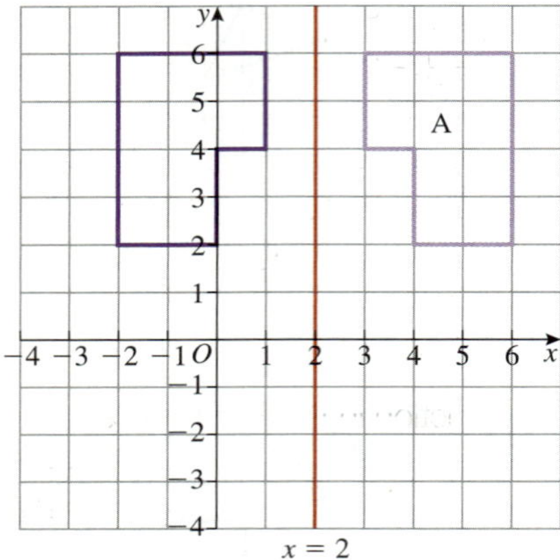

b

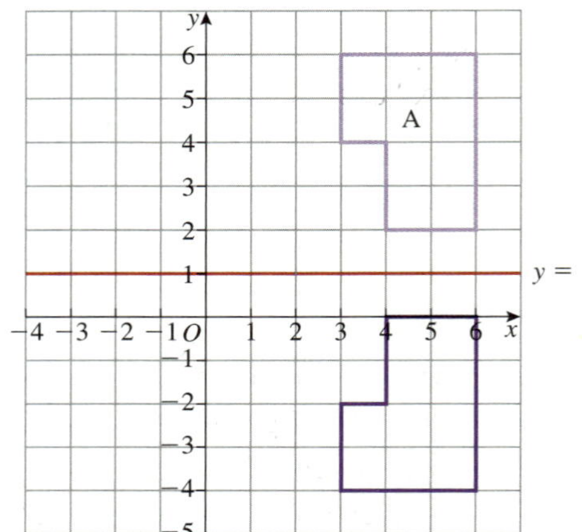

Example 5

Draw the image of the shape after reflection in the line $y = x$.

Solution 5

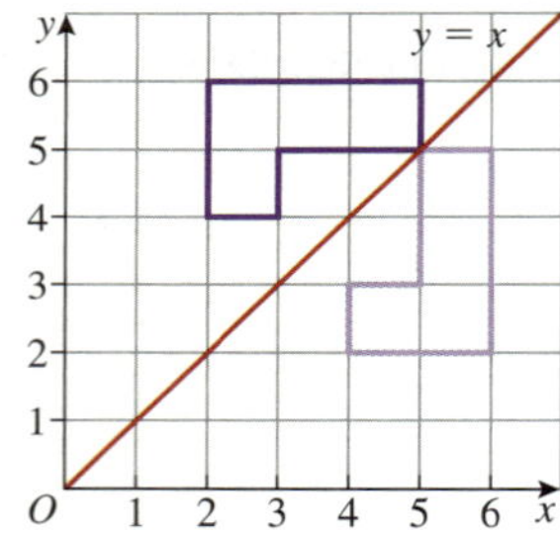

Example 6

Describe the single transformation that moves triangle A to triangle B.

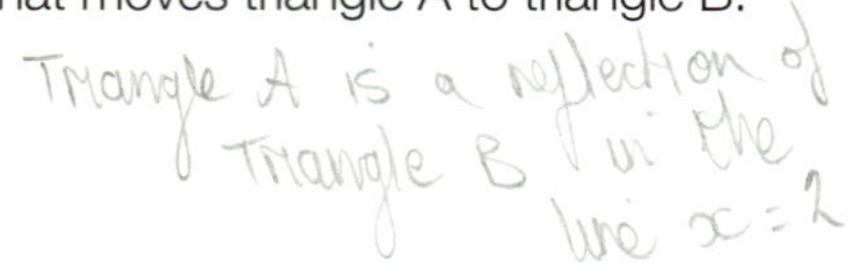

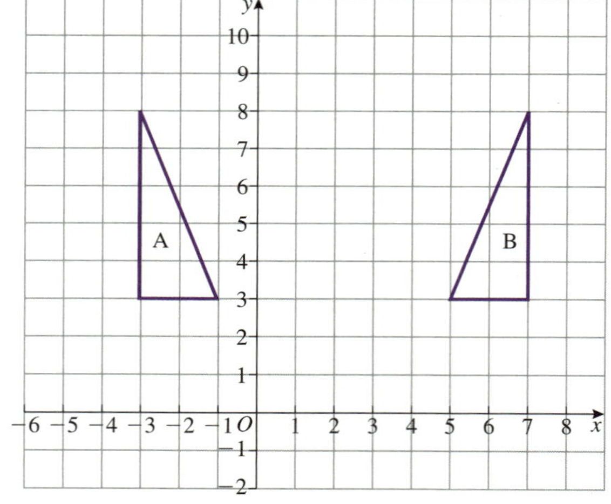

Solution 6

Triangle B is a reflection of triangle A.
The mirror line is halfway between matching points on A and B.
The mirror line is $x = 2$
Triangle B is a reflection of triangle A in the line $x = 2$

Exercise B

1 Copy this diagram.

a Draw the reflection of the shape in the line $x = 1$ Label this shape A.

b Draw the reflection of the shape in the line $y = -1$ Label this shape B.

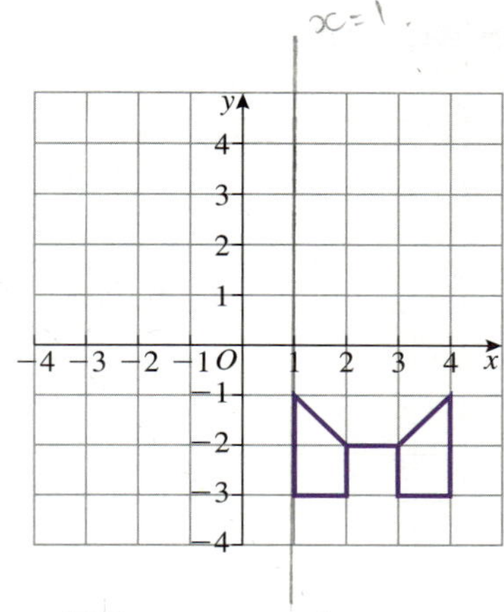

2 Copy the following diagrams onto squared paper.
For each diagram draw the image of shape A after reflection in the line $y = -x$.

a

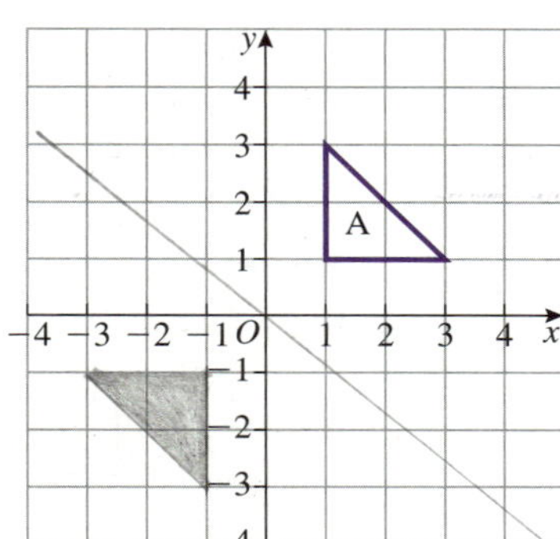

b

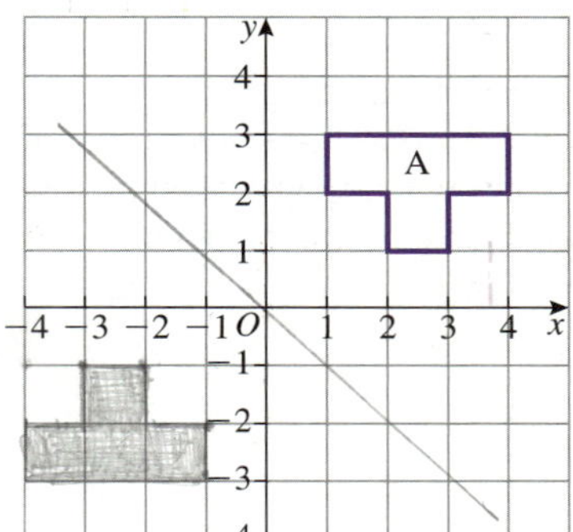

3 For each of the following diagrams:

i copy the diagram onto squared paper

ii draw the image of shape A after reflection in the line $x = -1$

a

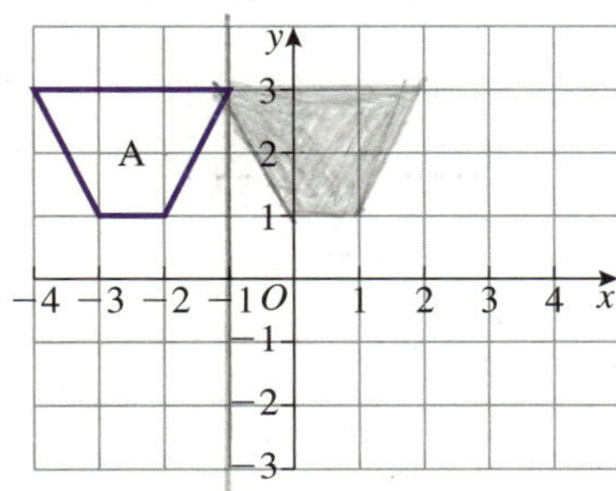

b

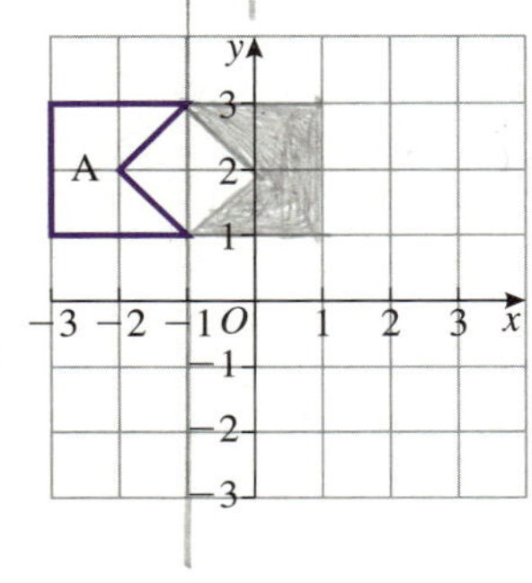

4 Copy each of these diagrams.
Draw the image of each shape after reflection in the line $y = x$.

a

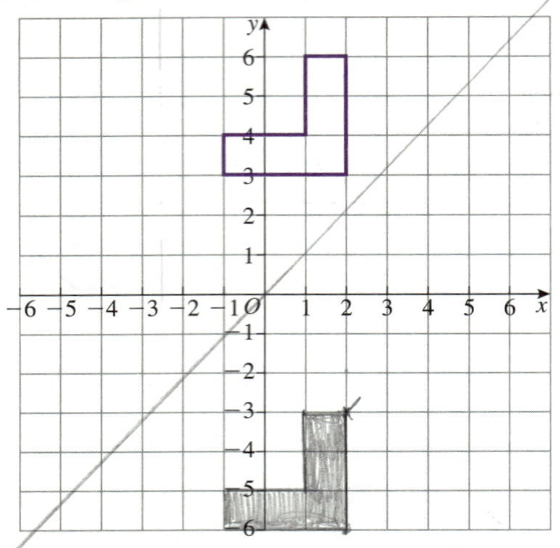

b

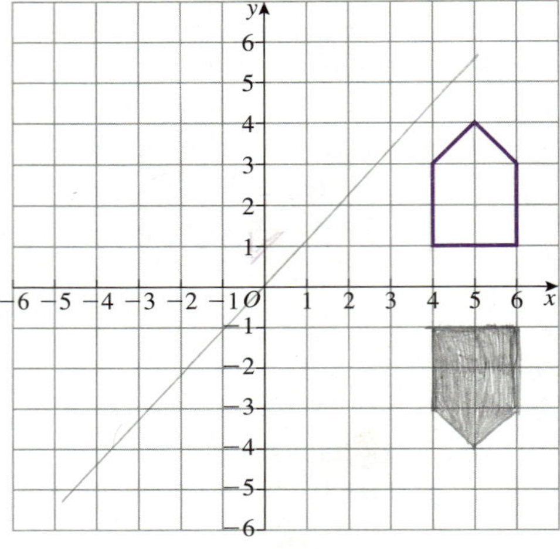

5 Look at these diagrams.

a Describe the single transformation which moves shape A to shape B. reflection in the line $y = 0$

b Describe the single transformation which moves shape A to shape C. reflection in the line $x = 0$

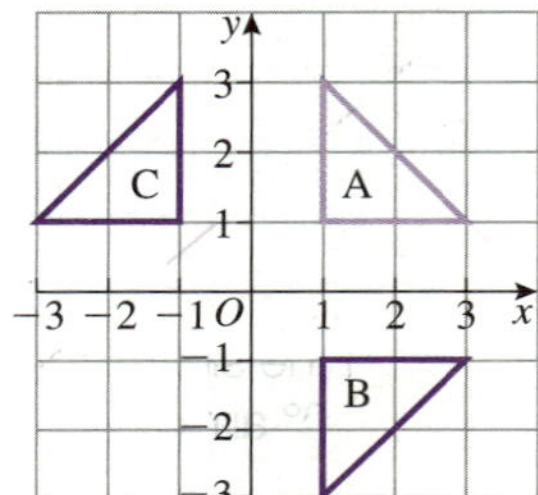

6 Describe fully the single transformation which moves object A to image B in each of these diagrams.

a

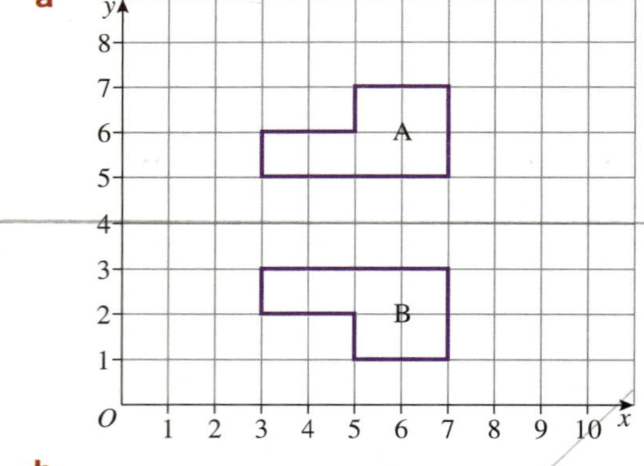

reflection in the line $y = 4$

b

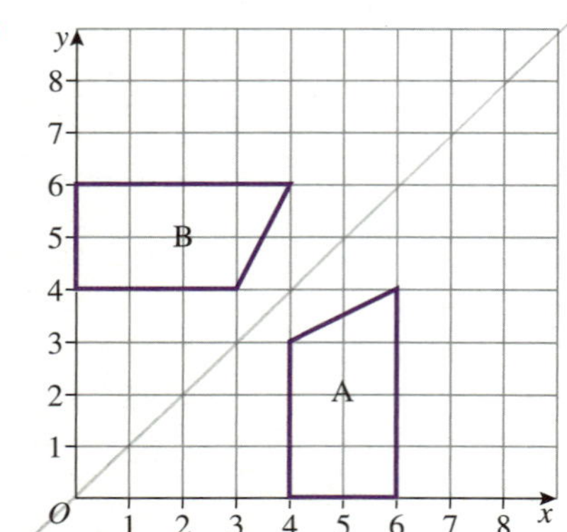

reflection in the line $y = x$

22.2 Rotations

CAN YOU REMEMBER

- A quarter turn is a rotation of 90°, a half turn is a rotation of 180°, a full turn is 360°?
- The meaning of 'clockwise' and 'anticlockwise'?
- Congruent shapes are exactly the same shape and size?

IN THIS SECTION YOU WILL

- Transform a shape by rotating it about a centre of rotation.
- Learn how to find a centre of rotation.
- Describe transformations which involve rotations.
- Transform shapes using a combination of reflection and rotation.

A *rotation* turns a shape about a fixed point, called the *centre of rotation*.
The angle of rotation can be given as a fraction of a turn or in degrees.

When an object is rotated the image is the same shape and size as the object.
The object and the image are *congruent*.

Example 1

Write down the single transformation that is equivalent to a rotation of 120° clockwise followed by a rotation of 50° anticlockwise.

Solution 1

It is equivalent to a rotation of 70° clockwise.

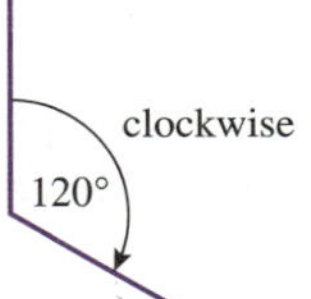

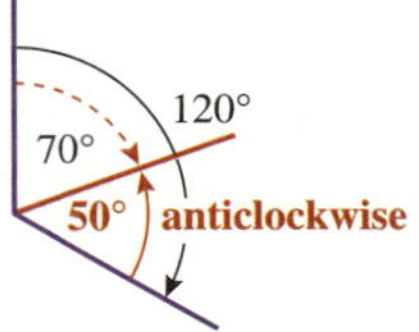

Tracing paper is useful when rotating shapes.

Example 2

Rotate triangle A through a quarter turn clockwise about the origin.

Solution 2

Trace the shape and the axes onto tracing paper.
Use a pencil point to hold the tracing paper on the centre of rotation (0, 0).
Rotate the tracing paper through a quarter turn clockwise to show the position of the image.
Draw the image on the grid.

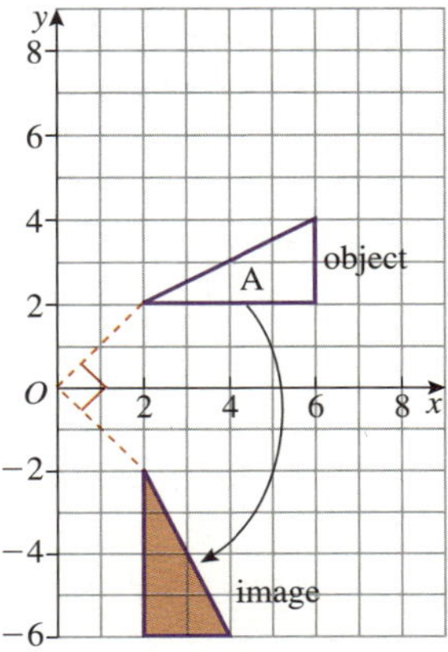

Example 3

Rotate shape B through 180° about (0, 0).

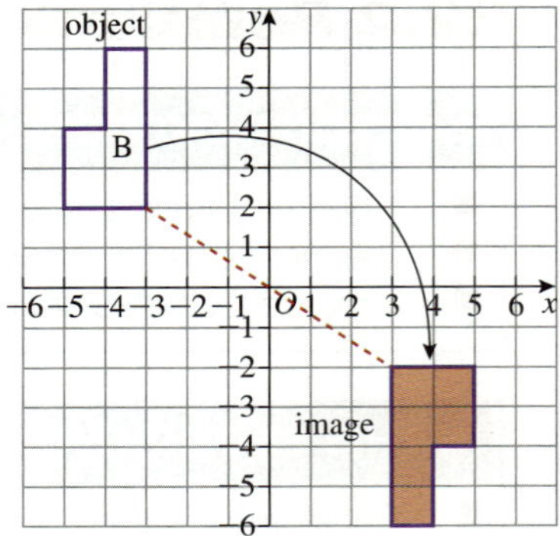

Solution 3

The direction is not given because 180° clockwise is the same as 180° anticlockwise.
The centre of rotation is (0, 0).

Exercise A

1 Copy and complete the following sentences:

- **a** A rotation of 40° clockwise is equivalent to a rotation of .... anticlockwise.

- **b** A rotation of 135° clockwise is equivalent to a rotation of .... anticlockwise.
- **c** A rotation of 200° clockwise is equivalent to a rotation of .... anticlockwise.
- **d** A rotation of 100° anticlockwise is equivalent to a rotation of .... clockwise.
- **e** A rotation of 50° anticlockwise is equivalent to a rotation of .... clockwise.
- **f** A rotation of 280° anticlockwise is equivalent to a rotation of .... clockwise.

2 Here is a list of angles:

45° 50° 60° 90° 120° 135° 270° 300°

From the list, write down an angle which is equivalent to:

a a quarter turn **b** $\frac{1}{6}$ of a turn **c** $\frac{1}{3}$ of a turn **d** $\frac{1}{8}$ of a turn.

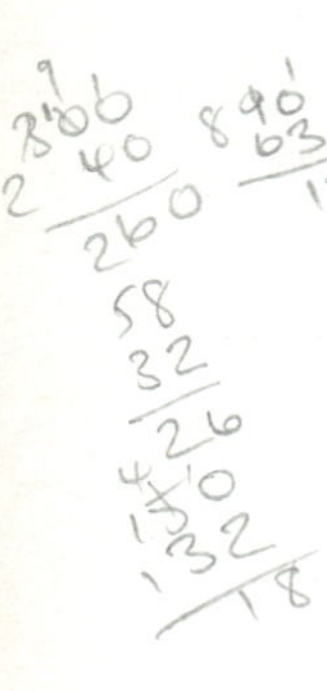

3 Copy and complete the following sentences:

- **a** A rotation of 90° clockwise followed by 63° anticlockwise is equivalent to a single rotation of ....
- **b** A rotation of 300° clockwise followed by 40° anticlockwise is equivalent to a single rotation of ....
- **c** A rotation of 58° clockwise followed by 32° clockwise is equivalent to a single rotation of ....
- **d** A rotation of 132° clockwise followed by 150° anticlockwise is equivalent to a single rotation of ....

4 Copy the diagram onto squared paper.
Rotate shape P a quarter turn anticlockwise about (0, 0).

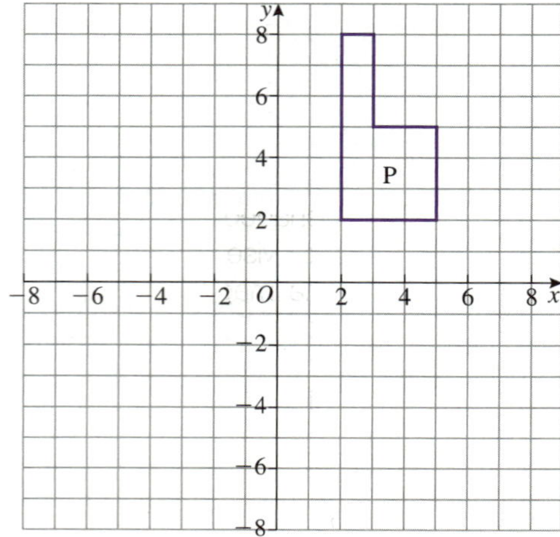

5 Copy the diagram onto squared paper. Rotate shape Q a half turn about the origin.

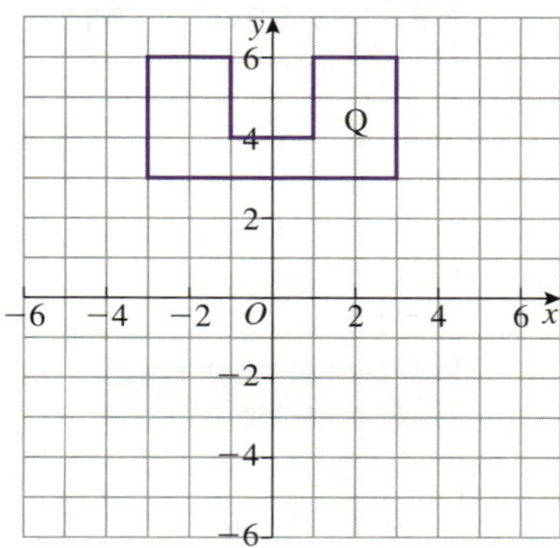

6 Which of the following shapes are rotations of the shaded shape?

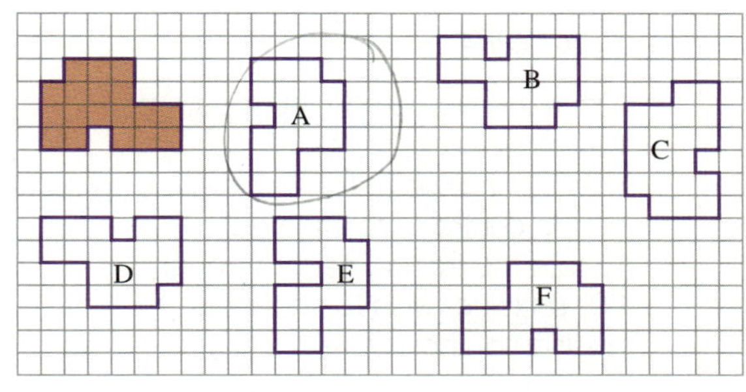

7 Rotate the shaded shape:

a 90° clockwise about (0, 0). Label the image A.

b 180° about (0, 0). Label the image B.

c 90° anticlockwise about (0, 0). Label the image C.

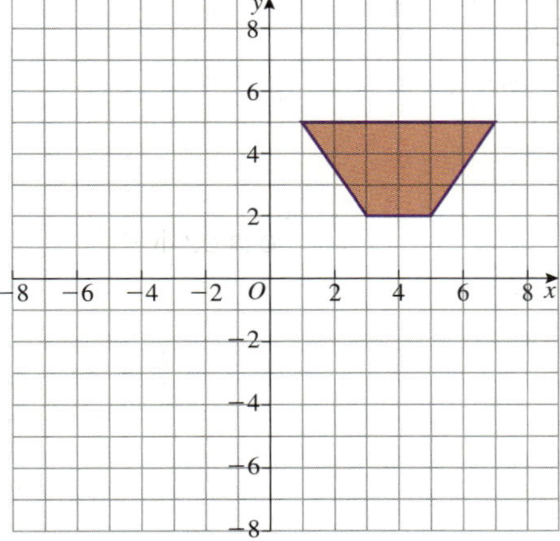

8 Rotate the shaded shape:

a a quarter turn anticlockwise about the origin. Label the image A.

b a half turn about the origin. Label the image B.

c a quarter turn clockwise about the origin. Label the image C.

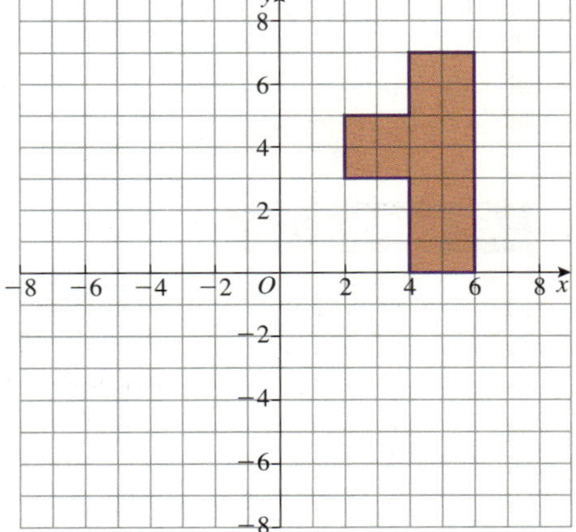

9 Rotate the shaded shape:

a 90° clockwise about (0, 0). Label the image A.

b 180° about (0, 0). Label the image B.

c 90° anticlockwise about (0, 0). Label the image C.

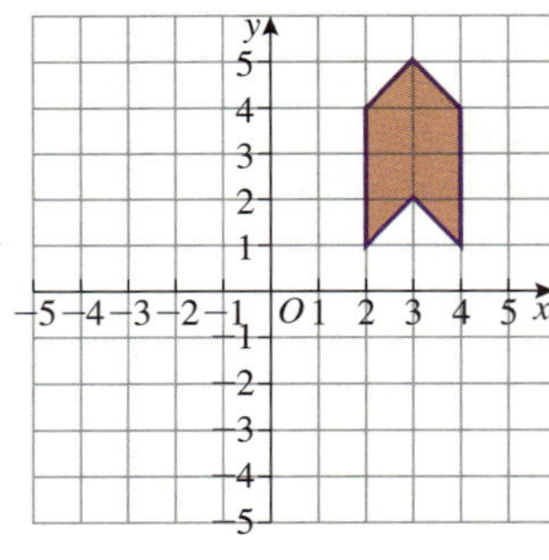

10 Rotate each of these shapes as described.

a

45° anticlockwise about O.

b

$\frac{1}{6}$ of a turn clockwise about O.

c

$\frac{1}{3}$ of a turn clockwise about O.

Example 4

Rotate the shaded shape 90° anticlockwise about (−1, 1).

Solution 4

Trace the shape and the axes onto tracing paper.
Use a pencil point to hold the tracing paper on the centre of rotation (−1, 1).
Rotate the tracing paper through 90° anticlockwise to show the position of the image.
Draw the image on the grid.

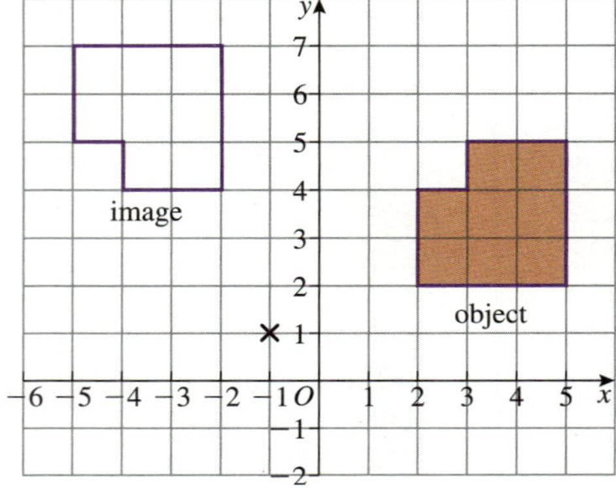

A description of a rotation must include:

- the angle through which it turns
- the direction of the turn
- the centre of rotation
- the word 'rotation'.

why not also a reflection

Example 5

The diagram shows two identical shapes A and B.
Describe fully the single transformation which takes shape A to shape B. Reflection of Triangle A in the line y = 0.

Solution 5

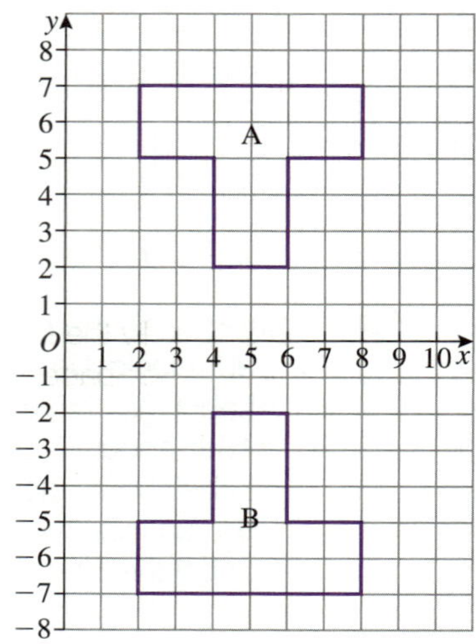

The transformation is a rotation.
Trace shape A and rotate it through different turns, to see which size of turn gives shape B.
The rotation is through 180°, so the direction of rotation is not needed.
To find the centre of rotation, rotate the tracing using different pivot positions. When the tracing is held at (5, 0), shape A fits exactly onto shape B.

The transformation is a rotation of 180° about (5, 0).

When a shape is rotated about one of its vertices, that vertex does not move.

Example 6

Describe the single transformation which takes the shaded shape to shape A.

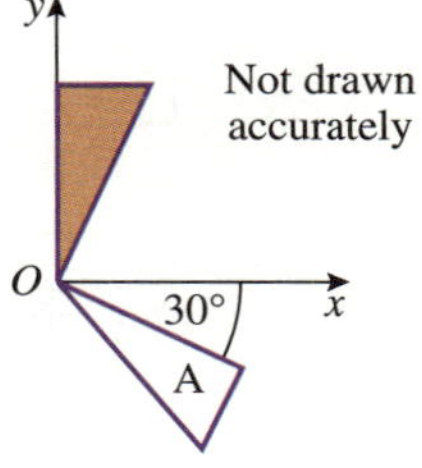

Solution 6

The vertex of the triangle at O has not moved, so O is the centre of rotation.
The vertical line has been rotated 90° + 30° clockwise.
The single transformation is a rotation 120° clockwise about O.

Exercise B

For questions **1** to **4**, use the resource sheet.

1 **a** Rotate shape A through 90° clockwise about (−1, 1). Label the image B.
b Rotate shape A through 180° about (−1, 1). Label the image C.

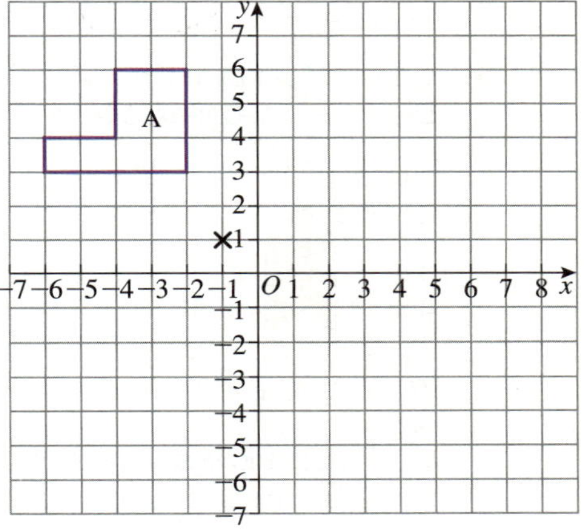

2 Rotate shape A 180° about (6, 2). Label the image B.

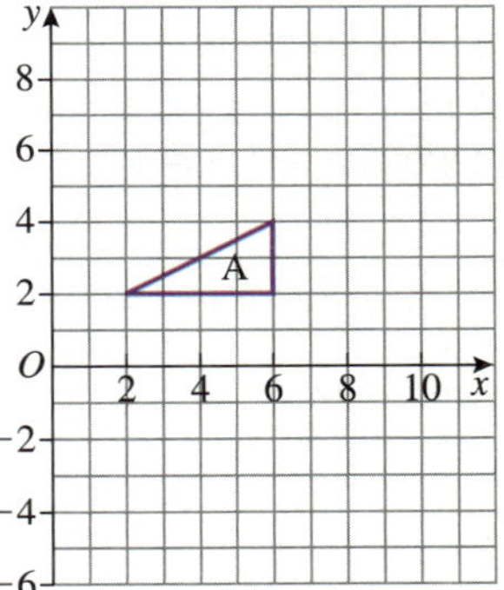

3 The diagram shows two identical shapes, A and B.
Describe fully the single transformation which takes shape A to shape B.

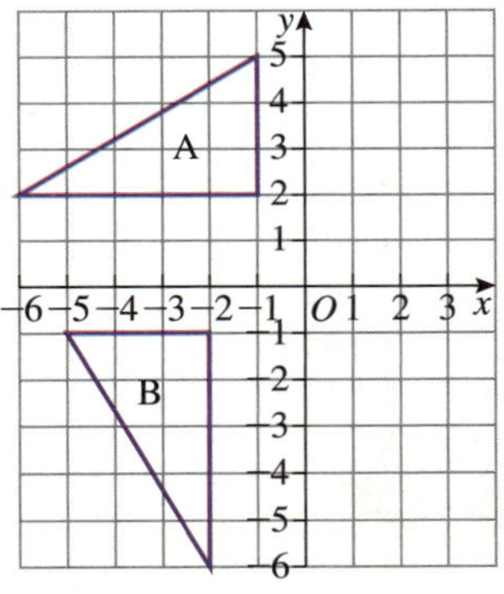

4 The diagram shows two identical shapes, A and B.

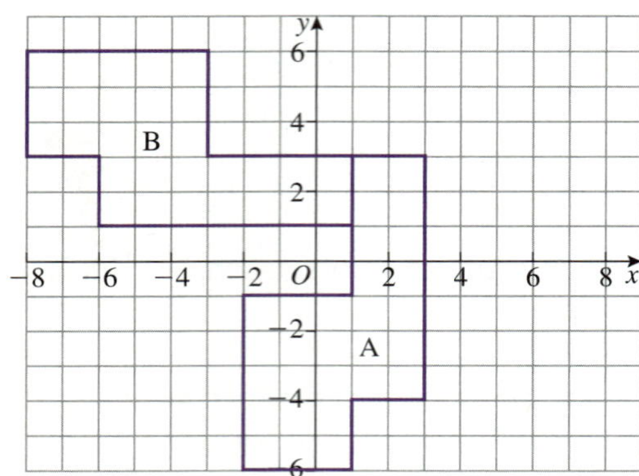

Describe fully the single transformation which takes shape A to shape B.

5 Copy the diagram onto squared paper.
Draw the x and y-axes from -5 to $+5$

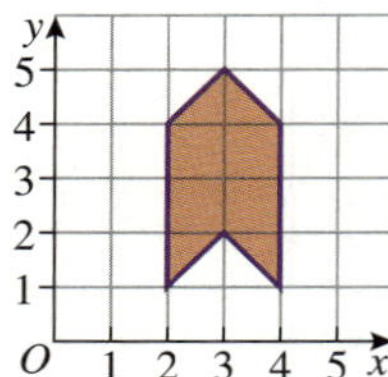

a Rotate the shaded shape 180° about (3, 0).
Label this shape A.

b Rotate shape A 90° clockwise about (0, 0).
Label this shape B.

c Describe fully the single transformation which will take shape B back to the shaded shape.

6 Describe the single transformation which will take the shaded triangle to triangle T.

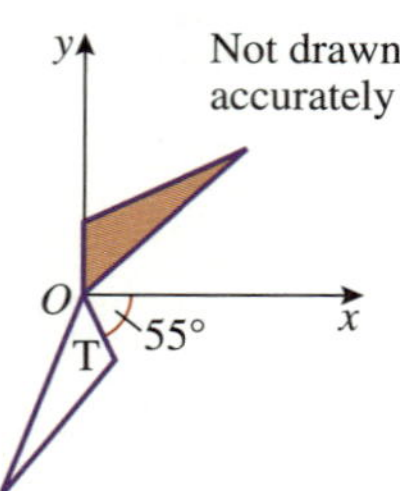

7 Describe fully the single transformation which will take shape A to shape B.

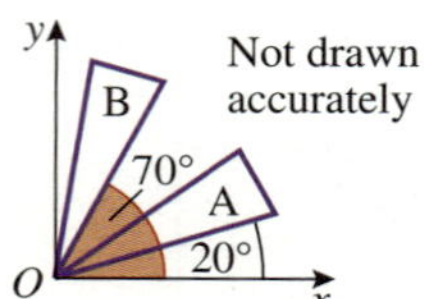

8

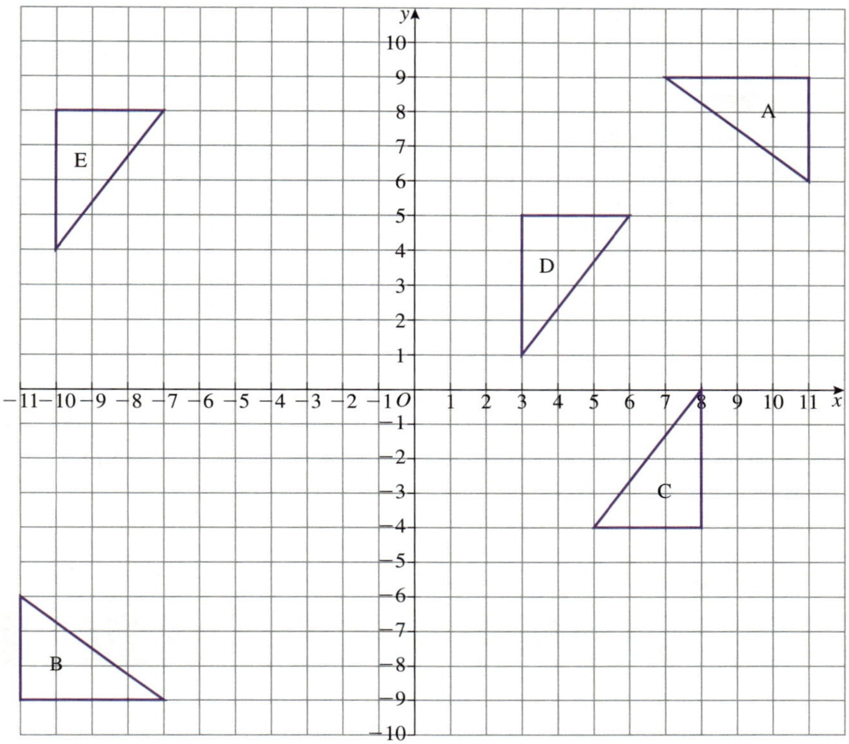

a Triangle C is rotated 90° anticlockwise about (−4, 3).
Which triangle is the image of C under this transformation?

b Triangle C is rotated 180° about (5.5, 0.5).
Which triangle is the image of C under this transformation?

9 Copy this diagram onto squared paper.

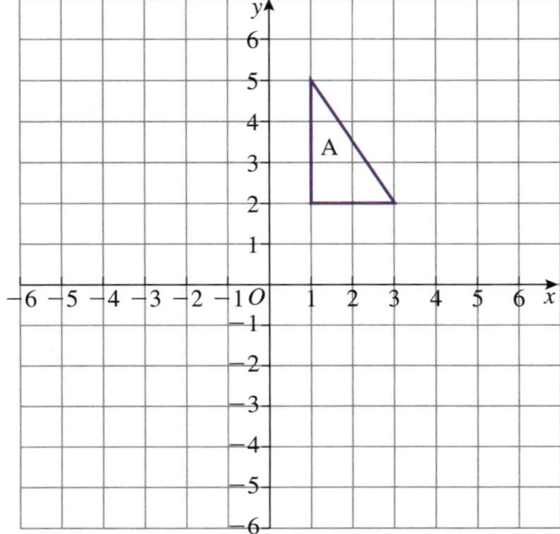

a Draw the reflection of triangle A in the x-axis. Label the image B.

b Draw the reflection of triangle B in the line $x = -1$. Label the image C.

c Describe fully the single transformation which will take triangle C to triangle A.

10 Copy this diagram onto squared paper.

a Draw the reflection of triangle P in the x-axis. Label the image Q.

b Rotate triangle Q 90° anticlockwise about (0, 0). Label the image R.

c Describe fully the single transformation which will take triangle R to triangle P.

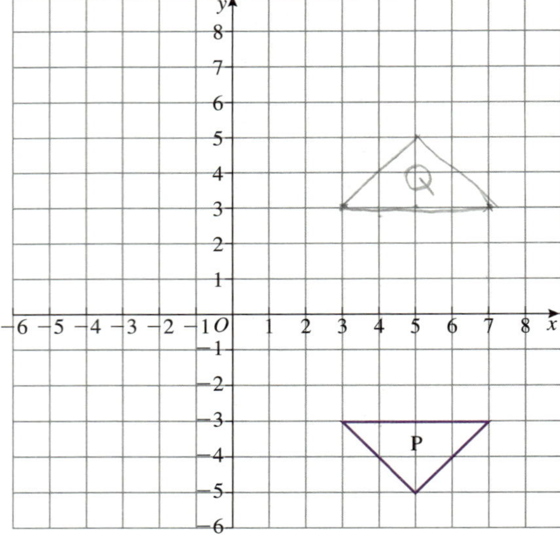

22.3 Translations

CAN YOU REMEMBER

- Congruent shapes are exactly the same shape and size?
- The meaning of 'object' and 'image'?

IN THIS SECTION YOU WILL

- Learn the meaning of the term 'translation'.
- Translate shapes by a given distance in the x-direction and the y-direction.
- Learn how to use column vectors to translate shapes.
- Describe translations in words and using column vectors.

A *translation* is the movement of a shape in the x-direction (horizontally) and the y-direction (vertically).

Every point in the shape moves in the same direction and through the same distance.

The object and its image are congruent.

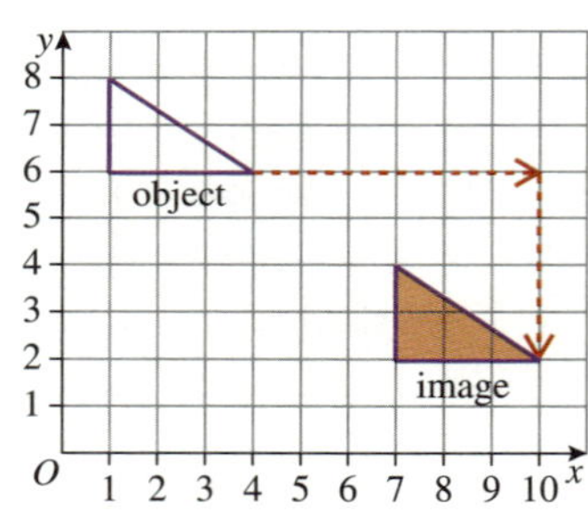

Example 1

Draw the image of $ABCD$ after a translation of five squares to the right and one square up.

Solution 1

From vertex A of the object, move five squares to the right and one square up and plot vertex A' for the image. Repeat for the other vertices.

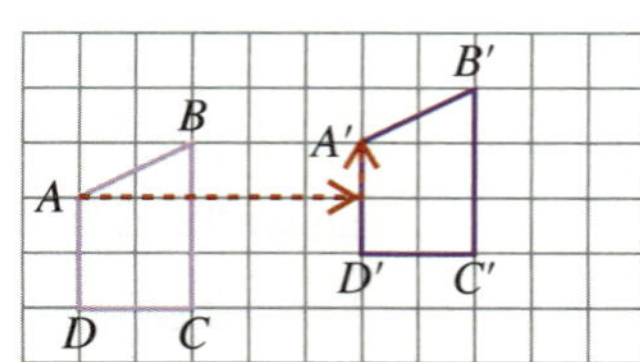

Example 2

Describe the transformation that takes shape A to shape B.

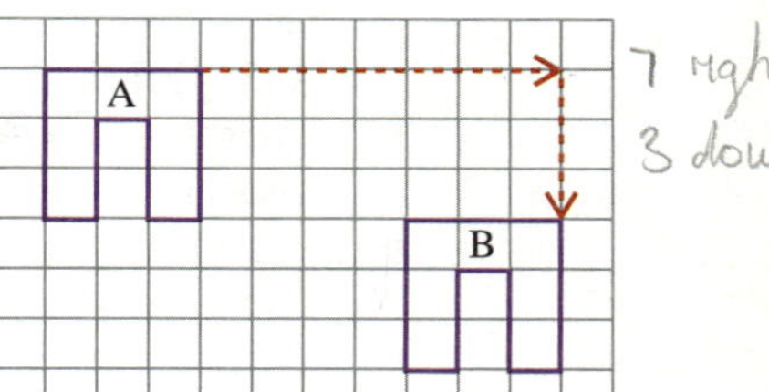

Solution 2

Choose a vertex on shape A. Count the squares across and down to the matching vertex on shape B. The shape has moved seven squares to the right and three squares down.
Translation of 7 units to the right and 3 units down.

Exercise A

1 Copy this diagram onto squared paper.
Draw the x and y-axes to 15
Translate the shaded shape:

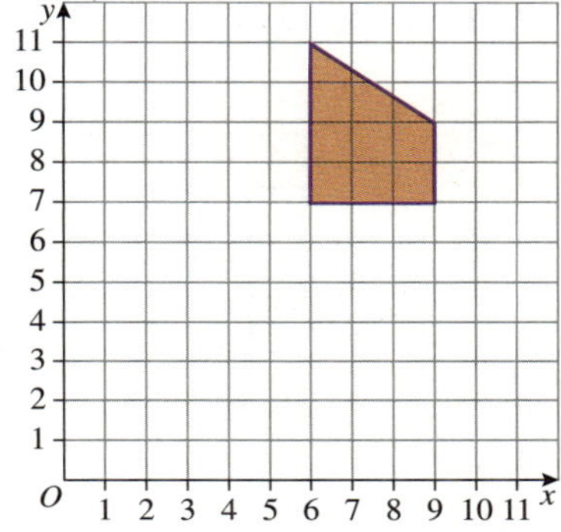

- **a** 4 units to the right and 4 units up. Label this image A.
- **b** 3 units to the right and 4 units down. Label this image B.
- **c** 6 units to the left and 3 units down. Label this image C.
- **d** 4 units to the left and 5 units up. Label this image D.

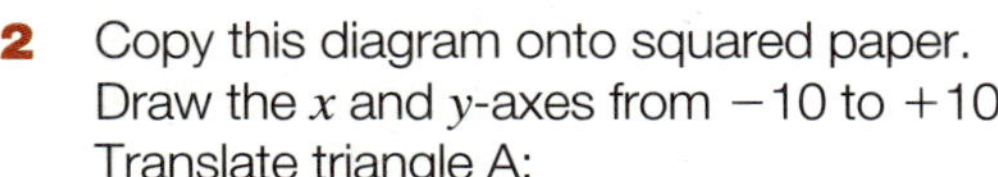

2 Copy this diagram onto squared paper.
Draw the x and y-axes from -10 to $+10$
Translate triangle A:

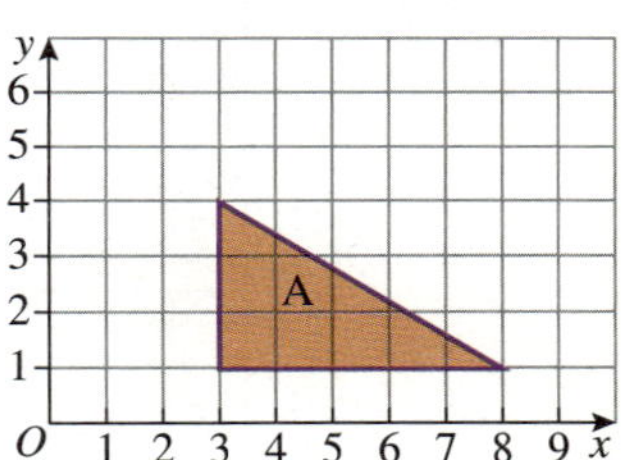

- **a** 2 units to the right and 5 units up. Label this triangle B.
- **b** 3 units to the right and 8 units down. Label this triangle C.
- **c** 10 units to the left and 6 units down. Label this triangle D.
- **d** 13 units to the left and 4 units up. Label this triangle E.

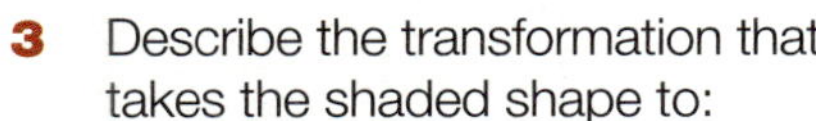

3 Describe the transformation that takes the shaded shape to:

- **a** shape A
- **b** shape B
- **c** shape C
- **d** shape D
- **e** shape E.

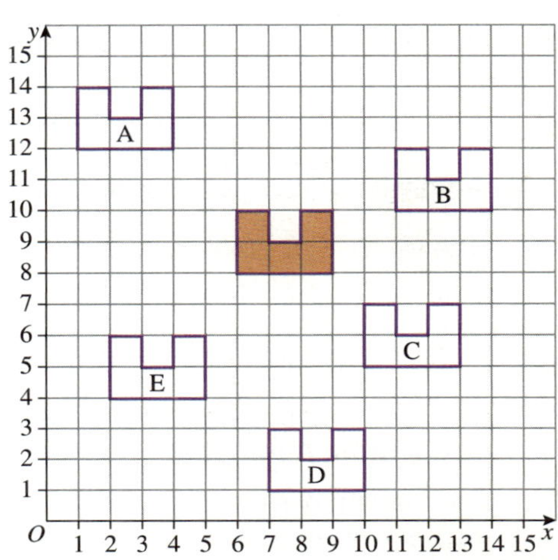

4 On squared paper draw and label x and y-axes from -10 to $+10$

a Draw the rectangle with coordinates
A (3, 1) B (3, 3) C (7, 3) D (7, 1).

b Draw the image of $ABCD$ after a translation of 2 units to the right and 5 units up.
Label this image P.

c Draw the image of $ABCD$ after a translation of 3 units to the right and 8 units down.
Label this image Q.

d Draw the image of $ABCD$ after a translation of 9 units to the left and 6 units down.
Label this image R.

e Draw the image of $ABCD$ after a translation of 13 units to the left and 4 units up.
Label this image S.

f Describe the transformation of shape P to shape Q.

g Describe the transformation of shape S to shape R.

5 Describe the transformation that takes the shaded shape to:

a shape B **b** shape C **c** shape D **d** shape E **e** shape F.

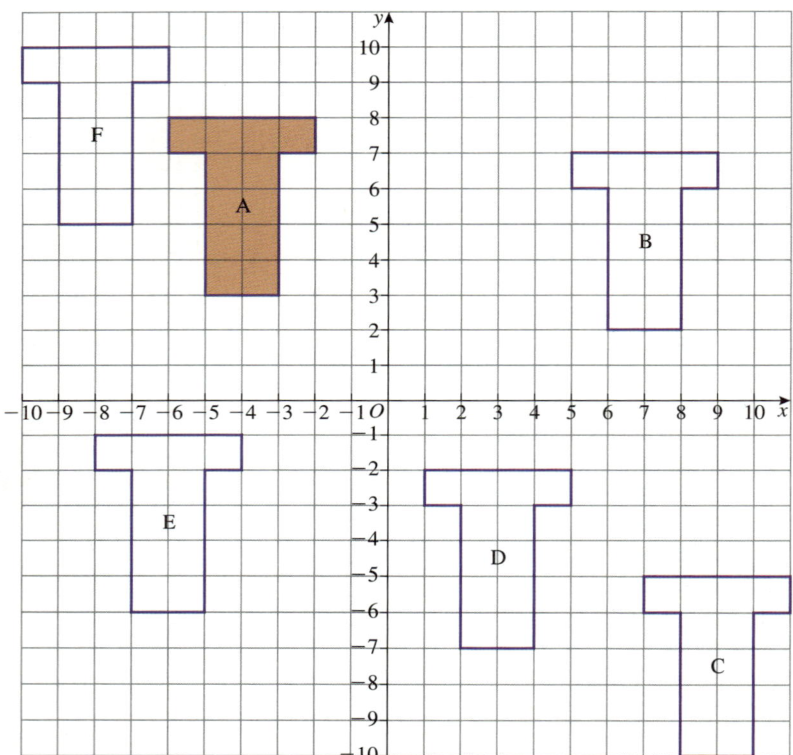

A translation can be described using a *vector*.

The vector $\begin{pmatrix} 2 \\ -3 \end{pmatrix}$ moves a point 2 units to the right and 3 units down.

The vector $\begin{pmatrix} -1 \\ 4 \end{pmatrix}$ moves a point 1 unit to the left and 4 units up.

The top number always describes movement in the x-direction. A **positive** value means movement to the **right**. A **negative** value means movement to the **left**.

The bottom number always describes movement in the y-direction. A **positive** value means movement **up**. A **negative** value means movement **down**.

Example 3

Write the following translations as vectors:

a 3 units to the right and 2 units up

b 8 units to the left and 5 units up

c 4 units to the left and 0 units up

d 2 units to the left and 6 units down.

Solution 3

a $\begin{pmatrix} 3 \\ 2 \end{pmatrix}$ **b** $\begin{pmatrix} -8 \\ 5 \end{pmatrix}$ **c** $\begin{pmatrix} -4 \\ 0 \end{pmatrix}$ **d** $\begin{pmatrix} -2 \\ -6 \end{pmatrix}$

Example 4

a Transform the shaded shape by a translation of $\begin{pmatrix} 0 \\ 7 \end{pmatrix}$.

Label the image A.

b Transform the shaded shape by a translation of $\begin{pmatrix} -3 \\ 4 \end{pmatrix}$.

Label the image B.

c Describe the transformation from shape A to shape B.

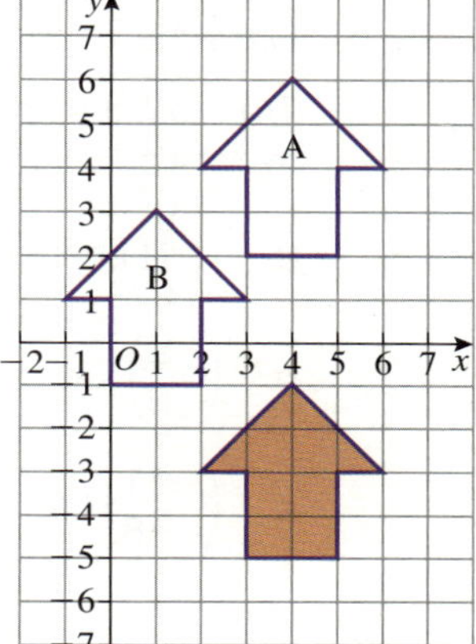

Solution 4

a Vector $\begin{pmatrix} 0 \\ 7 \end{pmatrix}$ moves the shaded shape 0 units to the right and 7 units up.

b Vector $\begin{pmatrix} -3 \\ 4 \end{pmatrix}$ moves the shaded shape 3 units to the left and 4 units up.

c Shape A to shape B is a translation of $\begin{pmatrix} -3 \\ -3 \end{pmatrix}$.

Exercise B

1 Write the following translations as vectors:

a 4 units to the right and 9 units up

b 6 units to the right and 5 units up

c 10 units to the left and 3 units up

d 7 units to the left and 1 unit down

e 8 units to the right and 9 units down

f 3 units to the left and 3 units up.

2 Describe in words the translations given by the following vectors.

a $\begin{pmatrix} 2 \\ -9 \end{pmatrix}$ **b** $\begin{pmatrix} -4 \\ 4 \end{pmatrix}$ **c** $\begin{pmatrix} 10 \\ 3 \end{pmatrix}$

d $\begin{pmatrix} 2 \\ 0 \end{pmatrix}$ **e** $\begin{pmatrix} -1 \\ -1 \end{pmatrix}$ **f** $\begin{pmatrix} 5 \\ -4 \end{pmatrix}$

3 Use vectors to describe these translations.

a A to B **b** A to D
c A to F **d** A to H
e G to E **f** G to C
g G to B **h** D to H
i H to C **j** F to B
k H to F **l** H to A

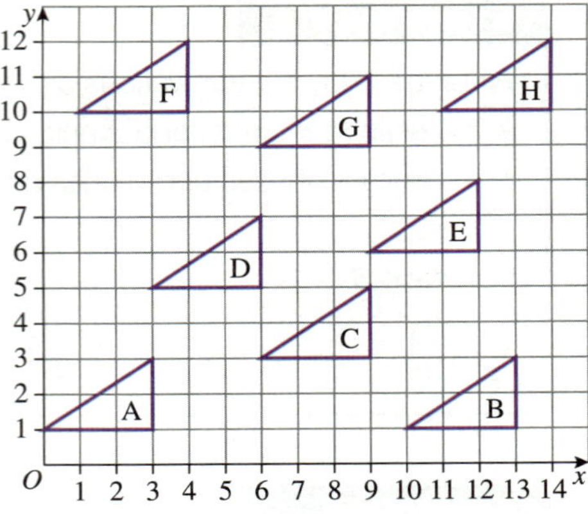

4 Copy the diagram onto squared paper.
Draw the x and y-axes from -10 to $+10$

Translate the shaded shape using the following translation vectors.

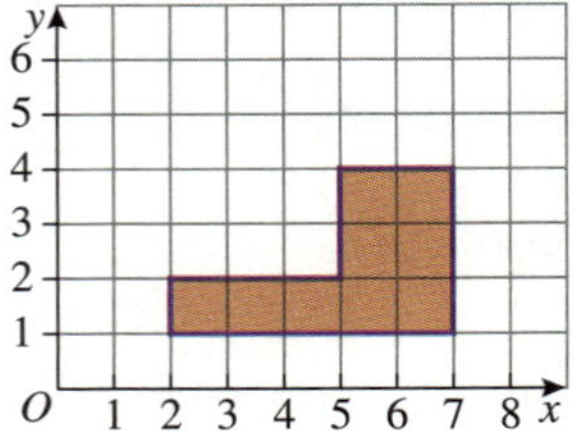

a $\begin{pmatrix}3\\6\end{pmatrix}$ Label the image A.

b $\begin{pmatrix}-9\\3\end{pmatrix}$ Label the image B.

c $\begin{pmatrix}-11\\-8\end{pmatrix}$ Label the image C. **d** $\begin{pmatrix}3\\-6\end{pmatrix}$ Label the image D.

5 Write down the vector for the translation which moves:

a $A(1, 1)$ to $P(4, 7)$ **b** $A(1, 1)$ to $Q(5, -2)$
c $A(1, 1)$ to $R(-3, 6)$ **d** $A(1, 1)$ to $S(-2, -4)$

6 The diagram shows a quadrilateral $ABCD$.
Write down the coordinates of D after the shape has been translated by the vector:

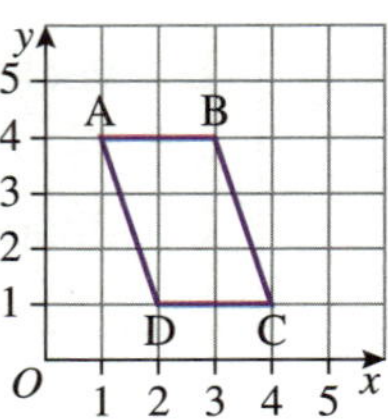

a  $\begin{pmatrix}2\\5\end{pmatrix}$ **b** $\begin{pmatrix}1\\-3\end{pmatrix}$ **c** $\begin{pmatrix}-4\\2\end{pmatrix}$ **d** $\begin{pmatrix}-3\\-2\end{pmatrix}$ **e** 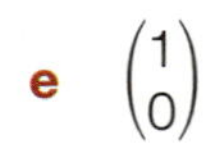 $\begin{pmatrix}1\\0\end{pmatrix}$

7 Look at this diagram.

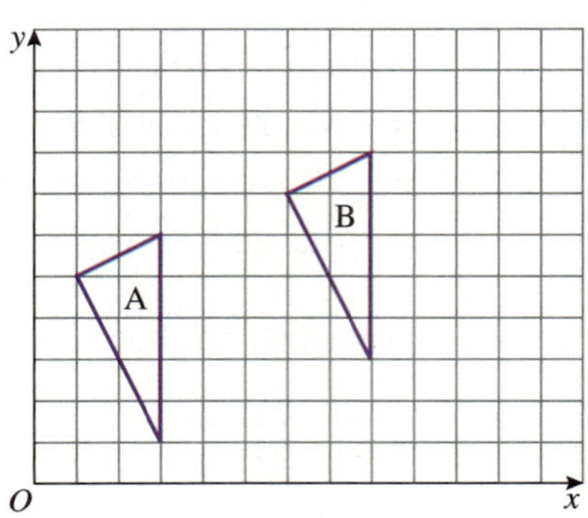

a **i** Write down the vector for the translation that takes triangle A to triangle B.
ii Write down the vector for the translation that takes triangle B to triangle A.
iii What do you notice about these two vectors?

b Triangle A is translated by vector $\begin{pmatrix}3\\-4\end{pmatrix}$ to give triangle C.

Write down the vector for the translation that takes triangle C to triangle A.

22.4 Enlargements

CAN YOU REMEMBER

- How to find the perimeter of a shape made from rectangles?
- The meaning of 'object' and 'image' in transformations?

IN THIS SECTION YOU WILL

- Enlarge shapes using positive and negative integer scale factors and positive fractional scale factors.
- Identify the scale factor of an enlargement.
- Work out the lengths of sides of enlarged shapes.
- Understand the effect of enlargement on perimeter and area of a shape.

An *enlargement* is a transformation that increases or decreases the size of a shape.
When a shape is enlarged:

- its angles remain unchanged
- its lengths are changed in proportion; this means that the lengths are multiplied by the same amount (for example, doubled, trebled, multiplied by 4).

For the rectangles shown, each length on the object has been multiplied by 2
The *scale factor* of the enlargement is 2

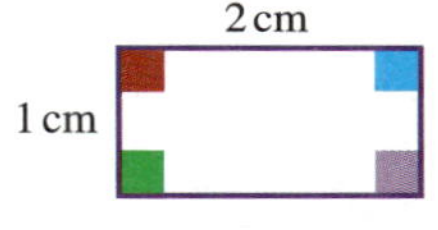

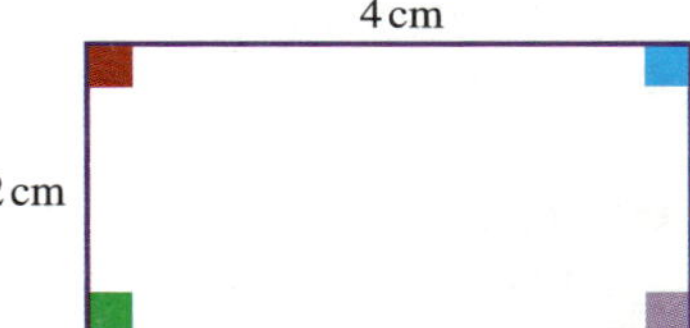

When one shape is an enlargement of another they are *similar.*
This means that they are the same shape, with the same angles, but a different size.

Example 1

a Enlarge shape A by scale factor 2
b Compare the perimeter of the object and the image.

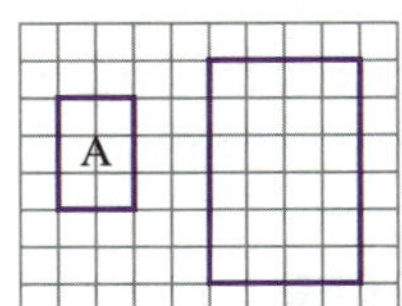

Solution 1

a Scale factor 2 means that the length of each side of the object is multiplied by 2
The object is a rectangle with width 2 and length 3
The image will be a rectangle with width $2 \times 2 = 4$ and length $2 \times 3 = 6$

b Perimeter of object $= 2 + 3 + 2 + 3 = 10$
Perimeter of image $= 4 + 6 + 4 + 6 = 20$
Perimeter of image is two times the perimeter of the object.
The perimeter is multiplied by the scale factor of the enlargement.

An object can be enlarged about a *centre of enlargement.*
An enlargement about a centre fixes the position of the image.

Example 2

Enlarge this triangle by scale factor 2 with centre of enlargement (0, 0).

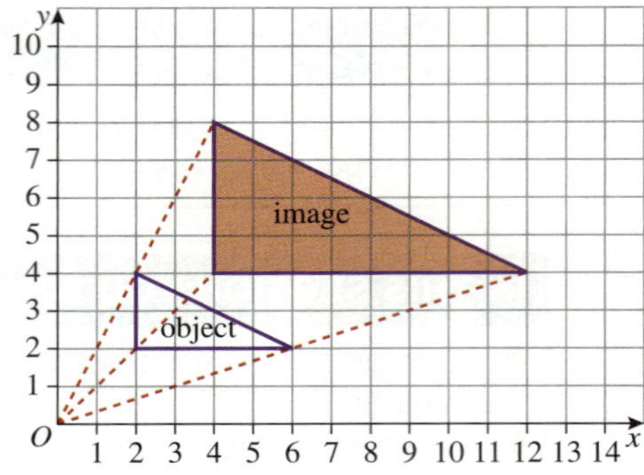

Solution 2

For an enlargement of scale factor 2:

- the length of each side of the triangle is multiplied by 2
- the distance from the centre of enlargement to each point on the object is multiplied by 2

Example 3

Enlarge this triangle by scale factor 3 with centre of enlargement (−5, 4).

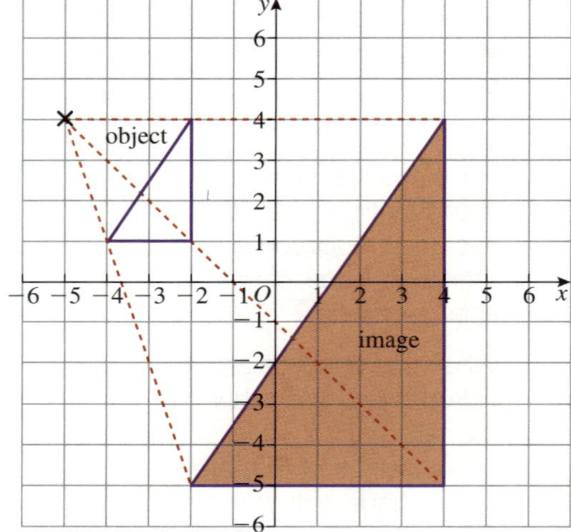

Solution 3

For an enlargement of scale factor 3:

- the length of each side of the triangle is multiplied by 3
- the distance from the centre of enlargement to each point on the object is multiplied by 3

A description of an enlargement about a centre must include:

- the word 'enlargement'
- the scale factor of the enlargement
- the centre of enlargement.

Example 4

a Describe the single transformation that transforms the object to the image.

b How many times bigger is the area of the image than the area of the object?

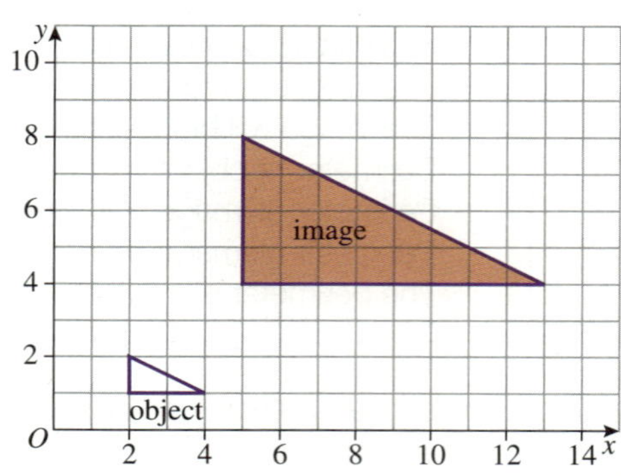

Solution 4

a The lengths of the sides of the image are four times the lengths of the object.
The scale factor of the enlargement is 4
The centre of enlargement is at the point of intersection of lines drawn through corresponding points on the object and image.
The centre of enlargement is (1, 0).
The transformation is an enlargement, scale factor 4, centre of enlargement (1, 0).

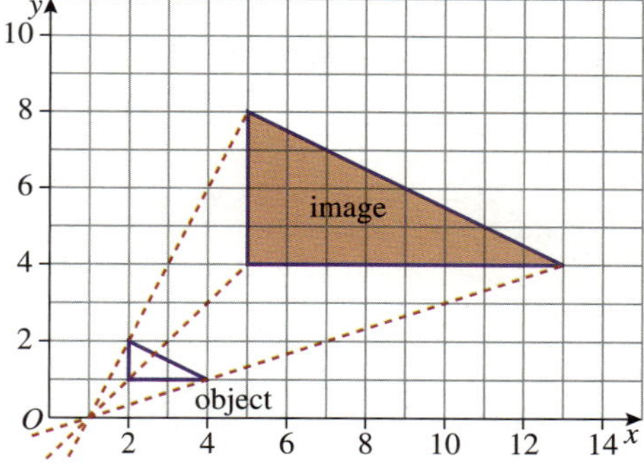

b Counting squares:
area of object = 1 square unit,
area of image = 16 square units
The area of the object is 16 times the area of the image.

Exercise A

1 Enlarge each shape by scale factor 2 with centre of enlargement (0, 0).

a

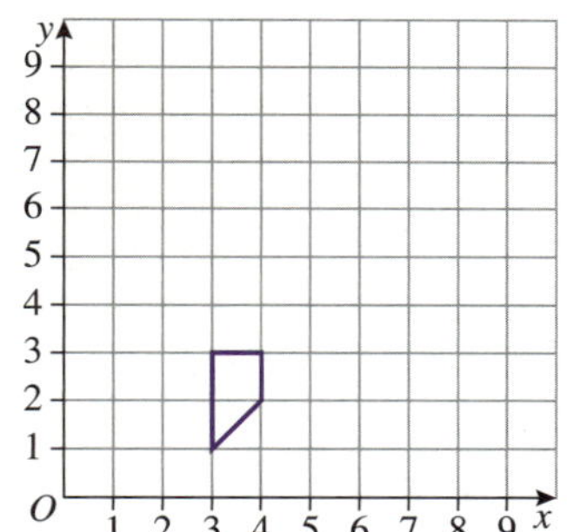

b

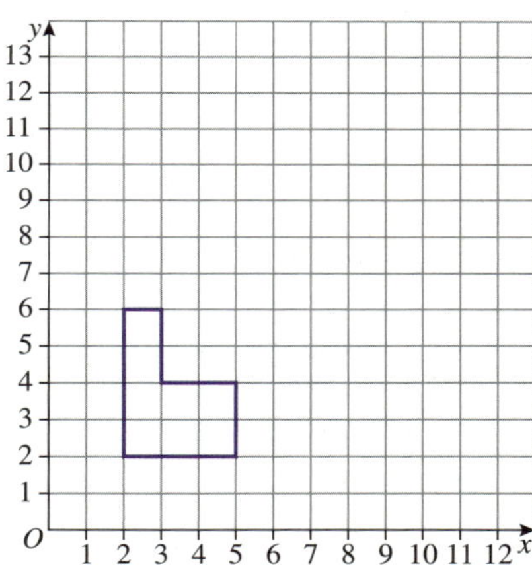

2 Enlarge the triangle by scale factor 3 with centre of enlargement (0, 0).

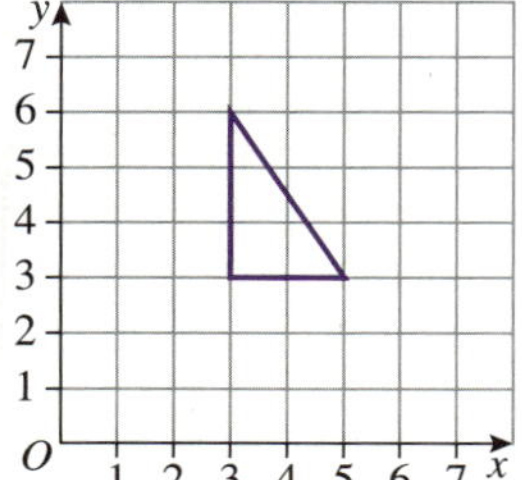

3 Enlarge each of the following diagrams using the given scale factor and centre of enlargement.

a Scale factor 3, centre of enlargement (4, 1).

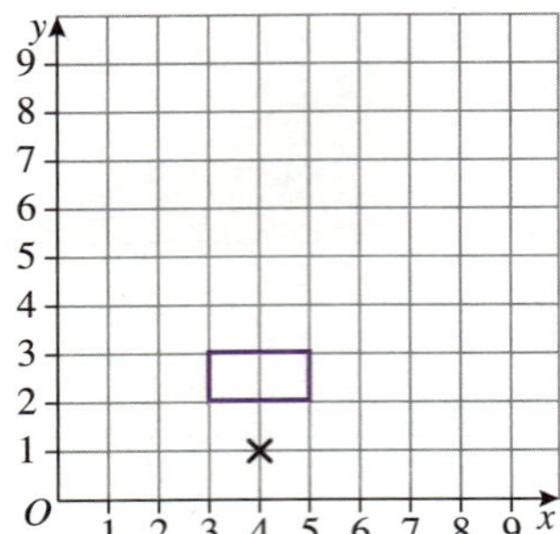

b Scale factor 2, centre of enlargement (−3, −2).

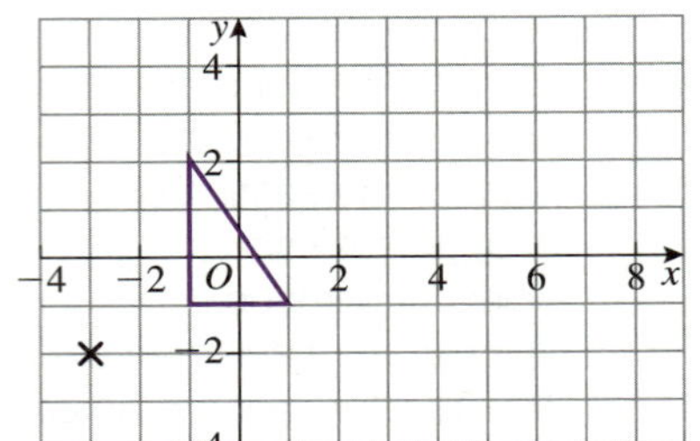

c Scale factor 3, centre of enlargement (1, 2).

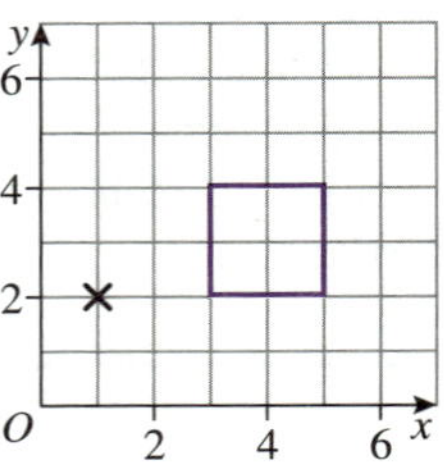

4 **a** **i** Enlarge this shape by scale factor 3

ii How many times bigger is the area of the image than the area of the object?

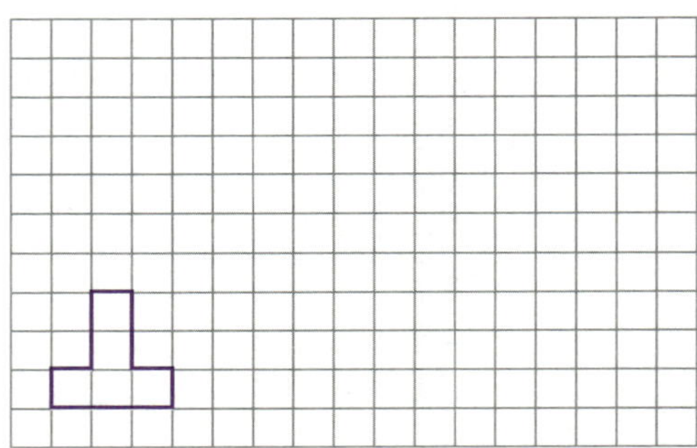

b **i** Enlarge the shape by scale factor 2

ii How many times bigger is the area of the image than the area of the object?

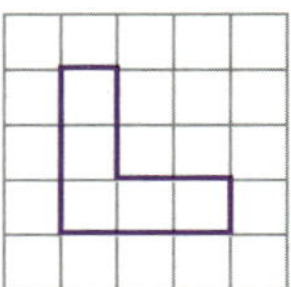

5 For each diagram describe fully the single transformation that transforms the shape A to the shape B.

a

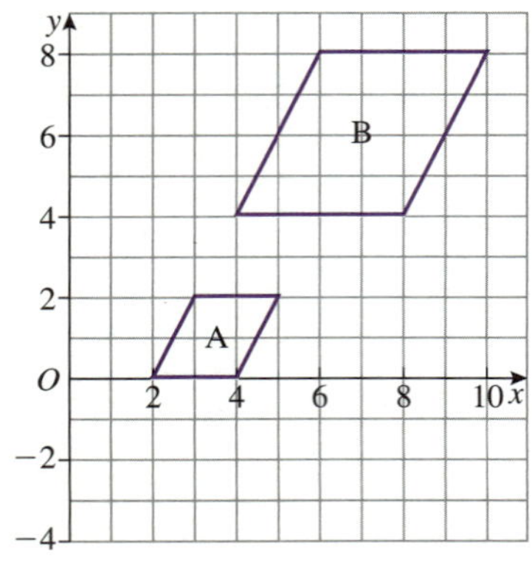

b

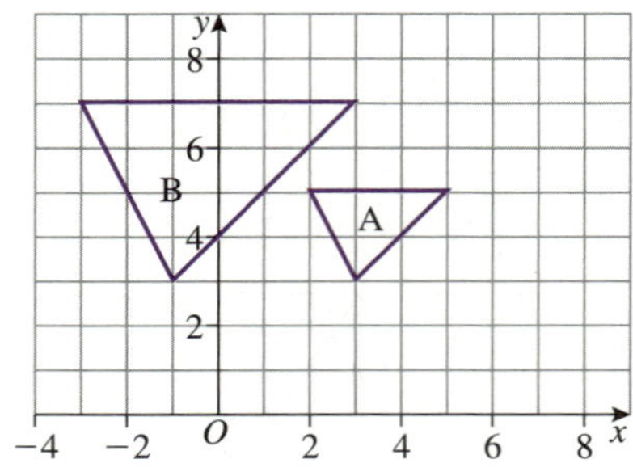

c

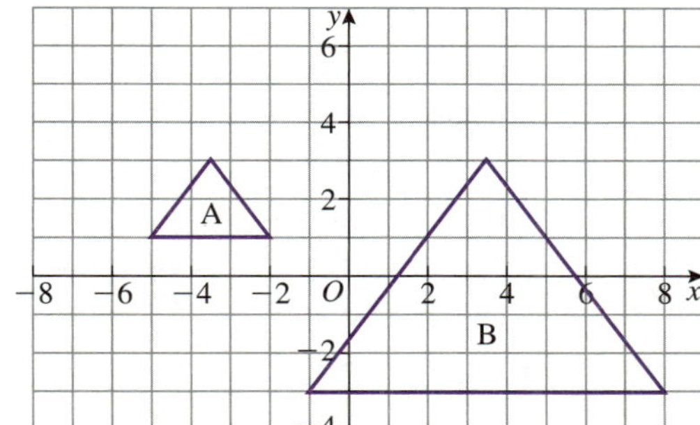

d

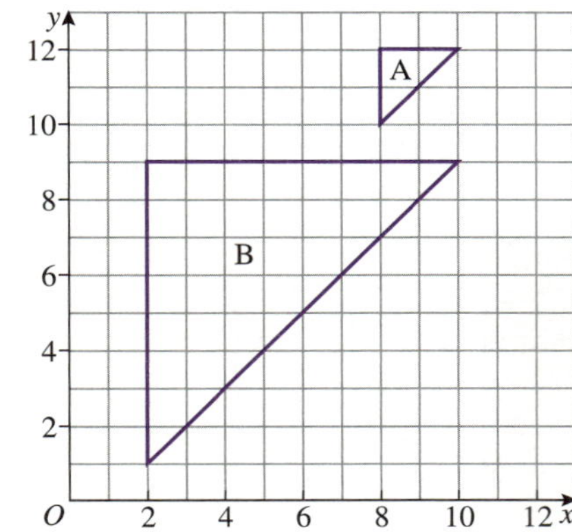

When the scale factor is a value between 0 and 1 the image of the shape will be *smaller* than the object.

Example 5

Enlarge this triangle by scale factor $\frac{1}{3}$ with centre of enlargement (1, 1).

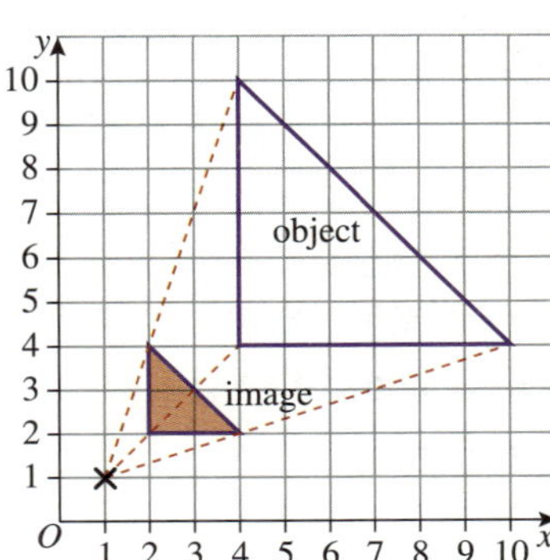

Solution 5

For an enlargement of scale factor $\frac{1}{3}$:

- the length of each side of the triangle is multiplied by $\frac{1}{3}$
- the distance from the centre of enlargement to each point on the object is multiplied by $\frac{1}{3}$

When the scale factor is negative the image is *inverted* and on the opposite side of the centre of enlargement.

Example 6

Draw an enlargement of this shape with scale factor −2 and centre of enlargement (1, 2).

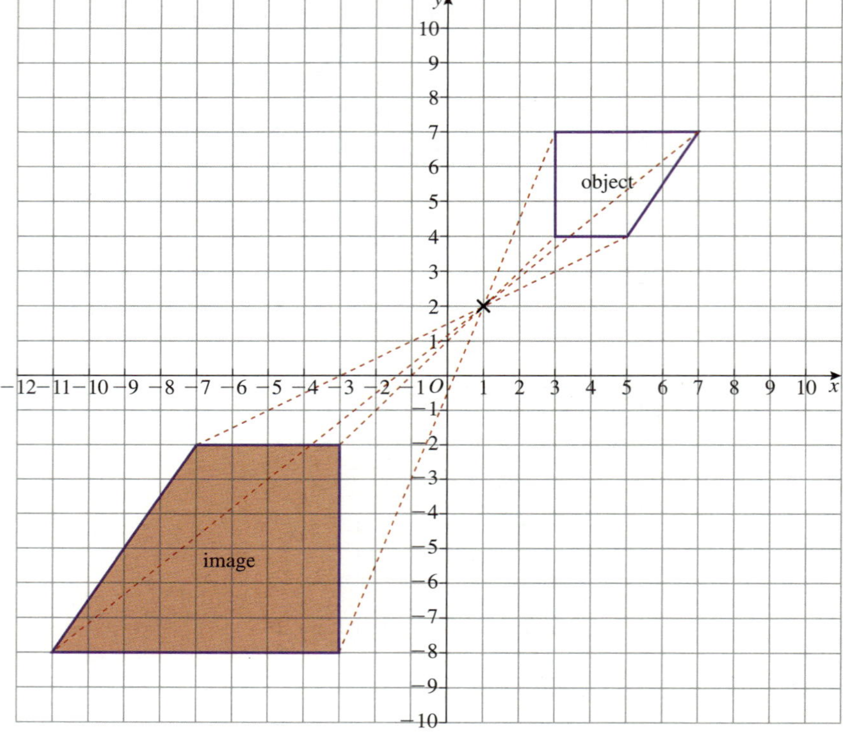

Solution 6

For an enlargement scale factor −2:

- the length of each side of the triangle is multiplied by 2
- the distance from the centre of enlargement to each point on the object is multiplied by 2 and in the opposite direction.

Exercise B

Copy each diagram onto squared paper.
Enlarge each shape by the given scale factor and centre of enlargement.

1 Scale factor $\frac{1}{2}$, centre of enlargement (1, 2).

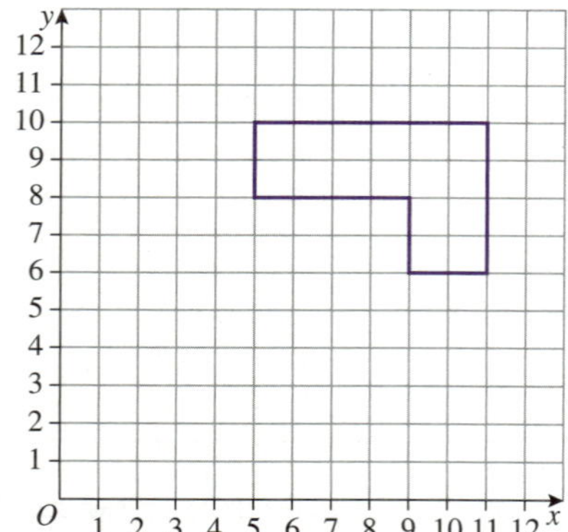

2 Scale factor −1, centre of enlargement (0, 0).

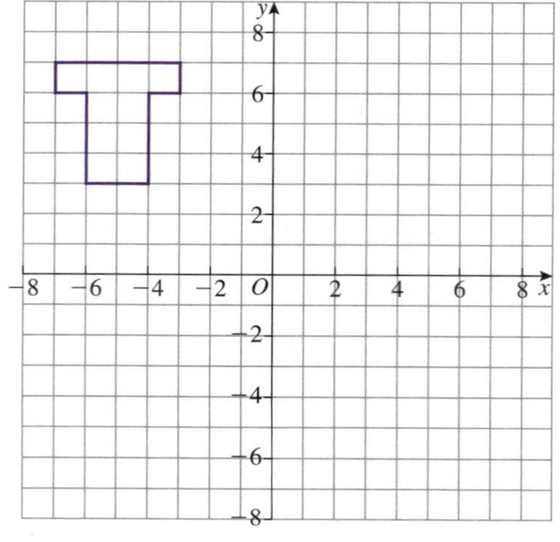

3 Scale factor $\frac{1}{3}$, centre of enlargement (0, 0).

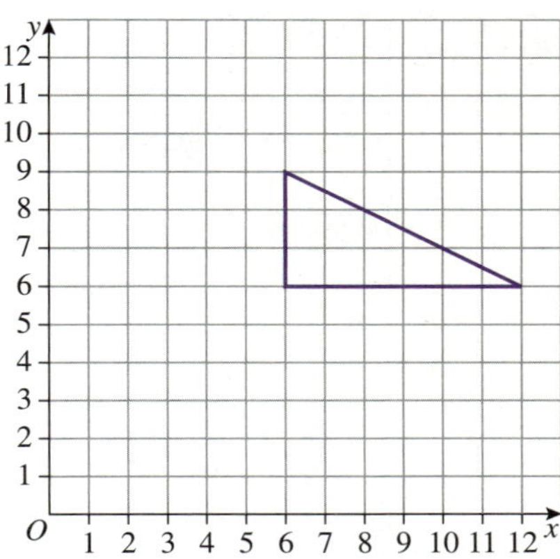

4 Copy the diagram onto a square grid.
Draw the x and y-axes from −6 to +9
Enlarge this shape by scale factor −2 with centre of enlargement (3, 0).

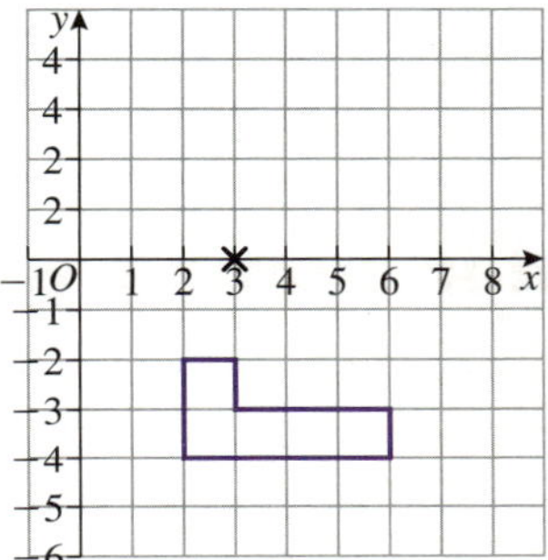

5 Copy the diagram onto a square grid.
Draw the x and y axes from −6 to +10
Enlarge this triangle by scale factor $-\frac{1}{2}$ with centre of enlargement (1, 1).

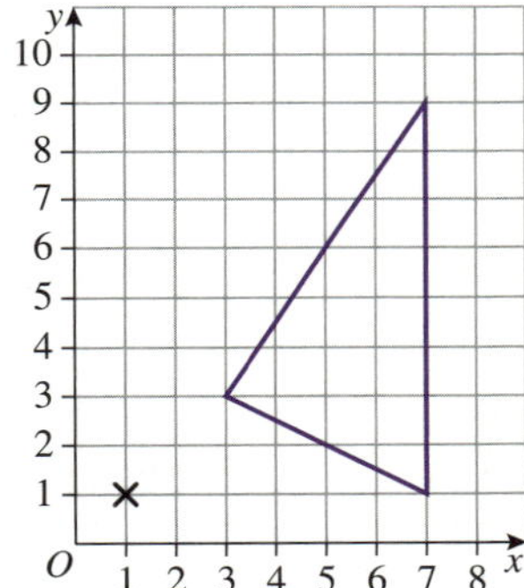

6 Describe fully the single transformation which transforms object A to image B in each diagram.

a

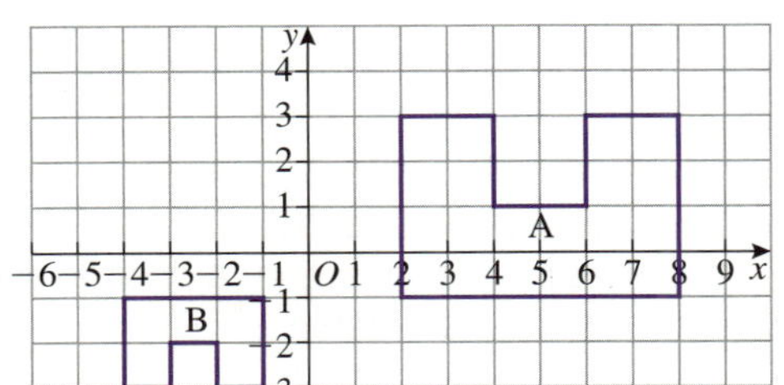

b

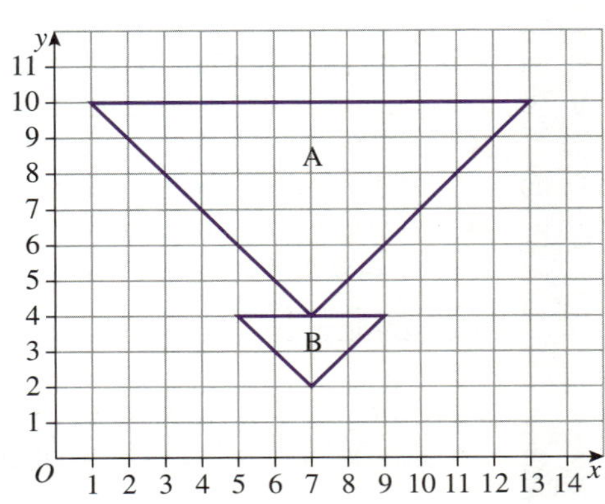

c

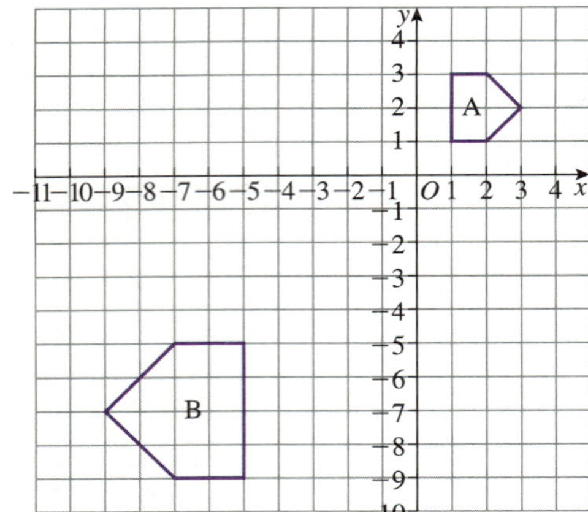

Chapter summary

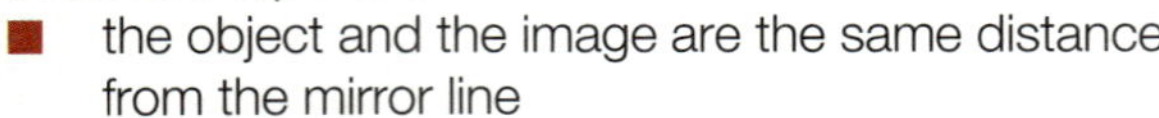

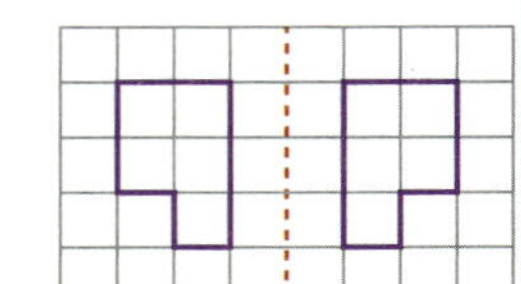

- When a shape is reflected:
  - the object and the image are the same distance from the mirror line
  - the object and the image are congruent.
- A point on the mirror line is reflected onto itself.
- A description of a reflection must include:
  - the word 'reflection'
  - the name of the mirror line, e.g. $y = 2$, the x-axis.
- A rotation turns a shape about a fixed point, called the centre of rotation.
- The angle of rotation can be given as a fraction of a turn or in degrees.
- Rotations can be in a clockwise or anticlockwise direction.
- A description of a rotation must include:
  - the word 'rotation'
  - the angle through which it turns
  - the direction of the turn
  - the centre of rotation.
- To find the centre of rotation, pivot a tracing of the object around different points until it fits exactly onto the image.
- When a shape is rotated about one of its vertices, that vertex does not move.
- A translation can be described using a vector:
  - the top number always describes movement in the x-direction. A positive value means movement to the right. A negative value means movement to the left.
  - the bottom number always describes movement in the y-direction. A positive value means movement up. A negative value means movement down.

  For example, $\begin{pmatrix} 2 \\ -3 \end{pmatrix}$ moves a point 2 units to the right and 3 units down.
- When an object is translated the object and the image are congruent.
- An enlargement is a transformation that increases or decreases the size of a shape.

- When a shape is enlarged:
  - its angles remain unchanged
  - its lengths are changed in the same proportion; this means that all the lengths are multiplied by the same amount
  - when one shape is an enlargement of another they are similar; this means that they are the same shape, with the same angles, but a different size.
- The scale factor of the enlargement is the number all lengths on the object are multiplied by to give the lengths on the image.
  For example, a scale factor of 2 doubles all the lengths on the image.
- The perimeter of the image is also increased by the scale factor.
- An object can be enlarged about a centre of enlargement.
- An enlargement about a centre fixes the position of the image:
  - the length of each side of the shape is multiplied by the scale factor
  - the distance from the centre of enlargement to each point on the object is multiplied by the scale factor.
- When the scale factor is between 0 and 1 the image of the shape will be smaller than the object.
- When the scale factor is negative the image is inverted and on the opposite side of the centre of enlargement.
- A description of an enlargement about a centre must include:
  - the word 'enlargement'
  - the scale factor of the enlargement
  - the centre of enlargement.

Chapter review

1 Copy the shape and mirror line.
Draw a reflection of the shape in the mirror line.

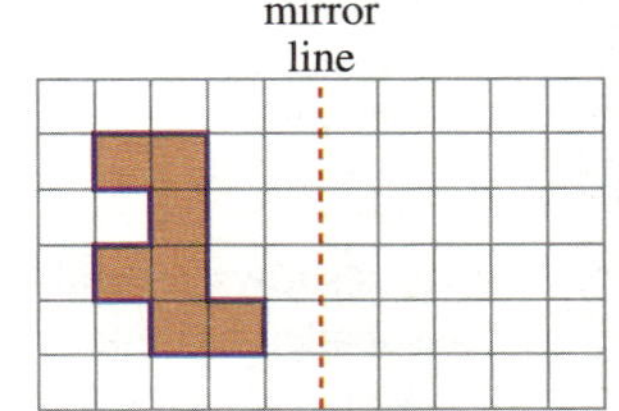

2 **a** The diagram shows two shapes, P and Q.
Describe fully the single transformation which takes shape P onto shape Q.

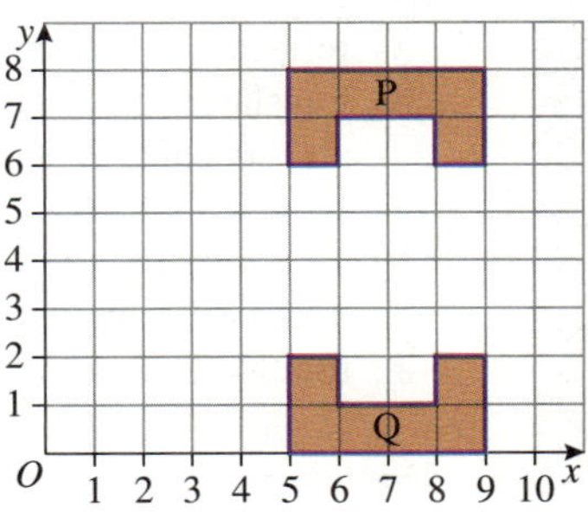

b Copy the grid and triangle R below.
The vertices of triangle R are (2, 1), (2, 3) and (5, 1).

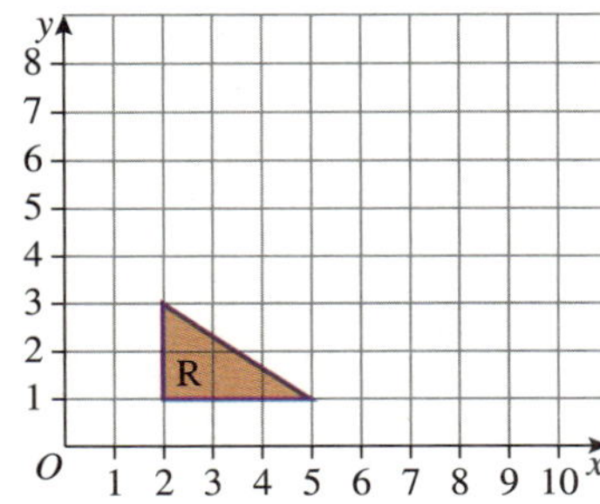

Enlarge triangle R by scale factor 2 with (0, 0) as the centre of enlargement.

3

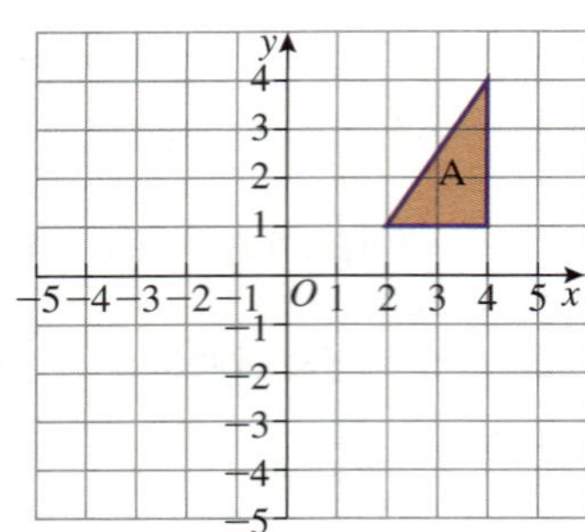

Copy the grid and triangle A.

a Reflect the triangle in the y-axis. Label the triangle B.

b Rotate triangle A 90° clockwise about the origin O. Label the triangle C.

4 Copy the grid and triangle A. Draw the new position of triangle A after a rotation of 90° clockwise about the origin.

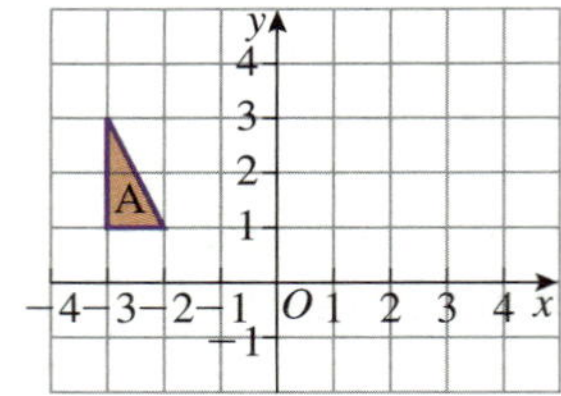

5 Copy the grid and shape A.

a On the graph, draw the finishing position when:

- **i** shape A is reflected in the line $y = 1$
- **ii** shape A is rotated through 180° about the origin.

b Describe fully the transformation which will map shape A onto shape B.

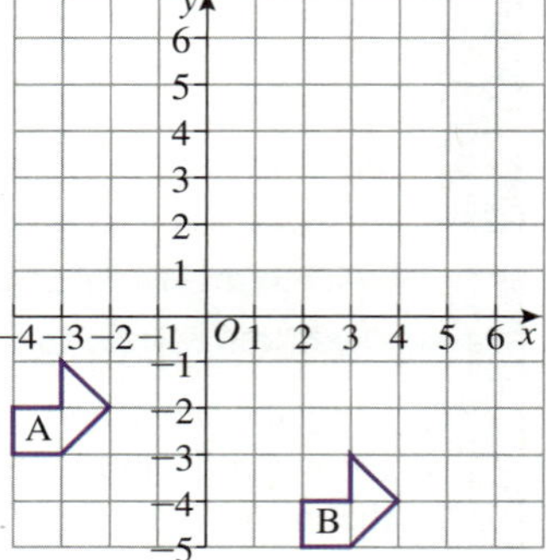

6 The grid shows several transformations of the shaded triangle.

a Write down the letter of the triangle after the shaded triangle is:

- **i** reflected in the line $y = 1$
- **ii** translated three squares to the right and six squares down
- **iii** rotated 180° about the point (0, 2).

b Describe **fully** the transformation which takes:

- **i** triangle H onto triangle D
- **ii** triangle E onto triangle G.

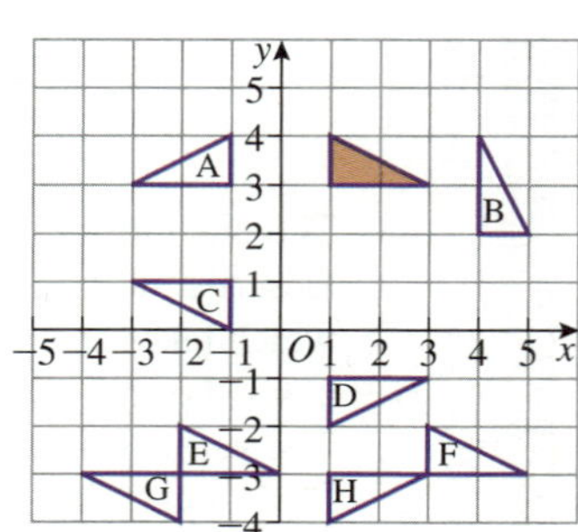

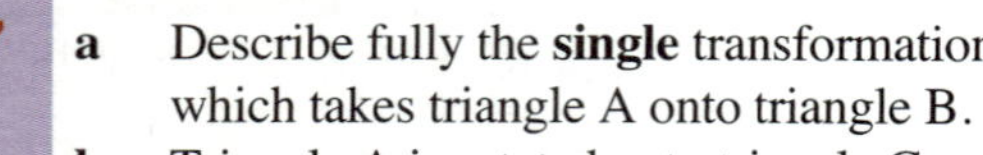

7 **a** Describe fully the **single** transformation which takes triangle A onto triangle B.

b Triangle A is rotated onto triangle C.

- **i** Write down the angle of rotation.
- **ii** Write down the coordinates of the centre of rotation.

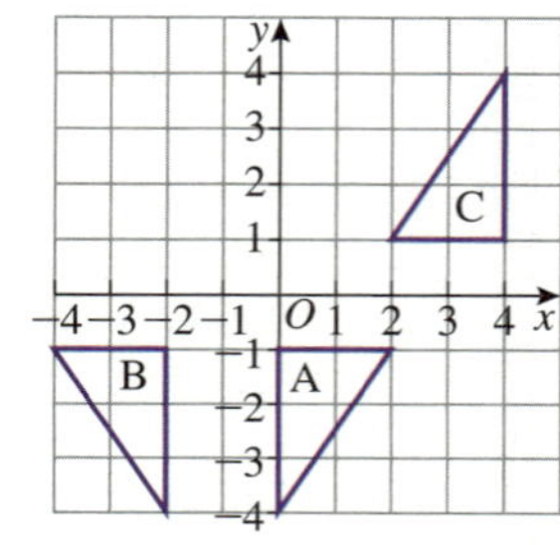

c Copy the grid and triangle D.

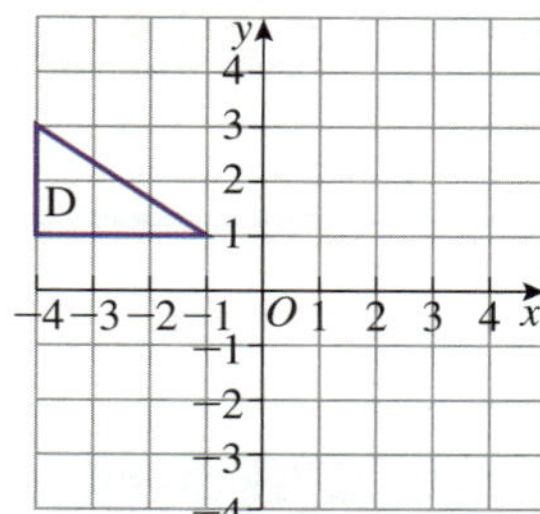

Triangle D is translated by the vector $\begin{pmatrix} 3 \\ -5 \end{pmatrix}$.

Draw the new position of triangle D.

8 **a** Describe fully the single transformation which maps shape A to shape B.

b Copy the grid and shape A.

i Draw shape A after it has been rotated through 180° about the origin O.
Label the shape C.

ii Translate shape A by the vector $\begin{pmatrix} 2 \\ -6 \end{pmatrix}$.

Label the new shape D.

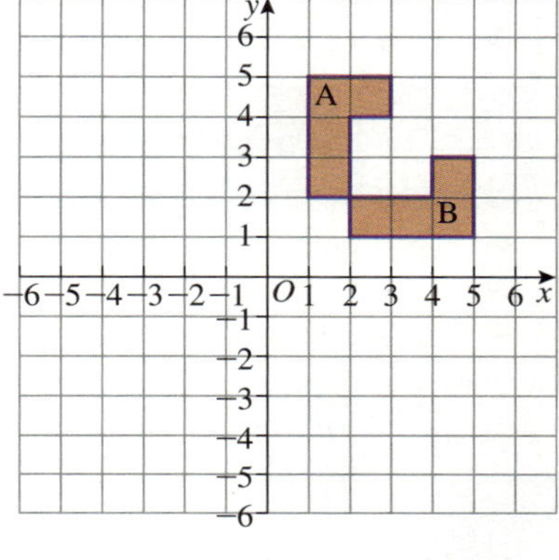

9 Enlarge the shaded shape by scale factor $\frac{1}{3}$ with centre of enlargement $(-2, -1)$.

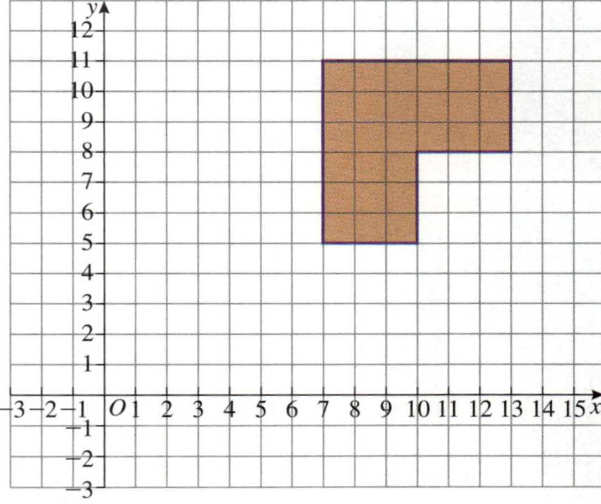

10 **a** On a copy of the graph, draw the finishing position when:

i Shape A is reflected in the line $y = 1$

ii Shape A is rotated through 180° about the point $(1, 1)$.

b Describe fully the transformation which will map shape A onto shape B.

c Describe fully the **single** transformation which will map shape B onto shape C.

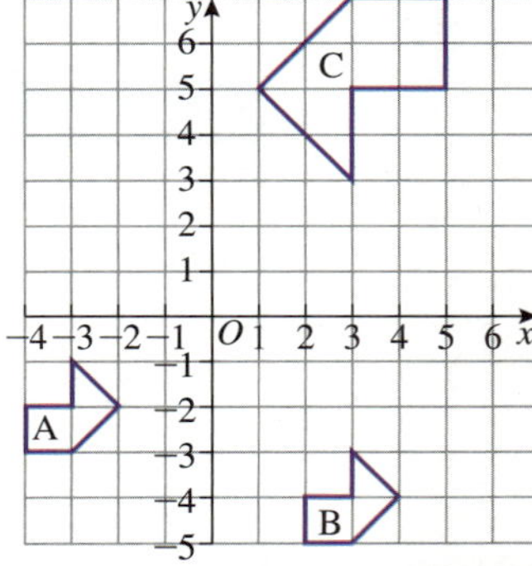

CHAPTER

23

Time series data

23.1 Time series

CAN YOU REMEMBER

- How to plot points on a graph?
- How to work out the mean, mode, median and range of data?

IN THIS SECTION YOU WILL

- Understand the meaning of 'time series'.
- Learn to draw and interpret line graphs for time series.
- Learn when to use time series graphs to make estimates and predictions.

A graph with a time scale along the horizontal axis is called a *time series*.
A time series graph has data whose values change over time.
The time period could be minutes, hours, weeks, months or years.
The points in a time series graph are joined by straight lines.

To interpret a time series, look carefully at the scale.
These two graphs show the same data.

Graph A makes it look as if sales are increasing rapidly.

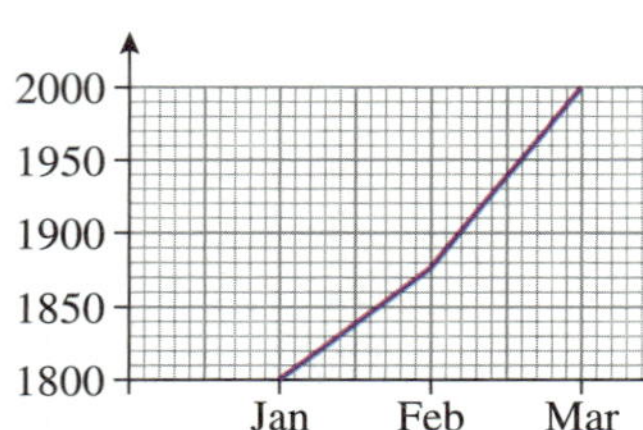

Graph B shows the same increase, but gives a more accurate picture.

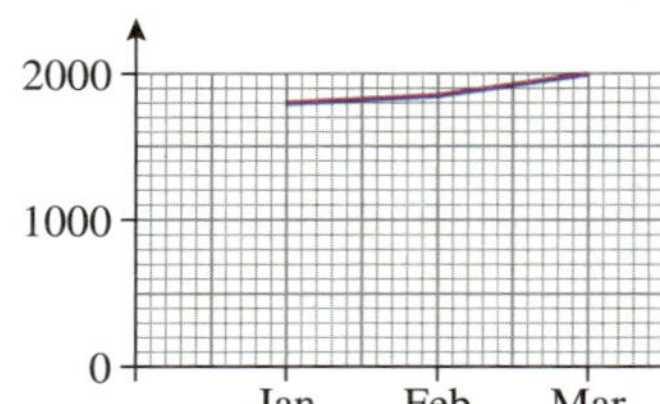

Two sets of data can be compared by drawing their time series on the same axes.

Example 1

The table shows the average maximum daytime temperatures for two cities in Canada.

City	Average maximum daytime temperatures °C			
	January	April	July	October
Montreal	−6	11	26	13
Quebec	−8	8	25	11

a Draw time series graphs for the two cities on the same axes.
b Which city is generally warmer throughout the year?
c What is the range of temperature for Quebec?

Solution 1

a Plot the point −6 at January, 11 at April and so on.
Repeat for Quebec using a different colour.
Use a key to explain which colour represents which city.

b The temperature for Montreal is always higher than the temperature for Quebec.
So Montreal is warmer than Quebec.

c Quebec: lowest temperature = −8°C
highest temperature = 25°C
Range = 25 − −8 = 33°C

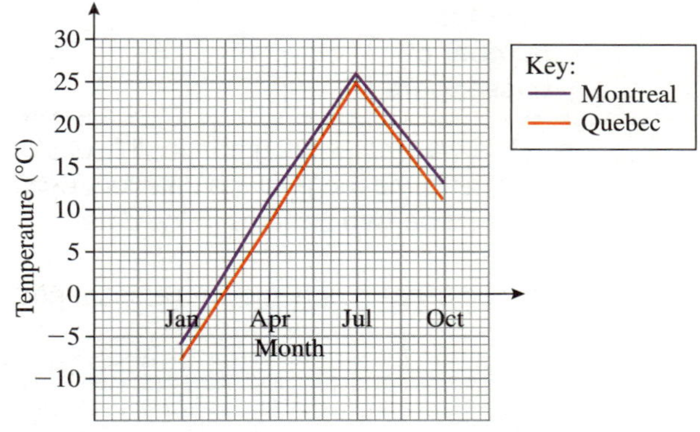

Exercise A

1 The heating bills, in pounds, over two years for a terraced house are shown in the table.

Quarter to	Jul 04	Oct 04	Jan 05	Apr 05	Jul 05	Oct 05	Jan 06	Apr 06
Heating costs (£)	25	38	55	75	32	43	68	70

a Draw a time series graph.
b Which bill was the highest?

2 The weekly attendances at a cinema are shown in the following table.

Week	1	2	3	4	5	6	7	8	9	10
Attendance	250	245	160	220	260	275	300	265	195	220

a Draw a time series graph.
b Which week had the highest attendance?
c Work out the range of these attendances.

3 The number of patients missing appointments at a doctor's surgery each day over a two-week period is shown in the table.

	Week 1					**Week 2**				
Day	Mon	Tues	Wed	Thurs	Fri	Mon	Tues	Wed	Thurs	Fri
Number of patients	5	8	12	2	1	6	9	10	3	2

a Draw a time series graph of this data.
b Describe any pattern shown by the time series graph.
c Calculate the mean number of patients per day missing appointments.

4 The average number of passengers catching the first Doncaster to London Kings Cross train is recorded for each quarter. The table shows the results for 3 years.

Year	2003				2004				2005			
Quarter	1	2	3	4	1	2	3	4	1	2	3	4
Average number of passengers	56	68	82	75	61	74	90	88	72	80	104	99

a Draw a time series graph for this data.
b What is the range of the data for 2005?
c Describe **two** patterns in the data.

5 The time series graph shows the share price, in pence, of a retail company.

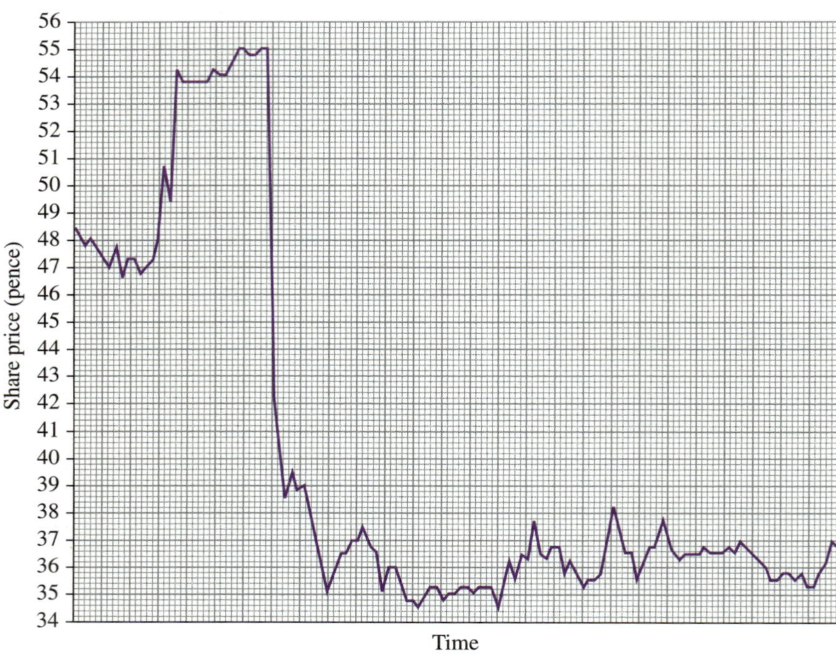

a What was the maximum price of this share over this period?
b After a takeover bid that failed, the price of the share dropped dramatically. By how much did the share price fall before it rose again?
c Calculate the range of this share price.
d In what way is the graph misleading?

6 Geoff and Betty are both traffic wardens.
The table shows the number of parking tickets they issued over a six-day period.

Day	1	2	3	4	5	6
Geoff	23	16	19	25	21	20
Betty	8	32	11	13	28	10

a Draw two time series graphs on the same axes.
b Compare the numbers of tickets given by Geoff and Betty.

Time series graphs can be used to estimate missing data values.
Estimates within the range of data given (interpolation) are fairly reliable.
Estimates outside the range of data given (extrapolation) may not be reliable, as the pattern may not continue in the same way.

Example 2

A newborn baby is weighed at birth and every week for the first eight weeks of its life.
The table shows the results in kilograms for baby Niles with two results missing.

Week	0	1	2	3	4	5	8
Weight (kg)	5.2	4.9	5.1	5.4	5.7	6.0	6.6

a Draw a time series graph for this data.
b Estimate baby Niles's weight after seven weeks.
c Predict Niles's weight after nine weeks.
d Which of the answers to parts **c** and **d** is more reliable? Explain your answer.

Solution 2

a

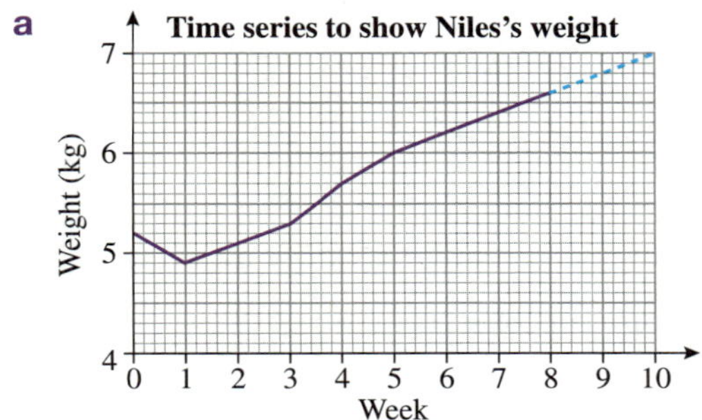

c Draw an extension to the line (shown dashed).
Estimate for nine weeks is 6.8 kg.

d The estimate for seven weeks is more reliable because it is within the given data (interpolation).
The estimate for nine weeks is less reliable, as it is outside the given data (extrapolation). It is not certain that the previous pattern in the data will continue beyond week eight.

b About 6.4 kg.

Exercise B

1 Each week a baby rabbit is weighed.
The graph shows its weekly weight up to week five.
In week six the rabbit weighed 107 g and in week ten its weight was 125 g.

a Copy and complete the graph.
Join the points with straight lines.

b Use the graph to estimate the rabbit's weight in:
  i week seven
  ii week 11

c Explain why it would not be sensible to use the graph to estimate the weight of the rabbit in week 20

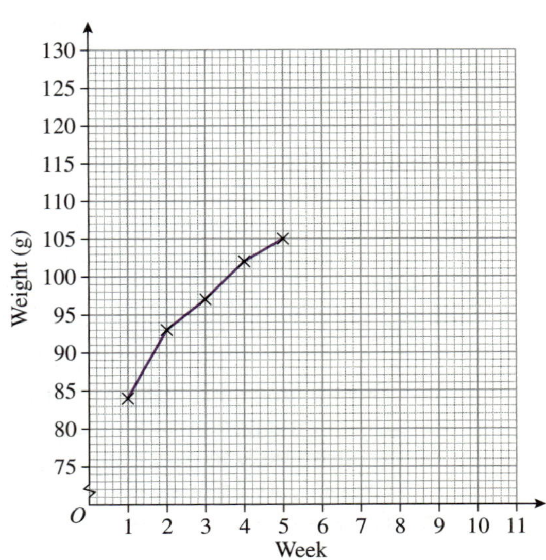

2 The graph shows the cost of insuring a car over an eight-year period.

a For how many years did the cost fall?

b Give a reason why the cost may have risen again after year 6

c In year 9 the cost doubled from that in year 8
In years 10 and 11 the cost then fell slightly each time.
Sketch how the graph may look for years 9–11.

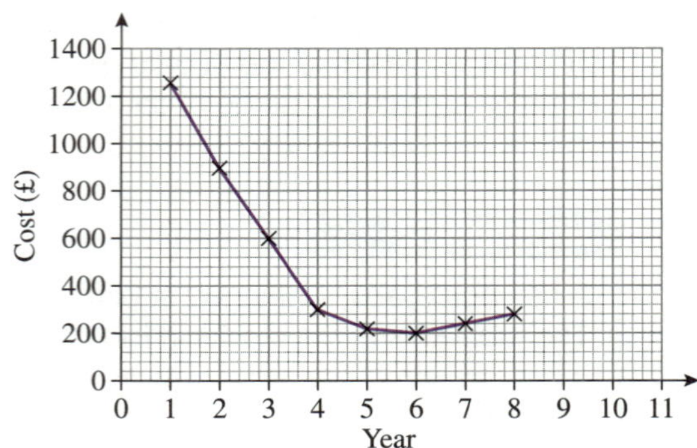

3 Josh records the amount of money that he spends each month on his credit card. His results for 11 months of 2005 are shown in the time series graph.

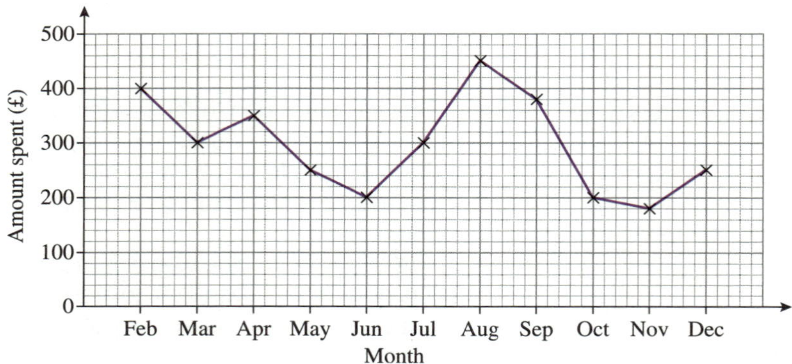

a Calculate the range of the amounts spent.

b Calculate the mean amount spent.

c Use your mean value in part **b** to estimate how much Josh spends in January 2006

d Plot the mean value from part **b** as an estimate for the amount spent in January 2006

e Why might your estimate in part **d** be unreliable?

4 Each day Jayne records the time it takes her to complete the Rubik's cube puzzle.
The times are shown in the table.

Day	1	2	3	4	5	6	7	8	9	10
Time (s)	360	340	320	285	240	120	135	100	95	100

a Draw a time series graph for this data.

b Describe a pattern in the data.

c Is Jayne likely to ever complete the puzzle in under 60 seconds? Explain your answer.

d Explain why it is not sensible to calculate the average of these times and use it to estimate the time to complete the puzzle for day 11

5 Use the information and graphs below to answer the following questions.

a Calculate the greatest difference between the maximum and minimum monthly temperatures in Cologne.

b Calculate the range of the maximum daily temperatures in Cologne in the period 11–25 August 2005

c **i** Draw two time series graphs on the same axes to show the average maximum temperatures in °C for Torrejon and Madrid.

ii Compare the average maximum temperatures in Torrejon and Madrid.

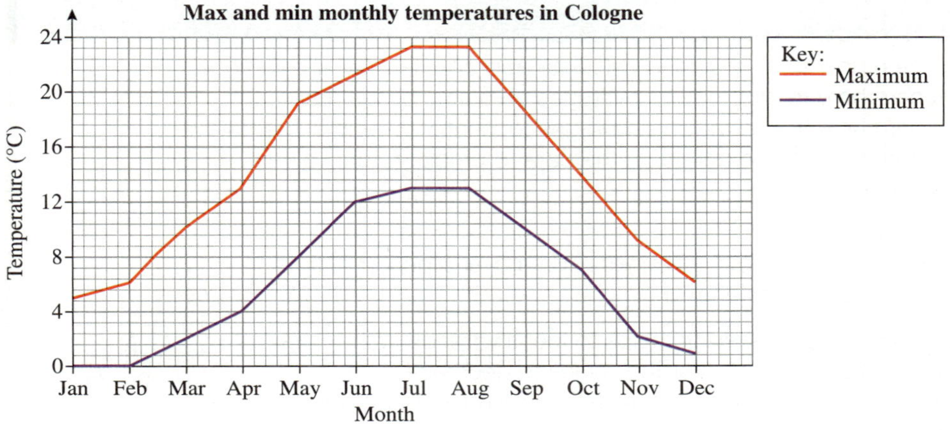

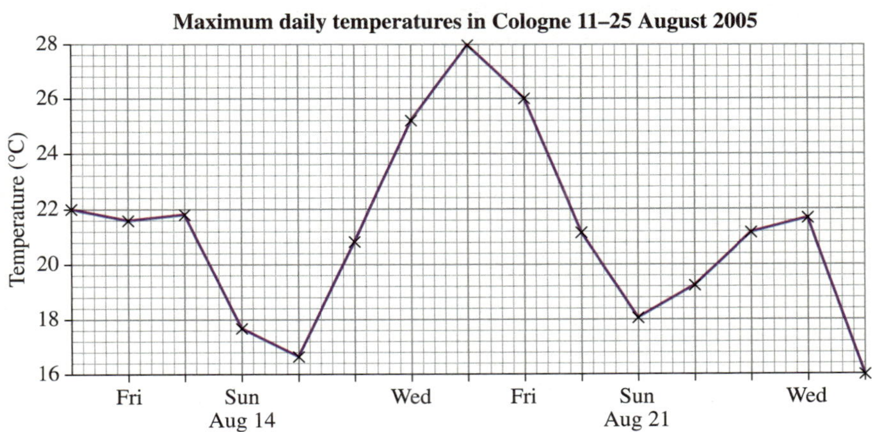

	Jan	Feb	Mar	Apr	May	Jun	Jul	Aug	Sep	Oct	Nov	Dec
Torrejon temperature (°C)	9.7	11.9	15.0	17.2	23.0	27.0	31.8	31.2	26.7	19.3	12.8	9.5
Madrid temperature (°C)	5.3	6.7	9.7	12.0	16.1	20.8	24.6	23.9	20.5	14.7	9.3	6.0

23.2 Moving averages

CAN YOU REMEMBER

- How to find the mean of a set of data?
- How to draw a time series graph?
- How to draw a line of best fit through a set of points?

IN THIS SECTION YOU WILL

- Learn how to choose and calculate appropriate moving averages.
- Learn how to plot moving averages on a time series graph.
- Learn how to use moving averages to identify a trend in the data.
- Learn how to use a trend in the data to predict future values.

A time series graph shows changes in data over a period of time. The data values may vary a lot.

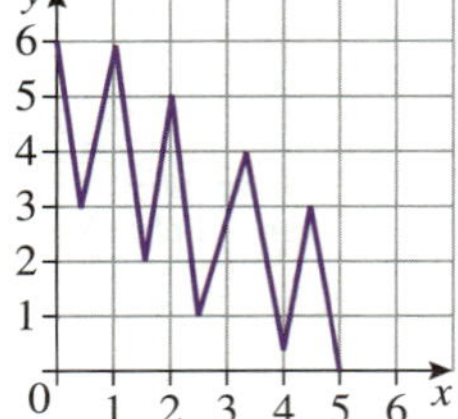

Calculating a *moving average* helps to identify trends in the data. For this graph, the trend is for the values to decrease.
A moving average is found by calculating the mean of a given number of values or points, then moving one data item along and calculating the next mean. For example, for three-point moving averages:

4 8 6 5 3 7 9 6 4

First three-point moving average

$= \frac{4 + 8 + 6}{3}$

4 8 6 5 3 7 9 6 4

Second three-point moving average

$= \frac{8 + 6 + 5}{3}$

4 8 6 5 3 7 9 6 4

Third three-point moving average

$= \frac{6 + 5 + 3}{3}$

Example 1

For the data values 3, 7, 8, 6, 10, 4 find:

a the first three-point moving average
b the second three-point moving average
c the third three-point moving average.

Solution 1

a The first three-point moving average is the mean of the first three values:

$$= \frac{3 + 7 + 8}{3} = 6$$

b The second three-point moving average is the mean of the second, third and fourth values:

$$= \frac{7 + 8 + 6}{3} = 7$$

c The third three-point moving average is the mean of the third, fourth and fifth values:

$$= \frac{8 + 6 + 10}{3} = 8$$

It is important to choose an *appropriate* moving average which takes into account the number of values in a particular time period. Then the moving averages show the overall trend and are not affected by trends in the different collection periods. The table gives some examples.

Data collected	Moving average
Twice yearly	two-point
Each school term	three-point
Quarterly	four-point
5-day week	five-point
7-day week	seven-point

Moving averages can be plotted on a time series graph. Each moving average is plotted in the middle of the time period for which it is calculated.
A line of best fit drawn through the moving averages shows the trend in the data.

Example 2

The table shows the sales (in £) for two weeks in a take-away which is open for five days per week.

	Week 1					**Week 2**				
Day	Tue	Wed	Thu	Fri	Sat	Tue	Wed	Thu	Fri	Sat
Sales	145	153	130	208	244	162	158	140	225	275

a Draw a time series graph to show the data.
b Explain why five-point moving averages should be calculated.
c Calculate the set of five-point moving averages.
d Plot the moving averages on the time series graph.
e Draw a line of best fit for the moving averages.
f Describe any trend in the data.

Solution 2

a, d, e

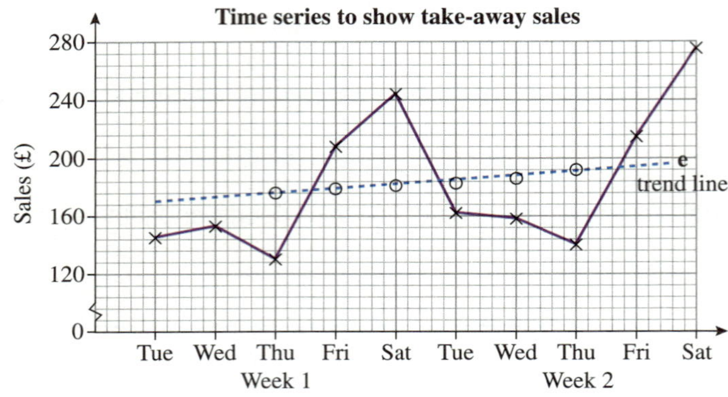

b The data has five readings per week, so five-point moving averages include one value from each of Tuesday to Saturday. This means there will be no daily effects on the moving averages, only overall trend effects.

c First five-point moving average $= \dfrac{145 + 153 + 130 + 208 + 244}{5} = 176$

It is calculated for the time period Tuesday to Saturday, which has midpoint Thursday. Plot the value 176 for Thursday.
Continuing in this way gives the remaining five-point moving averages and the days they are plotted against:

	Week 1					Week 2				
Day	Tue	Wed	Thu	Fri	Sat	Tue	Wed	Thu	Fri	Sat
Sales	145	153	130	208	244	162	158	140	225	275
Moving average			176	179.4	180.4	182.4	185.8	192		

d The moving average points are plotted as circles to distinguish them from the original data.
f The line of best fit shows a slight upward trend, indicating a slight increase in sales over the two weeks.

Exercise A

1 For the data set: 10, 12, 11, 16, 18, 15
- **a** find the first three-point moving average
- **b** find the second three-point moving average
- **c** find the third three-point moving average.

2 Find the set of four-point moving averages for the following data:

8 6 7 5 10 8 11

3 The number of pupils absent from Raimi's class over two weeks is given below.

3 2 4 3 1 0 2 2 1 0

- **a** Explain why a five-point moving average would be most suitable in this situation.
- **b** Find the set of five-point moving averages for this data.

4 Sukie's café is open three mornings per week.
Her takings for the last three weeks are given in the table below.

	Week 1			Week 2			Week 3		
Day	1	2	3	1	2	3	1	2	3
Takings (£)	50	80	50	20	50	65	35	20	35

a Plot this data on a time series graph.
b Calculate the set of three-point moving averages.
c Plot the moving averages on the graph.

Hint: remember to plot the values in the middle of the period so the first value needs to be plotted on the week 1 day 2 point.

5 Andy's gas bill is calculated quarterly (four times per year).
The table shows Andy's gas bills for the last two years.

	Year 1				Year 2			
Quarter	1	2	3	4	1	2	3	4
Bill (£)	100	80	40	90	120	90	60	100

a Plot this data on a time series graph.
b Calculate the set of four-point moving averages.
c Plot the moving averages on the graph.

Hint: remember to plot the values in the middle of the period so the first value needs to be plotted in between the points for quarters 2 and 3 in year 1

6 The number of passengers on the last bus each weekday evening for the last two weeks is given below.

	Week 1					Week 2				
Day	Mon	Tue	Wed	Thu	Fri	Mon	Tue	Wed	Thu	Fri
Number of passengers	8	11	15	20	52	6	8	12	21	43

a Plot the data as a time series.
b Calculate appropriate moving averages for this data, which is given for five days each week.
c Plot the moving averages on the time series graph.

7 City's last ten home match attendances were as follows:

23 184 18 905 22 675 25 438 30 000
27 553 21 873 30 000 24 004 28 488

a Plot the data as a time series.
b Calculate the set of four-point moving averages.
c Plot the moving averages on the time series graph.
d Identify a trend in the data.

8 Zaheer recorded the number of days he worked away from home for each period of four months over four years. His results are given in the table.

Year	2002			2003			2004			2005		
Period	1	2	3	1	2	3	1	2	3	1	2	3
Days worked	8	27	11	10	31	15	14	33	17	16	35	20

a Plot the data as a time series.
b What size moving average should be calculated to find any possible trend in the data? Explain your answer.
c Calculate these moving averages and plot them on the graph.
d Zaheer's wife complained that he was spending more time away from home each year. Is she correct? Explain your answer.

If it can be assumed that the trend the data shows will continue into the future, the moving averages trend line can be used to predict future values.
In cases where the trend might not continue, it is not appropriate to predict future values.

Example 3

The number of arrests made in a town centre during each quarter over a period of two years is given below.

Year	2004				2005			
Quarter	1	2	3	4	1	2	3	4
Arrests	32	45	86	49	26	33	76	42

a Plot the data as a time series graph.
b Calculate appropriate moving averages for the data.
c Plot the moving averages on the graph.
d Draw in a trend line and comment on the trend in the data.
e Use your trend line to estimate the number of arrests made in quarter 1 of 2006

Solution 3

a, c, d
b There are four data values per year so a four-point moving average is appropriate.

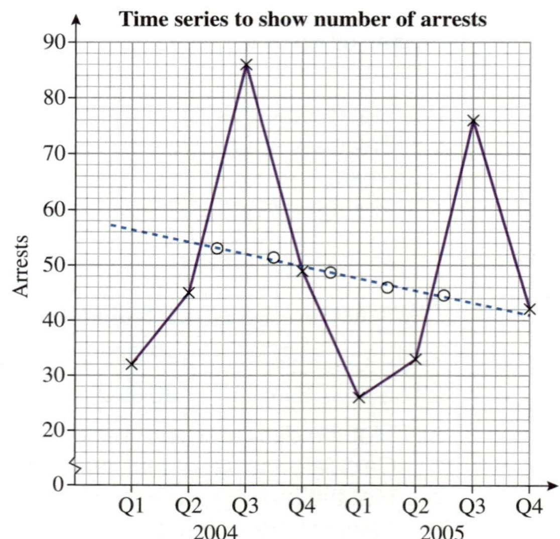

Year	2004				2005			
Quarter	1	2	3	4	1	2	3	4
Arrests	32	45	86	49	26	33	76	42

Moving average 53 51.5 48.5 46 44.25

First moving average is $\frac{(32 + 45 + 86 + 49)}{4} = 53$

Plot between quarter 2 and quarter 3 on the graph.

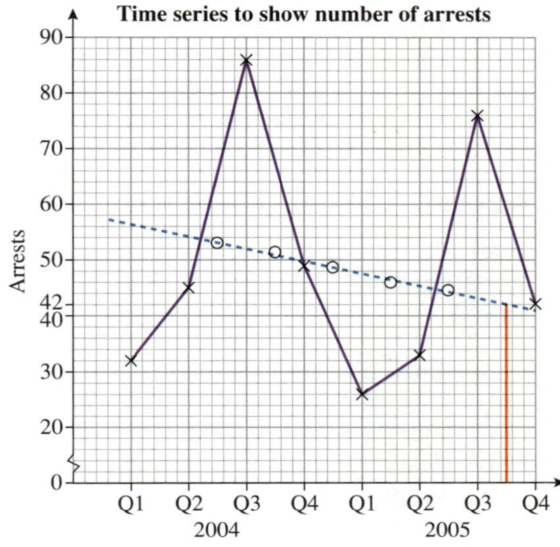

d The trend is for the number of arrests to decrease.

e Step 1: Extend the trend line.

Step 2: The next moving average would be halfway between Q3 and Q4, at 42

Step 3: Next moving average is $\frac{33 + 76 + 42 + x}{4} = 42$ where x is the predicted number of arrests made in quarter 1 of 2006

Step 4: $151 + x = 42 \times 4$ Multiply both sides by 4

$151 + x = 168$

$x = 17$

Estimate for quarter 1 2006 = 17

Exercise B

1 Penny is given a bonus by her company every six months. Her bonus for the last four years is shown below.

Year	2002		2003		2004		2005	
Bonus (£)	240	280	250	300	270	320	300	340

a Illustrate the data on a time series graph.

b Calculate the set of two-point moving averages.

c Plot the moving averages on the graph.

d Draw a line of best fit for the moving average data.

e Comment on any trend in the data.

f Predict Penny's first bonus for 2006

2 The number of bags of potatoes produced by a small farm over seven years is given in the table below.

Year	1999	2000	2001	2002	2003	2004	2005
Bags	28	29	34	36	41	44	46

a Illustrate the data on a time series graph.
b Calculate the set of three-point moving averages.
c Plot the moving averages on the graph.
d Draw a line of best fit on the graph and use it to comment on the trend in the data.
e Estimate the number of bags of potatoes produced by the farm in 2006

3 Natalie says 'My Bentley seems to be using more and more petrol as it gets older.'
She kept a record of the fuel consumption in miles per gallon for 2005

Month	Jan	Feb	Mar	Apr	May	Jun	Jul	Aug	Sep	Oct	Nov	Dec
Fuel consumption (mpg)	17.2	17.0	16.9	16.7	16.4	16.4	16.2	16.0	15.9	15.8	15.5	15.3

a Draw a time series graph of the data.
b Calculate four-point moving averages for the data.
c Plot the moving averages on the graph.
d Draw in a line of best fit and comment on Natalie's statement.
e Predict the fuel consumption for:
i January 2006 **ii** February 2006
f Which of your estimates in part **e** is the more reliable?
Give a reason for your answer.

4 Pia pays her gas bill every quarter.
Her bills for the last three years are given in the table.

	2003				**2004**				**2005**			
Quarter	1	2	3	4	1	2	3	4	1	2	3	4
Bill (£)	85	64	23	66	92	69	30	70	101	79	35	81

a Calculate appropriate moving averages for the data.
b Plot the original data and the moving averages on the axes.
c Draw a line of best fit on the graph and describe the trend.
d Predict Pia's total bill for the first half of 2006

Chapter summary

- A time series graph shows data whose values change over time.
- Time series graphs can be used to estimate or predict missing data values. Estimates within the range of data given (interpolation) are fairly reliable. Estimates outside the range of data given (extrapolation) may not be reliable, as the pattern may not continue in the same way.
- Calculating a moving average helps to identify trends in the data.
- For a three-point moving average, calculate the mean of the first three values, then move one data item along and calculate the next mean of the next three values, and so on.

- An appropriate moving average takes into account the number of data values in a particular period. Then the moving averages show the overall trend and are not affected by trends in the different collection periods. For example, for quarterly data use a four-point moving average; for a five-day week data use a five-point moving average.
- Moving averages can be plotted on a time series graph. Each moving average is plotted in the middle of the time period for which it is calculated.
- A line of best fit drawn through the moving averages shows the trend in the data.
- If it can be assumed that the trend the data shows will continue into the future, the moving averages trend line can be used to predict future values.
- In cases where the trend might not continue, it is not appropriate to predict future values.

Chapter review

1 For the data set 8, 10, 9, 14, 16, 13

a find the first three-point moving average
b find the second three-point moving average
c find the third three-point moving average.

2 The number of pupils given detention from George's class over two weeks is given below.

0 1 3 2 0 1 3 3 4 2

a Explain why a five-point moving average would be most suitable in this situation.
b Find the set of five-point moving averages for this data.
c What do the moving averages reveal about the trend in the number of detentions given in George's class?

3 Thomas's electricity bill for each quarter of the last two years is shown.

	Year 1				**Year 2**			
Quarter	1	2	3	4	1	2	3	4
Bill (£)	60	30	20	50	80	40	40	80

a Plot this data on a time series graph.
b Calculate the set of four-point moving averages.
c Plot the moving averages on the graph.

4 Sun Lee owns a company.
The company publishes its profits every six months.
The profit for the last four years is shown below.

Year	2002		2003		2004		2005	
Profit (£000s)	200	220	240	280	250	320	270	360

a Illustrate the data on a time series graph.
b Calculate the set of two-point moving averages.
c Plot the moving averages on the graph.
d Draw a line of best fit for the moving average data.
e Comment on any trend in the data.
f Predict Sun Lee's company's profit for the first six months of 2006

5 The number of apples picked from Roger's prize apple tree has been recorded for many years. The data for the last seven years is given below.

Year	1999	2000	2001	2002	2003	2004	2005
Apples	78	84	86	90	97	76	104

a Plot the data as a time series graph.

b In which year was there a drought which affected apple production?

c Calculate three-point moving averages up to but not including the drought year.

d Plot the values from part **c** on the time series graph.

e Draw a trend line.

f How many apples may have been lost due to the drought?

6 The table shows the amount paid by a company for the water supplied to it.

Date of bill	Jan 2001	Apr 2001	Jul 2001	Oct 2001	Jan 2002	Apr 2002	Jul 2002	Oct 2002
Amount (£)	40	58	112	190	54	60	130	200

The times series graph shows this data.

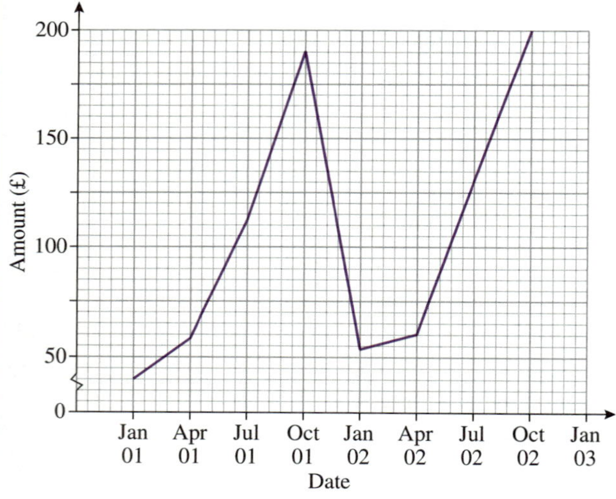

a Calculate the first value of the four-point moving average for the data.

The remaining values of the four-point moving average are: 103.5, 104, 108.5, 111

b Copy the graph and plot all five values of the moving average on the graph.

c Using the trend line, or otherwise, estimate the four-point moving average that would be plotted in January 2003

d Use the value from part **c** to calculate a prediction of the amount the company will have to pay for water in January 2003

7 Tina lives in a remote farmhouse which has frequent power cuts.
The number of power cuts for each period of four months over the last four years is given in the table.

Year	2002			2003			2004			2005		
Period	1	2	3	1	2	3	1	2	3	1	2	3
Power cuts	10	3	8	13	5	12	17	8	15	21	11	17

a Plot the data as a time series.

b What size moving average should be calculated to find any possible trend in the data? Explain your answer.

c Calculate these moving averages and plot them on the graph.

d Tina complains that there are increasing numbers of power cuts.
Is she correct?
Explain your answer.

8 The number of applications per quarter for licenses to run food outlets in the United Kingdom, over a period of two years, is given below.

Year	2004				2005			
Quarter	1	2	3	4	1	2	3	4
Applications	1085	1242	986	858	1022	1163	900	793

a Plot the data as a time series graph.

b Calculate appropriate moving averages for the data.

c Plot the moving averages on the graph.

d Draw in a trend line and comment on the trend in the data.

e Use your trend line to estimate the number of applications made in quarter 1 of 2006

9 Owen kept a record of the amount he spent on his credit card over the course of one year.

Month	Jan	Feb	Mar	Apr	May	Jun	Jul	Aug	Sep	Oct	Nov	Dec
Amount spent (£)	55	72	66	66	78	94	86	105	83	109	115	170

a Draw a time series graph of the data.

b Calculate 4-point moving averages for the data.

c Plot the moving averages on the graph.

d Draw in a line of best fit and comment on the trend.

e Estimate the amount Owen would spend in January the following year if the trend continued.

f Comment on the validity of this estimate.

10 The time series graph shows the number of appointments missed by patients at a doctor's surgery over two weeks.

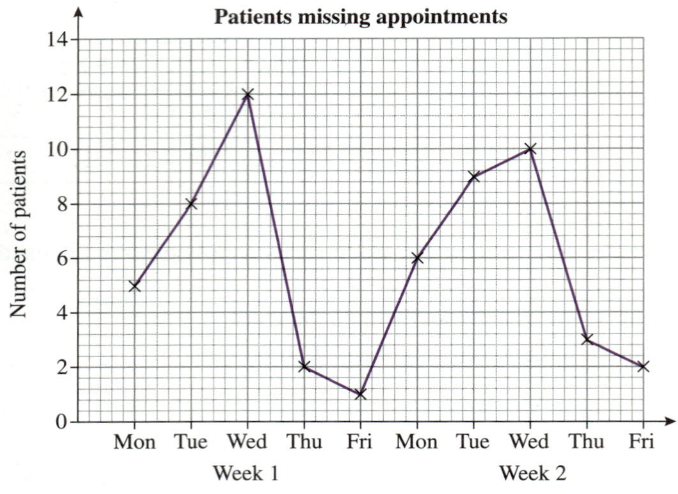

a Calculate appropriate moving averages for this data.
b Plot the moving averages on a copy of the graph.
c Use a line of best fit to estimate the number of missed appointments on the Monday of week 3

11

a Calculate, and plot on a copy of the graph, appropriate moving averages for this data.
b Estimate from the trend line the number of passengers to London in:
i Q1 2007 **ii** Q2 2007
c Which of your estimates in part **b** is more reliable? Explain your answer.

Hint: extend graph to Q2 2007 to prepare for part **b**.

CHAPTER 24

Linear graphs

24.1 Gradients

CAN YOU REMEMBER

- The meaning of 'gradient' and how to work out the gradient of a simple linear graph for positive integer gradients?
- That parallel lines have the same gradient?
- How to draw graphs of linear functions?
- How to draw and interpret distance–time and speed–time graphs?

IN THIS SECTION YOU WILL

- Reinforce and extend skills in finding the gradient of a straight line.
- Find gradients of distance–time graphs and speed–time graphs.
- Learn about the gradients of lines that are perpendicular to each other.

The *gradient* of a line describes how steep it is.

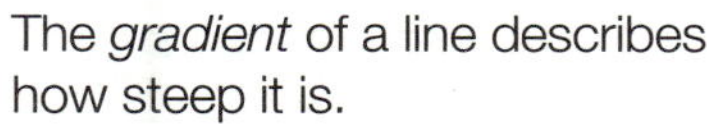

$$\text{Gradient} = \frac{\text{distance up or down}}{\text{distance across}}$$

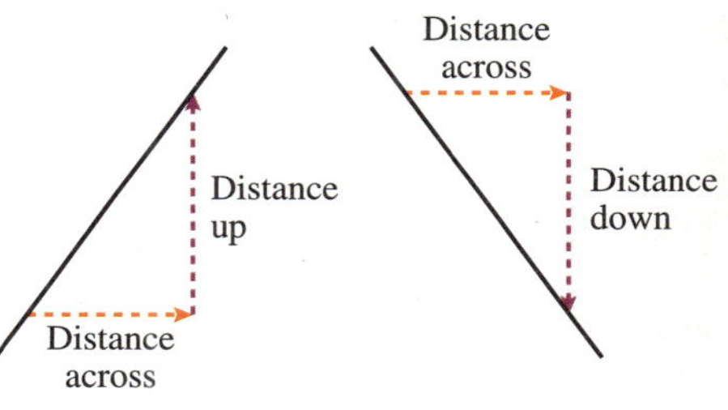

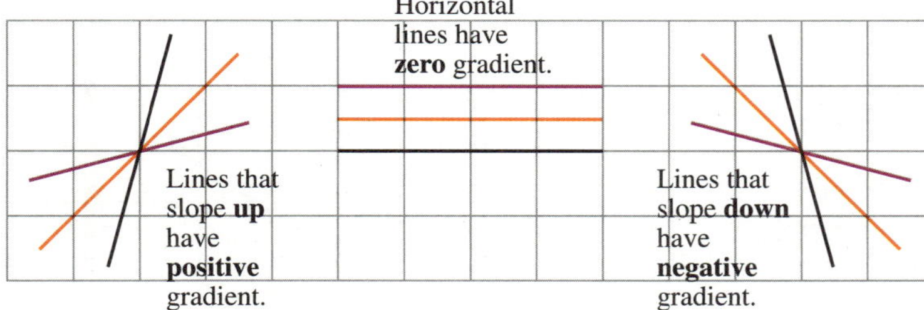

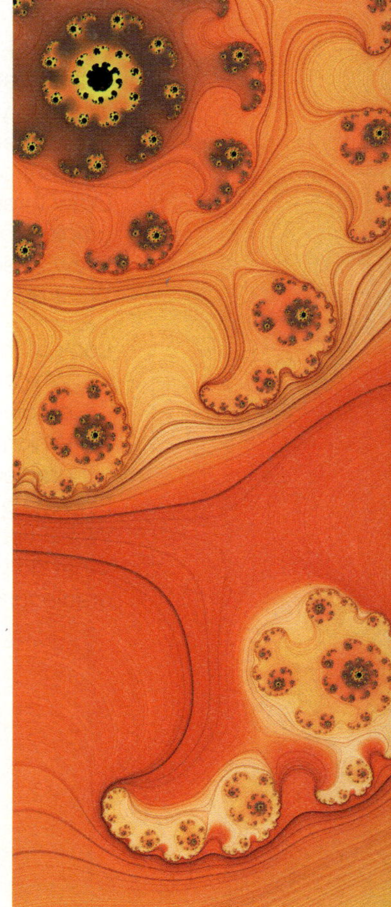

Example 1

a Find the gradient of the line joining the points (1, 1) and (4, 3).
b Draw a line passing through the point (−2, 3) with gradient −5

Solution 1

a The line slopes **up** so the gradient is positive.
Distance across from $x = 1$ to $x = 4$ $\quad 4 - 1 = 3$

Distance **up** from $y = 1$ to $y = 3$ $3 - 1 = 2$
Gradient = $\frac{2}{3}$

b The gradient is negative so the line slopes **down**.

$$-5 = \frac{\text{distance down}}{\text{distance across}} = \frac{-5}{1}$$

A line with gradient -5 goes **across 1** and **down 5**

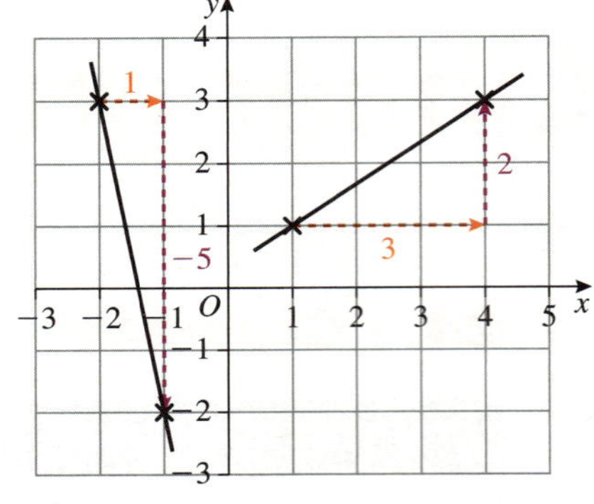

Exercise A

1 Find the gradient of each line drawn on the grid on the right.

2 On a grid, draw lines with the following gradients:

a	6	**b**	-6
c	$\frac{1}{4}$	**d**	$-\frac{1}{4}$
e	$\frac{2}{7}$	**f**	$-\frac{2}{7}$

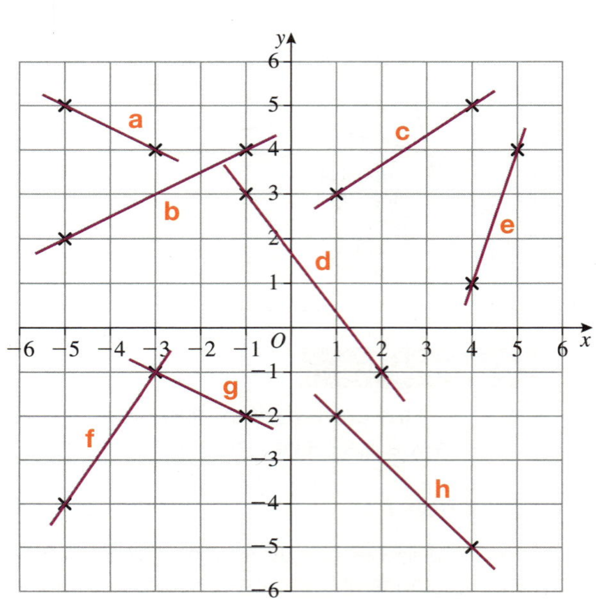

3 **a** On a grid, draw three lines with a gradient of 2
What do you notice?
b Draw three lines with a gradient of $\frac{2}{3}$
c Draw three lines with a gradient of -2
d Draw three lines with a gradient of $-\frac{2}{3}$
e What do you notice about the sets of lines you drew in parts **b**, **c** and **d**?

4 **a** Look at the grid opposite.
i Which lines have a positive gradient?
ii Which lines have a negative gradient?
b Find the gradient of each line.
c Which two of the lines are parallel?
d What do you notice about their gradients?

5 Find the gradient of the lines joining the points with the following pairs of coordinates:

a	(1, 2) and (9, 6)	**b**	(3, 1) and (4, 5)	**c**	(1, 1) and (2, 5)
d	(0, 3) and (10, 11)	**e**	(1, 1) and (6, 7)	**f**	(−2, −3) and (0, 3)
g	(−3, 2) and (3, −1)	**h**	(2, 5) and (4, −1)	**i**	(−4, 3) and (−2, −2)

6 **a** Draw the line passing through the point (1, 2) with gradient −2
b Draw the line passing through the point (−3, 1) with gradient $\frac{1}{2}$
c Show that the line passing through (1, −1) with gradient $-1\frac{1}{2}$ also passes through the point (−3, 5).

7 The opposite vertices of a quadrilateral have coordinates (3, 3) and (9, 7).
One pair of opposite sides has gradient 3
The other pair of opposite sides has gradient $\frac{1}{5}$
a Draw the quadrilateral on a grid.
b What is the special name of the quadrilateral?

8 The line through the point (−3, 1) with gradient $\frac{1}{2}$ crosses the line through the point (3, −3) with gradient −3
Find the coordinates of the point of intersection.

9 Find the gradient of the straight lines joining the following pairs of points:

a	(0, 0) and (a, a)	**b**	$(2b, 2b)$ and $(0, b)$
c	$(-c, 0)$ and $(0, -2c)$	**d**	$(3d, -2d)$ and $(d, 3d)$

The gradient on a distance–time graph measures speed.
Typical units of speed are m/s or metres per second and km/h or kilometres per hour.
The gradient on a speed–time graph measures acceleration.
Negative acceleration is called *deceleration*.
Typical units of acceleration are m/s^2 or metres per second per second and km/h^2 or kilometres per hour per hour.

Example 2

This distance–time graph shows a bus journey.

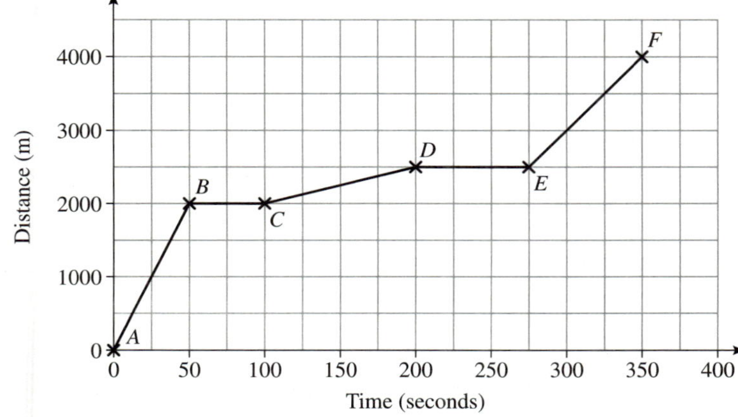

a Calculate the speed of the bus on each part of its journey.
b Calculate the average speed of the bus over the complete journey.

Solution 2

a AB: distance (up) = 2000 m, time (across) = 50 seconds

gradient = speed = $\frac{2000}{50}$ = 40 m/s

BC: distance = 0 m, time = 50 seconds

gradient = speed = 0 m/s

CD: distance = 500 m, time = 100 seconds

gradient = speed = $\frac{500}{100}$ = 5 m/s

DE: gradient = speed = 0 m/s

EF: distance = 1500 m, time = 75 seconds

gradient = speed = $\frac{1500}{75}$ = 20 m/s

b Average speed = total distance/total time

Total distance travelled = 4000 m, total time taken = 350 seconds

Average speed = $\frac{4000}{350}$ = 11.43 m/s

Example 3

This graph shows the speed of a bicycle during a short journey.

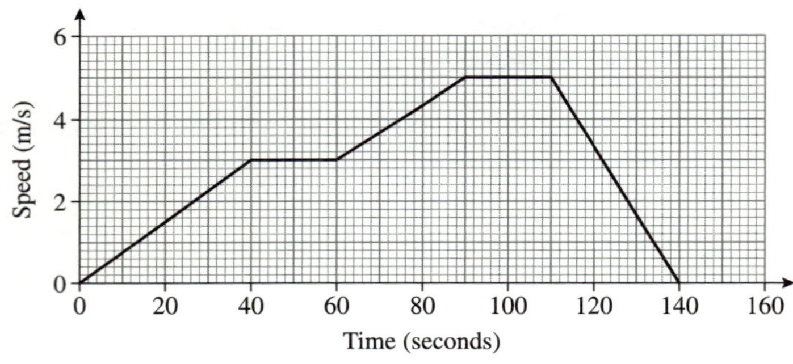

a In what parts of the journey is the speed constant?

b Calculate the acceleration of the car between:

i 0 and 40 seconds **ii** 110 and 140 seconds.

Solution 3

a The speed is constant when the gradient is zero. The gradient is zero between 40 and 60 seconds, and between 90 and 110 seconds.

b **i** Between 0 and 40 seconds:

Increase in speed = 3 m/s, increase in time = 40 seconds

Gradient = acceleration = $\frac{3}{40}$ = 0.075 m/s^2

ii Between 110 and 140 seconds:

Decrease in speed = 5 m/s, increase in time = 30 seconds

Gradient = acceleration = $\frac{-5}{30}$ = −0.167 m/s^2

Parallel lines have the same gradient.

Line A is *perpendicular* to line B.

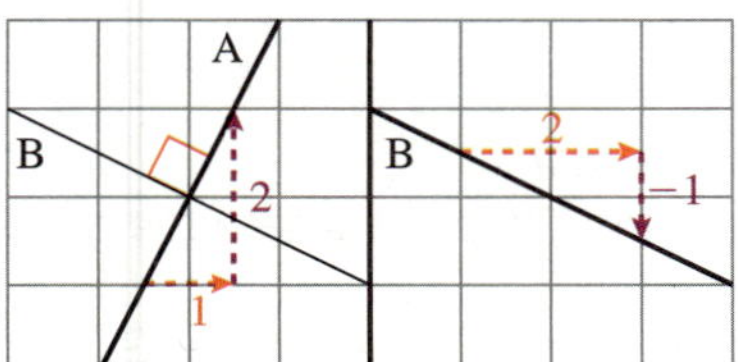

Line C is perpendicular to line D.

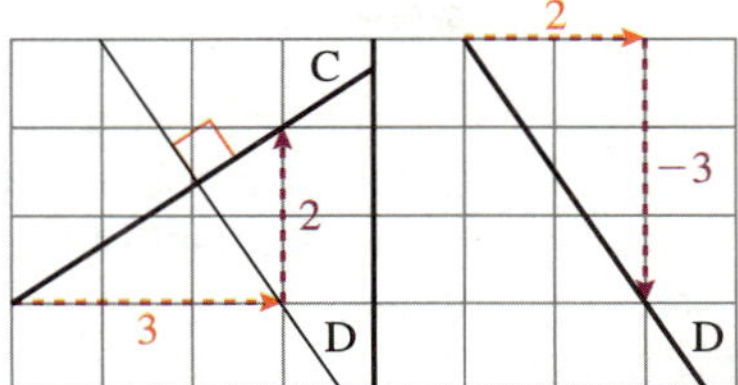

Line A

Gradient $= \dfrac{2}{1}$

$= 2$

Line B

Gradient $= \dfrac{-1}{2}$

$= -\frac{1}{2}$

Line C

Gradient $= \dfrac{2}{3}$

$= \frac{2}{3}$

Line D

Gradient $= \dfrac{-3}{2}$

$= -1\frac{1}{2}$

From lines A and B $\quad 2 \times -\frac{1}{2} = -1$

From lines C and D $\quad \frac{2}{3} \times -\frac{3}{2} = -1$

The gradients of perpendicular lines have a product of -1

A line perpendicular to a line of gradient m has a gradient of $-\dfrac{1}{m}$

This is the negative reciprocal of m.

Example 4

a Line M has gradient 5
Line N is perpendicular to line M.
What is the gradient of line N?

b Line P has gradient $-2\frac{1}{2}$
Line Q is perpendicular to line P.
What is the gradient of line Q?

Solution 4

a The gradient of line M = 5, so the gradient of line N is $-\frac{1}{5}$

Check: $5 \times -\frac{1}{5} = -1$

b $-2\frac{1}{2} = -\frac{5}{2}$

The gradient of line P $= -\frac{5}{2}$, so the gradient of line Q is $\frac{2}{5}$

Check: $-\frac{5}{2} \times \frac{2}{5} = -1$

Exercise B

1 Amita says that the gradient of a line joining the points (1, 1) and (3, 2) is 2
What has Amita done wrong?

2 The cards below show the gradients of different lines.
Match each line with the line perpendicular to it.

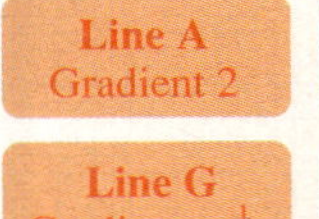

Line A Gradient 2	Line B Gradient −3	Line C Gradient $\frac{3}{5}$	Line D Gradient $-\frac{2}{9}$	Line E Gradient $-\frac{4}{5}$	Line F Gradient −2
Line G Gradient $-\frac{1}{2}$	Line H Gradient $-\frac{1}{2}$	Line I Gradient $\frac{1}{3}$	Line J Gradient $-1\frac{2}{3}$	Line K Gradient $4\frac{1}{2}$	Line L Gradient $\frac{1}{2}$

3 **a** **i** Complete the table for $y = 2x - 1$

x	−2	0	2
y			

ii Draw the graph of $y = 2x - 1$ for values of x from −2 to 2

iii Write down the gradient of the graph of $y = 2x - 1$ and the point where the graph crosses the y-axis.

b Draw a graph of each of the functions in the table for values of x from −3 to +3

Function	Gradient of graph	Coordinates where graph cuts y-axis
$y = 2x + 5$		
$y = 3x + 4$		
$y = 2 - 3x$		
$y = 3 - 2x$		
$y = \frac{1}{2}x - 3$		
$y = \frac{1}{4}x - 2$		
$y = 4 - \frac{1}{2}x$		
$y = 5 - \frac{1}{4}x$		

c For each graph complete the table by working out:

i the gradient

ii the coordinates of the point where the graph crosses the y-axis.

d What do you notice?

4 Amina says that lines with gradients $\frac{2}{7}$ and $3\frac{1}{2}$ are perpendicular. Explain why Amina is wrong.

5 Find the gradients of lines perpendicular to the lines joining each pair of points in Exercise A Question 5

6 Make a copy of this grid and the lines A, B, C and D.

a Work out the gradients of lines A, B, C and D.

b Work out the gradients of lines perpendicular to lines A, B, C and D.

c Draw lines passing through the point:

i (−3, 3) perpendicular to line A

ii (3, 3) perpendicular to line B

iii (−1, −3) perpendicular to line C

iv (1, −3) perpendicular to line D.

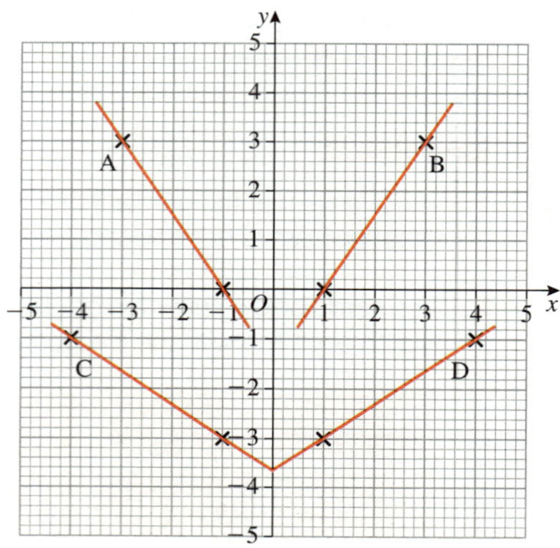

7 **a** What does the gradient of a distance–time graph represent?
b The distance–time graph shows David's journey as he walks from home to a local shop.

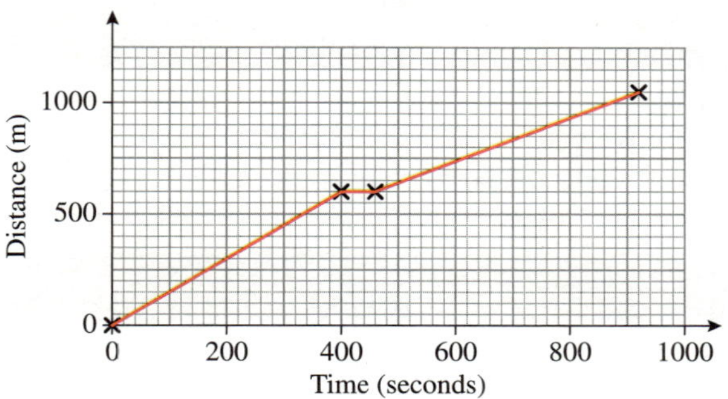

i Work out David's speed on each stage of his journey.
ii Work out David's average speed.

8 The diagram shows the speed–time graph of a car travelling between two sets of traffic lights.

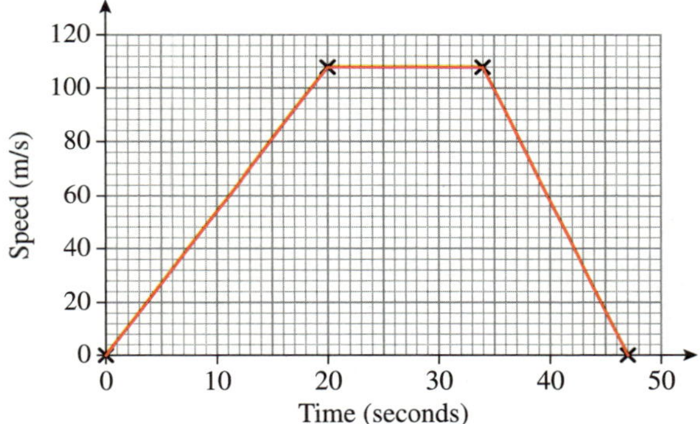

Calculate the acceleration of the car on each stage of the journey.

9 The distance–time graph shows a race between Tom and Said around a running track.

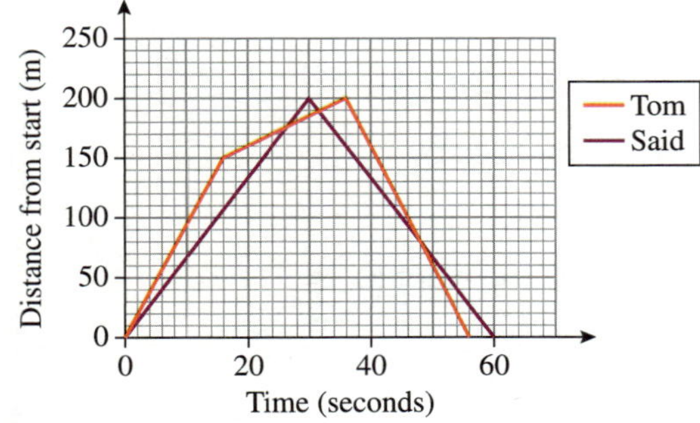

Describe in detail what happens during the race.
Hints: Work out the speeds in each part of the race.
Who is in the lead?
Who overtakes who and when?
How long is the race?

24.2 Linear functions of the form $y = mx + c$

CAN YOU REMEMBER

- The meaning of 'linear function'?
- How to find the gradient of a straight line?
- How to find the gradients of parallel and perpendicular lines?

IN THIS SECTION YOU WILL

- Extend skills in drawing the graphs of linear functions of the form $y = mx + c$.
- Learn how to write linear functions from their graphs.
- Learn about functions that give parallel and perpendicular lines.
- Learn how to use the gradient and y-intercept to help interpret real-life graphs.

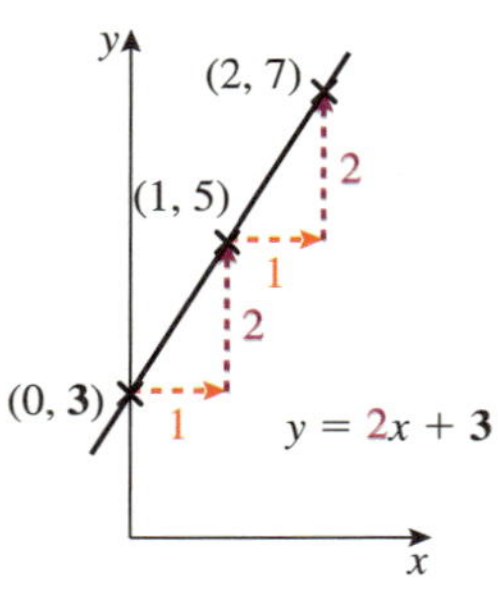

In the function $y = 2x + 3$
When $x = 0$, $y = 3$
When $x = 1$, $y = 2 + 3$
When $x = 2$, $y = 4 + 3$

x	0	1	2
y	3	5	7

As x increases by **1**, y increases by **2**

Gradient $= \frac{2}{1} = 2$

The graph passes through the point (0, **3**).

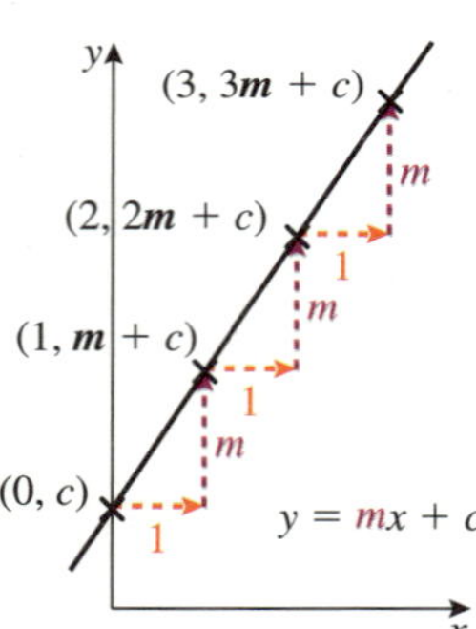

In the function $y = mx + c$
When $x = 0$, $y = c$
When $x = 1$, $y = m + c$
When $x = 2$, $y = 2m + c$
When $x = 3$, $y = 3m + c$

x	0	1	2	3
y	c	$m + c$	$2m + c$	$3m + c$

As x increases by **1**, y increases by m

Gradient $= \frac{m}{1} = m$

The graph passes through the point (0, c)

All graphs of functions of the form $y = mx + c$ are linear.

m is the *gradient* of the graph.

The graph crosses the y-axis at the point (0, c).

c is called the y-intercept.

$y = mx + c$ is a function, but it is often called the equation of a straight line.

Example 1

a Write down the gradient and y-intercept of the graph of $y = \frac{3}{4}x + 2$

b Hence draw the graph of $y = \frac{3}{4}x + 2$

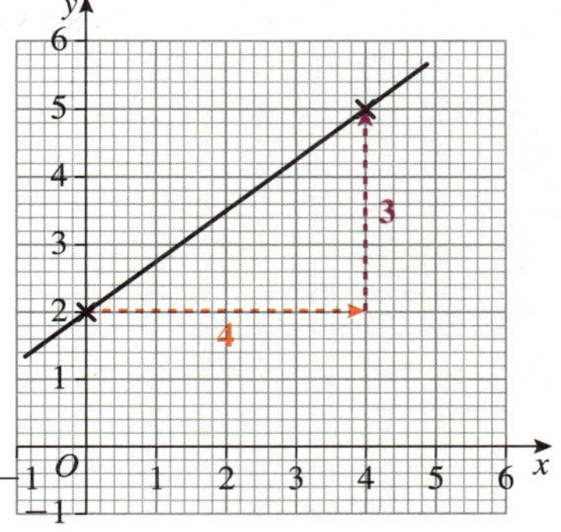

Solution 1

a Compare $y = \frac{3}{4}x + 2$ with $y = mx + c$
Gradient $(m) = \frac{3}{4}$, y-intercept $(c) = 2$

b The graph of $y = \frac{3}{4}x + 2$ is a straight line through (0, 2) with gradient $\frac{3}{4}$
To draw the graph, plot (0, 2) and go **across 4** and **up 3** to the next point.
Draw and extend the line through the two plotted points.

Example 2

What is the equation of the graph shown?

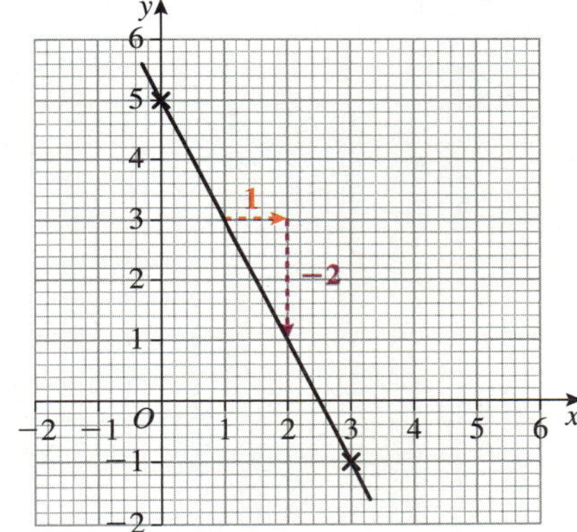

Solution 2

The graph is a straight line that passes through the point (0, 5).
So $c = 5$
The gradient of the line is $-\frac{2}{1} = -2$, so $m = -2$
The equation is $y = -2x + 5$ (or $y = 5 - 2x$).

Exercise A

1 **a** Write down the gradient and y-intercept for the graphs of:

i $y = 2x + 3$ **ii** $y = 4x - 1$ **iii** $y = 3x - 4$
iv $y = 2 - x$ **v** $y = \frac{1}{2}x + 7$ **vi** $y = -x + 2$
vii $y = \frac{1}{2}x + 7$ **viii** $y = \frac{2}{3}x - 1$ **ix** $y = 4 - \frac{1}{3}x$

b Use the gradient and y-intercept to draw each graph.

2 Match each function to its graph.

i $y = x + 2$ **ii** $y = 2x + 3$
iii $y = x$ **iv** $y = 3 - x$

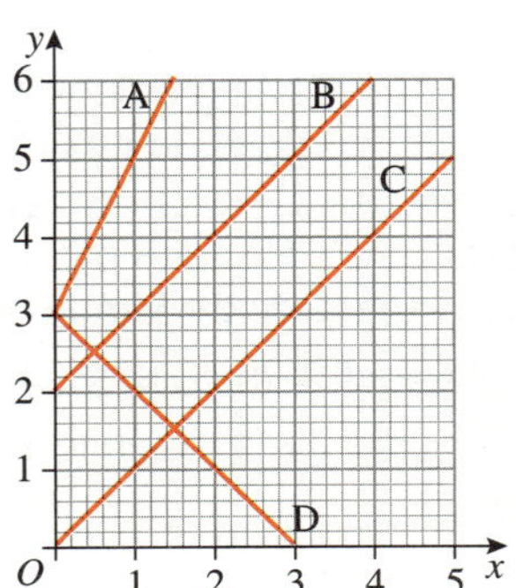

3 Match each function to its graph.

i $y = 2x - 3$ **ii** $y = 3x - 2$

iii $y = 2 - 3x$ **iv** $y = 3 - 2x$

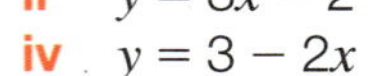

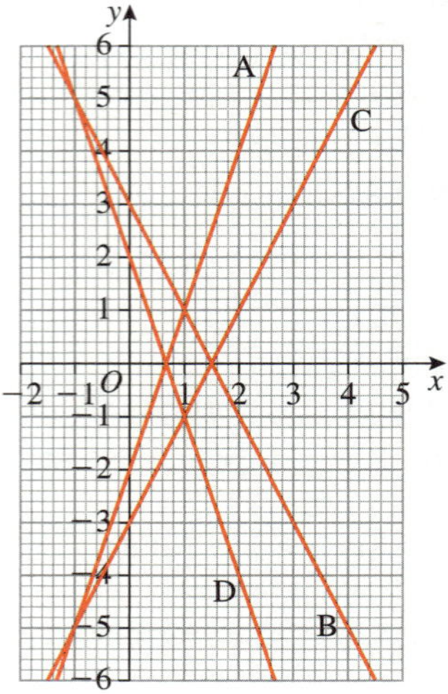

4 Work out the equations for each of the graphs shown on the grid.

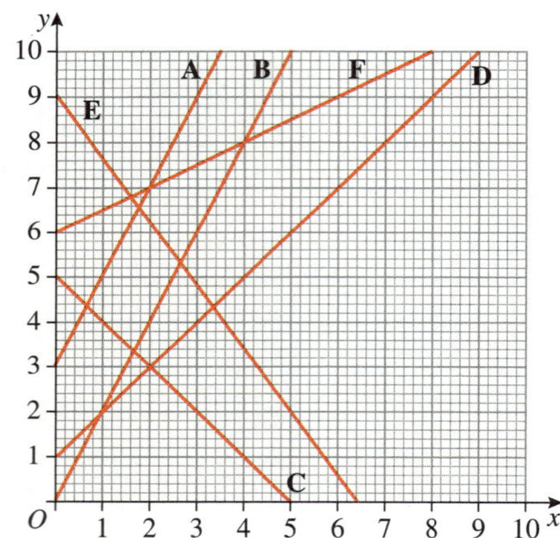

5 Work out the equations for each of the graphs drawn on the grid.

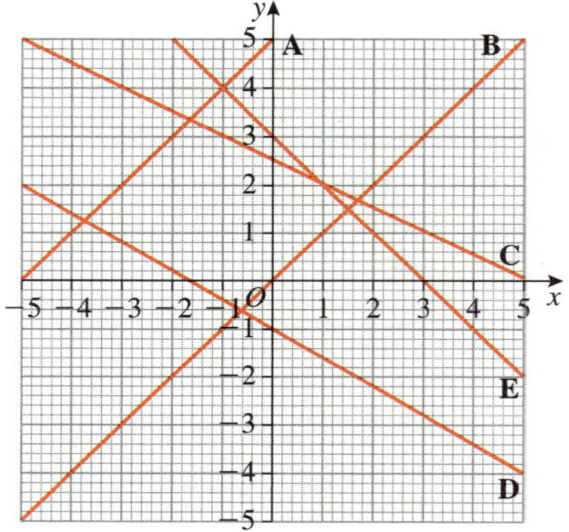

6 What functions give the straight lines passing through the following pairs of points? You may use a sketch to help you.

a (0, 2) and (1, 3) **b** (0, 4) and (4, 0) **c** (0, 3) and (2, 7)

d (1, 2) and (3, 8) **e** (2, 6) and (4, 7) **f** (−3, 1) and (0, 2)

g (−4, 6) and (2, 3)

7 **a** A straight line has gradient 2 and passes through the point (0, 4).
What is the equation of this line?
You may use a sketch to help you.

b Repeat part **a** for each of the following straight lines:

i gradient −3, through (0, 0) **ii** gradient −1, through (5, 0)

iii gradient 2, through (3, 4) **iv** gradient $-\frac{1}{2}$, through (1, 1)

v gradient $1\frac{1}{2}$, through (6, 3) **vi** gradient $-\frac{1}{4}$, through (4, 1)

Some real-life situations can be represented by graphs of the form $y = mx + c$.
On linear real-life graphs, the gradient and the y-intercept have a meaning.

Example 3

In an experiment, different weights (w kg) are attached to a spring and the length of the spring (l cm) is measured each time.
The graph shows the results.

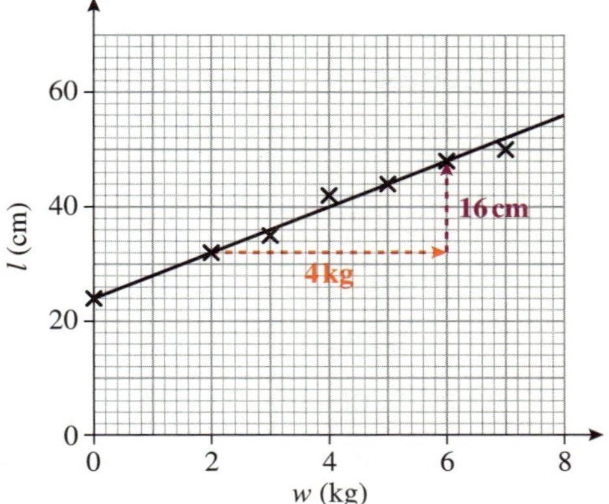

a What is the length of the spring with no weight attached?

b **i** Find the gradient of the graph.
ii What does the gradient represent?

c The relationship between l and w is of the form $l = aw + b$
What are the values of a and b?

d Estimate the weight needed to stretch the spring by 50 cm.

Solution 3

a Reading from the graph, when $w = 0$, $l = 24$ cm.

b **i** Distance up = 16 cm, Distance **across** = 4 kg
Gradient = 16 cm ÷ 4 kg = 4 cm/kg
ii The gradient represents the increase in length of the spring for each kilogram added.

c a is the gradient: $a = 4$ cm/kg
b is the value of l when $w = 0$: $b = 24$ cm

d $l = 4w + 24$
When the spring is stretched by 50 cm, $l = 24 + 50 = 74$ cm
Substitute $l = 74$ in $l = 4w + 24$
$74 = 4w + 24$
$4w = 50$
$w = 12.5$ kg

Example 4

Line A is the graph of $y = 3x + 4$
Line B is parallel to line A.
Line C is perpendicular to line A.
Lines B and C both pass through the origin.
What are the equations of lines B and C?

Solution 4

For line A, the gradient (m) = 3
Line B is parallel to line A and passes through (0, 0).
So for line B, $m = 3$ and $c = 0$, so B is the graph of $y = 3x$.
Line C is perpendicular to line A and passes through (0, 0).
So for line C, $m = -\frac{1}{3}$ and $c = 0$, so C is the graph of $y = -\frac{1}{3}x$

Example 5

A line is perpendicular to the line $y = 5x + 1$ and passes through the point (5, 2).
What is the equation of this line?

Solution 5

The gradient of a line perpendicular to $y = 5x + 1$ is $-\frac{1}{5}$

Method 1

Draw a line passing through (5, 2) with gradient $-\frac{1}{5}$
From the graph $c = 3$

This gives $y = -\frac{1}{5}x + 3$

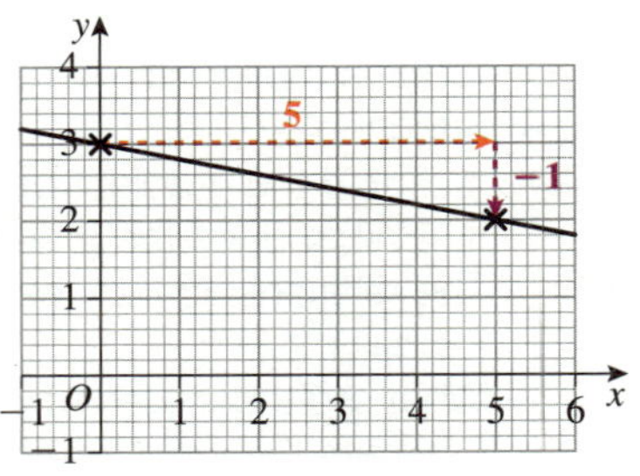

Method 2

The equation of the line is $y = -\frac{1}{5}x + c$

The line passes through (5, 2).

Substitute $x = 5$ and $y = 2$ into $y = -\frac{1}{5}x + c$

$2 = -\frac{1}{5} \times 5 + c$

$2 = -1 + c$

$c = 3$

This gives $y = -\frac{1}{5}x + 3$

Exercise B

1 The cards below show the functions for different straight lines.
Match each line with the line perpendicular to it.

Line A	Line B	Line C	Line D	Line E	Line F
$y = 2x + 7$	$y = -x$	$y = 3x + 4$	$y = 5x + 1$	$y = \frac{1}{3}x - 2$	$y = 5 - 2x$
Line G	**Line H**	**Line I**	**Line J**	**Line K**	**Line L**
$y = \frac{1}{2}x - 1$	$y = -\frac{1}{3}x + 6$	$y = -3x + 5$	$y = -\frac{1}{2}x - 1$	$y = -\frac{1}{5}x$	$y = x$

2 A is the line $y = 2x + 9$
Line B is parallel to line A and passes through the point (4, 0).
Line C is perpendicular to line A and also passes through the point (4, 0).
What are the functions for lines B and C?

3 State whether each of the following pairs of lines are parallel, perpendicular or neither.

a $y = 2x + 6$ and $y = \frac{1}{2}x + 3$

b $y = 3x - 4$ and $y = -\frac{1}{3}x$

c $y = 1 - \frac{2}{3}x$ and $y = 4 - \frac{2}{3}x$

d $y = \frac{1}{5}x - 4$ and $y = 3 + 5x$

e $y = 5 - 3\frac{1}{2}x$ and $y = \frac{2}{7}x + 1$

4 **a** A line is perpendicular to the line $y = 4x - 2$ and passes through the point (0, −2).
Find the equation of this line.

b A line is perpendicular to the line $y = -\frac{1}{2}x + 3$ and passes through the point (1, 5).
Find the equation of this line.

5 A quadrilateral has vertices at (1, 6), (5, 8), (7, 4) and (3, 2).
Show that the quadrilateral is a square.
Find the equations for each of its sides.

6 Explain why the gradient of the line $x = 4$ cannot be worked out using a calculator.

7 Work out the gradient of a line that is perpendicular to a line with gradient -0.315
Give your answer to two decimal places.

8 The graph shows how the monthly wage of a salesperson is made up of a basic wage plus a commission that depends on sales.

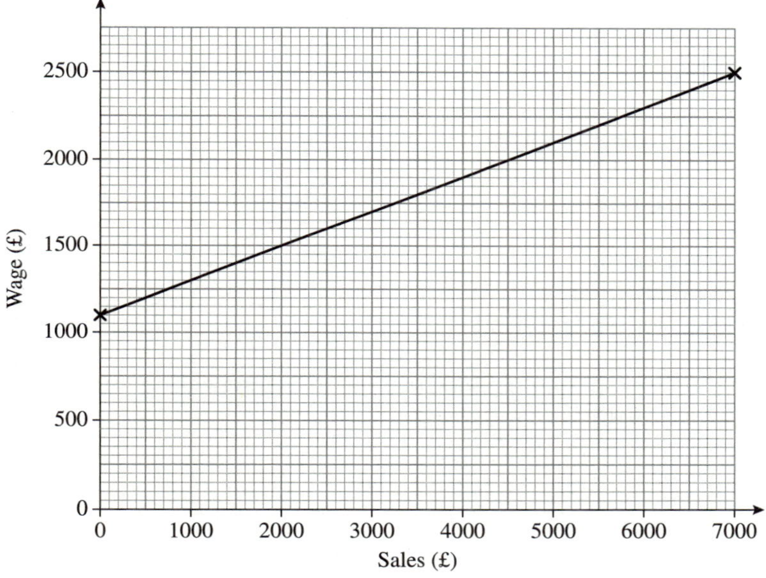

- **a** What is the basic wage?
- **b** **i** Work out the gradient of the graph.
  - **ii** What does the gradient of the graph represent?
- **c** Find the equation of the line in the form $y = ax + b$.
- **d** How much does the salesperson earn when sales are £10 800?

9 The charge for repairing a dishwasher is made up of a fixed charge plus a fee that depends on the time taken.

- **a** What is the fixed charge for a repair?
- **b** Find the gradient of the line.
- **c** What does the gradient represent?
- **d** What is the equation of the line?
- **e** Calculate the cost of a repair that takes 2 hours.

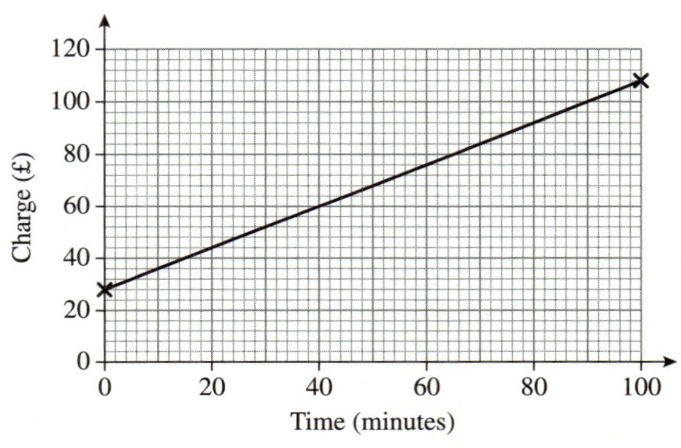

24.3 Linear functions of the form $px + qy = r$

CAN YOU REMEMBER

- The meaning of m and c in a linear function of the form $y = mx + c$?
- How to draw graphs of linear functions written in the form $px + qy = r$?
- How to change the subject of a formula?

IN THIS SECTION YOU WILL

- Find the y-intercept and gradient of lines with equations of the form $px + qy = r$.

The function for a linear graph may be given in the form $px + qy = r$.
For example, $2x + 3y = 18$

Example 1

The diagram shows a sketch of the graph of
$4x + 3y = 18$
The graph passes through the points with coordinates $(0, a)$ and $(b, 0)$.

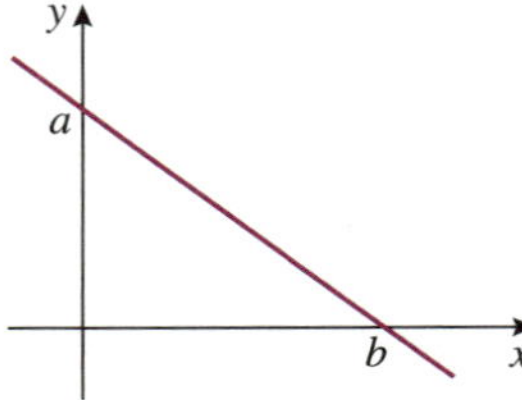

a Calculate the values of a and b.
b Work out the gradient of the graph.
c Write down the function for the graph in the form $y = mx + c$.

d Write down the function for the line perpendicular to the graph passing through
  i $(0, a)$ **ii** $(b, 0)$.

Solution 1

a At the point $(0, a)$, $x = 0$ and $y = a$.
Substituting these values in $4x + 3y = 18$
$4 \times 0 + 3a = 18$
$3a = 18$
$a = 6$

At the point $(b, 0)$, $x = b$ and $y = 0$
Substituting these values in $4x + 3y = 18$
$4b + 3 \times 0 = 18$
$4b = 18$
$b = 4\frac{1}{2}$

b Gradient = distance down ÷ distance across
Gradient $= -\frac{6}{4.5} = -\frac{12}{9} = -\frac{4}{3}$

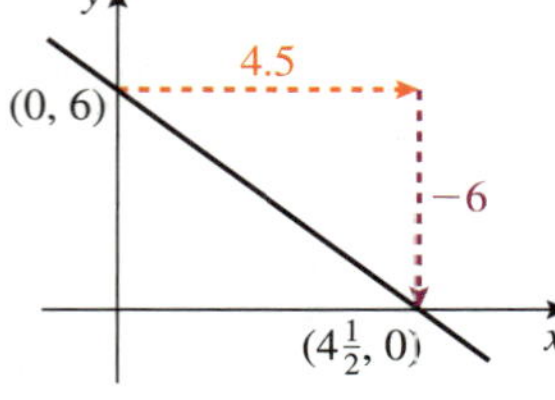

c Gradient $(m) = -\frac{4}{3}$ and y-intercept $(c) = 6$
So the function in the form $y = mx + c$ is $y = -\frac{4}{3}x + 6$

d The gradient of any line perpendicular to the line $y = -\frac{4}{3}x + 6$ is $\frac{3}{4}$
  i For the line through $(0, a) = (0, 6)$ the y-intercept is 6
  The function for the perpendicular line through $(0, 6)$ is
  $y = \frac{3}{4}x + 6$
  ii For the line through $(b, 0) = (4\frac{1}{2}, 0)$, the function is of the form $y = \frac{3}{4}x + c$.
  Substituting the values $x = 4\frac{1}{2}$, $y = 0$ gives
  $0 = \frac{3}{4} \times 4\frac{1}{2} + c$
  $0 = \frac{27}{8} + c$
  So $c = -\frac{27}{8}$
  The function for the perpendicular line through $(4\frac{1}{2}, 0)$ is $y = \frac{3}{4}x - \frac{27}{8}$

Exercise A

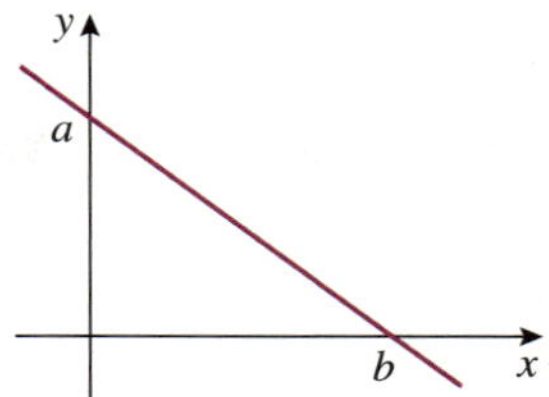

1 The diagram shows a sketch of a graph of the form $px + qy = r$ where p, q and r are positive integers.

a Find, for each function in the table below:

i the values of a and b

ii the gradient (m) and y-intercept (c)

iii the function in the form $y = mx + c$.

	Function	p	q	r	a	b	m	c	$y = mx + c$
a	$2x + 3y = 6$	2	3	6					
b	$3x + 2y = 6$	3	2	6					
c	$2x + 3y = 12$								
d	$3x + 2y = 18$								
e	$2x + 5y = 10$								
f	$5x + 2y = 10$								
g	$2x + 5y = 15$								
h	$5x + 2y = 20$								
i	$x + 4y = 8$								
j	$4x + y = 8$								
k	$x + 4y = 12$								
l	$4x + y = 2$								

Record your results in a copy of the table.
What do you notice?

b In the table below are more functions of the form $px + qy = r$ where p, q and r are positive or negative integers.
Copy and complete the table.

	Function	p	q	r	a	b	m	c	$y = mx + c$
a	$2x - 3y = 6$	2	-3	6					
b	$3x - 2y = 6$	3	-2	6					
c	$2x + 3y = -12$								
d	$3x - 2y = 18$								
e	$5x - 4y = 20$								
f	$5x - 4y = -10$								
g	$4x + 5y = -20$								
h	$5x + 2y = 20$								
i	$x + 2y = 8$								
j	$2x - y = 12$								
k	$x + 2y = -6$								
l	$-2x + y = 4$								

c Match the functions in part **b** to one of these graphs.

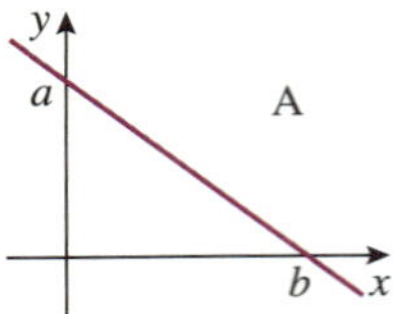

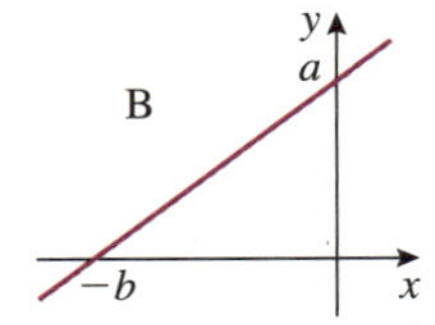

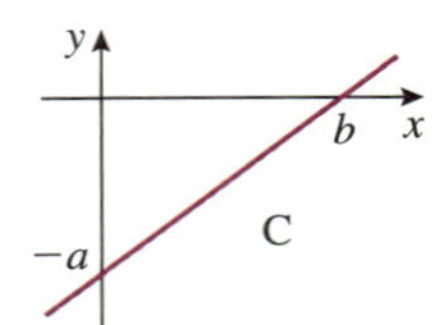

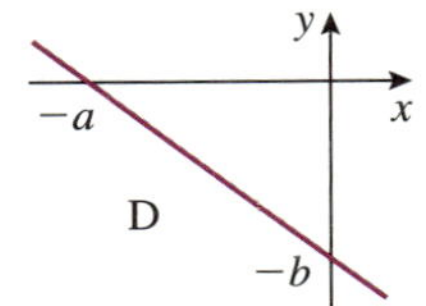

2 Find the equation of the graph perpendicular to the graph of $2x - 4y = 6$ passing through (0, 5).

3 Find the equation of the graph perpendicular to the graph of $5x - 6y = 30$ passing through (5, −2).

A linear function written in the form $px + qy = r$ can be rearranged so that it is in the form $y = mx + c$ and vice versa.

Example 2

a **i** Rearrange the function $3x + 4y = 12$ to the form $y = mx + c$.
ii Write down the gradient and y-intercept of $3x + 4y = 12$

b Rewrite the function $y = \frac{2}{3}x - 5$ in the form $px + qy = r$.

Solution 2

a **i** $3x + 4y = 12$

$4y = 12 - 3x$ — Subtract $3x$ from both sides.

$y = 3 - \frac{3}{4}x$ — Divide both sides by 4

ii The gradient of $3x + 4y = 12$ is $-\frac{3}{4}$ and the y-intercept is (0, 3).

b $y = \frac{2}{3}x - 5$

$3y = 2x - 15$ — Multiply both sides by 3

$-2x + 3y = -15$ — Subtract $2x$ from both sides.

To find the gradient and y-intercept of a line with equation $px + qy = r$ rearrange the equation into the form $y = mx + c$ (i.e. make y the subject).

Example 3

Show that the lines $y = 2x + 5$ and $2y = 4 - x$ are perpendicular.

Solution 3

The gradient of the line $y = 2x + 5$ is 2
Rearrange $2y = 4 - x$ to the form $y = mx + c$.
$2y = 4 - x$
$y = 2 - \frac{1}{2}x$ — Divide both sides by 2
The gradient of the line $2y = 4 - x$ is $-\frac{1}{2}$
$2 \times -\frac{1}{2} = -1$
The product of the gradients is −1, so the lines are perpendicular.

Exercise B

1 Write each of the following functions in the form $y = mx + c$.

a	$2x - y = 6$	**b**	$3x + 4y = 2$	**c**	$6x - 15 = 2y$
d	$x - 2y = -16$	**e**	$6x + 4y = -3$	**f**	$2x + 7y = 14$
g	$7x - 2y = 28$	**h**	$3x + 5y = 15$	**i**	$5x + 3y = -15$

2 Write each of the following functions in the form $px + qy = r$.

a	$y = \frac{1}{2}x - 2$	**b**	$y = \frac{1}{3}x - 4$	**c**	$y = \frac{2}{3}x + 1$
d	$y = 5 - \frac{1}{2}x$	**e**	$y = \frac{3}{4}x + 2$	**f**	$y = 6 - \frac{3}{5}x$
g	$y = 1 - \frac{3}{10}x$	**h**	$2y = \frac{4}{5}x - 3$	**i**	$4y = 7 - \frac{1}{3}x$

3 Sort the following cards into sets of three.
In each set there should be:

- a function in the form $y = mx + c$
- the same function written in the form $px + qy = r$
- a function of a line that is perpendicular to the other function.

A	B	C	D	E	F
$y = \frac{1}{3}x + 7$	$y = \frac{2}{5}x - 3$	$y = 2x + 3$	$y = \frac{1}{2}x + 7$	$y - 2x = 3$	$3y - x = 21$
G	**H**	**I**	**J**	**K**	**L**
$2x - 5y = 15$	$2y - x = 14$	$2x + y = 6$	$2y + x = -2$	$2y = 3 - 5x$	$y + 3x = 5$

4 Sally says that the lines with functions $3y = 2x + 6$ and $4x - 6y = 15$ are parallel.
Show that she is correct.

5 Tim says that the lines with functions $6x + 5y = 15$ and $5x + 6y = 15$ are perpendicular.
Show that he is wrong.

6 Show that the lines $3x + y = 7$ and $2y - 6x = 1$ are not perpendicular.

7 Show that the lines $2x + y = 6$, $2y - x = 6$, $y = 10 - 2x$ and $4y - 2x = -3$ intersect to form a rectangle.

8 Show that the lines $3y - 2x = 15$ and $2y + 3x = 23$ are perpendicular and that both pass through the point (3, 7).

9 Rearrange the function $px + qy = r$ to give y in terms of x.
Hence write the gradient and y-intercept in terms of p, q and r.

Chapter summary

- The gradient of a line describes how steep it is.
  gradient = distance up or down ÷ distance across
- Lines that slope **up** have **positive** gradient.
  Horizontal lines have zero gradient.
  Lines that slope **down** have **negative** gradient.
- The gradient on a distance–time graph measures speed.
  The gradient on a speed–time graph measures acceleration.
  Negative acceleration is called deceleration.
- Parallel lines have the same gradient.

- The product of the gradients of two perpendicular lines equals -1
- A line perpendicular to a line of gradient m has a gradient of $-\frac{1}{m}$
- All graphs of functions of the form $y = mx + c$ are linear.
  m is the gradient of the graph.
  The graph crosses the y-axis at the point $(0, c)$. c is called the y-intercept.
- To find the gradient and y-intercept of a line with equation $px + qy = r$ rearrange the equation into the form $y = mx + c$ (i.e. make y the subject).
- On linear real-life graphs, both the gradient and intercept have a meaning.

Chapter review

1 Find the equations of these lines.

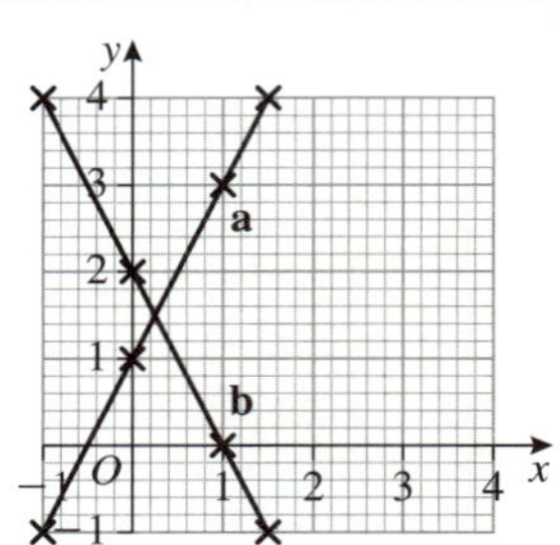

2 **a** Copy this grid and draw a line through the point $(-2, 4)$ with gradient $-\frac{1}{2}$

b What is the equation of this line?

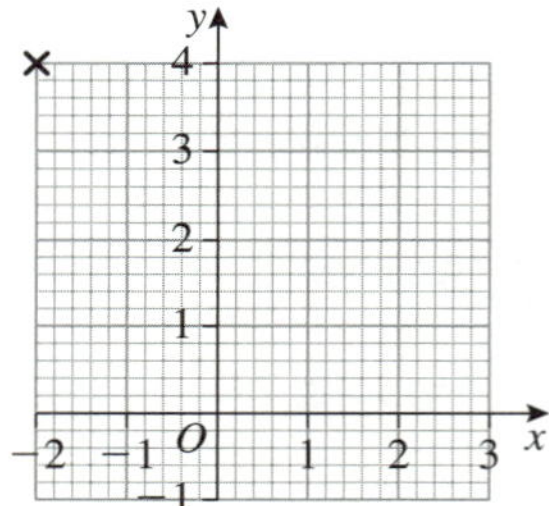

3 A sketch of the graph of a straight line is shown.
The equation of the line can be written in the form $y = mx + c$.
Find the values of m and c.

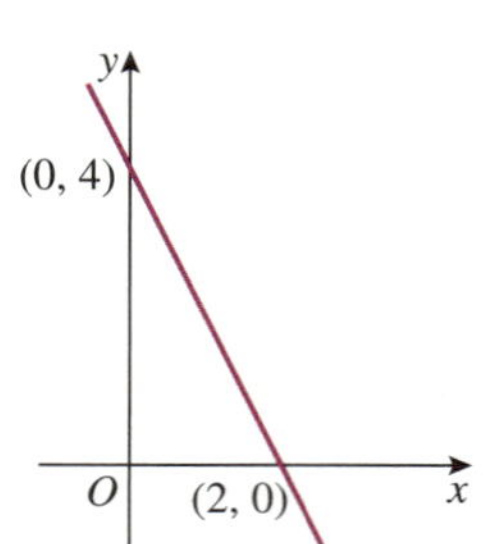

4 The diagram shows a sketch of the graph of $2y = x + 6$

a What are the coordinates of the point A?

b What is the gradient of the line $2y = x + 6$?

c Another line is drawn on the diagram.
It is parallel to the line $2y = x + 6$
What is its gradient?

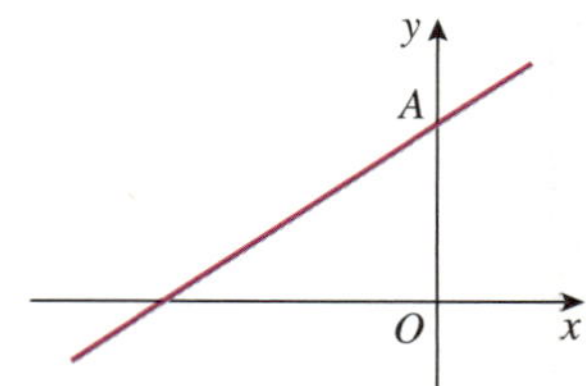

5 The diagram shows a sketch of the line $3x + 2y = 6$
The line crosses the y-axis at A and the x-axis at B.

a Find the coordinates of A.
b Find the gradient of the line AB.
c Find the gradient of a line perpendicular to AB.

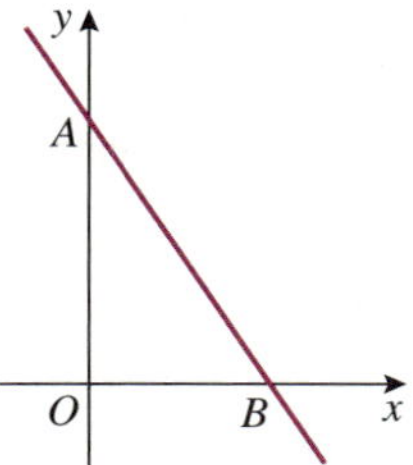

6 The diagram shows a sketch of the line $y = ax + b$.
The line passes through the points P $(-4, 0)$ and Q $(0, 3)$.

a Find the values of a and b.
b Find the equation of a line passing through Q that is perpendicular to PQ.

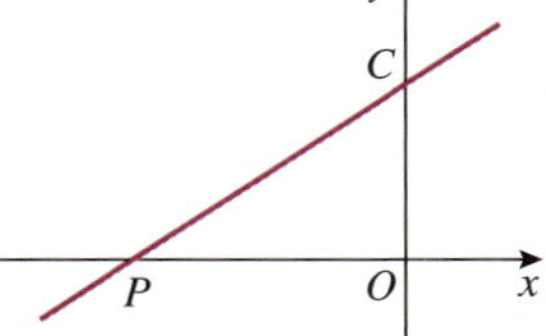

7 The line l has the equation $2x - 3y = 6$

a By first re-arranging the equation, show that the gradient of l is $\frac{2}{3}$

Equations A to D represent straight lines.

A: $3y = 2x + 10$ B: $2x + 3y = 10$
C: $3x + 2y = 10$ D: $3x - 2y = 10$

b Which of the equations A to D represents a line parallel to l?
c Which of the equations A to D represents a line perpendicular to l?

8 Line A has equation $2y = 3x - 5$
Line B has equation $6y + 4x = 12$

a Show that lines A and B are perpendicular.
b Find the function for the line parallel to line A passing through the point $(3, 5)$.

9 **a** Rearrange the function $8x - 3y = 12$ so that it is in the form $y = mx + c$.
b Hence find the function that has a graph perpendicular to the graph of $8x - 3y = 12$ and that passes through the point $(2, -1)$.

10 The distance–time graph shows a train journey.

a Find the speed of the train between each station.
You **must** show your working.
b Work out the average speed of the train for the complete journey.
Explain why this is less than the average of the speeds between the stations.

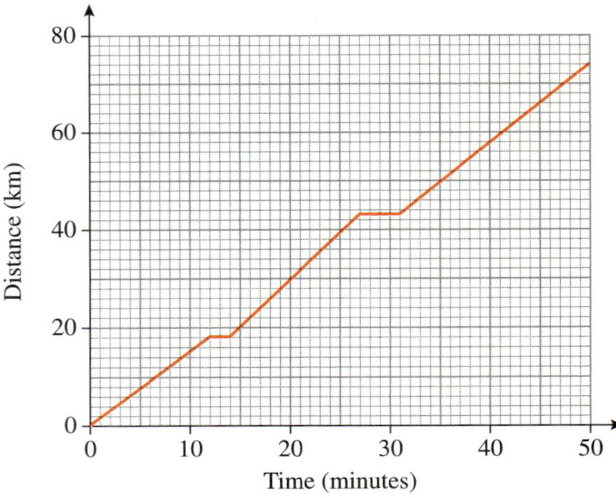

11 The graph shows the cost of printing business cards.

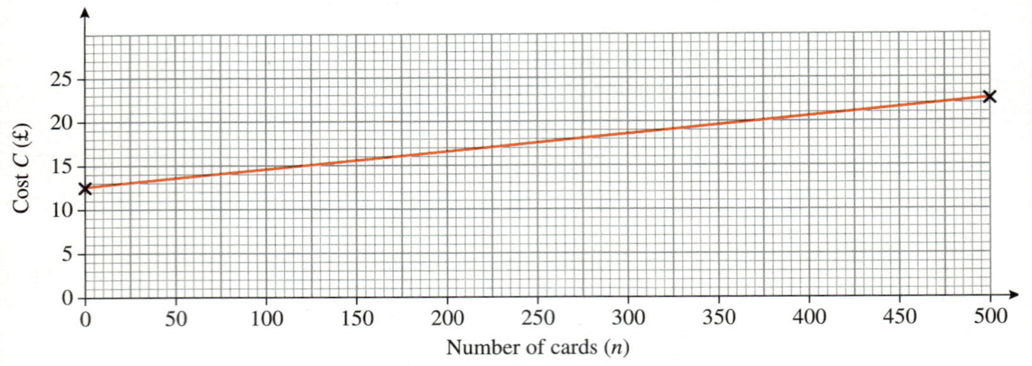

a Find the equation of the line in the form $C = mn + c$.

b Mary has 1000 business cards printed.
How much do they cost?

CHAPTER 25

More percentages

25.1 Compound interest

CAN YOU REMEMBER

- How to work out a percentage of a quantity?
- How to increase or decrease by a percentage?
- How to use a multiplier?

IN THIS SECTION YOU WILL

- Learn how to calculate compound interest by adding on yearly interest.
- Learn how to calculate compound interest using a multiplier.
- Learn how to calculate compound interest using a formula.

Most banks and building societies pay *compound interest.* The interest paid is added to the sum invested. Then the next interest payment is calculated on the new sum invested. So the interest payment increases each time.

Example 1

£1000 is invested in this account. Calculate the total amount in the account after two years.

INVEST £1000

Interest paid annually at a compound interest rate of 5% per year.

Solution 1

5% of £1000 = 0.05 × £1000 = £50, so £50 interest is paid at the end of the first year.
£1000 + £50 = £1050 is now invested for the second year.
5% of £1050 = 0.05 × £1050 = £52.50
So £52.50 interest is paid at the end of the second year.
Total in the account after two years = £1050 + £52.20 = £1102.50

The total value of an investment that earns compound interest can also be calculated using a formula.

$$A = P\left(1 + \frac{R}{100}\right)^T$$

where A is the final value of the investment
P is the amount invested
R is the rate of compound interest
and T is the time invested.

Example 2

Mr Hope invests £500 for two years in a bank account paying 4% compound interest.
Calculate the value of his investment after two years.

Solution 2

Using the formula $A = P\left(1 + \frac{R}{100}\right)^T$,

$P = £500$, $R = 4\%$, $T = 2$ years

$A = 500\left(1 + \frac{4}{100}\right)^2 = 500 \times 1.04^2 = £540.80$

When a population grows by a percentage, the new members are added to the total number in the population. So population growth (or decay) can be calculated in the same way as compound interest, using the multiplier method.

Example 3

There are 2000 fish in a pond.
The number of fish increases by 8% each year.
How many years will it take for the number of fish to increase to over 2500?

Solution 3

Original number of fish = 100%
Increase = 8%
Number of fish after one year = 100% + 8% = 108%
108% written as a decimal = 1.08, so the multiplier = 1.08
Use a calculator to work out the number of fish each year, rounding to the nearest whole number.
Number of fish after one year = 2000 × 1.08 = 2160
Number of fish after two years = 2160 × 1.08 = 2332
Number of fish after three years = 2332 × 1.08 = 2519
It takes three years for the number of fish to increase to over 2500

Exercise A

1 Work out the compound interest on each of the following after:
i one year **ii** two years.

a £500 at 10% per year
b £400 at 5% per year
c £2000 at 3% per year
d £5000 at 4% per year
e £600 at 7% per year
f £1000 at 8% per year
g £200 at 2.5% per year
h £1500 at 4% per year

2 There are 600 trees in a small wood.
The number of trees is decreasing by 10% each year.
How many trees will there be after three years?

3 The number of parking spaces in a village is increased by 20% each year.
If there are 50 spaces now, how many spaces will there be in three years?

4 Work out the value of the following compound interest investments after two years.

a £300 at 10% per year | **b** £500 at 2% per year
c £1000 at 5% per year | **d** £500 at 6% per year
e £1200 at 4% per year | **f** £800 at 3% per year
g £100 at 2.5% per year | **h** £2500 at 7% per year

5 A colony of ants is increasing at the rate of 15% per day.
How many days will it take the ants to increase the colony by 50%?

Exercise B

1 Which **two** of the following is the value of investing £1000 at 3% compound interest for two years?

£1000 × 3 × 3   £1000 × 1.03^2 £1000 × 1.03 × 1.03
£2000 × 1.03   £1000 + £30 + £30

2 Sarah invests £2000 in a savings account.
Compound interest of 3% is added to the account every year.
Explain why the amount in the account after three years is £2000 × 1.03^3

3 Write down a calculation for the total amount when £400 is invested at 5% compound interest for six years. You do not need to work out the answer.

4 The number of birds on an island is decreasing by 10% each year.
Explain why the number of birds will **not** have decreased by 30% in three years.

5 **a** The population of Growland is 18 million.
Each year the population increases by 10%.
How many years will it take for the population to double?

b The population of Shrinkland is also 18 million.
Each year the population decreases by 10%.
How many years will it take for the population to halve?

6 **a** Work out 1.2^4

b Use your answer to part **a** to state the number of years to double an investment at 20% compound interest.

7 Which is the better investment?

Explain your answer.

8 Chloe buys a violin for £950
Every six months the value of the violin decreases by 7% of the value at the beginning of the six months.
Work out the value of the violin after two years.
Give your answer to the nearest pound.

25.2 Overall percentage change

CAN YOU REMEMBER

- How to use a multiplier?

IN THIS SECTION YOU WILL

- Learn how to calculate overall percentage change using multipliers.
- Learn how to calculate overall percentage change using nominal amounts.

The *overall percentage change* is the change as a percentage of the starting value.

Example 1

The population of a small town increases by 5% one year and then by a further 10% of the new amount in the second year.
Calculate the overall percentage change.

Solution 1

Let the initial population be N.
First year increase = 5%
Population after one year = 100% + 5% = 105%
Multiplier = 1.05
Population at end of first year = $1.05N$
Second year increase = 10%
Multiplier for second year = 1.10 — 100% + 10% = 110%
Population at end of second year = $1.10 \times 1.05N$
Overall percentage change for the two years = $1.05 \times 1.10 = 1.155$
1.155 = 115.5% = 100% + 15.5%
Overall percentage change = 15.5%

Example 2

A shop sells items to make a profit of 25%.
In a sale the prices are reduced by 10%.
Calculate the percentage profit on the items sold in the sale.

Solution 2

Profit = 25%
Multiplier for profit = 1.25 — 100% + 25%
Sale reduction = 10%
Multiplier for reduction = 0.90 — 100% − 10% = 90%
Overall multiplier = $1.25 \times 0.90 = 1.125$
1.125 = 112.5% = 100% + 12.5%
Overall percentage profit = 12.5%

Exercise A

1 Use a calculator to work out the overall percentage change of the following.

a A 10% increase followed by a 20% increase.
b A 5% increase followed by an 8% increase.
c A 10% decrease followed by a 25% decrease.
d A 4% decrease followed by a 12% decrease.
e A 10% increase followed by a 15% decrease.
f A 20% decrease followed by a 25% increase.

2 A loan is charged at 10% compound interest per year for two years.
Work out the interest charged as a percentage of the loan.

3 The number of cars in a city has increased by 20% of the number in the previous year for the last two years.
Work out the overall percentage increase over the two years.

4 The price of a dress is reduced by 10% in a sale. The sale price is then reduced by 5%.
Work out the overall percentage reduction.

5 Match up a pair of the red multiplier cards with each of the yellow combined multiplier cards.
The first one has been done for you.

6 A lorry increases its speed by 8% in one mile downhill and then decreases its speed by 15% in one mile uphill.
Work out the overall percentage change in speed for the lorry.

One way of working out overall percentage change is to use a *nominal amount* to represent the original price. A simple nominal amount such as 1 or 100 makes calculations easier.

Example 3

The cost of a loaf of bread is reduced by 10%.
The shop sells 20% more loaves than normal.
Calculate the percentage increase in its takings.

Solution 3

Method 1: multiplier
Multiplier for cost of loaf = 0.90
Multiplier for sales = 1.20
Combining the multipliers = 0.90 × 1.20 = 1.08
Percentage increase in takings = 8%

Method 2: nominal amounts
Let the cost of a loaf = £1
New cost = 90p
Let the normal number of loaves sold = 100
New sales = 120
Original takings = 100 × £1 = £100
New takings = 120 × 90p = £108
Percentage increase in takings = 8%

Exercise B

1 Explain why increasing the contents of a box of chocolates by 10% and then decreasing the new contents by 10% does not return the contents to the original amount.

2 Compare the overall price of an item using method 1 and method 2.
Method 1: Increase the price by 10% and then reduce the new price by 10%.
Method 2: Decrease the price by 10% and then increase the new price by 10%.

3 For each of three years the number of ants in a colony increases by 10% of the number in the previous year.
After three years an epidemic kills half of the ants.
What percentage of the original number of ants remain?

4 A cycle shop reduces its price by 20%.
As a result it sells 30% more cycles than usual.
Calculate the percentage increase in its takings.

5 In a toffee factory, 2% of toffees are rejected.
Of the rejected toffees 75% are sold as seconds.
What percentage of the toffees produced in the factory are sold as seconds?

6 Bob estimates the number of bricks needed to build a wall.
His estimate is 25% too many.
He also estimates the cost of each brick.
This estimate is 10% less than the actual cost.
How much is the actual cost of the wall below his estimate?
Give your answer as a percentage of his original estimate, to one decimal place.

7 Jenny underestimates the distance that she runs each day by 4%.
She overestimates the time that she spends running each day by 10%.
Calculate her estimated average speed as a percentage of her actual average speed.

25.3 Reverse percentages

CAN YOU REMEMBER

- How to work out an increase or decrease by a percentage?
- How to divide by a decimal?

IN THIS SECTION YOU WILL

- Learn how to calculate reverse percentages.
- Learn how to solve reverse percentage problems.

Reverse percentage problems involve finding an original value when the value after a given percentage increase or decrease is known.
Examples include:

- finding the original cost of an item before it was reduced in a sale
- finding the cost of an item without the VAT
- finding the population last year given this year's population and the percentage change from last year.

Example 1

What was the cost of the doll before the sale?

Solution 1

The original price = 100%
The sale price is 100% – 10% = 90% of the original price.
90% = 0.9
Original price × 0.9 = sale price

Original price $= \frac{£18}{0.9} = £20$

Example 2

The price of a kettle is £9.40
This price includes VAT at 17.5%.
What is the price of the kettle without the VAT?

Solution 2

The original price without the VAT = 100%.
The price including the VAT is 100% + 17.5% = 117.5% of the original price.
117.5% = 1.175
Original price × 1.175 = price including VAT

Original price $= \frac{£9.40}{1.175} = £8$

Exercise A

1 A special offer box of chocolates contains 10% extra than the normal box.
The special offer box contains 330 grams of chocolate.
How much does the normal box contain?

2 The average number of vehicles in a car park has increased by 20% since last year.
The average number is now 240
What was the average number last year?

3 The price of a coat is reduced by 10% in a sale.
The sale price is £45
What was the price of the coat before the sale?

4 The number of students studying Mathematics in a college increased by 50% this year.
The number now studying Mathematics is 300
How many students studied Mathematics last year?

5 A travel card entitles the holder to 50% off the normal cost of a journey.
A particular journey costs £1.80 using the card.
What is the cost for this journey without the card?

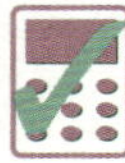

6 A computer is advertised at £658 including VAT at 17.5%.
Work out the cost of the computer before the VAT was added.

7 A taxi driver drives 23 000 miles in a year.
He says this is 15% more than last year.
How many miles did he drive last year?

8 Trevor says that he has grown 5% this year.
He is now 1.575 metres tall.
How tall was he last year?

9 The attendance at a hockey match is 1431
This is an increase of 6% on last week.
How many attended last week?

10 Toys at a car boot sale are reduced by 25%.
A toy is now on sale at £6.75
What was the price before the reduction?

Example 3

The population of Rotherstone increased by one quarter to 750 this year.
What was the population of Rotherstone last year?

Solution 3

One quarter = 25%
The original population = 100%
The population including the increase = 100% + 25% = 125% of the original population.
Original population × 1.25 = population including the increase

125% = 1.25

Original population $= \dfrac{750}{1.25} = 600$

Exercise B

1 The number of items for sale at an auction this week has fallen by one third to 1600
How many items were for sale last week?

2 A ticket machine issues one quarter more tickets today than yesterday.
The number of tickets issued today is 2175
Which of the following gives the number of tickets issued yesterday?

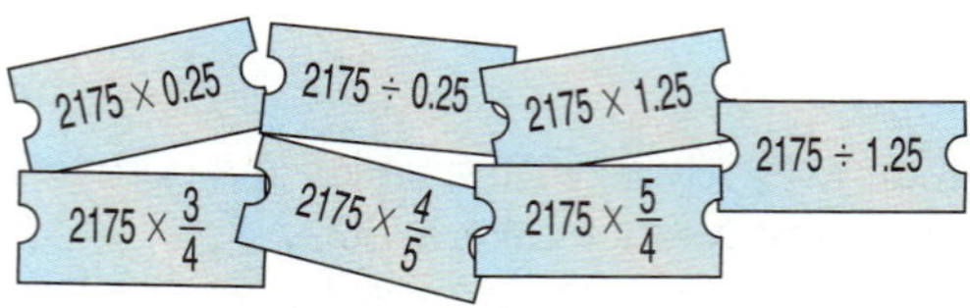

3 The number of fish in a pond has fallen by 10% of the previous year's total each year for the last two years.
There are now 405 fish in the pond.
- **a** How many fish were in the pond last year?
- **b** How many fish were in the pond two years ago?

4 The ice and snow cover of the Himalayas has shrunk 30% over the last 30 years.
Adnan says this means that there is now seven tenths of the amount of ice and snow cover of 30 years ago.
Is he correct? Explain your answer.

5 The same tool set is for sale at two shops.
VAT is $17\frac{1}{2}$%.
Which is the better offer? Show your working.

6 The retail price index (RPI) rose 4% last year.
- **a** Use the retail price index (RPI) to calculate last years' prices of the following:
  - **i** fish and chips costing £3.38 this year
  - **ii** an office chair costing £83.20 this year.
- **b** Explain why the retail price index may **not** be appropriate to use in every case.

7 The number of visitors to a restaurant in a week is 540
The manager says this is exactly 10% more than the previous week.
Explain why he cannot be correct.

8 A cricket set is reduced by 10% to £12.60
Claire says 10% is £1.26, so the original price was £12.60 + £1.26 = £13.86
Explain why she is **not** correct.

Chapter summary

- With compound interest, the interest paid is added to the sum invested. Then the next interest payment is calculated on the new sum invested. So the interest payment increases each time.
- The total value of an investment that earns compound interest can also be calculated using a formula

$$A = P\left(1 + \frac{R}{100}\right)^T$$

where A is the final value of the investment
P is the amount invested
R is the rate of compound interest
and T is the time invested.
- Population growth (or decay) can be calculated in the same way as compound interest, using the multiplier method.
- The *overall percentage change* is the change as a percentage of the starting value.

- Overall percentage change can be calculated by combining the two percentages.
  For example, a 10% increase followed by a 5% decrease = $1.10 \times 0.95 = 1.045$
  So overall percentage increase = 4.5%.
- Overall percentage change can be calculated using a nominal value.
  For example, a 10% increase followed by a 5% decrease on a nominal value of 100 gives
  $0.95 \times (1.10 \times 100) = 104.5$
  So overall percentage increase = 4.5%.
- *Reverse percentage* problems involve finding an original value, given the value after a given percentage increase or decrease.
  For example:
  - finding the original cost of an item before it was reduced in a sale
  - finding the cost of an item without the VAT
  - finding the population last year given this year's population and the percentage change from last year.

Chapter review

1 A mouse mat is being sold in a sale.
What is the normal price of the mouse mat?

2 David put £5000 in a savings account on 1 January 2006
Compound interest is added at 3% per year.

a How much money will David have in the account on 1 January 2007?

b David says that each year the interest will be the same amount.
Is he correct? Explain your answer.

3 The number of dogs at a kennels increases by 5% in January but then decreases by 10% in February.
What is the overall percentage change for the two months?

4 The population of Bramside fell by 10% to 4500 this year.
The population of Sunniley was 4800 last year.
Which place had the greater population last year?

5 A shop reduces the price of certain items in a sale by 25%.
The number of these items sold increases by 100%.
Work out the percentage increase in the shop's takings for these items.

6 Abdul has just been promoted in his job.
When he was promoted, his pay was increased by 25%.
Abdul now earns £6.40 an hour.
How much did he earn per hour before he was promoted?

7 The cost of a television set is reduced in a sale by 15%.
The cost in the sale is £722.50
How much was the television before the price reduction?

8 A telescope is priced at £893 including VAT at 17.5%.

a How much is the telescope without the VAT?

b The price of a different telescope is £100 less when the prices without the VAT are compared.

How much less is the price of this telescope when VAT is included in the comparison?

9 The table shows the percentage of people passing two stages of an audition.

First audition	10% of those attending
Second audition	50% of those passing first audition

If 14 people were selected after the second audition, how many people attended the first audition?

10 Dawn invested some money in a savings account.
After one year she had £2194.50 in the account.
Compound interest was paid at 4.5% per year.
How much did she invest?

11 The table shows some data about the number of people attending a show.

Day 1	Number attending = 160
Day 2	Number attending = 5% more than day 1
Day 3	Number attending = 48 less than day 2
Day 4	Number attending = $\frac{1}{2}$ of number on day 3

What was the overall percentage change in the attendance over the 4 days?

CHAPTER 26

Further triangle properties

26.1 Congruence

CAN YOU REMEMBER

- That for parallel lines, corresponding angles are equal and alternate angles are equal?

IN THIS SECTION YOU WILL

- Recognise congruent shapes.
- Find length of sides and size of angles of congruent triangles.
- Use congruence definitions to prove that two triangles are congruent.

Two shapes are *congruent* when they are exactly the same shape and size.
One shape will fit exactly over the other shape.
These shapes are all congruent.

Congruent triangles have three pairs of equal sides and three pairs of corresponding equal angles (opposite the same sides).

For example:
angle A = angle P
angle B = angle Q
angle C = angle R
$BC = QR$ = 11 cm
$AC = PR$ = 5 cm
$AB = PQ$ = 8 cm

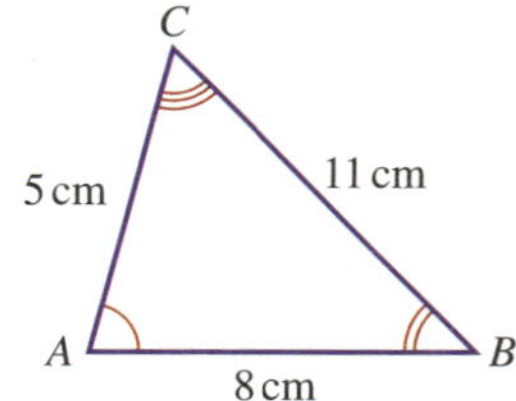

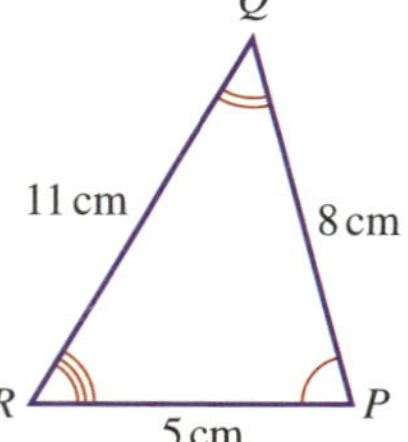

Triangle ABC is congruent to triangle PQR.
This can be written $\triangle ABC \equiv \triangle PQR$.
Note that the letter order matches the equal angles.

Example 1

These triangles are congruent.
Write down the values of x, y and z.

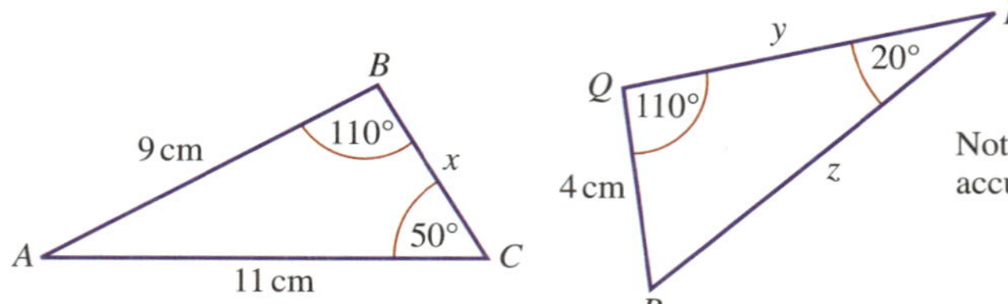

Solution 1

Angle A corresponds to angle P so $A = 20°$
Angle R corresponds to angle C so $R = 50°$
x is side BC.
BC corresponds to side QR (opposite the 20° angle), so $x = 4$ cm.
y is side PQ.
PQ corresponds to side AB (opposite the 50° angle), so $y = 9$ cm.
z is side PR.
PR corresponds to side AC (opposite the 110° angle), so $z = 11$ cm.

Exercise A

1 Write down which pairs of shapes are congruent.

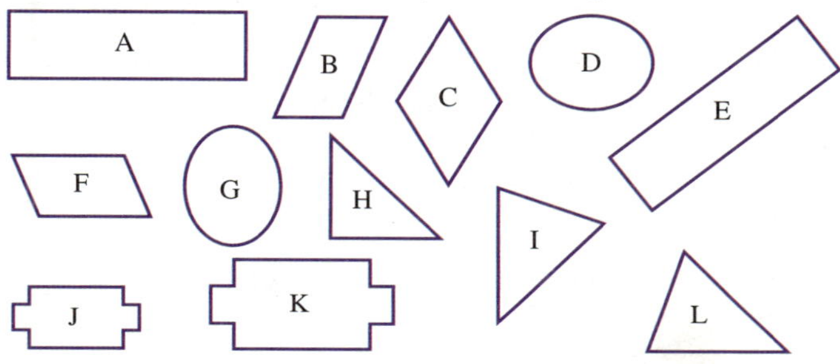

2 Which pairs of triangles are congruent?

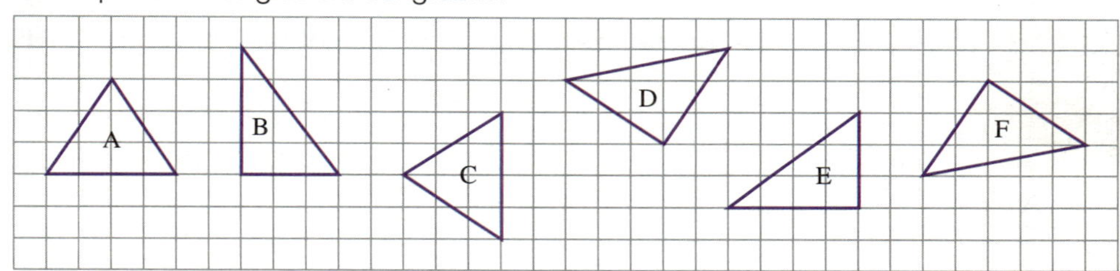

3 Triangles LMN and PQR each have angles of 56°, 78° and 46°
Explain why these triangles may **not** be congruent.

4 Two of these triangles are congruent.
Write down the letters of the congruent pair.

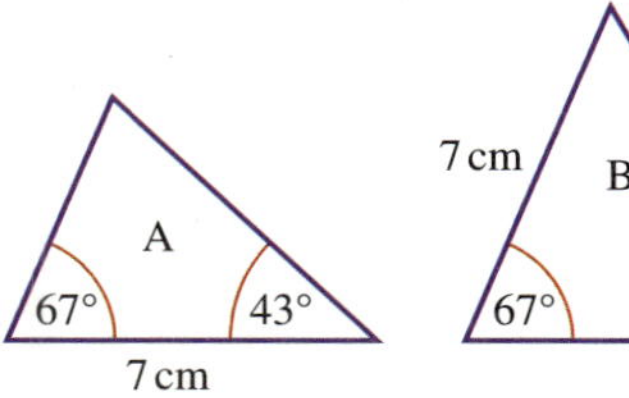

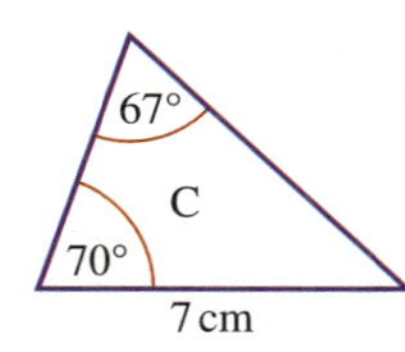

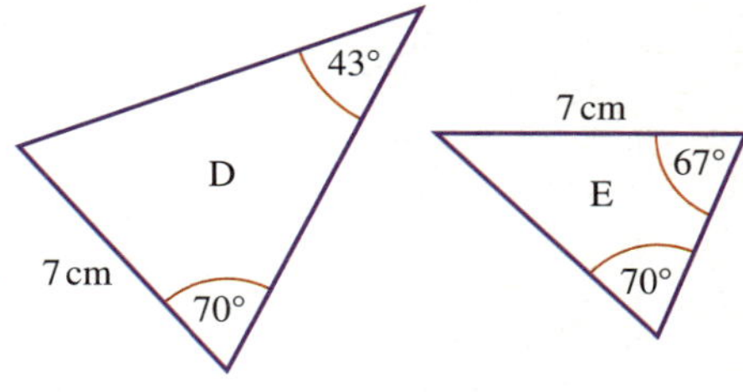

5 These two triangles are congruent.
Write down the values of x, y and z.

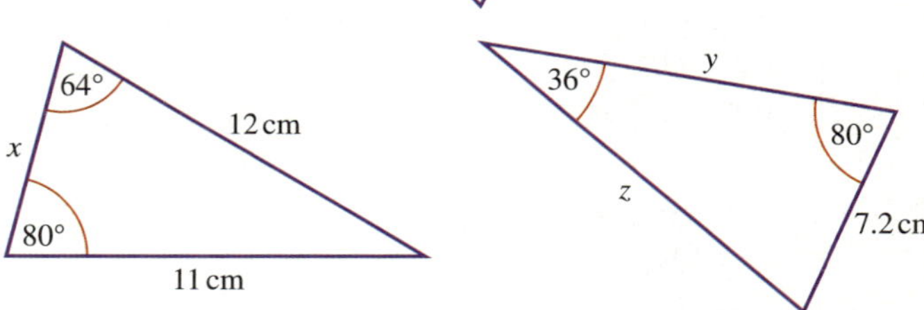

6 Triangles LMN and PQR are congruent.

a Write down the size of:

i angle R

ii angle P

b Write down the length of:

i side LM

ii side QR

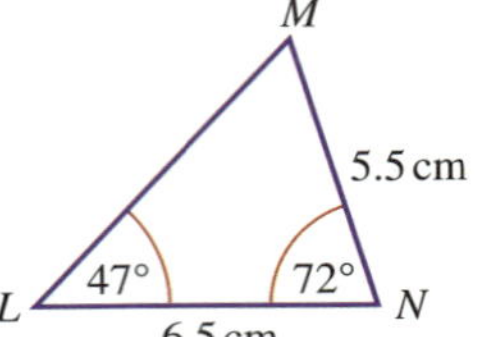

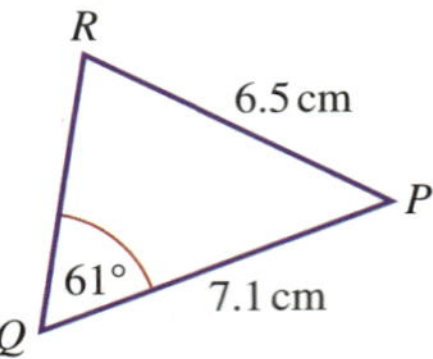

There are four ways to show that a pair of triangles are congruent.
These are called *conditions of congruence.*

- Three pairs of sides are equal – **SSS**.

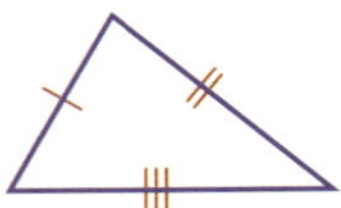
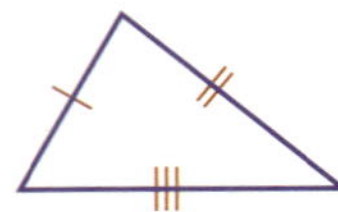

- Two pairs of sides and the angle between them are equal – **SAS**.

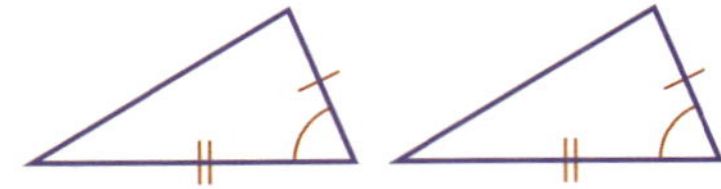

- Two pairs of angles and a corresponding side are equal – **ASA** or **AAS**.

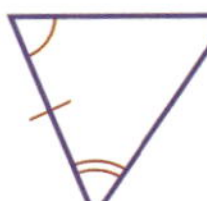
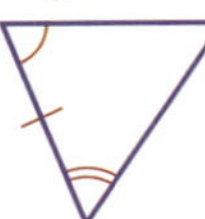

or

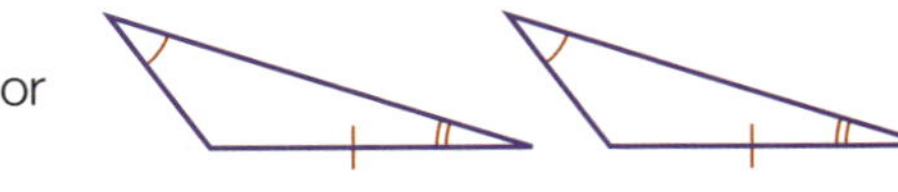

- For a right-angled triangle, the hypotenuse and one other pair of sides are equal – **RHS**.

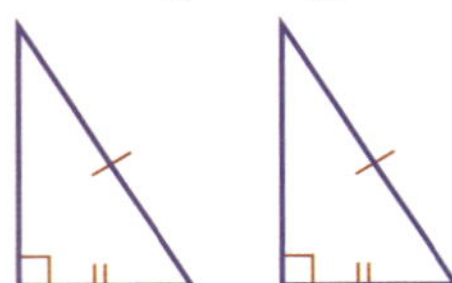

Example 2

Show that triangles LMN and PQR are congruent.
Give a reason for your answer.

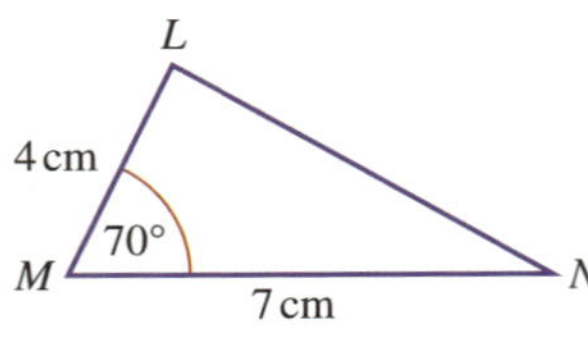

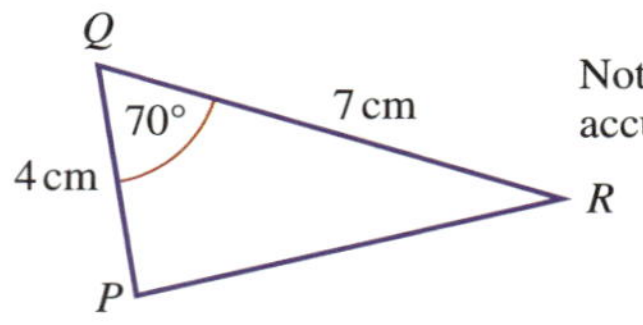

Not drawn accurately

Solution 2

$LM = PQ$ Both sides equal 4 cm.

$MN = QR$ Both sides equal 7 cm.

angle LMN = angle PQR Both angles equal 70° and are in corresponding positions between corresponding sides.

Two sides and the included angle are equal – SAS.
So $\triangle LMN$ is congruent to $\triangle PQR$.

Exercise B

1 State whether each pair of triangles is congruent.
When triangles are congruent give reasons.

a

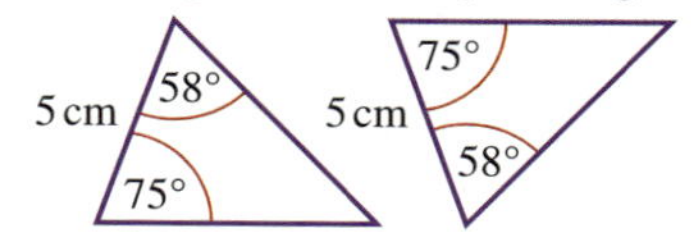

b

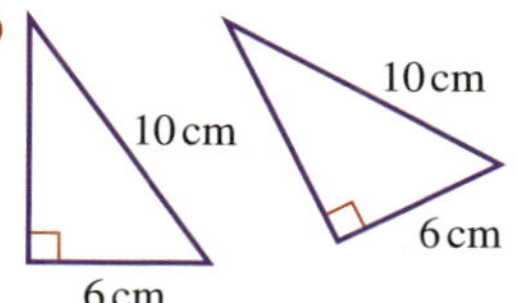

c

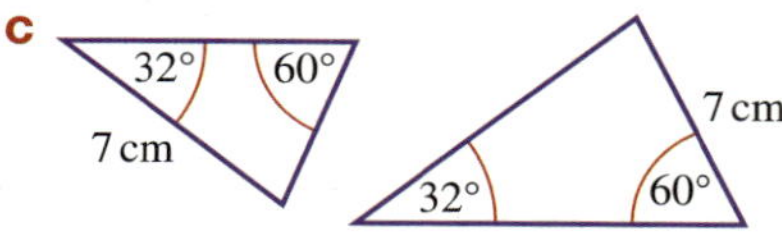

Not drawn accurately

2 Which two of these triangles are congruent?
Give reasons for your answer.

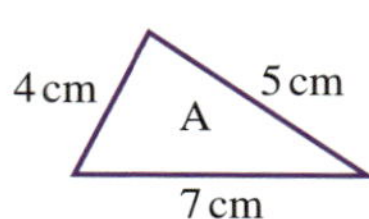

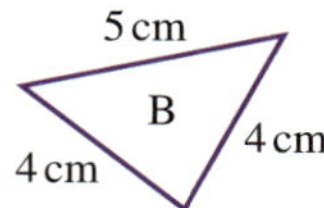

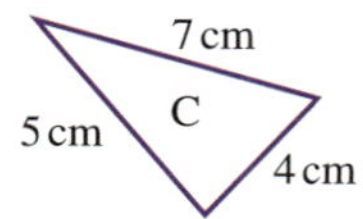

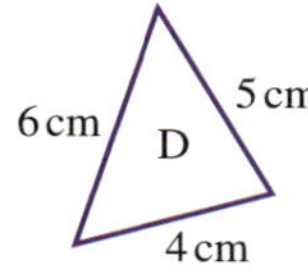

Not drawn accurately

3 The following triangles are not drawn accurately.
State whether each pair is congruent or not, giving reasons for each congruent pair.

a

b

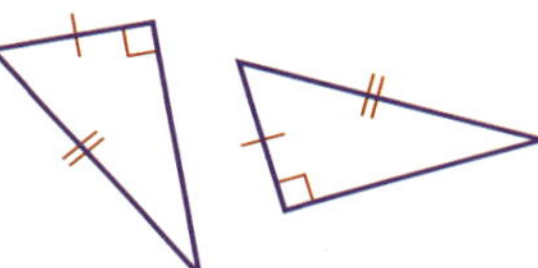

c

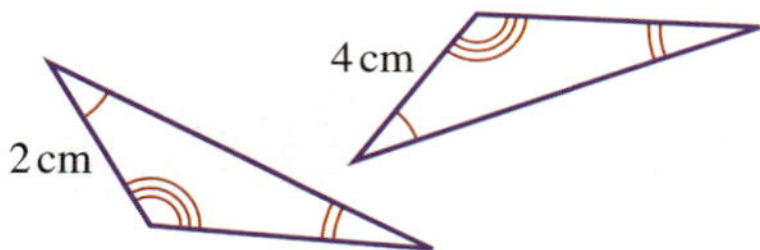

d

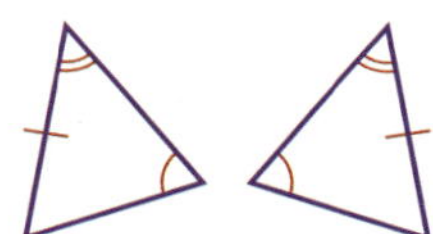

4 The diagram shows a rectangle which has been divided into five triangles.
Write down three congruent triangles.

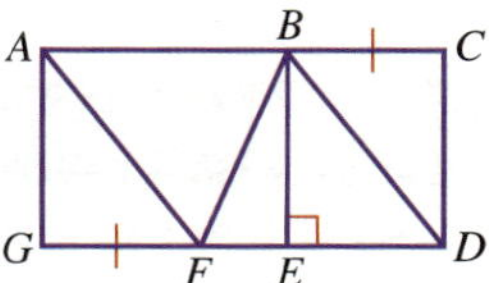

5 In the diagram $PQ = ST$

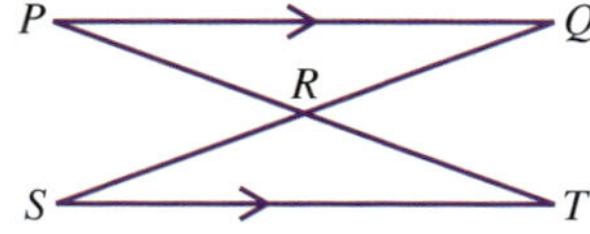

Prove that triangles PQR and RST are congruent.

6 Show that triangles ABC and DEF are congruent.

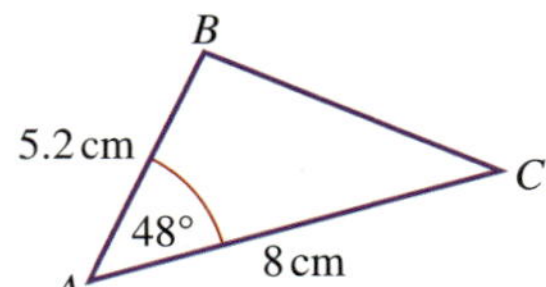

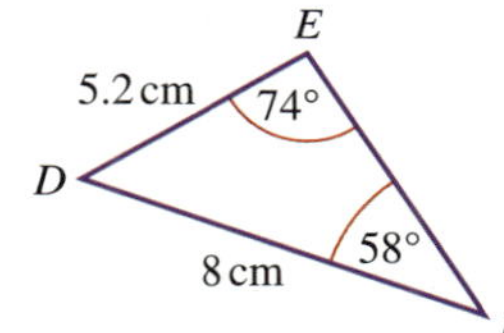

7 In the diagram on the right, AD is parallel to BC.

  a Write down the size of angle DAC.

  b Show that triangles ABC and ADC are congruent.

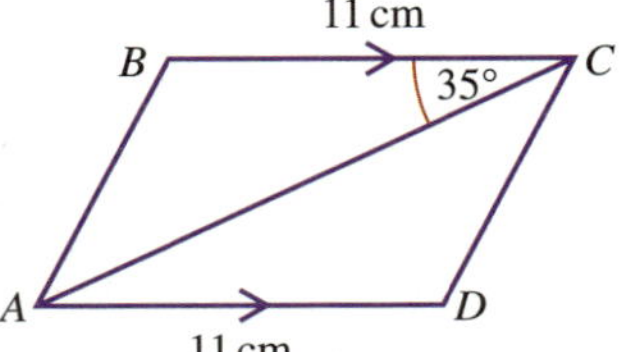

8 Show that triangles ABC and DEF are congruent.

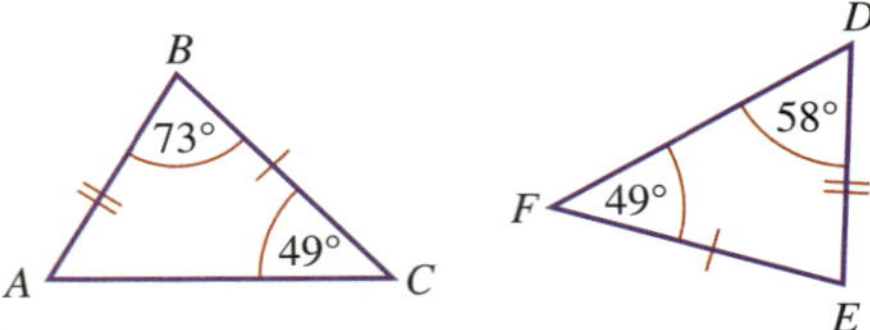

9 Here are two triangles.
Stuart says that the triangles are congruent.
Explain why he is **not** correct.

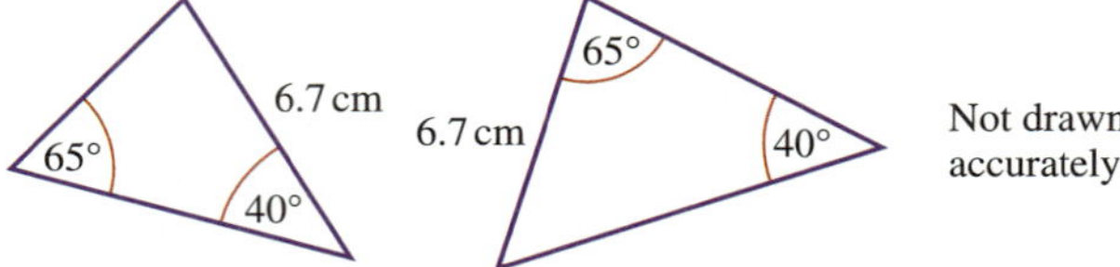

26.2 Similar figures

CAN YOU REMEMBER

- That the scale factor of an enlargement is the ratio of the lengths of corresponding sides?
- That in parallel lines, alternate and corresponding angles are equal?

IN THIS SECTION YOU WILL

- Show that two shapes are similar.
- Work out angles and sides of similar shapes.
- Calculate areas of similar shapes and volumes of similar solids.

Two shapes are *similar* if one shape is an enlargement of the other.
When two figures are similar:

- their shapes are the same
- the corresponding angles are equal
- the lengths of the corresponding sides are in the same ratio – this ratio is the scale factor of the enlargement.

For example, in these two rectangles the corresponding angles are equal as all the angles are 90°.

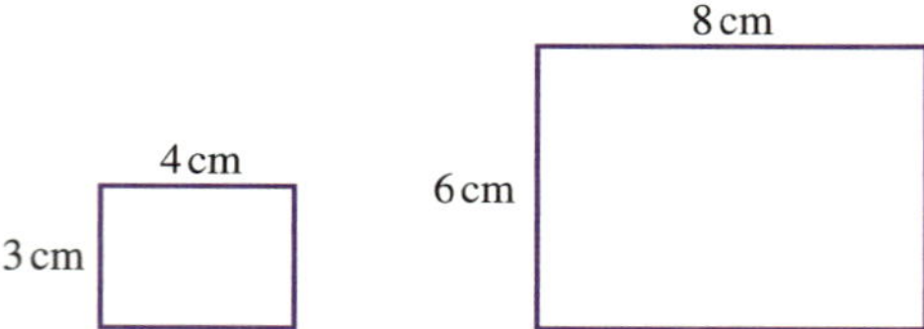

The lengths of the sides of the large rectangle are double the lengths of the sides of the small rectangle. The large rectangle is an enlargement of the small rectangle by scale factor 2
The ratio of length to width is also the same for each rectangle.
$8:6 = 4:3$ or $\frac{8}{6} = \frac{4}{3}$
So the two rectangles are similar.

Example 1

Show that triangles ABC and DEF are similar.

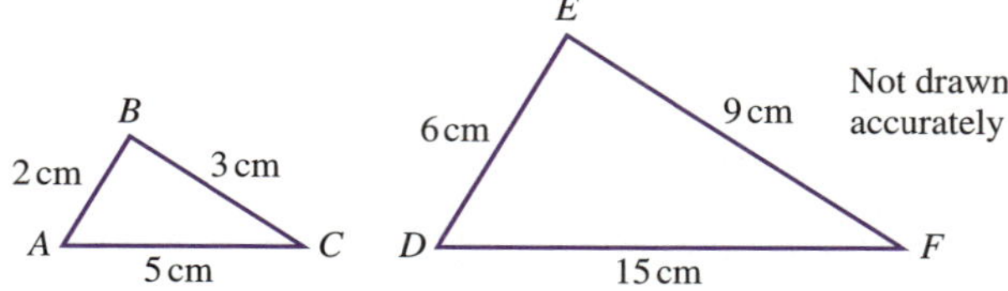

Solution 1

For the triangles to be similar the corresponding sides must be in the same ratio.

$DE:AB = EF:BC = DF:AC$ or $\frac{DE}{AB} = \frac{EF}{BC} = \frac{DF}{AC}$

Substituting in the lengths of the sides:

$\frac{6}{2} = \frac{9}{3} = \frac{15}{5} = 3$

The triangles are similar.

Example 2

These two quadrilaterals are similar.

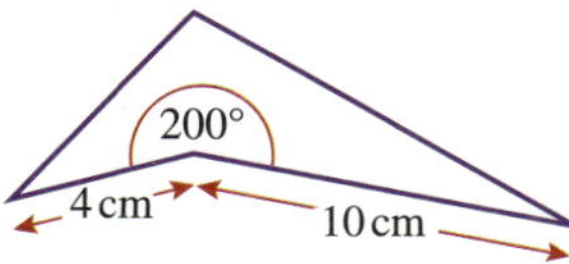

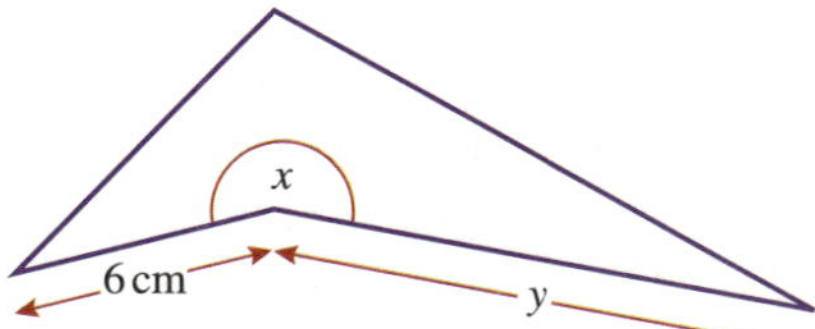

Find the values of x and y.

Solution 2

The quadrilaterals are similar so corresponding angles are equal.
So $x = 200°$
The ratio of corresponding sides is equal
$6:4 = y:10$

So $\frac{6}{4} = \frac{y}{10}$

$\frac{6}{4} \times 10 = y$ — Multiply both sides by 10

$15 = y$

$y = 15$ cm

Exercise A

1 a Each of these pair of shapes is similar.
Work out the values marked with letters.

Not drawn accurately

i

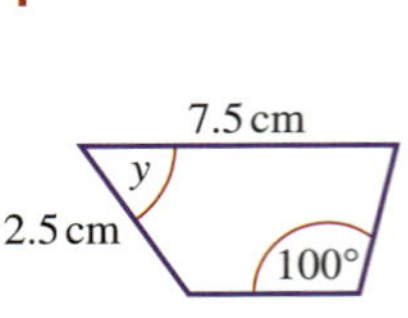

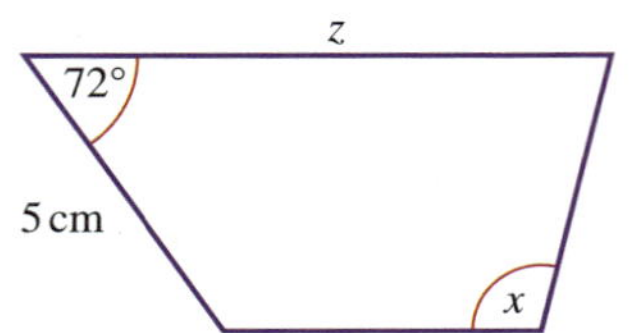

ii

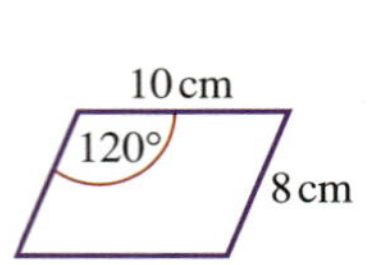

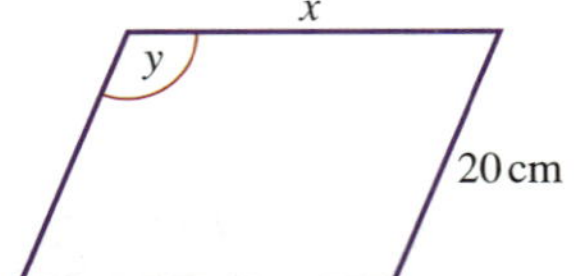

b Two rectangles are similar. Rectangle A has length 24 cm and width 15 cm. Rectangle B has width 5 cm.
Work out the length of rectangle B.

2 Each of these pairs of triangles are similar.
The equal angles are shown with matching arcs.
Work out the lengths of the sides marked with letters.

a

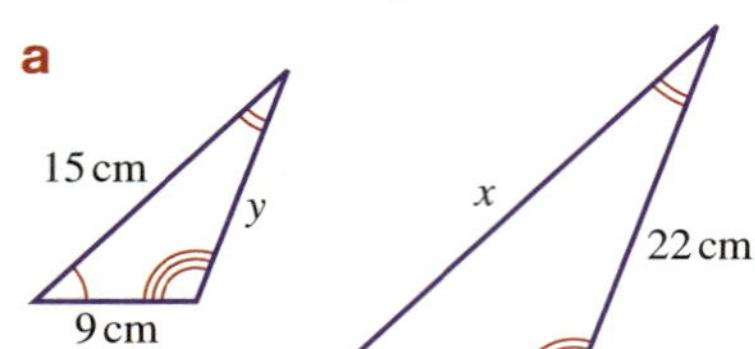

b

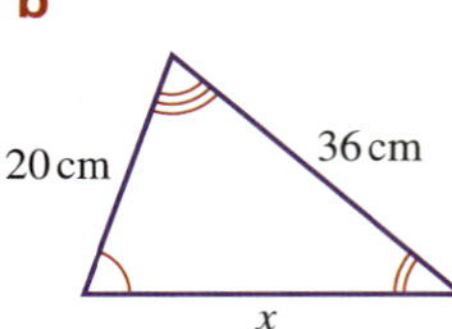

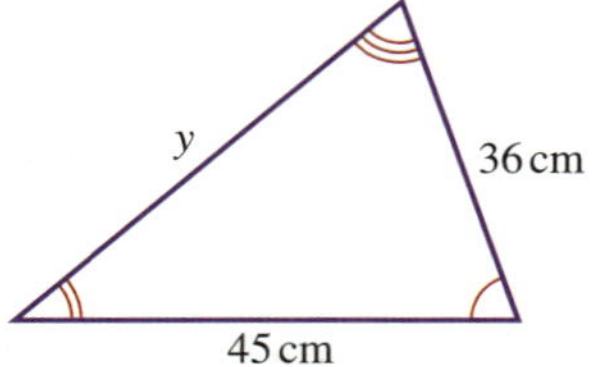

Not drawn accurately

3 In the diagram BC is parallel to DE.

a Explain why triangles ABC and ADE are similar.

b Work out the length of BC.

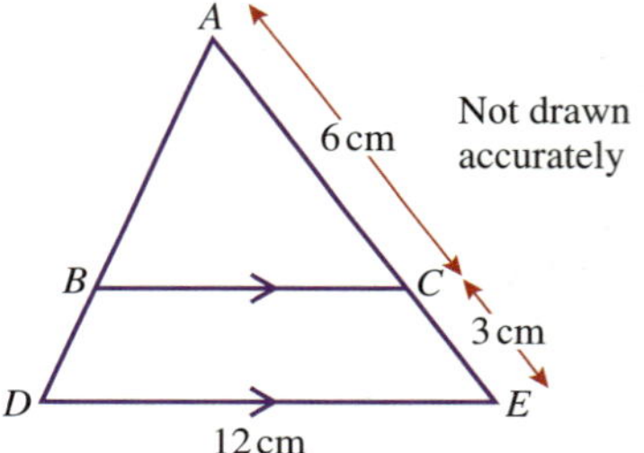

4 In the diagram PQ is parallel to ST.

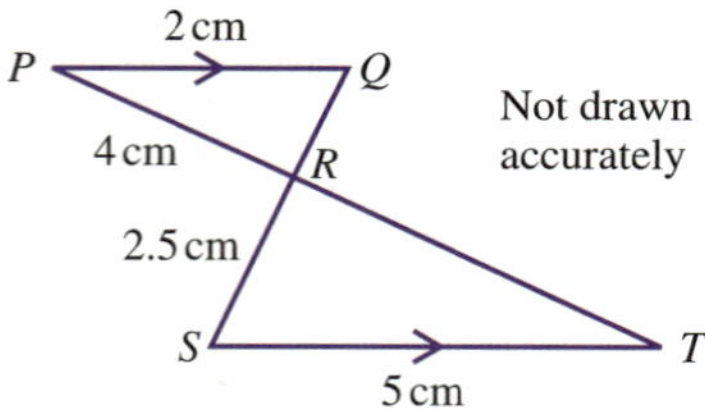

a Show that triangles PQR and TSR are similar.

b Work out the length of:

i RT **ii** QR.

5 Calculate the third angle in each of these triangles.
Hence write down three pairs of similar triangles.

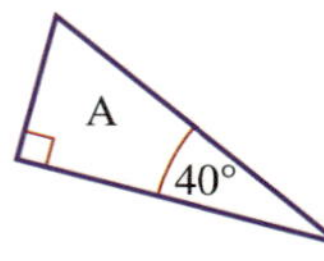

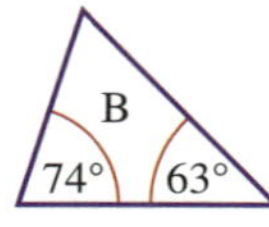

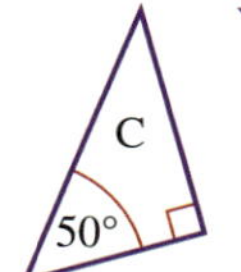

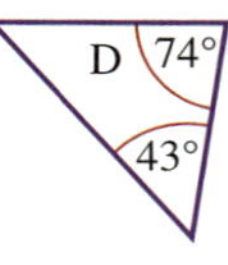

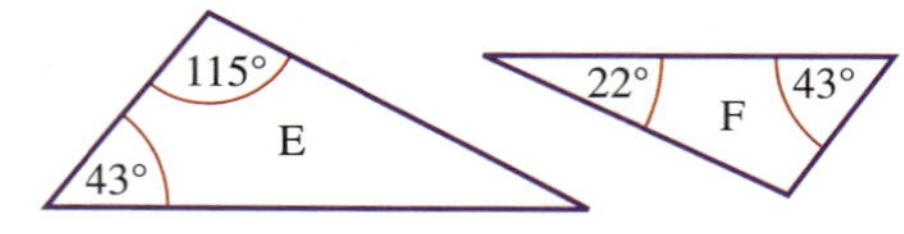

6 **a** Show that triangles ABC and ADE are similar.
b Calculate the length of DE.

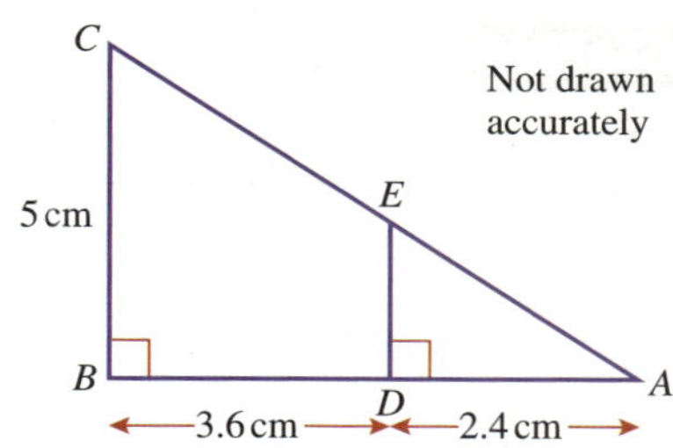

7 Two photographs are similar rectangles.
The smaller photograph measures 3.5 cm wide by 6.2 cm high.
The larger photograph is 8.4 cm wide.
Calculate the height of the larger photograph.

The large square is an enlargement of the small square with scale factor 3
Area of small square = 1 × 1 =1 cm^2
Area of large square = 3 × 3 = 9 cm^2
The area is enlarged by scale factor $\frac{9}{1} = 9 = 3^2$

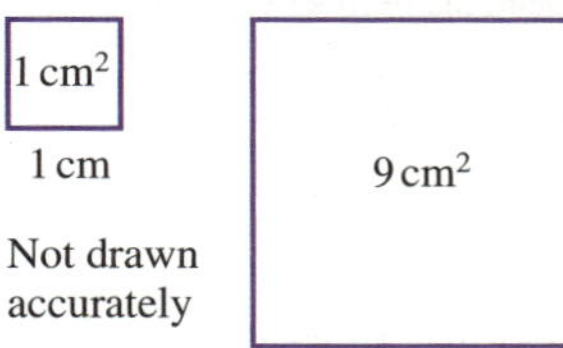

Volume of small cube = 1 × 1 × 1 = 1 cm^3
Volume of large cube = 3 × 3 × 3 = 27 cm^3
The volume is enlarged by scale factor $\frac{27}{1} = 27 = 3^3$

When a shape is enlarged by scale factor k:
- the area is enlarged by scale factor k^2
- the volume is enlarged by scale factor k^3

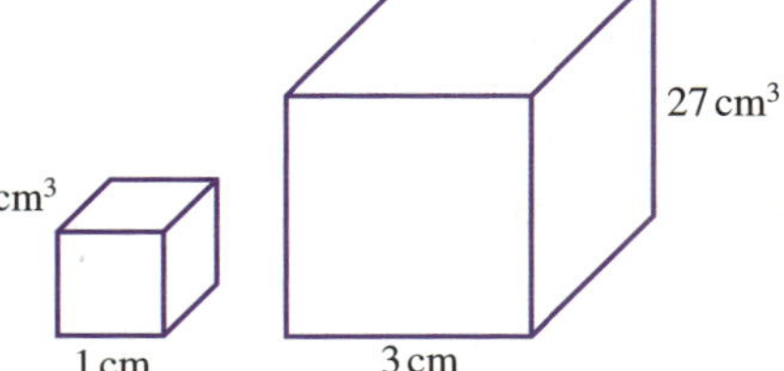

Example 3

Two triangles are similar. Triangle A has base 4 cm and triangle B has base 8 cm.
The area of triangle A is 11 cm^2
Work out the area of triangle B.

Solution 3

Scale factor of the lengths is $\frac{8}{4} = 2$
So area scale factor is $2^2 = 4$
Area of triangle B = 4 × area of triangle A = 4 × 11 = 44 cm^2

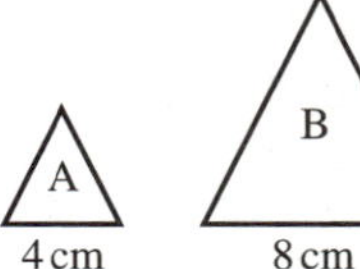

Example 4

Cone A is 14.2 cm high and has a volume of 210 cm^3.
Calculate the volume of a similar cone B of height 7.1 cm.

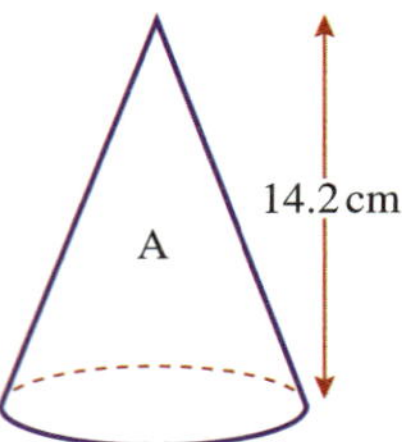

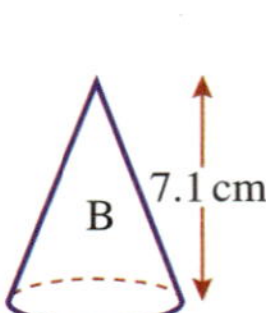

Solution 4

Scale factor of lengths $= \dfrac{7.1}{14.2} = \dfrac{1}{2}$

Scale factor of volumes $= \left(\dfrac{1}{2}\right)^3 = \dfrac{1}{8}$

Volume of cone B is $\dfrac{1}{8}$ of the volume of cone A $= \dfrac{1}{8} \times 210 = 26.25$ cm^3

Example 5

Two rectangles R and S are similar.
R has width 4 cm and area 30 cm^2
S has area 187.5 cm^2
Calculate the width of rectangle S.

Solution 5

Area scale factor $= \dfrac{187.5}{30} = 6.25$

Length scale factor $= \sqrt{6.25} = 2.5$
Width of rectangle S $= 2.5 \times$ width of rectangle R $= 2.5 \times 4 = 10$ cm

4 cm

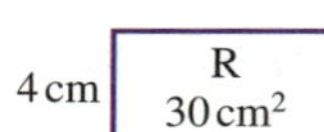

S
187.5 cm^2

Exercise B

1 A rug is 15 cm long and has an area of 90 cm^2
Work out the area of a similar rug of length 30 cm.

2 Kieran draws two rectangles.
Rectangle R has length 12 cm and width 7 cm.
Rectangle S has length 30 cm and width 21 cm.
Kieran says that the two rectangles are similar.
Is he correct?
Explain your answer.

3 A cuboid has height 3 cm and volume 60 cm^3
Work out the volume of a similar cuboid of height 6 cm.

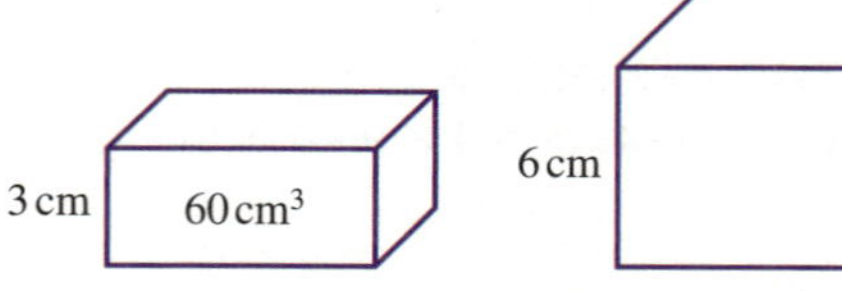

4 Two triangles are similar.
Triangle A has base 9 cm and area 54 cm^2
Triangle B has area of 6 cm^2
Work out the length of the base of triangle B.

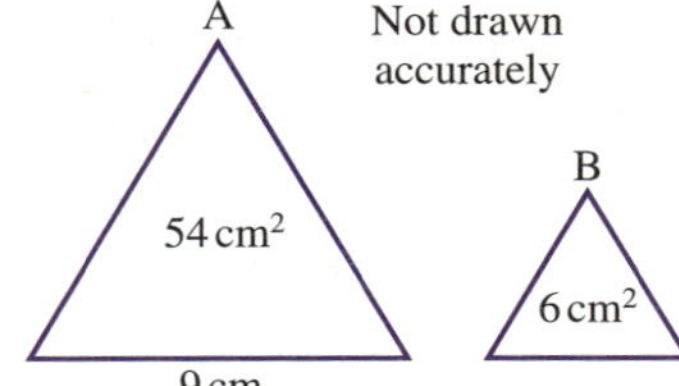

5 A box of height 4 cm has a surface area of 76 cm^2 and a volume of 40 cm^3
A similar box has height 2 cm.
For the second box, work out:
a its surface area **b** its volume.

6 Two paintings are similar rectangles.
Painting A has length 5.5 cm and area 44 cm^2
Painting B has area 176 cm^2
Work out the length of painting B.

7 P and Q are two similar parallelograms.
P has base 8 cm and area 56 cm^2
Q has base 12 cm.
Calculate the area of Q.

8 A square-based pyramid with a base of side 2.5 cm has volume 15 cm^3
What is the volume of a similar square-based pyramid with a base of side 7.5 cm?

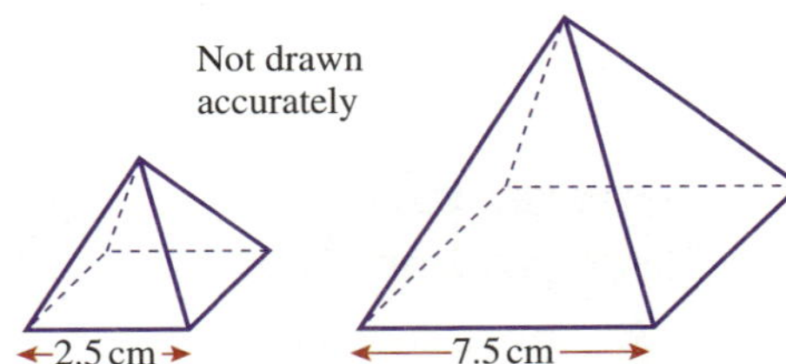

9 Orange juice is sold in two similar cans of different sizes.
The small size can has height 6 cm and holds 150 ml of orange juice.
The large can has height of 9 cm.
How much orange juice does the large can hold?

Chapter summary

- Two shapes are congruent when they are exactly the same shape and size.
- There are four *conditions of congruence.*
  - Three pairs of sides are equal – **SSS**.

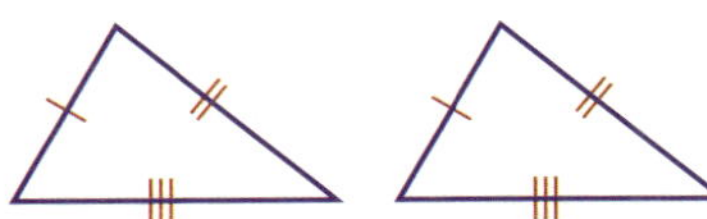

  - Two pairs of sides and the angle between them are equal – **SAS**.

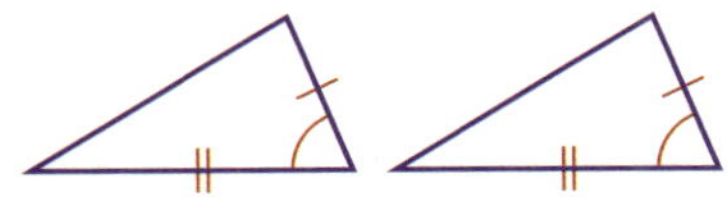

- Two pairs of angles and a corresponding side are equal – **ASA** or **AAS**.

 or 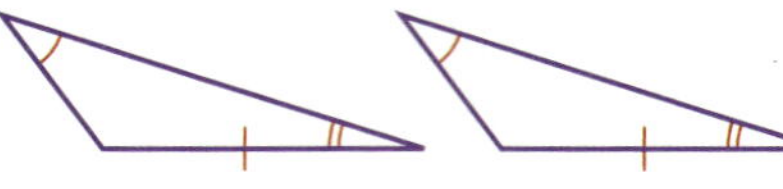

- For a right-angled triangle the hypotenuse and one other pair of sides are equal – **RHS**.

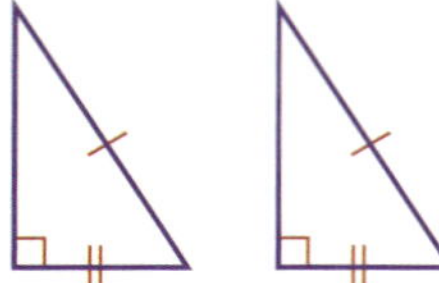

- When two figures are similar:
  - the corresponding angles are equal
  - the lengths of the corresponding sides are in the same ratio – the scale factor of the enlargement.
- When a shape is enlarged by scale factor k
  - the area is enlarged by scale factor k^2
  - the volume is enlarged by scale factor k^3

Chapter review

1 Two congruent triangles are shown.
Angle B = angle F.

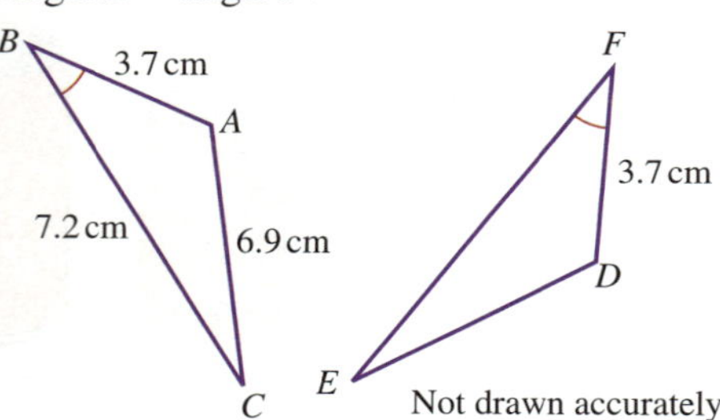

a Write down the length of DE.
b Explain why angle C = angle E.

2 Triangles P and Q are congruent.

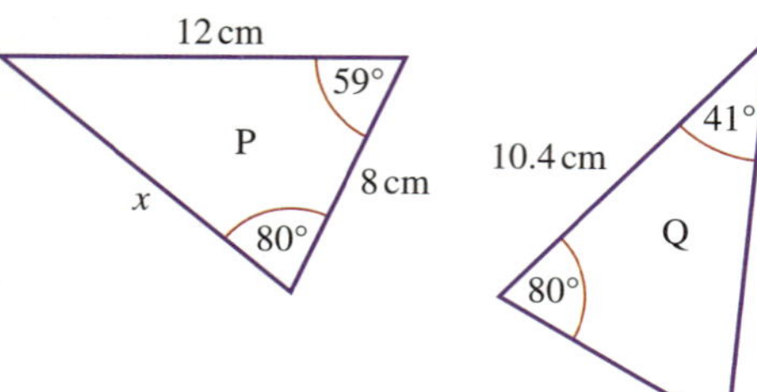

Write down the values of x and y.

3 Triangles ABC and DEF are similar.
Angle C = angle F.

a Calculate the length of DF.

b Calculate the length of BC.

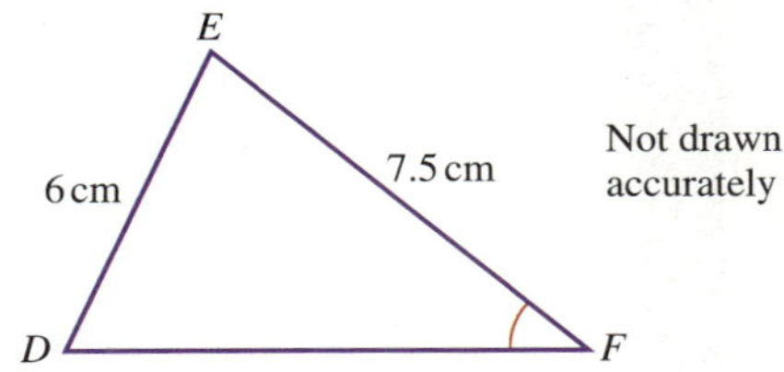

4 Triangle T and triangles A, B, C, D and E are not drawn accurately.

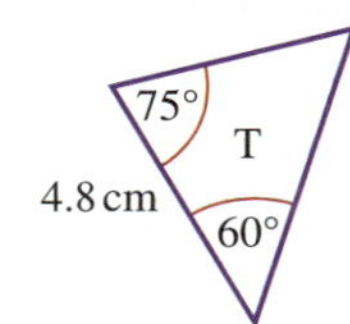

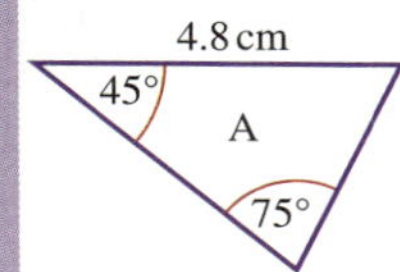

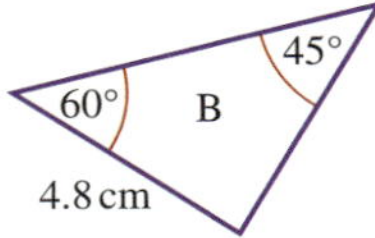

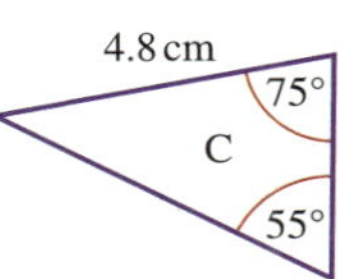

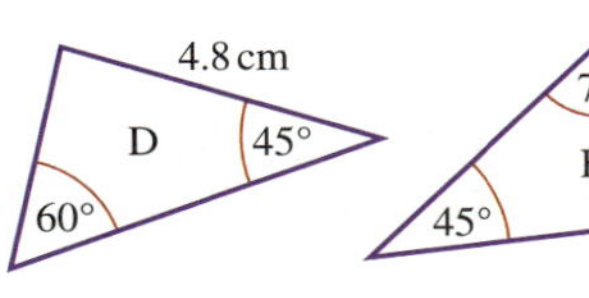

Which two of triangles A, B, C, D and E are congruent to triangle T?

5 Show that triangles ABC and DEF are congruent.

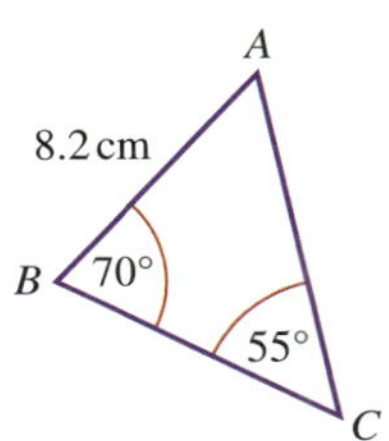

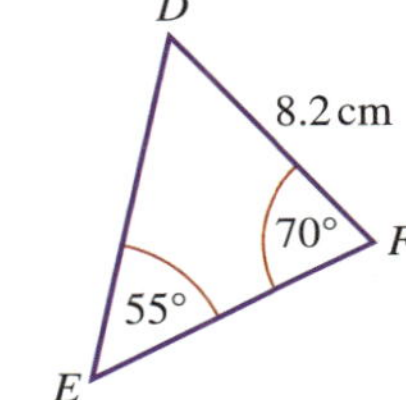

6 Triangles PQR and PRS are similar.

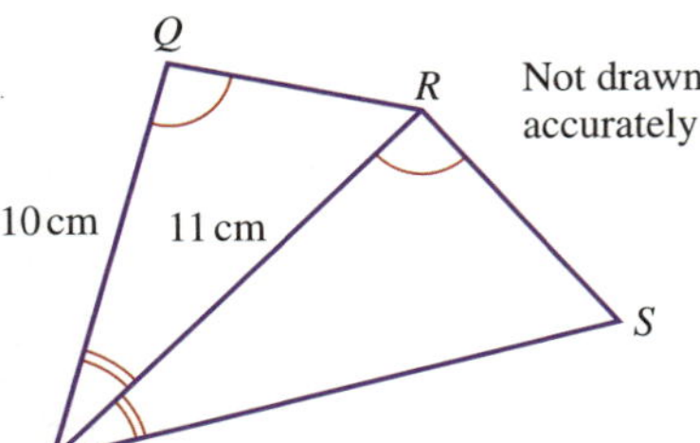

Calculate the length of PS.

7 $ABCD$ is a rectangle.
ADE is a straight line.
Angle ACE is 90°.

a Explain why triangles ABC and ACE are similar.

b Find the length of AE giving your answer to one decimal place.

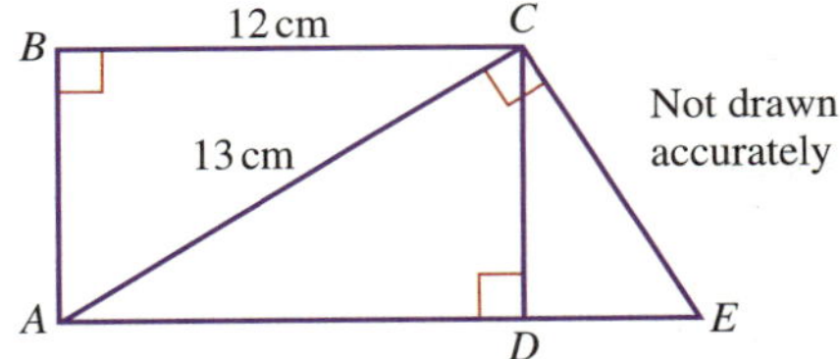

8 The diagram shows triangles ABC and ADE.
DE is parallel to BC.
Calculate the length of BD.

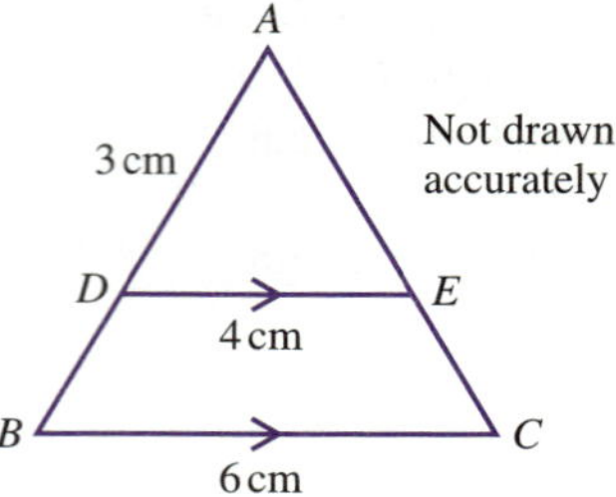

9 A square-based pyramid with base of side 3 cm has surface area 19.5 cm^2
What is the surface area of a similar square-based pyramid with a base of side 9 cm?

10 A company produces mugs in two sizes.
Small mugs are 6 cm high and can hold 108 cm^3 of liquid.
Large mugs are 8 cm high and are identical in shape to small mugs.
To calculate the volume of a large mug, the volume of a small mug must be multiplied by the number k.

a Express k as an exact fraction.

b Calculate the volume of a large mug.

Simultaneous linear equations

CHAPTER 27

27.1 Using a graphical method

CAN YOU REMEMBER

- How to draw linear graphs of the form $y = mx + c$ and $px + qy = r$?
- That straight lines with the same gradient are parallel?

IN THIS SECTION YOU WILL

- Learn about simultaneous equations.
- Learn how to use graphs to solve a pair of simultaneous equations.
- Use simultaneous equations to solve problems.

There are many pairs of values of x and y that satisfy $x + y = 8$
For example, (0, 8), (1, 7), (2, 6), (3, 5), …
There are also many pairs of values of x and y that satisfy $y = 3x$.
For example, (0, 0), (1, 3), (2, 6), (3, 9), …
From these lists you can see that $x = 2$ and $y = 6$ satisfy **both** $x + y = 8$ and $y = 3x$.

The graphs show that this is the **only** pair of values of x and y that satisfy both functions.
The lines cross at the point (2, 6) and nowhere else.
$x + y = 8$ and $y = 3x$ are called *simultaneous equations*.
Their solution is $x = 2$ and $y = 6$
The solution of a pair of simultaneous equations is the pair of values of the two unknowns that satisfy **both** equations.

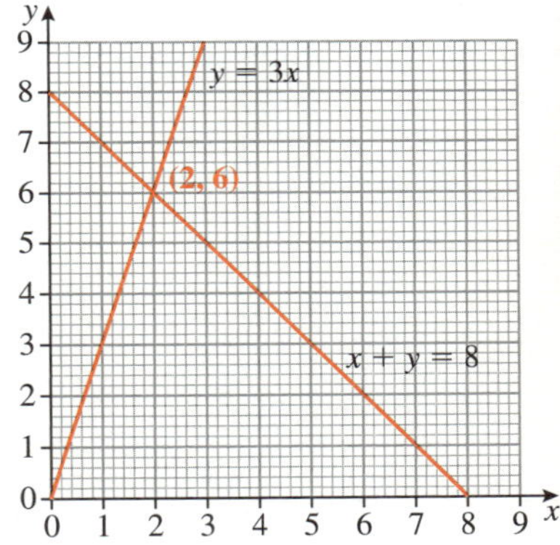

Example 1

Use a graphical method to solve the simultaneous equations:
$y - 2x = 1$ $\qquad$ $y + 2x = 5$

Solution 1

Draw the graphs of both functions on the same grid.

Method 1
$y - 2x = 1$ can be rearranged to $y = 2x + 1$
$y = 2x + 1$ has gradient 2 and y-intercept 1

$y + 2x = 5$ can be rearranged to $y = -2x + 5$
$y = -2x + 5$ has gradient -2 and y-intercept 5

Method 2

x	0	$-\frac{1}{2}$
y	1	0

The graph of $y - 2x = 1$ passes through (0, 1) and ($-\frac{1}{2}$, 0).

x	0	$2\frac{1}{2}$
y	5	0

The graph of $y + 2x = 5$ passes through (0, 5) and ($2\frac{1}{2}$, 0).
The graphs cross at the point (1, 3).
The solution is $x = 1$ and $y = 3$
Check: Substitute $x = 1$ into both equations:

$y - 2x = 1$	$y + 2x = 5$
$y - 2 = 1$	$y + 2 = 5$
$y = 3$	$y = 3$ ✓

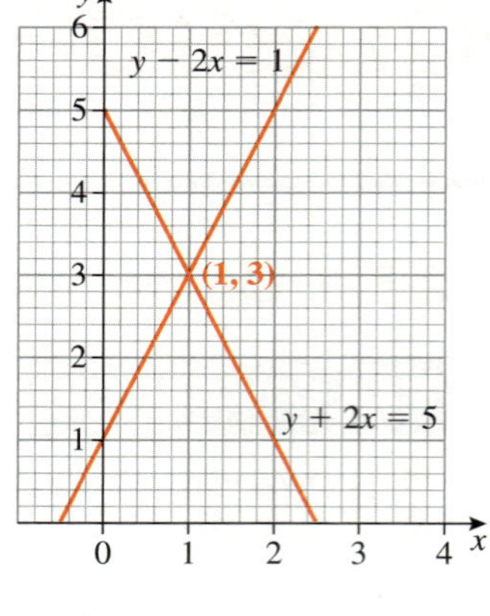

Exercise A

1 The graphs of $y = x - 1$, $y = 2x + 1$ and $x + y = 1$ are shown on the grid.
Use the graphs to solve the simultaneous equations:

a $y = x - 1$
$y = 2x + 1$

b $x + y = 1$
$y = x - 1$

c $x + y = 1$
$y = 2x + 1$

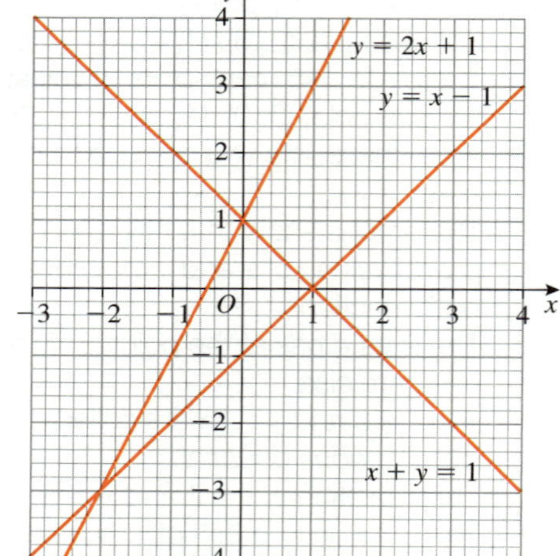

2 Copy the graph of $3y - x = 3$ shown on the grid.
By drawing another graph on the same grid solve the simultaneous equations
$3y - x = 3$
$2y + x = 7$

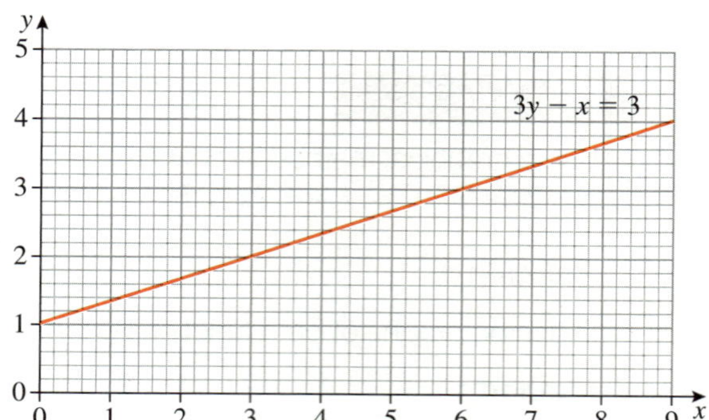

3 Draw the graph of $2y + x = 2$ for values of x from -4 to 3
By drawing another graph on the same grid solve the simultaneous equations:
$2y + x = 2$ $\quad$ $2x - y = -6$

4 Draw and label a grid with the x-axis from 0 to 4 and the y-axis from 0 to 6
On the grid draw graphs to solve the simultaneous equations:
$y - 2x = 1$ $\quad$ $y - x = 3$

5 Draw and label a grid with the x-axis from -3 to 4 and the y-axis from -2 to 6
On the grid draw graphs to solve the simultaneous equations:
$2y + x = 2$ $\quad$ $2x - y = -6$

6 Use graphs to solve each of the following pairs of simultaneous equations.
In each case you will need to draw a suitable grid.

a $y = 3x - 2$
$x + 2y = 10$

b $2y - 3x = 6$
$x + y = 8$

c $y - 4x = 1$
$y - 2x = 3$

d $y + 3x = 2$
$y - 2x = -3$

e $y - 2x = -1$
$y + 2x = 5$

f $2x - y = -3$
$x + 2y = -4$

Example 2

Explain why the simultaneous equations $6x + 4y = 12$ and $3x + 2y = 9$ have no solution.

Solution 2

Method 1
Draw the graphs of both lines.
$6x + 4y = 12$ passes through the points (0, 3) and (2, 0).
$3x + 2y = 9$ passes through the points (0, 4.5) and (3, 0).

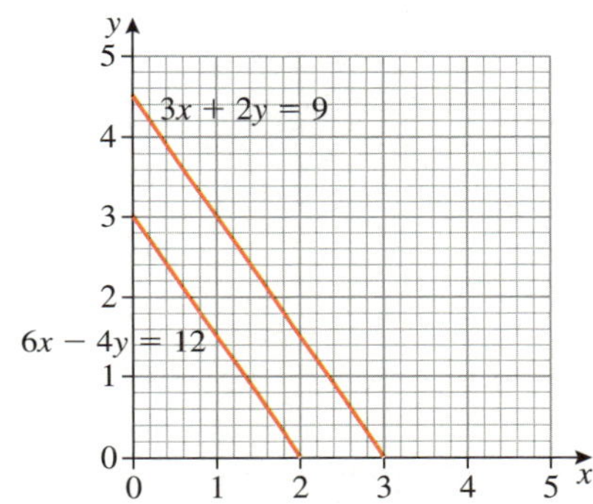

Method 2
Rearrange both equations into the form $y = mx + c$.

$6x + 4y = 12$	Subtract $6x$ from both sides.
$4y = -6x + 12$	Divide both sides by 4
$y = -1.5x + 3$	
$3x + 2y = 9$	Subtract $3x$ from both sides.
$2y = -3x + 9$	Divide both sides by 2
$y = -1.5x + 4.5$	

The rearranged equations show that both lines have gradient -1.5
Both methods show that the lines are parallel.
Parallel lines do not intersect so there is no solution.

Simultaneous equations that produce parallel graphs have no solution.
Simultaneous equations can be used to solve problems.

Example 3

On Monday Trevor buys four cups of tea and two cups of coffee. He pays £3.60
On Tuesday Trevor buys two cups of tea and five cups of coffee. He pays £4.60
On Wednesday morning Trevor buys four cups of tea and five cups of coffee.
Using a graphical method, work out how much change Trevor gets from a £10 note.

Solution 3

Step 1: Assign a letter symbol to each variable.
Let t pence stand for the cost of a cup of tea.
Let c pence stand for the cost of a cup of coffee.

Step 2: Write functions to represent the situations in the problem.
£3.60 = 360 pence and £4.60 = 460 pence
Monday: $4t + 2c = 360$ Tuesday: $2t + 5c = 460$
Step 3: Draw the graphs of each function on the same grid.
$4t + 2c = 360$
When $t = 0$, $c = 180$: this gives the point (0, 180).
When $c = 0$, $t = 90$: this gives the point (90, 0).
$2t + 5c = 460$
When $t = 0$, $c = 92$: this gives the point (0, 92).
When $c = 0$, $t = 230$: this gives the point (230, 0).

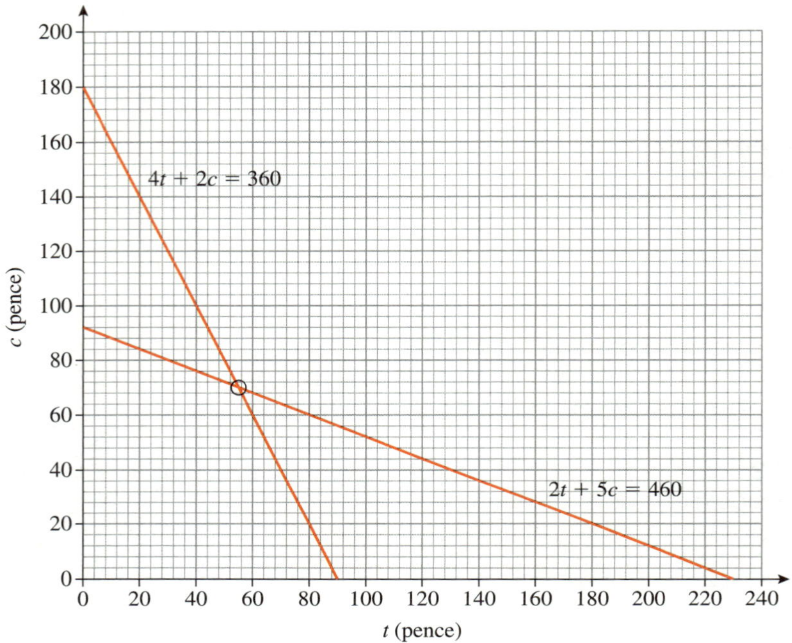

Step 4: Use the graph to find t and c
The lines cross at (55, 70)
$t = 55$ and $c = 70$
Check: Substitute $t = 55$ into both equations.

$4t + 2c = 360$	$2t + 5c = 460$
$220 + 2c = 360$	$110 + 5c = 460$
$2c = 140$	$5c = 350$
$c = 70$ ✓	$c = 70$ ✓

Step 5: Solve the problem.
$4t + 5c = 4 \times 55 + 5 \times 70 = 570$
On Wednesday Trevor pays £5.70
His change from £10 is £4.30

Exercise B

1 Explain why each of the following pairs of simultaneous equations do **not** have a solution.

a $\frac{1}{2}x - y = 4$
$2y - x = 10$

b $y - 3x = 9$
$3y = 9x + 1$

c $8y - 6x = 12$
$4y = 3x + 24$

You **must** show your working.

2 Which of the pairs of simultaneous equations on these cards has no solution? Explain your answer.

$4x - y = 4$ $4y - x = 1$	$y - 4x = 1$ $4y - x = 4$
$y + 4x = 1$ $4y + x = 4$	$y + 4x = 4$ $y = -4x + 1$

3 Samantha uses a graphical method to solve this pair of simultaneous equations.
$x + 2y = 4$
$2x + y = 5$
Her work is shown on the right.
Samantha has made errors in her work.
Find Samantha's errors and correct them.

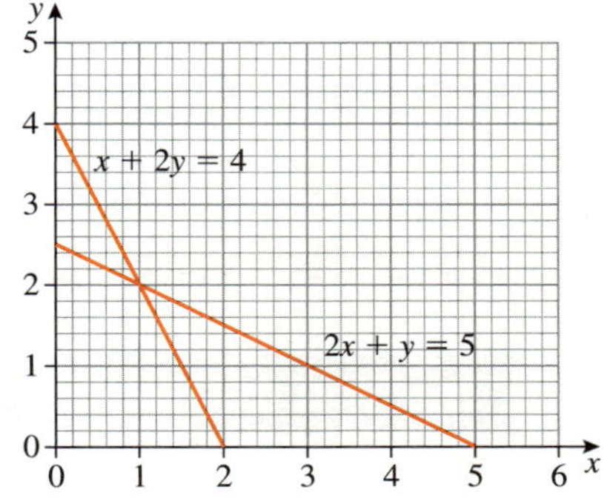

The solution is $x = 2$ and $y = 1$

4 The sum of two numbers, x and y, is 8 where y is the bigger number. The difference between the two numbers is 3
- **a** Write down two equations involving x and y.
- **b** Draw the graphs of both equations on a grid with both x and y from 0 to 9
- **c** Use your graphs to work out the values of x and y.

5 Amina buys three doughnuts and two sticky buns for a total cost of 60 pence.
Bryony buys two doughnuts and four sticky buns for a total cost of 80 pence.
Let x be the cost of one doughnut and y the cost of one sticky bun.
- **a** Use the information to write two equations in x and y.
- **b** On a copy of this grid draw graphs for each of the equations.
- **c** Use the graphs to find the values of x and y.

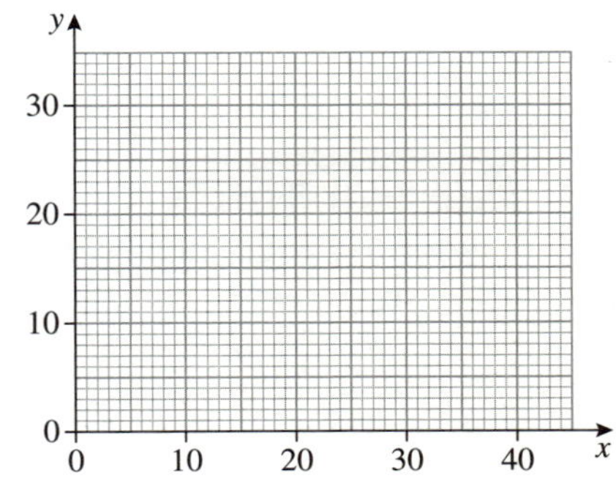

6 Ben goes on a short run.
- **a** On the outward leg he runs uphill for x metres at a speed of 5 m/s.
  He then runs downhill for y metres at a speed of 10 m/s.
  He takes a total of 50 seconds.
  - **i** Explain why $\frac{x}{5} + \frac{y}{10} = 50$
  - **ii** Re-write this equation without fractions.
- **b** On the return leg Ben runs in the opposite direction.
  He runs uphill for y metres at a speed of 5 m/s.
  He runs downhill for x metres at a speed of 10 m/s.
  He takes a total of 55 seconds.
  Write an equation for the return leg.
- **c** Draw graphs of the equations for the outward and return legs of Ben's run.
  Use a grid with both x and y from 0 to 600 with a scale of 50 m to 1 cm.
- **d** Use your graphs to work out how far Ben runs uphill on his run.

7 Billy sets Jessica a 'think of a number' puzzle.

a Jessica uses simultaneous equations and a graphical method to solve the puzzle.
Show Jessica's solution.

b Explain why Billy has to give Jessica two clues.

27.2 Solving simultaneous equations algebraically

CAN YOU REMEMBER

- How to use the balance method to solve linear equations?

IN THIS SECTION YOU WILL

- Learn how to solve simultaneous equations using the elimination method.
- Extend skills in using simultaneous equations to solve problems.

Simultaneous equations can be solved algebraically.
The balance method is used to *eliminate* one of the two variables in the equations.

Example 1

Solve the simultaneous equations.

a $4x + y = 15$
$x + y = 12$

b $4x + y = 6$
$3x - y = 8$

Solution 1

a **Step 1:** Label each equation.
$4x + y = 15$ A
$x + y = 12$ B
Step 2: The y terms match and they have the **s**ame signs.
Eliminate the y terms by **s**ubtracting the equations.
$3x = 3$ A − B
Step 3: Solve this equation to find x.
$x = 1$
Step 4: Substitute $x = 1$ into equation A to work out y.
$4 + y = 15$
$y = 11$
Step 5: Check the solution by substituting $x = 1$ and $y = 11$ into equation B.
$x + y = 1 + 11 = 12$ ✓
The solution is $x = 1$ and $y = 11$

b **Step 1:** Label each equation.
$4x + y = 6$ A
$3x - y = 8$ B
Step 2: The y terms match but they have **d**ifferent signs.
Eliminate the y terms by a**d**ding the equations.
$7x = 14$ A + B
Step 3: Solve this equation to find x.
$x = 2$
Step 4: Substitute $x = 2$ into equation A to work out y.
$8 + y = 6$
$y = -2$
Step 5: Check the solution by substituting $x = 2$ and $y = -2$ into Equation B.
$3x - y = 3 \times 2 - -2 = 6 - -2 = 8$ ✓
The solution is $x = 2$ and $y = -2$

Sometimes one of the equations has to be multiplied to make the x terms or y terms the same.

Example 2

Solve the simultaneous equations.

a $3x + 2y = 10$
$x + 4y = 5$

b $2x - 3y = 9$
$4x + y = 4$

Solution 2

a **Step 1:** Label each equation.
$3x + 2y = 10$ A
$x + 4y = 5$ B
There are two possible methods.

Method 1: Eliminate the y terms.
Step 2: To make the y terms match multiply equation A by 2
$6x + 4y = 20$ A × 2
$x + 4y = 5$ B
Step 3: The y terms have the **s**ame signs. Eliminate the y terms by **s**ubtracting the equations.
$5x = 15$ A × 2 − B
$x = 3$
Step 4: Substitute $x = 3$ into equation A to work out y.
$9 + 2y = 10$
$2y = 1$
$y = \frac{1}{2}$

Method 2: Eliminate the x terms.
Step 2: To make the x terms match multiply equation B by 3
$3x + 2y = 10$ A
$3x + 12y = 15$ B × 3
Step 3: The x terms have the **s**ame signs. Eliminate the x terms by **s**ubtracting the equations.
$10y = 5$ B × 3 − A
$y = \frac{1}{2}$
Step 4: Substitute $y = \frac{1}{2}$ into equation A to work out x.
$3x + 1 = 10$
$3x = 9$
$x = 3$

Step 5: Check the solution by substituting $x = 3$ and $y = \frac{1}{2}$ into Equation B.
$x + 4y = 3 + 4 \times \frac{1}{2} = 3 + 2 = 5$ ✓
The solution is $x = 3$ and $y = \frac{1}{2}$

b **Step 1:** Label each equation.
$2x - 3y = 9$ A
$4x + y = 4$ B
Again there are two possible methods. However, there is less chance of making an error if terms are eliminated by a**d**ding.
So eliminate the y terms because they have **d**ifferent signs.

Step 2: To make the y terms match multiply equation B by 3

$2x - 3y = 9$ A

$12x + 3y = 12$ B × 3

Step 3: Eliminate the y terms by adding.

$14x = 21$ A + B × 3

Step 4: Solve this equation to calculate the value of x.

$x = \frac{21}{14} = 1\frac{1}{2}$

Step 5: Substitute $x = 1\frac{1}{2}$ into equation A to work out y.

$3 - 3y = 9$

$-3y = 6$

$y = -2$

Step 6: Check the solution by substituting $x = 1\frac{1}{2}$ and $y = -2$ into equation B.

$4x + y = 4 \times 1\frac{1}{2} + -2 = 6 + -2 = 4$ ✓

The solution is $x = 1\frac{1}{2}$ and $y = -2$

Exercise A

1 Solve the simultaneous equations.

a $x + y = 12$, $x - y = 2$ **b** $x + 2y = 10$, $x - 2y = 2$ **c** $x + 3y = 7$, $x - 3y = 1$ **d** $2x + y = 3$, $2x - y = 1$

e $4x + 3y = 11$, $-4x - y = -9$ **f** $5x + y = 14$, $x - y = 4$ **g** $a + 6b = 4$, $5a - 6b = -16$ **h** $3r + 2s = 10$, $5r - 2s = 14$

i $4p + q = 0$, $6p - q = 5$ **j** $8m + 3n = 10$, $4m - 3n = -13$ **k** $-3c + 2d = -9$, $3c - d = 4$

2 Solve the simultaneous equations.

a $x + 3y = 10$, $x + 2y = 7$ **b** $3x + 4y = 10$, $3x + 2y = 8$ **c** $3x + 2y = 19$, $x + 2y = 9$ **d** $3x + y = -8$, $3x + 10y = 1$

e $-5x + 8y = 2$, $x + 8y = -10$ **f** $6x + 4y = 15$, $2x + 4y = 13$ **g** $a + 3b = 3$, $a + 6b = 2$ **h** $r - 2s = 8$, $3r - 2s = 12$

i $-p + q = 8$, $-p + 5q = 36$ **j** $11m - 5n = 12$, $4m - 5n = 5$ **k** $13c - 7d = 21$, $6c - 7d = 21$

3 Solve the simultaneous equations.

a $2x + 3y = 20$, $2x - 3y = -16$ **b** $x + 3y = 11$, $x - 3y = -13$ **c** $5x + 3y = -5$, $2x + 3y = 19$ **d** $a + b = 0$, $a - b = -1$

e $-2p + 3q = 0$, $p + 3q = 0$ **f** $3c + 2d = 2$, $3c - 2d = 0$

4 Solve the simultaneous equations.

a $4x + 3y = 7$, $x - y = 0$ **b** $7x + 3y = 27$, $5x - y = 13$ **c** $4x + 3y = -2$, $x - y = 3$ **d** $2x + 6y = -23$, $4x + y = -2$

e $-x + 2y = 11$, $9x + y = -23$ **f** $a + 10b = -2$, $-3a + 20b = 1$ **g** $2r + s = 11$, $3r - 2s = 6$ **h** $p + q = 7$, $11p - 4q = 2$

i $2m + 3n = 5$, $4m - n = 17$ **j** $2c + 4d = 7$, $6c + d = -1$

5 Solve the simultaneous equations.

a $2x + y = 15$, $6x - 2y = 40$ **b** $2x + 3y = 12$, $5x - 6y = 3$ **c** $x + 7y = 6$, $3x - y = -4$ **d** $8x + y = 4$, $-2x + 3y = -1$

e $x + 4y = -8$, $2x - 12y = -1$ **f** $3a + 2b = 9$, $6a + b = 6$ **g** $4r + s = 5$, $-2r + 3s = -6$ **h** $7p + 4q = 1$, $14p - q = -16$

i $9m + 2n = 19$, $3m - 4n = 4$ **j** $c + 4d = 10$, $6c + d = -9$

Sometimes **both** equations have to be multiplied to make terms match.

Example 3

Solve the simultaneous equations.

a $3x + 2y = 1$
$5x + 3y = 3$

b $2x - 3y = 11$
$3x + 4y = -\frac{1}{2}$

Solution 3

a **Step 1:** Label each equation.
$3x + 2y = 1$ A
$5x + 3y = 3$ B
There are two possible methods.

Method 1: Eliminate the x terms.
Step 2: Make the x terms match by multiplying equation A by 5 and equation B by 3
$\mathbf{15x} + 10y = 5$ A × 5
$\mathbf{15x} + 9y = 9$ B × 3
Step 3: The x terms have the **s**ame signs so they can be eliminated by **s**ubtracting the equations.
$y = -4$ A × 5 − B × 3
Step 4: Substitute $y = -4$ into equation A to work out y.
$3x + -8 = 1$
$3x = 9$
$x = 3$

Method 2: Eliminate the y terms.
Step 2: Make the y terms match by multiplying equation A by 3 and equation B by 2
$9x \mathbf{+ 6y} = 3$ A × 3
$10x \mathbf{+ 6y} = 6$ B × 2
Step 3: The y terms have the **s**ame signs so they can be eliminated by **s**ubtracting the equations.
$x = 3$ B × 2 − A × 3
Step 4: Substitute $x = 3$ into equation A to work out y.
$9 + 2y = 1$
$2y = -8$
$y = -4$

Step 5: Check the solution by substituting $x = 3$ and $y = -4$ into equation B.
$5x + 3y = 5 \times 3 + 3 \times -4 = 15 + -12 = 3$ ✓
The solution is $x = 3$ and $y = -4$

b **Step 1:** Label each equation.
$2x \mathbf{- 3y} = 11$ A
$3x \mathbf{+ 4y} = -\frac{1}{2}$ B
Again, there are two possible methods. However, there is less chance of making an error if terms are eliminated by a**d**ding.
So eliminate the y terms because they have **d**ifferent signs.
Step 2: To make the y terms match, multiply equation A by 4 and equation B by 3
$8x \mathbf{- 12y} = 44$ A × 4
$9x \mathbf{+ 12y} = -1\frac{1}{2}$ B × 3
Step 3: A**d**d the equations to eliminate the y terms.
$17x = 42\frac{1}{2}$ A × 4 + B × 3
Step 4: Solve this equation to calculate the value of x.
$x = \frac{42.5}{17} = 2\frac{1}{2}$
Step 5: Substitute $x = 2\frac{1}{2}$ into equation A to work out y.
$5 - 3y = 11$
$-3y = 6$
$y = -2$
Step 6: Check the solution by substituting $x = 2\frac{1}{2}$ and $y = -2$ into equation B.
$3x + 4y = 3 \times 2\frac{1}{2} + 4 \times -2 = 7\frac{1}{2} + -8 = -\frac{1}{2}$ ✓
The solution is $x = 2\frac{1}{2}$ and $y = -2$

Example 4

The line with equation $px + qy = 30$ passes through the points $(2, -5)$ and $(14, 10)$.
Find the values of p and q.

Solution 4

Step 1: Assign a letter symbol to each unknown.
The unknowns are p and q.
Step 2: Write equations to represent the situations in the problem.
The line passes through $(2, -5)$, so when $x = 2$, $y = -5$
Substituting in $px + qy = 30$ gives $p \times 2 + q \times -5 = 30$
This gives the equation $2p - 5q = 30$
Similarly, the point $(14, 10)$ gives the equation $14p + 10q = 30$
Step 3: Solve the equations.
$2p - 5q = 30$ A
$14p + 10q = 30$ B
Eliminate the q terms because they have **d**ifferent signs.
To make the q terms match multiply equation A by 2
$4p - 10q = 60$ A × 2
$14p + 10q = 30$ B
To eliminate the q terms a**d**d the equations.
$18p = 90$ A × 2 + B
$p = 5$
Substitute $p = 5$ into equation A to work out q.
$10 - 5q = 30$
$-5q = 20$
$q = -4$
Check the solution by substituting the values into equation B.
$14p + 10q = 14 \times 5 + 10 \times -4 = 70 + -40 = 30$ ✓
The solution is $p = 5$ and $q = -4$
Step 4: Answer the problem.
The equation of the line is $5x - 4y = 30$

Exercise B

1 Solve the simultaneous equations.

a $3x + 4y = 11$, $4x - 3y = -2$
b $2x + 5y = 11$, $5x - 3y = 12$
c $10x + 7y = 22$, $3x - 4y = 31$
d $5x + 11y = -5$, $7x - 5y = -7$
e $10x - 3y = 14$, $3x + 5y = -13.5$
f $4x + 2y = -9$, $3x - 6y = -10.5$
g $3r + 4s = 2$, $2r - 5s = 9$
h $2p + q = 4$, $p - \frac{1}{2}q = 4$
i $2m + 3n = -3\frac{1}{2}$, $3m + 2n = -9$
j $2c + 4d = 8$, $3c + 5d = 9$

2 Solve the simultaneous equations.

a $2x + 3y = 5$, $3x + 2y = 5$
b $x + 3y = 7$, $3x + y = 13$
c $4x + 3y = 3$, $2x + 6y = 24$
d $23x + 2y = 44$, $8x + 3y = 13$
e $7x + 3y = -11$, $5x + 2y = -8$
f $4a + 3b = 0$, $6a + 2b = \frac{5}{6}$
g $2r + \frac{1}{4}s = -4$, $3r - 2s = -25$
h $4p - 3q = 7$, $5p - 4q = 9$
i $-2m + 5n = 11\frac{1}{2}$, $3m + 2n = -3$
j $2c + 4d = 2\frac{1}{3}$, $5c + 3d = 3\frac{1}{2}$

3 Matthew saves x five-pence coins and y two-pence coins.
Altogether he saves 50 coins.
The total value of the coins is £1.90
a Write down **two** equations in x and y.
b Solve the equations to calculate x and y.

4 200 tickets for a concert are sold for a total of £720
Tickets cost £5 for adults and £3 for children.
How many tickets of each type are sold?

5 A graph with equation $y = ax^2 + bx$ passes through the points (2, 8) and (3, 15).
Find the values of a and b.

6 There are x seats in a first-class carriage and y seats in a standard-class carriage.
A train leaves Newcastle at 0815. It has three first-class carriages and five standard-class carriages and a total of 595 seats.
Another train leaves Newcastle at 1035. It has two first-class carriages and six standard-class carriages and a total of 610 seats.
Use an algebraic method to find the values of x and y.

7 Tim cycles to school.
He goes uphill for x metres and then downhill for y metres.
On his return from school he cycles y metres uphill and x metres downhill.
Tim cycles at a speed of 20 m/s downhill and 10 m/s uphill.
He takes a total of 3 minutes to get to school and 4 minutes to cycle home.
Find the values of x and y.

Chapter summary

- The solution of a pair of simultaneous equations is the pair of values of the two unknowns that satisfy **both** equations.
- The solution to a pair of simultaneous equations can be found graphically by drawing the graph of each equation and finding the coordinates of the point where they cross.
  If the graphs cross at the point (a, b), the solution is $x = a$ and $y = b$.
- If the graphs of two simultaneous equations are parallel, they do not intersect and the simultaneous equations do not have a solution.
- Simultaneous equations can also be solved algebraically using the method of elimination.
  - Step 1: Decide which of the unknowns to eliminate.
  - Step 2: If necessary multiply one or both of the equations to make the terms to be eliminated match.
  - Step 3: Eliminate the unknown by adding or subtracting the two equations with matching unknown terms.
  - Step 4: Solve the resulting equation to find the value of the other unknown.
  - Step 5: Substitute this value into one of the original equations to find the other unknown.
  - Step 6: Use the other equation to check the solution.
- Simultaneous equations can be used to solve problems involving two unknowns.
  First use the information given to write two simultaneous equations.
  Solve the simultaneous equations using either a graphical or algebraic method.

Chapter review

1 The graph shows the function $x + 3y = 6$

a On a copy of the same grid draw the graph of $y = \frac{1}{3}x$

b Use your graph to solve the simultaneous equations $x + 3y = 6$ and $y = \frac{1}{3}x$

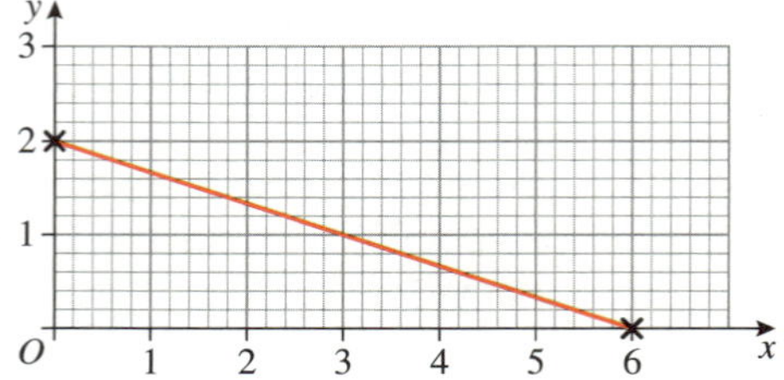

2 Use a graphical method to solve the simultaneous equations:

$2x + 3y = 12 \qquad 3x - 2y = 5$

3 The sum of two numbers, x and y, is 26
The difference of the two numbers is 8

a Write down two equations in terms of x and y.

b Solve the equations to work out the two numbers.

4 Solve the simultaneous equations.

a $x + 2y = 12$
$x - 2y = 8$

b $3x + 4y = 11$
$4x - 2y = 11$

c $2x + 3y = 5$
$5x + 9y = 11$

Do **not** use trial and improvement.
You **must** show your working.

5 Solve the simultaneous equations.

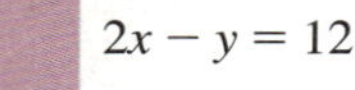

$2x - y = 12 \qquad 3x + 4y = 7$

6 A school canteen sells apples and bananas.
A group of students buy 12 apples and 3 bananas.
The total cost is £6.90
A different group of students buy 5 apples and 8 bananas.
The total cost is £6.25
How much does it cost to buy 3 apples and 7 bananas?

7 Solve the simultaneous equations.

$14x + 9y = 7 \qquad 6x + 2y = 16$

Do **not** use trial and improvement.
You **must** show your working.

8 Three fish and four portions of chips costs £9.75
Two fish and five portions of chips costs £9.65
What is the cost of one fish and one portion of chips?

Working with exact numbers

CHAPTER 28

28.1 Terminating and recurring decimals

CAN YOU REMEMBER

- How to convert a fraction to a decimal and a decimal to a fraction?
- Simple fractions and their equivalent decimals?
- The meaning of 'prime factor'?

IN THIS SECTION YOU WILL

- Learn the meaning of 'terminating decimal' and 'recurring decimal'.
- Learn how to distinguish between fractions which convert to terminating decimals and fractions which convert to recurring decimals.
- Convert a recurring decimal to a fraction.

A *terminating decimal* has a fixed number of decimal places, for example 0.123 or 6.75

A *recurring decimal* does not have a fixed number of decimal places and has a repeating pattern, for example 0.333… or 7.412 121 2…

All fractions can be converted into either a terminating or recurring decimal.

For example:

Fraction	$\frac{1}{2}$	$\frac{1}{3}$	$\frac{1}{4}$	$\frac{1}{5}$	$\frac{1}{6}$	$\frac{1}{7}$	$\frac{1}{8}$	$\frac{1}{9}$	$\frac{1}{10}$
Decimal	0.5	0.333…	0.25	0.2	0.1666…	0.142 857 142 857…	0.125	0.111…	0.1
Terminating (T) or recurring (R)	T	R	T	T	R	R	T	R	T

Fractions with denominators whose only prime factors are 2 or 5 are terminating decimals, for example, $\frac{1}{2}$, $\frac{1}{4}$, $\frac{1}{5}$, $\frac{1}{10}$

Fractions with denominators whose prime factors are **not** only 2 or 5 are recurring decimals, for example, $\frac{1}{3}$, $\frac{1}{6}$, $\frac{1}{7}$, $\frac{1}{9}$

Example 1

Which of these fractions convert to terminating decimals and which convert to recurring decimals?

$\frac{3}{4}$ $\quad$ $\frac{5}{6}$ $\quad$ $\frac{2}{7}$ $\quad$ $\frac{7}{10}$ $\quad$ $\frac{1}{13}$ $\quad$ $\frac{11}{100}$

Solution 1

$\frac{3}{4}$: denominator = 4, only prime factor of 4 is 2 so it is a terminating decimal.
$\frac{5}{6}$: denominator = 6, only prime factors of 6 are 2 and 3 so it is a recurring decimal.
$\frac{2}{7}$: denominator = 7, only prime factor of 7 is 7 so it is a recurring decimal.
$\frac{7}{10}$: denominator = 10, only prime factors of 10 are 2 and 5 so it is a terminating decimal.
$\frac{1}{13}$: denominator = 13, only prime factor of 13 is 13 so it is a recurring decimal.
$\frac{11}{100}$: denominator = 100, only prime factors of 100 are 2 and 5 so it is a terminating decimal.

Recurring decimals can be written using dot notation.
For example 0.333 333… can be written $0.\dot{3}$
5.047 474 7… can be written $5.0\dot{4}\dot{7}$
12.901 901 901… can be written $12.\dot{9}0\dot{1}$
The dots mean that the digits continue repeating in the same pattern.

Exercise A

1 Which of these fractions convert to terminating decimals and which convert to recurring decimals?

$\frac{2}{3}$ $\quad\frac{3}{10}$ $\quad\frac{1}{9}$ $\quad\frac{4}{5}$ $\quad\frac{9}{11}$ $\quad\frac{19}{20}$ $\quad\frac{8}{15}$ $\quad\frac{7}{30}$ $\quad\frac{13}{50}$ $\quad\frac{1}{25}$

2 Write each of these recurring decimals using dot notation.
a 0.111… **b** 0.121 212… **c** 0.123 123 123…
d 4.676 767… **e** 8.023 232 3… **f** 17.009 999 999…
g 3.190 490 490 4 **h** 4.213 535 35…

3 **a** Use a calculator to convert $\frac{1}{7}$ to a decimal.
Write your answer using dot notation.
b Repeat part **a** for $\frac{2}{7}$, $\frac{3}{7}$, $\frac{4}{7}$, $\frac{5}{7}$ and $\frac{6}{7}$
Describe the pattern in your answers.

4 **a** Use a calculator to convert $\frac{1}{9}$ to a decimal.
Write your answer using dot notation.
b Repeat part **a** for $\frac{2}{9}$, $\frac{3}{9}$ up to $\frac{8}{9}$
Describe the pattern in your answers.

5 **a** Use a calculator to convert $\frac{1}{11}$ to a decimal.
Write your answer using dot notation.
b Repeat part **a** for $\frac{2}{11}$, $\frac{3}{11}$ up to $\frac{10}{11}$
Describe the pattern in your answers.

6 Match up the decimals to the fractions.

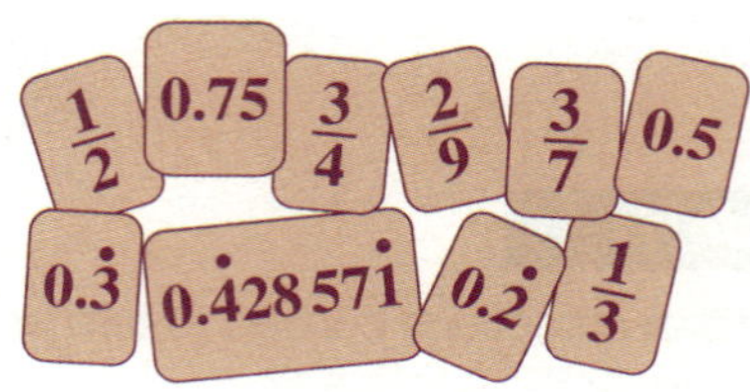

7 Explain how you know that $\frac{5}{18}$ is a recurring decimal.

Recurring decimals can be converted to fractions using patterns or algebra.
The pattern method can be used when a question asks for a recurring decimal to be written as a fraction. For example 'Express $0.8\dot{2}\dot{3}$ as a fraction in its simplest form.'

The pattern method
Use these facts about recurring groups of 1, 2 and 3 digits.
When one digit recurs immediately after the decimal point the denominator is 9
(See question **4** in Exercise A.)
$0.\dot{1} = \frac{1}{9}$, $0.\dot{2} = \frac{2}{9}$, $0.\dot{3} = \frac{3}{9}$, $0.\dot{4} = \frac{4}{9}$ and so on.
Similarly when two digits recur immediately after the decimal point the denominator is 99
For example, $0.\dot{1}\dot{2} = \frac{12}{99}$, $0.\dot{2}\dot{5} = \frac{25}{99}$
When three digits recur immediately after the decimal point the denominator is 999
For example, $0.\dot{1}2\dot{3} = \frac{123}{999}$

Example 2

Write each decimal as a fraction.

a $0.\dot{7}$ **b** $0.0\dot{7}$ **c** $0.\dot{1}7\dot{4}$ **d** $0.3\dot{2}\dot{8}$

Solution 2

Use the pattern method.

a $0.\dot{7} = \frac{7}{9}$ — Using the pattern of ninths for one recurring digit.

b $0.0\dot{7} = 0.\dot{7} \div 10 = \frac{7}{9} \div 10 = \frac{7}{90}$

c $0.\dot{1}7\dot{4} = \frac{174}{999}$ — Using the pattern for three recurring digits.

d $0.\dot{2}\dot{8} = \frac{28}{99}$ — Using the pattern for two recurring digits.

so $0.0\dot{2}\dot{8} = 0.\dot{2}\dot{8} \div 10 = \frac{28}{99} \div 10 = \frac{28}{990}$

now $0.3\dot{2}\dot{8} = 0.3 + 0.0\dot{2}\dot{8}$

$= \frac{3}{10} + \frac{28}{990}$

$= \frac{3 \times 99}{990} + \frac{28}{990}$ — Writing with a common denominator.

$= \frac{297}{990} + \frac{28}{990} = \frac{325}{990}$

$= \frac{65}{198}$ — Cancelling

Using algebra
The algebra method can be used to convert any recurring decimal to a fraction. It **must** be used when a question asks for a *proof* that a recurring decimal is equal to a particular fraction.
For example, 'Prove (or show) that $0.8\dot{2}\dot{3} = \frac{163}{198}$'

Example 3

Use algebra to convert the following recurring decimals to fractions.

a $0.\dot{6}$ **b** $0.\dot{1}\dot{7}$ **c** $0.\dot{8}4\dot{9}$

Solution 3

Use the algebra method.

a Let $x = 0.\dot{6}$ (1)
Then $10x = 6.\dot{6}$ (2) — For one recurring digit multiply by 10
$10x - x = 6.\dot{6} - 0.\dot{6}$ — Subtract equation (1) from equation (2).
$9x = 6$
$x = \frac{6}{9} = \frac{2}{3}$ — Divide both sides by 9
$0.\dot{6} = \frac{2}{3}$

b Let $x = 0.\dot{1}\dot{7}$ (1)
Then $100x = 17.\dot{1}\dot{7}$ (2) — For two recurring digits multiply by 100
$100x - x = 17.\dot{1}\dot{7} - 0.\dot{1}\dot{7}$ — Subtract equation (1) from equation (2).
$99x = 17$
$x = \frac{17}{99}$ — Divide both sides by 99
$0.\dot{1}\dot{7} = \frac{17}{99}$

c $x = 0.\dot{8}4\dot{9}$ (1)
Then $1000x = 849.\dot{8}4\dot{9}$ (2) — For three recurring digits multiply by 1000
So $999x = 849$ — Subtract equation (1) from equation (2).
$x = \frac{849}{999} = \frac{283}{333}$ — Divide both sides by 999
$0.\dot{8}4\dot{9} = \frac{283}{333}$

The algebra method can be summarised as follows.
Step 1: Write the equation $x =$ the recurring decimal.
Step 2: Multiply the equation in Step 1 by:

10	if there is one recurring digit
100	if there are two recurring digits
1000	if there are three recurring digits

Step 3: Subtract the equation in Step 1 from the equation in Step 2 to give a new equation.
Step 4: Rearrange the equation from Step 3 to obtain $x =$ fraction, cancelling if necessary.

Exercise B

Give all fractions in their simplest form in this exercise.

1 Use patterns to convert each of the following to fractions.
a $0.\dot{8}$ **b** $0.\dot{2}$ **c** $2.\dot{7}$ **d** $0.\dot{2}\dot{4}$
e $3.\dot{6}\dot{5}$ **f** $12.\dot{9}\dot{1}$ **g** $7.\dot{1}9\dot{2}$ **h** $45.\dot{2}3\dot{4}$

2 Use patterns to convert each of the following to fractions.
a $0.0\dot{3}$ **b** $0.0\dot{6}$ **c** $0.00\dot{1}$ **d** $0.00\dot{4}$
e $0.0\dot{3}\dot{1}$ **f** $0.0\dot{2}\dot{9}$ **g** $0.00\dot{4}\dot{2}$ **h** $0.0\dot{9}7\dot{5}$

3 Repeat questions **1** and **2** using the algebra method.

4 Use any method to express each recurring decimal as a fraction.
a $0.2\dot{4}$ **b** $0.6\dot{3}\dot{9}$ **c** $0.2\dot{7}\dot{1}$ **d** $0.1\dot{5}\dot{3}$

5 Prove that $0.9\dot{7}\dot{1} = \frac{481}{495}$

6 Prove that $0.1\dot{6}\dot{3} = \frac{9}{55}$

7 **a** Write $0.\dot{1}\dot{2}$ as a fraction in its simplest form.
b Hence or otherwise express $0.3\dot{1}\dot{2}$ as a fraction.

28.2 Multiplying and dividing mixed numbers

CAN YOU REMEMBER

- That a mixed number has a whole number part and a fraction part?
- How to multiply and divide by a fraction?
- How to convert mixed numbers to improper fractions?
- How to use a calculator for fraction calculations?

IN THIS SECTION YOU WILL

- Learn how to multiply and divide mixed numbers.
- Check answers using a calculator.

To multiply mixed numbers follow these steps:
Step 1: Convert the mixed numbers to improper fractions.
Step 2: Write the multiplication as a single fraction.
Step 3: Simplify by cancelling any common factors.
Step 4: Multiply the numerators and multiply the denominators.
Step 5: Write the answer as a mixed number.

Example 1

Work out $4\frac{1}{5} \times 2\frac{3}{4}$

Solution 1

Step 1: Convert the mixed numbers into improper fractions.

$$4\frac{1}{5} = \frac{21}{5} \qquad 2\frac{3}{4} = \frac{11}{4}$$

Step 2: Write the multiplication as a single fraction.

$$4\frac{1}{5} \times 2\frac{3}{4} = \frac{21}{5} \times \frac{11}{4} = \frac{21 \times 11}{5 \times 4}$$

Step 3: There are no common factors to cancel.
Step 4: Multiply the numerators and multiply the denominators.

$$\frac{21 \times 11}{5 \times 4} = \frac{231}{20}$$

Step 5: Write the answer as a mixed number.

$$\frac{231}{20} = 11\frac{11}{20}$$

$$4\frac{1}{5} \times 2\frac{3}{4} = 11\frac{11}{20}$$

To divide two mixed numbers follow these steps.

Step 1: Convert the mixed numbers to improper fractions.

Step 2: Change the division to a multiplication by inverting the second fraction and then write as a single fraction.

Step 3: Simplify by cancelling any common factors.

Step 4: Multiply the numerators and multiply the denominators.

Step 5: Write the answer as a mixed number.

Example 2

Work out $3\frac{1}{8} \div 2\frac{1}{4}$

Solution 2

Step 1: Convert the mixed numbers into improper fractions.

$$3\frac{1}{8} = \frac{25}{8} \qquad 2\frac{1}{4} = \frac{9}{4}$$

$$3\frac{1}{8} \div 2\frac{1}{4} = \frac{25}{8} \div \frac{9}{4}$$

Step 2: Change the division to a multiplication by inverting the second fraction and then write as a single fraction.

$$3\frac{1}{8} \div 2\frac{1}{4} = \frac{25}{8} \div \frac{9}{4} = \frac{25}{8} \times \frac{4}{9} = \frac{25 \times 4}{8 \times 9}$$

Step 3: Simplify by cancelling any common factors.

$$\frac{25 \times \cancel{4}^{1}}{{}_{2}\cancel{8} \times 9}$$

Step 4: Multiply the numerators and multiply the denominators.

$$\frac{25 \times 1}{2 \times 9} = \frac{25}{18}$$

Step 5: Write the answer as a mixed number.

$$\frac{25}{18} = 1\frac{7}{18}$$

$$3\frac{1}{8} \div 2\frac{1}{4} = 1\frac{7}{18}$$

Exercise A

1 Work out:

a $3\frac{1}{2} \times 1\frac{3}{4}$ **b** $5\frac{1}{4} \times 1\frac{1}{2}$ **c** $3 \times 2\frac{4}{5}$ **d** $8\frac{1}{4} \times 1\frac{7}{11}$

e $9\frac{1}{3} \times 4$ **f** $4\frac{3}{8} \times 2\frac{1}{10}$ **g** $7\frac{3}{5} \times 2\frac{1}{2}$ **h** $6\frac{1}{8} \times 1\frac{4}{9}$

2 Work out:

a $5\frac{1}{2} \div 1\frac{3}{4}$ **b** $7\frac{1}{2} \div 1\frac{1}{2}$ **c** $15 \div 1\frac{1}{5}$ **d** $3\frac{3}{4} \div 5$

e $4\frac{1}{3} \div 2$ **f** $6\frac{1}{8} \div 2\frac{1}{3}$ **g** $1\frac{3}{5} \div 1\frac{1}{7}$ **h** $9\frac{1}{3} \div 1\frac{1}{3}$

3 Use a calculator to check your answers to questions **1** and **2**

Exercise B

1 A rectangular photograph is $3\frac{1}{2}$ inches tall and $5\frac{1}{4}$ inches wide.
Calculate its area.

2 Work out $(2\frac{1}{2})^2$

3 The area of a circle is 154 cm^2
Taking π as $3\frac{1}{7}$, find the radius of the circle.

Area of a circle $= \pi r^2$

4 How many sixths are in one and a half?

5 A bag of flour weighs $1\frac{1}{2}$ kg.
A box containing bags of flour weighs $27\frac{1}{2}$ kg.
The box weighs 500 grams.
How many bags of flour are in the box?

6 A machine produces $3\frac{1}{5}$ tonnes of metal per hour.
How long does the machine take to produce 116 tonnes of metal?
Give your answer in hours and minutes.

7 Use a calculator to check your answers to questions **1** to **5**

28.3 Surds

CAN YOU REMEMBER

- Square numbers?
- The meaning of 'square root'?
- How to find factor pairs?

IN THIS SECTION YOU WILL

- Learn the meaning of 'surd' and 'rationalise'.
- Rationalise a denominator such as $\frac{1}{\sqrt{3}}$.
- Simplify surds.

A *surd* is a square root that does **not** have an exact value.
For example, $\sqrt{2}$ and $\sqrt{3}$ are surds, but $\sqrt{4}$ and $\sqrt{9}$ are **not** surds.
$\sqrt{a \times b} = \sqrt{a} \times \sqrt{b}$
This fact can be used to simplify surds when the number under the square root sign has a factor that is a square number.

Example 1

Simplify $\sqrt{18}$

Solution 1

Factors of 18 are 1, 2, 3, 6, 9 and 18
The factor pair of 18 containing a square number is 9×2
$\sqrt{18} = \sqrt{9 \times 2} = \sqrt{9} \times \sqrt{2} = 3\sqrt{2}$

Surds may appear in the denominator of a fraction, for example $\frac{1}{\sqrt{3}}, \frac{10}{\sqrt{5}}, \frac{2}{\sqrt{7}}$

To simplify these, multiply the numerator and denominator by the surd.
This is called *rationalising the denominator.* The surd will now appear in the numerator.

Example 2

Rationalise the denominator and simplify if possible.

a $\frac{1}{\sqrt{3}}$ **b** $\frac{10}{\sqrt{5}}$ **c** $\frac{2}{\sqrt{32}}$

Solution 2

a $\frac{1}{\sqrt{3}} = \frac{1}{\sqrt{3}} \times \frac{\sqrt{3}}{\sqrt{3}} = \frac{1 \times \sqrt{3}}{\sqrt{3} \times \sqrt{3}} = \frac{\sqrt{3}}{3}$

$\sqrt{3} \times \sqrt{3} = 3$

b $\frac{10}{\sqrt{5}} = \frac{10}{\sqrt{5}} \times \frac{\sqrt{5}}{\sqrt{5}} = \frac{10 \times \sqrt{5}}{\sqrt{5} \times \sqrt{5}} = \frac{10\sqrt{5}}{5}$
$= 2\sqrt{5}$

$\sqrt{5} \times \sqrt{5} = 5$

c **Method 1:** Rationalise first.

$\frac{2}{\sqrt{32}} = \frac{2}{\sqrt{32}} \times \frac{\sqrt{32}}{\sqrt{32}} = \frac{2 \times \sqrt{32}}{\sqrt{32} \times \sqrt{32}} = \frac{2\sqrt{32}}{32} = \frac{\sqrt{32}}{16} = \frac{\sqrt{2 \times 16}}{16}$

$= \frac{(\sqrt{2} \times \sqrt{16})}{16} = \frac{(4\sqrt{2})}{16} = \frac{\sqrt{2}}{4}$

Method 2: Simplify the surd first.

$\sqrt{32} = \sqrt{16 \times 2} = \sqrt{16} \times \sqrt{2} = 4\sqrt{2}$

$\frac{2}{\sqrt{32}} = \frac{2}{4\sqrt{2}} = \frac{2}{4\sqrt{2}} \times \frac{\sqrt{2}}{\sqrt{2}} = \frac{2 \times \sqrt{2}}{4\sqrt{2} \times \sqrt{2}} = \frac{{}^{1}\cancel{2}\sqrt{2}}{4 \times \cancel{2}_{1}} = \frac{\sqrt{2}}{4}$

Example 3

Simplify: **a** $\sqrt{6} \times 4\sqrt{3}$ **b** $\sqrt{24} + \sqrt{54}$

Solution 3

a $\sqrt{6} \times 4\sqrt{3} = 4 \times \sqrt{6} \times \sqrt{3} = 4\sqrt{6 \times 3} = 4\sqrt{18} = 4\sqrt{9 \times 2}$
$= 4 \times \sqrt{9} \times \sqrt{2} = 4 \times 3 \times \sqrt{2} = 12\sqrt{2}$

b $\sqrt{24} = 2\sqrt{6}$ $\sqrt{54} = 3\sqrt{6}$
So $\sqrt{24} + \sqrt{54} = 2\sqrt{6} + 3\sqrt{6} = 5\sqrt{6}$

Exercise A

1 Simplify:

a $\sqrt{8}$ **b** $\sqrt{20}$ **c** $\sqrt{27}$ **d** $\sqrt{50}$
e $\sqrt{45}$ **f** $\sqrt{75}$ **g** $\sqrt{200}$ **h** $\sqrt{128}$

2 Rationalise the denominator and simplify if possible.

a $\frac{1}{\sqrt{2}}$ **b** $\frac{1}{\sqrt{7}}$ **c** $\frac{3}{\sqrt{3}}$ **d** $\frac{5}{\sqrt{6}}$
e $\frac{15}{\sqrt{5}}$ **f** $\frac{8}{\sqrt{2}}$ **g** $\frac{4}{\sqrt{8}}$ **h** $\frac{3}{\sqrt{7}}$

3 Simplify:

a $\sqrt{3} \times \sqrt{3}$ **b** $\sqrt{5} \times \sqrt{10}$ **c** $2\sqrt{7} \times 3\sqrt{3}$

d $4\sqrt{6} \times \sqrt{2}$ **e** $\sqrt{200} + \sqrt{18}$ **f** $\sqrt{45} - \sqrt{20}$

g $\sqrt{6} + \sqrt{24}$ **h** $\sqrt{50} - 4\sqrt{2}$ **i** $\sqrt{125} - \sqrt{45}$

4 A rectangle is $\sqrt{45}$ cm long and $\sqrt{180}$ cm wide.
Work out the area.

Example 4

Show that $\sqrt{12}(\sqrt{18} - \sqrt{2}) = 4\sqrt{6}$

Solution 4

$\sqrt{12} = \sqrt{4 \times 3} = 2\sqrt{3}$ $\quad \sqrt{18} = \sqrt{9 \times 2} = 3\sqrt{2}$

So $\sqrt{12}(\sqrt{18} - \sqrt{2}) = 2\sqrt{3}(3\sqrt{2} - \sqrt{2}) = 2\sqrt{3} \times 2\sqrt{2} = 4\sqrt{6}$

Example 5

The radius of a circle is $(1 + \sqrt{2})$ centimetres.
Work out the area.

a Give your answer in its simplest exact form.

b Give your answer to two decimal places.

Solution 5

Area of circle $= \pi r^2$

a Area $= \pi(1 + \sqrt{2})^2 = \pi(1 + \sqrt{2})(1 + \sqrt{2}) = \pi(1 + \sqrt{2} + \sqrt{2} + 2)$
$= \pi(3 + 2\sqrt{2})$ cm^2

b Using a calculator, area = 18.31 cm^2 (to 2 d.p.)

Exercise B

1 **a** Simplify $\sqrt{8} \times \sqrt{2}$

b Show that $\dfrac{\sqrt{8} - \sqrt{2}}{\sqrt{8} + \sqrt{2}} = \dfrac{1}{3}$

2 Show that $\dfrac{\sqrt{128} + \sqrt{18}}{2\sqrt{75} + \sqrt{3}} = \dfrac{\sqrt{6}}{3}$

3 Show that $\sqrt{20}(\sqrt{45} - \sqrt{5}) = 20$

4 **a** Expand and simplify $(4 + \sqrt{2})^2$

b Hence or otherwise show that $(4 + \sqrt{2})$ is a solution of the equation $x^2 - 8x + 14 = 0$

5 Find the values of a and b such that $(3 + \sqrt{5})(6 - \sqrt{5}) = a + b\sqrt{5}$

6 Rationalise the denominator of $\dfrac{1 + \sqrt{7}}{\sqrt{7}}$

7 **a** Simplify $\sqrt{24} + \sqrt{150}$

b Hence simplify $\sqrt{3}(\sqrt{24} + \sqrt{150})$
Give your answer in its simplest surd form.

8 Express $\sqrt{63} + \sqrt{28}$ in the form $a\sqrt{7}$

9 The radius of a circle is $(2 + \sqrt{3})$ centimetres.
Work out the area.
a Give your answer in exact form. Simplify your answer.
b Give your answer to two decimal places.

Chapter summary

- A *terminating decimal* has a fixed number of decimal places, for example 0.123 or 6.75
- A *recurring decimal* does not have a fixed number of decimal places and has a repeating pattern, for example 0.333… or 7.412 121 2…
- Fractions with denominators whose only prime factors are 2 or 5 are terminating decimals, for example, $\frac{1}{2}, \frac{1}{4}, \frac{1}{5}, \frac{1}{10}$
- Fractions with denominators whose prime factors are not only 2 or 5 are recurring decimals, for example, $\frac{1}{3}, \frac{1}{6}, \frac{1}{7}, \frac{1}{9}$
- When a question asks for a decimal converted to a fraction, use either the pattern method or the algebra method.
- **Pattern method** – use these patterns of ninths.
  - When one digit recurs immediately after the decimal point the denominator is 9
    $0.\dot{1} = \frac{1}{9}$, $0.\dot{2} = \frac{2}{9}$, $0.\dot{3} = \frac{3}{9}$, $0.\dot{4} = \frac{4}{9}$ and so on
  - When two digits recur immediately after the decimal point the denominator is 99
    For example $0.\dot{1}\dot{2} = \frac{12}{99}$, $0.\dot{2}\dot{5} = \frac{25}{99}$
  - When three digits recur immediately after the decimal point the denominator is 999
    For example $0.\dot{1}2\dot{3} = \frac{123}{999}$
- When a question asks for a proof that a decimal converts to a given fraction, use the **algebra method**.
  - **Step 1:** Write the equation x = the recurring decimal.
  - **Step 2:** Multiply the equation in Step 1 by

10	if there is one recurring digit
100	if there are two recurring digits
1000	if there are three recurring digits

  - **Step 3:** Subtract the equation in Step 1 from the equation in Step 2 to give a new equation.
  - **Step 4:** Rearrange the equation from Step 3 to obtain x = fraction, cancelling if necessary.
- To multiply mixed numbers follow these steps:
  - **Step 1:** Convert the mixed numbers to improper fractions.
  - **Step 2:** Write the multiplication as a single fraction.
  - **Step 3:** Simplify by cancelling any common factors.
  - **Step 4:** Multiply the numerators and multiply the denominators.
  - **Step 5:** Write the answer as a mixed number.

- To divide mixed numbers follow these steps:
  - **Step 1:** Convert the mixed numbers to improper fractions.
  - **Step 2:** Change the division to a multiplication by inverting the second fraction and then write as a single fraction.
  - **Step 3:** Simplify by cancelling any common factors.
  - **Step 4:** Multiply the numerators and multiply the denominators.
  - **Step 5:** Write the answer as a mixed number.
- A *surd* is a square root that does **not** have an exact value.
  For example $\sqrt{2}$ and $\sqrt{3}$ are surds, $\sqrt{4}$ and $\sqrt{9}$ are **not** surds.
- $\sqrt{a \times b} = \sqrt{a} \times \sqrt{b}$
  This fact can be used to simplify surds when the number under the square root sign has a square number factor.
- Surds may appear in the denominator of a fraction, for example $\frac{1}{\sqrt{3}}, \frac{10}{\sqrt{5}}, \frac{2}{\sqrt{7}}$
  To simplify these, rationalise the denominator – multiply the numerator and denominator by the surd.

Chapter review

1 Work out $5\frac{1}{2} \times 6\frac{1}{3}$

2 **a** Express $0.\dot{3}\dot{4}$ as a fraction in its simplest form.
b Express $0.2\dot{3}\dot{4}$ as a fraction in its simplest form.

3 Prove that $0.3\dot{7} = \frac{17}{45}$

4 Write $0.\dot{3}\dot{6}$ as a fraction in its simplest form.

5 Prove that the recurring decimal 1.324 324 324… is equal to $1\frac{12}{37}$

6 Work out $9\frac{3}{4} \div 6\frac{1}{5}$

7 Rationalise the denominator and simplify $\frac{12}{\sqrt{3}}$

8 Show that $\frac{\sqrt{200} + \sqrt{50}}{\sqrt{200} - \sqrt{50}} = 3$

9 An insect walks $1\frac{2}{5}$ kilometres every day.
How many days will it take the insect to walk 10 kilometres?
Give your answer to the nearest day.

10 A square has sides of length $6\frac{1}{5}$ cm.
Work out the area of the square.

11 The area of a rectangle is $14\frac{7}{8}\text{ cm}^2$
The length of the rectangle is $3\frac{1}{2}$ cm.
Work out the perimeter of the rectangle.

12 Explain why $\frac{9}{40}$ is not a recurring decimal.

13 **a** Explain why $\frac{11}{42}$ is a recurring decimal.
b Use your calculator to work out $\frac{11}{42}$ as a recurring decimal.
Write your answer using dot notation.

CHAPTER 29

Trigonometry

29.1 Lengths of sides

CAN YOU REMEMBER

- That the longest side of a right-angled triangle is called the hypotenuse?
- That in similar triangles the ratios of corresponding sides are equal?

IN THIS SECTION YOU WILL

- Learn definitions for sine, cosine and tangent.
- Use these ratios to work out the lengths of sides in a right-angled triangle.

Trigonometry is used to find the lengths of sides and the sizes of angles in a right-angled triangle.
The sides of a right-angled triangle are named as shown.

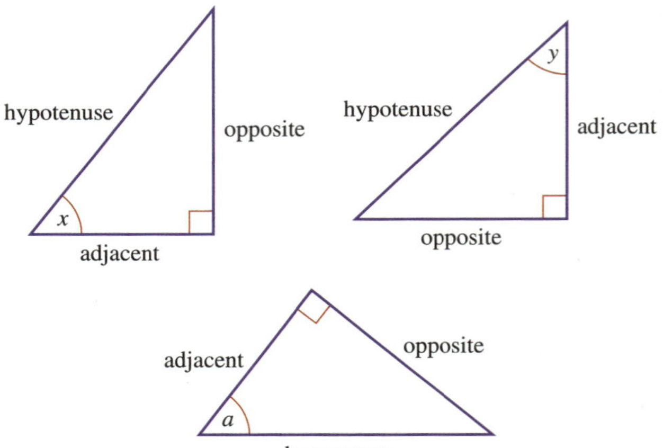

The *hypotenuse* is opposite the right angle.
The *opposite* side is opposite the angle being used.
The *adjacent* side is next to the angle being used.
Triangles BAC and DAE are similar.

So $\frac{BC}{DE} = \frac{AB}{AD}$ which rearranges to

$\frac{BC}{AB} = \frac{DE}{AD}$

BC and DE are opposite angle A.
AB and AD are the hypotenuses.

So the ratio $\frac{\text{opposite}}{\text{hypotenuse}}$ is the same for all right-angled triangles with this angle A.

This is the *sine* ratio for a right angled triangle.

$\sin A = \dfrac{\text{opposite}}{\text{hypotenuse}}$

Similar ratios for the other two pairs of sides are as follows.

The *cosine* of angle A is the ratio $\dfrac{\text{adjacent}}{\text{hypotenuse}}$

$\cos A = \dfrac{\text{adjacent}}{\text{hypotenuse}}$

The *tangent* of angle A is the ratio $\dfrac{\text{opposite}}{\text{adjacent}}$

$\tan A = \dfrac{\text{opposite}}{\text{adjacent}}$

Each formula links an angle and two sides.
If two of these values are known, the third can be calculated.
The sine, cosine and tangent values of any angle can be found using the sin, cos and tan buttons on a calculator.

Example 1

Work out the length of x.

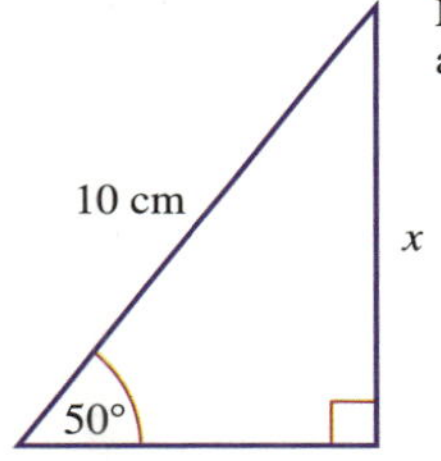

Angle	Sine	Cosine	Tangent
40°	0.643	0.766	0.839
50°	0.766	0.643	1.192

Solution 1

The given angle is 50°
The hypotenuse is 10 cm.
Length x is the side **opposite** the given angle.
Using the sine ratio:

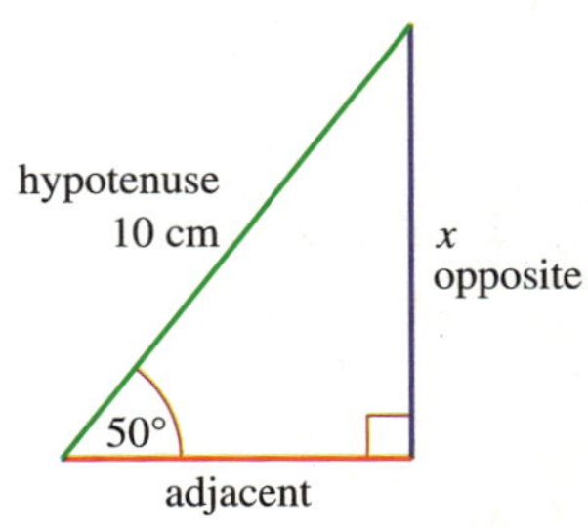

$\sin 50° = \dfrac{\text{opposite}}{\text{hypotenuse}} = \dfrac{x}{10}$

$10 \times \sin 50° = x$ Multiplying both sides by 10

From the table of data given, sin 50° = 0.766 (this value can also be found from a calculator).
$x = 10 \times 0.766 = 7.66$ cm.

Example 2

Find the length of x.

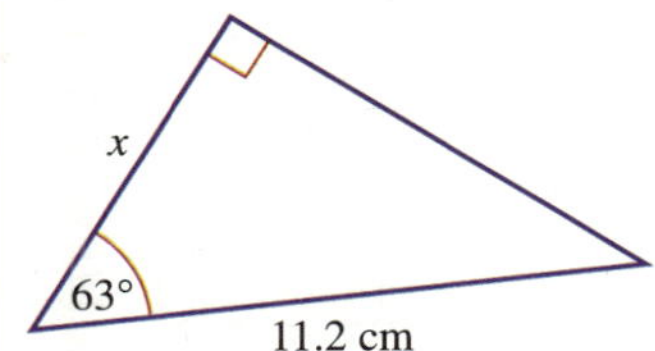

Solution 2

The given angle is 63°
The hypotenuse is 11.2 cm.
Side x is the side **adjacent** to the given angle.
Using the cosine ratio:

$$\cos 63° = \frac{\text{adjacent}}{\text{hypotenuse}} = \frac{x}{11.2}$$

$11.2 \times \cos 63° = x$ Use a calculator.
$x = 5.08$ cm (to 3 s.f.)

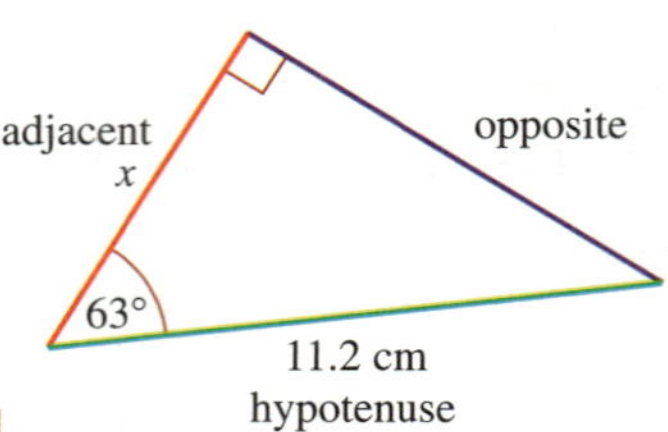

Exercise A

Diagrams are not drawn accurately.

1 Name all the sides in each of these triangles in relation to angle A.

a 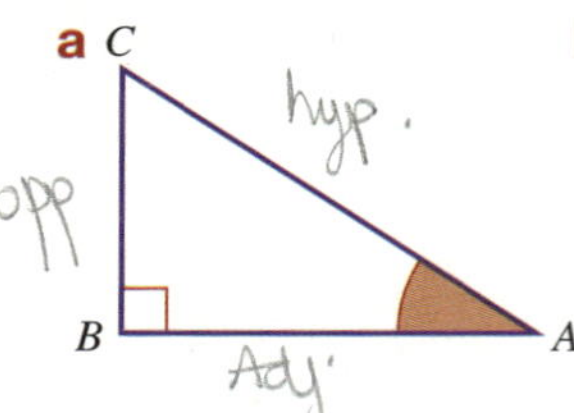

b 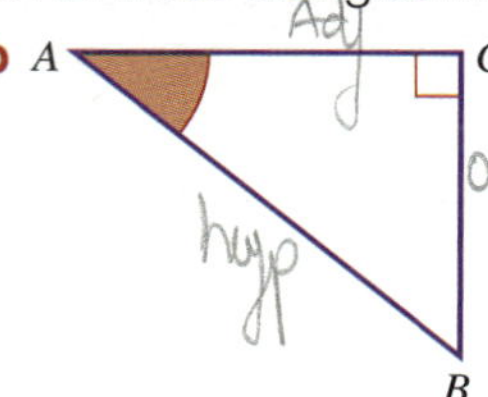

c 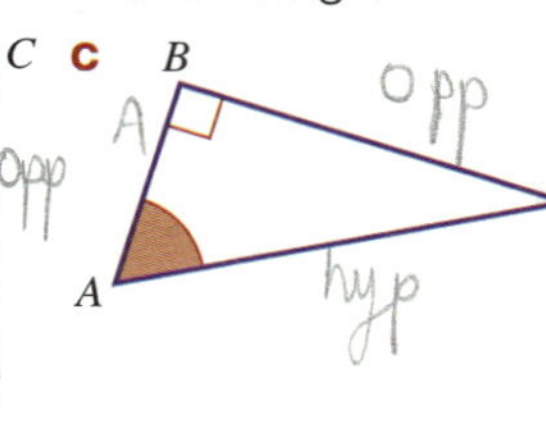

d 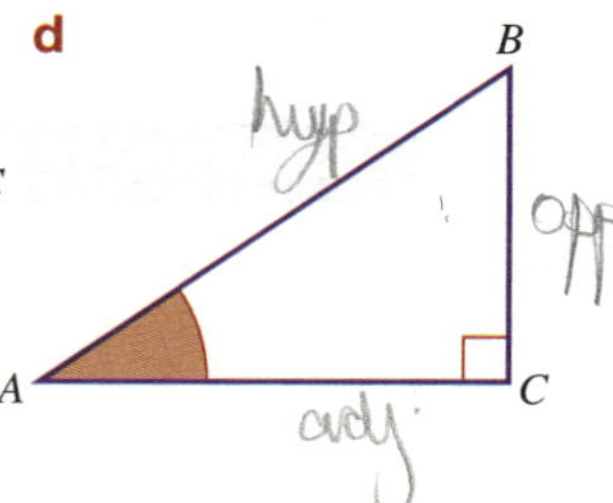

Use the values in this table to answer questions **2–4**

Angle	Sine	Cosine	Tangent
30°	0.5	0.866	0.577
35°	0.574	0.819	0.7
45°	0.707	0.707	1
55°	0.819	0.574	1.428
60°	0.866	0.5	1.732

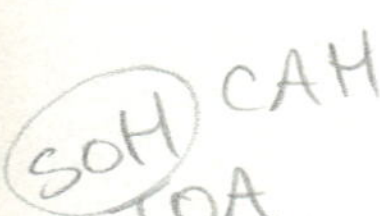

2 Work out the length of x.

a 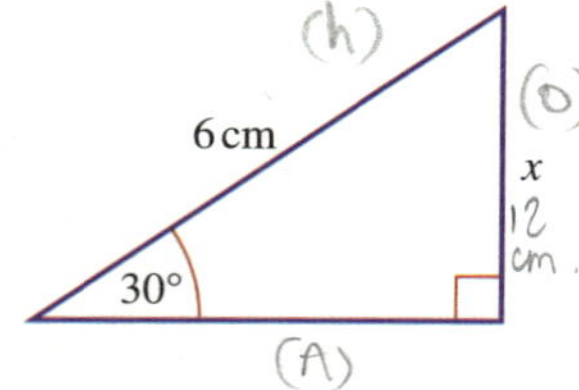

b 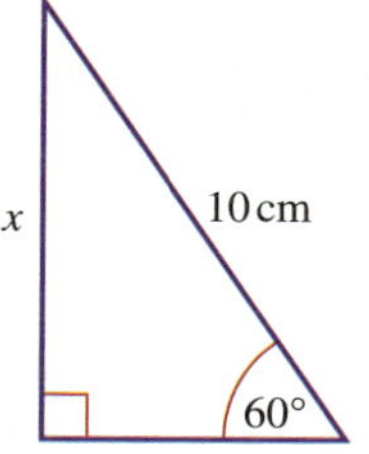

c 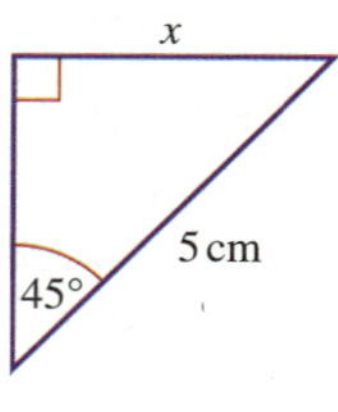

3 Find the length of the side marked x.

a 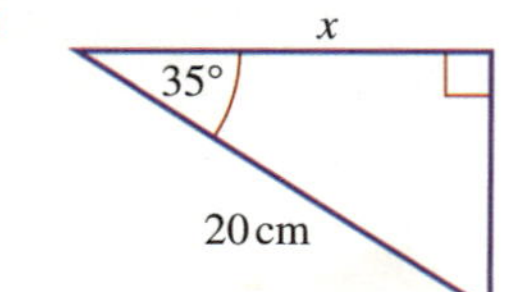

b 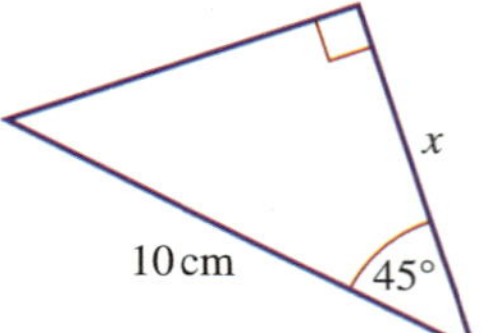

c 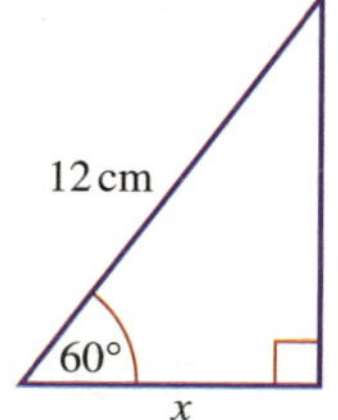

4 Find the length of x.

a

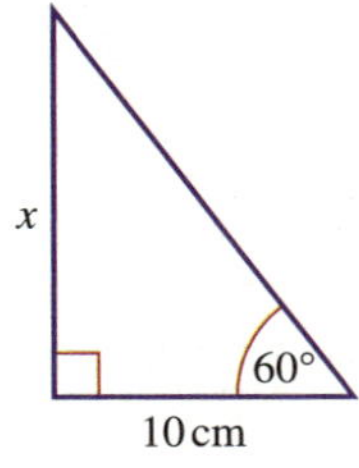

b

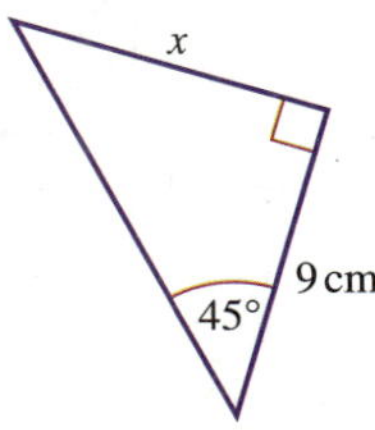

c

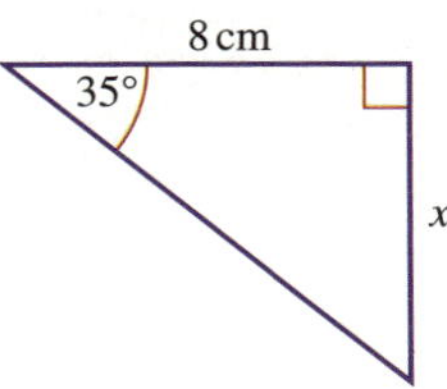

5 Use a calculator to write down the values of the following, to 3 s.f.

a	sin 20°	**b**	tan 37°	**c**	sin 56°	**d**	cos 80°	**e**	tan 74°
f	cos 32°	**g**	sin 65°	**h**	tan 25°	**i**	cos 48°	**j**	tan 44°

6 Calculate the length of the sides marked with letters.
Give your answers to 3 s.f.

a

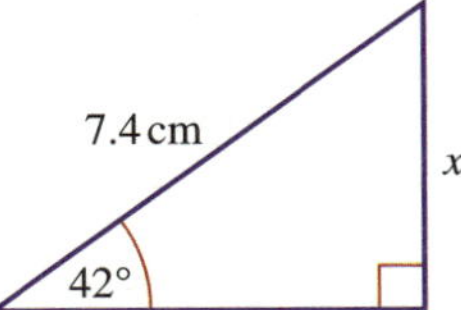

b

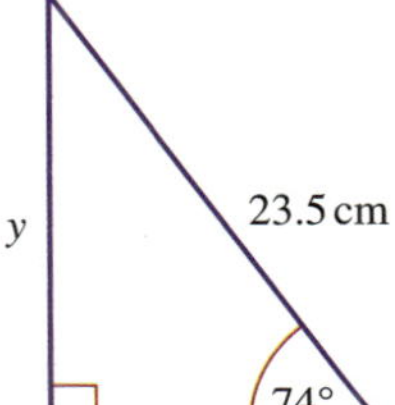

c

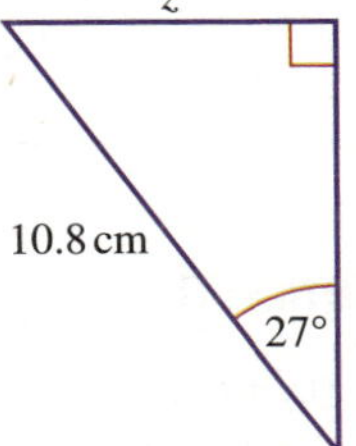

7 Calculate the length of the sides marked with letters.
Give your answers to 3 s.f.

a

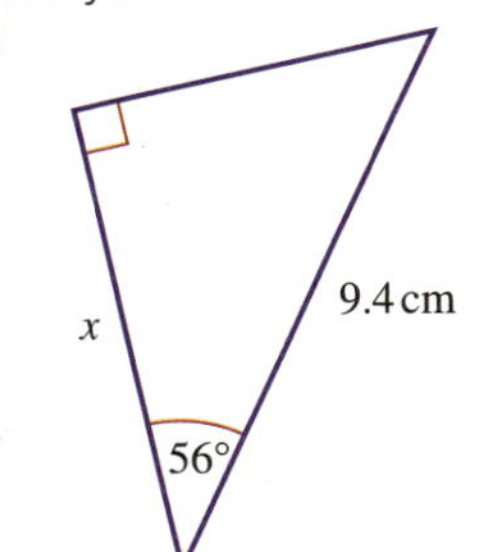

b

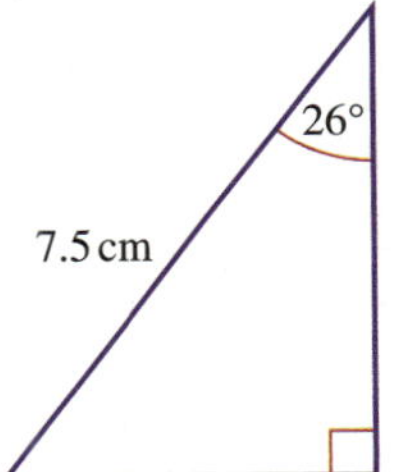

c

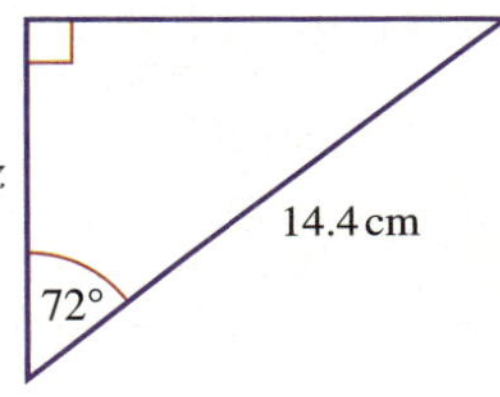

8 Calculate the length of the sides marked with letters.
Give your answers to 3 s.f.

a

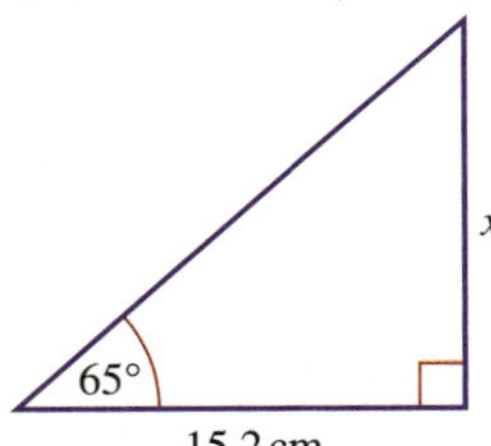

b

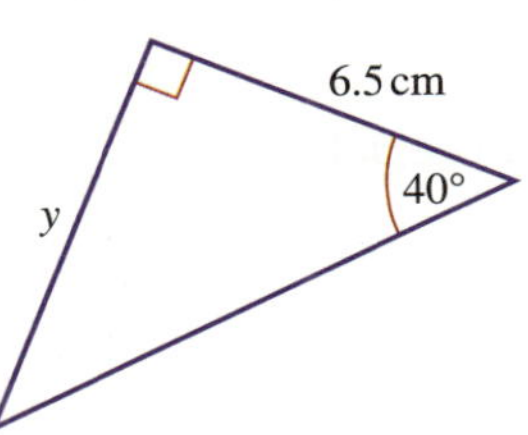

c

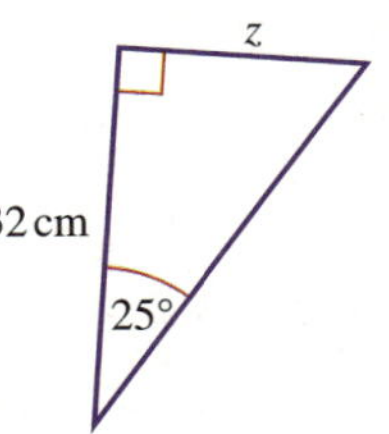

9 Calculate the length of each side marked with a letter.
Give your answers to an appropriate degree of accuracy.

a

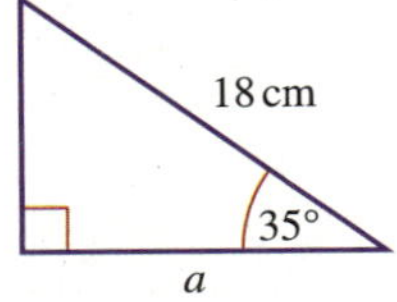

b

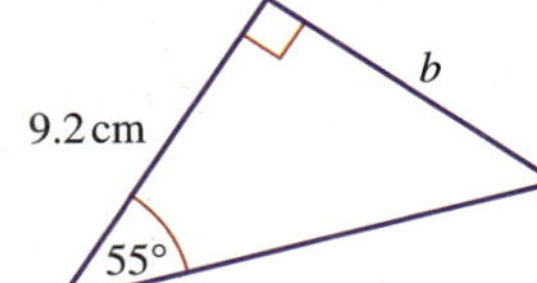

c

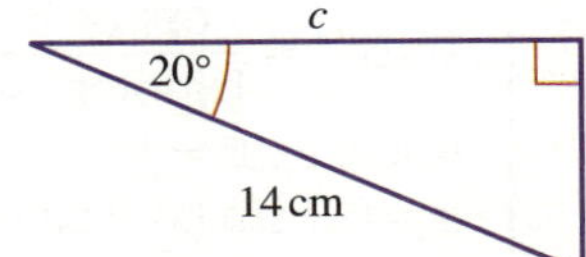

d

32 cm
62°
d

e

25°
12.5 cm
e

f

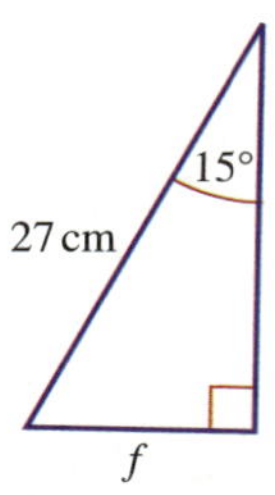

Example 3

Find the length of x.

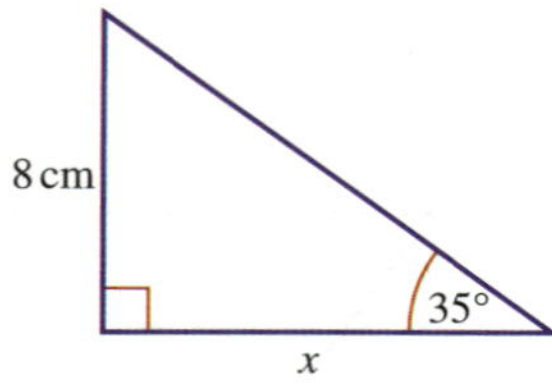

Solution 3

The given angle is 35°
The opposite side is 8 cm.
Side x is the side **adjacent** to the given angle.
Using the tangent ratio:

$$\tan 35° = \frac{\text{opposite}}{\text{adjacent}} = \frac{8}{x}$$

$$x \times \tan 35° = 8$$

$$x = \frac{8}{\tan 35°} = 11.4 \text{ cm}$$

Example 4

An isosceles triangle has two equal sides of length 8 cm and two equal angles of 50°
Calculate the height of the triangle.

Solution 4

Draw a sketch, marking in the height.

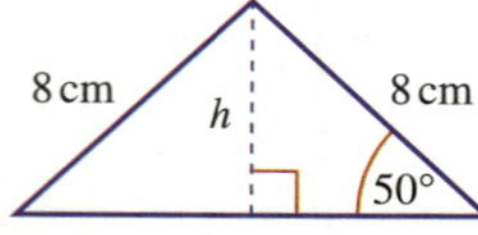

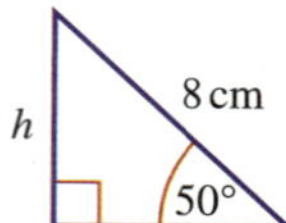

Each half of the isosceles triangle is a right-angled triangle.
The hypotenuse is 8 cm and the given angle is 50°
h is the **opposite** side.

$$\sin 50° = \frac{\text{opposite}}{\text{hypotenuse}} = \frac{h}{8}$$

$$8 \times \sin 50° = h$$

$h = 6.1$ cm (to 2 s.f.)

Exercise B

Diagrams are not drawn accurately.

1 In each triangle find the length of AC.
Give your answers to an appropriate degree of accuracy.

a 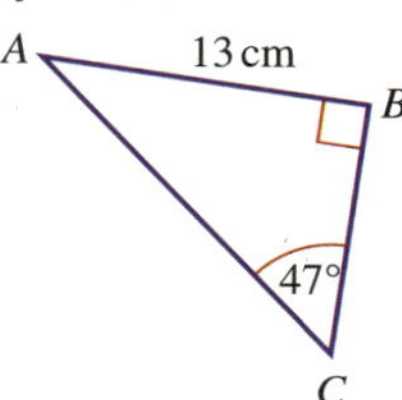

b 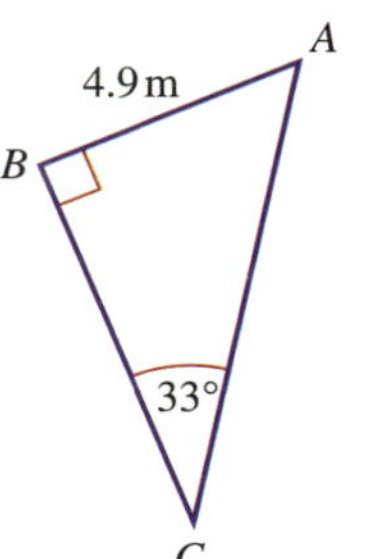

c 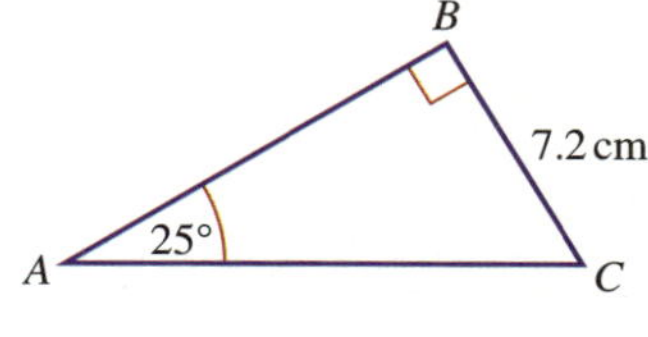

2 In each triangle find the length of BC.
Give your answers to 3 s.f.

a 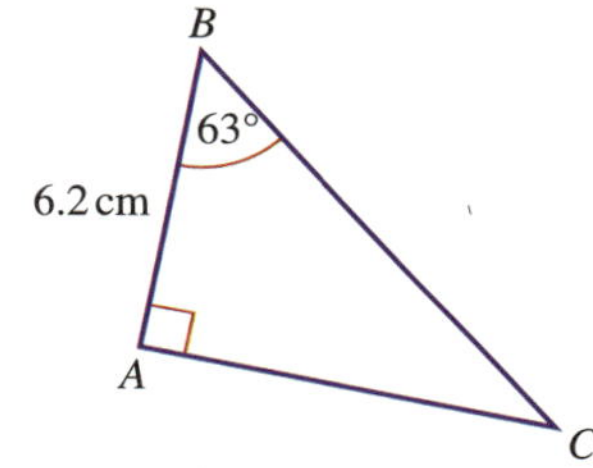

b 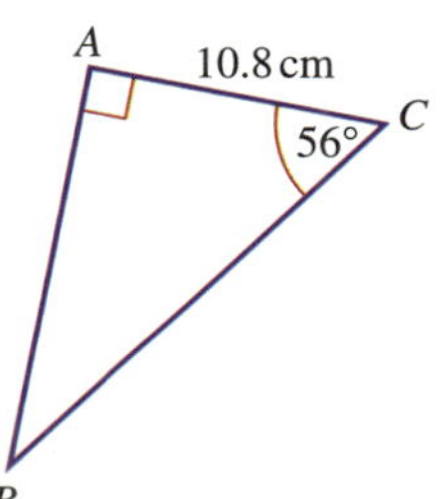

c 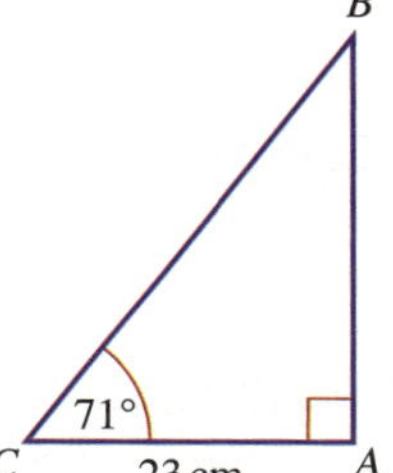

3 In each triangle find the length of the side marked x.
Give each answer to an appropriate degree of accuracy.

a 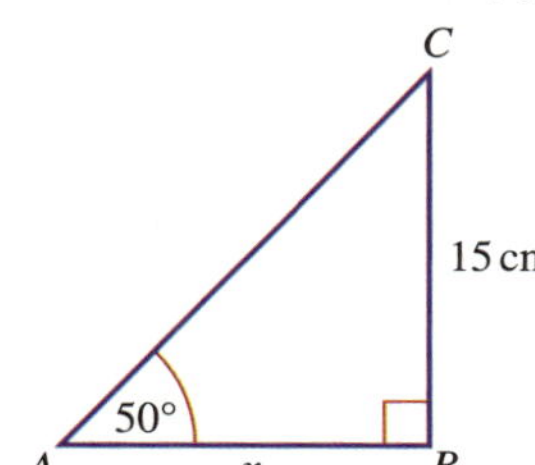

b 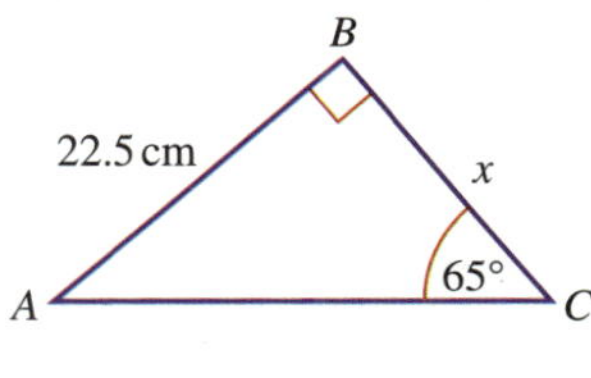

c 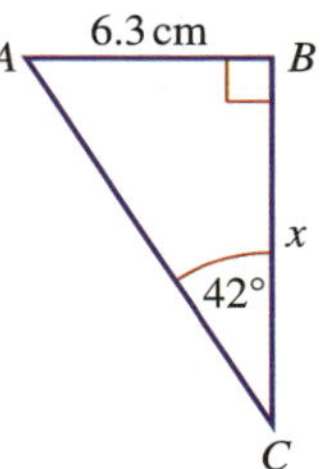

4 Find the length of the side marked with a letter.

a 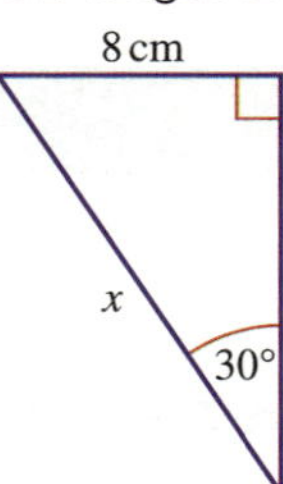

b 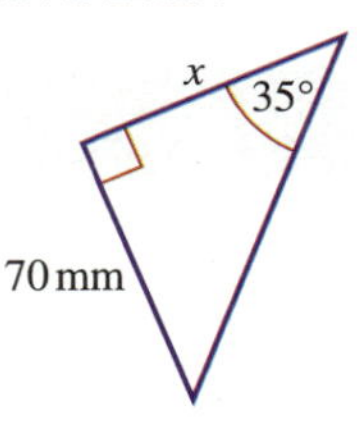

c 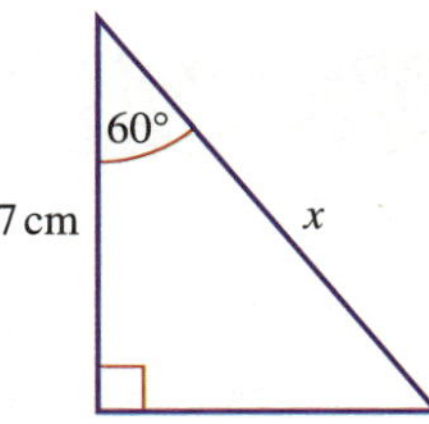

5 In triangle ABC, angle $B = 90°$

- **a** If $\angle BAC = 34°$ and $AB = 8.9$ cm, calculate the length of BC.
- **b** If $\angle ACB = 57°$ and $BC = 17.5$ cm, calculate the length of AC.
- **c** If $\angle ACB = 29°$ and $AC = 4.67$ m, calculate the length of AB.
- **d** If $\angle CAB = 73°$ and $BC = 19.4$ cm, calculate the length of AB.

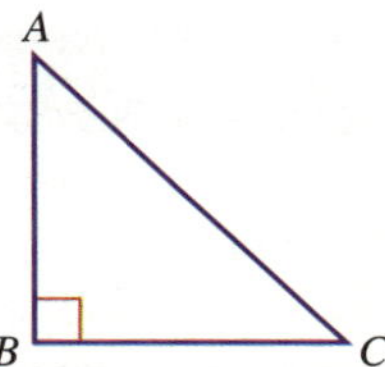

6 A ladder 5 m long rests at an angle of 70° to a wall.
Calculate the distance of the foot of the ladder from the wall (marked d on the diagram).
Give your answer to 2 s.f.

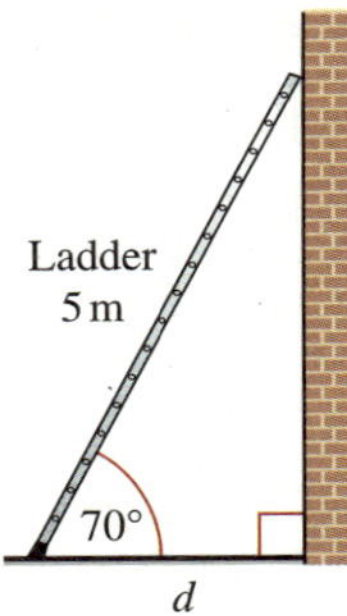

7 A wire is attached to the top of a flagpole 6 m high as shown.
Calculate the length of the wire.

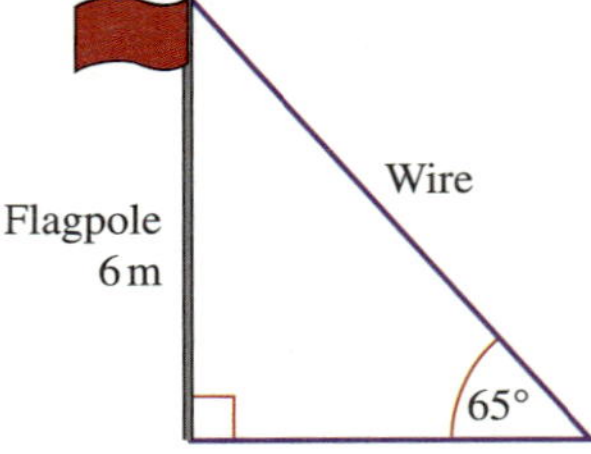

8 Calculate the height of this isosceles triangle.

9 The ladder is leaning against a wall.
Find how far up the wall the ladder reaches.

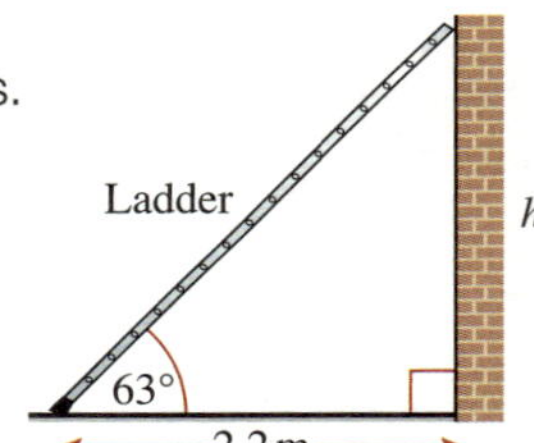

29.2 Finding an angle

CAN YOU REMEMBER

- The three trigonometric ratios:
  $\sin A = \dfrac{\text{opposite}}{\text{hypotenuse}}$, $\cos A = \dfrac{\text{adjacent}}{\text{hypotenuse}}$, $\tan A = \dfrac{\text{opposite}}{\text{adjacent}}$?
- That three figure bearings are measured from north in a clockwise direction and are written as e.g. 136°, 058°?

IN THIS SECTION YOU WILL

- Use trigonometric ratios to find the size of angles in right-angled triangles.
- Learn about inverse trigonometric ratios and the notation to represent them.
- Apply trigonometry to problems involving right-angled triangles and bearings.

The size of an unknown angle in a right-angled triangle can be calculated if the lengths of two sides are known.

The size of the angle is found using an *inverse* trigonometric ratio.

For example, if $\sin A = 0.6$, then A is the inverse sine of 0.6. This is written as
$A = \text{inv}\sin 0.6$ or $\sin^{-1} 0.6$ or $\arcsin 0.6$

So $A = 37°$ (to 2 s.f.)

Using a calculator.

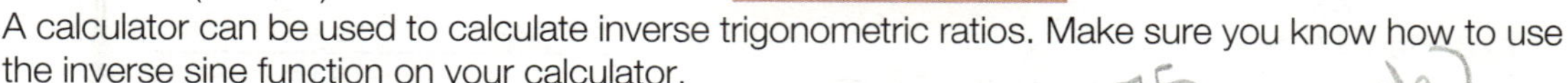

A calculator can be used to calculate inverse trigonometric ratios. Make sure you know how to use the inverse sine function on your calculator.

Example 1

Calculate the size of angle A.

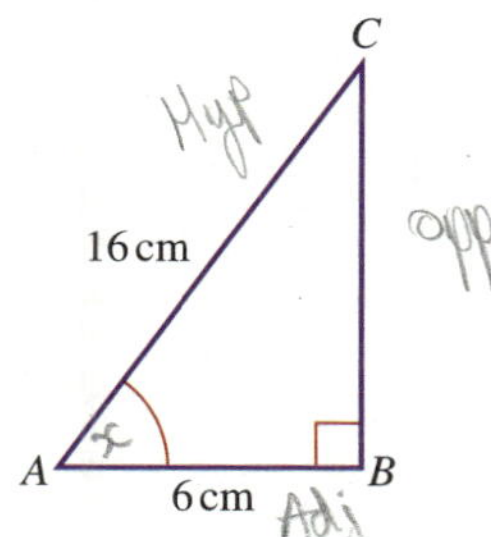

Solution 1

The adjacent side is 6 cm and the hypotenuse is 16 cm.

Using $\cos A = \dfrac{\text{adjacent}}{\text{hypotenuse}}$

$\cos A = \frac{6}{16} = 0.375$

$A = \cos^{-1} 0.375$

Using a calculator gives $A = 68°$

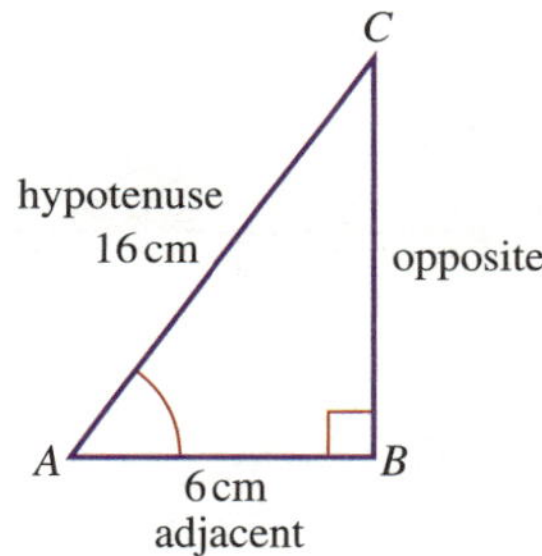

Angle of elevation and angle of depression

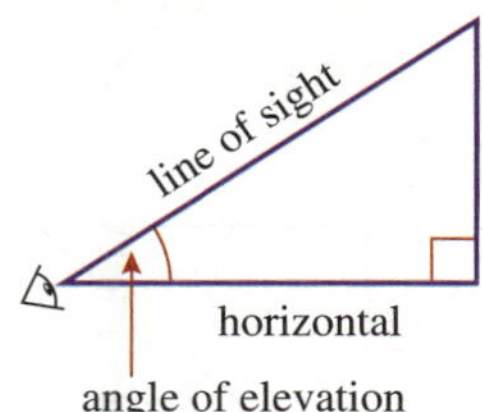

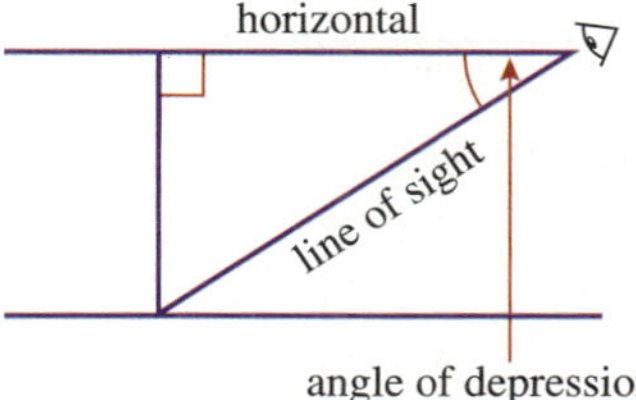

Example 2

A boy is standing at B, 43 m away from the foot of a flagpole.

The flagpole is 6.8 m high.

Calculate x, the angle of elevation of the top of the flagpole from B.

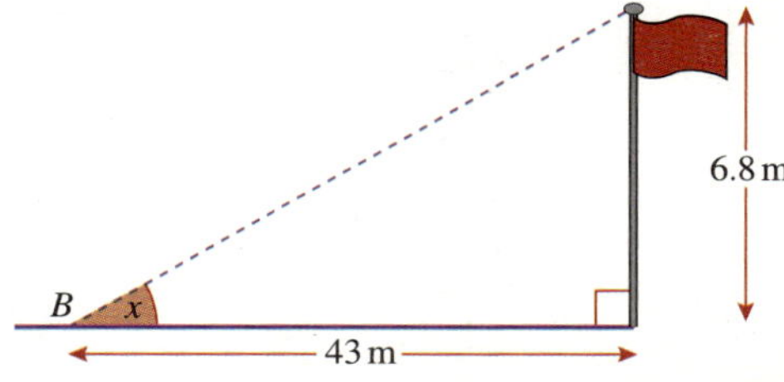

Solution 2

The opposite side is 6.8 m and the adjacent side is 43 m.

$\tan x = \dfrac{\text{opposite}}{\text{adjacent}}$

$\tan x = \dfrac{6.8}{43} = 0.158$

$x = \tan^{-1} 0.158$

$x = 9°$

Using a calculator.

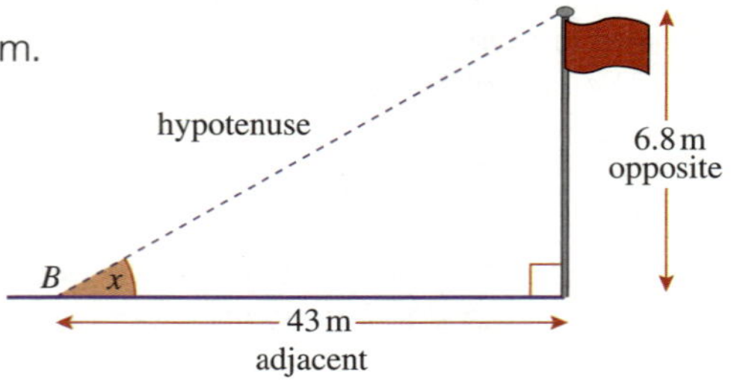

Exercise A

1 Use the data in the table to find angle x.

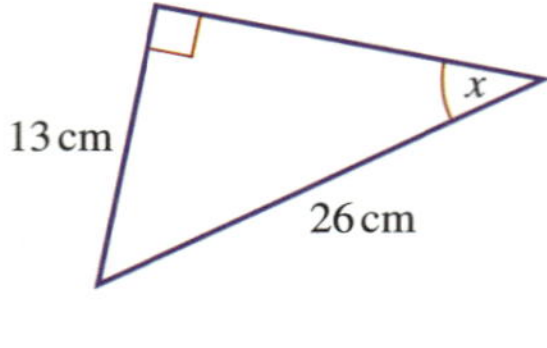

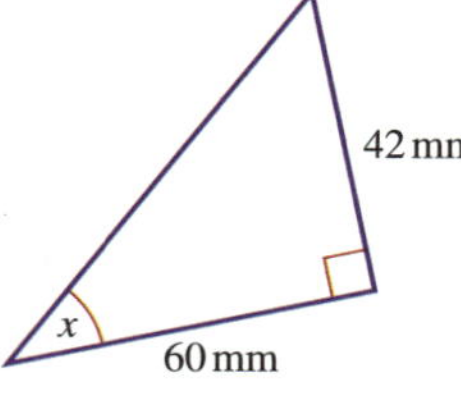

Angle	Sine	Cosine	Tangent
30°	0.5	0.866	0.577
35°	0.574	0.819	0.7

2 Calculate the value of the shaded angle in each triangle.

a

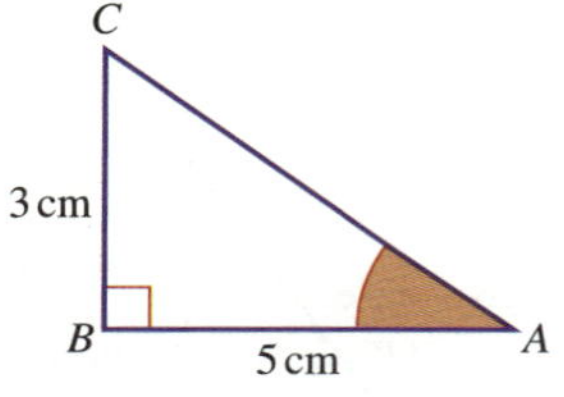

b

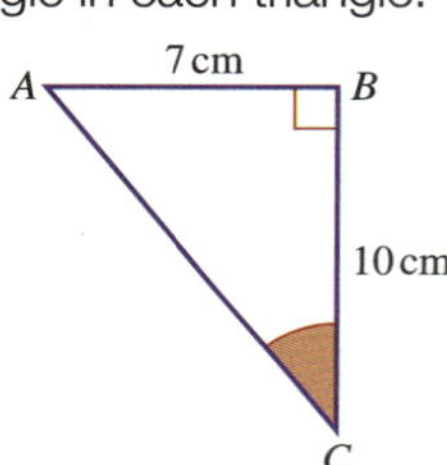

c

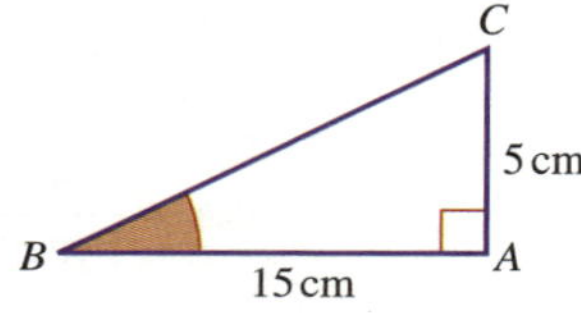

d

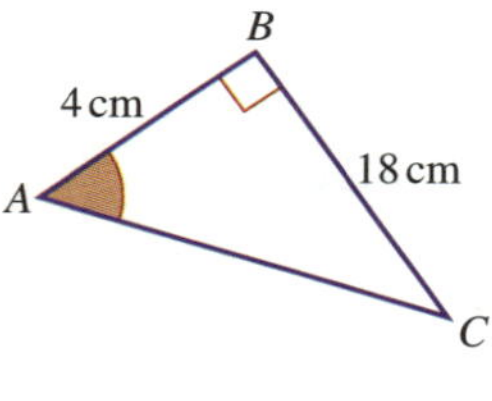

e

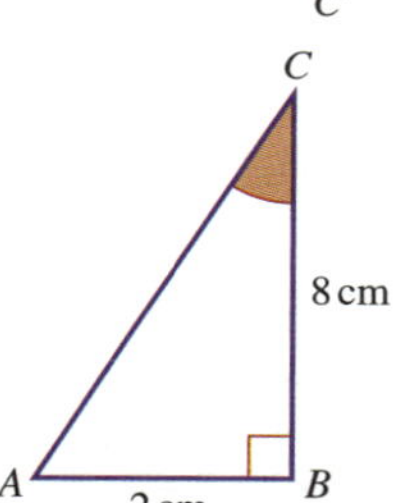

f

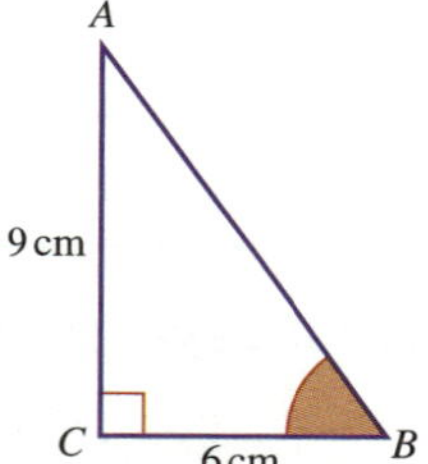

3 Work out the size of the angle marked with a letter.

a

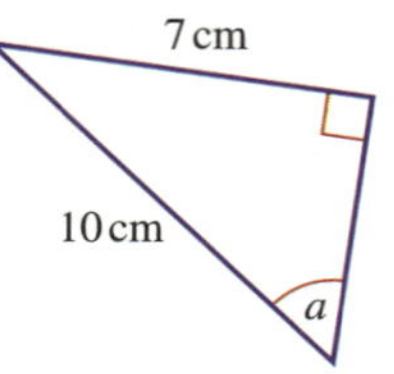

b

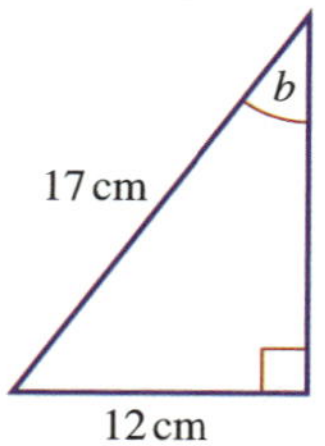

c

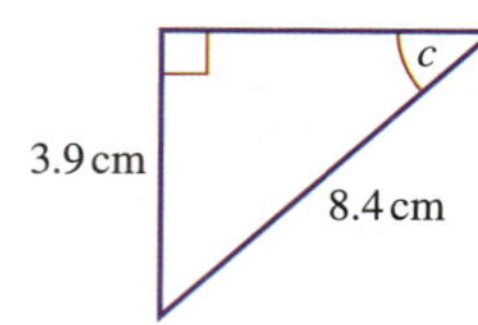

d

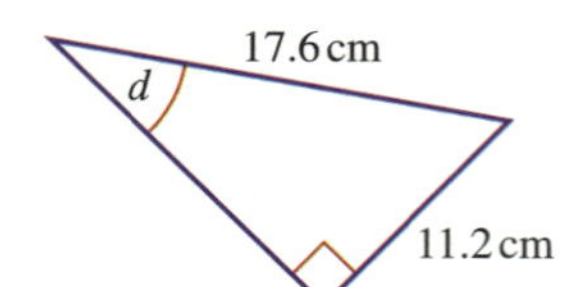

e

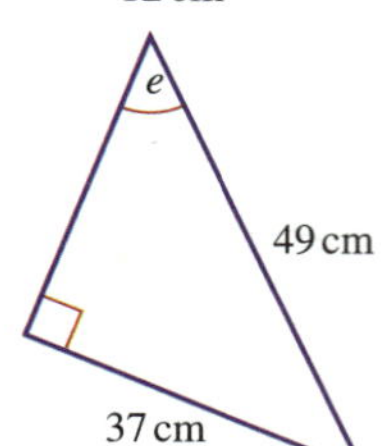

f

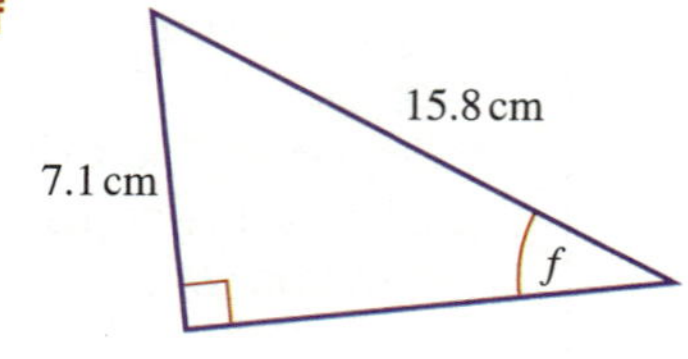

4 Calculate the size of the angle marked with a letter.

a

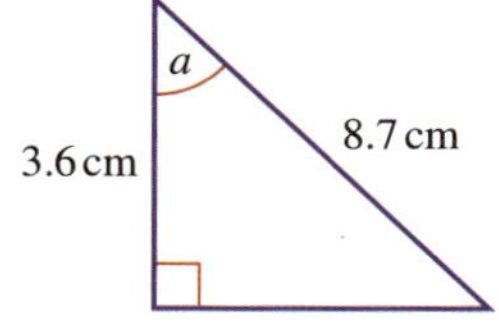

b

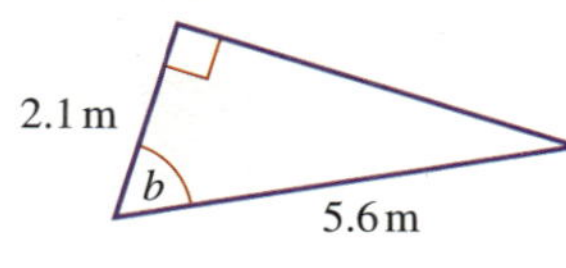

c

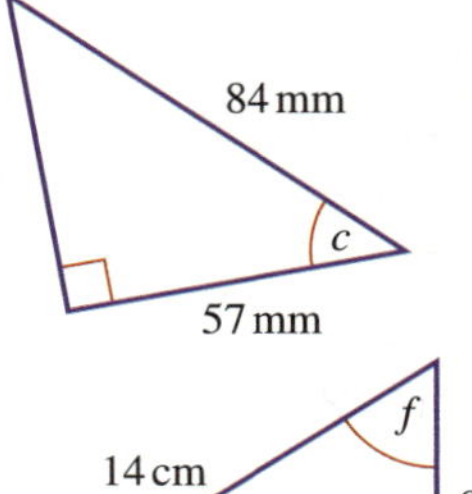

d

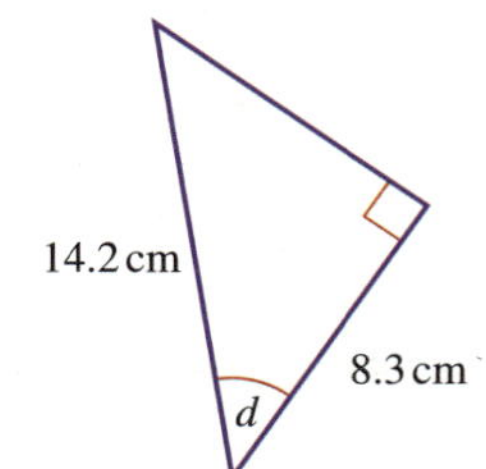

e

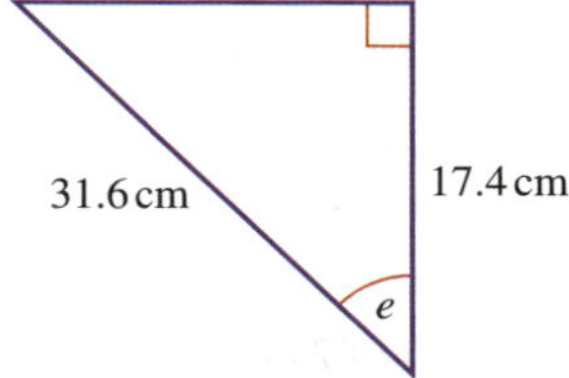

f

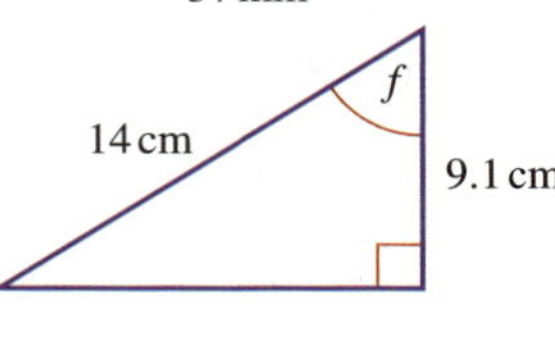

5 Find the marked angle.

a

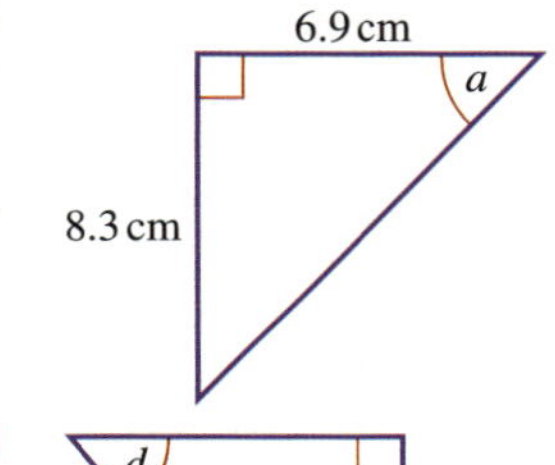

b

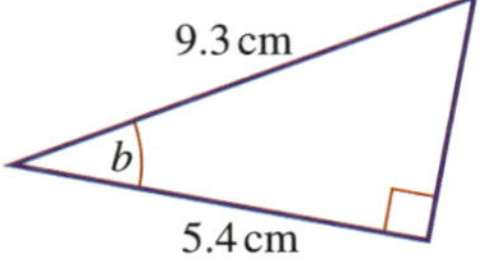

c

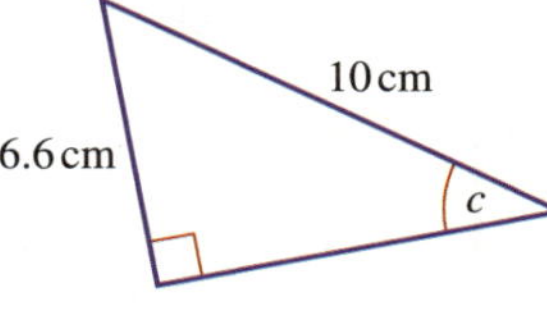

d

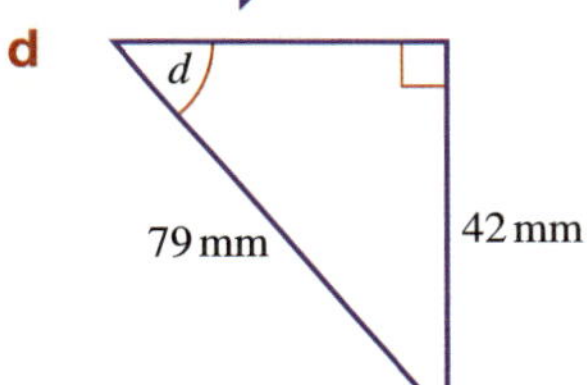

e

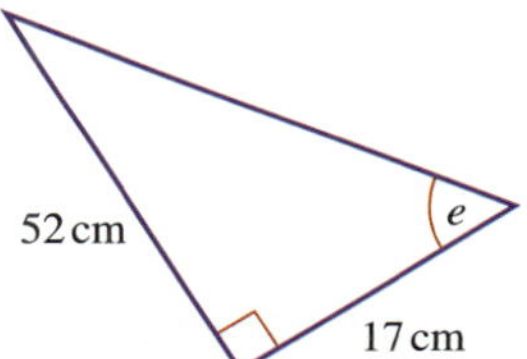

f

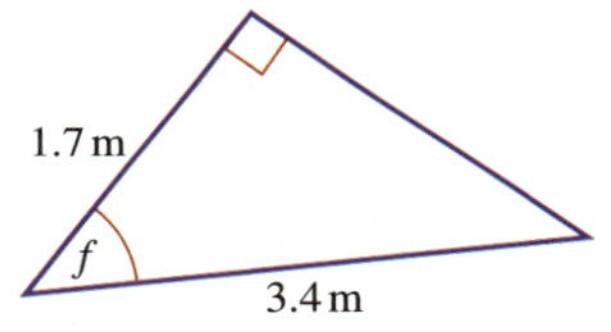

6 A ladder 7.2 m long leans against a wall. The top of the ladder is 4.5 m from the ground.

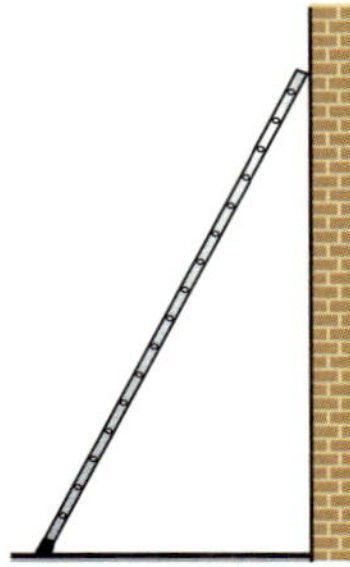

What angle does the ladder make with the ground?
Give your answer to the nearest degree.

7 A girl is standing at G, 58 m away from the foot of a radio mast.
The radio mast is 76 m high.
Calculate x, the angle of elevation of the top of the radio mast from G.
Give your answer to the nearest degree.

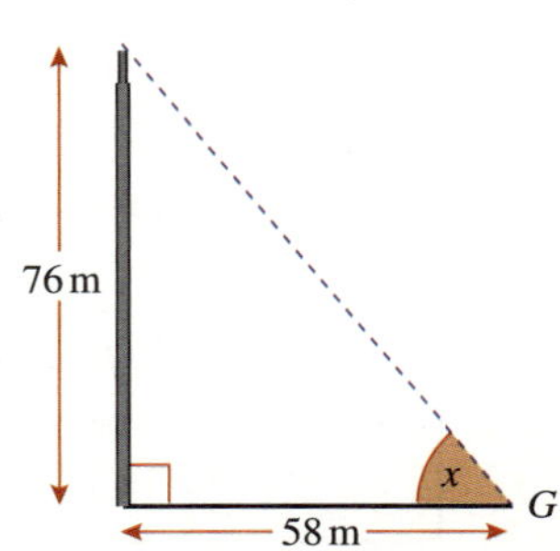

8 A coastguard standing on a cliff at point C sees a boat, S, in the sea below.

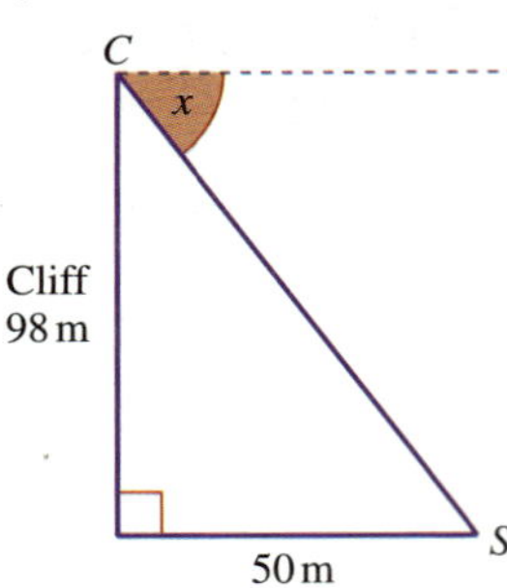

The cliff is 98 m high and the boat is 50 m away from the cliff.
Calculate the angle of depression of the boat from the top of the cliff (marked x in the diagram).

Example 3

Find the values of: **a** angle x **b** angle y.

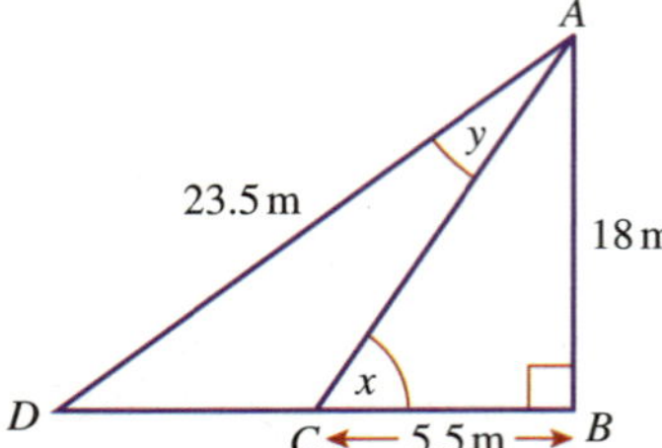

Solution 3

a In triangle ABC, the opposite side is 18 m and the adjacent side is 5.5 m.

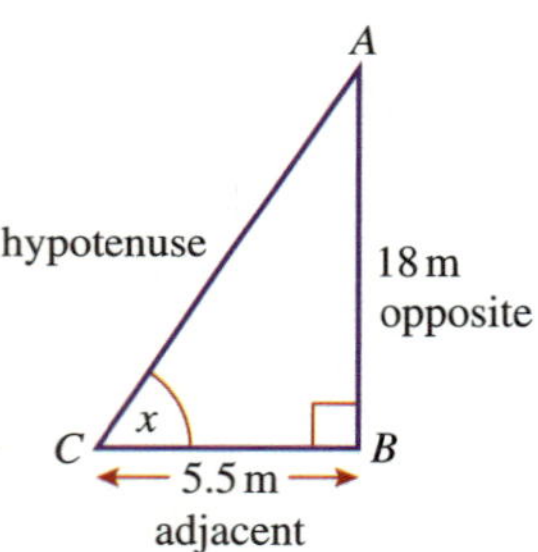

$$\tan x = \frac{\text{opposite}}{\text{adjacent}} = \frac{18}{5.5} = 3.2727...$$

$$x = \tan^{-1} 3.2727... = 73°$$

b First find angle BAD.
In triangle ABD the adjacent side to angle BAD is 18 m.
The hypotenuse is 23.5 m.

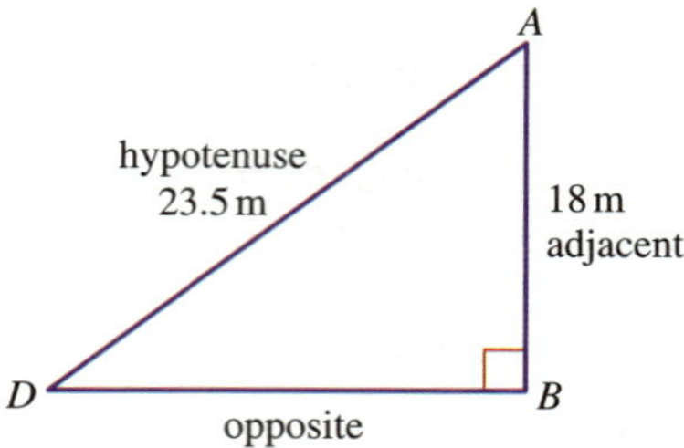

$$\cos BAD = \frac{\text{adjacent}}{\text{hypotenuse}} = \frac{18}{23.5}$$

$$= 0.7659...$$

Angle BAD = inv cos 0.7659... = 40°
Since angle BAC = 17° (angles in a triangle = 180°)
$y = 40° - 17° = 23°$

Example 4

A man leaves point A and walks 2.7 km due north. He then turns and walks 3 km due east to point B.
Find the bearing of B from A to the nearest degree.

Solution 4

Draw a sketch.
The bearing of B from A is marked x.
3 km is the opposite side and 2.7 km is the adjacent side.

$\tan x = \dfrac{\text{opposite}}{\text{adjacent}} = \dfrac{3}{2.7} = 1.11...$

$x = \tan^{-1} 1.11... = 48°$

The bearing of B from A is 048°

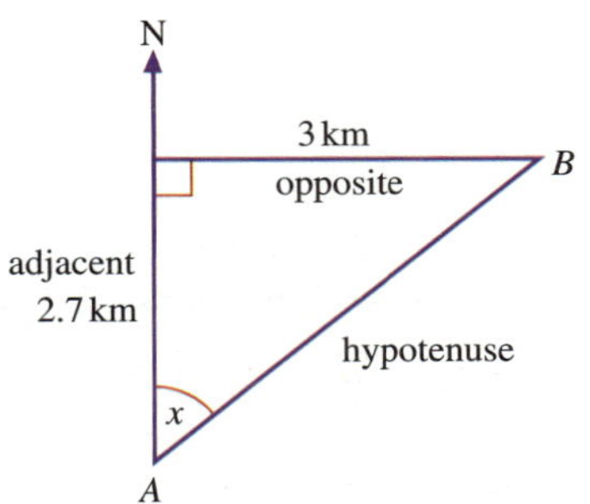

Exercise B

1 The diagram shows two right-angled triangles joined along RP.
 a Calculate the length of PR.
 b Calculate the length of RT.

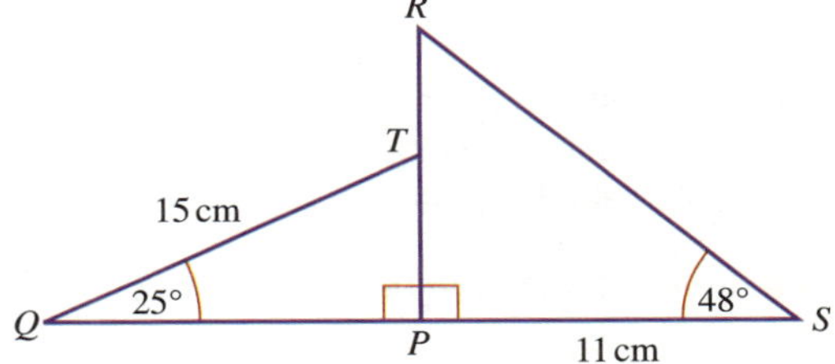

2 In the rectangle $ABCD$, the diagonal BD is 24 cm long and the side AD is 10.5 cm long. Sketch the rectangle and calculate the size of angle BDC.

3 After take-off an aeroplane flies 18 km in a straight line to climb to a height of 7 km.
Calculate the angle at which it climbs.

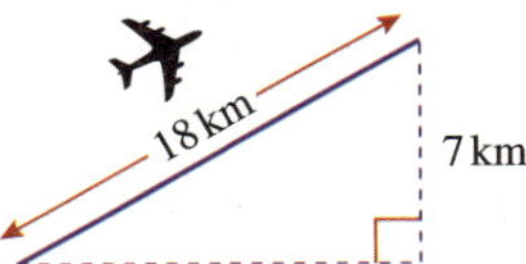

4 The diagram shows part of the framework for a roof.
Calculate the length of AD.

Hint: first find the length of BC.

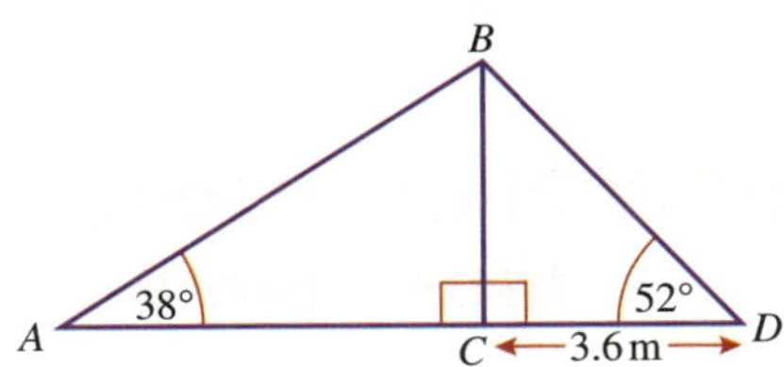

5 Calculate the sizes of angles x and y.
Give your answers to the nearest degree.

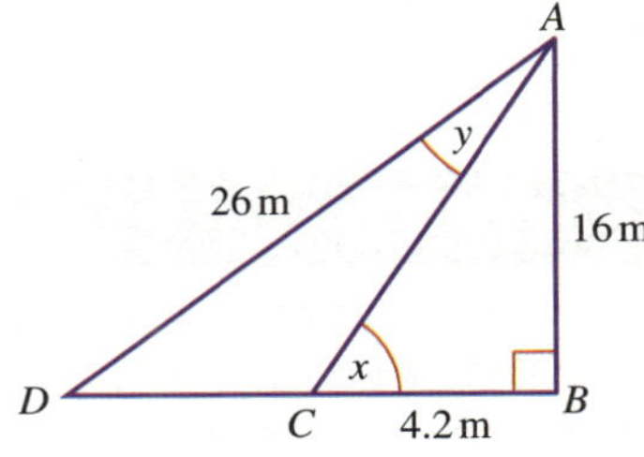

6 A farmer walks from his farmhouse F due north for 0.75 km, and then 1.4 km due east to reach a barn B. Calculate the bearing of the barn from the farmhouse.

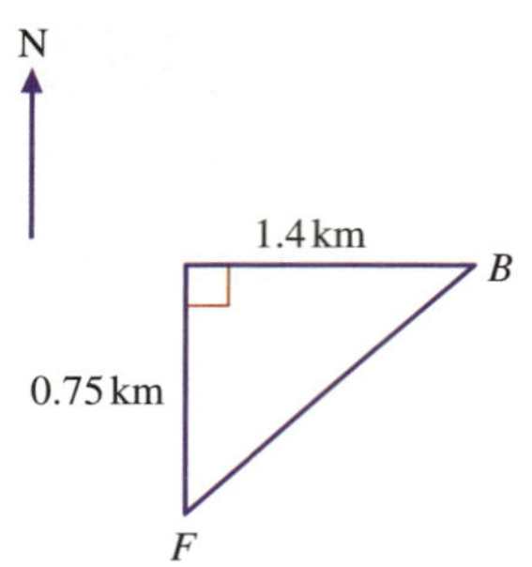

7 An isosceles triangle has $AB = AC = 18.1$ cm and $BC = 11.2$ cm. Calculate the three angles of the triangle.

8 A boy stands at B, 75 m from the foot of a tower. The angle of elevation of the top of the tower, T, from B is 40°.

a Calculate the height of the tower. Give your answer to one decimal place.

b The boy walks towards the tower until the angle of elevation of T is 50°. How far does he walk?

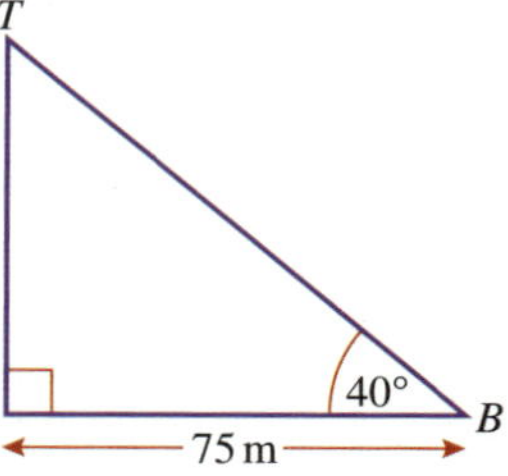

9 Rychester is 7 km due south of Ormcliffe.
Lunford is 10 km due east of Rychester.
Calculate the three-figure bearing of Lunford from Ormcliffe.

10 In the diagram PQR and PSQ are right-angled triangles.

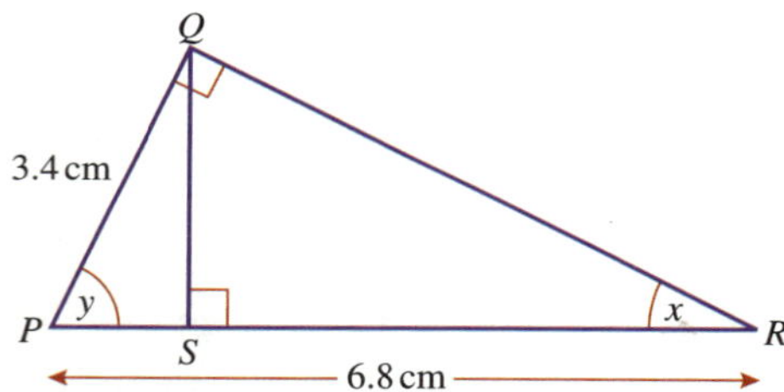

a Calculate the value of angle x.

b Hence write down the value of angle y.

c Calculate the length of RS.

29.3 Finding lengths and angles in three-dimensional shapes

CAN YOU REMEMBER

- How to use Pythagoras' theorem to work out the length of a side in a right-angled triangle?

IN THIS SECTION YOU WILL

- Use Pythagoras' theorem to calculate the lengths of lines in 3-D shapes.
- Use sine, cosine and tangent ratios to calculate sizes of angles in 3-D shapes.

Many problems in three dimensions involve finding the length of a line joining two points. If the length forms one side of a right-angled triangle, Pythagoras' theorem can be used.
For example, in the cuboid on the right, the length HB is the hypotenuse of the right-angled triangle HDB.

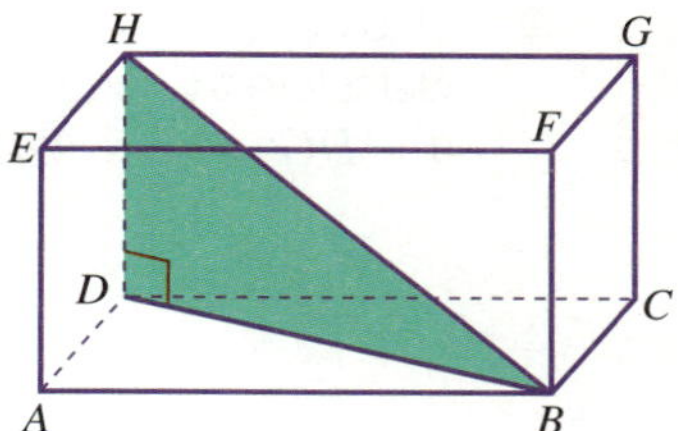

Example 1

This cube has sides of length 6 cm.
Calculate the length of the diagonal AG.

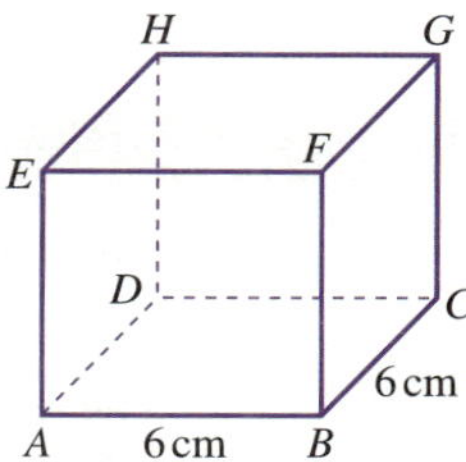

Solution 1

Sketch the right-angled triangle AGC.
$GC = 6$ cm but AC and AG are unknown.
To find length AC, use triangle ABC.

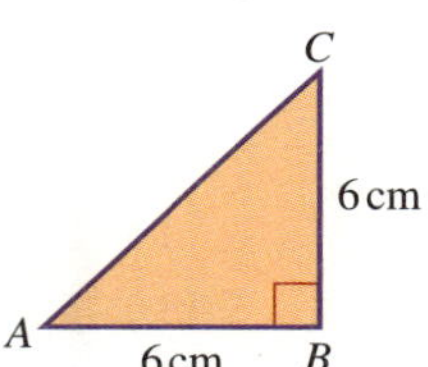

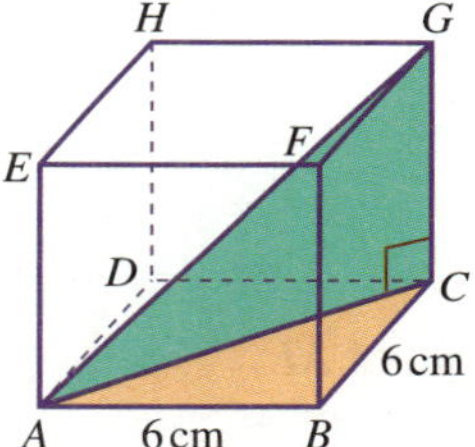

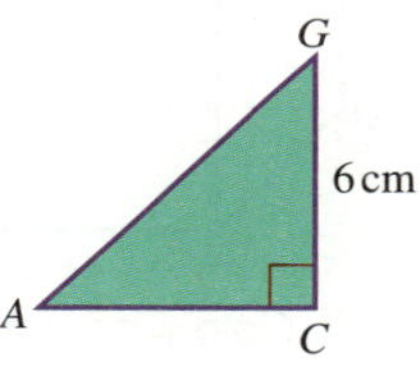

Using Pythagoras' theorem:
$AC^2 = AB^2 + BC^2$
$AC^2 = 6^2 + 6^2 = 36 + 36 = 72$
$AC = \sqrt{72}$ As this value will be squared in the next part of the solution, leave it as a square root here.
Now, using triangle ACG:
$AG^2 = AC^2 + GC^2 = (\sqrt{72})^2 + 6^2 = 72 + 36 = 108$
$AG = \sqrt{108} = 10.4$ cm (1 d.p.)

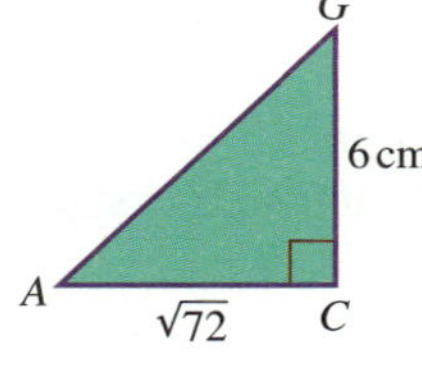

Exercise A

1 The diagram shows a cuboid.
  a Copy these triangles and label the known lengths.
  b Work out the length of:
  i AC **ii** FC.
  Leave your answers as square roots.

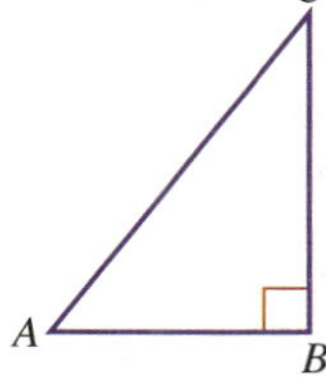

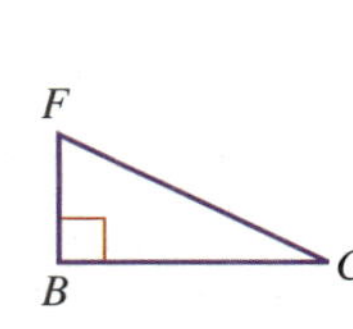

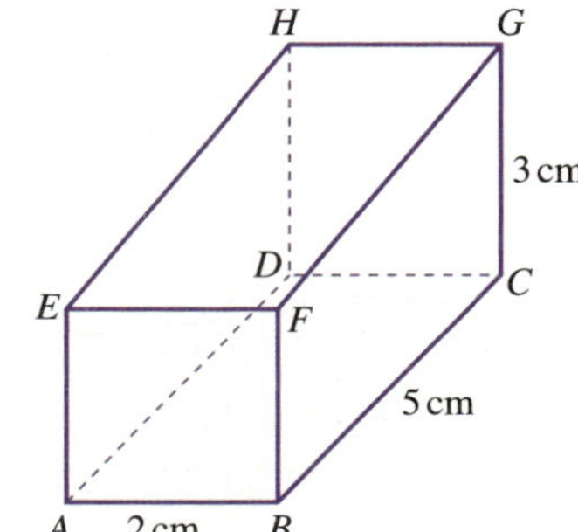

2 This cube has sides of length 10 cm.
Calculate the lengths of:
a DG **b** FD.

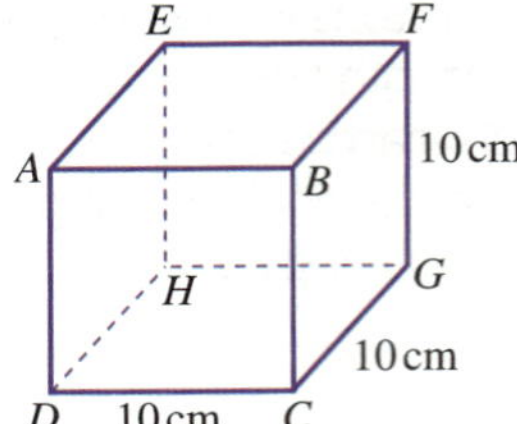

3 The diagram shows a pyramid with a square base of side 5 cm.
The vertical height of the pyramid is 10 cm.
Calculate:
a the length of AC
b the length of AE.

Hint: The *vertical* height always meets the base of a solid shape at 90°

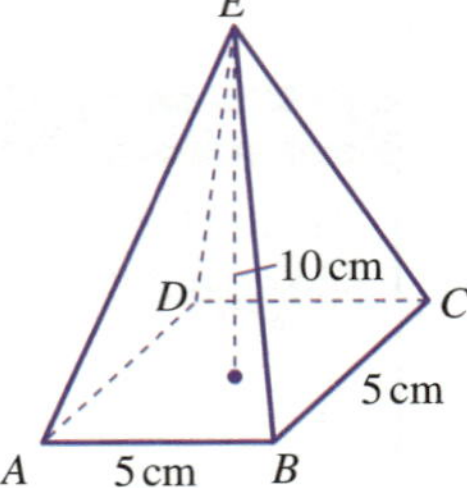

4 This cube has sides of length 7 cm.

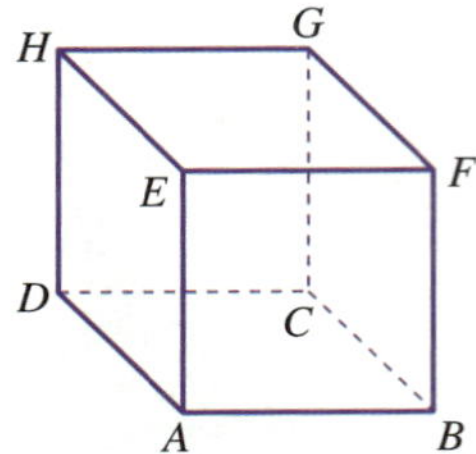

a Calculate the length of AF.
b Write down the length of AC.
c Calculate the length of the diagonal AG.

5 A triangular prism is 20 cm long.
The ends are isosceles triangles such that $AC = BC$ and $AB = 8$ cm.
The perpendicular height of the prism is 12 cm.
Calculate:
a the length BC
b the length of the diagonal CE.

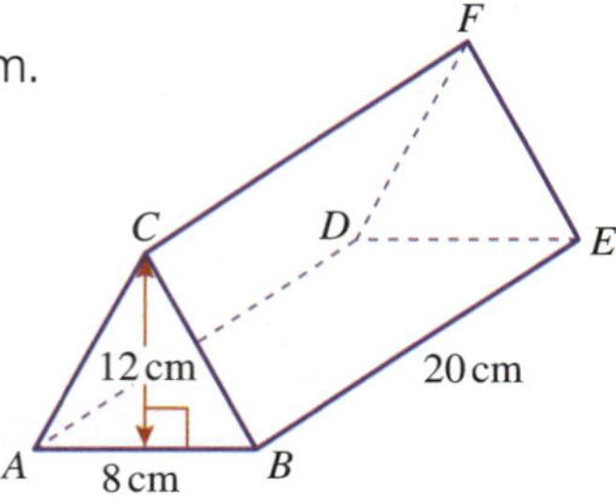

6 The diagram shows a pyramid with a rectangular base.

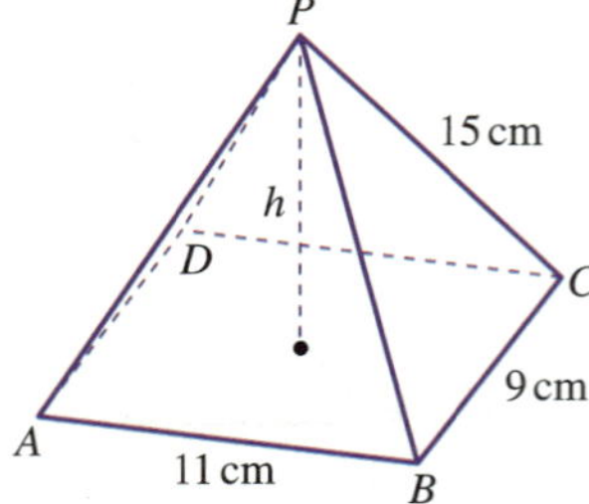

Edges PA, PB, PC and PD are 15 cm long.
Work out the vertical height of the pyramid.

When a problem in three dimensions involves finding the size of an angle between a line and a plane, trigonometry can be used.
For example, in this diagram, the line PQ intersects the plane at Q.
Draw PR perpendicular to the plane to form a right-angled triangle PRQ.
Angle PQR is the angle between the line and the plane.

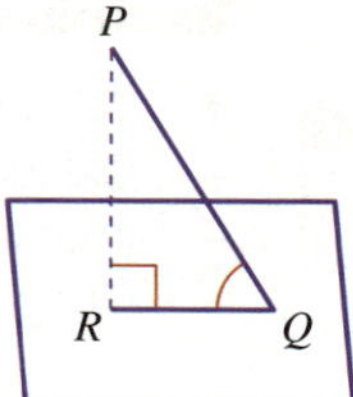

Example 2

The diagram shows a ramp.
Calculate:

a angle CAB

b the angle between DA and the base $ABEF$.

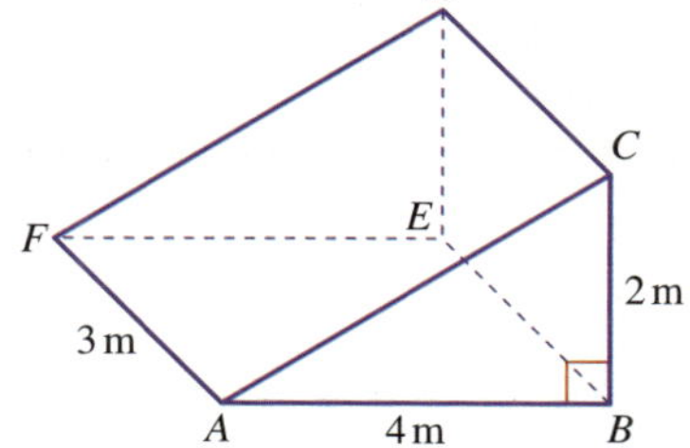

Solution 2

a Using triangle ABC:

$\tan A = \frac{\text{opposite}}{\text{adjacent}} = \frac{2}{4} = 0.5$

$A = \tan^{-1} 0.5 = 26.6°$

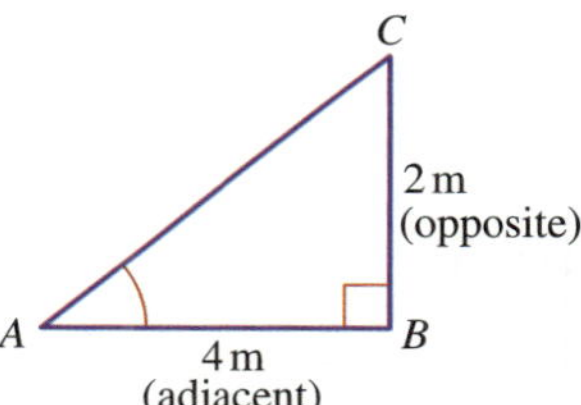

b Sketch triangle ADE.

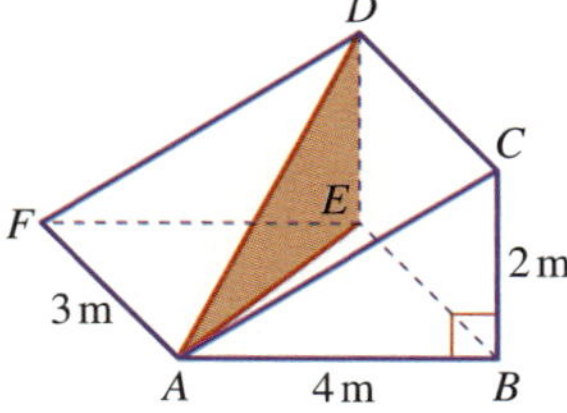

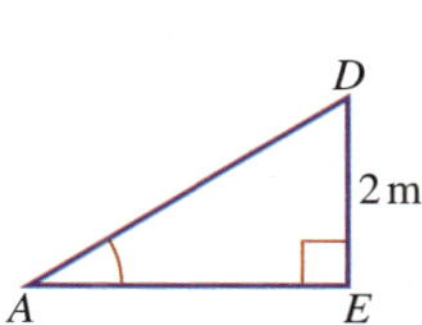

The angle between DA and the base is angle DAE.
To find this angle two sides are needed.
Use Pythagoras' theorem in triangle ABE to find the length of AE.

$AE^2 = 3^2 + 4^2 = 9 + 16 = 25$

$AE = \sqrt{25} = 5\text{ m}$

Now two sides are known in triangle AED.

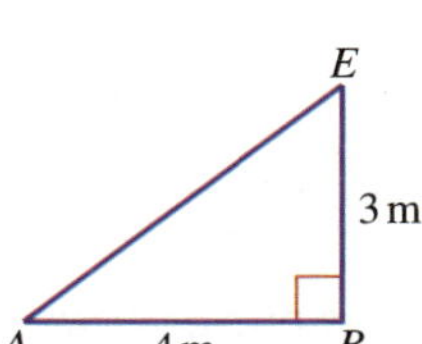

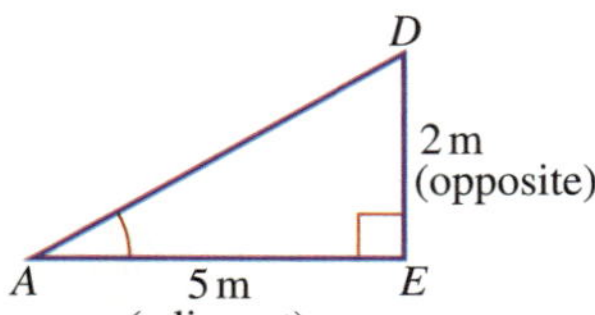

$\tan A = \frac{2}{5} = 0.4$

$A = \text{inv}\tan 0.4 = 21.8°$

The angle between the line AD and the base $ABEF$ is 21.8°

Exercise B

1 This cube has side length 14 cm.
Calculate the angle between the diagonal AG and the base $ABCD$ (marked x on the diagram).
Give your answer to the nearest degree.

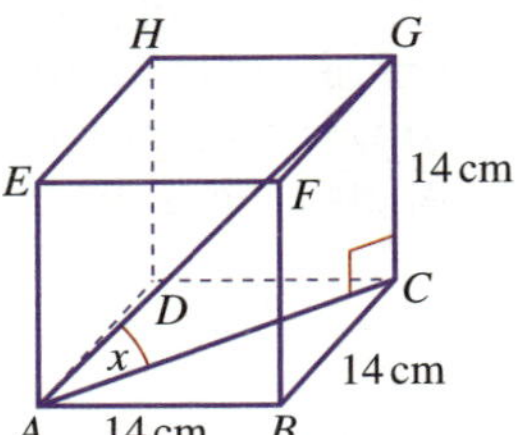

2 A square-based pyramid has vertical height 8 cm and a base of side 6 cm.
Calculate the angle between the edge EB and the base $ABCD$.
Give your answer to the nearest degree.

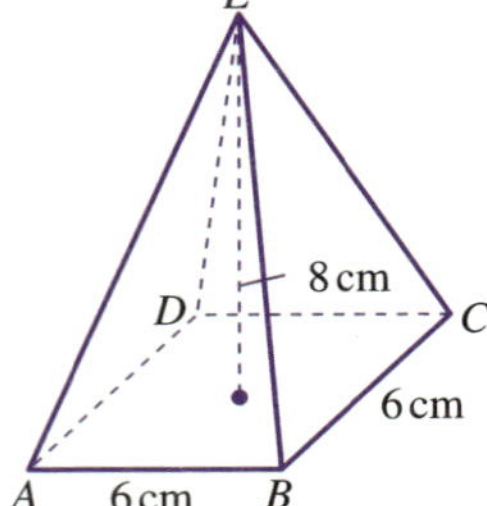

3 The diagram shows a ramp.

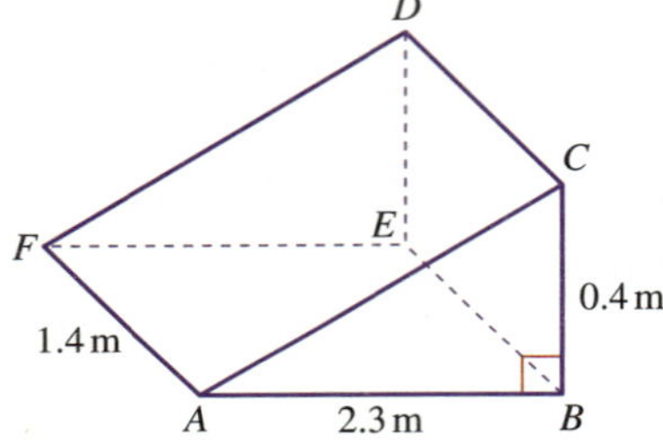

Calculate:

a the length of AC

b the angle between the diagonal CF and the base of the ramp.

4 This pyramid has a rectangular base.

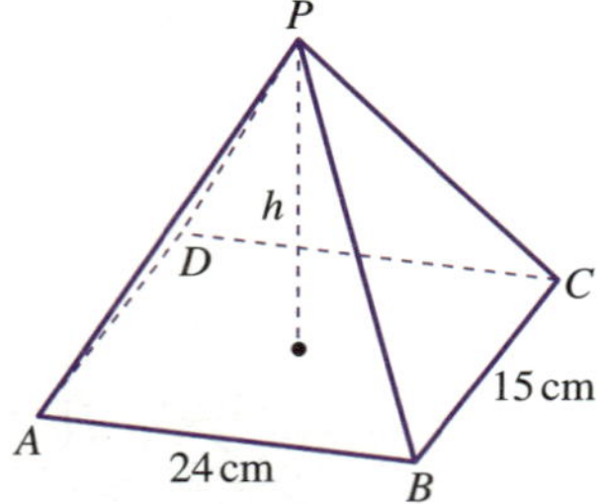

The angle between the edge PB and the base is 35°. Calculate:

a the vertical height of the pyramid

b the length of PB.

5 A box is in the shape of a cuboid with dimensions as shown.
Daniel says that he can fit a wooden pole of length 80 cm in the box.
Is he correct?
Show your working.

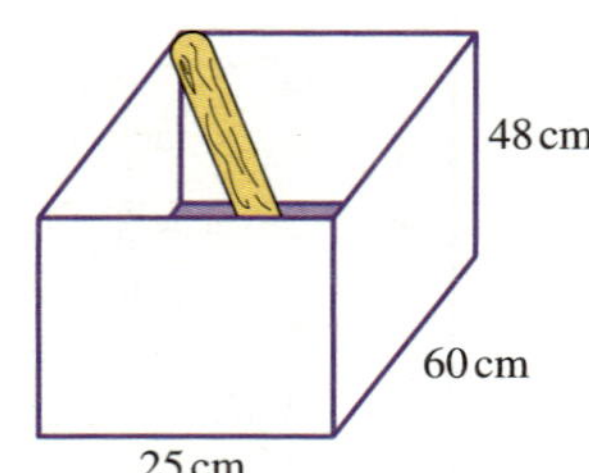

Chapter summary

- For any right-angled triangle the sides can be named as shown.
- The sine, cosine and tangent of a are given by the ratios:
  - $\sin a = \dfrac{\text{opposite}}{\text{hypotenuse}}$
  - $\cos a = \dfrac{\text{adjacent}}{\text{hypotenuse}}$
  - $\tan a = \dfrac{\text{opposite}}{\text{adjacent}}$

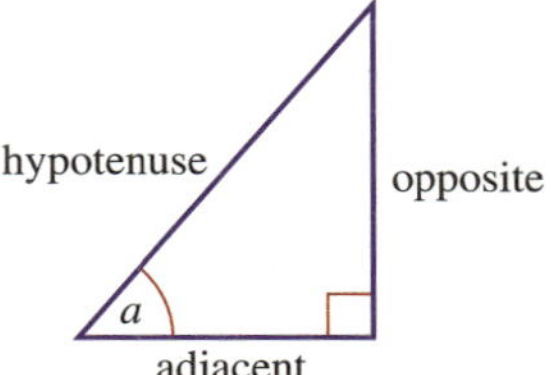

- Each formula links an angle and two sides. If two of these values are known the third can be calculated.
- The size of an unknown angle in a right-angled triangle can be calculated if the lengths of two sides are known.
- The size of the angle is found using the inverse trigonometric ratio.
  For example, if $\sin A = 0.6$, then A is the inverse sine of 0.6, written
  $A = \text{inv}\sin 0.6$ or $\sin^{-1} 0.6$ or $\arcsin 0.6$
- In some contexts angles may be called angles of elevation or angles of depression.
- Many problems in three dimensions involve finding the length of a line joining two points. If the length forms one side of a right-angled triangle, Pythagoras' theorem can be used.
- When a problem in three dimensions involves finding the size of an angle between a line and a plane, trigonometry can be used.
- Angle PQR is the angle between PQ and the plane.

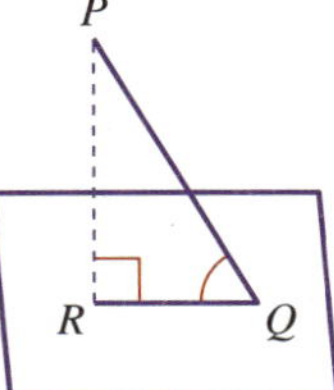

Chapter review

Use data from this table to answer questions **1–3**.

Angle	Sine	Cosine	Tangent
30°	0.5	0.866	0.577
40°	0.642	0.766	0.839
50°	0.766	0.642	1.192
60°	0.866	0.5	1.732
70°	0.94	0.342	2.75

1 The diagram shows a triangle ABC.
Angle $A = 40°$ and $AB = 10$ cm.
Work out the height AC.

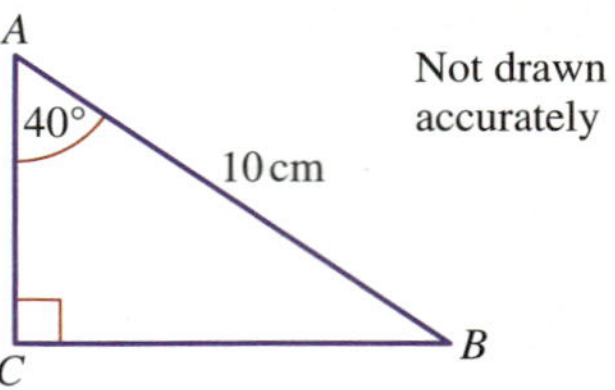

2 The diagram shows a triangle PQR.
$PQ = 6$ cm and $PR = 12$ cm.

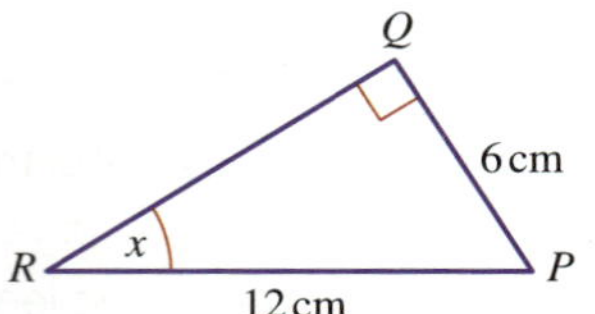

Work out the size of angle x.

3 The diagram shows a tower TW and a viewpoint V.
The viewpoint is 40 m from the foot of the tower.
From the viewpoint, the angle of elevation of the top of the tower is 70°
Work out the height of the tower.

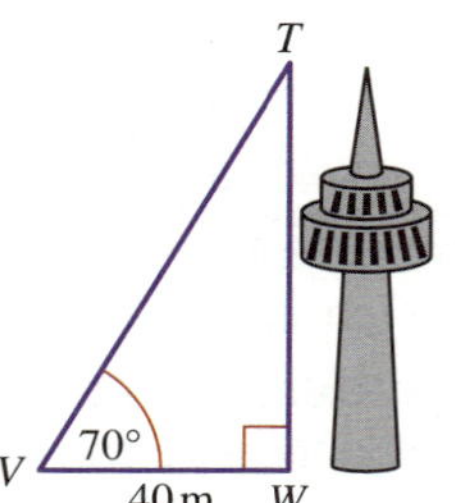

4 In triangle ABC, angle ABC is a right angle, $AC = 5.3$ cm and $BC = 4.7$ cm.

a Calculate the length of AB.

b Calculate the value of x.

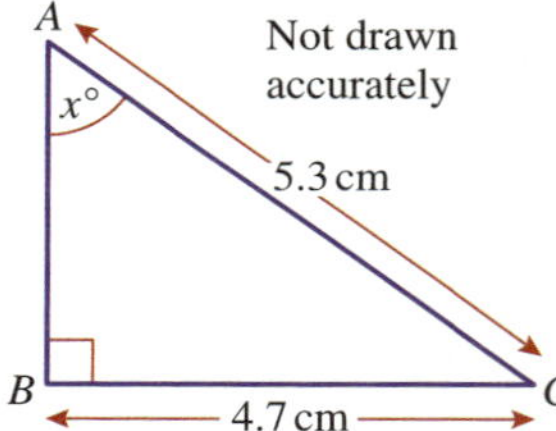

5 In the diagram, $AC = 3.2$ cm, $CD = 4.3$ cm, angle $BAC = 62°$ and angle ACD is a right angle.

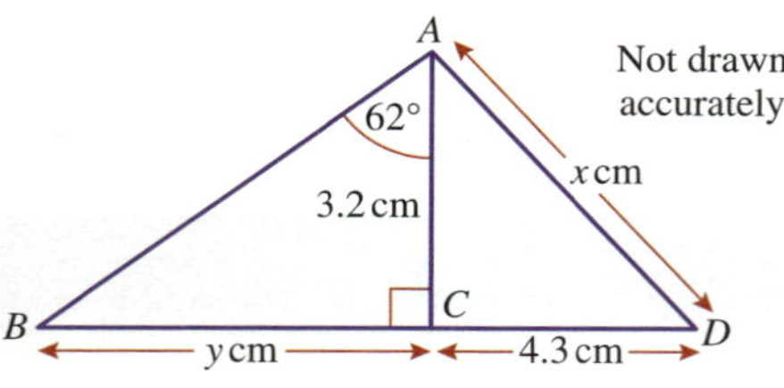

a Find the value of x.

b Find the value of y.

6 In the diagram $AC = 8$ cm and $BD = 3$ cm and angle $A = 20°$
Calculate the length of AD.
Give your answer correct to two decimal places.

7 A ship sets off from a port P and sails 15 km due south to a point S.
It then changes direction and sails on a bearing of 35° to a point T.
If T is due east of P, calculate the distance ST.
Give your answer correct to one decimal place.

8 $VPQRS$ is a pyramid on a square base of side 12 cm.
V is vertically above the centre of the square.
$VP = VQ = VR = VS = 16$ cm
Calculate the angle between the edge VP and the base $PQRS$.
Give your answer to the nearest integer.

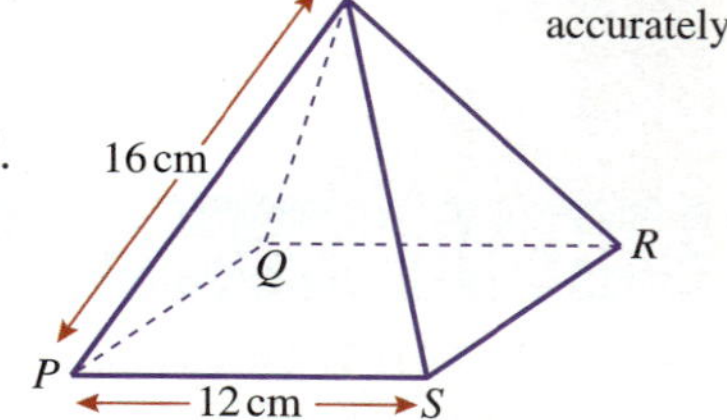

9 The diagram shows a door-wedge with a rectangular base $ABCD$.
The sloping face $ABEF$ is also rectangular.
$AB = 3.5$ cm, angle $CBE = 8°$ and the height $CE = 2.8$ cm.
Calculate the length of the diagonal FB.
Give your answer correct to two decimal places.

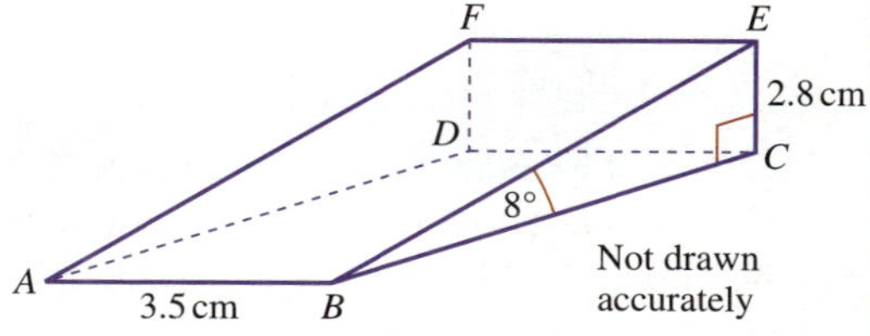

10 $ABCDEFGH$ is an open tank in the shape of a cuboid. $AB = 50$ cm, $AE = 60$ cm and $BC = 80$ cm.
A straight rod rests in the tank with its ends at B and H, as shown in the diagram.

a Calculate the length of the rod.

b Calculate the angle that the rod makes with the line BC.

c Calculate the angle that the rod makes with the plane $ABCD$.

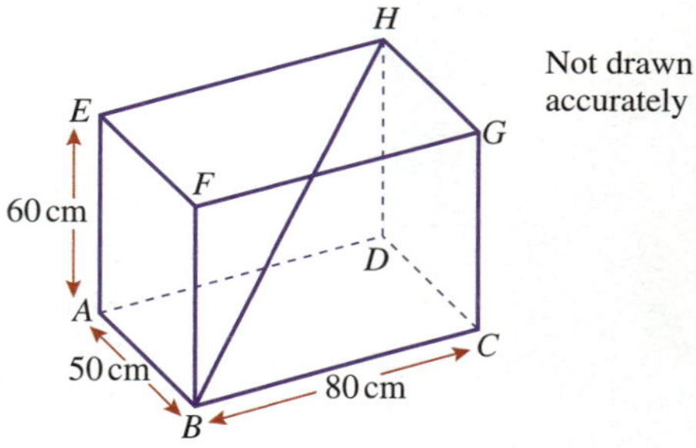

CHAPTER 30

Probability 2

30.1 Further probability

CAN YOU REMEMBER

- How to calculate simple probabilities?
- How to show the outcomes of two events in a table?
- The meaning of the notation P(event)?

IN THIS SECTION YOU WILL

- Understand the meaning of 'mutually exclusive outcomes'.
- Learn that the sum of the probabilities of all of the mutually exclusive outcomes is equal to 1
- Learn how to calculate probabilities for mutually exclusive outcomes.
- Learn the 'OR' rule or addition rule for mutually exclusive probabilities.

Outcomes that cannot happen at the same time are called *mutually exclusive outcomes*.

Examples of mutually exclusive outcomes are:

The dice is rolled. It shows 5
The dice is rolled again. It shows 2
These events cannot both happen at the same time.
They are mutually exclusive.

One disc is taken at random from the bag.
The possible outcomes are 1, 2, 3, 4, 5, 6, 7, 8, 9 and 10
Only one number can occur at a time.
These outcomes are mutually exclusive.

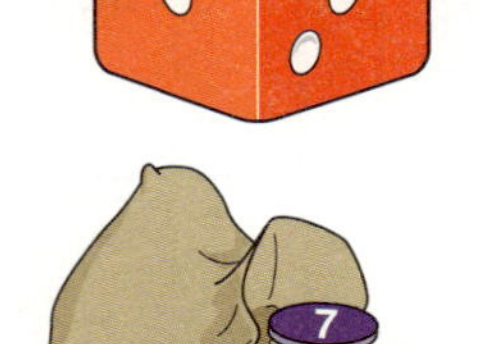

The coin is flipped. It shows heads.
The coin is flipped again. It shows tails.
'Heads' and 'tails' are mutually exclusive events.

Example 1

Here are some events from rolling an ordinary dice.
A: rolling a 6 ✓
B: rolling an even number
C: rolling a number less than 3
D: rolling a number greater than 0 ✓
Which two events are mutually exclusive? Explain your answer.

Because the ticked options have only one outcome.

Solution 1

Events A and C are mutually exclusive events because they cannot happen at the same time.
Any other pair of events can occur at the same time.

- A and B both occur if a 6 is rolled
- A and D both occur if a 6 is rolled
- B and C both occur if a 2 is rolled
- B and D both occur if a 2, 4 or 6 is rolled
- C and D both occur if a 1 or 2 is rolled.

A fair spinner has six equal sections.
One section is green, two are yellow and the rest are white.
The spinner is spun once.
The outcomes are green, yellow and white.
These are mutually exclusive outcomes.
The table shows the probabilities of each of these outcomes.

Outcome	Green	Yellow	White
Probability	$\frac{1}{6}$	$\frac{2}{6}$	$\frac{3}{6}$

$$\frac{1}{6}+\frac{2}{6}+\frac{3}{6}=\frac{6}{6}=1$$

The total probability of all the mutually exclusive outcomes of an event is 1
An event cannot happen and not happen at the same time. 'The event happens' and 'the event does not happen' are mutually exclusive.
So

$$P(\text{event happens}) + P(\text{event does not happen}) = 1$$

This can be rearranged as:

$$P(\text{event happens}) = 1 - P(\text{event does not happen})$$

Example 2

The probability that a fair spinner lands on a yellow section is 0.4

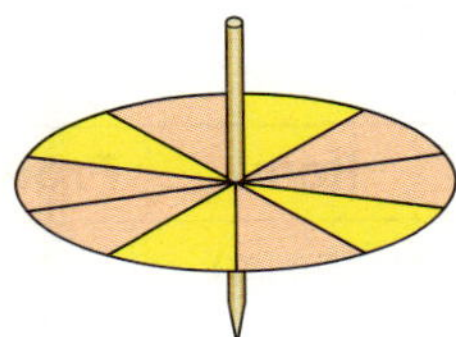

Calculate the probability that the spinner lands on a section that is **not** yellow.

Solution 2

$P(\text{not yellow}) = 1 - P(\text{yellow}) = 1 - 0.4 = 0.6$

Example 3

David takes an apple, an orange or a pear to work every day.
The table shows some of the probabilities for the fruit that he takes to work.
Calculate the probability that David takes a pear to work next Monday.

Fruit	Probability
Apple	0.5
Orange	0.3
Pear	

Solution 3

The probability that David takes a pear to work on Monday
= 1 − the probability that he does not take a pear to work on Monday
= 1 − (0.5 + 0.3) = 1 − 0.8 = 0.2

Exercise A

1 The probability that a girl at St Joseph's school has blond hair is 0.3
Work out the probability that a girl chosen at random from St Joseph's does **not** have blond hair.

2 Joe and Steve play a game. There is only one winner.
The probability that Joe wins is 0.6
Work out the probability that Joe does **not** win.

3 Katy has a bag of beads. One quarter of the beads are red.
Katy picks a bead from the bag.
Work out the probability that the bead she picks is **not** red.

4 The probability that Peter, a darts champion, hits the bullseye with his first throw is 0.7
Work out the probability that Peter misses the bullseye with his first throw.

5 The probability that Simon misses the bus to college is 0.5
Work out the probability that he does **not** miss the bus to college.

6 On a packet of Bixy cereals it states that there is a 10% chance that the packet will contain a prize.
Work out the probability that a packet of Bixy cereals chosen at random does **not** contain a prize.
Give your answer as a percentage.

7 The table shows some of the probabilities of patients arriving early, on time or late for a doctor's appointment.
Work out the probability that a patient arrives late.

Patient arrives	Probability
Early	0.1
On time	0.6
Late	

8 Penny often goes to the cinema. She always buys one item from the shop.
The table shows some of the probabilities for the item she buys.
Work out the probability that Penny buys crisps on her next visit to the cinema.

Item	Probability
Popcorn	0.2
Drink	0.4
Ice cream	0.3
Crisps	

9 The probability that Susan does **not** hand in her Mathematics homework on time is 0.52
Calculate the probability that Susan does hand her Mathematics homework in on time.

10 The table shows some of the probabilities of the type of people entering a shopping centre.
Calculate the probability that the next person to enter the shopping centre will be a boy.

Person	Probability
Man	0.21
Woman	0.36
Boy	
Girl	0.32

Example 4

Two ordinary fair dice are thrown.
The numbers shown on the dice are added to give a score.

a Draw a table to show all possible scores.
b Calculate the probability that the score is 7
c Calculate the probability that the score is **not** 7

Solution 4

a

Second dice \ First dice	**1**	**2**	**3**	**4**	**5**	**6**
1	2	3	4	5	6	**7**
2	3	4	5	6	**7**	8
3	4	5	6	**7**	8	9
4	5	6	**7**	8	9	10
5	6	**7**	8	9	10	11
6	**7**	8	9	10	11	12

b Probability of an event happening $= \dfrac{\text{number of successful outcomes}}{\text{total number of outcomes}}$

$P(\text{score is 7}) = \dfrac{6}{36} = \dfrac{1}{6}$

c **Method 1**

$P(\text{score is } \textbf{not } 7) = 1 - P(\text{score is 7}) = 1 - \dfrac{1}{6} = \dfrac{5}{6}$

Method 2

Count up all the outcomes that are not 7. There are 30

$P(\text{score is } \textbf{not } 7) = \dfrac{30}{36} = \dfrac{5}{6}$

If two events, A and B, are mutually exclusive:
$P(A \text{ or } B) = P(A) + P(B)$
This is known as the 'OR' rule or addition rule for mutually exclusive probabilities.

Example 5

A bag contains coloured counters marked with symbols.
There are 10 red counters, four with circles, the rest with squares.
There are 12 blue counters, seven with circles, the rest with squares.
There are five green counters, all with circles.
A counter is taken from the bag at random.
Find the probability that the counter is:

a red with a circle or blue with a circle
b red or with a circle.

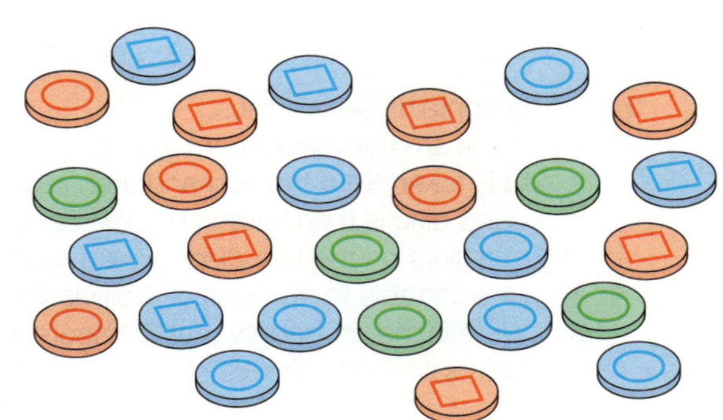

Solution 4

a The events 'red with a circle' and 'blue with a circle' are mutually exclusive so
P(red with a circle **or** blue with a circle) = P(red with a circle) + P(blue with a circle)
$= \frac{4}{27} + \frac{7}{27} = \frac{11}{27}$

b The events 'red' or 'circle' are not mutually exclusive as they can happen at the same time so the separate probabilities must not be added.
Instead, count the total of red or circles separately.
10 red + 7 circles (blue) + 5 circles (green) = 22
so the probability $= \frac{22}{27}$

Exercise B

1 A five-sided spinner has sections numbered 1, 2, 3, 4 and 5
The spinner is spun twice.
The numbers that the spinner lands on are added to give a score.

a Copy and complete the table to show all possible scores.

First throw

Second throw		1	2	3	4	5
	1	2				
	2	3				
	3					
	4					
	5				9	10

b Calculate the probability that the score is:
i 6 **ii** **not** 6

2 A fair six-sided dice and a coin are thrown.
If the coin shows heads the score is double the number shown on the dice.
If the coin shows tails the score is one less than the number shown on the dice.

a Copy and complete the table to show the possible scores.

b Calculate the probability that the score is:
i 0
ii odd
iii even.

Dice

Coin		1	2	3	4	5	6
	Heads	2					12
	Tails	0					5

3 A bag contains seven discs.
The discs are numbered from 1 to 7
A disc is taken from the bag and then replaced in the bag.
A second disc is then taken from the bag.
The numbers on the two discs are added to give a score.

a Draw a table to show all of the possible scores.
b What is the probability that the score is 14?
c Calculate the probability that the score is 12 or more.
d Use your answer to part **c** to calculate the probability that the score is less than 12

4 In a raffle for a new car 200 tickets were sold.
Andrew buys one ticket. James buys five tickets.
Write down the probability that the car is won by
a Andrew **b** James **c** neither Andrew nor James.

5 68% of the population own a mobile phone.
a Write down the percentage of the population that do **not** own a mobile phone.
In a survey of under 12s it was found that 75% do **not** have a mobile phone.
b Write down the percentage of under 12s that have a mobile phone.
c Explain why there is a difference between the population figures and the survey figures.

6 The table shows some of the probabilities of the number of cars queuing for petrol at a petrol station.

Number of cars	0	1	2	3	4 or more
Probability	0.23	0.28	0.14	0.11	

a Calculate the probability that the number of cars queuing is:
i 4 or more **ii** less than 2 **iii** more than 1
b What is the most likely number of cars queuing?

7 Mr and Mrs Smith and their daughter Jane live together.
Mr Smith has a 40% chance that a phone call to their house is for him.
Mrs Smith says she has a probability of 0.6 that a phone call is for her.
Jane claims that, on average, one in every 20 calls is for her.
a Explain why these probabilities cannot be correct.
In fact only Mrs Smith's probability of getting a phone call is incorrect.
b Calculate the correct probability that Mrs Smith receives a phone call at her house.

8 The probability that a fair ten-sided dice, numbered from 1 to 10, lands showing an even number is 0.5
The probability that this dice lands showing 6, 7 or 8 is 0.3
Tanya says that the probability the dice shows either an even number or 6, 7 or 8 is
$0.5 + 0.3 = 0.8$
a Explain why Tanya is wrong.
b Work out the correct probability.

9 A field contains ten white sheep, four black sheep, 20 black cows and six brown cows.
One random animal escapes.
Find the probability that the animal which escapes is:
a a black animal **b** **not** a sheep **c** a white animal or a sheep.

30.2 Independent events

CAN YOU REMEMBER

- How to calculate probabilities for equally likely events?
- The meaning of the notation *P*(event)?

IN THIS SECTION YOU WILL

- Learn the meaning of 'independent' and 'exhaustive'.
- Learn how to calculate the probability of two or more independent events happening.
- Learn the 'AND' rule or multiplication rule for independent events.

Two events are *independent* when the probability of one event happening is not affected by the outcome of the other event.

Example 1

Which of the following pairs of events are independent?
Explain your answers.

a Roll a dice.
Event A: the dice shows an even number.
Event B: the dice shows a 4

b Roll a dice and flip a coin.
Event A: the dice shows a number more than 3
Event B: the coin shows tails.

c Go outside.
Event A: it is raining.
Event B: it is windy.

Solution 1

a A and B are not independent. The dice showing an even number affects the probability of it showing a 4 (makes it more likely).

b A and B are independent. Whatever the dice shows cannot affect what the coin shows.

c A and B are not independent. It is more often windy when it is raining than when it is not raining.

To find the probability of independent events both happening, multiply the individual probabilities together.
If A and B are independent events
$P(\text{A and B}) = P(\text{A}) \times P(\text{B})$
This is sometimes called the 'AND' rule or multiplication rule.

Example 2

A coin is flipped and a dice is rolled.
What is the probability that the coin shows heads and the dice shows a 3?

Solution 2

On a coin, $P(\text{head}) = \frac{1}{2}$

On a dice, $P(3) = \frac{1}{6}$

P (head **and** 3) $= \frac{1}{2} \times \frac{1}{6} = \frac{1}{12}$

The probability of a head and a 3 $= \frac{1}{12}$

Example 3

The table shows the probability that Adam is late for work each weekday.

Day	Mon	Tue	Wed	Thu	Fri
P(late)	0.20	0.05	0.04	0.11	0.18

Work out the probability that he is only late on Wednesday in a particular week.
Assume each day is independent.

Solution 3

P(only late on Wednesday)
= *P*(not late Mon **and** not late Tue **and** late Wed **and** not late Thu **and** not late Fri)
$= 0.80 \times 0.95 \times 0.04 \times 0.89 \times 0.82 = 0.0222$ (4 d.p.)

Exercise A

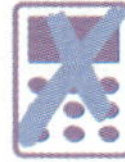

1 A coin is flipped and a dice is rolled.
What is the probability of the coin showing a tail and the dice showing an odd number?

2 Which of these pairs of events are independent?
Explain your answers.

a A red dice is rolled and a blue dice is rolled.
Event A: the red dice shows a 5
Event B: the blue dice shows a 4

b You go to a café.
Event A: you buy a cup of tea.
Event B: you buy a cold drink.

c You pick two counters out of a bag which contains ten red and ten blue counters. The first is replaced before the second is taken out.
Event A: the first counter is red.
Event B: the second counter is blue.

d You pick two counters out of a bag which contains ten red and ten blue counters. The first is **not** replaced before the second is taken out.
Event A: the first counter is red.
Event B: the second counter is blue.

3 The probability that Steve walks to work on a given day is 0.6
What is the probability he walks to work on two consecutive days?
Assume consecutive days are independent.

4 Betty and Jane both work in the same office.
The probability that Betty is late for work on a given day is 0.1
The probability that Jane is late for work on a given day is 0.2
- **a** What is the probability that both of them are late for work on the same day?
- **b** What assumption was necessary in answering part **a**?

5 Jeff spins three fair coins.
- **a** What is the probability that they all show heads?
- **b** What assumption was necessary in answering part **a**?

6 Each week the probability that Chris gets Maths homework is 0.75
Calculate the probability he gets homework for three consecutive weeks.
Assume each week is independent.

7 In any particular game Mr Hiassat's football team has an 80% chance of winning. What is the probability that his team:
- **a** win the next two games
- **b** fails to win any of the next three games?
- **c** Comment on the assumption you had to make to answer parts **a** and **b**.

8 The probability that Darren goes to the cinema in two consecutive weeks is 0.0576
Each week is independent.
What is the probability he goes to the cinema in any given week?

9 The table gives the probability of the morning train being late each day of the week.

Day	**Mon**	**Tue**	**Wed**	**Thu**	**Fri**
P(late)	0.3	0.1	0.2	0.15	0.25

Each day is independent of any other.
Find the probability that the train is:
- **a** **not** late on Monday
- **b** late on Monday, Tuesday and Wednesday
- **c** late every day
- **d** only late on Thursday.

10 **a** The probability Paul eats out on a particular weekend is 0.7
Show that the probability he eats out exactly once in two weekends is 0.42
Assume each weekend is independent.
- **b** The probability that Sally eats out on a particular weekend is x.
What is the probability that she eats out exactly once in two weekends?
Assume each weekend is independent.

Tree diagrams

Independent events and their probabilities can be shown on a tree diagram. Each event is represented by a 'branch'.

Example 4

The probability that Gerry drives to work on a particular day is 0.6
Successive days are independent.
- **a** Show on a tree diagram the possible outcomes for two days.
- **b** Use the tree diagram to find the probability that on two consecutive days, Gerry:
  - **i** drives both days
  - **ii** drives on exactly one day

Solution 4

a

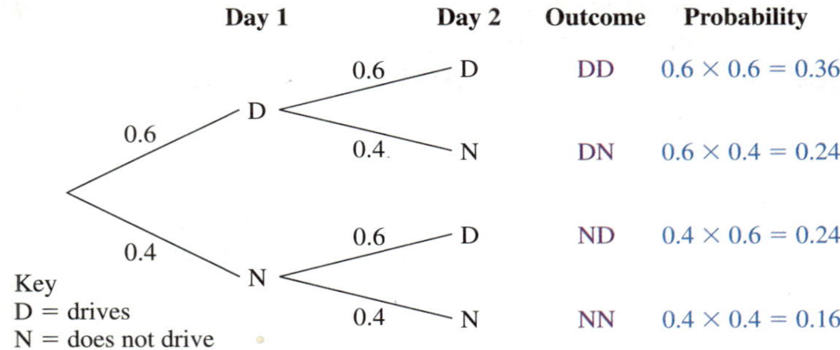

Note that on each pair of branches the two events are *exhaustive* – only one or the other will happen. Therefore their probabilities add to 1

Thus $P(\text{D}) = 0.6$ gives $P(\text{N}) = 1 - 0.6 = 0.4$

b **i** P(drives on both days) = P(drives on day 1 **and** drives on day 2)
= P(DD) = 0.36

ii P(drives on exactly one day)
= P(drives on day 1 **and** does not drive on day 2)
or P(does not drive on day 1 **and** drives on day 2)
= P(DN **or** ND) = 0.24 + 0.24 = 0.48

Exercise B

1 Oscar has a 0.1 chance of missing his bus in the morning.
Different days are independent.
Copy and complete the tree diagram to show the outcomes and probabilities for two days.

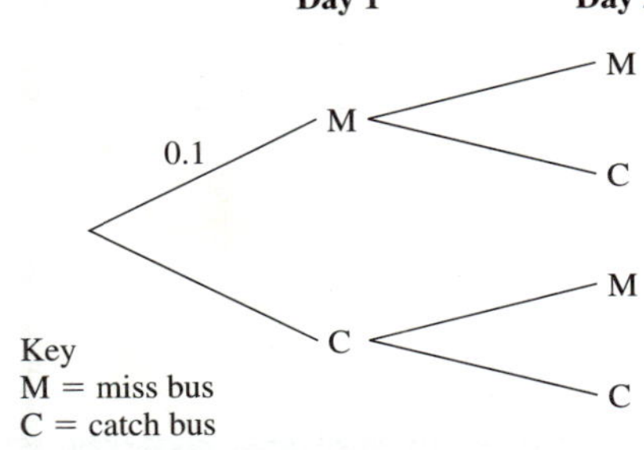

2 A fair coin is flipped twice.

a Copy and complete the tree diagram.

b Use the tree diagram to find the probability of:

i two heads
ii two tails
iii a head and a tail
iv at least one head.

Flip 1 Flip 2 Outcome Probability

H: H, T
T: H, T

Key
H = heads
T = tails

3 There is a 20% chance that it will rain on a day in January.

a Draw a tree diagram to show the outcomes and probabilities for rain on two days in January.

b Work out the probability that on two days in January it will rain:

i on both days **ii** on at least one day.

4 There is a chance of 0.3 that a given oyster will contain a pearl.
- **a** Construct a tree diagram for the possible outcomes and their probabilities for two oysters.
- **b** Use the tree diagram to find the probability that, of two oysters:
  - **i** both will contain a pearl
  - **ii** exactly one will contain a pearl.

5 77% of Britons can drive a car.
Use a tree diagram to find the probability that, of two Britons chosen at random:
- **a** both can drive a car
- **b** neither can drive a car
- **c** exactly one can drive a car
- **d** at least one can drive a car
- **e** at most one can drive a car.

6 A cat food manufacturer claims that the probability a cat will eat its food is 99%.
Two cats are chosen at random.
Use a tree diagram to help find the probability that at least one of the cats will **not** like the food.

7 Three dice are rolled.
- **a** Draw a tree diagram to show the possible outcomes and probabilities for the event getting a 5 or not on each dice.
- **b** Use the diagram to find the probability that there are exactly two 5s in these three dice rolls.

8 To gain a place at Scotter University, applicants have to pass three separate stages: their A levels, the admission test and the interview. The stages are completed in that order and failure at any stage means the student does not attempt the next stage.
The table shows the probability that a random applicant passes each stage.

Stage	A levels	Test	Interview
Probability of passing	0.45	0.15	0.24

- **a** Complete a fully labelled tree diagram showing all the possible outcomes and the probabilities of each outcome happening.
- **b** Use the tree diagram to find the probability that an applicant does not have an interview.
- **c** There are 3000 places at Scotter University available each year.
  Approximately how many applicants do they have?

30.3 Conditional probability

CAN YOU REMEMBER

- How to calculate probabilities for equally likely events?
- How to construct a tree diagram?

IN THIS SECTION YOU WILL

- Learn the meaning of 'conditional probability'.
- Learn how to calculate conditional probabilities.
- Learn how to use tree diagrams to calculate conditional probabilities.

When two events are not independent, the probability of one happening is affected by the other. This is *conditional probability*.

For example, the probability of rolling a 5 on a fair six-sided dice is $\frac{1}{6}$

However, if it is known that the outcome is an odd number there are now only three possible outcomes (1, 3 and 5). The conditional probability of a 5, given the score is an odd number, is $\frac{1}{3}$

Example 1

A fair eight-sided dice is rolled.
Given that the outcome is even, what is the probability that the dice shows:

a 7 **b** 4?

Solution 1

a The outcome is even, so 7 is impossible so $P(7) = 0$

b There are four even numbers on the dice so $P(4) = \frac{1}{4}$

Many probability questions involve counters being picked from bags.
For example, a counter is picked at random from a bag and its colour recorded. The counter is **not** replaced. This is known as *sampling without replacement*.

Example 2

A bag contains five red counters and ten blue counters.
One counter is taken out at random and the colour recorded.
The first counter is **not** replaced.
A second counter is then taken out at random and the colour recorded.
Work out the probability that both counters are red.

Solution 2

P(both counters red) = P(first counter red **and** second counter red)
= P(first counter red) × P(second counter red)

$P(\text{first counter red}) = \frac{5}{15}$

P(second counter red) is conditional probability, given that the first was red.
There are now only 14 counters in the bag and only 4 of those are red.

So, $P(\text{second counter red}) = \frac{4}{14}$

Now, $P(\text{first counter red}) \times P(\text{second counter red}) = \frac{5}{15} \times \frac{4}{14} = \frac{2}{21}$

'Without replacement' problems involve conditional probabilities.

Exercise A

1 A fair six-sided dice is rolled.
Given that the outcome is odd, what is the probability of a:

a 5 **b** 2?

2 A card is taken from a standard pack of 52 cards.
Given that the card is red, what is the probability that the card is a heart?

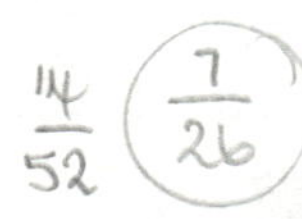

3 There is a 60% chance that dinner will include chips when Sol's dad cooks. This probability is halved when Sol's mum cooks.
What is the probability that Sol's mum will cook chips for dinner on two consecutive occasions when she cooks?

4 A bag contains discs numbered from 1 to 25
One disc is chosen at random from the bag.
- **a** Given that the disc has an odd number on it what is the probability of a single-digit number?
- **b** Given that the disc has a square number on it what is the probability of an odd number?
- **c** Given that the disc has a prime number on it what is the probability of a number above 15?

5 A bag contains three black counters and two white counters.
One counter is taken out at random and the colour recorded.
The first counter is **not** replaced.
A second counter is then taken out at random and the colour recorded.
Find the probability that:
- **a** both counters are white
- **b** both counters are black
- **c** there is one counter of each colour.

6 The chance of a machine in a factory breaking down is 0.06
If it has already broken down that week this rises to 0.2 for a second breakdown that week.
After two breakdowns the machine is turned off.
What is the probability that the machine will:
- **a** **not** break down in a week
- **b** break down twice in a week
- **c** break down just once in a week?

7 At a party every child gets a balloon to take home.
There are 40 purple balloons and 20 green balloons.
Find the probability that the first two children both get a purple balloon.

8 A bag contains balls numbered from 1 to 40
Three balls are drawn out without replacement.
The first two are 16 and 8
What is the probability that the third ball:
- **a** is a square number
- **b** is the largest or smallest of the three balls drawn?

9 Each person in an audience at a play is given a ticket.
Two tickets will be chosen at random for the winners to meet the actors.
There are 210 members of the audience, 96 of whom are men.
What is the probability that both winners are women?

10 Six numbers from 1 to 49 are drawn at random without replacement in the National Lottery.
Work out the probability of the six numbers being 1, 2, 3, 4, 5 and 6

Conditional probabilities can be calculated using tree diagrams.

Example 3

Horace keeps all his clean socks in a bag.
There are ten black and six white socks in the bag.
He takes out two socks from the bag at random and puts them on without looking.

a Draw a tree diagram to show the possible outcomes for the colours of each sock and their probabilities.

b Use the tree diagram to find the probability that he is wearing:

i a matching pair **ii** one black sock and one white sock.

Solution 3

a

First sock	Second sock	Outcome	Probability
$\frac{10}{16}$ B	$\frac{9}{15}$ B	BB	$\frac{10}{16} \times \frac{9}{15} = \frac{3}{8}$
	$\frac{6}{15}$ W	BW	$\frac{10}{16} \times \frac{6}{15} = \frac{1}{4}$
$\frac{6}{16}$ W	$\frac{10}{15}$ B	WB	$\frac{6}{16} \times \frac{10}{15} = \frac{1}{4}$
	$\frac{5}{15}$ W	WW	$\frac{6}{16} \times \frac{5}{15} = \frac{1}{8}$

Key
B = black sock
W = white sock

b **i** P(matching pair) = P(both black **or** both white)

$= P(\text{BB}) + P(\text{WW}) = \frac{3}{8} + \frac{1}{8} = \frac{1}{2}$

ii P(one white **and** one black)

$= P(\text{BW}) + P(\text{WB}) = \frac{1}{4} + \frac{1}{4} = \frac{1}{2}$

Example 4

Bag A contains two blue and three red balls.
Bag B contains three red and one blue balls.
One ball is taken at random from bag A and placed in bag B.
The balls in bag B are then mixed up and one ball is drawn at random from bag B.
Find the probability that this ball is red.

Solution 4

There are two possibilities for the ball from bag A:

- putting a red ball from bag A into bag B
- putting a blue ball from bag A into bag B.

Use a tree diagram:

$P(\text{red}) = P(\text{RR or BR}) = P(\text{RR}) + P(\text{BR})$

$= \frac{3}{5} \times \frac{4}{5} + \frac{2}{5} \times \frac{3}{5} = \frac{18}{25}$

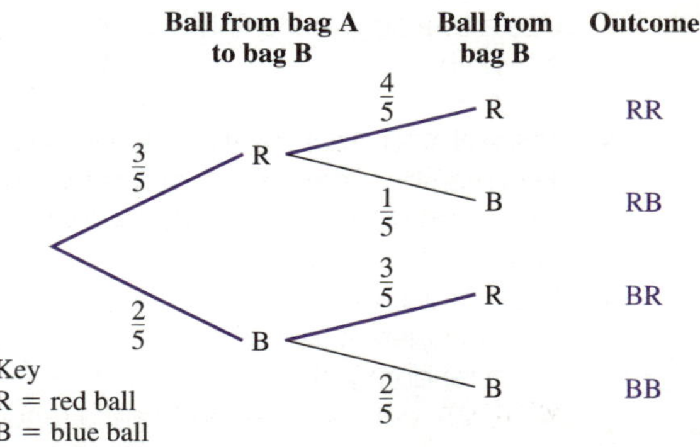

Exercise B

1 Joe and Kim are twin brothers working at the same firm.
They pick from the same shirts for work each morning.
One morning there are ten plain shirts and four striped ones.
Joe picks a shirt at random, then Kim picks a shirt at random.

a Complete the tree diagram to show the outcomes and probabilities for which type of shirt they both choose.

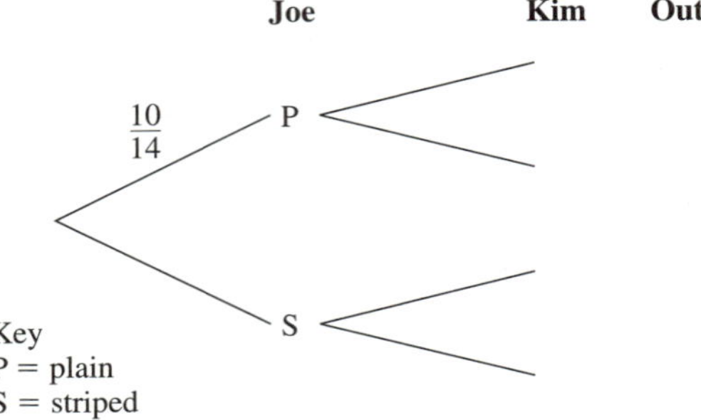

b Find the probability that they wear the same type of shirt.

c Find the probability that they wear a different type of shirt.

2 Mike and Lynn are eating from a box of chocolates.
There are six soft centres and four hard centres left.

a Draw a tree diagram to show the possible outcomes and probabilities if Mike and then Lynn choose and eat a chocolate chosen at random from the box.

b Calculate the probability that they eat:

i one hard and one soft centre
ii two of the same type of centre
iii at least one hard centre.

3 The probability that Javine goes to the gym at least once from Monday to Friday is 0.2
At the weekend, the probability she goes is 0.4 if she has been during the week and 0.7 if she has **not** been during the week.

a Illustrate this information on a fully labelled tree diagram.

b Work out the probability that Javine will:

i go during the week and at the weekend
ii go during the week or at the weekend but not both.

4 Sunita has a box containing 17 working light bulbs and five broken ones.
One day Sunita needs to change two light bulbs in her house.
She picks two bulbs at random from the box.
Use a tree diagram to find the probabilities that of the two bulbs she picks:

a both work **b** only one works **c** neither work.

5 There are 100 members of a small club. 45% are female.
Two members are chosen at random to arrange a party for members.
Use a tree diagram to find the probability that they are both male.

6 In a football division of 20 clubs, eight clubs play in red.

a Complete a tree diagram showing the possible outcomes for the colours of the two teams in a randomly chosen match.

b Work out the probability that a randomly chosen match will have one of the teams changing kit colour because they both play in red.

7 At a fair a prize can be won on the tombola stall by picking a ticket which ends in a digit five.
The tickets are numbered 1–100
Tickets are drawn without looking and not replaced.
Of the first 20 people who bought a ticket, only one won a prize.
Use a tree diagram to calculate the probability that the next two people to buy a ticket will both win prizes.

8 A bag contains 30 discs coloured red or blue in the ratio 3 : 2
One disc is drawn at random without replacement and then a second disc is drawn.
What is the probability that the second disc is red when the first disc drawn is blue?

9 A bag contains x red balls and y blue balls.
Two balls are chosen from the bag without replacement.
Find an expression for the probability that both balls are red.

10 A field contains 34 sheep and 15 cows.
Three random animals escape through a hole in the fence.
Find the probability that they are all sheep.

Chapter summary

- Mutually exclusive outcomes cannot happen at the same time.
  For example, a coin can only show 'heads' or 'tails'.
- The total probability of all the mutually exclusive outcomes of an event is 1
- An event cannot happen and not happen at the same time. 'The event happens' and 'the event does not happen' are mutually exclusive.
- P(event happens) + P(event does not happen) = 1
- P(event happens = 1 − P(event does not happen)
- If two events, A and B, are mutually exclusive:
  P(A or B) = P(A) + P(B)
  This is known as the 'OR' rule or addition rule for mutually exclusive probabilities.
- Two events are independent when the probability of one event happening is not affected by the outcome of the other event.
- To find the probability of independent events both happening, multiply the individual probabilities together.
- If A and B are independent events
  P(A and B) = P(A) × P(B)
  This is sometimes called the 'AND' rule or multiplication rule.
- Independent events and their probabilities can be shown on a tree diagram.
- When events are exhaustive, their probabilities add up to 1.
- When two events are not independent, the probability of one happening is affected by the other. This is conditional probability.
- 'Without replacement' problems involve conditional probabilities.
- Conditional probabilities can be calculated using tree diagrams.

Chapter review

1 **a** Explain the meaning of the term 'mutually exclusive'.

b A bag contains discs with the numbers 1 to 20 on them.
There is one of each disc.
Which of these events are mutually exclusive?
Event A: the disc is numbered 6
Event B: the disc is numbered with a factor of 30
Event C: the disc is numbered with a prime number.
Explain your answer.

2 Matt has eight plain shirts and two striped shirts.
He also has four plain and three striped ties.

a Complete the tree diagram to show the possible outcomes and probabilities for a shirt and tie combination.

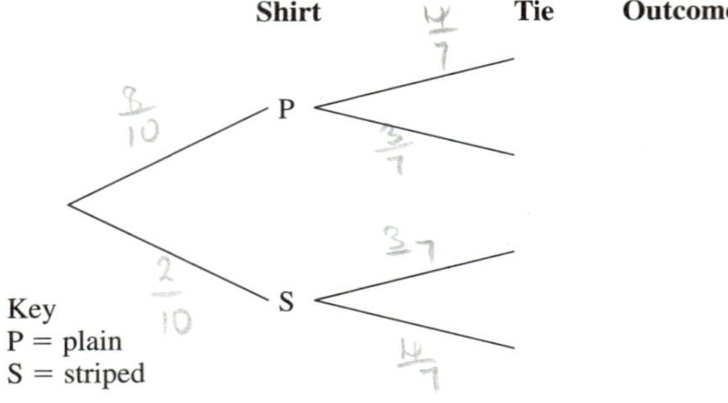

b Calculate the probability that Matt wears a combination where:
i both are plain **ii** both are striped
iii one is striped and one is plain.

3 A single bead is drawn at random from a container with 26 beads which have the letters of the alphabet (A to Z) on them.
Find the probability that this bead has:

a a letter from the word 'mutually' on it

b a letter from the word 'exclusive' on it.

c a letter from either of the words 'mutually' or 'exclusive' on it.

4 When Ambrose and Zahir play each other at darts, the probability that Zahir wins is 0.6. A draw is not possible.
Ambrose and Zahir play two games of darts.

a Copy and complete the probability tree diagram to show the possible outcomes.

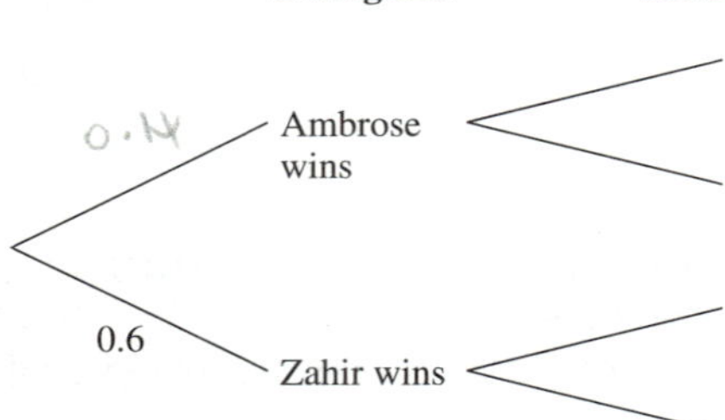

b Calculate the probability that each of them wins only one game.

5 Jack is a golfer who does not play very well if it is windy.
The probability he hits a straight shot is 0.8 if it is not windy but only 0.3 if it is windy.
The probability that it is windy on a given day is 0.1

a Copy and complete the tree diagram for this situation.

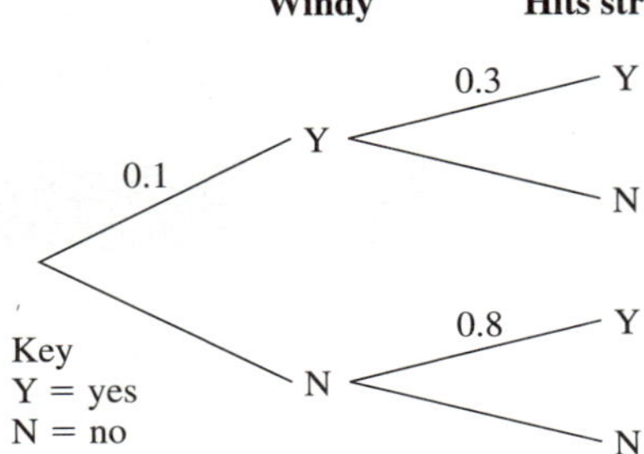

b What is the probability that on a randomly chosen day he will hit his first shot straight?

6 A fair six-sided dice is rolled twice.
The scores are added to make a total.
Given that the total is above 8, what is the probability it is above 10?

7 Each night Chan works as a security guard.
There is a 23% chance on a given night that he will fall asleep.
Work out the probability that he falls asleep on two of the next three nights.

8 Harry plays darts. He hits a single, a double or a treble with each dart he throws.
The probability of each outcome is shown in the table.

Outcome	Single	Double	Treble
Probability	0.64	0.17	0.19

He throws two darts.

a Draw a tree diagram showing all outcomes and their probabilities calculated in full.

b What is the probability that the player:

i hits two singles

ii hits the same outcome with both darts

iii hits a treble and a double.

9 The table shows the probabilities of some outcomes when an integer is randomly chosen from the list 1–50
Explain whether the following are true or false.

Outcome	Odd	Even	Square	Prime
Probability	0.5	0.5	0.14	0.3

a $P(\text{odd or even}) = 1$

b $P(\text{not square}) = 0.86$

c $P(\text{odd or square}) = 0.64$

d $P(\text{square or prime}) < 0.44$

10 A fair coin is flipped three times.
Use a tree diagram to find the probability of exactly two heads.

11 Bag A contains x red balls, $x + 3$ green balls and $x - 4$ blue balls.
Bag B contains $x + 1$ red balls and $x - 2$ blue balls.
One ball is transferred at random from bag A to bag B.
The balls in bag B are now mixed up and one is drawn out at random.
Write an expression for the probability that this ball is red. Give your expression in its simplest form.

CHAPTER 31

Mensuration

31.1 Arc length and area of a sector

CAN YOU REMEMBER

- The circumference of a circle $= 2\pi r$ or πd
- The area of a circle $= \pi r^2$
- The meaning of 'sector', 'arc', 'chord' and 'segment'.

IN THIS SECTION YOU WILL

- Learn how to calculate the arc length of a circle.
- Learn how to calculate the area of sectors and segments of circles.

The diagram shows a quarter circle, radius r.
The angle at the centre is 90°

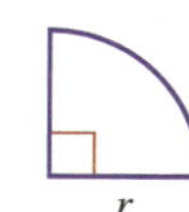

A quarter circle is $\frac{90}{360}$ of a whole circle.

Arc length $= \frac{90}{360} \times$ circumference $= \frac{90}{360} \times 2\pi r$ **or** $\frac{90}{360} \times \pi d$

Area of sector $= \frac{90}{360} \times$ area of circle $= \frac{90}{360} \times \pi r^2$

The area of the sector will be $\frac{1}{4}$ the area of the circle.

In general, for a sector of angle $a°$

Arc length $= \frac{a}{360} \times$ circumference $= \frac{a}{360} \times 2\pi r$

Arc of sector $= \frac{a}{360} \times$ area of circle $= \frac{a}{360} \times \pi r^2$

When a circle is divided into two sectors the smaller sector is called the *minor* sector and the larger sector is called the *major* sector.

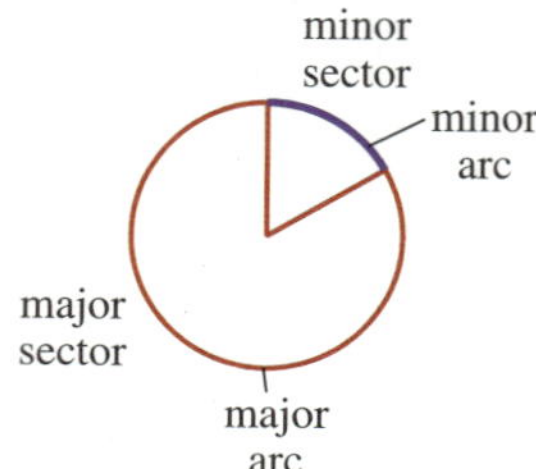

Example 1

The diagram shows a sector of a circle.
Find:

a the length of the arc
b the area of the sector.

Give your answers in terms of π.

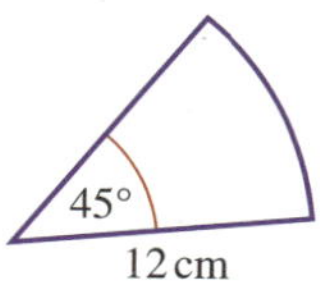

Solution 1

a Arc length $= \frac{a}{360} \times 2\pi r = \frac{\overset{1}{\cancel{45}}}{\underset{8}{\cancel{360}}} \times 2 \times \pi \times 12$

$= \frac{24\pi}{8} = 3\pi$

Arc length $= 3\pi$ cm

b Area of sector $= \frac{a}{360} \times \pi r^2 = \frac{\overset{1}{\cancel{45}}}{\underset{8}{\cancel{360}}} \times \pi \times 12^2 = \frac{1}{8} \times \pi \times 144$

$= \frac{144\pi}{8} = 18\pi$

Area of sector $= 18\pi\ \text{cm}^2$

Exercise A

1 The diagrams show sectors of circles.
Calculate the arc length and area of each sector shown.
Give your answers in terms of π.

a
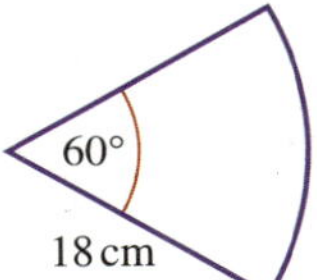

b
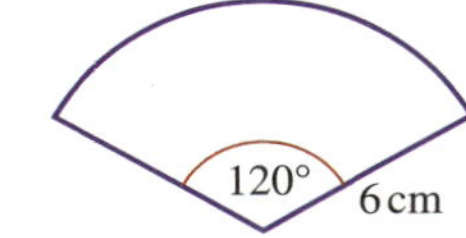

c
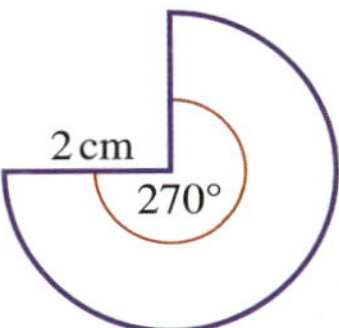

d
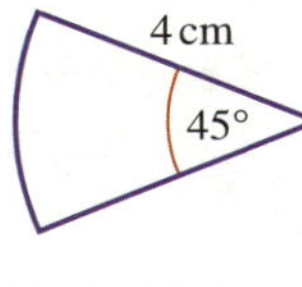

e
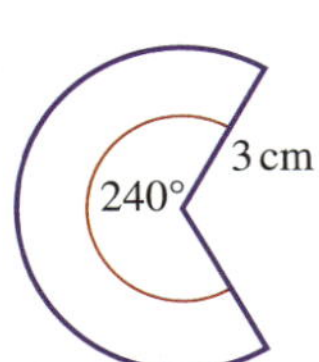

f
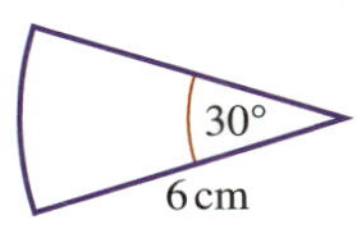

g
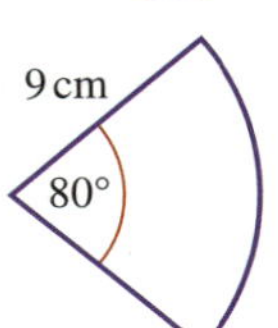

h
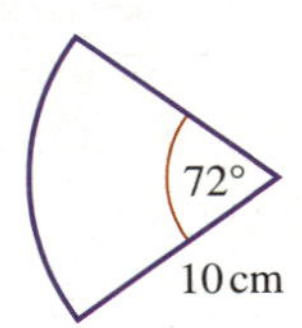

2 The length of the arc of this sector is 3π cm.
Work out the size of angle AOB.

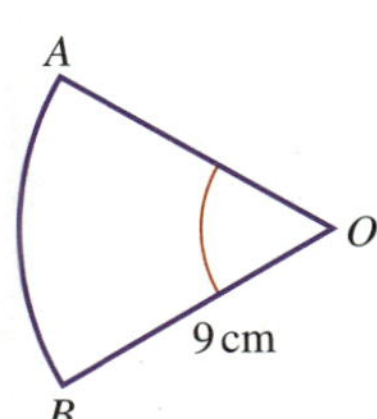

3 The area of this sector is $\frac{1}{2}\pi\ \text{cm}^2$
Calculate the size of angle XOY.

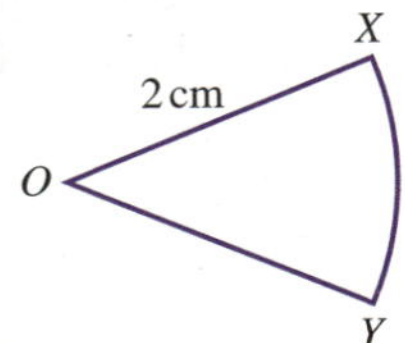

4 Calculate the arc length and area of each sector shown.
Give each answer to 3 s.f.

a

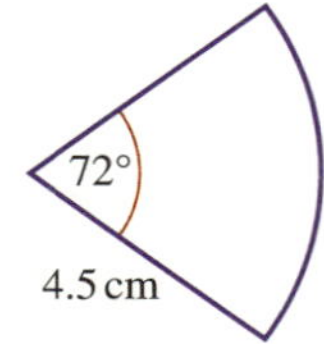

b

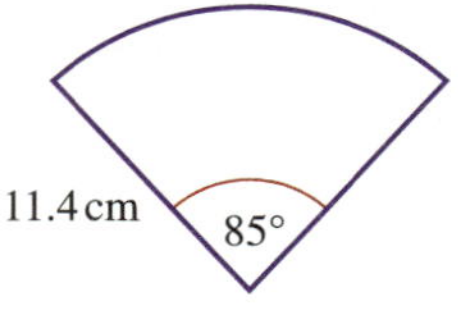

c

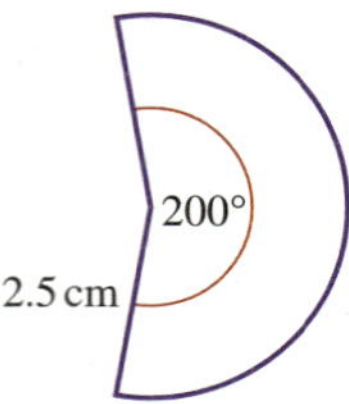

d

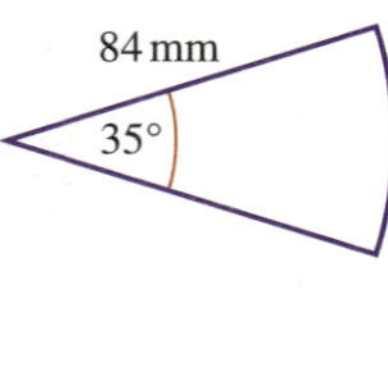

e

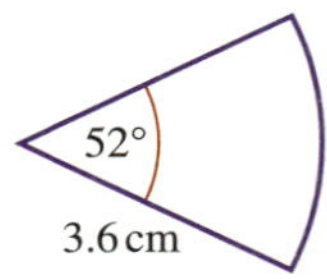

f

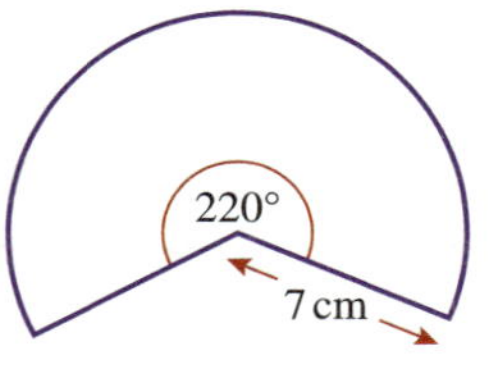

g

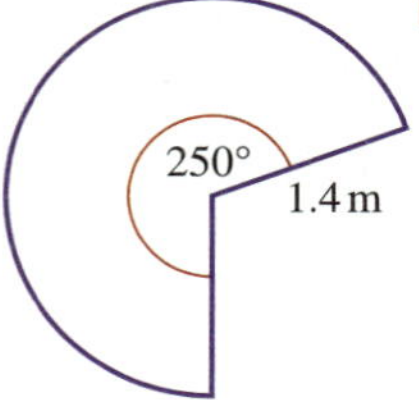

h

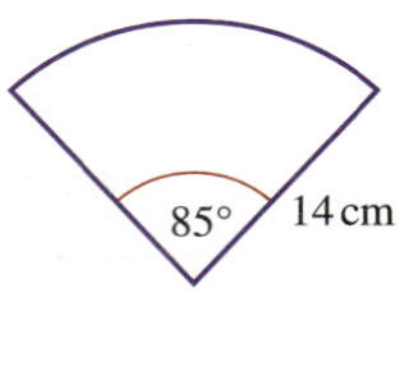

5 A sector of area 35.4 cm^2 has a radius of 4.2 cm.
Calculate the angle of this sector.
Give your answer to the nearest degree.

6 The angle of a sector of a circle is 24°. The length of the arc of this sector is 7.31 cm.
Calculate the radius of the circle. Give your answer to two decimal places.

Example 2

For the shaded part of this sector calculate:

a the perimeter **b** the area.

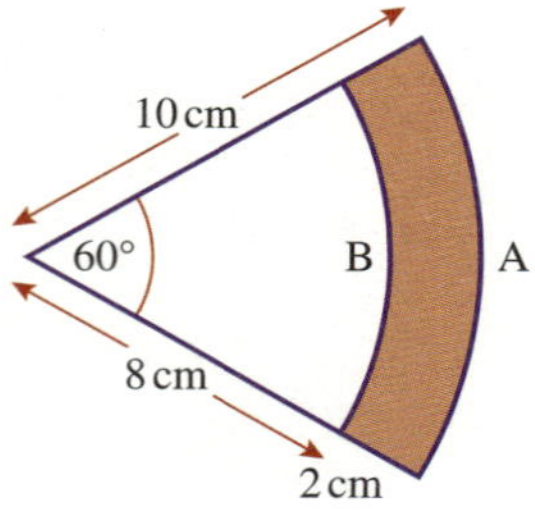

Solution 2

a Perimeter of shaded part
= length of arc A + length of arc B + 2 cm + 2 cm

length of arc A = $\frac{60}{360} \times 2 \times \pi \times 10 = 10.47\ldots$ cm

length of arc B = $\frac{60}{360} \times 2 \times \pi \times 8 = 8.37 \ldots.$ cm

Perimeter of shaded section = 10.47... + 8.37... + 2 + 2 = 22.8 cm (to 1 d.p.)

b Area of shaded section = area of sector of radius 10 cm − area of sector of radius 8 cm

$= \left(\frac{60}{360} \times \pi \times 10^2\right) - \left(\frac{60}{360} \times \pi \times 8^2\right) = 52.35\ldots - 33.51\ldots$

Area shaded = 18.8 cm^2 (to 1 d.p.)

Exercise B

1 The diagrams show sectors of circles.
Calculate the perimeter and area of each shaded section.
Give your answers to the nearest integer.

a

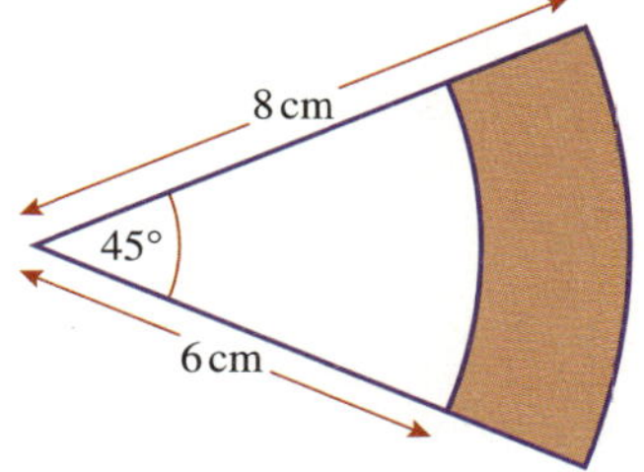

b

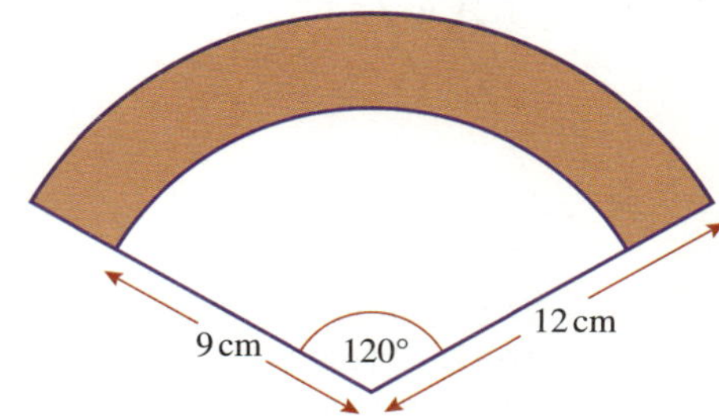

2 The diagram shows a quarter circle of radius 3.4 cm.

a Calculate the area of the sector.

b Calculate the area of triangle OAB.

c Hence calculate the area of the shaded segment.
Give your answer correct to one decimal place.

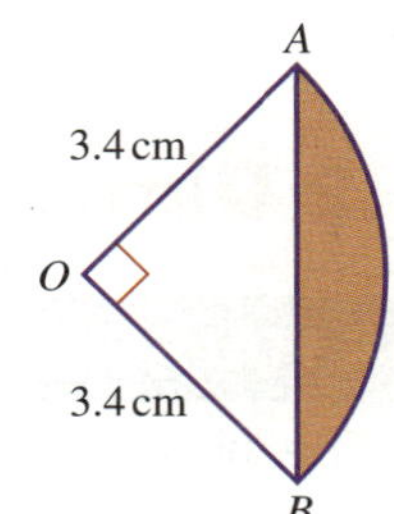

3 A garden lawn is 7.5 m long and 3.2 m wide.
A flowerbed in the shape of a sector of a circle of radius 1.8 m is cut in the lawn.
Calculate:

a the area of the flowerbed

b the area of the remaining lawn.

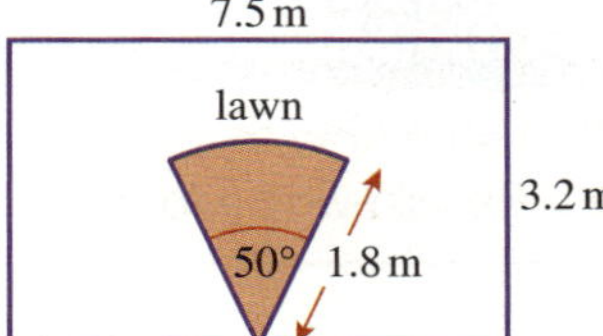

4 For the shaded section calculate:

a the perimeter **b** the area.

Give each answer correct to three significant figures.

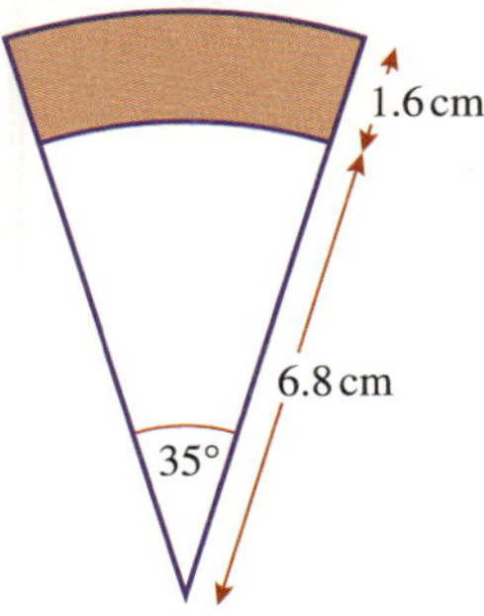

5 The diagram shows a quarter circle of radius 28 mm.
Calculate the area of the shaded segment.

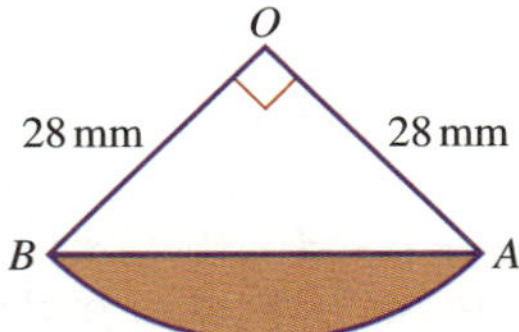

6 A keyhole has a shape formed from two sectors.
One sector has an angle of 72° and a radius of 11 mm.
The other sector has a radius of 5 mm.
Calculate the area of the keyhole.
Give your answer to the nearest integer.

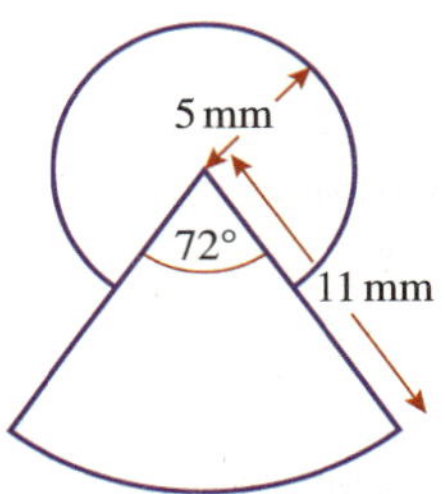

7 A metal badge is in the shape of two identical sectors of a circle of radius 2.5 cm.

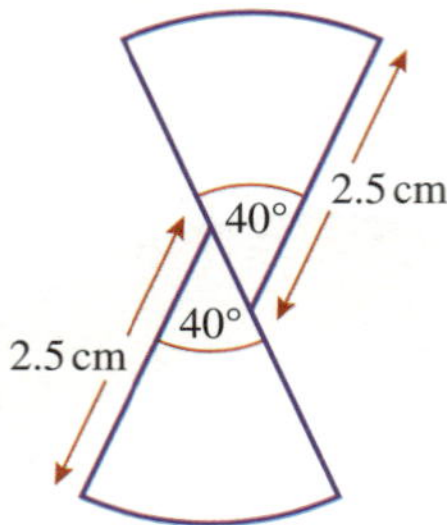

a Work out the perimeter of the badge.

b The badge is cut from a rectangular piece of metal of length 5 cm and width 3 cm.
Calculate the area of metal wasted.

31.2 Dimensional analysis

CAN YOU REMEMBER

- The meaning of 'length', 'area' and 'volume'?

IN THIS SECTION YOU WILL

- Learn how to distinguish between formulae for length, area and volume.
- Explain why a formula represents length, area, volume or none of these.

The dimensions of an expression can be analysed to work out whether a formula represents length, area, volume or none of these.
A line has one dimension.
The diagram shows a line in two sections.
The length of the line is $a + b$.
Each term in the expression $a + b$ has one dimension.
Adding (or subtracting) two lengths gives another length.
Length formulae have one dimension.
These expressions also represent length:

$4a$ $\quad a + b + c + d$ $\quad 2\pi r$

Remember, π is just a number and numbers have no dimensions.

An area has two dimensions.
The diagram shows a rectangle of length l and width w.
The area of the rectangle $= l \times w$ or lw
This expression has two lengths multiplied together.
The result is an area, with two dimensions.
length × length = area
Area formulae have two dimensions.
These expressions also represent area:

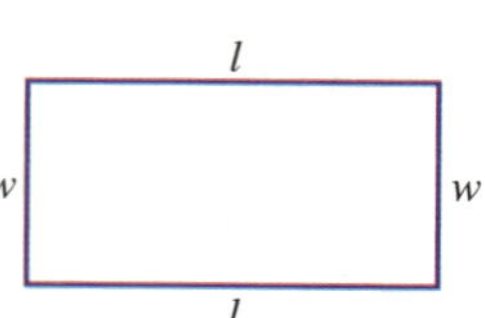

$3ab$ $\quad x^2$ $\quad \pi r^2$ $\quad \frac{1}{2}bh$

What does the formula $\frac{1}{2}(a + b)h$ represent?
$(a + b)$ is a length which is then multiplied by another length (h). This is a formula for area. It is, of course, the formula for the area of a trapezium.

A volume has three dimensions.
The diagram shows a cuboid of length l, width w and height h.
The volume of the cuboid $= l \times w \times h$ or lwh
This expression has three lengths multiplied together so has three dimensions.
length × length × length = volume
Volume formulae have three dimensions.
These expressions also represent volume:

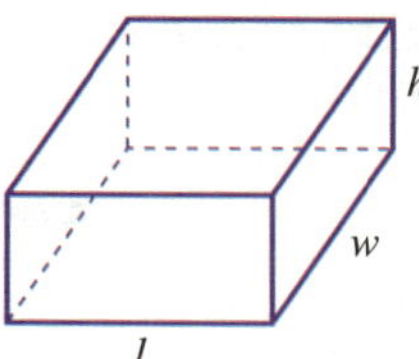

abc a^3 $\pi r^2 h$ $\frac{4}{3}\pi r^3$

It is not possible to add lengths, areas and volumes so the following expressions do **not** represent length, area or volume:
$a + bc$ $a^2b + ac$ $x + xy + xyz$ $3x + 2y + 3z^2$

Example 1

w, x, y and z represent lengths.
State whether each expression could represent a length, area, volume or none of these.

a $2x + 3y$ **b** $x^2y + 2x^2$ **c** $\frac{xyz}{w}$

Solution 1

a $2x$ is a length and $3y$ is a length.
$2x + 3y =$ length + length = length
The expression $2x + 3y$ represents a length.

b $x^2y = x \times x \times y =$ length × length × length = volume
$2x^2 = 2 \times x \times x = 2 \times$ length × length = area
As one term is volume and one term is area the expression $x^2y + 2x^2$ does not represent length, area or volume.

c $\frac{xyz}{w} = \frac{\text{length} \times \text{length} \times \text{length}}{\text{length}} = \text{length} \times \text{length}$
The expression $\frac{xyz}{w}$ represents area.

Exercise A

1 w, x, y and z represent lengths.
State whether each expression represents length, area, volume or none of these.

a $xy + wz$ **b** $3(x + y + z)$ **c** $w + x$ **d** $x + y + z$
e xz **f** x^2 **g** $y(x^2 + z^2)$ **h** $4\pi r^2$
i $2x + 3yz + 5w$ **j** $\frac{yz}{w}$ **k** x^2y^2 **l** $\frac{wxyz}{z}$
m $y^2 + z^3$ **n** $z^2 + xyz$ **o** $\frac{1}{2}(w^2 + y^2 + z^2)$ **p** $2x^2y + 3y^2z$

2 Match each expression to the type of formula it could represent.

length area volume none

$x^2 + yz$ $2x(y + 3)$ $3(a + b + c)$ $\frac{a^2b^2}{a}$

3 The expressions in the table can be used to calculate lengths, area or volumes of some shapes. The letters l, b, h and r represent lengths.

	Length	Area	Volume
$\pi r^2 h$			
$2(l + b)$			
$2\pi r$			
$\frac{1}{2}bh$			
lbh			
$2\pi r(h + r)$			
l^3			

Copy the table and put a tick in the table to show what each expression represents.

4 The letters l and w represent lengths.
Explain why the expression $l + w + lw$ cannot represent a length.

Exercise B

1 The diagram shows a football.
Which of the following expressions could represent the volume of the football?
Give a reason for your answer.

πd^2 $\qquad$ $\frac{1}{6}\pi d^3$ $\qquad$ $2\pi d + \pi d$

2 In these expressions p, q and r represent lengths.
Candice says that all the expressions represent areas.
Is she correct? Explain your answer.

$pq + qr$ $\qquad$ $\frac{p^3}{q}$ $\qquad$ $6p + 3q^2$ $\qquad$ $4pq + r^2$

3 a, b, c and d are all lengths on this triangular prism.
Which of the following expressions represents:

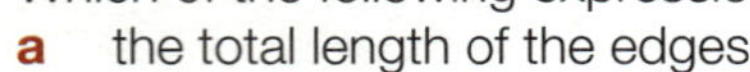

a the total length of the edges
b the surface area of the prism
c the volume of the prism.

$\frac{1}{2}abd$ $\qquad$ $2(a + b + c) + 3d$ $\qquad$ $ab + ad + bd + cd$

a b c d

4 The diagram shows an ellipse of width a cm and height b cm.
Three students are trying to remember the formula to find the area of an ellipse.

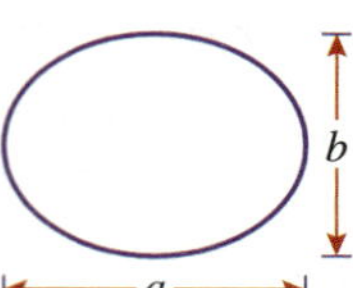

Jake says the formula is $\pi a^2 b$
Teri says the formula is $\pi(a + b)$
Ali says the formula is $\frac{\pi ab}{4}$
Only one of the students is correct.

a Write down the name of the student who is correct.
b Explain how you can tell from the formula that this student must be correct.

5 The diagram shows a prism where p, q, r, s and t are all lengths.
Here are some formulae connected with the prism.

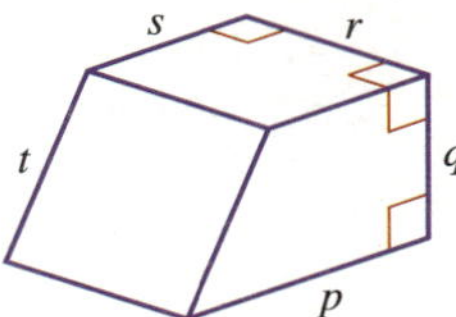

$rs + rp$ $\qquad \frac{1}{2}qr(s + p)$ $\qquad \frac{q(s + p)}{2}$ $\qquad 2(p + q + 2r + s + t)$

a Which of these formulae represents length?
b Which of these formulae represent volume?

Chapter summary

- For a sector of angle $a°$:
  - arc length $= \frac{a}{360} \times$ circumference $= \frac{a}{360} \times 2\pi r$
  - area of sector $= \frac{a}{360} \times$ area of circle $= \frac{a}{360} \times \pi r^2$
- The dimensions of an expression can be analysed to work out whether a formula represents length, area or volume:
  - length formulae have one dimension, e.g. $2x + 2y$
  - area formulae have two dimensions, e.g. $3ab$, πr^2
  - volume formulae have three dimensions, e.g. a^3, x^2y, $\frac{1}{3}\pi r^2 h$

Chapter review

1 The diagram shows a sector of a circle of radius 12 cm.
Find the arc length of the sector.
Give your answer in terms of π.

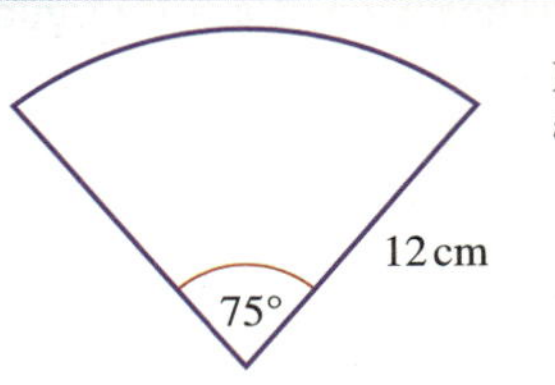

Not drawn accurately

2 The expressions in the table can be used to calculate length, area or volume of some shapes.
The letters a, b and c represent lengths.
Copy the table and put a tick in the box under the expressions that represent area.

$\frac{c}{2}(a + b)$	a^2b	$\frac{bc}{2}$	πab	$b^2(a + c)$	$3(a + b)$

3 Cones are made from card. The card is in the shape of a sector of a circle of radius 9 cm.
The angle of the sector is 240°
Find the area of card needed to make a cone.

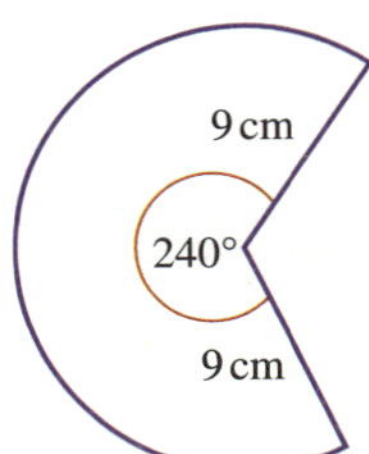

4 Rupert is using the formula $A = \pi x(y + z)$ to calculate an area.
He knows that x, y and z are all lengths measured in cm.
Becky says, 'You shouldn't be using that formula to calculate an area. It hasn't got any squares in it.'
Is Becky correct? Explain your answer.

5 The circle, centre O, has a radius of r cm.
The length of the minor arc AB is 10 cm.

a Form an equation in r and solve it to find the radius of the circle, giving your answer in terms of π.

b Find, in terms of π, the area of the minor sector OAB.

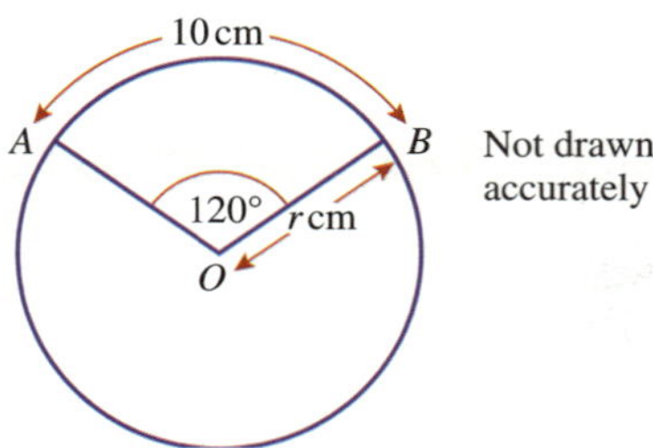

6 A sector of a circle has a radius of 6.5 cm.
The angle of the sector is 52°
Calculate the perimeter of the sector.
Give your answer correct to one decimal place.

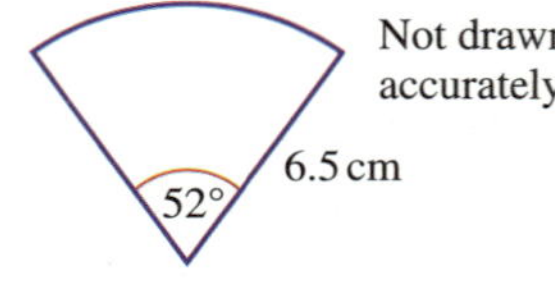

7 The diagram shows a sector of a circle.
The angle of the sector is 25°
Calculate the area of the shaded part of this sector.

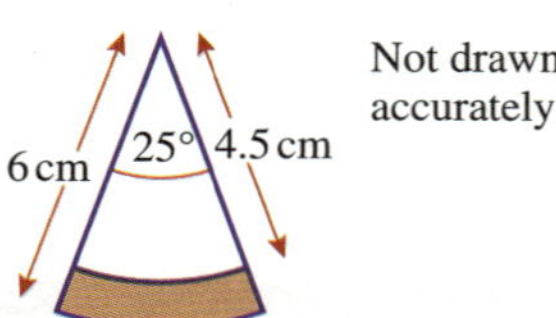

8 The shape of a solid figure is determined by two lengths, a cm and b cm.
Which of the following could not be the formula used for working out the volume of the shape?
Give a reason for your answer.

A: $a^2(a + b)$ B: $a(a^2 + b^2)$ C: a^3b D: a^2b

9 AOB is a sector of a circle of radius 8 cm.
The arc length of the minor sector AOB is 7.54 cm.
Calculate the size of angle AOB.

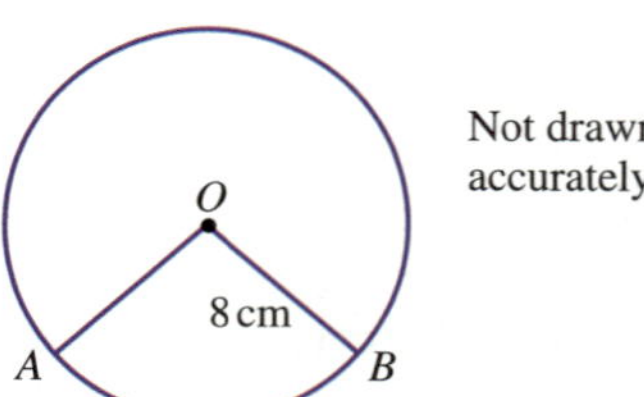

10 The diagram shows a quarter circle of radius 7.2 cm.
Calculate the area of the shaded segment.

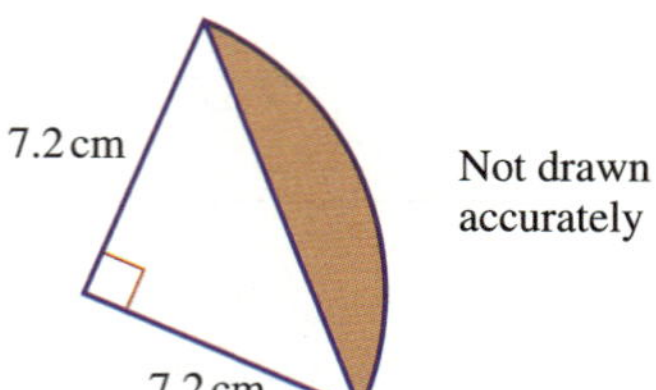

CHAPTER 32

Further graphs

32.1 Drawing and recognising non-linear graphs

CAN YOU REMEMBER

- The meaning of 'function'?
- How to use tables of values to find points on quadratic graphs?
- What a quadratic graph looks like?

IN THIS SECTION YOU WILL

- Extend skills in drawing the graphs of quadratic functions.
- Learn how to draw and recognise the graph of a simple cubic function, the reciprocal function, the exponential function and the circular functions $y = \sin x$, $y = \cos x$ and $y = \tan x$.
- Learn that $x^2 + y^2 = r^2$ is the equation of a circle with radius r and centre (0, 0).

Any function of the form $y = ax^2 + bx + c$ where $a \neq 0$ is a *quadratic function*. The graph of a quadratic function has a distinctive smooth U-shaped curve with a vertical line of symmetry and a maximum or a minimum point.

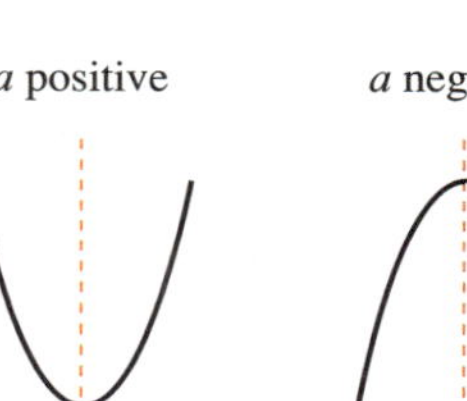

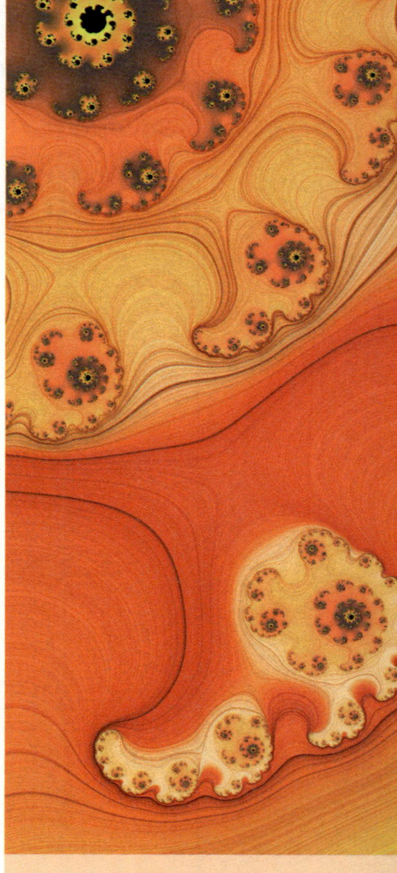

Example 1

a Complete the table for $y = 2x^2 - 3x - 1$

x	−2	−1	0	1	2	3
y	13		−1	−2		8

b Draw the graph of $y = 2x^2 - 3x - 1$ for values of x from −2 to 3

Solution 1

a When $x = -1$, $y = 2 \times (-1)^2 - 3 \times (-1) - 1 = 4$
When $x = 2$, $y = 2 \times 2^2 - 3 \times 2 - 1 = 1$

x	−2	−1	0	1	2	3
y	13	4	−1	−2	1	8

b

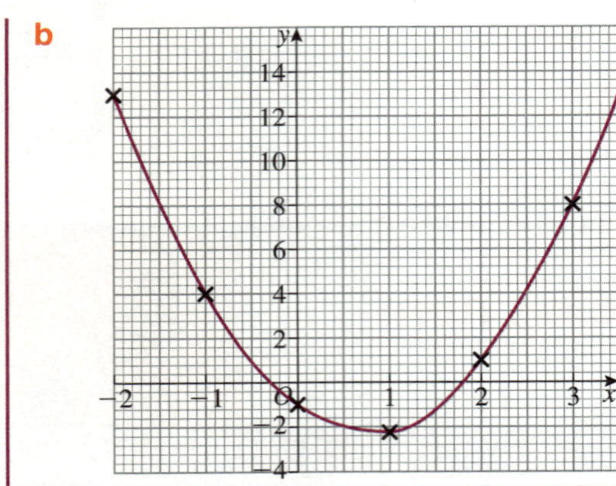

Any function of the form $y = ax^3 + bx^2 + cx + d$ where $a \neq 0$ is a *cubic function*. The graph of a cubic function has a distinctive curve with rotational symmetry. If a is positive, the cubic graph looks like one of these.

Example 2

a Complete the table for $y = x^3 - x^2 - 12x$

x	−4	−3	−2	−1	0	1	2	3	4
y	−32		12	10	0	−12	−20	−18	

b Draw the graph of $y = x^3 - x^2 - 12x$ for values of x from −4 to 4

Solution 2

a When $x = -3$, $y = (-3)^3 - (-3)^2 - 12 \times (-3) = -27 - 9 + 36 = 0$
When $x = 4$, $y = 4^3 - 4^2 - 12 \times 4 = 64 - 16 - 48 = 0$

x	−4	−3	−2	−1	0	1	2	3	4
y	−32	0	12	10	0	−12	−20	−18	0

b

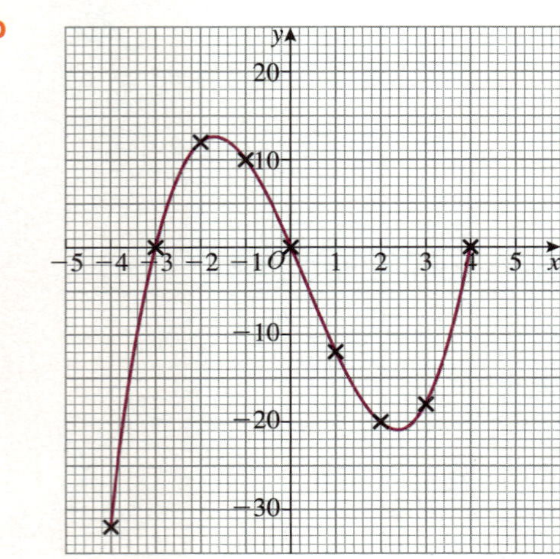

Any function of the form $y = \frac{a}{x}$ is called a *reciprocal function*.

The graph of a reciprocal function has a distinctive two-part curve.
As x approaches zero, y becomes very large.
Similarly, as y approaches zero, x becomes very large.
This means that points do not exist at either $x = 0$ or $y = 0$
If a is positive a reciprocal graph looks like this.

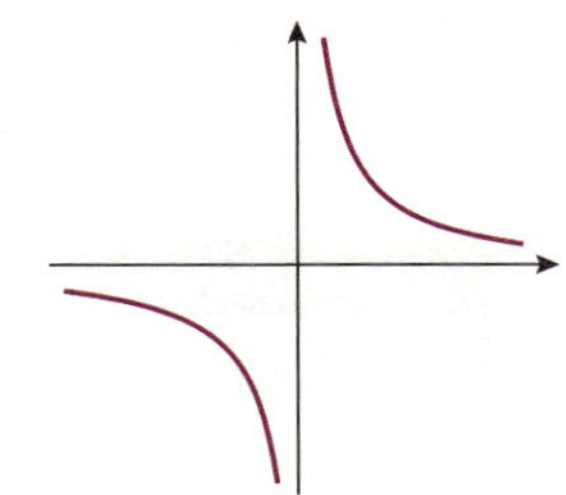

Example 3

a Complete the table for $y = \frac{6}{x}$

x	−6	−4	−3	−2	−1	1	2	3	4	6
y	−1	−1.5		−3	−6	6	3	2		1

b Why is there no point at $x = 0$?

c Draw the graph of $y = \frac{6}{x}$ for values of x from −6 to 6

Solution 3

a When $x = -3$, $y = 6 \div -3 = -2$
When $x = 4$, $y = 6 \div 4 = 1.5$

x	−6	−4	−3	−2	−1	1	2	3	4	6
y	−1	−1.5	−2	−3	−6	6	3	2	1.5	1

b When $x = 0$, $y = 6 \div 0$
Division by zero is impossible.

c

Any function of the form $y = a^x$ is called an *exponential function*.
Exponent is an alternative term for power or index.
All exponential functions pass through the point (0, 1).

Example 4

a Complete the table for $y = 2^x$

x	0	1	2	3	4	5
y		2	4	8	16	

b Draw the graph of $y = 2^x$ for values of x from 0 to 5

Solution 4

a When $x = 0$, $y = 2^0 = 1$
When $x = 5$, $y = 2^5 = 32$

x	0	1	2	3	4	5
y	1	2	4	8	16	32

b

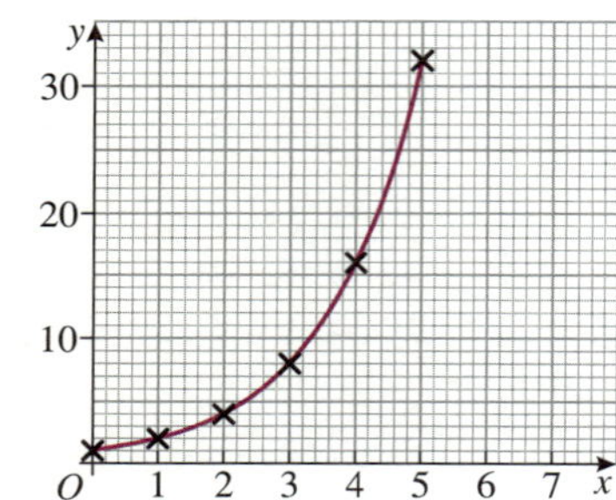

Exercise A

1 **a** Copy and complete the table for $y = 3x^2 + 2x - 12$

x	−3	−2	−1	0	1	2	3
y	9		−11	−12	−7		21

b Draw and label a grid with the x-axis going from −3 to 3 and the y-axis going from −15 to 20
Use a scale of 1 cm to 5 units on the y-axis

c Draw the graph of $y = 3x^2 + 2x - 12$ for values of x from −3 to 3

2 **a** Copy and complete the table for $y = 2x^2 + 3x - 7$

x	−4	−3	−2	−1	0	1	2
y		2				−2	

b Draw the graph of $y = 2x^2 + 3x - 7$ for values of x from −4 to 2

3 **a** Complete the table for $y = 2x^2 - x - 6$

x	−3	−2	−1	0	1	2	3
y							

b Draw the graph of $y = 2x^2 - x - 6$ for values of x from −3 to 3

4 **a** Complete the table for $y = -2x^2 + 3x + 2$

x	−2	−1	0	1	2	3	4
y							

b Draw the graph of $y = -2x^2 + 3x + 2$ for values of x from −2 to 4

5 **a** Copy and complete the table for $y = x^3 - 2x^2$

x	−1	0	1	2	3	4
y		0				32

b Draw the graph of $y = x^3 - 2x^2$ for values of x from −1 to 4

6 Draw the graph of $y = 2x^3 + x^2 - 4x + 3$ for values of x from −3 to 2

7 **a** Draw the graph of $y = \frac{4}{x}$ for values of x from −4 to 4

b Draw the graph of $y = \frac{12}{x}$ for values of x from −6 to 6

c Draw the graph of $y = \frac{1}{2x}$ for values of x from −6 to 6

8 **a** Draw the graph of $y = 3^x$ for values of x from 0 to 4

b Draw the graph of $y = 0.8^x$ for values of x from 0 to 4

9 **a** Match each graph to an equation.

Equation a	**Equation b**	**Equation c**	**Equation d**	**Equation e**
$y = 1 - 2x$	$y = 2 - x^2$	$y = \frac{2}{x}$	$y = x^3 + 1$	$y = x^2 - 2$

Graph 1 Graph 2 Graph 3 Graph 4

b Sketch the missing graph.

10 Match each equation to a graph.

Equation a	**Equation b**	**Equation c**	**Equation d**	**Equation e**
$y = \frac{3}{x}$	$y = x^3 + 3x$	$y = 4^x$	$y = -x^2 + 3x + 5$	$y = 2x^2 + x - 6$

Graph A

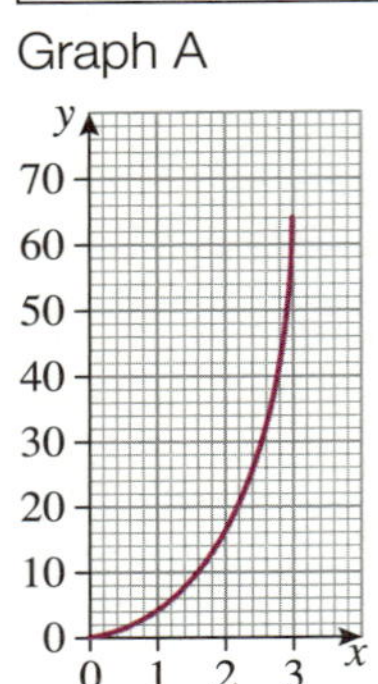

Graph B

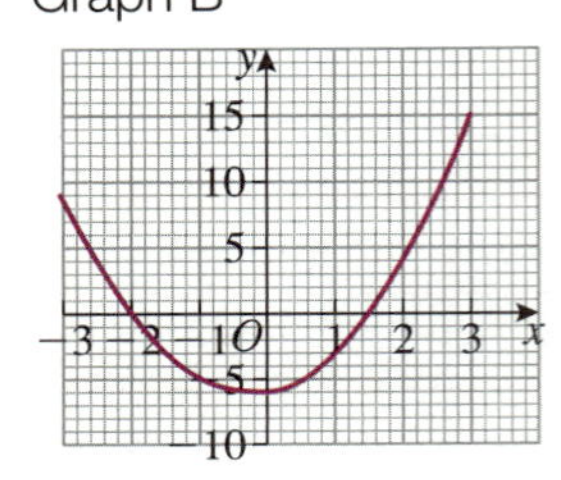

Graph C

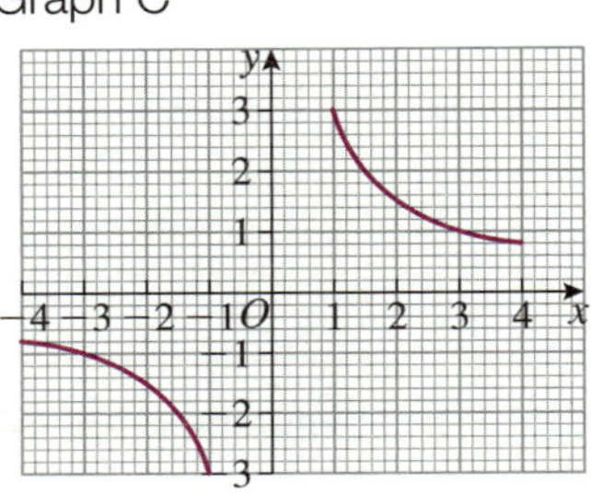

Graph D

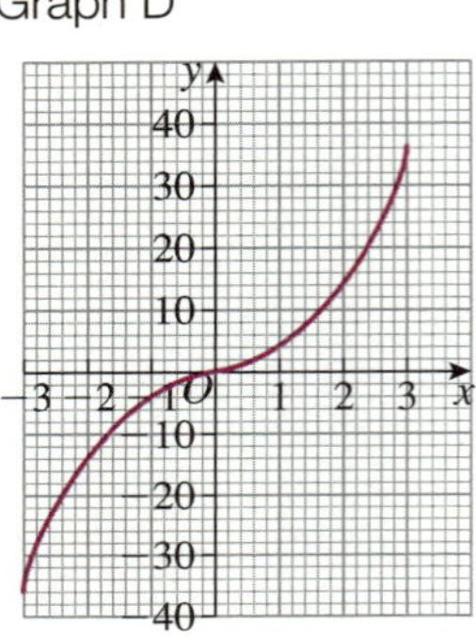

Graph E

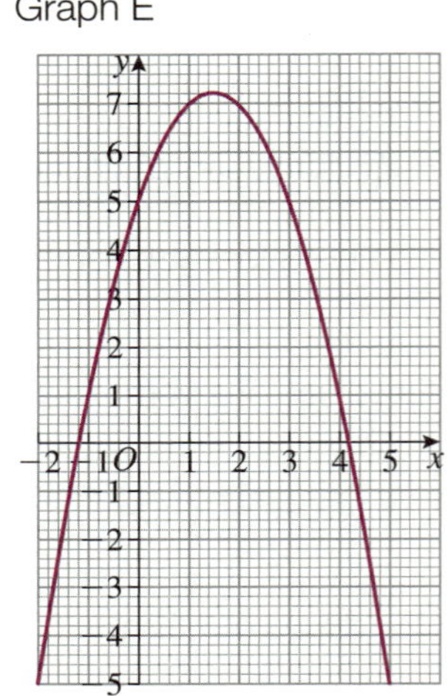

Trigonometric functions

Sines, cosines and tangents of angles are used to solve problems in triangles.
However, $\sin x°$ has a value for any value of x as has $\cos x°$ and $\tan x°$ has a value for most values of x.
These values can be found using a scientific calculator.
For example, the table shows values of $\sin x°$ to an accuracy of two significant figures from $x = 0°$ to $360°$.

x	0	30	60	90	120	150	180	210	240	270	300	330	360
$\sin x°$	0	0.5	0.87	1	0.87	0.5	0	−0.5	−0.87	−1	−0.87	−0.5	0

Sketches of the graphs of $y = \sin x°$, $y = \cos x°$ and $y = \tan x°$ for values of x from 0° to 360° are shown below.

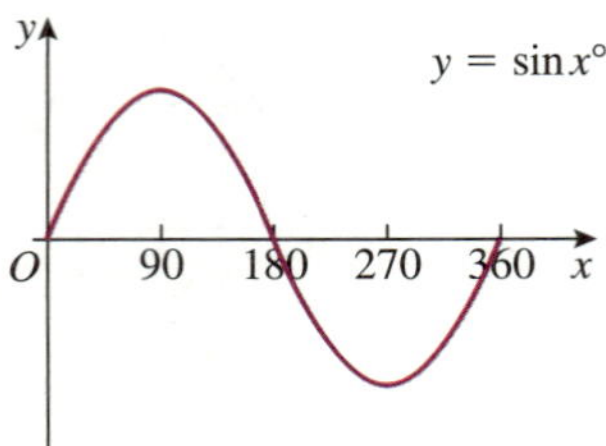

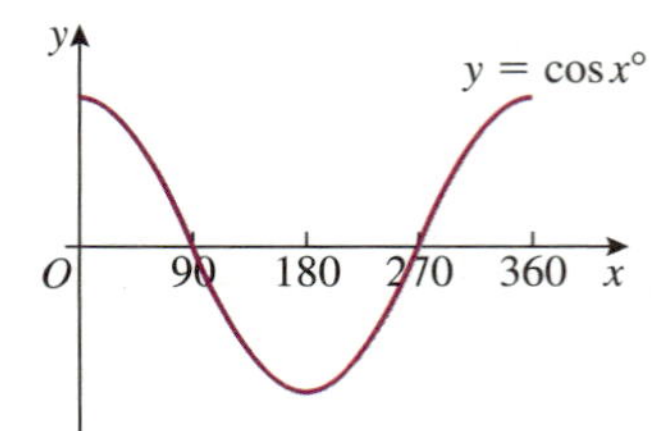

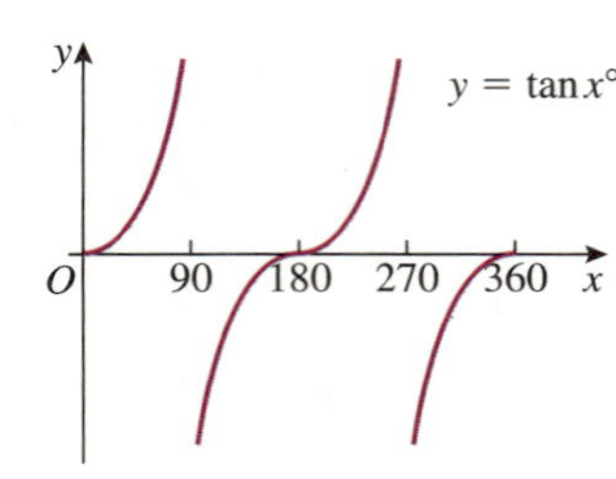

Example 5

a Draw the graph of $y = \sin x$ for $0° \leqslant x \leqslant 360°$.

b From the graph write down:

  i the values of x in the range $0° \leqslant x \leqslant 360°$ for which $\sin x = 0$

  ii the maximum and minimum values of $\sin x$.

Solution 5

a

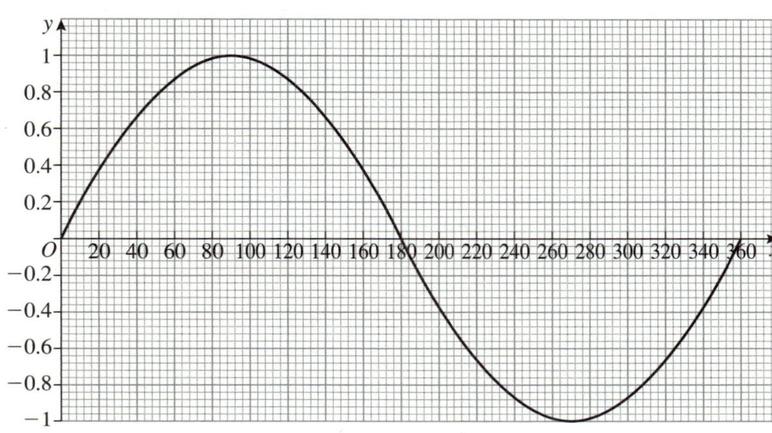

b **i** $\sin x = 0$ when $x = 0°$, $180°$ and $360°$

  ii The maximum value of $\sin x$ is 1 which occurs when $x = 90°$.
  The minimum value of $\sin x$ is -1 which occurs when $x = 270°$.

$x^2 + y^2 = r^2$ is the general equation of a circle radius r and centre (0, 0).
For example, the graph of $x^2 + y^2 = 16$ is a circle centre (0, 0) with radius 4
All points on the circle have coordinates (x, y), where the values of x and y satisfy the equation of the circle.

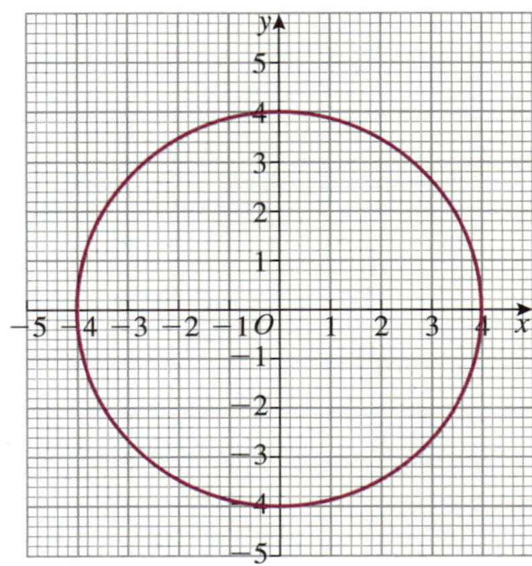

Example 6

a Show that the point $(-2, 3)$ lies on the circle with radius $\sqrt{13}$ and centre (0, 0)

b Find some more points with integer coordinates that lie on this circle.

c Show that the point $(-2, 3)$ lies on the line $3y - 2x = 13$

d Find the gradient of the line $3y - 2x = 13$

e Draw a grid with x and y from -7 to 7

  i Use your answers to **b** to help draw the circle on the grid.

  ii Draw the line $3y - 2x = 13$ on the grid.
  What do you notice?

Solution 6

a The equation of a circle of radius $\sqrt{13}$ passing through (0, 0) is $x^2 + y^2 = 13$
At the point with coordinates (−2, 3), $x = -2$ and $y = 3$
$(-2)^2 + 3^2 = 13$ — Substituting in $x^2 + y^2 = 13$
$4 + 9 = 13$
This is true, so the point with coordinates (−2, 3) lies on the circle.

b Square numbers are always positive.
This means that any combination of 2 and −2 with 3 and −3 satisfy $x^2 + y^2 = 13$
So the points (2, 3), (3, 2), (−2, 3), (−3, 2), (2, −3), and (−2, −3) all satisfy $x^2 + y^2 = 13$ and lie on the circle.
These points can also be found using the symmetry of the circle.

c At the point with coordinates (−2, 3), $x = -2$ and $y = 3$
$3 \times 3 - 2 \times (-2) = 13$ — Substituting in $3y - 2x = 13$
$9 - (-4) = 13$
This is true, so the point with coordinates (−2, 3) lies on the line $3y - 2x = 13$.

d Rearrange $3y - 2x = 13$ to the form $y = mx + c$
$3y - 2x = 13$ — Add $2x$ to both sides.
$3y = 2x + 13$ — Divide both sides by 3
$y = \frac{2}{3}x + \frac{13}{3}$
The gradient of $3y - 2x = 13$ is $\frac{2}{3}$

e The line $3y - 2x = 13$ passes through (−2, 3)
with a gradient $\frac{2}{3}$
This is shown on the grid.
The line $3y - 2x = 13$ is a tangent to the circle $x^2 + y^2 = 13$

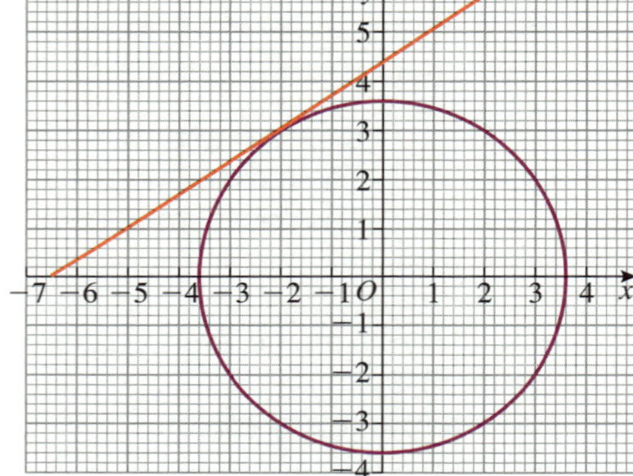

Exercise B

1 The stopping distance, d metres, of a car travelling at a speed of v km/hour is given by
$d = \frac{v^2}{150} + \frac{v}{5}$

a Copy and complete the table of values for $d = \frac{v^2}{150} + \frac{v}{5}$

v (km/hour)	0	15	30	45	60	75	90	105	120
d (metres)									

b Draw the graph of $d = \frac{v^2}{150} + \frac{v}{5}$ for values of v from 0 to 120

c The stopping distance of a car is 100 metres. Use the graph to estimate the speed of the car.

2 Draw the diagrams in this question on a grid with the x-axis from 0 to 100 and the y-axis from 0 to 30 using a scale of 1 centimetre to 5 metres on both axes.

The path that a javelin takes through the air is given approximately by the function $y = x - \frac{x^2}{d}$

where x is the horizontal distance travelled by the javelin y is the height of the javelin d is the distance travelled by the javelin.

a Copy and complete this table when $d = 50$ metres

x (metres)	0	10	20	30	40	50
y (metres)						

b Draw a graph to show the path of the javelin for $y = x - \frac{x^2}{d}$.

c Complete a table and use it to draw a graph to show the path of a javelin when $d = 80$ metres.

d Use your graphs to find the difference in maximum height between the paths of the javelins in parts **b** and **c**.

3 The Tyne Bridge in Newcastle upon Tyne has a parabolic arch in the approximate shape of the quadratic function $y = \frac{7x}{5} - \frac{7x^2}{800}$

a Copy and complete the table for $y = \frac{7x}{5} - \frac{7x^2}{800}$

x (metres)	0	20	40	60	80	100	120	140	160
y (metres)									

b Draw the graph of $y = \frac{7x}{5} - \frac{7x^2}{800}$

c What is the approximate maximum height of the parabolic arch?

4 a Draw the graph of $y = \frac{20}{x}$ from $x = -10$ to 10

b Find the x-coordinates of the points where the graph of $y = \frac{20}{x}$ and the line $x - 2y = 2$ intersect. Give your answer to one decimal place.

5 a Draw the graph of $y = x^2 - 1$ from $x = -2$ to 4

b Find the coordinates of the points where the graph $y = x^2 - 1$ meets the line $y = 2x + 2$

6 a Draw the graph of $y = x^3 + 2x^2 - 5x + 8$ for x values from -3 to 3

b Find the coordinates of the points of intersection of $y = x^3 + 2x^2 - 5x + 8$ and the line $y = 15 - 9x$

7 Find the coordinates of the points of intersection of the graphs $y = x^2 + 1$ and $y = x^3 + 1$

8 a Find the centre and radius of the circle with equation $x^2 + y^2 = 49$

b A circle has centre (0, 0) and radius 10 cm. Write down its equation.

9 a Show that the point (4, -1) lies on the circle radius $\sqrt{17}$ centre (0, 0).

b **i** Find seven more integer coordinates that lie on this circle.

ii Draw the circle on a grid with x and y from -7 to 7

c Show that the point (4, -1) lies on the line $4x - y = 17$

d Find the gradient of the line $4x - y = 17$

e **i** Draw the line $4x - y = 17$ on the grid.

ii What do you notice?

10 a Show that the line $5y - 3x = 34$ is a tangent to the circle $x^2 + y^2 = 34$

b Show that the line perpendicular to the line $5y - 3x = 34$ from the point where the line touches the circle passes through the centre of the circle.

11 a Copy and complete the table for $y = \cos x$ to an accuracy of two significant figures.
b Draw the graph of $y = \cos x$ for $0 \leqslant x \leqslant 360$

x	0	30	60	90	120	150	180	210	240	270	300	330
$\cos x°$												

c Use your graph to write down:
i The values of x for $0 \leqslant x \leqslant 360$ for which $\cos x° = 0$
ii The maximum and minimum values of $\cos x°$.

32.2 Solving quadratic equations graphically

CAN YOU REMEMBER

- How to draw quadratic graphs?
- How to solve equations of the form $x^2 + bx + c = 0$ graphically?

IN THIS SECTION YOU WILL

- Extend skills in solving quadratic equations graphically.

Quadratic functions are functions of the form $y = ax^2 + bx + c$, where $a \neq 0$
For example, $y = x^2 - 1$, $y = x^2 + 5x$ and $y = 2x^2 + 3x - 5$ are quadratic functions.
Quadratic equations are formed when a quadratic function is made equal to:

- a number, for example $x^2 - x = 3$
- a linear expression in the same variable, for example $x^2 - 5 = 2x + 1$
- another quadratic function in the same variable, for example $3x^2 + 3x - 5 = x^2 - 2$

Quadratic equations can be solved graphically. It is difficult to read accurate values from a graph, so solutions found graphically are *estimates*.

Example 1

Use a graphical method to estimate the solutions of:

a $x^2 - 2x - 1 = 0$ **b** $x^2 - 2x - 1 = 3$

Solution 1

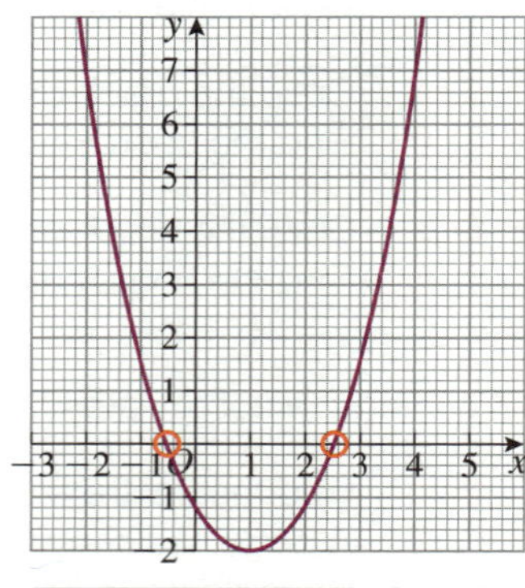

a The graph of $y = x^2 - 2x - 1$ is drawn on the grid.
To solve the equation $x^2 - 2x - 1 = \mathbf{0}$ find the points where the graph of $y = x^2 - 2x - 1$ intersects the line $y = \mathbf{0}$ (the x-axis).
The **approximate** solutions are $x = -0.4$ and $x = 2.4$

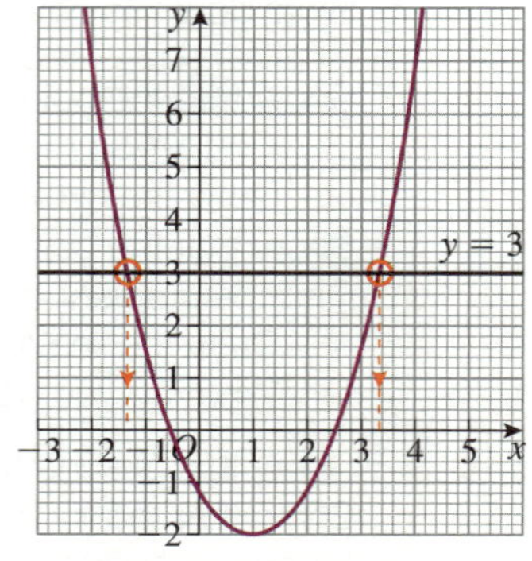

b Find the points where the graph of $\mathbf{y = x^2 - 2x - 1}$ intersects the line $\mathbf{y = 3}$
The approximate solutions are $x = -1.2$ and $x = 3.2$

Example 2

Use a graphical method to find the approximate solutions of the equation $2x^2 - x - 2 = 2x + 5$

Solution 2

The solutions are the x-coordinates of the points where the graph of $y = 2x^2 - x - 2$ and the line $y = 2x + 5$ intersect.

Step 1: Complete a table of values for $y = 2x^2 - x - 2$

x	−2	−1	0	1	2	3
y	8	1	−2	−1	4	13

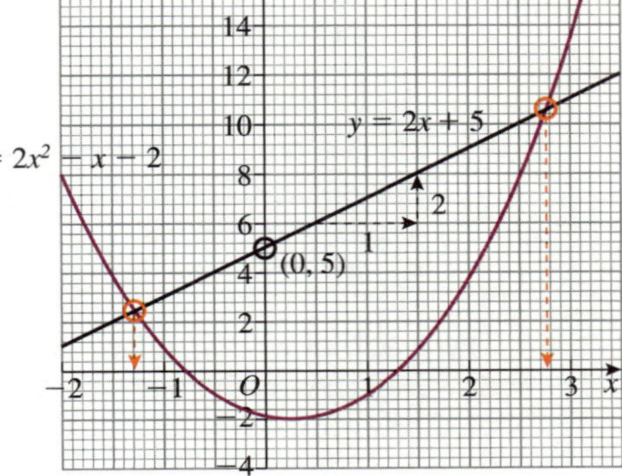

Step 2: Draw the graphs of $y = 2x^2 - x - 2$ and $y = 2x + 5$ on the same grid. The line $y = 2x + 5$ passes through (0, 5) with gradient 2

Step 3: Find the x-coordinates of the points where the graph intersects the line.
The solutions are $x = -1.3$ and $x = 2.8$

Exercise A

1 **a** Copy and complete the table of values for $y = 2x^2 - 4x - 3$

x	−2	−1	0	1	2	3	4
y	13		−3		−3	3	

b On a copy of the grid, draw the graph of $y = 2x^2 - 4x - 3$ for values of x from −2 to 4

c An approximate solution of the equation $2x^2 - 4x - 3 = 0$ is $x = 2.6$

i Explain how this can be found from the graph.

ii Use the graph to find another solution of this equation.

d Use the graph to estimate solutions to the following equations.

i $2x^2 - 4x - 3 = 8$

ii $2x^2 - 4x - 3 = 3x - 1$

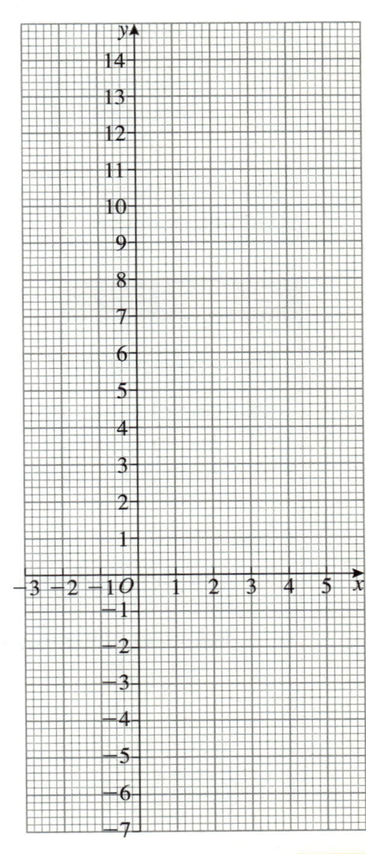

2 Answer these questions on a grid with x from −3 to 6 and y from −8 to 16
Use a graphical method to estimate the solutions of the following equations.

a $x^2 - 3x - 4 = 0$

b $x^2 - 3x - 4 = 5$

c $x^2 - 3x - 4 = \frac{1}{2}x + 1$

3 Use a graphical method to find the approximate solutions of the equation $3x^2 - x - 2 = x + 5$

4 **a** Copy and complete the table for $y = 4x^2 - 5x - 6$

x	-3	-2	-1	0	1	2	3	4
y								

b Draw the graph of $y = 4x^2 - 5x - 6$ for values of x between -3 and 4. Use a scale on the y-axis of 1 cm to 5 units.

c Use the graph to find approximate solutions to the following equations.

i $4x^2 - 5x - 6 = 0$ **ii** $4x^2 - 5x - 6 = -4$

iii $4x^2 - 5x - 6 = 2x + 3$

5 **a** Draw the graph of $y = 2x^2 - x - 3$ for values of x between -2 and 3

b Use the graph to find approximate solutions, **if possible**, to these equations. If no solution is possible explain why not.

i $2x^2 - x - 3 = 7$ **ii** $2x^2 - x - 3 = -4$

iii $2x^2 - x - 3 = 5x^2$ **iv** $2x^2 - x - 3 = x + 2$

6 The graph of $y = 2x^2 - 3x - 1$ is shown below.

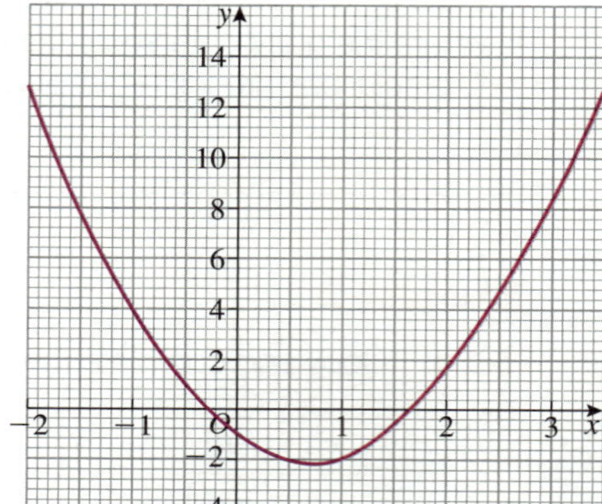

a Explain why there are no solutions to $2x^2 - 3x - 1 = -3$

b **i** Use the graph to read off the approximate negative solution to the equation $2x^2 - 3x - 1 = 10$

ii How many more solutions are there to this equation? Explain your answer.

c Estimate the value of k such that $2x^2 - 3x - 1 = k$ has exactly **one** solution.

7 **a** Draw the graph of $y = (x - 2)^2$

b Show that the equation $(x - 2)^2 = 3 - 2x$ has one solution.

Pairs of equations that can be rearranged to give a quadratic equation can be used to solve the quadratic equation.

Example 3

The x-coordinates of the points of intersection of the graphs of $y = 3x + 1$ and $y = \frac{5}{x}$ give the solutions of the equation $3x^2 + x - 5 = 0$

a Use an algebraic method to show that this is true.

b Use a graphical method to show that this is true.

Solution 3

a The x-coordinates of the points of intersection of the graphs of $y = \mathbf{3x + 1}$ and $y = \frac{\mathbf{5}}{\mathbf{x}}$ are the solutions of the equation $\mathbf{3x + 1} = \frac{\mathbf{5}}{\mathbf{x}}$

$\mathbf{3x + 1} = \frac{\mathbf{5}}{\mathbf{x}}$ — Multiply both sides by x.

$x(3x + 1) = 5$ — Expand the brackets.

$3x^2 + x = 5$ — Subtract 5 from both sides.

$3x^2 + x - 5 = 0$

So the equation $3x + 1 = \frac{5}{x}$ is equivalent to the equation $3x^2 + x - 5 = 0$

This means that the x-coordinates of the points of intersection of the graphs of $y = 3x + 1$ and $y = \frac{5}{x}$ are the solutions of the equation $3x^2 + x - 5 = 0$

b The graphs of $y = 3x + 1$, $y = \frac{5}{x}$ and $y = 3x^2 + x - 5$ are shown on the grid.
The points of intersection of the graphs of $y = 3x + 1$ and $y = \frac{5}{x}$ have the same x-coordinates as the points of intersection of the graph of $y = 3x^2 + x - 5$ and the x-axis.

This also shows that the solutions of the equation $3x^2 + x - 5 = 0$ can be found from the points of intersection of the graphs of $y = 3x + 1$ and $y = \frac{5}{x}$

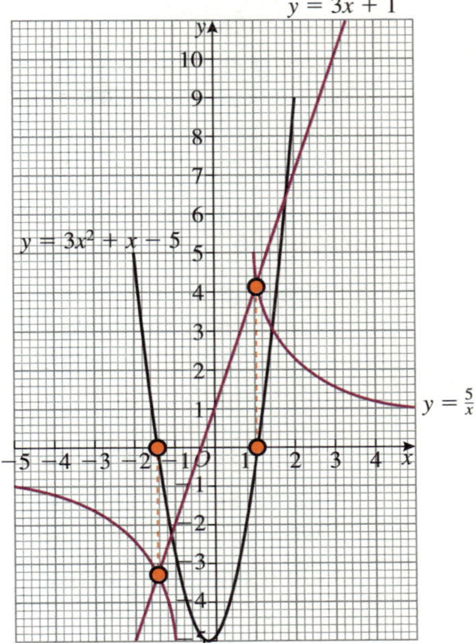

Example 4

The circle $x^2 + y^2 = 2$ and the line $y = 2x + 1$ are shown on the grid.

a Show that the line and the circle can be used to solve the quadratic equation $5x^2 + 4x - 1 = 0$

b Use the graph to estimate the solutions of $5x^2 + 4x - 1 = 0$

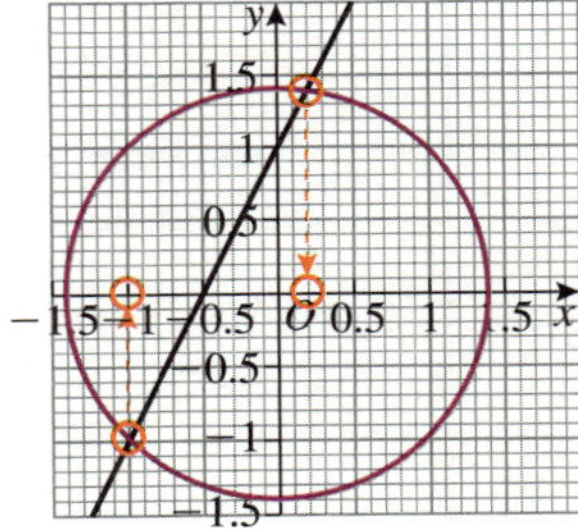

Solution 4

a The x-coordinates of the points where the line $y = 2x + 1$ and the circle $x^2 + y^2 = 2$ intersect satisfy the following simultaneous equations.

$y = 2x + 1$ A

$x^2 + y^2 = 2$ B

To solve these simultaneous equations, the method of substitution can be used.

Step 1: Substitute $y = 2x + 1$ from A into B.

$x^2 + (2x + 1)^2 = 2$

Step 2: Expand $(2x + 1)^2$

$x^2 + (4x^2 + 4x + 1) = 2$

Collect like terms and subtract 2 from both sides.

Step 3: Simplify and rearrange.

$5x^2 + 4x - 1 = 0$

So the x-coordinates at the points of intersection satisfy the quadratic equation $5x^2 + 4x - 1 = 0$

b The x-coordinates of the points of intersection of the circle and the line are $x = -1$ and $x = 0.2$
These are the solutions of the equation $5x^2 + 4x - 1 = 0$

Example 5

You are given the graph of $y = x^2 - 3x - 1$
Find the equations of the straight lines that can be used with this graph to solve:

a $x^2 - 3x - 2 = 0$
b $y = x^2 - x - 5$

Solution 5

a **Method 1:**

Let the required straight line have the equation $y = mx + c$
At the points of intersection:

$x^2 - 3x - 1 = mx + c$ — Subtract mx and c from both sides.
$x^2 - 3x - mx - 1 - c = 0$ — Factorise the x and number terms.
$x^2 - x(3 + m) - (1 + c) = 0$

Compare $x^2 - x(3 + m) - (1 + c) = 0$
with $x^2 - 3x - 2 = 0$

Comparing the x terms: $-(3 + m) = -3$
$m = 0$
Comparing the number terms: $-(1 + c) = -2$
$c = 1$
So the required straight line has equation $y = 1$

Method 2:

Change $x^2 - 3x - 2$ to the form $x^2 - 3x - 1 + ?$
$x^2 - 3x - 2 = x^2 - 3x - 1 - 1$
So $x^2 - 3x - 2 = 0$ can be written as
$x^2 - 3x - 1 - 1 = 0$ — Add 1 to both sides.
$x^2 - 3x - 1 = 1$

This is equivalent to $y = (x^2 - 3x - 1) - (x^2 - 3x - 2) = 1$
For convenience this can be written

$$\begin{array}{rl} & y = x^2 - 3x - 1 \\ - & 0 = x^2 - 3x - 2 \\ \hline & y = \qquad\qquad 1 \end{array}$$

Equation of given graph.
Equation to be solved.

The solution of $x^2 - 3x - 2 = 0$ can be found from the points of intersection of the graph of $y = x^2 - 3x - 1$ and the line $y = 1$

b

$$\begin{array}{rl} & y = x^2 - 3x - 1 \\ - & 0 = x^2 - \ \ x - 5 \\ \hline & y = \quad -2x + 4 \end{array}$$

Equation of given graph.
Equation to be solved.

The solution of $x^2 - 3x - 2 = 0$ can be found from the points of intersection of the graph of $y = x^2 - 3x - 1$ and the line $y = -2x + 4$ (or $y = 4 - 2x$).

Exercise B

1 Show that the graphs of $y = 4x - 3$ and $y = \dfrac{2}{x}$ can be used to solve a quadratic equation of the form $ax^2 + bx + c = 0$
Find the values of a, b and c.

2 **a** Show that the graphs of $y = 2x - 1$ and $y = \frac{5}{x} + 2$ can be used to solve a quadratic equation of the form $ax^2 + bx + c = 0$
Find the values of a, b and c.

b Solve graphically the equation $2x - 1 = \frac{5}{x} + 2$

3 **a** Draw a grid with x and y from -3 to 3
On the grid draw the circle $x^2 + y^2 = 5$ and the line $y = 3x - 1$

b Show that the line and the circle can be used to solve the quadratic equation $5x^2 - 3x - 2 = 0$

c Use the graph to estimate the solutions of $5x^2 - 3x - 2 = 0$

4 A graph has equation $y = x^2 - 4x + 8$

a Jim uses the graph to solve the equation $x^2 - 4x + 8 = 3x - 2$
What is the equation of the line Jim draws on the graph to do this?

b Anna uses the graph to solve the equation $x^2 - 7x + 10 = 0$
What is the equation of the line Anna draws on the graph to do this?

c Suki uses the graph to solve the equation $x^2 - 5x + 4 = 0$
What is the equation of the line Suki draws on the graph to do this?

5 The graph of $y = x^2 + 2x - 6$ is drawn on the right for values of x from -5 to 5
Use the graph to find approximate solutions of:

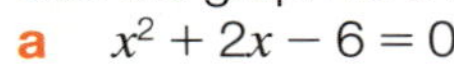

a $x^2 + 2x - 6 = 0$

b $x^2 + 2x - 5 = 0$

c $x^2 + 2x - 4 = x$

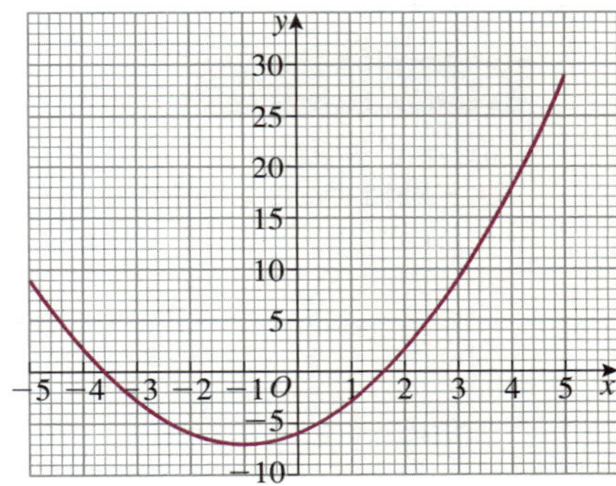

6 **a** Draw a grid with x and y from 0 to 5 using a scale of 2 cm to 1 unit.

b On the grid, draw the graphs of $y = \frac{1}{x}$ and $y = 4 - 4x$.

c Explain why the graphs of $y = \frac{1}{x}$ and $y = 4 - 4x$ show that the equation $4x^2 - 4x + 1 = 0$ has only **one** solution.

d Use the graph to estimate the solution.

7 Use the graph of $y = (x + 1)^2$ to find which of the following equations have exactly **one** solution.

a $(x + 1)^2 = x$ **b** $(x + 1)^2 = 4x + 1$ **c** $(x + 1)^2 + 2x + 3 = 0$

8 **a** Draw the graph of $y = 2x^2 - x - 3$ for values of x from -2 to 3

b Use the graph to find approximate answers to:

i $2x^2 - x - 3 = 1$ **ii** $2x^2 - x - 4 = 0$

iii $2x^2 - x - 3 = x + 2$ **iv** $2x^2 - x = x + 5$

9 **a** Draw the graph of $y = x^2 - 7x$ for values of x from 0 to 7

b Draw suitable straight lines on the graph to find approximate solutions to:

i $x^2 - 7x + 8 = 0$ **ii** $x^2 - 9x + 14 = 0$

10 **a** Draw the graph of $y = x^2 + 3x - 1$ for values of x from -5 to 2

b Hence solve graphically:

i $x^2 + 3x = 7$ **ii** $x^2 + 3x - 3 = x$ **iii** $2x^2 + 3x = 1$

32.3 Transformations of graphs

CAN YOU REMEMBER

- The distinctive shapes of the graphs of linear, quadratic, sine and cosine functions?

IN THIS SECTION YOU WILL

- Learn how to apply simple transformations to graphs.
- Learn about function notation.

Function notation can be used to show a relationship between two variables.
$f(x)$ means a **function of x**.
$f(x) = x^2$ is another way of writing $y = x^2$ where y is a function of x.
This can be shown on a number machine.

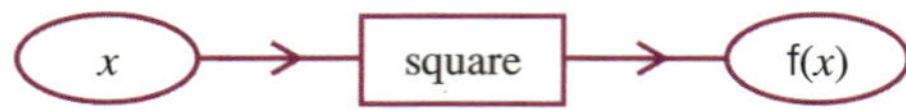

Example 1

$f(x) = x^2 + 2x$

a Find the value of:

i $f(3)$ **ii** $f(-4)$

b Write in terms of x:

i $f(x) + 1$ **ii** $f(x) + a$ **iii** $f(x) + 1$ **iv** $f(x + a)$

Solution 1

a **i** $f(3) = 3^2 + 2 \times 3$
$= 9 + 6 = 15$

ii $f(-4) = (-4)^2 + 2 \times (-4)$
$= 16 + -8 = 8$

b **i** $f(x) + 1 = x^2 + 2x + 1 - (x + 1)^2$

ii $f(x) + a = x^2 + 2x + a$

iii $f(x + 1) = (x + 1)^2 + 2(x + 1)$
$-x^2 + 2x + 1 + 2x + 2$
$-x^2 + 4x + 3 = (x + 3)(x + 1)$

iv $f(x + a) = (x + a)^2 + 2(x + a)$
$-x^2 + 2ax + a^2 + 2x + 2a$
$-x^2 + 2x(a + 1) + a(a + 2)$

The graph of a function can be transformed by changing either its position or its shape.
The equation of a transformed graph is related to the equation of the original graph.

Translating a graph

When a graph is translated all points on the graph move through the same distance and in the same direction.

Example 2

a On the same grid show the graph of $y = f(x)$ and $y = f(x) + 3$ where $f(x) = 2x - 1$

b Write down the equation of the transformed graph in the form $y = mx + c$

c Repeat parts **a** and **b** for:

i $y = f(x) - 2$ **ii** $y = f(x + 3)$ **iii** $y = f(x - 2)$

a The graph of $f(x) = 2x - 1$ has gradient 2 and y intercept -1
To find the coordinates of a point on $y = f(x) + 3$, pick points on $y = f(x)$ and **add 3** to their y-coordinates.
$(-1, -3) \rightarrow (-1, 0)$, $(0, -1) \rightarrow (0, 2)$, $(1, 1) \rightarrow (1, 4)$, ...
The graph of $y = f(x) + 3$ is a **translation** of **3** units **up** from the graph of $y = f(x)$.

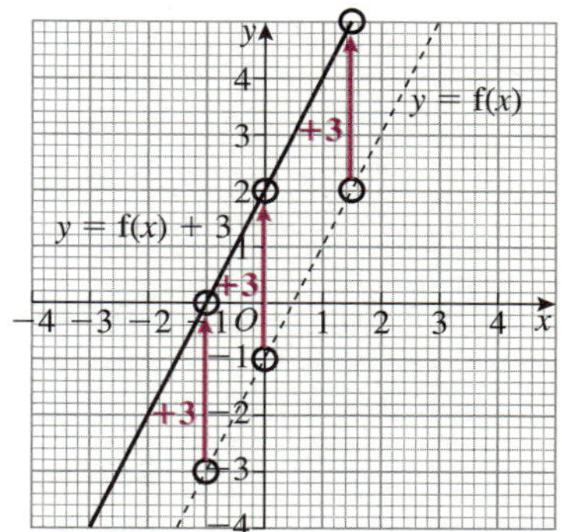

b **Method 1**
Substitute $2x - 1$ for $f(x)$ in $y = f(x) + 3$
$y = 2x - 1 + 3$
$y = 2x + 2$
Method 2
A translation of 3 up means that the gradient stays the same and the y intercept increases by 3
So for the graph of $y = f(x) + 3$:
gradient $(m) = 2$
y intercept $(c) = -1 + 3 = 2$
So $y = 2x + 2$

c **i** To find the coordinates of a point on $y = f(x) - 2$, pick a point on $y = f(x)$ and **subtract 2** from its y-coordinate.
$(0, -1) \rightarrow (0, -3)$, $(1, 1) \rightarrow (1, -1)$, $(2, 3) \rightarrow (2, 1)$, ...
The graph of $y = f(x) - 2$ is a **translation** of **2** units **down** from $y = f(x)$.
To find the equation of the transformed graph, substitute $2x - 1$ for $f(x)$ in $y = f(x) - 2$
$y = 2x - 1 - 2$
$y = 2x - 3$

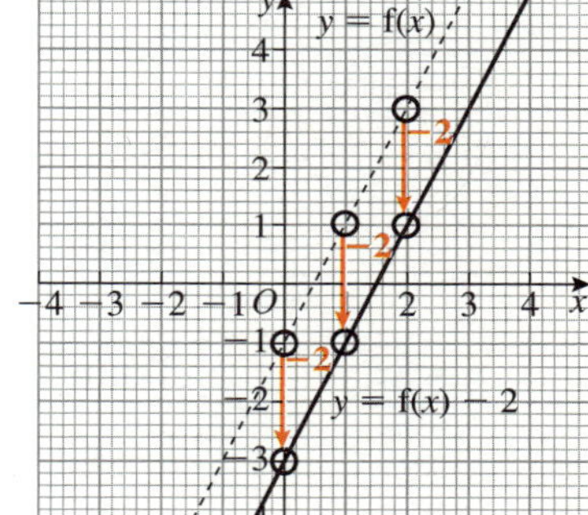

ii To find the coordinates of a point on $y = f(x + 3)$, pick a point on $y = f(x)$ and **subtract 3** from its x-coordinate
$(2, 3) \rightarrow (-1, 3)$, $(1, 1) \rightarrow (-2, 1)$, $(0, -1) \rightarrow (-3, -1)$, ...
The graph of $y = f(x + 3)$ is a **translation** of **3** units **left** from $y = f(x)$.
To find the equation of the transformed graph, substitute $(x + 3)$ for x in $y = 2x - 1$
$y = 2(x + 3) - 1$
$y = 2x + 6 - 1$
$y = 2x + 5$

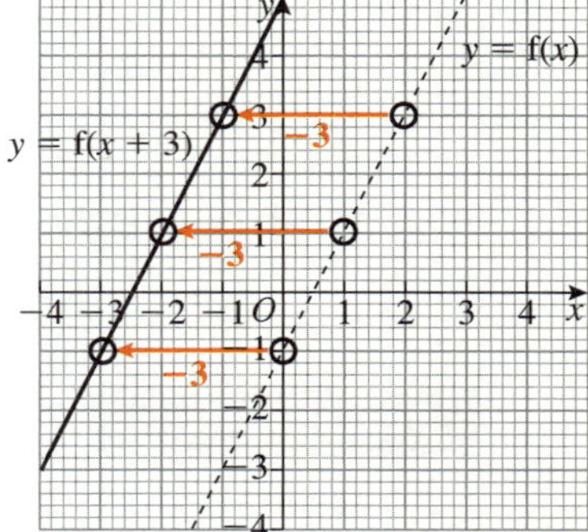

iii To find the coordinates of a point on $y = f(x - 2)$, pick a point on $y = f(x)$ and **add 2** to its x-coordinate.
$(-1, -3) \rightarrow (1, -3)$, $(0, -1) \rightarrow (2, -1)$, $(1, 1) \rightarrow (3, 1)$, ...
The graph of $y = f(x - 2)$ is a **translation** of **2** units **right** from $y = f(x)$.
To find the equation of the transformed graph, substitute $(x - 2)$ for x in $y = 2x - 1$
$y = 2(x - 2) - 1$
$y = 2x - 4 - 1$
$y = 2x - 5$

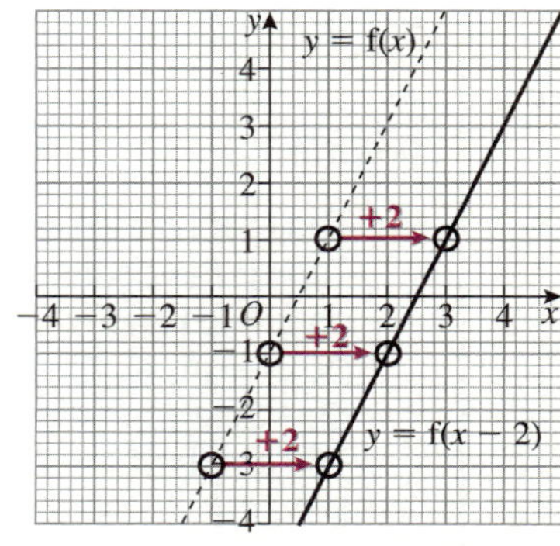

Original equation	**Transformation**	**New equation**	**Original graph → New graph**
$y = f(x)$	Translation a units **up** Column vector $\begin{pmatrix} 0 \\ a \end{pmatrix}$ **Add** a to all the y-coordinates of points on the original graph.	$y = f(x) + a$	$y = f(x) + a$; $y = f(x)$
$y = f(x)$	**Translation** a units **down** Column vector $\begin{pmatrix} 0 \\ -a \end{pmatrix}$ **Subtract** a from all the y-coordinates of points on the original graph.	$y = f(x) - a$	$y = f(x)$; $y = f(x) - a$
$y = f(x)$	**Translation** a units **left** Column vector $\begin{pmatrix} -a \\ 0 \end{pmatrix}$ **Subtract** a from all the x-coordinates of points on the original graph.	$y = f(x + a)$	$y = f(x + a)$; $y = f(x)$
$y = f(x)$	**Translation** a units **right** Column vector $\begin{pmatrix} a \\ 0 \end{pmatrix}$ **Add** a to all the x-coordinates of points on the original graph.	$y = f(x - a)$	$y = f(x)$; $y = f(x - a)$

A graph can be stretched either from the y-axis parallel to the x-axis or from the x-axis parallel to the y-axis.

Example 3

a On the same grid show the graph of $y = f(x)$ and $y = 2f(x)$ where $f(x) = x - 2$

b Write down the equation of the transformed graph in the form $y = mx + c$

c Repeat parts **a** and **b** for $y = f(3x)$.

Solution 3

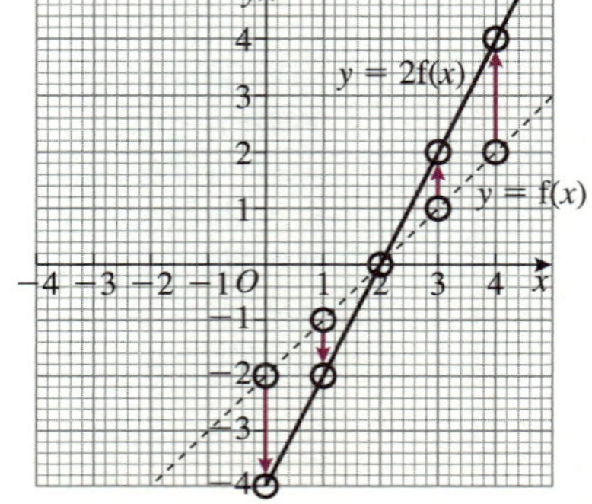

a The graph of $f(x) = x - 2$ has gradient 1 and y intercept -2
To find the coordinates of a point on $y = 2f(x)$, pick a point on $y = f(x)$ and **multiply** its y-coordinate by **2**
$(4, 2) \rightarrow (4, 4)$, $(3, 1) \rightarrow (3, 2)$, $(1, -1) \rightarrow (1, -2)$, $(0, -2) \rightarrow (0, -4)$, …
The graph of $y = 2f(x)$ is a **stretch** of the graph of $y = f(x)$ from the x-axis with scale factor **2**

b To find the equation of the transformed graph, substitute $x - 2$ for $f(x)$ in $y = 2f(x)$
$y = 2(x - 2)$
$y = 2x - 4$

c To find the coordinates of a point on $y = f(3x)$, pick a point on $y = f(x)$ and **divide** its x-coordinate by **3**
$(0, -2) \rightarrow (0, -2)$, $(3, 1) \rightarrow (1, 1)$ …
The graph of $y = f(3x)$ is a **stretch** of the graph of $y = f(x)$ from the y-axis with scale factor $\frac{1}{3}$
To find the equation of the transformed graph, substitute $3x$ for x in $y = x - 2$
$y = 3x - 2$

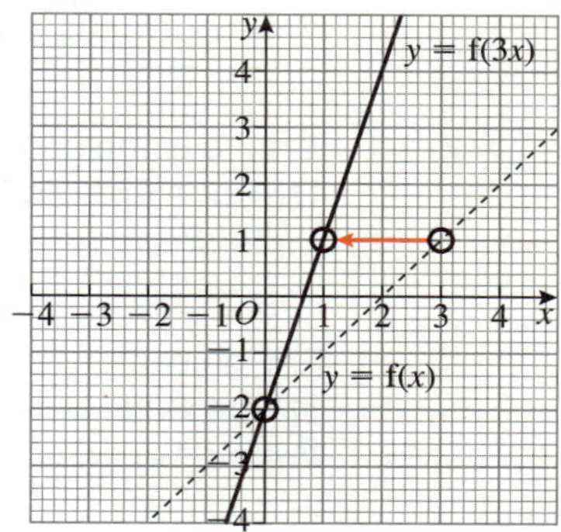

Original equation	Transformation	New equation	Original graph → New graph
$y = f(x)$	**Stretch** from the x-axis parallel to the y-axis, scale factor a. **Multiply** all y-coordinates on the original graph by a.	$y = af(x)$	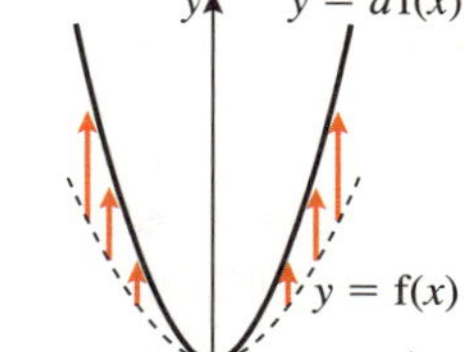
$y = f(x)$	**Stretch** from the y-axis parallel to the x-axis, scale factor $\frac{1}{a}$. **Divide** all x-coordinates on the original graph by a.	$y = f(ax)$	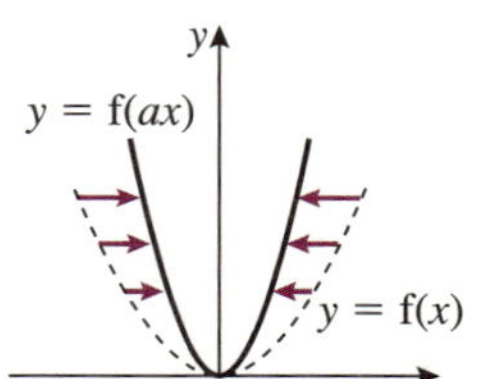

Example 4

The diagram shows the graph of $y = f(x)$ and the graphs of four other functions each of which is a different transformation of $y = f(x)$.
Describe each transformation.
Write the equation of each graph in terms of $f(x)$.

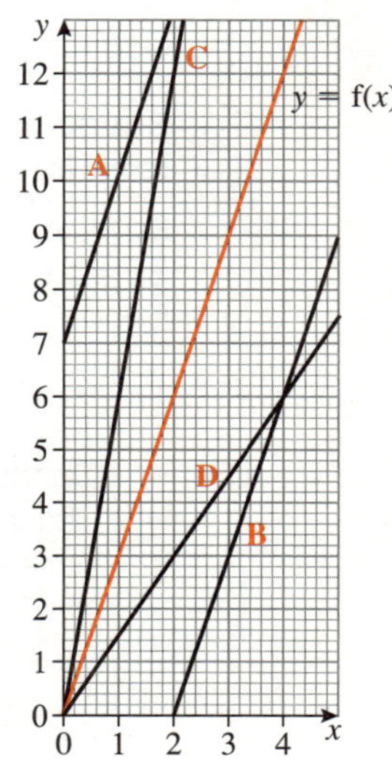

Solution 4

Graph **A**: the transformation is a translation of **7** units **up** from the graph of $y = f(x)$
Add 7 to $f(x)$, so $y = f(x) + 7$
Graph **B**: the transformation is a translation of **2** units **right** from the graph of $y = f(x)$
Replace x with $(x - 2)$, so $y = f(x - 2)$
Graph **C**: the transformation is a stretch of $y = f(x)$ from the ***x*-axis** scale factor 2
Multiply $f(x)$ by 2, so $y = 2f(x)$
Graph **D**: the transformation is a stretch of $y = f(x)$ from the ***y*-axis** scale factor 2
Replace x with $\frac{1}{2}x$, so $y = f(\frac{1}{2}x)$

Exercise A

1 **a** On the same grid show the graph of $y = f(x)$ and $y = f(x) + 5$ where $f(x) = x + 1$
b Describe the transformation.
c Write down the equation of the transformed graph in the form $y = mx + c$.

2 **a** On the same grid show the graph of $y = f(x)$ and $y = 3f(x)$ where $f(x) = x + 3$
b Describe the transformation.
c Write down the equation of the transformed graph in the form $y = mx + c$.

3 **a** On the same grid show the graph of $y = f(x)$ and $y = f(\frac{1}{2}x)$ where $f(x) = 3x - 2$
b Describe the transformation.
c Write down the equation of the transformed graph in the form $y = mx + c$.

4 **a** On the same grid show the graph of $y = f(x)$ and $y = \frac{1}{2}f(x)$ where $f(x) = 2x + 3$
b Describe the transformation.
c Write down the equation of the transformed graph in the form $y = mx + c$.

5 The diagram on the right shows the graph of $y = f(x)$ and the graphs of four other functions each of which is a different transformation of $y = f(x)$.
Describe each transformation.
Write the equation of each graph in terms of $f(x)$.

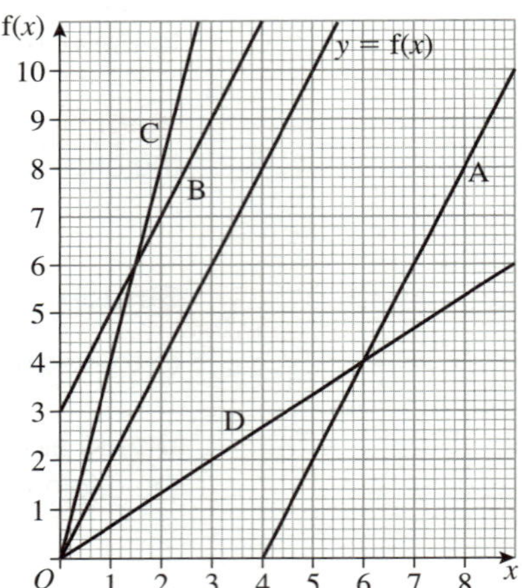

6 The table shows the equations of some graphs before and after a transformation.
Copy and complete the table.

Equation before transformation	Equation after transformation	Transformation
$f(x) = 3x$	$f(x) = 3x + 4$	
$f(x) = 2x + 1$	$f(x) = 4x + 1$	
$f(x) = x - 3$		**Translation:** 4 units left
	$f(x) = 6x + 8$	**Stretch:** from the x-axis, scale factor 2

7 **a** On the same grid show the graph of $y = f(x)$ and $y = 4f(x)$ where $f(x) = 3 - x$.
b Describe the transformation.
c Write down the equation of the transformed graph in the form $y = mx + c$.

8 Describe the transformation in each case for the lines shown on the graph on the right.

a line 1 to line 2
b line 2 to line 1
c line 3 to line 4
d line 4 to line 3
e line 3 to line 5
f line 5 to line 3

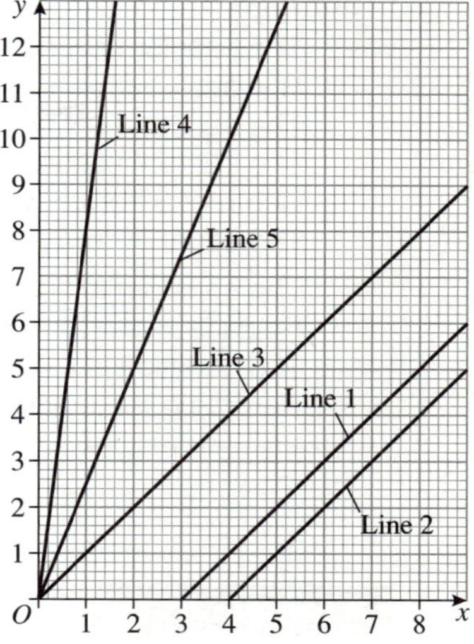

9 **a** Draw the graph of $y = x^2$ for values of x from -2 to $+2$

b On the same grid, draw the transformation of $y = x^2$ after:

i a translation 2 units down
ii a translation 2 units to the left
iii a stretch from the y-axis, parallel to the x-axis, with scale factor 2
iv a stretch from the x-axis, parallel to the y-axis, scale factor $\frac{1}{2}$

c For each of the transformations in part **b**, write down the equation of the transformed graph.

Example 5

The diagram shows the graph of $y = x^2$ for values of x from -2 to 2

Each of the graphs below is a transformation of this graph. Write down the equation of each graph.

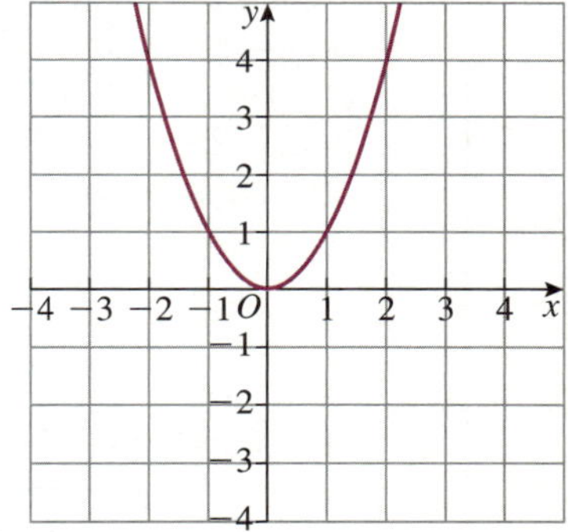

a

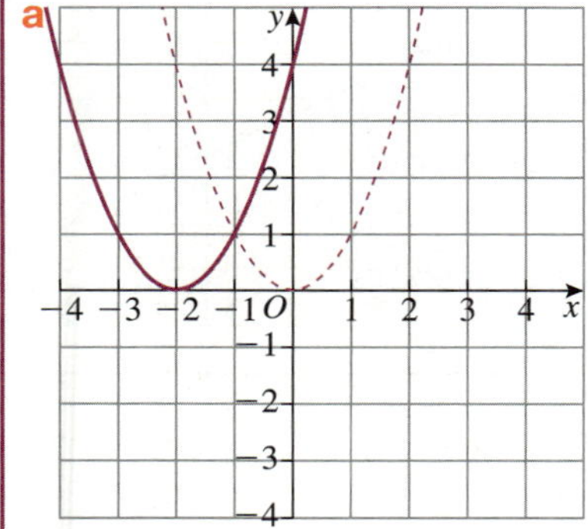

b

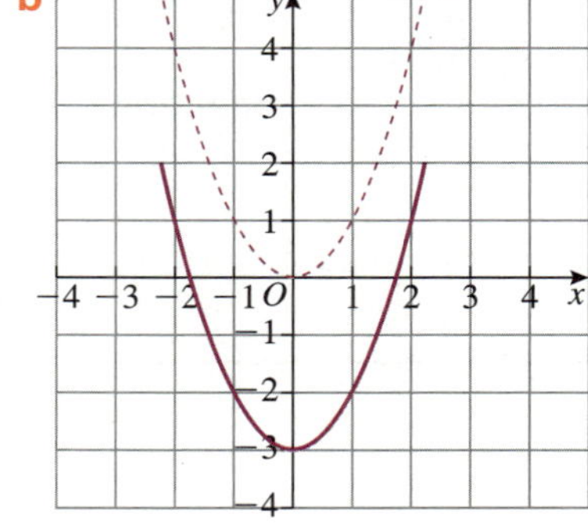

c

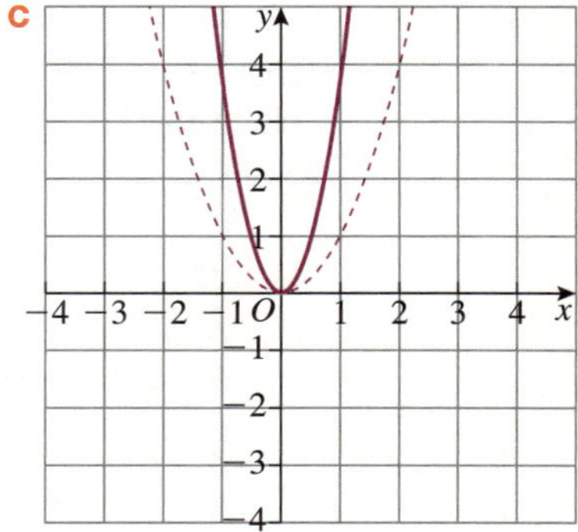

Solution 5

a The transformation is a translation of **2** units **left**.
Replace x with $x + 2$ in $y = x^2$
The equation is $y = (x + 2)^2$

b The transformation is a translation of **3** units **down**.
Subtract 3 from x^2 in $y = x^2$
The equation is $y = x^2 - 3$

c The transformation is a stretch from the y-axis with scale factor $\frac{1}{2}$
Replace x with $2x$ in $y = x^2$
The equation is $y = (2x)^2$
Removing the brackets gives $y = 4x^2$

Example 6

a On the same grid, show the graph of $y = \text{f}(x)$ and $y = -\text{f}(x)$ where $\text{f}(x) = \frac{1}{2}x - 1$

b On the same grid, show the graph of $y = \text{f}(x)$ and $y = \text{f}(-x)$ where $\text{f}(x) = \frac{1}{2}x - 1$

Solution 6

a The graph of $\text{f}(x) = \frac{1}{2}x - 1$ has gradient $\frac{1}{2}$ and y intercept -1
The graph of $y = -\text{f}(x)$ is a **stretch** of the graph of $y = \text{f}(x)$ from the x-axis with scale factor **−1**
To find the coordinates of a point on $y = -\text{f}(x)$, pick a point on $y = \text{f}(x)$ and **multiply** its y-coordinate by **−1**
$(4, 1) \rightarrow (4, -1)$, $(2, 0) \rightarrow (2, 0)$, $(0, -1) \rightarrow (0, 1)$,
$(-2, -2) \rightarrow (-2, 2)$, $(-4, -3) \rightarrow (-4, 3)$ …
This transformation is equivalent to a **reflection** in the x-axis.

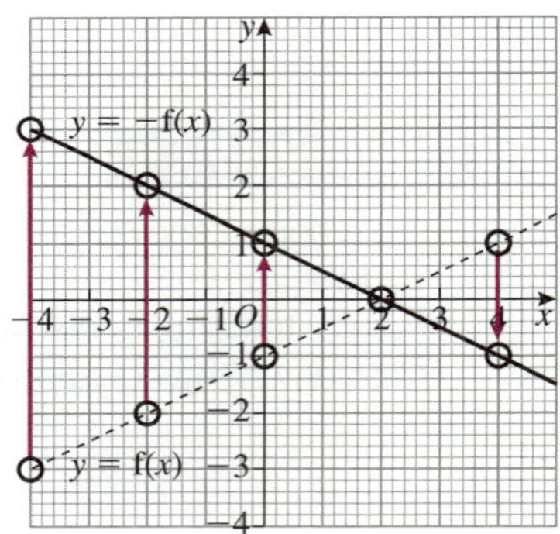

b The graph of $y = \text{f}(-x)$ is a stretch of the graph of $y = \text{f}(x)$ from the y-axis with scale factor **−1**
To find the coordinates of a point on $y = \text{f}(-x)$, pick a point on $y = \text{f}(x)$ and **divide** its x-coordinate by **−1**
$(-4, -3) \rightarrow (4, -3)$, $(-2, -2) \rightarrow (2, -2)$, $(0, -1) \rightarrow (0, -1)$,
$(2, 0) \rightarrow (-2, 0)$, $(4, 1) \rightarrow (-4, 1)$ …
This transformation is equivalent to a **reflection** in the y-axis.

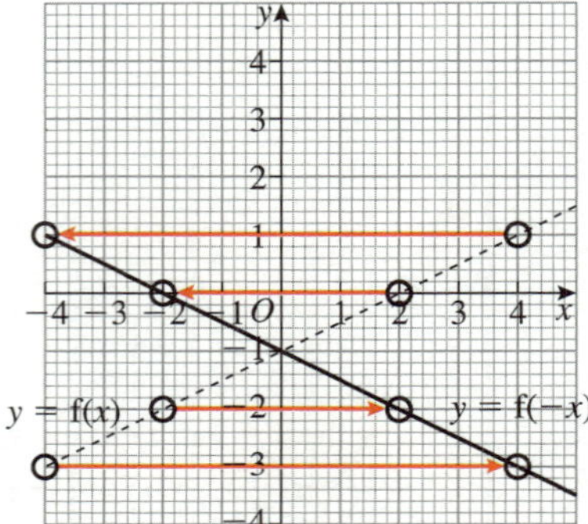

Original equation	Transformation	New equation	Original graph → New graph
$y = \mathrm{f}(x)$	**Stretch** from the x-axis parallel to the y-axis, scale factor **−1** **Reflection** in x-axis **Multiply** all y-coordinates on the original graph by **−1**	$y = -\mathrm{f}(x)$	$y = \mathrm{f}(x)$ $y = -\mathrm{f}(x)$
$y = \mathrm{f}(x)$	**Stretch** from the y-axis parallel to the x-axis, scale factor **−1** **Reflection** in y-axis **Divide** all x-coordinates on the original graph by **−1**	$y = \mathrm{f}(-x)$	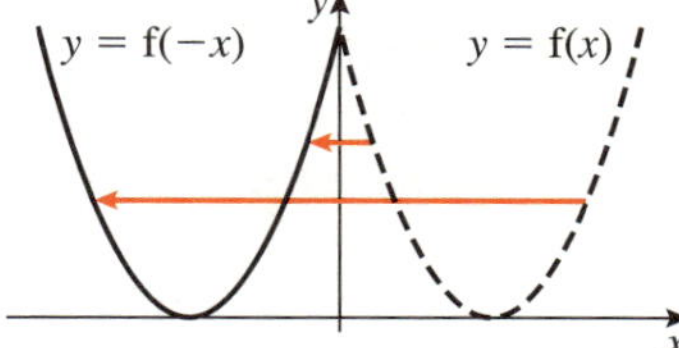

Exercise B

1 The diagram shows the graph of $\mathrm{f}(x) = x^2$ for values of x from −2 to 2
Copy the graph and on the same grid draw and label the graphs of:

a $y = \mathrm{f}(x) - 3$
b $y = \mathrm{f}(x - 2)$
c $y = \frac{1}{2}\mathrm{f}(x)$
d $y = \mathrm{f}\left(\frac{1}{2}x\right)$

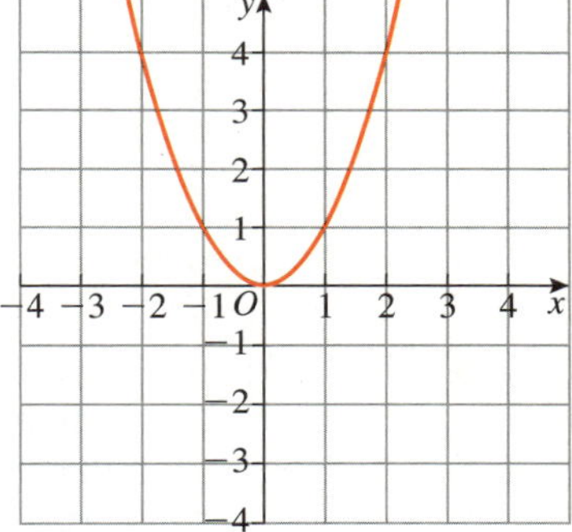

2 The graph of $y = \sin x$ with values of x from 0° to 360° is shown on the grid.

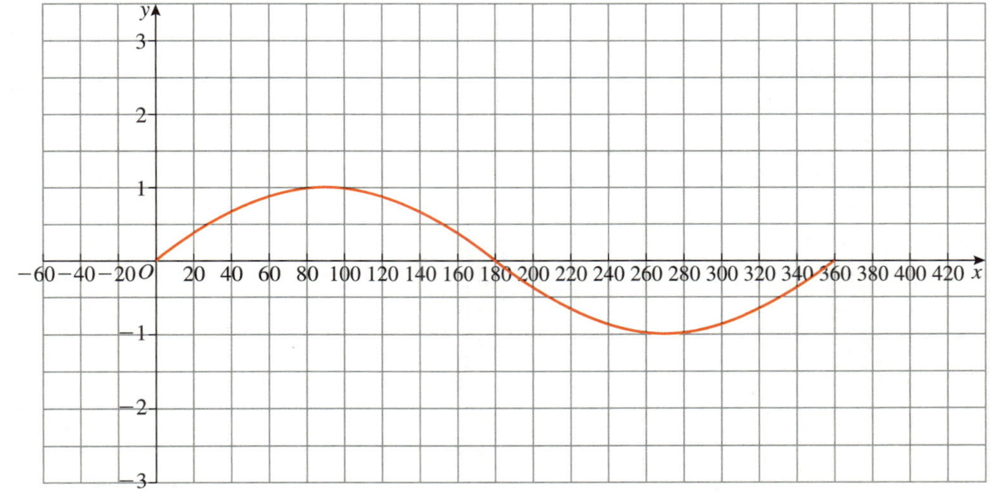

a Copy the graph and sketch the following transformed graphs.
  i $y = 2 + \sin x$ **ii** $y = \sin(x + 60)$ **iii** $y = 3 \sin x$ **iv** $y = \sin 3x$

b For each graph:
  i label the values of **all** points where the graph crosses the axes
  ii write down the coordinates of the transformed position of the point (90, 1).

3 **a** Draw the graph of $y = x^2 - 5$ for values of x from -3 to $+3$

b On the same grid, draw the transformation of $y = x^2 - 5$ after:
  i a translation 3 units up **ii** a translation 3 units to the left
  iii a stretch from the y-axis, parallel to the x-axis, with scale factor 2
  iv a stretch from the x-axis, parallel to the y-axis, scale factor $\frac{1}{2}$

c For each of the transformations in part **b** write down:
  i the equation of the transformed graph.
  ii the coordinates of the transformed position of the point $(0, -5)$.

4 The graph of $y = x^3 + x$ for values of x from -2 to 2 is shown on each of the following grids together with a transformation of the graph.
Write down the equations of the transformed graphs, A, B, C and D.

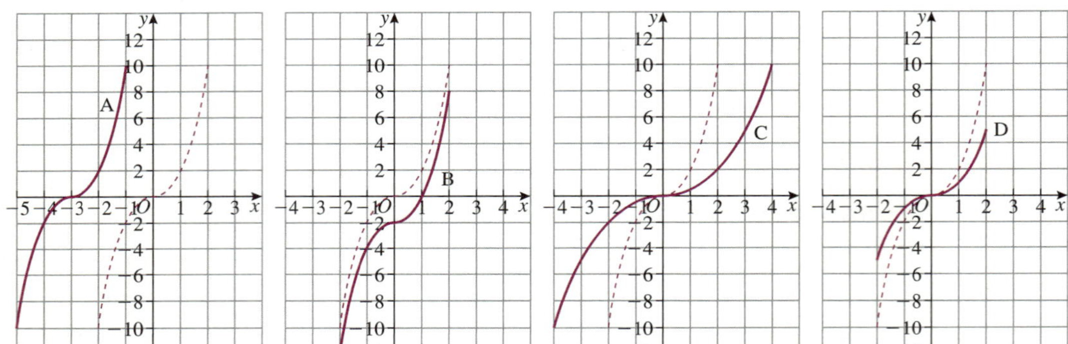

5 The diagram shows the graph of $y = x^2 + 1$ for x from -2 to 2
For each of the graphs below:
i describe the transformation
ii work out the equation of the transformed graph.

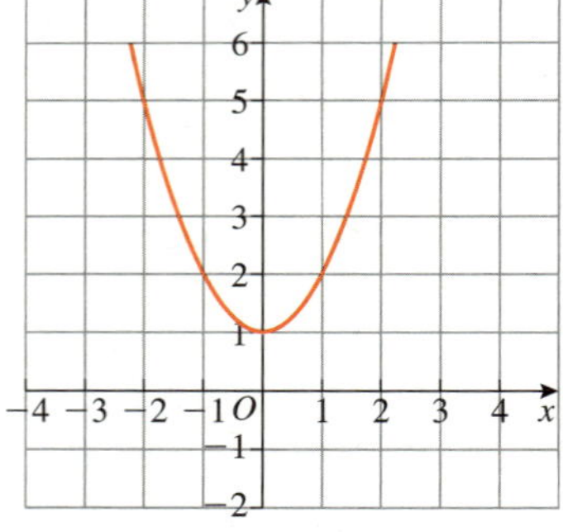

a

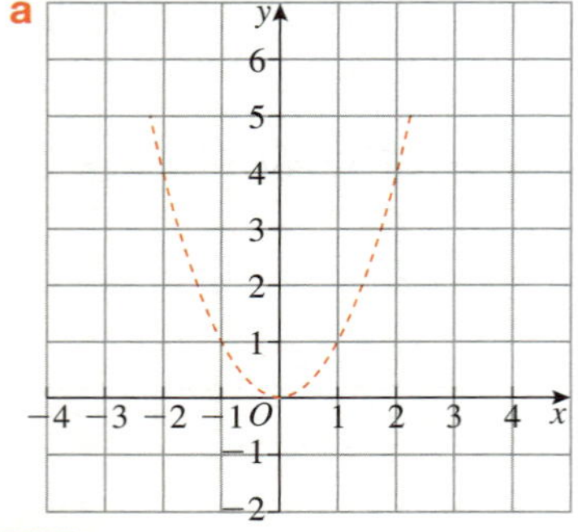

b

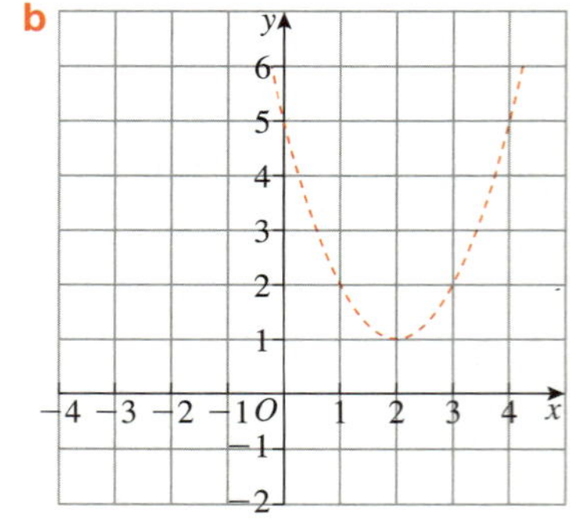

c

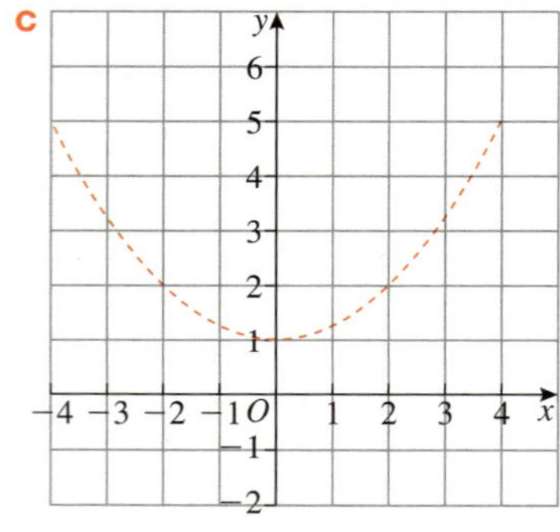

6 Answer this question on a grid with both the x-axis and y-axis from -6 to 6

- **a** $f(x) = 3x + 1$
  Draw the graphs of $y = f(x)$ and $y = -f(x)$ on the same grid.
- **b** $f(x) = 2x - 1$
  Draw the graphs of $y = f(x)$ and $y = f(-x)$ on the same grid.

7 The diagram on the right shows the graph of $f(x) = x^2$ for values of x from -2 to 2

- **a** Copy the graph and on the same axes draw and label the graphs of:
  - **i** $y = -f(x)$
  - **ii** $y = f(-x)$
- **b** What do you notice about the answers to part **a**?

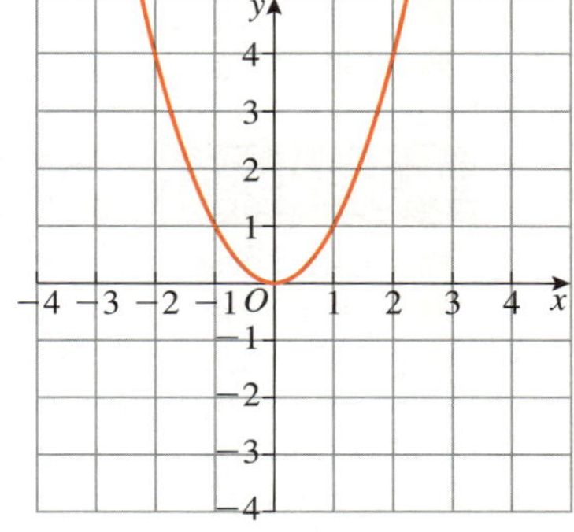

8 The grid shows the graph of $y = 3x^2 - x - 3$ for values of x between -2 and 2

- **a** Sketch the transformation of $y = 3x^2 - x - 3$ after a stretch:
  - **i** from the x-axis parallel to the y-axis with scale factor -1
  - **ii** from the y-axis parallel to the x-axis with scale factor -1
- **b** What is the equation of each of the transformed graphs in part **a**?

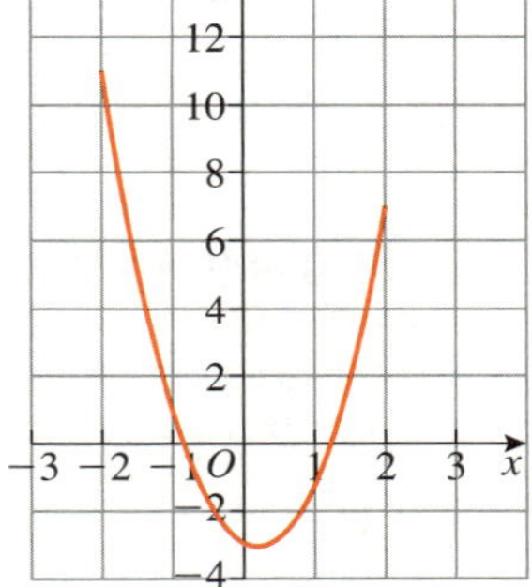

9 Use your knowledge of the graphs of $y = \sin x$ and $y = \cos x$ to decide whether the following statements are true or false.
Give a reason for each answer.

- **a** The graph of $y = \sin x$ is the same as the graph of $y = \cos x$ after a translation of 90 units right.
- **b** The graph of $y = \cos x$ is unchanged by a stretch from the y-axis parallel to the x-axis, scale factor -1

10 Katie says that the graph of $y = \sin 2x$ is a curve which varies between the values -2 and $+2$ on the y-axis.
Nikki disagrees. She thinks it is the graph of $y = 2\sin x$ that varies between the values -2 and $+2$ on the y-axis.
Without drawing the curves, explain who is correct.

32.4 More about quadratic equations and their graphs

CAN YOU REMEMBER

- The distinctive shape of a quadratic graph?
- How to change the quadratic expression $x^2 + bx + c = 0$ to the form $(x + p)^2 + q$?
- How to solve a pair of simultaneous equations?

IN THIS SECTION YOU WILL

- Learn how to find the minimum (or maximum) value of a quadratic expression.
- Learn what the values of p and q represent in a quadratic graph with equation $y = (x + p)^2 + q$.
- Learn how to use simultaneous equations to find the equation of a quadratic graph that passes through known points.

The graph of $y = x^2$ is transformed by the **translation p units left**.
The equation of the transformed graph is $y = (x + p)^2$
The coordinates of the minimum point are $(-p, 0)$.

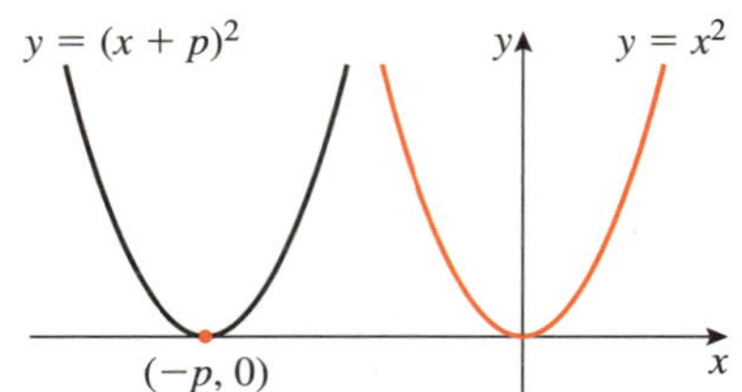

The graph of $y = (x + p)^2$ is transformed by the **translation q units up**.
The equation of the transformed graph is $y = (x + p)^2 + q$.
The coordinates of the minimum point are $(-p, q)$.

A quadratic expression of the form $(x + p)^2 + q$ has a *minimum* value of q.
A quadratic expression of the form $-(x + p)^2 + q$ has a *maximum* value of q.
These both occur when $(x + p)^2 = 0$ and $x = -p$.
This means that the minimum or maximum point has coordinates $(-p, q)$.

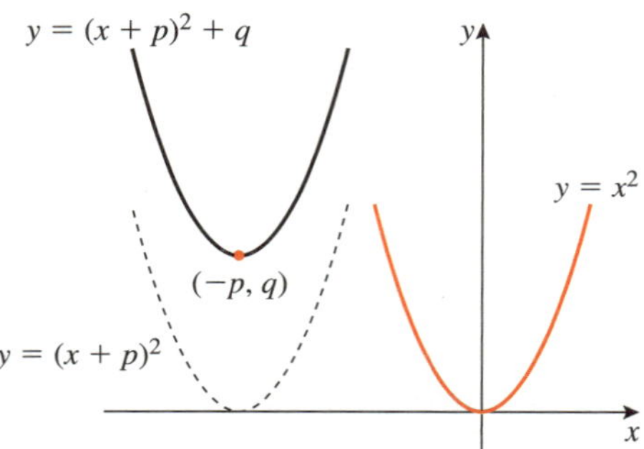

Example 1

Write the quadratic expression $x^2 + 2x - 5$ in the form $(x + p)^2 + q$.
Hence find the minimum value of $x^2 + 2x - 5$ and the coordinates of the minimum point.

Solution 1

$x^2 + \mathbf{2}x - 5$

$\frac{1}{2}$ of **2** = **1**

$(x + \mathbf{1})^2 \equiv x^2 + \mathbf{2}x + 1$

$x^2 + 2x - 5 \equiv x^2 + 2x + 1 - 6$

$x^2 + 2x - 5 \equiv (x + 1)^2 - 6$ — This is $(x + p)^2 + q$ with $p = 1$ and $q = -6$

The minimum value of $(x + 1)^2 - 6$ is -6
So the minimum value of $x^2 + 2x - 5$ is -6
The minimum point has coordinates $(-1, -6)$.

The vertical line of symmetry of a quadratic graph passes through its minimum or maximum point.
For example, $x^2 + \mathbf{4}x + 3 \equiv (x + \mathbf{2})^2 - 1$
So for the graph of $y = x^2 + 4x + 3$:

- the coordinates of the minimum point are $(-2, -1)$
- the vertical line of symmetry has equation $x = -2$

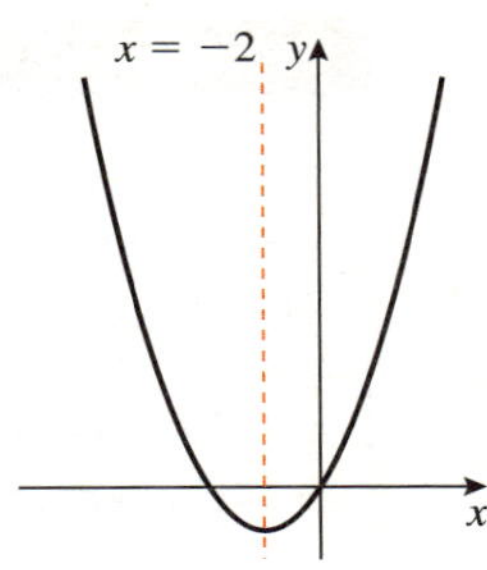

Exercise A

1 **a** Find the values of a and b such that $x^2 - 4x - 45 \equiv (x - a)^2 - b$.
Hence find the minimum value of $x^2 - 4x - 45$

b Write $x^2 - 10x + 24$ in the form $(x + p)^2 + q$.
Hence, find the minimum value of $x^2 - 10x + 24$

2 **a** Find the value of a such that $x^2 - 22x + 121 \equiv (x + a)^2$
Hence, write down the equation of the line of symmetry of the graph $y = x^2 - 22x + 121$

b Write $x^2 - 6x - 3$ in the form $(x + p)^2 + q$.
Hence write down the equation of the line of symmetry of the graph.

3 Calculate the minimum point and vertical line of symmetry of each of these graphs.

a $y = x^2 - 2x + 3$ **b** $y = x^2 + 8x - 2$

c $y = x^2 - 10x + 4$ **d** $y = x^2 - 4x + 12$

4 The diagram shows a sketch of the graph of $y = x^2 - 10x + 12$
Work out the coordinates of the point marked A on the graph.

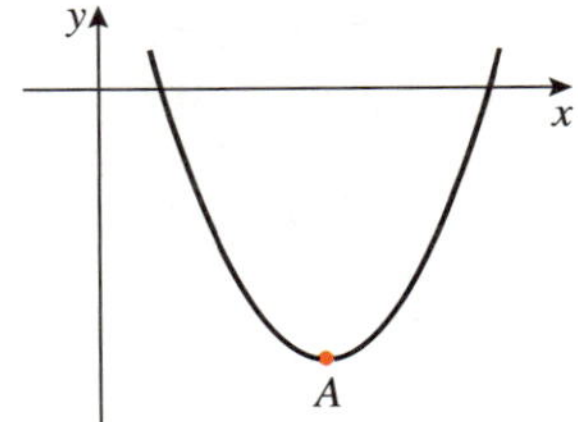

5 The diagram shows a sketch of the graph of $y = 7 + 2x - x^2$
Work out the coordinates of the point marked B on the graph.

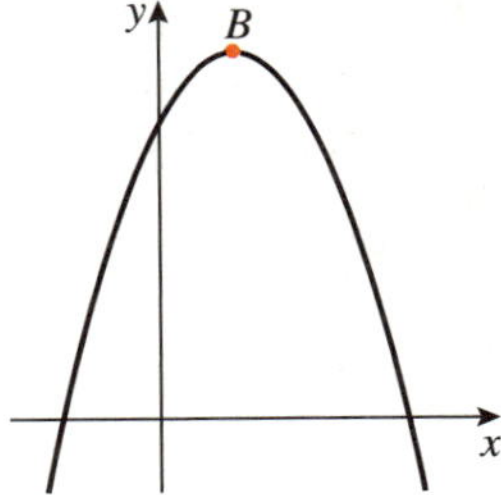

The equation of the graph can be worked out if the coordinates of two points on a quadratic graph are known.

Substituting the coordinate values into the equation $y = x^2 + bx + c$ gives two equations, which can be solved simultaneously to find the values of b and c.

Example 2

The diagram shows a sketch of a graph with equation of the form
$y = x^2 + bx + c$.
The graph intersects the x-axis at the points with coordinates $(-2, 0)$ and $(3, 0)$.

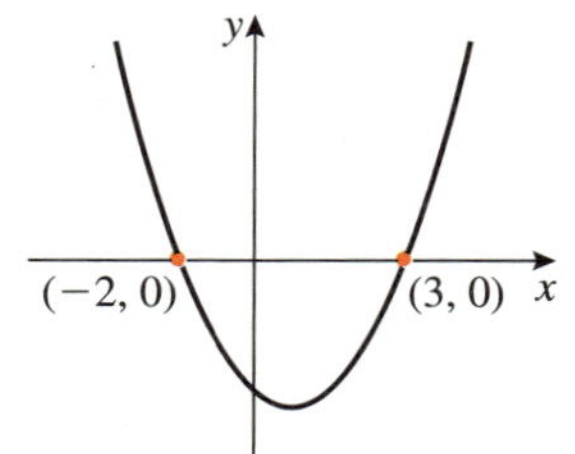

a Find the values of b and c.

b By factorising $x^2 + bx + c$, write the equation in the form
$y = (x + m)(x + n)$
What do you notice about the values of m and n?

Solution 2

a The graph passes through $(-2, 0)$
$0 = (-2)^2 + b \times (-2) + c$ — Substitute $x = -2$ and $y = 0$ in $y = x^2 + bx + c$.
$0 = 4 - 2b + c$
The graph passes through $(3, 0)$
$0 = 3^2 + b \times 3 + c$ — Substitute $x = 3$ and $y = 0$ in $y = x^2 + bx + c$.
$0 = 9 + 3b + c$
Substituting the coordinate values gives two simultaneous equations.
$0 = 4 - 2b + c$ A — Label the equations.
$0 = 9 + 3b + c$ B
$0 = 5 + 5b$ B − A — Subtract to eliminate c.
$b = -1$
$0 = 9 + 3 \times (-1) + c$ — Substitute $b = -1$ in B.
$0 = 6 + c$
$c = -6$

b $y = x^2 + bx + c = x^2 - x - 6$
$y = (x - 3)(x + 2)$ — $x^2 - x - 6 \equiv (x - 3)(x + 2)$
$m = -3$ and $n = 2$
The values of $-m$ and $-n$ are the solutions of the equation $y = x^2 - x - 6$
So $-m$ and $-n$ are the x-values where the graph of $y = x^2 - x - 6$ cuts the x-axis.

Exercise B

1 The graph with equation $y = x^2 + bx + c$ intersects the x-axis at the points $(-4, 0)$ and $(3, 0)$. Find the values of b and c.

2 The graph with equation $y = x^2 + bx + c$ intersects the x-axis at the points $(-1, 0)$ and $(2, 0)$. Find the values of b and c.

3 The graph with equation $y = x^2 + bx + c$ intersects the x-axis at the point $(-2, 0)$ and passes through $(1, 15)$.
a Find the values of b and c.
b Find the minimum value and the equation of the line of symmetry of this graph.

4 The graph with equation $y = x^2 + bx + c$ intersects the x-axis at the point $(3, 0)$ and passes through $(4, 9)$.
a Find the values of b and c.
b Find the minimum point and line of symmetry of this graph.

5 The graph with equation $y = x^2 + bx + c$ passes through the x-axis at the points $(2, 18)$ and $(-3, 3)$. Find the minimum value and the equation of the line of symmetry of this graph.

6 The diagram shows the graph of the equation $y = x^2 + bx + c$.
The graph passes through the points (3, 0) and (−2, 5).

a Find the values of b and c.

b Work out the coordinates of P, the other point where the graph intersects the x-axis.

c Work out the coordinates of Q, the point where the graph intersects the y-axis.

d Work out the coordinates of R, the minimum point on the graph.

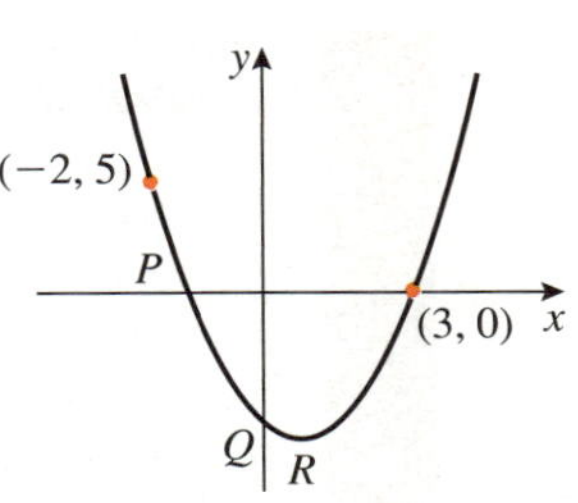

Chapter summary

- Any function of the form $y = ax^2 + bx + c$ where $a \neq 0$ is a quadratic function.
  The graph of a quadratic function has:
  - a distinctive smooth U-shaped curve
  - a vertical line of symmetry
  - a maximum or a minimum point.

a positive a negative

- Any function of the form $y = ax^3 + bx^2 + cx + d$ where $a \neq 0$ is a cubic function.
  The graph of a cubic function has a distinctive curve with rotational symmetry.
- If a is positive, a cubic graph looks like one of these.

- Any function of the form $y = \frac{a}{x}$ is called a reciprocal function.
  As x approaches zero, y becomes very large.
  Similarly, as y approaches zero, x becomes very large.
  This means that points do not exist at either $x = 0$ or $y = 0$
  If a is positive, a reciprocal graph looks like this:

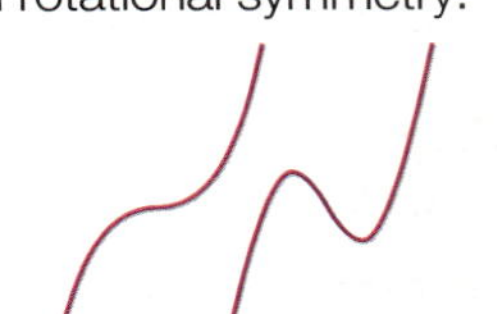

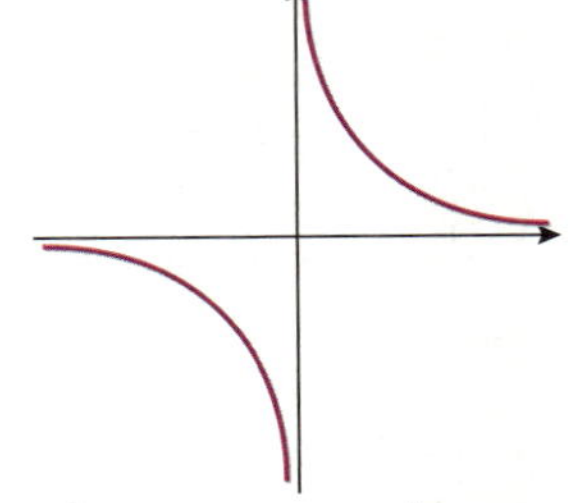

- Any function of the form $y = a^x$ is called an exponential function.
  All graphs of exponential functions pass through the point (0, 1).

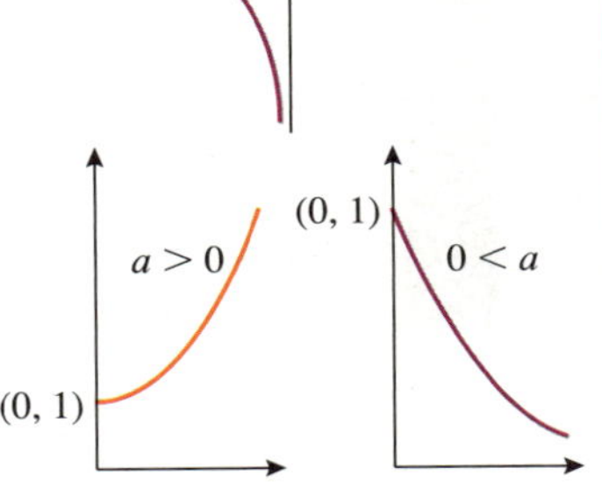

- The graphs of $y = \sin x°$, $y = \cos x°$ and $y = \tan x°$ for values of x from 0° to 360° are shown below.

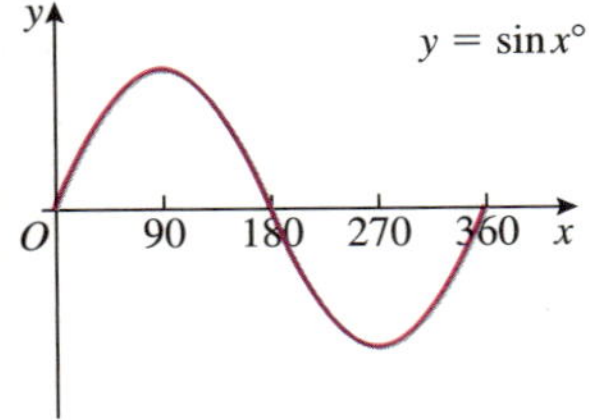

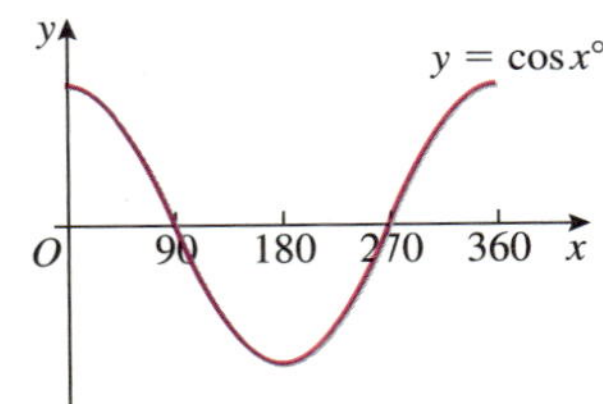

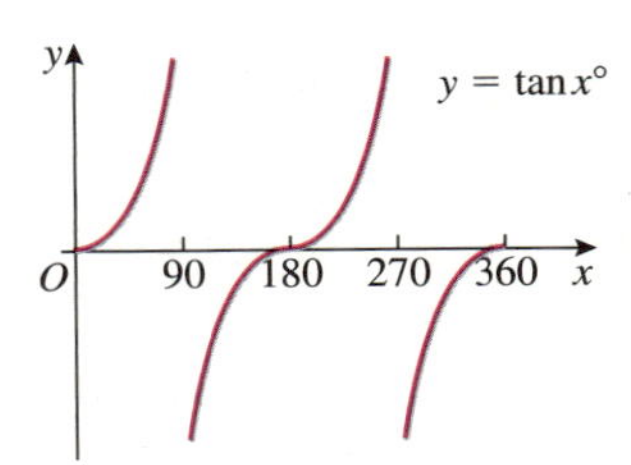

- A quadratic equation is an equation of the form $y = ax^2 + bx + c$, where $a \neq 0$
  Quadratic equations can be solved graphically.
  For example, the solutions of the equation $ax^2 + bx + c = k$ are the x-coordinates of the points where the graph of $y = ax^2 + bx + c$ intersects the line $y = k$.
  Pairs of equations that can be rearranged to give a quadratic equation can be used to solve the quadratic equation.
- Function notation can be used to show a relationship between two variables.
  $f(x)$ means a **function of x**.
  $f(x) = x^2$ is another way of writing $y = x^2$ where y is a function of x.
- The graph of a function can be transformed by changing either its position or its shape.
  The equation of a transformed graph is related to the equation of the original graph.

Transformation	Change to equation
Translation a units **up**	$y = f(x) \rightarrow y = f(x) + a$
Translation a units **down**	$y = f(x) \rightarrow y = f(x) - a$
Translation a units **right**	$y = f(x) \rightarrow y = f(x - a)$
Translation a units **left**	$y = f(x) \rightarrow y = f(x + a)$
Stretch from x-axis, scale factor a	$y = f(x) \rightarrow y = af(x)$
Stretch from y-axis, scale factor a	$y = f(x) \rightarrow y = f(\frac{1}{a}x)$
Stretch from the x-axis parallel to the y-axis, scale factor **−1**. **Reflection** in x-axis	$y = f(x) \rightarrow y = -f(x)$
Stretch from the y-axis parallel to the x-axis, scale factor **−1**. **Reflection** in y-axis	$y = f(x) \rightarrow y = f(-x)$

- A quadratic expression of the form $(x + p)^2 + q$ has a minimum value of q.
  A quadratic expression of the form $-(x + p)^2 + q$ has a maximum value of q.
  These both occur when $(x + p)^2 = 0$ and $x = -p$.
  This means that the minimum or maximum point has coordinates $(-p, q)$.
  The vertical line of symmetry of a quadratic graph passes through its minimum or maximum point.
- The equation of a quadratic graph can be worked out if the coordinates of two points on a quadratic graph are known.
  Substituting the coordinate values into the equation $y = x^2 + bx + c$ gives two equations.
  These can be solved simultaneously to find the values of b and c.

Chapter review

1 Each of the graphs represent one of the following equations.
Write down the letter of the equation represented by each graph.

A	B	C	D	E
$y = 3 - 2x$	$y = 3 - x^2$	$y = 1.5^x$	$y = x^3 - 1$	$y = 2x - 3$

Graph 1 **Graph 2** **Graph 3** **Graph 4**

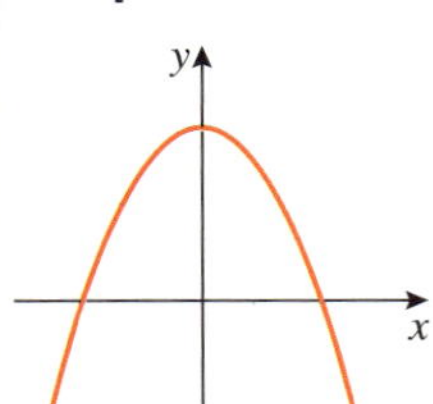

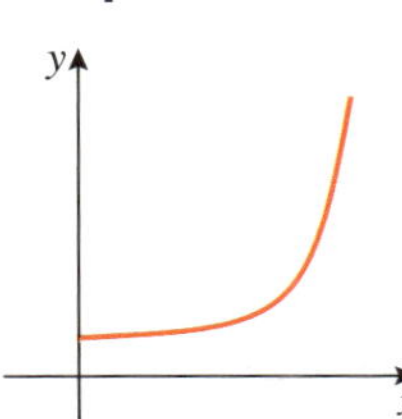

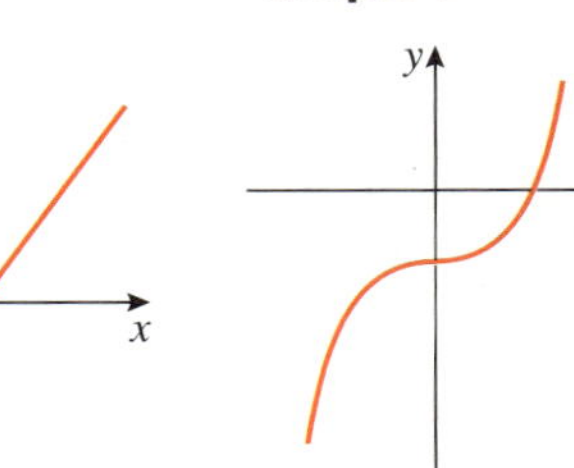

2 **a** Write down the equation of a circle with centre (0, 0) and radius 8 cm.
b What is the diameter of the circle with equation $x^2 + y^2 = 121$?

3 The diagram shows the graph of $y = 8 - x - 2x^2$ for values of x from -3 to 3

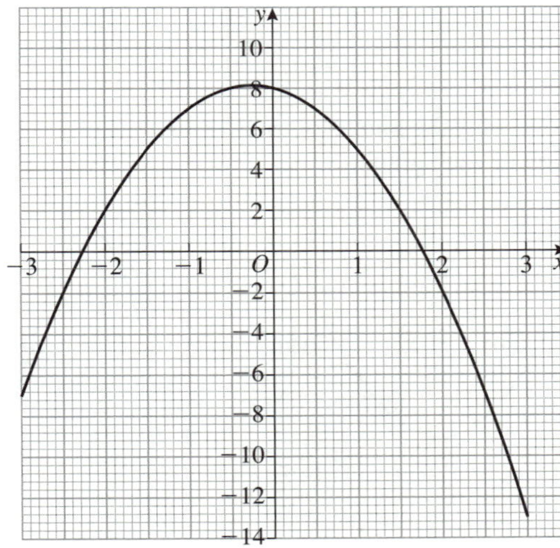

a Use the graph to solve the equations:
i $8 - x - 2x^2 = 0$ **ii** $8 - x - 2x^2 = 4$ **iii** $8 - x - 2x^2 = 1 - 2x$

b Emma wants to use the graph to solve the equation $2x^2 + 2x - 3 = 0$
What is the equation of the line she needs to draw?

4 The graph of $y = x^2 - 2x - 1$ and a graph of the form $y = ax + b$ can be used to solve the equation $x^2 - 5x + 2 = 0$
Find the values of a and b.

5 Write the equation $y = x^2 - 4x - 3$ in the form $y = (x + a)^2 + b$.
Hence, write down the minimum value of y and the line of symmetry of the graph of $y = x^2 - 4x - 3$

6 The diagram shows a sketch of the graph $y = x^2 + bx + c$.
The graph passes through the points $(1, 0)$ and $(0, -2)$.
Find the values of b and c.

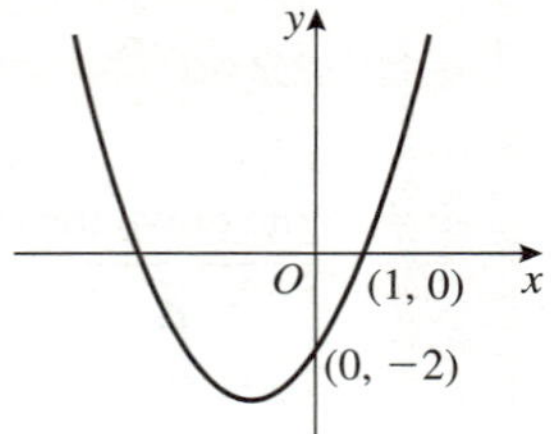

7 The diagram shows a sketch of the graph of $y = x^2$
On a copy of the diagram sketch the following graphs:

a $y = x^2 + 1$
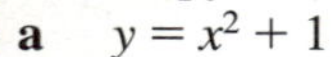

b $y = (x + 1)^2$

c $y = \frac{1}{2}x^2$

8 The diagram shows the graph of $y = \sin x°$
for $0 \leqslant x \leqslant 360$

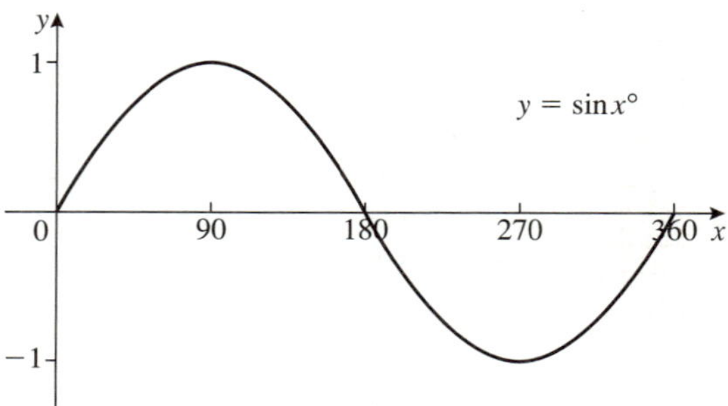

The two diagrams below show the graphs of transformations of $y = \sin x°$.
Write down the equation of each graph.

a

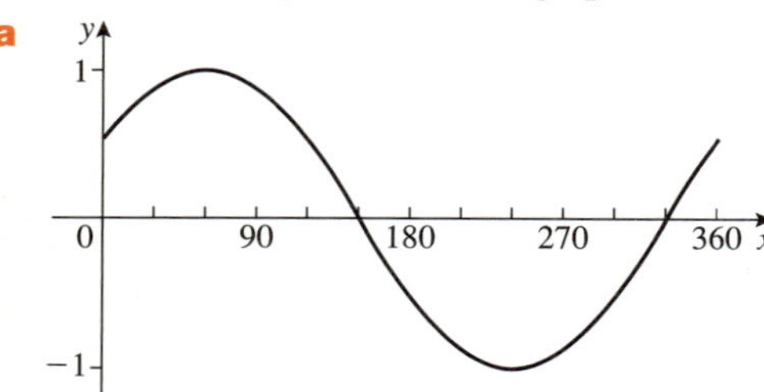

b

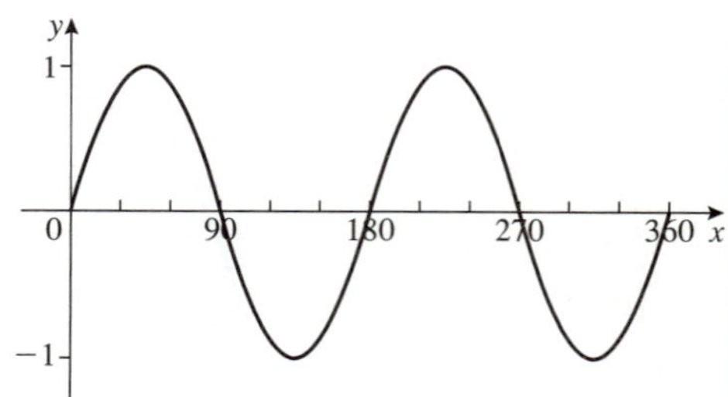

9 The diagram shows the graph of $y = f(x)$ where $f(x) = \cos x$ and four other graphs A, B, C and D.
Graphs A, B, C and D represent four different transformations of $y = f(x)$.

a Find the equations of each of the graphs, A, B, C and D.

b Write down the equations of the transformed graphs A to D in terms of $f(x)$.

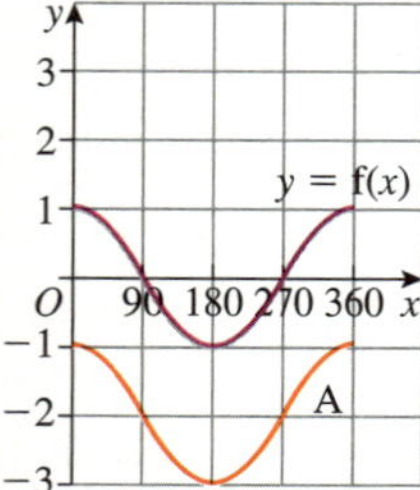

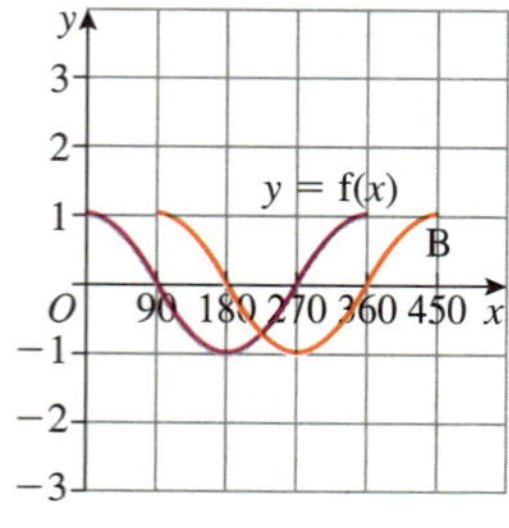

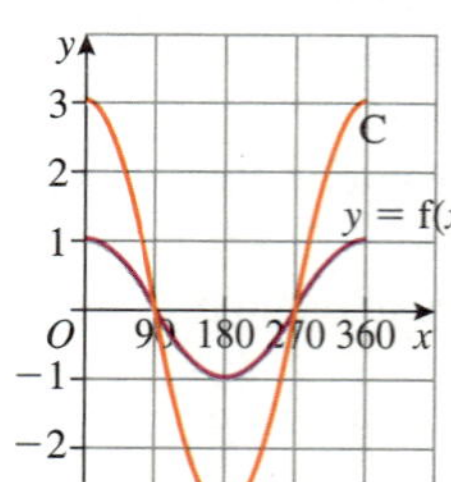

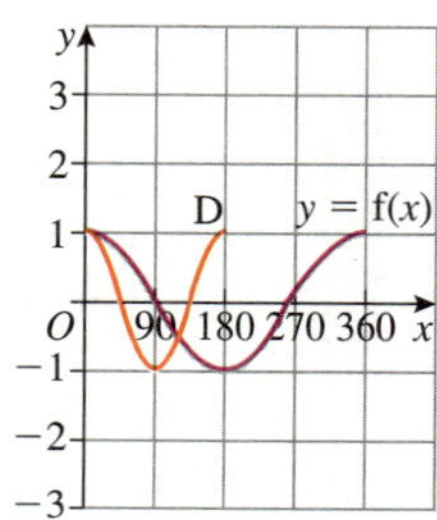

10 **a** Draw the graph of $y = x^2 - 2x + 3$ with values of x from -1 to 3

b By drawing an appropriate straight line on the graph of $y = x^2 - 2x + 3$ solve the equation $x^2 - x - 1 = 0$

11 **a** Copy and complete the table of values for $y = 4x^3 - 5x - 1$

x	−1.5	−1	−0.5	0	0.5	1	1.5
y	−7		1	−1	−3	−2	

b **i** Draw a grid with x from -1.5 to 1.5 with a scale of 1 cm to 0.5 units and y from -8 to 4 with a scale of 1 cm to 1 unit.

ii On the grid draw the graph of $y = 4x^3 - 5x - 1$ for values of x from -1.5 to 1.5

12 **a** Complete the table of values for $y = (0.7)^x$

x	0	1	2	3	4
y			0.49	0.343	0.2401

b Draw a grid with values of x from 0 to 4 with a scale of 2 cm to 1 unit and values of y from 0 to 1 with a scale of 1 cm to 0.1 units.

c On the grid draw the graph of $y = (0.7)^x$ for values of x from 0 to 4

d Use the graph to explain why there is no positive solution to the equation $(0.7)^x = 2$

CHAPTER 33

Further three-dimensional shapes

33.1 Surface area and volume of a pyramid

CAN YOU REMEMBER

- The area of a triangle $= \frac{1}{2} \times$ base $\times$ perpendicular height?
- How to draw the net of a square-based pyramid?
- How to use Pythagoras' theorem to work out the length of a side in a right-angled triangle?

IN THIS SECTION YOU WILL

- Learn how to calculate the surface area of a square-based pyramid.
- Learn how to calculate the volume of a pyramid.
- Solve problems involving surface areas and volumes of pyramids.

A square-based pyramid has five faces – a square base and four triangular sides.

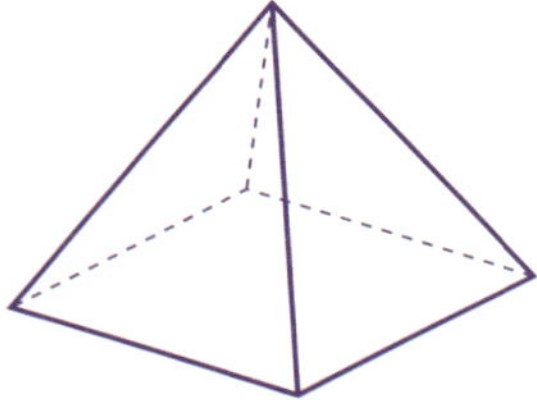

The total surface area is equal to the sum of the areas of the four triangles plus the area of the base.
The formula for the volume of a pyramid is:
$V = \frac{1}{3} \times$ area of base $\times$ perpendicular height.

Example 1

The diagram shows a pyramid with a square base of side 6 cm.
The other faces are triangles of perpendicular height 8 cm.
Calculate the total surface area of the pyramid.

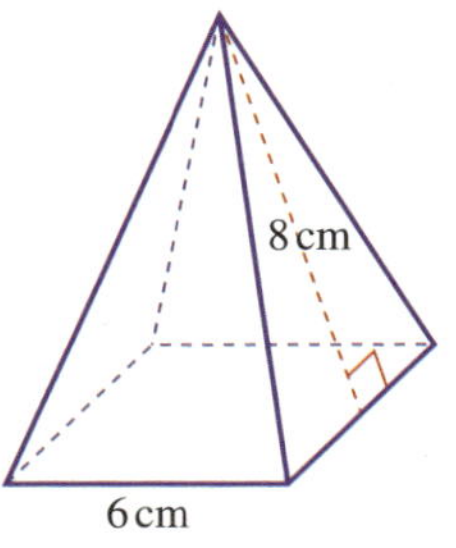

Solution 1

Sketch a net of the pyramid.
The pyramid has five faces.
The base is a square of side 6 cm.
Area of the base = $6 \times 6 = 36$ cm^2
The other four faces are triangles of base 6 cm and perpendicular height 8 cm.
Area of each triangle = $\frac{1}{2} \times$ base $\times$ perpendicular height
$= \frac{1}{2} \times 6 \times 8 = 24$ cm^2
Total surface area of pyramid = $36 + (4 \times 24) = 132$ cm^2

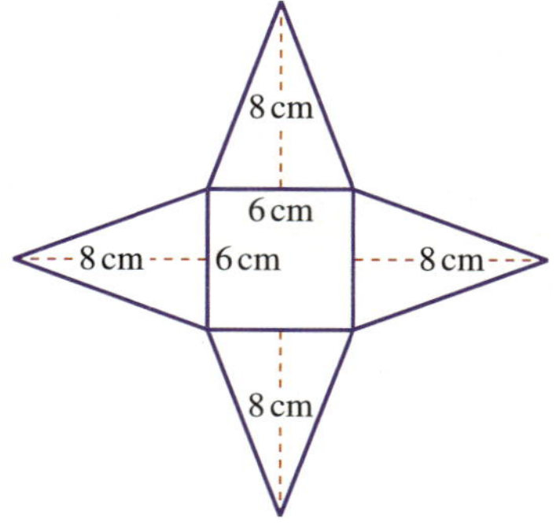

Example 2

The diagram shows a pyramid with a rectangular base.
The perpendicular height of the pyramid is 7 cm.
Calculate the volume of the pyramid.

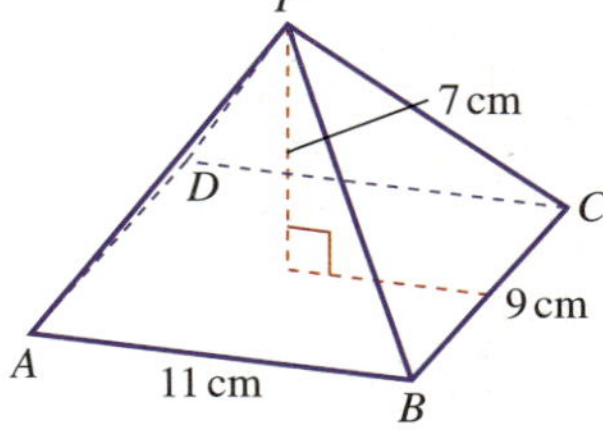

Solution 2

Volume of pyramid = $\frac{1}{3} \times$ area of base $\times$ perpendicular height.
Area of base = $11 \times 9 = 99$ cm^2
Perpendicular height = 7 cm
Volume = $\frac{1}{3} \times 99 \times 7 = 231$ cm^3

Exercise A

1 The diagram shows the net of a pyramid.
Work out the total surface area of the pyramid.

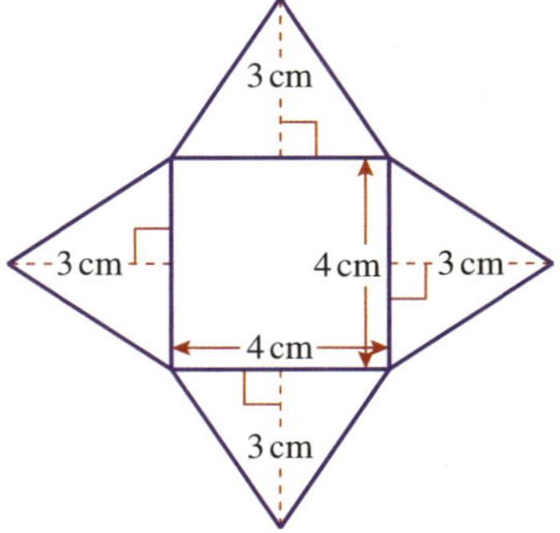

2 The diagram shows a pyramid with a square base of side 9 cm.
Every other face is a triangle of perpendicular height 10 cm.
a Sketch a net of the pyramid.
b Work out the total surface area of the pyramid.

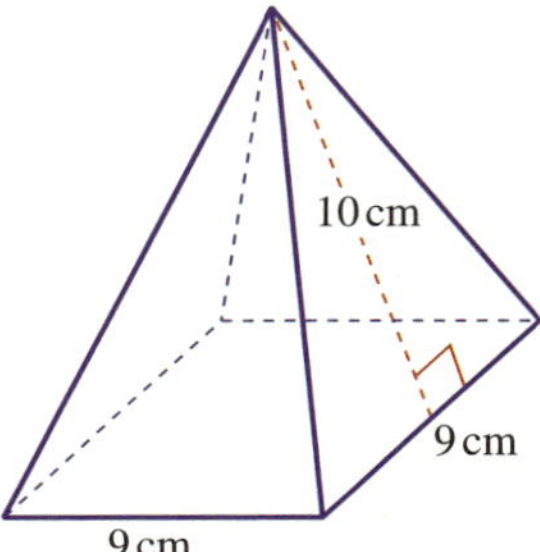

3 The diagram shows a rectangular-based pyramid.

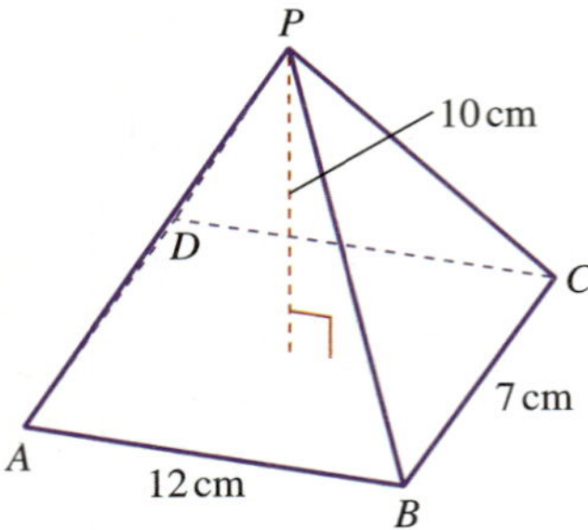

The perpendicular height of the pyramid is 10 cm.
Work out the volume of the pyramid.

4 A pyramid has a square base of side 8 cm. Its triangular faces have a perpendicular height of 5 cm.

a Sketch a net of the pyramid.

b Work out the total surface area of the pyramid.

5 A pyramid has a square base of side 12 cm.
The perpendicular height of the pyramid is 10 cm.
Work out the volume of the pyramid.

6 Calculate the volume of the following pyramids.

a Square base of side 4.2 cm, perpendicular height 5.5 cm.

b Square base of side 8.5 cm, perpendicular height 12 cm.

c Rectangular base of length 9.1 cm and width 3.8 cm, perpendicular height 8.5 cm.

7 The diagram shows a regular tetrahedron.

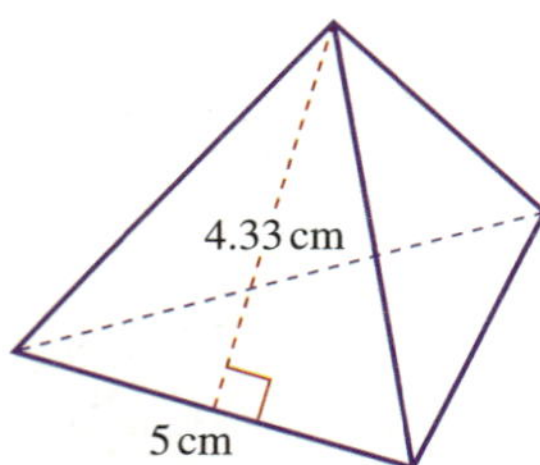

Each face is an equilateral triangle of base 5 cm and perpendicular height 4.33 cm.
Calculate the surface area of the tetrahedron.

8 Calculate the total surface area of this pyramid.

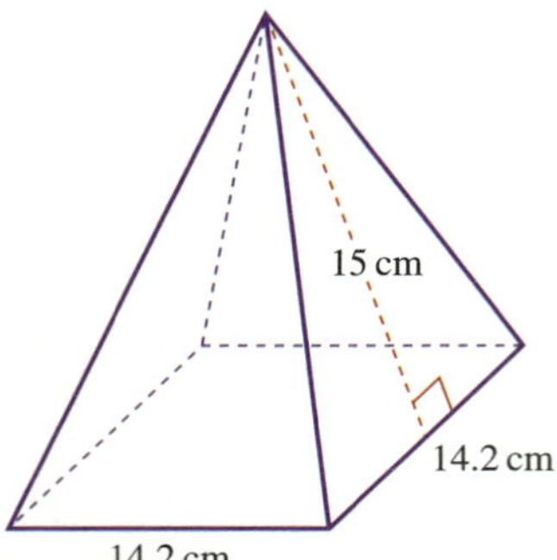

Example 3

A wooden block is in the shape of a square-based pyramid on top of a cuboid.
The height of the pyramid is 2 cm.
Calculate the volume of the block.

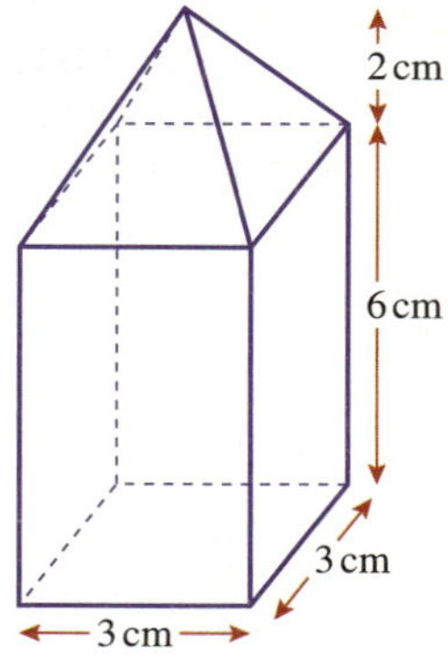

Solution 3

Volume of cuboid $= 3 \times 3 \times 6 = 54\text{ cm}^3$
Volume of pyramid $= \frac{1}{3} \times$ area of base $\times$ height
$= \frac{1}{3} \times (3 \times 3) \times 2 = 6\text{ cm}^3$
Volume of block $= 54 + 6 = 60\text{ cm}^3$

Example 4

A square-based pyramid has a base of edge 4 cm.
The vertex of the pyramid (P) is directly over the midpoint of the base.
The volume of the pyramid is 51.2 cm^3
Find the length of the slant edge of the pyramid (marked x in the diagram).

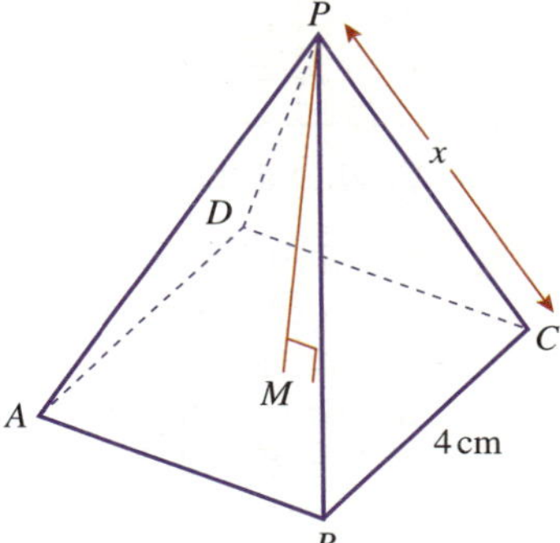

Solution 4

Length x is the hypotenuse of triangle PMC.
To find the length of x, first find the lengths of PM and MC.
$MC = \frac{1}{2}AC$
AC can be found from triangle ABC using Pythagoras' theorem.
$AC^2 = AB^2 + BC^2 = 4^2 + 4^2 = 16 + 16 = 32$
$AC = \sqrt{32}$

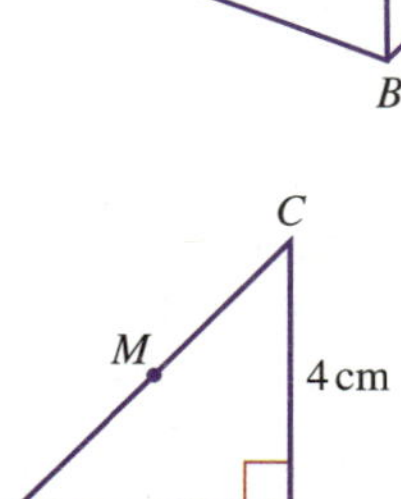

$$MC = \frac{\sqrt{32}}{2}$$

PM is the perpendicular height of the pyramid.
Using volume $= \frac{1}{3} \times$ area of base $\times$ perpendicular height
$51.2 = \frac{1}{3} \times (4 \times 4) \times PM$

$$\frac{51.2 \times 3}{16} = PM$$

$PM = 9.6$ cm
Now using Pythagoras' theorem in triangle PMC:
$x^2 = PM^2 + MC^2$

$$= 9.6^2 + \left(\frac{\sqrt{32}}{2}\right)^2 = 9.6^2 + \frac{32}{4} = 100.16$$

$x = \sqrt{100.16} = 10$ cm (to 1 d.p.)

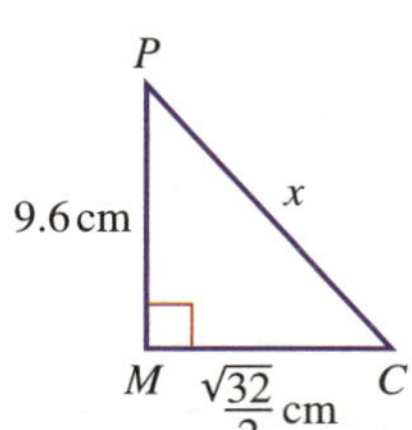

Exercise B

1 A child's building block is in the shape of a rectangular-based pyramid on top of a cuboid.
The height of the pyramid is 5 cm.
Work out the volume of the block.

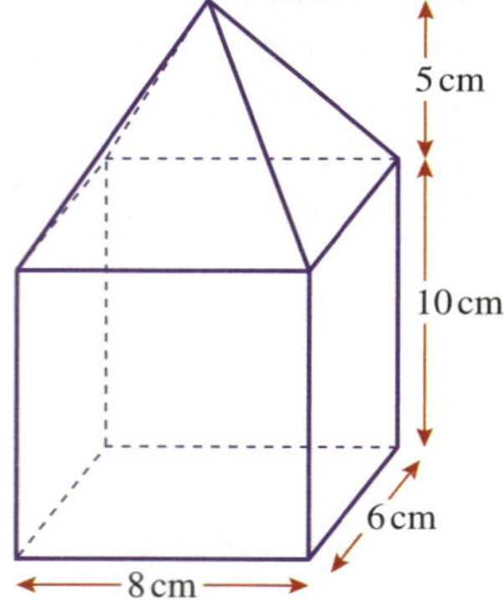

2 A juice container is in the shape of a pyramid with a square base of side 8 cm.
The container holds 192 ml of juice. (Hint: 1 cm^3 = 1 ml)

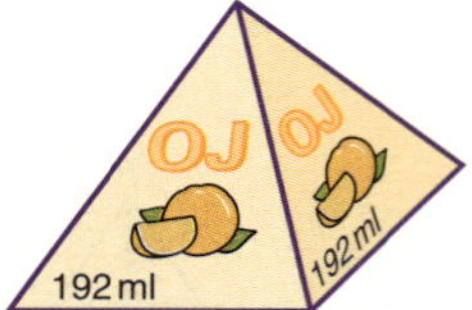

Work out the height of the container.

3 The roof of a building is in the shape of a pyramid 2 m high.
The roof is 8 m long and 7.5 m wide.
a Work out the volume enclosed by the roof.
b 65% of this volume is available for storage.
Work out the number of cubic metres available for storage.

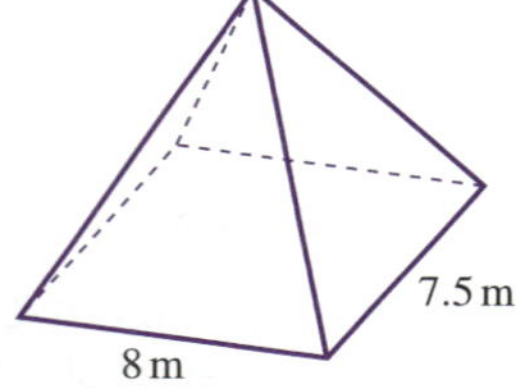

4 A pyramid has a rectangular base of length 7.5 cm and width 4.2 cm.
The volume of the pyramid is 207.9 cm^3
Calculate the perpendicular height of the pyramid.

5 A square-based pyramid has a perpendicular height of 12 cm.
The volume of the pyramid is 361 cm^3
Calculate the length of the base of the pyramid.

6 A hanging plant pot is in the shape of an inverted pyramid with a square top of side 10.5 cm.

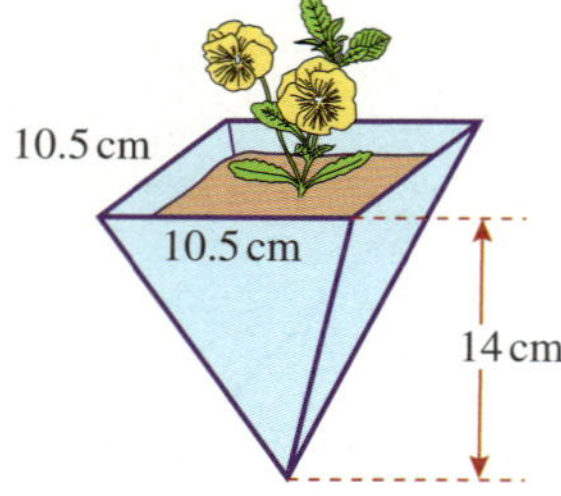

The pot is 14 cm deep.
Calculate the volume of soil needed to fill the pot three-quarters full.
Give your answer to the nearest cubic centimetre.

7 A square-based pyramid has a base of edge 14 cm. The vertex of the pyramid (P) is directly over the midpoint of the base.
The volume of the pyramid is 784 cm^3
Find the length of the slant edge of the pyramid (marked x in the diagram).
Give your answer correct to one decimal place.

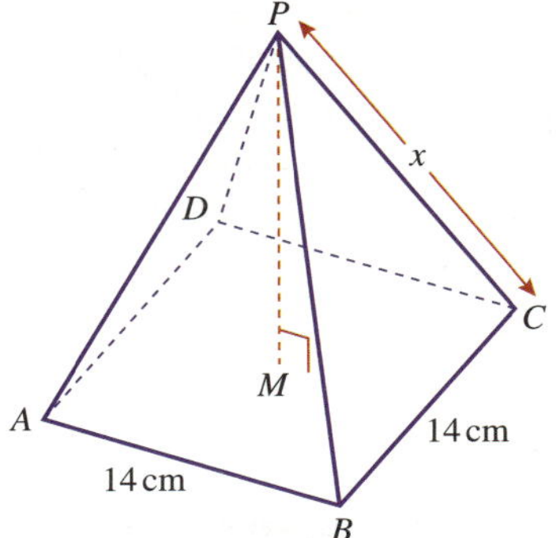

8 A fence post is in the shape of a cuboid on top of an inverted pyramid.
The cuboid has a square base of side 10 cm and is 2 m long. The height of the pyramid is 15 cm.
Calculate the volume of the fence post in cubic metres.

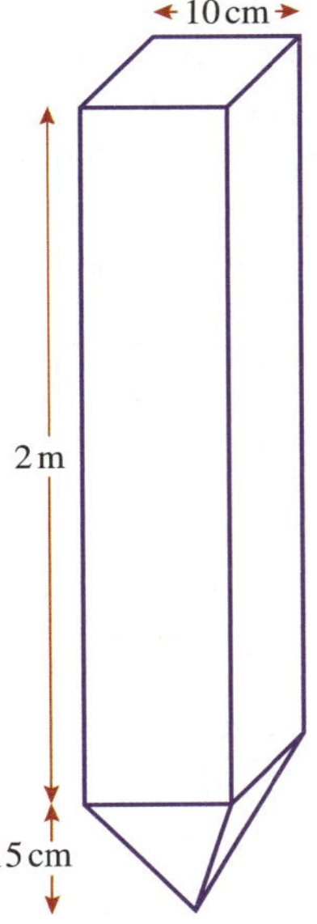

33.2 Surface area and volume of a cone

CAN YOU REMEMBER

- How to use Pythagoras' theorem to work out the length of a side in a right-angled triangle?
- The area of a circle $= \pi r^2$?
- The curved surface area of a cylinder $= 2\pi rh$ and volume of a cylinder $= \pi r^2 h$?
- If similar solids have lengths in the ratio a:b, their volumes are in the ratio a^3:b^3?

IN THIS SECTION YOU WILL

- Learn how to calculate the surface area of a cone.
- Learn the meaning of 'frustum'.
- Learn how to calculate the volume of a cone and of a frustum of a cone.
- Solve problems involving surface areas and volumes of cones.

The following diagram shows a cone with a circular base of radius r.
The perpendicular height of the cone is h and the slant height is l.
Volume of a cone $= \frac{1}{3} \times$ area of base $\times$ perpendicular height.

Area of circular base = πr^2
So volume of cone = $\frac{1}{3}\pi r^2 h$
A cone has a curved surface and a circular base.
Curved surface area = πrl and base area = πr^2
Total surface area of a cone is equal to $\pi rl + \pi r^2$

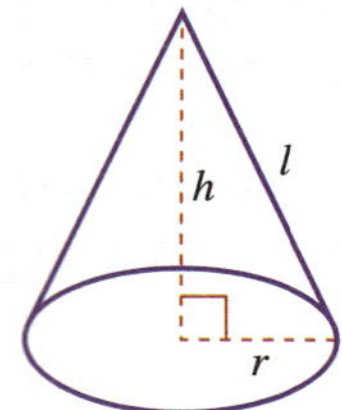

Using Pythagoras' theorem
$l^2 = h^2 + r^2$

Example 1

The diagram shows a cone of radius 5 cm and perpendicular height 12 cm.

a Work out the slant height of the cone.
b Hence calculate the curved surface area of the cone.
c Calculate the volume of the cone.

Remember to state the units of your answer.

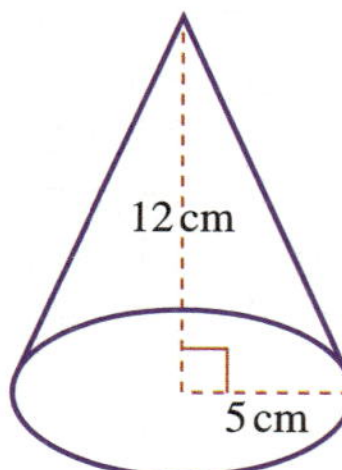

Solution 1

a Using Pythagoras' theorem
$l^2 = h^2 + r^2$
$l^2 = 12^2 + 5^2 = 144 + 25 = 169$
$l = \sqrt{169} = 13$ cm

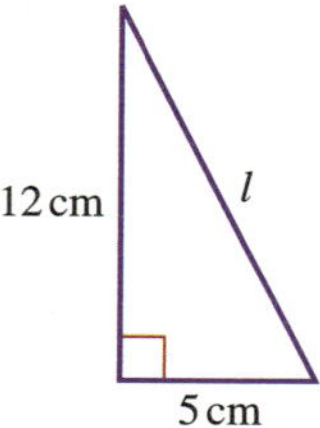

b Curved surface area = πrl
$= \pi \times 5 \times 13 = 204.2$ cm^2

c Volume = $\frac{1}{3}\pi r^2 h$
$= \frac{1}{3} \times \pi \times 5^2 \times 12 = 314.2$ cm^3 (to 1 d.p.)

Exercise A

1 Calculate the volume of each of these cones.
Leave your answers in terms of π.

a radius 3 cm, perpendicular height 5 cm
b radius 2 cm, perpendicular height 8 cm
c radius 7 cm, perpendicular height 10 cm
d radius 5 cm, perpendicular height 12 cm

2 For each cone, calculate:

i the curved surface area
ii the total surface area.

Give your answers in terms of π.

a

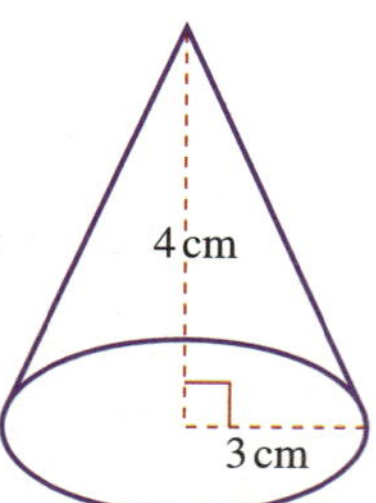

b

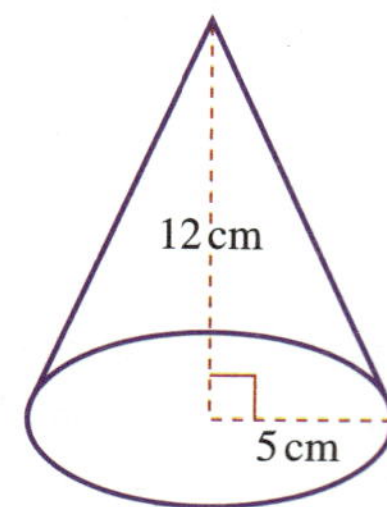

c

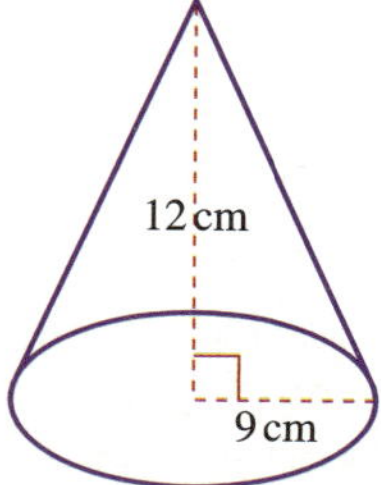

3 Calculate the volume of each of these cones. Give each answer correct to the nearest integer.
- **a** Radius 2.8 cm, perpendicular height 8.4 cm.
- **b** Radius 13.5 cm, perpendicular height 32 cm.
- **c** Diameter 48.4 cm, perpendicular height 18 cm.

4 Calculate the curved surface area of these cones.
Give each answer correct to one decimal place.
- **a** Radius 5.2 cm, perpendicular height 10.6 cm.
- **b** Radius 2.3 cm, perpendicular height 9.4 cm.
- **c** Diameter 30 mm, perpendicular height 27 mm.

5 Calculate the total surface area of these cones.
Give each answer to an appropriate degree of accuracy.
- **a** Radius 0.75 m, perpendicular height 2.5 m.
- **b** Radius 7 cm, perpendicular height 24 cm.
- **c** Diameter 12.84 cm, perpendicular height 15.74 cm.

6 A training cone has a height of 48 cm and a base diameter of 34 cm.
Calculate the volume of the cone.

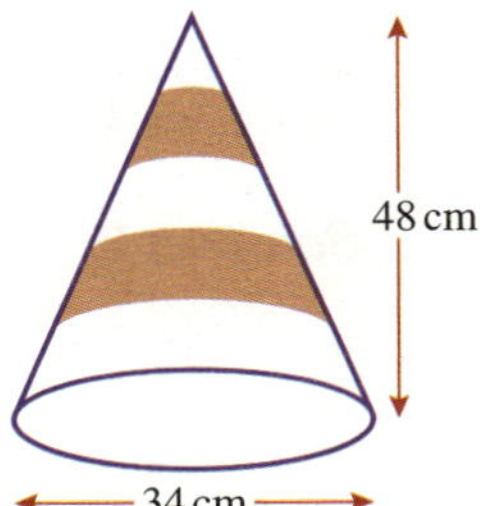

7 Sand is poured into a conical pile 1.4 m high and 6 m wide at the base.

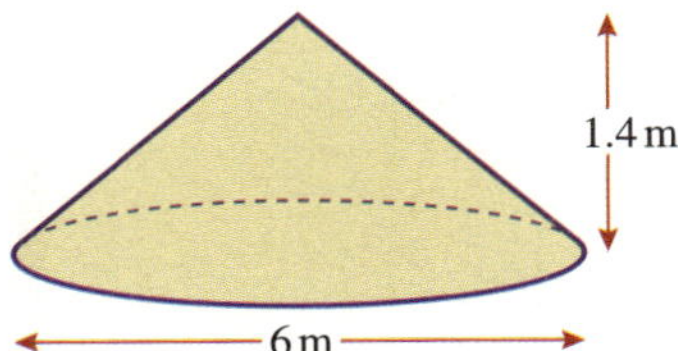

Find the volume of sand in the pile.

8 A vinegar bottle is in the shape of a cone of radius 2.1 cm and height 9 cm.
- **a** Calculate the volume of vinegar needed to fill the bottle.
- **b** How many vinegar bottles can be filled from a 500 ml container of vinegar?

(Hint: 1 cm^3 = 1 ml)

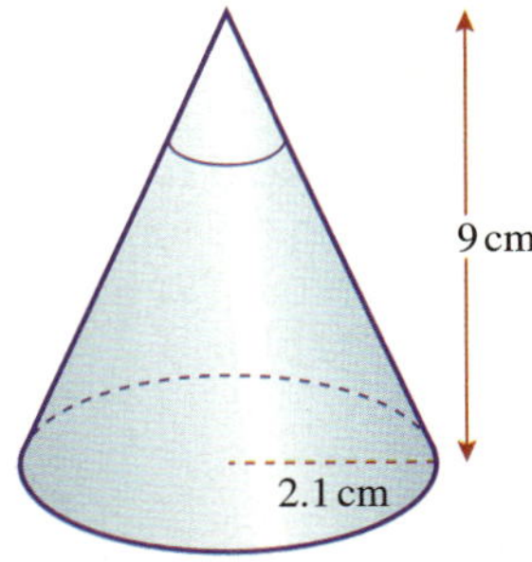

A *frustum* of a cone is formed by removing the top of the cone with a cut parallel to its base. The original cone and the cone removed are similar shapes.

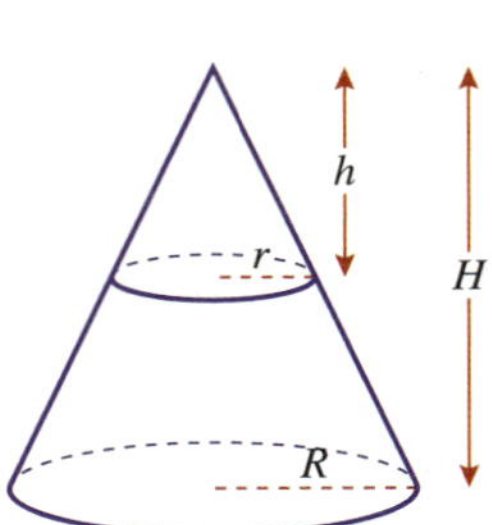

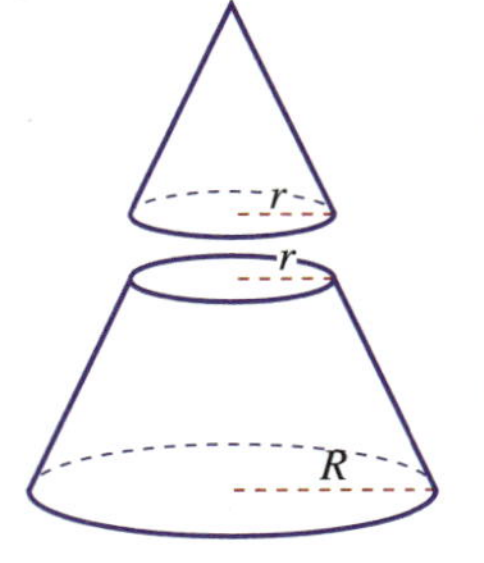

Volume of frustum = volume of complete cone − volume of cone removed
$= \frac{1}{3}\pi R^2 H - \frac{1}{3}\pi r^2 h$

Example 2

A cone has a radius of 15 cm and a height of 27 cm. A smaller cone of radius 5 cm is cut from the top of this cone to leave a frustum.

a Calculate the volume of the large cone.
b Calculate the volume of the small cone.
c Hence find the volume of the frustum.

Give each answer to the nearest integer.

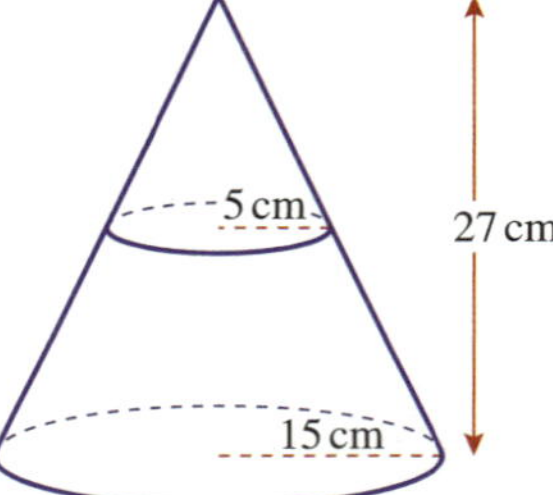

Solution 2

a Volume of large cone $= \frac{1}{3}\pi r^2 h$
$= \frac{1}{3} \times \pi \times 15^2 \times 27 = 6362\text{ cm}^3$

b The large cone and small cone are similar shapes.
Ratio of lengths = 15 : 5 = 3 : 1

Method 1

Height of small cone $= \frac{1}{3} \times 27 = 9\text{ cm}$
Volume of small cone $= \frac{1}{3}\pi r^2 h = \frac{1}{3} \times \pi \times 5^2 \times 9 = 235.619 = 236\text{ cm}^3$

Method 2

Ratio of lengths = 3:1
So ratio of volumes = $3^3:1^3$ = 27:1

The volume of the small cone is $\frac{1}{27}$ of the volume of the large cone.

Volume of small cone $= \frac{1}{27} \times 6362 = 235.629 = 236\text{ cm}^3$ to the nearest integer.

c Volume of frustum $= 6362 - 236 = 6126\text{ cm}^3$

Exercise B

1 The diagram shows the frustum of a cone formed by cutting the top off the cone.
Work out the volume of the frustum giving your answer in terms of π.

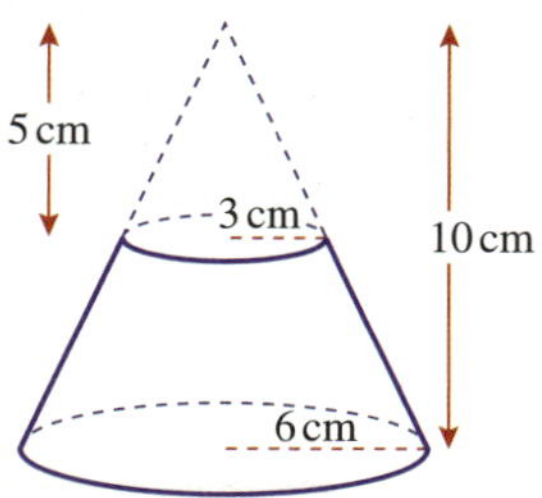

2 A wooden block is made from a cone and a cylinder as shown.
Work out the total volume of the block.
Give your answer in terms of π.

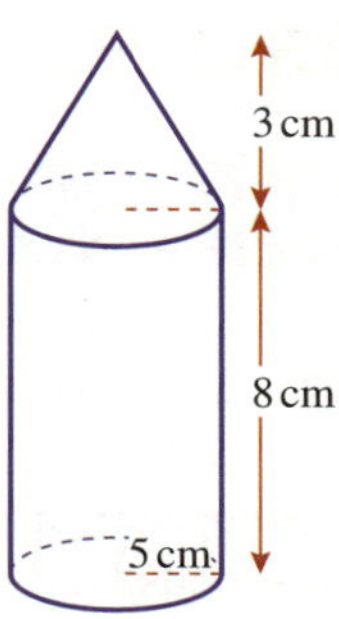

3 A cone has a volume of 460 cm^3 and a perpendicular height of 8.9 cm.
Calculate the radius of the cone.

4 Three cubic metres of sand are poured into a conical pile of diameter 2.1 m.
Show that the height of the pile of sand is 2.6 m (to 1 d.p.)

5 The diagram shows a cone of base radius 9 cm and perpendicular height 12 cm.
A smaller cone of radius 4.5 cm and height 6 cm is cut off the bottom to leave a frustum.

a Find the volume of the frustum.

b The frustum has the same volume as another cone of perpendicular height 6.5 cm.

Calculate the radius of this cone. Give your answer correct to one decimal place.

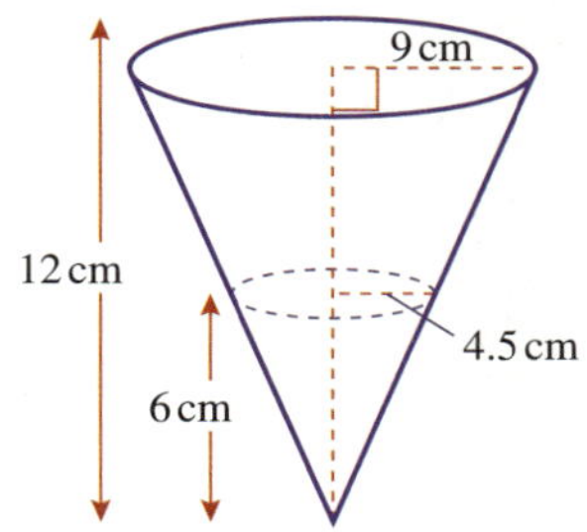

6 A bucket is in the shape of a frustum of a cone.
The bucket has a base diameter of 18 cm and a top diameter of 32 cm. The height of the bucket is 40 cm.
Calculate the capacity of the bucket in litres.
(Hint: 1000 cm^3 = 1 litre)

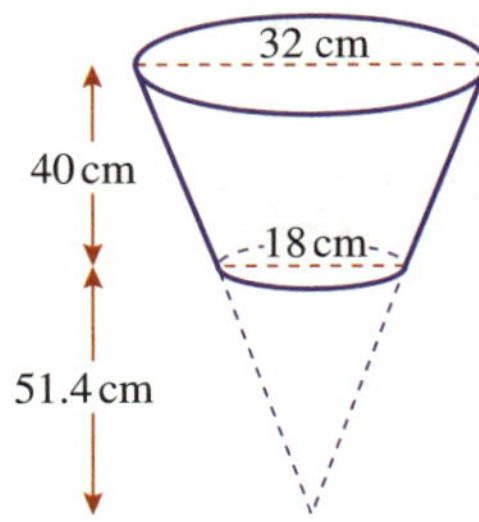

7 A garden centre sells wooden gate posts in the shape of a cone on top of a cylinder.
The gate posts, including the base, are painted with varnish.
One tin of varnish will cover 11 m^2 of wood.
How many gate posts can be painted with one tin of varnish?
Show your working.

33.3 Surface area and volume of a sphere

CAN YOU REMEMBER

- The curved surface area of a cylinder $= 2\pi rh$ and volume of a cylinder $= \pi r^2h$?
- The curved surface area of a cone $= \pi rl$ and volume of a cone $= \frac{1}{3}\pi r^2h$?

IN THIS SECTION YOU WILL

- Learn how to calculate the surface area of a sphere.
- Learn how to calculate the volume of a sphere.
- Solve problems involving surface areas and volumes of spheres.

The diagram shows a sphere of radius r.

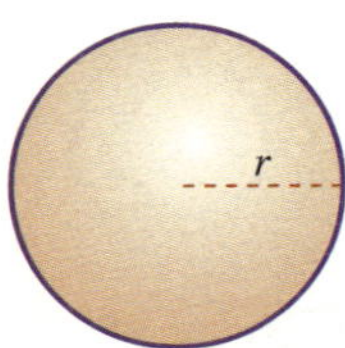

Surface area of a sphere $= 4\pi r^2$

Volume of a sphere $= \frac{4}{3}\pi r^3$

A *hemisphere* is half a sphere.

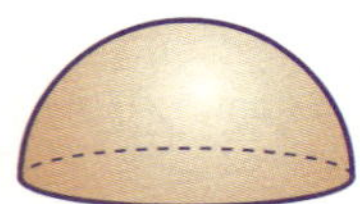

The surface area of a hemisphere is equal to half the surface area of a sphere plus the area of the circular base.
Surface area of a hemisphere $= 2\pi r^2 + \pi r^2 = 3\pi r^2$
Volume of a hemisphere = half the volume of a sphere $= \frac{2}{3}\pi r^3$

Example 1

A sphere has a radius of 5 cm. Calculate the surface area and volume of the sphere.

Solution 1

Surface area $= 4\pi r^2 = 4 \times \pi \times 5^2 = 4 \times \pi \times 5 \times 5 = 314.2\text{ cm}^2$

Volume $= \dfrac{4}{3}\pi r^3 = \dfrac{4}{3} \times \pi \times 5^3 = \dfrac{4}{3} \times \pi \times 5 \times 5 \times 5 = 523.6\text{ cm}^3$

Example 2

A hemisphere has a radius of 3 cm. Calculate:

a the total surface area **b** the volume

of the hemisphere. Give your answers in terms of π.

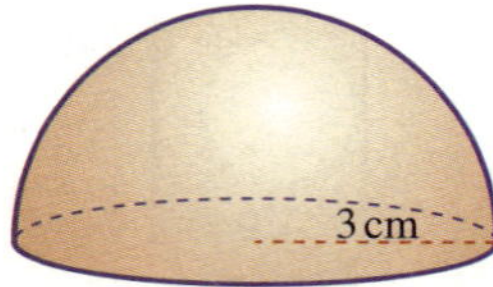

Solution 2

a Total surface area $= 3\pi r^2 = 3 \times \pi \times 3^2 = 3 \times \pi \times 9 = 27\pi\,\text{cm}^2$

b Volume $= \frac{2}{3}\pi r^3 = \frac{2}{3} \times \pi \times 3^3 = \frac{2}{\cancel{3}_1} \times \pi \times \cancel{3}^1 \times 3 \times 3$

$= 2 \times \pi \times 3 \times 3 = 18\pi\,\text{cm}^3$

Exercise A

For questions **1–4** give your answers in terms of π.
State the units of your answer.

1 Calculate the volume of the following spheres:
- **a** radius 3 cm
- **b** radius 6 cm

2 Calculate the surface area of each of these spheres:
- **a** radius 4 cm
- **b** radius 7 cm
- **c** radius 10 cm

3 Calculate the volume of a hemisphere of diameter 60 cm.

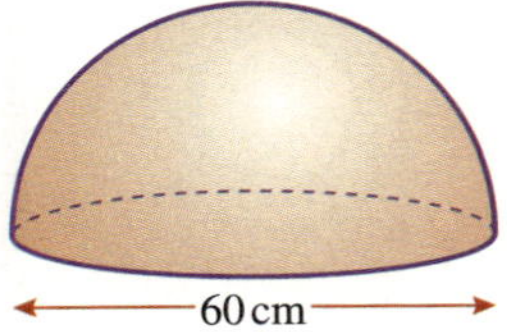

4 Calculate the total surface area of these hemispheres:
- **a** radius 12 cm
- **b** diameter 18 cm
- **c** radius 20 cm

5 For each of these spheres, calculate:
- **i** the volume
- **ii** the surface area
- **a** radius 4.5 cm
- **b** radius 28 mm
- **c** diameter 1.2 m
- **d** diameter 18.4 cm

6 Calculate the volume of each of these hemispheres:
- **a** radius 11.2 cm
- **b** radius 2.75 cm
- **c** diameter 86 mm
- **d** diameter 3.8 m

7 Calculate the curved surface area of each of these hemispheres:
- **a** diameter 21 mm
- **b** radius 8.2 cm
- **c** radius 0.7 m

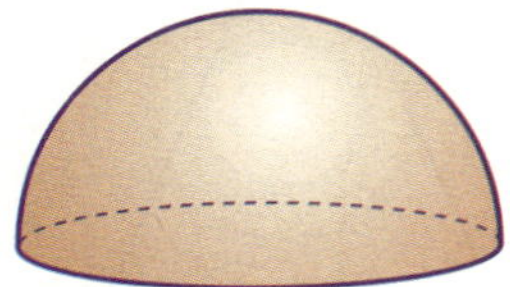

8 Calculate the total surface area of each of these hemispheres:
- **a** radius 3.6 m
- **b** diameter 12.4 cm
- **c** radius 23 mm

Example 3

A spherical football of diameter 22 cm is packed into a box which is a cube of side 30 cm.
Calculate the volume of the space around the football.

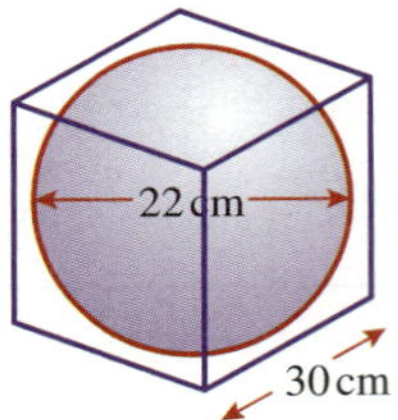

Solution 3

Volume of the box $= 30 \times 30 \times 30 = 27\,000\ \text{cm}^3$

Volume of football $= \frac{4}{3}\pi r^3 = \frac{4}{3} \times \pi \times 11^3 = 5575.3\ \text{cm}^3$

Volume of space $= 27\,000 - 5575.3 = 21\,424.7\ \text{cm}^3$

Example 4

A globe has a volume of $11\,494\ \text{cm}^3$

Calculate the radius of the globe.

Solution 4

Volume of globe $= \frac{4}{3}\pi r^3 = 11\,494$

$4\pi r^3 = 34\,482$ — Multiply both sides by 3

$\pi r^3 = 8620.5$ — Divide both sides by 4

$r^3 = 2744$ — Divide both sides by π.

$r = \sqrt[3]{2744} = 14$ cm — Take the cube root of both sides.

The radius of the globe is 14 cm.

Exercise B

1 A toy is in the shape of a cone on top of a hemisphere. The diameter of the hemisphere is 12 cm and the height of the toy is 25 cm.

a Calculate the volume of the toy.

b Calculate the surface area of the toy.

Give each answer correct to the nearest integer.

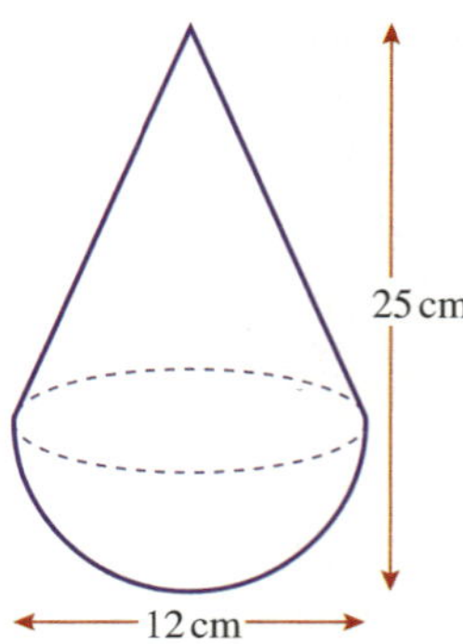

2 The diagram shows two ice-cream containers.
One container is a hemisphere of radius 5 cm and the other container is a cone of radius 4 cm and height 15 cm.

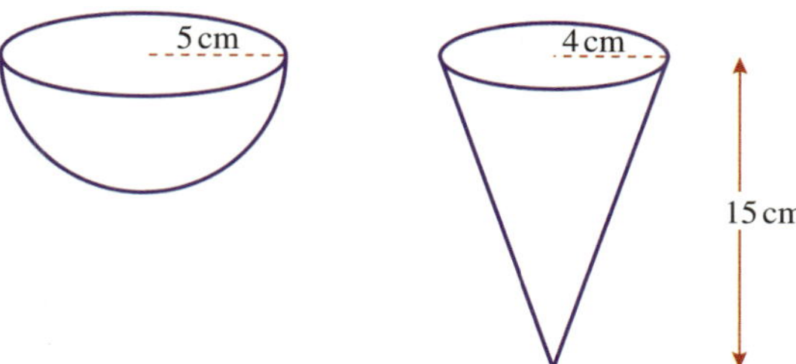

Which container has the largest capacity?
Show your working.

3 The diagram shows a balloon which is spherical in shape.
The volume of air in the balloon is 1450 cm^3
Calculate the radius of the balloon correct to the nearest integer.

4 A laboratory flask is formed from a sphere and a cylinder as shown in the diagram.
Calculate the capacity of the flask.

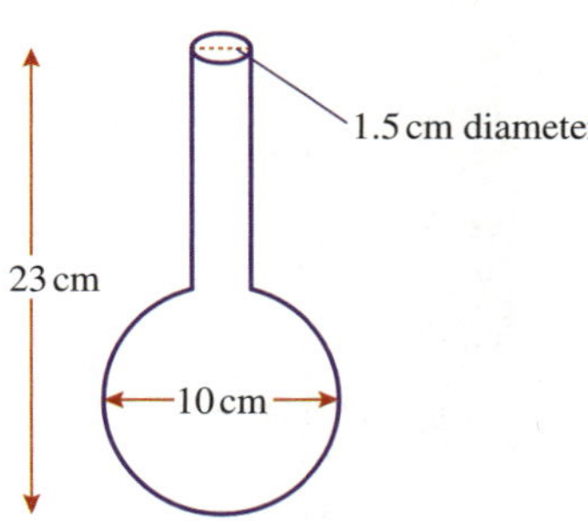

5 A wooden fruit bowl is in the shape of a hemisphere.

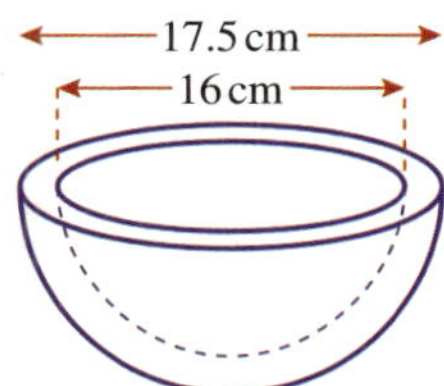

Calculate the volume of wood in the fruit bowl.

6 A sugar shaker is formed from a cylinder and a hemisphere as shown.
Calculate:

a the capacity
b the surface area

of the sugar shaker.

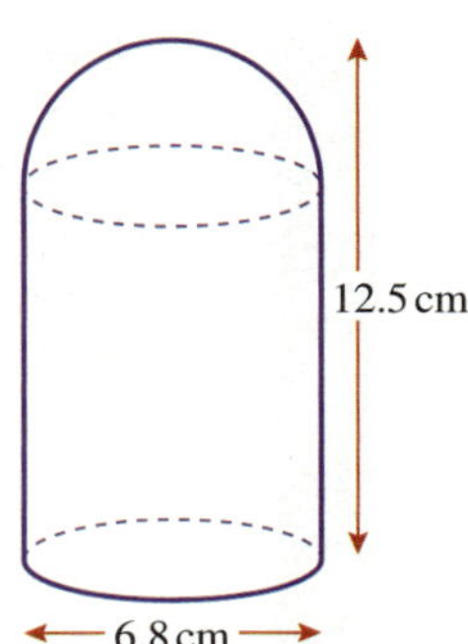

7 A piece of metal of length 8 cm, width 5 cm and depth 2 cm is melted down and made into ball bearings of radius 0.75 cm.
Calculate the number of ball bearings that can be made from this piece of metal.
Show your working.

8 A water tank is 48 cm long, 25 cm wide and 30 cm high.
It contains water to a depth of 21 cm.
Two spheres of diameter 22 cm are placed in the tank and sink to the bottom.
Will the water overflow?
Give reasons for your answer.

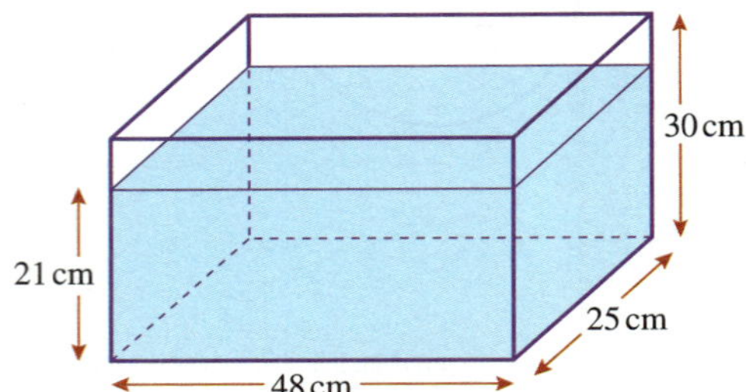

Chapter summary

- The total surface area of a square-based pyramid is equal to the sum of the areas of the four triangular faces plus the area of the base.
- Volume of a pyramid $= \frac{1}{3} \times$ area of base $\times$ perpendicular height.
- For a cone with circular base of radius r and perpendicular height h the slant height l is given by $l^2 = h^2 + r^2$ (Pythagoras' theorem).
- Volume of a cone $= \frac{1}{3} \times$ area of base $\times$ perpendicular height $= \frac{1}{3}\pi r^2 h$
- A cone has a curved surface and a circular base.
  Curved surface area $= \pi r l$ and base area $= \pi r^2$
  Total surface area of a cone is equal to $\pi r l + \pi r^2$

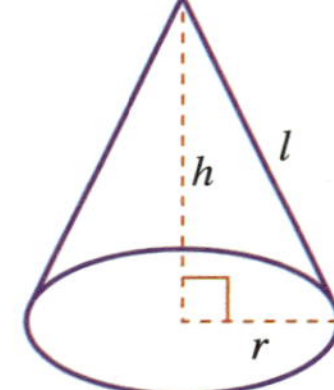

- The frustum of a cone is formed by removing the top of the cone with a cut parallel to the base. The original cone and the cone removed are similar shapes.

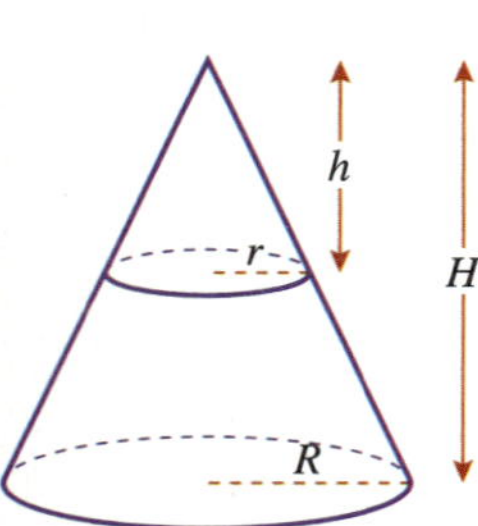

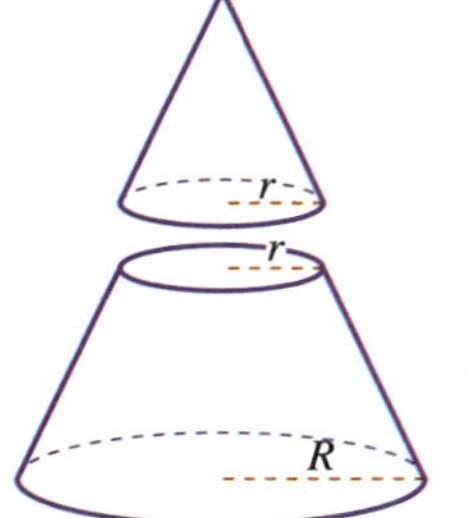

cone removed

frustum

- Volume of frustum = volume of complete cone − volume of cone removed
  $= \pi R^2 H - \pi r^2 h$
- Surface area of a sphere $= 4\pi r^2$
- Volume of a sphere $= \frac{4}{3}\pi r^3$
- A hemisphere is half a sphere.
- Surface area of a hemisphere is equal to half the surface area of a sphere plus the area of the circular base:
  surface area $= 2\pi r^2 + \pi r^2 = 3\pi r^2$
- Volume of a hemisphere = half the volume of a sphere $= \frac{2}{3}\pi r^3$

Chapter review

1 A globe has a diameter of 16 cm.
Work out the surface area of the globe giving your answer in terms of π.

2 A solid block of wood is a cube of side 10 cm.
A square-based pyramid of side 10 cm and vertical height 9 cm is cut from the cube.
Work out the volume of wood remaining.

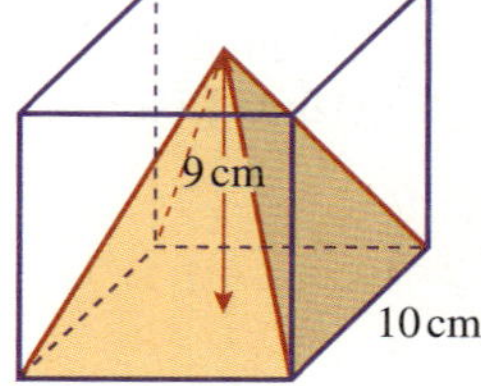

3 A cone has a radius of 5 cm and a slant height of 13 cm.

a Work out the perpendicular height of the cone.

b Hence work out the volume of the cone giving your answer in terms of π.

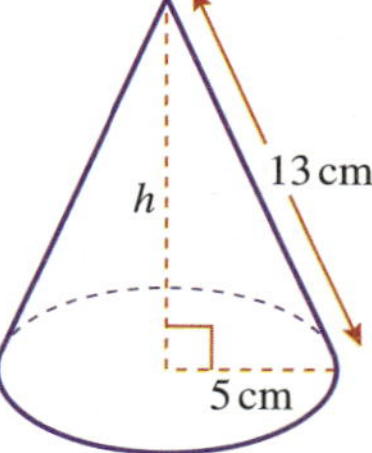

4 A pyramid has a square base of side 6 cm. The volume of the pyramid is 108 cm^3.
Work out the height of the pyramid.

5 A cone has a radius of 6 cm and a perpendicular height of 8 cm.
Work out the curved surface area of the cone.
Give your answer in terms of π.

6 A cone has a radius of 6 cm and a height of 21 cm. A smaller cone of radius 2 cm is cut from the top of this cone to leave a frustum.

a Calculate the volume of the small cone.

b Calculate the volume of the frustum.

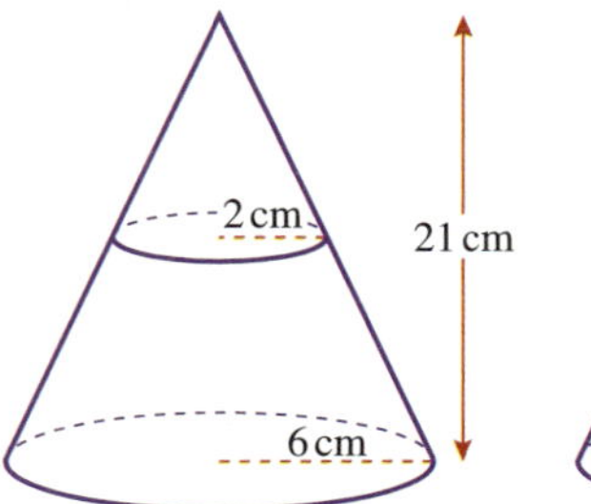

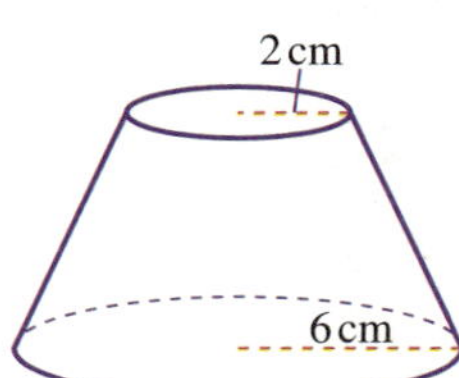

7 A box for table tennis balls is in the shape of a cuboid of length 19.5 cm, width 10 cm and height 5 cm.
The box holds eight table tennis balls, each of radius 2.4 cm, as shown in the diagram.
Calculate the volume of the space in the box.

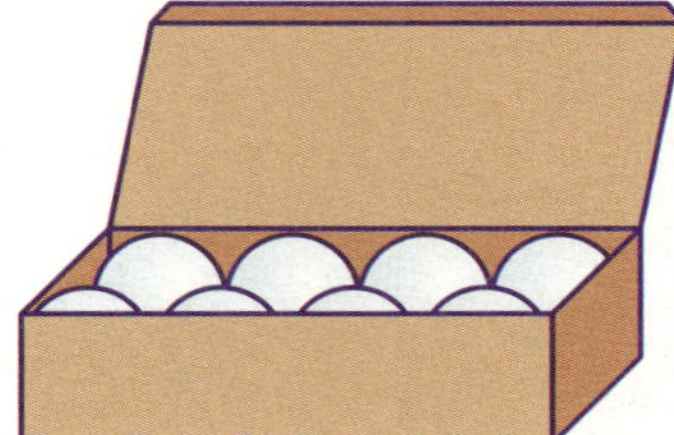

8 A sweet container is formed from a cylinder with a hemisphere removed from one end.
The diameter of the container is 5.5 cm and the length is 18 cm.
Calculate the volume of the container.
Give your answer to the nearest integer.

9 A drinking glass is in the shape of a frustum of a cone as shown.
Calculate the capacity of the glass in millilitres.
(Hint: 1 cm^3 = 1 ml)

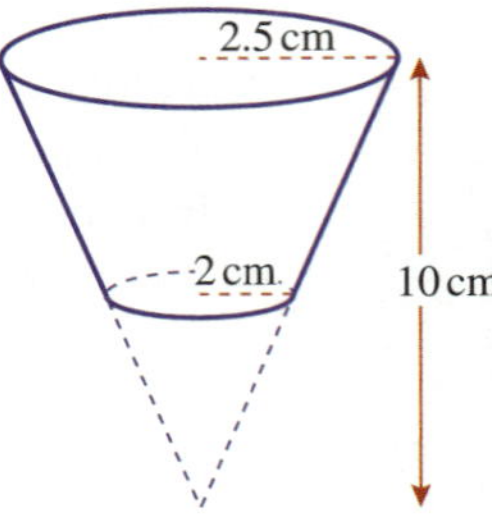

10 Conutto ice creams consist of a thin paper cone filled with ice cream, with a hemisphere of ice cream on top of the cone, as shown in the diagram.
The height of the cone is twice the radius of the hemisphere.

a Show that the amount of ice cream in the cone is the same as the amount in the hemisphere.
A Conutto contains 200 cm^3 of ice cream.

b Find the radius r cm, of the hemisphere.

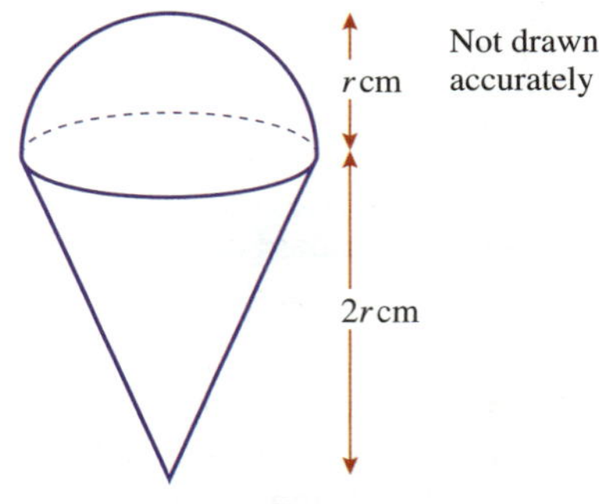

CHAPTER 34

Distributions

34.1 Comparing distributions using frequency polygons

CAN YOU REMEMBER

- How to draw and interpret a frequency polygon?
- How to find measures of average and spread from a frequency polygon?

IN THIS SECTION YOU WILL

- Learn how to use frequency polygons to compare two distributions.
- Compare distributions by comparing the shapes of frequency polygons.

Frequency polygons can be used to compare two or more sets of data. The spread, modal class and median can be found from the polygons and compared.

Example 1

The frequency polygons represent the heights, in metres, of trees in a park (black line) and trees in a wood (red line).
Compare the two sets of data.

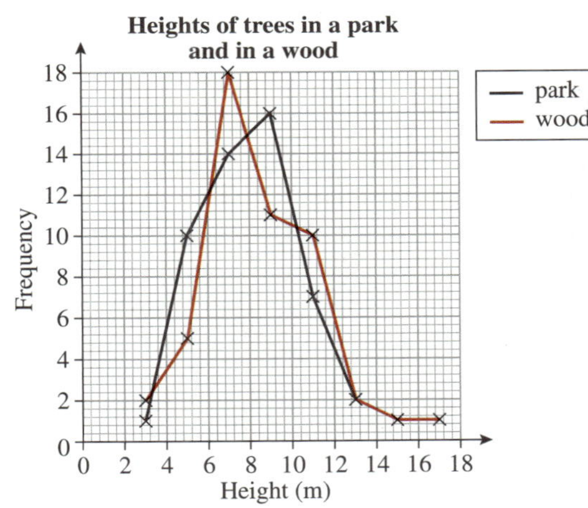

Solution 1

For the trees in the park, the point plotted at (3, 1) represents the class interval 2–4 metres, and so on. So the point at (13, 2) represents the class interval 12–14 metres.
An estimate for the range of heights is $16 - 2 = 14$ metres. The exact value cannot be calculated as the exact minimum and maximum data values are not known.
For the trees in the wood, an estimate for the range of heights is $18 - 2 = 16$ metres.

The tree heights in the wood are more spread out than the tree heights in the park.

The modal class for the trees in the park is height 8–10 metres.
The modal class for the trees in the wood is height 6–8 metres.
The modal height for trees in the park is taller than the modal height for trees in the wood.

Example 2

The frequency polygon shows the heights of 50 men from a university.

The heights of 50 women from the same university have a range of 105 cm and a median of 150 cm.
Compare the heights of the men and the women.

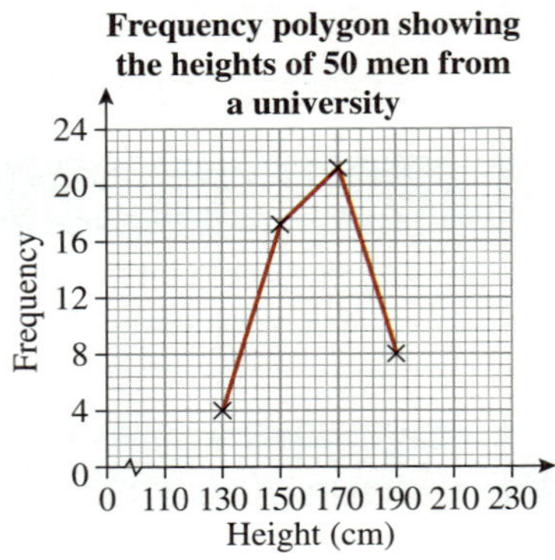

Solution 2

From the polygon:

- the men's heights vary from approximately 120 to 200 cm
- the range of the men's heights is around 80 cm
- therefore the women's heights are more spread out than the men's heights.

The median male height is the height of the $\frac{50 + 1}{2}$ = 25.5th man, which is in the 160–180 cm range.

Therefore on average the males are taller than the females.

Exercise A

1 The frequency polygon shows the weight of the pumpkins entered for a show in 2005
In 2004 the average pumpkin weighed 2.6 kg and the range of the weights was 3 kg.
Compare the weights of pumpkins in 2004 and 2005

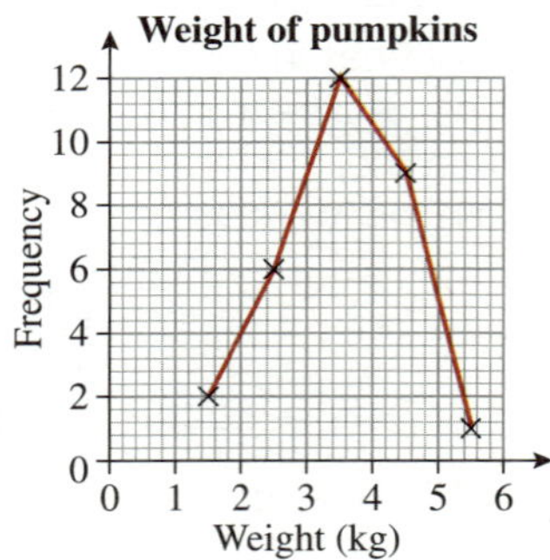

2 The frequency polygon shows the time taken for Abu to get on-line using his Internet connection.
Tracey takes an average of 75 seconds to get on-line with a range of 2 minutes.
Compare the times taken for Abu and Tracey to get on-line with their Internet connections.

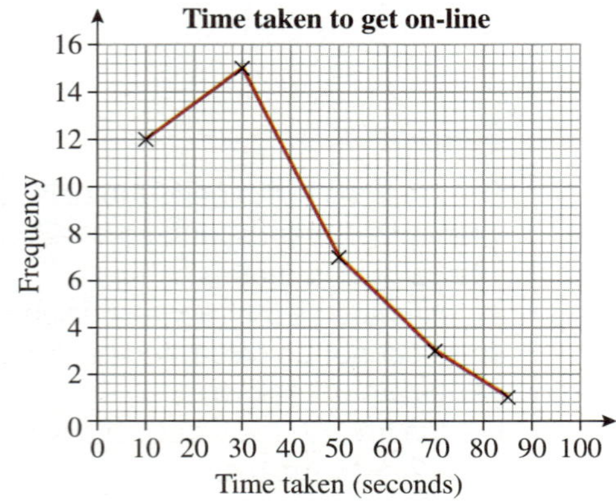

3 The frequency polygon shows the time taken for a group of students to complete a sponsored walk.
The teachers' times for the sponsored walk had a range of 23 minutes with a modal time of 50–60 minutes.
Compare the times taken by the teachers and students.

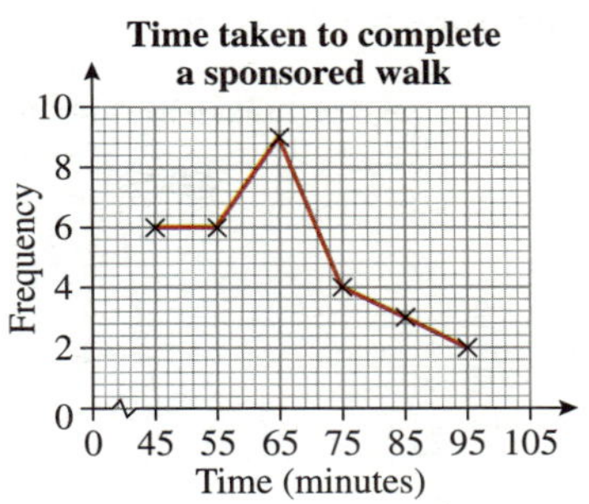

4 The frequency polygons show the actual size of angle drawn when a group of Year 7 students (blue line) and a group of Year 10 students (red line) were asked to draw an angle of 38 degrees without a protractor.
Compare the two distributions.

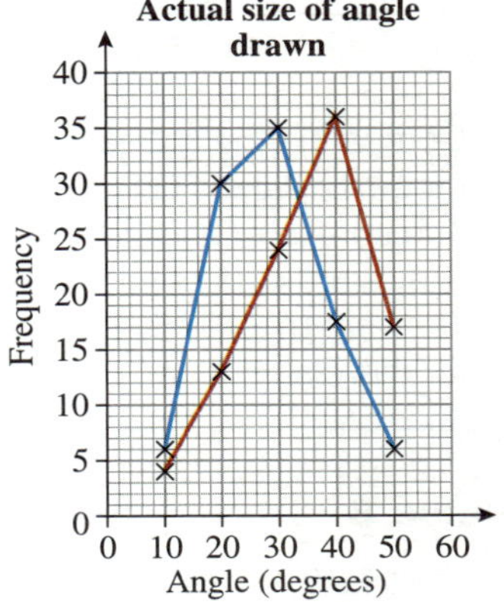

The shapes of two frequency polygons can be compared. The shape of a frequency polygon shows the modal class and how the data is spread out.

Example 3

The times taken for food to be served in two restaurants are recorded in the tables below.

Jake's Grill

Length of time, t (min)	Frequency, f
$10 \leqslant t < 15$	1
$15 \leqslant t < 20$	7
$20 \leqslant t < 25$	34
$25 \leqslant t < 30$	54
$30 \leqslant t < 35$	19
$35 \leqslant t < 40$	2

Amy's Place

Length of time, t (min)	Frequency, f
$10 \leqslant t < 15$	6
$15 \leqslant t < 20$	14
$20 \leqslant t < 25$	66
$25 \leqslant t < 30$	6
$30 \leqslant t < 35$	5
$35 \leqslant t < 40$	3

a On the same axes draw frequency polygons to display the data.

b Compare the time taken for food to be served at the two restaurants.

c Tom and Rebecca go to one of the restaurants.
They wait 29 minutes for their food to be served.
State, with a reason, which restaurant they are more likely to have visited.

Solution 3

a

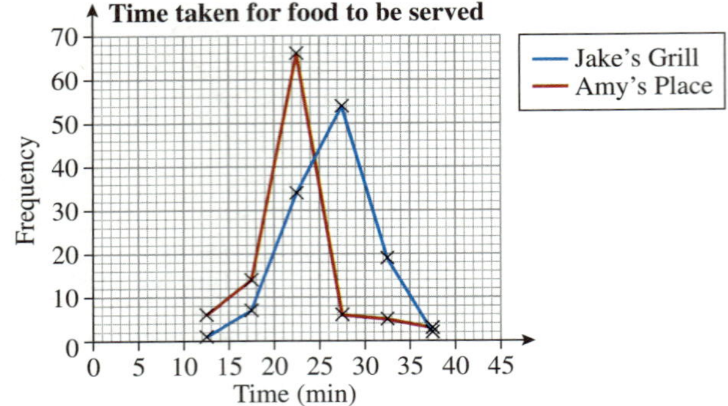

b Comparing the shapes of the polygons, the mode for Amy's Place is a shorter time than the mode for Jake's Grill. So on average the service is quicker at Amy's Place.
The spread of service times is about the same at both restaurants but most of the times for Amy's are concentrated between 15 and 30 minutes.

c They are most likely to have gone to Jake's Grill as the time of 29 minutes is in the modal class for this distribution.

Exercise B

1 A small factory has two machines which pack crisps into packets.
Data is obtained showing the weight of 200 packets packed by each machine.

Machine A

Weight of packet, w (g)	Frequency, f
$29 \leqslant w < 30$	21
$30 \leqslant w < 31$	109
$31 \leqslant w < 32$	63
$32 \leqslant w < 33$	7

Machine B

Weight of packet, w (g)	Frequency, f
$28 \leqslant w < 29$	15
$29 \leqslant w < 30$	62
$30 \leqslant w < 31$	84
$31 \leqslant w < 32$	39

a On the same axes, draw two frequency polygons to illustrate the data.
b Hence compare the weights of packets produced by each machine.
c The packets are labelled 'weight 30 g'.
Comment on the performance of each machine.

2 The tables show the age of the staff at two schools, one a comprehensive school, one a grammar school.

Comprehensive school

Age (years)	Frequency
$21 \leqslant x < 30$	27
$31 \leqslant x < 40$	42
$41 \leqslant x < 50$	20
$51 \leqslant x < 60$	11

Grammar school

Age (years)	Frequency
$20 < x \leqslant 30$	6
$30 < x \leqslant 40$	30
$40 < x \leqslant 50$	34
$50 < x \leqslant 60$	23
$60 < x \leqslant 70$	7

a On the same axes, draw two frequency polygons to illustrate the data.
b Hence compare the ages of staff at the two schools.
c A 23-year-old newly qualified teacher who works at one of the schools is chosen at random. Estimate the probability that this teacher works at the grammar school.

3 Kaye makes lots of phone calls to her friends.
She uses either her mobile phone which she pays the bill for, or her parents' house phone which they pay the bill for.
The table shows the length of the last 100 calls made using each phone.

Time of call (minutes)	Frequency (for Kaye's mobile phone)	Frequency (for her parents' house phone)
$0 \leq t < 5$	23	5
$5 \leq t < 10$	35	15
$10 \leq t < 15$	20	35
$15 \leq t < 20$	18	28
$20 \leq t < 25$	4	10
$25 \leq t < 30$	0	7

a On the same axes, draw two frequency polygons to illustrate the data.
b Hence compare the lengths of the phone calls made on the two phones.
c Kaye's parents tell her she will have to pay 50p for every call longer than 10 minutes made on her parents' phone.
Explain why her parents chose the value 10 minutes.

4 The frequency polygon shows the weights of 50 people before and after a special diet aimed at losing weight.
Explain whether the following statements are definitely true, probably true, definitely false or you cannot tell.
a On average the people involved lost weight during the diet.
b Every person lost weight during the diet.
c Those who did lose weight, did so because of the diet.
d The spread of the weights decreased after the diet.

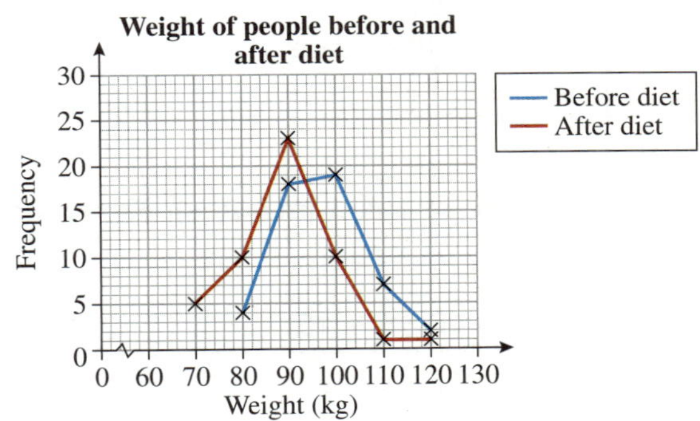

34.2 Histograms with unequal intervals

CAN YOU REMEMBER

- How to draw a histogram for data with equal class sizes?

IN THIS SECTION YOU WILL

- Learn how to draw a histogram for data with unequal class sizes.
- Learn the meaning of the term 'frequency density'.

A *histogram* is a frequency diagram for grouped continuous data.
Each group or class is represented by a bar. There are no gaps between the bars.
The *area* of each bar is proportional to the *frequency* of the class it represents.
There are two methods for drawing histograms.

Method 1: Frequency density

This method uses the formula:

$$\textit{frequency density} = \frac{\text{frequency}}{\text{class width}}$$

The frequency density is calculated for each class and gives the height of each bar.
The vertical axis of the histogram is labelled 'frequency density'.

Method 2: Using a key

Choose a number of squares on the histogram to represent a number of items in the data table.
Draw the bars to this scale.
Draw a key to show the scale.
The vertical axis is left unlabelled.

Example 1

The table shows the length of calls to a customer complaint line.
Draw a histogram to show the data.

Length of call, x (minutes)	Frequency, f
$0 \leqslant x < 10$	5
$10 \leqslant x < 15$	15
$15 \leqslant x < 20$	18
$20 \leqslant x < 30$	16

Solution 1

Method 1

Add a third column for class width and a fourth column for frequency density to the table.
Calculate the frequency density for each class interval using:

$$\text{frequency density} = \frac{\text{frequency}}{\text{class width}}$$

The group $0 \leqslant x < 10$ has a class width of 10, the group $10 \leqslant x < 15$ has a class width of 5 and so on.

Length of call, x (minutes)	Frequency, f	Class width (minutes)	Frequency density
$0 \leqslant x < 10$	5	10	$5 \div 10 = 0.5$
$10 \leqslant x < 15$	15	5	$15 \div 5 = 3$
$15 \leqslant x < 20$	18	5	$18 \div 5 = 3.6$
$20 \leqslant x < 30$	16	10	$16 \div 10 = 1.6$

Draw the axes for the histogram.
Label the horizontal axis with a continuous scale.
Label the vertical axis 'Frequency density'.
Draw the bars using frequency density as the height.

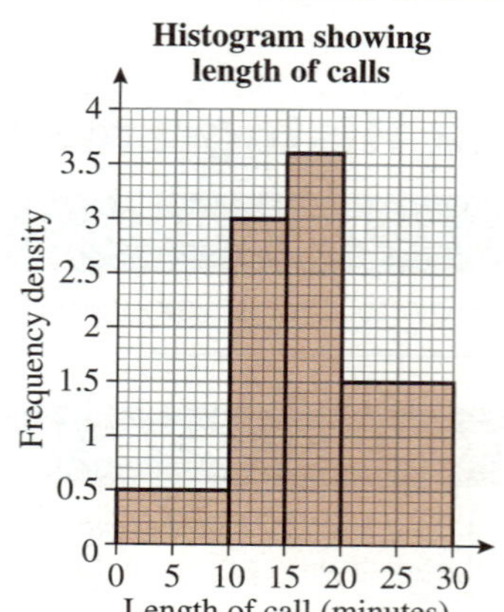

Method 2: Using a key

Let one large square on the grid represent two calls.
The frequencies in the data table are 5, 15, 18 and 16
Using this scale the four classes need to have area 2.5, 7.5, 9 and 8 squares.
The $0 \leqslant x < 10$ class is two squares wide, so for area 2.5 squares the bar needs to be 1.25 squares tall.
The $10 \leqslant x < 15$ class is one square wide, so for area 7.5 squares the bar needs to be 7.5 squares tall.
The $15 \leqslant x < 20$ class is one square wide, so for area 9 squares the bar needs to be 9 squares tall.
The $20 \leqslant x < 30$ class is two squares wide, so for area 8 squares the bar needs to be 4 squares tall.
For this method, the vertical scale is not labelled, but a key is needed.

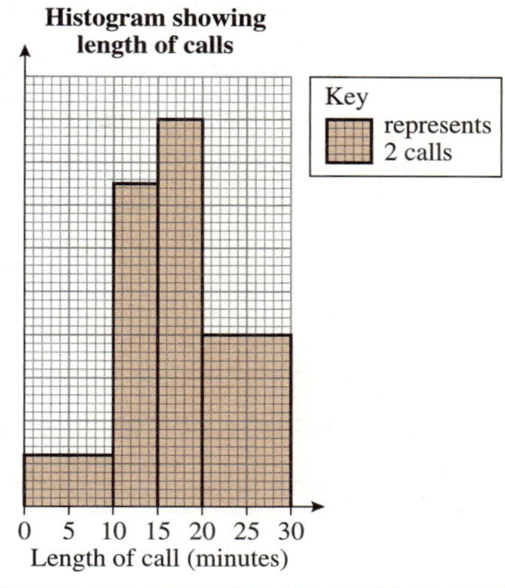

Exercise A

For each data set, draw a fully labelled histogram to represent the data.
Use the method of your choice, adding a key if necessary.

1 The table shows the speed of vehicles passing a speed camera in a town centre.

Speed, s (mph)	Frequency, f
$20 \leqslant s < 24$	12
$24 \leqslant s < 26$	12
$26 \leqslant s < 28$	16
$28 \leqslant s < 34$	18

2 The table shows the heights of 100 athletes.

Height, h (cm)	Frequency, f
$120 \leqslant h < 150$	27
$150 \leqslant h < 160$	34
$160 \leqslant h < 180$	32
$180 \leqslant h < 200$	7

3 The table shows the length of 100 political speeches.

Length of time, t (min)	Frequency, f
$1 \leqslant t < 5$	8
$5 \leqslant t < 10$	12
$10 \leqslant t < 15$	34
$15 \leqslant t < 20$	27
$20 \leqslant t < 30$	10
$30 \leqslant t < 60$	9

4 The table shows the weight of small bags of tomatoes.

Weight of tomatoes, w (g)	Frequency, f
$20 \leqslant w < 45$	5
$45 \leqslant w < 50$	16
$50 \leqslant w < 55$	13
$55 \leqslant w < 65$	22
$65 \leqslant w < 100$	3

5 The table shows the time taken to drink a pint of water.

Time taken, t (seconds)	Frequency, f
$5 \leqslant t < 12$	4
$12 \leqslant t < 15$	12
$15 \leqslant t < 17$	14
$17 \leqslant t < 20$	13
$20 \leqslant t < 30$	16
$30 \leqslant t < 60$	9

If a histogram has no key, and the vertical axis is unlabelled, use the total number of items to work out what each square on the histogram represents.

Example 2

The histogram shows the weights of 100 hospital patients.

a How many of the patients weighed 70 kg or over?

b Estimate the number of patients who weighed between 45 kg and 65 kg.

c One of these patients is chosen at random. Estimate the probability that the patient weighs less than 60 kg.

d Two of the patients are chosen at random. Estimate the probability that they **both** weigh at least 80 kg.

e Give an estimate of the median weight.

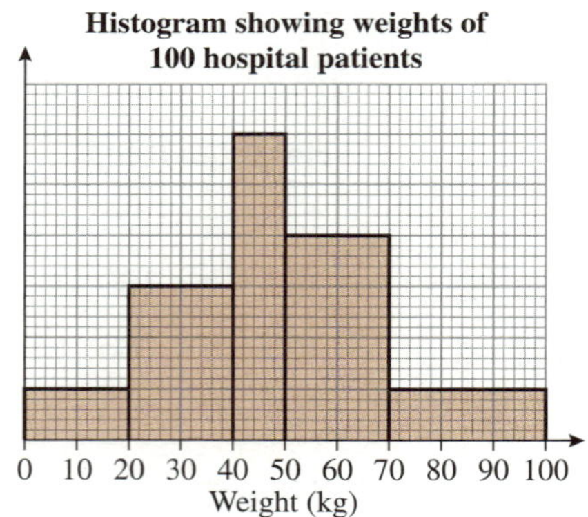

Solution 2

There is no frequency density scale or key, so to interpret the histogram, use the fact that there are 100 patients.

The histogram covers a total of 25 large squares, so each square represents $100 \div 25 = 4$ patients.

a Three squares represent '70 kg or over', so the number of patients is $3 \times 4 = 12$

b Between 45 kg and 65 kg is 9 squares which represents 9×4 patients $= 36$

c The histogram does not show how the patients' weights are distributed in the 50–60 kg group. An estimate for the patients less than 60 kg is:

18 squares $= 18 \times 4 = 72$ patients

so $P(\text{less than 60 kg}) = \frac{72}{100} = \frac{18}{25}$

d An estimate for the patients that are at least 80 kg is:
$2 \text{ squares} = 2 \times 4 = 8$ patients
Probability that first patient is at least 80 kg $= \frac{8}{100}$
Probability that second patient is at least 80 kg $= \frac{7}{99}$
Probability that both patients are at least 80 kg $= \frac{8}{100} \times \frac{7}{99} = \frac{56}{9900} = \frac{14}{2475}$

e In a histogram, the median divides the area under the bars into two equal parts.
There are 25 squares, so the median is 12.5 squares along the histogram.
The 40–50 bar contains squares 9–14
The median is approximately $\frac{2}{3}$ along the 40–50 bar.
Estimate of median = 47

Exercise B

1 The histogram shows the weight of 50 apple pies entered into the UK Apple Pie baking championships.

a Estimate the number of pies that weighed under 180 g.

b How many pies weighed more than 220 g but less than 270 g?

c Estimate the probability that the winning pie was over 200 g in weight.

d What assumption was made in answering part **c**?

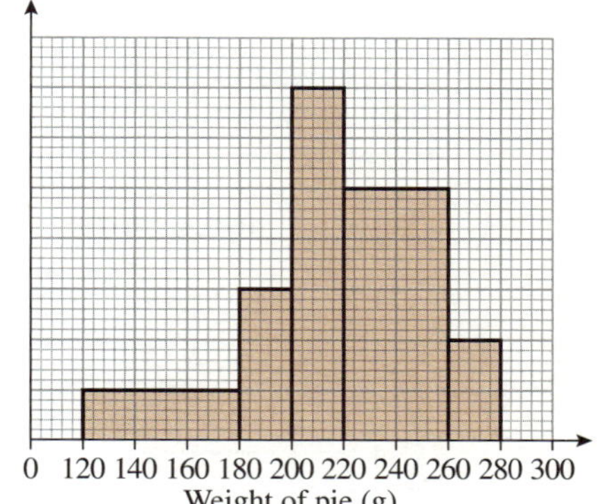

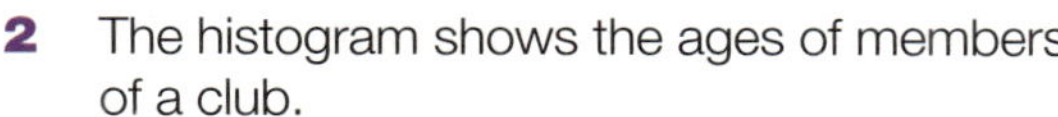

2 The histogram shows the ages of members of a club.

a How many members are aged 70 or over?

b How many members are in their fifties?

c What is the probability that the treasurer of the club is under 50 years old?

d The President of the club is over 60
What is the probability that the President is over 70?

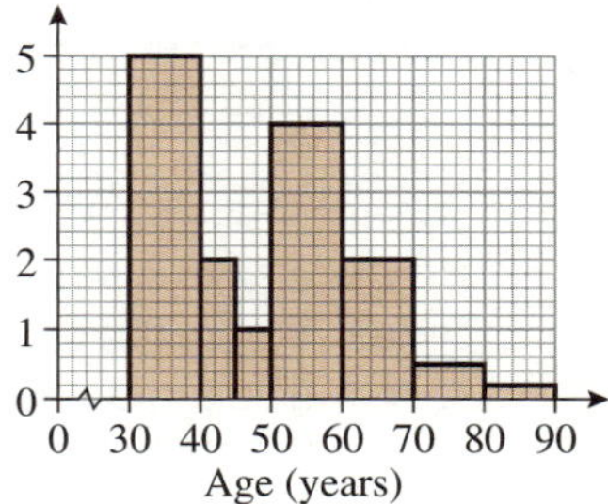

3 The histogram shows the weights of 60 newborn babies.

a The first bar has a height of 0.5 and represents one baby. Explain why the final bar which has a height of 0.8 represents two babies.

b Copy and complete the grouped frequency table for the weights of the newborn babies.

Weight of baby, w (kg)	Frequency, f
$0 \leqslant w < 2$	1
$2 \leqslant w < 3$	
$3 \leqslant w < 3.5$	
$3.5 \leqslant w < 4$	
$4 \leqslant w < 5$	
$5 \leqslant w < 7.5$	2

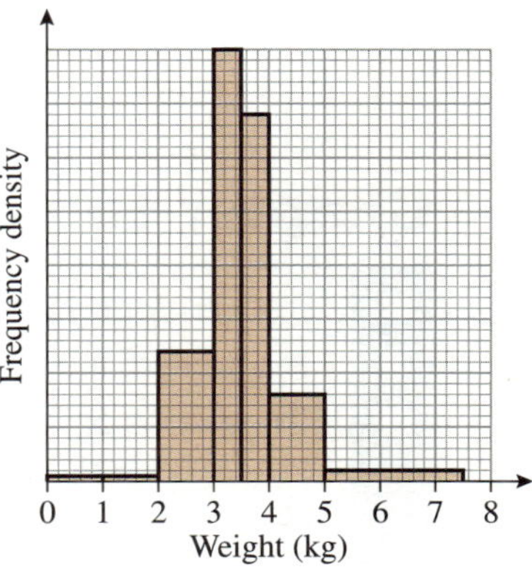

4 The incomplete table and incomplete histogram each partly represent the length (in cm) of 40 French sticks in a bakery.

Length of French sticks, l (cm)	**Frequency, f**
$30 \leqslant l < 40$	
$40 \leqslant l < 45$	11
$45 \leqslant l < 50$	
$\leqslant l < 60$	13

0 25 30 35 40 45 50 55 60
Length of French stick (cm)

Copy and complete both the table and the histogram.

5 Dougie was looking at the two histograms below.
They show the weights of the tomatoes he grew without fertiliser and the weights of the tomatoes he grew with fertiliser.

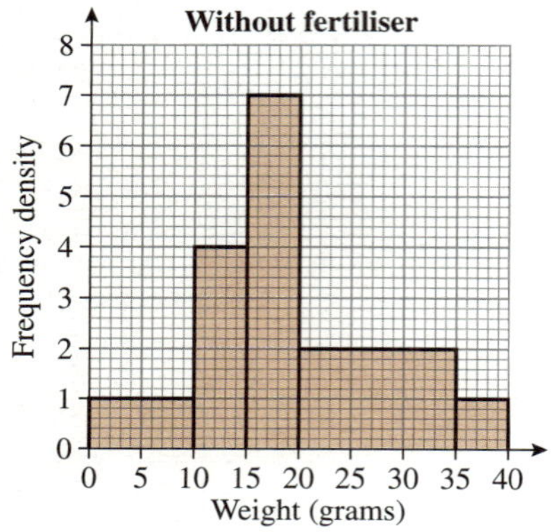

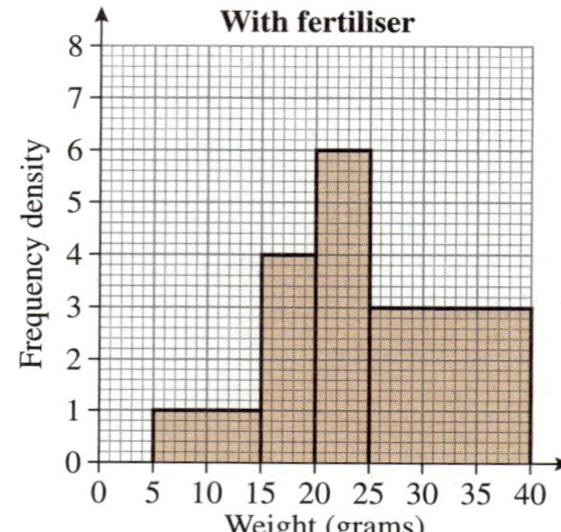

State, with a reason, whether each of Dougie's statements below is correct.

a I grew the same number of tomatoes with and without fertiliser.
b The tomatoes with fertiliser seemed to be heavier than those without.
c The tomatoes had a similar range of weights whether they were given fertiliser or not.
d The median weight of tomato without fertiliser was 15 grams.

Chapter summary

- Frequency polygons can be used to compare two or more sets of data.
- The spread, the modal class and the median can be found from the polygons and compared.
- The shapes of the frequency polygons can be compared. The shape of a frequency polygon shows the modal class and how the data is spread out.

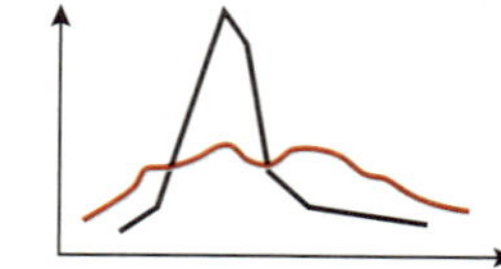

- A histogram is a frequency diagram for grouped continuous data.
- Each group or class is represented by a bar. There are no gaps between the bars.
- The area of each bar is proportional to the frequency of the class it represents.

- There are two methods for drawing histograms.
  - **Method 1: Frequency density**
    Calculate the frequency density $\left(= \frac{\text{frequency}}{\text{class width}}\right)$ for each class and the frequency density gives the height of each bar.
    The vertical axis of the histogram is labelled 'Frequency density'.
  - **Method 2: Using a key**
    Choose a number of squares on the histogram to represent a number of items in the data table. Draw the bars to this scale.
    Draw a key to show the scale.
    The vertical axis is left unlabelled.
- If a histogram has no key, and the vertical axis is unlabelled, use the total number of items to work out what each square on the histogram represents.

Chapter review

1 The histogram shows the ages of 68 people at a dance class.

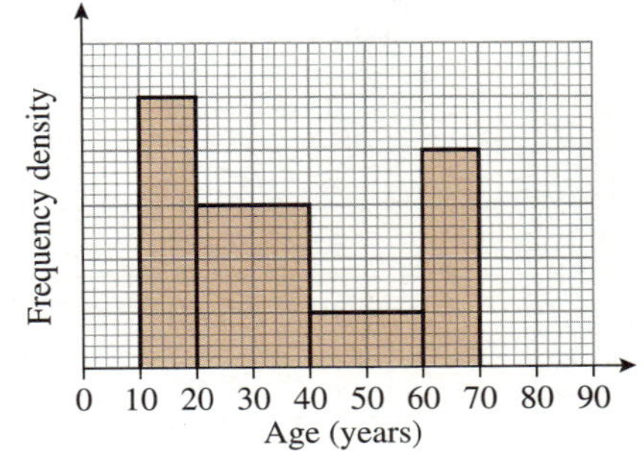

a How many people are aged 60 or over?

b What is the probability that a person chosen at random is aged between 10 and 20 years old?

c **i** Estimate the number of people aged under 25 years old.

ii Explain why your answer to part **c i** is an estimate.

2 Mica used a sample of 50 pupils to investigate the amount of time they spent watching television on one evening.
The histogram shows her results.
12 pupils watched television for less than half an hour.
2 pupils watched television for longer than 3 hours. They both watched for over 5 hours.

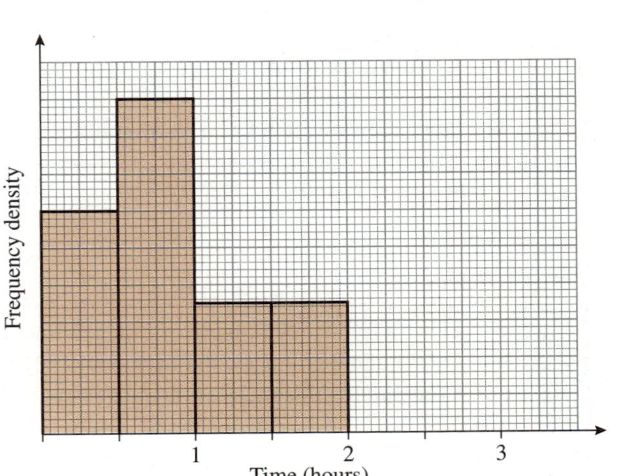

a Calculate the number of pupils who watched television for between 2 and 3 hours.

Mica drew a histogram to represent the times. Because their times were not representative of the rest of the sample, she did not include the times for the pupils who watched for more than 5 hours.

b Copy the histogram and add a column to illustrate the pupils who watched television for between 2 and 3 hours.

3 The table summarises the heights of 20 winter plants.

Height, h (centimetres)	Number of plants
$0 < h \leqslant 5$	1
$5 < h \leqslant 15$	10
$15 < h \leqslant 25$	6
$25 < h \leqslant 40$	3

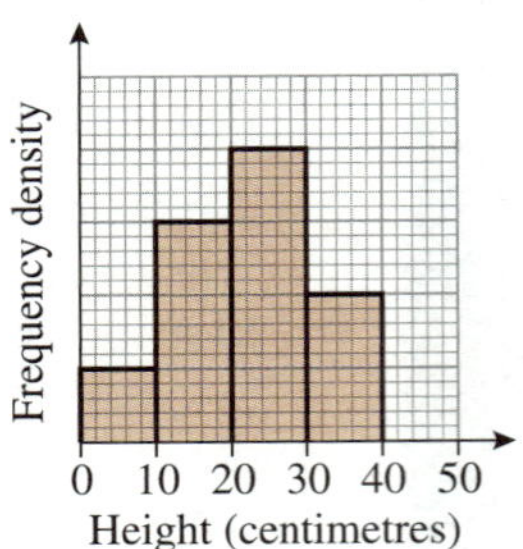

a Draw a histogram to represent this data.

b The heights of 20 summer plants are represented by the histogram on the right. Write down a comparison between the heights of the winter plants and the heights of the summer plants.

4 The diagram shows a frequency polygon of times for 20 boys to complete a task.

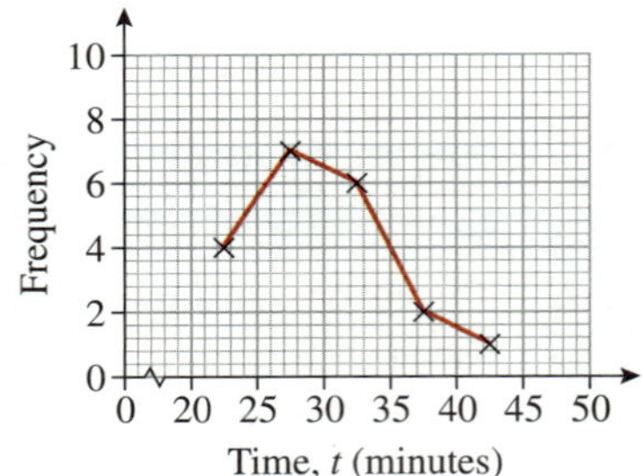

The times for 20 girls to complete the same task are shown in the table.

Time, t (minutes)	Frequency
$20 < t \leqslant 25$	8
$25 < t \leqslant 30$	3
$30 < t \leqslant 35$	2
$35 < t \leqslant 40$	1
$40 < t \leqslant 45$	6

a Copy the frequency polygon for the boys' data. On the same grid draw the frequency polygon for the girls.

b Compare the results for the boys and the girls.

5 The table shows the thickness, T, in millimetres, of 25 maths and 25 science textbooks.

Thickness, T (mm)	$0 < T \leqslant 10$	$10 < T \leqslant 20$	$20 < T \leqslant 30$	$30 < T \leqslant 40$
Maths	3	12	6	4
Science	1	10	9	5

a Draw a frequency polygon for the thickness of maths textbooks.

b On the same grid draw the frequency polygon for the thickness of science textbooks.

c Compare the thickness of the maths and science textbooks.

6 The distribution of the weights of 125 men is summarised in the table on the right. Draw a histogram to represent these data.

Weight, w (kg)	Frequency
$60 \leqslant w < 70$	16
$70 \leqslant w < 75$	30
$75 \leqslant w < 80$	37
$80 \leqslant w < 100$	42

7 The table shows a summary of the lengths l, in minutes, of 12 tracks on a CD.

Length, l (min)	$0 < l \leqslant 3$	$3 < l \leqslant 3.5$	$3.5 < l \leqslant 5$
Frequency	2	7	3

Draw a histogram to represent the data.

8 A survey of the annual mileage of 50 privately owned and 50 company owned cars is carried out. The results are summarised in the table.

Mileage	0–10 000	10 001–15 000	15 001–25 000	25 001–35 000
Privately owned	6	24	15	5
Company owned	2	14	15	19

a Draw a frequency polygon for the annual mileage of the privately owned cars.
b On the same grid draw the frequency polygon for the annual mileage of the company owned cars.
c Compare the mileages.

9 The histogram shows a summary of the distances that 36 people travel to work.
a How many people travel more than 30 miles to work?
b Estimate the number of people who travel less than 15 miles to work.
c The median distance travelled divides the area of a histogram into two equal parts.
Which of these statements is most likely to be correct?
i The median distance is 25 miles.
ii The median distance is greater than 25 miles.
iii The median distance is less than 25 miles.
Explain your answer.

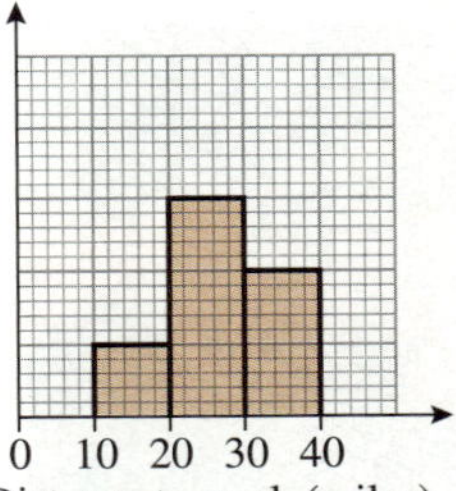

CHAPTER 35

Circle theorems

35.1 Angle theorems

CAN YOU REMEMBER

- That the angles on a straight line total 180° and in a full circle total 360°?
- The properties of an isosceles triangle?

IN THIS SECTION YOU WILL

- Learn facts about angles in a circle and how to prove them.
- Use the facts to find the size of angles within a circle.
- Learn the meaning of 'cyclic quadrilateral'.

Here are some useful angle properties of circles.
Each fact can be proved to be true in all situations.
In all diagrams O is the centre of the circle.

Fact: angle in a semicircle = 90°

Proof: let angle $CAB = x°$

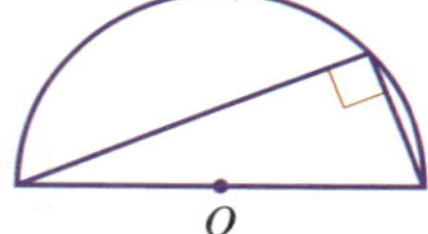
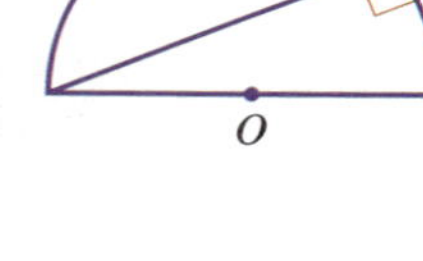

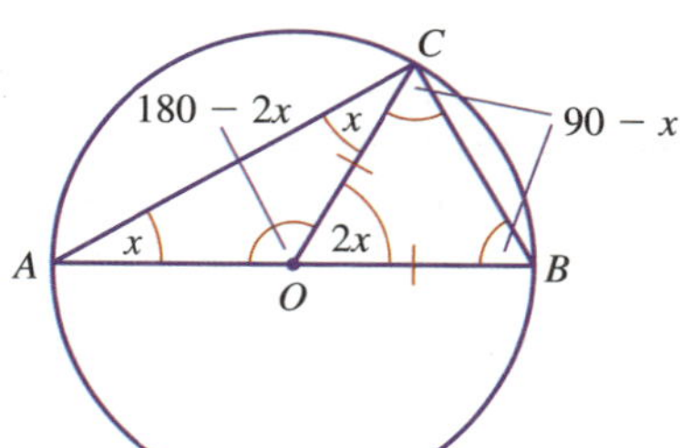

Angle $ACO = x°$ — Triangle AOC is isosceles.

Angle $AOC = (180 - 2x)°$ — Angles in a triangle add up to 180°

Angle $COB = 2x°$ — Angles on a straight line add up to 180°

Angle OCB = Angle OBC
$= (90 - x)°$ — Triangle COB is isosceles.

Angle $ACB = x° + (90 - x)° = 90°$

Example 1

AB is the diameter of the circle.
Work out angle x.
Give reasons for your answer.

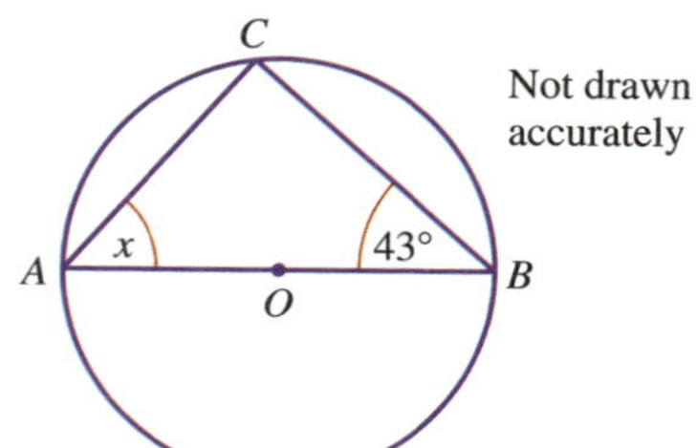

Solution 1

angle $ACB = 90°$
$x = 180° - (90° + 43°)$
$= 180° - 133° = 47°$

Angle in a semicircle = 90°

Angles in a triangle add up to 180°

Fact: angle at centre of circle = twice angle at circumference of circle
Proof: let angle $ABO = x°$ and angle $CBO = y°$.

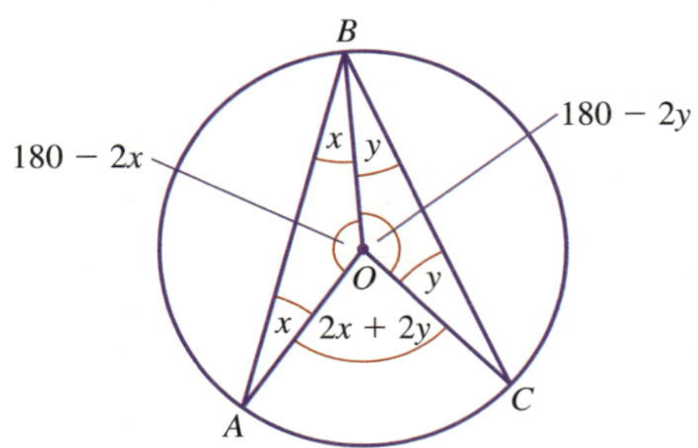

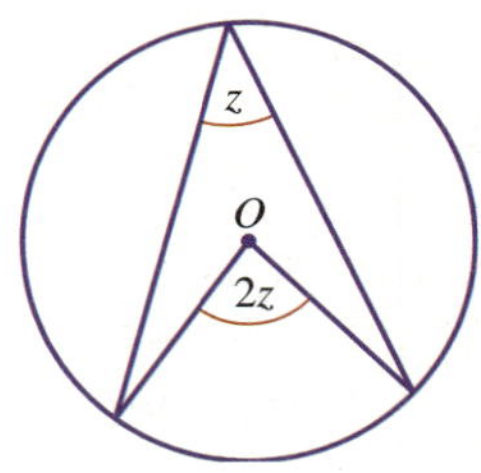

Angle $BAO = x°$ and angle $BCO = y°$
Angle $BOA = (180 - 2x)°$ and angle BOC
$= (180 - 2y)°$
Angle $AOC = 360° - (180 - 2x)° - (180 - 2y)°$
$= (2x + 2y)° = 2(x + y)°$
Angle $ABC = (x + y)°$
So angle $AOC = 2 \times$ angle ABC

Triangles BAO and BCO are isosceles.

Angles in a triangle add up to 180°

Angles at a point add up to 360°

Example 2

Work out the size of angle x giving reasons for your answer.

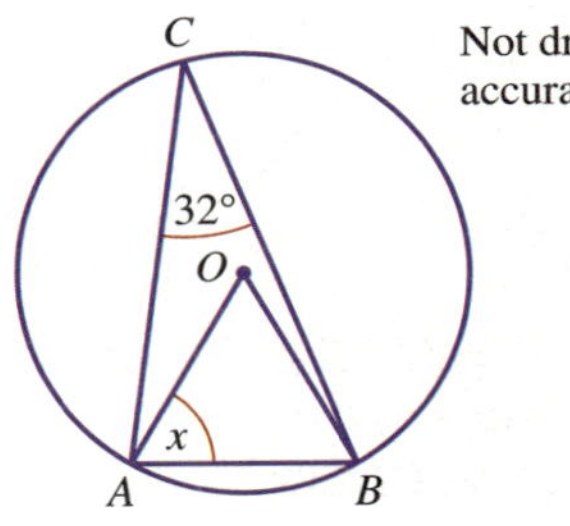

Solution 2

Angle $AOB = 2 \times 32° = 64°$
$180° - 64° = 116°$
angle x = angle $OBA = 116° \div 2$
$x = 58°$

Angle at centre is twice angle at circumference.

Isosceles triangle.

Fact: angles on the same arc (or chord) are equal.
Proof: let angle $AOB = 2x°$

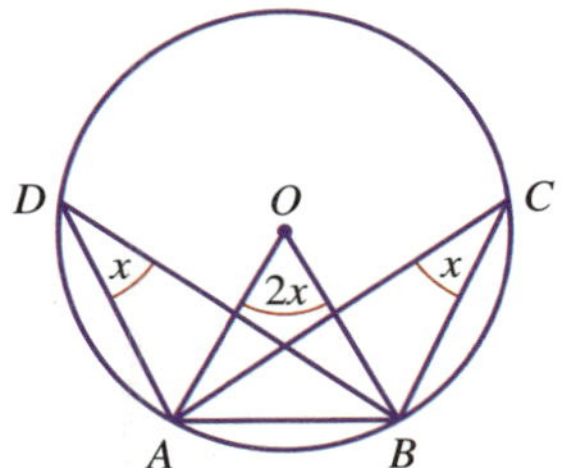

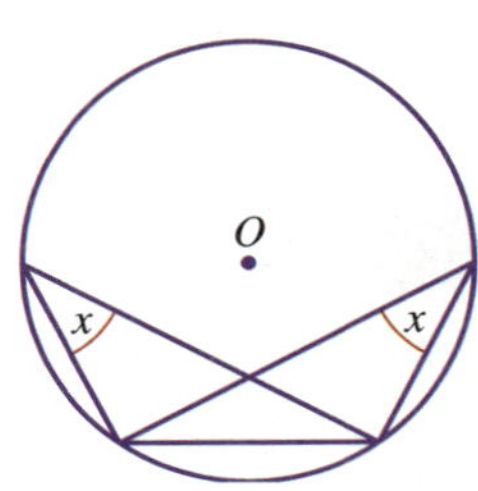

Angle $ACB = x°$
Angle $ADB = x°$
Angle ADB = angle ACB

Angle at centre = twice angle at circumference

Angle at centre = twice angle at circumference

Example 3

Find angle x giving a reason for your answer.

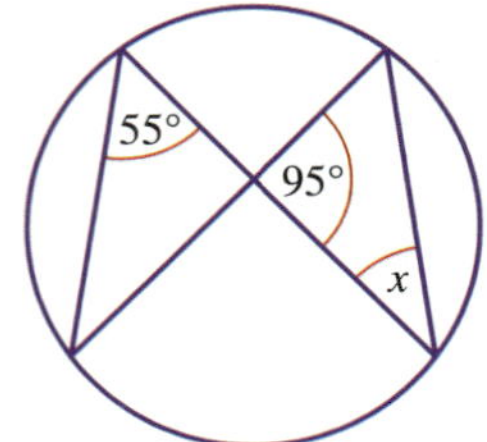

Not drawn accurately

Solution 3

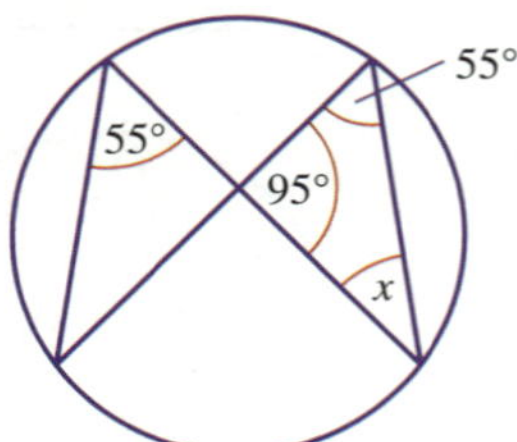

Write in the other angle of 55°

$x = 180° - (95° + 55°) = 30°$

Angles on same arc or chord are equal.

Angles in a triangle add up to 180°

A *cyclic quadrilateral* is a quadrilateral drawn inside a circle with all four vertices on the circumference.

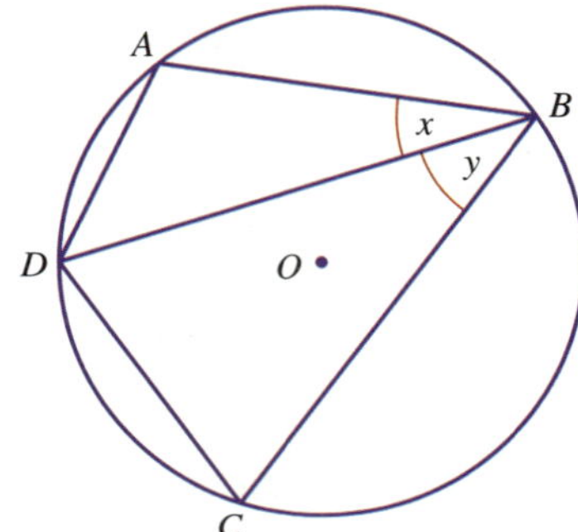

Fact: opposite angles in a cyclic quadrilateral add up to 180°

Proof: let angle $ABD = x°$ and angle $CBD = y°$

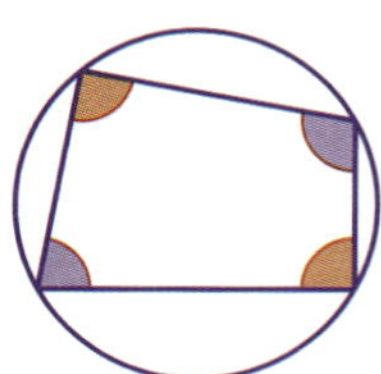

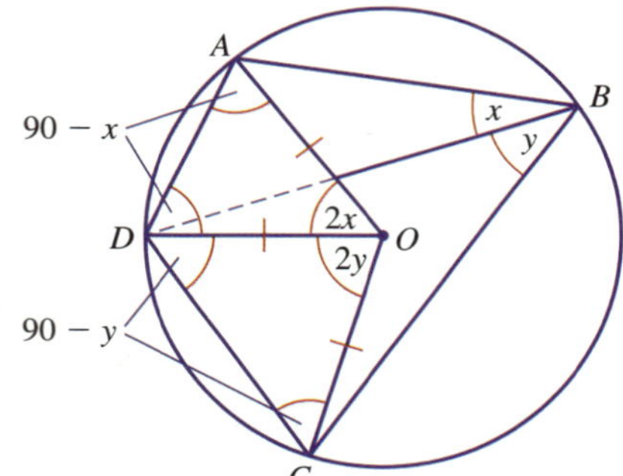

Angle $AOD = 2x°$ and angle $DOC = 2y°$

Angle $ADO = (180 - 2x)° \div 2 = (90 - x)°$ and angle $CDO = (180 - 2y)° \div 2 = (90 - y)°$

Angle ADC = angle ADO + angle CDO

$= (90 - x)° + (90 - y)° = (180 - x - y)°$

Angle ABC + Angle ADC

$= (x + y)° + (180 - x - y)° = 180°$

Angle at centre = twice angle at circumference

Angles in isosceles triangles

Example 4

Work out the sizes of angles x and y.

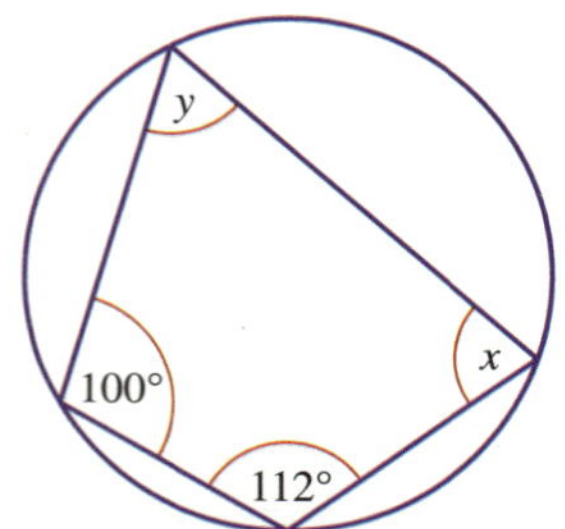

Not drawn accurately

Solution 4

Opposite angles of a cyclic quadrilateral add up to 180°

$x = 180° - 100° = 80°$

$y = 180° - 112° = 68°$

Exercise A

In this exercise the diagrams are not drawn accurately.
In all diagrams O is the centre of the circle.

1 Find the value of the angles marked with letters.

a
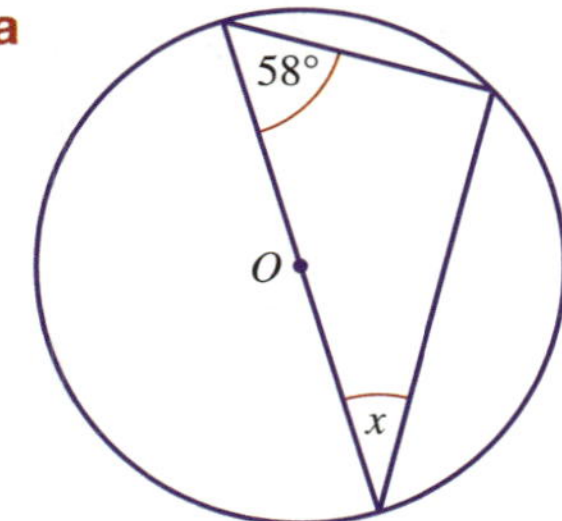

b
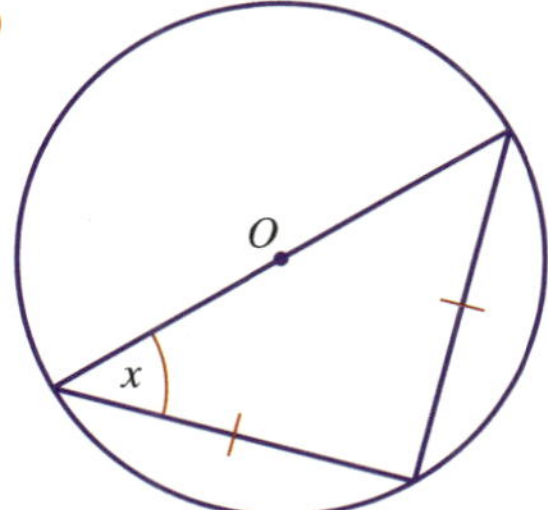

c
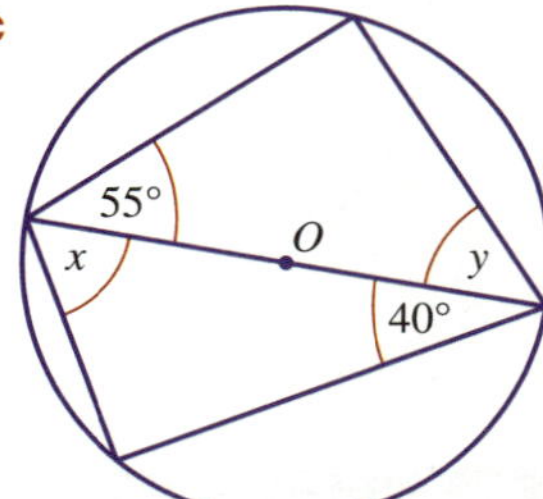

2 Find the values of x and y giving a reason for your answer.

a
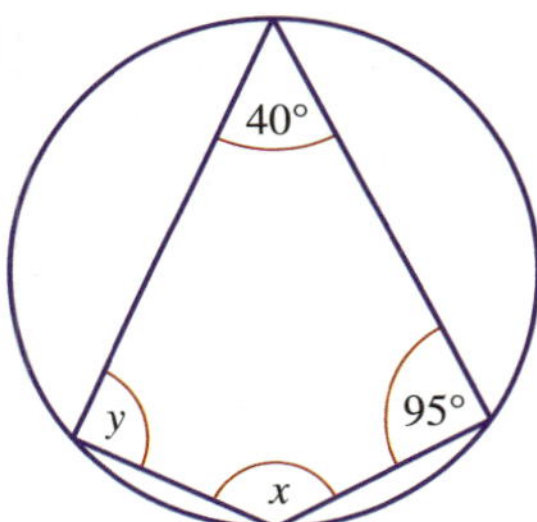

b
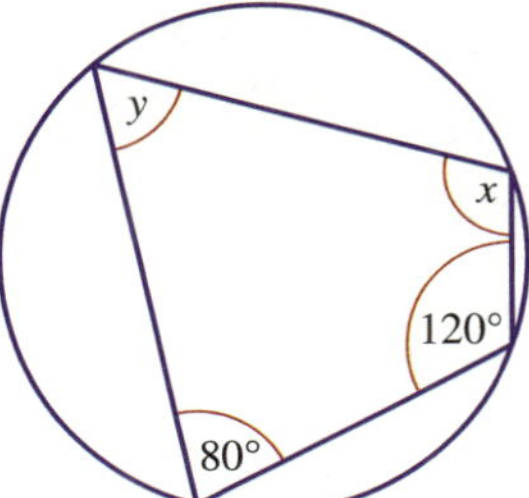

c
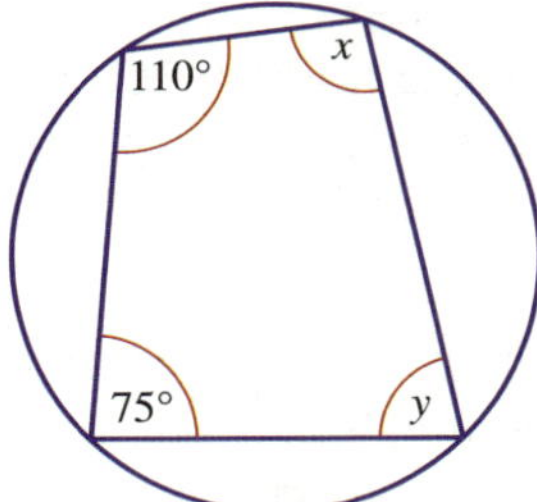

3 Work out angle x giving reasons for your answer.

a
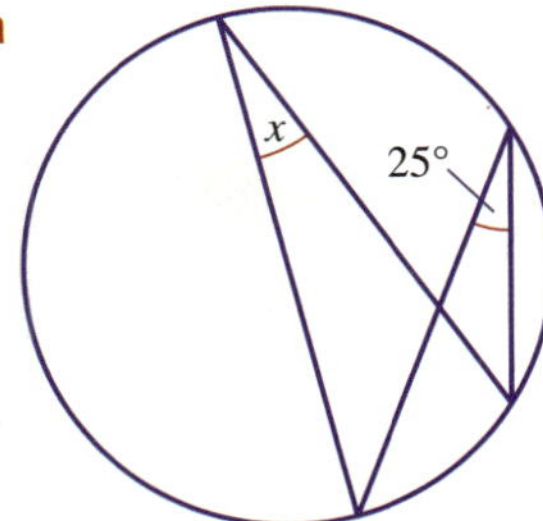

b
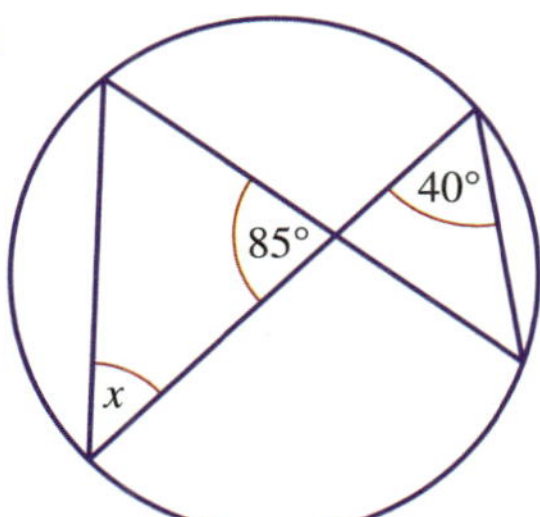

c
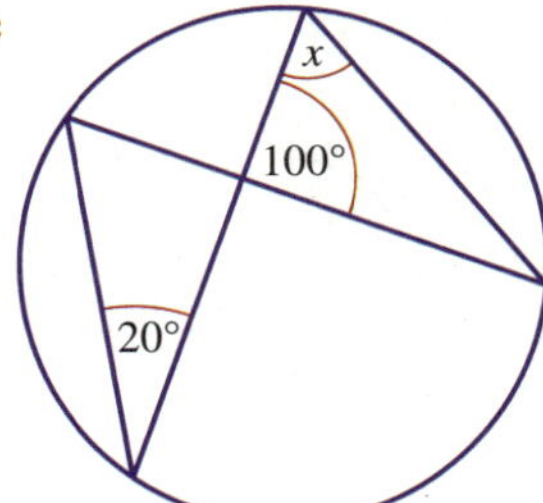

4 Write down the size of angle x.

a
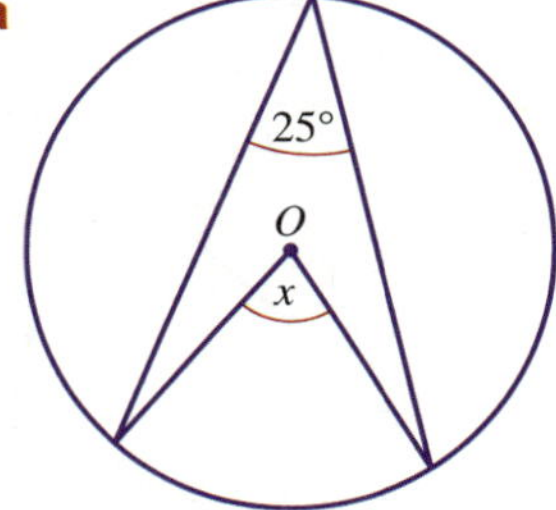

b
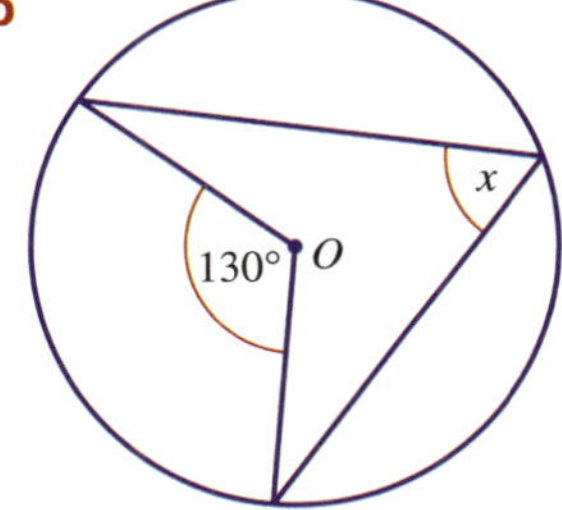

c
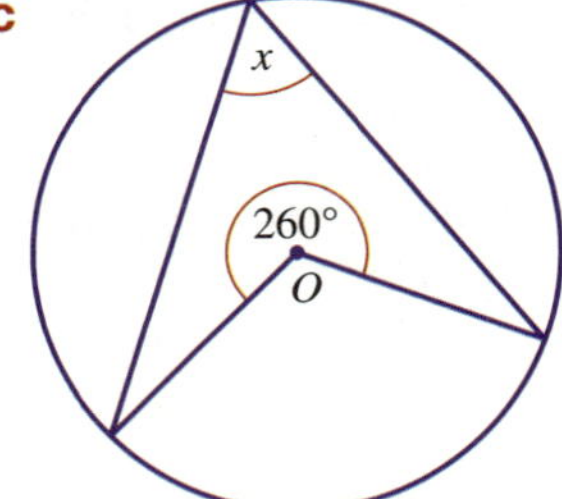

5 Calculate the sizes of the angles marked with letters.

a

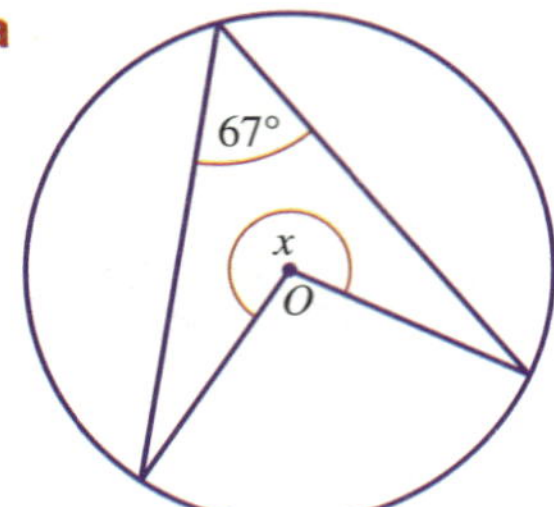

b

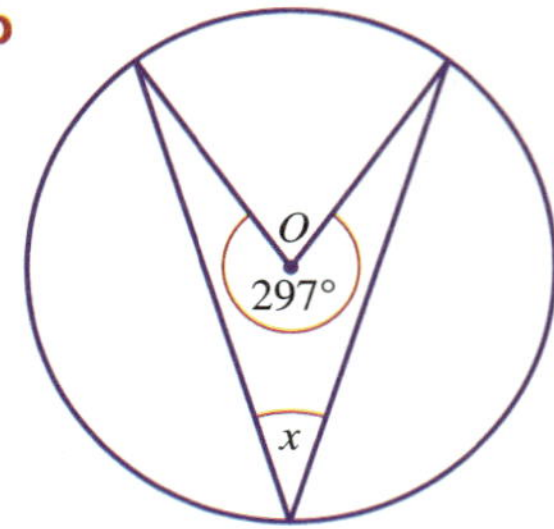

c

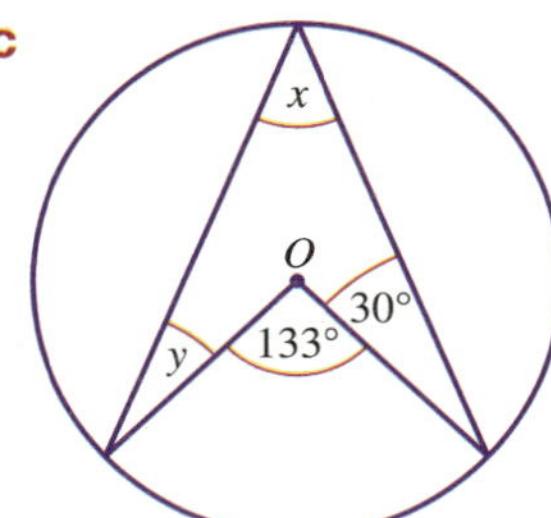

Example 5

Find the sizes of the angles marked with letters.

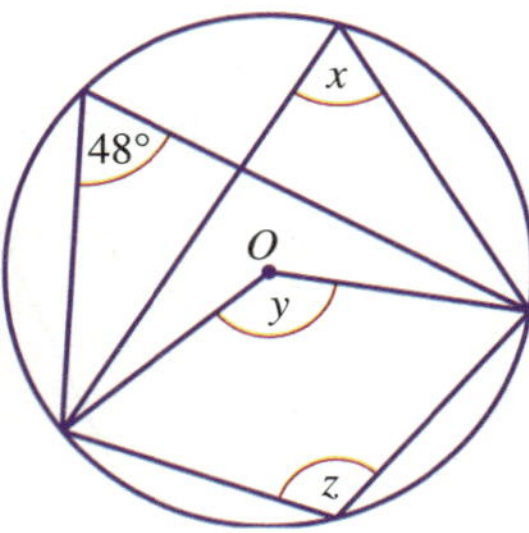

Solution 5

$x = 48°$	Angles on the same arc are equal.
$y = 2 \times 48° = 96°$	Angle at centre is twice angle at circumference.
$z = 180° - 48° = 132°$	Opposite angles of cyclic quadrilateral total 180°

Exercise B

The diagrams in this exercise are not drawn accurately.
In all diagrams O is the centre of the circle.

1 Work out the size of the angles marked with letters.
Give reasons for your answers.

a

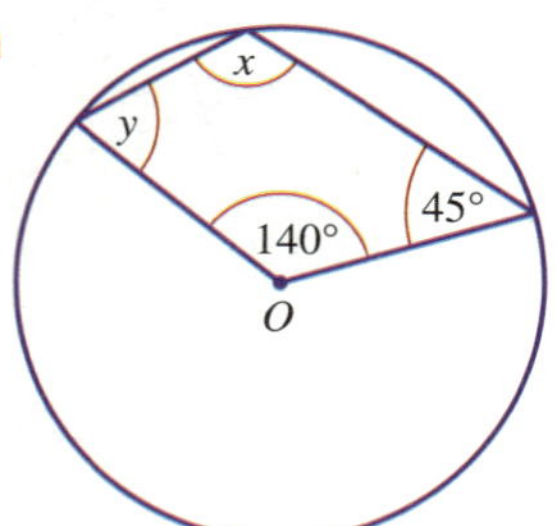

b

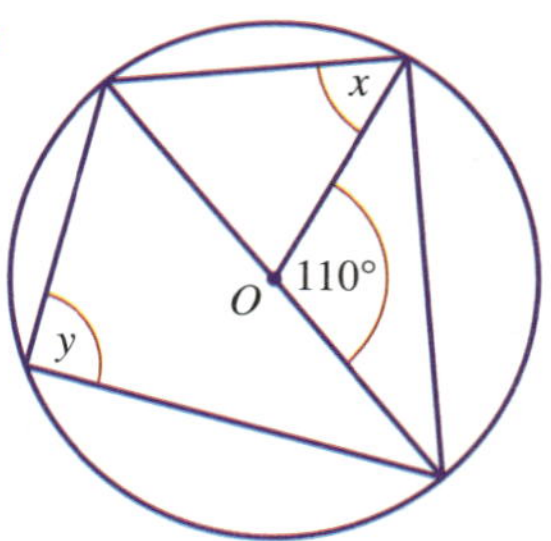

2 In the diagram angle $OCA = 35°$ and angle $OCB = 40°$
Prove that angle $AOB = 150°$

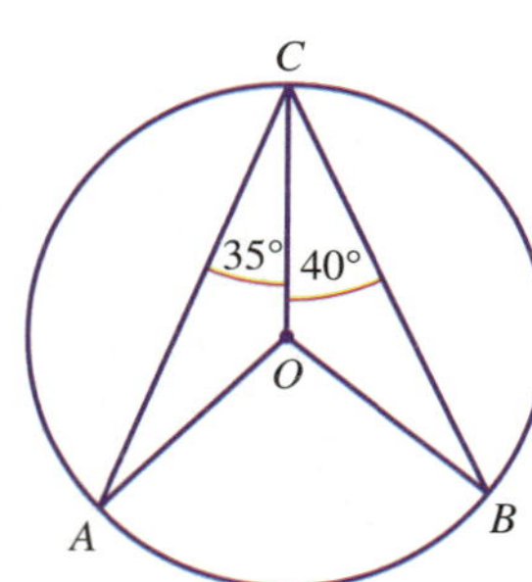

3 Work out the values of x and y giving a reason for each answer.

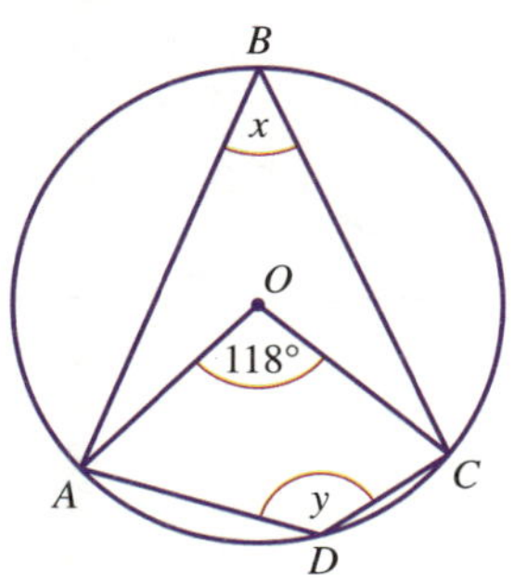

4 Points P, Q, R and S lie on a circle.
$PQ = QR$
Angle $PQR = 108°$
Explain why angle $QSR = 36°$

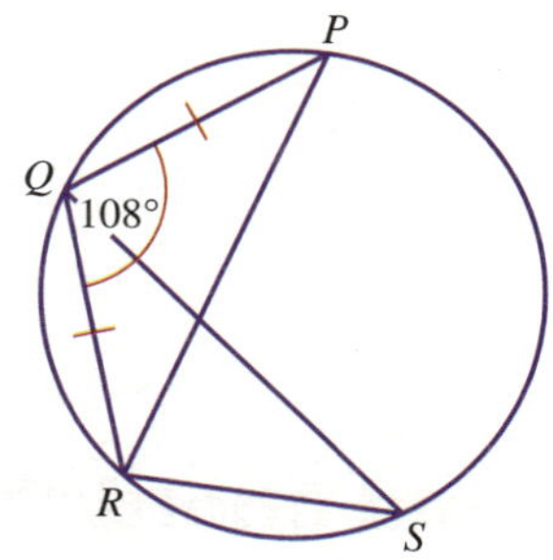

5 In the diagram BD is a diameter of the circle.
Angle $BDC = 57°$

a Write down the value of x.

b Calculate the value of y.

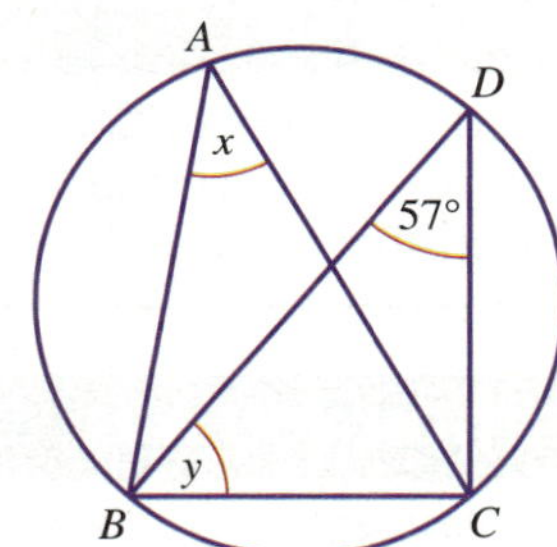

6 P, Q, R and S are four points on the circumference of a circle.
Angle $RPS = 41°$ and angle $QSR = 56°$
Calculate the following angles giving reasons for your answers.

a angle QPR **b** angle QRS

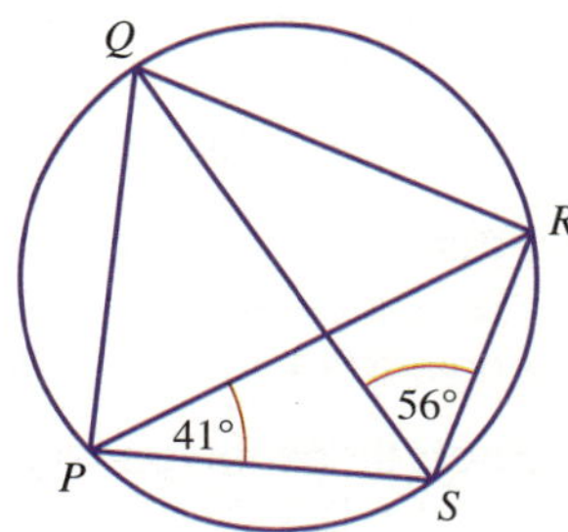

7 In the diagram below P, Q, R and T lie on a circle.
QRS and PTS are straight lines.
Calculate the size of angle RTS. Give a reason for each step of your working.

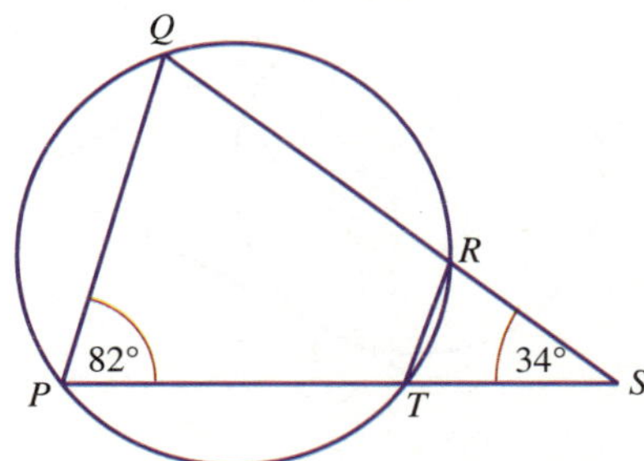

8 In the diagram on the right, B, C, D and E lie on a circle.
ABC and AED are straight lines.
Angle $BAE = x$, angle $BCD = y$
Work out an expression for angle ABE in terms of x and y.

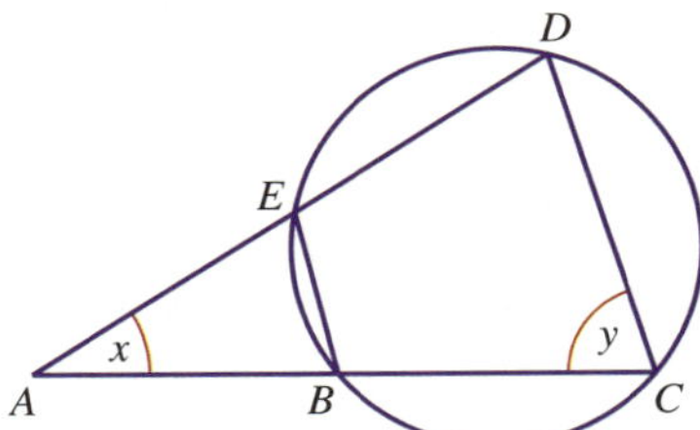

9 In the diagram angle $BAC = 27°$
Prove that angle $ACB = 90°$

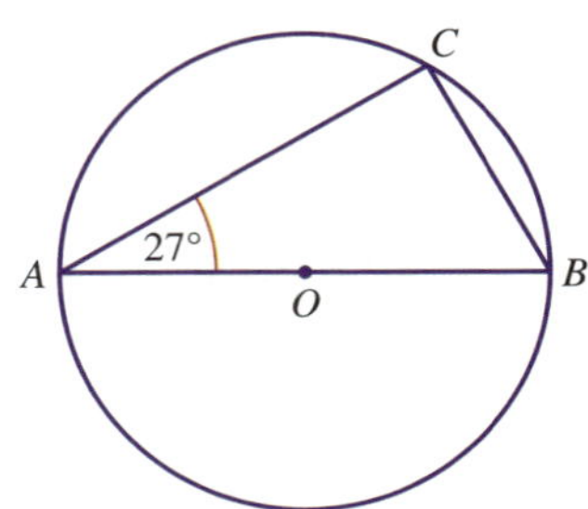

35.2 Tangent and chord theorems

CAN YOU REMEMBER

- The meaning of 'tangent', 'chord', 'sector' and 'segment'?
- That the angle in a semicircle = 90°?
- The conditions for congruency in triangles – SSS, SAS, ASA, RHS?

IN THIS SECTION YOU WILL

- Learn and use facts about tangents, chords and circles.
- Prove and use the alternate segment theorem.

The diagram shows a tangent AB which touches a circle at P.

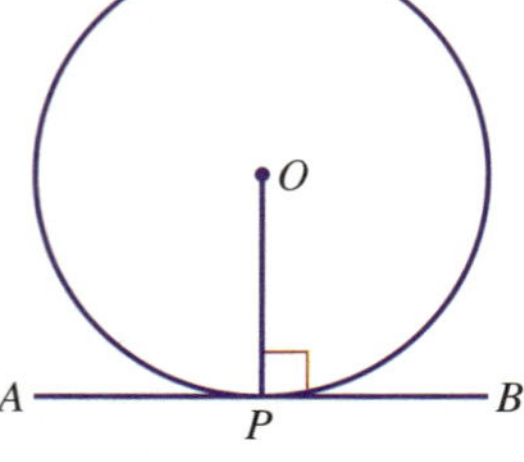

Fact: the angle between the tangent to the circle and the radius at this point is 90°
Angle BPO = angle $APO = 90°$ Using symmetry.

Fact: tangents drawn to a circle from the same point are always equal in length.

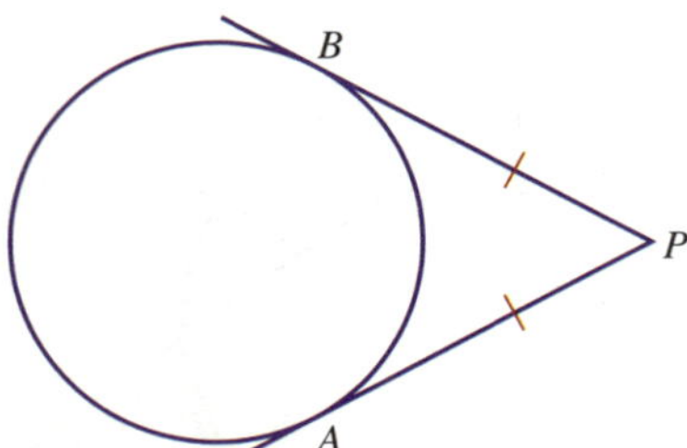

$PA = PB$ Using symmetry.

Fact: the perpendicular from the centre of a circle to a chord bisects the chord.

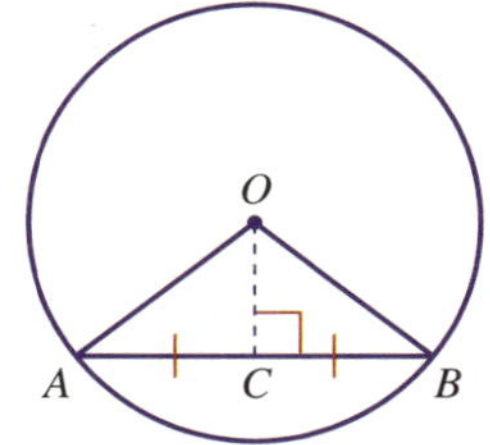

Proof:

$OA = OB$ — Radii of circle.

$OCA = OCB = 90°$ — OC is perpendicular to AB and OAB is an isosceles triangle.

OC is common to triangles OCA and OCB.

Triangles OCA and OCB are congruent. — SAS

So $AC = AB$

Example 1

The diagram shows a tangent to a circle of centre O.
Work out the value of x.

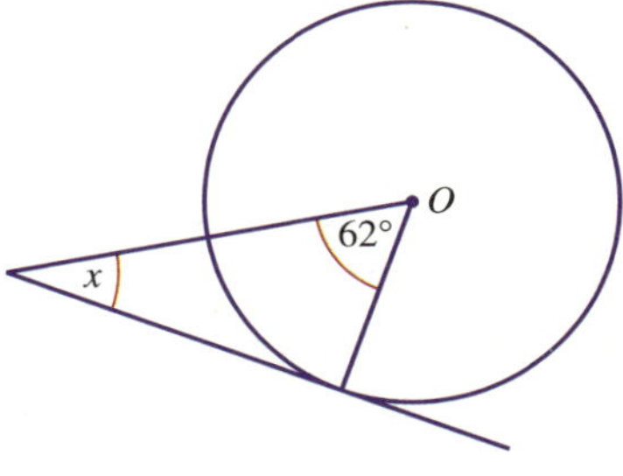

Solution 1

The angle between the tangent and the radius $= 90°$

angle $x = 180° - (90° + 62°) = 28°$ — Angles in a triangle add up to 180°

Example 2

The diagram shows two tangents drawn from point P to a circle, centre O.
Work out the size of angle x.

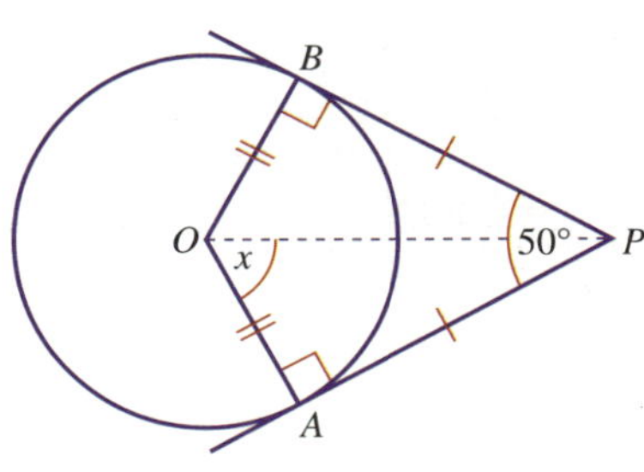

Solution 2

Triangles OAP and OBP are congruent. — SAS

Therefore angle OPB = angle OPA, which means that the line OP bisects angle APB. Similarly, the line OP bisects angle AOB.

Angle $APO = 25°$, angle $OAP = 90°$

Angle $x = 180° - (25° + 90°) = 65°$ — Angles in a triangle add up to 180°

Exercise A

In this exercise the diagrams are not drawn accurately.
O is the centre of the circle.

1 Work out the value of the angle marked with a letter.

a

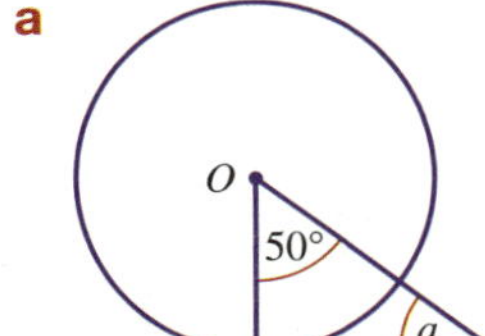

b

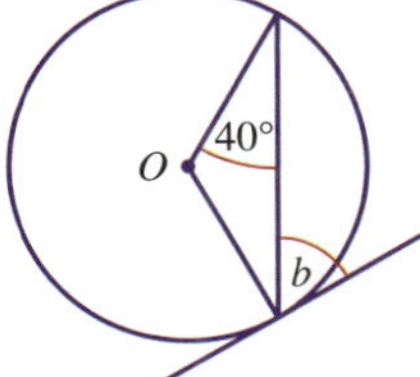

c

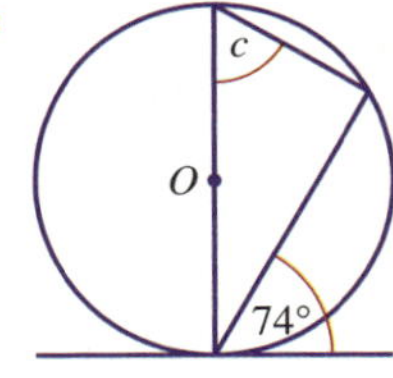

d

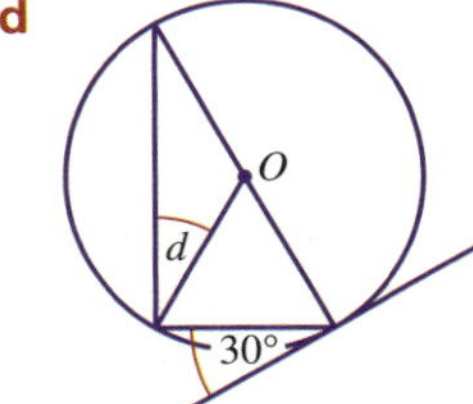

2 Work out the value of the angles marked with letters.

a

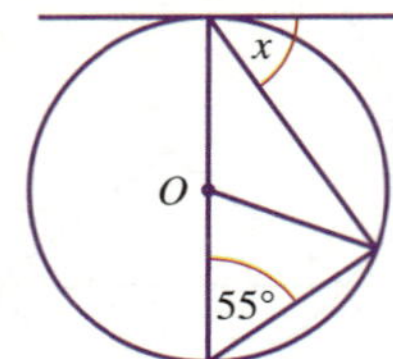

b

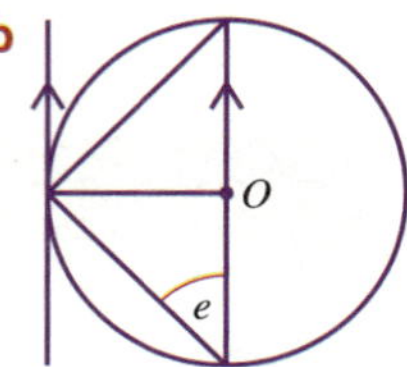

c

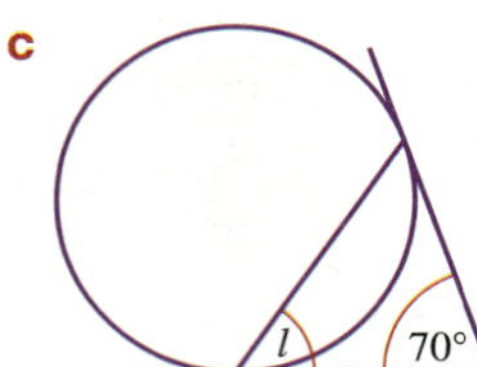

d

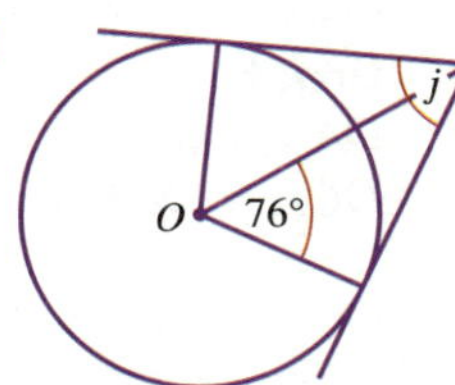

3 Calculate the size of the angles marked with letters.

a

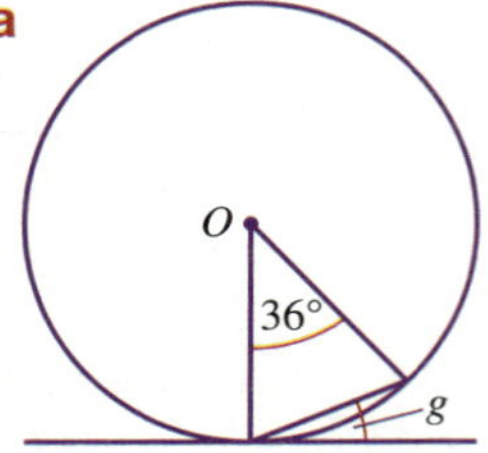

b

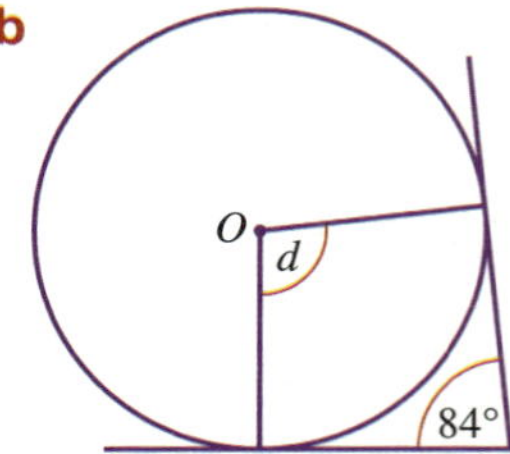

4 The diagram on the right shows two tangents to a circle.
Calculate the value of m.

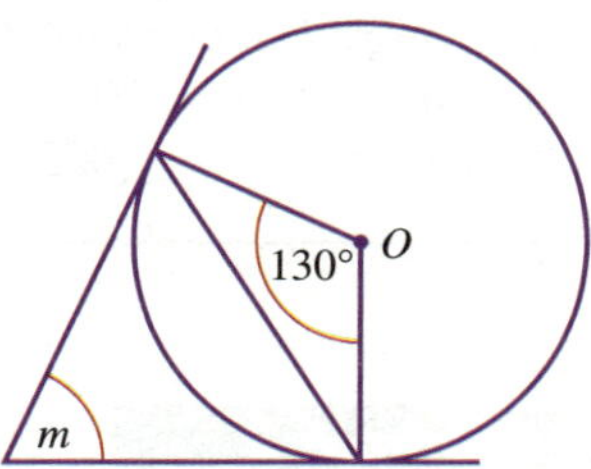

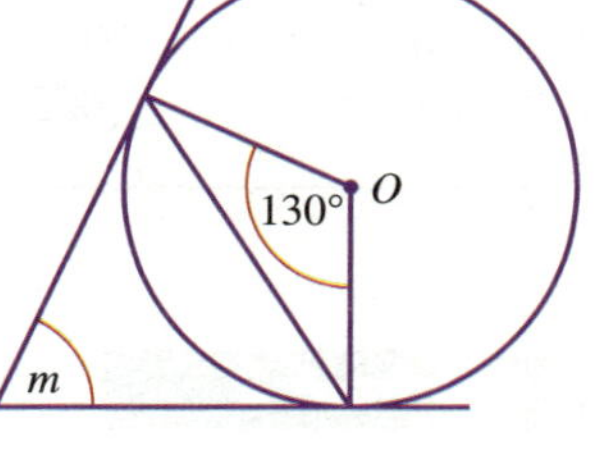

5 The diagram shows a tangent AB to a circle of centre O.
OM is perpendicular to PQ.
Calculate the size of:

a angle OPM **b** angle MPB.

Q
O
71°
M
A P B

6 A tangent is drawn to a circle as shown in the diagram.
Calculate the value of h.

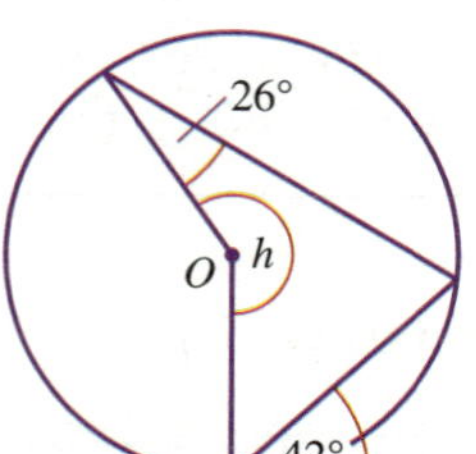

7 Two tangents are drawn from the same point to a circle.
Calculate the size of the angle marked i.

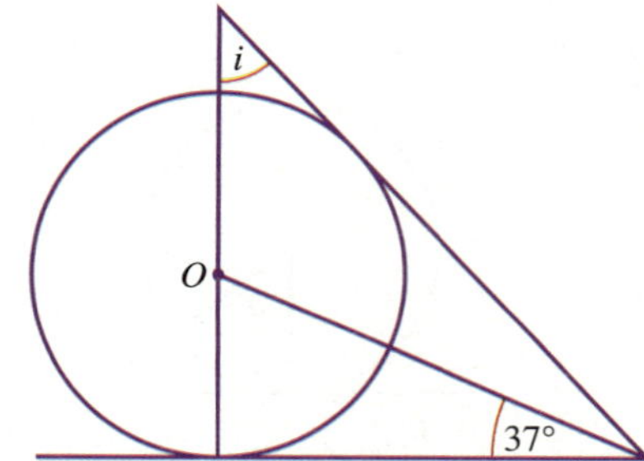

Alternate segment theorem
The angle between a tangent and a chord is equal to any angle in the alternate segment formed from the same chord.
Proof: let angle $AST = x°$.

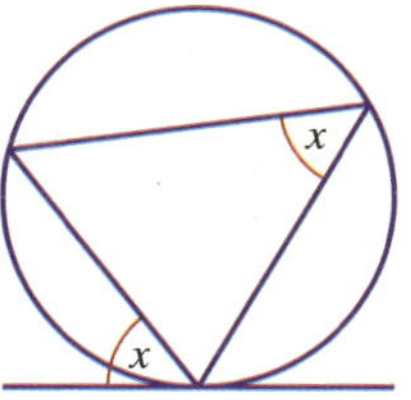

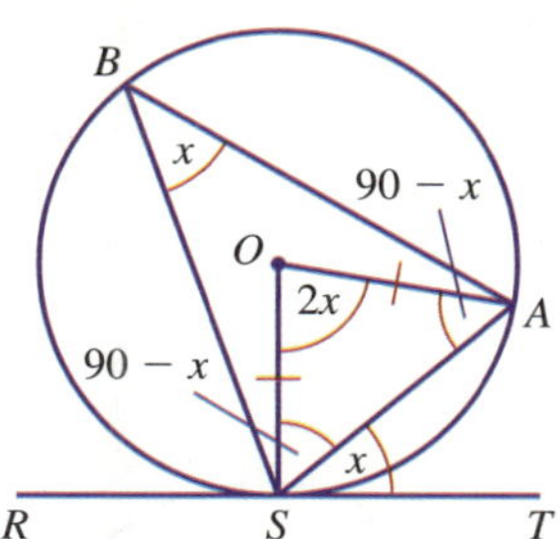

Angle $OST = 90°$	Tangent at any point is perpendicular to radius.
Angle $OSA = (90 - x)°$	
Angle $OAS = (90 - x)°$	Isosceles triangle.
Angle $SOA = 2x$	Angles in triangles add up to 180°.
Angle $ABS = x$	
Angle AST = Angle ABS	Angle at centre = twice angle at circumference

Example 3

Write down the values of a and b giving reasons for your answers.

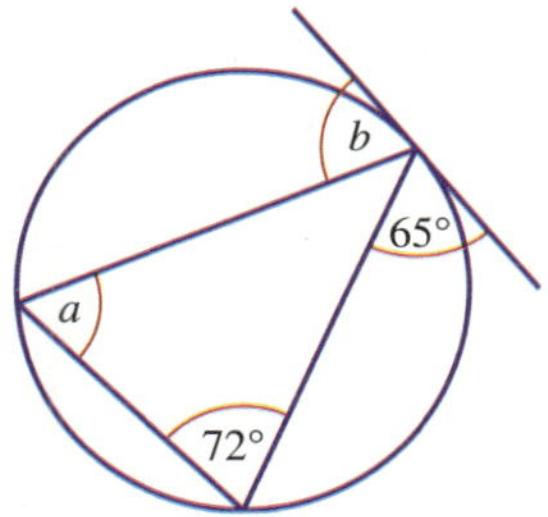

Solution 3

$a = 65°$	Alternate segment theorem.
$b = 72°$	Alternate segment theorem.

Exercise B

In this exercise the diagrams are not drawn accurately.

1 Write down the value of the angles marked with a letter.

a

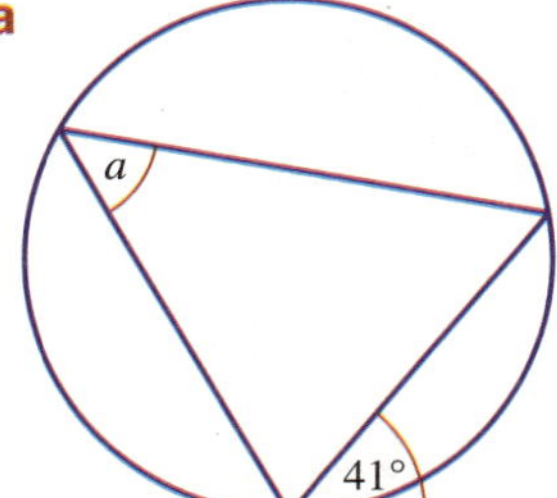

b

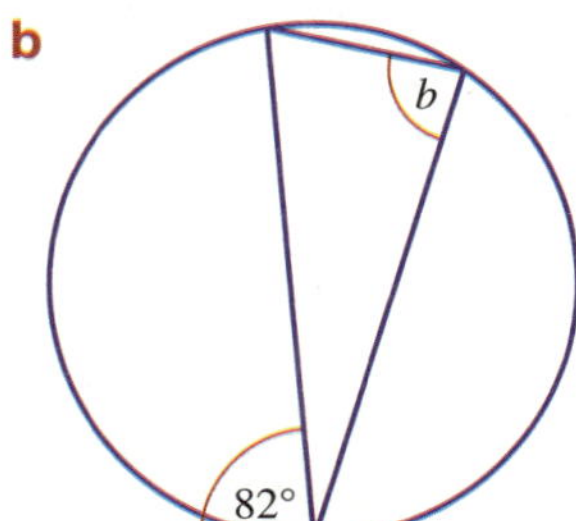

2 Write down the value of angles c and d. Give a reason for your answers.

a

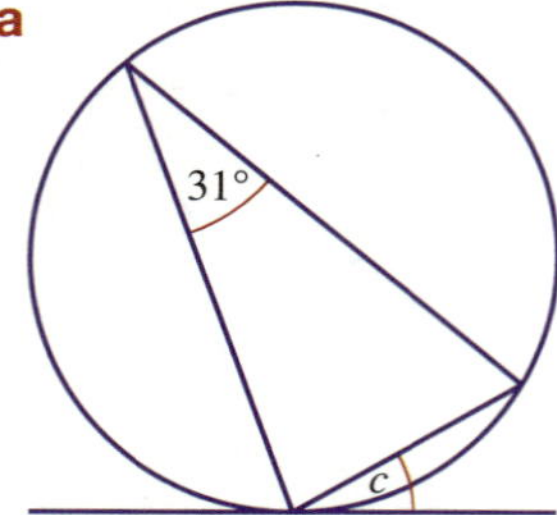

b

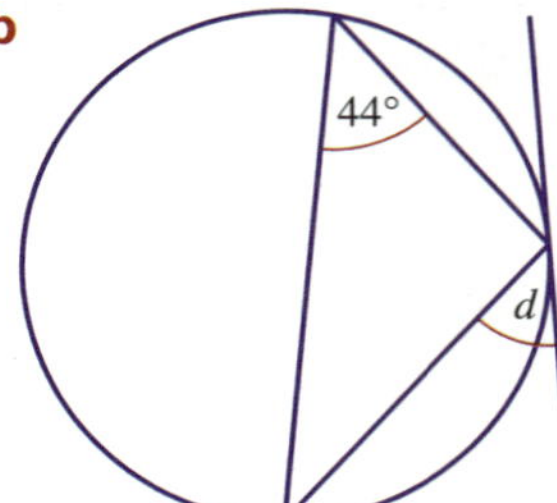

3 The diagram shows a tangent to a circle of centre O.

a Write down the value of e. Give a reason for your answer.

b Work out the value of f. Give a reason for your answer.

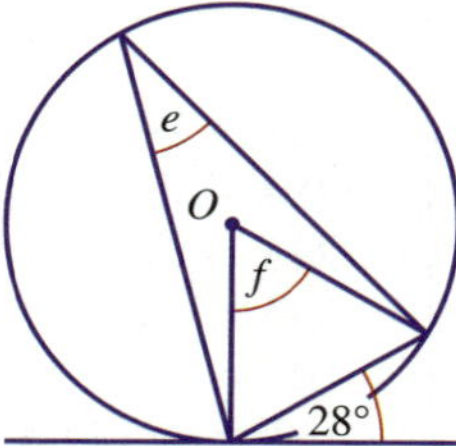

4 Work out the value of y.

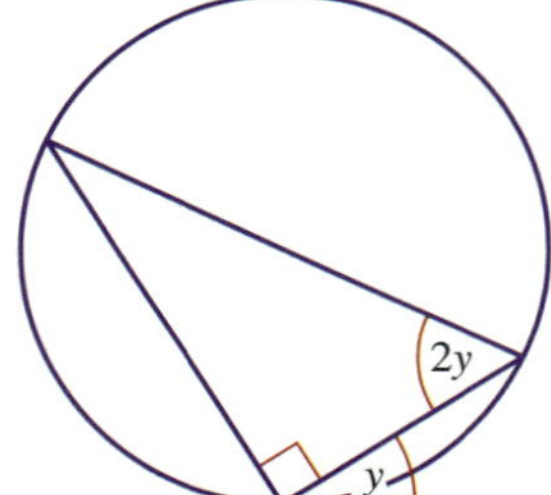

5 The diagram shows a tangent to a circle of centre O.

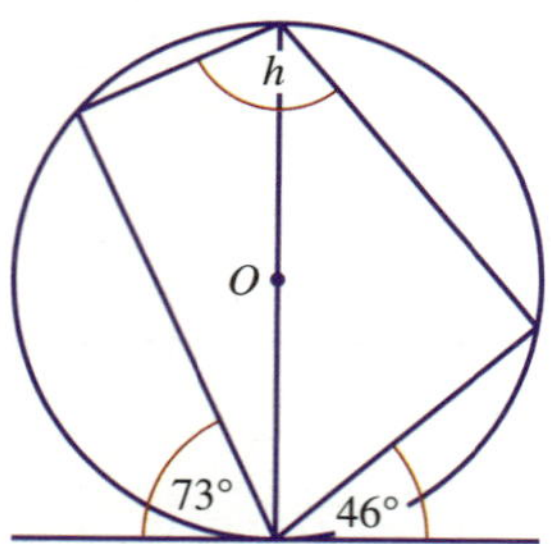

Calculate angle h.

6 In the diagram on the right, the lines marked with arrows are parallel.
Calculate the angle marked i.

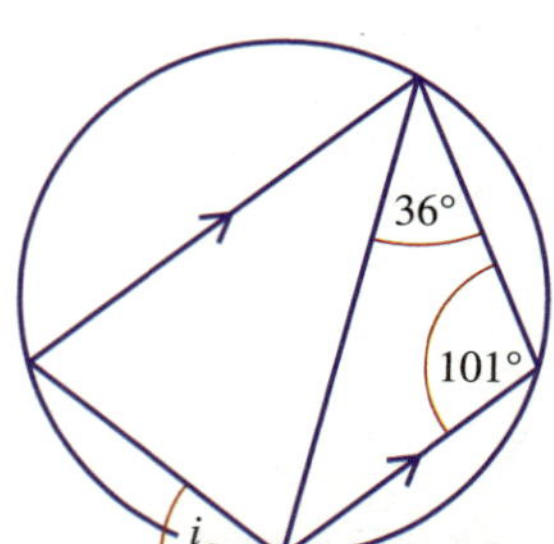

7 A tangent is drawn to a circle of centre O.

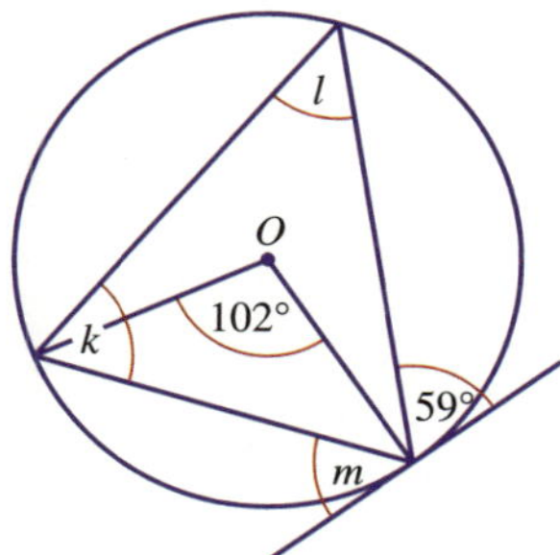

Calculate the size of angles k, l and m giving reasons for your answers.

8 Calculate the sizes of angles p, q and r in the diagram below.

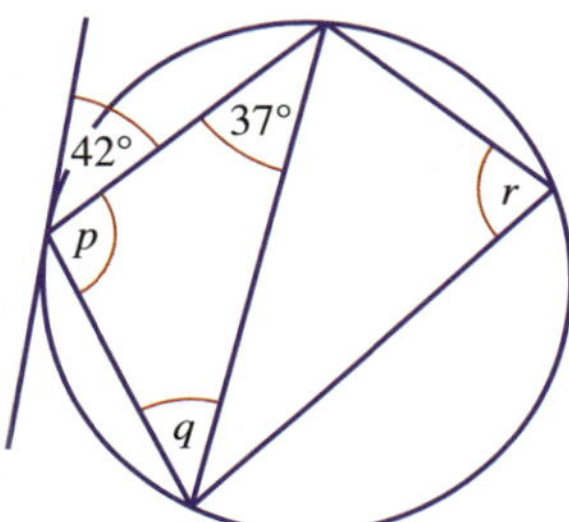

Chapter summary

- The angle in a semicircle is 90°

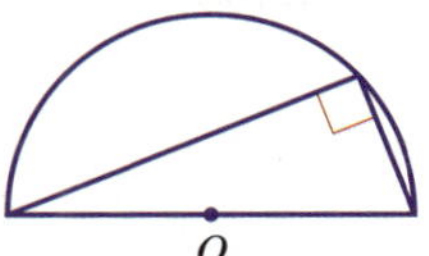

- The angle at the centre of a circle is twice the angle at the circumference of the circle.

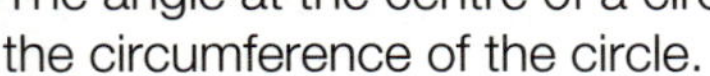

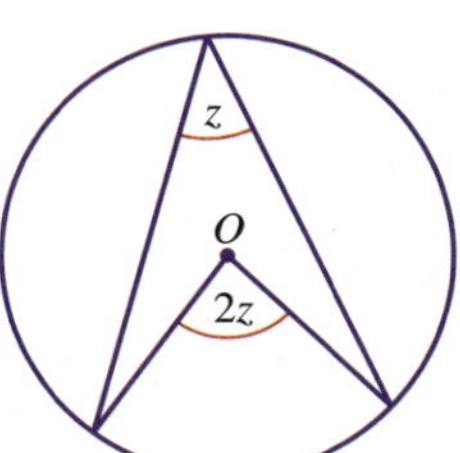

- Angles on the same arc (or chord) are equal.

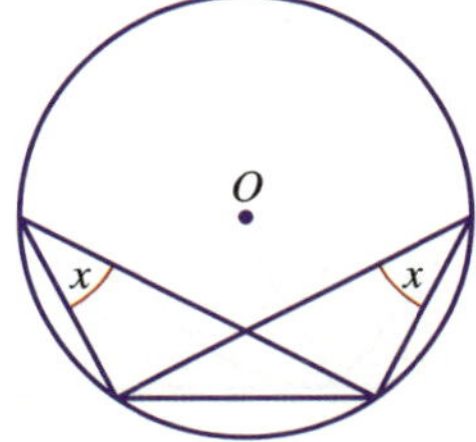

- A cyclic quadrilateral is a quadrilateral drawn inside a circle with all four vertices on the circumference.

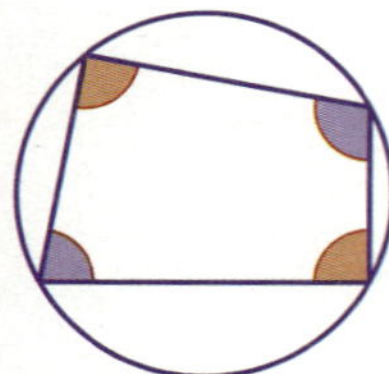

- Opposite angles in a cyclic quadrilateral add up to 180°
- The proofs of these facts need to be known.
- The angle between the tangent to the circle and the radius at this point is 90°.

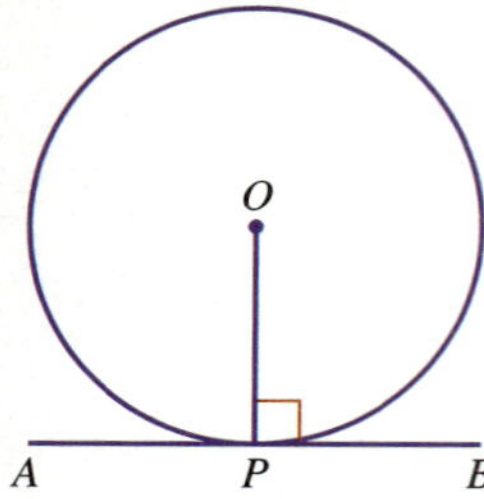

- Tangents drawn to a circle from the same point are always equal.

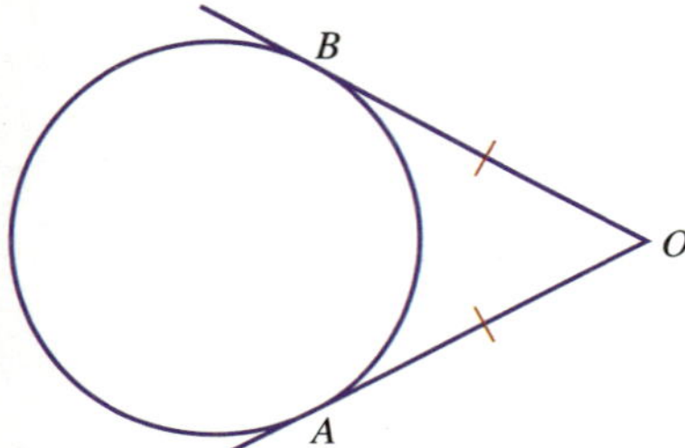

- The perpendicular from the centre of a circle to a chord bisects the chord.

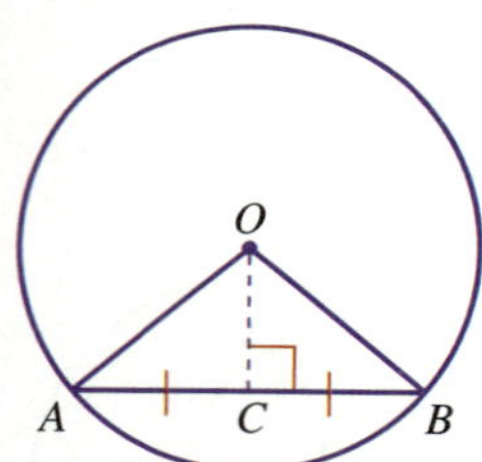

- The angle between a tangent and a chord is equal to any angle in the alternate segment formed from the same chord.
  This is known as the alternate segment theorem.

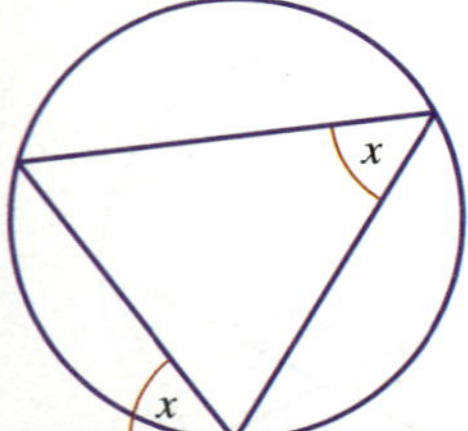

Chapter review

1 **a** The diagram shows a circle with centre O.

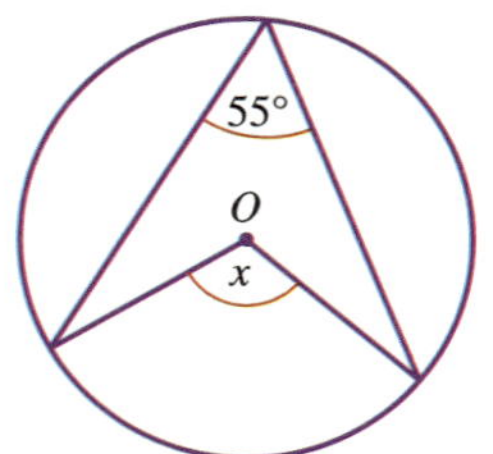

Work out the size of the angle marked x.

b The diagram on the right shows a different circle with centre O.
Work out the size of the angle marked y.

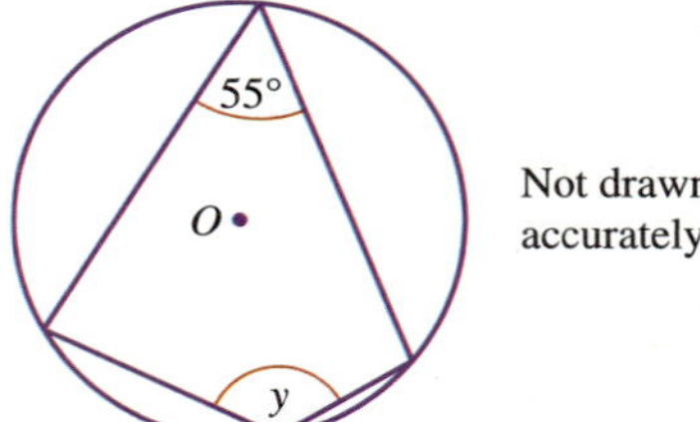

2 **a** O is the centre of the circle.

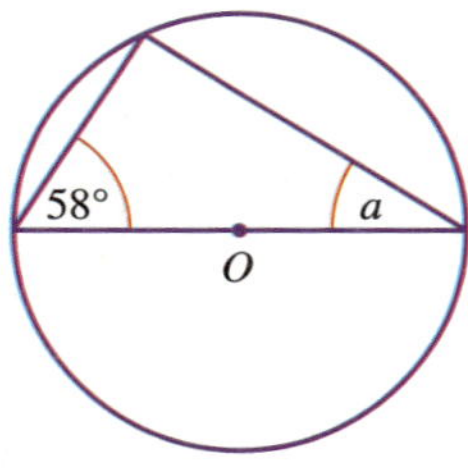

Calculate the value of a.

b O is the centre of the circle.
A, B, C and D are points on the circumference.
Angle $AOC = 146°$

i Calculate the value of x.

ii Calculate the value of y.

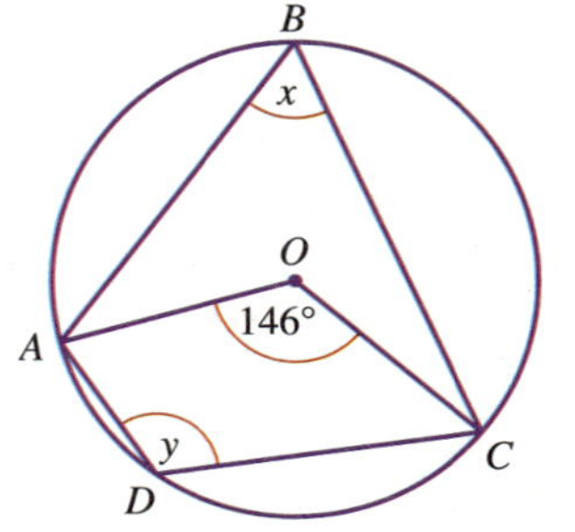

3 In the diagram on the right, points A, B, C and D lie on a circle.
$AB = BC$. Angle $ABC = 104°$
Explain why angle $BDC = 38°$

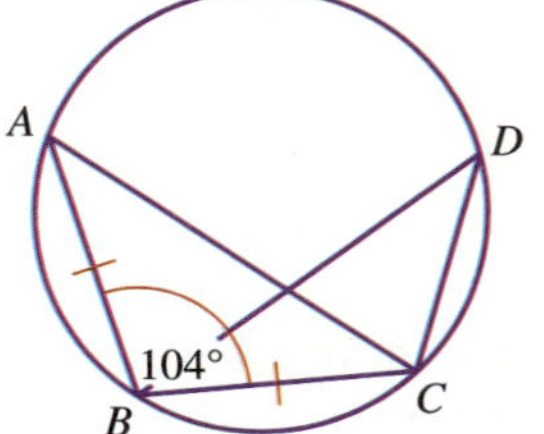

4 In the diagram below, PA and PB are tangents to the circle, whose centre is O. Prove that triangles OAP and OBP are congruent.

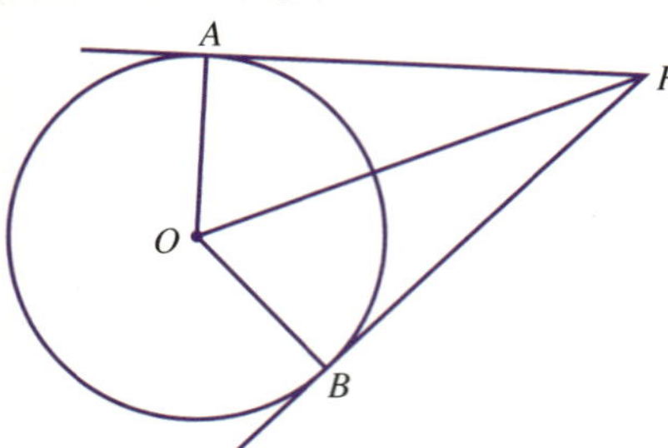

5 The figure shows a circle whose centre is at O. A, B, C and P are points on the circumference of the circle. Angle $CAO = x°$ and angle $BAO = y°$

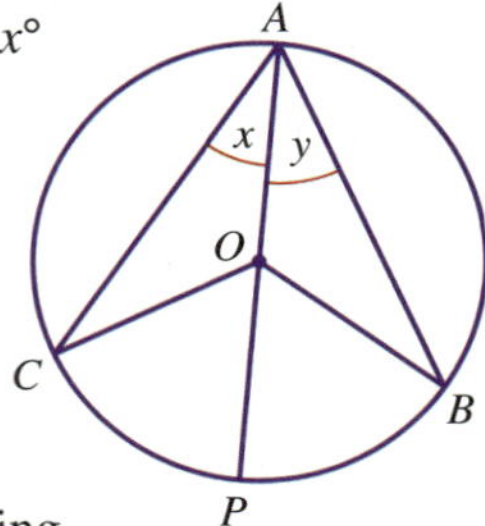

a Using only facts about angles in triangles, express angle AOC in terms of x. Explain your method.

b Hence write down, in terms of x and y, angle COB.

c What fact about angles in circles is proved by your answer to part **b**?

d What fact about angles in circles can be proved by making $(x + y)°$ equal to $90°$?

6 In the diagram on the right, AB is a diameter of the circle and O is the centre of the circle. Angle $BAC = 73°$

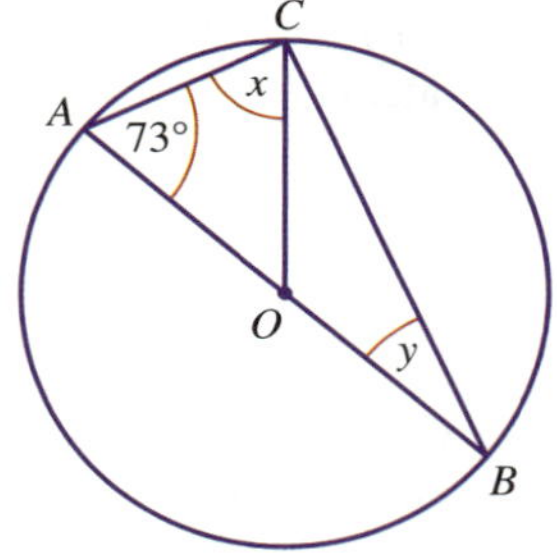

a Calculate the value of x, giving a reason for your answer.

b Calculate the value of y, giving a reason for your answer.

7 A, B and C are three points on the circumference of a circle, ABD is a straight line and the line DC is a tangent to the circle.
Angle $BAC = x°$ and angle $ACB = y°$
$AB = 7$ cm and $BD = 8$ cm.

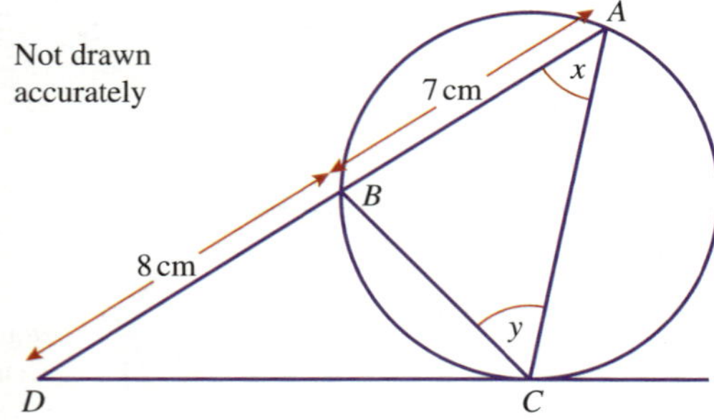

Find, in terms of x and y,

a angle BCD **b** angle DBC.

8 The diagram shows a circle, centre O.
TP is a tangent to the circle at P.
Angle $QPT = 85°$ and angle $QPR = 47°$

a Calculate the size of angle QOR.

b Calculate the size of angle ORP.

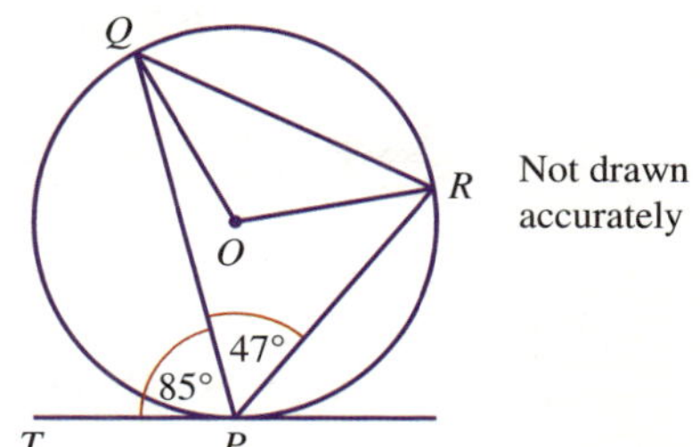

9 R, S and T are points on the circumference of the circle.
PRQ is the tangent to the circle at R.
Calculate the value of x.
Give a reason for each step of your working.

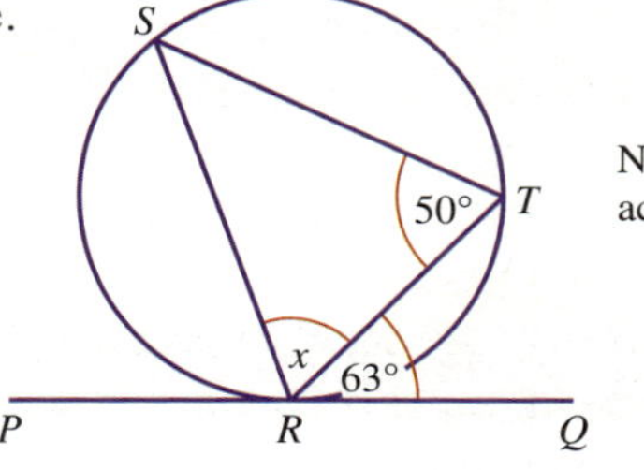

10 The diagram shows a cyclic quadrilateral $ABCD$.
The straight lines BA and CD are extended and meet at E.
$EA = AC$
Angle $ABC = 3x$
Angle $ADC = 6x$
Angle $DAC = 2x$

a Show that $x = 20°$

b Calculate the size of angle DAE.

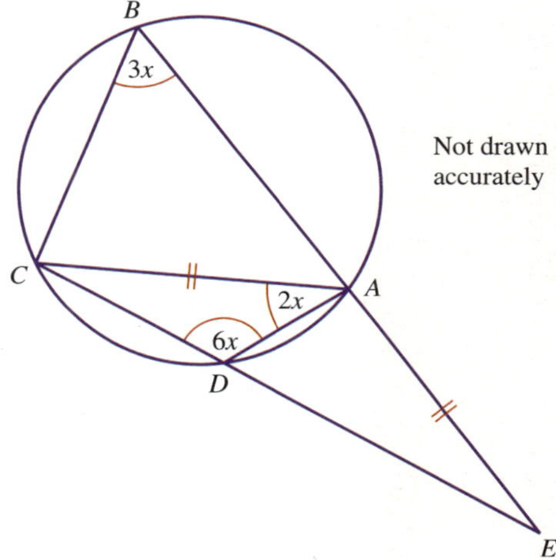

CHAPTER

36 Quadratic expressions and equations

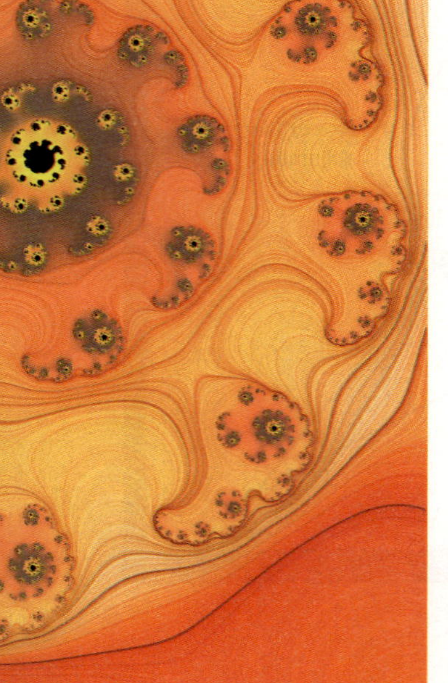

36.1 Solving by factorising

CAN YOU REMEMBER

- How to factorise a quadratic expression, including the special cases of the difference of two squares and perfect squares?

IN THIS SECTION YOU WILL

- Learn how to solve a quadratic equation by factorising.
- Solve problems by setting up and solving quadratic equations.

A *quadratic equation* is an equation of the form $ax^2 + bx + c = 0$, where $a \neq 0$

One way of solving a quadratic equation is by factorising the expression $ax^2 + bx + c$.

For example, $x^2 + 5x - 6 \equiv (x + 6)(x - 1)$

So the equation $x^2 + 5x - 6 = 0$ is equivalent to $(x + 6)(x - 1) = 0$

For $(x + 6)(x - 1)$ to equal zero, either $(x + 6) = 0$ or $(x - 1) = 0$

This gives two solutions, $x = -6$ and $x = 1$

These solutions can be checked by substituting $x = -6$ and $x = 1$ into $x^2 + 5x - 6$

Check: When $x = -6$, $x^2 + 5x - 6 = (-6)^2 + 5 \times (-6) - 6$
$= 36 + -30 - 6 = 0$ ✓

When $x = 1$, $x^2 + 5x - 6 = 1^2 + 5 \times 1 - 6$
$= 1 + 5 - 6 = 0$ ✓

Example 1

Solve $2x^2 - 5x = 0$

Solution 1

Step 1: Factorise $2x^2 - 5x$

$2x^2 - 5x \equiv x(2x - 5)$

Step 2: Rewrite the quadratic equation in factorised form.

$x(2x - 5) = 0$

Step 3: Make each expression in the product equal to zero.

Either $x = 0$ or $2x - 5 = 0$ so $2x = 5$, giving $x = 2.5$

Check: When $x = 0$, $2x^2 - 5x = 2 \times (0)^2 - 5 \times (0) = 0$ ✓

When $x = 2.5$, $2x^2 - 5x = 2 \times (2.5)^2 - 5 \times (2.5)$
$= 12.5 - 12.5 = 0$ ✓

The solutions of $2x^2 - 5x = 0$ are $x = 0$ and $x = 2.5$

Example 2

Solve $x^2 - 6x + 9 = 0$

Solution 2

Step 1: Factorise $x^2 - 6x + 9 = 0$

Method 1 $x^2 - 6x + 9 \equiv x^2 - 2 \times 3 \times x + 3^2$

$x^2 - 6x + 9 \equiv (x - 3)^2$

This is a perfect square.

Method 2 $x^2 - 6x + 9 \equiv (x - p)(x + q)$

$p + q = -6$ and $pq = 9$

$p + q$ is negative and pq is positive, so both p and q are negative.

p	q	pq	$p + q$
-3	-3	$-3 \times -3 = 9$ ✓	$-3 + -3 = -6$ ✓

So $p = q = -3$

So $x^2 - 6x + 9 \equiv (x - 3)^2$

Step 2: Rewrite the quadratic equation in factorised form:

$(x - 3)^2 = 0$

Step 3: Make each expression in the product equal to zero.

$x - 3 = 0$, so $x = 3$

When the quadratic expression is a perfect square there is only one solution.

Check: When $x = 3$, $x^2 - 6x + 9 = 3^2 - 6 \times 3 + 9 = 9 - 18 + 9 = 0$ ✓

The solution of $x^2 - 6x + 9 = 0$ is $x = 3$

Example 3

Solve: **a** $2x^2 - 9x + 10 = 0$ **b** $9x^2 - 4 = 0$

Solution 3

a **Step 1:** $2x^2 - 9x + 10 \equiv (2x + p)(x + q)$

$p + 2q = -9$ and $pq = 10$

$p + 2q$ is negative and pq is positive, so both p and q are negative.

The possible pairs of values of p and q are:

$\times$	$2x$	p
x	$2x^2$	px
q	$2qx$	pq

p	q	$pq (=10)$	$p + 2q$
-1	-10	$-1 \times -10 = 10$	$-1 + 2 \times -10 = -21$ ✗
-10	-1	$-10 \times -1 = 10$	$-10 + 2 \times -1 = -12$ ✗
-2	-5	$-2 \times -5 = 10$	$-2 + 2 \times -5 = -12$ ✗
-5	-2	$-5 \times -2 = 10$	$-5 + 2 \times -2 = -9$ ✓

$p = -5$ and $q = -2$

So $2x^2 - 9x + 10 \equiv (2x - 5)(x - 2)$

Step 2: $(2x - 5)(x - 2) = 0$

Step 3: Either $2x - 5 = 0$, so $2x = 5$ and $x = 2.5$ or $x - 2 = 0$, so $x = 2$

Check: When $x = 2.5$, $2x^2 - 9x + 10 = 2 \times 2.5^2 - 9 \times 2.5 + 10$

$= 12.5 - 22.5 + 10 = 0$ ✓

When $x = 2$, $2x^2 - 9x + 10 = 2 \times 2^2 - 9 \times 2 + 10 = 8 - 18 + 10 = 0$ ✓

The solutions of $2x^2 - 9x + 10 = 0$ are $x = 2.5$ and $x = 2$

b **Step 1:** $9x^2 - 4 \equiv (3x)^2 - 2^2 \equiv (3x - 2)(3x + 2)$ This is the difference of two squares.

Step 2: $(3x - 2)(3x + 2) = 0$

Step 3: Either $(3x - 2) = 0$, so $3x = 2$ and $x = \frac{2}{3}$

or $(3x + 2) = 0$, so $3x = -2$ and $x = -\frac{2}{3}$

Check: When $x = \frac{2}{3}$, $9x^2 - 4 = 9 \times \left(\frac{2}{3}\right)^2 - 4 = 9 \times \frac{4}{9} - 4 = 0$ ✓

When $x = -\frac{2}{3}$, $9x^2 - 4 = 9 \times \left(-\frac{2}{3}\right)^2 - 4 = 9 \times \frac{4}{9} - 4 = 0$ ✓

Exercise A

1 Solve the following quadratic equations.

a $x^2 - x = 0$ **b** $x^2 - 2x = 0$ **c** $x^2 - 5x = 0$
d $x^2 + x = 0$ **e** $x^2 + 3x = 0$ **f** $x^2 + 6x = 0$
g $2x^2 - x = 0$ **h** $3x^2 - 2x = 0$ **i** $3x^2 - 8x = 0$
j $6x^2 + x = 0$ **k** $5x^2 + 3x = 0$ **l** $10x^2 + 7x = 0$
m $x^2 - \frac{1}{3}x = 0$ **n** $\frac{1}{2}x^2 + x = 0$ **o** $\frac{1}{2}x^2 - \frac{1}{5}x = 0$

2 Solve the following quadratic equations.

a $(x - 1)(x - 2) = 0$ **b** $(y - 6)(y - 4) = 0$ **c** $(z + 8)(z - 1) = 0$
d $(x - 7)(x + 2) = 0$ **e** $(2t - 1)(t + 4) = 0$ **f** $(2x - 3)(3x + 4) = 0$
g $(6x - 1)(6x + 1) = 0$ **h** $(4w + 7)(2w - 9) = 0$

3 Solve the following equations.

a $q^2 + 5q + 6 = 0$ **b** $r^2 + 3r + 2 = 0$ **c** $s^2 + 9s + 8 = 0$
d $t^2 + 2t + 1 = 0$ **e** $u^2 + 9u + 20 = 0$ **f** $v^2 + 8v + 16 = 0$
g $w^2 + 4w + 4 = 0$ **h** $x^2 + 11x + 30 = 0$ **i** $y^2 + 11y + 28 = 0$
j $z^2 + 12z + 35 = 0$

4 Solve the following equations.

a $x^2 - 5x + 4 = 0$ **b** $x^2 - 6x + 5 = 0$ **c** $x^2 - 2x + 1 = 0$
d $x^2 - 10x + 25 = 0$ **e** $x^2 + 5x - 6 = 0$ **f** $x^2 - 4x - 12 = 0$
g $x^2 - 7x - 30 = 0$ **h** $x^2 + x - 12 = 0$ **i** $x^2 - x + 56 = 0$
j $x^2 + 7x - 18 = 0$

5 Solve the following equations.

a $x^2 + 5x = 0$ **b** $7x^2 - 2x = 0$ **c** $2x^2 - \frac{1}{4}x = 0$
d $x^2 + 12x + 27 = 0$ **e** $x^2 - 7x + 10 = 0$ **f** $x^2 + 3x - 18 = 0$
g $x^2 - 14x - 15 = 0$ **h** $x^2 - 9 = 0$ **i** $x^2 - 100 = 0$
j $x^2 - 1 = 0$ **k** $x^2 - 64 = 0$

6 Solve the following equations.

a $2x^2 + 5x + 3 = 0$ **b** $3x^2 + 5x + 2 = 0$ **c** $2x^2 + 9x + 10 = 0$
d $5x^2 + 6x + 1 = 0$ **e** $2x^2 + 7x + 3 = 0$ **f** $3x^2 + 19x + 20 = 0$
g $3x^2 + 10x + 7 = 0$ **h** $7x^2 + 23x + 6 = 0$ **i** $4x^2 + 4x + 1 = 0$
j $4x^2 + 5x + 1 = 0$

7 Solve the following equations.

a $2a^2 - 5a + 2 = 0$ **b** $3b^2 - 14b + 15 = 0$ **c** $5c^2 - 6c + 1 = 0$
d $6d^2 - 5d + 1 = 0$ **e** $2e^2 - 7e - 4 = 0$ **f** $3f^2 + 13f - 10 = 0$
g $4g^2 - 1 = 0$ **h** $25h^2 - 4 = 0$ **i** $15i^2 - 2i - 1 = 0$
j $2j^2 + 3j - 20 = 0$ **k** $3k^2 + 17k - 6 = 0$ **l** $2l^2 - l - 21 = 0$
m $5m^2 + 12m - 9 = 0$ **n** $4n^2 - 9 = 0$ **o** $6p^2 + p - 1 = 0$
p $7q^2 + 60q - 27 = 0$

8 Solve the following quadratic equations.

a $6x^2 + 5x - 6 = 0$ **b** $15x^2 - 17x - 4 = 0$
c $8x^2 - 6x - 9 = 0$ **d** $9x^2 - 9x - 28 = 0$

9 Solve the following equations.

a $x^2 - 12x = 0$ **b** $5x^2 + x = 0$ **c** $(x + 6)(2x - 1) = 0$
d $(3x + 11)(5x - 4) = 0$ **e** $x^2 + 17x + 72 = 0$ **f** $x^2 - 12x + 32 = 0$
g $x^2 + 2x - 63 = 0$ **h** $x^2 - x - 42 = 0$ **i** $3x^2 - 7x + 4 = 0$
j $11x^2 + 54x - 5 = 0$ **k** $2x^2 - 9x - 56 = 0$ **l** $15x^2 + 16x + 4 = 0$
m $25x^2 - 9 = 0$ **n** $49x^2 - 25 = 0$

Quadratic equations must always be rearranged to the form $ax^2 + bx + c = 0$ before they can be solved.

Example 4

The equation $\frac{3}{x} = 2x - 5$ can be rearranged to give an equation of the form $ax^2 + bx + c = 0$

Use this to solve the equation $\frac{3}{x} = 2x - 5$

Solution 4

$\frac{3}{x} = 2x - 5$ — Multiply both sides by x.

$3 = x(2x - 5)$ — Expand brackets on right hand side.

$3 = 2x^2 - 5x$ — Subtract 3 from both sides.

$0 = 2x^2 - 5x - 3$

$2x^2 - 5x - 3 \equiv (2x + 1)(x - 3)$

$(2x + 1)(x - 3) = 0$

Either $2x + 1 = 0$, so $x = -\frac{1}{2}$ or $x - 3 = 0$, so $x = 3$

Check: When $x = -\frac{1}{2}$, $\frac{3}{x} = 3 \div -\frac{1}{2} = 3 \times -2 = -6$

$$2x - 5 = 2 \times \left(-\frac{1}{2}\right) - 5 = -1 - 5 = -6 \checkmark$$

When $x = 3$, $\frac{3}{x} = 3 \div 3 = 1$

$$2x - 5 = 2 \times 3 - 5 = 6 - 5 = 1 \checkmark$$

So the solutions of the equation $\frac{3}{x} = 2x - 5$ are $x = -\frac{1}{2}$ and $x = 3$

Many problems can be solved by setting up and then solving a quadratic equation.
Sometimes, one of the solutions of the quadratic equation is not a sensible solution to the problem.
This should be explained in the solution.

Example 5

The hypotenuse of a right-angled triangle is 4 cm longer than the shortest side and 2 cm longer than the other side.
Find the lengths of the sides.

Solution 5

Step 1: Show the information on a diagram and set up the equation.

Let the shortest side $= x$ cm — Call the unknown quantity x.

hypotenuse $= (x + 4)$ cm — The hypotenuse is 4 cm longer than the shortest side.

other side $= (x + 2)$ cm — The hypotenuse is 2 cm longer than the other side.

$(x + 4)^2 = x^2 + (x + 2)^2$ — Using Pythagoras' theorem.

Step 2: Rearrange the equation to the form $ax^2 + bx + c = 0$

$(x + 4)^2 \equiv x^2 + 8x + 16$ — Expanding the brackets.

$(x + 2)^2 \equiv x^2 + 4x + 4$

So $x^2 + 8x + 16 = x^2 + x^2 + 4x + 4$ — Rewriting the equation.

$x^2 - 4x - 12 = 0$ — Rearranging.

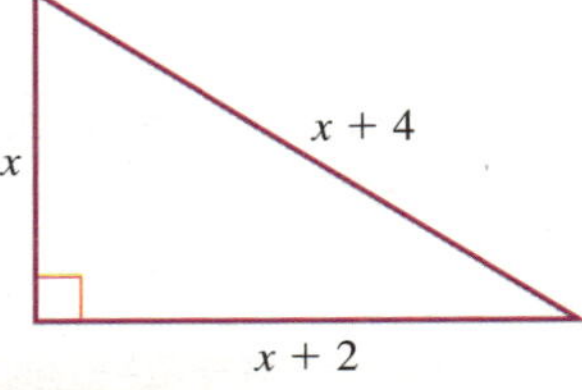

Step 3: Solve the equation. — Factorising.

$x^2 - 4x - 12 = 0$

$x^2 - 4x - 12 = (x + p)(x + q)$ — $pq = -12$ and $p + q = -4$, $p = -6$ and $q = 2$

$(x - 6)(x + 2) = 0$

Either $(x - 6) = 0$, so $x = 6$ or $(x + 2) = 0$, so $x = -2$

Step 4: Solve the problem.

The triangle cannot have a negative length, so $x = 6$ cm.

The sides of the triangle are 6 cm, 8 cm and 10 cm.

Check: Using Pythagoras' theorem, $10^2 = 8^2 + 6^2$

$100 = 64 + 36$ ✓

Exercise B

1 Solve each of the following equations.

a $x^2 = 6x - 5$
b $x^2 = x + 2$
c $2x^2 + 3x + 4 = x^2 + 2$
d $x^2 = 10 - 3x$
e $3x^2 + 7 = 2x^2 + 2x + 22$
f $3x^2 + 11x - 10 = x^2 + 2x + 8$
g $(x + 2)(x + 7) = 4(2x - 1)^2$
h $5x(x - 1) = 2(x^2 + x - 1)$

2 Solve each of the following equations.

a $x = \frac{(x + 6)}{x}$
b $2x - 5 = \frac{12}{x}$
c $x = \frac{6x - 8}{x}$
d $x - 4 = -\frac{3}{x}$
e $x = \frac{1}{x}$
f $4x = \frac{5}{x + 2}$
g $-\frac{7x}{2} = 3x^2 + 1$
h $4x = \frac{3}{x + 1}$

3 The sum of two numbers is 17

a One of the numbers is x.
Write an expression for the other number in terms of x.

b The product of the two numbers is 60
Show that $x^2 - 17x + 60 = 0$

c Solve $x^2 - 17x + 60 = 0$ and find the two numbers.

4 Two numbers differ by 5

The product of the two numbers is $18\frac{3}{4}$

a Show that $4x^2 - 20x - 75 = 0$, where x is the bigger of the two numbers.

b Solve $4x^2 - 20x - 75 = 0$ to find the two numbers.

5 Rectangle A has length $(3x + 20)$ cm and width $(x + 4)$ cm.
Rectangle B has length $(5x - 4)$ cm and width $(x + 4)$ cm.

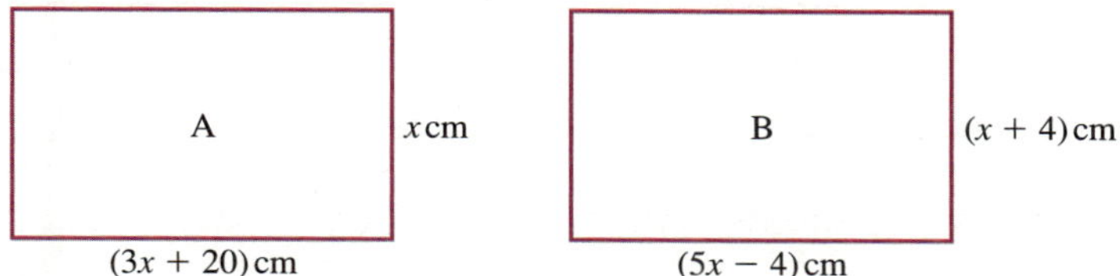

The areas of rectangles A and B are equal.
Calculate the value of x.

6 The diagram shows a right-angled triangle.

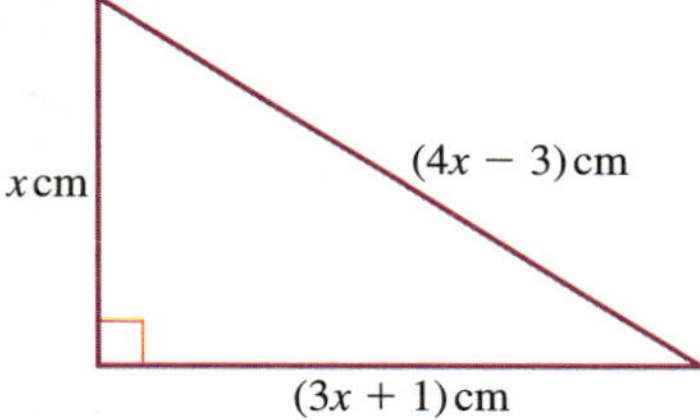

The lengths of the sides are x cm, $3(x + 1)$ cm and $(4x - 3)$ cm.
Find the value of x.

7 Shanti is 6 years older than Trevor.
David is two years younger than Shanti.
Let Trevor's age = x years.
The product of David and Trevor's age is 45

a Show that $x^2 + 4x - 45 = 0$

b Find Shanti's age.

8 Mason, Ali and Paul go fishing.
Mason catches twice as many fish as Paul.
The number of fish that Ali catches is the product of the numbers that Mason and Paul catch.
Paul catches x fish.
Altogether Mason, Ali and Paul catch 27 fish.

a Show that $2x^2 + 3x - 27 = 0$

b How many fish did Mason catch?

36.2 Completing the square and the quadratic formula

CAN YOU REMEMBER

- How to recognise quadratic expressions that are perfect squares?
- How to change a quadratic expression of the form $ax^2 + bx + c$ to the form $(x + p)^2 + q$?
- How to simplify surds?

IN THIS SECTION YOU WILL

- Learn how to solve quadratic equations by completing the square.
- Learn how to solve quadratic equations using the quadratic formula.
- Extend skills in using quadratic equations to solve problems.

Quadratic equations can involve quadratic expressions that cannot be factorised.
However, many of these equations have solutions. This can be seen from their graphs.
For example $x^2 + 2x - 1$ cannot be factorised.
The graph of $x^2 + 2x - 1$ is shown.
There are two solutions, which can be estimated from the graph.
These solutions can also be found by *completing the square*.
This method uses identities of the form $x^2 + bx + c \equiv (x + p)^2 + q$.

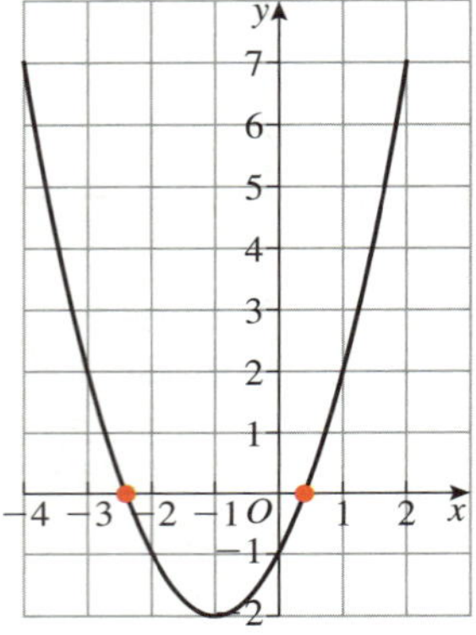

Example 1

Solve the equation $x^2 + 2x - 1$ by rewriting $x^2 + 2x - 1$ in the form $(x + p)^2 + q$.
Give your answer to an accuracy of two decimal places.

Solution 1

Step 1: Rewrite $x^2 + 2x - 1$ in the form $(x + p)^2 + q$.
Look at $x^2 + \mathbf{2}x$

$\frac{1}{2}$ of $\mathbf{2} = \mathbf{1}$ and $(x + \mathbf{1})^2 \equiv x^2 + 2x + 1$

$x^2 + 2x - 1 \equiv x^2 + 2x + 1 - 2$
So $x^2 + 2x - 1 \equiv (x + 1)^2 - 2$

Step 2: Rewrite the equation using $x^2 + 2x - 1 \equiv (x + 1)^2 - 2$
$(x + 1)^2 - 2 = 0$

Step 3: Solve the equation.
$(x + 1)^2 - 2 = 0$ — Add 2 to both sides.
$(x + 1)^2 = 2$ — Take the square root of both sides.
The square root of 2 is both $+\sqrt{2}$ and $-\sqrt{2}$ because $(\sqrt{2})^2 = (-\sqrt{2})^2 = 2$
$+\sqrt{2}$ and $-\sqrt{2}$ can be written $\pm\sqrt{2}$
$x + 1 = \pm\sqrt{2}$ — Subtract 1 from both sides.
$x = -1 \pm\sqrt{2}$
Either $x = -1 - 1.41 = -2.41$ or $x = -1 + 1.41 = 0.41$
The solutions of $x^2 + 2x - 1 = 0$ to two decimal places are $x = -2.41$ and 0.41

Any quadratic equation written in the form $ax^2 + bx + c = 0$ can be solved using the *quadratic formula*

$$x = \frac{-b \pm \sqrt{b^2 - 4ac}}{2a}$$

The formula is derived from $ax^2 + bx + c = 0$ by completing the square.
Solutions to quadratic equations found by completing the square or using the quadratic formula can be given either in surd form or to a given degree of accuracy, for example two decimal places.

Example 2

a Solve the equation $x^2 + 4x - 2 = 0$
Give your answer in surd form.

b Solve the equation $3x^2 = 2x + 2$
Give your answer to an accuracy of two decimal places.

Solution 2

a $x^2 + 4x - 2 = 0$

Step 1: Write down the values of a, b and c.
In the equation $x^2 + 4x - 2 = 0$, $a = 1$, $b = 4$ and $c = -2$

Step 2: Substitute the values of a, b and c in the quadratic formula.

$$x = \frac{-4 \pm \sqrt{4^2 - 4 \times 1 \times (-2)}}{2 \times 1}$$

Step 3: Evaluate the formula

$$x = \frac{-4 \pm \sqrt{16 + 8}}{2}$$

$$x = \frac{-4 \pm \sqrt{24}}{2}$$

$\sqrt{24} = \sqrt{(4 \times 6)} = \sqrt{4} \times \sqrt{6} = 2\sqrt{6}$

$$x = \frac{-4 \pm 2\sqrt{6}}{2}$$

Divide numerator and denominator by 2

$x = -2 \pm \sqrt{6}$

The solutions of $x^2 + 4x - 2 = 0$ in surd form are $x = -2 + \sqrt{6}$ and $x = -2 - \sqrt{6}$

b $3x^2 = 2x + 2$

Step 1: Rewrite the equation in the form $ax^2 + bx + c = 0$

$3x^2 = 2x + 2$

Subtract $2x$ and 2 from both sides

$3x^2 - 2x - 2 = 0$

Step 2: Write down the values of a, b and c.
$a = 3$, $b = -2$ and $c = -2$

Step 3: Substitute the values of a, b and c in the quadratic formula

$$x = \frac{-(-2) \pm \sqrt{(-2)^2 - 4 \times 3 \times (-2)}}{2 \times 3}$$

Step 4: Evaluate the formula.

$$x = \frac{-4 \pm \sqrt{28}}{6} = \frac{-4 \pm 5.2915\ldots}{6}$$

Either $x = (-4 - 5.2915\ldots) \div 6 = -1.548\ldots$ or $x = (-4 + 5.2915\ldots) \div 6 = 0.215\ldots$
The solutions of $3x^2 - 2x - 2 = 0$ to two decimal places are $x = -1.55$ and $x = 0.22$

Exercise A

1 **a** **i** Write $x^2 + 2x - 3$ in the form $(x + p)^2 + q$.
ii Hence, solve the equation $x^2 + 2x - 3 = 0$
b **i** Find the values of a and b such that $x^2 + 6x - 16 \equiv (x + a)^2 + b$.
ii Hence, solve the equation $x^2 + 6x - 16 = 0$
c Solve the equation $x^2 + 5x - 24 = 0$ by first writing $x^2 + 5x - 24$ in the form $(x + p)^2 + q$.

2 Solve the equations by first rewriting them in the form $(x + p)^2 + q = 0$
Give your answers in surd form.
a $x^2 + 2x - 4 = 0$ **b** $x^2 + 4x + 1 = 0$ **c** $x^2 + 2x - 7 = 0$
d $x^2 + 6x + 9 = 0$ **e** $x^2 + 8x - 6 = 0$ **f** $x^2 + 4x - 6 = 0$
g $x^2 + 6x + 1 = 0$ **h** $x^2 + 10x + 15 = 0$ **i** $x^2 + 10x - 1 = 0$
j $x^2 + 2x - 9 = 0$

3 Use the quadratic formula to solve the quadratic equations in question **2**
Leave your answers in surd form.

4 Solve the following equations by factorising.
Check each solution using the quadratic formula.
a $2x^2 - 3x - 5 = 0$ **b** $2x^2 - 5x + 2 = 0$
c $3x^2 + 2x - 1 = 0$ **d** $5x^2 + 8x + 3 = 0$

5 Use the quadratic formula to solve each of the following quadratic equations.
Give your answers in surd form.
a $4x^2 - 3x - 2 = 0$ **b** $3x^2 + 5x + 1 = 0$ **c** $2x^2 - x - 3 = 0$
d $x^2 + x - 4 = 0$ **e** $2x^2 - 5x - 1 = 0$ **f** $2x^2 - 5x + 1 = 0$
g $x^2 - 5x + 3 = 0$ **h** $3x^2 + 3x - 2 = 0$ **i** $5x^2 + 8x + 2 = 0$
j $3x^2 - 4x - 2 = 0$ **k** $4x^2 - 2x - 1 = 0$ **l** $7x^2 - 8x + 2 = 0$

6 Solve these quadratic equations using the method of completing the square.
Give your answers to two decimal places.
a $x^2 - 7x + 3 = 0$ **b** $x^2 + 6x + 2 = 0$ **c** $x^2 - 9x - 3 = 0$
d $x^2 - 4x + 1 = 0$ **e** $x^2 - 8x + 4 = 0$ **f** $x^2 + 7x - 7 = 0$
g $x^2 - x - 10 = 0$ **h** $x^2 + 2x - 9 = 0$ **i** $x^2 + 9x + 5 = 0$
j $x^2 + 11x + 6 = 0$ **k** $x^2 + 13x + 10 = 0$ **l** $x^2 - 15x + 20 = 0$

7 Solve these quadratic equations using the quadratic formula.
Give your answers to two decimal places.
a $2x^2 - 6x + 3 = 0$ **b** $2x^2 + x - 8 = 0$ **c** $3x^2 - 4x + 1 = 0$
d $5x^2 - 2x - 1 = 0$ **e** $4x^2 - 9x + 4 = 0$ **f** $3x^2 - 6x + 2 = 0$
g $7x^2 - 12x + 4 = 0$ **h** $4x^2 - x - 6 = 0$ **i** $3x^2 + 7x + 2 = 0$
j $10x^2 - 8x - 1 = 0$ **k** $6x^2 - 2x - 7 = 0$ **l** $3x^2 + 7x + 3 = 0$

8 Solve these quadratic equations.
Give your answers to two decimal places where necessary.
a $x^2 = 3x - 1$ **b** $6x^2 + 6 = 13x$ **c** $2x^2 - 13x = 7$
d $x^2 = 1 + 4x$ **e** $3x^2 - 8 = 4x$ **f** $2(x^2 - 7) = 9x$
g $5(x^2 - 1) = 3x$ **h** $4(x^2 - 1) = 7x$ **i** $2x(x + 1) = 4$
j $5x(x - 2) = 6$ **k** $5(x^2 - 2) = 2(x^2 + 3x)$ **l** $2(x^2 - 5) = (x + 1)$
m $2(x - 3) = 7/x$ **n** $4(x - 2) = 1/x$ **o** $7x - 27 = 4/x$
p $5/3x = 4x + 2$

To complete the square for a quadratic equation where $a \neq 1$, rewrite $ax^2 + bx + c$ in the form $a(x + p)^2 + q$.

Example 3

a Show that $2x^2 - 8x - 3 \equiv 2(x - 2)^2 - 11$

b Hence, solve the equation $2x^2 - 8x - 3 = 0$
Give your answer to two decimal places.

Solution 3

a Rewriting $2x^2 - 8x - 3$ in the form $a(x + p)^2 + q$ gives

$2x^2 - 8x - 3 \equiv 2(x^2 - 4x) - 3$ — Complete the square for $x^2 - 4x$.

$\frac{1}{2}$ of $4 = 2$, $(x - 2)^2 \equiv x^2 - 4x + 4$ — $x^2 - 4x \equiv x^2 - 4x + 4 - 4$
$\equiv (x - 2)^2 - 4$

$2x^2 - 8x - 3 \equiv 2(x^2 - 4x) - 3$ — Substitute $x^2 - 4x \equiv (x - 2)^2 - 4$ in $2(x^2 - 4x) - 3$

$2x^2 - 8x - 3 \equiv 2((x^2 - 2^2) - 4) - 3$ — Expand the brackets.

$2x^2 - 8x - 3 \equiv 2(x - 2)^2 - 8 - 3 \equiv 2(x - 2)^2 - 11$

b $2x^2 - 8x - 3 = 0$ — Rewrite $2x^2 - 8x - 3$ as $2(x - 2)^2 - 11$

$2(x - 2)^2 - 11 = 0$ — Add 11 to both sides.

$2(x - 2)^2 = 11$ — Divide both sides by 2.

$(x - 2)^2 = \frac{11}{2} = 5.5$ — Take the square root of both sides.

$x - 2 = \pm\sqrt{5.5}$ — Add 2 to both sides.

$x = 2 \pm \sqrt{5.5}$

Either $x = 2 + \sqrt{5.5} = 4.35\ldots$ or $x = 2 - \sqrt{5.5} = -0.35\ldots$

The solutions are $x = 4.35$ and -0.35 to two decimal places.

Example 4

The length of a rectangle is 8 cm more than its width.
The area of the rectangle is 60 cm^2.
Calculate the perimeter of the rectangle to an accuracy of two decimal places.

Solution 4

Step 1: Show the information on a diagram and set up the equation.

Let the width of the rectangle $= x$ cm — Call the unknown quantity x.

Length $= (x + 8)$ cm — The length is 8 cm longer than the width.

Area $= x(x + 8) = 60$ — Area = length × width

Step 2: Rearrange the equation to the form $ax^2 + bx + c = 0$

$x(x + 8) \equiv x^2 + 8x$ — Expanding the brackets.

$x^2 + 8x = 60$ — Subtract 60 from both sides.

$x^2 + 8x - 60 = 0$

x

$x + 8$

Step 3: Solve the equation.
$a = 1$, $b = 8$ and $c = -60$

$$x = \frac{-8 \pm \sqrt{8^2 - 4 \times 1 \times (-60)}}{2 \times 1} = \frac{-8 \pm \sqrt{304}}{2}$$

$x = (-8 + 17.435) \div 2 = 4.7175$ and $x = (-8 - 17.435) \div 2 = -12.7175$
Step 4: Solve the problem.
The rectangle cannot have a negative length, so $x = 4.7175$ cm.
The sides of the rectangle are 4.7175 cm and 12.7175 cm.
Check: Area $= 4.7175 \times 12.7175 = 59.9948$ cm^2 ✓
The perimeter $= 2 \times 4.7175 + 2 \times 12.7175 = 9.435 + 25.435 = 34.87$
The perimeter $= 34.87$ cm to two decimal places.

Exercise B

1 **a** **i** Write $2x^2 - 4x - 1$ in the form $2(x + q)^2 + r$.
ii Hence, solve the equation $2x^2 - 4x - 1 = 0$
Give your answer to two decimal places.
b Repeat part **a** for $2x^2 + 12x - 3 = 0$
c **i** Show that $4x^2 - 8x - 1 \equiv 4(x - 1)^2 - 5$
ii Hence, solve the equation $4x^2 - 8x - 1 = 0$
Give your answer to two decimal places.

2 Solve the equation $(3x - 2)(x + 1) = (x - 1)(x + 1)$

3 Solve the equation $(3x - 2)^2 = (2x - 1)(2x + 1)$
Give your answer to an accuracy of two decimal places.

4 Rectangles A and B have equal area.

(3x − 5) cm
(x + 3) cm
A

(x + 7) cm
(x + 1) cm
B

Find the difference between the perimeters of the rectangles.

5 The diagram shows a rectangular flower bed with a path on three sides.
The flower bed is $(3x + 1)$ metres long and 3 metres wide.
The path is x metres wide.
The area of the flower bed is equal to the area of the path.
Work out the width of the path to an accuracy of two decimal places.

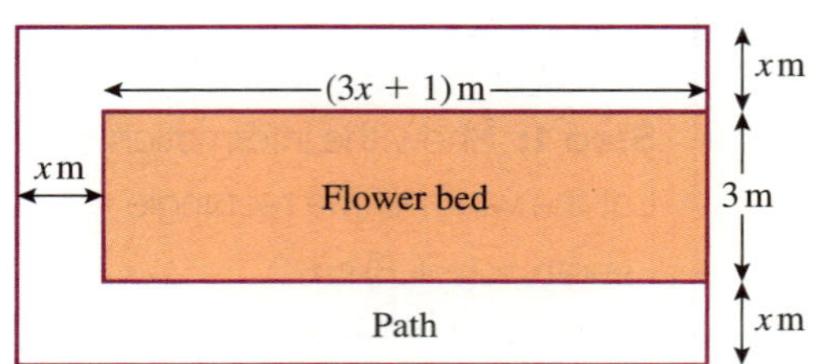

6 The sum of three consecutive square integers is 770
a If the first integer is x, show that $3x^2 + 6x - 765 = 0$
b Solve the equation $3x^2 + 6x - 765 = 0$ and find the three integers.

7 The diagram shows a right-angled triangle.
The lengths of the sides are $(2x + 5)$ cm, $(x + 3)$ cm and $(3x + 2)$ cm.

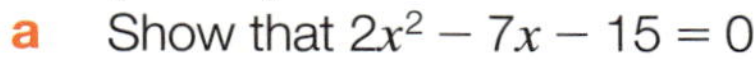

a Show that $2x^2 - 7x - 15 = 0$
b Solve the equation in part **a** to find the length of the hypotenuse.

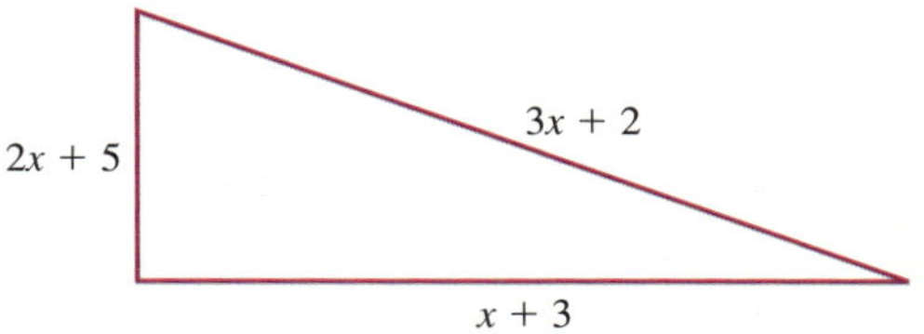

8 $ax^2 + bx + c \equiv 4x^2 - x + 5$
a Write down the values of a, b and c.
b **i** Work out the value of $b^2 - 4ac$.
ii Explain what your answer to part **i** tells you about the equation $4x^2 - x + 5 = 0$

9 Explain why it is not possible to solve the quadratic equation $3x^2 - x + 2 = 0$
What does this tell you about the graph of $y = 3x^2 - x + 2$?

36.3 Harder situations involving quadratics

CAN YOU REMEMBER

- How to solve quadratic equations including those that do not factorise?
- The meaning of least common multiple (LCM) and how to simplify a fraction?
- That the equation of a circle, centre the origin and radius, r, is $x^2 + y^2 = r^2$?

IN THIS SECTION YOU WILL

- Learn how to solve equations with fractions that have linear algebraic expressions in the denominators.
- Learn how to solve two simultaneous equations when one is linear and one is quadratic.
- Learn how to calculate the points of intersection of a line and a circle with centre the origin.

Some equations with algebraic fractions lead to quadratic equations.

Example 1

Solve the equation $\dfrac{3}{x+3} + \dfrac{2}{x-5} = 2$

Solution 1

The least common multiple (LCM) of the denominators is $(x + 3)(x - 5)$.
Multiply both sides by $(x + 3)(x - 5)$.

$$(x+3)(x-5) \times \frac{3}{x+3} + (x+3)(x-5) \times \frac{2}{x-5} = (x+3)(x-5) \times 2$$

Simplify each fraction.

$$\cancel{(x+3)}(x-5) \times \frac{3}{\cancel{(x+3)}} + (x+3)\cancel{(x-5)} \times \frac{2}{\cancel{(x-5)}} = (x+3)(x-5) \times 2$$

$3(x - 5) + 2(x + 3) = 2(x + 3)(x - 5)$ — Expand and collect like terms.
$3x - 15 + 2x + 6 = 2(x^2 - 2x - 15)$
$5x - 9 = 2x^2 - 4x - 30$ — Rearrange to the form $ax^2 + bx + c = 0$
$2x^2 - 9x - 21 = 0$ — Use the quadratic formula.

$a = 2$, $b = -9$ and $c = -21$

$$x = \frac{-(-9) \pm \sqrt{(-9)^2 - 4 \times 2 \times (-21)}}{2 \times 2} = \frac{9 \pm \sqrt{81 + 168}}{4} = \frac{9 \pm \sqrt{249}}{4}$$

$x = (9 + \sqrt{249}) \div 4 = 6.19$ or $(9 - \sqrt{249}) \div 4 = -1.69$

Check: When $x = 6.19$, $\frac{3}{(x+3)} + \frac{2}{(x-5)} = \frac{3}{9.19} + \frac{2}{1.19} = 2.00$ ✓

When $x = -1.69$, $\frac{3}{(x+3)} + \frac{2}{(x-5)} = \frac{3}{1.31} + \frac{2}{-6.69} = 1.99$ ✓

The solutions are $x = -1.69$ and $x = 6.19$ to an accuracy of two decimal places.

Example 2

A car and a van go on the same 96-kilometre journey.
The car's average speed is 16 km/h faster than the van's average speed.
The van takes $\frac{1}{2}$ hour longer than the car to complete the journey.

a The car travels at a speed of x km/h. Write down an expression in terms of x:
- **i** for the time the car takes to complete the journey
- **ii** for the time the van takes to complete the journey.

b Use your answers to **a** to show that $x^2 - 16x - 3072 = 0$

c Solve the equation $x^2 - 16x - 3072 = 0$
Use your solution to find how long the car takes to complete the journey.

Solution 2

a Time taken $= \frac{\text{distance}}{\text{average speed}}$

i Distance = 96 km and speed of car = x km/h

So the car takes $\frac{96}{x}$ hours.

ii Distance = 96 km and speed of van = $(x - 16)$ km/h

So the van takes $\frac{96}{(x-16)}$ hours.

b The van takes $\frac{1}{2}$ hour longer than the car.

$$\frac{96}{(x-16)} - \frac{96}{x} = \frac{1}{2}$$

The LCM of the denominators is $2x(x - 16)$

Multiply both sides by $2x(x - 16)$

$$2x(x-16) \times \frac{96}{(x-16)} - 2x(x-16) \times \frac{96}{x} = 2x(x-16) \times \frac{1}{2}$$

$$2x\cancel{(x-16)} \times \frac{96}{\cancel{(x-16)}} - 2\cancel{x}(x-16) \times \frac{96}{\cancel{x}} = \cancel{2}x(x-16) \times \frac{1}{\cancel{2}}$$

Simplify each fraction.

$2x \times 96 - 2(x - 16) \times 96 = x(x - 16)$
$192x - 192(x - 16) = x(x - 16)$

Expand and simplify.

$3072 = x^2 - 16x$

Subtract 3072 from both sides.

$0 = x^2 - 16x - 3072$
This can be written in the form $x^2 - 16x - 3072 = 0$

c Use the quadratic formula: $a = 1$, $b = -16$ and $c = -3072$

$$x = \frac{-(-16) \pm \sqrt{(-16)^2 - 4 \times 1 \times (-3072)}}{2 \times 1} = \frac{16 \pm \sqrt{256 + 12\,288}}{2}$$

$$= \frac{16 \pm 112}{2}$$

$x = (16 + 112) \div 2 = 64$ or $(16 - 112) \div 2 = -48$.

The car cannot have a negative speed, so $x = 64$ km/h.

The car completes the journey in $\frac{96}{64} = 1\frac{1}{2}$ hours

Check: Speed of car = 64 km/h, time taken = $1\frac{1}{2}$ hours

Speed of van = 64 − 16 = 48 km/h, time taken = $\frac{96}{48} = 2$ hours

The van takes $\frac{1}{2}$ hour longer than the car. ✓

$x^2 - 16x - 3072 \equiv (x - 64)(x + 48)$ could have been solved by factorising, but the factors are not easy to spot.

Exercise A

1 Solve the following equations.

a $\frac{4}{x} - \frac{5}{x+3} = 1$

b $\frac{8}{x} - \frac{6}{x+2} = 1$

c $\frac{2}{x} - \frac{4}{x+3} = 1$

d $\frac{4}{x} - \frac{1}{x-1} = 1$

e $\frac{9}{x} - \frac{8}{x+1} = 1$

f $\frac{8}{x-2} - \frac{15}{x+1} = 1$

g $\frac{6}{x+1} - \frac{1}{x-1} = 1$

h $\frac{5}{x+3} + \frac{1}{x-5} = 1$

2 Solve the following equations.

a $\frac{6}{x} + \frac{7}{x+1} = 2$

b $\frac{6}{x} - \frac{1}{x-1} = 2$

c $\frac{3}{x} + \frac{1}{x-1} = 2$

d $\frac{10}{x} + \frac{6}{x-3} = 5$

e $\frac{2}{x+2} + \frac{3}{2x+3} = 5$

f $\frac{7}{x} - \frac{5}{x+4} = 6$

g $\frac{8}{x+1} + \frac{5}{2x-1} = 3$

h $\frac{1}{2x-3} - \frac{3}{x-1} = -2$

3 **a** Set A contains x integers with a sum of 32
Write down an expression for the mean of set A.

b Set B contains $(x + 2)$ integers with a sum of 50
Write down an expression for the mean of set B.

c The mean of set B is one more than the mean of set A.
Show that $x^2 - 16x + 64 = 0$

d Find the mean of set A.

4 A field has an area of 600 m²
The length plus the width of the field is 50 m.
a Show that $x^2 - 50x + 600 = 0$ where x is the length of the field.
b Hence find the length and width of the field.

5 Jack's garden pond can be filled using two hose pipes in 3 hours.
The larger of the two hose pipes alone takes 8 hours less than the smaller hose pipe alone to fill the pond.
Let x be the time taken, in hours, for the smaller pipe alone to fill the pond.
a Find the fraction of the pond filled by the smaller pipe alone in 1 hour.
b Find the fraction of the pond filled by the larger pipe alone in 1 hour.
c When both hose pipes are used, what fraction of the pond can be filled in 1 hour?
d Use your answers to parts **a**, **b** and **c** to show that $x^2 - 14x + 24 = 0$
e Hence find the time in which the pond would be filled by each pipe on its own.

6 A group of holidaymakers hire a minibus to tour around the island they are staying on. The cost of hire is £120 to be shared equally amongst the holidaymakers. Two more people decide to join the tour. Each person now has to pay £2 less than before.
Find the original number of holidaymakers in the group.

7 Solve the following equations.

a $\dfrac{2}{x} + \dfrac{3}{(x+2)} = 4$ **b** $\dfrac{5}{x} + \dfrac{8}{(3x+7)} = 3$

c $\dfrac{3}{(x-1)} - \dfrac{2}{(x+1)} = 1$ **d** $\dfrac{5}{(x+2)} - \dfrac{4}{(2x-3)} = 5$

e $5 - \dfrac{3}{(x-2)^2} = 3$ **f** $\dfrac{7}{(x+1)} + \dfrac{2}{(x+1)^2} = 1$

8 The area of rectangle A is 20 cm²
The area of rectangle B is 36 cm²
The width of rectangle B is 2 cm greater than the width of rectangle A.
Let x cm be the width of rectangle A.
a Write down an expression for the length of rectangle A.
b Write down an expression for the length of rectangle B.
c The sum of the lengths of rectangles A and B is 11 cm.
Show that $11x^2 - 34x - 40 = 0$
d Calculate the value of x and show that rectangle B is a square.

9 The length and width of a rectangle are $(x + 4)$ cm and x cm respectively.
a Write down an expression for the perimeter of the rectangle.
b A square has the same perimeter as the rectangle.
Write down the length of the sides of the square.
c The sum of the areas of the square and the rectangle is 50 cm²
Show that $x^2 + 4x - 23 = 0$
d Find x.

It is possible to find the points of intersection of a straight line and the graph of a quadratic function graphically.
It is also possible to calculate the points of intersection by solving the equation of the straight line and quadratic graph simultaneously.

Example 3

The graphs of $y = x + 1$ and $y = x^2 + 2x - 3$ are shown on this grid. Calculate the coordinates of the points of intersection by solving the pair of simultaneous equations.

$y = x + 1$
$y = x^2 + 2x - 3$

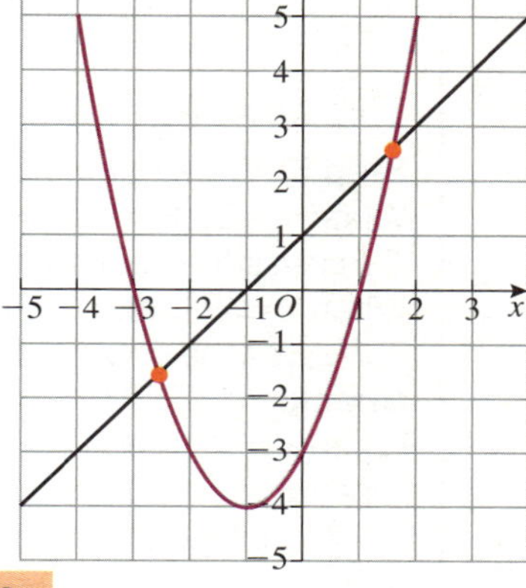

Solution 3

Step 1: Label the equations.

$y = x + 1$ A
$y = x^2 + 2x - 3$ B

Step 2: Substitute $y = x + 1$ from equation A into equation B.

$x + 1 = x^2 + 2x - 3$

Step 3: Rewrite the equation in the form $ax^2 + bx + c = 0$

$0 = x^2 + x - 4$ Subtract x and subtract 1 from both sides.

This gives $x^2 + x - 4 = 0$

Step 4: Use the quadratic formula to solve the equation, $a = 1$, $b = 1$ and $c = -4$

$$x = \frac{-1 \pm \sqrt{1^2 - 4 \times 1 \times -4}}{2 \times 1} = \frac{-1 \pm \sqrt{17}}{2}$$

$x = -2.56$ and 1.56 to two decimal places.

Step 5: Work out the coordinates.

When $x = -2.56$, $y = x + 1 = -1.56$
This gives the coordinates $(-2.56, -1.56)$.
When $x = 1.56$, $y = x + 1 = 2.56$
This gives the coordinates $(1.56, 2.56)$.

Check: Substitute in $y = x^2 + 2x - 3$

When $x = -2.56$, $y = (-2.56)^2 + 2 \times (-2.56) - 3 = -1.57$ ✓
When $x = 1.56$, $y = 1.56^2 + 2 \times 1.56 - 3 = 2.55$ ✓

The line intersects the curve at the points with coordinates $(-2.56, -1.56)$ and $(1.56, 2.56)$.

The points of intersection of a line and a circle can be calculated in the same way.

Example 4

Find the point of intersection of the line $y = 2x - 1$ and the circle with equation $x^2 + y^2 = 16$

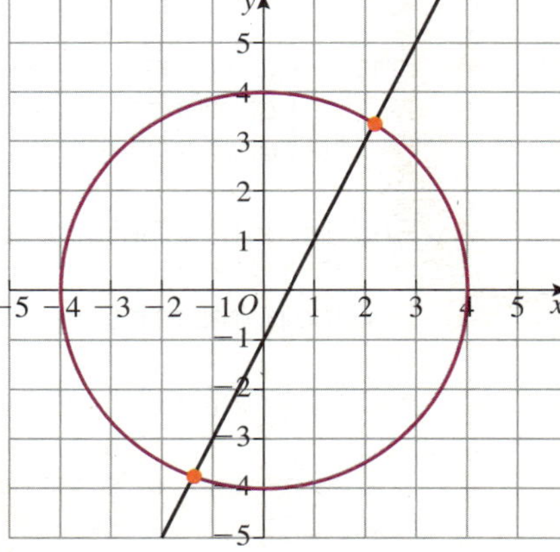

Solution 4

Step 1: Label the equations.

$y = 2x - 1$ A
$x^2 + y^2 = 16$ B

Step 2: Substitute $y = 2x + 1$ from equation A into equation B.

$x^2 + (2x - 1)^2 = 16$

Step 3: Rewrite the equation in the form $ax^2 + bx + c = 0$

$x^2 + (2x - 1)^2 = 16$ Expand the brackets.

$x^2 + 4x^2 - 4x + 1 = 16$ Collect like terms and subtract 15 from both sides.

$5x^2 - 4x - 15 = 0$

Step 4: Use the quadratic formula to solve the equation;

$a = 5$, $b = -4$ and $c = -15$

$$x = \frac{-(-4) \pm \sqrt{(-4)^2 - 4 \times 5 \times -15}}{2 \times 5} = \frac{4 \pm \sqrt{316}}{10}$$

$x = 2.18$ and -1.38 to 2 decimal places.

Step 5: Work out the coordinates.

When $x = 2.18$, $y = 2x - 1 = 2 \times 2.18 - 1 = 3.36$

This gives the coordinates (2.18, 3.36).

When $x = -1.38$, $y = 2x - 1 = 2 \times -1.38 - 1 = -3.76$

This gives the coordinates (−1.38, −3.76).

Check:

When $x = 2.18$ and $y = 3.36$, $x^2 + y^2 = 2.18^2 + 3.36^2 = 16.042$ ✓

When $x = -1.38$ and $y = -3.76$, $x^2 + y^2 = (-1.38)^2 + (-3.76)^2 = 16.042$ ✓

The line intersects the circle at the points with coordinates (−1.38, −3.76) and (2.18, 3.36).

Exercise B

1 Solve the pairs of simultaneous equations, giving your answers to two decimal places.

a $y = x + 3$, $y = x^2$
b $y = x + 9$, $y = x^2$
c $y = x + 5$, $y = 2x^2$
d $y = 2x + 1$, $y = x^2 + x$
e $y = 1 - x$, $y = 2x^2 + 3x - 4$
f $y = 2 + x$, $y = x^2 - 4$
g $y = 3x + 1$, $y = x^2 - 5x$
h $y = 2x - 3$, $y^2 = x^2 + x + 1$

2 Solve the pairs of simultaneous equations.
Give your answers to two decimal places.

a $y = 2x$, $x^2 + y^2 = 10$
b $y = 3x$, $x^2 + y^2 = 1$
c $y = 2x - 1$, $x^2 + y^2 = 20$
d $y = 1 - 3x$, $x^2 + y^2 = 5$
e $y = 1 - 2x$, $x^2 + y^2 = 25$
f $y = 4x - 5$, $x^2 + y^2 = 8$
g $y = 3 - x$, $x^2 + y^2 = 100$
h $y = 7 - 5x$, $x^2 + y^2 = 35$

3 Find the coordinates of the points of intersection of the line and curve where:

a the equation of the line is $y = 4 - 4x$ and the equation of the curve is $y = x^2$
b the equation of the line is $y = x + 5$ and the equation of the curve is $y = 2x^2 - 3x$

4 Find the coordinates of the points of intersection of the line and curve where:

a the equation of the line is $y = 3x - 4$ and the equation of the curve is $y = 2x^2 - x - 3$
b the equation of the line is $y = 5 - 2x$ and the equation of the curve is $y = 3x^2 + x - 7$

5 Find the points of intersection of the line $3x + y = 5$ and the circle $x^2 + y^2 = 25$

6 Find the points of intersection of the line $y + 2x = 9$ and the circle $x^2 + y^2 = 18$

7 Find the points of intersection of the line $x + y = -5$ and the circle $x^2 + y^2 = 32$

8 The centre of a circle has coordinates (0, 0).
The radius of the circle is 3
Calculate the points of intersection of this circle and the line $x + 2y = 4$

Chapter summary

- A *quadratic equation* is an equation of the form $ax^2 + bx + c = 0$, where $a \neq 0$
  Quadratic equations must always be rearranged to the form $ax^2 + bx + c = 0$ before they can be solved.
- To solve a quadratic equation:
  - If the expression $ax^2 + bx + c$ factorises, factorise $ax^2 + bx + c$ and rewrite the equation in the form $(mx + p)(nx + q) = 0$
    To find the solutions make each factor equal to zero.
  - If the expression $ax^2 + bx + c = 0$ does not factorise, use either completing the square or the quadratic formula.
    Completing the square:
    When $a = 1$, rewrite $ax^2 + bx + c$ in the form $(x + p)^2 + q$
    When $a \neq 1$, rewrite $ax^2 + bx + c$ in the form $a(x + p)^2 + q$
    The quadratic formula is:
    $$x = \frac{-b \pm \sqrt{b^2 - 4ac}}{2a}$$
  - Solutions to quadratic equations found by completing the square or the quadratic formula can be given either in surd form or to a given degree of accuracy, for example two decimal places.
- Problems can be solved by setting up and then solving a quadratic equation.
- The points of intersection of a straight line and the graph of a quadratic function can be calculated by solving the equation for the straight line and the quadratic graph simultaneously. To do this, substitute the expression for y from the linear equation into the quadratic equation.
- The points of intersection of a line and a circle can be calculated in a similar way.

Chapter review

1 **a** Solve $y^2 + 8y = 0$
b Solve $x^2 - 9 = 0$
c **i** Factorise $x^2 - 7x + 10$
ii Hence, or otherwise, solve the equation $x^2 - 7x + 10 = 0$

2 Solve the equations:
a $x^2 - 9x - 22 = 0$ **b** $5x^2 - 14x - 3 = 0$ **c** $3x^2 + 2x - 8 = 0$

3 **a** Solve the equation $4x^2 - 72 = 0$
Give your answer in surd form.
b Solve the equation $x^2 - 4x + 1 = 0$
Give your answer in surd form.

4 Solve the equation $\frac{5}{x} = 11 - 2x$

5 ABC is a right-angled triangle with a right angle at A.
$AB = (x + 2)$ cm
$AC = 6$ cm
$BC = 3x$ cm

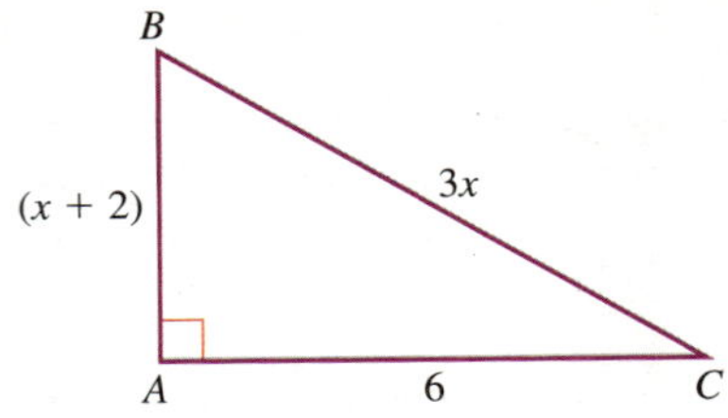

a Show that $2x^2 - x - 10 = 0$
b **i** Solve the equation $2x^2 - x - 10 = 0$
ii Write down the length of the hypotenuse of triangle ABC.

6 A class takes x weeks to collect £84 for charity.
The following week the class collects £20
a Write down the mean amount collected per week by the class after:
i x weeks **ii** $(x + 1)$ weeks
b The collection of £20 increases the mean amount collected per week by £1
Use your answers to part **a** to show that $x^2 - 19x + 84 = 0$
c Solve this equation to calculate x.

7 The centre of a circle has coordinates $(0, 0)$.
The radius of the circle is 5
Calculate the coordinates of the points of intersection of this circle and the line $2y - x = 2$

8 **a** Solve $x^2 - 3x - 3 = 0$
Give your answers to two decimal places.
b Solve $2x^2 + 2(x + 3)^2 = 73$

9 Solve the equation $2x^2 - 3x - 4 = 0$
Give your answers correct to two decimal places.

10 **a** Show that $x^2 - 6x - 13 \equiv (x - 3)^2 - 22$
b Hence, or otherwise, solve the equation $x^2 - 6x - 13 = 0$
Give your answers to two decimal places.

11 $x^2 - 10x + 14 \equiv (x + q)^2 + r$
a Calculate the values of q and r
b Hence, or otherwise, solve $x^2 - 10x + 14 = 0$
Give your answers to two decimal places.

12 Solve the equation

$$\frac{5}{(x + 2)} + \frac{1}{(2x - 5)} = 1$$

Give your answer to two decimal places.

13 Solve the simultaneous equations
$x^2 + y^2 = 16$
$y = 3x - 1$
Give your answer to two decimal places.

CHAPTER 37

Sampling

37.1 Random sampling

CAN YOU REMEMBER

- The meaning of 'random'?
- That obtaining information from every member of a population is called a census?

IN THIS SECTION YOU WILL

- Understand when and why sampling may be appropriate.
- Learn the meaning of 'sampling', 'representative' and 'random sample'.
- Learn how to obtain a random sample from a population.
- Understand how to use random numbers to obtain a random sample.

Obtaining information from part of a population is called *sampling*. Analysing data for every member of a population is not always practical. For example, a company producing light bulbs wants to find out the average lifetime of their light bulbs. If it tested the entire population there would be no bulbs left to sell! It needs to test a sample.

One method of sampling is to take a *random sample*.

In a random sample:

- every member of the population has an equal chance of being part of the sample
- every possible set of members of the population must have an equal chance of being the sample.

These two criteria are not the same.

For example, a sample of four is to be chosen at random from a class of 15 boys and 15 girls.

If the decision is made to pick two boys and two girls, this is not a random sample. Every person in the class has an equal chance of being in the sample but it is not possible to have, for example, three girls and one boy. So not every possible set of members of the population can make up the sample.

One way of selecting a random sample is to pick names or numbers from a hat.

Example 1

A bus company wishes to obtain opinions on the quality of its service.

a Explain why a sample of its customers should be taken rather than a census.

b The managing director suggests everyone on the number 51 bus on a Monday morning is questioned. Criticise this suggestion.

Solution 1

a It would be extremely time consuming and costly to question every single person who is a customer of the bus company.

b This is not a random sample. The people on this bus at this time may well be of a certain type, e.g. people on their way to work, and would certainly not be representative of all customers on all routes.

Example 2

Cara wants to ask people from her class at school what they think of their new school uniform.
She puts the names of the people from her class on separate pieces of paper, puts them in a bag and picks five pieces of paper out without looking.
Has Cara chosen a random sample?
Explain your answer.

Solution 2

Every member of the class has an equal chance of being selected.
All possible sets of five people could occur as the sample.
So, as both criteria for a random sample have been met, Cara has a random sample.

Exercise A

1 A tyre company wishes to test the number of miles its tyres run before the tread wears to below the legal minimum.
- **a** Explain why the company should test a sample rather than conduct a census.
- **b** The company tests the first 100 tyres produced one day.
  Criticise the choice of sample.

2 David wants to choose a sample of six from his class.
He writes down all the pupils' names on pieces of paper, puts all the boys' names in one bag and all the girls' names in another bag. He then chooses, without looking, three pieces of paper from each bag.
Has David obtained a random sample?

3 A sandwich company wants to taste-test a new type of sandwich.
The sandwich is produced by three machines A, B and C.
- **a** Explain why a sample of the sandwiches needs to be taste-tested.
- **b** The company selects 50 women from its workforce to test 100 sandwiches from machine A.
  Give **three** criticisms of the procedures.

4 A club has 508 members. A committee of five is to be chosen at random from the members.
State, with a reason, whether each one of these methods of choosing the committee is random.
- **a** The first five members in alphabetical order.
- **b** The five oldest members.
- **c** The five members whose birthdays fall earliest in the year.
- **d** Writing all names on cards and picking cards placed face down.

5 A village contains 1100 people. It is proposed to build a new fast food outlet in the village. Each person in the village is to be asked to fill in a questionnaire giving their opinion on the proposal. A small working group of five is to be set up to monitor the progress of the proposal if it is accepted.
- **a** Explain why the questionnaire is a census.
- **b** How could the questionnaires be used to obtain a random sample of villagers for the working party?

Another way to take a random sample is to use random numbers.
Random numbers can be obtained from printed tables or using the random function on a calculator.
Calculators can produce random numbers in groups of three, in decimal form.

0.173	three random digits 173
0.92	three random digits 920
0.014	three random digits 014

Make sure you know how to generate random numbers on your calculator.

Example 3

Use the random function on a calculator to obtain a random sample of three from the list of 11 colours.

black red white grey green blue brown pink purple yellow orange

Solution 3

Method 1

Number the population.

01 black	02 red	03 white	04 grey	05 green	06 blue
07 brown	08 pink	09 purple	10 yellow	11 orange	

A calculator gives the random numbers:
620 830 102 133 086 377 015
Write these as a string of digits:
620830102133086377015
Two-digit random numbers are needed, so take the digits in twos.
62 – unusable (no member of the population has this number)
08 – pink
30 – unusable
10 – yellow
21 – unusable
33 – unusable
08 – repeat
63 – unusable
77 – unusable
01 – black
The sample of three is pink, yellow and black.

Method 2

In Method 1, many of the two-digit numbers generated were unusable.
It is possible to assign more than one two-digit number to each population item.
black: 01, 02, 03, 04, 05, 06, 07, 08, 09
red: 11, 12, 13, 14, 15, 16, 17, 18, 19
white: 21, 22, 23, 24, 25, 26, 27, 28, 29
grey: 31, 32, 33, 34, 35, 36, 37, 38, 39
green: 41, 42, 43, 44, 45, 46, 47, 48, 49
blue: 51, 52, 53, 54, 55, 56, 57, 58, 59
brown: 61, 62, 63, 64, 65, 66, 67, 68, 69
pink: 71, 72, 73, 74, 75, 76, 77, 78, 79
purple: 81, 82, 83, 84, 85, 86, 87, 88, 89

yellow: 91, 92, 93, 94, 95, 96, 97, 98, 99
orange: 10, 20, 30, 40, 50, 60, 70, 80, 90
Only 00 is now unusable.
Using the same list of random numbers now gives:
62 – brown 08 – black 30 – orange 10 – orange (repeat)
This gives the random sample of brown, black and orange.

To take a random sample using random numbers:
Step 1: Number every member of the population.
Step 2: Obtain random numbers with the correct number of digits.
Step 3: Ignore repeats or unusable numbers.
Step 4: Select the members of the population with these numbers.
As a general guideline, it is often sensible to take a sample of between 5% and 10% of the population.

Example 4

A small town has a population of 5307
There are 685 children in the village.
A company is investigating average earnings for the adults in this town.
What size sample should be taken?

Solution 4

The adult population of the town is 5307 − 685 = 4622
5% of 4622 = 231.1, this is 231 to the nearest person.
10% of 4622 = 462.2, this is 462 to the nearest person.
The data would be quite difficult to collect as personal information is being asked for.
A sample of 200–250 would be appropriate.

Exercise B

For questions **1** and **2**, use the random number lists at the end of each question.

1 Joseph was setting a quiz. He wanted a random choice of letters which would form the answers to the quiz.
Obtain a random choice of four letters from the alphabet.
ABCDEFGHIJKLMNOPQRSTUVWXYZ
Random numbers: 432, 512, 880, 916, 657, 721, 800, 092

2 There are 40 families in a street. They live in houses numbered 1–40
Obtain a random sample of six families from the street.
Random numbers: 461, 178, 930, 034, 131, 322, 764, 126, 111

3 A village has a population of 3208
- **a** List the steps required to obtain a random sample of 30 from the village.
- **b** Comment on the size of the sample.

4 Use the random number function on a calculator to obtain a random sample of five from the list of towns and cities below.

Aberdeen	Belfast	Cardiff	Derby	Edinburgh	Glasgow
Huddersfield	London	Manchester	Norwich	Portsmouth	Reading
Scunthorpe	Worcester				

5 A machine can fill 20 000 tins with paint in one day.
The tins should contain 1 litre of paint.
The manager wants to check that the machine is filling the tins with the correct amount of paint.
How many tins should be sampled?

6 List all the people in your Maths class.
Obtain a random sample of the appropriate size for your group.

7 Obtain a list of 30 share prices for companies.
- **a** Obtain a random sample of five of the share prices.
- **b** Find the mean of your sample.
- **c** Find the mean of the entire list of share prices.
- **d** Comment on your answers to parts **b** and **c**.

37.2 Stratified sampling

CAN YOU REMEMBER

- How to write one number as a fraction of another?

IN THIS SECTION YOU WILL

- Learn the meaning of 'stratified sample'.
- Understand why stratified samples are used.
- Learn how to take stratified samples.

If a sample is to be *representative* and avoid *bias* it needs to reflect the nature of the population.
A population is *stratified* if it is divided up into distinct strata or groups. For example, in a human population, the two most common groupings are:
- males and females
- different age groups.

In a *stratified sample* each group is represented in the same proportion as in the overall population.
For example, if a Physics course has 75% female students and 25% male students, a stratified sample of students on the course has 75% females and 25% males.
Once the numbers for each group are decided, the 75% and 25% are selected using random sampling.

Example 1

In a factory there are three different-sized machines which produce components for a car.
Machine A produces 50% of the factory output.
Machine B produces 30% of the factory output.
Machine C produces the remainder of the output.
The components are to be sampled for checking.
- **a** Explain why a stratified sample should be taken.
- **b** The sample size is to be 1000
  How many components from each machine should be tested?

Solution 1

a A stratified sample takes into account the fact that the different machines produce different amounts of the component.

b Machine A produces 50% of output, so 50% of the sample should come from Machine A.
Machine A: 50% of 1000 = 500
Similarly for the other machines:
Machine B: 30% of 1000 = 300
Machine C: 20% of 1000 = 200
Total = 1000

Exercise A

1 A local council is made up of 80% men and 20% women.
A questionnaire is to be given to a stratified sample of councillors.
What percentage of men and women should be in the stratified sample?

2 A night school runs a course on flower arranging.
There are four times more women on the course than men.
The course leader wishes to ask a sample of the students whether they think it is good value for money.

a Explain why a stratified sample might be advisable.

b The sample size is to be 20
How many women and how many men should be in the sample?

3 In Scotter comprehensive school the teachers' ages are distributed as shown in the table.

Age	Number of teachers	Teachers in sample
Under 30	20	
31–40	40	
41–50	30	
Over 50	10	

Copy and complete the table to show the number of teachers from each age group in a stratified sample of 30
(Hint: Work out the percentage of teachers in each age group.)

4 A maternity ward asks a sample of new mothers how they feel about their experiences.
The percentages of first-time mothers and those who have had previous children is as given in the table.

Type of mother	Percentage	Number in sample
First time	45	
1 previous child	30	
2 previous children	20	
3+ previous children	5	

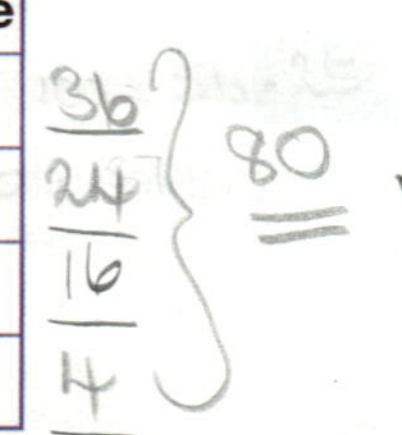

a Explain why a stratified sample would be better than a simple random sample in this case.

b The sample size is to be 80
Copy and complete the table.

5 On a particular commuter train, there are twice as many male adult passengers as female adult passengers. There are also six times as many adults as children.
How many male adults, female adults and children should there be in a stratified sample of 140?

6 A factory has 150 shop floor workers, 12 supervisors and four managers.
What percentage of each type of worker should be in a stratified sample?

Example 2

The number of students in each year of a large comprehensive school is given in the table.

Year	7	8	9	10	11
Number in year	201	182	244	195	221

A stratified sample of size 100 is to be taken from the students in the school.
Calculate the number of students in each year to be included in the sample.

Solution 2

Step 1: Find the total number of students in the school.
$201 + 182 + 244 + 195 + 221 = 1043$
Step 2: Find each group as a fraction of the total.
Year 7: $\frac{201}{1043}$ Year 8: $\frac{182}{1043}$ Year 9: $\frac{244}{1043}$ Year 10: $\frac{195}{1043}$ Year 11: $\frac{221}{1043}$
Step 3: Work out these fractions of the total sample size required.
Year 7: $\frac{201}{1043} \times 100 = 19.27$ Year 8: $\frac{182}{1043} \times 100 = 17.45$
Year 9: $\frac{244}{1043} \times 100 = 23.39$ Year 10: $\frac{195}{1043} \times 100 = 18.70$
Year 11: $\frac{221}{1043} \times 100 = 21.19$
Step 4: Round the answers to the nearest integer.

Year	7	8	9	10	11
Number in sample	19	17	23	19	21

Step 5: Check that the total sample number is as required.
$19 + 17 + 23 + 19 + 21 = 99$
This is not the required total of 100
Step 6: Adjust the rounding to give the required total.
An extra student is required, so one of the numbers which was rounded down needs to be rounded up instead. Out of the numbers rounded down, Year 8 with 17.45 was closest to being rounded up.
So the final sample numbers are:

Year	7	8	9	10	11
Number in sample	19	18	23	19	21

Exercise B

1 The table shows the number of each type of worker in a very large factory.

Type of worker	Labourer	Supervisor	Manager
Number	500	100	10

How many of each type of worker should be present in a stratified sample of 61?

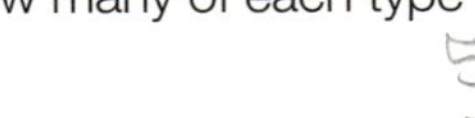

2 The age distribution of a village is as shown.

Age	Under 18	18–30	31–50	51–70	Over 70
Number in village	154	298	542	365	71

A stratified sample of 100 people is to be taken from the village.
Calculate the number from each age group in the sample.

3 A school is to ask a sample of students about changes to the school day.
The year and gender distribution of the school is given in the table on the right.

Year \ **Gender**	Male	Female
7	122	143
8	117	104
9	98	149
10	127	121
11	135	126

a The school decides to carry out a stratified sample of 50 based on gender.
Calculate the number of male and female students who should be in this sample.

b Later, it is decided that it would be better to use a stratified sample based on school year and increase the sample size to 100
Copy and complete the table showing the numbers in the sample for each year.

Year	7	8	9	10	11
Number in sample					

c Which of the samples in parts **a** and **b** is more representative of the school? Explain your answer.

4 A swimming pool is considering changing its opening times.
The pool is used by 435 members, 326 of whom are female.
The manager is going to ask members their views on the proposals.
How many males should be in a stratified sample of size 55?

5 A local council wants to put double yellow lines on both sides of a street. The council wants to obtain the views of the residents in the street.
The table shows some details about the 35 families in the street.

Family number	01	02	03	04	05	06	07	08	09	10	11	12	13
Own car?	Y	Y	Y	N	N	Y	Y	N	Y	N	Y	Y	Y
Have children?	Y	Y	Y	Y	N	Y	N	N	Y	Y	N	N	N

Family number	14	15	16	17	18	19	20	21	22	23	24	25	26
Own car?	Y	Y	N	N	Y	Y	Y	N	Y	Y	Y	N	Y
Have children?	Y	Y	Y	Y	N	N	Y	Y	N	N	N	Y	Y

Family number	27	28	29	30	31	32	33	34	35
Own car?	Y	Y	N	Y	Y	Y	N	Y	Y
Have children?	N	Y	Y	Y	Y	N	Y	N	Y

a How many car owners should be in a stratified sample of ten based on car ownership?
b How many families without children should be in a stratified sample of 15 based on children?
c Copy and complete the table which shows the number of families having (or not having) cars and children.

Car \ Children	Y	N
Y	13	
N		

d Construct a new table for a stratified sample of 20 based on **both** criteria.

6 A school has 227 pupils in Year 9
In a sample stratified by year, 13 Year 9 pupils were included.
In the same stratified sample, 16 Year 10 pupils were included.
Stratified numbers may have been rounded.
Estimate the number of pupils there are in Year 10.

Chapter summary

- Obtaining information from part of a population is called sampling.
- Analysing data for every member of a population is not always practical.
  Sampling may be appropriate.
- One method of sampling is to take a random sample.
- In a random sample:
  - every member of the population has an equal chance of being part of the sample
  - every possible set of members of the population must have an equal chance of being the sample.
- To obtain a random sample:
  - pick numbers or names from a hat
  - use random numbers from a calculator or a table.
- To take a random sample using random numbers:
  - **Step 1:** Number every member of the population.
  - **Step 2:** Obtain random numbers with the correct numbers of digits.
  - **Step 3:** Ignore repeats or unusable numbers.
  - **Step 4:** Select the members of the population with these numbers.
- As a general guideline, it is often sensible to take a sample of between 5% and 10% of the population.
- A population is stratified if it is divided up into distinct strata or groups.
  For example, in a human population, the two most common groupings are:
  - males and females
  - different age groups.
- In a *stratified sample* each group is represented in exactly the same proportion as in the overall population.

Chapter review

1 A train company wishes to obtain opinions on the quality of its service.

a Explain why it should take a sample of its customers rather than a census.

b The managing director suggests that everyone on the 08:37 train on a Monday morning is questioned. Criticise this suggestion.

2 Davina wants to choose a sample from her Maths set.
She writes down all the names of people in her Maths set onto pieces of paper and puts them into two bags, one for the boys and one for the girls.
She then pulls out, at random, two pieces of paper from each bag and notes the names.
Has Davina taken a random sample of:

a two boys in her Maths set

b two girls in her Maths set

c four people in her Maths set

d four people in her school?

3 The crowd at a football match is made up of 68% adult males, 14% adult females and the rest children.
A stratified sample of 200 is to be taken from the crowd.
Copy and complete the table.

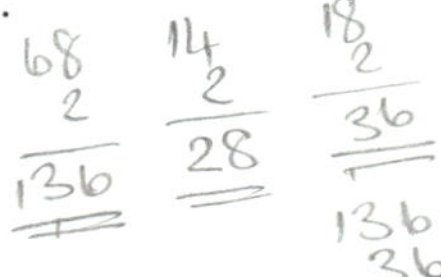

	Number in sample
Adult males	
Adult females	
Children	
Total	200

4 There are 65 teachers in a school.
List the steps required to find a random sample of an appropriate size from the school.

5 The table shows the number of three types of machine in a very large factory.

Type of machine	Automatic electric	Manual electric	No power
Number	250	140	30

How many of each type of machine should be sampled in a stratified sample of 42?

6 Use the random number function on a calculator to obtain a random sample of four from the list of football teams below.

Arsenal	Aston Villa	Birmingham	Blackburn
Bolton	Chelsea	Derby County	Everton
Fulham	Gillingham	Huddersfield Town	Ipswich
Liverpool	Manchester City	Manchester United	Middlesbrough
Norwich	Oldham	Portsmouth	QPR
Rotherham	Scunthorpe United	Southampton	Tottenham
Watford	West Ham United	Wolves	Yeovil

7 In a primary school, there are 71 pupils in Year 4, 43 pupils in Year 5 and 50 pupils in Year 6
A teacher wants to choose a sample of 20 pupils from these classes.

a Explain why the teacher should use stratified sampling.

b The teacher decides to use stratified sampling. Calculate the number of pupils that should be selected from each year.

8 The head teacher of a school wants to give a sample of students, stratified by year, a questionnaire about the amount of homework they receive.

a Explain why it is a good idea to use a stratified sample.

b The table shows the number of students in each year.

Year	7	8	9	10	11	12	13
Number of students	280	216	243	208	237	112	99

The total sample size is to be 100

Copy and complete this table.

Year	7	8	9	10	11	12	13
Number in sample							

9 A TV watchdog wishes to monitor the amount of sport on terrestrial TV.

Ten days from one month are to be selected to find the amount of sport being shown.

a Would random or stratified sampling be better for this purpose?
Explain your answer.

b Comment on the choice of ten days over one month.

10 **a** Use a telephone directory to obtain a random sample of ten people from the telephone directory with the surname Brown.

b Does a sample from a telephone directory give a representative sample of the overall population.
Explain your answer.

11 The table shows the occupation types of members of a club.

Occupation type	**Number**
Professional	86
Manual	204
Self-employed	54
Unemployed	29

A sample of 40, stratified by occupation, is to be questioned on proposed increases to membership fees.

a Why is stratification by occupation to be used here?

b Copy and complete the table.

Occupation type	**Number in sample**
Professional	
Manual	
Self-employed	
Unemployed	

CHAPTER 38

Further trigonometry

38.1 Using trigonometric graphs to solve equations

CAN YOU REMEMBER

- The graphs of sin x, cos x and tan x for values of x from 0° to 360°?
- How to use a calculator to find values of sin x, cos x and tan x and their inverses?

IN THIS SECTION YOU WILL

- Learn that the graphs of sin x, cos x and tan x are periodic and can be extended to cover all values of x.
- Solve simple trigonometric equations using trigonometric graphs.

In chapter 32, the graphs of sin x, cos x and tan x were shown for values of x from 0° to 360°.

These graphs can be extended for **any** values of x as shown below.

$y = \sin x$

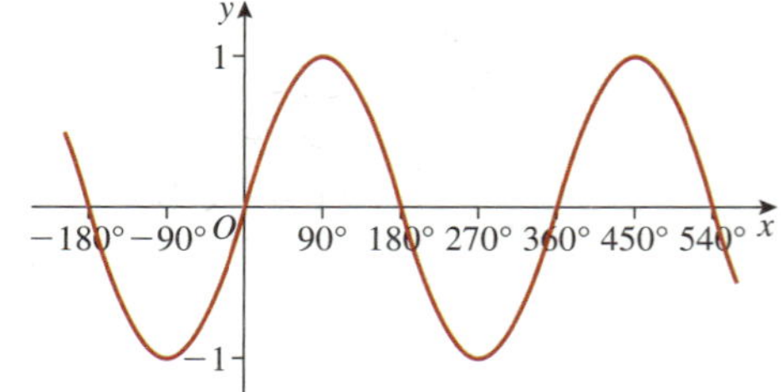

$y = \cos x$

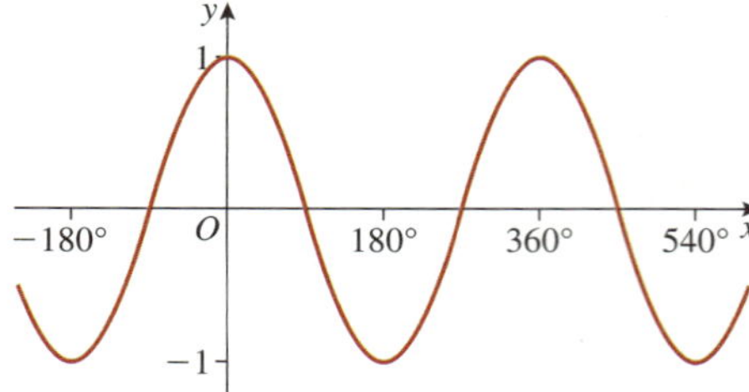

$y = \tan x$

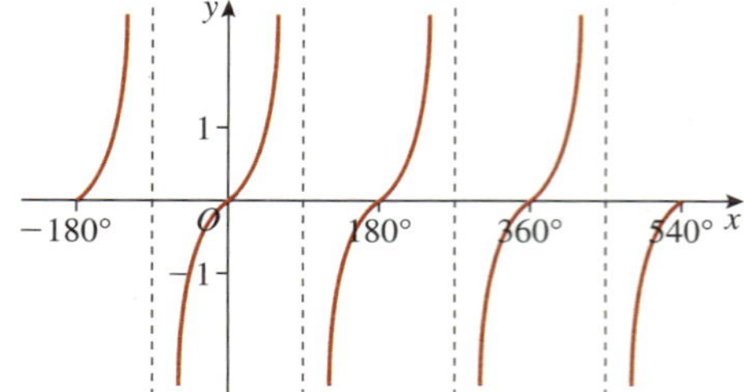

In each graph, the pattern repeats an infinite number of times. The number of degrees before the pattern repeats is called the *period* of the function. The functions sine, cosine and tangent are called *periodic functions*.
Sin x and cos x have period 360°. Tan x has period 180°.

Graphs can be used to solve trigonometrical equations such as $\sin x = 0.5$
Using a calculator gives $\sin^{-1} 0.5 = 30°$.
However there are an infinite number of angles which have a sine value of 0.5

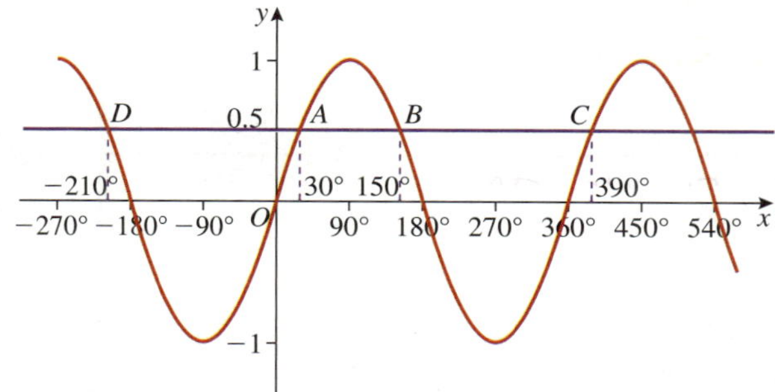

A is 30°. Using the symmetry of the graph,
$B = 180° - 30° = 150°$
$C = 360° + 30° = 390°$
$D = -180° - 30° = -210°$

Example 1

a Sketch the graph of $\cos x$ for $0° \leqslant x \leqslant 360°$.
Find the values of x in this range for which $\cos x = 0.39$

b Find the values of x for which $\cos x = -0.39$

Solution 1

a From a calculator, $\cos^{-1} 0.39 = 67°$.
$A = 67°$ and using the symmetry of the graph,
$B = 360° - 67° = 293°$
The values of x are 67° and 293°.
Check: using a calculator, $\cos 293° = 0.39$ ✓

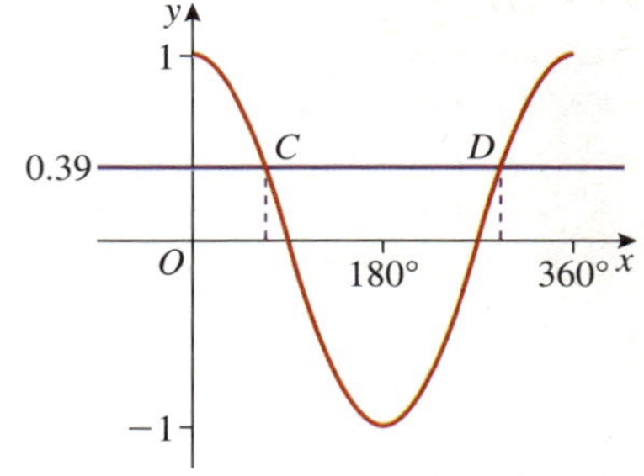

b

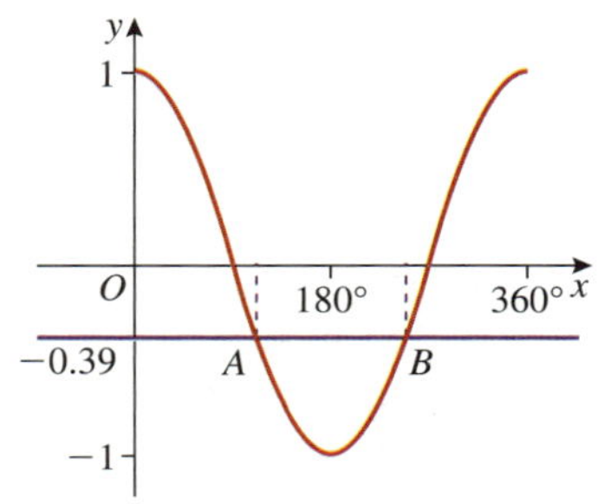

Using the symmetry of the graph, $C = 180° - 67° = 113°$ and $D = 180° + 67° = 247°$
The values of x are 113° and 247°.

Example 2

Given that $\tan x = 0.7$ has a solution $x = 35°$, write down the other solutions of this equation within the range $-180° \leqslant x \leqslant 180°$

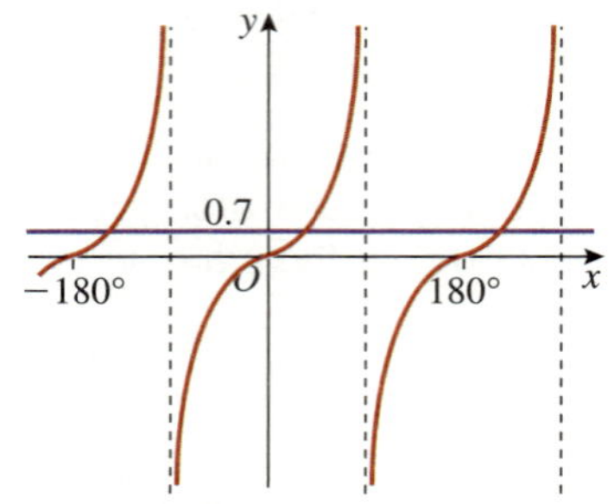

Solution 2

The line at $y = 0.7$ on the graph shows that there are two possible solutions within the range $-180° \leqslant x \leqslant 180°$
As one solution is given as 35°, by symmetry the other solution is $-180° + 35° = -145°$

Exercise A

1 **a** Sketch the graph of $y = \sin x$ for values of x from 0° to 360°.
b Given that $\sin x = 0.53$ has a solution $x = 32°$, work out the other solution of this equation in this range.

2 **a** Sketch the graph of $y = \cos x$ for $0° \leqslant x \leqslant 360°$.
b Given that $\cos 52° = 0.616$, solve the equation $\cos x = 0.616$ for $180° \leqslant x \leqslant 360°$.

3 **a** Sketch the graph of $\tan x$ for values of x from 0° to 360°.
b Given that one solution of the equation $\tan x = 3.27$ is $x = 73°$, work out the other solution within this range.

4 Find all the solutions of the following equations for $0° \leqslant x \leqslant 360°$, giving answers correct to the nearest degree.
a $\sin x = 0.259$ **b** $\sin x = 0.777$ **c** $\sin x = -0.97$

5 Find all the solutions of the following equations for $0° \leqslant x \leqslant 360°$, giving answers correct to the nearest degree.
a $\cos x = 0.695$ **b** $\cos x = 0.956$ **c** $\cos x = -0.56$

6 Find all the solutions of the following equations for $-180° \leqslant x \leqslant 180°$, giving answers correct to the nearest degree.
a $\tan x = 1$ **b** $\tan x = 2.6$ **c** $\tan x = -1$

Example 3

a $2\sin x = 0.94$
i Work out the acute angle that satisfies this equation.
ii Use your answer to part **i** to find another solution to the equation in the range $x = 0°$ to $x = 360°$.
b Find a solution of $\cos(x - 30°) = 0.342$

Solution 3

a **i** $2\sin x = 0.94$
$\sin x = 0.94 \div 2 = 0.47$
$x = \sin^{-1} 0.47 = 28°$
ii A second solution is $180° - 28° = 152°$

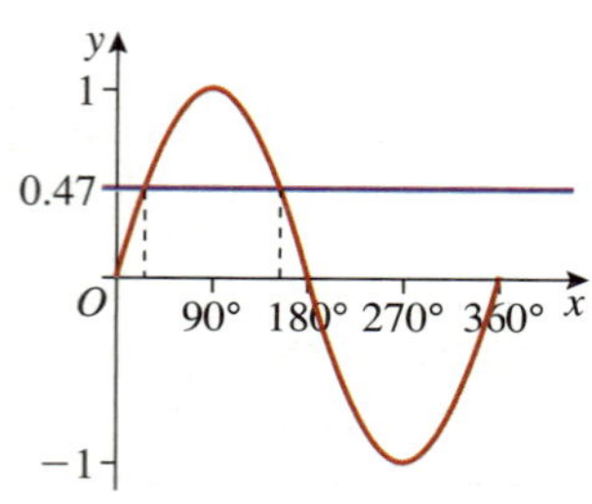

b $\cos(x - 30°) = 0.342$

$x - 30° = \cos^{-1} 0.342 = 70°$

$x = 70° + 30°$ — Add 30° to both sides.

$x = 100°$

Exercise B

1 For each of the following:

i work out the acute angle that satisfies the equation

ii use your answer to part **i** to find another solution to the equation.

a $3\sin x = 0.624$ **b** $2\cos x = 0.584$ **c** $4\cos x = -0.9$

2 You are given that $\cos x = 0.5$
Sandy says that cos 120° is also 0.5. Is she correct? Explain your answer.

3 Find a solution for each of these equations.

a $\sin(x + 25°) = 0.743$ **b** $\tan(x - 40°) = 4.7$

4 Find all the solutions of the following equations for $0° \leqslant x \leqslant 360°$.
Give each answer to the nearest degree.

a $2\sin x = -0.878$ **b** $\cos(x - 15°) = -0.309$

38.2 Sine rule and area of a triangle

CAN YOU REMEMBER

- That in a right-angled triangle with an angle A, $\sin A = \dfrac{\text{opposite}}{\text{hypotenuse}}$?
- The area of a triangle $= \frac{1}{2} \times$ base $\times$ perpendicular height?
- How to draw diagrams to scale?

IN THIS SECTION YOU WILL

- Use the sine rule to calculate the lengths of sides and sizes of angles in triangles.
- Find the area of a triangle using the formula $A = \frac{1}{2}ab\sin C$.
- Use scale drawings and the sine rule to solve problems.

In a triangle ABC, side a is opposite angle A, side b is opposite angle B and side c is opposite angle C.

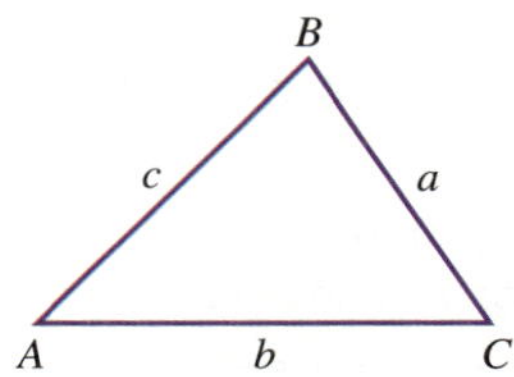

The diagram shows a triangle ABC. The perpendicular height, h, divides the triangle into two right-angled triangles.

In triangle BDA

$\frac{h}{c} = \sin A$ so $h = c\sin A$

In triangle BDC

$\frac{h}{a} = \sin C$ so $h = a\sin C$

h is common to both triangles so $h = c\sin A = a\sin C$

Rearranging the equation:

$$\frac{a}{\sin A} = \frac{c}{\sin C}$$

This can be extended to use side b and angle B:

so $\frac{a}{\sin A} = \frac{b}{\sin B} = \frac{c}{\sin C}$ or $\frac{\sin A}{a} = \frac{\sin B}{b} = \frac{\sin C}{c}$

This is known as the *sine rule*. To use the sine rule, one side and its opposite angle must be known together with another side or angle.

Example 1

Calculate the length of side a in triangle ABC.

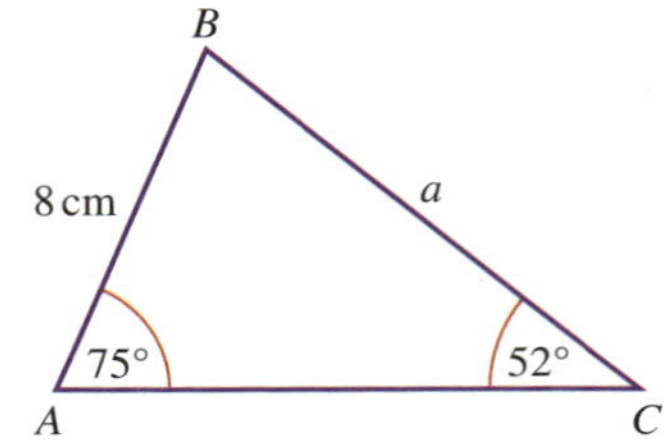

Solution 1

Side c, angle C and angle A are known.
The sine rule can be used.

Using $\frac{a}{\sin A} = \frac{c}{\sin C}$ gives $\frac{a}{\sin 75°} = \frac{8}{\sin 52°}$

$a = \frac{8}{\sin 52°} \times \sin 75°$ Multiply by sin 75°.

$a = 9.8$ cm (to 1 d.p.)

Example 2

The diagram shows triangle ABC.
Calculate the size of angle C.

Solution 2

Side a, angle A and side c are known.
The sine rule can be used.

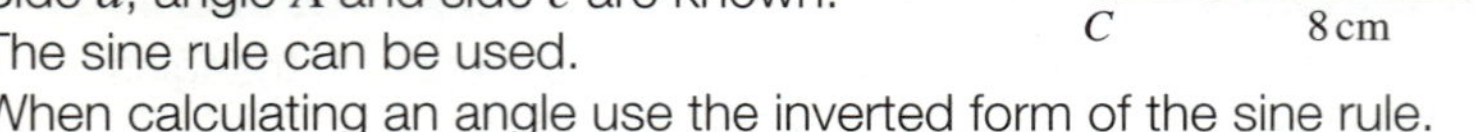

When calculating an angle use the inverted form of the sine rule.

Using $\frac{\sin A}{a} = \frac{\sin C}{c}$ gives $\frac{\sin 70°}{8} = \frac{\sin C}{3.5}$

$3.5 \times \frac{\sin 70°}{8} = \sin C$ Multiply by 3.5°

$0.411 = \sin C$

$C = \sin^{-1} 0.411 = 24.3°$

Note that $\sin^{-1} 0.411$ also gives an angle of $180° - 24.3° = 155.7°$. However, in this example, side c is smaller than side a so angle C must be smaller than angle A.

Example 3

In triangle ABC, angle $A = 22°$, $BC = 4.5$ cm and $AC = 7.2$ cm.
Calculate the size of angle B.

Solution 3

BC = side a, AC = side b

Using $\frac{\sin B}{b} = \frac{\sin A}{a}$ gives $\frac{\sin B}{7.2} = \frac{\sin 22°}{4.5}$

$\sin B = \frac{\sin 22°}{4.5} \times 7.2 = 0.6$

$B = \sin^{-1} 0.6 = 37°$ or $143°$ (to the nearest degree)
Both angles are possible and give two possible triangles, as shown.

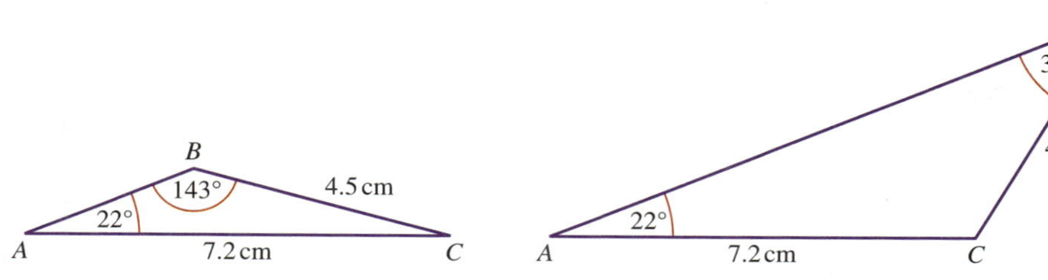

Exercise A

1 Calculate the length of side a in each of these triangles.

a
A
58°
7 cm
42°
C
a
B

b
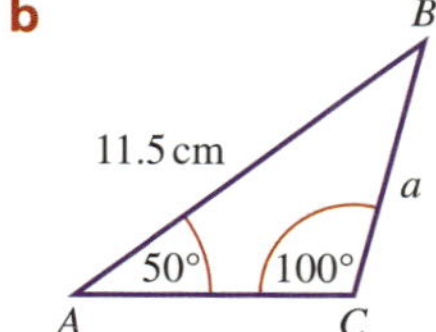

c
B
6.2 cm
a
105°
32°
A
C

d
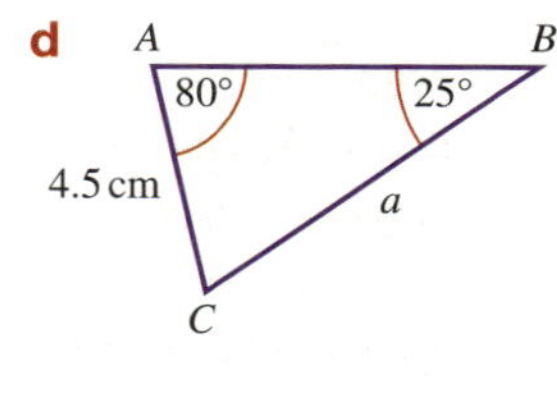

2 Calculate the length of the side marked by a letter.

a
A
8 cm
B
35°
b
80°
C

b
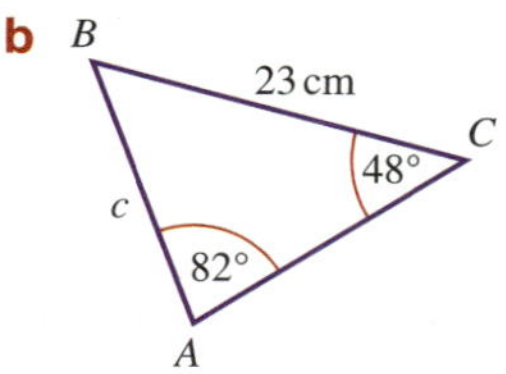

c
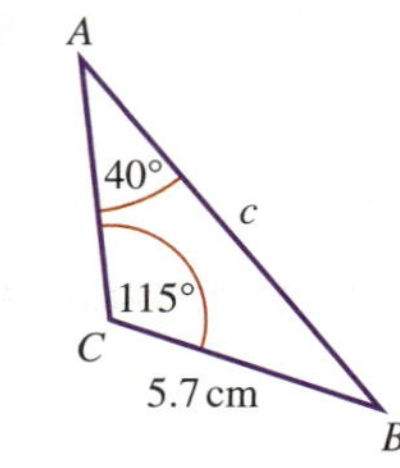

d
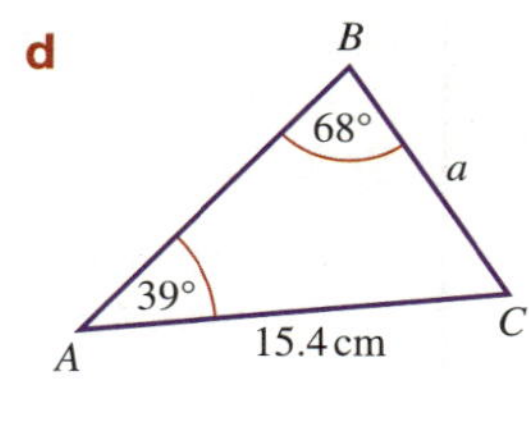

3 Calculate the size of angle B in each of these triangles.

a
C
105°
4.8 cm
B
12.5 cm
A

b
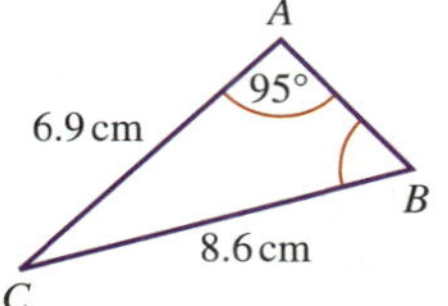

c
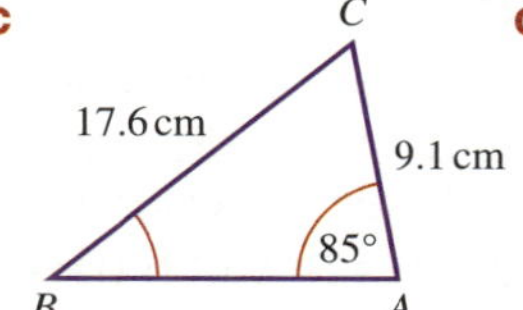

d
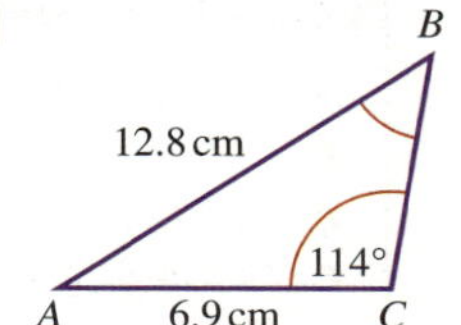

4 **a** Calculate the size of the obtuse angle A in this triangle. Give your answer correct to the nearest degree.

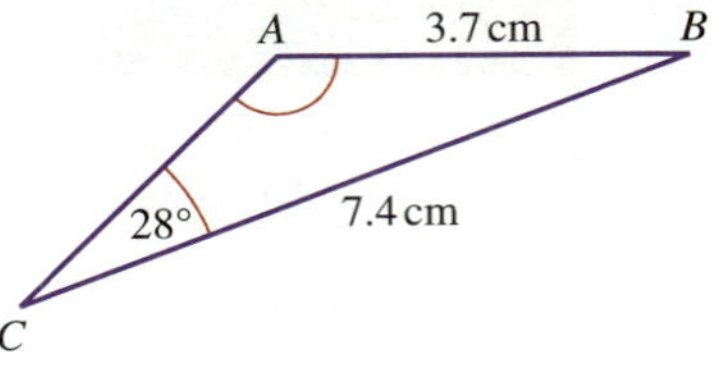

b In triangle ABC below, angle C is acute. Calculate the size of angle C, giving your answer correct to one decimal place.

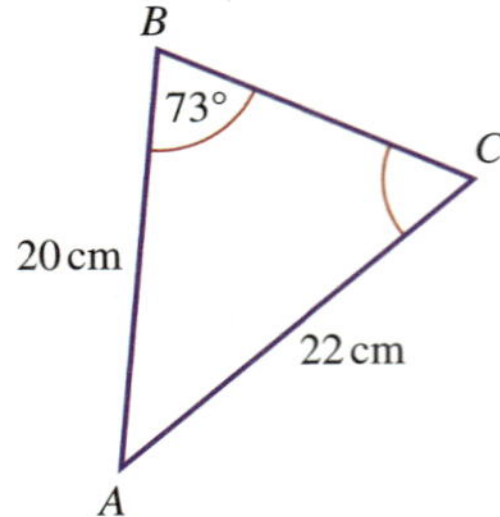

5 In triangle PQR angle $P = 34°$, $QR = 7.5$ cm and $PR = 8.2$ cm. Calculate the two possible values of angle Q and sketch both triangles.

Look again at triangle ABC.

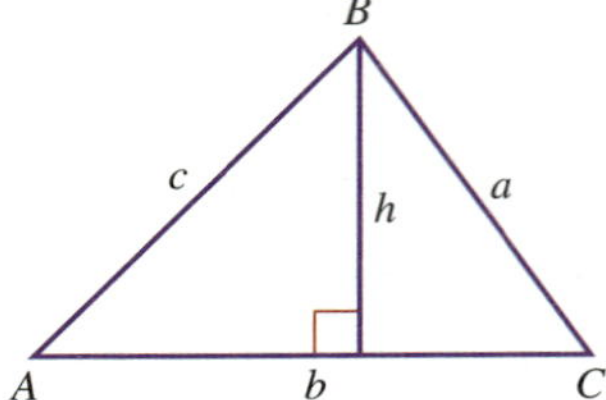

The area of triangle ABC can be found using the formula

area $= \frac{1}{2} \times$ base $\times$ perpendicular height

area $= \frac{1}{2}bh$

But $h = a\sin C$ so the formula can be written

area $= \frac{1}{2}ab\sin C$

Using other sides as the base also gives

area $= \frac{1}{2}bc\sin A$ or $\frac{1}{2}ac\sin B$

Example 4

Find the area of triangle ABC.

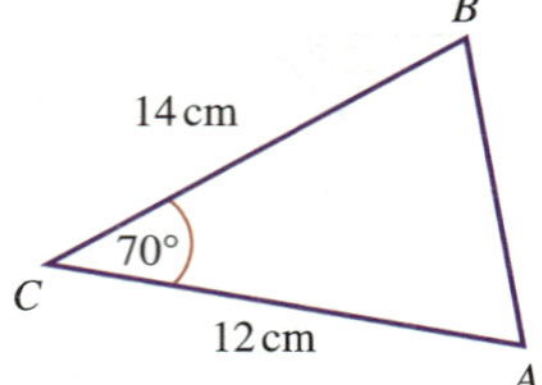

Solution 4

area $= \frac{1}{2}ab\sin C$

$= \frac{1}{2} \times 14 \times 12 \times \sin 70° = 78.9\text{ cm}^2$ (to 1 d.p.)

Example 5

A triangular island PQR has angle $QPR = 120°$, angle $PQR = 33°$, length $PR = 10$ km and $PQ = 8$ km.

a Make an accurate scale drawing of the island using a scale of 1 cm to 2 km.

b Use your drawing to work out the length of RQ.

c Check your answer to part **b** using the sine rule.

Solution 5

a

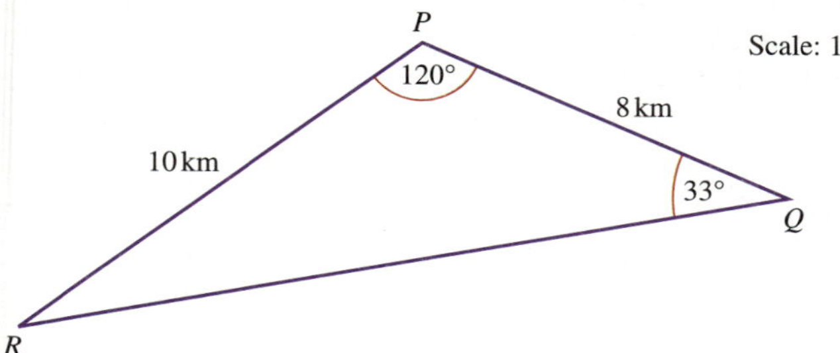

b On the diagram the length RQ is 7.9 cm.
The actual distance $RQ = 7.9 \times 2 = 15.8$ km.

c By the sine rule $\dfrac{RQ}{\sin P°} = \dfrac{PR}{\sin Q°}$ so $\dfrac{RQ}{\sin 120°} = \dfrac{10}{\sin 33°}$

$RQ = \dfrac{10}{\sin 33°} \times \sin 120° = 15.9$ km (to 1 d.p.)

Note that the sine rule answer is the accurate answer.

Exercise B

1 Given that $\sin 65° = 0.91$, $\sin 49° = 0.75$ and $\sin 30° = 0.5$, work out the area of each of these triangles.

a

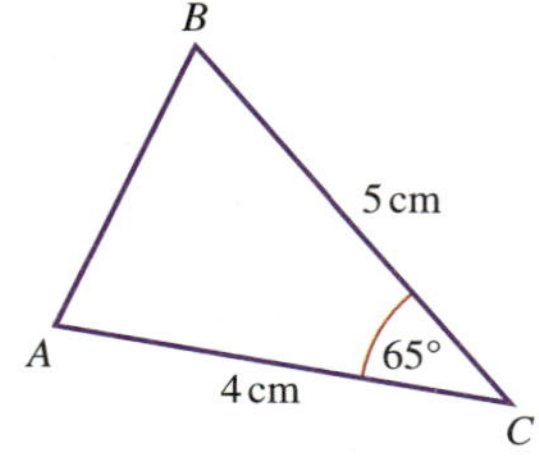

b

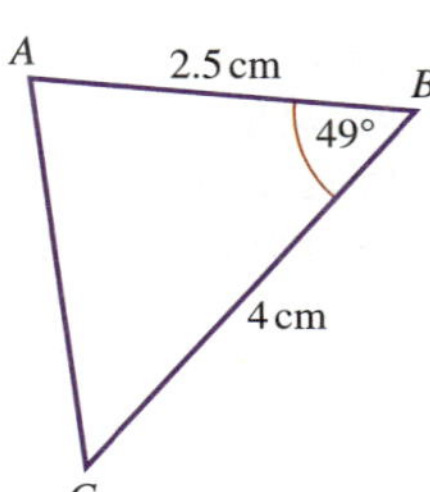

c

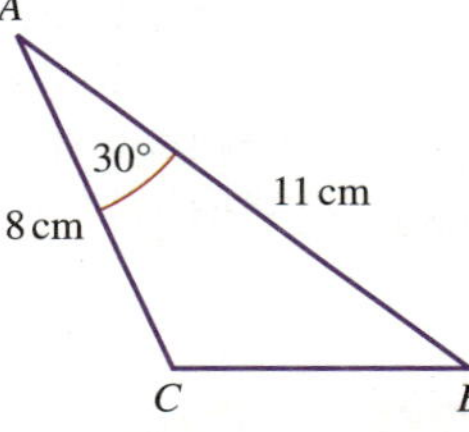

2 Find the area of each of these triangles.

a

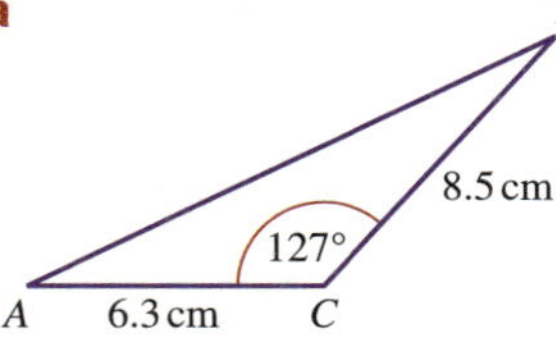

b

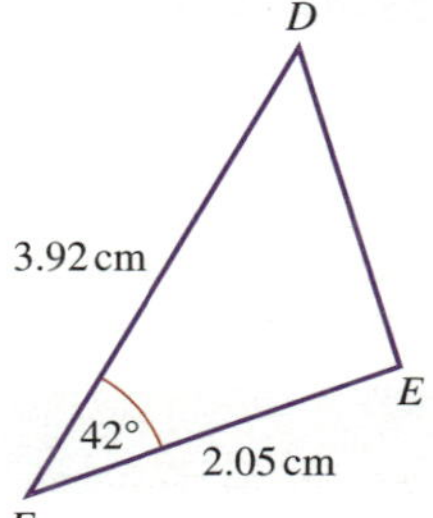

c

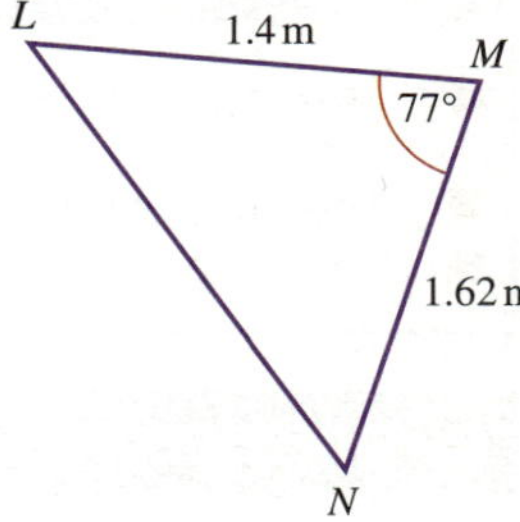

3 Calculate the area of an equilateral triangle of side 7 cm.

4 The diagram shows a parallelogram $PQRS$.
Calculate the area of the parallelogram.

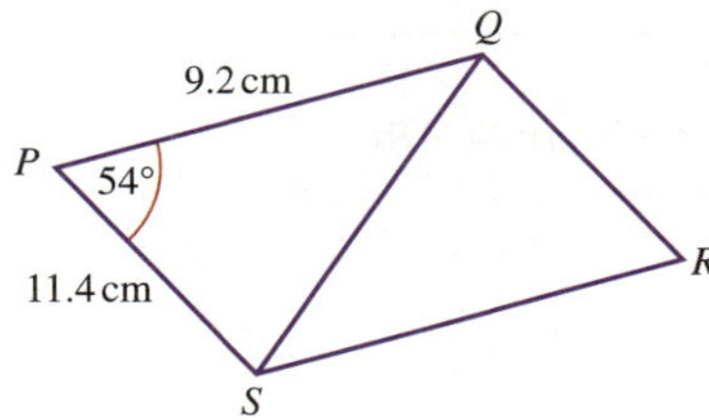

5 Triangle ABC has $AB = 12$ m, $AC = 7.5$ m and angle $BAC = 70°$.
- **a** Make an accurate scale drawing of the triangle using a scale of 1 cm to 3 m.
- **b** Calculate the area of the triangle in m^2.
- **c** Use your diagram to work out the actual length of BC to one decimal place.
- **d** Given that angle $ABC = 37°$, use the sine rule to check your answer to part **c**.

6 The diagram shows a quadrilateral $ABCD$.
- **a** Calculate the length of BD.
- **b** Calculate the area of the quadrilateral, giving your answer to an appropriate degree of accuracy.

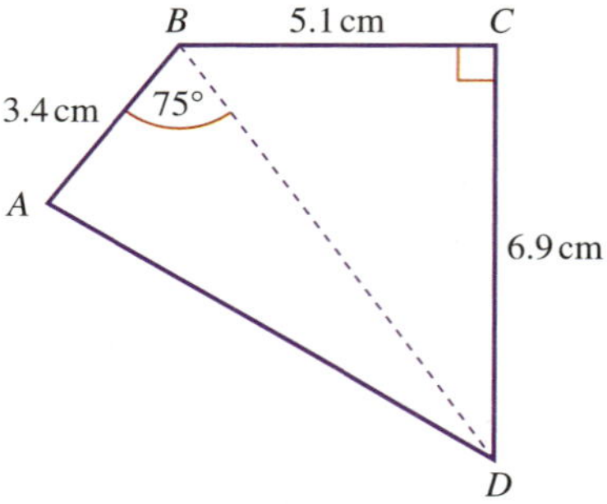

7 In a triangle RST, $RS = 7$ cm and $RT = 9.2$ cm. The area of the triangle is 27.3 cm^2. Calculate angle SRT, given that it is acute. Give your answer to the nearest degree.

8 An isosceles triangle, ABC, has an area of 17.9 cm^2.
Angle $BAC = 74°$ and $AB = AC$.
- **a** Calculate the lengths of AB and AC.
- **b** Calculate the length of BC.

9 The diagram shows a sector of a circle of radius 8 cm.
- **a** Calculate the area of the sector.
- **b** Calculate the area of triangle OAB.
- **c** Hence calculate the area of the shaded segment.
Give your answer to an appropriate degree of accuracy.

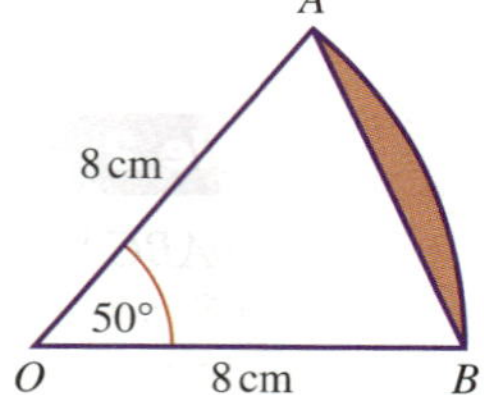

38.3 Cosine rule

CAN YOU REMEMBER

- The sine rule: $\frac{a}{\sin A} = \frac{b}{\sin B} = \frac{c}{\sin C}$?
- The area of a triangle $= \frac{1}{2}ab\sin C$?
- That three figure bearings are measured clockwise from north?

IN THIS SECTION YOU WILL

- Use the cosine rule to calculate the length of sides and sizes of angles in triangles.
- Solve problems using the sine and cosine rules, including the use of bearings and scale drawings.

In any triangle ABC
$a^2 = b^2 + c^2 - 2bc \cos A$

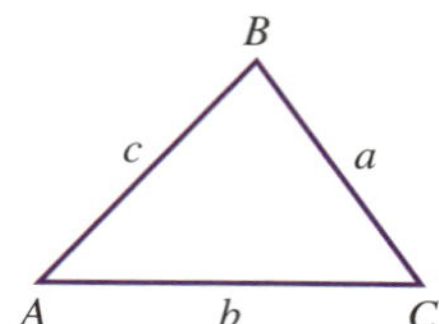

Rotating the letters in the cosine rule formula gives
$b^2 = a^2 + c^2 - 2ac\cos B$
$c^2 = a^2 + b^2 - 2ab\cos C$
This is known as the *cosine rule*.
The cosine rule can be used to find the third side of the triangle if two sides and the angle between the two sides are known.
If three sides are known, the cosine rule can be used to find the angles.

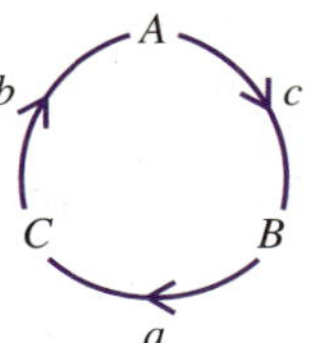

Rearranging the cosine rule formula gives:

$$\cos A = \frac{b^2 + c^2 - a^2}{2bc} \text{ or } \cos B = \frac{a^2 + c^2 - b^2}{2ac} \text{ or } \cos C = \frac{a^2 + b^2 - c^2}{2ab}$$

Example 1

The diagram shows a triangle ABC.
Calculate the length of AB.

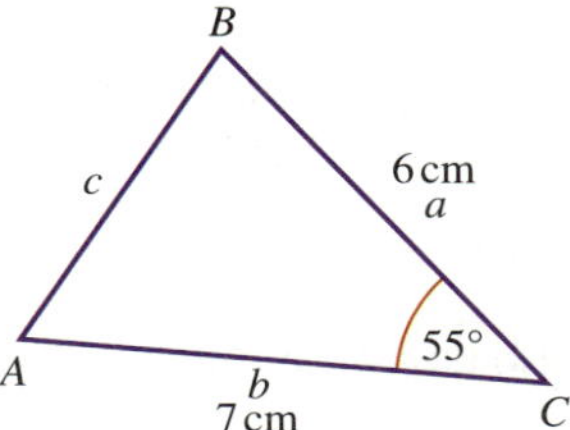

Solution 1

$c^2 = 6^2 + 7^2 - (2 \times 6 \times 7 \times \cos 55°)$
$= 36 + 49 - 48.18 = 36.8196$
$c = \sqrt{36.8196} = 6.0679 = 6.1$ cm to 1 d.p.

Example 2

Triangle ABC has side lengths $AB = 5.2$ cm, $BC = 4.8$ cm and $AC = 7.1$ cm.
Calculate the size of angle BAC.

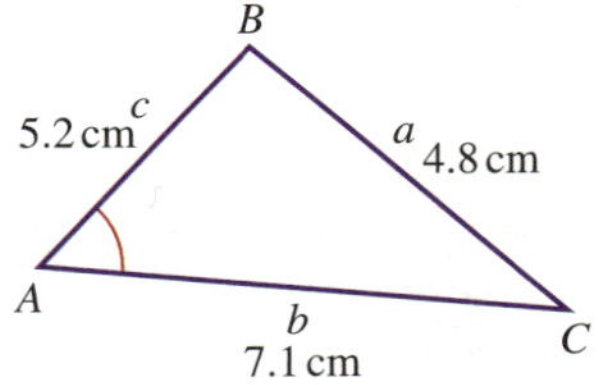

Solution 2

Sketch the triangle and label the sides.

$$\cos A = \frac{b^2 + c^2 - a^2}{2bc}$$

$$\cos A = \frac{7.1^2 + 5.2^2 - 4.8^2}{2 \times 7.1 \times 5.2} = \frac{54.41}{73.84} = 0.7369$$

$A = \cos^{-1} 0.7369 = 42.5°$

Exercise A

1 Given that $\cos 60° = 0.5$, work out the length of a in each triangle.
Leave each answer as a square root.

a

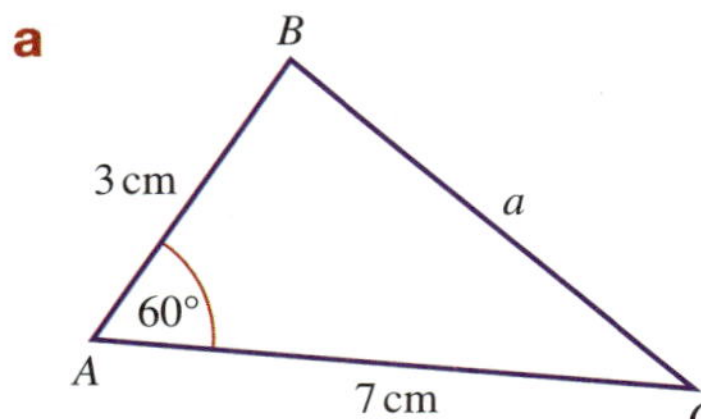

b

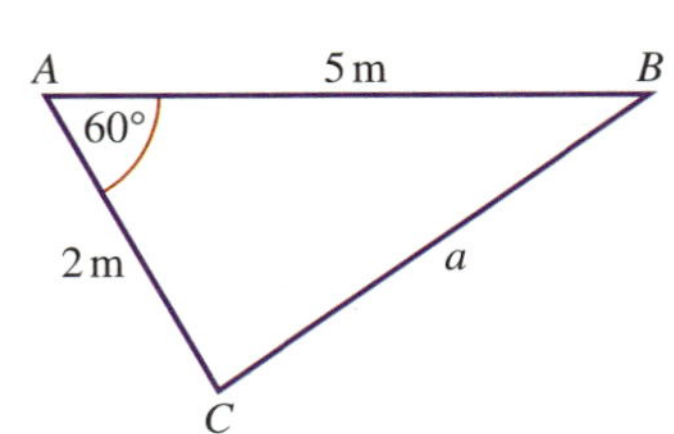

2 Calculate the length of side b in each triangle.

a

B, 37°, 11.6 cm, 5.2 cm, A, b, C

b

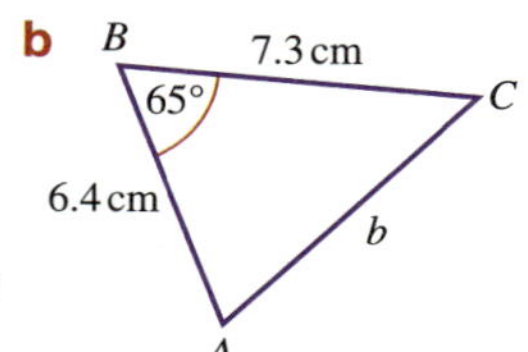

c

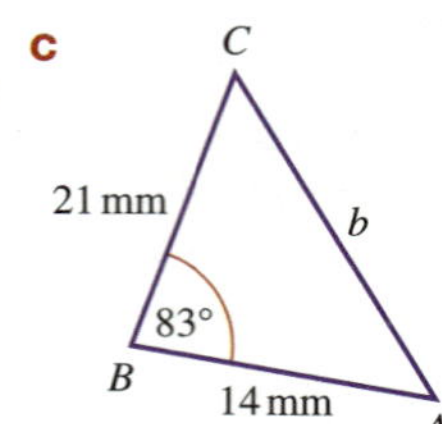

d

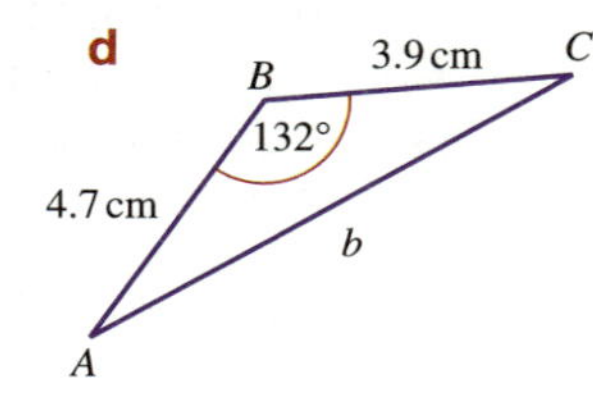

3 Calculate the size of angle A in each triangle, giving your answers correct to the nearest degree.

a

B, 11.4 cm, 9.7 cm, A, 12.6 cm, C

b

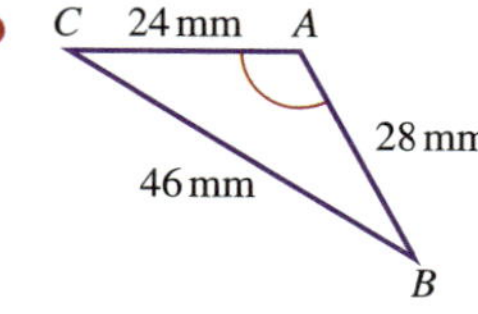

c

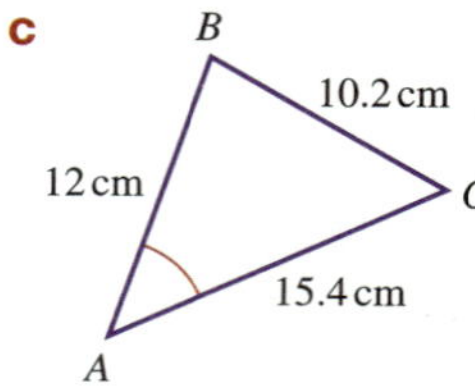

d

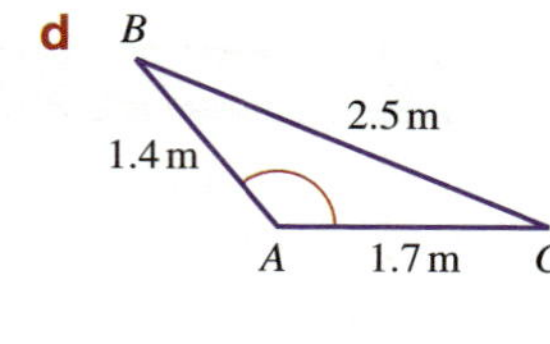

4 Find the length of the side marked with a letter.

a

A, c, B, 27 mm, 35 mm, 41°, C

b

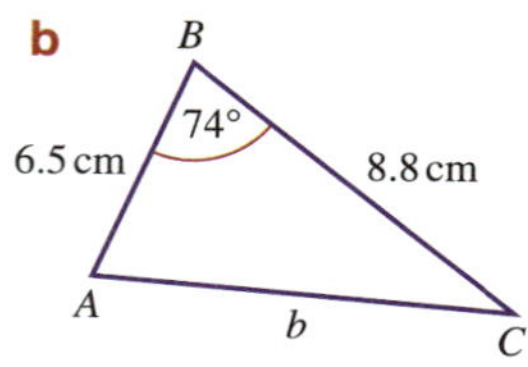

c

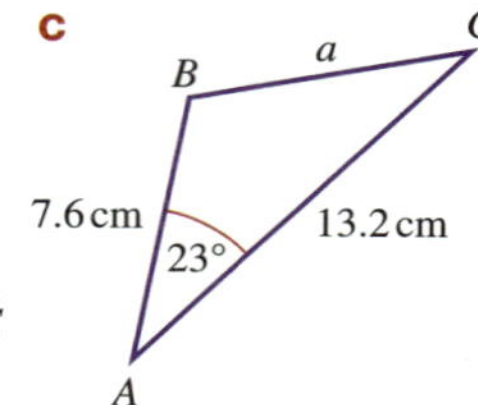

d

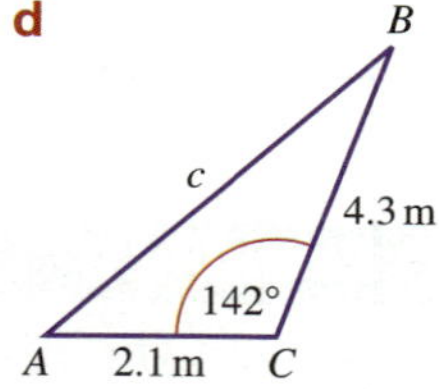

5 **a** In triangle ABC, $AB = 8.2$ cm, $BC = 4.5$ cm and $AC = 7.3$ cm. Calculate the size of angle ABC.

b In triangle PQR, $PQ = 23$ mm, $PR = 17$ mm and $QR = 38$ mm. Calculate the size of angle QPR.

c In triangle LMN, $LM = 3.4$ m, $MN = 2.7$ m and $LN = 1.9$ m. Calculate the size of angle LMN.

Example 3

A ship leaves a port and sails on a bearing of 120° for 4 km.
The ship then changes course and sails on a bearing of 245° for 5 km.
Use the cosine rule to find the distance of the ship from the port.

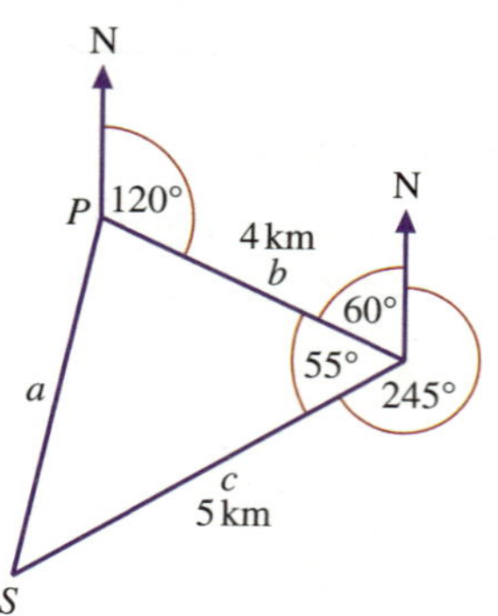

Solution 3

Draw a sketch as shown on the right.

$a^2 = 4^2 + 5^2 - (2 \times 4 \times 5 \times \cos 55°)$

$a^2 = 16 + 25 - 22.94 = 18.0569$

$a = \sqrt{18.0569} = 4.25$ km (2 d.p.)

Example 4

The diagram shows the quadrilateral $ABCD$.
Calculate the value of the obtuse angle BDC, marked x on the diagram.

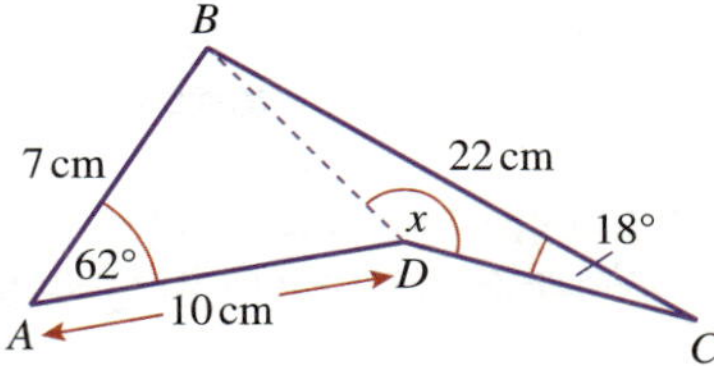

Solution 4

Find BD using triangle BDA and the cosine rule.
$BD^2 = 7^2 + 10^2 - (2 \times 7 \times 10 \times \cos 62°) = 49 + 100 - 65.726 = 83.274$
$BD = \sqrt{83.274} = 9.13$ cm (2 d.p.)
Now the sine rule can be used to find angle x.

$$\frac{\sin x}{22} = \frac{\sin 18}{9.13}$$

$$\sin x = \frac{\sin 18}{9.13} \times 22 = 0.7446$$

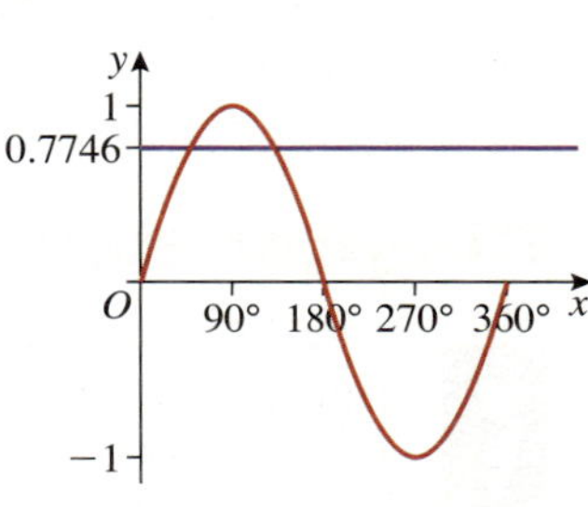

Using a calculator, $\sin^{-1} 0.7746 = 48.1°$
therefore $x = 48.1°$ or by symmetry $180° - 48.1° = 131.9°$
As x is obtuse, $x = 131.9°$.

Exercise B

1 Tony leaves home and drives on a bearing of 035° for 25 km. He then changes direction and drives on a bearing of 115° for 20 km before stopping.
- **a** Make an accurate scale drawing of his route using a scale of 1 cm to 5 km.
- **b** Use your scale drawing to work out the distance Tony is from home.
- **c** Check your answer to part **b** using the cosine rule.

2 The diagram shows a quadrilateral $PQRS$.
Calculate the size of angle PSR.

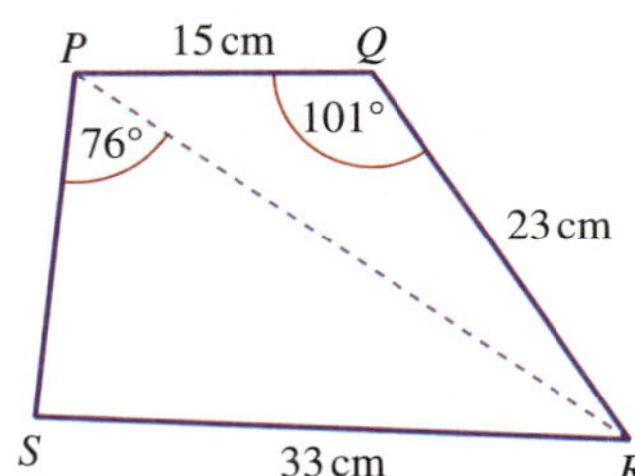

3 Two ships, S and T, leave port at 9 am.
Ship S travels at a speed of 28 km/h on a bearing of 075°.
Ship T travels at a speed of 36 km/h on a bearing of 140°.
Calculate the distance between the ships at 11 am. Give your answer to the nearest kilometre.

4 The diagram shows a field $ABCD$.
A footpath runs across the field from corner B to corner D.
- **a** Calculate the length of the footpath giving your answer to three significant figures.
- **b** Calculate the perimeter of the field.

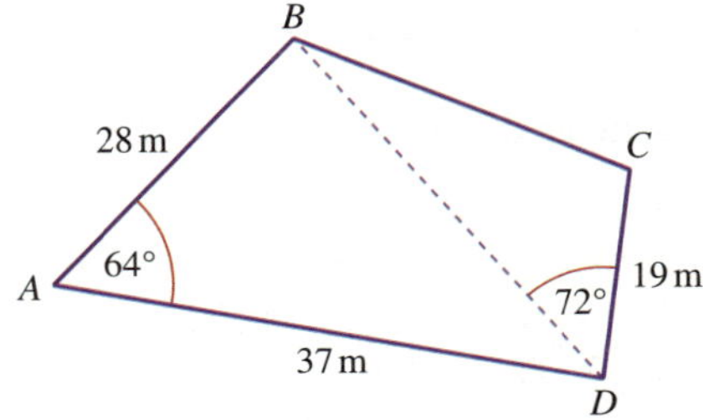

5 A watch has a minute hand which is 6 mm long and an hour hand which is 3.5 mm long.
Calculate the distance between the ends of the hands when the watch shows 5 o'clock.

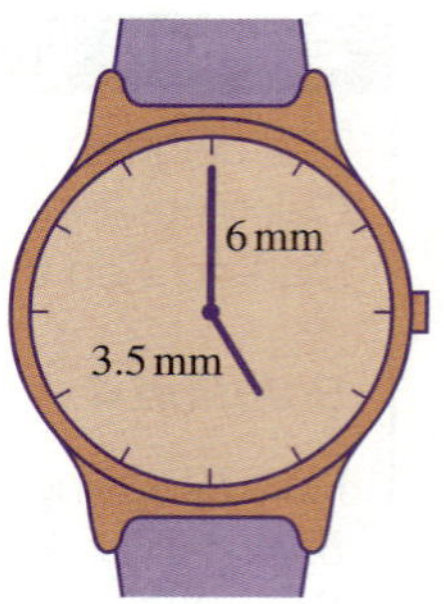

6 A triangle has side lengths of 7 cm, 12 cm and 15 cm.
Calculate the area of the triangle.

7 A triangle has sides of 6 cm, 8 cm and 10 cm.
Use the cosine rule to prove that the triangle is right-angled.

Chapter summary

- The graphs of $\sin x$, $\cos x$ and $\tan x$ can be extended for **any** values of x.
- The number of degrees before the pattern repeats is called the period of the function. The functions sine, cosine and tangent are called periodic functions.
- $\sin x$ and $\cos x$ have period 360°. $\tan x$ has period 180°.
- The sine rule states that $\frac{a}{\sin A} = \frac{b}{\sin B} = \frac{c}{\sin C}$ or $\frac{\sin A}{a} = \frac{\sin B}{b} = \frac{\sin C}{c}$
- To use the sine rule, one side and its opposite angle must be known, together with another side or angle.
- Area of a triangle $= \frac{1}{2}ab\sin C$
- In any triangle ABC, $a^2 = b^2 + c^2 - 2bc\cos A$ or $b^2 = a^2 + c^2 - 2ac\cos B$ or $c^2 = a^2 + b^2 - 2ab\cos C$
This is known as the cosine rule.
- The cosine rule can be used to find the third side of the triangle if two sides and the angle between the two sides are known.
- If three sides are known the cosine rule can be used to find the angles.
Rearranging the cosine rule formula gives:
$\cos A = \frac{b^2 + c^2 - a^2}{2bc}$ or $\cos B = \frac{a^2 + c^2 - b^2}{2ac}$ or $\cos C = \frac{a^2 + b^2 - c^2}{2ab}$

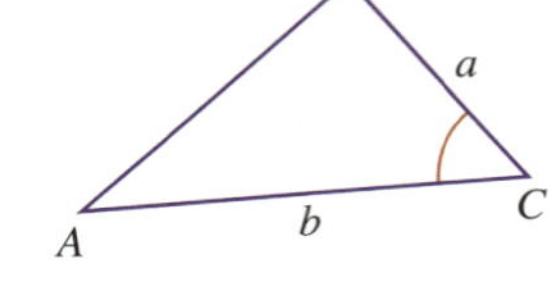

Chapter review

1 **a** Sketch the graph of $y = \sin x$ for $0° \leqslant x \leqslant 360°$.
b Use your graph to find two solutions of the following equations:
i $\sin x = 0.891$ **ii** $\sin x = -0.891$

2 PQR is a triangle. $PQ = 20$ cm, $PR = 26$ cm, $QR = 38$ cm.
Calculate the size of angle QPR.

Q
Not drawn accurately
20 cm
38 cm
P
26 cm
R

3 Find the acute angle for which $2\cos x = 0.484$

4 The diagram shows a sector of a circle of radius 6.5 cm.
Calculate the area of the shaded segment.

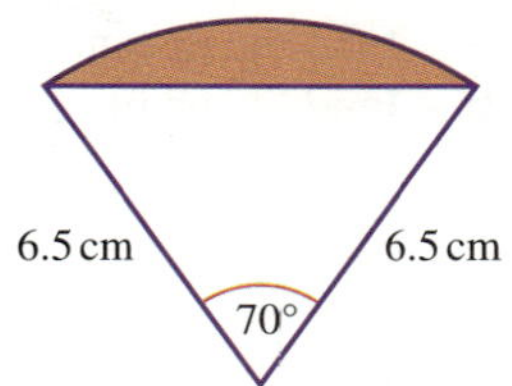

5 In a triangle ABC, $AB = 8$ cm, $BC = 7$ cm and $AC = 6$ cm.
Calculate the area of the triangle.

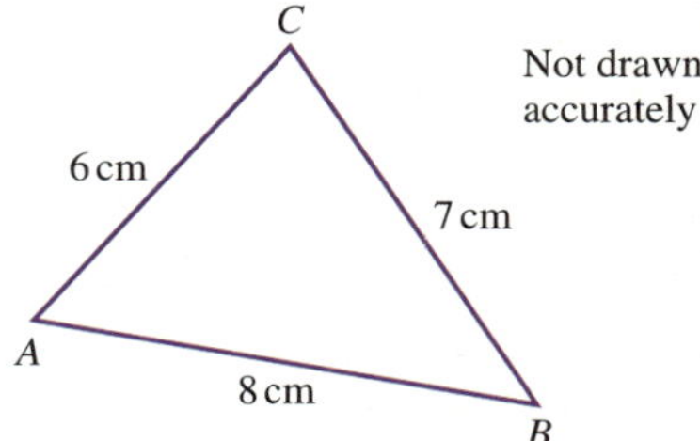

6 The diagram shows a block of flats.

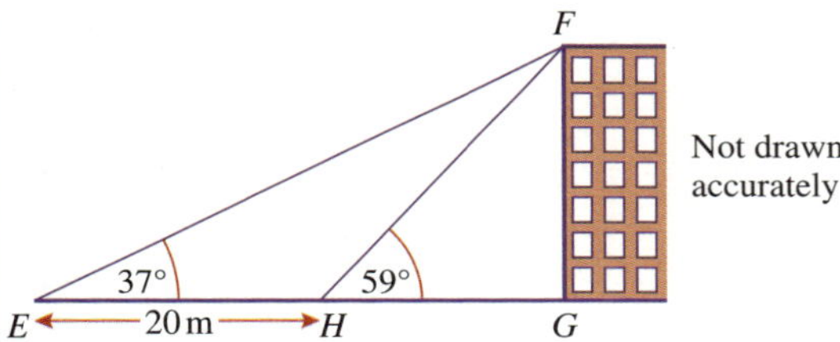

At E the angle of elevation of the top of the building is 37°.
At H the angle of elevation of the top of the building is 59°.
Calculate the height of the block of flats.

7 The diagram shows the quadrilateral $ABCD$.

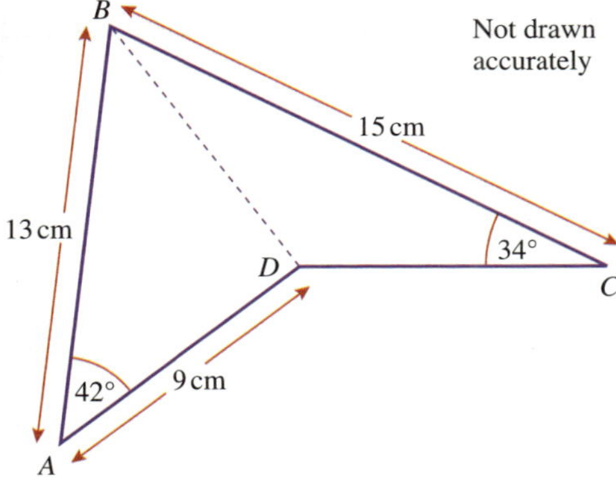

Angle BDC is obtuse.
Calculate angle BDC.

8 The diagram shows part of a rough map which illustrates the relationship between the positions of three villages marked A, B and C.
B is 3.3 km due north of A and C is 2.9 km from A on a bearing of 052°.

a Find the distance BC.

b Find the bearing of C from B.

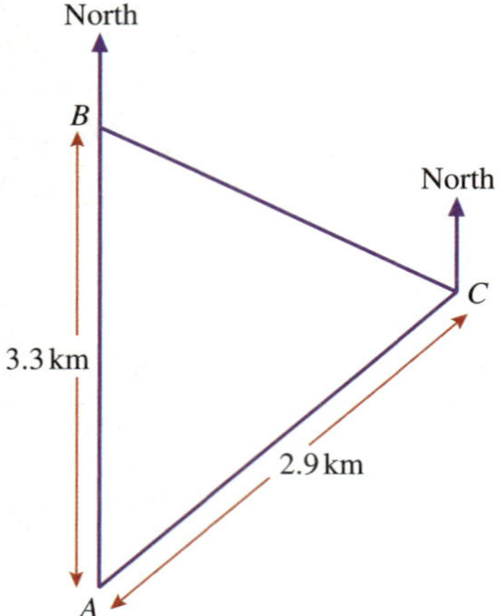

9 The diagram shows an animal enclosure $PQRS$.
Work out the perimeter of the enclosure.

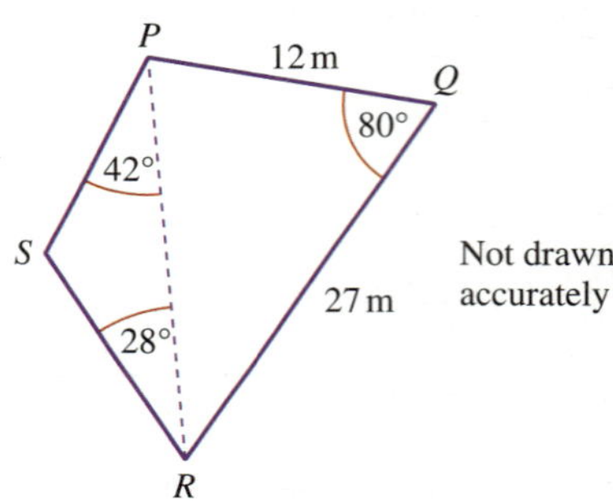

10 Two boats, A and B, leave port at 10 am.
Boat A travels at a constant speed of 12 km/h on a bearing of 075°.
Boat B travels at a constant speed of 8 km/h on a bearing of 136°.
Calculate the distance between the two boats at 10:30 am.

CHAPTER 39

Direct and inverse proportion

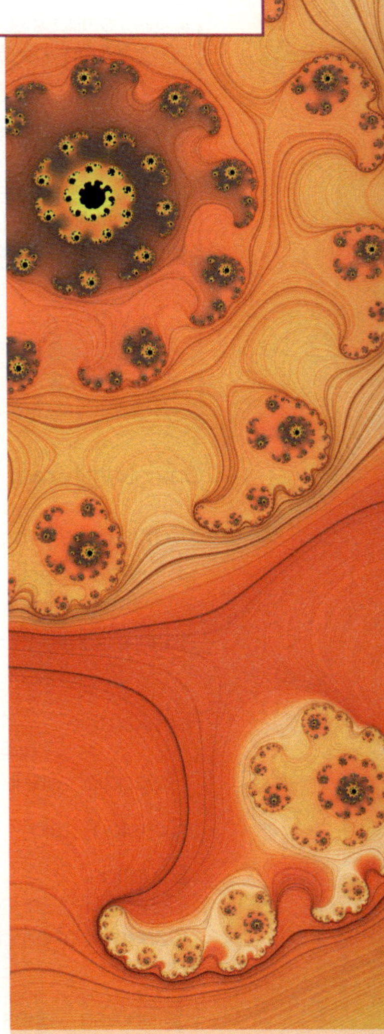

39.1 Direct proportion

CAN YOU REMEMBER

- How to simplify a ratio?

IN THIS SECTION YOU WILL

- Learn the meaning of 'direct proportion'.
- Learn how to find an equation or formula connecting quantities that are in direct proportion.
- Use direct proportion to solve problems.
- Identify graphs representing direct proportion.

Jim walks at a constant speed of 1.5 metres per second.
The table shows the distance that Jim walks for various times up to 1 minute.

Time, t (seconds)	0	10	20	30	40	50	60
Distance, d (metres)	0	15	30	45	60	75	90

The table shows

- When $t = 0$, $d = 0$
- The ratio of $t : d$ in its simplest form is always $2 : 3$

When any two quantities x and y are such that:

- when $x = 0$, $y = 0$
- the ratio $y : x$ is always the same

then y is said to be *directly proportional* to x.

This relationship can be written in symbols: $y \propto x$
$\propto$ means 'is directly proportional to'.
The relationship can also be expressed as an equation: $y = kx$
where k is the *constant of proportionality*.

The value of k is $\frac{y}{x}$

Example 1

The table shows values of p and q where q is directly proportional to p.

p	2	5	6	10	12	b
q	1.2	3	3.6	6	a	0.3

a **i** What happens to q when p doubles from 5 to 10?
ii What happens to q when p trebles from 2 to 6?
b Find the values of a and b.

Solution 1

a **i** When p **doubles** from 5 to 10, q **doubles** from 3 to 6
ii When p **trebles** from 2 to 6, p **trebles** from 1.2 to 3.6

b **Method 1:** Use equivalent ratios.
$q \propto p$, so the ratio $p : q$ is always the same.
When $p = 6$, $q = 3.6$ and when $p = 12$, $q = a$
$6 : 3.6 \equiv 12 : a$
$12 = 6 \times \mathbf{2}$
So $a = 3.6 \times \mathbf{2} = 7.2$
When $p = 5$, $q = 3$ and when $p = b$, $q = 0.3$
$5 : 3 \equiv b : 0.3$
$0.3 = 3 \div \mathbf{10}$
So $b = 5 \div \mathbf{10} = 0.5$

Method 2: Find the equation connecting p and q.
$q \propto p$
$q = kp$
To find k substitute corresponding values of p and q into $q = kp$
When $p = 5$, $q = 3$
$3 = k \times 5$ — Divide both sides by 5

$$k = \frac{3}{5} = 0.6$$

So the equation connecting p and q is $q = 0.6p$.
When $p = 12$
$p = 0.6 \times 12 = 7.2$
$a = 7.2$

When $q = 0.3$
$0.3 = 0.6 \times p$
$b = 0.5$

One quantity may be directly proportional to the **power** or **root** of another quantity.

In this case, when any two quantities x and y are such that:

- when $x = 0$, $y = 0$
- the ratio $y : x^n$ is always the same

then y is said to be *directly proportional* to x^n.

For example

Proportionality in symbols	$y \propto x$	$y \propto x^2$	$y \propto x^3$	$y \propto \sqrt{x}$
Constant ratio	$y : x$	$y : x^2$	$y : x^3$	$y : \sqrt{x}$
Equation	$y = kx$	$y = kx^2$	$y = kx^3$	$y = k\sqrt{x}$
Constant of proportionality	$k = \frac{y}{x}$	$k = \frac{y}{x^2}$	$k = \frac{y}{x^3}$	$k = \frac{y}{\sqrt{x}}$

The phrase 'varies directly with' is sometimes used instead of 'is directly proportional to'.

Example 2

Find an equation for y in terms of x for each of these situations.

a y varies directly with x^3 and $y = 18$ when $x = 2$

b y varies directly with $\sqrt{x}$ and $y = 18$ when $x = 9$

Solution 2

a $y \propto x^3$
$y = kx^3$
When $x = 2$, $y = 18$
$18 = k \times 2^3$
$18 = k \times 8$
$k = \frac{18}{8} = \frac{9}{4}$
The equation is $y = \frac{9}{4}x^3$

b $y \propto \sqrt{x}$
$y = k\sqrt{x}$
When $x = 9$, $y = 18$
$18 = k \times \sqrt{9}$
$18 = k \times 3$
$k = 6$
The equation is $y = 6\sqrt{x}$

Example 3

y is proportional to the square of x where x and y are positive integers.
When $x = 2$, $y = 100$

a Find y when $x = 4$

b Find x when $y = 2500$

Solution 3

Find the equation for y in terms of x
$y \propto x^2$
$y = kx^2$
When $x = 2$, $y = 100$
$100 = k \times 2^2 = k \times 4$
$k = 25$
$y = 25x^2$

a When $x = 4$, $y = 25 \times 4^2 = 25 \times 16 = 400$
So when $x = 4$, $y = 400$

b When $y = 2500$, $2500 = 25x^2$
$x^2 = 2500 \div 25 = 100$
$x = \sqrt{100} = 10$
So when $y = 2500$, $x = 10$

Exercise A

1 Express the following statements as mathematical equations.

a r is proportional to s.

b w varies directly with the cube root of z.

2 In each of the following tables of values y is proportional to x.

a

x	5	12	25	50
y	3	7.2	15	?

b

x	2	0.4	1	10
y	5	1	2.5	?

c

x	10	15	35	?
y	18	27	63	90

For each table:

i find the ratio $y : x$ in its simplest form

ii express y in terms of x

iii work out the missing value.

3 In each of the following tables of values b is proportional to a^2.

a

a	1	2	5	10
b	5	20	125	?

b

a	2	6	10	15
b	3.2	28.8	80	?

c

a	0.5	2.5	5	?
b	0.5	12.5	50	288

For each table:

- **i** find the ratio $b : a^2$ in its simplest form
- **ii** work out the constant of proportionality for each table
- **iii** express b in terms of a
- **iv** work out the missing value.

4 In the table a varies directly with b.

- **a** Express b in terms of a.
- **b** Copy and complete the table.

a	2.5	6	
b	12.5		75

5 a $y \propto x^2$

The constant of proportionality is 5

- **i** Calculate y when $x = 2$
- **ii** Calculate x when $y = 500$

b $y \propto \sqrt{x}$

When x is 25, $y = 10$

What is the constant of proportionality?

6 In the table y is directly proportional to the square of x.

- **a** Express y in terms of x.
- **b** Copy and complete the table.

x	4	2	
y	24		54

7 a y is directly proportional to x.

When $x = 5$, $y = 20$

- **i** Calculate y when $x = 6$
- **ii** Calculate x when $y = 50$

b x is a positive integer.

y varies directly with the square of x.

When $x = 2$, $y = 16$

- **i** Form an equation for y in terms of x.
- **ii** Work out the value of y when $x = 3$
- **iii** Work out the value of x when $y = 1$

8

s	5	10	20
t	1.25	5	20

u	2	6	10
v	10	30	50

w	0.5	1	2
x	0.375	3	24

y	1	9	16
z	0.5	1.5	2

Bill has worked out these statements for the tables but has got the powers mixed up.

$t \propto s^{0.5}$ $\quad v \propto u^2$ $\quad x \propto w$ $\quad z \propto y^3$

Correct the statements.

9 The distance D in metres that a stone falls in time t seconds is given by the formula $D = 5t^2$

- **a** Copy and complete the sentences.
  The distance D is directly proportional to the .... of the time.
  The constant of proportionality = ...
- **b** Calculate the distance that a stone falls in 15 seconds.
- **c** A stone falls 500 m.
  For how many seconds does it fall?

10 y is directly proportional to the square root of x.

When $x = 64$, $y = 2$

- **a** Form an equation for y in terms of x.
- **b** Find the value of y when $x = 100$
- **c** Find the value of x when $y = 12.25$

Many quantities in real life are in proportion.

Example 4

The weight of an elephant, W, is approximately proportional to its height, h, cubed.
The height of an elephant in the zoo is 3 m, and its weight is 4050 kg.

a Find a formula that can be used to estimate W in terms of h.

b **i** The height of a baby elephant is 1.5 m.
Estimate its weight to the nearest 10 kg.

ii The weight of an elephant is 3000 kg.
Estimate its height to the nearest 10 cm.

Solution 4

a $W \propto h^3$
$W = kh^3$
When $h = 3$, $W = 4050$
$4050 = k \times 3^3$
$4050 = k \times 27$
$k = 4050 \div 27 = 150$
The formula is $W = 150h^3$

b **i** $W = 150 \times 1.5^3 = 506.25$ kg
The weight of the elephant to the nearest 10 kg is 510 kg.

ii $3000 = 150 \times h^3$
$h^3 = 3000 \div 150 = 20$
$h = \sqrt[3]{20} = 2.7144\ldots$
The height of the elephant to the nearest 10 cm is 2 metres 70 cm.

The sketch graphs show y against x when $y \propto x^n$ for different values of n.

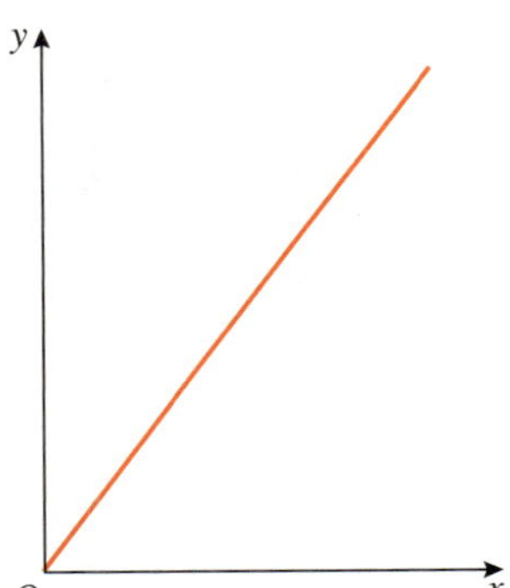

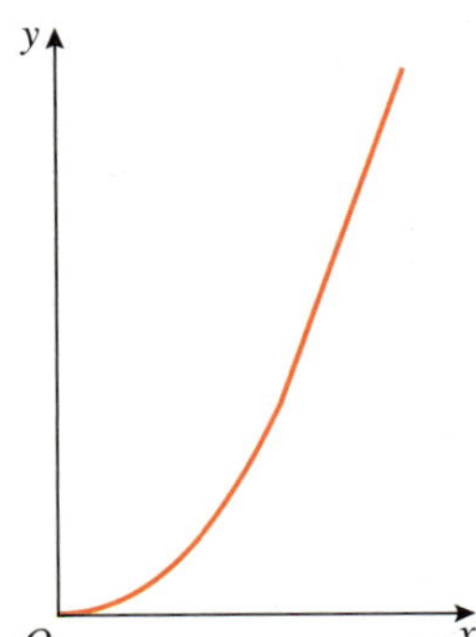

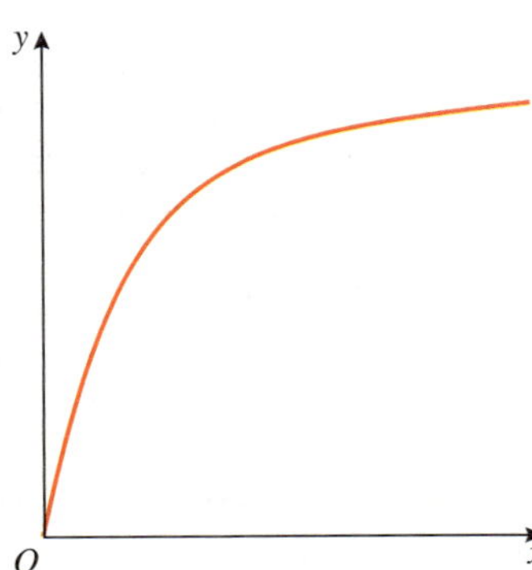

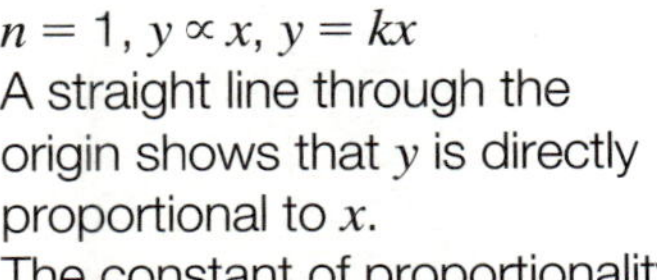

$n = 1$, $y \propto x$, $y = kx$
A straight line through the origin shows that y is directly proportional to x.
The constant of proportionality equals the gradient.

$n = 2$, $y \propto x^2$, $y = kx^2$
This is typical of the shape of the graph when $y \propto x^n$ and $n > 1$
As x increases by a constant amount, y increases by an increasing amount.

$n = \frac{1}{2}$, $y \propto \sqrt{x}$
This is typical of the shape of the graph when $y \propto x^n$ and $0 < n < 1$
As x increases by a constant amount, y increases by a decreasing amount.

Example 5

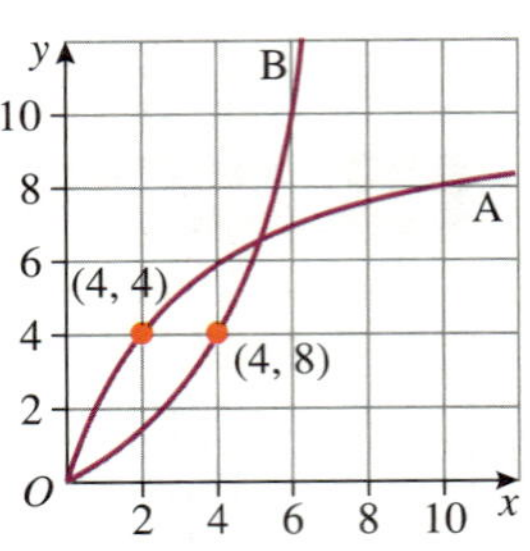

Graphs A and B show different relationships between x and y.
On one of the graphs $y \propto \sqrt{x}$ and on the other $y \propto x^2$
Graph A passes through the point (4, 8).
Graph B passes through the point (4, 4).
Find the equation of each graph.

Solution 5

Graph A is the graph showing $y \propto \sqrt{x}$
$y = k\sqrt{x}$
When $x = 4$, $y = 4$
$4 = k \times \sqrt{4}$
$4 = k \times 2$
$k = 2$
The equation of graph A is $y = 2\sqrt{x}$

Graph B is the graph showing $y \propto x^2$
$y = kx^2$
When $x = 4$, $y = 8$
$8 = k \times 4^2$
$8 = k \times 16$
$k = 0.5$
The equation of graph B is $y = 0.5x^2$

Exercise B

1 **a** The area of a circle, A, is proportional to the square of its radius, r.
  i Write a formula expressing A in terms of r.
  ii What does the constant of proportionality represent?
b Distance, d, varies directly with time, t.
  i Write a formula expressing d in terms of t.
  ii What does the constant of proportionality represent?

2 Tiaz is swinging a conker on a string in a circle.
The force, F, acting on the conker is proportional to the square of its speed, v.
a Find the increase in F when v is doubled.
b Find the decrease in F when v is halved.

3 **a** A set of cones have the same base radius.
The volume of the cones, V, varies directly with the height, h.
  i One of the cones has a height of 4 cm and a volume of 24.8 cm^3
  Express V in terms of h.
  ii What does the constant of proportionality represent?
b A different set of cones have the same height, h.

The volume of the cones, V, varies directly with the square of the base radius, r.
  i One of the cones has a radius of 3 cm and a volume of 40.5 cm^3
  Express V in terms of r.
  ii What does the constant of proportionality represent?

4 Match each graph to one of the statements below.

Graph 1

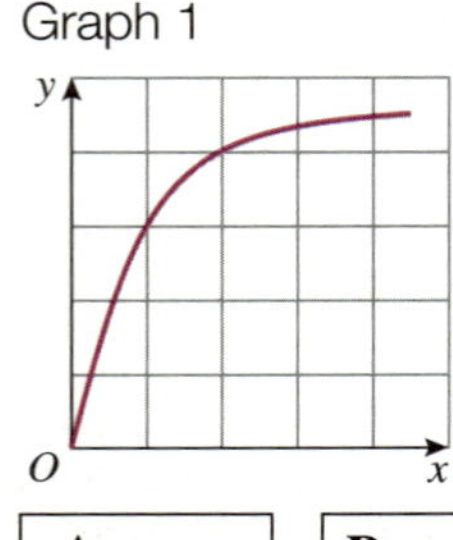

Graph 2

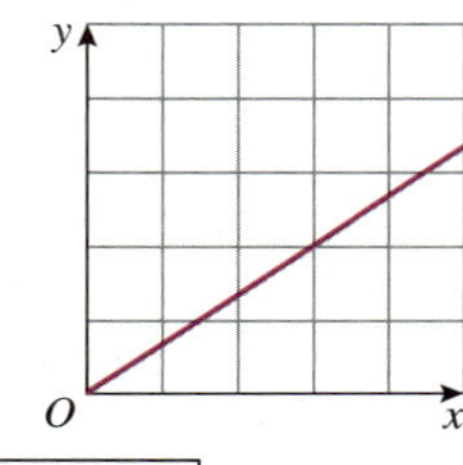

Graph 3

A: $y \propto x$ **B:** $y \propto \sqrt{x}$ **C:** $y \propto x^2$

5 $y \alpha x^2$

- **a** What happens to y when x is doubled?
- **b** What happens to y when x is increased by 10%?
- **c** What happens to y when x is decreased by 20%?

6 The area, A cm², of a circular puddle varies directly with the square of the radius, r cm.
When $r = 10$ cm, $A = 314$ cm²

- **a** Work out the constant of proportionality and comment on your answer.
- **b** Find A when $r = 12$ cm.
  Give your answer to an appropriate degree of accuracy.

7 Match each statement to one of the tables below.

1: $y \alpha x$ | **2:** $y \alpha \sqrt{x}$ | **3:** $y \alpha x^2$ | **4:** $y \alpha x^3$

Table A

x	1	2	3
y	0.35	2.8	9.45

Table B

x	1	4	25
y	6.5	13	32.5

Table C

x	1	4	10
y	0.7	2.8	7

Table D

x	1	6	10
y	0.1	3.6	10

8 Sam does an experiment with a conker on a string.
He measures the time, t, it takes for the conker to swing backwards and forwards ten times.
He does this for different lengths of string, l.
Here are his results.

l (cm)	20	30	40	50	60
t (s)	7.16	8.76	10.12	11.31	12.39

Show that $t \propto \sqrt{l}$

9 The weight, W grams, of a spherical ball is proportional to the cube of its radius, r cm.
When $r = 4$ cm, $W = 300$ grams.

- **a** Find the weight of the ball when $r = 5$ cm.
- **b** Find the value of r when $W = 150$ grams.

Give your answers to three significant figures.

10 The number of days, D, taken to build a bridge is proportional to the number of man hours, h, worked per day.

- **a** It takes 50 days to build a bridge if 900 man hours are worked per day.
  - **i** Find an equation connecting D and h.
  - **ii** How many man hours per day are needed to complete a bridge in 40 days?
- **b** Sketch a graph which shows that D is proportional to h.

39.2 Inverse proportion

CAN YOU REMEMBER

- How to represent direct proportion as a statement of proportionality using the symbol $\propto$ and as an equation?
- The meaning of 'reciprocal'?
- The meaning of 'negative integer' and 'fractional indices'?

IN THIS SECTION YOU WILL

- Learn the meaning of 'inverse proportion'.
- Learn how to find an equation or formula connecting quantities that are inversely proportional.
- Use inverse proportion to solve problems.
- Identify graphs for equations representing inverse proportion.

The time taken to build a wall depends upon the number of bricklayers working on it, as shown in this table.

Number of bricklayers, n	1	2	4	5	8	10
Number of days, d	10	5	2.5	2	1.25	1

The table shows that:

- as n increases, d decreases
- the ratio of $d : \frac{1}{n}$ in its simplest form is always 10 : 1
- the product $d \times n$ is constant and equal to 10

When any two quantities x^n and y are such that:

- when x increases, y decreases
- the ratio $y : \frac{1}{x^n}$ is always the same

then y is said to be *inversely proportional* to x^n.

This relationship can be written in symbols: $y \propto \frac{1}{x^n}$

The relationship can also be expressed as an equation: $y = \frac{k}{x^n}$ where k is the *constant of proportionality*.
The value of k is $x^n y$.
If y is inversely proportional to x^n, y is proportional to the reciprocal of x^n.

Example 1

p	2	4	5	8	10	20
q	8	4	3.2	2	1.6	x

r	0.5	1	2	5	10	y
s	200	50	12.5	2	0.5	0.125

a i Show that q is inversely proportional to p.
ii Calculate the value of x.

b i Show that s is inversely proportional to the square of r.
ii Calculate the value of y.

Solution 1

a **i** If q is inversely proportional to p then $q = \frac{k}{p}$ and qp is constant.

$qp = 2 \times 8 = 4 \times 4 = 5 \times 3.2 = 8 \times 2 = 10 \times 1.6 = 16$
qp has a constant value of 16
So q is inversely proportional to p.

ii $q = \frac{k}{p}$ where $k = qp = 16$

So $q = \frac{16}{p}$

When $p = 20$, $q = x$

$x = \frac{16}{20} = 0.8$

b **i** If s is inversely proportional to the square of r then $s = \frac{k}{r^2}$ and sr^2 is constant.

$sr^2 = 0.5^2 \times 200 = 1^2 \times 50 = 2^2 \times 12.5 = 5^2 \times 2 = 10^2 \times 0.5 = 50$
sr^2 has a constant value of 50
So s is inversely proportional to the square of r.

ii $s = \frac{k}{r^2}$ where $k = sr^2 = 50$

When $r = y$, $s = 0.125$

$y^2 = \frac{50}{0.125} = 400 \quad y = 20$

The phrase 'varies inversely with' is sometimes used instead of 'is inversely proportional to'.

Example 2

R and S are positive quantities.
R varies inversely with the square root of S.
When $S = 4$, $R = 1$
Express R in terms of S.

Solution 2

$R \propto \frac{1}{\sqrt{S}}$ — Write the proportionality in symbols

$R = \frac{k}{\sqrt{S}}$ — Write as an equation

When $S = 4$, $R = 1$ — Substitute corresponding values into the equation

$1 = \frac{k}{\sqrt{4}}$

$1 = \frac{k}{2}$ — Multiply both sides by 2

$k = 2$

$R = \frac{2}{\sqrt{S}}$ — Substitute $k = 2$ in $R = k\sqrt{S}$

Exercise A

1 Write down an equation in terms of x, y and a constant of proportionality k for each of the following:

a y is inversely proportional to the square of x

b y is inversely proportional to the square root of x

c y is inversely proportional to x.

2 In each of the following tables, y is inversely proportional to x.

a

x	0.1	0.4	1	50
y	100	25	10	?

b

x	0.2	0.4	1	10
y	5	2.5	1	?

c

x	0.1	0.4	1	?
y	40	10	4	0.5

d

x	0.1	0.5	1	?
y	500	100	50	10

For each table:

i find the ratio $y : \frac{1}{x}$ in its simplest form

ii express y in terms of x

iii work out the missing value.

3 In each of the following tables, b varies inversely with a^2.

a

a	0.2	0.4	1	10
b	25	6.25	1	?

b

a	0.2	0.4	1	10
b	100	25	4	?

c

a	0.2	0.4	1	?
b	500	125	20	0.2

d

a	0.1	0.4	1	?
b	50	3.125	0.5	0.005

For each table:

i find the ratio $b : \frac{1}{a^2}$ in its simplest form

ii work out the constant of proportionality for each table

iii express b in terms of a

iv work out the missing value.

4 **a** $P \propto \frac{1}{Q}$

When $Q = 4$, $P = 0.2$

Write an equation connecting P and Q.

b $r \propto \frac{1}{s^2}$

When $s = 5$, $r = 0.4$

Write an equation connecting r and s.

c $m \propto \frac{1}{n^3}$

When $n = 2$, $m = 4$

Write an equation connecting m and n.

5 y varies inversely with x.
When $x = 2$, $y = 6$

a Find an equation connecting y and x.

b Work out the value of y when $x = 3$

c Work out the value of x when $y = \frac{1}{4}$

6 R is inversely proportional to v^2
When $v = 10$, $R = 20$

a Find an equation connecting R and v.

b Work out the value of R when $v = 5$

c Work out the value of v when $R = 5$

7 $T = \frac{k}{\sqrt{l}}$

When $l = 81$, $T = 5$

a Work out the value of T when $l = 10$
Give your answer to three significant figures.

b Work out the value of l when $T = 15$

8 The variables a, b, c, d, e, f, g and h are related as follows.

$b \propto a$ $\quad$ $d \propto \frac{1}{c}$ $\quad$ $f \propto e^2$ $\quad$ $h \propto \frac{1}{g^2}$

a Match each table of values to a proportionality statement.

i

?	1	2	5	10
?	0.5	2	12.5	

ii

?	1	2	5	10
?	5	2.5	1	

iii

?	1	2	5	
?	36	9	1.44	0.09

iv

?	1	2	5	
?	0.4	0.8	2	4

b Calculate the missing value in each table.

9 y varies inversely with the square root of x.
When $x = 16$, $y = 1$

a Find an equation connecting y and x.

b Work out the value of y when $x = 25$

c Work out the value of x when $y = \frac{1}{2}$

10 y is inversely proportional to the square of x.
When $x = 6$, $y = 4$

a Find an equation connecting y and x.

b Work out the value of y when $x = 3$

c Work out the value of x when $y = 9$

Many quantities in real life are in inverse proportion.

Example 3

The intensity of light, I, provided by a lamp is inversely proportional to the square of the distance, d, from the lamp.
When $d = 10$, $I = 20$

a Find an equation expressing I in terms of d.

b **i** Find the value of I when d is 20

ii Find the value of d when I is 80

Solution 3

a $I \propto \dfrac{1}{d^2}$

$I = \dfrac{k}{d^2}$

When $d = 10$, $I = 20$

$20 = \dfrac{k}{10^2}$

$20 = \dfrac{k}{100}$ Multiply both sides by 100

$k = 2000$

$I = \dfrac{2000}{d^2}$

b **i** When $d = 20$

$I = \dfrac{2000}{20^2} = \dfrac{2000}{400} = 5$

ii When $I = 80$

$80 = \dfrac{2000}{d^2}$

$d^2 = \dfrac{2000}{80} = 25$

$d = \sqrt{25} = 5$

This is typical of the shape of the graph when $y \propto \dfrac{1}{x^n}$

Inverse proportionality can be written as direct proportionality using negative powers. For example

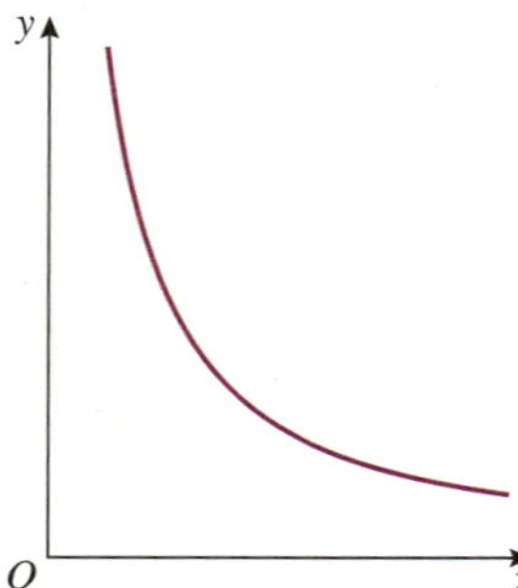

$y \propto \dfrac{1}{x}$ can be written $y \propto x^{-1}$

$y \propto \dfrac{1}{\sqrt{x}}$ can be written $y \propto x^{-\frac{1}{2}}$

$y \propto \dfrac{1}{x^n}$ can be written $y \propto x^{-n}$

As x increases by a constant amount, y decreases by a decreasing amount.

Example 4

The diagram shows the graph of x against y where $y \propto x^n$ where n is a positive or negative integer.
Find the equation of the graph.

Solution 4

As x increases, y decreases, so the graph shows inverse proportionality

$y \propto \dfrac{1}{x^n}$

$y = \dfrac{k}{x^n}$ where k is the constant of proportionality

The graph passes through the point (1, 8)

Substitute $x = 1$ and $y = 8$ in $y = \dfrac{k}{x^n}$

$8 = \dfrac{k}{1^n}$

$8 = \dfrac{k}{1}$

$k = 8$

So $y = \dfrac{8}{x^n}$

The graph passes through the point (2, 2)

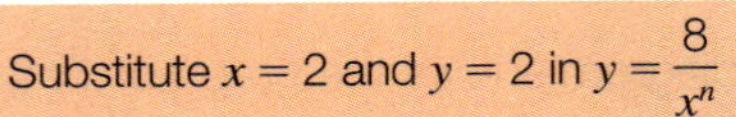

Substitute $x = 2$ and $y = 2$ in $y = \dfrac{8}{x^n}$

$2 = \dfrac{8}{2^n}$

Multiply both sides by 2^n

$2 \times 2^n = 8$

Divide both sides by 2

$2^n = 4$

So $n = 2$

The equation of the graph is $y = \dfrac{8}{x^2}$

Exercise B

1 The electrical resistance per metre of a circular wire, R, varies inversely with the square of its radius, r.
When $R = 0.5$ ohms per metre, $r = 3$ mm.

- **a** Find an equation expressing R in terms of r.
- **b** **i** What is the electrical resistance of a wire of diameter 4 mm?
  - **ii** The resistance of a wire is 0.125 ohms per metre.
    Calculate r.

2 Newton's law of gravitation states that the force of attraction between two objects, F, is inversely proportional to the square of their distance apart, d.
When $d = 100$ km, $F = 4$ units of force.

- **a** Find an equation expressing F in terms of d.
- **b** **i** Calculate F when $d = 50$ km.
  - **ii** Calculate d when $F = 25$ units of force.

3 The fuel consumption in miles per gallon, C, of a car is inversely proportional to its speed in miles per hour, s.
When $C = 30$ mpg, $s = 50$ mph.

a Find an equation expressing C in terms of s.

b **i** Calculate C when $s = 75$ mph.

ii Calculate s when $C = 60$ mpg.

4 X and Y are positive quantities
Y is inversely proportional to the square of X.
When $X = 2$, $Y = 16$
Find the value of X when $Y = X$.

5 $p \propto q^{-0.5}$
When $q = 6.25$, $p = 3$

a Complete the statement: 'As q increases, p ....'

b Find an equation for p in terms of q.

c **i** Calculate p when $q = 4$

ii Calculate q when $p = 2.5$

6 In the table of values y varies inversely with the cube of x.

x	0.5		8.2
y	149.2	22.8	

Complete the table to an accuracy of three significant figures.

7 The diagram shows the graph of x against y where $y \propto x^n$ where n is a positive or negative integer.
The graph passes through the points (0.25, 12), (0.5, 3) and (1, 0.75)
Find an equation expressing y in terms of x.

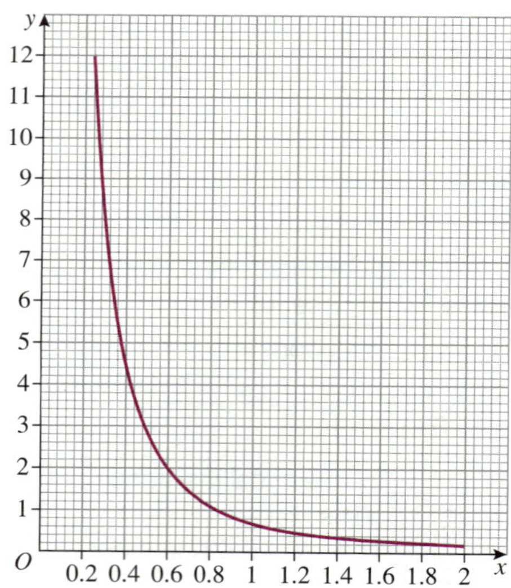

8 The diagram shows the graph of x against y where $y \propto x^n$ where n is a positive or negative number.
The graph passes through the points (0.25, 0.125), (1, 0.25) and (4, 0.5)
Find an equation expressing y in terms of x.

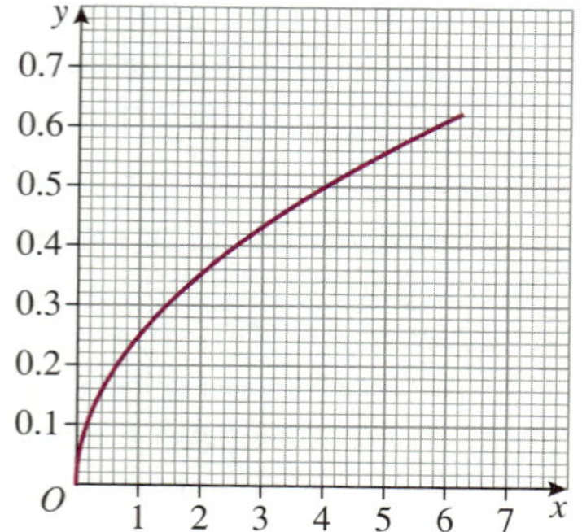

9 W and X are positive quantities.
X is inversely proportional to the cube of W.
When $W = 2$, $X = 16$
Find the value of W when $2X = W$.

10 b is directly proportional to a^3
a is inversely proportional to the square root of c.
When $a = 2$, $b = 10$
When $b = 80$, $c = 25$
Find the value of c when $a = 5$

Chapter summary

- When any two quantities x^n and y are such that:
  - when $x^n = 0$, $y = 0$
  - when x increases, y increases
  - the ratio $y : x^n$ is always the same

  then y is said to be *directly proportional* to x^n.
- The relationship y is directly proportional to x^n can be written in symbols as $y \propto x^n$, where $\propto$ means 'is proportional to' or 'varies directly with'.
- The relationship can also be expressed as an equation, $y = kx^n$, where k is the constant of proportionality. The value of k is $\frac{y}{x^n}$
- When any two quantities x^n and y are such that:
  - when x increases, y decreases
  - the ratio $y : \frac{1}{x^n}$ is always the same

  then y is said to be *inversely proportional* to x^n.
- The relationship y is inversely proportional to x^n can be written in symbols as $y \propto \frac{1}{x^n}$ or $y \propto x^{-n}$
- These relationships can also be expressed as an equation $y = \frac{k}{x^n}$ or $y = kx^{-n}$, where k is the constant of proportionality. The value of k is $x^n y$.
- If y is inversely proportional to x^n then y is proportional to the reciprocal of x^n.
- Quantities in real life are often in direct or inverse proportion.
- The diagrams show the sketches of graphs of y against x^n for different values of n.

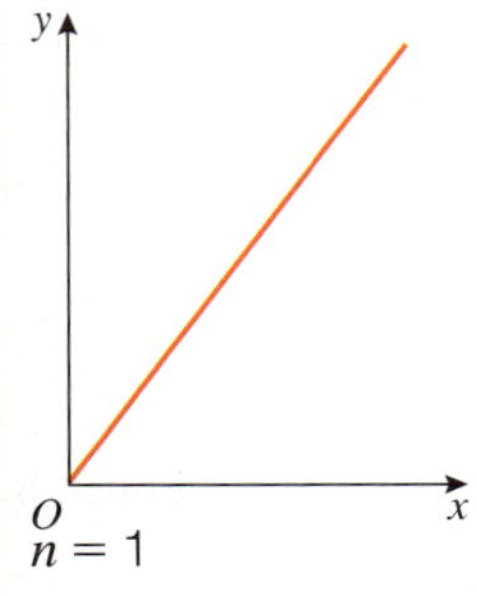

$n = 1$

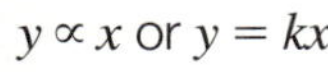
$y \propto x$ or $y = kx$

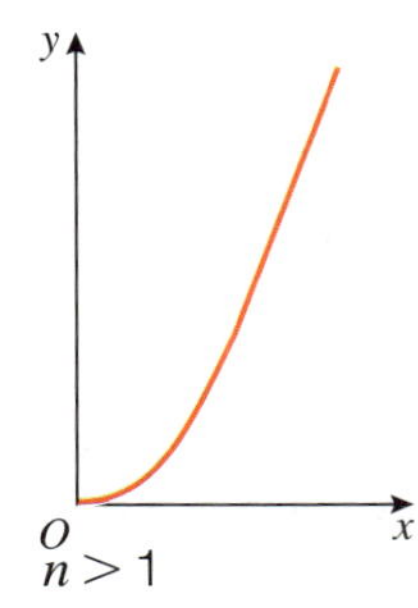

$n > 1$

For example, $y \propto x^2$ or $y = kx^2$

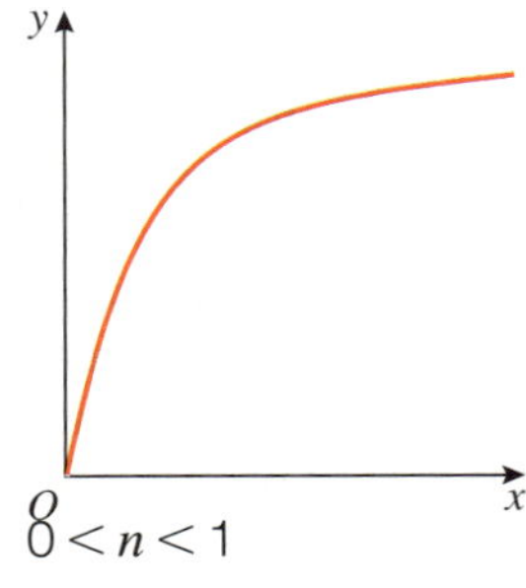

$0 < n < 1$

For example, $y \propto \sqrt{x}$ or $y = kx^{1/2}$

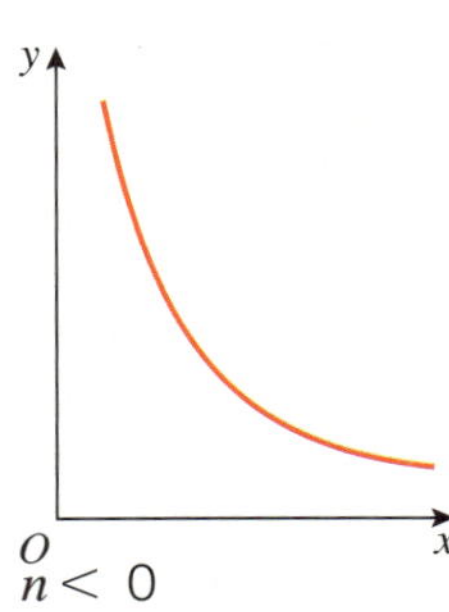

$n < 0$

For example, $y \propto \frac{1}{x}$ or $y = kx^{-1}$

Chapter review

1 y is directly proportional to the square root of x.

x	100	25	
y	7		14

Copy and complete the table.

2 y is directly proportional to x^3
$y = 216$ when $x = 3$
Find the value of x when $y = 1000$

3 B is inversely proportional to c^2
When $B = 16, c = 3$
a Find c when $B = 25$
b Which of the following graphs represents the relationship between B and c.
Give a reason for your answer.

Graph 1

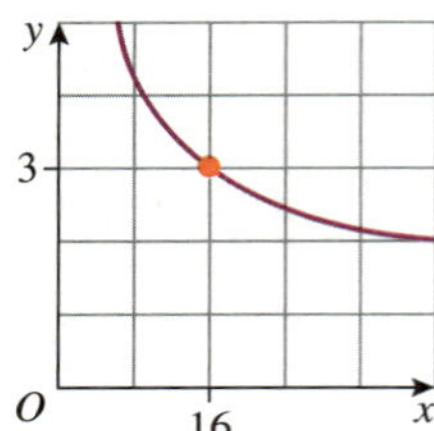

Graph 2

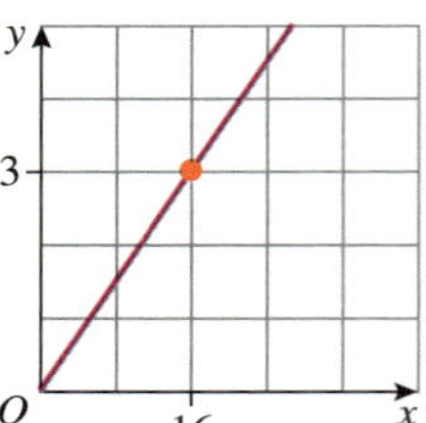

Graph 3

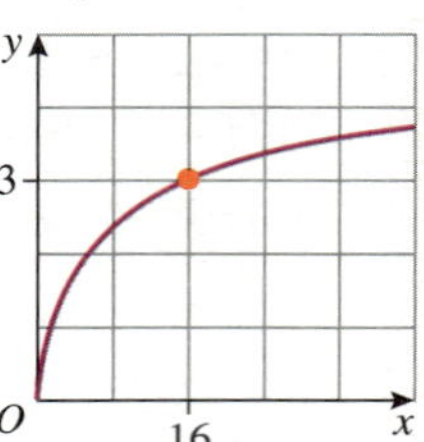

4 The area, A, of an advertising sign is directly proportional to the square of its height, h.
A sign with height 5 metres has area 8 m^2
a Find an equation connecting A and h.
b Find the area of an advertising sign of height 2.5 metres.

5 In an electrical circuit, the resistance, R, varies inversely with the current, I.
When $R = 20$ ohms, $I = 15$ amps.
a Find an equation that gives R in terms of I.
b Find I when $R = 5$ ohms.

6 You are given that $y \propto x^n$ when $x > 0$
a Write down the value of n when:
- **i** y is directly proportional to x
- **ii** y is proportional to the square of x
- **iii** y varies inversely with x
- **iv** y is inversely proportional to the square root of x.

b Sketch a graph for each of the relationships when the constant of proportionality equals 1

7 A company produces mugs in two sizes.
Small mugs are 6 cm high and can hold 108 cm^3 of liquid.
Large mugs are 8 cm high and are identical in shape to small mugs.
To calculate the volume of a large mug, the volume of a small mug must be multiplied by the number k.
a Express k as an exact fraction.
b Calculate the volume of a large mug.

8 In the following tables, $q \propto p^n$ and $s \propto r^n$

a For each table, find the value of:

  i n

  ii the constant of proportionality.

b Hence, or otherwise, copy and complete the tables.

Table 1			
p	1	4	6
q	4	256	

Table 2			
r	1	4	5
s	8	0.5	

9 The table shows the range of sizes of circular badges made by a company.

Size	Radius, r (cm)
Small	3
Standard	4
Large	5
Giant	10

The cost, C pence, of making each badge is proportional to the square of its radius, r cm.
A small badge costs 13.5 pence.

a Find an equation that connects C to r.

b Work out the cost of making a giant badge.

c The company make a special badge.
They sell the special badge for 99 pence and make a 10% profit.
What is the radius of the special badge?
Give your answer to an appropriate degree of accuracy.

10 The diagram shows a sketch of a graph where $y \propto kx^n$.
The graph passes through the points (1, 15) and (8, 30)

a Find the values of the constant of proportionality.

b Find the value of n.

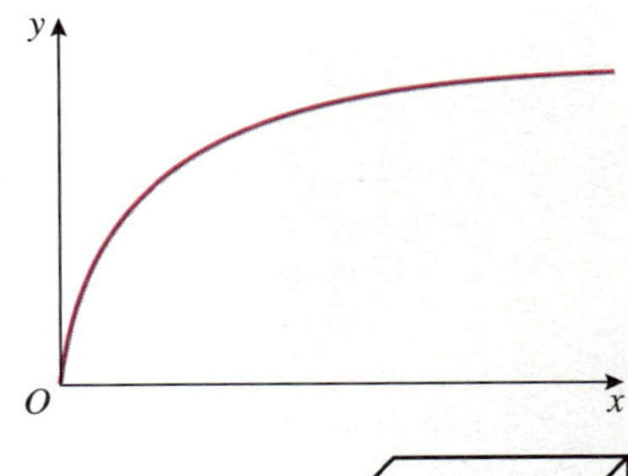

11 Tom is investigating a set of similar gift boxes.
He measures the length, L, area of base, A, and volume, V, of each box.

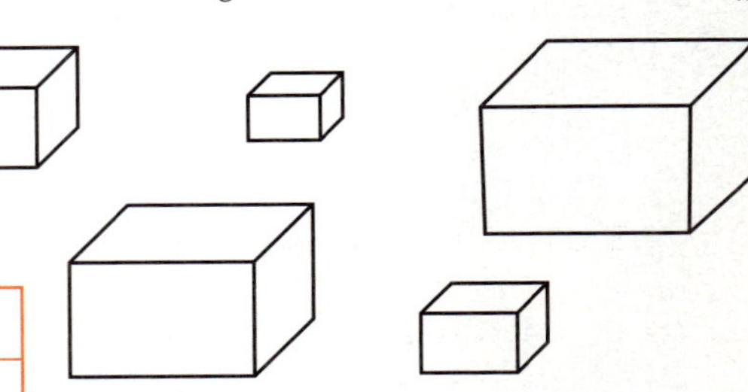

L (cm)	2	3	4		
A (cm^2)	3	6.75	12		75
V (cm^3)	3	10.125	24	81	

a Complete these statements.

A is proportional to the .... of L

V is proportional to the .... of L

L is proportional to the .... of A

L is proportional to the .... of V

b Find an equation that gives

  i V in terms of L

  ii L in terms of A

  iii A in terms of V

In **ii** and **iii** leave the constant of proportionality in surd form.

c Copy and complete the table.

CHAPTER 40

Vectors

40.1 Vector arithmetic

CAN YOU REMEMBER

- That column vectors can be used to describe the translation of points or shapes?
- A column vector $\begin{pmatrix} x \\ y \end{pmatrix}$ represents a move of x units in the horizontal direction and y units in the vertical direction?

IN THIS SECTION YOU WILL

- Understand and use vector notation.
- Learn how to add and subtract vectors and multiply by a scalar.
- Learn how to find the resultant of two vectors by arithmetic and graphically.

Quantities that have **size** only are called *scalars*; for example distance, area and temperature.

Quantities that have both **size** and **direction** are called *vectors*; for example 25 m due north or 7 mph south west.

Vectors can be represented by line segments with arrows. The length of the line represents the size, and the arrow represents the direction.

Vectors can be labelled in the following ways:

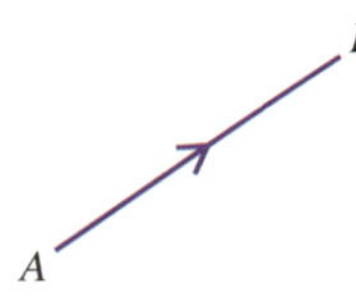

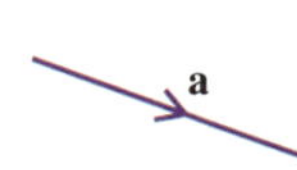

vector $\overrightarrow{AB}$ vector $\mathbf{a}$

Two vectors are *equal* if they have the same length and are in the same direction.

A vector with the same length but the *opposite* direction to a vector $\mathbf{a}$ is the vector $-\mathbf{a}$

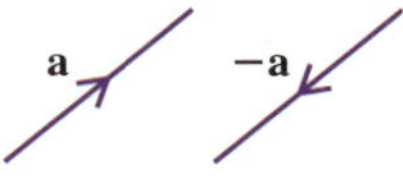

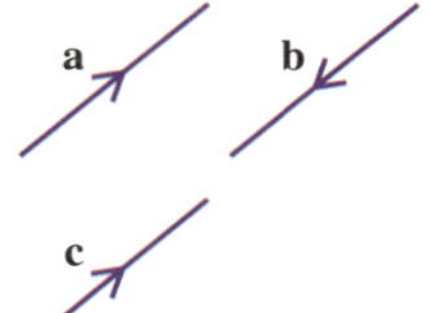

These three vectors are all the same length. $\mathbf{a}$ and $\mathbf{c}$ have the same direction but $\mathbf{b}$ is in the opposite direction.

$\mathbf{a} = \mathbf{c}$ $\quad$ $\mathbf{a} = -\mathbf{b}$ or $\mathbf{b} = -\mathbf{a}$ $\quad$ $\mathbf{c} = -\mathbf{b}$

Column vectors

Column vectors are used to describe the length and direction, or *displacement*, of a vector in the same way as they are used to describe translations.

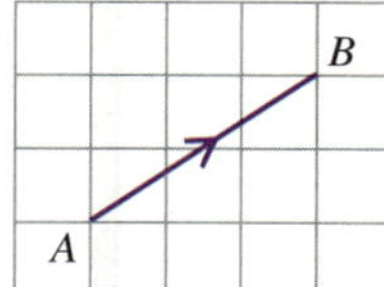

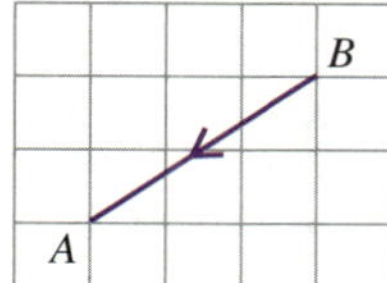

The displacement from A to B is 3 units to the right and 2 units up.

$\overrightarrow{BA} = -\overrightarrow{AB} = \begin{pmatrix} -3 \\ -2 \end{pmatrix}$

Vector $\overrightarrow{AB}$ can be represented by the column vector $\begin{pmatrix} 3 \\ 2 \end{pmatrix}$.

Example 1

Write down the column vectors for **a**, **b**, **c**, **d**, **e**, **f** and **g**.

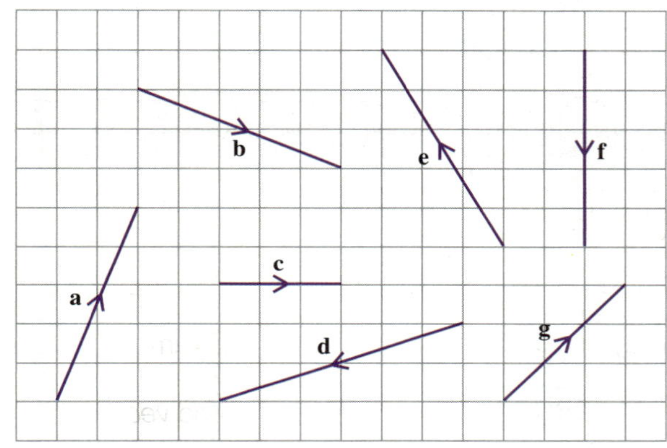

Solution 1

$\mathbf{a} = \begin{pmatrix} 2 \\ 5 \end{pmatrix}$ $\mathbf{b} = \begin{pmatrix} 5 \\ -2 \end{pmatrix}$ $\mathbf{c} = \begin{pmatrix} 3 \\ 0 \end{pmatrix}$ $\mathbf{d} = \begin{pmatrix} -6 \\ -2 \end{pmatrix}$ $\mathbf{e} = \begin{pmatrix} -3 \\ 5 \end{pmatrix}$ $\mathbf{f} = \begin{pmatrix} 0 \\ -5 \end{pmatrix}$ $\mathbf{g} = \begin{pmatrix} 3 \\ 3 \end{pmatrix}$

Multiplying a vector by a scalar

The diagram shows vectors **a** and **b**.

Both vectors have the same direction but different lengths.
Vectors with the same direction are either parallel or in a straight line.

$\mathbf{a} = \begin{pmatrix} 3 \\ -2 \end{pmatrix}$, $\mathbf{b} = \begin{pmatrix} 6 \\ -4 \end{pmatrix}$

Vector **b** is twice the length of vector **a**.

$\mathbf{b} = \begin{pmatrix} 2 \times 3 \\ 2 \times -2 \end{pmatrix}$ or $2 \times \begin{pmatrix} 3 \\ -2 \end{pmatrix} = 2 \times \mathbf{a}$

so $\mathbf{b} = 2\mathbf{a}$

Example 2

The diagram shows four vectors **a**, **b**, **c** and **d**. Express **b**, **c** and **d** in terms of **a**.

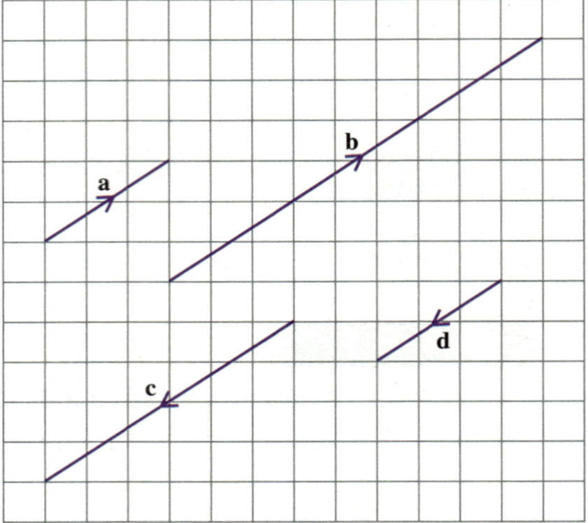

Solution 2

b is in the same direction as **a** and three times the length of **a**.
$\mathbf{b} = 3\mathbf{a}$
c is in the opposite direction to **a** and twice the length of **a**.
$\mathbf{c} = -2\mathbf{a}$
d is in the opposite direction to **a** and the same length.
$\mathbf{d} = -\mathbf{a}$

Example 3

$\overrightarrow{AB} = \begin{pmatrix} 3 \\ 2 \end{pmatrix}, \overrightarrow{BC} = \begin{pmatrix} 2 \\ -4 \end{pmatrix}$

Work out vectors to represent the following:

a $3\overrightarrow{AB}$ **b** $\overrightarrow{BA}$ **c** $2\overrightarrow{BC}$ **d** $\frac{1}{2}\overrightarrow{BC}$

Solution 3

a $3\overrightarrow{AB} = 3 \times \begin{pmatrix} 3 \\ 2 \end{pmatrix} = \begin{pmatrix} 9 \\ 6 \end{pmatrix}$

b $\overrightarrow{BA} = -\overrightarrow{AB} = \begin{pmatrix} -3 \\ -2 \end{pmatrix}$

c $2 \times \begin{pmatrix} 2 \\ -4 \end{pmatrix} = \begin{pmatrix} 4 \\ -8 \end{pmatrix}$

d $\frac{1}{2} \times \begin{pmatrix} 2 \\ -4 \end{pmatrix} = \begin{pmatrix} 1 \\ -2 \end{pmatrix}$

Exercise A

1 Write down the column vector for each of the vectors in the diagram.

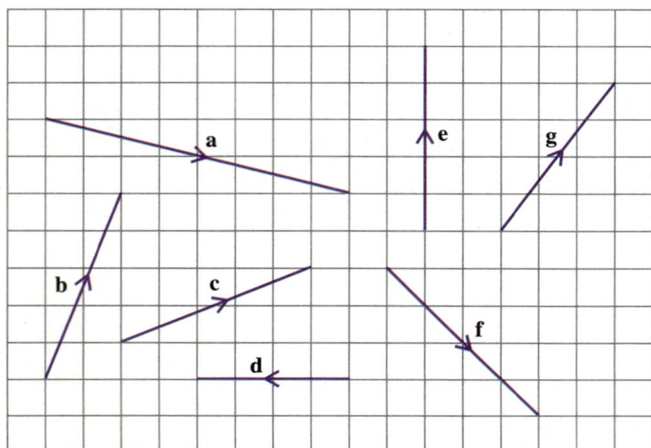

2 Draw each of the following vectors on squared paper.

$\mathbf{a} = \begin{pmatrix} -3 \\ 2 \end{pmatrix}$ $\mathbf{b} = \begin{pmatrix} -6 \\ 0 \end{pmatrix}$ $\mathbf{c} = \begin{pmatrix} 1 \\ 5 \end{pmatrix}$ $\mathbf{d} = \begin{pmatrix} 5 \\ -2 \end{pmatrix}$ $\mathbf{e} = \begin{pmatrix} 2 \\ 1 \end{pmatrix}$

$\mathbf{f} = \begin{pmatrix} 5 \\ 5 \end{pmatrix}$ $\mathbf{g} = \begin{pmatrix} 0 \\ -7 \end{pmatrix}$ $\mathbf{h} = \begin{pmatrix} -6 \\ -3 \end{pmatrix}$ $\mathbf{i} = \begin{pmatrix} -3 \\ 4 \end{pmatrix}$ $\mathbf{j} = \begin{pmatrix} 2 \\ 6 \end{pmatrix}$

3 Write down the pairs of equal vectors on this diagram.

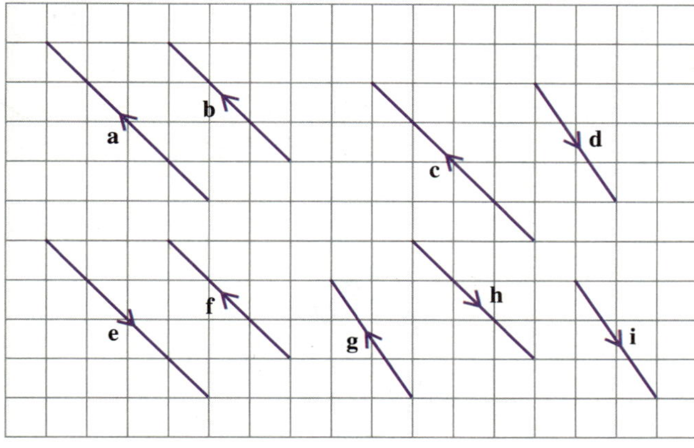

4 The diagram shows five vectors **a**, **b**, **c**, **d** and **e**.

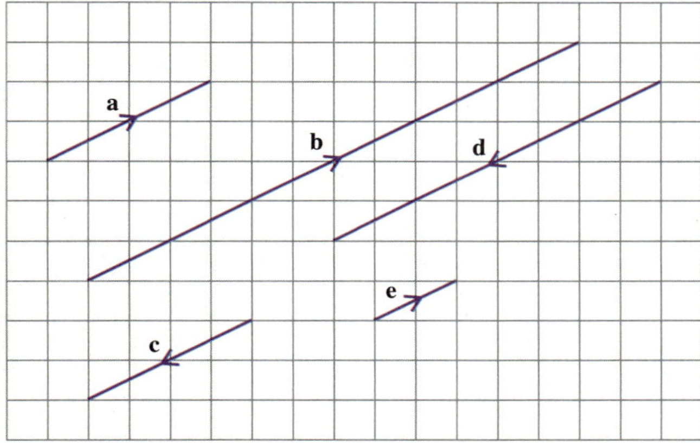

a Write the column vectors for **a** to **e**.
b Express vectors **b**, **c**, **d** and **e** in terms of **a**.

5 $\mathbf{a} = \begin{pmatrix} -3 \\ -2 \end{pmatrix}$, $\mathbf{b} = \begin{pmatrix} -1 \\ 2 \end{pmatrix}$, $\mathbf{c} = \begin{pmatrix} 4 \\ 1 \end{pmatrix}$

On squared paper draw vectors to represent the following:

i $2\mathbf{a}$ **ii** $-\mathbf{b}$ **iii** $3\mathbf{c}$ **iv** $4\mathbf{b}$ **v** $-2\mathbf{c}$ **vi** $-3\mathbf{a}$

6 $\overrightarrow{AB} = \begin{pmatrix} -3 \\ -1 \end{pmatrix}$, $\overrightarrow{BC} = \begin{pmatrix} 4 \\ 2 \end{pmatrix}$

a Work out the column vectors for:
i $2\overrightarrow{BC}$ **ii** $4\overrightarrow{AB}$ **iii** $-3\overrightarrow{BC}$

b On squared paper, draw vectors to represent:
i $2\overrightarrow{AB}$ **ii** $\frac{1}{2}\overrightarrow{BC}$ **iii** $-\overrightarrow{AB}$

The diagram shows three points A, B and C.
A man walks from A to B and then from B to C.
The result is the same as walking directly from A to C.

So $\overrightarrow{AB} + \overrightarrow{BC} = \overrightarrow{AC}$

Vectors can be subtracted in the same way
$\overrightarrow{AB} - \overrightarrow{BC} = \overrightarrow{AB} + \overrightarrow{CB}$ (since $\overrightarrow{CB}$ is in the opposite direction to $\overrightarrow{BC}$)

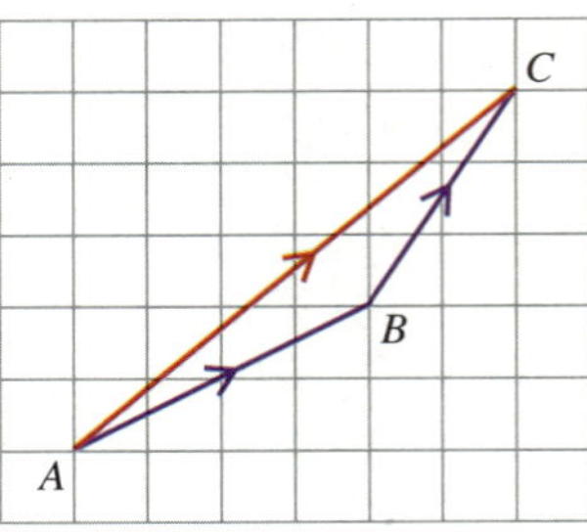

The result of vector addition or subtraction is called the *resultant vector*.

Vector addition
$\mathbf{a} + \mathbf{b}$

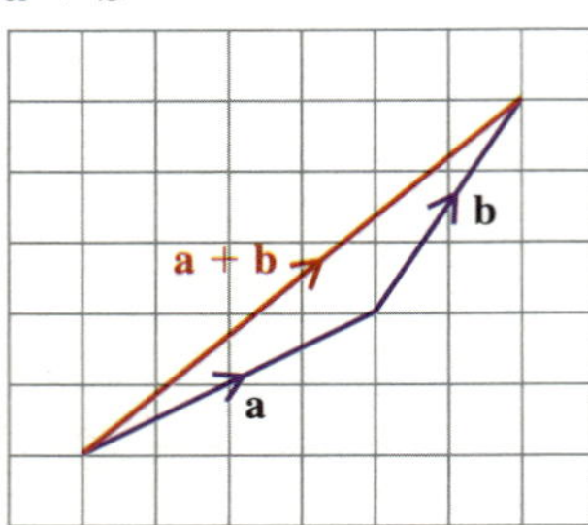

Vector subtraction
$\mathbf{a} - \mathbf{b}$ can be written as $\mathbf{a} + -\mathbf{b}$

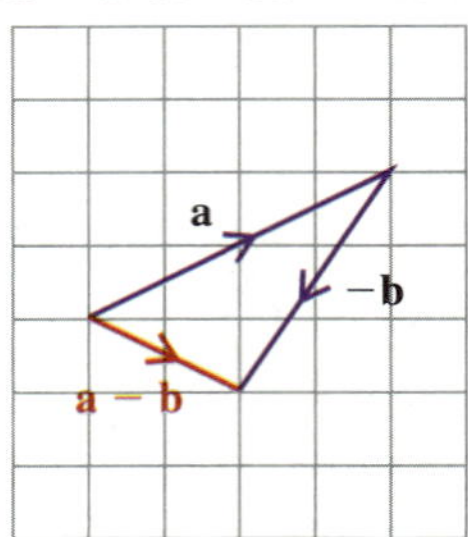

Vectors may be added or subtracted by adding or subtracting the column vectors.

$\mathbf{a} = \begin{pmatrix}4\\2\end{pmatrix}$ and $\mathbf{b} = \begin{pmatrix}2\\3\end{pmatrix}$ $\quad$ $\mathbf{a}+\mathbf{b} = \begin{pmatrix}4\\2\end{pmatrix} + \begin{pmatrix}2\\3\end{pmatrix} = \begin{pmatrix}6\\5\end{pmatrix}$ $\quad$ $\mathbf{a}-\mathbf{b} = \begin{pmatrix}4\\2\end{pmatrix} - \begin{pmatrix}2\\3\end{pmatrix} = \begin{pmatrix}2\\-1\end{pmatrix}$

Example 4

The diagram shows vectors **a** and **b**.

a Draw diagrams to show:

i $\mathbf{a} - \mathbf{b}$ **ii** $3\mathbf{a} + \mathbf{b}$ **iii** $2\mathbf{a} - 2\mathbf{b}$

b What do you notice about the resultant vectors for part **a i** and **iii**?
What does this tell you about the relationship between the vectors $\mathbf{a} - \mathbf{b}$ and $2\mathbf{a} - 2\mathbf{b}$?

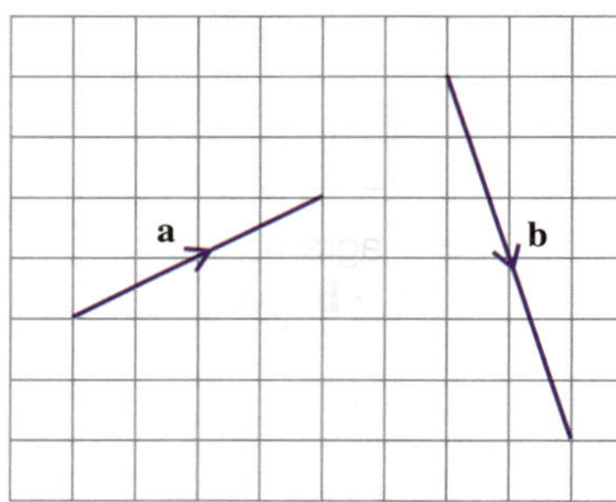

Solution 4

a i

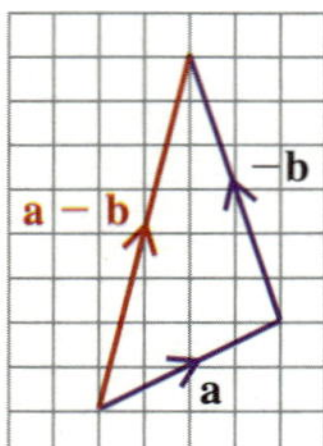

ii

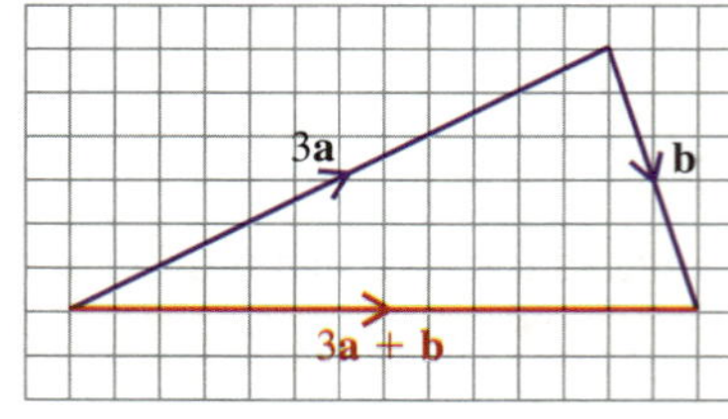

iii

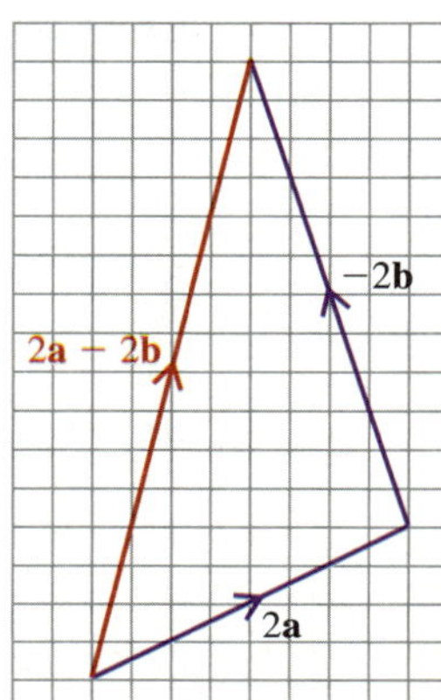

b The vector $2\mathbf{a} - 2\mathbf{b}$ is in the same direction as $\mathbf{a} - \mathbf{b}$ and is twice as long.
So $2\mathbf{a} - 2\mathbf{b} = 2(\mathbf{a} - \mathbf{b})$

Exercise B

1 Work out the resultant vector for each pair of vectors.

a $\begin{pmatrix}3\\-4\end{pmatrix}+\begin{pmatrix}2\\5\end{pmatrix}$ **b** $\begin{pmatrix}1\\4\end{pmatrix}+\begin{pmatrix}-3\\2\end{pmatrix}$ **c** $\begin{pmatrix}5\\2\end{pmatrix}-\begin{pmatrix}1\\3\end{pmatrix}$

d $\begin{pmatrix}0\\6\end{pmatrix}+\begin{pmatrix}5\\-7\end{pmatrix}$ **e** $\begin{pmatrix}8\\-2\end{pmatrix}-\begin{pmatrix}-1\\-3\end{pmatrix}$ **f** $\begin{pmatrix}-4\\-5\end{pmatrix}-\begin{pmatrix}-2\\3\end{pmatrix}$

2 $\overrightarrow{AB}=\begin{pmatrix}-3\\5\end{pmatrix}$, $\overrightarrow{BC}=\begin{pmatrix}6\\-1\end{pmatrix}$

On squared paper draw diagrams to represent the following:

a $\overrightarrow{AB}+\overrightarrow{BC}$ **b** $\overrightarrow{AB}-\overrightarrow{BC}$ **c** $2\overrightarrow{AB}+2\overrightarrow{BC}$ **d** $2(\overrightarrow{AB}+\overrightarrow{BC})$

3 $\mathbf{a}=\begin{pmatrix}3\\-4\end{pmatrix}$, $\mathbf{b}=\begin{pmatrix}1\\5\end{pmatrix}$, $\mathbf{c}=\begin{pmatrix}-2\\2\end{pmatrix}$

Find the resultant vectors:

i $\mathbf{a}+\mathbf{b}$ **ii** $2\mathbf{b}-\mathbf{c}$ **iii** $3\mathbf{a}+2\mathbf{b}$ **iv** $\mathbf{a}+\mathbf{b}+\mathbf{c}$ **v** $2\mathbf{c}-\mathbf{a}$ **vi** $2(\mathbf{b}+\mathbf{c})$

4 The diagram shows vectors **a**, **b**, and **c**.

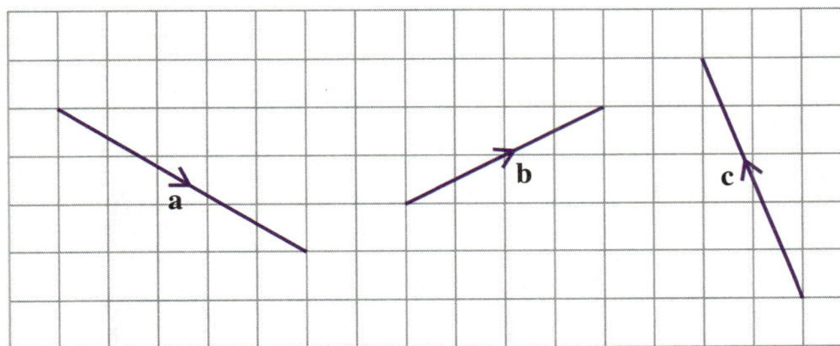

Draw diagrams to show:

i $2\mathbf{a}+\mathbf{b}$ **ii** $\mathbf{b}+\mathbf{c}$ **iii** $\mathbf{c}-\mathbf{a}$ **iv** $\mathbf{a}+2\mathbf{b}$ **v** $\mathbf{a}+\mathbf{b}+\mathbf{c}$ **vi** $-2\mathbf{b}+\mathbf{c}$

5 $\mathbf{a}=\begin{pmatrix}2\\-3\end{pmatrix}$, $\mathbf{b}=\begin{pmatrix}-1\\4\end{pmatrix}$

i Draw vector diagrams to show that $\mathbf{a}+\mathbf{b}=\mathbf{b}+\mathbf{a}$

ii Draw vector diagrams to show that $2(\mathbf{a}+\mathbf{b})=2\mathbf{a}+2\mathbf{b}$

6 $\overrightarrow{AB}=\begin{pmatrix}3\\1\end{pmatrix}$, $\overrightarrow{BC}=\begin{pmatrix}-2\\4\end{pmatrix}$, $\overrightarrow{CD}=\begin{pmatrix}1\\3\end{pmatrix}$

Find: **i** by adding column vectors **ii** by drawing a diagram

a $\overrightarrow{AC}$ **b** $\overrightarrow{BD}$ **c** $\overrightarrow{AD}$

7 A man drives 8 km south and then 5 km west.

a Represent this information in a vector diagram.

b Calculate the direct distance of the man from his starting point. Give your answer to two decimal places.

40.2 Vector geometry

CAN YOU REMEMBER

- Vectors have both size and direction?
- Two vectors are equal if they have the same length and are in the same direction?
- The vector $-\mathbf{a}$ has the same length but is in the opposite direction to vector $\mathbf{a}$?

IN THIS SECTION YOU WILL

- Use vectors to solve problems in geometry.

Parallel lines have the same direction so are multiples of the same vector.

In the diagram, $\overrightarrow{RS}$ is in the same direction as $\overrightarrow{PQ}$ but is twice the length of $\overrightarrow{PQ}$.

$\overrightarrow{PQ} = \mathbf{a}$ $\quad\overrightarrow{RS} = 2\mathbf{a}$

Vectors can be used to show that lines are parallel.

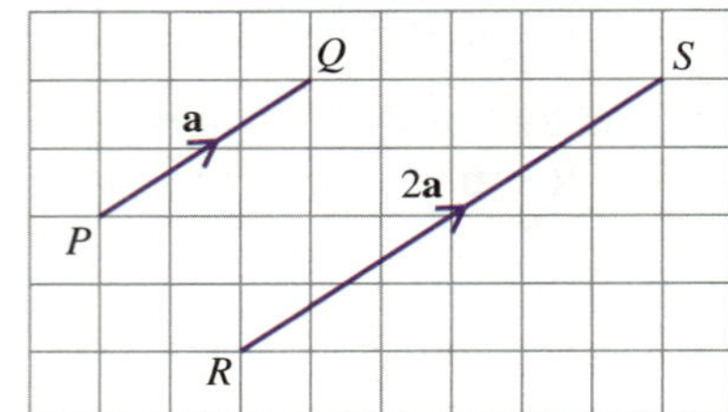

Example 1

OAB is a triangle. $\overrightarrow{OA} = \mathbf{a}$ and $\overrightarrow{OB} = \mathbf{b}$.
M is the mid-point of AB.
Write down the vectors:

a $\overrightarrow{AO}$

b $\overrightarrow{AB}$ in terms of $\mathbf{a}$ and $\mathbf{b}$

c $\overrightarrow{AM}$ in terms of $\mathbf{a}$ and $\mathbf{b}$

d $\overrightarrow{OM}$ in terms of $\mathbf{a}$ and $\mathbf{b}$.

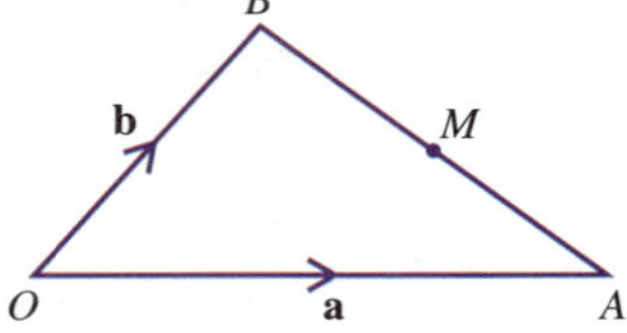

Solution 1

a $\overrightarrow{AO}$ is the opposite direction to $\overrightarrow{OA}$ so $\overrightarrow{AO} = -\mathbf{a}$

b $\overrightarrow{AB} = \overrightarrow{AO} + \overrightarrow{OB} = -\mathbf{a} + \mathbf{b}$ or $\mathbf{b} - \mathbf{a}$

c $\overrightarrow{AM} = \frac{1}{2}\overrightarrow{AB} = \frac{1}{2}(\mathbf{b} - \mathbf{a})$

d $\overrightarrow{OM} = \overrightarrow{OA} + \overrightarrow{AM} = \mathbf{a} + \frac{1}{2}(\mathbf{b} - \mathbf{a}) = \mathbf{a} + \frac{1}{2}\mathbf{b} - \frac{1}{2}\mathbf{a} = \frac{1}{2}\mathbf{a} + \frac{1}{2}\mathbf{b}$ or $\frac{1}{2}(\mathbf{a} + \mathbf{b})$

Example 2

$OABC$ is a parallelogram.
$\overrightarrow{OA} = \mathbf{a}$, $\overrightarrow{OC} = \mathbf{c}$
D is the mid-point of OB.

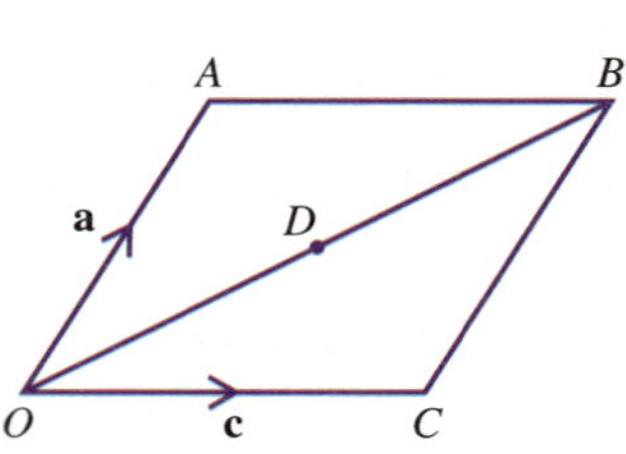

a Write down the vector $\overrightarrow{OB}$ in terms of $\mathbf{a}$ and $\mathbf{c}$.

b Write down the vector $\overrightarrow{AD}$ in terms of $\mathbf{a}$ and $\mathbf{c}$.

c Write down the vector $\overrightarrow{AC}$ in terms of $\mathbf{a}$ and $\mathbf{c}$.

d What do the answers to parts **b** and **c** tell you about the position of D?

Solution 2

a $\overrightarrow{OB} = \overrightarrow{OA} + \overrightarrow{AB}$

$\overrightarrow{AB}$ is parallel to $\overrightarrow{OC}$ and equal length so $\overrightarrow{AB} = \mathbf{c}$.

$\overrightarrow{OB} = \mathbf{a} + \mathbf{c}$

b $\overrightarrow{AD} = \overrightarrow{AO} + \overrightarrow{OD}$

$\overrightarrow{AO} = -\overrightarrow{OA} = -\mathbf{a}$

$\overrightarrow{OD} = \frac{1}{2}\overrightarrow{OB} = \frac{1}{2}(\mathbf{a} + \mathbf{c})$

So $\overrightarrow{AD} = -\mathbf{a} + \frac{1}{2}(\mathbf{a} + \mathbf{c}) = -\mathbf{a} + \frac{1}{2}\mathbf{a} + \frac{1}{2}\mathbf{c} = \frac{1}{2}\mathbf{c} - \frac{1}{2}\mathbf{a} = \frac{1}{2}(\mathbf{c} - \mathbf{a})$

c $\overrightarrow{AC} = \overrightarrow{AO} + \overrightarrow{OC} = -\mathbf{a} + \mathbf{c} = \mathbf{c} - \mathbf{a}$

d $\overrightarrow{AD} = \frac{1}{2}\overrightarrow{AC}$

So AD is in the same direction as AC. Both AD and AC pass through the point A, so A, D and C are in a straight line. The length AD is half the length AC, so D is the mid-point of AC.

If two vectors are in the same direction and pass through the same point, they are part of the same straight line.

Exercise A

1 $OABC$ is a parallelogram. M is the mid-point of AB.

$\overrightarrow{OA} = \mathbf{a}$, $\overrightarrow{OB} = \mathbf{b}$

a Write down the vector $\overrightarrow{AB}$.

b Write down the vector $\overrightarrow{AM}$.

c Write down the vector $\overrightarrow{OM}$ in terms of $\mathbf{a}$ and $\mathbf{c}$.

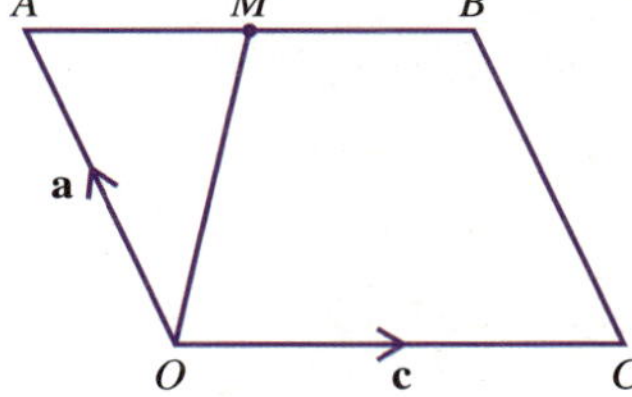

2 OBC is a straight line. $OB = BC$

$\overrightarrow{OA} = \mathbf{a}$, $\overrightarrow{OB} = \mathbf{b}$

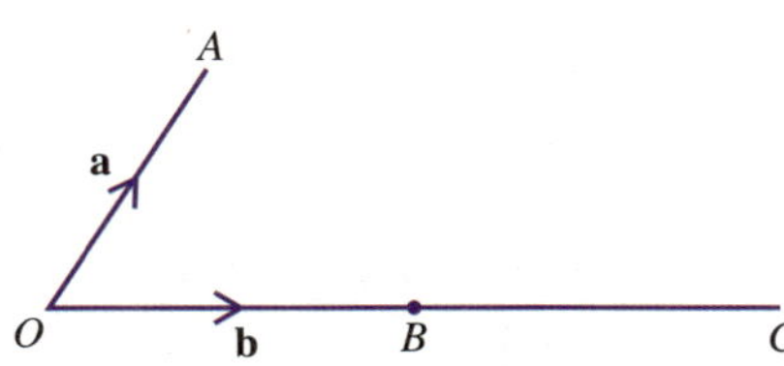

Write down, in terms of $\mathbf{a}$ and $\mathbf{b}$, expressions for:

a $\overrightarrow{BC}$ **b** $\overrightarrow{CO}$ **c** $\overrightarrow{CA}$

3 $OABC$ is a parallelogram.

$\overrightarrow{OA} = \mathbf{a}$, $\overrightarrow{OC} = \mathbf{c}$

M is the mid-point of AB.

Write down, in terms of $\mathbf{a}$ and $\mathbf{c}$, the vectors:

a $\overrightarrow{OM}$ **b** $\overrightarrow{OB}$ **c** $\overrightarrow{MC}$

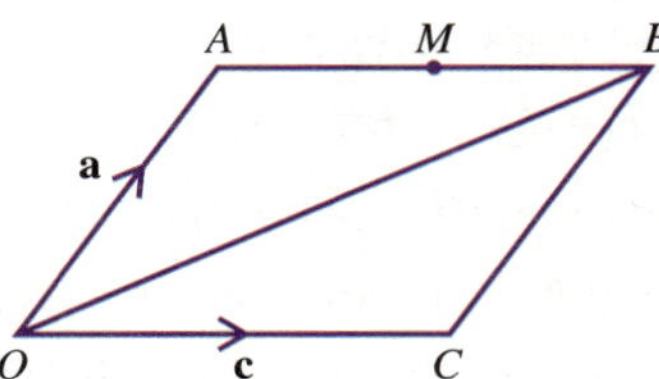

4 *OABC* is a parallelogram.
$\overrightarrow{OA} = \mathbf{a}$, $\overrightarrow{OC} = \mathbf{c}$
Write down, in terms of $\mathbf{a}$ and $\mathbf{c}$, expressions for:
a $\overrightarrow{OB}$ **b** $\overrightarrow{OM}$ **c** $\overrightarrow{AM}$

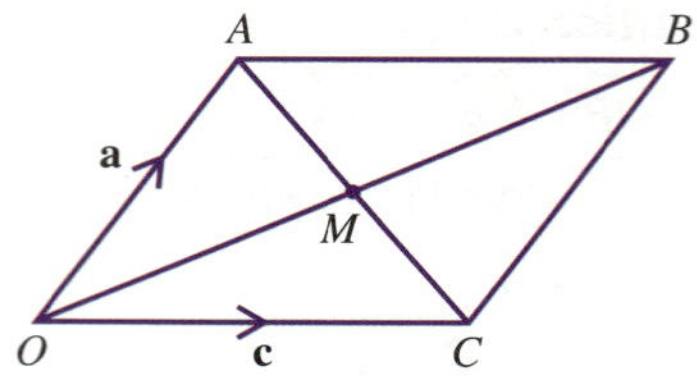

5 *OABCD* and *OWXYZ* are straight lines.
$\overrightarrow{OA} = \overrightarrow{AB} = \overrightarrow{BC} = \overrightarrow{CD} = \mathbf{a}$
$\overrightarrow{OW} = \overrightarrow{WX} = \overrightarrow{XY} = \overrightarrow{YZ} = \mathbf{w}$
a Find, in terms of $\mathbf{a}$ and $\mathbf{w}$, expressions for:
i $\overrightarrow{AW}$ **ii** $\overrightarrow{BX}$ **iii** $\overrightarrow{CY}$ **iv** $\overrightarrow{DZ}$
b Copy and complete the sentences.
i Line .... is twice the length of line *BX*.
ii Line .... is three times the length of line *AW*.

6 The diagram shows a triangular grid.
Mark on a copy of the grid the points:

A such that $\overrightarrow{OA} = \mathbf{t} + \mathbf{s}$
B such that $\overrightarrow{OB} = \mathbf{t} - \mathbf{s}$
C such that $\overrightarrow{BC} = 2\mathbf{t}$

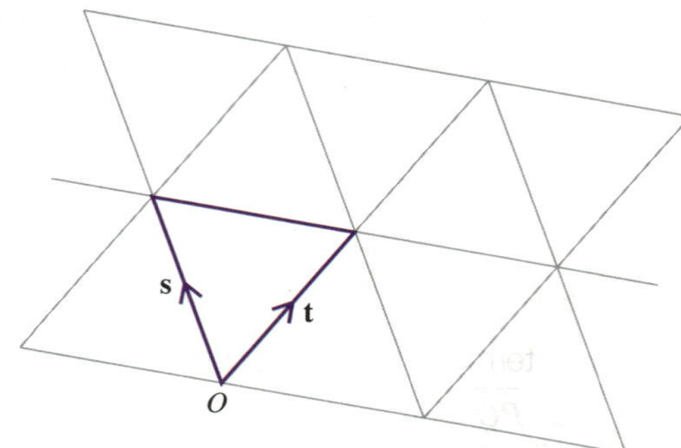

Vector methods can be used to solve geometrical problems.

Example 3

OABC is a quadrilateral.
P, *Q*, *R* and *S* are the mid-points of *OA*, *AB*, *BC* and *OC*, respectively.
$\overrightarrow{OP} = \mathbf{a}$, $\overrightarrow{AQ} = \mathbf{b}$, $\overrightarrow{OS} = \mathbf{c}$
a Find, in terms of $\mathbf{a}$, $\mathbf{b}$ and $\mathbf{c}$ expressions for:
i $\overrightarrow{PQ}$ **ii** $\overrightarrow{QR}$
iii $\overrightarrow{SR}$ **iv** $\overrightarrow{PS}$
b Use your results from part **a** to show that *PQRS* is a parallelogram.

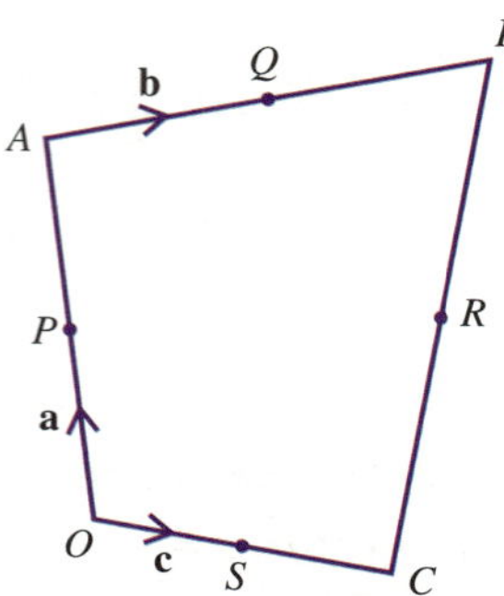

Solution 3

a **i** $\overrightarrow{PQ} = \overrightarrow{PA} + \overrightarrow{AQ} = \mathbf{a} + \mathbf{b}$
ii $\overrightarrow{QR} = \overrightarrow{QB} + \overrightarrow{BR} = \overrightarrow{QB} + \frac{1}{2}\overrightarrow{BC}$
$\overrightarrow{BC} = -\overrightarrow{AB} - \overrightarrow{OA} + \overrightarrow{OC} = -2\mathbf{b} - 2\mathbf{a} + 2\mathbf{c}$
So $\frac{1}{2}\overrightarrow{BC} = \mathbf{c} - \mathbf{b} - \mathbf{a}$
This gives $\overrightarrow{QR} = \mathbf{b} + \mathbf{c} - \mathbf{b} - \mathbf{a} = \mathbf{c} - \mathbf{a}$

iii $\overrightarrow{SR} = \overrightarrow{SC} + \overrightarrow{CR}$

$\overrightarrow{CR} = -\frac{1}{2}\overrightarrow{BC} = -\mathbf{c} + \mathbf{b} + \mathbf{a}$ or $\mathbf{a} + \mathbf{b} - \mathbf{c}$

This gives $\overrightarrow{SR} = \mathbf{c} + \mathbf{a} + \mathbf{b} - \mathbf{c} = \mathbf{a} + \mathbf{b}$

iv $\overrightarrow{PS} = \overrightarrow{PO} + \overrightarrow{OS} = -\mathbf{a} + \mathbf{c} = \mathbf{c} - \mathbf{a}$

b $\overrightarrow{PQ} = \overrightarrow{SR} = \mathbf{a} + \mathbf{b}$

$\overrightarrow{QR} = \overrightarrow{PS} = \mathbf{c} - \mathbf{a}$

PQRS has two pairs of equal and parallel sides so it is a parallelogram.

Exercise B

1 *OACB* is a parallelogram.
P, *Q*, *R* and *S* are the mid-points of the sides of the parallelogram.
$\overrightarrow{OS} = \mathbf{x}$, $\overrightarrow{OP} = \mathbf{y}$

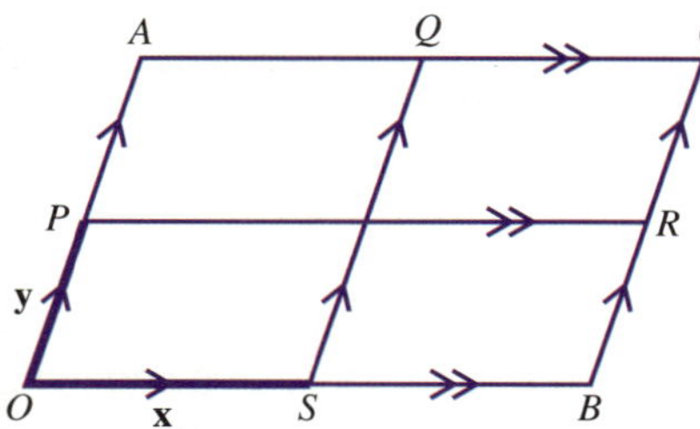

Find, in terms of **x** and **y**, expressions for:

a **i** $\overrightarrow{PQ}$ **ii** $\overrightarrow{OC}$ **iii** $\overrightarrow{SR}$

b Write down one fact about lines *PQ*, *OC* and *SR*.

2 *OXWV* and *OYUX* are parallelograms.

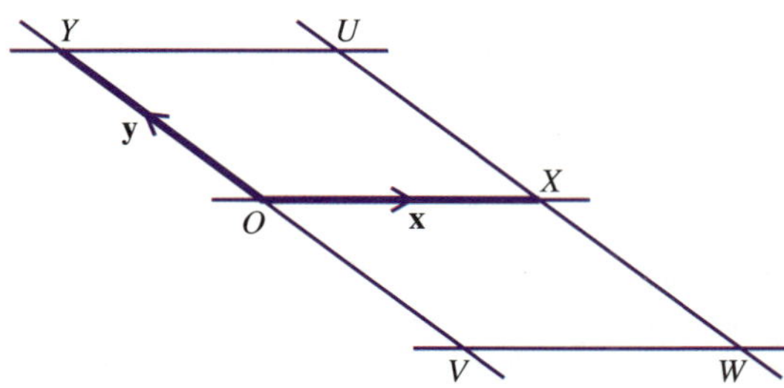

a Write down, in terms of **x** and **y**, expressions for:

i $\overrightarrow{OU}$ **ii** $\overrightarrow{UV}$

b The point *S* is such that *YUVS* is a parallelogram.
Write down the vector $\overrightarrow{OS}$ in terms of **x** and **y**.

3 *OAB* is a triangle.
$\overrightarrow{OA} = \mathbf{a}$, $\overrightarrow{OB} = \mathbf{b}$
M is the mid-point of *OA* and *N* is the mid-point of *AB*.

a Write down, in terms of **a** and **b**, expressions for:

i $\overrightarrow{AB}$ **ii** $\overrightarrow{AN}$ **iii** $\overrightarrow{MN}$

b Write down the special name of quadrilateral *OBNM*.

4 *OAB* is a triangle.
M is the mid-point of *OA*.
$OM = \mathbf{a}$ and $AN = \mathbf{c}$.
N and *P* are points on *AB* such that $AN = NP = PB$.

a Find, in terms of **a** and **c**, expressions for:

i $\overrightarrow{AB}$ **ii** $\overrightarrow{MN}$ **iii** $\overrightarrow{OP}$

b What shape is *OMNP*?
Give a reason for your answer.

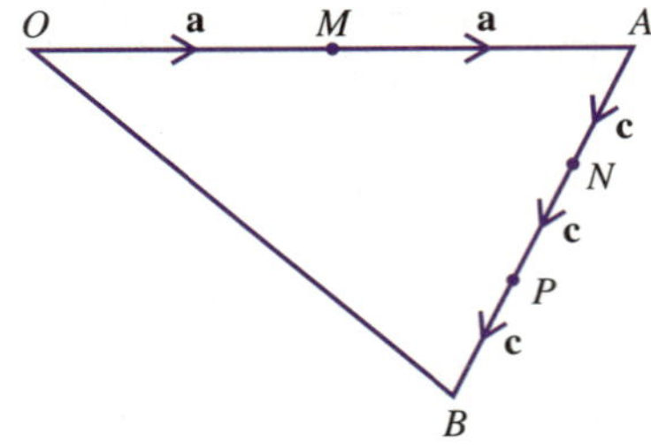

5 *ABCD* is a parallelogram.
X is the mid-point of *AC*.
$\overrightarrow{OA} = \mathbf{a}$, $\overrightarrow{OB} = \mathbf{b}$
BXY is a straight line.
X is the mid-point of *BY*.

a Express, in terms of **a** and **b**:

i $\overrightarrow{BX}$ **ii** $\overrightarrow{BY}$ **iii** $\overrightarrow{OY}$

b Write down one fact about the positions of *O*, *A* and *Y*.

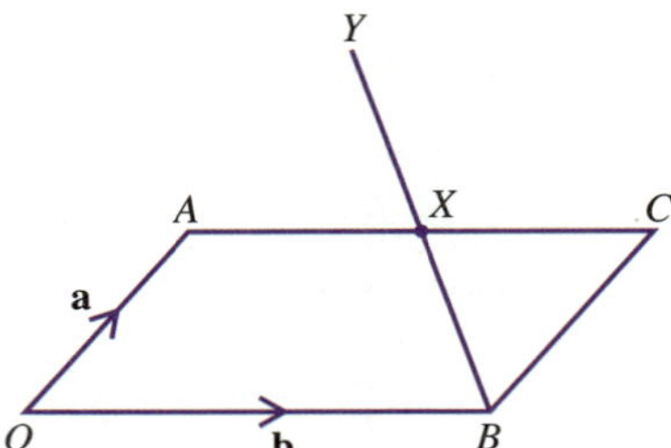

Chapter summary

- Quantities that have **size** only are called scalars; for example, distance, area and temperature.
- Quantities that have both **size** and **direction** are called vectors; for example 25 m due north or 7 mph south west.
- Vectors can be represented by line segments with arrows. The length of the line represents the size, and the arrow represents the direction.

- Vectors can be labelled in the following ways:

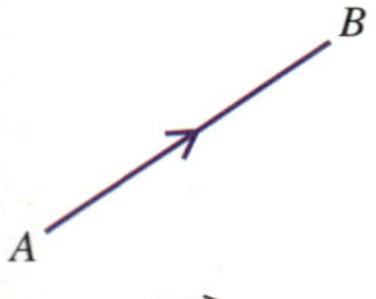

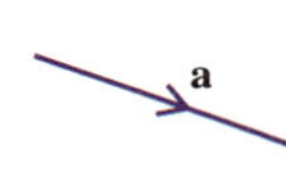

vector $\overrightarrow{AB}$ vector **a**

- Two vectors are equal if they have the same length and are in the same direction.
- Vectors with the same direction are either parallel or in a straight line.
- A vector with the same length but the opposite direction to a vector **a** is the vector $-\mathbf{a}$.
- Column vectors, e.g. $\begin{pmatrix}3\\2\end{pmatrix}$, are used to describe the length and direction or displacement of a vector.
- Vectors may be added or subtracted by adding or subtracting the column vectors.
  - Vector addition

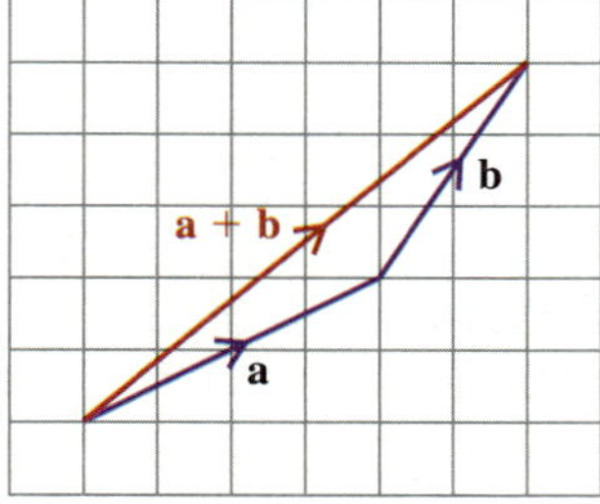

- Vector subtraction: **a** − **b** can be written as **a** + −**b**

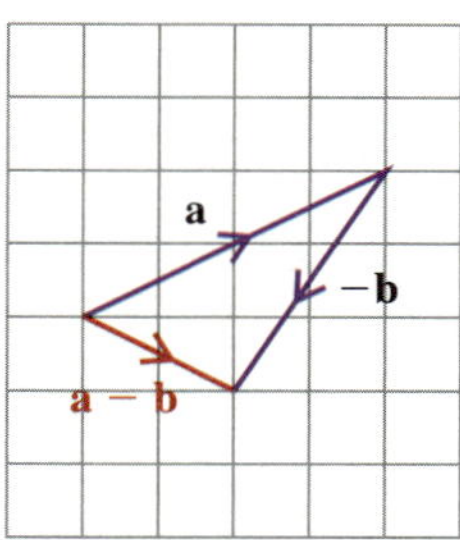

- The result of vector addition or subtraction is called the resultant vector.
- Parallel lines have the same direction so are multiples of the same vector.
- If two vectors are in the same direction and pass through the same point, they are part of the same straight line.
- Vector methods can be used to solve geometrical problems.

Chapter review

1 The diagram shows vectors **a**, **b**, **c**, **d** and **e**.

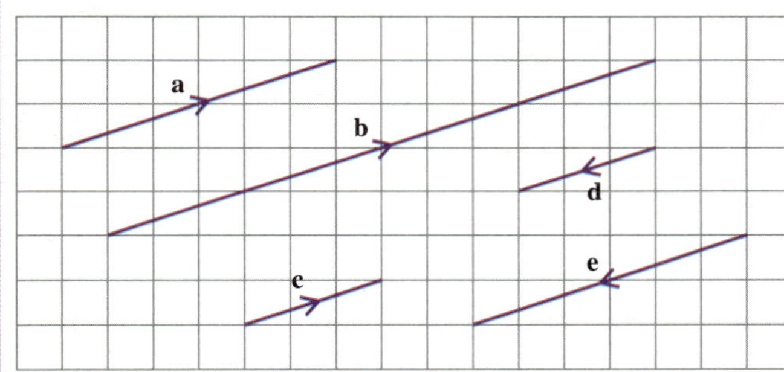

a Write the column vectors for **a** to **e**.
b Express vectors **b**, **c**, **d** and **e** in terms of **a**.

2 $\mathbf{a} = \begin{pmatrix} 1 \\ -3 \end{pmatrix}, \mathbf{b} = \begin{pmatrix} -2 \\ 2 \end{pmatrix}, \mathbf{c} = \begin{pmatrix} 3 \\ 4 \end{pmatrix}$

On squared paper draw vectors to represent the following:
i 2**a** **ii** −**b** **iii** −2**c** **iv** $\frac{1}{2}$**b** **v** −3**a**

3 The diagram shows three vectors **a**, **b** and **c**.
On squared paper draw vectors to represent:
i **a** + **b**
ii **b** − **c**
iii 2**a** + **b** + **c**

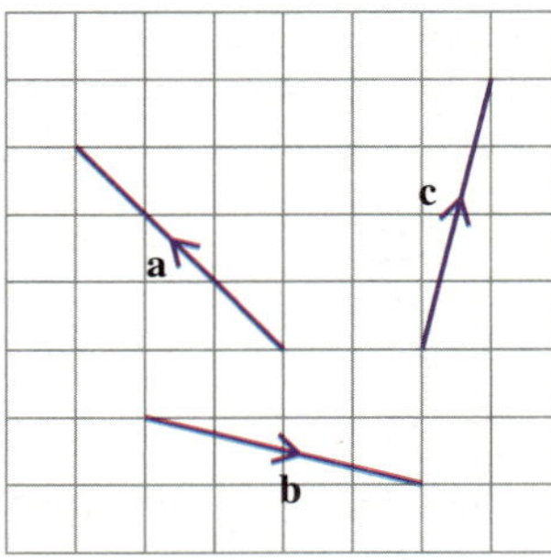

4 $\overrightarrow{AB} = \begin{pmatrix} -4 \\ 6 \end{pmatrix}, \overrightarrow{BC} = \begin{pmatrix} 1 \\ -3 \end{pmatrix}$

a Work out the column vectors for:

i $2\overrightarrow{BC}$ **ii** $-\overrightarrow{AB}$ **iii** $-3\overrightarrow{BC}$

b On squared paper draw vectors to represent:

i $\frac{1}{2}\overrightarrow{AB}$ **ii** $2\overrightarrow{BC}$ **iii** $\overrightarrow{AB} + \overrightarrow{BC}$

5 $\overrightarrow{AB} = \begin{pmatrix} 3 \\ 6 \end{pmatrix}, \overrightarrow{BC} = \begin{pmatrix} 4 \\ 2 \end{pmatrix}, \overrightarrow{CD} = \begin{pmatrix} 2 \\ -5 \end{pmatrix}$

On squared paper draw diagrams to represent the following:

a $\overrightarrow{AB} + \overrightarrow{BC}$ **b** $\overrightarrow{AB} - \overrightarrow{BC}$ **c** $\overrightarrow{AB} + \overrightarrow{BC} + \overrightarrow{CD}$

6 *OABC* is a parallelogram. *M* is the mid-point of *BC*.

$\overrightarrow{OA} = \mathbf{a}$, $\overrightarrow{OC} = \mathbf{c}$

Write down, in terms of **a** and **c**:

a $\overrightarrow{OB}$ **b** $\overrightarrow{OM}$ **c** $\overrightarrow{AM}$

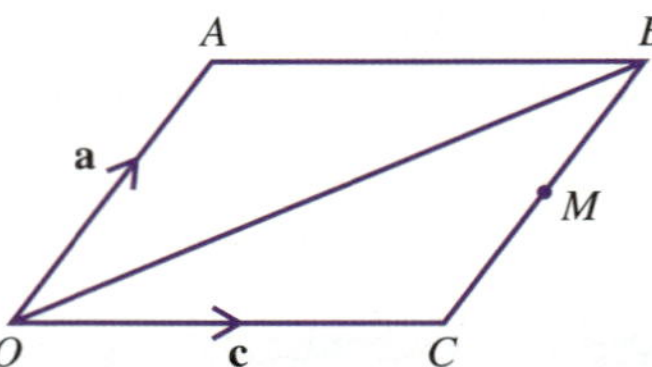

7 The diagram shows triangle *OAB*.

OAT is a straight line.

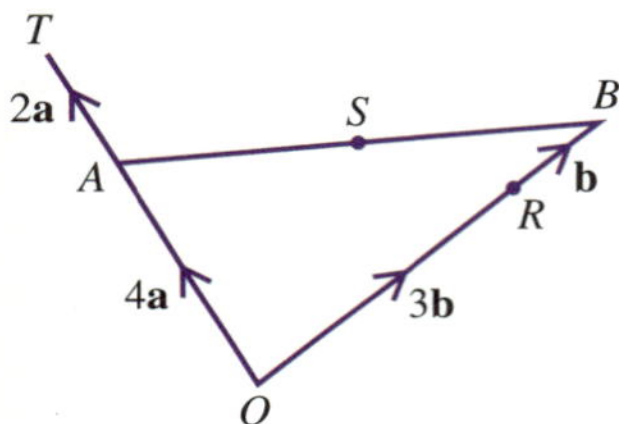

S is the mid-point of *AB* and *R* is the point such that $OR = 3RB$.

a Write down, in terms of **a** and **b**, vectors to represent the following:

i $\overrightarrow{BA}$ **ii** $\overrightarrow{RS}$ **iii** $\overrightarrow{ST}$

b What do your answers to **ii** and **iii** tell you about the positions of *R*, *S* and *T*?

8 *ABCD* is a quadrilateral.

$\overrightarrow{AP} = \overrightarrow{PB} = \mathbf{p}$

$\overrightarrow{BQ} = \overrightarrow{QC} = \mathbf{q}$

$\overrightarrow{AS} = \overrightarrow{SD} = \mathbf{s}$

R is the mid-point of *DC*.

a Find, in terms of **p**, **q** and **s**, expressions for:

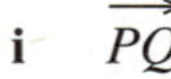

i $\overrightarrow{PQ}$

ii $\overrightarrow{DC}$

iii $\overrightarrow{DR}$

iv $\overrightarrow{SR}$

b What shape is quadrilateral *PQRS*?

Explain your answer.

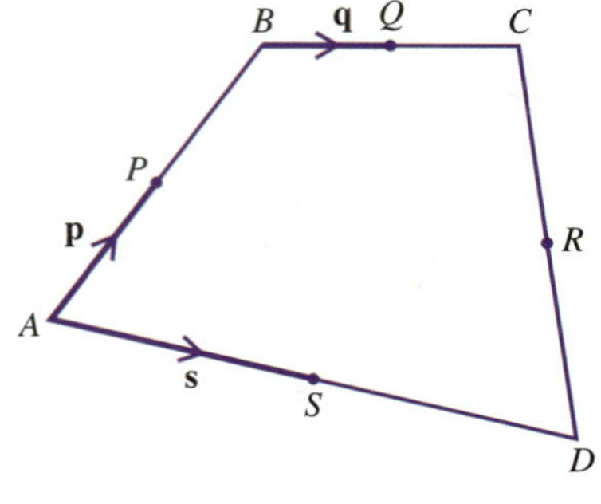

9 *OABC* is a parallelogram. *M* is the mid-point of *AB*. $\overrightarrow{OA} = \mathbf{p}$ and $\overrightarrow{OC} = \mathbf{q}$.

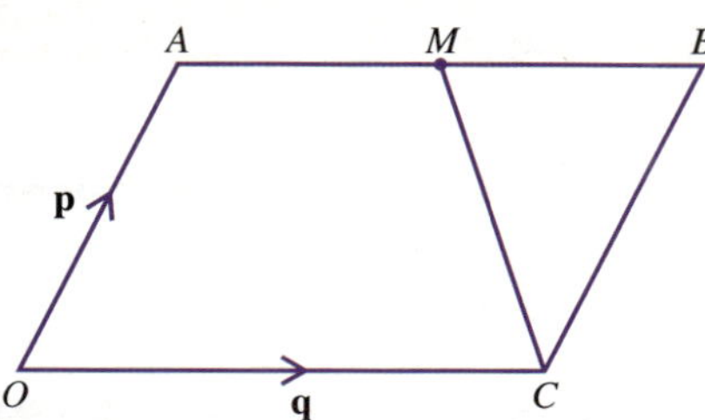

a Find, in terms of **p** and **q**, expressions for the following vectors.

i $\overrightarrow{OB}$ **ii** $\overrightarrow{AM}$ **iii** $\overrightarrow{MC}$

R is a point on *MC* such that $MR = \frac{1}{3}MC$.

b Find, in terms of **p** and **q**, expressions for:

i $\overrightarrow{MR}$ **ii** $\overrightarrow{OR}$

c Describe fully what your expression for $\overrightarrow{OR}$ tells you about the position of *R*.

10 *OABC* is a parallelogram. $\overrightarrow{OA} = \mathbf{p}$ and $\overrightarrow{OC} = \mathbf{q}$. *R* is a point outside the parallelogram such that $\overrightarrow{OR} = 2\mathbf{q} - \mathbf{p}$.

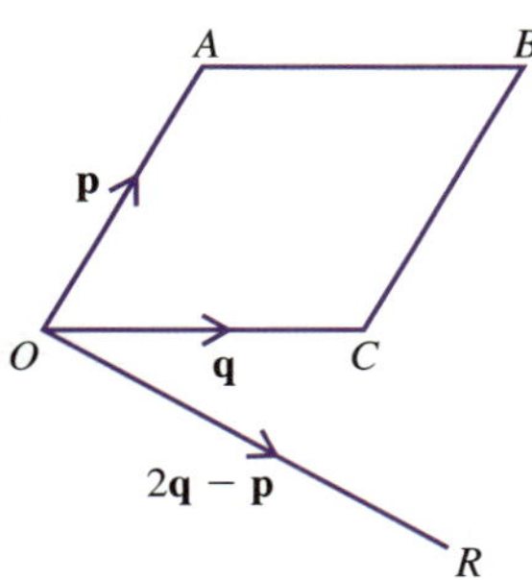

a Find, in terms of **p** and **q**, expressions for:

i $\overrightarrow{OB}$ **ii** $\overrightarrow{AC}$ **iii** $\overrightarrow{CR}$

b Describe fully what your answers to part **a** tell you about the position of *R*.

CHAPTER

41 Algebraic identities 2

41.1 Algebraic fractions

CAN YOU REMEMBER

- How to simplify a fraction by dividing numerator and denominator by their highest common factor?
- How to add, subtract, multiply and divide fractions?
- How to simplify algebraic expressions by collecting like terms, expand brackets and factorise algebraic expressions?

IN THIS SECTION YOU WILL

- Learn how to simplify algebraic fractions.
- Learn how to add, subtract, multiply and divide algebraic fractions.

An *algebraic fraction* can be simplified if the numerator and denominator have a common factor.

Example 1

Simplify:

a $\dfrac{2x^2 + 4x}{x^2 + 5x + 6}$ **b** $\dfrac{2x^2 - x - 3}{4x^2 - 9}$

Solution 1

a $\dfrac{2x^2 + 4x}{x^2 + 5x + 6} \equiv \dfrac{2x(x + 2)}{(x + 2)(x + 3)}$ Factorise $2x^2 + 4x$ and $x^2 + 5x + 6$

$\dfrac{2x\cancel{(x + 2)}}{\cancel{(x + 2)}(x + 3)} \equiv \dfrac{2x}{x + 3}$ Cancel the common factor $(x + 2)$.

b $\dfrac{2x^2 - x - 3}{4x^2 - 9} \equiv \dfrac{(2x - 3)(x + 1)}{(2x - 3)(2x + 3)}$ Factorise $2x^2 - x - 3$ and $4x^2 - 9$

$\dfrac{\cancel{(2x - 3)}(x + 1)}{\cancel{(2x - 3)}(2x + 3)} \equiv \dfrac{x + 1}{2x + 3}$ Cancel the common factor $(2x - 3)$.

Algebraic fractions can be multiplied and divided.

Example 2

Simplify:

a $\dfrac{x^2}{x-2} \times \dfrac{x^2-4}{x^5}$ **b** $\dfrac{5x^2+9x-2}{x+3} \div \dfrac{x^2-x-6}{x^2-9}$

Solution 2

a Factorise $x^2 - 4$

Factorise $x^2 - 4$

$$\frac{x^2}{x-2} \times \frac{x^2-4}{x^5}$$

$$\frac{x^2}{x-2} \times \frac{(x-2)(x+2)}{x^5}$$

Cancel the common factors $x - 2$ and x^2

$$\frac{\cancel{x^2}}{\cancel{x-2}} \times \frac{\cancel{(x-2)}(x+2)}{\cancel{x^5}} \equiv \frac{x+2}{x^3}$$

b $\dfrac{5x^2+9x-2}{x+3} \div \dfrac{x^2-x-6}{x^2-9}$

To divide by a fraction, multiply by its reciprocal.

$$\frac{5x^2+9x-2}{x+3} \times \frac{x^2-9}{x^2-x-6}$$

Factorise $5x^2 + 9x - 2$, $x^2 - 9$ and $x^2 - x - 6$

$$\frac{(5x-1)(x+2)}{x+3} \times \frac{(x-3)(x+3)}{(x-3)(x+2)}$$

$$\frac{(5x-1)\cancel{(x+2)}}{\cancel{x+3}} \times \frac{\cancel{(x-3)}\cancel{(x+3)}}{\cancel{(x-3)}\cancel{(x+2)}}$$

Cancel the common factors $(x + 2)$, $(x - 3)$ and $(x + 3)$.

$$\frac{5x^2+9x-2}{x+3} \div \frac{x^2-x-6}{x^2-9} \equiv 5x - 1$$

Exercise A

1 Simplify:

a $\dfrac{x^7}{x^2}$ **b** $\dfrac{x(x+2)}{x^3(x-2)}$ **c** $\dfrac{x^5(x+3)}{x^3(x+3)}$ **d** $\dfrac{(y-5)(y+7)}{(y+2)(y-5)}$

e $\dfrac{4y^4(y+1)}{2y(y-1)}$ **f** $\dfrac{9y^9(y-1)}{6y^6(y-1)}$ **g** $\dfrac{10y^5(y+3)}{25y^7(y-3)}$ **h** $\dfrac{12y^3(2y-3)}{8y^7(2y-3)}$

2 Simplify:

a $\dfrac{2x+4}{x+2}$ **b** $\dfrac{6x^2+3x}{3x}$ **c** $\dfrac{4x^3+6x^2}{2x+3}$ **d** $\dfrac{12x^3+8x^2}{6x^2+4x}$

e $\dfrac{10y^2+5y}{5(2y+1)}$ **f** $\dfrac{(18y^3+12y)(2y-1)}{3(4y-2)}$

g $\dfrac{(5xy-15y)(3xy-9x)}{15xy}$ **h** $\dfrac{16x^2y^3+12xy}{(4xy^2+3)(x+y)}$

3 Simplify:

a $\frac{2x-4}{x^2-3x+2}$ **b** $\frac{x^2+3x}{x^2+7x+12}$ **c** $\frac{2x^2+8x}{x^2+2x-8}$ **d** $\frac{x^2y-3xy}{x^2-8x+15}$

e $\frac{x^2-1}{x-1}$ **f** $\frac{x^2-4}{x+2}$ **g** $\frac{x^2-3x-4}{x+1}$ **h** $\frac{5x-10}{x^2-11x+18}$

i $\frac{x+5}{x^2-2x-35}$ **j** $\frac{3x-12}{x^2-3x-4}$

4 Simplify:

a $\frac{x^2+5x-14}{x^2-x-2}$ **b** $\frac{x^2+3x-70}{x^2-100}$ **c** $\frac{x^2-7x-8}{x^2-2x-3}$ **d** $\frac{x^2+6x-16}{x^2-6x+8}$

e $\frac{x^2-9}{x^2-5x+6}$ **f** $\frac{2x^2-8}{x^2-3x-10}$ **g** $\frac{3x^2-12}{x^2-9x+14}$ **h** $\frac{x^2-25}{x^2-10x+25}$

i $\frac{x^2-4x+4}{x^2+x-6}$ **j** $\frac{x^2-16x+64}{x^2-64}$

5 Simplify:

a $\frac{2x+3y}{4x^2-9y^2}$ **b** $\frac{2x^2+9x+10}{5x^2-20}$ **c** $\frac{x^3-16x}{x^2-10x-16}$ **d** $\frac{3x^2-5x-2}{5x^2-9x-2}$

e $\frac{2x^2-x-1}{3x^2-4x+1}$ **f** $\frac{2x^2-3x-2}{2x^2-5x-3}$ **g** $\frac{3x^2+14x-5}{3x^2+16x+5}$ **h** $\frac{4x^2-81}{2x^2-7x-9}$

6 Simplify:

a $\frac{x^2}{y^3}\times\frac{y}{x}$ **b** $\frac{y}{y-1}\times\frac{y^2-1}{3y^2}$

c $\frac{3b-6}{8b+4}\times\frac{2b+1}{b^2-4}$ **d** $\frac{x^2-3x+2}{10xy-15y}\times\frac{5y}{x-2}$

e $\frac{x}{x+4}\times\frac{x^2-16}{x^3}$ **f** $\frac{x+2}{x^2-6x+9}\times\frac{x-3}{2x+4}$

g $\frac{3x^2+x-2}{4x}\times\frac{2x^2-4x}{x+1}$ **h** $\frac{3x^2-2x-3}{x^2-5x+6}\times\frac{x^2+2x-6}{3x^2+13x+4}$

7 Simplify:

a $\frac{x+3}{x}\div\frac{x^2-2x-15}{2x^2}$ **b** $\frac{6x^2y}{x^2-y^2}\div\frac{2xy}{x+y}$

c $\frac{8x^2-18}{5-2x}\div\frac{2x+3}{2x-5}$ **d** $\frac{x^2-x-20}{x^2+8x+16}\div\frac{x^2-10x+25}{x^2-2x-24}$

e $\frac{2x^2-x-3}{x^2-6x-7}\div\frac{3x^2-10x+7}{x^2-4x+3}$

Algebraic fractions can be added and subtracted.

Example 3

Simplify:

a $\dfrac{4}{x-3} - \dfrac{3}{x+3}$ **b** $\dfrac{2x}{x-1} + \dfrac{x-3}{(x-1)^2}$

Solution 3

a Find the least common multiple (LCM) of the denominators.

The LCM of $(x-3)$ and $(x+3)$ is $(x-3)(x+3)$

Write each fraction with $(x-3)(x+3)$ as the common denominator.

$$\frac{4}{x-3} - \frac{3}{x+3} \equiv \frac{4(x+3)}{(x-3)(x+3)} - \frac{3(x-3)}{(x-3)(x+3)}$$

Write the expression as a single fraction.

$$\frac{4(x+3)}{(x-3)(x+3)} - \frac{3(x-3)}{(x-3)(x+3)} \equiv \frac{4(x+3)-3(x-3)}{(x-3)(x+3)}$$

Expand brackets in the numerator and simplify.

$$\frac{4(x+3)-3(x-3)}{(x-3)(x+3)} \equiv \frac{4x+12-3x+9}{(x-3)(x+3)} \equiv \frac{x+21}{(x-3)(x+3)}$$

b The least common multiple (LCM) of $(x-1)$ and $(x-1)^2$ is $(x-1)^2$

$$\frac{2x}{x-1} + \frac{x-3}{(x-1)^2} \equiv \frac{2x(x-1)}{(x-1)^2} + \frac{x-3}{(x-1)^2}$$

$$\frac{2x(x-1)}{(x-1)^2} + \frac{x-3}{(x-1)^2} \equiv \frac{2x(x-1)+x-3}{(x-1)^2}$$

$$\frac{2x(x-1)+x-3}{(x-1)^2} \equiv \frac{2x^2-x-3}{(x-1)^2}$$

Factorise $2x^2-x-3$

$$\equiv \frac{(2x-3)(x+1)}{(x-1)^2}$$

Exercise B

1 Simplify:

a $\dfrac{1}{x} + \dfrac{1}{x+1}$ **b** $\dfrac{1}{x+2} + \dfrac{1}{x+1}$ **c** $\dfrac{1}{x+3} + \dfrac{1}{x+1}$ **d** $\dfrac{1}{x+2} + \dfrac{1}{x+3}$

e $\dfrac{1}{x+2} + \dfrac{1}{x-1}$ **f** $\dfrac{1}{x-2} + \dfrac{1}{x-1}$ **g** $\dfrac{1}{x+4} - \dfrac{1}{x+3}$ **h** $\dfrac{1}{x+4} - \dfrac{1}{x-3}$

i $\dfrac{1}{x-4} - \dfrac{1}{x-3}$ **j** $\dfrac{1}{x-4} - \dfrac{1}{x-5}$

2 Simplify:

a $\dfrac{3}{x} + \dfrac{2}{2x+1}$ **b** $\dfrac{2}{x+2} + \dfrac{3}{x-1}$ **c** $\dfrac{5}{2x+3} - \dfrac{2}{x+1}$ **d** $\dfrac{3}{3x+2} + \dfrac{2}{2x+3}$

e $\frac{5}{3x-2} - \frac{1}{x-1}$ **f** $\frac{2}{x-2y} + \frac{2}{x-y}$ **g** $\frac{x}{x+4} - \frac{3}{2x+3}$ **h** $\frac{5}{x+4} - \frac{3}{x-3}$

i $\frac{x}{x-4} - \frac{4x}{4x-1}$ **j** $\frac{2x}{x-4} - \frac{4}{3x-5}$

3 Simplify:

a $\frac{3x}{x+2} + \frac{x}{x-6}$ **b** $\frac{x^2}{x^2-1} + \frac{x}{x+1}$ **c** $\frac{x-1}{x+2} + \frac{x+5}{x-2}$

d $\frac{2x-1}{x+3} - \frac{x+5}{3x-2}$ **e** $\frac{4x-3}{3x+2} - \frac{3x+1}{5x-2}$

4 A rectangle has length $\frac{x+1}{x-1}$ and width $\frac{x-5}{x^2-1}$.

Show that the perimeter of the rectangle is $\frac{x+4}{x-1}$.

5 **a** Explain why the least common multiple (LCM) of $x^2 - 1$ and $x^2 - 3x + 2$ is $(x-1)(x+1)(x-2)$.

b Hence, show that

$$\frac{x}{x^2-3x+2} - \frac{x+3}{x^2-1} \equiv \frac{6}{(x-1)(x+1)(x-2)}$$

6 **a** Find the least common multiple of $x^2 + 3x + 2$ and $x^2 + 5x + 6$

b Hence, simplify $\frac{1}{x^2+3x+2} + \frac{1}{x^2+5x+6}$

7 Show that: $\frac{1}{a-b} + \frac{1}{a-c} + \frac{1}{b-c} \equiv \frac{a(a+b-c) - b(b-c) + c(c-2a)}{(a-b)(a-c)(b-c)}$

41.2 Algebraic proof

CAN YOU REMEMBER

- The meaning of 'identity'?
- How to simplify and add, subtract, multiply and divide algebraic fractions?
- How to simplify algebraic expressions by collecting like terms, expand brackets and factorise algebraic expressions?

IN THIS SECTION YOU WILL

- Use algebra to prove simple rules.
- Use a range of algebraic skills to prove algebraic identities.

Algebra is often used to establish the truth of a general statement in mathematics.
For example, the truth of the statement 'the sum of two consecutive positive integers is an odd number' can be **demonstrated** with examples such as $1 + 2 = 3$, $14 + 15 = 29$, $101 + 102 = 203$ …
However, the fact that the statement is true for some particular cases does not mean it is true for **all** pairs of consecutive integers.

The statement can be **proved** by picking **any** two consecutive integers n and $n + 1$
Then the sum of the two integers is $n + n + 1 = 2n + 1$
$2n$ is the nth term for the multiples of 2
$2n + 1$ is one more than the multiples of 2, the odd numbers.
This *proves* that the statement is always true for any value of n.

Example 1

Anna and Ben are working on a problem.
There are some marbles in bag A.
Bag B contains four more marbles than bag A.
Bag C contains twice as many marbles as bag B.
Prove that this rule gives the total number of marbles in bags A, B and C:

Add three to the number of marbles in bag A and then multiply by 4

Ben chooses some values for the number of marbles in bag A to see if the rule works.
a Try Ben's method for 10 marbles in bag A.
b Does Ben's method prove the rule for all possible values for the number of marbles in bag A?
Anna lets the number of marbles in bag A equal x and uses algebra to prove the rule.
c Show Anna's method.
d Explain why Anna's method proves the rule.

Solution 1

a Bag A contains 10 marbles. Bag B contains $10 + 4 = 14$ marbles.
Bag C contains $14 \times 2 = 28$ marbles.
Total number of marbles $= 10 + 14 + 28 = 52$ marbles.
Using the rule: $(10 + 3) \times 4 = 52$
The rule works for 10 marbles in bag A.
b Ben's method shows that the rule works for one particular case, but not for all cases, so it does not prove the rule.
c Let the number of marbles in bag A be x marbles.
In bag B, there are $x + 4$ marbles.
In bag C, there are $2(x + 4)$ marbles.
Total number of marbles $= x + x + 4 + 2(x + 4) \equiv 4x + 12 \equiv 4(x + 3)$
d This shows that the rule works for all values of x.
Because x can take **any** value, Anna's method **proves** the rule.

Finding examples that agree with a statement does not prove the statement.
However, a statement can be **disproved** by finding a single example that does **not** agree with it.
This is called finding a *counter example*.

Example 2

Terri says, 'The sum of five consecutive integers is always odd.'
Find a counter example to show that this is not true.

Solution 2

$1 + 2 + 3 + 4 + 5 = 15$
The sum in this case is odd. This supports the truth of the statement but does **not** prove it.
$2 + 3 + 4 + 5 + 6 = 20$
The sum is even. This is a counter example and disproves the statement.

Algebraic skills can be used to prove an algebraic *identity*.

Example 3

Prove that $(2 + 3x)^2 + (6 - x)^2 \equiv 10(x^2 + 4)$

Solution 3

$(2 + 3x)^2 + (6 - x)^2 \equiv 4 + 12x + 9x^2 + 36 - 12x + x^2$
$\equiv 10x^2 + 40 \equiv 10(x^2 + 4)$

Expanding brackets.

Exercise A

1 Bag A contains some marbles.
Bag B contains three fewer marbles than bag A.
Bag C contains four times as many marbles as bag B.
Bag D contains the square of the number of marbles in bag B.
Prove that the total number of marbles in bags A, B, C and D is six less than the square of the number of marbles in bag A.

2 Andy has some £1 coins.
Billy has six more £1 coins than Andy.
Clare has three times as many £1 coins as Billy.
David has four fewer £1 coins than Clare.
Prove that the total number of £1 coins that Billy and David have is two more than the total number Andy and Clare have.

3 The sum of two consecutive odd numbers is a multiple of 4
This is how Beth and Dilip try to prove this statement.
Beth's work:

> The odd numbers are 1, 3, 5, 7, 9 …
> $1 + 3 = 4, 3 + 5 = 8, 5 + 7 = 12$ …
> This always gives a multiple of 4
> The sum of two consecutive odd numbers is always a multiple of 4

Dilip's work.

> The nth odd number is $2n - 1$
> The next odd number $= 2n - 1 + 2 = 2n + 1$
> **Any** two consecutive odd numbers are $2n - 1$ and $2n + 1$
> The sum of two consecutive odd numbers is $2n - 1 + 2n + 1 = 4n$
> $4n$ is the nth multiple of 4
> The sum of two consecutive odd numbers is **always** a multiple of 4

a Whose work, Beth's or Dilip's, proves the statement?
Explain your answer.
b Prove that the sum of four consecutive odd numbers is a multiple of 8

4 Prove each of the following statements.
a The sum of three consecutive integers is a multiple of 3
b The sum of five consecutive integers is a multiple of 5
c The product of two consecutive even numbers is a multiple of 4

5 Prove each of the following statements.

a The sum of two consecutive square numbers is an odd number.

b The sum of three consecutive square numbers is one less than a multiple of 3

6 Lilin says that $(x - y)^2 \equiv x^2 - y^2$
Use a counter example to show that this is not true.

7 Prove that $a(x + y) - b(x - y) \equiv x(a - b) + y(a + b)$

8 Prove that:

a $(a + b)^2 + (a - b)^2 \equiv 2(a^2 + b^2)$ **b** $(a + b)^2 - (a - b)^2 \equiv 4ab$

9 Prove that:

a $(p + qx)^2 + (pq - x)^2 \equiv (q^2 + 1)(x^2 + p^2)$ **b** $(p + qx)^2 - (pq + x)^2 \equiv (q^2 - 1)(x^2 - p^2)$

10 Prove that:

a $(x + y)(x^2 - xy + y^2) \equiv x^3 + y^3$ **b** $(x - y)(x^2 + xy + y^2) \equiv x^3 - y^3$

11 Brad is investigating the difference, D, between consecutive cube numbers.
$D = 2^3 - 1^3 = 8 - 1$
$D = 10^3 - 9^3 = 1000 - 729 = 271$
Brad says that D is always a prime number.
Find a counter example to show that this is not true.

Example 4

Tim uses this diagram to obtain an identity for x^2
$x(x - y) + y(x - z) + yz \equiv x^2$

a Explain how Tim obtains the identity from the diagram.

b Use algebra to prove the identity.

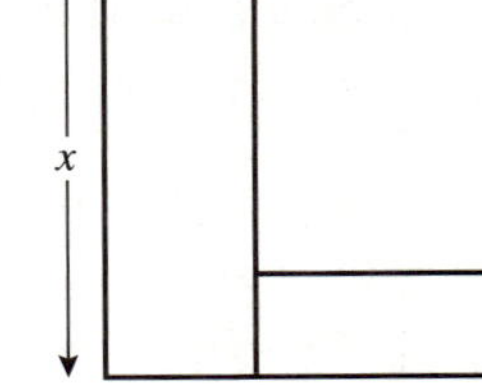

Solution 4

a The x by x square has been divided into three rectangles.
The area of each of these rectangles is $x \times (x - y)$, $y \times (x - z)$ and $y \times z$
The total area of these rectangles is $x \times x$

b $x(x - y) + y(x - z) + yz \equiv x^2 - xy + xy - yz + yz \equiv x^2$

Example 5

Prove that $(x - 1)^3 \equiv x^3 - 3x^2 + 3x - 1$

Solution 5

$(x - 1)^3 \equiv (x - 1)(x - 1)^2 \equiv (x - 1)(x^2 - 2x + 1)$

Method 1

$\equiv x(x^2 - 2x + 1) - (x^2 - 2x + 1)$
$\equiv x^3 - 2x^2 + x - x^2 + 2x - 1$
$\equiv x^3 - 3x^2 + 3x - 1$

Method 2

$(x - 1)(x^2 - 2x + 1)$ can be expanded using a multiplication grid.

	x^2	$-2x$	1
x	x^3	$-2x^2$	x
-1	$-x^2$	$2x$	-1

$\equiv x^3 - 3x^2 + 3x - 1$

Exercise B

1 The diagram shows a square of side length x split into four rectangles A, B, C and D.

a Write expressions in terms of x, y and z for the areas of the four rectangles.

b Hence, write an identity for x^2

c Prove the identity.

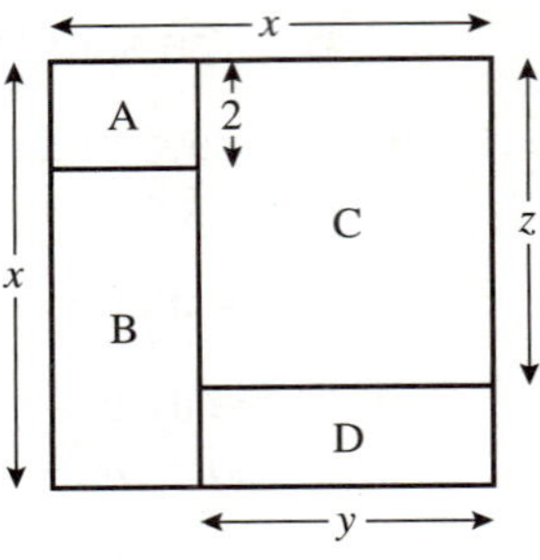

2 Repeat question **1** for the following dissections of an x by x square.

a

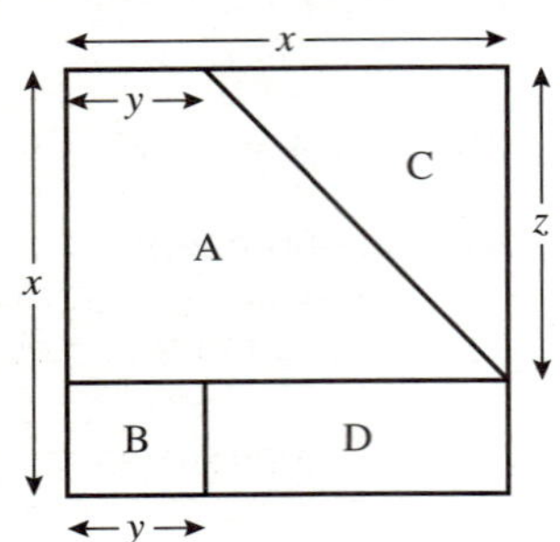

b

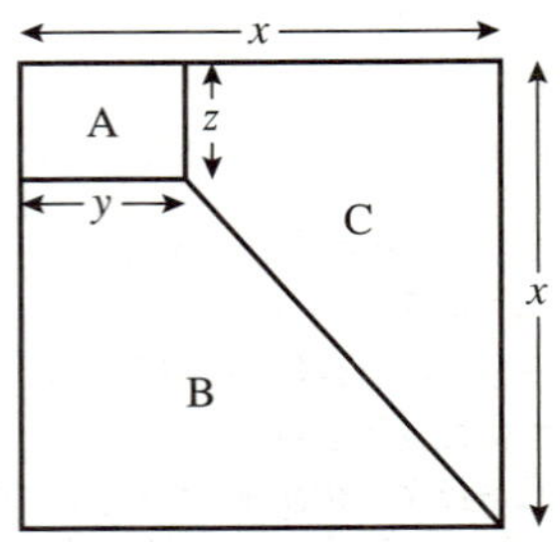

3 The diagram shows a square dissected into four congruent triangles with base y and height x and a smaller square. Show that the area of the larger square is $x^2 + y^2$
Use the result to prove Pythagoras' theorem.

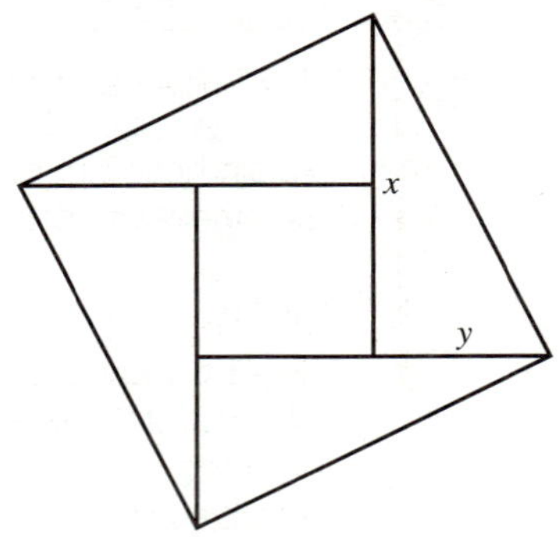

4 The diagram shows a trapezium.
Prove that its area is $\frac{1}{2}(a + b)h$

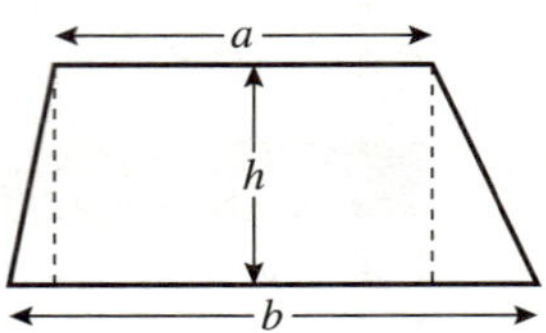

5 **a** The first 10 terms of the sequence with $a = 3$ and $d = 4$ are
3, 7, 11, 15, 19, 23, 27, 31, 35, 39 …
Pick any three consecutive terms in the sequence.
Let these have values x, y and z.
Calculate $\sqrt{(y^2 - xz)}$
For example, $x = 7$, $y = 11$ and $z = 15$
$\sqrt{(y^2 - xz)} = \sqrt{(11^2 - 7 \times 15)} = 4$
Repeat for other values of x, y and z.
What do you notice?
Prove that this **always** happens.

b Repeat part **a** for five consecutive odd terms in the sequence where x and z are the first and last of the five terms and y is the middle term of the five terms.

c Repeat parts **a** and **b** for the sequence with $a = 2$ and $d = 5$

6 Prove that:

a $\dfrac{x+1}{x-1} + \dfrac{x-1}{x+1} \equiv \dfrac{2(x^2+1)}{x^2-1}$

b $\dfrac{x+1}{x-1} - \dfrac{x-1}{x+1} \equiv \dfrac{4x}{x^2-1}$

7 Prove that:

a $(x-2)^3 + 6(x-2)^2 + 12(x-2) + 8 \equiv x^3$

b $2(x-1)(x-2)^2 + 2(x-2)^2 + 8(x-1)(x-2) + 8(x-1) + 8(x-2) + 8 \equiv 2x^3$

c $(nx-2)(x-2)^2 + 2(x-2)^2 + 4(nx-2)(x-2) + 4(nx-2) + 8(x-2) + 8 \equiv nx^3$

8 Prove that: $\dfrac{2x^2+3x-2}{5x^2-26x+5} \times \dfrac{3x^2-17x+10}{2x^2+5x-3} \div \dfrac{3x^2+4x-4}{5x^2+14x-3} \equiv 1$

Chapter summary

- An algebraic fraction is in its simplest form if there are no common factors in the numerator and denominator.
  To simplify an algebraic fraction factorise expressions in the numerator and/or denominator and then cancel by any common factors.
- To multiply an algebraic fraction, factorise expressions in the numerator and/or denominator and then cancel by any common factors before multiplying.
- To divide by a fraction, change to multiplication by its reciprocal.
- To add or subtract algebraic fractions:
  - Find the LCM of the denominators
  - Write the addition/subtraction as a single fraction with the LCM as common denominator.
  - Expand any brackets in the numerator and simplify.
  - If possible, factorise the numerator and cancel any common factors.
- The truth of a general statement can be **demonstrated** by finding examples that agree with the statement.
- Algebra can be used to **prove** the truth of a statement.
- A statement can be disproved by finding a counter example. This is an example that does **not** agree with the statement.
- Algebraic skills can be used to prove an algebraic identity.

Chapter review

1 Simplify fully:

a $\dfrac{x^2+2x}{x^2-4}$ **b** $\dfrac{2x^2-32}{x+4}$ **c** $\dfrac{x^2-9}{x^2-3x}$

2 Simplify fully:

a $\dfrac{2x-8}{3x^2-11x-4}$ **b** $\dfrac{8x^2+24x}{2x^2+5x-3}$

c $\dfrac{5x^2+4x-1}{x^2-2x-3}$

3 Simplify fully $\dfrac{x^3 - 4x}{3x^2 + 2x - 8}$

4 Simplify: **a** $\dfrac{x^2 - 4}{2x - 4}$ **b** $\dfrac{x^2 - 4}{x^2 - 3x + 2}$

5 **a** Write as a single fraction $\dfrac{2}{x} - \dfrac{1}{x + 1}$

b Simplify $\dfrac{x}{x - 1} - \dfrac{1}{x + 1}$

6 Show that:

a $\dfrac{x + 1}{x^2 - x - 2} \times \dfrac{x^2 - 5x + 6}{x - 3} \equiv 1$ **b** $\dfrac{2x^2 + 9x - 5}{x + 5} \div \dfrac{2x^2 - 7x + 3}{x - 3} \equiv 1$

c $\dfrac{8}{2x - 1} - \dfrac{4}{x} \equiv \dfrac{4}{2x^2 - x}$ **d** $\dfrac{3}{x - 5} + \dfrac{2}{2x + 3} \equiv \dfrac{8x - 1}{2x^2 - 7x - 15}$

7 **a** A rectangle has length x cm and area 10 cm^2

Show that its perimeter in centimetres is $\dfrac{2(x^2 + 10)}{x}$.

b Add $\dfrac{x}{y}$ to its reciprocal and write down the reciprocal of the answer in its simplest form.

8 The dimensions of these two shapes are as shown.

a Show that the shapes have equal area.

b Show that the total area of both shapes is $(a + b)^2 + a^2 + b^2$

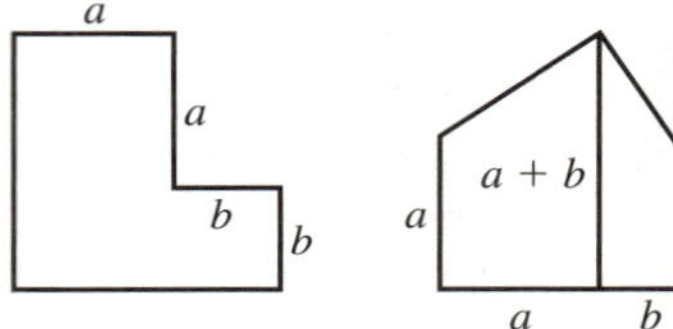

9 **a** Show that $x^3 - x \equiv x(x - 1)(x + 1)$

b Hence, explain why

i $x^3 - x$ is always a multiple of 3 when x is an integer > 1

ii $x^3 - x$ is always a multiple of 24 when x is an **odd** integer > 1

10 Show that $(2ax + b)^2 - (ax + 2b)^2 \equiv 3(a^2x^2 - b^2)$

11 **a** Prove that the difference between two consecutive square numbers is an odd number.

b The nth triangle number is $\frac{1}{2}n(n + 1)$

i Write down an expression for the $(n + 1)$th triangle number.

ii Prove that the sum of two consecutive triangle numbers is a square number.

12 Tim says that $(x + 1)^2 - (x - 1)^2 \equiv 2x + 2$

a Find a counter example to show that Tim is wrong.

b Use an algebraic method to find show that Tim is wrong.

13

Pat is investigating the function $y = x^2 - x + 11$
Find a counter example to prove that Pat is wrong.

Index

Published by: Pearson Education Limited, Edinburgh Gate, Harlow, Essex CM20 2JE, England
www.longman.co.uk

First published 2006
ISBN-10: 1-405-81633-3
ISBN-13: 978-1-405-81633-5

Concept design by Mick Harris. Cover design by Juice Creative Ltd. Index by John Holmes.

Typeset by Tech-Set, Gateshead

Printed in the U.K. by CPI

The publisher's policy is to use paper manufactured from sustainable forests.

Live Learning, Live Authoring and Live Player are all trademarks of Live Learning Ltd.

The Publisher wishes to draw attention to the Single-User Licence Agreement below.
Please read this agreement carefully before installing and using the CD-ROM.

We are grateful to the following for permission to reproduce photographs:
Britain On View: pg549 (©Roger Coulam); **Construction Photography**: pg672 (©Adrian Sherratt); **Education Photos**: pg212 (educationphotos.co.uk/walmsley; **Getty Images**: pg414 (Ralph Morse); **Punchstock Royalty-Free Images**: pg7 (digitalvision), pg465 (digitalvision); **Royalty-Free Images**: pg206 (PhotoDisc Vol.44 - Nature, Wildlife & the Environment 2)

Picture Research by Karen Jones. Figurative illustration by Joanne Kerr.

Every effort has been made to trace the copyright holders and we apologise in advance for any unintentional omissions. We would be pleased to insert the appropriate acknowledgement in any subsequent edition of this publication.

Crown copyright material is reproduced with permission of the Controller of HMSO.
